Contemporary
Literary Criticism

Guide to Gale Literary Criticism Series

For criticism on	Consult these Gale series
Authors now living or who died after December 31, 1959	*CONTEMPORARY LITERARY CRITICISM (CLC)*
Authors who died between 1900 and 1959	*TWENTIETH-CENTURY LITERARY CRITICISM (TCLC)*
Authors who died between 1800 and 1899	*NINETEENTH-CENTURY LITERATURE CRITICISM (NCLC)*
Authors who died between 1400 and 1799	*LITERATURE CRITICISM FROM 1400 TO 1800 (LC)* *SHAKESPEAREAN CRITICISM (SC)*
Authors who died before 1400	*CLASSICAL AND MEDIEVAL LITERATURE CRITICISM (CMLC)*
Black writers of the past two hundred years	*BLACK LITERATURE CRITICISM (BLC)*
Authors of books for children and young adults	*CHILDREN'S LITERATURE REVIEW (CLR)*
Dramatists	*DRAMA CRITICISM (DC)*
Hispanic writers of the late nineteenth and twentieth centuries	*HISPANIC LITERATURE CRITICISM (HLC)*
Native North American writers and orators of the eighteenth, nineteenth, and twentieth centuries	*NATIVE NORTH AMERICAN LITERATURE (NNAL)*
Poets	*POETRY CRITICISM (PC)*
Short story writers	*SHORT STORY CRITICISM (SSC)*
Major authors from the Renaissance to the present	*WORLD LITERATURE CRITICISM, 1500 TO THE PRESENT (WLC)*
Major authors and works from the Bible to the present	*WORLD LITERATURE CRITICISM SUPPLEMENT (WLCS)*

ISSN 0091-3421

Volume 106

Contemporary Literary Criticism

Excerpts from Criticism of the Works
of Today's Novelists, Poets, Playwrights,
Short Story Writers, Scriptwriters, and
Other Creative Writers

Deborah A. Schmitt
EDITOR

Jeffrey W. Hunter
CLC COORDINATOR

Tim Akers
Pamela S. Dear
Daniel Jones
John D. Jorgenson
Jerry Moore
Polly Vedder
Timothy White
Thomas Wiloch
Kathleen Wilson
ASSOCIATE EDITORS

GALE

DETROIT · NEW YORK · LONDON

Library of Congress Catalog Card Number 76-46132
ISBN 0-7876-2029-7
ISSN 0091-3421

Printed in the United States of America
10 9 8 7 6 5 4 3 2 1

Contents

Preface vii

Acknowledgments xi

Louis Althusser 1918-1990 1
   French Marxist philosopher

Jorge Amado 1912- 52
   Brazilian novelist, short story writer, and nonfiction writer

André Brink 1935- 93
   South African novelist, essayist, dramatist, and translator

Blaise Cendrars 1887-1961 147
   Swiss-born French poet, novelist, autobiographer, editor, and essayist

Pier Paolo Pasolini 1922-1975 200
   Italian poet, novelist, essayist, critic, editor, short story writer, screenplay writer,
   film director, and actor

Alan Paton 1903-1988 276
   South African novelist, nonfiction writer, short story writer, autobiographer, biographer,
   dramatist, essayist, and poet

May Swenson 1919(?)-1989 312
   American poet, translator, author of children's books, dramatist, and critic

Andrew Vachss 1942- 353
   American novelist, short story writer, poet, essayist, and nonfiction writer

Literary Criticism Series Cumulative Author Index   371

Literary Criticism Series Cumulative Topic Index   439

CLC Cumulative Nationality Index   449

CLC-106 Title Index   465

Preface

A Comprehensive Information Source
on Contemporary Literature

Named "one of the twenty-five most distinguished reference titles published during the past twenty-five years" by *Reference Quarterly,* the *Contemporary Literary Criticism (CLC)* series provides readers with critical commentary and general information on more than 2,000 authors now living or who died after December 31, 1959. Previous to the publication of the first volume of *CLC* in 1973, there was no ongoing digest monitoring scholarly and popular sources of critical opinion and explication of modern literature. *CLC,* therefore, has fulfilled an essential need, particularly since the complexity and variety of contemporary literature makes the function of criticism especially important to today's reader.

Scope of the Series

CLC presents significant passages from published criticism of works by creative writers. Since many of the authors covered by *CLC* inspire continual critical commentary, writers are often represented in more than one volume. There is, of course, no duplication of reprinted criticism.

Authors are selected for inclusion for a variety of reasons, among them the publication or dramatic production of a critically acclaimed new work, the reception of a major literary award, revival of interest in past writings, or the adaptation of a literary work to film or television.

Attention is also given to several other groups of writers-authors of considerable public interest—about whose work criticism is often difficult to locate. These include mystery and science fiction writers, literary and social critics, foreign writers, and authors who represent particular ethnic groups within the United States.

Format of the Book

Each *CLC* volume contains about 500 individual excerpts taken from hundreds of book review periodicals, general magazines, scholarly journals, monographs, and books. Entries include critical evaluations spanning from the beginning of an author's career to the most current commentary. Interviews, feature articles, and other published writings that offer insight into the author's works are also presented. Students, teachers, librarians, and researchers will find that the generous excerpts and supplementary material in *CLC* provide them with vital information required to write a term paper, analyze a poem, or lead a book discussion group. In addition, complete bibliographical citations note the original source and all of the information necessary for a term paper footnote or bibliography.

Features

A *CLC* author entry consists of the following elements:

- The **Author Heading** cites the author's name in the form under which the author has most commonly published, followed by birth date, and death date when applicable. Uncertainty as to a birth or death date is indicated by a question mark.

- A **Portrait** of the author is included when available.

- A brief **Biographical and Critical Introduction** to the author and his or her work precedes the excerpted criticism. The first line of the introduction provides the author's full name, pseudonyms (if applicable), nationality, and a listing of genres in which the author has written. To provide users with easier access to information, the biographical and critical essay included in each author entry is divided into four categories: "Introduction," "Biographical Information," "Major Works," and "Critical Reception." The introductions to single-work entries—entries that focus on well known and frequently studied books, short stories, and poems—are similarly organized to quickly provide readers with information on the plot and major characters of the work being discussed, its major themes, and its critical reception. Previous volumes of *CLC* in which the author has been featured are also listed in the introduction.

- A list of **Principal Works** notes the most important writings by the author. When foreign-language works have been translated into English, the English-language version of the title follows in brackets.

- The **Excerpted Criticism** represents various kinds of critical writing, ranging in form from the brief review to the scholarly exegesis. Essays are selected by the editors to reflect the spectrum of opinion about a specific work or about an author's literary career in general. The excerpts are presented chronologically, adding a useful perspective to the entry. All titles by the author featured in the entry are printed in boldface type, which enables the reader to easily identify the works being discussed. Publication information (such as publisher names and book prices) and parenthetical numerical references (such as footnotes or page and line references to specific editions of a work) have been deleted at the editor's discretion to provide smoother reading of the text.

- Critical essays are prefaced by **Explanatory Notes** as an additional aid to readers. These notes may provide several types of valuable information, including: the reputation of the critic, the importance of the work of criticism, the commentator's approach to the author's work, the purpose of the criticism, and changes in critical trends regarding the author.

- A complete **Bibliographical Citation** designed to help the user find the original essay or book precedes each excerpt.

- Whenever possible, a recent, previously unpublished **Author Interview** accompanies each entry.

- A concise **Further Reading** section appears at the end of entries on authors for whom a significant amount of criticism exists in addition to the pieces reprinted in *CLC*. Each citation in this section is accompanied by a descriptive annotation describing the content of that article. Materials included in this section are grouped under various headings (e.g., Biography, Bibliography, Criticism, and Interviews) to aid users in their search for additional information. Cross-references to other useful sources published by Gale Research in which the author has appeared are also included: *Authors in the News, Black Writers, Children's Literature Review, Contemporary Authors, Dictionary of Literary Biography, DISCovering Authors, Drama Criticism, Hispanic Literature Criticism, Hispanic Writers, Native North American Literature, Poetry Criticism, Something about the Author, Short Story Criticism, Contemporary Authors Autobiography Series,* and *Something about the Author Autobiography Series.*

Other Features

CLC also includes the following features:

- An **Acknowledgments** section lists the copyright holders who have granted permission to reprint material in this volume of *CLC*. It does not, however, list every book or periodical reprinted or consulted during the preparation of the volume.

- Each new volume of *CLC* includes a **Cumulative Topic Index,** which lists all literary topics treated in *CLC, NCLC, TCLC,* and *LC 1400-1800.*

- A **Cumulative Author Index** lists all the authors who have appeared in the various literary criticism series published by Gale Research, with cross-references to Gale's biographical and autobiographical series. A full listing of the series referenced there appears on the first page of the indexes of this volume. Readers will welcome this cumulated author index as a useful tool for locating an author within the various series. The index, which lists birth and death dates when available, will be particularly valuable for those authors who are identified with a certain period but whose death dates cause them to be placed in another, or for those authors whose careers span two periods. For example, Ernest Hemingway is found in *CLC,* yet F. Scott Fitzgerald, a writer often associated with him, is found in *Twentieth-Century Literary Criticism.*

- A **Cumulative Nationality Index** alphabetically lists all authors featured in *CLC* by nationality, followed by numbers corresponding to the volumes in which the authors appear.

- An alphabetical **Title Index** accompanies each volume of *CLC.* Listings are followed by the author's name and the corresponding page numbers where the titles are discussed. English translations of foreign titles and variations of titles are cross-referenced to the title under which a work was originally published. Titles of novels, novellas, dramas, films, record albums, and poetry, short story, and essay collections are printed in italics, while all individual poems, short stories, essays, and songs are printed in roman type within quotation marks; when published separately (e.g., T. S. Eliot's poem *The Waste Land),* the titles of long poems are printed in italics.

- In response to numerous suggestions from librarians, Gale has also produced a **Special Paperbound Edition** of the *CLC* title index. This annual cumulation, which alphabetically lists all titles reviewed in the series, is available to all customers and is typically published with every fifth volume of *CLC.* Additional copies of the index are available upon request. Librarians and patrons will welcome this separate index: it saves shelf space, is easy to use, and is recyclable upon receipt of the next edition.

Citing *Contemporary Literary Criticism*

When writing papers, students who quote directly from any volume in the Literary Criticism Series may use the following general forms to footnote reprinted criticism. The first example pertains to material drawn from periodicals, the second to material reprinted in books:

[1]Alfred Cismaru, "Making the Best of It," *The New Republic,* 207, No. 24, (December 7, 1992), 30, 32; excerpted and reprinted in *Contemporary Literary Criticism,* Vol. 85, ed. Christopher Giroux (Detroit: Gale Research, 1995), pp. 73-4.

[2]Yvor Winters, *The Post-Symbolist Methods* (Allen Swallow, 1967); excerpted and reprinted in *Contemporary Literary Criticism,* Vol. 85, ed. Christopher Giroux (Detroit: Gale Research, 1995), pp. 223-26.

Suggestions Are Welcome

The editors hope that readers will find *CLC* a useful reference tool and welcome comments about the work. Send comments and suggestions to: Editors, *Contemporary Literary Criticism,* Gale Research, Penobscot Building, Detroit, MI 48226-4094.

Acknowledgments

The editors wish to thank the copyright holders of the excerpted criticism included in this volume and the permissions managers of many book and magazine publishing companies for assisting us in securing reproduction rights. We are also grateful to the staffs of the Detroit Public Library, the Library of Congress, the University of Detroit Mercy Library, Wayne State University Purdy/Kresge Library Complex, and the University of Michigan Libraries for making their resources available to us. Following is a list of the copyright holders who have granted us permission to reproduce material in this volume of *CLC*. Every effort has been made to trace copyright, but if omissions have been made, please let us know.

COPYRIGHTED EXCERPTS IN *CLC*, VOLUME 106, WERE REPRODUCED FROM THE FOLLOWING PERIODICALS:

African Literature Today, v. 14, 1984 for "`Ah, But Your Land is Beautiful'" by Christopher Heywood. © Heinemann Educational Books 1984. Reproduced by permission of the author.—*The American Poetry Review,* May-June, 1980 for "Blaise Cendrars: An Interview," by Michel Manoll, translated by Bertrand Mathieu/ v. 23, September-October, 1994 for "Life's Miracles: The Poetry of May Swenson" by Grace Schulman. Copyright © 1980, 1994 by World Poetry, Inc. Reproduced by permission of the author.—*Américas,* v. 36, May/June, 1984; v. 44, 1992. © 1984, 1992, Américas. Both reprinted by permission of Américas, a bimonthly magazine published by the General Secretariat of the Organization of American States in English and Spanish.—*Arcadia,* v. 10, 1975 for "Alan Paton's `Cry, the Beloved Country' and Maxwell Anderson's/ Kurt Weill's `Lost in the Stars': A Consideration of Genres" by Myron Matlaw. © 1975 by Walter de Gruyter & Co. Reproduced by permission of the author.—*Book World--The Washington Post,* November 5, 1978; v. XVIII, May 22, 1988; v. XXII, March 15, 1992; January 2, 1994. © 1978, 1988, 1992, 1994, The Washington Post. All reproduced by permission of the publisher.—*Booklist,* v. 90, July, 1994. Reproduced by permission.—*boundary 2,* v. 22, Spring, 1995. Copyright © boundary 2, 1995. Reproduced by permission.—*Chicago Tribune,* June 11, 1989. © copyrighted 1989, Chicago Tribune Company. All rights reserved. Used with permission.—*Chicago Tribune,* September 5, 1993 for "André Brink Bawy Romp" by Charles R. Larson/ October 16, 1994 for "African Realities: Andre Brink Blents Truth, Fable and Colonial Crimes" by David Plott. © copyrighted 1993, 1994, Chicago Tribune Company. All rights reserved. Both reproduced by permission of the authors.—*Chicago Tribune--Books,* November 21, 1993 for "The Wages of Virture: Jorge Amado's Novel of Familiar Enchantments, Casual Miracles" by James Polk. © copyrighted 1993, Chicago Tribune Company. All rights reserved. Reproduced by permission of the author.—*Critique,* v. XXXIV, Fall, 1992. Copyright © 1992 Helen Dwight Reid Educational Foundation. Reproduced with permission of the Helen Dwight Reid Educational Foundation, published by Heldref Publications, 1319 18th Street, NW, Washington, DC 20036-1802.—*The Durham University Journal,* v. LXXVI, June, 1984. Reproduced by permission.—*English Studies in Africa,* v. 24, March, 1981 for "Poetic Truth in `Too Late The Phalarope'" by J. B. Thompson/ v. 32, 1989 for "Paton and the Silence of Stephanie" by Myrtle Hooper. © Witwatersrand University Press 1981, 1989. Both reproduced by permission of the publisher.—*Film Comment,* v. 3, Fall, 1965. Copyright © 1965 by Film Comment Publishing Corporation. Reproduced by permission of the Film Society of Lincoln Center.—*Film Society Review,* v. 4, January, 1969 for "Pier Paolo Pasolini: Poetry As A Compensation" by John Bragin. Copyright © 1965 by Film Comment Publishing Corporation. Reproduced by permission of the author.—*Forum Italicum,* v. IX, December, 1975. Copyright © 1975 by Forum Italicum. Reproduced by permission.—*The French Review,* v. 69, May, 1996. Copyright 1996 by the American Association of Teachers of French. Reproduced by permission.—*Hispania,* v. 67, May, 1984 for "Structural Ambiguity in Jorge Amado's A Morte E A Morte De Quincas Berro Dágua," by Earl E. Fitz. © 1984 The American Association of Teachers of Spanish and Portguese, Inc. Reproduced by permission of the publisher and the author.—*The Horn Book Magazine,* v. LXIX, May-June, 1993. Copyright, 1993, by The Horn Book, Inc., 11 Beacon St., Suite 1000, Boston, MA 02108. All rights reserved. Reproduced by permission.—*The International Fiction Review,* v. 8, Winter, 1981. © copyright 1981 International Fiction Association. Reproduced by permission.—*Italian Quarterly,* v. XXI & XXII, Fall-Winter, 1980-81. Copyright © 1980 by Italian Quarterly. Reproduced by permission.—*Journal of Latin American Lore,* v. 2, Summer, 1976. Reproduced by permission.—*The Kenyon Review,* v. XVI, Summer, 1994 for "A Mysterious and Lavish Power: How Things Continue To Take Place in the Work of May Swenson," by Sue Russell. Copyright 1984

COPYRIGHTED EXCERPTS IN *CLC,* VOLUME 106, WERE REPRODUCED FROM THE FOLLOWING BOOKS:

PHOTOGRAPHS AND ILLUSTRATIONS APPEARING IN *CLC,* VOLUME 106, WERE RECEIVED FROM THE FOLLOWING SOURCES:

Louis Althusser
1918-1990

French Marxist philosopher.

The following entry presents an overview of Althusser's career.

INTRODUCTION

Louis Althusser was a French Marxist philosopher who had a strong following as a serious and intellectual interpreter of Marxism. A troubled personal life overshadowed his intellectual achievements, however, when he was committed to a psychiatric hospital after he murdered his wife. Since then his abilities and accomplishments have been much reviewed and debated, with his place and importance to Marxist philosophy left unclear.

Biographical Information

Althusser was born in Algeria on October 16, 1918. He was named after his father's brother, with whom his mother had been in love. After his uncle was killed in World War I, his mother married Althusser's father. Althusser always felt inadequate in the shadow of his uncle's memory. Details about his early childhood are unclear and come mostly from his autobiography written after his wife's murder. His parents were Catholics and Althusser felt a strong attachment to Catholicism, an attachment which continued even after he joined the Communist Party. His family moved to Marseilles in 1930 and then to Lyons in 1936. Althusser entered a provincial school which enabled him to prepare for study at the Ecole Normale Superieure, but he was called to military service in World War II. By the spring of 1940 Althusser was captured by the Germans and remained in a prison camp until 1945. When Althusser returned to Paris he entered the Ecole, where he was trained as a philosopher. Althusser spent most of his life at the Ecole Normale Superieure, first as a student and then as an instructor. In 1948 he joined the Communist Party, and communism became the subject of his intellectual interest. Althusser's outspoken ideas about Marxism often conflicted with the French Communist Party. His involvement with Hélène Legotien, a former activist in the Resistance during the war who was denied admittance in the French Communist Party, further complicated his relationship with the Party. Althusser's relationship with Legotien was also a complicated one. She was older than him and dominating. Throughout their marriage their relations became increasingly volatile. In addition to his troubled marriage, Althusser suffered from severe bouts of depression

throughout his adult life. His followers and employers at the Ecole tried to hide his troubles, but in November 1980 Althusser's psychological problems became public. Althusser strangled his wife and was committed to a psychiatric hospital after being judged mentally unfit to stand trial for her murder. He remained in the asylum until 1984 when he wrote his memoirs, *L'avenir dure longtemps* (1992) in an attempt to answer for his crime, an opportunity he never had in court. He died in Paris in 1990.

Major Works

Althusser's two major works were his collection of essays entitled *Pour Marx* (*For Marx;* 1965) and a collaborative effort with his students *Lire "Le Capital"* (*Reading "Capital";* 1965). Althusser asserted that it was necessary to clear away what people thought of as Marxism and start fresh by re-examining the writings of Karl Marx, the German political philosopher who inspired twentieth-century communism. It was Althusser's contention that Marx discovered historical materialism and dialectical materialism. Althusser also rejected the idea of a Marxist humanism which had become popular after the 1953 death of Joseph Stalin. Instead of focusing on the individual worker, Althusser's work examines the overall structure of society. Humanism asserts that humans, or subjects, are the initiators of change, but the structuralism Althusser expounded presumed that humans are actually shaped by societal structures. Althusser's *For Marx* and *Reading "Capital"* assert that Marx himself abandoned the idea of humanism found in his early works and turned instead to what Althusser called a "science of history" to explain societal change. Humanistic concerns over individuals suffering from alienation became less important to Marx than understanding the structure that caused this alienation. The resulting science of history, according to Althusser, consisted of tracing the causes of social phenomena to economic, political, ideological, and theoretical factors that often act independently of one another. In addition, structural change is rooted in an "overdetermination"—a term Althusser borrowed from Sigmund Freud—of events from these four factors. Specifically, change occurs through an "overdetermination of contradiction," which means that when a society's structural components include opposing forces, the contradiction is resolved through a change in the structure. Hence, change arises not from individual achievement but from large-scale struggle and contradiction, an idea Althusser derived in part from Marx's concept of history as class struggle.

Critical Reception

Critical reception of Althusser's work has been mixed and has changed over the years. Initial response to his ideas was favorable. He offered a fresh approach to Marxist philosophy which was gratefully embraced by a generation of young communists. Humanist Marxists, however, have always taken exception with Althusser's lack of concern with the individual and question the validity of Althusser's approach. One major criticism of Althusserianism referred to what Althusser called his "symptomatic reading" of Marx. Tony Judt complained that a symptomatic reading meant "they took from him what they needed and ignored the rest." Criticism and discussion addressing Althusser's work since the murder of his wife has concentrated on the value of studying the work of a madman rather than the specifics of his philosophy. Most of this discussion has arisen out of Althusser's confession in his autobiography that he was a fraud and did not even read all of Marx's original writings. Paul Mattick, Jr. states that "Of course, the truth is more complex: Althusser was neither a genius nor just a nut." Other critics try to avert attention from Althusser the man and point to what his work has contributed to Marxist philosophy. Susan James asserts that "his views have moulded the character of much recent social theory and changed the direction of current debate. His startling claims about the emergence of Marx's ideas have provoked a rejuvenating, hermeneutic interest in Marx's own texts."

PRINCIPAL WORKS

Montesquieu: La Politique et l'histoire ["Montesquieu: Politics and History"] (essays) 1959
Pour Marx [*For Marx*] (essays) 1965
Lire "Le Capital." 2 Volumes. [with Jacques Ranciere and Pierre Macherey in Volume I; with Etiene Balibar and Roger Establet in Volume II] [*Reading "Capital"*] (essays) 1965
Lenine et la philosophie [*Lenin and Philosophy, and Other Essays*] (essays) 1969
L'Eglise aujourd'hui [As L. Althusser, with J. M. Domenach, M.D., M. D. Chenu, M. Marechal, and others] (essays) 1969
Response a John Lewis (essay) 1973
Elements d'autocritique ["Elements of Self-Criticism"] (essays) 1974
Philosophie et philosophie spontanee des savants, 1967 [*Philosophy and the Spontaneous Philosophy of the Scientists, and Other Essays*] (essays) 1974
Positions, 1964-1975 (essays) 1976
Vingt-deuxieme Congres (essays) 1977
Ce qui ne peut plus durer dans le Parti communiste (articles) 1978
Essays on Ideology (essays) 1984
L'avenir dure longtemps [*The Future Lasts Forever*] (autobiography) 1992

CRITICISM

Susan James (essay date 1988)

SOURCE: "Althusserian Materialism in England," in *Studies in Anglo-French Relations: Imagining France,* edited by Ceri Crossley and Ian Small, London: MacMillan Press, 1988, pp. 187-209.

[*In the following essay, James discusses the influence Althusser's conception of materialism has had on other thinkers and points out some of the problems with his arguments.*]

Hearing that I was about to write this essay, a friend recently remarked to me that he no longer felt ashamed at not knowing about the work of Louis Althusser—a reaction which has become, I think, quite common among English and American philosophers and social scientists. During the 1970s, when Althusser was a star of the kind that shines only from Paris, many intellectuals were excited by his brilliance, and ignorance was a source, if not of shame, at least of regret. Some people studied his views and others did not; but for all of them his reputation stood high, and he was acknowledged as the author of a serious and important contribution to the interpretation of Marxism. Now that the star has waned, however, the name of Althusser is no longer one to conjure with. In France and elsewhere his claims have been criticised on both philosophical and political grounds, so that his period of popular fame is sometimes represented as nothing but a season's fancy, without lasting consequences for either the theory or the practice of Marxism.

Only by cleansing our minds of Marx*ism*, [Althusser] suggests, and looking afresh at what Marx actually wrote, can we hope to appreciate his unprecedented but obscured originality, and understand the development of his thought.
—*Susan James*

Twenty years on, it is of course true that Althusser's work is neither so fashionable nor intellectually novel as it was, and self-avowed Althusserians are hard to come by. Nevertheless, a dismissive response to this state of affairs, which looks only superficially at the contours of Althusser's public career, is deeply insensitive to the ways in which his views have moulded the character of much recent social theory and changed the direction of current debate. His startling claims about the emergence of Marx's ideas have provoked a rejuvenating, hermeneutic interest in Marx's own texts. And his insistence on the need for a materialist interpretation of these ideas, allied to an appreciation of their consequences for many of our everyday conceptions of society, has inspired a new fascination with the relation between 'structure' and 'agency' in social explanation, evident in the work of Marxists and non-Marxists alike. Althusser's significance as a social theorist is therefore not in doubt, and he has duly taken his place in the textbooks. But, to understand why his ideas have been at once so influential and so little accepted on their own terms in the English-speaking world, one must first learn a little about them.

Louis Althusser, who was born in Algeria in 1918, has spent his life as an academic. Trained as a philosopher, he taught until 1980 at the Ecole Normale Supérieure, from where he published a series of essays on Rousseau, Montesquieu and Hegel, and where he also pursued a deep interest in the work of Spinoza. In 1948 he joined the French Communist Party, and gradually became known as one of its most distinctive and outspoken intellectuals. His great reputation, however, is founded on two collections of essays which unite these scholarly and political commitments. The first—*Pour Marx*—appeared in 1965, signalling, among other things, the emergence of a comparatively relaxed attitude to intellectual debate on the part of the French Communist Party. For

at a time when the Party officially expounded a 'humanist' brand of Marxism, Althusser began to outline a strongly contrasting materialism, at once stimulating and heretical. The dissonance between his position and the Party line grew still sharper later in the same year, when Althusser gave a series of seminars with Etienne Balibar on the text of *Das Kapital;* in these papers (which were published in 1968 as ***Lire le Capital***) he laid out in detail a series of radical interpretative and philosophical claims about Marx's *magnum opus,* portraying Marx himself as the stumbling but triumphant discoverer of the science of historical materialism.

It may at first seem curious that Althusser chose to present his ideas in the form of a commentary on a particular text; yet this approach is in fact an integral part of his project. Only by cleansing our minds of Marx*ism,* he suggests, and looking afresh at what Marx actually wrote, can we hope to appreciate his unprecedented but obscured originality, and understand the development of his thought. This last point is important to Althusser, as he uses his study of *Capital* to provide further support for an earlier claim, originally made in the essays in ***Pour Marx,*** that there is an epistemological break in Marx's writings, a particular point, marked by *The German Ideology* of 1845, when Marx shuffled off the coil of Hegelianism and started to formulate historical materialism proper. More generally, however, Althusser's reliance on the text also fulfils the function of underpinning his radical interpretation of this very theory.

Althusser offers an account of historical materialism which is designed to avoid two unsatisfactory extremes. On the one hand, he wishes to clear Marx of the charge of holding the crude and implausible belief that the base determines the superstructure; on the other he obviously eschews the non-Marxist view that the superstructure is no more dependent on the base than the base is on it. To steer between these dangers, Althusser attributes to Marx a sophisticated and flexible account of society as 'a complex whole, structured in dominance', made up of 'practices'. Practices, the basic building-blocks of Marx's theory, are themselves complex entities modelled on the analysis of the economic mode of production given in *Capital.* Like the economic mode of production, they are seen as processes comprising raw materials, means of production and products. But, in addition to economic practice, Althusser identifies politico-legal practice, ideological practice and—in his earlier work—theoretical practice. These *ensembles* are said to be found in all societies and, importantly, are invariably interdependent. For example, Althusser points out that among the relations of production of capitalist societies are the buying and selling of labour power by capitalists and workers. These relations, which are part of economic practice, can only exist in the context of a legal system which establishes individual agents as buyers and sellers. And this arrangement, in turn, may have to be maintained by political or ideological means. Certain aspects of economic practice therefore depend upon the so-called superstructure, as well as the other way round, and Althusser emphasises that it is a serious mistake to neglect this aspect of Marx's theory. 'The whole superstructure of the society considered is thus implicit and present in a specific way in the relations of production, i.e., in the fixed structure of the distribution of means of production and economic functions between determinate categories of production agents.

Societies are therefore to be seen as 'complex wholes' constructed out of interdependent practices; but, if Althusser's model is to be able to explain social change as well as social structure, some more elaborate account of the relations between practices will be needed. For this, Althusser relies on the notions of contradiction and non-contradiction, which are, he claims, in turn illuminated by the notion of the complex, structured whole. Contradiction and non-contradiction are themselves ideal types, standing at opposite ends of the spectrum of possible relations between practices, so that practices are contradictory when they grate on one another, so to speak, and non-contradictory when they are mutually supporting. Althusser is not in the least apologetic about describing these relations metaphorically. Philosophy, he believes, is bound to be metaphorical, since this is the only way of breaking the bounds of established usage and grasping ideas which are not already intuitively familiar. He does, however, throw a little more light on the notions of contradiction and non-contradiction, while at the same time doing obeisance to Lenin, by showing how they are incorporated into the latter's analysis of the Russian Revolution.

Lenin wished to explain why it was that, although the 'peaceable mask' of capitalism had been torn off in all the countries of Western Europe by the end of the nineteenth century and popular discontent was widespread, it was only in Russia that a successful revolution occurred. He suggests that this was due to the fact that Russia was the 'weak link' in a 'collection of imperialist states', by virtue of the fact that it contained 'all the contradictions which were then possible within a single state'. The explanation of the Revolution is consequently traced to two sets of circumstances. The first are conditions within Russia, such as large-scale exploitation in cities, suburbs, mining-districts, and so on; the disparity between urban industrialisation and the medieval condition of the countryside; and the lack of unity of the ruling class. The second deals with the relation of Russia to the rest of the world, and includes the existence of an elite of Russians, exiled by the Tsar, who had become sophisticated socialists, as well as those aspects of foreign policy which played into the hands of revolutionaries.

Althusser uses this case to support his claim that Marx held a complex view of social change, and did not regard it as the outcome of a single contradiction between the forces and

relations of production. He appeals to the differences between events in Russia and those in Western Europe to show that, while a contradiction between the forces and relations of production may be a necessary condition of a situation in which revolution is 'the task of the day', it is clearly not sufficient to bring about a revolution proper:

> If this contradiction is to become *'active'* in the strongest sense, to become a ruptural principle, there must be an accumulation of 'circumstances' and 'currents' so that whatever their origin and sense (and many of them will *necessarily* be paradoxically foreign to the revolution in origin and sense, or even its 'direct opponents'), they *'fuse'* into a *ruptural unity:* when they produce the result of the immense majority of the popular masses *grouped* in an assault on a regime which its ruling classes are *unable to defend.*

And then he claims that the list of circumstances above were among the factors needed to produce the revolution in Russia. Furthermore, these circumstances are said to be essentially heterogeneous, so that they cannot be seen as aspects of one large contradiction; each is a contradiction within a particular social totality:

> If, as in this situation, a vast accumulation of 'contradictions' comes into play *in the same court,* some of which are radically heterogeneous—of different origins, different sense, different *levels* and *points* of application—but which nevertheless 'merge' into a ruptural unity, we can no longer talk of the sole, unique power of the general 'contradiction'.

Althusser therefore concludes that Marx's concept of contradiction is inseparable from that of a social whole, and borrows a Freudian term to describe the relations between various states of affairs. Changes in social structure are said to be *overdetermined* by numerous contradictions.

This reading, if it is correct, certainly demolishes the charge that Marx is a vulgar materialist. As it stands, however, it is equally destructive of the claim that he is any kind of materialist at all, since there is so far no suggestion that economic practice has any special role to play. To correct this impression, Althusser introduces the idea that the complex whole is 'structured in dominance'; one of its practices dominates the others, in the sense that it has more effect on them than they have on it, and therefore stands out as being of particular significance. This most prominent aspect of society (which is held to be religious in feudal formations and economic in capitalist ones) is called the 'dominant instance', and Althusser argues that it is in turn determined 'in the last instance' by the economy. That is to say, the economic practice of a society determines which other aspect of it dominates that society as a whole.

The idea of determination in the last instance is therefore vital to Althusser's analysis of historical materialism, but one may still wonder why there must always *be* a dominant instance determined by economic practice. The answer is to be found, I think, in the underlying belief that any mode of production which distributes wealth away from its producers will not survive unless it can somehow be made acceptable. The *dominant* instance of a society is then that aspect of it which sustains the existing economic system by controlling and justifying its allocation of income and resources. And, granted that particular modes of production will be more effectively legitimated by some practices than by others, the exact character of an economy will determine which instance is dominant.

According to Althusser, the analysis of society as a complex whole was one of Marx's greatest achievements. To appreciate its significance, however, it is not enough to regard it, as we have so far done, as a relatively straightforward account of social organisation and change; instead, one must look more deeply into the epistemological assumptions underlying it. For the extraordinary innovativeness of Marx's insights only becomes clear once we realise that he constructed a theory quite unlike those of his predecessors and of a kind of hitherto unknown, a science of historical materialism comparable in originality to the mathematics of Thales or the cosmology of Galileo.

Althusser's discussion of the birth of historical materialism and the analogy he draws between Marx and these mathematical and scientific geniuses owes a good deal to the work of one of his teachers, Gaston Bachelard. Himself an extremely eminent philosopher of science, Bachelard held that a scientific theory proper emerges out of a collection of pre-scientific techniques and beliefs, and incorporates its own epistemological standards—a set of criteria for testing and judging propositions, on the basis of which some are regarded as known to be true. These standards change with the theories of which they are a part: modern science, for instance, relies on mathematical techniques, and, as these develop, new ways of expressing and testing them have to be found. The epistemological criteria used to generate scientific knowledge are therefore not fixed, but are at any time a function of a particular set of theories.

When Althusser argues that Marx transcended the 'pre-scientific' assumptions of classical political economy to institute, in historical materialism, a science of history, he conceives this transition along roughly Bachelardian lines. As a new *science,* historical materialism will not merely be a modification of earlier economic theories. It will bring with it its own conception of knowledge and how to get it. This

attempt to formulate the philosophical and methodological precepts on which *Capital* is founded is not in itself new. Korsch, Lukács, Marcuse, della Volpe, Sartre and Adorno had all pointed to the need to extract a method from Marx's works, which could then be applied and refined. Althusser's attempt to do this is unusual, however, in its scope and boldness, characteristics which have bred both intense excitement and genuine perplexity. The claim that Marx was a thoroughgoing materialist was a heady antidote to the prevailing humanism. Yet what *was* the vast epistemological change that Marx had wrought?

Althusser's reply to this central question begins by enumerating what Marx is not: he is *not* an empiricist, an idealist or a pragmatist. Of these demons, the most insinuating is empiricism (a term which Althusser employs in an unusually broad sense). The empiricist conception of knowledge, he says, presupposes the existence of a subject and an object, and regards the subject as gaining knowledge of the object by extracting its essential from its inessential properties. The function of knowledge is thus to 'separate, in the object, the two parts which exist in it, the essential and the inessential—by special procedures whose aim is to *eliminate the inessential real* . . . and to leave the knowing subject only the second part of the real which is its essence, itself real'. Once the problem is set up in this way, the task of epistemology is to offer some sort of guarantee that the object of knowledge corresponds to the real object, that its essence has been successfully extracted, and Althusser argues that the major traditions of modern philosophy, however disparate they appear, should all be seen in this light. Like the eighteenth-century tradition 'from Locke to Condillac', the idealist solution of identifying the real object with the thought object is 'in principle simply a variant of the confusion which characterises the problematic of empiricism', as is pragmatism when it offers practice as the criterion of knowledge. All these traditions make the same mistake: they address a 'problem of knowledge' which is presented as a genuine quest for enlightenment, but is actually limited by the need to maintain the pre-established categories of subject and object. Anything that is to count as a solution to the problem must leave these intact; yet this requirement may render it—in another sense—insoluble.

By the standards of most twentieth-century philosophy, this analysis appears monstrously unfair and shockingly ignorant. To flatten out the differences between opposed schools, to suggest that idealists and empiricists are both committed to the categories of subject and object, is enough to make one a laughingstock. Althusser is of course aware of this, and lumps such a broad spectrum of epistemological positions together the better to contrast them with Marxism. For the innovativeness of Marx's view is said to consist precisely in his break with the categories of subject and object, on the one hand, and with the idea of identifying some sort of process guaranteed to produce knowledge, on the other.

Of these two connected ideas, the abandonment of the notions of subject and object—the abolition of the subject, as Althusser calls it—is the most fundamental. What Marx means to transform here is our everyday conception of the human agent (the subject) whose desires, motives and beliefs are cited as the explanation for social events and states of affairs. Rather than being regarded as actors who make their own history, individuals are to be seen as the 'supports' of social practices which maintain and reproduce them. As Althusser puts it,

> The structure of the relations of production determines the *places* and *functions* occupied and adopted by the agents of production, who are never anything more than the occupants of these places, insofar as they are the 'supports' (*Träger*) of these functions. The true 'subjects' (in the sense of constitutive subjects of the process) are therefore not these occupants or functionaries, are not, despite all appearances, the 'obviousness' of the 'given' of naïve anthropology, 'concrete individuals', 'real men'—but *the definition and distribution of these places and functions*.

This is not to deny, of course, that individuals are causal subjects: they fill various social roles, engage in the work of production, and thereby bring about changes in the social world. But their intentional properties are to be regarded as consequences, rather than causes, of social practice.

Having established history as a process without a subject, Marx has, in Althusser's view, got free of empiricist epistemology and its search for guarantees.
—*Susan James*

The view that individuals are determined by social practice is, of course, familiar enough, but it remains to see how Althusser fills it out. First of all, because conditions vary from society to society, the social practices in which particular individuals engage will depend on time and place. This much is uncontentious, and provides a defence of the claim that the properties of individuals are not constant, so that—as Althusser puts it—each class has 'its' individuals, whose beliefs and behaviour are founded upon their experiences. However, Althusser also argues that not only do the manifestations of subjecthood change from society to society, but the concept of subjecthood itself changes. What it is to be an individual subject fluctuates from ideology to ideology:

> Where only a single subject (such and such an individual) is concerned, the existence of the ideas of his belief is material in that *his ideas are his material actions inserted into material practices governed by material rituals which are themselves defined by the material ideological apparatus from which derive the ideas of that subject.* . . . It therefore appears that the subject acts insofar as he is acted by the following system: . . . ideology existing in a material ideological apparatus, prescribing material practices governed by a material ritual, which practices exist in the material actions of a subject acting in all consciousness according to his belief.

A central part of our common-sense view of individual agents is our conviction that there is an explanatory link between belief and action. But Althusser argues that this, too, is the fruit of practice:

> The ideological representation of ideology is itself forced to recognise that every 'subject' endowed with a 'consciousness' and believing in the 'ideas' that his 'consciousness' inspires in him and freely accepts, must '*act* according to his ideas', must therefore inscribe his own ideas as a free subject in the actions of his material practice. If he does not do so, 'that is wicked'. . . . In every case, the ideology of ideology thus recognises, despite its imaginary distortion, that the 'ideas' of a human subject exist in his actions, or ought to exist in his actions, and if that is not the case, it lends him other ideas corresponding to the actions (however perverse) that he does perform.

Within bourgeois society the human individual is generally regarded as a subject with a certain range of properties, including that of being a self-conscious agent. However, people's capacity for perceiving themselves in this way is not innate; it is acquired within a framework of established social practices which impose on them the role (*forme*) of a subject. Each set of social practices not only determines the characteristics of the individuals who engage in it but also supplies them with a conception of the range of properties they can have, and of its limits. For example, individuals brought up in a truly Marxist society would presumably not regard themselves as the subjects of history, whereas those in bourgeois society believe that they are intentional agents.

Having established history as a process without a subject, Marx has, in Althusser's view, got free of empiricist epistemology and its search for guarantees. Instead, Marx asks what mechanism enables the process of knowledge, which takes place entirely in thought, to produce the cognitive appropriation of its real object, which exists outside thought in the real world? But how, one might ask, does this search for a mechanism differ from the old search for a guarantee? (Indeed, might not the discovery of a mechanism *be* such a guarantee?)

The difference between the two approaches is said to lie in the fact that Marx sees knowledge as the outcome of a production process which unites raw materials, means of production, and so on, instead of as a relation between a subject and an object. Knowledge therefore has to be seen as the product of a structure, and it is only by studying the characteristics of this structure that we can come to know what knowledge is. The change is from 'things as they are' (their essences) to things as they are *produced*.

Althusser originally argued that Marx's historical materialism had not only shaken off empiricist epistemology, but had at the same time got free of ideology and established a new science. Whereas ideologies were illusory representations, designed to sustain a particular theoretical account (as bourgeois epistemology sustains the categories of subject and object) and are thus arranged to produce an answer known in advance, scientific inquiry is genuinely open and critical. Sciences are also able, so Althusser originally argued, to tell you what the world is really like; historical materialism, as well as being revolutionary, is also *true*.

This distinction between realist science and illusory ideology is, needless to say, extremely crude, and it is unsurprising that Althusser later abandoned it in favour of a more complex analysis of the relations between science, ideology and the subject. Rather than being straightforwardly a source of illusions, ideological practice (itself composed of ideological state apparatuses or ISAs) has an important role to play in constituting subjects:

> [It] 'acts' or 'functions' in such a way that it 're-cruits' subjects among the individuals (it recruits them all), or 'transforms' the individuals into subjects (it transforms them all) by that very precise operation which I have called *interpellation* or hailing, and which can be imagined along the lines of the most commonplace everyday police (or other) hailing: 'Hey, you there!'

The 'precision' of this mechanism leaves something to be desired. But Althusser elaborates it a little, using the example of Christianity, where the religious practice is said to 'hail' the individual and provide him with his status as a subject:

> It [Christian religious ideology] says: I address myself to you, a human individual . . . in order to tell you that God exists and that you are answerable to Him . . . This is your origin, you were created by God for all eternity, although you were born in the

1920th year of Our Lord! This is your place in the world! This is what you must do! . . . God thus defines himself as the Subject *par excellence*, he who is through himself and for himself ('I am that I am'), and he who interpellates his subject.

This case is supposed to show not only how Christianity works as an ideology, but how ideology works in general, and Althusser denies the need for a more detailed account on the grounds that, 'as the formal structure of all ideology is always the same, I shall restrict my analysis to a single example, one accessible to everyone, that of religious ideology, with the proviso that the same demonstration can be produced for ethical, legal, political, aesthetic ideology, etc.' With this reassurance he moves on.

Quite apart from the exegetical question of whether it is to be found in Marx's mature work, Althusser's interpretation of historical materialism has given rise to an enormous amount of philosophical debate among both Marxists and non-Marxists. In the English-speaking world (and particularly in Britain) his doctrine of the abolition of the subject and the epistemology associated with it have provoked a plethora of reactions, most of them strong: it has been heralded as the Truth, dismissed as risible, condemned as scandalous and welcomed as the rejuvenation of Marxist theory. On the whole, however, it is fair to say that hostile responses have come to outweigh the friendly ones, so that it is easy to see the reception of Althusser's ideas as a flirtation, now firmly suppressed in the name of family values.

The reasons for this are far from simple—after all, the same trajectory has been followed in France. However, the tradition of Anglo-American social philosophy is peculiarly resistant to theses such as Althusser's, which challenge its deeply embedded individualism. It is therefore unsurprising that many people should have regarded his views as barely intelligible or downright dangerous, and examples of both are easy to find. On the one hand, a number of theorists accustomed to viewing society as the outcome of both actions and structural constraints had difficulty in grasping quite what Althusser was saying. They criticised him for over-emphasising the role of structures and for failing to give due weight to the part played by agents in the construction of society, not fully realising that his view aimed to undercut the very dichotomy on which their objection rested. The individualist assumption that, whatever the constraints under which people labour, social organisation and change is still to be explained as the outcome of individual actions which are in some sense free, proved extremely durable. On the other hand, theorists who understood the implications of Althusser's view felt at once incredulous and—for a variety of reasons—threatened. In some cases the threat was primarily a political one. The idea of the abolition of the subject conjured up a picture of impersonal and uncontrollable practices embarked upon an inevitable historical process, which was thought tantamount to Stalinism. Although this objection was voiced by critics with various political allegiances, the most clamorous and hysterical was undoubtedly the historian E. P. Thompson, whose tract *The Poverty of Theory* alleges that 'Althusserianism *is* Stalinism reduced to the paradigm of Theory. It is Stalinism at last, theorised as ideology'. This charge provoked Perry Anderson to a stern, though also rather high-handed, reply, in which the supposed affinity between Althusser and Stalin is minutely investigated. In many ways, as Anderson shows, Thompson's allegation is grossly unjust: for example, Althusser was far from being a supporter of bureaucratic unity within the French Communist Party; his brand of materialism contrasts starkly with that of Stalin; and there is no evidence that he felt any sympathy for the ruthless repressive policies which give Stalin's name its dark evaluative load. Despite its unfairness, however, the charge does draw attention to a series of problems in Althusser's deterministic reading of Marx which remain to be confronted. Anderson tries to sweep these aside by valiantly asserting the compatibility of determinism and free will:

> If Thompson had allowed a normal historical consciousness to inform his attention to Althusser, he would perhaps have recalled that in the history of philosophy there is no intrinsic relation between a causal determinism and a callous amoralism. If anything, the contrary is true. The most radical and implacable determinist of all, Baruch Spinoza, was known in his own lifetime as the noblest and gentlest of men, and was canonised by his successors as the 'saint of philosophers'.

But Spinoza's saintliness is not the point. First, while it is perfectly true that being a determinist does not entail having a nasty character, this reply does not capture the full weight of Thompson's charge; for when he accuses Althusser of being a Stalinist he is primarily condemning not Althusser himself, but his views. Second, while Anderson is also right to imply that the determinism defended by Althusser is true now if it is true at all and is therefore compatible with our current conception of ourselves as agents, he neglects the fact that Althusser does not propose to leave this comfortable state of affairs intact. If we were to come to believe that Marx's theory, as interpreted by Althusser, is true about us, we should presumably come to see ourselves, not as agents, but as the supports of social practices. It is the implications of this—the fact that, as one commentator puts it, Althusser presents 'human individuality as the fantasy of a creature constitutionally unable to apprehend its rigidly social location'—which many of his critics find threatening, and, while their nervousness may stand in the way of inquiry, they have at least seen what is at stake. For many of our current moral and political ideas are built around the assumption that in-

dividuals are agents. Why, after all, do we often regard citing somebody's action as a sufficient explanation for some state of affairs? Because, to put it roughly, we assume that their action was autonomous. We could go on to list various constraints which narrowed the range of available alternatives, but we believe, nevertheless, that within these constraints many actions are freely chosen. If we abandon this idea, as Althusser urges us to do, we obviously lose one commonplace form of explanation. But at the same time—and this is what worries many of Althusser's opponents—we lose our moral conception of individual responsibility. If there are no subjects, no autonomous agents, then there are, by the same token, no responsible agents, and we no longer have the ability to distinguish between states of affairs for which people are responsible and those for which they are not, and thus between states of affairs for which they can be blamed and those for which they can be praised. Much of our everyday morality, not to say legality, therefore disappears.

Faced with so radical a position, many of Althusser's English readers have simply retreated into their intuitively established individualist views. Such a crazy view, they think, just cannot be right, and does not require serious rebuttal and argument. I have argued elsewhere that the hegemonal position of individualism in English social theory has the consequence that it is assumed rather than argued for—a fact obviously disappointing to holists in general, and particularly to those as tenacious as Althusser. However, a number of theorists have taken Althusser's views seriously, and have produced a sustained discussion of the epistemological tenets he attributes to Marx.

Of the various criticisms levelled at Althusser's argument, some of the most serious are those aiming to convict it of begging the question. Paul Hirst raised the interesting objection that, in his account of the ISAs which are supposed to constitute subjects, Althusser illicitly presupposes that subjects exist. The individuals or groups who are interpellated by ISAs have to be able to perceive, listen, recognise and then internalise the discourses which these apparatuses convey; but in order to do this they must already be subjects. Something in this argument is absolutely right, but it is difficult to tell from Althusser's own discussion of interpellation whether he is really as vulnerable to it as his critics believe. To start with the kernel of truth, if people are to be constituted as subjects, they must be capable of forming beliefs about themselves as a result of being exposed to discourses. And, in order to form beliefs about themselves, it seems that they must already have some conception of 'self' as opposed to 'other'. This is what Hirst points out. Rather than being conclusive in themselves, however, his observations raise a series of further questions.

First, Althusser would presumably not deny that people acquire some sense of the difference between 'self' and 'other' early on in their lives. But, when he talks about 'the constitution of subjects', he has in mind, as we have seen, both the constitution of the occupants of particular roles, and the constitution of *agents*. The question of whether people can be *constituted* as agents (or whether, as Hirst argues, any account of this process is bound to presuppose they just *are* agents) obviously depends on what you understand by the notion of an agent. For Althusser, as I have already suggested, this seems to consist in the capacity to act autonomously: to decide, choose, change your mind, and so on. Exactly what this involves is the subject of continuing lively debate within all the traditions of European philosophy. But, for the charge brought by Hirst to stick, it would have to be shown that the idea of being constituted as a choosing, deciding subject, is incoherent. This is certainly not obvious. Babies, for example, might perhaps have a sense of themselves as the subjects of events (things that happen to them are distinguished from things that happen to others) whilst still lacking a conception of choice. Any serious attempt to grapple with this problem, however, requires a clearer conception of the 'subject' than any offered by Althusser, as well, no doubt, as a talent for developmental psychology.

Secondly, the widespread belief that many of our most fundamental ideas about ourselves as subjects are formed in early childhood gives rise to a further set of questions about interpellation. The ISAs which figure most prominently in Althusser's account are—relatively speaking—ones which enter into our lives quite late. By the time we are in a position to be interpellated by religious or educational practice we already have quite a developed sense of self—five-year-olds, for example, are perfectly good at making choices, and are in many ways established agents. So we need to be able to see the constitution of the subject as a historical process, in which certain ISAs—pre-eminently the family—play an overwhelmingly important part. For they presumably do much of the work of constituting the self as agent, preparing the ground for its later constitution as an agent of a certain sort—as a member of a particular class, as having a certain gender, as having a particular nationality.

Althusser's claim that all this is done by ISAs implies, of course, that the whole story could be different; different ideological discourses could and would constitute subjects who would not, by our standard, be subjects at all, since they would have a radically different sense of their own identities and capacities. Besides prompting the obvious inquiry 'What on earth would that be like?' and causing Kantians to hop up and down, this picture may be incompatible with others of Althusser's claims. I have argued, against Hirst, that Althusser may conceivably be able to give an account of the constitution of the subject which does not presuppose the existence of a *subject* in the relevant sense. But any such account must make some presuppositions and these may be more substantial than Althusser intends.

This doubt is pursued by another critic, who argues that Althusser begs the question in a different way, by assuming some fixed traits of human nature. By allotting such a major place to ideological practice, Althusser supposes that people must somehow be cajoled, duped or persuaded into roles which do not reflect their true interests. In order for a capitalist mode of production to perpetuate itself, for example, a majority of capitalists and workers alike must fail to comprehend it. But why should this be so? Only because it is assumed that if people understood the system in which they were involved they would not put up with it, and it would not go on. But this is to assume that humans have a natural capacity to recognise and reflect on their interests, and that they will only stand so much injustice.

As a rebuttal of Althusser's account of the relation between individuals and structured totalities, this objection is incomplete. Ideologies *may* be needed to neutralise 'natural' human characteristics which apply to all practices. But they might also serve to overcome properties of the individual members of a society which are themselves the result of other social practices. If this were so, the existence of ideologies could be explained without resorting to an 'anthropological dimension'. Furthermore, an Althusserian who faces this criticism directly will surely reply that there is no question of individuals who have 'real interests' being 'duped' by ideology; to talk in this way to revert to the very problematic Marx was striving to transcend. The function of ideological practice is not to 'deceive' ready-made subjects, but to constitute individuals as subjects. So, although a different totality might produce subjects who were neither exploiters nor exploited, such individuals cannot be produced within capitalist societies. For they would have to have escaped the very apparatuses which constitute subjects and thus would not be subjects at all.

This is a strong answer to the question in hand, but it releases a sea of epistemological troubles. First, as we have already noticed, Althusser's account must somehow explain the enormous variety of beliefs and judgements, many of them damaging to the *status quo,* that are found in capitalist societies (and others, for that matter). For example, if the only way to be a subject is to be constituted by the existing ISAs, how are we to explain the fact that many theorists are so convinced of the necessity of intentional subjecthood, while Althusser views it as a contingency? Did the ISAs slip up in Althusser's case? He might perhaps attribute the incompleteness of his account to the fact that he is bourgeois subject, who can only glimpse an alternative view of the individual; but this defence is still a problem, for even a glimpse suggests that the ISAs of the capitalist totality may be more or less effective and this variation will have to be explained. His reply, as I have imagined it, turns away the suggestion that ISAs somehow 'persuade' people into views and roles which do not reflect their real interest, on the grounds that these apparatuses constitute subjects rather than manipulating them. But social practices only need legitimating if there is some chance that they may be rejected. So it seems that this is a further reason for Althusser to allow that the process of constitution may be more or less successful.

If Althusser's view is to remain true to the tenets of traditional Marxism, his belief that social change is to be explained by appealing to the practices which constitute subjects and constrain social affairs must be reconciled with the notion of social classes.
—*Susan James*

On the face of it, two lines of defence are seen to be open to him. One alternative is to distinguish the constitution of individuals as intentional subjects who reason, choose and decide, from their constitution as capitalists, workers or *Lumpenproletariat,* and to argue that it is the particular roles of a society which give rise to the need for legitimation. But it is unlikely that Althusser would welcome such an option, because, as we have seen, he is anxious to reject this very distinction. The other alternative is to claim that the very constitution of individuals as intentional subjects serves to legitimate capitalist modes of production, for only if individuals perceive themselves as free agents will these alienating arrangements seem tolerable. The constitution of subjects, and the simultaneous constitution of the occupants of particular roles would then both be seen as forms of legitimation. This approach to the problem looks the more promising of the two, but breeds its own epistemological difficulties, which I shall mention presently.

As we have seen, Althusser presents his argument at a high level of abstraction, in outline rather than in detail, and, without a more precise idea of the subject and the practices that are supposed to constitute it, it is hard to know how to go on. For some readers this sketchiness has been a source of discouragement. Others, however, have found it a challenge, and the enthusiasm of a number of social theorists has resulted in a spate of work informed or inspired by Althusser's materialism. By asking a series of more specific questions about, for example, the analysis of over-determination, or the nature of political practice, writers such as Erik Olin Wright and Nicos Poulantzas have aimed to formulate claims and hypotheses ripe for investigation and development. At the same time, some of them have demonstrated the limits of our present ability to give Althusserian analyses of social organisation and change, thereby highlighting the extent

to which Althusser's own work is programmatic. Poulantzas, for example, offers an elaborate account of the capitalist state, designed both to display the interconnections between political practice and the various other practices of the complex whole, and to show how the state responds to changing class relations. This latter ambition is dear to Althusser's heart, for he too is anxious to integrate his image of society as a whole with the role played by the class struggle. If Althusser's view is to remain true to the tenets of traditional Marxism, his belief that social change is to be explained by appealing to the practices which constitute subjects and constrain social affairs must be reconciled with the notion of social classes. On one account, these are simply to be seen as the outcome of structural constraints; their members see the world as existing ideological practices bid them see it, and act accordingly. But this thoroughgoing determinism is not easy to reconcile with the idea that the revolutionary working class may precisely be able to see through the ideological practice of capitalist society, and, taking matters into its own hands, bring about the revolution.

In trying to accommodate these two aspects of Marxist theory, both Althusser and Poulantzas encounter grave difficulties. For Althusser the problem takes an epistemological form. If we are constituted as subjects, including as class-members, how *can* we ever 'take matters into our own hands', as Marx seems to require? Furthermore, if our beliefs about society are the outcome of ideological practices, which form us in ways of which we are unaware, how can we know that Althusser's claims about the relation between individuals and structural totalities are right? How can we be sure that they are not an ideological representation like all the others? Althusser's later work offers a reply to these questions: since we cannot expect to gain untainted knowledge of ourselves and our relation to social practices, the claims of a subjectless epistemology must be assessed, like their competitors, by the standards we habitually employ. But what standards are these? And has Althusser not slid into a relativism far removed from Marx's science of historical materialism?

Poulantzas' approach to the issue of class struggle suggests that he does not find Althusser's explanations by appeal to practices satisfactory. For him, it is not enough to explain social change by appealing to variations in social structures. In order to understand the history of capitalist societies one must look in addition at the balance of power between classes and the way this power is exercised. What actually happens depends to some extent on the strategies that classes pursue and on the unity with which they organise themselves and seize opportunities to strengthen their positions. How, though, is the class struggle to be analysed? In particular, can Poulantzas explain the shifting relations between classes without tacitly relying on some sort of voluntarism? Unfortunately, although he does not admit any difficulty of this kind, his appeals to class strategy are treacherous, and reintroduce the conception of the subject that both he and Althusser are so anxious to stamp out.

Scattered throughout Poulantzas' studies of the phases of capitalism are appeals to the strategies adopted by classes in order to realise their interests. At first glance these appear anachronistic, for our ordinary understanding of the term 'strategy' embodies the idea of intentional action. If a class is to lay plans there must be a strategist who assesses the circumstances, evaluates possible outcomes and decides what to do; and, while these properties can be attributed to groups as well as individuals, an agent (what Poulantzas would call a subject) is needed in both cases. Strategy, in this everyday sense, is incompatible with the abolition of the subject, and it is therefore reasonable to suppose that Poulantzas is not proposing to explain the course of the class struggle in terms of the ingenuity exercised by classes and class-members in realising their goals. But to avoid this return to voluntarism he must have in mind some further conception of strategy, and it is not surprising to find him talking about it in what might be called its objective sense: the strategy of a class—the course of action which will best enable it to gain power over other classes—is estimated in the light of its objective interests and its position in the formation, and is detached from the beliefs and aspirations of its members. In discussing the rise of fascism in Germany, for example, Poulantzas claims that, 'with the end of the First World War, a genuinely revolutionary period opened in Germany and Italy. Revolution was on the agenda, in the sense that there were conjunctions of objectively revolutionary situations. But the working class failed to take state power . . . and to secure its objectives in critical situations.' The strategy of the working class is therefore worked out in terms of the opportunities open to it in a particular situation—or rather in terms of the opportunities that Poulantzas claims would have been open to it had the class itself been different. But strategy of this sort, while it is a useful analytic tool, does not contribute much to historical explanation. For we still have to understand what makes the difference between situations where classes pursue their objective interests and situations where they stray from them.

Perhaps the most obvious course is to elucidate the strategy of classes by appealing to the constraints under which they labour. Given its position in the struggle and the structures of the capitalist formation, a class may not be left with many options. And, as long as its strategy conforms to one or some of these, the task of explanation is relatively well defined. Some of the explanations given by Poulantzas fit this pattern. Others, however, do not. He argues, for instance, that German National Socialism 'handled its main enemy, the working class and the latter's relation to other popular classes, by a calculated plan to divide it'. But calculation, in the ordinary sense, requires individuals to assess, judge, choose and decide. Since we are familiar with Poulantzas' rejection of voluntarism, we shall assume that this in turn is to be explained in a way that avoids treating either individuals or classes as subjects. The choices, assessments and selections which go into forming a strategy, and the ingenuity or crassness displayed in implementing it, must themselves be shown to be determined by factors other than intentions.

This, though, is where Poulantzas lets his readers down. For instead of taking the final explanatory step he leaves them with an unanalysed notion of class strategy. They know how *not* to analyse it, it is true, but are given no positive guidance which will enable them to get around the menace of voluntarism. If we now ask how we are able to get any grasp of the explanatory role of class strategy in Poulantzas' theory, the answer is that we rely on our everyday, voluntarist understanding of it. We use this to cast light on a metaphor of which we are given no other interpretation.

This inability to realise the aspirations which Althusser attributes to Marx undoubtedly constitutes a serious criticism of both theorists. It does not, however, destroy the significance of either, as the extent of Althusser's influence testifies. More than anyone else, he is responsible for the widespread current preoccupation with both materialism and ideology—preoccupations which extend far beyond the bounds of Marxism and embrace theorists of every political stamp. The problems posed by these phenomena may well elude any quick solution. But they are extremely interesting none the less.

Mark Lilla (review date 25 September 1992)

SOURCE: "Marx and murder: Althusser's demon and the flight from subjectivity," in *TLS,* No. 4669, September 25, 1992, pp. 3-4.

[*In the following review, Lilla discusses the implications that details from Althusser's life have on his work.*]

On a grey November morning in 1980, the French Marxist philosopher Louis Althusser strangled his wife Hélène in their apartment at the École Normale Supérieure in Paris. Within hours he was whisked away by ambulance to a psychiatric hospital, where he was subsequently confined by court order after having been judged mentally unfit to stand trial for an act he said he could not remember. At the time, many in Paris suspected a plot by former *normaliens* to protect their former teacher and exculpate him. But soon it became known that Althusser had spent much of his adult life in states of severe depression and had divided his time almost equally between the École and various psychiatric clinics. This revelation ensured that the case did not become an "affair", and it soon fell from public attention. At most, the Althusser murder was remembered along with Nicos Poulantzas's suicidal leap from the Tour Montparnasse and Michel Foucault's death from AIDS as another morbid episode in the dénouement of *la pensée 68.*

For all intents and purposes, Althusser's act was a murder-suicide. He took no part in public or professional life after the event, spent most of the next ten years in clinics, and died quietly in 1990. By then he was nearly forgotten, and not only because of the murder. Althusser's moment on the French public stage was actually quite short. It began noisily in 1965, when he published two highly influential books: *Pour Marx,* a collection of his essays, and a collaborative work with his students titled *Lire le Capital.* These works earned him a reputation as the leading philosophical Marxist of his generation. But by the late 1970s, after the publication of Solzhenitsyn's *gulag* books and the butchery of Cambodia, the French largely abandoned Marx. Althusser was still widely read and discussed by Italian and Latin American communists, and also revered by left-wing academics in America and Great Britain. But to the few thousand Parisians who constitute *le monde entier* of every French intellectual, he had already ceased to exist.

It came as some surprise, then, to learn that Althusser, his writings and his "act" had been heatedly debated in France last spring. Behind the commotion was the publication of no less than two Althusser autobiographies. The first, a short one called *Les Faits* written in 1975, is a riveting document mixing lucidity with moments of wild delirium in which Althusser recounts imaginary meetings with Pope John XXIII and de Gaulle, fantasies about robbing a bank, and fears of being pursued by the Red Brigades. The second memoir is a longer one entitled *L'Avenir dure longtemps,* and was composed in 1985 to "explain" how his early psychological experiences set the stage for his crime. It is a cagier and far more equivocal work. It is also something of a public disrobing, in which Althusser presents himself as an intellectual faker who had read little Marx, less Freud, and no Nietzsche. Accompanying these two very different memoirs was the first volume of a massive biography written by one of his students, Yann Moulier Boutang, and which gives yet a third account of his early life. A number of polemical articles have now been published on the new Althusser case, and Clément Rosset's slight book on the matter will probably be followed by other, more substantial ones.

The prurient interest in these Marxist "Mémoires d'outre-tombe" is obvious. But whatever one's view of Althusser's Marxism, there is good reason to be sceptical about using such material to conduct yet another investigation into the biographical sources of a philosopher's thought. After the Heidegger case (where the stakes are high) and the de Man case (where they were pitifully low), one wonders whether anything can be learned by picking over the bones of a relatively minor thinker who was, by all accounts, profoundly sick and dangerous.

Surprisingly, the answer is yes. Quite apart from their value as psychological documents—these are, after all, authentic diaries of an intelligent madman—the Althusser volumes permit a rare glimpse into the back-rooms of post-war French intellectual life. And like a number of recent biographies and memoirs, they confirm that the radical French philosophies of the period had less to do with grand history or our "postmodern" condition than with the shared obsessions of a small group of thinkers working in the highly centralized French context. Anyone interested in these thinkers will want to read the Althusser books, despite the atmosphere of scandal surrounding them, in order to familiarize himself with the intimate historical background to the way we think now.

Louis Althusser was born in his grandparents' Algerian home in 1918 and remained within the *pied noir* enclave there until 1930, when the family moved to Marseilles. As a young teenager he began to show signs of intellectual promise, and when the family moved to Lyons in 1936, he was able to enter one of the respectable provincial schools that prepare students for the École Normale. He did exceptionally well at Lyons, arriving near the top of his class and gaining the respectful friendship of his teachers. Foremost among these were the philosopher Jean Guitton and the conservative historian Jean Lacroix, strict Catholics both. Indeed, one of the revelations of Boutang's biography is the depth of Althusser's youthful attraction to monarchism and Catholicism, and the continuing presence of the latter in his private life until the early 1950s, well after his adherence to the Communist Party. By the time he left Lyons in 1939, he was like any other right-leaning, church-going boy of the period preparing to join the aristocracy of adolescence that has ruled France since the Third Republic.

Was Althusser's normal childhood? A great deal is made to rest on the question in these biographical writings, though they do surprisingly little to answer it persuasively. One reason is that Althusser himself paints two very different pictures of his early family life, the second under the burden of providing the psychological profile of a murderer. In the 1975 memoir, he portrays his parents as a stiff Catholic couple brought together almost by chance in a mistaken marriage and their family life as somewhat cold. Yet they were clearly devoted to him in their own awkward way, making the necessary sacrifices for his education and keeping up an unbroken correspondence after he left home. Excerpts from these letters collected by his biographer are not lacking in reciprocal affection.

As Boutang remarks, nothing on the surface of Althusser's childhood reflects an underlying Faulknerian chaos. So what is one to make of his 1985 memoir, which places most of the blame for his psychological distress—and, indirectly, for his criminal act—squarely on the shoulders of *maman* and *papa?* These pages are painful reading, combining as they do a reprehensible ingratitude with an utterly conventional analysis of his own sexual maturation (or lack thereof). It is astonishing to read a man famed for his intellectual sophistication and skepticism repeating the platitudes of his last psychoanalyst in the style of "Freud raconté aux jeunes filles". Perhaps Althusser, so steeped in Marxism, had lost the habit of considering human beings in any light other than that of class and ideology. He nearly says as much at the beginning of his second memoir, when he admits "surprise" at his inability to employ his earlier Marxist theoretical categories "pour comprendre ce qui m'est advenu". Such a confession by such a committed thinker is a troubling sign that vulgar Freudianism will outlast vulgar Marxism as an intellectual and cultural force in our time.

Whether Althusser's early family life was in fact the original source of his later psychological disintegration must remain forever in doubt. One important reason is that the natural course of his private and professional lives was abruptly altered by a singular historical event that neither Freudianism nor Marxism could explain: the Second World War. Although Althusser had been received into the École Normale for the fall of 1939, he was called into active military service before he could matriculate. By the spring of 1940, he had already been captured by the Germans and would remain in a Schleswig-Holstein prison camp until 1945. Althusser devotes surprisingly little reflection to this period in his memoirs, apart from noting his relative comfort and his first encounters with young men outside his class (including Communists). But Boutang finds evidence in letters and interviews that Althusser's depressions began here, and that he had already begun to withdraw into the care of doctors and the security of the hospital bed. It was during this period as well that he lost his religious faith, an event he passes over in silence.

Whatever the combination of causes may have been, it is clear that in late 1945 Althusser arrived in Paris a fragile, almost broken young man. And it was at this precise moment of psychological weakness that he entered into the three relationships that would define his adult existence. One of the virtues of Boutang's otherwise over-written biography is that he manages to establish the connections between these relations—with the École Normale, with his future wife Hélène Legotien, and with the Communist Party—and to show why they constituted a single, inseparable bloc in Althusser's mind.

Of the three, Althusser's dealings with the École were the most stable and satisfactory because they permitted him to fulfil his intellectual ambitions within strict psychological limitations. Those limitations already appeared midway through his second year at the École, when he fell into a menacing depression that required treatment. To their credit, the school authorities reacted quickly and placed him in a separate room in the infirmary, a room where he (like Michel Foucault after him) would frequently seek psychological refuge. Despite his mood swings, Althusser's brilliance soon made him a school favorite, and when the position of *caïman* in philosophy fell vacant in 1948, he received it without contest. Like everything else about the École Normale, the position of *caïman* is unique. It is not a professorship, since the École is not a university. Officially, its holder is simply responsible for supervising students' work in one field and preparing them for the national *agrégation.* The position demands only occasional teaching, and this schedule permitted Althusser to absent himself frequently for psychiatric treatment. Yet given the École's central place in French intellectual life, and the extreme importance placed on the philosophy *agrégation,* the philosophy *caïman* is by default one of the most powerful figures in the French intellectual establishment. This means that from 1948 until 1980, two generations of French philosophers and intellectuals passed under Althusser's manic-depressive tutelage.

Althusser was fortunate to have found an understanding "parent" in the École, for his relations with Hélène and the Communist Party were extremely rocky. As biographical writings attest, one is obliged to treat these two relationships together for reasons that are peculiar to Althusser's make-up. He and his future wife first met shortly after his arrival in Paris when he looked to be little more than a depressed, Catholic, conservative, and relatively unworldly young student. Hélène Legotien was his opposite in almost every respect—active, Jewish, Communist, and with more political experience than Althusser could ever hope to acquire. Several years his senior, she had been involved in left-wing politics since the 1930s, had worked for Jean Renoir, and had spent the war in the Resistance, where she befriended Albert Camus and Louis Aragon. Although the Liberation had left Hélène with more memories than prospects, she was the most exotic thing Althusser had ever encountered. *Coup de foudre.*

Althusser's relations with Hélène might have ended after she robbed him of his virginity in the École infirmary, had she not also (or so he thought) saved his life. When Althusser's depression was first diagnosed in Paris, he was nearly committed to an asylum, a prospect that understandably terrified him, since lifetime incarcerations were then not uncommon. Hélène refused to accept this diagnosis and secretly arranged a second examination with a doctor who recommended shock treatments, which seemed the lesser evil. These restored him to his senses, at least temporarily, and kept him a free man. After helping to liberate France, Hélène had, as it were, liberated Althusser. However sexually and ideologically promiscuous he would later become, Althusser would not forget these nearly simultaneous liberations, and in the following decades neither reason, common sense, nor an instinct for self-preservation could separate him from Hélène or the Party.

Who was Hélène Légotien? Boutang's portrait of her is anything but flattering. Very little can be confirmed about her past, except that she had abandoned her given name, Rytmann, in contempt of her Jewish roots. Boutang tells us repeatedly that she was physically unattractive, personally abrasive, and incapable of getting along with Althusser's students and friends. Althusser himself fought often and violently with her, and they were frequently separated. None the less, they always returned to his claustrophobic apartment at the École and continued to suffer there together until that November morning in 1980.

And suffer they did, both in private and public. Certainly the most historically significant chapters of the biography concern the Althussers' joint struggle with the PCF in the decade after the war, and in them Boutang does a good job of evoking the eerie Stalinist mentality of the period. The background to this little drama is still shrouded in mystery. It seems that immediately after the war the Party had refused Hélène admittance, charging her with involvement in gruesome "purification" murders in Lyons during the Liberation. Hélène steadfastly denied the charges, and Althusser of course believed her. (Boutang intimates that the Party may have known something.) For the rest of their lives together, the couple were engaged in the demeaning task of clearing her name and begging for admission. Letters were written, meetings held, but even Althusser's prestigious academic position failed to move the Party leaders. Humiliation followed humiliation. When, for example, a meeting of the local Communist cell was held on the question in 1950, Althusser actually voted against her out of Stalinist solidarity. ("Je le savais depuis longtemps, j'étais bien un lâche.") Later that year, Althusser himself was called before the cell of Communist students in the École to explain his liaison and was ordered to break with her. He agreed, only to recant the next day. (Emmanuel Le Roy Ladurie and Michel Foucault were both cell members at the time.)

Boutang's first volume breaks off in early 1956, three years before Althusser published his first book. This is a sensible stopping-point, since both the political situation and Althusser's public profile would change radically thereafter. For the French Communist Party, 1956 was a watershed: Khrushchev's secret speech, the failed Hungarian uprising, and the PCF's hesitant embrace of something called Communist "humanism". Althusser opposed such a reorientation of the Party, and it was this opposition in the name of a theoretically pure, anti-humanistic Marxism that would make his reputation over the following decade. The next volume will no doubt pay closer attention to Althusser's intellectual de-

velopment during this period, to his doctrinal quarrels with the PCF, his discovery of a *coupure* between the early and late Marx, his "theory of theoretical practice", and his flirtations with Leninism, Maoism, and liberation theology. In short, it should present an Althusser more familiar to us.

Whether Boutang will find a similar *coupure* between the early and late Althusser remains to be seen. It is possible that his second volume will restore some lustre to the later philosophical writings in this way, but it is difficult to imagine how they can survive the brutal psychological reduction to which Althusser himself subjects their author. If his first memoir is to be believed, Althusserian Marxism is defensible, but its author was mad. If the second is to be believed, Althusserian Marxism did not exist, since Althusser was not responsible for his actions—not for his writings, nor for Hélène's murder. Perhaps his illness means that neither memoir should be believed, but then where does that leave us? The paradox of Althusser, like that of the Cretan liar, looks insoluble.

And in the end it may not matter. Althusserian Marxism was an ephemeral philosophical development unimaginable—indeed inexplicable—outside the *petit monde* of Paris in the 1960s and that unique intellectual Petri dish, the École Normale Supérieure. Yet the morality lurking behind this philosophy persists and has proved remarkably adaptable, as Althusser's own case shows. His earliest political teaching, elaborated in his writings on Marx, was that man is not the "subject" of historical activity but only the "bearer" of a history which ideology and social structures produce through him. This became an article of faith in *la pensée 68,* which sought to drive "subjectivity" and "humanism" from every intellectual domain. When Althusser's anti-humanistic Marx failed to enlighten him about the murder, he had no trouble changing horses and adopting an anti-humanistic Freud to make the same moral point: man is not his own subject.

In fact, Louis Althusser was not the subject of himself. He was possessed by something he could not control, a demon that tormented him for over forty years and drove him to kill the only person he loved. No one reading these doleful confessions will reach any other conclusion. But are we all so possessed? Althusser's work today appears as one extended effort to make us share his condition, to persuade us not only that modern capitalism mesmerizes through the "Ideological Apparatuses of the State", but, as he later puts it in his last memoir, that "the most terrible, unbearable, and frightening of all Ideological Apparatuses of the State is the family". Biography now permits us to see what a profoundly intimate meaning the philosophical flight from subjectivity and the attack on humanism had for Althusser, as it did for Foucault. Why their quest for self-erasure then found resonance among an entire generation of Western intellectuals is a puzzle which historians must confront when they come to write about the time in which we live.

Morton G. Wenger (review date Summer 1993)

SOURCE: A review of *Philosophy and the Spontaneous Philosophy of the Scientists and Other Essays,* in *Science and Society,* Vol. 57, No. 2, Summer, 1993, pp. 240-43.

[*In the following review, Wenger asserts that "If the reader follows the unfolding of Althusser's logic with care, it is evident that while he is not correct about everything he analyzes, most of what he says is powerful and compelling."*]

An important set of questions might now be asked about Louis Althusser by current theorists of "what is left of the Left," with the least interesting being the empirical matter of the extent and character of his contemporary readership, and the more significant being: who *should* now read Louis Althusser, if anyone, and why? This collection, with Gregory Elliott's excellent introduction, is probably sufficient grounds to reach conclusions regarding the ongoing salience of Althusser in the current period of socialist retreat and theoretical disarray.

The various writings presented in this book in chronological order were either previously untranslated, had become unavailable in English, or were incomplete in their earlier versions. Thus, this assemblage of many of Althusser's explicitly "philosophical" arguments, that is, those done as an overt intervention in philosophical discourse, is of interest to "Althusserologists" (such as may currently exist), historians of ideas, and "Marxological" students of Marxist theory. However, taken by themselves, the further edification and gratification of the bibliophiliac and bibliographic desires of these small and continually diminishing constituencies would hardly be sufficient reason to announce the existence of this book. Indeed, if these were the sole *raisons d'etre* for this volume, its promulgation would probably have caused Althusser great pain. Happily, there is considerably more to recommend it, not the least being a lucidity sometimes foreign to many of Althusser's more widely disseminated works. This is likely due to the fact that almost all of these works had a didactic character, being uttered as lectures, defenses, conference presentations, self-clarifications, etc., and sometimes to non-Marxist but erudite audiences. This is not to say that this work will be easy even for those with more than a passing acquaintance with Althusser's major categories and his terminological conventions; rather, it is to assure the non-philosopher that with some effort, it is ultimately accessible.

Almost all of Althusser's main concepts and positions are

revisited and made part of a structured whole in these essays: the assertion of the dual character of Marxist science, subdivided into historical and dialectical materialism; the notion of the epistemological break in science represented by an internal rupture in Marx's thought; the spirited denial of History with a Subject (*any* subject) and, corollary to this, the categorical rejection of the possibility of a Marxist humanism; overdetermination and underdetermination; the "relative" autonomy of the state and, more here than perhaps elsewhere in Althusser's *ouevre,* that of the sphere of ideology. What is most striking is the clarity with which the editor is able to systematically assemble these diverse conceptualizations into a coherent whole, particularly when it is understood that these writings were produced over more than a decade. The most significant thread that binds them is more than the common terminological-syllogistic schema they exhibit. Of far greater interest is the specific, ongoing development of Althusser's rejectionist view of philosophy in general and as it has hitherto existed in Marxism. This radical representation of the totality of philosophy is the common textual element in all these essays, and it is in order to highlight this stance that Elliott brought these works together.

Althusser's position on philosophy shifted and evolved over the course of the years these essays span (1965-1978), but his overarching goal is unswerving: to dissolve philosophy into a mode of ideology. He asserts in some of the middle points of his development that in its essence philosophy is the manifestation in theoretical practice of idealism, and thus a manifestation of the hegemonic and/or dominant ideology of ruling classes, which wishes to deny the material nature of existence so as to mask the class nature of society. At later points he presents philosophy as the process by which the internal contradictions of historically developed ruling ideologies are rendered internally consistent. Early on, he asserts that philosophy is politics in the realm of theory. For all this mutability, possibly evolution, in his views, Althusser is clear in his central thesis: the deployment of idealist categories in the philosophical act is a form of ideological domination. However, a sub-text which is foregrounded in the later essays is that the reduction of Marxist theory to a mode of philosophy *by Marxists,* such as Stalin, is as damaging to the objective interests of the proletariat as is the propagation of bourgeois ideology. By producing a dogmatic Marxism, some Marxists have not only violated the nature of Marxist science, but have produced specific disasters, primary among them the Stalin period in the Soviet Union and its aftermath, which is still with us, and which is still catastrophic when seen from the perspective of the proletariat.

It is when Althusser begins an auto-analysis of his own philosophical interventions, that the unity of his thought becomes most apparent. He situates his own theoretical/philosophical activities in the context of first demonstrating the "relatively autonomous" role of theory in the construction of post-revolutionary societies. He then embeds his ideas in the conjectural matrix of that which he labels a "leftist" critique of Stalinism, which tendency he feels was absent from the Twentieth Party Congress "rightist" analysis presented by Khrushchev. In this way he frames his belief in the ongoing developmental possibilities of a prophylactic Marxist theory. That is, for Althusser the *practical* failure of the now formerly existing socialist societies was a failure of theory and/ or "line," and the possibility of any future revolutionary success depends on a rectification thereof. Althusser seeks to lift this position out of the realm of the partisan struggle over doctrine, and show the logical necessity of correct Marxist theorization, while simultaneously demonstrating the political necessity of his particular corrective. His ultimate aspiration, which accounts for much of the path he follows in his development as an intellectual, is to establish that there is no real difference between correct theory and correct line, even though he seems uncomfortable with such elisions in the earlier days.

It is in his belief that theoretical sufficiency equals political correctness that Althusser is perhaps most vulnerable. Although in the course of his magisterial syllogistic development he generates scores of remarkable theoretical and metatheoretical insights, he is forced by his theoretico-practical stance to rely on an extremely rationalistic model of human activity, wherein humans act on the basis of symbolico-material "values" and ideas which they receive from ideological "apparatuses." Although laudatory toward Freud in passing here, as in more detail elsewhere, Althusser fails to confront the insights of the Frankfurt School(s), not to ill effect in eschewing their subjectivism, but rather suffering some harm by ignoring the question of the actual material formation of the mechanisms of mental life which process sensation and "apply" ideology. In other words, he does not deal fully here with humans as real objects, even while frequently extolling the assertions of the *German Ideology.* Even sympathetic readers of Althusser might ask of his analysis whether its treatment of the relationship between theory, line, and revolutionary action is not itself noticeably tinged with idealism.

In closing, the answer to the implied question framed at the outset as to whether Marxists in 1992 should read Althusser in general or, more specifically, the Althusser found in this volume, is in the strong affirmative. Althusser's self-clarifications are simultaneously clarifications of many of the fundamental theoretical problems which all Marxist theoreticians face, and which any possible future Marxist politics must also confront. If the reader follows the unfolding of Althusser's logic with care, it is evident that while he is not correct about everything he analyzes, most of what he says is powerful and compelling. Therefore, entering into dialectic with this body of thought makes further clarification and development unavoidable on the part of any who confront it. Until the ideas propounded here have been negated in their own terms, which is an uncertain prospect, they cannot be laid to rest, no matter how much they may be consigned, in Engels' words, "to the gnawing criticism of the mice."

Martin Bright (review date 10 December 1993)

SOURCE: "Invisible man," in *New Statesman and Society,* December 10, 1993, pp. 38-9.

[*In the following review, Bright discusses Althusser's* The Future Lasts a Long Time *and asserts that "it is when he writes about his dreadful upbringing that he is at his most passionate."*]

When the French Marxist philosopher, Louis Althusser, wrote his autobiography in 1985, he knew that it would not be published in his lifetime. Five years earlier, he had strangled his wife Hélène during a severe bout of depression. His state of mind at the time meant that he was never tried for the murder. Instead he was granted a *non-lieu,* a special dispensation for someone who is deemed unfit to stand trial. In return, all his civil liberties were removed.

So for ten years Althusser lived in total obscurity, mostly in the Sainte-Anne psychiatric hospital in Paris, unable to sign his own name on official documents and forbidden from publishing any of his writings. To all intents and purposes, Althusser ceased to exist after the murder, though in fact he did not die until 1990.

Perhaps this sounds like a good deal. But as Althusser points out at the beginning of *The Future Lasts a Long Time,* he did not even have the basic rights of a "normal" criminal. He was not allowed to repay his debt to society by serving a prison sentence, and until the publication of this book he was not even permitted to answer for his crime.

Individual identity in the public arena is somewhat less developed in Britain than it is in France. Recent resistance to John Major's identity card proposals and, before that, people's readiness to disappear from the electoral roll rather than pay the poll tax would seem to show that we rather like it that way. In France, where one's identity as a rational, responsible citizen is carefully controlled and monitored, what you *are* is fixed from a very early age by a rigid education system and a blithely interventionist state.

This proved to be a problem for Louis Althusser, whose sense of his own identity was pretty frail from the outset. He was named Louis after his uncle, a dashing airman who had been his mother's sweetheart before he was killed in the first world war. When people said his name, the effeminate young Althusser often imagined they were saying "lui" (him—referring to the uncle) and that he, the younger Louis, was invisible.

Even when Althusser became one of the most respected *maitres à penser* of French intellectual life, he was still haunted by the feeling that he was living in a void: "Since I did not really exist, I was simply a creature of artifice, a non-being, a dead person who could only love and be loved by means of artifice and deception."

In his autobiography, Althusser tries to come clean about this artifice and deception. He admits vast gaps in his reading: he knew nothing about Aristotle or Kant, had read only a little Hegel. He even says that he had only studied a few passages of Marx in detail. He also confesses that he invented quotations to score philosophical points.

At no point, however, does Althusser suggest that this duplicity undermined the concept at the heart of his work—that the ideological machinery of the modern state (the family, the church, the education system, political parties *et al*) encourages in us the acceptance of our own oppression. But then Althusser himself was the living proof. In *The Future Lasts a Long Time,* we see him being eaten up and spat out by each of the Ideological State Apparatuses, as he liked to call them.

Worst of all for Althusser was the family, "that most frightful and appalling and horrifying of the Ideological State Apparatuses". And it is when he writes about his dreadful upbringing that he is at his most passionate. In one passage where he tells of how his parents refused to let him play with other children, his fury is uncontainable: "They did it in order to instill in me as a small child the supreme values prevailing in the society in which I was growing up: absolute respect for authority and above all for the state, which since Marx and Lenin we have come to recognise, thank God, as a terrible 'machine'."

Much has been made of Althusser's madness and badness in relation to his politics. It was, to say the least, unfortunate for the European left that the most prominent modern reinterpreter of Marx turned out to be a deluded wife-killer. In the present political atmosphere it is hard to imagine the excitement that was once generated by books with titles such as *For Marx* and *Reading Capital.* But if Althusser could rework Marx's ideas for a whole generation in the 1960s, it was because he felt their truth so deeply in his own life.

Philip Goldstein (essay date Winter 1994)

SOURCE: "Althusserian Theory: From Scientific Truth to Institutional History," in *Studies in Twentieth-Century Literature,* Vol. 18, No. 1, Winter, 1994, pp.15-26.

[*In the following essay, Goldstein asserts that "[Tony] Bennett's account of literary studies gives Althusserian theory the Foucaldian history that its postmodern opponents deny it."*]

The spectacular collapse of the USSR and other Communist states has only exacerbated the hostile relationship of Marxism and postmodern theory. On the one hand, Marxists complain that postmodern theorists refuse to see society as a whole or to preserve culture's autonomous ideals. On the other hand, postmodern theorists fear that Marxism cannot overcome its totalitarian nature or answer its poststructuralist opponents. Even the innovative theory of Louis Althusser suffers from this debilitating opposition. Scientific realists praise the Althusser who fears that liberal humanist beliefs destroy the objectivity of Marxist theory; theoretical rationalists esteem the Althusser who defends the autonomous norms of formal thought, but postmodern theorists complain that Althusser, along with the Marxist tradition, cannot assimilate the twentieth century world of discourse, media, and high-tech communications. I mean to show that, in addition to the scientific and the rationalist stance, Althusserian theory develops a postmodern stance that resists the totalitarian character of its predecessors and elaborates a Foucauldian account of knowledge. Moreover, the literary theory of Tony Bennett, who criticizes traditional and Marxist aesthetics in these Foucauldian terms, outlines the rich implications of this Althusser for cultural study.

> In *Reading Capital,* Althusser . . . says that Marxist philosophy is a circular hermeneutic, not a transcendent truth.
> —*Philip Goldstein*

Objective, scientific, but hardly postmodern, the first Althusser emerges in *Pour Marx,* which brings together his essays on the young Marx, dialectics, theater, science, and humanism. When he wrote these essays in the late 1950s and the early 1960s, Marxism-Leninism, the French Communist party, and the French Left enjoyed a high prestige inconceivable in post-Communist America. At the same time, the ongoing revelations of Stalinist dogma and brutality led Althusser to fear that an intrusive, non-scientific humanism was corrupting Marxist theory.

To defend the integrity of a scientific Marxism, he critiques humanist accounts of Karl Marx. He grants that Feuerbach's humanism influenced the young Marx, but he argues that Marx repudiated this speculative humanism and adopted a scientific outlook. A critic of established religion, Feuerbach argued that by attributing society's powers to God, religion alienates human kind from its essential powers or "species-being." Even though a society's art, science, industry, government, or education produced impressive works, the established religion attributed these achievements to God's will, divine providence, or some equally mystical figure, not to humanity's social powers. A critic of Hegel, Feuerbach also argued that what Hegel called the "cunning of reason" mystified social forces in a similar way; they simply develop the pre-determined rationality of the world spirit, not the potentiality of their own powers. Althusser admits that this secular, humanist critique of religion and Hegel allowed Marx "to think the contradiction between the essence of the state [reason] and its existence [unreason]" (my translation). Still, Althusser insists that in *The German Ideology* Marx discovered the fault of Feuerbach's theory: it remains speculative. Like Hegel, Feuerbach does not abstract the theoretical concepts of the mind from the nature of empirical reality. He idly deduces empirical reality from the mind's concepts and denies, as a result, the authenticating force of what Marx calls "sensuous human activity." Marx recognizes that Feuerbach repudiates Hegel's alienated reconstruction of society's essential powers but not Hegel's speculative reconstruction of scientific concepts. Althusser suggests that, unlike Feuerbach, Marx rejects this speculative self-consciousness and goes on to develop a purely scientific Marxism. As Althusser says, the "rupture with . . . all philosophical humanism is not a secondary detail; it is one with the scientific discovery of Marx."

Some critics say that this account of Marx's rupture with Hegelian theory justifies the unjustifiable dogmas of Marxism-Leninism, the French Communist Party, or the Stalinist USSR. Other critics say that this account of a Marxist science rejects only Stalinist "humanism," not all Hegelian theory. These contrary views misconstrue Althusser's account of Marx's rupture with Feuerbach and, more generally, Hegelian humanism. Primarily philosophical, this account assumes that Marxist theory is a hermeneutic practice subverting the theoretical self-consciousness of Hegelian theory. In *Reading Capital,* Althusser, whose colleague at the École Normale Superieure was Jacques Derrida, says that Marxist philosophy is a circular hermeneutic, not a transcendent truth. Marxist philosophy construes knowledge in a phenomenological manner, as a circular application of the very beliefs which the traditional humanist expects the external world to betray. At the same time, Althusser denies that this metaphysical closure contains scientific theory. Scientific theory does not simply describe what lies outside the circle of western metaphysics; this theory escapes the hermeneutic circle because Marx's rupture with Hegelian humanism opens up a radically new space, the positive space of history.

Some critics complain that this account fails to identify the specific point at which Marx breaks with Hegelian humanism and develops this new scientific theory. This objection is well-known but misleading: a hermeneutic practice that deconstructs the metaphysical language of Hegelian theory does not divide Hegelian humanism and scientific theory so neatly. Other critics object that a phenomenological hermeneutics favors indeterminacy, free play, and difference. To retain scientific truth, especially the well-known, economic determination, is to repress the indeterminacy fostered by this hermeneutics. This objection is forceful but one-sided: Althusser's hermeneutics is rationalist, not Heideggerian nor Derridean. In a Cartesian manner Althusser allows the skeptical doubt of the phenomenologist but preserves the objective truths of the scientist.

The rationalist Althusser does not abandon the scientific objectivity of Marxist theory; he assimilates the science to the rationalist's theoretical norms. That is to say, he defines science in a formal, not in a dogmatic way: it can grasp reality only if it rigorously develops its concepts and its terms, not if it conforms with practice, fact, or truth. In these formal terms, scientific theory establishes its own criteria of truth. By contrast, what Althusser calls ideology imposes the familiar conformity of theory and practice or ideas and facts. This anti-humanist conformity is not altogether negative. It is well known that he endowed ideology with a positive role: it constructs ("interpellates") a subject. Ideology does not represent falsehood or misrepresentation; ideology explains the subject's role in a society's socio-economic structure— what Althusser calls the subject's relation to the relations of production. Nonetheless, because theory preserves its own criteria of validity, he claimed that theory resists this ideological interpellation and effectively grasps the nature of reality. As scholars have shown, Althusser believed that precise, scientific theory escapes the corrosive force of discourse and reflects the true nature of the real.

Some critics say that this account of a scientific theory betrays the rationalist's unduly optimistic belief that some preordained harmony brings nature and reason together. Other scholars object that this notion of theory renders it autonomous, if not neutral. As Dominick LaCapra says, Althusser favors a subtle "positivist" scientism that denies the ideological character of objective science. Still other scholars accept Althusser's account of a scientific theory but reject his account of the subject and its ideologies. These scholars complain that this account reduces "virtually any aspect of contemporary society" to "a symptom of 'bourgeois' ideology," fragments and fetishizes the subject and inflates and absolutizes language, or imposes a robotlike, "functionalist" conformity with established discourse.

Michèle Barrett suggests that while Foucault's account of discourse answers such objections well enough, they destroy not only Althusser's account of ideology and science but the broad Marxist account as well. I admit that Althusser does not answer them. Still, he does respond to them, and his responses outline a third, poststructuralist self-extending Marxist theory. In **Pour Marx** he clearly defends the rationalist belief that theory possesses formal criteria of validity enabling it to distinguish scientific from ideological claims. Still, in **Reading Capital,** where he distinguishes between philosophy and science, he repudiates the "foundational" rationalism of **Pour Marx,** vehemently insisting that he does not seek any such guarantees of a theory's truth. He does not give up the idea that theory grasps reality, but he denies that theory reduces practice to a slavish instrument of an autonomous mind. He argues that theory follows its own practices, and practice presupposes its own theory. Indeed, the widespread belief that theory and practice form a harmonious unity he considers a ridiculous myth perpetuated by Hegelian or Sartrian humanists.

Moreover, in his later works he repudiates the autonomous norms enabling theory to subvert ideology. He calls the defense of these norms the error of "theoreticism," and, rejecting the broad distinction between theory and ideology, he argues that economics, history, philosophy, mathematics, science, and other disciplines and practices establish their own "inner" criteria of validity and produce their own legitimate objects and discourses. These disciplines create what Althusser calls a "knowledge effect," not cognitive truths nor autonomous facts. He means that an authoritative exponent of a discipline considers a particular theory legitimate knowledge because the theory conforms with the discipline's conventions, languages, procedures, or protocols, not with an external reality. What Althusser terms a "problematic," which is this ensemble of a discipline's conventions and discourses, explains why the exponents of a discipline accept certain theories at one time and other theories at another time. Just as Foucault assumes that the episteme structuring a discipline explains the cognitive force of its discourses, so Althusser argues that the problematics of a discipline explain its "knowledge-effects."

I do not mean to imply that this Foucauldian account of knowledge resolves the difficulties of Althusser's scientific or rationalist stances. I mean to say that, even though this stance may not be consistent with the other stances, this Foucauldian stance gives Althusser the poststructuralist self that Barrett and others deny him. My reader may object that these scholars do not simply ignore his Foucauldian theory; they consider Marxism a closed, outmoded doctrine as viable and compelling as Ptolomaic astronomy and Greek divination. I grant this objection. In *Foucault, Marxism and History,* Mark Poster says that Marxism describes past eras, when production, factories, machines, and workers were central, whereas poststructuralists depict the modern era, in which communication, ideology, and discourse are central.

Similarly, in *The Politics of Truth* Michèle Barrett, who defends the traditional humanist belief that political movements require agency, intention, and human nature, insists that Karl Marx's unwavering commitment to scientific truth and class struggle establishes the essentially anti-feminist, totalitarian nature of any and all Marxisms.

The work of Tony Bennett, who rejects the theoretical ideals of the scientists and the rationalists, challenges this belief in an unchanging, outdated Marxism. In literary terms, Bennett denies the aesthetic grounds of textual analyses and emphasizes the historical and institutional contexts of literary reception. In *Outside Literature,* Bennett says that literary theory cannot tell critics what correct readings must look like. Like Stanley Fish, who has argued that theory cannot produce valid interpretations or resolve critical disputes, Bennett insists that theoretical norms cannot regulate interpretive practices. Moreover, he claims that scholars who make theory such a criterion of truth accept what he calls bourgeois aesthetics, which requires a critic to show that his or her judgments of value possess universal validity. Bennett argues that this aesthetic theory does not successfully overcome the opposition between universal values and the critic's subjective taste. David Hume admits that different persons, cultures, and eras show a remarkable diversity of taste, but he still insists that humankind shows an equally remarkable uniformity of judgment. He argues that the distinct character of the authoritative critic ensures that his or her judgements are universally valid, yet he grants that even these authoritative critics differ. Bennett also says that in Kant's view, individual judgments of value must employ the universal terms "good" and "bad," even though these judgments are subjective and hypothetical. Critics talk as though everyone must share their taste, but only the hypothetical assumption of a common human nature or a common sense gives these judgments their universality.

Bennett also suggests that Marxist humanists imitate these "bourgeois" aestheticians. For example, he says that Hegelian Marxists like Georg Lukács and Lucien Goldmann explain canonical works in profound, socio-historical terms but ignore the canon's origins, reception, and exclusions. Adopting the established canon, these critics assume that the immanent value of canonical works will become clear and plain in the communist era, when a rational subject will finally emerge. Aesthetic judgments can escape the historical relativity of the established canon because Marxist theory ensures that when history ends, the universality of the texts' values will be self-evident.

Bennett says that scientific Althusserians also seek to overcome the traditional uneasiness with arbitrary or subjective judgments. However, the Althusserians argue that a scientific stance exposes the ideological incoherence, distortion, and gaps hidden by a text and, as a result, aesthetic judgments acquire the objectivity of socio-historical truths. Althusserian critics grant literary forms the quasi-scientific ability to expose ideology's incoherence and gaps, but the Althusserian faith in scientific theory preserves the rationalist belief that objective truth lies outside cultural discourse.

Bennett denies not only that aesthetic norms justify this ideological critique but also that totalizing, theoretical self-consciousness undermines institutions or produces historical change. However, while most postmodern scholars take this repudiation of theory to destroy ideological criticism, Bennett's Althusserian stance preserves it. For example, like Bennett, Richard Rorty insists that theory does not ground knowledge, but Rorty critiques traditional epistemology, not aesthetics. In *The Consequences of Pragmatism,* for example, he complains that while Platonists, empiricists, and Kantians fiercely oppose each other's views, they all defend epistemological criteria of truth. The Platonist argues that the unity and autonomy of Being justifies his belief that the rational mind can escape its subjective predispositions and grasp the objective nature of reality. The empiricist argues that sense data, raw feels, distinct impressions or strong intuitions can expose the metaphysical character of nonsense and ground the positive assertions of legitimate theory. The Kantian, who seeks a third way between Platonist and empiricism, argues that the presuppositions of knowledge represent universal rules enabling an individual to escape his or her subjectivity and to establish the universal framework of knowledge. Rorty complains that, despite these epistemological differences, the Platonist, the empiricist, and the Kantian all assume that epistemological criteria enable one to escape one's determinate historical context or "vocabularies" and to grasp certain, objective truth.

Like Bennett, Rorty forcefully debunks this traditional quest for epistemological certainty. However, an unredeemed liberal, he considers postmodern theorists like Derrida and Foucault self-conscious ironists, not public theorists. His argument is that these theorists do not make propositional kinds of argument; they critique our vocabularies, denying that any vocabulary and, hence, any rules or conventions are final. As a consequence, their "ironizing" does not escape their private subjectivity. In his view, "[i]ronist theorists like Hegel, Nietzsche, Derrida, and Foucault seem to me invaluable in our attempt to form a private self-image, but pretty much useless when it comes to politics." Moreover, identifying literary criticism with this "ironizing," he claims that criticism too is "largely irrelevant to public life." Nancy Fraser rightly objects that Rorty would "require us to turn our backs on the last hundred years of social history."

By contrast, Bennett shows that postmodern theory undertakes valuable ideological criticism. In *Bond and Beyond,* he and Janet Woollacott argue that a literary text functions as a passive arena within which the proponents of different "intertextual" strategies make their views prevail. As Bennett and Woollacott say, "[t]exts constitute sites around which the pre-eminently social affair of the struggle for the production of meaning is conducted." The intentions of an author or the figures of a text do not reveal the objective truth or constrain the activity of readers. Rather, what Bennett and Woollacott call the "production of meaning" is a "pre-eminently social affair" because readers are situated within and constructed by subjective institutional structures or, to use his term, "reading formations." To interpret a text is to contest its terrain, to vindicate one's methods and ideologies, and, by implication if not by explicit assertion, to debunk opposed methods and ideologies.

Stanley Fish and Barbara Herrnstein Smith also favor a subjective account of literary criticism. They believe that the beliefs and the values of the reader explain his or her interpretation of a text. Smith argues that the traditional "axiology" of David Hume, Immanuel Kant, and other modern aestheticians seeks but fails to impose absolute norms of universal value. She asserts that these aestheticians do not successfully overcome the subjectivity of individual taste and the relativity of individual beliefs. However, Smith emphasizes the individuality of the reader, whose interpretations express his or her personal "economy" of values. Fish argues that interpretive communities govern the practices of readers but not of individuals, who circulate among diverse communities. Bennett also says that the reading formations embedded in literary institutions govern the interpretations of individual readers, but, more Foucauldian than either Fish or Smith, Bennett claims that these reading formations enable schools and universities to discipline readers, ensuring that they constitute proper political/ethical subjects.

In other words, Bennett assumes that embedded in distinct institutions literary discourse produces its own social relations and does not simply mimic or distort them. In the nineteenth century, when the schools turned literature into what Bennett calls a "moral technology," the ideal teacher and, subsequently, the many-layered text, made the reader's interpretive activity the basis of his or her unending improvement. Bennett says that while traditional "bourgeois" criticism takes this technology to produce ethical improvement, Marxist criticism assumes that it provides ideological correction. However, both the bourgeois and the Marxist critic ignore the technology's power to constitute the subject.

Some opponents of this view might object that in a postmodern fashion it emphasizes the inescapable present, not theoretical critique, local academic interests, not the underlying social totality. Certainly Fredric Jameson, who dismisses the Foucauldian problematic of power as anti-Marxist, harshly condemns what he calls Bennett's "sinister variant" of a widespread "anti-intellectualism." As

Jameson says, Bennett "does not seem to realize how ob-scene American readers are likely to find his proposals." In effect, Jameson reduces Bennett's theory to the "obscene" proposal that radicals ought to support Jesse Jackson, Bill Clinton, and the Democratic party. But Bennett's institutional history also bears on pedagogic issues, including the status of the Anglo-American canon, the place of cultural studies, the neglect of popular culture, the teacher-centered charac-ter of the classroom, and the gross inadequacies of state and federal funding. Jameson assumes, as does Theodor Adorno, that the instrumental rationality dominating modern society makes theoretical critique the only revolutionary force. But these pressing issues clearly require not only an engaged, institutional politics, but a historical analysis as well.

I have argued that Bennett's account of literary studies gives Althusserian theory the Foucauldian history that its postmodern opponents deny it, and yet, a skeptic could still refuse to believe that Althusserian theory is Foucauldian or postmodern. After all, without the social totality, theoreti-cal critique, scientific truth, or class conflict very little of this Althusser looks or sounds like the Marxism that we know and love (or hate). Bennett suggests that our trying to answer this objection may not be worth the effort. Still, the objection is misleading. It assumes that we have defined once and for all the "true" nature of Marxism. The many schol-ars who consign Marxism to the dustbin of history accept this assumption, but Althusser, who insists that Marxism is a scientific field and not a set of doctrines, denies it. Bennett may not definitively establish the postmodern character of Althusserian theory, but he shows us what a poststructuralist Marxism might look like. This outline of the poststructuralist Althusser may be less conventional than the scientific or the rationalist Althusser, but this Althusser is not, on that ac-count, the less important.

Chip Rhodes (essay date Winter 1994)

SOURCE: "Ideology Takes a Day Off: Althusser and Mass Culture," in *Studies in Twentieth-Century Literature,* Vol. 18, No. 1, Winter, 1994, pp. 39-54.

[*In the following essay, Rhodes discusses Althusser's work on ideology and the aesthetic as it applies specifically to mass culture. In addition he analyzes the movie* Ferris Bueller's Day Off *in relation to an Althusserian approach to mass culture.*]

In the move within cultural studies toward the effacement of the distinction between high and low culture, the Althusserian theory of ideology has become something that one moves beyond. In this theory's implications many crit-ics have detected the creeping specter of the culture

industry's conception of popular texts, with its supposed vi-sion of the masses as lambs led unwittingly to the slaughter. In its place, a variety of modes of "reading the popular" (in John Fiske's phrase) have gained popularity that focus on empowerment, use value, and utopian bribes and seek to bring what Fredric Jameson calls "dialectical criticism" into the study of mass culture.

It will be the argument of this paper that these two recog-nizable poles of cultural criticism—the conspiracy theories of massive interpellation of an essentially docile public, and the populist theories of a more savvy public that picks and chooses according to its needs and desires—represent a false choice between structuralism without agency and humanism with. In this reduction, Althusser's groundbreaking work on ideology, structural causality, relative autonomy and overdetermination is either ignored or misconstrued. Using these conceptual tools, this essay will attempt the following: first, to articulate an Althusserian approach to mass culture that draws on both Althusser's work on ideology *and* his less influential work on the aesthetic; second, to update much of what Althusser says specifically about the contours of ide-ology under capitalism, focusing in particular on the rise of mass culture.

I will begin with a discussion of a standard critique of Althusser and then move on to those alternative models that focus largely on struggle at the level of consumption. Then I will discuss a popular film (*Ferris Bueller's Day Off*) at length because it points in the direction that an elaboration of Althusser's work must go in order to deal with the increas-ingly dominant role played by mass culture within the ISAs [ideological state apparatuses] as a whole. More concretely, I hope to use the film to show how mass culture's widespread success in producing consumer desire in contemporary America requires a revamped Althusserian theory of ideo-logical interpellation that *includes* the aesthetic. This project, again, need not import concepts from outside Althusserian Marxism. It is quite consistent with Althusser's model of ide-ology in general, even if it takes issue with some of its par-ticulars. The ultimate goal is to produce knowledge about what he calls in **Reading Capital** the "mechanism of pro-duction of the *society effect* in the capitalist mode of pro-duction."

Criticisms of Althusser are not hard to find. They have come from post-structuralists and orthodox Marxists alike. Perry Anderson, who used Althusserian tools himself in *Lineages of the Absolutist State,* explains the ill-fated union of struc-turalism and Marxism this way: "Rather than resisting this move [the structuralist rejection of the humanist subject], Althusser radicalized it, with a version of Marxism in which subjects were abolished altogether, save as the illusory ef-fects of ideological structures." Anderson's point is simple. The union was a mistake for Marxism from the start because its displacement of the constituting subject from the historical process necessarily precludes collective political action toward revolutionary change. In terms of the study of mass culture, the point is equally straightforward. The decentering of the subject denigrates the individual, turning her/him into little more than the "illusory effects of ideological structures," passive repositories without any capacity for resistance.

The either/or logic underpinning this now familiar critique of Althusser runs roughly as follows: either there are no constituting subjects, individual or collective, and we may as well let history and the class struggle take their course, or there are real possibilities of conscious intervention through organised political action. If the argument is formulated in this way (as it usually is by Marxist Humanists), then political action and its agents must be privileged. The fear of the loss of the subject (individual or collective) as the constituting historical agent is thus the underlying issue we must bear in mind in trying to make sense of the polarized debate over mass culture mentioned above. This fear is also largely responsible, I think, for the shift in emphasis from production to consumption. As Meaghan Morris has argued, the "banality" of culture studies today is its view of consumption as a separate sphere "rather than [as] one of the necessary, complex, variable *phases* of a productive process." Morris attributes this development to the facility with which struggle can be found in consumption and the difficulty finding it in an increasingly complicated, deindustrialized global economy.

Warren Montag has argued in a similar vein that Jameson's conception of postmodernism denies the possibility for struggle at the level of production. Jameson's approach to mass culture seems to follow logically from this dispiriting conclusion. Indeed, because conflict can no longer be found in production proper, Jameson seeks and finds it elsewhere in the subject's interaction with popular texts. However, both the denial of production and the affirmation of consumption can be traced to the same source. Both derive from a single theory of history. For Jameson, history is a totalization with a totalizer, a developmental narrative by which men caught in the realm of necessity yearn for the realm of freedom. In other words, history is a process *with* a subject—an idealist theory Althusser attributes to Hegel.

It should be pointed out up front that Jameson's approach to the popular and Althusser's are not diametrically opposed. Both agree that the practice of popular culture is not a univocal, but a contradictory one. The difference between these two theories lies in the complexion and complexity of this contradiction. Consider the logic underpinning this passage from Jameson's essay, "Reification and Utopia in Mass Culture":

[T]he hypothesis is that the works of mass culture cannot be ideological without at one and the same time being implicitly or explicitly Utopian as well: they cannot manipulate unless they offer some genuine shred of content as a fantasy bribe to the public about to be so manipulated . . . the deepest and most fundamental hopes and fantasies of the collectivity.

History, in this passage, is something of an unnatural ruse that thwarts and manipulates a collectivity that has sought throughout the course of time to realize its deepest desires, the purest pre-social expressions of human nature. Popular texts then articulate the repressed desires of the people, the real subjects of history. The public is consequently drawn to those popular texts that narrate its collective story.

Instead of focusing on a utopian dimension as a bribe to a pre-existing subject, a strict Althusserian approach should conceive of texts and subjects both as the bearers of structures.
—*Chip Rhodes*

However much sympathy we may feel for this as an *ideology,* it is just that: an ideology, and not an explanation of the structural practices that determine its shape and function. In its refusal to abandon the humanist subject, Jameson's formulation sacrifices its potential to make sense of the conflicts within the structures that determine that very subject. As Michel Pêcheux has indicated, there exist "relations of contradiction-unevenness-subordination" among and within these structures that can and often do produce resistance. But Jameson's subject-based discourse does not make the epistemological break that Althusser attributes to the later Marx, a break that allows for an understanding of history as a process *without* a subject.

An Althusserian approach to popular texts necessarily conceives of such texts as overdetermined. Texts, like subjects, are the product of intersecting (and conflicting) material practices. Instead of focusing on a utopian dimension as a bribe to a pre-existing subject, a strict Althusserian approach should conceive of texts and subjects both as the bearers of structures. Both are sites of a complex interplay among multileveled material practices that includes but is not reducible to economic practice. To operationalize this approach to the text, Althusser recommends what he calls symptomatic reading. This method decisively rejects Jameson's humanist ideology that affirms the existence of a subject that can be distinguished from its social context in favor of a discourse that reads the text for "specific structures of historicity" that are immanent in the text in their effect.

Terry Lovell has argued that such anti-humanist knowledge is ultimately disabling to political action because it sees the subject as constituted by ideology and not constitutive of history. Indeed, this too is a familiar criticism, and it is one that Althusser himself acknowledged in his later essays. It is true that Althusser did not fully formulate an account of how the working class might make history. But as Althusserians like Pêcheux, Goran Therborn and Catherine Belsey have shown, Althusser's work on ideology can provide the basis for a cultural politics that does. Pêcheux's work is particularly valuable for our purposes because it stresses the absolute necessity of hard empirical work to determine the balance of class forces and the structural features of capitalist society at any given historical moment. Only after this work has been done can the progressive or reactionary charge of any given popular artifact be determined.

When Althusser writes in **"On the Materialist Dialectic"** that contradiction is the motive force of history, he is suggesting (as any Marxist should) that each of the multiple contradictions that exists in the complex whole in dominance means "a real struggle, real confrontations, precisely located within the structure of the complex whole." Theories of mass culture like Jameson's and Lovell's imply that this motive force derives from the subject (instead of constituting it) because individuals will always and instinctively fight against exploitation. As a result, however, the specificity of any given conjuncture gets lost in the rush to treat the culture industry dialectically. The cultural critic finds this essential conflict time and again, and history becomes a continuous narrative produced by human intentionality. The Althusserian subject does indeed 'make history' too, but always in ways that exceed its intent. Montag puts it this way:

> We act within a specific conjuncture only to see that conjuncture transformed beneath our feet, perhaps by our intervention itself, but always in ways that ultimately escape our intention or control, thereby requiring new interventions *ad infinitum*.

This need for on-going intervention presupposes a resisting subject, but not a humanist one. Moreover, it implies that the ideologically constituted subject is decentered because ideology is structured like language, a point that Michael Sprinker has made. This is why ideology is eternal and why the subject is constantly being hailed, constantly being interpellated by the ISAs. This is also why the subject is overdetermined, in process and thus always susceptible to interpellation by competing ideologies like communism.

Consequently, any investigation of mass culture must carefully situate it in relation to other ideological practices—ones like the family and the schools that have traditionally played a more crucial role in fulfilling ideology's function. The relations among these practices is not predetermined, but rather always shifting—and always possessing the potential for a reshuffling that operates to transform the productive relations. The fact that these relations cannot be known *a priori* is implicit in the ISA essay. In it, Althusser says that under capitalism the schools have replaced the church as the dominant apparatus. However, as we will see in a moment when we turn to *Ferris Bueller,* the schools no longer hold this privileged position, having relinquished it to mass culture.

Lovell and John Fiske find elitism in Marxist approaches to the popular that do not grant consumers the ability to decide for themselves. They point out that the consumer still determines whether a high-budget Hollywood film, for example, will be a blockbuster or a bust. Lovell turns to Marx's concept of use value to theorize the individual's ability to use the commodities foisted upon him or her for contrary purposes. In buying, in other words, the subject resists. In choosing to watch a particular television show or attend a particular film, the subject is asserting its ability to fight back against its oppressors. And yet, however much we may wish to stress the subversive potential of popular texts, we don't want to forget the overall social effect of mass culture. Although we may indeed struggle politically at the level of consumption, we are continually reminded that this struggle is not waged on a level playing field. In general, mass culture displaces antagonism far more often than it condenses or instigates it. Here surely Althusser's notion of "last instance determination" is a helpful (if sobering) reminder that these texts are commodities delimited by the economic interests that finance them and reap the profits. Theories of culture that dwell on empowerment and resistance too often read like apologies for the culture industry. The point isn't that no struggle goes on at this level, but that this struggle is only *relatively* autonomous. As such, it must always be studied as one among many phases of a complicated production process.

Although Althusser always included the aesthetic among the ISAs, he saw it as a sort of second-order signifying system that "internally distantiates" ideology and allows the spectator/reader to "see, perceive and feel" the discrepancy between the imaginary relation of ideology and the real relation of the productive relations.
—*Chip Rhodes*

In a moment, I will concretize this investigation by turning to *Ferris Bueller's Day Off,* a film that can be read as a critical allegory of Althusser's theory of ideology. More specifically, it takes as its subject matter the complex role of mass culture in subject interpellation. Our discussion of the particular function of mass culture must acknowledge that this apparatus was not sufficiently theorized by Althusser. While it is true that other apparatuses generally seek to construct *producing* subjects prepared to enter the work force without complaint, mass culture is tied so heavily to consumption that the subjects it seeks to construct are more *consuming* subjects characterized by classlessness. Here, it might be argued that in his broader assertions concerning ideology Althusser did not always adhere to his own caution to respect the relative autonomy of different material practices. While the cumulative effect of ideology as Althusser saw it in the ISAs essay was a "free" producing subject, a mass culture-dominated ideological matrix seems to form something very different: a nonproductive, "free" consuming subject. True, these two subjects are both first and foremost "misrecognizing" subjects, seeing themselves as their own cause—a process Pêcheux calls the "Münchhausen" effect after the immortal baron who lifted himself into the air by pulling his own hair. Moreover, it can be argued that the producing and consuming subjects are complementary. In order to acquire the consumer items that will express one's unique individuality, one must enter the work force to make the necessary capital. But if mass culture's ascendance comes at the expense of the schools' legitimacy (as indeed it does in *Ferris Bueller*) then an ideological crisis might be in the offing. If education is the ideological practice that teaches the skills needed to participate in the labor force, its denigration by mass culture jeopardizes ideology's overarching function.

Althusser did not provide for the radical alteration of the ideological terrain that mass culture's ascendance in the United States has brought about. I've already mentioned its denigration of the educational apparatus and complication of the production side of capitalism. But it has also swallowed up the aesthetic. Although Althusser always included the aesthetic among the ISAs, he saw it as a sort of second-order signifying system that "internally distantiates" ideology and allows the spectator/reader to "see, perceive and feel" the discrepancy between the imaginary relation of ideology and the real relation of the productive relations. This theory has been criticized often enough for its ostensible privileging of the avant-garde and its dismissal of classical realism. I will not rehash this argument. I only wish to suggest that it is no longer a particularly relevant one because mass culture itself has erased the dividing line between the two aesthetic modes. *Ferris Bueller's Day Off* confronts the Althusserian aesthetic with a mocking dilemma: it is a cynical, enormously popular film that appears to lay its own practice bare. It thus renders the Althusserian division between "real" art and mass culture meaningless. But it also points the way toward a revised Althusserian approach to cultural artifacts that is capable of making sense of mass culture in the postmodern age.

The choice of *Ferris Bueller's Day Off* is not an arbitrary one. The film speaks volumes about teen films in particular and mass culture in general because it takes as its very subject the ideological function of such discourses. It presents us with a literalization of the interpellative process that Althusser outlines in the ISA essay. Ferris Bueller—the consummate teenage trickster figure—doesn't merely outwit school administrators and parents; he also teaches his best friend Cameron and the audience how to be individuals in a capitalist society. His day of fun and frolic in Chicago is only a pretense to pass along this valuable lesson. Ferris is something of a filmic figure for the Absolute Subject in whose name individuals are interpellated as subjects by ideology. Cameron is a filmic figure for the "hailed" subject that only exists in and through ideology. To pursue this schematic outline, the relationship between Ferris and Cameron allegorizes two processes: first, transhistorically how what Althusser calls ideology in general functions, has always functioned, and always will function—even after class distinctions have been erased. Consequently, the self-originating subject of humanism is the determinate absence of the film. It is revealed instead to be the bearer of structures; and second, historically how the relations of contradiction-unevenness-subordination among the ideological apparatuses that serve to shape individuals as subjects have shifted. In the realigned relations that can be read symptomatically from the film, the schools (the apparatus Althusser argued was the dominant apparatus in capitalist society) and the family are subordinate to and in contradiction with the mass culture apparatus that has become increasingly hegemonic. This is particularly true in youth culture, the segment of the population that has yet to take up its position within the productive relations. This shift in the complex constellation of ideological practices parallels a shift in a subject defined by its identity as a producer to a subject defined as a consumer—a shift from a free wage laborer to a consumer expressing his/her freedom in the marketplace of leisure. This shift also suggests that the ISAs function in late capitalism no longer to fulfill ideology's role of reproducing the productive relations in the way Althusser envisioned when he wrote the ISA essay.

From the opening shot, the spectator is positioned as a sort of silent pupil quite explicitly by Ferris, who has just conned his parents into believing that he is too sick to go to school. As the door of Ferris' bedroom shuts behind them, Ferris turns directly to the camera (thus breaking the fourth wall so precious to classic realism) and says, "They bought it. The worst performance of my life and they never doubted it for a second." There is nothing shocking about this rupture of the diegetic space, however. No alienation effect is produced. Through a combination of exaggerated point of view shots from Ferris' perspective and aided by his unctuous overacting, the spectator is led to recognize that what she/he is witnessing is purely performative.

In the series of tableaux that follow, Ferris gives the camera a primer on how to bring off a similar deception. As we tag along, Ferris takes a shower during which he offers up what is supposed to be the film's message. Here, as elsewhere, director John Hughes gives his audience little credit, presenting this thematization as the filmic equivalent of the Cliff Notes they no doubt read instead of the books themselves:

> I do have a test today. That wasn't bullshit. It's on European Socialism. I mean, really, what's the point? I'm not European. I don't plan on being European, so who gives a crap if they're Socialists? They could be fascist anarchists for all I care and it still wouldn't change the fact that I don't have a car. Not that I condone fascism. Or any ism for that matter. Isms, in my opinion, are not good. A person should not believe in an ism, he should believe in himself. I quote John Lennon: "I don't believe in Beatles, I just believe in me."

Ferris seems to be saying that ideologies are not just uniformly bad, they're irrelevant. The subject who "believes in himself" is outside of the apparatus through which ideology realizes itself. Schools (in addition to the family, which is also not to be taken seriously judging by the case with which Ferris outsmarts his parents) here stand as the pre-eminent purveyors of the kind of "ism" Ferris deplores. Interspersed with this lesson on how to resist the dominant ideological apparatus, the viewer is treated to a series of shots from classrooms. The contrast is clear. While Ferris moves around the house freely, dancing to themes from MTV and "Bewitched" and then sipping a tropical drink by the family pool, his peers are staring glassy-eyed at unspeakably boring teachers droning on about the Great Depression and symbolism in some unspecified novel.

This segment erects the fundamental distinction upon which the film's ideological project depends: the distinction between the subject and the social structure that demands allegiance—between two spaces, the ideological and the nonideological. According to Ferris and the film, there are subjects who exist within ideology (like those who submit to school authority and take the test on European Socialism), and those who elude its grasp by believing in themselves. The spectator ends up in the interesting position, soon to taken up by Cameron within the film, of a student being taught how to be herself or himself. But as Althusser argues, such a distinction is the precondition for the practice of ideology. "What really takes place in ideology seems to take place outside it. That is why those who are in ideology believe themselves by definition outside ideology: ideology never says, 'I am ideological.'" So far, the film is keeping to Althusser's model of ideology in general. But we should recognize that Ferris' modes of expressing this vaguely ar-

ticulated belief in oneself are (and will be throughout the film) all mass cultural, consumer-oriented activities. While the ideological work done in the formerly dominant schools is clearly at odds with the reality of the existence of its subjects, mass culture presents the "nonideological" liberation of leisure and consumption. Ferris *chooses* all these activities. Conversely, the apathy on the students' faces in the schools bespeaks the consequence of their refusal to exercise individual choice. A change in the dominant apparatus is figured here that in turn constructs a different subject. It is no longer a willing worker, but a consumer in the democratic marketplace. Of course, this is an imaginary relation inasmuch as it denies the reality of unequal distribution of the capital necessary to express this individuality. Thus the shift from a producer-oriented ideological matrix to a nonproductive, consumer culture also seeks fictively to deny the reality of class (which emanates from the productive relations).

One point on ideology in general: the seductiveness of Ferris' monologue clearly is suggestive in some unexpected ways. If we accept Althusser's contention that there will always be ideology and thus subjects, then Ferris' manner of presentation could be used in very different ways. If, instead of reciting an ode to consumption, Ferris were to begin inculcating the beliefs of historical materialism and explaining the social construction of identity, might the film serve a more radical political aim? If, as Slajov Zizek has argued, you don't believe in communism because you understand Marx, but rather you understand Marx because you believe in communism, then might Ferris' example suggest an initial procedure for bringing subjects to internalize an ideological system? Of course, the film probably would not have been produced (let alone have been successful) if its ideological raw material hadn't been familiar and safe. The next crucial allegorical section of the film involves the introduction of Cameron, Ferris' best friend, who really is too sick to go to school. When we meet Cameron for the first time, he is lying motionless in bed, covered from head to toe by blankets. The phone rings and Cameron's voice is heard from under the bed covers moaning monotonously. We then hear Ferris' voice speaking through the answering machine, telling Cameron to pick up the receiver because Ferris knows he's there. It is only after several moments that Cameron picks up the phone, and even then the camera cannot make out his face beneath the blankets. All we can hear is Cameron's voice chanting, "Let my Cameron go," over and over. Read allegorically, this scene is a temporalization of the process of entry into subjectivity Althusser describes. Only when Ferris hails him does Cameron recognize that it is really he, Cameron, who is the subject of Ferris' hailing; only then does he accept his social existence.

Ferris's motives are two-fold. On the one hand, he claims to be rescuing Cameron from the malaise that has resulted from the contradictory effects of interpellation in the family and the schools. In both the family and the schools, the degraded position of subordination Cameron inhabits has produced alienation and cynicism. However, Cameron's apathy can also be read as the result of a disjunction between an ideology of a productive subject appropriate to an early phase of capitalism and the reality of a nonproductive, commodity-oriented economy. The latter is represented by the only employment options the film presents: real estate agent and advertising executive (held by Ferris' mother and father respectively). Both jobs are lucrative, but neither produces any value. This gap thus suggests the unevenness of the relations among ideological apparatuses. The schools and the family have lagged behind a shift in the U.S. economy that has thrown the fictiveness of ideology into relief and diminishes its effectiveness. Ferris is an agent of the now dominant ideology of free consumption more appropriate to this new phase. On the other hand, we must remember that Ferris has a particular reason for calling Cameron: he *needs* him, needs his car to turn his plan of a "day off" into a reality. Similarly, the ideology of consumption that mass culture legitimizes needs the capital that a constructed, desiring consumer will spend to perpetuate itself.

The structures that determine the subject thus become the very subject matter of *Ferris Bueller.* In the action that follows Ferris' phone call to Cameron, we see Cameron trying to decide whether or not to give in to Ferris' demand that he pick him up in his car. But much of the humor of this segment derives from the fact that Ferris and the camera guess—always correctly—what Cameron is thinking to himself. At one point, just as Cameron is about to drive to Ferris' house, he abruptly turns the car off, gets out and disappears back into the house. As the viewer watches Cameron through the back window storming away, the camera never leaves the car seat Cameron has abandoned. It waits patiently for Cameron to return and go get Ferris. Like Ferris, the camera knows what Cameron does not. What appears to be an internal dilemma that Cameron as an autonomous subject must resolve is determined by the ideological structure that dominates him. Evidence supporting this conclusion will accumulate through the course of the film until, at the very end, it serves to undermine Cameron's declarations of self-determination. Thus, while the viewer does indeed come to identify with Cameron, this identification includes the fact that human nature is the end product of a process of internalization, not the source of meaning. In this sense, the film clearly illustrates Pierre Macherey's thesis that the work of art does not so much express ideology as it endows it with aesthetic figuration that ends up enacting the latter's unmasking and self-criticism. Thus, a film that offers a developmental narrative of a character coming to terms with himself unmasks the very process that makes this mystification possible.

After Ferris bullies Cameron into letting him "borrow"

Cameron's father's limited edition 1961 Ferrari to pick up Ferris' girlfriend Sloane from school, the three head into Chicago for the day. After parking the car in a garage, they go to an upscale restaurant at which Ferris impersonates Abe Froman, the sausage king of Chicago. Then they go to a Cubs game, to the Art Institute and finally to a parade. What is worth noting about these scenes is that each takes place in an ideological space that is in no way innocent of the charge levelled explicitly at the schools and implicitly at the family. The presention of the school scenes and Cameron's description of his home life have figured ideology as a repressive force. At the school, boring teachers who pass on stale ideology share space with vindictive administrators like Principal Ed Rooney whose sole purpose appears punitive. At home, parents are either domineering like Cameron's commmodity-fetishizing father (he "loves this car more than life itself," says Cameron) and children are subordinate and fearful or parents are eminently gullible like Ferris' loving, cliché-spewing parents, and children get away with murder. In neither case is there any room for "free" expression and autonomy. The "day off" is the antidote to the alienation that characterizes the schools and the family. But the antidote costs money (especially the restaurant where Ferris even feels the need to slip some money to the snotty maître d'), and the process whereby money is made and distributed unequally falls outside the film's purview.

When Cameron finally appears to be letting go and actually enjoying himself in the way Ferris encourages, he stops worrying for the first time about the condition of his father's favorite fetishized commodity, the Ferrari. The car is literally that and figuratively a condensation point for the contradictions that traverse Cameron's subjectivity. As they are driving home, Cameron notices that the odometer reads over 100 miles higher than it should. The odometer presents inescapable proof of the principal contradiction that has run through the film—the incompatibility of the actions Ferris compels Cameron to undertake as a free subject and the actions expected of Cameron as a dutiful son by his father. Put another way, the odometer registers the contradiction between the imaginary relation to existence that represses class differences and the real relation to existence that is based upon a class-based power discrepancy. Ferris represents the former imaginary relation; the father as "absent cause" is the source of the latter real one. When this contradiction disrupts the forward movement of the narrative, Cameron's (and the viewer's) interpellation is also disrupted. As a result, Cameron lets out a blood-curdling scream, which is sustained as the camera disappears down his open throat. When it reemerges, Cameron is catatonic. For the moment, the contradiction that traverses the ideological apparatus of the social formation has made acting as a "free" subject impossible.

It seems fair to read this moment as an aporia of sorts. Read on its own terms, the film depicts Cameron's process of coming to understand and accept his status as a subject who "works by himself," in Althusser's words. But the film also generates a second reading that suggests that contradiction is a condition of narrative, a condition of ideology. It is the antagonistic relation between these two readings that leads to Cameron's momentary paralysis. From this point on, the film works to recuperate this rupture. And so, the problem of Cameron's subject formation is transformed into one of abstract, psychologized fear. Cameron thus decides to take the heat for the car debacle, despite Ferris' rather lackluster protests. When Cameron claims that he is responsible for his own actions and Ferris smiles, Cameron says, "it is possible to say no to Ferris Bueller, you know." This statement is a reiteration with a difference of Ferris' earlier claim that it is possible for the individual to get outside ideology in leisure activity and consumerism. Only now the invalidity of such a claim is evident. The statement is a false reconciliation of the contradiction that surfaced when Cameron saw the odometer.

Later, when the film proper is over and the credits have rolled, Ferris returns to the screen and tells the audience with feigned irritation that the film is over. "Go on, go home, it's over," he says with a dismissive wave. This suggests that the consumer subject thus constituted through mass culture is a desiring subject based on lack. It suggests that as long as mass culture reigns supreme among the ISAs, the subject will indeed act in the contradictory fashion of Cameron—denying her/his subordination in the productive relations and proving her/his freedom by spending money on leisure pursuits and films like *Ferris Bueller.*

The film in general and the last tableau in particular testify to Hughes' cynicism. Self-reflexivity, now a stock postmodern technique, increases the film's own smirky appeal. It also renders inescapable the erasure of Althusser's distinction between the aesthetic and plain ideology. *Ferris Bueller* produces no alienation effect. Nor does it distantiate the film's own ideology. Rather, it takes consumerism as a given and assumes an audience raised on television and Hollywood. Hughes reinforces this ideology by figuring it as nonideological and contrasting it to the now outmoded school and family that offer obviously subordinate subject positions.

The implication for further work in the Althusserian tradition should now be evident. We need to start with a theory of ideology that exists only in and through subjects, but we must be continually aware of the fact that the configuration of the ISAs is dynamic. While ideology in general is eternal, ideologies are always changing. Moreover, we should resist the trendy temptation to consider postmodernism as "the end of all crises, the end of all narratives, the end of resistance and revolutionary transformation," in Montag's words. The effect of any ideological practice on the specta-

tor cannot be known ahead of time. It will vary according to the different overdetermined and contradictory, constructions of different audiences. *Ferris Bueller* will be most likely to contradict the imaginary and real relations of audience members who don't happen to be white, male and middle-class suburbanites—a contradiction that might potentially lead to spectator resistance to Ferris' "call." But the possibilities for resistance that any cultural artifact might elicit can't be determined solely with the help of theory. They can only be determined through the kind of empirical work necessary to comprehend the text's historical specificity. Althusser provides us with some of the tools for such work, but these alone will not determine what we may find.

Any text of mass culture like *Ferris Bueller* will necessarily bear the marks of contradiction and conflict that traverse the historical moment of its production even if it ends in mystification. These marks are not, however, the unavoidable result of the arbitrariness of language or the impossibility of achieving semantic closure. They are the mark of the history of multiple social struggles. Consumption marks one such social struggle, but only one. To focus exclusively on consumption obscures as much as it illuminates. The prominence of consumption in my reading of *Ferris Bueller* does not contradict this assertion. Consumption is the effect of ideological production, not the antidote. It is an ideology with a history (specifically, emerging at the turn of the century to meet increased industrial production). Shaped by the specific modality of filmic form, the consumer ideal of individuality that Ferris embodies narrates its own unmasking in Cameron's imminent punishment at the hands of his father (which is not shown, of course) and the underlying reality that he will have to get a job someday. The ideology of uninhibited consumerism is thus contradicted most fundamentally by the necessity of employment to make the money necessary to exercise it. It is a banal fact for much of the population, however, that even employment does not lead to free-wheeling spending. More often than not, it brings simple subsistence.

This is the primary contradiction in the film. But it is overdetermined by an educational system that seeks to establish the predispositions appropriate to the division of labor of the economic system and a domestic sphere that is built upon a "natural" and "legitimate" power disparity between adults and teenagers. From an Althusserian perspective, *Ferris Bueller's Day Off* is a cultural artifact that allows for the provisional construction of a model of its society. Such an approach to mass culture rejects belief in either the pure hegemony of the ruling classes or the heroic resistance of exploited men and women who "make their own history." For the key to this famous quotation from *The 18th Brumaire* lies in the next few words: "but they do not make it just as they please." The dialectic between acquiescence and resistance that characterizes mass culture in particular and the

ISAs in general is the Marxist dialectic of history. This dialectic is driven forward continually by conflict and contradiction. In a Marxist theory of history, it could not be otherwise.

George Steiner (review date 21 February 1994)

SOURCE: "Stranglehold," in *The New Yorker,* Vol. LXX, No. 1, February 21, 1994, pp. 115-19.

[*In the following review, Steiner asserts that the scandal surrounding Althusser's life has overshadowed his work.*]

There are moments when bad taste is the last refuge of common sense. Let me be in bad taste. Perhaps philosophers *should* strangle their wives. The name of Socrates' wife has passed into the language as that of an ignorant shrew. Philosophy is an unworldly, abstruse, often egomaniacal obsession. The body is an enemy to absolute logic or metaphysical speculation. The thinker inhabits fictions of purity, of reasoned propositions as sharp as white light. Marriage is about roughage, bills, garbage disposal, and noise. There is something vulgar, almost absurd, in the notion of a Mrs. Plato or a Mme. Descartes, or of Wittgenstein on a honeymoon. Perhaps Louis Althusser was enacting a necessary axiom or logical proof when, on the morning of November 16, 1980, he throttled his wife.

But the master ironist, the joker, is life itself. It is likely that Althusser's writings on Hegel and Marx are already fading into cold dust. Paradoxically, what has vitality in his work is only his collapse into murder and derangement. It is this hideous coda which continues to fascinate, to inspire biography, and to motivate the publication—and, now, the translation into English—of Althusser's apologetic memoir. In French, the title is **L'Avenir Dure Longtemps.** The English title is a gross mistranslation, *longtemps* being, very precisely, not "forever." Either way, the title is more than a touch pretentious and vacuous, as is so much of Althusser's philosophic prose. The haunting marvel, and what will endure *longtemps,* is the initial two and a half pages. I know of no document like them. Ideally, they ought to be cited in full.

"I shall describe what happened—between two zones of darkness, the unknown one from which I was emerging and the one I was about to enter. Here is the scene of the murder just as I experienced it," they begin, and Althusser sets down his recollection with uncanny detail. Often he would massage the neck of his wife, Hélène, he explains. This time, he was massaging the front of her neck:

> I pressed my thumbs into the hollow at the top of
> her breastbone and then, still pressing, slowly

moved them both, one to the left, the other to the right, up towards her ears where the flesh was hard. I continued massaging her in a V-shape. The muscles in my forearms began to feel very tired; I was aware that they always did when I was massaging.

Hélène's face was calm and motionless; her eyes were open and staring at the ceiling.

Never before had Louis Althusser "looked into the face of someone who had been strangled." Utter terror seized him. He screamed "I've strangled Hélène!" and rushed into the empty courtyard (it was a Sunday) of the École Normale, France's hothouse of intellect, in which he made his almost legendary home. He roused the school doctor: "I kept on screaming that I had strangled Hélène and pulled him by the collar of his dressing-gown insisting he come and see her, otherwise I would burn the École down. Étienne did not believe me, saying 'It's impossible.'" Alone for a moment back in his apartment, Althusser took a strip from the tattered window curtains—the couple cultivated deprivation—and "placed it diagonally across Hélène's chest, from her right shoulder to her left breast." A curious gesture: part academic decoration—the hood of an honorary degree—and part pathetic valediction. The doctor came, and gave Althusser an injection. In Althusser's study "someone (I do not know who) was removing books I had borrowed from the École library." This is a Shakespearean touch, unendurably exact in its intimations of academic priorities. What is mere homicide compared with unreturned library books?

The assassin sank into darkness. He came to in Sainte-Anne's, the hospital for the mentally diseased, "I am not sure when." The French mandarinate had swung into action. *Normaliens* are the freemasonry of cultural politics. The Minister of Justice was, of course, an alumnus. By the time the police arrived, Althusser had been spirited to bleak safety. No warrant could be served on a man in a state of total mental collapse. Two months after the murder, legal proceedings were dropped. The philosopher stayed in mental hospitals until 1983. He was then allowed to live alone in the north of Paris, seeing a very few faithful friends and acolytes. Rumor has it that he would now and again stroll the gray streets and call out to passersby, "I am the great Althusser!" He died, of cardiac failure, in a clinic outside Paris on October 22, 1990; he was seventy-two. During the years of isolation and twilight, he composed voluminous autobiographical texts, this book among them. They qualify, correct, and embellish one another. But the same cry of questioning despair rings through them: "Why did I kill Hélène? I cannot find any coherent answer. Nor can the psychiatrists who are now my familiars and contact with reality. Reader, can you?" And it is that cry and the overwhelming truth of the narrative of the deed which compel attention.

Who was *le grand Althusser,* and what formed him? A conventional bourgeois background; fervent Catholicism during adolescence and early manhood; the characteristic Gallic reflex of seeking out confessors and "masters of thought" among his teachers. Captured in June of 1940, at the age of twenty-one, Althusser spent more than four and a half years as a prisoner of war in a *Lager* in Schleswig-Holstein. Material on this period is still to be published, but it may well have been during this long captivity that the first shadows fell. So far as is known, Althusser strove for neither repatriation nor escape. His attitude appears to have been one of resignation and inertia. The truth or the strategic legend of an enduring fatigue—a melancholy and miasma of the soul—caused by these years of impotence attached itself to the rest of Althusser's career. At the École Normale, which he entered after the war, Althusser found a cadre and a climate of sensibility uniquely fitted to his gifts. After completing his studies, he rapidly established himself as a tutor in philosophy and a master in residence. In each successive class, or *promotion,* many of the most brilliant students clustered around the young guru. His tutorials and seminars acquired an almost mystical aura. Some students, however, were repelled. In a recently published memoir by one of them, an incisive French metaphysician, we read, "It was obvious to me from the start that Louis Althusser was mad."

In a twofold motion emblematic of the later nineteen-forties and the nineteen-fifties in the Paris intelligentsia, Althusser joined the Communist Party and went into analysis. As a student at the École, he had undergone bouts of electroshock therapy. Black depressions alternated with periods of formidable, charismatic literary and pedagogic activity. A public debate in which Althusser pulverized Sartre (the detested father figure) established his celebrity at large. With the publication, in 1965, of *Pour Marx* and *Lire "Le Capital,"* two tracts put together with members of his seminars, Althusser's influence was at its greatest. It declined rapidly, owing both to the derisive hostility of official French Communism and to Althusser's ambiguous—indeed, inert—role during the 1968 student uprising.

In 1946, during one of his periods of weariness and enervation, Althusser had met Hélène Rytmann, who in the Resistance had taken the name Légotien. The facts of this crucial relationship remain opaque despite—or, rather, because of—the volume of narrative and conjecture it has generated. Poignantly, Althusser tells of their shared *misère,* of the bruising needs that bound them. If one reads his recollections closely, it appears that she initiated him sexually and represented the only substantive eros in a life otherwise cloistered. Yann Moulier Boutang, the first volume of whose devoted but scrupulously penetrating biography of Althusser has already appeared, says otherwise. There were other and contrastively radiant women in Althusser's life, Moulier Boutang writes, but Hélène's insane suffering when she

sensed or stumbled on these episodes only served to augment her devouring grip. Ugly, neurotic, obsessional in every way, Hélène was also fascinating in her asceticism, in her courage, in her uncompromising intellectuality. (Imagine trying to live with Simone Weil.) Althusser's dependence on her was that of an addict. She ruled his life. Around 1970, she simply moved into his quarters at the École. In what Althusser calls his "hypomanic states," he would turn fiercely on his guardian demon, only to come back to her in penitential despair. A long inferno out of Strindberg, but manifestly indispensable to both parties.

To make matters worse, Hélène had been excluded from the Party. The circumstances are murky in the extreme. (Moulier Boutang hints at fresh light in his second volume.) In any event, this anathema paralyzed Hélène. She demanded of Althusser that he sacrifice whatever time, energies, political pressures he could to her reinstatement. Did he himself know the facts? Gossip—and outside the Vatican there is none more venomous than that in the Communist Party labyrinths—hinted at some unauthorized, possibly sadistic vendetta in which Comrade Légotien had been critically implicated just before or just after the Liberation in Lyons. Whatever the facts, Althusser failed to obtain reparation or Party amnesty for her. This, in turn, aggravated his own sense of isolation and the hysterical litigations between them. Yet his worship remained unshaken. According to him, Hélène's language was more inventive than that of James Joyce. "The softness of her laugh was irresistible." (Others recall an acid cackle.) "Through her ability to listen, her understanding of the human heart, and her genius for understanding she was indeed the equal of the greatest who lived." A classic tale of the unreason of love sings through these pages:

> But what moved me more than anything were her hands, which never changed. They had been fashioned by work and bore the marks of hard physical labour, yet her touch had a wonderful tenderness which betrayed her heartbreak and helplessness. They were the hands of a poor, wretched old woman who had nothing and no one to turn to yet who found it in her heart to go on giving. I was filled with such sorrow at the suffering engraved on them. I have often wept into these hands and they have often made me weep, though I never told her why. I feared it would cause her pain.
>
> Hélène, my Hélène . . .

Here is an historical but genuine descendant of Augustine and Rousseau. If anything of Althusser persists, it will be passages such as this.

In his professional life, Althusser set out to prove that Marxism had been misread not only by the bureaucrats of

Stalinism and by the French Communist Party but by philosophers everywhere. It was not an ideology at all, he maintained, but a rigorous scientific theory (in the sense in which econometrics may be held to be the rigorous scientific theory of our social structure and conduct): Marxism yielded laws of material and social evolution as predictive as those being discovered by Lévi-Strauss in structural anthropology, by Chomsky in generative grammar, by Lacan in psychoanalysis. What mattered more was that such laws entailed political actions—they underwrote a revolutionary praxis as systematic as that of thermodynamic reactions. Political adventurism, "spontaneism," libertarian rhetoric, and the hot air of "humanism" were the enemy. Althusser's disciples thrilled to the promise of a true science of revolution. Cannily, Althusser's style of exposition melds that spice of obscurity essential to recent French doctrines with a contemptuous harshness. His works are "little red books" on a magisterial, canonic level. The very fact that the Party poured derision on these "ivory tower vaporings" only increased their spell.

The misreading is, largely, Althusser's. Marxism is not, and has never been, a rigorous science. Its predictions and theoretical dogma have in the main turned out to be false. Marxism is, rather, a messianic dream of immanent justice. Its source is twofold: the Judaic prophetic vision of human redemption, and the millenarian promise of the French Revolution and European Romanticism. Marx's peers are not the exact scientists but the panoptic dreamers of historical progress and fulfillment, such as Hugo, Michelet, and Wagner. *Pace* Althusser, it is Marx's incensed humanism that has inspired millions of men and women even unto sacrificial death, and it is the recent collapse of that humanistic impulse that has left a black hole in the history of hope.

Did Althusser himself come to realize this? There is substantial testimony that during his late years of dishevelment he tried for some kind of arrangement with the Roman Catholicism of his youth. In 1979, he sought an audience with John Paul II. There is method in the madness. In their doctrinal absolutism, their organization, and their altruistic ideals, Catholicism and utopian Marxism are akin. But then there is hardly an issue on which Althusser did not exhibit divided, possibly schizophrenic sentiments. Various modes of psychoanalysis and psychotherapy punctuated his wretched state. He published a collection of turgid meditations on psychoanalysis, accompanied by letters exchanged with Lacan, and for a long time Lacan was a key presence. Yet in 1980 Althusser turned on the magus with public ferocity.

That Louis Althusser possessed intellectual and pedagogic powers of an unusual order is obvious. So is the role that he played, albeit briefly, in the life of the mind of a certain French élite during the nineteen-sixties. His writings on

Montesquieu, on the continuities between the early and the mature Marx, on the perennial dilemma of the relations between Marxist theories of history and current political practice, especially in regard to the industrial working class, exercise a certain authority, even where they are arbitrary and wrong-headed. The claim that he was among the most influential of Western thinkers on Marxism was for a decade certainly arguable. Today, it has all but faded. And what subsists, as the mere fact of this translation for readers who will never have glanced at the theoretical works of Althusser makes plain, is the piteous scandal of the life.

Why did Althusser kill Hélène?

There can be, as he says over and over in wild desolation, no coherent, summarizing answer. Douglas Johnson, an old friend, reports in the book's informative introduction that Althusser was a sleepwalker, and may have acted wholly unaware, repeating, this time fatally, the massage he frequently used to relieve Hélène's nervous tension. Others whisper that Hélène had decided to end their hermetic coexistence, and Althusser felt he could never endure the break. Romantic conjecture has it that Althusser's love for Hélène had reached pathological excess—that, apprehensive of his own darkening condition, he made certain that they would be together, and singular to one another, always. A few disenchanted observers have hinted that Althusser could no longer stand his companion's crazed possessiveness and the incessant blame she heaped on him for his failure to obtain her reintegration into the Party. She clawed at him until he snapped.

I have no knowledge of the matter. Perhaps each of these hypotheses is partly right. Or could it be that a man inebriate with abstraction, with the elixir of naked thought, will come to perceive that for him the only viable marriage is that with solitude?

Scott McLemee (review date March 1994)

SOURCE: "Breathless: Louis Althusser Loses His Grip," in *Voice Literary Supplement,* No. 123, March, 1994, p. 15.

[*In the following review, McLemee discusses the implications of Althusser's memoir,* The Future Lasts Forever, *on the reading of his work.*]

Marxism is dead, as everybody knows; so is Louis Althusser. And not for the first time, in either case. In 1978, after nearly two decades as the most provocative thinker in the French Communist Party, Althusser told a friend: "My universe of thought has been abolished. I can't think anymore." (No fate closer to death than that, for a philosopher.) The mind exhausted, his body lived on until 1990—collapsing sometime between the Berlin Wall and the Gorbachev regime.

In the interim, Althusser practically disappeared from public life. A popular book on "la pensée '68" relegated his ideas to the status of yesteryear's fad: Althusser's Marxism "irresistibly recalled a recent but evolved past, like the Beatles' music or the early films of Godard." The market in theoretical commodities was finished with him. And then, too, there had been that embarrassing incident, late in 1980, when Althusser strangled his wife to death.

Of the murder itself, Althusser remembered nothing. In *The Future Lasts Forever,* his memoir of the killing and its aftermath, he describes awakening from a blackout to find his fingers massaging Hélène Althusser's neck, her face "calm and motionless," the eyes "open and staring at the ceiling." The fog lifts from his mind. And when it clears, panic sets in: "I noticed the tip of her tongue was showing between her teeth and lips, strange and still."

This moment of unnerving lucidity fell, as Althusser writes, "between two zones of darkness, the unknown one from which I was emerging and the one I was about to enter." Friends would later reveal that Althusser had long suffered from manic depression and had been hospitalized numerous times. Injected with tranquilizers, hurried through the medical-legal process that declared him unfit to stand trial, transported to Sainte-Anne's Hospital, the philosopher then disappeared—or rather was transformed, in the eyes of the law and the press, into a madman.

Insanity, breaking into public space, is always a scandal. And all the more so in this case, for generations of the French cultural and political elites had studied under Althusser at the Ecole Normale, where his colleagues had for decades, it seemed, covered up the fact of his instability. For the French right, the speed with which Althusser was declared unfit for trial made the murder a political sensation. The political catcalls renewed in 1983 with Althusser's release from the hospital. A late photograph shows him with a pathetic, vacant look on his face. In the introduction to his old friend's memoir, Douglas Johnson describes Althusser during his final years, adrift in the streets of northern Paris, "a shabby, ageing figure [who] would startle passers-by as he shouted 'Je suis le grand Althusser.'"

Following his release, Althusser began to prepare the long memoir from which *The Future Lasts Forever* gets its title. It is in many senses a posthumous work, of almost indescribable morbidity. "I am neither alive nor dead. . . ," Althusser writes. "I am simply *missing,* which was Foucault's splendid definition of madness." The memoir was his effort "to remove the weight of the tombstone which lies over me." Composition of this manuscript occupied Althusser from

1985 until his death. To it the editor has appended a much shorter autobiographical fragment from 1976, "The Facts." Reading them together is apt to be unsettling for anyone who knows Althusser primarily through his *magna opera* of 1965, **For Marx** and **Reading "Capital."**

Denied by law the chance to testify in public, Althusser seeks desperately, interminably, to chart the genesis and structure of his mental disorders and to find some meaning in the violent act that ended his companion's life. Gregory Elliott's superb intellectual and political biography, *Althusser: The Detour of Theory,* barely mentions its subject's depressions and the murder. In the autobiography, for some 360 pages, they are the prism through which his entire life and career are figured.

Althusser writes like someone long accustomed to the therapeutically induced habit of rummaging through the lumber room of the preconscious, of memory and half-repressed fantasy. The texts make an exhaustive trip through the details of his childhood and adolescence, and prepare a carefully annotated catalogue of obsessions: with VD and sexual inadequacy; with self-loathing and a persistent sense of being a fraud; with his mother and (strangest by far) General De Gaulle. There is a certain amount of do-it-yourself Lacanian analysis here. The fact that young Louis bore the name of a father dead before his birth proves not merely significant but decisive. So does the fact that in his surname lurk Alsatian puns: "Althusser" equals both "old teeth" and "old houses." Seldom has Karl Krauss's maxim that psychoanalysis is the very disease for which it pretends to offer a cure seemed more apt.

A tragic inevitability suffuses all details of Althusser's relationship with Hélène. As Althusser recounts it, he first suffered a depression requiring hospitalization after their initial love making. Their marriage was, to understate it, tempestuous. Althusser (and others) often characterized Hélène as "difficult," while he was, he admits, a philanderer and emotionally cold. "To all appearances, which are so readily accepted (because it is so much easier!), we were a sado-masochistic couple, incapable of breaking the vicious circle of our own dramatic anger, hatred, and mutual destructiveness." Yet, in spite of its dogged efforts, Althusser's memoir never reveals any truth that this "appearance" might belie.

The murder emerges, in the final pages of *The Future Lasts Forever,* as a sort of displaced suicide. Someone trained in the clinical practice of attending to the discourse of manic depression might read such a text with the distance needed to bracket out its enormous affective charge. For anyone else, I suspect, *The Future Lasts Forever* will prove harrowing—and infuriating. Althusser appears in it as such a monster of self-absorption that one scarcely gets a sense of Hélène, his wife and his victim. And the overwhelming sense of fate that propels the narrative seems to preclude much depth of regret. The murder becomes purely a manifestation of that self-destructiveness for which Althusser has been searching, throughout the memoir, to find a source and a meaning.

After finishing this long, depressive text, it is a jolt to read **"The Facts"**—a jocular essay from the mid 1970s composed, evidently, during a manic period. It covers much the same material discussed in portions of *The Future Lasts Forever,* with strange discrepancies, not the least of which concerns whether Althusser voted to expel his wife from the Communist Party. (In *The Future,* he claims he voted for expulsion; in **"The Facts,"** against.) Althusser also claims to have had private channels to the Pope and De Gaulle and to have stolen a nuclear submarine.

In these memoirs, the cool, magisterial tone of his theoretical works all but disappears. Plainly Althusser was no master in the old house of the ego. And yet somehow he managed; only fairly late in his career did the delirium break wholly out of control. Bouts of severe depression were such a regular part of Althusser's life that he learned to work around them, between them, rushing to finish work before the next, inevitable crash. His writings and seminars from the 1960s and '70s had sought to transform Marx's ideas into a conceptual system as rigorous as mathematics, to purge them of any "humanist" or "historicist" taint. Now, in retrospect, the theorist's drive for precision seems like a desperate effort to contain, and to repress, that violence suffusing the memoirist's narratives.

The Future Lasts Forever unfortunately renders such overneat, "psychologistic" interpretation of Althusser's major writings almost irresistibly tempting—particularly (as I must admit in my own case) for someone already pretty dubious about their conceptual and philological rigor. Throughout the book, Althusser reveals a deep ambivalence about his own work: confidence about its contribution to Marxist thought mixed with the most self-lacerating admissions of how little of Hegel or Marx he had actually read. He claims to have read the first volume of *Capital* just in time to conduct a seminar on it—no crime for a minor professor, but rather pathetic coming from the Communist Party's great theoretical hope.

"Phrases I came across or picked up," Althusser explains, "were like 'philosophical core samples,' on the basis of which I was easily able to determine (using analytical methods) what the deeper levels of a particular philosophy were. Then, and only then, was I able to read the text from which the sample came. Thus I read a limited number of texts extremely closely, and naturally as rigorously as I could, without knowing in advance any semantic or syntagmatic details." Issuing a flow of discourse without knowledge of

"semantic or syntagmatic details" is a practice familiar enough from the academic world, where it is sometimes called bullshitting.

Had *The Future Lasts Forever* appeared during the Cold War, one would have expected a sustained campaign around it in the right-wing press here: the Communist as murderer, the Marxist as lunatic. And in Britain—where his theoretical work left its stamp not only on the cultural-studies movement but also on some intellectuals in the Labour Party—Althusser's memoir received vicious attentiveness in the papers. His impact on the nonacademic left in the United States was slight, although it was debated in the pages of dissident communist journals such as *Urgent Tasks, Theoretical Review,* and *Line of March* some years ago. Today, of course, every theory junky knows his essays on the Ideological State Apparatuses, plus maybe a couple of others. If our Hilton Kramers and William Bennetts take notice of Althusser's memoirs at all, it will be to bait not U.S. communists but the multiculturati—our comrades in armchairs who pursue, as Althusser did in his prescient way, the long march through the institutions. A preemptive campaign may be in order. Hands off Althusser! Leave the poor, crazy, dead man in peace.

Tony Judt (review date 7 March 1994)

SOURCE: "The Paris Strangler," in *The New Republic,* Vol. 210, No. 10, March 7, 1994, pp. 33-7.

[*In the following review, Judt states that in Althusser's* The Future Lasts Forever *"We are presented not only with a man who is on the edge of insanity, obsessed with sexual imagery . . . dreams of grandeur and his own psychoanalytical history, but also with a man who is quite remarkably ignorant."*]

I was brought up a Marxist. Nowadays that is not much of a boast, but it had its advantages. Parents and grandparents were imbued with all of the assumptions and some of the faith that shaped the European Socialist movement in its heyday. Coming from that branch of East European Jewry that had embraced Social Democracy and the Bund (the Jewish Labor organization of early twentieth-century Russia and Poland), my own family was viscerally anti-Communist. In its eyes, Bolshevism was not only a dictatorship, it was also—and this, too, was a serious charge—a travesty of Marxism. By the time I went to university, I had been thoroughly inoculated with all the classical nineteenth-century texts; and as a result I was immune to the wide-eyed enthusiasm with which Marxist revelations were greeted by those of my freshmen peers who were discovering them for the first time.

Thus, when I arrived in Paris as a graduate student in the late '60s, I was skeptically curious to see and to hear Louis Althusser. In charge of the teaching of philosophy at the Ecole Normale Supérieure, the French elite academy for future teachers and leaders, Althusser was touted by everyone I met as a man of extraordinary gifts, who was transforming our understanding of Marx and reshaping revolutionary theory. His name, his ideas, his books were everywhere. Sitting in on his crowded and sycophantic seminar, I was utterly bemused. For Althusser's account of Marxism, to the extent that I could make any sense of it, bore no relation to anything I had ever heard. It chopped Marx into little bits, selected those texts or parts of texts that suited the master's interpretation and then proceeded to construct the most astonishingly abstruse, self-regarding and ahistorical version of Marxist philosophy imaginable. The exercise bore no discernible relationship to Marxism, to philosophy or to pedagogy. After a couple of painful attempts to adapt myself to the experience and to derive some benefit from it, I abandoned the seminar and never went back.

Returning to the subject many years later, and constrained for professional reasons to read Althusser's mercifully few published works, I understood a little better what had been going on, intellectually and sociologically. Althusser was engaged in what he and his acolytes called a "symptomatic reading" of Marx, which is to say that they took from him what they needed and ignored the rest. Where they wished Marx to have said or meant something that they could not find in his writings, they interpreted the "silences," thereby constructing an entity of their own imagination. This thing they called a science, one that Marx was said to have invented and that could be applied, gridlike, to all social phenomena.

Why invent a Marxist "science" when so much was already at hand, the Marxist "theory of history," "historical materialism," "dialectical materialism" and the rest? The answer is that Althusser, like so many others in the '60s, was trying to save Marxism from the two major threats to its credibility: the grim record of Stalinism and the failure of Marx's revolutionary forecasts. Althusser's special contribution was to remove Marxism altogether from the realm of history, politics and experience, and thereby to render it invulnerable to any criticism of the empirical sort.

In Althusser-speak, Marxism was a theory of structural practices: economic, ideological, political, theoretical. It had nothing to do with human volition or agency, and thus it was unaffected by human frailty or inadequacy. These "practices" determined history. Their respective importance, and their relationship to one another, varied with circumstances; the "dominant structure" was sometimes "economic practice" and sometimes "political practice," and so on. Of particular significance was the notion of "theoretical practice." This

oxymoronic phrase, which came to be chanted, mantralike, all over Europe in those years, had the special charm of placing intellectuals and intellectual activity on the same plane as the economic organizations and the political strategies that had preoccupied earlier generations of Marxists.

> **Althusser's account of Marxism, to the extent that I could make any sense of it, bore no relation to anything I had ever heard. It chopped Marx into little bits, selected those texts or parts of texts that suited the master's interpretation and then proceeded to construct the most astonishingly abstruse, self-regarding and ahistorical version of Marxist philosophy imaginable.**
> **—Tony Judt**

This subjectless theory of everything had a further virtue. By emphasizing the importance of theory, it diverted attention from the embarrassing defects of recent practice. In such an account, Stalin's crime was not that he had murdered millions of human beings, it was that he had perverted the self-understanding of Marxism. Stalinism, in short, was just another mistake in theory, albeit an especially egregious one, whose major sin consisted of its refusal to acknowledge its own errors. This was important to Althusser, who was a member of the French Communist Party and who sought to admit the embarrassing history of that organization without undermining whatever remained of its claim to revolutionary omniscience. The Party's leadership itself had responded to this conundrum by belatedly treating Stalin as an unfortunate but parenthetical episode in the otherwise unblemished record of communism. His crimes were a mere deviation born of the cult of personality. But Althusser went one better by showing that "Stalin" and his works constituted only a collective analytical error. This performed the double service of keeping personalities out of the matter and reiterating the centrality of concepts.

It is hard, now, to recapture the mood of the '60s in which this absurd dialectical joust seemed appealing. But Althusser unquestionably filled a crucial niche. He gave young Maoists an impressively high-flown language in which to be "antihumanist" Communists, dismissive of the "Italian road" to socialism. At the time this was a matter of some importance: the early works of Marx, notably the *Economic and Philosophical Manuscripts,* had only recently entered the canon, having for many years languished unknown and untranslated. Placed alongside his other youthful writings, they suggested a rather different Marx from the conventional image passed down from Engels via the popularizers of the early European Socialist movements; a man more interested in Romantic-era philosophy than in classical economics, an idealist whose agenda was not simply social revolution but the moral transformation of mankind. The interest in this "humanist". Marx had been aroused both by the recent French rediscovery of Hegel and by a new generation of radical intellectuals seeking to locate Marx in something other than the lineage imposed upon the European left by the doctrinaire positivism of Leninism.

Taking his cue from the growing fashion for "structuralism" (initially confined to linguistics and anthropology, but by the early '60s seeping into sociology and philosophy), Althusser worked hard to excommunicate this humanist and understandably more appealing Marx as "unscientific." In his view, to emphasize the moral condition and responsibilities of individual men was to detract from an appreciation of the larger, impersonal forces at work in history, and thus to delude the workers, or anyone else, into believing they could act on their own behalf, instead of accepting the authority of those who spoke and thought for them. In his words, "only theoretical anti-humanism justifies general practical humanism."

To flesh out his structuralist account, Althusser invented something that he and his followers called "Ideological State Apparatuses." In his heyday these were confined to the public and political world. In his memoirs, however, his attention was diverted to more personal matters. Althusser informs us that "it is an irrefutable fact that the Family is the most powerful State Ideological Apparatus" (obligatory capitals), and in reflecting upon his experience in the mental hospital he wonders "what can now be done to free the mentally ill from the Hell created for them by the combined operations of all the Ideological State Apparatuses." In Althusserian dogma the presence of these repressive and all-embracing ogres was held particularly responsible for the inconvenient stability and durability of liberal democracy. Of special note was the announcement that the university was, of all of these, the dominant one for our era. "Theoretical practice" in the academic arena was thus the site of ideological battle; and philosophy was absolutely vital as the "class struggle in theory." Scholars in their seminars were on the front line, and need feel guilty no more.

Althusser borrowed a term from the philosopher Gaston Bachelard and announced that an "epistemological break" in Marx's writings had occurred somewhere in the mid-1840s. Everything he wrote before the break was neo-Hegelian humanist flannel and could be ignored. Henceforth left-wing students and lecturers were free to jettison those bits of (the early) Marx that seemed to speak of alienation, reconciliation, human agency and moral judgment. This was hard for many people in the '60s to swallow. In Italy and in the English-speaking world, most young left-wingers were more attracted to the idea of a gentler, kinder Marx. In France, however, where the sordid political compromises of the Socialists and Communists during the battle over decolonization had left a sour taste among some of their younger supporters, this static, structuralist Marx sounded analytically pure and politically uncompromising.

By the end of the '70s, however, Althusser's star was on the wane. He had been absent during the events of May 1968, and had showed little interest in the political developments of that year. His only direct comment on the "failed revolution" of 1968 was characteristic and revealing: "When revolt ends in defeat without the workers being massacred, it is not necessarily a good thing for the working class which has no martyrs to mourn or commemorate." Even his erstwhile followers admitted that he had nothing new to offer, and his rigid stance in defense of Marxism, communism and "the revolution" made him appear irrelevant in a decade that saw the publication in France of *The Gulag Archipelago,* the tragedy in Cambodia, the eclipse of Mao and the steady loss of radical faith among a generation of French intellectuals. Had matters been left there, Althusser could have looked forward to a peaceful and obscure old age, a curious relic of a bizarre but forgotten era.

But then, on November 16, 1980, he murdered his wife Hélène in their apartment at the Ecole Normale. Or, as the jacket copy of The New Press's translation of his memoir coyly puts it, "while massaging his wife's neck [he] discovered he had strangled her." (To be fair, this is how Althusser himself explained the event; but it is curious to find the claim reproduced unattributed on the book.) Althusser was examined by doctors, found to be mentally unfit to stand trial and locked away in a psychiatric hospital. Three years later he was released and spent his last years in a dreary flat in north Paris, emerging occasionally to startle passers-by with "Je suis le grand Althusser!" It was in these years that he drafted two versions of an autobiography. They were found after his death in 1990, and first published in French, as a single book, in 1992.

These "memoirs" are curious. Althusser would have us read them as Rousseau-like confessions, but that is hard to do, and the comparison is embarrassingly unflattering to their author. They are clearly an attempt on Althusser's part to make sense of his madness, and to that extent they are indeed revealing; by his own account he wrote them "to free myself from the murder and above all from the dubious effects of having been declared unfit to plead" (it is ironic that their posthumous impact on any unprejudiced reader will surely be to confirm the original forensic diagnosis). As a genre, however, they really come closer to magical realism. The book, especially a short early draft incongruously titled "The Facts," is full of fantasies and imagined achievements, so much so that it is sometimes hard to disentangle the fictive Althusser from the rather mundane creature whose sad story emerges in these pages.

That story is soon told. Althusser was born in 1918, the eldest child of middle-class French parents in Algeria. His father was a banker whose career took him back to Marseilles in Louis's adolescent years. The young Althusser had an utterly uneventful early career. Academically promising, he was sent to the lycée in Lyons to prepare for the entrance exam to the Ecole Normale. He passed the exam, but had to postpone his higher education when he was drafted into the army in 1939. Like many French soldiers, he had a futile war; his company was rounded up by the Germans in 1940, and he spent the next five years in a prisoner of war camp. About the only interesting thing that seems to have happened to him there was that he learned, somewhat belatedly, the pleasures of masturbation. (He was not to make love for the first time until he was 29.)

Finally admitted to the Ecole upon his return to France, Althusser did well there, coming second in the national philosophy examinations. Having spent his adolescence and his youth as an active young Catholic, he discovered left-wing politics at the Ecole and joined the Communist Party in 1948, which was about the time when other young intellectuals, nauseated and shocked by its Stalinist culture and tactics, were beginning to leave it. Shortly after graduating, Althusser obtained a teaching post at the Ecole and settled into the quiet, secure life of an academic philosopher. He was to stay in the same post until being forcibly retired in the aftermath of the scandal that ended his career.

It was during his student years that Althusser met his future wife, Hélène Légotien (she had abandoned her family name, Rytmann, during the war), a woman nine years his senior who had played an active part in the Communist Resistance. As he acknowledges in his memoir, it was a troubled, even tormented relationship. They were held together by bonds of mutual destructiveness. By 1980, he writes, "the two of us were shut up together in our own private hell." Hélène seems to have been an unhappy woman, insecure, tormented and bitter—and with good reason. The Communist Party abandoned her after the war, falsely accusing her of some obscure act of betrayal during the Resistance. Uneasy with her own immigrant Jewish background, and desperate for the love and attention of her husband, she put up with his moods, his women-friends and his colleagues, most of whom looked down on her from the very great height of their own vaunted intellectual standing. She was clearly not a person comfortable with herself or others; and Althusser's own bizarre personality can only have made matters worse.

For what emerges clearly from his own account is that Althusser was always a deeply troubled person. This memoir is warped and curdled by his morbid self-pity, by his in-

security and the repeated invocation of Lacanian clichés to account for his troubles. Indeed, the book's main theme is his own psychological and social inadequacy, a defect for which he naturally holds his parents responsible, in equal parts. His mother's insistence on naming him for a dead uncle is blamed for his lifelong sense of "not existing": Louis being homonymic with the word "lui," meaning "him," the young Althusser's name rendered him impersonal and anonymous. (He seems not to have given much thought to the millions of happy Louis among his fellow countrymen.) According to Althusser, his mother "castrated" him with her excessive care and attention; hence his belated discovery of women and his inability to form satisfactory relations with them. And so it goes, for page after page. Small wonder that when Louis does away with his wife, after forty years of manic-depressive bouts, hospitalization, treatment and analysis, we learn that he was taking his revenge on the older woman who not only brought him to Communism but substituted, as he admits, for mother and father alike.

There is a human tragedy here, but it is presented in a breathtakingly narcissistic key. Althusser wrote this memoir not in order to comprehend why he killed his wife, but to show himself and others that he was sane. He had been, as he puts it, "deprived of his status as a philosopher" by being declared unfit to plead, and this final loss of identity, this fear that once again he would "not exist," seems to have been the driving compulsion behind his autobiography. (Other, less exalted murderers have suffered rather greater deprivations, of course, but this, too, our author overlooks.) If we take him at his word, this fear of "not existing" was the very engine that propelled his life's work. By elaborating a doctrine in which human volition and human action counted for nought, in which theoretical speculation was the supreme practice, Althusser could compensate for a life of gloomy, introspective inaction by asserting and legitimizing his existence in the arena of the text. As he says, "I . . . emerged as the victor, in the realm of pure thought."

This much, at least, we can learn from the memoir, and it casts interesting new light on the otherwise inexplicably murky and self-referential quality of the earlier philosophical writings. Althusser was reconstructing Marx to give his own life a shape with which he could live, and one that could stand respectable comparison with those of his father (a successful banker) and his wife (a Resistance fighter). We thus learn from this book that Althusser was conscious, in every sphere of his life, of "having practiced a great deception," though it never seems to have occurred to him that this insight bodes ill for the credibility of his intellectual legacy. Unfortunately for its author, however, the book reveals much more. We are presented not only with a man who is on the edge of insanity, obsessed with sexual imagery (a stick of asparagus is "stiff as a man's penis" and so on), dreams of grandeur and his own psychoanalytical history, but also with a man who is quite remarkably ignorant.

He seems to know nothing of recent history. (Among his howlers is an indictment of the "Polish fascist" Pilsudski for starting the Second World War.) He seems only late in life to have discovered Machiavelli and other classics of Western philosophy, and he even admits to a skimpy and partial acquaintance with Marx's texts (something one might have inferred from his published work). He is also unsophisticated to the point of crudity in his political analysis. He seems to have learned nothing and to have forgotten nothing in the last twenty years of his life. Thus there is much talk of "the hegemony of bourgeois, imperialist capitalism"; and he is dismissive of the dissidents of the Soviet bloc ("cut off from their own people") and contemptuous of writers like André Glucksmann for "putting around unbelievable horror stories of the Gulag." Those words were written in 1985!

One puts down this depressing book with an overwhelming sense of bewilderment. How could it be that so many intelligent and educated people were taken in by this man? Even if we allow that his manic fancies met some widespread need in the '60s, how are we to account for the continuing fascination that he exercises in certain circles today? In France he is largely forgotten, though the jacket blurb by Didier Eribon describes the autobiography as "magnificent" and explains that "madness [is] the inevitable price of philosophy." It is a conclusion whose deductive logic and historical accuracy are truly in the Althusserian tradition; but Eribon is a French journalist who has made a career of playing the fawning hyena to the preening lions of Parisian intellectual life, and he is not representative.

In the United States, however, there are still university research centers that devote time and money to the study of Althusser's thought, and mount expensive conferences at which professors lecture one another earnestly about "Althusserianism" in everything from linguistics to hermeneutics. Meanwhile respectable English-language publishers continue to market books with titles like *The Althusserian Legacy, Althusser and the Detour of Theory, Reading Althusser, Althusser and the Renewal of Marxist Social Theory* and, inevitably, *Althusser and Feminism,* most of them unreadable excursions into the Higher Drivel.

Althusser was not a charlatan. He himself really believed that he had discovered something significant—or was about to discover something significant—when his illness struck. It is not because he was mad that he was a mediocre philosopher; indeed, the recognition of his own intellectual mediocrity may have contributed to his depressions, and thence to his loss of sanity. If there is something humiliating about the Althusserian episode in intellectual history, then, the humiliation is not his alone. He was a guru, complete with

texts, a cult and true believers; and he showed occasional insight into the pathos of his followers, noting that they imitated his "smallest gestures and inflections."

Althusser's work and his life, with his drugs, his analysts, his self-pity, his illusions and his moods, take on a curiously hermetic quality. He comes to resemble some minor medieval scholastic, desperately scrabbling around in categories of his own imagining. But even the most obscure theological speculation usually had as its goal something of significance. From Althusser's musings, however, nothing followed. They were not subject to proof and they had no intelligible worldly application, except as abstruse political apologetics. What does it say about modern academic life that such a figure can have trapped teachers and students for so long in the cage of his insane fictions, and traps them still?

Alice Kaplan (review date 13 March 1994)

SOURCE: "A Living Death," in *The Los Angeles Times Book Review,* March 13, 1994, pp. 4, 8.

[*In the following review, Kaplan asserts that "The lucidity of a man condemned by his madness to a living death is perhaps what gives* [The Future Lasts Forever] *its chilling edge."*]

On Nov. 16, 1980, Louis Althusser, the leading philosophical and political theorist of French Marxism, strangled his wife, Hélène Rytman, in their suite at the Ecole Normale Superieure, an elite institute for the training of the French professoriate where he had lived, first as a student, then as a professor, for 34 years.

Many received the news of his crime as a symbol of the demise of European communism. Those who knew Althusser understood that whatever fit of madness induced him to strangle Hélène was not brought on by the world of politics. The elegant theorist, the man who redefined the concept of "ideology" as "our imaginary relationship to real conditions of existence" and who fought against a purely economistic interpretation of the works of Marx, had shuttled back and forth between the Ecole Normale and the psychiatric Hospital Sainte Anne at regular intervals for many, many years.

As a result of the murder of his wife, Louis Althusser was declared unfit to stand trial by reason of insanity—in French, this is called a *non-lieu.* This verdict preceded and preempted a trial. The *non-lieu* saved Althusser from the nightmare of a trial, and possible condemnation, but its consequences were enormous. As a person deemed unfit to plead, he lost his right to a trial—that is the right to testify and be held responsible for his actions; he lost his right to enter into contract (his affairs would be handled by a legal guardian) and hence by extension—at least symbolically—his signature, his authorship.

Althusser, calling himself a "missing person," claims to be writing his memoir from this "non-place." He writes not as some latter-day Chateaubriand, from beyond the grave: He writes buried alive.

Following the murder, Althusser was committed to psychiatric internment for a period of three years, after which he retired quietly to an apartment far from the Ecole Normale. There he wrote the second of the two memoirs published in this volume, which were donated after his death in 1990 to the IMEC, the Institute for the Memory of Contemporary Publishing in Paris. (The IMEC houses archives of a number of French writers, including Celine, Genet and Paulhan). Olivier Corpet, the director of the IMEC, prepared the Althusser manuscripts for posthumous publication along with Yann Moulier Boutang, Althusser's biographer.

Their editors' forward, like the introduction to a very good mystery tale, frames what follows with a statement of the basic facts and with provocative questions for the reader: "How is it that such a story can move into the realm of madness, yet its author remain so aware? How does one come to terms with the author of a book of this kind?"

Althusser's story, they argue, is both the work of a madman and of a philosopher, both a work of imagination and a document about contemporary French intellectual history. Part I, **"The Future Lasts a Long Time,"** was written in 1985. It is structured as a flashback, beginning with the scene of crime—the night of the strangulation—and moving backward to Althusser's relationship with his mother, his upbringing, his relationship with Hélène, his intellectual formation and the escalating mental illness that would lead to the murder. Part II, **"The Facts,"** written before the murder in 1976, is straightforward and condensed, reiterating the themes of part one in a lighter mode.

The lucidity of a man condemned by his madness to a living death is perhaps what gives this book its chilling edge. Althusser's sense, since childhood, of his own nonexistence is at its core. He was named after his mother's great love: When Louis died at Verdun in World War I, Althusser's mother would marry Louis' brother, Charles, and name their son for the dead love. Althusser is a brilliant close reader of his given name:

> For a long time, Louis was a name I literally detested. It was too short . . . and ended in the sharp "ee" sound which offended me. . . . Doubtless it also said yes [*oui*] a little too readily on my behalf,

and I rebelled against this "yes," which corresponded to my mother's desire rather than to mine. Above all, it contained the sound of the third person pronoun (*lui*) which deprived me of any personality of my own, summoning as it did an anonymous other. It referred to my uncle, the man who stood behind me: "Lui" [him] was Louis. It was him my mother loved, not me. . . . My mother's love, directed through me to someone who was dead, made it impossible for me to exist in my own right.

Douglas Johnson, a former student of Althusser's, argues in an introduction designed for readers outside France that one should not take Althusser too seriously when he insists that he was something of a fraud as a thinker. This is just the kind of joke, Johnson surmises, that brilliant Ecole Normale students like to make about never having to study. He's doubtless right on target about students at the Ecole, but not about Althusser.

The sensation of fraudulence was deeply bound up with Althusser's self-definition, his depression, his imagination. The passages where he explores his own success, and his concomitant feelings of being a fake (his ability to charm, to reduce things to a formula), are among the most critical moments in the book. He writes: "In fact my philosophical knowledge of texts was rather limited. . . . I felt (what an illusion!) that I was capable of working out, if not the specific ideas at least the general drift or direction of an author or a book I had not read, on the basis of a simple turn of phrase. I obviously had certain intuitive powers as well as a definite ability for seeing connections, or a capacity for establishing theoretical oppositions, which enabled me to reconstruct what I took to be an author's idea on the basis of the authors to whom he was opposed."

This confession does not lessen our sense of Althusser's contribution to the history of philosophy—his theories, by now, have taken on a life of their own, separate from his life—but it heightens our sense of his self-loathing. Each successful writing project would be followed by anguish, and a breakdown.

What Althusser proves in *The Future Lasts Forever* is that in addition to his talents for theoretical work, he had a real genius for storytelling. The feeling of having "gotten away with murder" all his life is what makes the literal murder of his wife make such terrifying good sense. His writing ranks with Gide's for narcissistic self-condemnation and with James M. Cain's for sheer creepiness and a sense of evil. The clarity of his French formulations are inevitably somewhat muted in English, but Richard Veasey's British translation works. I liked the choice of *The Future Lasts Forever* as the title for the two-part volume, instead of the original French, which would have translated literally as *The Future Lasts a Long Time Followed by the Facts: Autobiographies.*

The idea of a future lasting forever captures perfectly our sense that Althusser was condemned by his murder to a living death. As a reader I had the uncanny feeling of inhabiting Althusser's thoughts; repulsed and fascinated by him, as he was by himself, I was terrified and compelled to read on. Who, I kept asking myself, was Hélène, the woman portrayed on Page 1, already dead, the tip of her tongue showing between her teeth and lips?

I learned that after the first time Althusser made love to her (he was a virgin at age 30; she was 38) he vowed never to do it again and needed to be hospitalized for anguish; that she was purged from the French Communist Party on suspicion of betraying the Resistance and that Althusser didn't believe the charges but voted to purge her in a moment of cowardice; that he tortured her by seducing other women in her presence; that his friends resented her; that, with the pressure of taking care of him, she became every bit the witch they imagined. We may need to wait for the translation of Yann Moulier Boutang's biography to learn more about Hélène Rytman's own story. The way Althusser himself tells it, the real incentive for murder was all hers. . . .

Paul Mattick Jr. (review date 25 May 1994)

SOURCE: "Murder, He Wrote," in *The Nation,* Vol. 258, No. 16, May 25, 1994, pp. 566-68.

[*In the following review, Mattick analyzes Althusser's attempt to understand his murder of his wife, but asserts that "Unfortunately, the book must be judged a failure as an effort at self-understanding."*]

The publication of the English translation of Louis Althusser's memoir has provoked a lively response among the local intelligentsia. People are talking about it, and it has been widely reviewed. This interest is no doubt traceable in part at least to the sensational aspect of the French philosopher's story: his 1980 strangling of his wife, Hélène, in their apartment in the École Normale, the elite university where he had taught and lived since getting his degree there soon after World War II. This was not a matter of some unknown academic beating a prostitute to death with a hammer (as a Tufts professor did some years ago, inspiring interest mostly among true-crime devotees) but the burning fall of a world-class intellectual. It is not so often that someone moves like a comet from the Parisian heights of Theory into the tabloid domain of the Bobbitts and the Menendez brothers, and this is bound to excite.

Most commentary, however, has not stressed the lurid angle. Writing in *The New Yorker,* George Steiner suggested a high-toned defense, weirdly wondering whether *all* philosophers shouldn't strangle their wives—"There is something vulgar, almost absurd, in the notion of a Mrs. Plato or a Mme. Descartes, or of Wittgenstein on a honeymoon." How could a man "inebriated with abstraction" bear to live with . . . a woman? Scott McLemee pleads in *The Village Voice* with future commentators to "leave the poor, crazy, dead man in peace." Tony Judt, New York University expert on French intellectuals, devoted most of his *New Republic* review to the inanity of Althusser's version of Marxist theory, which amounted to no more than "abstruse . . . apologetics" for the Communist Party. The strangling, and the evidence of the memoir, only confirmed for Judt the diagnosis suggested by the theoretical works. For him the *cas Althusser* chiefly raises the question, "What does it say about modern academic life that such a figure can have trapped teachers and students for so long in the cage of his insane fictions, and traps them still?" (Judt doesn't, alas, try to answer this interesting question, which one might well extend to wonder about the mass acceptance of such theoretically and practically ineffective fields as economics, or the apologetic character—abstruse or crude—of most political science.)

Althusser was actually already disappearing from scholarly view by the end of 1980, when the murder took place. Foucault, and to a lesser degree Lacan, had decisively conquered the francophile center stage, and Bourdieu was waiting in the wings. This was quite a change: Just five years earlier, Althusser's name had decorated bibliographies throughout the humanities and the social sciences and was invoked by left-wingers even outside the professoriate. The decline of his renown is not to be traced to growing sophistication about Marxist theory generally or powerful critiques of Althusser's reading of *Capital* in particular (despite the splendid effort of E. P. Thompson in his *The Poverty of Theory*). It was due, rather, to the ebbing of social movements, in particular among students, in the course of the 1970s. This reflux brought a steady loss of interest in radical theory, especially when centered on the concept of class. As they withdrew deeper into the university system academics kept alive some sense of their earlier high spirits by dressing commonplaces of yesteryear in the new clothes of deconstruction and Lacanian theory, and by concentrating the force of discourse on sexuality and "the body," always exciting topics. Marxism-Leninism, even in its obscure Althusserian form, had to go.

The strangling seems in a manner of speaking to have brought Althusser back from the dead, even as it consigned his wife to the real thing and himself to the twilight zone of mental hospitals. He hadn't gone away; now like a zombie he haunted the groves of academe, the scandal of his act stirring some awareness of the scandal of the subjection of intellectual life to fashion. Perhaps after all he was a genius, too smart for this world; or he was a nut all along, and only the foolishness of the sixties let people who refused to accept the failures of Marxism be taken in.

Of course, the truth is more complex: Althusser was neither a genius nor just a nut. As he tells the story in his memoir, he was born in Algeria in 1918 to middle-class French parents, who returned to France as his father moved up the hierarchy in the bank he worked for. He passed the entrance examination for the École Normale, but was drafted into the army in 1939 and didn't enter the school until after the war, which he spent in a German P.O.W. camp. An active Catholic as a youth, he entered the Communist Party in 1948; around the same time he met Hélène, who was expelled from the party on dubious charges. (In *The Future Lasts Forever* he says he joined in the vote to expel; in a briefer memoir printed along with it he hints that he didn't.) This inevitably painful situation for the couple fitted all too easily into the tormented pattern of their relationship. Prone throughout his life to periods of severe depression, Althusser seems to have been both dependent on and cruel to a wife with serious troubles of her own. Nonetheless, he professes a lifetime of love on the way to killing her.

Meanwhile, he had become an academic star. In his 1965 volumes *For Marx* and *Reading Capital,* Althusser argued that Marxist philosophers should not elaborate a general worldview but provide a foundation for a science of history. For young Communists, this brought welcome relief from the French party's promotion of "proletarian science," long including Lysenkoist biology. While thus aiding de-Stalinization, Althusser's analysis aimed at modernizing Marxism-Leninism, reframing it in structuralist terms and borrowing the fashionable concept of the "epistemological break" from the philosophy of science to emphasize the discontinuities between Marxism and earlier theory (to relate this to American developments: Althusser spoke of "problematics" where Thomas Kuhn invoked "paradigms"). His opposition to "humanism" not only preserved the traditional insistence that Marxism is a science but established connections with the critique of human subjecthood being worked out in different frameworks by Foucault and others.

Althusser claims in *The Future Lasts Forever* that at the time he published those two books he "knew almost nothing about the history of philosophy or about Marx." Whether he is bragging or confessing, it is true that in his writings insights lie side by side with striking errors, and his contribution to the understanding of Marx's work is finally a slight one. Nevertheless, his work was taken up by students, especially those attracted to Maoism by the myth of the Cultural Revolution. Disciplined by the party in 1966 for doctrinal independence, Althusser turned to a more conventional conception of Marxist-Leninist philosophy as "class struggle in

theory." He also accepted the party's line in May-June 1968, when, as he says in his memoir, "out of fear of the masses and fear of losing control (reflecting its permanent obsession with the primacy of organization over popular movements), the Party did all it could to break the popular movement." He quit the organization only after he killed Hélène, because he "did not want to burden the Party with a dangerous 'murderer.'" Aside from the idea of reforming it from within—a conception he rightly describes as "megalomaniac"—he justifies his remaining in the party for so long with the curious argument that "as an active member it was possible to get an extremely clear idea of the Party's practices and of the obvious contradictions between those practices and its . . . principles." Whatever his reasoning, the decision to knuckle under, together with his absence from Paris while the young were in the streets (he spent the time in a mental hospital), certainly accelerated the decline of his stock among French students.

Politics and philosophy are not the center of *The Future Lasts Forever.* The book is primarily Althusser's attempt to make some sense of the murder of his wife, "to assume responsibility for what I was doing" when he found himself (as he reports things) with his fingers on his dead wife's neck. Judged unfit to plead, he could neither accept nor defend himself against the accusation of murder; he was confined for three years as an insane person, a status that indeed, as Althusser says, "raises a number of legal, penal, medical, analytical, institutional, and ultimately ideological and social questions." These questions are not explored; they are overwhelmed by Althusser's anguish over the mess he made of his life, not to mention his wife's, and the inadequacy of the conceptual and institutional means available to him to deal with it.

Unfortunately, the book must be judged a failure as an effort at self-understanding. It is quite clear that despite all his thirty years of psychoanalysis, Althusser had only the most formulaic grasp of his problems; his case might well do for Parisian analysis what Woody Allen's did for New York. Though there's no reason here to think that any of his analysts noticed it, the information he provides is highly suggestive of serious childhood trauma in the area of sexuality. An early memoir finds him sitting on his mother's knee as she awaits her husband's return; her "half-exposed breasts disgusted me and made me feel ashamed." As a psychologist specializing in child abuse observed to me, such a negative reaction on an infant's part seems a response to misplaced sexual behavior on his mother's part. This tallies with later experiences of her as "brutally intrusive" in sexual matters. For instance, when she congratulated him for his first wet dreams, she "had invaded my privacy, the most intimate part of my naked body . . . just as if she had looked into my pants or grabbed hold of my penis to show it off." One hesitates to make too much of a narrative that is often incoherent, studded with evident fantasy and marked by neo-Freudian clichés, but such thoughts are consistent with Althusser's lifelong sexual phobia toward women. The most striking example of this is the "profound state of anguish" and "violent and deep-seated feeling of repulsion" provoked in him by his first sexual experience, initiated by the ill-fated Hélène. While he comforts himself after the murder with the thought, suggested (he says) by a doctor friend, that he had fulfilled his own death wish "while at the same time doing her the immense service of killing her," it seems more plausible to find the roots of Althusser's act in the fear and repulsion he had experienced all his life with women, and with his wife to an apparently unbearable degree.

The Future Lasts Forever is the memoir of a frustrated, miserable man, whose craving for influence in the world was matched (he says) by a conviction of worthlessness. I never admired his work, and his life indeed makes a terrible tale, and yet I found myself moved by the pathos of his will to understand that tale. That he failed at this too makes the story all the sadder.

Edith Kurzweil (review date Summer 1994)

SOURCE: "Althusser's Madness: Theory or Practice?" in *Partisan Review,* Vol. LXI, No. 3, Summer, 1994, pp. 514-17.

[*In the following review, Kurzweil discusses Althusser's focus on his personal past as opposed to his philosophy in his* The Future Lasts Forever.]

From this lucid and gripping memoir the average American reader would not realize that Louis Althusser, "the world-renowned French philosopher" who murdered his wife on November 16, 1980, was the preeminent theoretician of the Communist Party in the 1960s and 1970s, or that he incited the French student revolts of 1968. Nor would anyone familiar with his distinctive and heavy theoretical prose have thought him capable of producing such a lyrical and allusive account of his lonely life. His allusions begin with the title, *L'avenir dure longtemps,* correctly translated as lasting "a long time" rather than "forever." Is he referring to his future without Hélène Rytman, the life-long companion he had killed, or to the ideal future he foresaw and that took so long in arriving—the dream of freedom in the communist world he had dedicated his life to bring about? (The book consists of the autobiography featured in the title [1986] and another one, *The Facts* [1976], both written before the disintegration of the Soviet Union.) Or has the fact that being declared insane saved him from the murder trial which might well have become a take-off on a Stalinist-type show trial and would at least have touched on the irrepa-

rable flaws in his theoretical enterprise? If ever we will get any answers to these questions, Althusser's memoirs do not provide them.

The casual reader will keep wondering whether Althusser was mad when he kept massaging his wife's neck until she stopped breathing, or whether the fact that his fingers left no mark on her is an indication that he had planned her death. But the reader familiar with Michel Foucault's publication of another memoir, *I, Pierre Rivière, having killed my mother, my sister and my brother. . . ,* will wonder whether Althusser purposely emulated Rivière who, in confinement in 1831, wrote the tale of the murders he committed. (Rivière had confessed, but the jurors at his trial could not decide whether he had been mad or had committed a crime.) Althusser's doctors and intimates rushed him into a mental clinic even before the police arrived. Did he get such special treatment because he had been one of the foremost guides of France's left intelligentsia, or because some of its luminaries at the time of the murder had leading positions in government?

In any event, we now learn that Althusser had been in and out of mental institutions all his life—at least fifteen times, he states at one point—but maybe much more often if we were to add up the separate instances he recalls throughout the book. This fact in itself is not shocking. But it makes us wonder why his friends, and these included communists and fellow-travellers, insisted on keeping their theoretician's state of mind such a closely guarded state secret. (Because Althusser is so brutally honest he ought to be diagnosed as sane. And yet, when he tells us that this "succession of memories by association [includes] hallucinations . . . [as] facts," we have our doubts.)

In the first sentence to the introduction, his former fellow student and neighbor at the Ecole Normale, Douglas Johnson, calls Althusser "one of the most original and controversial of French intellectuals: with Antonio Gramsci he was the most influential of Western thinkers on Marxism." Although this statement is superficially correct, it leaves out that Althusser pitted himself against reformist, humanist and existential Marxists, social democrats and socialists, and that, with the help of a "structuralist" rereading, he promised to discover the "scientific" Marx by focusing on Marx's later works alone. Raymond Aron ranked him as the "second-best" imaginary Marxist, immediately after Sartre. Obviously, "Althusser usually aroused strong feelings," and more so after the killing. However, contrary to Althusser's and Johnson's assumption that the newspapers kept commenting on the killing because it provided food for scandal-mongering, they were inquiring why he seemed to be getting away with murder thanks to powerful friends and his position at the Ecole Normale. Although his general influence had declined, he retained enough of an international coterie which still believed that his allegedly subjectless "theoretical practice" might engender a new universal consciousness.

In 1968, the most radical students had followed Althusser's thought in initiating a revolutionary movement and, soon thereafter, had faced his silence rather than his support. Johnson calls that "the mistake of history," because Althusser "believed that the student movement [that] touched off the general strike should not cause one to imagine that . . . [it] was more important than the workers movement." He goes on to discuss this point in line with the position then taken by Hélène, and by the officials of the Communist Party—without ever differentiating between history as event and history as the making of the coming revolution, or referring to anything more than "difficulties in the theory." Still, Douglas is insightful when he locates the key to Althusser's impersonal philosophy in the conflicts he had within the Communist Party and those due to the emotional remnants of his early Catholicism.

Althusser begins the memoir by stating that the precise memory of that unforgettable November morning is forever engraved in his mind. It is a sort of *plaidoyer,* as well as explanation, wish for expiation, and psychoanalytic inquiry into his tortured psyche. His insights into his love and life with Hélène are replete with self-accusations, with reproaches to friends who saw her only as a difficult and abrasive person, as the older woman who induced him to join the Communist Party, who kept dominating him. He asserts throughout that this is far from true, that his victim loved him, helped him and made him emotionally whole, although he recounts the many difficulties in their relationship which could have led those who knew them as a couple to come away with the impression that she was a shrew. When they met, in 1946, they "were two extremely lonely people, both in the depths of despair . . . [and] kindred spirits, sharing the same sense of anguish, of suffering, of loneliness, and the same desperate longing." They also were poor. Althusser recounts that he was extremely unfaithful, that he flaunted his infidelities, made advances in front of Hélène, and often invited his mistresses to meet her. Yet even though they had many fights over these matters, she always forgave him. A few paragraphs later, he recalls, lovingly, their courtship: "How cheerful and proud I was listening to the sound of my footsteps echoing down the deserted rue Saint-Jacques [after visiting her]. . . . I would not have changed my supreme good fortune, my treasure, my love, my joy, for anything in the world." One is left to wonder about these mood swings and about whether his friends felt they had to protect him from such swings or from Hélène who, he states, "was infinitely superior to me and did me a favour by introducing me to a world (of communism) I did not know." But he had "phases of violent arguments with his analyst as well, especially around 1976-77," the period that coincides with his writing

of *The Facts* and of his *Essays in Self-Criticism;* when he apparently revolted against Party discipline.

Althusser does not introduce philosophy, politics and his position within the Party until page 160 of the book. And then he does so parenthetically, with much emphasis on his student experiences with Bachelard, Desanti, Merleau-Ponty and many other luminaries among the French intellectual elite at the Ecole Normale. In this "'womblike' place, [he] felt warm and at home and was protected from the outside world." His doctor and psychiatrist were nearby, and so were such students as Etienne Balibar, Pierre Macherey, Régis Debray, Robert Linhart and Dominique Lecourt—all names we are familiar with from the neo-Althusserian works they wrote. He mentions having been influenced by Georges Canguilhem, having appointed Jacques Derrida. Friend and foe alike crossed his path, leading us to marvel at how internal are the French jokes, intellectual deliberations and rhetoric which years later, outside Paris and shorn of their native idiom, were turned into the theories that have animated much of American academic life.

In the course of this self-analysis Althusser repeatedly states that he does not want to address the contradictions and overdetermination within his theories because he did so in his books. Instead, he "seek[s] to elucidate if possible the deep-seated, personal motives, both conscious and especially unconscious, which underpinned this whole undertaking." He has succeeded in this task. But that does not mean that, finally, we know whether he was sane or insane at the time of the murder. We do know, however, that he was a better autobiographer than philosopher, whether or not we believe that he wrote about Marx's economics without having read *Das Kapital:* although he was "not sure whether humanity will ever experience communism"—that is, "the absence of relationships based on the market, on class exploitation and the domination of the state"—he clung to Marx's dictum that "history is more imaginative than we are." Altogether, Althusser's memoir focuses on the personal past: on his literally life-long psychoanalysis; his identification with a patriarchal grandfather; his rejection of parents who were not made for each other; the unconscious reasons for his emotional ups and downs; and the depressive states that so frequently induced him to sign himself into mental clinics. But if the year 1979-80 looked promising because he "resisted the early stages of depression," why was he suicidal enough to enter yet another clinic in June 1980?

Ultimately, one gets the eerie feeling that not only Althusser's mental state before and after the murder, but his habits as well, were on a continuum. After Hélène no longer could come to see him, other women friends took her place; and his philosopher friends continued to give him emotional support. Whether or not they will continue to pursue his "scientific Marxism," or are inventing yet another variant of it, is a moot issue. But we should note that the memoir, in its unacknowledged subjectivity, refutes Althusser's theoretical endeavor; and that nevertheless some of its components and assumptions are inherent in the current theories of so-called postmodernism which, though passé in Paris, have found their home in our universities.

Richard Block (essay date Spring 1995)

SOURCE: "Second Reads: Althusser Reading Marx Reading Hegel (After 1989)," in *Boundary 2,* Vol. 22, No. 1, Spring, 1995, pp. 211-33.

[*In the following essay, Block analyzes the relationships between the works of Althusser, Marx, and Hegel.*]

The English translation of Louis Althusser's *Le future dure longtemps* presents a curiosity. *Longtemps,* for the most part, has been rendered as forever, as if, after 1989, the promise of Althusserian Marxism had been displaced into an irretrievable or unrealizable future. One need only refer to the many recent dismissive reviews of the book to note how such judgments extend to Althusser's thought in general. Martin Bright, for example, writes that "in the present political atmosphere it is hard to imagine the excitement that was once generated by books with titles such as *For Marx* and *Reading Capital.*" George Steiner remarks that "it is likely that Althusser's writings on Hegel and Marx are already fading into cold dust." Similarly, Paul Mattick, Jr., notes that "Marxism-Leninism, even in its obscure Althusserian form, had to go." And Tony Judt summarizes these sentiments most succinctly when he describes Althusser's work as "abstruse apologetics for Communism."

In light of these reviews, it is perhaps time to revisit Althusser's instructions for reading *Capital* in the opening pages of *Reading Capital,* and to consider just what it is about the future that lasts a long time, or, as Althusser might remark, why the last instance never comes. A key to that riddle, with unexpected consequences for Marxism after 1989, is, I will argue, in the instructions themselves: "to read the text itself . . . line by line" and "to return ten times to the first chapters." As we will see, what Althusser insists upon is a reading that goes beyond exegesis to the "symptomatic" discourse hidden in the text's lacunae. For Althusser, the revolutionary break Marx made "to settle accounts with [his] erstwhile philosophical consciousness" remained incomplete, and it is left now to readers of *Capital* to construct the "Theory" of his theoretical practice. This emphasis on a practice of reading that does not merely collate materials and juxtapose them against a master text is, in fact, consistent with Marx's own call to resist mere interpretation and seek, instead, to change the world to which interpretation otherwise refers. In other words, the practice of reading, "its particular labor," in which that practice breaks away from an original text, assigns, for Althusser, this labor of reading a critical role, whereby reading's own relation (or nonrelation) to its text serves as a model for moving beyond sheer interpretive practices to "practical-critical" activities destined to alter the world.

Although numerous studies have been devoted to Althusser's thought, none, to date, has attended the central function that reading, as a productive practice, assumes in both *For Marx* and *Reading Capital.* More than providing a scientific basis, akin to a psychoanalytic one, for assessing critically the rather unscientific data that serve as a premise for materialist thought, the notion of reading practice resituates or locates those material markers within the theoretical or philosophical enterprise itself; it no longer divorces the theoretical project from considerations of its own materiality. Stated more broadly, the emphasis on reading as practical-critical activity responds to the two most persistent challenges leveled against Althusserian Marxism: its apparent privileging of theory as an autonomous practice and the inability to account for traces of Hegel in Marx long after the *1844 Manuscripts.*

The first of these objections was most convincingly argued by E. P. Thompson in "The Poverty of Theory." For Thompson, Althusserian Marxism is symptomatic of a "conceptual lethargy" that is "now bringing down upon our heads its necessary revenge." The role theory plays in Althusser is, according to Thompson, a product of a false mode of empiricism that fails to consider that one dialogue "out of which our knowledge is formed" is that between "the theoretical organization of evidence, on the one hand," and "the determinate character of its object, on the other." By pursuing Althusser's thought as it relates to his practice of reading, I intend to show how Althusser is, in fact, engaged in that very dialogue Thompson assures us his epistemology silences. Althusser simply locates the determinate character of the object in the text to be read. Attending to the material production inseparable from, but often suppressed in, "reading" is already underlined by Althusser in his reference to the psychoanalytic model shortly after the passage in *Reading Capital* cited above:

> Only since Freud have we begun to suspect what listening, and hence, what speaking (and keeping silent mean [*veut dire*]); that this meaning [*vouloir dire*] of speaking and listening reveals beneath the innocence of speech and hearing the culpable depth of a second, quite different discourse, the discourse of the unconscious. I dare maintain that only since Marx have we had to begin to suspect what, in theory at least, reading and hence writing means [*veut dire*].

What Althusser emphasizes by invoking the psychoanalytic model so early in his argument is the requirement of enacting reading, of regarding it as a writing of its own text. Just as the psychoanalytic reading promises a break from the misprision of an original text, so too, does Marx's reading of history signal a break from the mystifications of bourgeois ideologies. Although the full importance of productive reading will become clear only once Althusser's entire reading of Marx has been reconstructed, the conditions he enunciates for that reading in no way conflict with what Marx presents in the postface to the second edition of *Capital:*

> Of course the method of presentation must differ in form from that of inquiry. The latter has to appropriate the material in detail, to analyze its different forms of development and to track down their inner connection. Only after this work has been done can the real movement be appropriately presented. If this is done successfully, if the life of the subject-matter is now reflected back in the ideas, then it may appear as if we have before us *a priori* construction.

More than merely reemphasizing the need to avoid a mimetic rendering of history, this passage underscores the importance not just of receiving the object but also of constructing it so as to provoke change. Therein lies the basis for disputing what Thompson presumes is Althusser's "conceptual lethargy."

The consequence of the second challenge leveled against Althusser, namely his inability to account for residues of Hegelian thought so evident, for example, in the opening chapter of *Capital,* seems to consign Althusserian Marxism to a pre-Hegelian mode of idealist thinking about the thing-in-itself. Althusser's reading, to be sure, names, but ultimately fails to provide definitive knowledge about, the determinate instance, or "thing," in its system. This does not imply, however, an eternization of a capitalist mode of production. The unnamed "thing-in-itself" does not exist apart from the material transformations of Althusser's reading, nor does it structure forever the same appearances or manifestations. Moreover, upon investigation into the origins (if one can ever speak of origins in an Althusserian context) of a Marxist science of history and its break with the philosophical consciousness of the past, one comes to recognize that Marx, rather than abandoning Hegel, came to embrace him precisely in the manner Althusser insists one read *Capital.* In other words, **Reading Capital** might be another name for Reading Hegel.

For Althusser, Marx is essentially two Marxes; the one before 1845, and the radically different author of *Capital* and founder of the science of history. The latter is not to be understood as the product of a progressive development.

Marx's revolution consists in a radical break from his youth, a change from ideology to science. The science Marx founded represents a radical discontinuity and rupture with previous systems of knowledge, "a massive leap and dislocation." What this leap constitutes is Marx's rejection of Hegel and Feuerbach, an abandonment of all attempts to explain history in terms of human history or an originary subject. What rises in its stead is an investigation into, and construction of, social formations and the mode of production. With this rupture from the past emerges "the reign of a new logic, which far from being a mere development, the truth or the inversion of the old one, literally takes its place." It is a complete departure from the "whole pattern and frame of reference" of the prescientific mode characteristic of the writings before 1845.

Why Althusser insists that the construction of this new science can be nothing other than a radical break from Marx's philosophical heritage is inextricably related to what, for him, is ideology. As pre-knowledge from which the new science severs itself, ideology masks the true character of the social formations that structure human existence. Ideology is the lived relation between human beings and the world, the system of "ideas or representations" that dominate society and serve to "reinforce or reproduce the existing set of social relations." As a system of mass representations, ideology is indispensable to any society if human subjects "are to be formed, transformed, and equipped to respond to the demands of their conditions of existence." In other words, unlike more traditional Marxisms that ascribe ideology only to class domination in capitalist society, ideology is, for Althusser, the necessary means by which individuals in all societies adapt to their social roles. Unlike science, which makes a revolutionary break from the prevailing ideology to render knowledge of how to change it, ideology privileges the "practico-social function" and relinquishes any concern with the "theoretical function (function as knowledge)." What this means is that Marxist science, to break from its own "practico-social" ideological interests, must establish and preserve a clear distinction between the object of knowledge and the real object. That is, if Marxist science merely abstracts from reality and posits these abstractions as truth, they become mere theoretical sublimations of ideology, unable to overcome or elude ideology's practical aims. For Marx, whose ideological heritage is German idealism, the practico-social interest is to root social formations and their history in man, to believe in the "omnipotence of man's liberty or of creative labor," which does nothing more than serve, in the final analysis, the interest of the ruling class. This, in fact, is the precise function the philosophies of Hegel and Feuerbach serve, albeit in different, but mutually reinforcing, ways. Both use the dialectic to mystify the social basis of capitalist production and to assert the primacy of human agency. Toward the practico-social ends of ideology, the two seek to render "transparent the opacity of social relations by relying on the phenomenal forms of those relations (whose form renders invisible the truth behind them)" and then by "relating those phenomenal forms to the subject, whether the terms be self-consciousness, man, or the concept of sensation." Existence is explained in terms of the appearance of existence, which, in turn, is explained in terms of the subject's alienated essence.

To trace Marx's break with the "mystical form" of the Hegelian dialectic, it is necessary to reconstruct that break according to two distinct moments. The mention of moments, however, should not seek to replace discontinuity with its opposite. Moreover, the first moment of the coming to terms with Hegel in the *1844 Manuscripts* presents a Marx still beholden to Feuerbach. It is only the failure of the manuscripts, the insoluble contradiction they run up against, that allows Marx to settle all accounts of his "erstwhile philosophical consciousness."

In the *1844 Manuscripts,* Marx undertakes a critique of Hegel from the perspective of Feuerbach, seeking to employ the Hegelian dialectic in terms of "man" and the alienation of "his" labor. And it is this critique of Hegel that explains, at the same time, the failure of this marriage. By confusing thought and being, by assuming that the object of thought is, in effect, the real object, Hegel fails to see the real qualitative transformations of real existence (*das Bestehende*). Material life is merely a ruse of reason, whose otherness, as a negation of the self, is eventually negated as other and recognized as self. "It is the alienation of self-consciousness [that] establishes thingness." All this negation of the negation affirms, however, is the alienated essence of man. Religion and the state, for example, are affirmed as the alienated essence of the subject, in that the self recognizes itself in this other. "When, for example, Hegel conceives wealth, the power of the state, etc., as entities estranged from the being of man, he conceives them only in their thought form. . . . They are entities of thought. . . . The entire history of alienation is therefore nothing more than the history of the production of abstract, i.e., absolute, thought, of logical, speculative thought." In other words, Hegel's crime is one of abstraction, which allows the essence of the self to experience and affirm itself in a state of alienation, as abstraction. He mistakes the object of thought for the real object.

This critique of Hegel, from within Feuerbach, however, is not without its own problems. In affirming the real, or material, basis of existence, Marx, according to Althusser, comes to recognize the failure of his own position. His attempt to adopt Feuerbach's anthropological model and explain all of political economy in terms of the alienation of human labor comes against very real and material obstacles. In the Hegelian model, each moment of consciousness "lives and expresses its own essence through all the echoes of the essence it has previously been. . . . Because the past is never

more than the internal essence of the future it encloses, the presence of the past is the present to consciousness of consciousness itself, and no true external determination." External determination, however, is precisely what frustrates Marx's attempts to employ Hegel in terms of Feuerbach. The social formations so work on and transform "alienated labor" that it becomes unthinkable that it could ever be returned to man. Any negation of this supposedly first negation of man's essence (or external determination) might return to or affirm something in that social formation of his alienated essence, but much more would remain unsublated to structure existence according to principles that do not reduce to man's essence. The underlying Hegelian model, even if we begin with "man," and not his abstract essence, is a simple contradiction. Hegel reduces "all the elements that make up the concrete life of a historical epoch (economic, social, political, and legal institutions, customs, ethics, art, religion, war, battles, defeats, and so on) to one principle of internal unity." But this is only possible "on the absolute condition of taking the whole concrete life of a people for the externalization-alienation (*Entäusserung/Entfremdung*) of an internal spiritual principle, which can never be anything but the most abstract form of that epoch's consciousness of itself"—that is to say, of its ideology. Whether that one principle of internal unity is the idea—as it is with Hegel—or "man" himself, the results are equally unsatisfactory. Historical materialism does not lend itself to such ideological descriptions premised on an internal unifying principle standing in simple contradiction to itself. When one takes up the materialist perspective, real constitutive conditions create equally constitutive transformations that render notions of a simple or dialectically "solved" contradiction a mere ruse of ideology.

This, Althusser insists, was precisely the problem Marx faced as he tried to complete the *1844 Manuscripts,* using the concept of alienated labor as his starting point. To do so, Marx himself was forced to employ a "phenomenological" approach, accepting political economy "precisely as it present[ed] itself without questioning the content of its concepts or their systematicity." What he was forced to suppress was the non-sublatable contradiction between the impoverishment of the working class and the simultaneous enrichment of the capitalist class. The unresolved question became how, and where, could one locate man as the essence of these two class formations. Only an investigation of the many distinct concrete practices that mutually determine one another could explain it. The notion of a simple contradiction between subject and object, "man" and his alienated labor no longer held the explanatory power to account for the differences between classes. As a result, Marx would be forced to consider, as he states in the sixth thesis on Feuerbach, the "ensemble of social relations." The failure of the *1844 Manuscripts* pointed to a need by Marx to abandon "man" as the center of his system and to seek a "new rigorous method of investigation, another method than that of a simple prospective or retrospective assimilation." Althusser's attribution of the failure of the manuscripts to their theoretical untenability thereby excludes the possibility of tying that failure and the ensuing shift in Marx's thought to the *real* failure of the revolution of 1848.

Another way to understand the problem implicit to the *1844 Manuscripts* is to rethink, for example, Hegel's section on "Sense-certainty" in the *Phenomenology*. The "this" or "here," which leaves behind its immediate referent to move toward perception, cannot, nonetheless, erase the markers of that material immediacy, much less the very real transformation they undergo in exclusion of Hegel's emerging concept. Hegel's model may account for the internal movement of the concept, but it can neither bring to a halt nor explain the changes, formations, and relations occurring outside, or external, to it. Likewise, Feuerbach points out the fact of religious self-alienation, "of the duplication of the religious world and secular one," but he fails to pose, much less to address, the question as to why. He fails to recognize that all social life is essentially practice, a complex of material practices and activities of transformation. He is no better than Hegel in that he attempts to explain, or interpret, what *is* in terms of an abstract concept of man. He does not recognize "that the abstract individual which he analyzes belongs to a form of society, civil society," which, through ideology, gives the impression that the individual relates immediately to his/her social, or material, world. For example, he concedes sensuousness only in the form of an object, as an intuition without practice. He sees religion as the alienated essence of man but does not examine its social formation. As Althusser writes, even the concept of fruit is not the production of an operation of abstraction performed by a subject, but "the product of distinct concrete practices—dietary, agricultural, or even magical and religious and ideological practices—in its origins."

What the failure of the *1844 Manuscripts* ultimately points to is the radical break toward a new science Marx outlines in the "Theses on Feuerbach" and delivers in *Capital.* He abandons the Hegelian and Feuerbachian model of abstraction and "inverts the dialectic" to "discover the rational kernel in its mystical shell. Once that shell is removed, the dialectic no longer is an internal unifying principle impervious to external factors and social and material transformations. The basic structures of the Hegelian dialectic, such as "negation, the negation of the negation, the identity of opposites, the supersession and the transformation of quantity into quality, [and] contradiction," are either abandoned or radically transformed. Instead of employing "alienated labor" as the key and unifying concept, Marx develops a new vocabulary to explore the mode of production and social relations. Instead of working with past ideologies that merely "register [and accept] the contradiction of the increasing

pauperization of the workers and the remarkable wealth of the modern world it celebrates," Marx founds a new science that critically questions social formation and seeks to change it. Just how different that structure becomes for Marx is, according to Althusser, evident by his break from the theoretical pretensions of all humanism, from all attempts to explain society and history in terms of free human subjects, of labor, of human desire, or of moral and political action. As Marx wrote in the *Grundrisse,* "A society is not composed of individuals"; or, as he wrote later in *Notes on Wagner's Textbook,* "My analytic does not start from Man but from the economically given period of society." Simple inversion of the dialectic produced Hegel in the anthropological garb of Feuerbach; removal of its mystical shell produced a science of social relations, which no longer involved only "men," but also "*things,* the means of production, derived from material nature."

To understand fully the genealogy of Marx's new science of history and its radical departure from the premises of his earlier works, it is important not only to elucidate its theoretical basis but also to underline the tension and drama of class conflict that permeate the *1844 Manuscripts.* Althusser's description of this conflict is critical: "They [working and capitalist classes] do not share the same world, they do not lead the same class struggle, and yet they do come into confrontation, and this certainly is a contradiction since the relation of confrontation reproduces the conditions of confrontation instead of transcending them in a beautiful Hegelian exaltation and reconciliation." The inability to suppress that conflict converts the manuscripts into a document "on the threshold, . . . as if, before the rupture, in order to achieve it, he [Marx] had to give philosophy every chance, its last, this absolute empire over its opposite, this boundless theoretical triumph that is, its defeat." By casting that confrontation in such dramatic terms, Althusser emphasizes the tension that leads to the rupture. Once the notion of a simple contradiction loses its ability to contain, account for, and suppress the ensemble of determinations underlying it, what follows is not a realignment or reconstruction of its terms but rather a complete separation from that framework. Without this complete break, the late Marx would have been unable to found his science; he would have remained chained to the ideological ground that, nonetheless, by dint of the pressure the *1844 Manuscripts* had forced upon them, had already given way. While for Althusser, Marxist "humanism" of the sort represented by Sartre often attempted to repair the damage through a last-ditch effort to see "man" as the originary ground, Althusser reconstructs the tensions that force that ground to give way. And that, in effect, is Marx's supreme accomplishment, his revolutionary break.

The ramifications of Althusser's reading of the young Marx and his insistence on an epistemological rupture become clearer upon examination of so-called traditional Marxists and their attempt(s) to apply the notion of a simple contradiction to a materialist base. While no singular account of traditional Marxists can justify the vast differences that exist between them, the tendency is to lend primacy to the forces of production in society and the contradiction that grows out of these forces in the simultaneous production of use- and exchange-values. The relations of production, according to Simon Clark, should not be seen as separate from material production, "as an externally derived form imposed upon a pre-existent content"; rather, production is "indissolubly social and material." But the unity of these two products is not harmonious, rather contradictory. At the root of capitalist production is a contradiction between production of use-value and the simultaneous production of social relations, which forces "capital beyond the immediate process of production in order to accomplish its valorization." Social relations, therefore, are all subsumed under the rubric of relations of production or ultimately have their ground in them. While these relations appear in historically different forms, economically, ideologically, and politically they are all determinations of the relations of production, which are based on a dominant, simple contradiction implicit to production. Marxism, therefore, is concerned with the concrete historical configuration of this contradiction. In its totality, capitalist society can be seen as the expression of this fundamental contradiction at the root of its production. The example often cited is the falling rate of profit and the consequent increased exploitation of the working classes. Simply stated, competition forces profits downward, leading to lower wages, longer working hours, or new technologies to increase efficiency. Capital becomes concentrated in the hands of a few, as smaller capitalists lack the means to keep pace. Crisis necessarily ensues, as overproduction idles workers and factories, and concentration of capital impoverishes the many. This contradiction between labor and capital in the mode of production in capitalist society eventually reaches a breaking point, ushering in a new age. As Marx himself put it, "At a certain stage of their development the material forces of production in society come into conflict with the existing relations of production. . . . From forms of development of the forces of production these relations turn into fetters. Thus begins the epoch of social revolution."

Althusser's break from this so-called traditional reading of Marx is nothing short of radical. Once he removes the mystical shell from Hegel's dialectic, what remains is no longer an organic unity whose dynamism is rooted in a contradiction introduced at the instant commencing production, rather a structured and self-compensating mechanism visible only in its overdetermined effects. Althusser relies heavily on this notion of overdetermination, a term he borrows from Freud, who used the term to show how "several simultaneous factors, each with some explanatory power, can contribute to the formation of a symptom." A dream, for example, typically has various determinant factors that render possible

various, often contradictory, notions. Applied to historical materialism, overdetermination suggests that the economic is not the sole determinant; not only are the base and superstructure, forces and relations of production and social relations, mutually determining, they also have a considerable degree of autonomy. If more "traditional" Marxisms evoke the concept of a totality, whereby each part is an expression of an internal essence of that totality, Althusser's Marx argues for an "accumulation of radically heterogeneous contradictions—of different origins, different sense, different levels and points of application." Although these may "nevertheless merge into a ruptural unity, we can no longer talk of the sole unique power of the general 'contradiction.'"

In opposition to the organic explanation of the base and superstructure, Althusser therefore introduces four distinct levels of what he calls the social practice: economic, political, ideological, and theoretical. The economic "transforms nature by human labor into social products; the political transforms social relations, through revolutions, the ideological transforms men's consciousness, and theory transforms ideology into science." The mode of production is no longer the forces and relations of production, with the superstructure seen as epiphenomenal, rather it includes all levels of practice and their interaction. With each level of practice enjoying some amount of autonomy, contradiction necessarily ensues at several levels due to what Althusser calls the law of uneven development. That is, the structured whole of society consists of several levels of practice and production that stand in uneven development to each other but that mutually condition one another. What lends this uneven development a structured unity is essentially the hierarchic relationship in which they stand to one another. Society is divided into determinant, dominant, and subordinate instances, each with its own degree "of specific effectivity":

> That one contradiction dominates the others presupposes that the complex in which it is featured is a structured unity, and that this structure implies the indicated domination-subordination of relations between contradictions. . . . Domination is not just an indifferent fact, it is a fact essential to the complexity itself. That is why complexity implies domination as one of its essentials; it is inscribed in the structure.

Althusser stresses that the whole is not a dominant contradiction, which serves as its essence with secondary contradictions as mere phenomena of that essence. On the contrary, the secondary contradictions are the conditions of the dominant one: "They constitute its condition of existence. The superstructure is not the pure phenomenon of the structure; it is also its condition of existence." In other words, each contradiction indicates in itself the structure of the complex whole, so when one speaks of the existing conditions of the whole, one speaks of its conditions of existence. If each contradiction indicates its relation to the unevenness of the whole, as well as to itself, it can no longer be said to be univocal. That is not to say it is equivocal; rather, as Smith points out, it is simply overdetermined. Since the structure in dominance exists only by virtue of these secondary or subordinate contradictions, which in turn reflect that structure, the determinate instance is missing. The mode of production, the structured whole in which these secondary contradictions are hierarchically ordered, is present only in its effects, in the ordering itself. The mode of production is an absent presence whose expression in actual production necessarily stands in overdetermined contradiction to the absence of the determinate moment to which it nonetheless refers. Each act of production is conditioned by the structure in which it occurs (without these acts of production, the structure would not exist), and, as an expression of that structure, it alters that structure by the very act of its production. It is always already a misreading or misrepresentation of the structure it seeks to prove. So, when Marx says there is "never production without society," without social relations, he is emphasizing, on the one hand, the pre-givenness of that structure. Production, in other words, is, among other things, the reproduction of the relations of production, which are always already present but are instantly altered by the facticity of the production that reproduces and reaffirms them. The "invariability" of the structure is known only by the "variability" of its effects. On the other hand, with that same statement, Marx also points to the lack of an originary ground, which, in turn, means that the ground of all contradiction is present only in its absence. That, in fact, is its contradiction, its overdetermination. It also explains the immense difficulty so many critics have had in trying to locate a precise source of the Althusserian notion of contradiction in the uneven development of the various levels of practice.

The psychoanalytical model also helps explain transition or change in Althusser's sense of a synchronic model of the mode of production. This, in fact, is, for many, the locus of the impasse of Althusser's reading of Marx, its apparent inability to account for transition from one mode of production to another. To be sure, Althusser presents an antihistorical model; history is nothing but a series of discontinuous permutations of the underlying structure. The impossibility of the "effects" ever fulfilling their debt to the absent-present to which they refer eliminates any achievable telos from the structure. There is no progression toward an end in sight, rather only an unlimited reconfiguration of capitalist relations of production, whose determinate moment by dint of its overdetermination cannot be located. As Marx writes,

> The capitalist production process considered in its
> inner connection (*Zusammenhang*), or as reproduc-

tion, produces not only commodities, not only surplus value, but it also produces and eternalizes the social relation between the capitalist and the wage-earner.

Since the structure of these relations is not static, can never be static, Althusser adapts the psychoanalytic terms of displacement and condensation to describe the dynamic of its reconfigurations. Freud used these terms to explain the representations of thoughts in dream. Displacement was the transferral of psychic energy from one image to another, while condensation was the "compression" of a number of dream-thoughts into one image. For Althusser, displacement describes the uneven development of contradictions within and among each level of practice when the tension of contradiction is sufficiently diffused so as to be nonantagonistic. In condensation, the reverse occurs. Secondary contradictions so converge, or fuse, onto a single level that a realignment in the dominant structure ensues; the existing unity dissolves. The contradictions within the economic, political, and ideological meet in a "nodal strategic point," which, as the locus of confrontation, prompts a new hierarchy among the contradictions. While condensation fuels political change, the overdetermined condition of the complex whole remains unaltered; its self-correcting mechanism merely expresses itself in more or less volatile effects. The complex whole can never escape the condition of its overdetermination. The simple contradiction of the economic, which Marx tells us determines in the last instance, is irretrievably displaced into the future: "the economic dialectic is never active in the pure state; in History, these instances, the superstructures, etc.—are never seen to . . . scatter before His Majesty the Economy as he strides along the royal road of the Dialectic. From the first moment to the last, the lonely hour of the 'last instance' never comes."

The psychoanalytic model also serves to illuminate the strict theoretical antihumanism of Althusser's Marxism. For Althusser, any philosophy of the subject is an intrusion of ideology: "For the corollary of theoretical Marxist antihumanism is the recognition and knowledge of humanism itself: as an ideology." Freud himself noted in the *Introductory Lectures on Psychoanalysis* that man's "naïve self-love" has been progressively "humbled by advances in science," from Copernicus, to Darwin, to his own model, which ousts the ego as "master in its own house." For Althusser, this progressive de-centering of the subject makes "man" no longer the subject of history; its movements and mechanistic operations defy all attempts to spotlight man at the center of the historical stage.

> The structure of the relations of production determines the places and functions occupied and adopted by the agents of production, who are never anything more than occupants of these places, in-

sofar as they are the supports (*Träger*) of these functions. The true subjects . . . are therefore not these
occupants or functionaries . . . but the definition and
distribution of these places and functions. The true
"subjects" are these definers and distributors: the
relations of production (and political and ideological social relations).

The Freudian model, which assigns unconscious desires the
power to undermine or erase conscious human intentionality, is clearly not far removed from Althusser's own model.
In both instances, terms such as *choice, intention, agency,*
and *decision* are virtually meaningless. Just as one is unable
in Freud to locate a unified center, so, Althusser would agree,
humans cannot locate themselves at the center of the critical or defining moments of social formation, or, for that matter, of their own lives.

In the final analysis, one might be forced to concede the limited explanatory power of the structured and complex whole
Althusser presents. Just as the lonely hour of the last instance
never arrives, so, too, is the moment in which the underlying structure of the social formation becomes transparent
barred to us. What we observe in each instant is an effect
of that structure, which, by reproducing the relations of that
system, by mirroring its complex whole in the structure of
its own contradiction, alters the very structure to which it
refers. The need or inherent claim of the structure to seek
its own reproduction may spawn an infinite number of effects or substitutions in a doomed quest to reach the last instance, but that instance will most surely never arrive. That
problem has prompted many observers to charge Althusser
with regressing to a pre-Hegelian mode of thought, of naming or finding a description for something that can never be
known. What such critics seem to be seeking is a defining
substrata of the structure, an originary or primary structure
obscured only by its endless permutations. The notion of
some originary form, however, ignores the consequences of
Marx's restructuring of the Hegelian dialectic: once removed
of its mystical shell, there is no kernel. There is no internal
or ultimate ground of the referent. To assert otherwise is to
convict Althusser of proposing the same organic, simple
Hegelian unity he quite obviously repudiates. To be precise,
the structure of overdetermination is the structure.

The more pertinent question, it seems, is how such an
antihumanist, antihistorical model fulfills Marx's demand to
change, and not merely to interpret, the world. Given the
mechanistic displacement of man as an agent of history and
the mercilessness with which structures in domination self-
compensate and adjust, how is the class struggle to be overcome? Where is the vehicle for change? Not surprisingly,
the riddle and its solution lie as much in the formation of
the objection as they do in Althusser's presentation.

What Marxist science works on and presents is not merely
a mimetic description of society; it is a particular construction of the ensemble of relations aimed at overcoming the
class struggle and one that was only possible, Althusser remarks, after Marx had taken up the position of the proletariat. Capitalist ideology presents the illusion that man is
center-stage, that he/she is the determinant agent. Such ideologies achieve an apparent reconciliation of the oppressed
worker with the very structure responsible for his/her impoverishment. The worker imagines a univocal relation to his/
her universe; conditions are an outcome of his/her actions.
The very establishing of a relationship, however, is by its
very nature reification, suppressing the otherness of that relation and blinding one to the (over)determinations that challenge the validity of that relation and the possibility of
freeing oneself from its constrictions. So, when Steven
Smith, for example, charges that the result of Althusser's
reading of Marx is to "evacuate the term [mode of produc-
tion] of all explanatory power, since what is used indiffer-
ently to explain everything must in the end explain nothing,"
he fails to recognize the perverse wisdom of his own critique. That is precisely the point—to reveal the absent
ground of all relations and unground the ideological basis
of capitalism. Althusser constructs a model that frees production, from the constraints of humanism, from the artificial ground of self-awareness and self-determination, from
the German idealist notion of l=l—all of which are nothing
but the motors of class oppression. There is no ground on
which the self may look back at and see itself standing; its
presence is only its absence.

Althusser's attempt to reconstruct a genealogy of Marxist
scientific practice suppresses, however, a contradiction of its
own—namely the one alluded to above between synchrony
and diachrony. The productive moment in which science
transforms an abstract ideological concept into a concrete
one in thought cannot, it would seem, be very distinct or tem-
porally dislocated from the moment of rupture itself. We
know that all productive acts necessarily alter the complex
whole from which they emanate, rendering them mere effects and, for scientific practice, a depiction, or representation, of a structure not quite what it was before the
productive act. Moreover, once that science contextualizes
itself, once it reestablishes a relationship with the structure
in dominance, it is difficult to see how it can resist attach-
ing itself and being subsumed under that structure. If
Althusser denies history any continuity or progression, the
same, not surprisingly, can be said of his science of history.
That is, Marxist science, which quite clearly requires
Althusser's reading of it, neither moves toward some teleo-
logical completion of itself nor does it subsume its results
under some interpretive, eternally valid superstructure. Its
status is precarious at best:

Finally . . . it was a question of recalling that knowledge of reality [Marxist science] changes something in reality because it *adds* to it precisely the fact that *it* is known, though everything makes it appear as if the addition canceled itself out in the result. Since knowledge of reality belongs in advance to reality, . . . it adds something to it only on the paradoxical condition of adding nothing to it, and once produced, reverts to it without need of sanction and disappears in it.

Scientific practice for Althusser is thus a continuous discontinuous practice. Knowledge is less a separate corpus of privileged insights adding continuously to its own truths, and more a practice dependent on, and visible only, in its break from a preexisting corpus. And while that knowledge is once again annulled or reabsorbed under the structure in dominance, it changes, in the process, what it broke from.

Althusser's charge, it seems, is to force ever anew the existing concepts, infected by the "truths" produced in the previous instance of scientific practice, to collapse under the weight of their determination, to dislodge from the ideological structure of univocal determinations. He is not offering, as Roy Edgley suggests, a map of reality to invoke as a blueprint to pinpoint the weak link in the structure in dominance. Marxist science is not a theoretical enterprise designed to render a telos or destination. That would reduce its execution to sheer interpretation—knowledge and practice subsumed under the rubric of a master script. Overdetermination, by its very definition, renders such strategies nugatory. Rather, Marxist theory is a theory of practice, an unending practice designed to defy conceptual reifications by rehearsing endlessly a break from the structure in dominance. This, in turn, is why Althusser was fond of noting Lenin's insistence on "the infinity of its object."

With that in mind it is now possible to understand the importance Althusser places on a productive reading of *Capital.* In its own moment of breaking with the text and thereby producing its own construction of the ensemble of social relations, that practice of reading produces a concrete in thought of such radical otherness that it defies "commodization"; no value can be assigned it. Since it severs, before its reabsorption and annulment, all conceptual relations, it can be exchanged for nothing. It has, to be sure, only use-value. And its (re)enactment not so much scripts for the proletariat the necessary moves to break from the structure of class domination as it does constitute a revolutionary break from the eternalized relations of the capitalist mode of production. Lenin was therefore entirely correct in asserting that without a revolutionary theory, there can be no revolution, so long as theory is understood as practice, as a loosening of the foundation in expectation of the last instance, which may never come. Why it never arrives is not because the promise is false, rather because the "last in-

stance" is always followed by another, one of reabsorption and annulment, by another structure in dominance. Nonetheless, the scientists of history must continue, as Althusser insists, to read *Capital,* to stage a productive reading of *Capital* and return, if necessary, to the opening passages ten times. But this reading, as his de-centering of the subject would imply, can have no author. It can refer to no center of its constellation nor seek to ground its determinations. Its meaning is its enactment, lest the reader fall prey to the ideological ruses of capitalism and project her-/himself as the agent of change:

> Now we can recall that highly symptomatic term *"Darstellung,"* compare it with this "machinery" and take it literally, as the very existence of this machinery in its effects: the mode of existence of the stage direction (*mise en scene*) of the theater which is simultaneously its own stage, its own scripts, its own actors, the theater whose spectators can, on occasion, be spectators only because they are first of all forced to be its actors, caught by the constraints of a script and parts whose authors they cannot be, since it is in essence *an authorless theater.*

In settling Marx's account with Kant, Althusser simultaneously opens another, with Hegel. Although, as I have shown, he devotes numerous passages in virtually all the major essays to explicate how the mystical shell of the Hegelian dialectic suppresses the real transformations of its material base, that critique is arguably directed at a reductivist Hegel seen through the eyes of Feuerbach. For what generates the whole movement of the *Phenomenology of Spirit,* it could be argued, is precisely a structure of overdetermination implicit to each stage of consciousness. The structure in dominance, or a moment of consciousness, is forced to move beyond itself, to readjust its hierarchic alignment or apprehension of its object precisely because an entire field of determinations condense or fuse in that object to force its restructuring. That is evident in the first moments of self-certainty, when the "this" or "here" breaks up into countless "thises" or "heres" and thereby forces the move to perception, which is prepared to take the "this" and "here" as universals.

Likewise, the section on "Force and Understanding" in the *Phenomenology* seems to point to unerased traces of Hegel in the mature Marx. Force is precisely that process in which dispersed or unrelated elements issue from a unity in which they were unexpressed or submerged only to lose themselves again in this unity. The independent, and now dispersed, elements are the manifestations of Force, while unexpressed Force is the unity out of which these manifestations emerge. The description of Force as expressing itself in appearing and then disappearing elements, as something known only in its appearance, cannot be far from the description Althusser offers of production or of productive *forces*. What is produced at each level of practice is an effect of the system, which bears witness to the forces and relations of production. And like the manifestations of force, these effects are nothing but the structure. Moreover, when Hegel asserts later in that same section that "the world of appearance" is the "essence of the supersensible beyond" and "its filling," he seems to anticipate Althusser's Marx, who asserts that production is only re-production and that the pre-given structure is known only in its effects. Just how close the two texts often are is apparent at the end of that section. Hegel posits a simple infinity—a unity that stands behind the infinite manifestations of apparent difference. It is infinite since it is bounded by no other thing, nothing from the outside delimits it. Difference is thus its self-diremption. Hegel goes on to assert that life is this simple infinity, which is known, of course, only in its infinite self-diremption. Life—or the production of difference that testifies to the simple infinity that is life—might therefore be as equally overdetermined for Hegel as it is for Althusser. For both a univocal schematic of determination is insufficient to explain appearance. (We must also not forget that critical to the *Phenomenology* is not merely transformation of the object of consciousness but also consciousness itself. The two mutually condition one another, just as in Marx's [for Althusser] ideology, the product of man's consciousness, reflects the complex whole and the complex whole reflects ideology. In both instances, uneven development might be used to describe the unequal relation between the two relata.)

This very brief sketch of Hegel's "Force and Understanding" is intended not to map out similarities between Hegel and Althusser but to establish a preliminary *basis* on which to validate posing the question of just how far apart the two are. Althusser's rejection of Hegel might, in fact, be better understood as a rejection of a dialectical structure that posits the beginning toward which the end aims as essential, somehow unchanged, and always awaiting self-realization. From the remarks on "Force" cited above, it seems certain that Hegel, as well, did not adhere to such a structure. The content of Force is indistinguishable from its manifestation; it is only in thought that its moments of "exteriorization" and "being driven back upon itself" are considered distinctly. Consciousness, as ideology is for Althusser, is only the result of a play of forces—no more or less essential than the forces themselves, whose play consciousness manifestly is. Might it not be more accurate to assert that what Althusser (and Marx) ultimately rejects is less Hegel and more a *Lebensphilosophie,* which mistakes life's essence or content as distinct from its manifestation? For Hegel, the essence is distinct only insofar as it is nothing; for Althusser, only insofar as it is absent. The heart of such an inquiry, it seems, might ultimately hinge on the role of the phenomenologist in Hegel and the scientist in Althusser. Despite Althusser's

claim that Hegel is merely abstracting from the real, there is undoubtedly an element of construction or production associated with the phenomenologist who is not far removed from the role of the scientist in Althusser. Hegel's "science" of consciousness is itself not science; *Bewußtsein* cannot be equated with *Wissen.* In the third thesis on Feuerbach, Marx himself asserts the privileged consciousness or role of the educator, who, in his superior role in society, is charged with "the changing of circumstance and of human activity." Hegel, in turn, says "we," the phenomenologist, must "step into the place of [consciousness] and be the Notion which develops and fills out what is contained in the result." The phenomenologist's role, it would seem, is far greater than merely receiving and interpreting the object. That function is reserved for consciousness, or, in Althusserian terms, ideology. Moreover, as Smith points out, Althusser imports into Marx Hegel's doctrine of immanent critique. Knowledge for both provides its own criterion. As Hegel remarks, "consciousness tests and examines itself." In a virtual echo of Hegel, Althusser remarks, "Theoretical practice is indeed its own criterion and contains in itself definite protocol with which to validate the quality of its product."

To be sure, the *Phenomenology* and *Capital* are two very different texts. The question is, Wherein lies the critical difference? Without pursuing the argument I promised not to, and without repeating what has been stated above, I would suggest once again that the heart of the inquiry is in the role of the phenomenologist and the Marxist scientist; the critical difference, however, is in their *reading.* That is, *Capital* is a reading of the *Phenomenology* under the very conditions Althusser issues for a reading of *Capital.* In constructing the conditions of self-consciousness, Hegel was able to negate negation, to assert "that differences which arose were not differences," but, in fact, were "self-same." In reading the *Phenomenology,* Marx could not help but keep running up against the traces of those sublated differences. Whereas for Hegel, the "contents of the moment of change" remained the same, for Marx, change brought with it qualitative transformations. Sublation did not annul difference but produced difference anew.

The point, however, is better understood, as I have mentioned above, in the Althusserian context of reading. Marx read the *Phenomenology* Hegel wrote. With the production of the *Phenomenology,* the mode of production (of self-consciousness) was thereby altered. By the very fact it was read and became known, the *Phenomenology,* like the science of history, altered the complex whole of which it was already an effect. By the time Marx read that text, it needed to be rewritten, could not help but be rewritten. It had become a material fact reflecting the complex whole that no longer was the same by virtue of its being produced, or, for that matter, by its being read. What Marx did was simply read the *Phenomenology* to the letter and chart its mode of production in each of its moments. Only this time, the new author did not "phenomenologize" its production; rather, he produced a reading of phenomenology that, conscious of itself as activity or production, could not but celebrate the material transformations of that reading, its radical break from the original text. Whether Hegel was aware that the production of the concept, that self-consciousness coming to consciousness of itself as self-consciousness, would require it to continue to come to consciousness of what it has just brought to self-consciousness in each of its moments, is another matter. In any case, absolute knowledge would always be something just less than absolute. That Marx, on the other hand, took it upon himself to do just that, we know from the seemingly endless and certainly unfinished document, *Capital.*

FURTHER READING

Criticism

Easthope, Antony. "Text and Subject Position after Althusser." *Studies in Twentieth-Century Literature* 18, No. 1 (Winter 1994): 83-96.
    Presents a new reading of Althusser's work and provides reasons for the importance of reexamining his work.

Lock, Graham. Review of *Schriften* Vol. 1 and 2, by Louis Althusser. *Ethics* 99, No. 1 (October 1988): 197.
    Asserts that "Political theorists should find many points of interest in this volume."

Ricoeur, Paul. "Althusser." In his *Lectures on Ideology and Utopia,* pp. 103-58. New York: Columbia University Press, 1986.
    Discusses the main changes in Marxist theory in relation to ideology and science.

Additional coverage of Althusser's life and career is contained in the following sources published by Gale: *Contemporary Authors,* Vols. 131 and 132.

Jorge Amado
1912-

Brazilian novelist, short story writer, and nonfiction writer.

The following entry presents an overview of Amado's career. For further information on his life and works, see *CLC*, Volumes 13 and 40.

INTRODUCTION

Jorge Amado is a best-selling author known for his novels which evoke the spirit of the people of Bahia, Brazil. A communist in an authoritarian-ruled nation, Amado spent many years fleeing government persecution and espousing communist ideals in his novels. Eventually Amado became disenchanted with the Communist Party and wrote from a more personal perspective about his region and its people. He became a well-loved national and much-acclaimed international novelist.

Biographical Information

Amado was born in Ilheus, Bahia, Brazil, on August 10, 1912. He grew up on his father's cocoa plantation and then attended a Jesuit boarding school. While interested in classical literature, Amado found it hard to concentrate on his studies. In 1930 Amado went to Rio de Janeiro to attend law school, where he earned a diploma which he never bothered to pick up. Amado published his first novel, *O paiz do carnaval* (1931), when he was nineteen. His second novel, *Cacau* (1933), made evident his political leanings and interest in the newly formed Brazilian Communist Party. The neofascist government headed by Getulio Vargas ordered that the book be removed from bookstores. Amado became a member of the National Liberation Alliance, a left-leaning political group which attempted a coup in 1935. Shortly after the coup failed, Amado was arrested and spent two months in jail. His adversarial relationship with the Brazilian government continued, and in 1937 the government staged a public book burning in which the majority of books destroyed were Amado's. Amado eventually fled to Argentina in 1941 and wrote a biography of the founder of the Brazilian Communist Party, Luiz Carlos Prestes, entitled *Vida de Luiz Carlos Prestes, o cavaleiro da esperança* (1942). He returned to Brazil, and his struggle with the government continued until Vargas was ousted from office. In 1945 Amado was elected federal deputy of São Paulo on the Communist Party ticket. Within a few years, however, the Party again became illegal, and in 1948 Amado decided to leave his country. He lived in France and Czechoslovakia for the next four years, then returned to Brazil again in 1952. After

Joseph Stalin's death there was much debate over the future and ideological position of the Brazilian Communist Party. In 1955 Amado left the party, and from then on his relationship with communism was ambiguous. His writing underwent a significant change, becoming less political and more universally recognized by critics. During the fall of 1971 Amado came to America as a visiting fellow at the Institute for the Arts and Humanistic Studies at Pennsylvania State University.

Major Works

Amado began his career trying to expose the problems of the northeast region of Brazil, specifically of his home state, Bahia. The works were more political in nature, but beginning with *Gabriela, cravo e canela* (1958; *Gabriela, Clove and Cinnamon*) his work turned more personal, focusing on specific people and how life in Bahia affected their individual lives. Amado's protagonists are antiheroes, often coming from the lower class and including whores and rogues. Amado's work is full of mystical elements: statues that come to life and walk away, as in *O sumiça da santa* (1988; *The*

War of the Saints); a protagonist who dies more than once, as in *A morte e a morte de Quincas Berro Dágua* (1962); and a dead husband returning, as in *Dona Flor e seus dois maridos* (1966; *Dona Flor and Her Two Husbands*). Amado's *Dona Flor and Her Two Husbands* is about a woman who falls in love with a rogue. He is passionate and exciting but hurts her with his wild exploits. When her husband dies, Dona Flor mourns but then goes on to remarry. This time her husband is respectable, responsible, and dull. While she knows her second husband is good for her, Dona Flor misses the passion her first love inspired in her. The first husband's spirit returns to her, and at first she resists him. Eventually she discovers happiness with the best of both husbands. The mystical nature of *Dona Flor and Her Two Husbands* resurfaces in *The War of the Saints,* in which the statue of Saint Barbara of the Thunder comes to life and simply walks away to tend to her people.

Critical Reception

Reviewers usually discuss Amado's career as having two phases, marked by the shift in Amado's career away from political-oriented works. Leftist critics ignore his later novels, but most reviewers agree the change was for the better. James Polk asserts, "His first works were embittered, pedantic tracts, weighted with social squalor and class struggle, resolved by a simplistic and highly romanticized brand of communism." Many critics have pointed out the importance of Bahian cultural forms in Amado's fiction, such as his use of the *candomblé* religious ritual and the Brazilian martial art *capoeira* in many of his stories. In addition they refer to his borrowing from Bahian's popular literary press, the *folhetos,* or songbooks. Reviewers often point out the mystical quality of his work and praise his ability to make supernatural events seem ordinary. Many reviewers call Amado a regionalist, but a few point to the general truths present in Amado's work and the popular appeal of his fiction. Amado is known for his strong female characters. A few critics mention his almost feminist views being in strong opposition to traditional Brazilian machismo. However Amado has been accused of inconsistency in his views. His public statements on sexism and racism in Brazil have sometimes conflicted with his presentation of those problems in his novels. Complaints about characterization range from assertions that portraying intimate or unspoken thoughts is not Amado's forte to charges that his characters are underdeveloped. Some reviewers have accused Amado of being a pornographer, but critics generally dismiss this label. Critical assessment of Amado's fiction is mixed. Some critics assert that he is a master storyteller with a great ability to evoke the images and soul of his native region. Others accuse him of being a hack, simply a writer of popular formulaic novels that lack any literary merit. Jon S. Vincent states, "Amado is anything but a simple spinner of yarns. His later novels are deceptively sophisticated fictions by a writer with a perfect ear for the right word, a flawless sense of dramatic and comic pace, and a keen sensibility for narrative pattern."

PRINCIPAL WORKS

O paiz do carnaval (novel) 1931
Cacau (novel) 1933
Suor (novel) 1934
Jubiabá (novel) 1935
Mar morto [*Sea of Death*] (novel) 1936
Captiães da areia [*Captains of the Sands*] (novel) 1937
A estrada do mar (novel) 1937
ABC de Castro Alves (novel) 1941
Vida de Luiz Carlos Prestes, o cavaleiro da esperança (nonfiction) 1942
Terras do sem fim [*The Violent Land*] (novel) 1943
São Jorge do Ilhéus [*George of Iltheus*] (novel) 1944
The Golden Harvest (novel) 1944
Bahia de todos os santos (travel essay) 1945
Homens e coisas do Partido Comunista (nonfiction) 1946
Seara vermelha (novel) 1946
O amor de Castro Alves (novel) 1947
O mundo da paz (nonfiction) 1950
Os subterrâneos da liberdade (novel) 1954
Gabriela, cravo e canela [*Gabriela, Clove and Cinnamon*] (novel) 1958
Os velhos marinheiros [*The Two Deaths of Quincas Wateryell* and *Home Is the Sailor*] (short stories) 1961
A morte e a morte de Quincas Berro Dágua (novel) 1962
Os pastores da noite [*Sheperds of the Night*] (novel) 1964
Dona Flor e seus dois maridos, história moral e de amor [*Dona Flor and Her Two Husbands*] (novel) 1966
Tenda dos milagres [*Tent of Miracles*] (novel) 1969
Tereza Batista, cansada de guerra [*Tereza Batista: Home from the Wars*] (novel) 1972
O gato malhado e a andorinha Sinhá [*The Swallow and the Tomcat*] (novel) 1976
Tieta do Agreste: Pastora de cabras [*Tieta the Goat Girl*] (novel) 1977
Farda, fardão, camisola de dormir [*Pen, Sword, Camisole*] (novel) 1979
A bola e o goleiro (novel) 1984
Tocaia grande [*Showdown*] (novel) 1984
O sumiça da santa [*The War of the Saints*] (novel) 1988
Chapada diamantina (novel) 1989
Navegação de cabotagem (memoir) 1992
A descoberta da América pelos Turcos (novel) 1994

CRITICISM

David Gallagher (review date 17 August 1969)

SOURCE: A review of *Dona Flor and Her Two Husbands,* in *The New York Times Book Review,* August 17, 1969, p. 33.

[*In the following review, Gallagher praises Amado's* Dona Flor and Her Two Husbands, *but complains that "It is a pity that Amado mars his achievement by often writing flatly, without discipline or tension."*]

For the average citizen of São Paulo or Rio, the North-East of Brazil is an area of calamitous suffering he is happy never to have visited. And if this vast, arid region, inhabited by nearly 17 million Brazilians, ever pricks his conscience, it will be to some extent due to the work of three novelists of the North-East, José Lins do Rego, Gracilano Ramos and Jorge Amado.

Amado's early books were renowned for the militant socialist realism he brought to bear, as a member of the Communist party and follower of Luis Carlos Prestes. The relative permissiveness of the Soviet thaw radically altered his writing over the last 13 years. In 1958, he wrote **Gabriela, Clove and Cinnamon,** an ebulliently exotic book in which social postures were abandoned and characters were paraded with more emphasis on their eccentricities than their suffering. **Dona Flor and Her Two Husbands,** a novel about sex and gambling, is in much the same vein.

The problems of the North-East are scarcely mentioned. This time, Amado has nothing to tell us about the dire consequences of mass labor migration to the cities. Nor does he record the agonizing effects of the North-East's droughts, or the fact that less than five per cent of the schoolchildren in the North-East finish their primary education. In his new novel, we see the North-East from the inside, through the eyes of its humbler inhabitants, people whose primary interests are the latest film at the local movie house, the prospects of success at roulette or with a handsome *mulatta,* the latest serial on the radio—and, not least, the marriage, widowhood and remarriage of everyone's favorite neighbor Dona Flor Dos Guimarães.

The novel's villain is Dona Rozilda, Dona Flor's mother, and her villainy lies in the fact that she is a scheming social climber. The hero is Dona Flor's reckless first husband, a handsome rogue named Vadinho, whom no *mulatta* has ever been known to resist, who is so charming that no man can refuse to lend him money. Usually, he lavishes the loan on a game of baccarat. If he wins, he throws a party; if he loses, that's too bad; another creditor will be found. When he dies, he dies dancing the samba.

No one who knows Brazil need be reminded that this is an immensely happy country, even in the North-East. Practically everyone in Amado's galaxy of characters exudes a reckless

joie de vivre. There are innumerable penniless playboys, pranksters and gamblers; dissolute mayors presiding over towns with retinues of voluptuous *mulattas;* lascivious priests; gossiping crones downing glasses of rum at their relatives' wakes. Among them all, Vadinho towers. When he dies, Dona Flor forgets the hours she lived in solitude, while he caroused with any woman in Bahia lucky enough to have him, or squandered money she had painfully saved for a new radio. She can remember only his artistry in bed.

A respected cooking instructress, expert at preparing stewed turtle and fricassee of lizard, she finds her bereavement hard to bear. Erotic nightmares invade her sleep. Widowhood, she finds, is "outwardly all chastity, inwardly a pool of dung." Fortunately the local pharmacist, Dr. Teodoro, is eager to console her, and Dona Flor is glad to accept his proposal of a second marriage.

Dr. Teodoro gives her stability and fidelity. Dr. Teodoro is a solemn man, determined to fulfill his marital obligations, albeit a little predictably: "On Wednesdays and Saturdays, at ten o'clock, give or take a minute, Dr. Teodoro took his wife in upright ardor and unfailing pleasure, always with an encore on Saturday, optional on Wednesday."

Despite which, Dona Flor continues to have lewd visions. Vadinho, a rascal even in death, appears stark naked and irresistible at the foot of her bed. Soon she is forced to yield to his lascivious ghost. For "Coupling is a blessed thing. It was God who ordered it. 'Go and couple, my children, go and have babies' was what He said, and it was one of the best things He did."

In the past few decades the shamanistic traditions of Latin America (usually in countries where there is a strong Negro influence or a living Indian culture) have been skillfully exploited in literature. Fantasy in many Latin American novels is a real, active dimension in the characters' lives—and, just as the characters themselves ignore the boundaries between reality and imagination, so for the reader, too, real events slip almost imperceptibly into magic. In **Dona Flor and Her Two Husbands** it is the Devil-God Exu who resuscitates the body of Vadinho and restores it to Dona Flor, to distract her from her second husband. "Exu," Amado tells us, "drinks only one thing—straight rum. At the crossroads, he waits sitting upon the night to take the most difficult road, the narrowest, the most winding, the bad road—for all Exu wants is to frolic, to make mischief. . . . Exu, Vadinho's patron deity." As Vadinho explains to Dona Flor, Dr. Teodoro "protects your virtue. He is your outward face, I your inner, the lover whom you can't bear to evade. . . . To be happy, you need both of us. . . . The rest is deceit and hypocrisy."

It is easy to see that the Yoruba deities of Brazil have done a therapeutic service to Dona Flor in resurrecting Vadinho and removing her deceitful inhibitions—a service performed by classical deities in much modern literature. Magic plays another role, that of wish-fulfilling retributions. Just as in Miguel Angel Asturias's novel *Strong Wind* a cyclone summoned by the local shaman levels the exploiting American banana plantations of Guatemala, so in **Dona Flor** the magic of Exu is deployed to avenge the exploitation of the local roulette wheel. During his lifetime, Vadinho lost a small fortune on his favorite number, 17. With magical powers acquired in death, he is able to ruin the casino by causing 17 to come up with miraculous regularity, after whispering to his cronies that they should stake every cent they can borrow on it.

Dona Flor and Her Two Husbands is a remarkable novel for the coolness with which the author is able to impose his extraordinary characters on us. Like them, we learn to take exoticism and magic in our stride. It is a pity that Amado mars his achievement by often writing flatly, without discipline or tension. His refreshing exuberance is diminished by the novel's almost aggressive repetitiveness. Cut to half its size, it would have been a better book.

Jorge Amado with J. C. Thomas (interview date 23 June 1975)

SOURCE: "Jorge Amado," in *Publishers Weekly*, Vol. 207, No. 25, June 23, 1975, pp. 20-1.

[*In the following interview, Amado discusses his presentation of women in his novels and his relationship to his home region of Bahia.*]

A regionalist who calls himself a materialist, Jorge Amado also describes himself as "a chronicler of the lives of the poor people of Bahia," a state in the northeast of Brazil. American readers know him best as the author of *Gabriela, Clove and Cinnamon;* now, with the publication shortly by Knopf of his latest novel, that audience will discover a different kind of liberated woman in **Tereza Batista.**

He is a stocky man of medium height, with leonine features that could easily belong to a Greek statue; however, he is not Hellenic but Brazilian—and strongly contemporary in his views about women and men and their sometimes loving, sometimes loathing dialogues. And, perhaps ironically, in Portuguese, the language in which he writes, the word for novel is "romance" and the name Amado is literally translated as "beloved."

"It is becoming more difficult each year to publish fiction in Brazil," he told *PW* in a recent interview at his home in Salvador, Bahia, speaking in Portuguese and being translated by Ivanka Ajdaric, a Yugoslavian lady now living in Bahia. "Yet I consider myself more of a journalist than a novelist, because I do not add anything to my writing about the people of Bahia that does not already exist in their lives. I simply transfer the reality of their lives to a literary plane and recreate the ambience of Bahia, and that is all."

Like Willy Loman, he knows the territory. Born in the city of Ilheus in southern Bahia 63 years ago, Amado grew up on his father's cocoa plantation, edited a self-published neighborhood newspaper when he was 10, became a full-time reporter at 15, and had just turned 19 when his first novel, **Land of Carnival,** was published. His latest, **Tereza Batista,** is book No. 19 in Brazil but only the eighth to appear in America. And despite his comment on present publication difficulties, he possesses a literary stability that must be envied by publisher-changing *Norteamericanos.* His Brazilian books have always been brought out under the imprint of Livraria Martins Editora in São Paulo, and only Knopf has published him in this country—the result of a serendipitous encounter with Blanche Knopf when she was traveling in Brazil after World War II. To the U.S. audience, his best-known books concern themselves with the tragicomic adventures of highly individualistic, extremely outspoken, uncompromisingly independent and definitely desirable women. *Gabriela* in 1962 . . . **Dona Flor and Her Two Husbands** in 1969—and now . . .

"Tereza Batista is an orphan living in a small town in the interior of Bahia," Amado explains in his rich voice. "At 13, she is sold as a common-law wife to a man who prefers to sleep with girls no older than 15. She then becomes a prostitute when she becomes a woman." He pauses, adding, "Yet she still earns the respect of the people in her community and, most important of all, she respects herself." It is almost as if Amado is a closet feminist in a *macho* country, an exponent of women's liberation in a land where divorce is still illegal.

"My feelings are that women have the same rights—and responsibilities—as men," he says. "Sometimes I treat the women in my books with more sympathy, but that is because they are often more interesting than the men." As for the marital situations of several of his heroines, "Thousands of Brazilians, due to the laws against divorce, are living together without benefit of marriage, most of them happily, I think."

And Bahians even more so. For Amado, like [William] Faulkner, is essentially a regional writer who extrapolates universal values from local characters. As he points out, "Brazil is like India, more a continent than a country, for regional differences here are very great. I feel that I know more about life in Bahia than in any other region, for I have lived here almost all of my life."

Bahia is also the Brazilian state where the true integration created by intermarriage is more evident than elsewhere. This theme is fully developed and strikingly demonstrated in **Tent of Miracles,** published in 1971. The protagonist, Pedro Archanjo, is a self-educated, street-smart *mulato* who achieves great renown—and recriminations—for the authorship of, among other self-published works, "Notes on Miscegenation in the Families of Bahia" and "African Influence on the Customs of Bahia." This is another unifying theme in Amado's writing, what he calls "the magical force of the people, being the result of the mixed blood of all Brazilians, including myself. It is the black people who have provided the thrust for our Brazilian culture as we know it today."

Not exactly a rallying call for black power, yet scarcely likely to endear him to those who pretend to be whiter than white. Nor do his views on power endear him to politicians, for he believes that "whoever is in power in any system often confuses the interests of the people with his own." Such realistic opinions did not sit well with Brazil's military government when Amado was a Federal Deputy in the 1940s. As he wryly comments, "I was obliged to leave the country in 1948. I lived in France and Czechoslovakia until I was allowed to return four years later."

> **I am a historical materialist; I believe in the reality of history in shaping people's lives. But in America you have a different meaning for that word, so perhaps I had better say that I am an optimist.**
> —*Jorge Amado*

And when he did, he returned to his daily writing ritual, six to 10 hours every day of the week, typing out draft after draft, month after month, until another book is finished. He was then, as he remains, the best-known author in Brazil, and was elected to the Brazilian Academy of Letters in 1961. However, Amado considers Machado de Assis "a better storyteller, a man who knows all of Brazil and thus is more of a national Brazilian author than myself." The young writer Joao Rebeiro has also attracted his attention. As for other South American writers, he describes Jorge Luis Borges as simply "a Spanish fantasist in the tradition of [Miguel de] Cervantes," though of course Borges is from Argentina. But his favorite writer and close friend was the late Chilean poet and diplomat Pablo Neruda, of whom he says, with great affection, "I wept with joy when he won the Nobel Prize." (Of contemporary American writers, Amado had little to say; his favorite remains Mark Twain and, no doubt for political and socioeconomic reasons, he mentioned the 1930s radical writer Mike Gold with approval.)

He has much to say, however, of *candomblé,* the religious ritual indigenous to Bahia in which Catholic saints are syncretized with African gods. Amado calls *candomblé* "the principal religion of the poor people of Bahia. From a historical point of view, it has helped the black people who came here as slaves to keep their African culture intact." Then he confides, "My father took me to see my first *candomblé* when I was 14, and I have been participating ever since." He is now one of twelve *Obas de Xango* in Brazil; a minister of Xango, the god of thunder.

Such exoticism no doubt contributed to his popularity when he was a Visiting Fellow at the Institute for the Arts and Humanistic Studies at Pennsylvania State University during fall 1971 (his first American visit since the Depression). Professor Stanley Weintraub was instrumental in persuading the Brazilian author and his wife Zelia to leave their beloved country for 10 weeks in America. There Amado participated in a weekly lecture series on his writing, speaking, as always, in Portuguese, with a different translator for each session selected from the students and faculty. These exchanges were less lecture than conversation, with questions and answers, culminating in late evening talking and drinking bouts that left no doubt that Amado needed no formal translation to communicate his feelings. (He seems unconcerned about translation of his works into other languages, for he has never met any of his translators into the many languages in which his books are on sale.)

In closing, the *PW* interviewer asks Amado if he would care to sum himself up in one word. He answers, "I am a materialist." Further clarification is immediately requested. "I am a historical materialist; I believe in the reality of history in shaping people's lives. But in America you have a different meaning for that word, so perhaps I had better say that I am an optimist." He smiles knowingly: "In this world, you are either an optimist or you believe the world is going to end, and in that case it makes no difference."

Nancy T. Baden (essay date Summer 1976)

SOURCE: "Popular Poetry in the Novels of Jorge Amado," in *Journal of Latin American Lore,* Vol. 2, No. 1, Summer, 1976, pp. 3-22.

[*In the following essay, Baden traces Amado's use of popular and oral verse forms in his novels.*]

The diverse aspects of Bahian popular culture manifest themselves as some of the most distinctive and important elements of the fiction of Jorge Amado. In effect, popular songs, stories, and customs are at the core of the underlying psychological structure of his novels. Naturally, many critics have referred to Amado's heavy borrowing from the *folhetos,* the popular literary press of Brazil's Northeast, as well as his extensive utilization of such aspects of popular Afro-Bahian culture as *candomblé* and *capoeira*. Little has been done, however, in the way of a systematic examination of the kinds of popular verse forms utilized, their origins, and their functions within the novels. Thus, it is my purpose here to study the role of popular poetry in Amadan fiction.

Amado's ties to the popular culture of Bahia are so well known that *Manchete,* one of Brazil's leading large-circulation magazines, featured an article entitled the "ABC de Jorge Amado." His life is presented in the manner of the popular narrative poems commonly used in the Brazilian Northeast, which exhalt the lives of bandits, saints, and other famous personages. Amado's extensive use of the ABC poems in his novels is so recognized in Brazil that no real explanation is necessary for the general reading public. Dorival Caymmi, a famous composer and longtime friend of the author, reveals Amado's intimate relationship with popular poetry when he says: "Aliás, a maior parte desses versos já estavam criados nos próprios livros, criados por Jorge sôbre a base folclórica dos abcs e das canções do cais que êle estudou quando estava para escrever seus romances." Certainly Amado is not a folklorist by training, nor does he have the reputation as a scholar in that field, as does Mário de Andrade; nevertheless, Câmara Cascudo, in his important *Dicionário do folclore brasileiro,* does not hesitate to use him as a source of reference.

When did Amado begin to use popular elements as part of his narrative? Actually, in his very first work, *País do carnaval* (1930), snatches of *sambas* are included to enhance his descriptions of *carnaval.* Popular culture was a major concern of the Generation of 1930, of which Amado was a part. Scholars such as Édison Carneiro, the ethnographer, and Artur Ramos were experts in the area of popular culture. Aspiring young writers such as Jorge Amado, Raquel de Queiroz, and José Lins do Rego utilized these elements to give expression to their concern for the social conditions of the Brazilian Northeast.

Concerned primarily with portraying the downtrodden workers, vagabonds, and prostitutes of the lower classes, Amado utilizes their culture, based predominantly on oral traditions and the *folhetos* of the popular press, to lend an air of authenticity to his tales.
—*Nancy T. Baden*

It is in his fourth novel, *Jubiabá* (1935), that folk and popular elements are combined in a pattern associated with his novelistic style over the ensuing forty years. Rather than simply including songs to create mood, he ties them to the development of the protagonist, thus weaving them into the very fabric of the novel. Following the publication of *Gabriela, cravo e canela* (1958), where Amado formally sheds the trappings of social realism and presents his social concerns in a comic vein, popular culture acquires added importance. In 1961 Clarivaldo Prado Valladeres quotes Amado as saying, "As preocupaçoes fundamentais de minha obra continuam a partir de *Gabriela:* a transposição para o plano literário da cultura popular." An examination of the verse forms found in the novels illustrates Amado's interest in transposing popular culture to a literary plane.

As one might suspect, poetic folklore and other elements of popular culture do not appear uniformly in the body of his fiction. That is to say, where the setting is Bahia and the class studied is the lower class, folklore appears frequently. Where the characters have a middle class orientation as in *A completa verdade sôbre as discutidas aventuras do Comandante Vasco Moscoso de Aragão, capitão de longo curso* (*Os velhos marinheiros,* 1961) or *Dona Flor e seus dois maridos,* the utilization of popular verse forms is less frequent. In the propaganda-laden novels like *Seara vermelha* (1946) and *Os subterrâneos da liberdade* (1954), which take place away from Bahia, these elements appear only occasionally.

Amado draws heavily upon his surroundings in creating mood in his fiction—so much so that Bahia (Salvador) and Amado have become almost synonymous in the eyes of many. He expresses his fondness for this city in his guidebook *Bahia de todos os santos.* This same sentiment permeates the novels. He frankly alludes to the magical qualities of his city when he says, "Sou materialista, não tenho preocupaçöes religiosas. Mas vivo aqui, na Bahia mágica e crio sôbre tal magia."

Concerned primarily with portraying the downtrodden workers, vagabonds, and prostitutes of the lower classes, Amado utilizes their culture, based predominantly on oral traditions and the *folhetos* of the popular press, to lend an air of authenticity to his tales. In order to convey the multifaceted popular culture of Bahia, Amado draws on many areas of popular culture, particularly from the popular literary press (*literatura de cordel*) of the Brazilian Northeast. Traditionally, written forms cannot be classified as folklore because they lack the requisites of definition for folklore such as anonymity. The Argentine Raúl Cortazar notes, however, that there is an undeniable interpenetration in this hazy, ill-defined area. He carefully differentiates between literary folklore, such as that used by Amado, and folk literature, emanating from the people. Amado uses the projection or outgrowth of folk literature as well as elements from the popular press as literary devices to enhance mood and local color. His is far more than a superficial incorporation of these elements; rather, he integrates popular poetry into the very fabric of his story. He uses verses of both European and African origin and borrows heavily from *literatura de cordel.* In addition, he pens his own verses in imitation of all these verse forms. The result is that it is almost impossible to distinguish his creations from his models. The reader becomes so caught up in the created world that the fine line between fiction and reality becomes blurred.

One of the most important functions of songs in the novels is to help build mood. *Mar morto,* for example, takes on a lyrical tone suggested by the interspersing of a *toada,* a rather melancholy and sentimental song found throughout most of Brazil. Written by Amado himself, the lines "É doce morrer no mar" appear at significant junctures to foreshadow the destiny of the seamen about whom he writes. Similar is the case of *Terras do sem fim,* which describes the opening of the cacao lands near Ilhéus. To underscore the epic quality of the saga, Amado chooses lines from a popular song collection (*cancioneiro*), "Eu vou contar uma história, uma história de espantar," which prepares the reader for the bloody battles to follow.

Another use of popular verse forms is simply to add a touch of local color and authenticity to a given scene. Such is the case of the songs related to the Christmas season, or those sung by beggars (*cantiga de cego*) on the streets. The following example from *Jubiabá* shows an elderly lady from the poor section of Salvador gathering her neighbors about her at dusk to tell or read stories in verse. This stanza begins the story of the accursed daughter (*filha maldita*) portion of the *literatura de cordel:*

> Leitores que caso horrível
> vou aqui vos relatar
> me faz o corpo tremer
> e os cabelos arrepiar
> pois nunca pensei no mundo
> existisse um ente imundo
> capaz de seus pais matar.

It is the reference to well-known songs and legends that helps in the creation of mood and involves the reader with the beliefs and superstitions of the poor hill people (*favelados*).

Given the eclectic nature of Amado's approach to the use of popular songs and oral traditions, it is difficult to strictly adhere to any given classification. Naturally, the *folhetos* emanating from the popular press will be treated separately. The classification of Brazilian songs set forth by Renato Almeida will be used to group the remaining songs and dances. The examples fall into the following general categories: religious songs of both Catholic and fetishist origins; *cantigas* comprising work songs; children's songs and rounds; and *cantigas de cego;* songs associated with recre-

ation, in this case *capoeira;* and a general category of miscellany ranging from sentimental *modinhas* to *sambas.*

The ABC, a song published by the popular press in the Brazilian Northeast, is one of the most commonly found verse forms in Amado's novels. These narrative poems, which laud the exploits of outlaws who fight the Establishment and become the heroes of the common people, fit naturally into the themes chosen by the author. *Jubiabá* shows the complete integration of the ABC into the plot as it relates to the development of the antihero, Antônio Balduíno. In the first part of this episodic novel, the young Antônio Balduíno, one of the orphaned black poor of Salvador, finds inspiration in the life of Lucas da Feira, a nineteenth-century Brazilian Robin Hood whose exploits were recorded in *literatura de cordel:*

> Homem pobre nunca robei
> pois não tinha o que roubar
> mas os ricos de carteira
> a nenhum deixei escapar.

Not only does the verse focus on the problem of social class, but Balduíno, whose father was an outlaw, finds a new hero in Lucas.

The idea of liberty, a common motif in Amadan fiction, is also reinforced through the songs as Antônio Balduíno seeks to overcome the oppressive forces of society. Later in the novel, when Balduíno becomes known as a songwriter, he attempts to write an ABC about Zumbi dos Palmares, the runaway slave whose fame is the subject of a legend. As the novel progresses, Balduíno takes on the stance of a political activist. His own personal feelings regarding freedom parallel the sentiment expressed in the song about Zumbi:

> Palmares onde eu briguei
> Lutei contra a escravidão
> Mil polícias aqui veio
> E nenhuma não voltou.

Although not an ABC, the "Cantiga de Vilela," from the *literatura de cordel,* is another song that heralds an outlaw. One evening as Balduíno plays the guitar while his sidekick Gordo sings, the people who have gathered listen attentively to the story of the bandit Vilela and his heroic struggle with the Alferes (Second Lieutenant):

> O Alferes foi valente
> E de valente enforcou-se,
> Mais valente foi Vilela
> Morreu, foi santo e salvou-se!

When he finally commits himself to the strike as a means of overcoming social oppression, Balduíno finds his destiny. The novel ends with the "A.B.C. de Antônio Balduíno," this time written by Amado himself. It is of interest to note that the name, *Antônio Balduíno* is, itself, the beginning of an ABC.

> Este é o ABC de Antônio Balduíno
> Negro Valente e brigão
> Desordeiro sem pureza
> mas bom de coração.

This ABC is typical of most of the songs that Amado writes for inclusion in the novels. He utilizes one or two stanzas—just enough to highlight the qualities of the protagonist. By subsequently referring to the manner in which *folhetos* are actually sold in markets, the narrator blends his own creation with those of the popular poets. "O ABC de Antônio Balduíno, trazendo na capa vermelha um retrato do tempo em que o negro era jogador de boxe, é vendido no cais, nos saveiros, nas feiras, no Mercado Modêlo, nos botequins. . . ."

Antônio Balduíno is not the only Amadan protagonist associated with the ABC. This type of song is built into the accounts of other protagonists, especially those involved in a social struggle. In *Mar morto,* Francisco, an old seaman, tells stories in verse about Rosa Palmeirão, a legendary figure among the seamen who is as adept at fighting as she is at making love:

> Rosa bateu em seis soldados
> Na noite de São João
> Chamaram seu delegado,
> Ele disse—não vou lá não.
>
> Veio tôda a puliça
> Ele puxou o punhal
> Foi medonho o rebuliço
> Foi uma noite fatal.

In *Seara vermelha* (1946) there is an outlaw (*cangaceiro*), Lucas Alvoredo, whose cruel exploits terrorize the towns-people of the hinterland (*sertão*):

> Lá vem Lucas Arvoredo,
> armado com seu fuzil . . .
> O sertão treme de medo.
> já matou pra mais de mil . . .

Os ásperos tempos, the first volume of the trilogy entitled *Os subterrâneos da liberdade* (1954), is set firmly within the philosophical framework of socialist realism. The repressed members of the Communist party struggle against the oppression of the Vargas regime at the onset of the Estado Novo in 1937. José Gonçalo, known as Gonçalão, is one of those faithful Communist party workers who strives to serve the people. When forced to flee Salvador to avoid a prison term, he is led to safety by our friend, Antônio

Balduíno, who sings the following ABC to celebrate Gonçalão's prowess:

> Dos índios capitão
> coronel da gente pobre,
> general da valentia,
> Zé Gonçalo ou Gonçalão
> Revoltoso perseguido,
> escondido na Bahia
> e condenado à prisão
> . . . .
> Nunca que prender vão
> Zé Gonçalo ou Gonçalão!

More recently, *Tereza Batista cansada de guerra* (1972) follows in the combative spirit found in the earlier novels. Tereza, having been sold into prostitution, struggles for her freedom. The idea of *literatura de cordel* is built into the very structure of the work, even though it is penned in prose rather than the traditional verse form. The dedication of the novel alludes to this when it says, "Peste, fome e guerra, morte e amor, a vida de Tereza Batista é uma história de cordel." An interesting phenomenon has occurred with regard to this novel. Tereza's struggle against injustice so intrigued the well-known popular poet Rodolfo Coelho Cavalcante that he wrote a *folheto* directly inspired by the novel. He frankly states this in the first and last stanzas, which are cited below:

> Inspirado no Romance
> Do Escritor Jorge Amado
> Dei o título do seu livro
> e no mesmo baseado
> Vou descrever com Ihaneza
> A história de Tereza
> Cujo drama foi narrado.
>
> Me desculpe Jorge Amado
> Se eu fui fraco trovador.
> Mas o drama de Tereza
> É o drama da minha dor,
> Hoje Cançado de Guerra
> Sofro aqui na sua terra
> CIDADE DO SALVADOR.

This clearly shows how Amado's protagonists who are caught up in a social struggle are in keeping with the spirit of the heroes lauded by the popular poets. The use of the ABCs and *folhetos* not only spotlights the development of these antiheroes, but also enhances the epic mood that characterizes these novels.

In the presentation of religious songs it is natural to expect the inclusion of both Catholic celebrations and fetishist cults associated with the *candomblé* of African origin. The role of the *candomblé* in Amadan fiction has been discussed by both Russell G. Hamilton, who traces the development of the Afro-Bahian cults in Amado's novels, and by Maria Luisa Nunes, who relates the *candomblé* to the preservation of African culture in Brazil. While both articles describe the rituals, neither discusses the use of the liturgical chants as a means of achieving verisimilitude in the fictional rendering of the ceremonies.

The dignified figure of the cult priestess, Mãe Aninha, comes to the fore in *Capitães da areia* (1937) to defend the poor against Omolu, the god of smallpox. The narrator describes the participants singing:

> Cabono
> aziela engoma.
> Quero vê couro zoá!
> Omolu vai pro sertão
> Bexiga vai espalhá.

In *Mar morto* ample reference is made to Iemanjá, African goddess of the waters. The sailors and dock workers portrayed in the novel consider Iemanjá, a most popular figure, as their guardian. Here the cult priestess (*mãe do terreiro*) sings of Iemanjá in Yoruba to give the reader the full flavor of the rites:

> A ode resse
> o ki é Iemanjá
> Akóta guê lêguê a cio
> Er fi rilá

Naturally, most of the description is of the dancing, but the inclusion of part of the liturgy adds an air of authenticity to the scenes.

In other instances, personages engaged in their daily tasks sing songs associated with the cults. Rufino, the black canoeman in *Mar morto,* sings to Iemanjá as he rows upriver:

> Eu me chamo Ogum de lê
> Não nego meu naturá
> Sou filho de águas claras
> Sou neto de Iemanjá

As the reader learns more of Iemanjá he senses the symbolic importance of the sea goddess to the people of Bahia.

The songs and popular processions that relate to the Christian calendar, particularly those associated with the Christmas season, are included in Amado's fiction to round out the cultural milieu. Of particular importance to the culmination of Christmas season activities is the Kings Day celebration (*Dia dos Reis*). Reference is made in this context

to shepherdesses (*pastorinhas*) in *São Jorge dos Ilhéus* where cacao worker Florindo dreams of an earlier procession when times were better. He remembers having played the part of Herod:

> ó rei Heródia
> respeita o menino
> que é nosso Deus . . .

On a lighter note, when the heroine of *Gabriela, cravo e canela* can not tolerate the restraints of the society New Years' dance (*Reveillón*), she leads the distinguished citizenry into the street to dance with Dora and the shepherdesses of her *terno:*

> Sou linda pastorinha
> venho Jesus adorar,
> No presépio de Belem
> os reis magos saudar.

In *Tenda dos milagres,* a work dedicated to popular culture, the protagonist, Lídio Corrió, Pedro Archanjo's friend and partner, directs the rehearsal of the shepherdesses. The verses included are those of the *entremez* of the little donkey (*entremez da burrinha*).

> Bote a burrinha pra dentro
> Pro sereno não molhar
> O selim é de veludo
> A colcha de tafetá.

Although the *pastoris* are in effect a dying, or dead, tradition, their inclusion in the novels is in keeping with Amado's desire to portray the customs of a given period. The action of *Gabriela, cravo e canela* takes place in 1925, while that of *Tenda dos milagres* occurs in 1968. The latter flashes back in time to depict the life of Pedro Archanjo, who was born in 1868. As a result, many of the incidents in the plot date back to the turn of the century when *pastoris* played a more important social role.

It is only natural to find work songs in novels whose setting is the Ilhéus area. The plots depict the society surrounding the rich cacao plantations that are so well known in the southern part of Bahia. In *Terras do sem fim* (1943), *São Jorge dos Ilhéus* (1944), and *Gabriela, cravo e canela* (1958), the plantation worker is consistently portrayed as one who suffers and labors under conditions that resemble those of serfdom.

Terras do sem fim deals with the power struggle that surrounded the opening up of the cacao lands about 1911. The action focuses on the fortunes of the powerful landowners (*Coronéis*) who ruthlessly sought to control the lucrative farmlands. In the section of the novel entitled "A Luta," a work song is used to foreshadow the conflict that will result in so many needless deaths:

> Minha sina é sem esperança . . .
> É trabalhar noite e dia . . .
>
> Minha vida é de penado
> Cheguei e fui amarrado
> nas grilhetas do cacau . . .

In another portion of the novel the workers sing as they trudge in the rain:

> O cacau é boa lavra . . .
> Já chegou a nova safra . . .

The sequel, **São Jorge dos Ilhéus,** shows the transfer of power in the cacao region from the old colonels to the exporters in the mid-1930s. Nevertheless, the plight of the worker remains unchanged. In this example Florindo works and sings as he harvests:

> Minha côr é do cacau,
> mulato de querer bem,
> mas ai! mulata, mas ai!
> sour amarelo emapuça'o,
> côr de maleita também.

Gabriela, cravo e canela, with its comic overtones and generally lighthearted mood, nevertheless contains more serious moments, as when the workers sing of their life of toil on the plantation of Coronel Melk Tavares:

> Dura vida, amargo fel,
> sou negro trabalhador
> Me diga, seu coronel,
> Me diga, faça o favor:
> quando é que eu vou colhêr
> as penas do meu amor?

These sad songs of the oral tradition show the worker as resigned to his destiny, very much as in the spirituals of the southern United States. They not only reinforce the social concerns expressed in the novels, but also serve to enhance their underlying tone.

> **Amado not only utilizes songs of the oral tradition, but also writes in imitation of them.**
> —*Nancy T. Baden*

As if in sharp contrast to more somber themes, the happy songs sung by children are sprinkled through Amado's later

novels. Naturally, the effervescent, youthful qualities of Gabriela immediately come to mind. The children's tune sung by Gabriela and Negrinho Tuísca is directly related to the heroine's name and emanates from the oral tradition:

> A rosa ficou doente,
> O cravo foi visitar,
> a rosa teve um desmaio
> o cravo pôs-se a chorar.

Shortly thereafter, Gabriela and Tuísca sing and dance the traditional *caranguejo* round:

> Palma, palma, palma,
> Pé, Pé, Pé,
> Roda, roda, roda . . .
> Caranguejo peixe é.

In **Dona Flor** again the heroine is involved in a children's round. This time it is imagined, and the dreamlike sequence highlights the dilemma that the attractive widow Dona Flor faces in choosing one of her many suitors. Flor is drawn into the circle of the children's game, ring-around-the-rosy (*ciranda-cirandinha*). Instead of children, however, the participants are candidates for her hand in marriage:

> Ai Florzinha Ai Florzinha
> Entrarás na roda
> E ficarás sòzinha

One of the suitors, a young man, enters the circle and sings the following traditional song:

> Tira tira o seu pèzinho
> Bota aqui ao pé do meu
> E depois não vá dizer
> Que você se arrependeu.

As with the ABC Amado not only utilizes songs of the oral tradition, but also writes in imitation of them. There are four songs that thematically tie together the sections of **Gabriela, cravo e canela,** and each is related to one of the four women important in the novel. The "Cantiga para Ninar Malvina" is dedicated to the ill-fated daughter of Melk Tavares, who flees from her tyrannical father and the constraints of Ilhéus society. This lullaby (*acalanto*), written by Amado, is reminiscent of the oral tradition:

> Dorme, menina dormida
> teu lindo sonho a sonhar
> No teu leito adormecida
> Partirás a navegar.

Alceu Maynard Araújo refers to the custom of blind beggars singing in the markets of the Northeast. This is another type of song that appears occasionally in the novels. In *Jubiabá,* Gordo, one of Antônio Balduíno's cohorts, is not blind, but very adept at imitating blind beggars in order to fleece the unsuspecting public:

> Esmola para sete ceguinhos . . .
> Eu sou o mais velho,
> êsse é o segundo,
> os outros estão em casa,
> Papai é aleijado
> Mamãe é doente,
> me dê uma esmola
> pra sete órfãozinhos
> são todos ceguinhos.

As a means of summing up the dramatic events of the land struggles in *Terras do sem fim,* the blind singers at the market recount the exploits of those who battled. Here, however, it is not a *cantiga de cego,* but an ABC. In *Tereza Batista cansada de guerra,* Belarmino, a blind man who has begged at a fixed place for twenty years, moves to the cathedral in hopes of finding a more receptive audience. The narrator reports that he changes his song in keeping with his new surroundings:

> Salve o menino Jesus
> em seu berço de luz
> e o Senhor São José
> protetor da nossa fé
> e Santa Virgem Maria
> com bondade e cortesia.

This is a song written by Amado in imitation of the *cantiga de cego.* Again, it is not surprising that Amado would choose these songs over other forms of traditional verse, for like the work songs, they serve to depict the plight of the poor, whose cause he champions.

Capoeira, the combat like sport, comes to mind when one thinks of songs that deal with recreation. As with many other facets of Afro-Bahian culture, Amado's interest in *capoeira* dates back many years. In his guidebook to the city of Salvador, entitled *Bahia de todos os santos,* he includes a chapter on the subject of *capoeira.* In *As sete portas da Bahia* he dedicates a *cantiga de capoeira* to his friend, the famous Argentine artist Carybé. According to Waldeloir Rego, Amado begins with a refrain from a *cantiga de capoeira* and proceeds to laud Carybé in imitation of the traditional form:

> Mestre de muitas artes,
> ê, ê camarado,
> quem é que é?
>
> Quem é que é,
> ê, ê, camarado,

da Bahia o filho amado?

> É Carybé, camarado?
> ê, camarado, ê.

Although many of Amado's male figures, from Balduíno in *Jubiabá* to Sete Voltas in *Gabriela,* excel in the sport, it is mentioned only in passing. In *Tenda dos milagres* (1970), however, he integrates the *cantiga de capoeira* into the plot, much in the way that ABCs were used in *Jubiabá.* Here his setting is the Pelourinho, an old section of Salvador that he refers to as the university of the people, or the popular territory. His hero, Pedro Archanjo, a *bedel* born in 1868, writes important documents, authenticating aspects of popular culture.

The *cantigas de capoeira* become an integral part of the action when they refer to Pedrito Gordo and his persecution of *capoeira* and other aspects of black culture so dear to Pedro Archanjo. In real life, he was Dr. Pedro de Azevedo Gordilho, a greatly feared member of the Bahian police force who, in the decade of the 1920s, persecuted *pais-de-santo* and others involved with *candomblé* and *capoeira.* His deeds so captivated the imagination of the people that an ABC was written about him at a time when ABCs were no longer common. Although Amado does not utilize stanzas from the "ABC de Pedrito," he does employ some *cantigas* in the story. One of these is called the warning (*aviso* or *cavalaria*), a special rhythmic beat (*toque*) used to warn participants of the arrival of the dreaded police.

> Não gosto de candomblé
> Que é festa de feiticeiro
> Quando a cabeça me dói
> Serei um dos primeiros.
>
> Acabe coeste Santo
> Pedrito vem aí
> Lá vem cantando ca ô cabieci
> Lá vem cantando ca ô cabieci.

The *cantigas de capoeira* permeate the novel, seemingly to heighten atmosphere. As one of the characters walks at night, he overhears the following song:

> Panhe a laranja no chão tico-tico
> Meu amôr foi simbora, eu não fico
> Minha toalha é de renda de bico
> Panhe a laranja no chão, tico-tico.

Waldeloir Rego indicates that this is one of the berimbau beats (*toque de berimbau*) that utilizes the name of a children's round (*roda infantil*) widespread in Brazil.

During the first part of this ritualized sport, known as the *canto de entrada,* it is customary to laud one's teacher. Many of the masters are very well known to the people of Bahia. The stanza below refers to Barroquinha.

> Menino quem foi seu mestre?
> Meu mestre foi Barroquinha
> Barba êle não tinha
> Metia o facão na polícia
> E paisano tratava bem.

Later in the chapter, Besouro Cordão de Ouro, another of Bahia's famous teachers of *capoeira,* is mentioned:

> Besouro antes de morrer
> Abriu a bôca e falou
> Meu filho não apanhe
> Que seu pai nunca apanhou.

Combined, these verses clearly aid in the development of the novel's thesis, as they are supportive of the black man as he seeks to preserve his cultural heritage.

Many other types of songs appear in Jorge Amado's novels, but because they do not appear in sufficient numbers and in a consistent pattern they do not merit a special category. Ranging from sentimental to satirical, the songs serve to illustrate the wide variety of sources the author draws from in creating his fictive world.

Most songs are definitely popular in origin with very Brazilian overtones. One ballad associated with the Portuguese tradition, however, is "Romance da Nau Catarineta."

> La vem a Nau Catarineta
> Que tem muito que contar.

This fragment is cited in *Jubiabá* as Balduíno expresses his love for Lindinalva, the daughter of a Portuguese Comendador, and brings the Lusitanian heritage clearly to the fore.

The *modinha* is a frequently appearing popular song that has had impact on both sides of the Atlantic. In *Dona Flor* Amado refers to the composer Cândido das Neves by name:

> Noite alta, céu risonho
> a quietude é quase um sonho
> e o luar cai sôbre a mata
> qual uma chuva de prata
> de raríssimo esplendor . . .
> Só tu dormes, não escutas
> o teu cantor . . .

Bits of this song, which was in vogue in the 1920s, are sung

by Vadinho to his beloved Flor in a serenade that was the talk of the neighborhood.

In both *Mar morto* and *Os velhos marinheiros,* where the action centers on the sea, the songs of the sailors appear to reinforce the theme and add authenticity to the scenes. As mentioned previously, Amado wrote the song used as a leitmotif in *Mar morto*—"É doce morrer no mar." He also uses traditional sea songs (*moda do mar*). The sad lyrics speak of death at sea, a common fate among these people.

> Êle ficou nas ondas
> êle se foi a afogar
> Eu vou por outras terras
> que meu amor já se foi
> nas ondas verdes do mar.

Included in *Os velhos marinheiros* is a famous popular song composed by Dorival Caymmi based on a folklore motif. Used as the narrator describes life aboard the coastal sailing vessels known as Itas, the title of the song, "Peguei um Ita no norte," is in keeping with the subject at hand.

As would be expected, snatches of *sambas* and *sambas-de-roda* are found, particularly when a lighter mood is prevalent. Similar to the *cantiga de capoeira,* these *sambas* are sung or heard as people mingle in the streets. Gabriela sings:

> Não vá lá, meu bem
> que lá tem ladeira
> escorrega e cai,
> quebra o galho da roseira.

As Dona Flor and her friend Norma leave church, they hear a group of street urchins (*moleques*) singing and beating out the rhythm of empty tins:

> Ó mulher do balaio grande!
> Ó do balaio grande!
> Bom balaio!

Since the novels are chronicles of the times, political songs that reflect the events of the period are included. In *Jubiabá,* as Antônio Balduíno nears the strike Amado includes a song composed during a strike against the Companhia Circular (Light) in 1934.

> Um sindicato
> de operários
> se levantou em greve
> para aumentar os seus salários
> aderiu tôdas as classes
> para reforçar
> E houve uma forte corrente
> Contra a Circular.

As the mysterious captain makes his rounds on board the Ita, in *Os velhos marinheiros,* the following *marchinha* is heard as it relates to the elections:

> O seu Tonico
> Do torrão do leite grosso,
> Ponha a cêrca no caminho
> Que o paulista é um colosso,
> Pega a garrucha,
> Finca o pé firme na estrada,
> Que com êsse puxa-puxa
> Faz-se do leite coalhada.

Occasionally Amado creates verses in a satirical vein when he wishes to poke fun at one of his characters. These scurrilous songs are very close in spirit to the Portuguese *cantiga de escárnio e maldizer.* Tonico, Gabriela's paramour, the dandy who deals the final blow to her already failing marriage, is the subject of such a satirical song:

> Ó Tonico Pinico
> don Juan de puteiro
> se fudeu por inteiro.
> —Tu és bem casada?
> —Eu sou é amigada.
> E levou bofetada
> ó Tonico Pinico.

In "A invasão do morro do Mata Gato ou amigos do povo," a portion of *Os pastores da noite,* the narrator, with tongue in cheek, lauds Jacó Galub, the journalist who stood by the people in their struggle to retain squatters rights on the lands of the Spanish millionaire Pepe Oitocentas.

> Herói do Mata Gato
> o jornalista Jacó
> ameaçado de assalto
> de ser jogado no pó
> foi o amigo do povo
> destemido campeão
> para lhe dar casa e pão
> Galub o amigo do povo.

The *double entendre* is perfectly clear to the reader, for Jacó is just as opportunistic as the other members of the so-called Establishment. Although not a full-scale attack, as in the case of Tonico, the satiric intention remains quite clear.

It can be seen that Amado works with a wide variety of verse forms from both the popular and oral traditions, ranging from ABCs to children's rounds. If one compares the forms utilized in the novels with the examples shown in José Calasans Brandão da Silva's *Folclore geo-histórico da Bahia e seu recôncavo,* it is evident that Amado has employed and adapted extensively from the rich traditions of the region in his portrayal of Bahian society.

> **When it comes to the understanding and transmitting of popular culture . . . Jorge Amado has few peers.**
> **—Nancy T. Baden**

It is also clear that he does not adapt from the Brazilian popular traditions alone, but incorporates a number of Lusitanian forms. Naturally the *literatura de cordel* and the Afro-Bahian songs predominate, but there are numerous songs of European origin as well. The *pastoris,* the children's songs, and others stem directly from this tradition.

Furthermore, Amado very carefully selects those songs that best support his themes. The ABCs, the sad songs of the sea, and the workers songs all attest to his overriding concern for the poor and their destiny. He also chooses songs from specific time periods to authenticate the political and social events of the era he wishes to portray.

This abundant use of popular and oral verse forms is obviously in keeping with Jorge Amado's determination to interpret the popular culture of Bahia through his novels. Amado's contribution to Brazilian letters has been vigorously debated and the discussion will, no doubt, continue. Those who praise him admire his loyalty to the people, the ease with which he weaves his tales, his poetic prose, and so forth. Those who deride him refer to shallow characterizations, overriding superficiality, and the exploitation of a successful formula used to sell books. All of these criticisms are probably true to some extent. When it comes to the understanding and transmitting of popular culture, however, Jorge Amado has few peers. There is no doubt that an important part of his effectiveness as a novelist has been his ability to assimilate, adapt, utilize, and to create in imitation of, the plethora of popular songs found in the Bahian area he so vividly portrays.

Earl E. Fitz (essay date May 1984)

SOURCE: "Structural Ambiguity in Jorge Amado's *A Morte e a Morte de Quincas Berro Dágua,*" in *Hispania,* Vol. 67, No. 2, May, 1984, pp. 221-28.

[*In the following essay, Fitz asserts that "in* A Morte e a Morte de Quincas Berro Dágua, *Jorge Amado offers tangible evidence of how technically sophisticated he can be, of how effectively he can combine the best features of literature's oral tradition with those of its written form."*]

While, as William Empson has demonstrated, a properly conceived and controlled ambiguity can add richness, complexity and depth to any literary work, Jorge Amado's *A Morte e a Morte de Quincas Berro Dágua* offers us a singular example of just how integral a role it can play in the structuring of an entire novel. Arguably Amado's finest overall technical achievement, the tale of the materially poor but spiritually rich vagabond, Quincas Berro Dágua, is a work all too often overlooked by scholars concerned with Amado's skill as a novelist. Part of the reason it has received relatively little critical attention is that it has been overshadowed by several of Amado's other, better known works, such as *Gabriela, Cravo e Canela, Dona Flor e seus dois Maridos* and *Tenda dos Milagres.* A related problem is that the story of Quincas and his companions deals with many of the same social types that we have grown accustomed to seeing, but in expanded versions, in other of the author's works. And, finally, this spare 1961 work simply does not have the same breadth and scope as do many of Amado's other novels, especially those coming from his post-1958 period. Given all these reservations, then, how is it that *A Morte e a Morte de Quincas Berro Dágua* may be said to constitute Amado's finest effort as a novelist? The answer to this question, which forms the basis of this essay, centers squarely on the author's skill in weaving a fundamental ambiguity concerning what "really happens" in the story into the actual structuring of the story itself. The result is a tightly written, highly cohesive tale composed of causally related events which, under the author's careful control, open themselves up to different interpretations.

When we evaluate the quality of a piece of fiction, we must, of necessity, come to grips with the issue of technique: how does the author select, organize and shape his material so as to achieve the desired effect? What aesthetic norms guide him in the creation of his fictive world? In the case of Jorge Amado, an author more widely praised for his vitality as a teller of tales than as a craftsman of the novel form, this crucial critical issue deserves more attention than it has so far received. And of all the many novels he has written, *A Morte e a Morte de Quincas Berro Dágua* stands out as the prime example of how well Amado has mastered the technical demands of not only the oral tradition, but those of the well-crafted novel as well. This work, a synthesis of both these modes of expression, is full of ribald and charming characters from Bahia's lower classes, yet it is also a carefully composed, rigorously ordered and sharply focused work of art, one that proves just how thoroughly Amado appreciates the importance of structure in the novel.

Closely related to the issue of technique is the question of structure in narrative, the order in which the events depicted are placed. And while this ordering is an undeniably important part of the structuring of *A Morte,* there is an additional element at work here as well, one which, more than anything else, gives this tale its unusual piquancy and charm. I refer to Amado's steady balancing of the plausible with the implausible, of events seemingly "real" in nature with those that, if taken in their literal context, seem wholly supernatural in nature. As suggested, for example, in the title itself, Quincas Berro Dágua, the protagonist, "dies" at least twice in this story: the first time, restively, in body, and, the second time, peacefully, in spirit. In the mundane, dully rational world of everyday human existence, we do not often get to expire as often as our hero here does, but then, happily, Quincas Berro Dágua is not an ordinary homo sapiens. And although much of the tale's structural tightness derives directly from the author's unwavering focus on Quincas, and on the fulfillment of a certain vow he makes, its uniqueness, indeed, its brilliance, lies in Amado's ability to counterbalance in an unobtrusive fashion events that are mimetically rendered with those that are utterly fantastic in nature. Also playing a vital role in this structural legerdemain is Amado's considerable talent for drawing the reader into the story and eliciting from him a sympathetic response concerning the protagonist's fate. This, of course, merely underscores Amado's repeatedly proven excellence as a storyteller, but in addition it illustrates how effectively he can control the sundry components of the novel as art form.

In terms of its internal organization, the novel's structural ambiguity, which, in its role as mediator between fact and fancy, provides the outstanding technical feature of the work, shows three distinct but closely interlocking levels of development: part one begins with the provocative epigram that opens the narrative and runs through chapter VIII. The narrative voice, which is never identified, quickly sets the stage for the events that will follow. It also establishes a deferentially self-conscious tone and, through it, suggests to the reader continuously that, in this story, nothing is impossible, that here, as in the human experience, it is difficult, if not impossible, to say with absolute certainty what is true and what is not; the second section, in which the turning point of the action appears, comprises chapters IX and X. The narrative voice here increasingly gives way to the characters themselves, allowing them, by means of their own words and actions, to carry the story to the reader. In these chapters, the signal feature, structurally speaking, is the delicate though omnipresent tension that Amado establishes between what really happened and what, given the circumstances, might have happened; finally, in the third section, made up of chapters XI and XII, we find the resolution of the basic conflict and a concluding statement that re-connects us with the uncertainty expressed in the introduction to part one. Here, the narrative voice judiciously re-enters the story in an active, participatory way, giving counsel to the reader and calling his attention to the "magical" qualities of the events recounted. This final, short section also carries the mixing of verisimilitude and fantasy to its zenith and, as noted earlier, links the enigmatic conclusion of the tale to the epigramatic statement about the essential mysteriousness of life that opens the book. Thus, on one level the novel exemplifies the classical pattern of plot development in the realistic novel: a rising action, which leads to a decisive moment, suddenly unravels itself in a logical denouement. But this is not exactly a "realistic" novel, at least not in terms of the most salient feature of its structuring. For in addition to the acknowledged realism of its style, which, as always with Jorge Amado, is earthy and demotic, *A Morte e a Morte de Quincas Berro Dágua* is "magically realistic" in much the same way as is Gabriel García Márquez's *Cien años de soledad.* In the story of Quincas Berro Dágua, as in the story of the Buendía family, the "magic" of the events described springs from and is a rational, entirely reasonable extension of the three-dimensional world of "normal" human existence. The "reality" of these works is thus rooted in two different levels of existence—the quotidian and the ideal.

By establishing this charming duality at the outset, the first part of the novel's plot structure is the longest because through it Amado's narrator must tell us what we need to know about the relationship between his protagonist's life (or lives) and death (or deaths). He does this immediately by citing, in a prefatory statement to the first chapter, what was allegedly one of Quincas' final utterances: "'Cada qual cuide de seu entêrro, impossível não há.' (Frase derradeira de Quincas Berro Dágua, segundo Quitéria que estava ao seu lado)."

The real meaning of these words, which imply that, in reading this narrative, we will not always be able to distinguish "fact" from "fiction," merges with what appears to be the unequivocal truth of a certain bit of evidence—the testimony of an eye-witness. By proceeding in this fashion, Amado deliberately blurs the distinction between "truth" and "falsity" in his story and, in so doing, immediately creates an aura of beguiling ambiguity that will be meticulously nurtured throughout the remainder of the work. Amado reinforces this basic, structurally based uncertainty by having his narrative voice then declare to the reader, as if in a disclaimer of responsibility for knowing "the truth" about "what really happened": "Até hoje permanece certa confusão em tôrno da morte de Quincas Berro Dágua. Dúvidas por explicar, detalhes absurdos, contradições no depoimento das testemunhas, lacunas diversas. Não há clareza sôbre hora, local e frase derradeira."

The author then calls upon his narrator to make a statement that, in one sense, is in perfect accord with his earlier statement but which questions, indirectly, the efficacy of being a reader who is overly accustomed to tales in which the "facts" are presented in a no-nonsense fashion. We read:

> Tantas testemunhas idôneas, entre as quais Mestre Manuel e Quitéria de Olho Arregalado, mulher de

uma só palavra, e, apesar disso, há quem negue todâ e qualquer autenticidade não só à admirada frase mas a todos os acontecimentos daquela noite memorável, quando, em hora duvidosa e em condiçoes discutíveis. Quincas Berro Dágua mergulhou no mar da Bahia e viajou para sempre, para nunca mais voltar. Assim é o mundo povoadodi de céticos e negativistas, amarrados, como bois na canga, à ordem e à lei, aos procedimentos habituais, ao papel selado.

Looking ahead to the rest of what he will be telling us, the narrative voice continues to entwine the factual with the not so factual, and to do so in a way that enables him increasingly to enhance the now firmly established ambiguity surrounding the events with which he is concerned. As he puts it, at one point: ". . . os acontecimentos posteriores—a partir do atestado de óbito até seu mergulho no mar—uma farsa montada por êle com o intuito de mais uma vez atazanar a vida dos parentes, desgostarlhes a existência, mergulhando-os na vergonha e nas murmuraçoes da rua."

Amado, completely in control not only of what he wants to say but, more importantly, of how he wants to say it, preserves the central ambiguity of the action by balancing contrastive but equally "appropriate" explanations of what is transpiring.

—Earl E. Fitz

These final words demonstrate, in particular, how careful Amado is to construct sentences and verb tenses which clearly indicate that Quincas actually did things even after he had "died." By utilizing this practice consistently, Amado builds into the textual core of the work phrases which, grammatically speaking, are unambiguous in terms of the actions they describe, but which, given the nature of the story, are quite ambiguous with respect to the relationships and situations they create. As with most technically accomplished writers, Amado is acutely aware that language does considerably more in literary art than merely communicate some arbitrary, conventional set of meanings. He is sensitive to the fact that words, especially as employed in literature, are arranged in such a way as to suggest the possibility of several meanings, all of which are at least potentially applicable to a given set of circumstances. This quality, the polysemy of language, is what I. A. Richards had in mind when he spoke of the "resourcefulness of language," its unique capacity to admit of several possible meanings, or interpretations, at one time, and it is precisely this aspect of language, or, rather, of the interplay between language, meaning and reality, that Amado exploits so successfully in this novel.

One important moment in the process by which he achieves this end occurs in chapter II, when Amado introduces what becomes a key leitmotif for the remainder of the tale, Quincas' real or imagined post-mortem smirk. The ambiguity involved here straddles the gap between the credible and the incredible because in each case, "what happens" can be quite reasonably explained in diverse ways, each of which has its own special appeal. In its initial appearance, for example, the smirk can be taken: as the rictus of death; as one of the peculiar ways Vanda, Quincas' conniving daughter, sees it; or as "proof" that Amado has abruptly entered a purely fantastic but entirely appropriate (and therefore acceptable) element into the text. Considering the nature of the story he tells here, this latter gambit would not involve, as one might well suppose, the insertion of an awkward Deus ex Machina into the story since the basic principle of uncertainty as to what took place that "magic" night had already been established by the narrative voice in an earlier section. Even Vanda's reaction to Quincas' smirk, which functions as a critical point of reference for the reader, is structured so that the essential plausibility of each of these three distinctive interpretations remains intact. This same issue comes to a head in chapter VI, when Quincas, now cleaned up by his petty, crass and invidious kin, is dressed in conformity with his erstwhile bourgeois role as Joaquim Soares da Cunha, a name and an existence that he had categorically rejected years earlier in favor of becoming the bohemian Quincas Berro Dágua. In this scene, which expands upon the possible interpretations inherent in the earlier one, Quincas seems not only to smirk at the vindictive Vanda, who is here alone with the "corpse," but to speak to her as well, indeed, to insult her, to antagonize her even as she and the rest of Quincas' image conscious family consign him to a cold grave. We read:

> Pousou os olhos no rosto barbeado. E levou um choque, o primeiro. Viu o sorriso. Sorriso cínico, imoral, de quem se divertia. O sorriso não havia mudado, contra especialistas da funerária. . . . Quincas ria daquilo tudo, um riso que se ia ampliando, alargando, que aos poucos ressoava na pocilga imunda. Ria com os lábios e com os olhos, olhos a fitarem o monte da roupa suja e remendada, esquecida num canto pelos homens da funerária. O sorriso de Quincas Berro Dágua. E Vanda ouviu, as sílabas destacadas com nitidez insultante, no silêncio fúnebre:—Jararaca!

At this point, the narrative adopts Vanda's point of view, with the result being that the reader, like Vanda, now feels strongly that Quincas is not dead at all, that he is alive and bent on extracting a final revenge on his unfaithful, undeserving family. The appeal of this interpretation derives from the fact that Vanda, along with the reader, knows full well of what she has been guilty, that, during his lifetime, she had

let her father down and sided with her shrewish mother against him. Now she lives in shame, mortified at what her father, assuming the identity of the lowly but honorable Quincas Berro Dágua, had chosen to become.

The supernatural quality of this crucial scene, however appropriate it may be to the tone of the story, is held in check by two "realistic" factors, the stifling heat of the room (Vanda had shut the window so the cool evening sea breeze would not come in and blow out the candles) and the heavy perfume the undertakers had poured so copiously on the body to mask any trace of an unpleasant odor. Even though the text clearly indicates that Quincas did smirk at Vanda, did insult her and that she responded in a markedly unflustered way to it, another, more "rational" view of things would argue that none of this really happened, that the heat and the perfume made Vanda, who was already suffering from exhaustion and emotional trauma due to the "death" of her father, momentarily lose control of her senses; due to the stress of the situation and to the condition of the room, which Amado takes pains to describe in detail, Vanda just imagines Quincas' "recovery." This possible but rather pedestrian interpretation is given additional credence by the sudden appearance of Aunt Marocas, who says to Vanda, "Você está abatida, menina. Também com o calor que faz nesse cubículo. . . ." But immediately, to restore the proper degree of ambiguity, Amado's narrator interrupts to tell us:

> Ampliou-se o sorriso canalha de Quincas ao enxegar o vulto monumental da irmã. Vanda quis tapar os ouvidos, sabia, por experiência anterior, com que palavras êle amava definir Marocas, mas que adiantam ãos sôbre as orelhas para conter voz de morto? Ouviu:—Saco de peidos! Marocas, mais descansada da subida em olhar sequer o cadaver, escancarou a janela.

The appearance of Tia Marocas here is important structurally because it represents a new, objective view of the unsure string of events that connect Quincas, Vanda and the reader. As we see in the passage just quoted, Vanda, in putting her hands over her ears so as not to "hear" the epithet she knows Quincas will hurl at the corpulent Marocas, seems fully to expect not only that Quincas will speak but that Marocas, too, will hear the outrageous things he says. If this were to happen, however, the scales would tip too much toward a clear-cut explanation of what is really taking place in this scene, and Amado, bent on maintaining his structural balance between "fact" and "fantasy," will not permit this to happen. The result is that Marocas is, or seems to be oblivious not only to the sly grin Quincas may or may not have on his face, but to the words he may or may not have said. The reasons for this obliviousness on her part, however, introduce an additionally possible interpretation, namely, that, like Vanda, Tia Marocas is not in the least surprised at Quincas' cantankerous behavior and so she does not react to it. But this view seems less likely than the other two possibilities noted, that Quincas actually has returned from the dead, or that the entire scene is only a figment of Vanda's overwrought imagination. In either case, the main point is that Amado, completely in control not only of what he wants to say but, more importantly, of how he wants to say it, preserves the central ambiguity of the action by balancing contrastive but equally "appropriate" explanations of what is transpiring.

Coming hard on the heels of this pivotal scene in the first movement of the story is the climactic moment in chapter X, the point at which Quincas' four cronies, Cabo Martim, Curió, Pé-de-Vento and Negro Pastinha, come to pay their last respects to their old friend. This section of the novel, lyrical in its poignancy and gentle humor, represents the high point of Amado's melding of fact and fantasy into a seamless web of probability and possibility. And just as in the first movement of the novel, where the primary interpretational question centered on the condition of the room (as opposed to the possibility that Quincas had actually become revivified), here the pivotal feature involves the introduction of alcohol into the action. This is important because, like the hot, stuffy room, the alcohol can be said to have addled the brains of Quincas' four friends, thereby calling into question the issue of their reliability as witnesses to all that took place that "magic evening." Martim, Curió, Pé-de-Vento and Negro Pastinha all use the third-person to speak about Quincas as if he were dead and gone, but they also, at times, speak directly to him, using the familiar second-person form of address. In these cases, the text itself implies that Quincas is, in fact, alive and well, that he is not dead and that his friends are conversing with him as if things were as they had always been. The narrator, himself noting the role alcohol might have played in regard to the friend's perspicacity in relating the events of that night, declares:

> . . . os quatro amigos mais íntimos de Quincas Berro Dágua . . . desciam a Ladeira do Tabuão em caminho do quarto do morto. Deve-se dizer, a bem da verdade, que não estavam êles ainda bêbedos. Haviam tomado seus tragos, sem dúvida . . . mas o vermelho dos olhos era devido às lágrimas derramadas, à dor sem medidas, ...

Then, while pretending to tell the complete truth and clarify matters, the narrator actually injects a further element of uncertainty into the group's experience with Quincas that night: "Quanto à garrafa que o Cabo Martim teria escondida sob a camisa, nada ficou jamais provado." Moreover, references to Quincas' rascally conduct in regard to Vanda occur steadily in the text right up to the arrival of the four comrades in the room where, we are led to believe, Quincas is anxiously awaiting them:

> Vanda lançava um olhar de desprêzo e reproche ao pai. Mesmo depois de morto, êle preferia a sociedade daqueles maltrapilhos.

> Por êles estivera Quincas esperando, sua inquietação no fim da tarde devia-se apenas à demora, ao atraso da chegada dos vagabundos.

By thus suggesting, through the text itself, that Quincas was restlessly waiting for his friends to come see him, Amado tips the scales between fact and fancy back toward fancy. Taking full advantage of his right as a storyteller to employ poetic license, Amado subtly brings together what, seemingly, "did happen" with what, in a more perfect world, "should have happened," and the resultant admixture strikes a deeply affective chord in the reader. It is as if to say that the regenerative powers of love, fidelity and comradeship can, in the final throw of the dice, overcome even death itself, that when we truly love someone they can never really die. This is perhaps Amado's most basic message here, and while it can be found in many of his other books, nowhere is it more simply or more beautifully presented than it is in this novel.

As the serious drinking and commiserating get into full swing, Private Martim, who, the text suggests, has just incurred Quincas' wrath by declaring his intention of taking over for Quincas in regard to his "departed" friend's love life, promptly declares, "Vamos dar um gole a êle também . . . propôs o Cabo, desejoso das boas graças do morto." With Quincas now an active (if not a necessarily willing) participant in the drinking, he seems to grow in his role as a perfectly normal character. Yet Amado, never allowing Quincas' "normalcy" to develop to the point that we can feel certain he is "alive," structures his telling of the story at this point so that the events related can be viewed in more than one way. Hence, when we read, "Abriram-lhe a bôca, derramaram-lhe a cachaça. Espalhou-se um pouco pela gola do paletó e o peito da camisa," we cannot be certain about what we are to make of this action. We can, on the one hand, reason that of course the cachaça would spill, since you can pour liquor into the mouth of a cadaver but you can't make it drink! But on the other hand, a reader more in harmony with Quincas and his worthies might conclude, as they do, that the spillage is simply a matter of positioning, the kind of thing that could give anyone trouble: "—Também nunca vi ninguém beber deitado. . . . —É melhor sentar êle. Assim pode ver as gente direito. Sentaram Quincas no caixão, a cabeça movia-se para um e outro lado."

The two actions described here, the change of Quincas' position in the coffin and the rolling of his head, serve to demonstrate Amado's awareness of the importance that an organized and integrated ambiguity makes to his story. A look at the first verb in the last sentence of the passage just cited shows clearly that Quincas' pals propped him up so that he might "drink" more successfully with them. As soon as they do this, however, Quincas' head begins to bob from side to side, this providing a rather picturesque detail that can be explained in basely physiological terms or in a more poetic manner, one, in fact, that is reinforced in the very next line, "Com o gole de cachaça ampliara-se seu sorriso." Particularly evident in this middle section of the novel, Amado's basic tactic, as we can readily see in the scene where Quincas "drinks" cachaça in his coffin, is entirely structural in its nature and function. He alternates, in an unbroken pattern, scenes that seem to demand a routinely "realistic" explanation with scenes that, often containing direct quotations from Quincas himself, make sense only when interpreted in terms of Quincas being alive. By means of this technique, Amado succeeds artistically in maintaining a nearly perfect equilibrium between a verisimilar representation of life and a supernatural one. He supplies us, one after another, with scenes which we are invited to interpret in both ways, scenes which, as with the one just noted, both advance the plot and increasingly lure the reader into the web of poetic uncertainty that slowly envelops the story.

Perhaps the outstanding example of this balancing process appears toward the end of chapter X, when Quincas and his confederates, now suffering hunger pangs, decide to set off through the dark streets of Old Salvador for Mestre Manuel's fish fry, which, they knew, was to be held that same evening at the wharf. In a structural sense, this seemingly off-hand decision to attend Captain Manuel's feed is actually the third in a four-step process by means of which Quincas will be able to "die" the second "Morte" mentioned in the title and, in so doing, bring the novel to a close. In chapter VII, the reader learned in a rather desultory manner that Quincas envisioned himself as a "velho marinheiro," and that, ". . . reservara ao mar a honra de sua hora derradeira, de seu momento final." In order for this carefully foreshadowed event to take place, Amado must arrange for Quincas first to die on land, which he does easily enough in chapter III, but then he must somehow be taken to the bay, where he can find his final resting place. Amado accomplishes this delicate maneuver in a way that is so smoothly done that we can easily miss it. The arrival of Quincas' four friends at his wake, an arrival anticipated by the narrative voice's reference to Quincas' impatience in waiting for them, allow Amado to provide Quincas with the means by which he can go—or be transported to—the seaside, ostensibly to "attend" Mestre Manuel's "moqueca." The hunger the group feels, after several rounds of drinks, reminds them that they should head off to Captain Manuel's fish fry, and since they decide, naturally, to take Quincas along, the reader suddenly realizes how Quincas will be able to arrive at his final, presaged destination. The beauty of Amado's technical skill here is that the fulfillment of Quincas' oath does not in any way intrude upon that part of the story which involves the delight-

fully ambiguous series of events that occur, in chapters IX and X, between Quincas, his friends and Vanda. In truth, the fulfillment of Quincas' final wish actually tightens the structure of the entire story, imparting to it a unity and cohesiveness it would not otherwise have had. Amado, fully in command of his story, is notably concise in his construction of the pivotal scene in which this section takes place. We read: "—Não era hoje de noite a moqueca de Mestre Manuel?—Hoje mesmo. . . . —E por que a gente não vai? Mestre Manuel é até capaz de ficar ofendido. . . . —A gente prometeu não deixar êle sòzinho.—Sòzinho? Por que? Ele vai com a gente. . . ."

Then, referring to the possibility that Quincas may be "too crippled" to move, Amado adds a fine ironic touch to what seems to be Quincas' assessment of his own situation: "Consultaram Quincas:—Tu quer ir?—Tou por acaso aleijado, pra ficar aqui?"

Quincas is then stood up on his feet, but once this is done he proves none too stable, the ambiguity here being that he totters either because he is a corpse or because he is drunk. Consistent with his basic technique, Amado now has Negro Pastinha deliver the words that tip the scales once again:

> Tá tão bêbedo que não se agüenta. Com a idade tá perdendo a fôrça pra cachaça. Vambora, paizinho.
>
> Curió e Pé-de-Vento saíram na frente. Quincas, satisfeito da vida, num passo de dança, ia entre Negro Pastinha e Cabo Martim, de braço dado.

So, in this turning point scene, which is both a moving statement about the indestructable bond between Quincas and his friends and the structural device that allows Quincas to get to the seaside for a final, peaceful death, Amado presents us with the wonderfully comic yet tender picture of Pastinha and Cabo Martim, themselves inebriated, staggering along and propping up between them someone whom we might fairly describe, using an English expression that seems particularly apt here, as being "dead drunk."

As the group heads out into what the narrator is careful to describe as a ". . . noite fantástica, quando a lua-cheia envolvia o mistério da cidade de Bahia. . . ," we sense that now anything is possible, that reality is no longer restricted to the corporeal realm, that now it is a relative concept, one that supercedes time and space. This lyrical, concluding movement of the tale establishes for the reader a deeply satisfying compromise between what is "realistically true" and what is "poetically true," this being precisely the goal that Amado has sought all along to attain. In terms of plot, this section of the story contains the climax, the final death of Quincas and his burial at sea, but, in terms of its structure, it continues to play out the novel's underlying ambiguity right through to the epilogue-like conclusion in chapter XII. By organizing the story in this manner, Amado succeeds in resolving the basic plot conflict at the same time that he succeeds in prolonging the structural ambiguity between what "really happened" and what "might have happened." In response to this attenuated balancing act, the reader, playing his role in the game of fiction, is drawn into the story as an active participant. He is, moreover, likely to be sympathetic to Quincas and his friends and, for that reason, is willing to suspend his rational or "realistic" interpretations of the events described in favor of more magically realistic, or poetic ones. Under the spell of Amado's skill as a teller of tales, the reader is led to feel that if this is not precisely the way it "really" was, then perhaps it should have been.

Upon completion of the reading of this remarkable novel [*A Morte e a Morte de Quincas Berro Dágua*], the reader, as usual, is struck by Amado's charm and enthusiasm as a spinner of good yarns. But, as amply evidenced here, he proves himself to be a good deal more than this as well.
—*Earl E. Fitz*

During the course of this "magic night," Quincas, aided—one way or another—by his pals, moves slowly, as if in a funeral procession, through the streets of his beloved city saying good-bye to everyone. As the narrator expresses it: "Por onde passavam, ouviam-se gritos chamando Quincas, vivando-lhe o nome. Ele agradecia com a cabeça, como um rei de volta a seu reino." Once again, the essential question is one of perspective; did Quincas voluntarily nod his own head to the crowds of well-wishers, or was his head—the head of a dead man being borne about by his drunken friends—merely lolling, uncontrollably, from side to side? The artfully structured text offers the reader no definitive answer, but, to the contrary, holds open the door for both interpretations. Later, as Quincas is "having a farewell drink" in the bar of yet another old crony, a brawl, "caused" by Quincas, erupts. When it is over, Quincas' questionable condition (he is stretched out on the floor, "unconscious"), is explained in a by now predictable fashion: ". . . Quincas encontrava-se estendido no chão, levara uns socos violentos, batera com a cabeça numa laje do passeio. . . ." Moments later, Quincas is "revived" in a scene that hearkens back to the important role that alcohol plays in the second and third movements of the book: "Quincas reanimou-se mesmo foi com um bom trago. Continuava a beber daquela maneira esquisita: cuspindo parte da cachaça, num esperdício. Não fosse dia de seu aniversário e Cabo Martim chamarlhe-ia a atenção delicadamente." As we can see, at first glance it appears that Quincas himself takes a healthy swig of cachaça, but when we consider how he just seems to spit it out, to

waste it, this action, given his fame as a connoisseur of good liquor and his reputation as a prodigious drinker, seems unthinkable. Thus, the essential ambiguity between what the text seems to say and what it suggests is not only maintained but intensified.

The final scene of the novel, Quincas' "burial" at sea, is arrived at economically, with no wasted motion. The "turma" arrives at the dock and everyone boards Captain Manuel's "saveiro," which is about to set sail for a moonlight cruise around the bay. The reader sees Quincas "moving about" the boat, but then, in another moment of narrative unreliability, we are told that, "Ninguém sabe como Quincas se pôs de pé, encostado à vela menor. . . . Só a luz do cachimbo do Mestre Manuel persistia, e a figura de Quincas, de pé, cercado pela tempestade, impassível e majestoso, o velho marinheiro." At this point, a storm, which, like the sweltering room of part one and the alcohol of part two, impairs the perception of the people around Quincas, suddenly blows up. The narrative voice then enters the story again "to explain" the uncertain circumstances surrounding the final moments of Quincas' "existence": "No meio do ruído, do mar em fúria, do saveiro em perigo, à luz dos raios, viram Quincas atirar-se e ouviram sua frase derradeira. Penetrava o saveiro nas águas calmas do quebra-mar, mas Quincas ficara na tempestade, envolto num lençol de ondas e espuma, por sua própria vontade."

Later in this concluding scene, the narrative voice tells us that the undertakers refused to take back the casket, thus implying that, for whatever the reason, Quincas had turned up missing from his own wake. But this same voice, our none too certain guide throughout the entire tale, also declares, "Quanto à frase derradeira há versões variadas. Mas, quem poderia ouvir direito no meio daquele temporal?" As noted earlier, this indefinite, open-ended conclusion recalls for us what the tentative, self-conscious narrator says at the beginning of the story, thereby imparting a sense of circularity to its overall organization. But seen exclusively in its structural context, it is a circularity based entirely on the meticulously balanced ambiguity at work in the story between the reader's ability to know with certainty what "really" happened as opposed to his interest and curiosity in speculating about "what might have happened."

Upon completion of the reading of this remarkable novel, the reader, as usual, is struck by Amado's charm and enthusiasm as a spinner of good yarns. But, as amply evidenced here, he proves himself to be a good deal more than this as well. In ***A Morte e a Morte de Quincas Berro Dágua***, Jorge Amado offers tangible evidence of how technically sophisticated he can be, of how effectively he can combine the best features of literature's oral tradition with those of its written form. This compact, tightly structured gem of a novel is worthy of attention by anyone interested in the organic relationship between form and content in narrative. The entire tale, composed in three distinct but closely orchestrated movements, leads us into a fictive world made believable, on one level, by an abundance of sharply drawn realistic detail, but one made enticing, on another level, by the delightful possibility that what we read is not necessarily what is meant. This pivotal ambiguity, which is a direct result of the manner in which Amado structures the text itself, establishes the vital link between the reader's perception of the story's literal truth and its figurative truth. Controlled and shaped throughout by Amado's finesse as a novelist, the ambiguity that exists between what seems to have happened and what may have happened emerges as the fundamental structural motif of the entire work, its defining characteristic. Like the great poets, with whom he has a great deal in common, Jorge Amado possesses a deep appreciation of how words, properly selected, composed and arranged, will stimulate several different streams of thought at once. Built largely on this concept, *A Morte e a Morte de Quincas Berro Dágua,* a novel too often overlooked by evaluators of Amado's expertise as a writer, spans the gap between poetry and prose and between oral and written literature. In so doing, it also goes a long way toward proving that Jorge Amado, long hailed as Brazil's most popular novelist, is one of its finest writers as well.

Jorge Amado with Berta Sichel (interview date May/June 1984)

SOURCE: "Jorge Amado," in *Américas,* Vol. 36, No. 3, May/June, 1984, pp. 16-9.

[In the following interview, Amado discusses his work and its relationship to other cultures, Brazil, and his own region of Bahia.]

If Gabriel García Márquez opened the way for Mario Vargas Llosa, Carlos Fuentes, Ernesto Cardenal and many other Latin American writers in Spanish, it was Jorge Amado who did the same for the Brazilian authors. This writer from Bahia, who doesn't like to talk about himself, was the first to tell the world of Bahia, of Brazil and its people. He was the first to demonstrate that Brazilian literature is less homogeneous than that produced in other Latin American countries since it is a product of the cultural diversity of a vast country.

In Brazil they say that Jorge Amado has done more for Brazilian culture than have all the government departments for the advancement of culture in the history of the republic. His work includes 26 titles, 684 Brazilian and 40 Portuguese editions, and 260 translations into over 40 languages. But as he turned 70 two years ago, he merely said of himself that

"I am a sensual and romantic Brazilian who lives the admirable life of the Bahian people."

[Sichel:] Could you give us a brief chronicle of how your works have fared abroad?

[Amado:] My books have been read in translation for many years. The first, *Cacau,* was translated into Spanish and published in Buenos Aires in 1935. . . . *Jubiabá,* in 1938, was the first French translation. . . . The first into Russian dates from 1937, and the first into English was in 1945. After World War II my books began to be widely translated into the major languages—French, English, German, Russian, Italian, Spanish, Chinese—as well as into more diverse and rare languages. In Russia my books are translated into some ten languages other than Russian. . . . I now am published in 42 languages. There are many pirated editions—in Greek, Arabic, Turkish and Persian, for example. Every now and then I learn that a book of mine has been translated into a rare language like Korean or Mongolian. In some languages I have a strong audience, I'm widely read; in others, literary success hasn't been matched by success in sales, at least for the time being. I think this happens to writers everywhere.

You opened the path to success for Brazilian literature in the United States. How do you see the invasion of the U.S. market by Brazilian authors?

I wonder if there is such an invasion. If there is one, it's just beginning, and it's a great thing to have happen. Before, very few Brazilian authors were published or had major or minor success—Machado de Assís, Erico Veríssimo, Gilberto Freyre, Graciliano Ramos, José Lins do Rego, Antônio Calado, José J. Veiga, and so forth. Today, other authors, veterans like Raquel de Queiroz, Lygia Fagundes Telles and Darcy Ribeiro, and young ones like João Ubaldo Ribeiro, Márcio de Souza, Ignacio de Loyola, Antônio Tôrres and Ivan Angelo, all excellent writers capable of attracting the interest of the U.S. public (and of other countries as well), are being translated and published. . . . I believe this interest is due to the growth of Brazil as a nation and the Brazilian people's affirmation of their struggle to build a free country capable of eliminating the huge social contradictions that make such a rich country live with such poverty and oppression.

Do you think that the translation of your work can serve a social purpose in the United States or in Europe?

The growing solidarity with our people can help. I think I win friends for Brazil—I know of many who became interested in Brazil after reading my books.

What can a foreigner—a European or a North American— learn about Brazil from reading your work?

I think they can get an idea of Brazilian reality with its immense contradictions, its dramatic poverty and its obstinate, invincible people born from the mix of bloods, races and cultures. My books reflect Brazilian reality and are portraits of my people.

Do you consider yourself a political writer?

Every writer is political, even those who think they have nothing to do with politics, since the mere act of writing is a political act—the writer exerts influence on the readers, and this is a political action. I am a writer who basically deals with social themes, since the source material for my creation is Brazilian reality. . . . [Many of my] novels narrate the life of the people, everyday life, the struggle against extreme poverty, against hunger, the large estates, racial prejudice, backwardness, underdevelopment. The hero of my novels is the Brazilian people. My characters are the most destitute, the most needy, the most oppressed—country and city people without any power other than the strength of the mestizo people of Brazil. They say that I am a novelist of whores and vagabonds, and there is truth in that, for my characters increasingly are anti-heroes. I believe that only the people struggle selflessly and decently, without hidden motives.

Do you believe that literature should have a commitment?

I believe every writer has the right to carry out his own literary work as he sees fit—whether or not he may have a political commitment, take a position on the struggle of the people, write about the social situation or the personal problems of a human being. Each one is master of his own way of existing and creating. Personally, I consider myself to be a writer with a commitment, a writer who is for the people and against their enemies, who develops his work around the reality of Brazil, discussing the country's problems, touching on the dramatic existence of the people and their struggle. I believe that commitment in no way diminishes the quality of the work. However, I also believe that the quality of literary work does not depend on the author's degree of commitment. The only thing of which I totally disapprove is official literature, from any side, for whatever regime it may serve. Literature commissioned as propaganda for governments or political parties will always be limited, momentary, incidental and dogmatic.

As a political writer, could you make a comparison between political literature of the 1930's and that of the 1970's?

I find the political literature of the 1930's was more romantic, broader, less manipulative. The political literature of the present is more limited, conventional, generally more dogmatic, at least as dogmatic as the literature in the 1950's that responded to Stalinism. Of course, there are exceptions. Lately in Brazil some books have been published that are

documents of genuine interest; some of them are powerful as well as beautiful, like the books of Gabeira, who is a real writer. It's also worth mentioning with regard to political literature of the 1930's (including early Soviet literature, so free, so strong and spontaneous, in contrast to the later, Stalinist literature) that it was creative literature—poetry, short stories, novels, theater. The current output is inclined to be documentary.

Is Brazil the only Latin American country that has diverse cultural centers? How do you fit into this heterogeneity?

Diverse cultural centers undoubtedly do exist in Brazil, and happily so. But there also exists a very strong national unity that is reflected in our literature. Erico Veríssimo is as Brazilian a writer as José Américo de Almeida, for even though they come from different cultural areas, they exhibit the same Brazilian spirit. It is necessary to understand this phenomenon in order to understand Brazil. I am a Brazilian writer who comes from the culture of Bahia. On the other hand, I don't believe in the existence of what's conventionally referred to as "Latin American literature." What does exist is literature from different countries in Latin America, each with its own characteristics. What the devil does an Argentine writer have in common with a writer from Cuba?

The critics classify your work as regionalist. How do you interpret this view?

Critics can be extremely funny when they're not [offensive]. All of us writers from the northeast have been tagged regionalists. Nevertheless, we are the ones who have had the most general impact.

What do you think of the current output of Brazilian literature?

I look at it optimistically. Much is being written and published. Naturally there are some bad things, but out of it all emerge writers of true quality. They will endure and move our literature ahead.

There is something magical in your work, something that penetrates not only Brazilian society but also others. To what do you attribute this?

The magic of the Brazilian people. Bahia, the principal setting for my books, is a magical land—the city as well as the state. We are a mestizo people, of an intense culture, and every one of us is a magician.

From your point of view, what role does your work play in the Brazilian context?

I influence the mass readership. I am a writer read by a large audience in my country. I transmit a positive message of confidence, struggle, resistance and hope.

What are the problems facing a Brazilian writer today?

The greatest problem is amateurism, despite a strong existing current that strives for professionalism. . . . There are many people writing and publishing, and there are many books in the bookstore. All that is necessary is that those books be of real interest to the existing Brazilian readership, which is growing daily. It is a large readership and can absorb a great amount of literature as soon as those books awaken an interest in the majority of those readers.

Nelson H. Vieira (essay date Winter 1986)

SOURCE: "Myth and Identity in Short Stories by Jorge Amado," in *Studies in Short Fiction*, Vol. 23, No. 1, Winter, 1986, pp. 25-34.

[*In the following essay, Vieira analyzes several of Amado's shorter works in order to illuminate common themes and universal truths found in all of Amado's work.*]

Overshadowed by the success of such bawdy, sweeping, lyrical, and socially-minded novels as *Gabriela, Clove and Cinnamon, Shepherds of the Night, Dona Flor and Her Two Husbands,* and *Tereza Batista Home From the Wars,* Jorge Amado's short fiction has understandably received little attention from readers and critics. Except for the highly acclaimed short story/novella, *A Morte e a Morte de Quincas Berro D'Água,* 1959 (*The Two Deaths of Quincas Wateryell*) and the fable, *O Gato Malhado e a Andorinha Sinhá* (*The Swallow and the Tom Cat: A Love Story*) first composed in 1948 but published in 1979, there has been scant commentary on the handful of Amado's short narratives which have been sporadically appearing since 1937 in literary magazines and short story collections. Forgotten in limited editions and issues that have not received wide readership, three out of six stories have been translated into English while only one of these has appeared in German, French and Spanish translations.

Paulo Tavares in his bio-bibliographical study, *O Baiano Jorge Amado e Sua Obra* catalogues only three works as short stories. To these we may add **"The Miracle of the Birds"** which appeared in *Harper's,* April, 1982 as well as *Berro D'Água* and the fable *The Swallow and the Tom Cat.* While we can safely attest to at least six narratives under the rubric of short fiction, our purpose here is not to present Jorge Amado as a short story writer, but rather as an author/narrator whose craft, aesthetics and literary vision, deftly developed in the novel, are, as well, notably evident in the

few short narratives that have appeared in published form. Therefore, since three of these narratives have been somewhat neglected, two having never been translated, it is our intent, on the one hand, to call attention to their existence, and on the other, to consider these stories as workable, capsulized sources for insights into Amado's thematic and narrative scheme.

By addressing Amado's overall aesthetics from the perspective of certain facets of the short story, excluding, naturally, such structural principles as length, we believe that these narratives can be viewed as artistic "sketches" or examples that parallel literary techniques apparent in the longer works. The practice of examining short story narratives to exemplify elements in the novel is adopted by David William Foster with his analysis of Latin American fiction in *Studies in the Contemporary Spanish-American Short Story.*

For our discussion of the short story, Charles E. May provides a theoretical frame of reference that will serve and justify our purpose in using elements within the short story to underscore key aspects of Amado's novels. May defines the short story as ". . . primarily a literary mode that embodies and recapitulates mythic perception itself." He goes on to clarify this perception as one centered around "emotion, intuition, and fleeting perceptions" and quotes Ernst Cassirer's theory of "intensive compression" and the "focusing of all forces on a single point" (similar to [Edgar Allan] Poe's single effect) as the "prerequisite for all mythical thinking and mythical formulation." In fact, for Amado's short stories, it is this issue of the *single point as myth*—that is the evocation and depiction of the grand and legendary values, beliefs and deeds of Brazil's *povo* (people)—that remind the reader of the mythical themes and images which consistently reappear in extensive and elaborate distribution throughout Amado's novels. These single points emerge as myths because they invariably center upon time-honored human values that immortalize Amado's heroic characters. If we consider Northrop Frye's view of myth as an "art of implicit metaphorical identity," we can further appreciate Amado's popular appeal and in particular, his narrative focus with its strong allegiance to and identity with Brazil's popular literature, its folk heroes, tales, and ideology.

Stemming from Brazil's oral tradition of folk literature as it appears today in the *folhetos* (songbooks) and *baladas* of the *literatura de cordel* of Brazil's Northeast, these cultural myths and their value system form the very ideological basis of an Amado story, novella or novel. Moreover, the exposition of these values and themes are relentlessly operating upon a dialectical, binary axis which recalls Amado's much-alluded-to, albeit elastic, Marxist aesthetics that earlier labeled him one of Brazil's notable proponents of Marxism, both as a public figure and as a novelist. Essentially, this dialectical framework sets the stage for a Marxian perspective in which the implication for change or conversion surfaces via the dynamic conflict of opposing forces—for example, Amado's frequent depiction of the high values of the proletariat or underdog vs. the false ones of the bourgeoisie or the oppressors. Interestingly, this dialectic is also a formal element inherent in the basic structure of the poetics in the *literatura de cordel.* According to Candace Slater, this antinomy is frequently embodied in opposing behavioral traits such as those of *firmeza* (steadfastness) and *falsidade* (falsity or deception) which translate into opposing forces of good and evil manifested invariably by characters of the lower and upper classes respectively. This seemingly simple, antithetical, dualistic formula is however expressed by complex, sometimes ambiguous, figures and scenes that project a multi-dimensional profile, but which nonetheless are structurally outlined into shades of good and evil—forces that reveal an intrinsic Manichaeistic nature, characteristic of popular culture and art forms such as those found in Brazil. These, in turn, unceasingly posit the less privileged vis-a-vis the ruling classes, or in political terms, place the oppressed Left against the oppressive Right.

Along these lines, we may take a cue from Fredric Jameson in his study, *The Political Unconscious,* which presents the notion of contradiction as central to any Marxist cultural analysis. Jameson refers to Claude Lévi-Strauss' work as the model for the interpretation of myth and aesthetic structure, one that harbors a basic analytical or interpretive principle wherein ". . . the individual narrative, or the individual formal structure, is to be grasped as the imaginary resolution of a real contradiction." As such, it follows that ". . . the production of aesthetic or narrative form is to be seen as an ideological act in its own right, with the function of inventing imaginary or formal 'solutions' to unresolvable social contradictions." Considering Daphne Patai's view of Jorge Amado's work as "Oscillating between socio-political criticism and romantic lyricism. . . ," we can further appreciate Jameson's reference to the association of Marxism and romance, and especially, to his allusion to Northrop Frye's paradigm of storytelling and narrative:

> On this view, the oral tales of tribal society, the fairy tales that are the irrepressible voice and expression of the underclasses of the great systems of domination, adventure stories and melodrama, and the popular or mass culture of our own time are all syllables and broken fragments of some single immense story.

With these considerations in mind, we may entertain the ultimate universal ramifications of Jorge Amado's Human Comedy with its implicit ethical and dialectical basis, a reason for the reader's magnetic identification with these stories and their dynamic interpretation of popular culture; in particular, the expression of values, virtues and conflicts of the economically and socially oppressed in Brazil and the world at large.

To draw upon another view to clarify our own theoretical presentation of Amado's stance and dialectical approach, we offer Sergei Eisenstein's "Dialectical Approach to Film Form" in which he refers to *conflict* ". . . as the fundamental principle for the existence of every art-work and every art-form." Intrinsic to this is the concept of Being as a constant evolution from the interaction of *two contradictory opposites* and the concept of Synthesis arising from the classic opposition between thesis and antithesis. In other words, we view Amado's *Weltanschauung* as pivoting upon this fundamental binary structure, i.e., an implicit ideological thematics of contradictory forces. Thus, we believe that this formal treatment is crucial to understanding Amado's art, that is, his integration of form into content, and furthermore, his role as a committed professional writer of the popular and the universal. Using this focus with the short stories, we will be able to address the wide, evolutionary spectrum of his artistic expression from his earlier proletariat novels of social realism to his "realismo maravilhoso" (magical realism). The latter naturally calls to mind a similar world of illusion, fantasy and reality found in Gabriel Garcia Marquez—a world which ultimately compels the reader to examine the responsibility for the socio-economic and political turmoil rampant in present-day Latin American societies.

For the rest of our discussion we will be focusing mainly upon two of the three lesser-known stories: **"História do Carnaval"** (**"A Carnaval Story"**), 1937 and **"De Como o Mulato Porciúncula Descarregou Seu Defunto"** (**"How the Mulatto Porciúncula Got the Corpse Off His Back"**), 1959. The third story, **"As Mortes e o Triunfo de Rosalinda"** (**"The Deaths and the Victory of Rosalinda"**), 1965, will be addressed briefly for its basic form and theme of socio-political conflict. These stories serve our purpose well for they embody the formal considerations we have previously outlined and also deal with a variety of subjects and techniques that will illustrate Amado's dialectical approach as well as his gallery of popular tales, heroes and myths.

As a member of the "generation of 1930," the Brazilian Regionalists, who espoused socialist esthetic theories that parallel such works as [John] Steinbeck's *Grapes of Wrath,* Jorge Amado published novels throughout the thirties which are representative of the proletarian and socialist fervor of the times. Appropriately, his first known short story, **"História do Carnaval,"** emerges from that period as a simple but incisive tale of class conflict and consciousness from the point of view of a poor girl who has the opportunity to rise above her social station via her possible marriage to a young lawyer who, not surprisingly, maintains very conventional views of women and social behavior. Maria dos

Reis' dilemma or conflict rests with her wanting to participate in the free-spirited festivities of Carnaval, specifically as a member of the joyous float, the "Felizes Borboletas" (Happy Butterflies) which is destined to win first prize. However, her *namorado,* (boyfriend) whom she met during the previous Carnaval, when she performed as an outstanding "borboleta," is now decidedly against her participation since their engagement is soon to be announced. In fact, he threatens to end their relationship if she goes against his wishes.

Told primarily from Maria's angle of vision, the third person narration is also related in a colloquial style suggestive of Maria's own voice as well as that of an oral narrator. This popular narrator, however, lends some perceptive distance to Maria's situation by subtle shifts in the point of view within dialogue and interior monologue. In so doing, the narrative conveys an oral quality in tune with Amado's chronicle-like and ironic storyteller style flagrantly apparent in his later fiction. However, for our purposes, the revealing and principal quality of this story lies within Amado's structural and ideological framework of juxtaposing, on the one hand, Maria's "alegria," her happiness and free-spirited nature, and her sense of freedom within the Carnaval metaphor, along with her happy friends (the Cordeiro sisters), especially the simpática Antonieta; and, on the other, the restrictive forces of her impending marriage, her solemn boyfriend Teodoro, and her future higher-class position. While Maria's mother and aunt appeal to Maria's common sense on such moral grounds as social propriety as well as the practical one of securing a husband, Maria wavers and momentarily skirts the real issue. However, the heart of the matter is unabashedly articulated by her frank girlfriend, Antonieta, as she confronts Maria's boyfriend:

> Então, seu Teodoro, não quer deixar a dos Reis sair na nossa prancha, hein? Só porque é prancha de gente pobre e a futura esposa de um advogado não pode sair misturada com as filhas de um escriturário do correio, não é? Se fosse a prancha dos Andrades, ela podia, não é? (So, Suh Teodoro, you don't want to let Maria go out on our float, huh? Just because it's a poor man's float and the future wife of a lawyer cannot go out and mix with the daughters of a mail clerk, isn't that so? If it were the float belonging to the Andrades, she'd be able to, right?)

Antonieta's direct accusations speak honestly to a class issue that instead has been clouded by Maria's family in terms of morality, decency and propriety. The family's implication that lower class girls are "bad" and "immoral" eventually forces Maria to compromise herself and her freedom even though her thoughts about her boyfriend's "brutishness" (*bruto, bruto, bruto*) tell her otherwise. Her final decision to follow the rules of convention projects a picture which suggests her future existence as a submissive, repressed wife.

After the "borboletas" win all the Carnaval prizes, the narrative shifts to Antonieta's point of view and ends with this final image of Maria dos Reis as the festive float and its metaphorical implication of happiness pass her by: "Antonieta descobriu Maria dos Reis que ia pelo braço do noivo, um lança-perfume na mão, atrás a mãe e a tia, solenes os quatro, marchando pelo Carnaval com passos medidos e rostos sérios." (Antonieta saw Mary of Kings clutching to her fiance's arm, a Carnaval favor in hand; in back, her mother and aunt, the four of them solemn, marching to the Carnaval beat with measured steps and serious faces.)

Amado's juxtaposition of freedom and social convention reveals his keen perception of the false social mores and the inherently complex, contradictory, socio-economic issues that come into play and that moreover dictate implacably the lives in a highly stratified society. Amado underscores this perception during the last paragraph where the point of view of the triumphant Antonieta becomes the main focus. Moreover, the subtle implication of social aspirations, inherent in Maria dos Reis' name (Mary of Kings) adds to Amado's intuitive portrayal of class consciousness and conflict. Furthermore, the added implication of Maria's *falsidade* and Antonieta's *firmeza* is basic and inescapable, but as we can see, this approach is not simplistic, because it signals to the reader perceptions into other multi-dimensional and complex issues such as the role of women, *machismo* and bourgeois behavior, all of which surface dualistically in contradictory situations. Thus, in a seemingly simple narrative, we have a considerably complex exposition of themes.

The next story under consideration is **"De Como Porciúncula Descarregou o Seu Defunto,"** first published in Rio in the monthly literary magazine *Senhor.* This story, translated and included in *The Eye of the Heart, Short Stories from Latin America,* 1973, serves as a fine illustration of Amado's consistent, conceptual framework as well as his adaptation of techniques from Brazil's popular poetry which later find their most notable expression and parallel in Amado's *Tereza Batista,* 1972. In fact, the character Tereza Batista is alluded to in this earlier 1959 narrative along with her sister Maria do Véu, one of the central figures in the story. This practice points to one of Amado's common literary devices—that of using the same characters across different narratives, thereby bestowing upon his world a sense of history and authenticity. This ploy, on the other hand, is also one of the more evident characteristics of the *folhetos* which mix history and fiction and purport to document only what has been "seen" or verified.

A close reading of **"Porciúncula"** will reveal all the major aspects of Amado's aesthetic mode; in particular, we notice his use of hyperbole and myth to characterize his own poetic and epic brand of "magical realism" that seeks to immortalize heroes who embody ethical and moral truths which encourage reader identity and above all represent basic human and universal values—ones that are depicted outside the confines of class, often in a marginal world not concerned with prejudice and appearances.

> **Drawing upon the oral tradition of storytelling and his lyrical treatment of love, Amado . . . infuses his narrative with fantasy in order to magnify the deeds of his heroes and elevate them in the eyes of the readers.**
> —*Nelson H. Vieira*

The first part of the narrative sets the stage for the drama between Porciúncula and his corpse, the dead Maria do Véu. Here, the narrator slips in the main theme before the actual development of the central story, a device common to the popular *folhetos* and one that draws the reader into the narrative and prepares him/her for the moral lesson that follows. In this case, the tale revolves around the mulatto's sense of duty and honesty as contrasted with its absence in two other characters: 1) a blond, cold-hearted Gringo who stabbed his adulterous wife and her lover to death, and 2) the son of a certain landowner, Coronel Barbosa, who deflowered Maria and promised to marry her in church with white gown and veil. These two men serve as bad examples for they never "get their corpses off their backs." The Gringo never confesses and consequently is visibly bent and weighed down by his burden, since he never paid for his sins before the law. The coronel's son simply used Maria, never expecting to fulfill his promise honorably. The reader learns that Porciúncula had told his story to the present narrator on a rainy night in a bar in the presence of several drinkers, one of whom is the aforementioned Gringo. This set-up helps to contrast the more honorable Porciúncula with the dishonest Gringo by having the mulatto "unburden" or confess the whole truth of his story even though the narrative does not always place him in a favorable light. We learn through the retelling of the story by the present narrator that Porciúncula cheats at cards, is a renowned storyteller in his own right, and whores around with Tibéria's "girls" in this madam's bordello. It is via Tibéria that Porciúncula meets Maria who, after being seduced and abandoned by the coronel's son, ends up in Tibéria's whorehouse. Porciúncula is immediately smitten by Maria's beauty and consequently falls madly in love. She, on the other hand, appears indifferent to his advances, preferring to spend most of her leisure time going to weddings, cutting out pictures of brides and dreaming of someday wearing a veil. This behavior is a result of her having witnessed the wedding of the young coronel's son to the daughter of another prominent coronel. So obsessed is she with this scene that she becomes known as Mary of the Veil and at one point vows to Tibéria: "Um dia há de chegar e

eu visto um vestido desses." (One of these days you'll see me in one of those gowns.)

Maria demonstrates no affection for any man except perhaps for the sincere Porciúncula whom she regularly sees since he persistently seeks her out: ". . . não passava noite sem procurar Maria na beira do mar, espiando seu requebrar, nela querendo naufragar." (A night didn't go by when he wasn't watching for Maria on the waterfront, trailing her, wanting to shipwreck himself on her.) However, Maria mysteriously refuses to sleep with Porciúncula despite (or rather on account of) his sincere love. Porciúncula's sincerity and honesty are held in high esteem by the macho narrator because he recognizes the fact that another man would have lied, never admitting that he failed to sleep with Maria. But, the confused Porciúncula eventually tires of this rejection and momentarily forgets Maria in the sensual arms of a voluptuous mulata, Carolina. Later, when he learns that Maria is dying of a fever and is calling for him, he devotedly rushes to her side only to find that she has already expired, but not before confiding to Tibéria one last wish. Designating Porciúncula as her bridegroom, she asked to be buried with wedding gown, veil and bouquet. Although a half-crazed wish, it is a corpse's request, and so, not wishing to abandon Maria again, the honorable Porciúncula responds accordingly. Everything is arranged by Tibéria and her "girls" who make up a bridal ensemble fit for a queen. Sitting on the bed next to the splendiferously dressed Maria, Porciúncula places on her finger a ring given by Clarice, another abandoned woman. As he holds her hand, he notices that Maria is smiling. Assuring his listeners that he had not touched a drop, Porciúncula further swears to another supernatural phenomenon—the transformation of Tibéria into a priest dressed in all the appropriate vestments: "um padre gordo, com jeito de santo" (a fat priest who looked saintly). The "magical" elements serve here to heighten Porciúncula's honesty and actions. The story ends with the present narrator commenting on the fact that by "getting the corpse off his back" through his storytelling, Porciúncula relieved himself of his burden. In other words, this act translates into his redeeming himself for momentarily abandoning Maria, but above all, it shows his profound sense of duty and love as her suitor, a deed or virtue heightened by the contrast between Porciúncula and the other two men.

Jorge Amado thus reinforces the virtues of the members of the lower class with his Marxian dialectical polarity of positing them in relation to their socio-economic oppressors. Drawing upon the oral tradition of storytelling and his lyrical treatment of love, Amado also infuses his narrative with fantasy in order to magnify the deeds of his heroes and elevate them in the eyes of the readers. At the same time, via simple language, he casts a critical view upon the upper class by the use of an ironic narrator armed with humor and satire. However, it is the insertion of the supernatural and magic in this story which stresses Amado's departure from mere referential regionalism and stark social realism toward an increased usage of fantasy, legend and illusion in order to distill an inner reality of mythical proportions, one that reverberates in his epic and universal vision of human values inherent in the people of the lower and marginal classes. For the reader, these basic values serve as *the* reference point for identification with the humanity in Amado's world.

Porciúncula, as we learn in the later novel, **Shepherds of the Night,** is actually the character Cabo Martim, a central figure in that 1964 novel and also one of **Berro D'Agua's** faithful companions during the hero's "second-death," the other short narrative also published in 1959, the year of the Porciúncula story. As a matter-of-fact, from this particular short story and its contemporary, **Two Deaths,** we can designate 1959 as an important turning point in Amado's imaginative use of fantasy. Moreover, this short story also serves as a clear, succinct example of how Amado employs a self-conscious narrative form to call attention to the art of storytelling as a process that is cathartic and instructive as well as entertaining. In so doing, he mirrors the popular poet's role as is most apparent in his following statement:

> Sou um contador de histórias, jamais fui outra coisa. Histórias aprendidas do povo, vividas numa vida ardente e recriadas depois para entregá-las novamente ao povo de onde elas vieram. Isso é o que pretendia fazer e o que tenho feito.
>
> (I'm a storyteller, I never was anything else. Stories I learned from the people, experienced during a passionate life and recreated later in order to return them again to the people from whence they came. That's what I intended to do and that's what I've done.)

In *Myth and Ideology in Contemporary Brazil,* Daphne Patai finds fault with Amado's use of myth and magic which she believes is contradictory to the Marxian premise that sets forth the need to abandon illusion in order to gain perceptive, rational knowledge. In this story, the narrative's fantasy is specifically set up for the reader's purpose so that he/she may in fact grasp metaphorically, thus rationally, the story's quintessential reality—that of Porciúncula's and Maria's *firmeza.* As we have delineated, Amado's *Weltanschauung* is ultimately directed at *registering* for the reader the *status quo* in a Third World society such as Brazil's. Henceforth, his legendary moments of truth serve to elicit from the reader perceptions that eventually lead to a clearer understanding of the underlying conflicts and injustices within a highly class-conscious society.

This is remarkably evident in the third short story. Here, it is sufficient to note that **"As Mortes e o Triunfo de Rosalinda"** is an anarchical, revolutionary fantasy that outlines the potential violence possible with class conflict. This monologue/harangue by an irreverent and lower-class narrator who relentlessly assails an array of imaginary readers with virulent, sarcastic and vituperative epithets, directed at their middle and upper-class selves, recalls Amado's dialectical approach and use of myth but, above all, appears to be a direct product of the political times—the period related to the 1964 military take-over. On the other hand, the narrative's revolutionary spirit and implicit call for violent action also bring to mind Amado's literary roots of the 30's and their Marxist stance, apparent in these words which he articulated during his acceptance speech at the Brazilian Academy of Letters in 1961: "Nasci para a literatura e o romance . . . quando os fundamentos do Brasil vinham de ser abalados por um movimento revolucionário de raízes populares." (I was born for literature and the novel . . . at a time when Brazil's very foundations were being shaken by a revolutionary movement of popular roots.) Here we are reminded of Amado's original literary impulse, one that, notwithstanding its later development, sophistication and tempered stance, has, in our opinion never really veered away from his popular and political perspective, but has in fact sparked and guided his aesthetics toward a more universal dimension. As Roger Bastide once noted, Jorge Amado seeks to defend the spontaneity of life against the illusory search for material riches or appearances of respectability. In short, Amado advocates individual freedom over the alienating forms of social oppression. This theme has undeniable appeal for everyone because it is the stuff of literature with which all readers can identify.

In conclusion, it appears that in these stories as well as in his novels, Jorge Amado is reaching for universal truths through his own particular version of the Brazilian Human Condition. Perhaps this is what Fritz Teixeira meant when speaking about the noble **Gabriela:** "E o que é **Gabriela,** senão um grande poema popular, uma rapsódia do povo, símbolo de uma humanidade que nasce—uma humanidade brasileira?" (And what is **Gabriela,** if not a great popular poem, a rhapsody of the people, symbol of a humanity that is coming to life—a Brazilian humanity?) The uniqueness of this Brazilian humanity or spirit is the reflective lens through which Jorge Amado strives to frame those universals and singular human values that ultimately transcend national boundaries and the oppressive barriers of class in an almost messianic search for the kind of Hope that will liberate Mankind.

Enrique Grönlund and Moylan C. Mills (essay date 1988)

SOURCE: "*Dona Flor and Her Two Husbands:* A Tale of

Sensuality, Sustenance, and Spirits," in *Film and Literature: A Comparative Approach to Adaptation,* Texas Tech University Press, 1988, pp. 165-78.

[*In the following essay, Grönlund and Mills praise Bruno Barreto's film adaptation of Amado's* Dona Flor and Her Two Husbands.]

Jorge Amado's novel **Dona Flor and Her Two Husbands: A Moral and Amorous Tale** tells the story of Floripedes, a raven-haired Brazilian beauty "with eyes shining like oil and skin the color of tea," and the two men she marries. This independent-minded woman of Bahia, who "had been born with the gift for seasoning," a teacher of culinary arts who runs her own school, marries first the man of her youthful dreams—someone blond, dashing and poor—in the person of Vadinho who, in addition to being blond, dashing and poor, is a gambler, a randy rake, a mischievous, yet charming, fake, as well as a sensitive, loyal, generous human being. His lust for life takes him away from home practically every night, sometimes for days at a time; it returns him home often drunk; and it creates for him a perpetual state of insolvency, which, at times, causes him to beat Flor for the sole purpose of stealing a few cruzeiros from her to pay for his revelries. Vadinho's gambling, drinking, and womanizing carry him to an early grave; he dies at age thirty-one, while dancing the samba early one Sunday morning of *Carnaval.*

He is mourned by his friends, to whom he remains a hero, an example of manhood; his caring and loyalty are warmly remembered. To the majority of the people who have not been touched by his charm and genuine optimism, Vadinho's death provides an opportunity to malign his character with impunity. Flor, who for seven years had tolerated her husband's dissolute ways, is a kind, forgiving wife whose painful, heartfelt grief is not completely abated until his return from the netherworld some two and one-half years later.

Although the marriage of Vadinho and Flor may not have been made in heaven, their sex life was, for it is the poetic eroticism of their lovemaking that is destined to symbolize their relationship. Tender and animal-like, fiery and sweet, it is never obstructed by social or moral conventions. When the desire strikes, it is readily satiated. If there is no bed available, the floor offers a handy substitute. Clothes and bedsheets are minor impediments to be discarded on the road to concupiscent bliss. And, if the neighbors can hear the sighs of passion because the doors and windows have been left open, well, their jealousy be damned.

By the conclusion of the proper year of mourning, Flor's inner suffering, caused by the absence of a conjugal life, has become intolerable. She is urged to remarry, which she does. This time the fortunate man is the local pharmacist, an up-

standing member of the community, a paragon of good-breeding, a man of means. All that and more is bassoon-playing Dr. Teodoro Madureira. This second marriage provides Flor with the economic security and social respect heretofore missing in her life. She travels in a new social world in which a regimented, straight-laced lifestyle is required in order to maintain superficial social airs. Yet, she is at peace with herself, happy with the new stable rhythms; she accepts the fact that there is a place for everything, and that everything is in its place. She seems content with the monotony of her new life. She learns to make love wearing nightclothes, always under the sheets, on "Wednesdays and Saturdays, at ten o'clock, ... with an encore on Saturday, optional on Wednesday," always modestly and quickly.

Flor has accomplished a marital Möbius loop by having shared her life with polar opposites. Everything that Vadinho was, Dr. Teodoro is not; everything that Dr. Teodoro has, Vadinho never possessed. In the end, although Flor respects and appreciates Dr. Teodoro for what he is and for what he provides, she, nevertheless, misses the spontaneity, the gaiety, the excitement of Vadinho.

The blood that brings to life Amado's creation is the language. It is at once humorous, touching, poignant, descriptive, and above all, lyrical. It weaves a tapestry rich in symbol, wit, sorcery, harmony, fragrance, poetic sexuality, and gastronomic delights.
—*Enrique Grönlund and Moylan C. Mills*

Her heart, her burning womb, call out to Vadinho. And, so, he returns, naked and roguish as ever, more alive than dead, to wreak havoc upon Flor's libido. Flor, always the proper lady, does not succumb to her first husband's advances without a moral and spiritual struggle. But, when she eventually does, her life is fulfilled: the benefits of both matrimonies join together to form a most unusual union.

Such is the skeletal essence of the novel's storyline, through which Amado seriously examines the relationship between men and women, the flesh and the spirit. The muscle provided by Amado is comprised of quirky subplots, anecdotal asides, dream sequences, haunting *candômblé* spiritism, telling observations on people and life, and last, but certainly not least, the myriad of unforgettable characters representing all areas of Bahian society: the good-natured gamblers and whores, the meddling gossips, and the stuffy upper crust, each a unique individual.

The blood that brings to life Amado's creation is the language. It is at once humorous, touching, poignant, descriptive, and above all, lyrical. It weaves a tapestry rich in symbol, wit, sorcery, harmony, fragrance, poetic sexuality, and gastronomic delights. This eloquent amalgamation of language, theme, plot, and character is pure magic. Within this context, the sensuosity, the *candômblé* spiritism, and the gastronomic elements can be addressed as they are reflected in both the novel and in the 1977 translation of **Dona Flor and Her Two Husbands** to the film medium.

During the seventeenth century, West-Central African Yoruba culture with its spiritism was one of the numerous and diverse cultural groups imported into Brazil by Portuguese slave-traders. Subsequently, Sudan-rooted Yoruba culture became the dominant African one in Bahia, a Northeastern province in Brazil, whose capital, Salvador, is the setting of the novel.

Within the label *Yoruba,* one can also identify various ethnic sub-cultures called nations, each united by similar customs, beliefs, language, etc., among which the Ketu is "the major group in Bahia" and, as such, is predominant in the *candômbés* of that province. Jorge Amado, the author, has become a lay protector (an *ogan*) as well as a minister (an *obá*) of the *candômbés* rituals as practiced by the Ketu nation in Bahia. Consequently, his presentation of Yoruba spiritism, Ketu in particular, is founded on personal knowledge and experience. Thus, the roles that various Yoruba spirits play throughout the course of **Dona Flor and Her Two Husbands** accurately reflect Ketu orthodoxy and lend credence to what may otherwise seem illogical goings-on during the course of the novel.

Although neither Dona Flor nor Vadinho worship non-Catholic dieties, they are, nevertheless, protected, unbeknownst to them, by Afro-Brazilian spirits. As a result, certain personality traits of Dona Flor and Vadinho, along with particular actions and beliefs of theirs, tend to reflect these spirits more so than any Christian omnipresence.

For example, Vadinho's protector is Exú, god "of doors, paths, and openings." Although among most Afro-Brazilian cultures, including the Yoruba, Exú is identified "with the devil," the Ketu nation has "faithfully preserved the African image (of a) god of orientation, a young boy, mischievous rather than spiteful." In addition, he "loves pranks and likes to play tricks," yet "he has a good heart in spite of all his nonsense." Above all, Exú "presides over the sexual act," and "eats anything in the way of food."

And mischievous Vadinho is. He met Flor after having gate-crashed an exclusive gala affair, pretending to be a government official rather than the penniless, indolent gambler he in fact was. His so-called gift of gab sustains his avocation, enabling him to sweet-talk people with money out of countless loans, most of which will go unpaid, and also rescues

him from equally countless situations when creditors come calling. On the other hand, whenever the number *17* comes up, lining his pockets with money, Vadinho spends lavishly on his friends and Flor. Moreover, upon his return to the world of the living, Vadinho delights his friends and cronies by having their bets win continuously, thus bringing the treasuries of the very same gambling establishments that so often emptied his own pockets perilously close to financial ruin. Not one to plan for the future, Vadinho views each day as a new life whose pleasures of gambling, whoring, eating, drinking, and loving Dona Flor must be enjoyed to the fullest. Thus the correlation between the monicker "Vadinho" and the Portuguese verb "vadiar"—to wander about, also to loaf—becomes evident. Amado's symbolic intent is clear in the original Portuguese.

Yet, Vadinho's failures on the gaming tables rarely interfere with his love for Flor. It is undeniable that, on rare occasions, he physically abuses his beloved wife in order to obtain money she has saved from her cooking school. But somehow his sexual prowess is so pleasing and satisfying that it overcomes all else. When it comes to making love, Vadinho has no peer. Neither clothes, nor clocks, nor furniture, nor social convention interfere with his sexual appetite. Bluntly stated, the man loves to screw and teaches Dona Flor to love screwing on an equal basis. As he, himself, states, "Screwing is a blessed thing. It was invented by God in Paradise." The language in Harriet de Onis's translation is considerably less to the point than its Portuguese counterpart, where, again, the verb "vadiar"—euphemistically, to fornicate—is ever present on Vadinho's lips, not as a negative epithet, but as an earthy natural desire. Once again, Amado's correlation between the Portuguese verb and the alliterative monicker cannot be ignored.

Although Vadinho expresses his masculinity and manhood by seducing women whenever possible, his favorite partner is Flor, who is protected by the goddess Oxun. Oxun is associated with water, especially sweet, "fresh water." Also, Oxun is the "goddess of sensual love," "the image of the eternal feminine," who practices "erotic magic." Hence, sex and water are integral elements that join forces at some of the critical moments in Flor's life. For example, Flor and Vadinho's premarital consummation of their love occurs in a cottage by the sea, with the sea howling "a hallelujah" of approval at the point of orgasm. Later, after her marriage to the straight-laced Dr. Teodoro, who makes love according to the calendar, Flor's honeymoon night is spent in a small hotel near the very same sea where she and Vadinho made love for the first time. Furthermore, Vadinho's return from the hereafter (answering Dona Flor's call) inevitably leads to his second seduction of Flor. On a "Saturday" night, which is, incidentally, Oxun's feast day, with "the rain pattering on the roof," Flor does not deny Vadinho "water to drink."

It is also important to consider Oxun's demeanor. To the unknowing, she is "gentleness itself . . . outwardly still water." Nevertheless, upon closer inspection, it is revealed that the goddess is "over proud," a woman unafraid to become concubine and wife to another god, rejecting her first husband. Oxun's exterior calmness, thus, is betrayed by her libidinous desires, which foment "inwardly, a squall."

Dona Flor, like Oxun, the "two-timer," has been married twice. Unlike Oxun, Flor's relationships are a result of death, not adultery. Now, after her first husband's death, Flor follows the requisite mourning code expected of her. The young, vibrant, sensual widow develops a "roaring blaze" inside her womb, which can be extinguished only by a man. Her demeanor becomes affected, for she is "outwardly, modesty personified. . . .meekness itself; inwardly, a raging fire." Dr. Teodoro, fortunately, extinguishes the conflagration. On the other hand, unfortunately, the doctor's systematic, controlled, and inhibited style of lovemaking provides, at best, temporary relief—very temporary. Consequently, although Flor is in love with her second husband, the lack of passion, spontaneity, and reckless abandon that defined her first marriage causes her to call out to Vadinho. His return from the hereafter is sponsored by his protector Exú, god of the crossroads. Vadinho's explanation that he has come in order "to prevent [Flor] from taking a lover and dragging [her] name and honor through the mud," confounds the "decent, respectable woman [who is] not going to betray [her] husband." After all, Flor understands fully why Vadinho has returned. As has been posited, like Oxun, whose "favorite meat" is "goat," Flor realizes that she might well be unfaithful. Yet, is it truly a case of adultery? After all, Flor does not fornicate out of wedlock. Besides, the horns of cuckoldry never manifest themselves upon the brow of the good doctor. In the end, both the outer and inner selves of Flor are satisfied: she has achieved complete fulfillment, she is one. Love has conquered all.

On a somewhat different level, Oxun's importance as a deity of the waters also evinces itself, provided that the generally accepted symbolism between water and life is agreed upon, in Dona Flor's prowess as an expert cook. As the name of her cooking school indicates, "Savor and Art" reflect the concern, care, and creativity with which she lends her expertise to provide sustenance for living. She gives of herself to the fruits of the earth and the sea with the same ardor and willingness with which she gives herself to Vadinho. Unabashedly, she flavors her recipes and lovemaking with the spices of life. And, in Vadinho, than whom "nobody had a more delicate palate," she has a man who relishes all of her offerings, and, also, like Exú, a man who eats anything.

So, it is not surprising when water and food join hands in the novel. *Moqueca de siri mole,* braised marinated soft-shell crabs, is Vadinho's "favorite dish," never to be made again by Flor after his death. *Siri,* Bahian for crab, occupies a different, yet no less important, place in Vadinho's frolicsome life. Expert dancer that he is, when the mood strikes him to burst the hypocritical balloon of social convention, Vadinho "with perfection and grace" performs the steps of the smuttily licentious *siri-boceta.* By imitating a crab's undulating and grinding movements as it attempts to dig itself into the sand, the dance becomes a racy representation of sexual intercourse. Interestingly enough, the word *boceta* is a Portuguese vulgarism for vagina. Thus, with *siri* and *boceta,* Vadinho's favorite foods are clearly designated, and Flor's are no doubt the best.

Oxun, water, and Flor intertwine once again during Flor's period of mourning. Again, the catalyst is a recipe, in this case *cágado guisado,* stewed fresh water turtle. In preparation of this dish, the animal is killed and carved up in a rather gruesome manner. This brutal procedure symbolizes Flor's current state of existence. Flor's spirit is encased in a moral shell furnished by social conventions and restrictions. If the shell were removed, an inner self mutilated by the violent struggle between Flor's desire to break free and her need to adhere to conventional morality would be revealed. Her thoughts are expressed thus:

> But if your guest wants even finer and more unusual game, if he is looking for the *ne plus ultra,* . . . the pleasure of the gods, then why not serve him up a young and pretty widow, cooked in her tears of suffering and loneliness, in the sauce of her modesty and mourning, in the moans of her deprivation, in the fire of her forbidden desire, which gives her the flavor of guilt and sin?
>
> Ah, I know of such a widow, of chile and honey, cooking over a slow fire every night, just ready to be served.

Like that of Oxun, Flor's calm demeanor projected externally is belied by her consuming inner passion. Fortunately, Dr. Teodoro will serve himself a sizable portion, even a second helping at times, of Flor's delectable ingredients.

Caviar, another product of the waters, is used to define Flor's sexual relationships with both husbands. At a reception following a concert in which Dr. Teodoro has played on the bassoon a composition honoring his wife, Flor and her best friend, Dona Norma, discuss the merits of caviar in the following exchange:

> Dona Norma: "This stuff has a rancid taste. I don't know how to describe it."
>
> Dona Flor (quoting Vadinho): "It tastes like tail . . . and it's very good."

In the original Portuguese, the word that has been translated as "tail" is *boceta*. This curiosity is not lost on Dona Norma, who acknowledges that Vadinho "understood those tastes."

Later that evening, Dona Norma, who has drunk a bit too much champagne, teasingly asks Dr. Teodoro: "'Did you like the caviar?'"

He responds: "'I know that it is a delicacy for the gods, . . . [but] I did not find it altogether to my liking.'"

Dona Norma persists: "'And what did it taste like to you?'"

Dr. Teodoro answers: "'To tell you the truth, I can't recall anything that tastes like it. . . . I thought it tasted awful.'"

And, Dona Norma finishes the discussion thus: "'But there are those who like it, aren't there, Flor?'"

This charmingly witty scene not only underlines the basic attitudinal differences toward sex between the two husbands, but also serves to return the presence of Vadinho to the forefront of the narrative. He has not been forgotten; he is spoken of openly once again. His return is foreshadowed. Dona Flor's life will finally be complete, thanks in part to Exú, god of the crossroads, who had aided Vadinho's transmutation. And it is through Amado's creative genius that water, food, and sex become one as a result of eating imported caviar.

This same sensuous amalgam of sex, food, music, and *carnaval* is used by Bruno Barreto to flavor his 1977 adaptation of the novel into a film, a film that has become the most successful film in the history of Brazilian cinema. **Dona Flor and Her Two Husbands** is, however, only one of the Brazilian films to have exploded on the international cinema scene in recent years with great impact. It might be in order, therefore, to point out briefly some of the attributes of Brazilian cinema that have contributed to this success, and also to place the film **Dona Flor** in context.

From the early part of the twentieth century through the 1960s, Brazilian films were very heavily influenced by Hollywood, and American films dominated Brazilian screens. It was during the late 1950s and early 1960s that the so-called Cinema Novo movement began in Brazil—with such films as *Black Orpheus, O Pagador de Promessas* (*The Given Word*), *Antonio das Mortes,* and others. These films explored in graphic terms the social conflicts and violence in Brazilian society, the cultural cost of progress, and the influence of Indian and African traditions on the European colonial cultures.

Typically, the Cinema Novo and subsequent films of the 1970s and 1980s employed:

—a very colorful *mise en scene,* taking great care in portraying the true Brazilian urban and rural landscapes;

—brilliant use of color to explore the rich *mise en scene* and to define the emotional concerns of the protagonists;

—effective utilization of the various techniques of international cinema, most notably those of the Italian Neo-Realists, the French New Wave auteurs, and individual filmmakers such as Welles, Losey, and Jansco;

—inventive use of lively and sensuous Brazilian music, especially that of Antonio Carlos Jobim and Luis Bonfa;

—very frank language; very candid depictions of nudity and sex;

—extensive utilization of Indian and African fables and rituals; and

—a focus on the social conditions of the country, often in a highly critical way.

Brazilian films are often flamboyant and extravagant in style. Indeed, this combination of social critique and stylistic vivacity is highly appropriate for expressing the lives of people perpetually in crisis and *carnaval.*

The film *Dona Flor* is, of course, an excellent exemplar of these attributes, all of which blend together to create a delightful and colorful romantic comedy that upon closer examination yields a meaning at once ironic and socially explosive: that to be totally happy one must have erotic freedom and fulfillment, as well as all of the more practical middle-class virtues and values.

Vadinho tells Flor in the novel: "[Teodoro] gives you: your own house, conjugal fidelity, respect, order, consideration, and security . . . his love is made up of these noble (and tiresome) things, and you need all of them to be happy." But Flor needs more, as she learns in the novel and film, and by a supreme act of will, she provides her own happiness by bringing Vadinho back from the dead to give her, as Vadinho points out, "impure, wrong, crooked love, dissolute and fiery, . . . to bring you joy, suffering, and pleasure."

In the film, director Bruno Barreto and the screenwriters Eduardo Coutinho and Leopoldo Serran deftly cut away most of the subplots that embellish the novel's narrative to concentrate on Flor and her involvement with the two men in her life. To achieve this intense concentration, Barreto excises certain extended episodes that appear in the novel, such as the pharmaceutical debate, the movie theatre excursion, the concert, and the buying of the house by Flor and Teodoro. This condensation is clearly related to Andre

Bazin's chandelier/usher's flashlight comparison wherein the novel is equated with the multiplicity of rays emanating from a chandelier, and the film adaptation is equated with the strong single beam of an usher's flashlight.

One of the film director's most noticeable cinematic techniques is his use of close and medium-close shots to bring the audience into an intimate relationship with Flor and her dilemma. Barreto is adroit in his use of the theory of proxemic distance, thus creating audience empathy with Flor and her confusions, dissatisfactions, and ultimate fulfillment. This theory suggests that the closer the camera gets to its subject, the more involved the audience becomes with that same subject. Barreto's camera lingers incessantly on the luminous copper-colored flesh of Flor and also on the golden blond body of Vadinho. Interestingly, Vadinho, who appears naked throughout the final third of the film, does not have a beautifully muscled athletic body. Instead he has the slight paunch of the sensualist, the man who loves food almost as much as he loves women and gambling.

Barreto uses the *mise en scene* very creatively. The film opens with a long shot of an empty square in Bahia, Dona Flor's house on one side, the local church on the other. The audience waits for the square to be populated, to be filled up, for the story to begin. The *mise èn scene* itself suggests the need for action to lead to fulfillment. The film ends appropriately with the same square in long shot, now filled with people, but also filled with the joy and satisfaction of Dona Flor, who has resolved the conflict between the giddy needs of the senses and the quotidian demands of the practical world. Barreto also uses the film's *mise en scene* to indicate the joyous but messy disorder of Flor's life with Vadinho and her ordered but dull existence with Teodoro. In the scenes with Vadinho, Flor and her friends stand in overlapping configurations. With Teodoro, Flor and her friends sit in ordered rows, each in her or his particular place. Barreto also contrasts the blonde Vadinho, naked and free, with Teodoro soberly clothed in his dark suit.

To understand the full command that Barreto has over his cinematic medium, one has only to recall a key scene near the beginning of the film. From close-ups of Flor's memory of her wedding night. Barreto gives his audience ecstatic close-ups of the glowing flesh of Flor and Vadinho, actually bathing the joyous couple in a golden light; then he films the love scene in a series of overlapping dissolves that prolong the ecstasy, emphasizing the delirium of the love-making, enforcing the fact that Flor will lose this ecstasy with the death of Vadinho. This erotic sequence establishes Flor's longing for this sensual joy, a longing that haunts her during the rest of the film, until her need, so strong, so insistent, brings Vadinho back, enabling Flor to complete her existence. The scene culminates in a close-up of Flor's face, her satisfaction manifest in her expression of postcoital ful-

fillment. Later she turns to Vadinho, to find him gone. The scamp has left his wedding bed for a night of gambling and whoring. Thus, the sequence epitomizes the various elements that lead to the story's subsequent conflicts and resolution.

Because Barreto has made his necessary deletions, certain moments that may be overlooked in the lengthy, episodic literary narrative stand out in the film. For instance, near the beginning of the film, Vadinho goes to the church to ask the priest for gambling money. While there, he comments on the lascivious look that a male angel is giving to a statue of Saint Clare. Later Flor looks at the same statue, notes the same flirtatious look on the angel's face and realizes the full impact of her longing for Vadinho. In the novel, Flor thinks to herself:

> Poor Saint [Clare]: her sanctity, however strong and fortified, however great in virtue, could not hold out against the lascivious eyes of that [angel] devil, the poor blessed creature succumbing to him, handing over to him her decency and her life, risking for him her salvation already gained, trading heaven for hell, for without him, what was heaven or life worth?

The film sacrifices Flor's interior monologue, but because the two scenes are now closer together, the audience recognition of their linkage is that much greater.

Because of his rich, poetic style and discursive structure—emphasizing anecdote, incident, digression, and a great number of colorful characters—Amado can be compared to the great English novelists of the eighteenth and nineteenth centuries.
—*Enrique Grönlund and Moylan C. Mills*

Another moment that adds to the characterization of Flor and underscores dramatically her desperate desire for Vadinho is the mad cry she emits after the *candômbé* that she has initiated to get rid of the reincarnated Vadinho begins to work, causing Vadinho to begin to fade away. The scream, mentioned only obliquely in the novel, erupts with full force on the screen followed by an extreme close-up. It is unequivocally clear that Flor's overwhelming need, made manifest in sound and image, keeps Vadinho in her life. This moment in particular underlines the strength of the film adaptation, indicating how faithfully Barreto cleaves to the essential narrative line, emphasizing always the madding dilemma of a human being attempting to resolve the disparate longings of all human beings for both security—economic and social—and sensual excitation and delirium. Incidentally, this scream repeats Flor's anguished outburst at the beginning of the film when she sees Vadinho's lifeless body spread out on the cobblestones of the square, and she realizes with horror that her adored husband is dead. Barreto designs a kind of visual parentheses with these screams. The difference, of course, is that after the first outcry, Flor loses Vadinho; after the second, she regains him for good.

The novel's unique intermingling of eroticism and gastronomy is manifested in the film through Barreto's tantalizing close-ups of food, especially the braised soft-shell crabs, and through his obsessive focus on the radiant face and succulent torso of Brazilian film star Sonia Braga. Thus, Barreto, following the dictates of Amado, interweaves in a very graphic way those two temptations, food and sex. There is, for instance, the director's unabashed realization of the moment in the nightclub when Flor asks Vadinho if he likes caviar, and he replies, "Of course, because it tastes just like your *boceta,*" Flor's "little box." And again, Barreto, by means of an artfully arranged, slow, reverse zoom shot of the supine and incandescently naked Sonia Braga, suggests visually the young widow simmering in her own tears, about to explode, so she says, if she does not soon find a man to give her sexual ecstasy and release.

The one element of the novel that is minimized in the film is Amado's emphasis on spiritism, relegated by Barreto to an atmospheric background element—for instance, in the opening carnaval sequence—and a plot device by which Flor tries to exorcise Vadinho after his sudden return to her life. Barreto, perhaps because of the influence of the Cinema Novo moment, underscores much more obviously the conflicts that Flor has with bourgeois social attitudes, even with the prevailing moral views of the Catholic Church. Barreto designs a striking visual juxtaposition by placing the imposing and very grand Catholic Church edifice on one side of the square in which much of the film's action takes place and by setting Flor and Vadinho's love nest on the other side of that same area, with the local prostitute's abode somewhere in between, creating a marvelous holy/unholy trinity. In fact, when Flor finally makes her decision to have her cake and eat it too, appearing in public, subsequently, arm-in-arm with her Sunday-suited second husband and her stark naked first husband, she boldly and happily flaunts her outrageous behavior on the steps of the very same sacred citadel. And to make his point even more visually explicit, Barreto, unlike Amado, places a large crucifix conspicuously over the bed blasphemously occupied by Flor and her two husbands. Another component that adds to the unique flavor of the film is the expressive, sensual beat of the Brazilian samba, used by Barreto and his composer Francis Hime as a constant reminder of the sexual tides that control and confound Flor in her quest for fulfillment. Appropriately, the musical track becomes less native and more classical as Teodoro becomes the dominant element in Flor's life.

Because of his rich, poetic style and discursive structure—emphasizing anecdote, incident, digression, and a great number of colorful characters—Amado can be compared to the great English novelists of the eighteenth and nineteenth centuries. In fact, whether Amado would agree or not, he might be termed the Brazilian [Charles] Dickens. Barreto, on the other hand, crafts a much more direct interpretation of Dona Flor's plight, never forgetting, of course, Amado's central and comical thematic concerns, which he brings to cinematic life by means of his own lushly evocative images.

If the film misses some of the subtlety and color of the novel, it provides enough *carnaval, candômbé,* and feverishness to give filmgoers the flavor of Amado's romance. If the film sacrifices the episodic, leisurely pace of the novel, the larger canvas, the seemingly endless roster of eccentric Bahians, it gains a certain intrinsic force because of its seamless narrative drive and because Barreto has cut to the essential spine of the novel, creating a film at once amusing, provocative, and enormously satisfying. Thus, Barreto's creation, which can be understood and enjoyed by a vast audience, has become the most popular and successful film in Brazilian cinema, grossing close to $40 million dollars at last count and having been seen by about 30 million people worldwide.

Although the film has great mass appeal, the more discerning filmgoer will discover and savor the underlying themes—discreetly placed within the more overtly sensational *ménage à trois* plot contrivances—which lead to the recognition that Flor's goal is the ultimate desire that many of us have: to possess outward and inner fulfillment, the yes and no of our beings, the completion of ourselves. The film ends with this triumphal image: the threesome—Flor and her two husbands—one naked and glowing, caressing his lover's buttocks; the other, soberly suited, dignified, supporting his wife with his strong, conservative arm. No words need accompany this last shot, no explanation. On every level of recognition, this image is all that is needed.

The final irony of the film and the novel, of course, is that this kind of paradise on earth occurs rarely and that these rare occurrences most often take place on the printed page or on the silver screen. It is unusual for a truly fine novel to be translated into a film of equal caliber; for example, one need only consider the films of *War and Peace, Crime and Punishment, The Stranger, The Great Gatsby, The Sun Also Rises,* even *Sophie's Choice.* Jorge Amado's sublimely sensual and sensible fable, **Dona Flor and Her Two Husbands**—beautifully and sensitively and carefully adapted to the screen by Bruno Barreto—may be one of the unique exceptions.

Paul West (review date 7 February 1988)

SOURCE: "Ambushed in the Cacao Groves," in *The New York Times Book Review,* February 7, 1988, pp. 3, 37.

[*In the following review, West lauds Amado's* Showdown.]

The only calendar in Tocaia Grande—it was a New Year's gift—hangs outside the dry-cacao storehouse, more a toy borrowed from the cradle of time than anything practical. It pictures a mountain snowscape and a big hairy dog under whose chin hangs a small cask. From the print there dangles a booklet of numbered leaves, a few of which old Gerino now and then peels away, mainly out of gratitude. No wonder life in this verdant riverside shantytown among the cacao groves of South Bahia remains "permanently behind time," thwarting not only those who need to clock the rains and the harvests along the Rio das Cobras, but also Fadul the Turk who owns the canteen and wants to collect punctually on his loans. Nobody even knows which day is Sunday.

That central image in Jorge Amado's new novel suggests that for many years nobody knew which year it was, but the calendar endured, a holy relic. *Showdown* tells how one green and pleasant place grew and died, then grew again, uplifted into squalid village and then suaver town by the grit and vision of successive settlers hell-bent on making a living from those who worked the cocoa crop. So, there had to be a provisions store, a brothel, a blacksmith and, later on, a dentist, a church and an exclusive club. Indeed, this might be the story of Brazil itself, seen through a dark glass lovingly, honed into a compact metaphor implying a whole nation's tumultuous vigor, its addiction to the life force in hyperbole and, most of all, the capacity for ecstasy of its poor, whose brand of Calvinism has had to let life be bleak and short, so long as it was picturesque. *Showdown* hoists into the light a country whose imagination is its finest crop, but one it cannot eat.

The book abounds in festively elegiac emblems. Each has a powerful effect on that part of the narrative in which it first appears, but all of them resonate throughout the book as well—like the ambush or showdown of the title. It haunts the mind throughout the novel because Tocaia Grande grew near to an improvised hill cemetery dug after a famous ambush in which one of two feuding colonels lost all 27 of his men.

Everyone in the town is to some extent ambushed by time, and by a quaint fecklessness that combines the mood of John Steinbeck's *Sweet Thursday* with that of James Hilton's *Lost Horizon.* They all dream and fornicate timelessly, and they are ambushed or "hidden in the bushes" forever, as if Mr. Amado were saying they belong as much to myth as to calendars. Being killed in an ambush by someone in hiding isn't much different from being killed by a deity in hiding too.

"Tocaia Grande" means "big ambush" or "showdown" anyway, and the place has already had more than its share of fame, from events to which there can be no comparable sequel. Or can there be? Mr. Amado's neatly designed chronicle obliges you to wonder which is the worse delusion: a calendar tossed capriciously aside unmarked, or one marked all over with appointments, trips, rendezvous and red-letter days. I can think of only one similarly powerful use of this image: in Jean Genet's *Miracle of the Rose,* we are told that a man serving a long sentence writes out the calendar of his entire sentence and pastes the sheets to the walls of his cell, thus getting one awful eyeful of his wasted days but at the same time possessing his doom physically, as if it were an artifact or even a person.

But that is not the mood of *Showdown.* Mr. Amado gives a portrait of the settlement every bit as beguiling and picturesque as the portrait of a woman was in his *Gabriela, Clove and Cinnamon.* This teeming scene is almost a palette-knife painting of a pioneer nation trapped between the ancient gods of the forest and the new ones of commerce, only to be overwhelmed (for a while) by the sheer force of a river in spate.

Showdown is a vital novel, more complex than it seems at first, written in a long series of ebullient lunges, none of them stylish or notably elegant or eloquent, but in sum haunting and massive. Mr. Amado's prose in his other books sometimes has all the elegance of a badly combed turnip, but here he creates something fecund and funny, tender and burly, as if his lively social conscience, under pressure, had yet again had to take the side of the human race. No doubt *Showdown* would make a compelling movie, but it is essentially a verbal performance. It is only in the words that you can savor Mr. Cicero Moura, a gonorrhea sufferer also known as "Dr. Permanganate," who rides "a slow and steady donkey" named Envelope; or such animals as Peba's rheas, seriemas and *currasows;* or woods called *putumuju,* pink peroba and jacaranda; and a conga line of whores named "Dalila, Epifânia, Bernarda, Zuleica, Margarida Cotó, Two-Ton Marieta, Cotinha, Dorita, Teté, and Silvia Pornambuco" (that name teems with both geography and lust). Only Jacinta Coroca, an overworked midwife, is omitted from the catalogue because "she was worth more than all the others put together" and because, when Aprígio made to pull his revolver, she kicked him in a place so private that his shriek was heard three and a half leagues away.

The atavistic pleasure in this novel comes from jungle words as well as jungle ways. The characters, almost too many to remember, are like revelers from the apocalyptic New Year in which Gerino received the first calendar. During a sudden flood the inhabitants save the children by passing them along a chain of people standing on the 12 wooden beams of the battered bridge, and after the flood they rebuild the settlement. Indeed, the book is almost a chain of tableaux dedicated to human resilience, but you don't mind because Mr. Amado grounds even the most minor character-drawing in anecdotal devotion to detail.

There are enough characters in **Showdown** to allow almost everyone to pick a favorite. Mine include Castor Abduim the black blacksmith, a horseshoer who turned horse doctor, and then dentist and busybody; Venturinha, the lawyer son of Col. Boaventura Andrade, who is unable to tear himself away from the fleshpots of Rio, where he endlessly trains himself to take over his father's lands; and Jussara, a widow and heiress whose body inflames Fadul the Turk, at least until he realizes she is trying to trick him into marriage, whereupon he thinks of giving her "the amount of money corresponding to the usual payment to a whore for an afternoon in bed."

Mr. Amado reveals Fadul at his most private, by the light of a small lamp counting his money and placing it in a big red bandanna, then putting his copper and nickel coins in two pieces of paper that go into a small leather bag. Off he goes to replace his stock of dried meats, cane liquor, brown sugar and cotton pants at the marketplaces. We get a similarly private view of him out in the woods: "He dove into the river, cleaning off the sweat, the stink of bedbugs and his nighttime visions. He cleaned his teeth by rubbing them with a plug of tobacco; he blew on the embers to revive the coals under the iron trivet, an Asian luxury acquired at cost in payment for a debt in Taquaras." Gazing at the so-called ladies' bidet, a river pool with a waterfall, where the whores bathe and do their laundry, he is "the Grand Turk surveying his empire."

Mr. Amado is not renowned for depicting people at their most intimate, or for intimating the unspoken thought that sinks back uncompleted into the slurry of consciousness where Nathalie Sarraute is queen; but sometimes, as in **Showdown,** he gets the reader close to his characters by observing keenly the externals of mental turnover rather than by probing directly. A mentally handicapped girl who runs after pigs wants so much to be a mother that she shoves clumps of sedge under her dress, at one point pretending to give birth to a piglet. She drowns in the flood, but a sky-blue flower mysteriously appears in her hands. One of the whores, writing to Fadul, inscribes "a number of commas, apostrophes, accent marks, exclamation points, and question marks" under her signature for him to distribute as he wishes throughout her unpunctuated letter.

The delicacy of Mr. Amado in such matters is the perfect foil for a novel whose dominant mode is histrionic and tumultuous. We are dealing as much with easygoing magic here as with psychology: we read that Dodô the birdman barber keeps a dove to pull gray hairs from his head as they

appear. Mr. Amado tips the horn of plenty with a practiced swing, not so much copying a world as creating it. And he is not without irony. The last incarnation of Tocaia Grande is a city named Irisópolis, with bungalows and villas, English cobblestones and a Masonic lodge, a social club and a literary society. About all that the narrator's comment is pithy enough: "*isn't worth mentioning, holds no interest.*"

Gregory Rabassa's translation from the Portuguese is nimble and robust. Mr. Amado doesn't give him much scope for subtle wordplay, but Mr. Rabassa's own sense of humor matches exactly that of the book.

The novel's final images of Tocaia Grande are of the "no-name fever" that "reduced the strongest man to a rag before killing him"; Venturinha giving his father a stroke by heading off for further studies at Oxford and the Sorbonne; the sea on the beaches of Ilhéus (a real town) turning to foam; confessionals being set up in the dry-cacao shed; pigs being shot in the streets with the arrival of law and order; and the final massacre in which Coroca leads the town's defenders against a military force led by a sergeant with a "big old nickel-plated pocket watch."

Much of this ribald, epic novel could not be quoted in this newspaper, but it evinces a compassion as big as Brazil itself. One leaves it as one leaves new, exciting friends, wondering how much of an accident it is that the dying Dadô produces from his bullet-riddled chest a bird.

Barbara Mujica (review date 1992)

SOURCE: "Passionate Tales," in *Américas,* Vol. 44, No. 5, 1992, pp. 60-1.

[*In the following review, Mujica praises Amado's* The Golden Harvest *and asserts that "Thanks to the superb translation by Clifford E. Landers, English-speaking audiences can now appreciate the skill and wit of the young Jorge Amado and gain insight into the evolution of a truly great novelist."*]

The creator of classics such as **Gabriela, Clove and Cinnamon, Dona Flor and Her Two Husbands, Tieta,** and **Tereza Batista,** Brazil's Jorge Amado is one of Latin America's greatest storytellers. Even in this 1944 novel, translated now for the first time into English, Amado's narrative powers are remarkable.

While the author's later works feature lusty women, macho men, juicy plots, and lots of humor, his early novels are highly political. The later novels provide a panoramic view of northern Brazilian society and capture the warmth and vitality of the people of Bahia, yet Amado remains a non-judgmental spectator. In *The Golden Harvest,* on the other hand, the author has an agenda. He is out to expose the corruption of the moneyed classes and the social injustice that has kept the Brazilian farm worker in a state of near servitude for centuries.

Like other Amado stories, *The Golden Harvest* takes place in Ilhéus, the port city of southern Bahia from which cacao is exported. The colonials, or cacao lords, took and held the rich lands surrounding Ilhéus by means of violence. They cleared the acres and cultivated the cacao crops, relying on impoverished peasants doubling as hired killers to work and protect it.

As Amado's story begins, the colonials have grown old, affluent and respectable. Still rough and rugged men at heart, their sons, who have not had to fight for their fortune, are spoiled, decadent fops. Motivated by greed, a powerful cabal of exporters, led by Carlos Zude, sets out to ruin the cacao growers and take over their lands. The plan is to force a rise in prices, thereby creating a boom. The unsophisticated colonials and their debauched offspring begin to squander money, running up huge bills and borrowing from the exporters against future sales of their cacao. When the exporters unexpectedly lower prices, thereby forcing a bust, the colonials are caught off-guard. With no further credit and no means of paying their debts, they are forced to sell their lands at ridiculously low prices. Zude's plan has worked perfectly. Or has it?

The Communists, who have been trying to organize the workers all along, are aided by the bust, which has put thousands of cacao workers out of a job. Formerly oblivious to the calls of the agitators, the unemployed hands join forces and show their collective muscle. Even worse for Zude is the fact that his wife, Julieta, is having an affair with a Communist sympathizer and winds up finding her husband's business tactics unbearably distasteful. A precursor of the good-hearted temptress-protagonists in Amado's later novels, Julieta is a bombshell who drives men mad, especially her own husband. In fact, it is for his wife that Zude devises his diabolical scheme for getting rich. But once Julieta takes up with her lover/poet, she starts to read and to think—no longer content to be just a sex object—and, eventually, to reject everything that Zude stands for.

Like Amado's later novels, *The Golden Harvest* portrays an entire society. This book includes a vast array of characters—rich colonials, small farmers, cacao workers, exporters and their children, wives, mistresses, and hired hands. It includes folk songs and customs of the working class, as well as a close look at the habits and values of the moneyed elite.

Although *The Golden Harvest* contains a harsh condemnation of exploitation on the cacao plantations as well as in the export houses, this is no political treatise. It is an engrossing romance whose political message never overpowers the plot. Thanks to the superb translation by Clifford E. Landers, English-speaking audiences can now appreciate the skill and wit of the young Jorge Amado and gain insight into the evolution of a truly great novelist.

James Polk (review date 21 November 1993)

SOURCE: "The Wages of Virtue," in *Chicago Tribune Books,* November 21, 1993, pp. 6-7.

[*In the following review, Polk discusses Amado's* War of the Saints *and states that "Amado has also found that his surest weapon against the related evils of puritanism and fascism is ridicule . . . he employs that weapon to sure and constant effect."*]

Jorge Amado (*Dona Flor and Her Two Husbands, Showdown, Gabriela, Clove and Cinnamon*) sets his latest novel, as he has most of his nearly 20 others, in his home territory, the Brazilian city and state of Bahia. A better stage for the crazy, intertwined dramas of *The War of the Saints* is hard to imagine.

A place "where everything is intermixed and commingled, where no one can separate virtue from sin, or distinguish the certain from the absurd or the line between truth and trickery, between reality and dream," Bahia is comfortable with the unexpected, familiar with the enchanted. The novel, too, is a great confusion of things, filled with casual miracles and grandly mixed metaphors.

Late one day "toward the end of the sixties or the beginning of the seventies, more or less," the cargo sloop Sailor Without a Port is under full sail, crossing the Bay of All Saints toward the city of Bahia. In addition to the usual conglomeration of things in her hold, the ship carries the much revered statue of St. Barbara of the Thunder, bound for the Museum of Sacred Art in the capital.

The venerated icon, subject of a just-published monograph by the museum's director, has been removed from her altar in the church of Santo Amaro only after much wrangling and protestation to serve as the centerpiece in an exhibition of religious art. But when the ship docks, unfortunately for waiting officials, the statue walks off and disappears into the crowded streets.

Why is this happening? Well, it seems that Barbara is venerated not just by Bahia's Christians. Known as "Barbara

Yansan," she is also an Afro-Brazilian saint and has gone to look after her other flock.

From the outside, that makes a certain amount of sense. But to many of those in the novel, especially to the unimaginative leaders of church and state who like to think of themselves as being in charge, the statue's disappearance is the work of thieves or, worse, of communists. Inept cops enter the case, envisioning evildoers under every bed in Bahia and valuable artworks on every flight out of the country. Accusations fly back and forth between various seats of power, and blame is scattered like seeds in the springtime. None of the frazzled authorities, of course, suspect the magical truth.

On the other hand, the black and mulatto communities of the city just as naturally take the magic for granted. When Barbara Yansan shows up at the Afro-Brazilian festival of the Washing of the Church of Bomfin, it logically follows, for that's where she belongs. Nor is anyone surprised when the saint begins making unannounced appearances around the city.

The multiple mysteries that so befog those who accept without question that water may become wine or that a couple of tiny fish might feed a multitude fit right in with the flexible cosmology of the supposed spiritual primitives.

While the search for the missing saint occupies the authorities of Bahia, in certain back alleys another, more personal drama is unfolding. The beautiful young Manela is falling for Miro, a handsome, dark-skinned taxi driver. Their feeling for one another is pure and innocent, a testament to youth and true love.

Not so to Adalgisa, the girl's aunt, guardian and personal inquisitor. Considering herself more Spanish (read: white) than Brazilian, Adalgisa sees it as her duty to raise her niece a proper Catholic, imbued with the correct European virtues, protected from the city's heathen and, most important, saved from the foulness of sex, which even after marriage does not "cease to be a cruel and obscene act." These ends the aunt pursues with demonic fury, aided by convenient doorlocks, a healthy set of lungs and a thick leather strap.

In Gregory Rabassa's fluid translation, *The War of the Saints* is about the struggle between sensuality and rigidity, innocence and guilt, sex and prudery. On the streets of Bahia it is fought out among those looking for Saint Barbara and those celebrating with Barbara Yansan. It is fought between the feisty spirit of Manela and the doctrinaire severity of Adalgisa. But most of all, the novel is about the battle raging within the chaotic soul of Adalgisa herself.

Amado has made her into the central character of the novel. An obvious symbol of repression and false piety, the woman is a terror, not only to Manela but also to her mild, put-upon husband Danilo, a former soccer star who has spent the long nights of their marriage hoping to perform the cruel and obscene act with his wife, only to repair, frustrated every time, to the local brothel.

But Adalgisa bears a secret, although she doesn't know it. Shortly after her own conception, her mother, a believer in the "fetishes" Adalgisa would later find so primitive and uncouth, had entered into a deep trance, and the child in her womb was born enchanted. In other words, this pure Catholic maiden has grown up carrying the seeds of hedonism and passion within her. Will they ever sprout? In Bahia, where "there were so many gods and such prodigious happenings that one lost count of miracles and no longer paid any attention to them," they probably will.

Readers of this laid-back, sexy, funny novel unfamiliar with the career of its author might be surprised to learn that when Amado first began publishing in the early 1930s, he labored diligently in the well-tilled fields of social realism. A practitioner of the hyperrealistic "novel of the northeast," his first works were embittered, pedantic tracts, weighted with social squalor and class struggle, resolved by a simplistic and highly romanticized brand of communism.

Not until the '50s did he begin finding his true voice—ironic, satirical, self-mocking and caged with subtleties. The message, however, remains much the same: Amado is still a battler against repression and reaction. But his fight has expanded to include those who repress the spirit as well as the body.

Leaving simplification behind, he has found, particularly in Bahia, where "all shades of color exist in the flesh of its inhabitants," that the human condition is hardly monochromatic. And Amado has also found that his surest weapon against the related evils of puritanism and fascism is ridicule. In this lively, seductive novel he employs that weapon to sure and constant effect.

Allen Josephs (review date 28 November 1993)

SOURCE: "The Stone Made Flesh," in *The New York Times Book Review,* November 28, 1993, p. 20.

[*In the following review, Josephs lauds Amado's* War of the Saints.]

As Jorge Amado's spectacular new novel, *The War of the Saints,* opens, St. Barbara—or, more properly, "a statue of St. Barbara of the Thunder, famed for her eternal beauty and miraculous powers"—has just been transported across the

Bay of All Saints to Bahia for an exhibition of religious art. Suddenly, just after the ship has docked, the statue takes life and steps from her litter, transformed into the living African deity St. Barbara Yansan. Waving politely to the nun and winking at the priest who have accompanied her, she disappears, with a sway of her hips, "into the midst of her people." Literal-minded readers will not get beyond this point, but believers in magic realism will be enthralled with the events of the next 48 hours.

Now 79 years old, the author of 21 novels, which have been translated into 46 languages, Mr. Amado has long been Brazil's best-known and most-loved novelist. Like many of his Latin American counterparts, he concerns himself with the mixing of race, religion and custom, with the syncretism that underpins much of magic realism. Bahia is particularly well suited as a setting for this fictional endeavor, since nowhere else in the Western Hemisphere have African and colonial cultures blended so thoroughly. Describing the process, Mr. Amado tells of Our Lord of Bomfim, who came from Portugal in the early days "riding on the mournful Catholic vow of a shipwrecked Portuguese sailor," and Oxalá, a deity who arrived "from the coast of Africa, during the time of the traffic in blacks, riding on the bloody back of a slave." Joined together "in the breasts" of the citizens of Bahia, they have become "a single uniquely Brazilian divinity."

> **If the mulatto culture of this part of Brazil, based on the commingling of Roman Catholicism and West African animism, is the underlying subject of the novel, it is clear that the author's sympathy lies almost entirely with the latter.**
> —*Allen Josephs*

If the mulatto culture of this part of Brazil, based on the commingling of Roman Catholicism and West African animism, is the underlying subject of the novel, it is clear that the author's sympathy lies almost entirely with the latter. *Candomblé*—defined in the useful, if incomplete, glossary as an "Afro-Brazilian religious ceremony partly of Yoruban origin"—is the book's true protagonist and the uncontested winner in Mr. Amado's deliciously described cultural struggle.

In his preface, the author says that he means to tell "the small tale of Adalgisa and Manela and a few other descendants of the love, between the Spaniard Francisco Romero Pérez y Pérez and Andreza da Anunciação, the beautiful Andreza de Yansan, a dark mulatto girl." Although this lush, dense tropical novel—translated from the Portuguese by Gregory Rabassa with his customary grace, facility and fluidity—is

far from a small tale, the other particulars suggest rather exactly the author's point of view and intentions.

Mr. Amado also warns that the events of the novel "couldn't have happened anywhere else" but Bahia. And, in fact, the setting is the source of much of the book's brilliance. Through the lighthearted, lively, rhythmical Carnaval atmosphere that Mr. Amado so engagingly evokes—as if he were synthesizing elements of primitive art within an intentionally naive style—he manages to animate the animistic side of his native land. As a result, even extreme magic realism seems perfectly normal in Mr. Amado's Bahia. When St. Barbara Yansan walks among her people spreading miracles, it is as right and believable as when the gods walk among the mortals in Homer or the witches and ghosts appear in Shakespeare.

St. Barbara Yansan has come to rescue the lovely Manela, a young girl who is in love with a taxi driver named Miro, from the puritanical clutches of her equally beautiful but devoutly Catholic (and distinctly coldhearted) aunt, Adalgisa. Being a goddess, St. Barbara Yansan naturally succeeds, although to explain how would spoil the story. Along the way, she permits her humble servant, the author, to create a triumphantly satirical epic that takes to pieces critics and professors, Marxists and fascists, generals and judges, priests and politicians and policemen—in short, anyone with any power in Brazil. And, at the same time, the novel lionizes the people of Bahia (many of them real), especially the artists, poets and musicians, the innocents and the lovers, the priests and priestesses of *candomblé.*

Many readers will be reminded of Marcel Camus's 1958 film, *Black Orpheus,* which does not go unmentioned in these pages. Indeed, the music, the merriment and the magic—the sense of time-out-of-time of Carnaval—and the celebration of life amid misery all create a similar atmosphere in Mr. Amado's book. But while *Black Orpheus* ends unavoidably in tragedy, **The War of the Saints** is unabashedly triumphant. Its long parade of Bahian saints and sinners will snake through your mind like a *candomblé* procession.

Mr. Amado's felicity does much more than soften his satirical blows; it also bathes a sometimes misunderstood aspect of African-Brazilian culture in the golden light of a tropical sunset. He made me want to head down to Bahia right away.

Ilán Stavans (review date Winter 1994)

SOURCE: A review of *The Golden Harvest,* in *World Literature Today,* Vol. 68, No. 1, Winter, 1994, p. 100.

[*In the following review, Stavans praises Amado's* Golden Harvest.]

Translated into English now for the first time, *The Golden Harvest,* in the realistic tradition of Europeans like Dickens and Balzac, is, simply put, a delight. Jorge Amado's first artistic period, ideologically committed, was concerned with class-struggle domination and the re-creation of social types from all segments of Brazilian society. Beginning with *Gabriela, Clove and Cinnamon* in 1958, notwithstanding, he broke toward more magical, lighthearted constellations of themes and characters.

Originally published in 1944 as *São Jorge doe Ilhéus* (this American edition was issued to coincide with the writer's eightieth birthday and his sixtieth year as a published writer, his first novel, *The Land of Carnival,* having appeared when he was only nineteen), *The Golden Harvest* indeed enlightens Amado's beginning as a novelist; it also astonishingly re-creates his childhood environment, the cacao plantation in the Ferradas district, in the countryside of the state of Bahia, where he was born in 1912. Playboys, whores, avaricious exporters, religious fanatics, and adventurous entrepreneurs—the multiple cast dissects a natural universe used and abused. (While reading the book, I kept invoking Mario Vargas Llosa's novel *The War of the End of the World.*) A traditionalist work that guides the reader without deliberate incongruences and needless experimentations, *The Golden Harvest,* in its labyrinthine plot twists and emotional ups and downs, is to unsophisticated readers a genuine treat full of melodramatic ingredients, a visit to south-of-the-border idiosyncrasy; more educated (and pedantic) ones might find the narrative an invaluable testament of Brazilian popular culture. Either way, there is little doubt that Jorge Amado is one of the consummate storytellers of the twentieth century.

Patricia Aufderheide (review date 2 January 1994)

SOURCE: "Blame It on Bahia," in *Book World—The Washington Post,* January 2, 1994, p. 8.

[*In the following review, Aufderheide discusses Amado's* War of the Saints *and his celebration of African-Brazilian culture.*]

Reading a new Jorge Amado novel is like eating yet another Brazilian dinner. The ingredients are predictably pleasant: the beans, the rice, the palm oil, seafood, a zesty dash of lime. The novelty is all in the mix and the company. There's something stale about the execution this time, but you can hardly be surprised.

Amado has juggled the ingredients he uses in *The War of the Saints* more than 20 times before. This is the latest novel in a career that began in 1933, with brutally social-realistic works written in the passion of leftish youth. Since then, Brazil has joined the world's top 10 industrial nations, and Amado has mellowed without losing a populist edge to his never-far-from-pulp storytelling.

His novels are usually set in or around Bahia, which as the colonial capital was a premier exporter of sugar and tobacco produced with African slave labor. The legacy of that past is evident—feudal countryside, an African majority, pronounced African elements in everything from language to food to religion, and endemic tension between Europhiles and Afrophiles.

Amado has become a widely revered celebrator of African-Brazilian culture. Although the son of a plantation owner, he is a spiritual leader in the syncretic African religious practices he often writes about. Amado's romantic melting-pot imagery—typically embodied in the figure of the sultry *mulata*—has been challenged by later generations of social critics. Today's rising black-pride movement, which charges that racism is part of Brazilian culture, has a far different take on Brazil's complex cultural heritage.

The War of the Saints proceeds as if, in matters multicultural, time has stopped. The novel is in fact set in the late '60s, the time of the generals, of torture, censorship, and student riots. With belated boldness (he began writing this in 1968, picking it up again two decades later), Amado refers to military brutalities and stupidities, American aid, radical priests, and the protest-and-rejoice music of Castano Veloso and Gilberto Gil.

The action is triggered by the arrival at the Bahian port of an antique statue of Santa Barbara, during *carnaval*. In the syncretic religious beliefs of the region she is also the African goddess Yansan. When the statue comes to life—this isn't magical realism, it's just garden-variety Amadoism—the fiercely sexy Yansan walks into and all over the lives of a cross section of Bahian society.

The luscious but puritanical Adalgisa—her African side brutally repressed after a lifetime of Spanish-influenced Catholicism—is trying to beat the passion out of her niece Manela, who wants only to become a devotee of Yansan and marry her black boyfriend. Meanwhile, a liberation-theology priest arrives in the city, tailed by a gunman with murder orders from a backlands landowner. Determined to seduce the priest is a mixed-blood beauty, impatient with silly old celibacy. In the shadows, a backlands schemer, eager for incriminating photos, can't wait for him to fall for her. Then there's the venerable German immigrant priest, Dom Maximiliano, whose future rests on the return of the mysteriously missing statue.

The intertwining of these and other lives becomes elaborate, as the author himself notes repeatedly in archly antiquarian asides. It also reinforces familiar dichotomies for Amado readers. African/European, men/women, rich/poor—there are no surprises.

It's easy to hate yourself in the morning after staying up to finish an Amado novel, but this one, like his best, does keep you reading. Translator Gregory Rabassa again virtually erases the gulf between Portuguese and English, while carefully preserving the sense of difference Amado wants for the African-based vocabulary (there's a glossary). Besides, underneath the piled-on adjectives, the habitual long lists of everything from regional delicacies to *capoeira* dancers, the oh-so-titillating sexual description, there are rewards.

Amado can perceptively sketch a situation from the point of view of often-opposed protagonists. So we quickly see why the hired killer can be seen as "a reliable professional, a good man," why Adalgisa finds marital sex repulsive, why the feudal landowner must defend his honor with murder. His fascination with Brazil's African side is contagious, even if it sometimes verges on the touristic. And the populist sensibility that grounds the tale can be touching. When stuffy old Dom Maximiliano, astonished, figures out what happened to the statue, a fellow priest reminds him, "Miracles happen . . . Isn't simply living under the conditions that people do a miracle—one of the greatest?"

Bondo Wyszpolski (review date 3 January 1994)

SOURCE: "Truth and Tomfoolery in the Tropics," in *The Los Angeles Times Book Review,* January 3, 1994, pp. 3, 7.

[*In the following review, Wyszpolski praises Amado's* War of the Saints, *which he calls "a novel so loud you can find it with the lights out."*]

Jorge Amado wrote his first novel in 1931 when he was 19-years-old. The title, **Carnival Country,** could be applied to the body of work he's been amassing ever since.

This is the Brazilian novelist who gave Dona Flor two husbands (one living; one dead, but livelier), and he's still mixing wry, ribald poetry with literary soap opera. Even now, Amado remains idealistic, boyishly romantic, a jester and a humanist whose compassion for the downtrodden is unstinting. What makes it all rather fun is that Balzac seems to be whispering into one ear while Henry Miller whispers into the other.

Now there's **The War of the Saints,** a novel so loud you can find it with the lights out. Over and around the story line, Amado has thrown together a one-man shindig for his beloved Salvador da Bahía. In the author's hands, this former capital of Brazil is like a chessboard; each piece, each character, is moved with gusto and a roaring generosity. Host or author, party or novel: good question, for everyone Amado has ever shaken hands with seems to put in an appearance.

The author confines his story to 48 hours and drops it into the early 1970s, during the gloomy nadir of Brazil's 21-year-long dictatorship. Not that there's any constraint in Amado's writing; he's just too zestful for that. Anyway, Dom Maximiliano von Grudin, director of the Museum of Sacred Art in Bahía, has assembled a jewel of an exhibit and acquired the loan of a priceless statue—Saint Barbara of the Thunder—which is transported down the Paraguacu River. However, "Before Master Manuel and Maria Clara had finished mooring the sloop and managed to lift out the saint, the saint herself got down from the litter, took a step forward, smoothed the folds of her cape, and walked off."

The mystery of the saint's disappearance and Dom Maximiliano's dark night of the soul (he'll tussle with humility and self-pride before Amado's through with him) are the first of several subplots already swimming off, to emerge periodically until the end of the book.

Three other subplots will sashay across the dance floor of love gained or regained. When their parents died, Mariety went to live with congenial Aunt Gildete, Manela with strict Aunt Adalgisa. Or, as Amado says, "in the lottery of orphanhood, it was Mariety who had won the grand prize." This sets up Manela as our sympathetic Juliet, her Romeo being the taxi driver Miro, poor but pure and brazenly Brazilian. Couple number one.

The second couple is Manela's Aunt Adalgisa and Uncle Danilo, an ex-soccer champ who rarely stands up to his wife and who'll only stand up for Manela when Adalgisa dumps her into a convent. That's a story in itself. Danilo and Adalgisa have a stalled-on-the-tracks 20-year marriage, but we'll see what a splash of Afro-Brazilian religious ritual can do about that.

Lastly, there's the young and untainted Father Abelardo Galvao gently pursued by Patricia das Flores, an aspiring actress and a knock-out, it appears, in both body and brains. An actress and a priest? Oh, my, what possibilities.

In each of these instances Saint Barbara will play a key role. Amado goes to great lengths to decorate the stage, and he won't be rushed: there's usually a payoff 200 pages down the line. He relishes his diversions and he lovingly dotes on his characters. Those in search of a straightforward, snappy narrative are advised to move on.

Amado has listened well to the song of the land and the song of its people, but this depiction of Bahía is closer to *Peter Pan* than to Hector Babenco's *Pixote.* For example, Amado's captains-of-the-sands,those abandoned youngsters who roam the waterfront, are not quite the lovable rascals he portrayed 50 years earlier. To his credit, he treats them all like grandchildren—neglecting to let on that in the city of Bahía some 80% of its inhabitants are underemployed, or not employed at all.

What he says instead is: "Anyone who wants to know more about these matters of saints, voodoo, *candomblé, macumba,* possessions, mixed blood, and *orixas* should try to put a little money together and take a trip to Bahía, the capital city of dreams." Hmmm, All that's lacking is the color insert and the travel coupons.

The War of the Saints is undermined somewhat by its diversions and its asides, which—and here's the dilemma—are not only funny but provide color and rhythm. Ultimately, they tend to deflect the main thrust of the novel, leaving behind handsome vignettes that—mostly—will soon disperse.

A mixed blessing, all this, with blessing decidedly emphasized. As a prose stylist whose flourishes descend with the accuracy of a Bob Hope punch line, Amado is quite an entertainer. His stereotypes, his tomfoolery and his formulas, trotted out again and again, may prevent his acclaim as a great novelist, but Amado is every bit a child of tropical Brazil. It pulsates in virtually every line. Whistling in disbelief—and we'll do a lot of that—is no deterrent to our wanting to find out what happens next.

Nelson H. Vieira (review date Winter 1996)

SOURCE: A review of *A Descoberta da América pelos Turcos,* in *World Literature Today,* Vol. 70, No. 1, Winter, 1996, pp. 173-4.

[*In the following review, Vieira asserts that "by creating a compelling sense of narrative [in* A Descoberta da América pelos Turcos] *Amado again proves himself to be a deft storyteller."*]

Labeled a "small novel" by the author and written for the Quincentenary celebration (1492-1992), *A Descoberta da América pelos Turcos* was originally a project commissioned in 1991 by an Italian state public-relations agency for a volume of stories, dramatizing the "encounter" between the Old and the New World, by best-selling authors such as

Norman Mailer, Carlos Fuentes, and Jorge Amado. Since the original project never came to fruition, the present book was completed prior to Amado's antimemoirs, *Navegação de Cabotagem* (1992), but only appeared in Brazil after published translations in French and Turkish. Inspired by characters from Amado's 1986 novel *Tocaia Grande: A face obscura* (Eng. *Showdown,* 1988) the novella proposes a very telluric New World encounter, one that mocks the testimonies of European chroniclers by deriding the historically noble notions of discovery and conquest of "virgin" territory. In so doing, Amado characterizes the polemic surrounding the 1992 commemoration in sexual as well as sociohistorical and geographic terms. With his bawdy theme of sexual "conquest" occurring in the interior of Bahia, Brazil, during the early 1900s, Amado questions the veracity of those who say they first "discovered" the New Land by representing his story as the Arabic discovery and conquest of what is still valued as virgin territory—in this case, women as well as the Bahian hinterland.

Purportedly not taking sides in this Old/New World polemic, the anonymous narrator, a Brazilian mestizo who considers himself a product of the discovery and of the conquest because he embodies cultural and racial mixture, in the first chapter nevertheless criticizes the concept of conquest by alluding to the experience of massacred Indians, enslaved blacks, and many cultures razed by mercenaries and missionaries carrying the Cross of Christ. On the other hand, the narrator ends the first chapter by praising the twentieth-century amalgamation of such peoples as backlanders, Jews, Turks (actually Arabs, Syrians, and Lebanese), and others who discovered and conquered the virgin backlands of Bahia. Labeling all these settlers Brazilian, Amado's narrator depicts Brazil as an ethnic, cultural, and racial democracy, suggestive of the newly touted concept of cultural hybridity.

In nineteen short, fast-paced chapters, with handsome illustrations based on classic paintings from the *Rubáiyát,* the novella focuses on the eventual betrothal of Adma, the ugly, unmarried elder daughter of Ibrahim Jafet, a morally righteous virgin who has made the life of her despondent but morally irresponsible father a living hell since the death of his wife. Believing the solution to his problems rests with finding a husband who will romantically and sexually tame or "conquer" Adma, Ibrahim sets out to engage able-bodied Arab-Brazilian bachelors capable of dominating her, even if their conquest entails a program of spankings and caresses. Unfortunately, the emphasis upon sexual conquest and Adma's surprising sexual gifts, explained as miraculous divine intervention by Jehovah *and* Allah, affirming again the supposedly rampant syncretism of the Brazilian religious experience, strains the author's attempted dramatization of cultural democracy, since gender is handled undemocratically, conveying an unrelenting sexist treatment of women. In this vein, it is unclear to what extent Amado is parodying patriarchal history and Brazilian machismo in order to debunk the seemingly inescapable manifestation of the "conquest" proclivity pervasive in traditional Brazilian culture. As an overall theme, the narrator heralds the mixture of Arab and Brazilian cultures by highlighting the New World syncretic predisposition in religion, customs, language, and food, the actual text representing a hybrid of historical chronicle, Brazilian Northeast customs, and Arab culture.

By creating a compelling sense of narrative, Amado again proves himself to be a deft storyteller who here infuses his tale with ironic humor, challenging fixed notions of a Brazilian monoculture while indirectly alluding to recurring authoritarian traits that have been implanted since 1500.

FURTHER READING

Criticism

Foster, David William, ed. "Jorge Amado." *Modern Latin American Literature.* New York: Frederick Ungar Publishing Co., 1975, pp. 30-42.
    Contains reviews of several of Amado's novels.

Additional coverage of Amado's life and career is contained in the following sources published by Gale: *Contemporary Authors,* **Vol. 77-80;** *Contemporary Authors New Revision Series,* **Vol. 35;** *Dictionary of Literary Biography,* **Vol. 113;** *DISCovering Authors Modules: Multicultural Authors* **and** *Novelists; Hispanic Literature Criticism;* **and** *Major Twentieth-Century Writers.*

André Brink

1935-

South African novelist, essayist, dramatist, and translator.

The following entry presents an overview of Brink's career. For further information on his life and works, see *CLC,* Volumes 18 and 36.

INTRODUCTION

Andre Brink's career has run parallel to developments which took his native South Africa from a state marked by the policy of apartheid to a dismantling of this systemic racial injustice. Through his work he has promoted an awareness of the problems of his society, explored their roots, expressed opposition to repressive authorities and now enjoys the freedom to explore a delight in storytelling. A writer who began from an existentialist position, citing Albert Camus among his significant influences, Brink developed a social conscience which was reinforced by strong reactions against his work, notably in the form of state censorship: he was the first Afrikaner writer to be censored (for *Kennis van die aand/ Looking on Darkness,* 1973). He is associated with the "Sestigers," a group of South African writers who came of age in the sixties and whose work is distinguished for its experimentation with forms and themes. Committed to expressing the concerns of his time, Brink's work is also rooted in the historical past, which is presented not simply as a series of facts, but in terms of personal experience. His characters are often rebels, writers or historical figures and his themes are history, myth, love, sex, race and politics. Although he is best known for his novels, beginning with *Looking on Darkness,* through to his most recent *Imaginings of Sand* (1996), he has written in several genres, including the essay and drama, and is an extraordinarily prolific translator. Brink has had an influential voice in his country's recent history and his work has been translated into more than twenty languages.

Biographical Information

André Philippus Brink was born in Vrede, Orange Free State, South Africa on May 29, 1935. His father was a magistrate, and Brink's family was repeatedly relocated with his father's new appointments. Brink studied at Potchefstroom University, which Brink described as "a small Calvinist university," where he took a B.A. in 1955, an M.A. in English in 1958 and another M.A. in Afrikaans and Dutch in 1959. From 1959-1961 he settled in France to do postgraduate work in comparative literature at the Sorbonne. Brink commented that this remote location and the witnessing from afar of the

Sharpeville massacres in South Africa of March 1960 forced him "to re-examine all the convictions and beliefs I had previously taken for granted." Returning to South Africa, he gained prominence as a spokesperson for the "Sestigers." In the late '60s Brink returned to Paris where, he relates, he found himself in the midst of the student revolt of 1968 and reevaluated the writer's role in society, concluding that he needed to return to South Africa to, as he put it, "assume my full responsibility for every word I write, within my society." *Looking on Darkness* resulted. The work brought intimidation and harassment in the form of censorship, (the book was banned under South Africa's comprehensive 1963 Censorship legislation) State confiscation of his typewriters, and death threats. These reactions served to strengthen his convictions, however, and he began to write all his work in English at this time, to permit publishing outside his country and to acquire a wider, international readership. His method has consisted of writing in both Afrikaans and English, translating back and forth. Brink was also a faculty member in the Afrikaans department at Rhodes University from 1961 until 1990, and became a Professor of English at the University of Cape Town in 1991. He was President of the Afrikaans Writers Guild (1978-80) and won recognition abroad with several awards, among them, the Médicis étranger prize (France) and the Martin L. King Memorial Prize (UK) for *Droe wit seisoen (1980; A Dry White Season)* in 1980. Further formal foreign recognition followed, especially in France where he was named Chevalier, Legion of Honor 1982 and Commander, Order of Arts and Letters in 1992, distinctions which have allowed him to take a place alongside fellow South African writers like J.M.Coetzee, Nadine Gordimer and Athol Fugard.

Major Works

Brink's early career was spent producing work in Afrikaans. The banning upon publication in 1973 of *Kennis van die aand* (*Looking on Darkness*) was a turning point which forced Brink to work in English in order to maintain a readership and helped him focus his subject: South African society, its roots, its realities. It marked the beginning of what led to the development of a style Brink has referred to as "African Magic Realism." *Looking on Darkness,* like many of his novels, involves a sexual relationship between a white and a black, in this case between Joseph Malan and Jessica Thomason, and deals boldly with sex and with racial conflict and persecution. *'N Oornblik in die wind* (1975; *An Instant in the Wind*) deals with the love affair of an 18th-century white woman, Elisabeth Larsson, and Adam Mantoor, a runaway black slave, in the interior of the Cape of Good Hope, and its interracial sexuality brought more trouble with the censors. *Gerugte van reen* (1978; *Rumours of Rain*), the story of Martin Mynhardt, an Afrikaans Nationalist, is a novel that presents a severe condemnation of South Africa's racist regime. This was followed by *'n Droe wit seisoen* (1979; *A Dry White Season*). Told in the words of a freelance writer who has inherited the papers of the protagonist, Ben Du Toit, it is set shortly after the Soweto riots of June 1976 and involves the political awakening of a trusting model citizen when confronted with the deceptions and brutality of white authorities. *Houd-den-Bek* (1982; *A Chain of Voices*) is set on a Boer farm in the Cape Colony during the pre-Trek 1820s where a small-scale revolt takes place is marked by an engaging experimental feature: the "voices" of the title are those of the archetypal characters. The voice in *The Wall of the Plague* (1985), is that of a writer who in his research for a film script on the plague turns up a metaphor for the condition of white Afrikaners in South Africa. *States of Emergency* (1989), set in 1985 when a state of emergency was declared in South Africa and subtitled 'Notes towards a Love Story,' deals with urgent emotional/personal states, as well as political ones at a time of crisis. In *An Act of Terror* (1991), called a political thriller by one critic, white photographer Thomas Landmanas has the misfortune of having the people he photographs turning up dead. The story, which has a love element in Thomas's involvement with an Afrikaner woman, was seen as revealing the self-destruction

of the Afrikaners. With the dismantling of Apartheid and the lifting of censorship, the politics in Brink's work receded slightly, and the storytelling began to take center-stage. *Cape of Storms: The First Life of Adamastor* (1993), a tale concocted from a mix of sources (François Rabelais, Luis Camões and Khoikhoi legends) weaves a magical historical love story. *On the Contrary* (1994) is the narrative of Etienne Barbier told in the words he writes while awaiting execution. Barbier was a French adventurer in the Cape of Good Hope in the 1730s who led rebel Afrikaner colonists in their struggle with the corrupt administration of the East India Company. The novel has a strong element of magic realism with the presence of mythical creatures and the voice of Jeanne-D'Arc. This magical, mythical strain continues in *Imaginings of Sand,* a novel that explores a feminine perspective. Set against the background of South African elections of 1994, the story is told through the eyes of Kristien Müller, a white South African woman who has returned from exile to be with her dying grandmother. The grandmother is a repository of stories of the South African past and promises her granddaughter who has been away too long, "I'll give you back your memory." Michael Kerrigan observes that this "rambling roundabout skein of stories . . .comprises the true history of the Afrikaners."

Critical Reception

Brink's essays are recognized as important statements on literature and politics. Commenting on these, Joseph Skvorecky places Brink among the writers who have labored under oppressive censorship "with considerable technical skill and almost the elaborateness of a Henry James, " while J.M. Coetzee, with whom Brink has published an anthology called *A Land Apart: A South African Reader* (1986), sees in Brink an example of a writer who is "an organ developed by society to respond to its need for meaning," and one whose "focus is now not on the existential duty of the writer but on the strategy of battle." The power of his novels is recognized by most critics. C.J. Driver speaking of *Looking on Darkness* points out that his work is "linguistically exciting, continually perceptive about a society gone mad, fiercely angry about cruelty." Frank Pike calls *An Instant in the Wind* "an ambitious work," that is "memorable by any standards, especially . . . in its evocation of the landscape." *Rumours Of Rain,* Jim Hoagland affirms, "takes the reader inside the reality" of its subject and "captures the spreading terror of the white man trapped within the vast spaces of Africa and surrounded by equally vast numbers of Africans." Mel Watkins detects in *A Dry White Season* a vehicle for Brink "to better focus our attention on the ruthlessly dehumanizing apparatus of the apartheid system itself," while Jim Crace, finds in *The Wall of the Plague* a novel that is "a courageous self-assessment" and "an interesting and pivotal work." Along with these praises, however, are some recurring complaints. Brink is often accused of melodrama and sensationalism. In *Looking on Darkness,* Driver finds "imaginative credibility slips, the control of the narrating 'I' wavers and pity becomes self-pity." Roger Owen in a review of *A Chain of Voices* complains that despite the "awesomeness of the subject matter" there are serious flaws, among them " derivativeness; a proneness to cliché; a striving for 'fine' writing; a certain woodenness of style." The depiction of sex is also a sore point. Crace accused the dialogue in such scenes of being "thinly motivated and rawly expressed," and declared Brink's observations on human sexuality as "farcically solemn." But, as Pike asserts, Brink himself is the uniting source of power in his work: "he is most successful as a writer when his own voice rather than those of his often artificial characters, dominates the scene."

PRINCIPAL WORKS

Kennis van die Aand [*Looking on Darkness*] (novel) 1974
An Instant in the Wind (novel) 1976
Rumours of Rain (novel) 1978
A Dry White Season (novel) 1979
A Chain of Voices (novel) 1982
The Wall of the Plague (novel) 1985
States of Emergency (novel) 1989
An Act of Terror (novel) 1991
Cape of Storms: The First Life of Adamastor (novel) 1993
On the Contrary (novel) 1994
Imaginings of Sand (novel) 1996

CRITICISM

C. J. Driver (review date 15 November 1974)

SOURCE: "Mixing the Colours," in *Times Literary Supplement,* No. 3793, November 15, 1974, p. 1278

[*In the following review of* Looking on Darkness *Driver comments on the novel's social context and assesses its artistic merits.*]

Looking on Darkness is the English translation (by the author himself) of an Afrikaans novel, **Kennis van die Aand,** which was banned on publication in South Africa: "If this is art", said the clerical Vorster, brother of the Prime Minister, "then a brothel is a Sunday school". It is not difficult to understand why it was banned: it is explicit about sex; it is explicit about torture in South African gaols; it is explicit about racial hatred and persecution, and about the way South Africans actually live and talk and feel; and it largely concerns the (illegal) love affair between a Cape Coloured man

and a (white) British girl. According to an Afrikaans saying, "a bird must not shit in its own nest": André Brink has done more than that—he has torn the nest to pieces.

Looking on Darkness is presented as the autobiography of a Cape Coloured actor, Joseph Malan, recounted in a series of extended flashbacks from the cell in which he awaits execution for the murder (committed as part of an unfinished suicide pact) of his white girl-friend, Jessica. We are told that he destroys what he writes as he completes it, which is rather confusing for the reader. He recalls the stories of his ancestors which he heard as a child; looks back on his friendships and loves, his schooling and university, his years in England—at RADA in provincial rep and at the RSC—his decision to go back to his own country and people; reviews his intellectual and dramatic interests, and so on. Public events obtrude: Sharpville and Langa; the deportation of a priest; the suicide of Malan's spiritual mentor, Dulpert Naidoo, while in solitary confinement.

But Malan is primarily an actor, and he works for his people's liberation and his own by forming a company to take on tour. The productions include a rewritten version of *Hamlet, SA!* (after Peter Brook's *US*), *Andorra* a version of *Tartuffe:* it is one of Brink's skills that he makes these sound both feasible and exciting. The company works well enough to bring down on itself the full weight of the police-state, in all its logical illogicality and crushing pettiness. Gradually Malan is forced back to his own drama, the idyllic and doomed love-affair with Jessica, and finally his present position. His heroism consists in his refusal to make the choices his white masters demand, and by the end of his story he has achieved a kind of freedom.

There are failings in the novel: imaginative credibility slips, the control of the narrating "I" wavers and pity becomes self-pity. The citing of intellectual parallels and authorities is too insistent (though it might be argued that Malan's habit of supporting every thought with a reference is both typical of his actor's mind and a defence against the racialists' cry that all blacks, however educated, remain barbarians). It interests me that Afrikaans writers seem to find it much easier to identify imaginatively with coloured than with black Africans. But within its context this is a brave and important novel, and in any terms a fine one—linguistically exciting, continually perceptive about a society gone mad, fiercely angry about cruelty. Even read safely in exile—midway between contexts—it is very disturbing, partly because of what it has to say about the condition of exile itself, but mainly because it (unfashionably) makes of self-abnegation a convincing ideal. Not that Joseph Malan denies himself experience, but the murder of Jessica is deliberate self-murder, and his decision not to commit suicide is, paradoxically, an act of commitment to the consequences, not simply of his actions, but of his history, his slave-ancestors' history, his refusal to say "baas". Not for nothing is St John of the Cross constantly cited: this is abnegation which moves to ecstasy. "And so I regret nothing. This is love", says Malan on the eve of his execution. "I was never sure whether I'd be able to endure it all, but I have. I haven't betrayed anyone: neither Jessica, nor Jerry, nor my history. This is joy."

Frank Pike (review date 17 September 1976)

SOURCE: "Veldanschauung," in *Times Literary Supplement,* No. 3888 September 17, 1976, p. 1147.

[*In the following review of* An Instant in the Wind, *Pike presents an outline of the elements of the novel and comments on its success in evoking an historical period.*]

Reminiscent of; if not inspired by Patrick White's *Voss,* this ambitious work takes the few recorded facts of an episode of the past to evoke the history and character of a country through the relationship of two individuals. In 1751, Elisabeth Larsson returned to Cape Town accompanied only by a runaway slave, Adam Mantoor, having set out nearly two years earlier on an expedition into the interior of the Cape of Good Hope with her newly married husband, the Swedish traveller Erik Larsson, an incompetent guide, and a complement of ox wagons and Hottentot bearers. The guide shot himself after a quarrel, most of the oxen were stolen, the bearers decamped, and finally Larsson walked off into the bush never to reappear. At this point Elisabeth was discovered by Adam Mantoor, and together they began the journey back to the sea.

In narrative terms this novel is simply an account of a relationship between a black man and a white woman, between them and a landscape, and between them and the historical currents which have set them together, almost at opposite ends of the social scale, in an embryonic civilization in southern Africa. As the journey proceeds the personal histories emerge: Elisabeth, a daughter of the evolving Cape Dutch petty bourgeoisie, resentful of the aspirations to gentility which restrict her desirable accomplishments to piano-playing and needlework, insisting on marrying Larsson to escape them; Adam, betrayed by his childhood playmate, the master's son, into a vicious flogging, and later banished to Robben Island for striking his master. In their struggling progress across the terrain, losing in succession wagon, oxen and almost everything else, the pair become a couple, a sexual idyll counterpointing the physical trials of sun, rain, cold or thirst.

It is a plot that might have been more than competently handled by Nevil Shute, especially as the author has sensibly avoided "period quality" in the dialogue, where only the

occasional contemporary vulgarism jars. Yet even if one evades pronouncing on the ultimate effectiveness of the historical and spiritual symbolism or the extent to which André Brink has achieved the kind of epic he was aiming at, there is much writing here that is memorable by any standards, especially but not exclusively in its evocation of the landscape. It is not merely the travel-poster decor of veld or mountain which is justified by an intensely communicated feeling for its plants, animals and birds (which Larsson's expedition set out to record and classify): there is a genuinely historical sense of the almost paradisal quality of the fertility and temperateness which the Cape must have had to the earliest settlers.

Jim Hoaglund (review date 5 November 1978)

SOURCE: "Storm Over Soweta," in *Washington Post Book World,* November 5, 1978, Sect. G, p. 8

[*In the following review of* Rumours of Rain, *Hoagland provides a brief overview of some of Brink's other work and considers the social relevance of the novel under review.*]

André Brink is a member of the only white tribe the African continent has ever produced—the 2.5 million Calvinist, Dutch-speaking Afrikaners descended of Europeans who first came to South Africa 300 years ago. Supported by two million English speaking whites, the Afrikaners rule the country's 20 million blacks through the harsh system of Apartheid.

Brink's birthright as an Afrikaner gives him a ringside seat at the racial Armageddon his book suggests is coming for South Africa, as surely as rain comes to wash away a parching drought. His courage and vision in describing his land's dilemmas have made him a tribal outcast, however. An earlier novel, ***Looking on Darkness,*** was banned in South Africa, and has come out in paperback in the United States, just as ***Rumours of Rain*** is being published here.

> **In *Rain* Brink captures the spreading terror of the white man trapped within the vast spaces of Africa and surrounded by equally vast numbers of Africans.**
> **—*Jim Hoaglund***

Taken together, the two books establish Brink as South Africa's most important novelist since Alan Paton. The contrast between the humanistic, eloquent and vaguely paternal English-speaking Paton and the angry, apocalyptic Brink is a cultural sign of the broader changes in South African realities over the past 30 years.

For Brink is a writer of violence and of terror. **Darkness,** written four years before the murder of Steve Biko in a South African police cell, takes the reader inside the reality of a black activist in the hands of white security police determined to break him. In **Rain** Brink captures the spreading terror of the white man trapped within the vast spaces of Africa and surrounded by equally vast numbers of Africans.

Brink himself is more interesting than many of the characters he has created in **Rain** to tell the story of what he suggests, in this complex and uneven novel, is a growing tribal death-wish. And he is most successful as a writer when his own voice rather than those of his often artificial characters, dominates the scene.

As his narrator-protagonist Brink has created Martin Mynhardt, a wealthy, sophisticated businessman who, like the majority of Afrikaners his age, has moved off the family farm into the city and into a position of power and prosperity. Mynhardt is a cardboard cutout figure of the detribalized Afrikaner whose conversion to modern capitalism, city life and international political manners was thought by many at the beginning of this decade to be South Africa's best chance for peaceful change in racial attitudes.

But the cold, insensitive Mynhardt fails at everything except making money. His narrative of a crucial weekend in his life, when he attempts to pressure his mother into selling the family farm so he can make a killing in a corrupt government land deal is a detailed portrait of a man failing his best friend, his wife, his son, his mistress—who calls Mynhardt tellingly "the man in the middle"—and ultimately his tribe.

The author suggests that the detribalized Afrikaner has become incapable of producing change. In his view the Afrikaner today who does not stand for violence—either to stop or to aid black revolution—has also become irrelevant.

"'Don't you think a man, especially if he's a highly sensitive and intelligent man, can be driven to the point where he sees violence as the only solution for a situation in which he has become expendable?'" Mynhardt is asked by his best friend, Bernard Franken, in a question that frames the moral context of the book.

Mynhardt turns away from the question, and his failure to address it defines him and much of Afrikaner society.

Franken is a lawyer who has been sentenced to life imprisonment for giving support to black revolutionaries. He is, in fact, a thinly disguised fictionalization of Afrikaner poet

Breyten Breytenbach, a close friend of Brink's, who was sent to jail on treason charges for nine years in 1976.

The final third of the book, unlike the clumsily crafted first 100 pages, is written tautly and with sharp impact. It revolves around the relationship between Mynhardt and his son Louis. Near the book's end, the two are driving back from the farm toward Johannesburg, when they hear broadcasts announcing that the 1976 Soweto uprising is beginning against the Afrikaner government that Mynhardt unquestioningly supports. During their ride, the father finally senses—too late—the deep alienation and anger of his son, who has been sent to the Angola War by that same South African government—the same government whose corruption is now destroying the family farm and is trying to destroy black political awareness in Soweto

Six years ago I ended a nonfiction book on South Africa with a metaphor of that country as Sisyphus, condemned to roll the rock of racial conflict but, if Camus was right, not condemned to despair. In a novel that is full of reporting as accurate as any you will read in newspapers, Brink suggests that there is another aspect of the ancient myth in the South African context that never entered my mind.

A black colleague of Mynhardt's tells him that the "'white Sisyphus operates in the dimension of metaphysics. My dimension is social . . . . On my way downhill to pick up the absurd rock again, I don't see anything metaphysical. What I see is my social condition, my oppressors. You may think in terms of suicide, if you wish to stick to Camus. Not I, because I exist socially. I've got to make the jump from suicide to murder.'"

Mel Watkins (review date 23 March 1980)

SOURCE: "A Novelist's Impassioned Indictment," in *New York Times Book Review,* Vol. 85, March 23, 1980, pp. 15, 20, 21.

[*In the following review Watkins examines the fictional devices Brink uses in* A Dry White Season *to expose some of the realities of living under Apartheid, while considering the novel alongside some of Brink's previous work.*]

In his previous novel, **Rumours of Rain,** André Brink, an Afrikaaner and head of the department of literature at Rhodes University at Grahamstown, South Africa, gave his audience a chilling glimpse into the inner sanctum of the South African ruling class. Through his portrayal of Martin Mynhardt, a calculating and philandering Afrikaans Nationalist, he dramatized the firmly entrenched attitudes of superiority and self-righteousness that brace his country's political posture. That novel, like his earlier works, was a direct indictment of South Africa's racist regime. Mr. Brink's latest book, *A Dry White Season,* his most impressive novel thus far, is perhaps even more censorious. The approach, however, is entirely different, and clearly Mr. Brink has discovered a much more compelling angle from which to view apartheid and its corrosive effect on all of South African society.

Ben Du Toit, a white Johannesburg schoolteacher, is the typical suburban family man—a model citizen with a wife and three children. And like most ordinary citizens, as his life moves forward with measured serenity, he is contentedly oblivious to the machinations of the ruling political regime. Shortly after the Soweto riots of June 1976, however, Ben's complacent life begins to crumble.

It begins harmlessly enough. Gordon, a black janitor at Ben's school, asks Ben to help him locate his son Jonathan, who has disappeared. He was last seen among the protestors at Soweto. Ben agrees, and with the aid of a lawyer they begin petitioning the police for information on Jonathan's whereabouts.

From the outset, the authorities stall and give them conflicting reports. At first they claim they know nothing of Jonathan. Then, after Gordon and Ben confront them with statements by black informants who have seen the boy in jail and in a hospital, the officials tell Gordon's lawyer that Jonathan had been detained after all, and that he has died of a heart attack. When Gordon attempts to claim his son's body, however, he encounters more evasiveness. Finally Gordon and Ben are told that all previous information was incorrect, and that Jonathan was fatally wounded on the day of the riots and buried a month later, after no one had claimed the body. The case, so far as the authorities are concerned, is closed.

For Ben, the word of the Special Police is enough; but Gordon is obsessed with his son's mysterious death, and continues the investigation on his own. Then he, too, is arrested, and the affidavits he has collected to prove that his son had been detained in jail are confiscated. When Gordon's wife pleads for Ben's assistance, he again agrees to help.

At this point the novel assumes a Kafkaesque sense of foreboding as Ben, totally convinced of the system's impartiality, presses to expedite Gordon's release and clarify the circumstances of Jonathan's death. But each time he moves closer to unraveling the matter, his efforts are frustrated by the Special Branch. For Ben it is a revelatory journey into a labyrinth of bureaucratic duplicity and official deceit, manipulation and violence. Witnesses who confirm that Jonathan had been detained and tortured disappear or fall victim to strange accidents; Gordon "confesses" to being a

terrorist and later, officials say, commits suicide. Ben's house is searched and his phone is tapped; he is blackmailed and forced to resign from his job. He receives a bomb in the mail and is shot at while driving to meet a friend of Gordon's. His friends and, eventually, his wife and family turn against him. His commitment to unearthing the truth, and thereby questioning the integrity of the authorities, has thrust him into a deadly conflict with "the invisible and shapeless power" that controls the state.

"I don't think I ever really knew before," he tells Stanley, a black friend of Gordon's. "Or if I did, it didn't seem to directly concern me. It was, well, like the dark side of the moon. Even if one acknowledged its existence it wasn't necessary to live with it . . . . The problem is: once you've caught a glimpse of it, once you've merely started suspecting it, it is useless to pretend it's different."

Ben's descent from respected family man to isolated pariah is dramatically the most arresting aspect of this novel. But in one sense, it is simply a vehicle for Mr. Brink to better focus our attention on the ruthlessly dehumanizing apparatus of the apartheid system itself. Through Ben's harrowing experience as an ordinary, essentially moral Afrikaaner who is drawn into the fray out of compassion, the brutal inflexibility of the system is exposed and indelibly imprinted on the reader.

Counterpoised against Ben's travail is the horror and degradation of the Kaffir shantytowns, where people disappear without a trace at the slightest infraction of state rules and the gratuitous violence of the Special Police is rampant. As in his previous novels, Mr. Brink describes these conditions explicitly; but here the exposition is perhaps more subtle, for we view this scene through Ben's eyes and the shock of its severity is buffered by his initial incredulity as well as his deep-rooted fear of the people he has set out to help:

"The awareness of disembodied sound grew overpowering. And once again, but more intensely than before, he had the feeling of being inside an enormous animal body with intestines rumbling, a dark heart beating, muscles contracting and relaxing, glands secreting their fluid. Only, in Stanley's absence, it acquired a more ominous, malevolent aspect, an amorphous menacing presence . . . . Exposed to pure anguish, he sat motionless, feeling the tiny cold pricks of perspiration on his face where the air touched him . . . . 'Now I know what this Black Peril is people are so scared of,' he said mockingly."

A Dry White Season demonstrates André Brink's continuing refinement of his fictional technique, without sacrificing any of the poignancy that his previous books have led us to expect. By telling the story in the words of a freelance writer who has inherited Ben's papers, notes and evidence collected during his investigation, the narrative achieves an objectivity, an almost documentary sense, that both heightens its effect and moderates the occasional lapses into bathos and tendentiousness that have marred Mr. Brink's earlier work. Yet the complex portrait of Ben Du Toit, with his genuine compassion and sincere but misguided belief in the basic justice of the South African regime, insures the novel's emotional impact.

Like many works by the Russian dissidents, *A Dry White Season* is both an exposé and a passionate appeal for social justice. At its core is a basic moral question: Do we continue resisting injustice and moral corruption even when resistance seems futile, or do we capitulate and become silent accomplices? Mr. Brink argues persuasively that the answer is ineluctable. One acts, one protests, or one simply forfeits his humanity.

Richard Eder (Interview/Profile date 23 March 1980)

SOURCE: "An Interview with André Brink," in *New York Times Book Review,* Vol. 85, March 23, 1980, pp. 15, 20.

[*In the following interview between Brink and Eder, the issues of writing under censorship and of writing in two languages are discussed.*]

To make laws is to make loopholes. Or, prohibition is the stepmother of invention. André Brink, an Afrikaans writer, has been creeping through and around South African censorship ever since one of his first books, *Looking on Darkness,* was banned in 1974.

Mr. Brink has devised a kind of private publishing system that is not strictly underground, nor quite overground either. It is a kind of hedge-hopping; and it sold 4,000 copies of *A Dry White Season* in South Africa before the censors caught up with it, banned it temporarily and then released it.

The 44-year-old author, who was here on his way to serve on a literary jury in Oklahoma, explained the workings of his system. The South African censorship generally exercises its functions after publication. In 1977, after he had written *An Instant in the Wind,* which dealt with the love affair of an 18th-century white woman and a runaway black slave, Mr. Brink had no reason to think that the censors would be any kinder to it than they were to the earlier *Looking on Darkness,* which told of a sexual relationship between a white woman and a black man. "We had the book printed privately," he said. "Instead of submitting it to a publisher, we advertised in the newspapers that it was available at a number of specified locations."

After his next book, *Rumours of Rain,* was held up for six months by the authorities before being allowed to circulate, Mr. Brink reverted to his private distribution system for *A Dry White Season.*"We had a subscription list of those who had bought the earlier books," he said, "and we worked from that. We sold about 4,000 copies that way." Late last year, in an apparent liberalization move, the censors gave approval to the book, so it could be released through formal publication. They also lifted the ban on Nadine Gordimer's *Burger's Daughter.*

"What with these few unbannings—I even had a meeting with the Minister of the Interior—I get the impression they are keen to open up a bit," Mr. Brink said. "But I'm not sure whether this will apply to all or just to the few who can write from an international position." He noted that shortly afterward a book by a black writer, Mtutuzell Matshoba, whom he called "one of the most talented writers in the country," had been banned. "It suggests they still don't give a damn about young writers, particularly black ones, who are vulnerable and can't talk back. In a sense it makes the situation even more inequitable if some are going to get preferential treatment."

If Mr. Brink has what he calls an international position, it is because he has found another way of getting through the censorship. For some time he has written his books simultaneously in Afrikaans and in English. Almost simultaneously, that is: he writes a draft or two in Afrikaans, then does an English version, and polishes back and forth.

Writing a book bilingually is most unusual. For Mr. Brink it has had the obvious advantage of allowing him to publish in Great Britain even when banned in South Africa, and it has other advantages as well: "It is a strange kind of dialogue I have with myself," he said. "The moment you translate your clichés they stand out. And sometimes there are things that work in one language and not in another; whole scenes, even. And since I am author as well as translator, I can take liberties with each version."

Despite these expedients, Mr. Brink finds the book-censorship system in his country both demoralizing and degrading. He is a teacher—a professor of Afrikaans at the predominantly English Rhodes University in Grahamstown—and he finds that the younger writers are badly affected. "They used to come to me and ask: Do you think this is good enough? Now the question is: Will this pass the censor? It puts our entire literature in jeopardy."

More damaging to literature than censorship is the system it supports, he said, noting that the white writers of South Africa, whether English or Afrikaans, find it impossible to write convincingly about blacks, and vice versa: "One of the inevitable results of apartheid is that it sets people so far apart in their formative years that one group cannot imagine the other well enough to write about it. Some of us grow together when we are grown up, but these very important childhood years are a closed book, one to the other."

Until the 1960's, those South African writers who set themselves against the racial policies of their country belonged to the English community: Alan Paton, Nadine Gordimer and others. Mr. Brink and others such as Etienne Lerroux and Breyten Breytenbach were a newer and unwelcome phenomenon to the closed community of Afrikaaners, who regarded their language and culture as an embattled island in a black sea: "For a while, I think, the Afrikaans writers who were critical could get away with more, but now I have the impression we are treated more severely," he said. "In a way, of course, we are more vulnerable than those who write in English. It is a small language, and if we are banned at home where else will we be read?"

By the older Afrikaaners, he says, he tends to be looked upon as a traitor. On the other hand, the fiercely anti-apartheid stand of his books has found a widespread response. "Writing as I've been doing has brought people together," he said. "There were a lot of individuals in the country who thought they were alone, but now they see they do share doubts and problems with many others."

He says he has found support among students and colleagues at his university, which maintains a liberal tradition, and in some sectors of the Afrikaans press, which has grown more liberal in recent years. Until recently, he even edited the book page of the largest weekly Afrikaans newspaper, *Rapport*.

Mr. Brink said he had seen signs that the authorities were beginning to realize the need to deal fairly with blacks—this was before the recent hard-line turn by Prime Minister Pieter Botha—and was moderately encouraged by this: "The problem is that the indications may be given, but unless they are substantiated by facts and actions, you will get disillusionment, and then what happened in Soweto will seem like child's play compared to what will be."

Bernard J. Toerien (review date Spring 1983)

SOURCE: A review of *A Chain of Voices and Houd-den-bek,* in *World Literature Today,* Vol. 57, no. 2, Spring 1983, pp. 339-40.

[*In the following review of* A Chain of Voices/Hou-den-bek, *Toerien points out the novel's strengths and failings and compares the English and Afrikaans versions.*]

Brink's new novel was simultaneously published in English and Afrikaans, the latter version under the title of the remote South African farm ("Shut Your Trap") where an abortive slave rebellion took place in the early nineteenth century. That rebellion provides the basis of the novel, which is presented as a series of monologues by a large cast of protagonists, most of whom are named in the actual indictment and verdict which frame the novel. Brink gives the participants flesh and blood and lets them speak for themselves.

The time is 1828, about thirty years after the Cape has been taken over by the British. Dutch colonists have been moving inland, displacing the indigenous Hottentots (Khoikhoin) and bringing with them their slaves imported from Batavia and Mozambique. The Hottentots, although nominally "free," had become economically enslaved and beholden to the whites—a situation which persists to this day. South African blacks are not featured in this uprising; they were situated on the faraway eastern border of the colony and had only recently been encountered by the colonists, leading to the countless "Kaffir wars." The region of the uprising in question is that of the Cold Bokkeveld (Cold Goat Country), a harsh, rocky and agriculturally poor area north of Cape Town but cut off from the rich agricultural lands by almost inaccessible mountains. It was natural for the settlers to become a law unto themselves, left to their own devices as they had been by the ineffective administration of the Dutch East India Company. The new British administration was trying hard to rule justly and to protect the rights of the indigenous inhabitants, and the abolition of slavery was in the air. The colonists naturally resented the interference of a central authority.

All these threads are woven into Brink's powerful novel and make for compelling reading. He is especially effective in probing the minds of the simple nonwhites and makes them the heroes of his book. This is almost revolutionary for Afrikaans writing and probably English South African writing as well. The first-person narration is skillfully handled on the whole, as Brink manages to infuse the story with a measure of excitement, in spite of the foregone conclusion. He therefore moves the narration forward together with the action and in this way is able to get the dead victims to tell their story as well. But I did find one thing bothersome: at what point in time are these persons speaking? How is it that the old woman Ma-Rose, introduced by Brink (and very successfully too) as a sort of Greek chorus, looks back on the complete events in the beginning of the book, whereas the other characters move forward bit by bit? And, more seriously, why do all these characters sound so much the same, all musing in full, complete and grammatically correct sentences? One often feels that the author's own thoughts and language are put in the mouths of his characters. Monotony sets in, and the second half of the book becomes progressively harder to finish.

Apart from substance, there is the problem of language. Brink wrote the English and Afrikaans versions at the same time, as he states in a *New York Times Book Review* interview. He made it clear that the English version is not a translation, as a direct comparison of the two texts bears out. There is no attempt at a faithful rendition; whole sentences and paragraphs are left out in either version, but more usually in the English. Whereas the Afrikaans voices are often colloquial and earthy, their English counterparts are usually bland, colorless and very much alike. One would expect more individuality in the characters' speech, more use, for example, of monosyllables or unfinished sentences. Even the characters born overseas, such as the Batavian and Mozambican slaves, speak correct English or Afrikaans.

My last reservation about the book is that the whites are painted as just too corrupt and mean, whereas the nonwhites have a romantic aura of nobility about them. Galant, the leader of the rebellion, is a full-fledged Hollywood hero, a dark Errol Flynn.

But this is nitpicking. The book is a considerable achievement, bold in concept and in execution. One can only admire Brink for always grappling with the form of the novel anew; in his earlier Afrikaans novel **Orgie** he had his characters speak at the same time, their speeches printed as in a play or rather a libretto; in **Looking on Darkness** . . . the book was written on paper and then swallowed by the accused in his cell to remove the evidence (but how did it get printed for us to read?), and so on. These ploys make his books immediate and exciting.

Josef Skvorecky (review date 30 April 1984)

SOURCE: "The Fear of Literature," in *The New Republic*, Vol. 190, No. 17, April 30, 1984, pp. 29-33.

[*In the following piece, the expatriate Czech novelist and essayist Josef Skvorecky reviews Brink's collection of essays* Writing in a State of Siege. *Skvorecky explores the similarities in political climate and state censorship between Brink's South Africa and Skvorecky's native Czechoslovakia.*]

Among the many remarkable features of **Writing in a State of Siege,** a collection of literary essays and speeches written between 1967 and 1982, one is particularly useful to us who know South Africa only from contemporary newspapers and from the false consciousness of television. That is the author's introduction. It sketches out the unique history of the white people of the southern tip of the African continent, and sheds light on what, for most of us, is the Afrikaner paradox, the mess that this heroic race of men and women find themselves in at present. After all, they spent their three

hundred years in Africa—as many as their American counterparts on this continent—repeatedly fighting for freedom.

The Afrikaners, like the Americans until 1783, were a classically oppressed people; like their transatlantic immigrant contemporaries, they mixed their sweat, and often their blood, with the soil of the land. In the course of those centuries they came to love the country, and defended it on the two classical fronts: against the overseas intruder, and against the domestic sectarian, the "loyalist," the disrupter of unity.

The bloody story began in the early part of the seventeenth century with a general uprising against the Dutch Governor Willem Adriaan van der Stel, one side effect of which was the shaping of Afrikaans as the national language. It continued throughout the nineteenth century, with the British as the enemy. The story's first climax was in the Great Trek, an exodus of Afrikaners from the Cape Colony, movingly modeled on the Old Testament, but executed without visible help from heaven. It was marred also by internecine struggles, which kept putting the fragile unity in jeopardy for the rest of the century. The second climax came with the Boer War, perhaps the first universally registered modern symbol of a small nation's fight for freedom against an overwhelming foreign oppressor. The war ended in bitter defeat and was followed by efforts to anglicize the entire South African way of life, first of all by eradicating the Afrikaans language, the main token of unity. Struggle again and disunity again, a lasting resentment of the foreign power that eventually led a sizable segment of the Afrikaner population to sabotage General Smut's war effort, thus earning them, for the first time I suppose, the opprobrium of being fascists.

> **The Afrikaners, like the Americans until 1783, were a classically oppressed people; like their transatlantic immigrant contemporaries, they mixed their sweat, and often their blood, with the soil of the land.**
>
> **—*Josef Skvorecky***

But at the beginning of this history, and for a considerable part of it, there was hardly any trace, even among prominent Afrikaners, of the notion that pigment, so useful for survival in hot climates, should be a sign of inferiority, or a mark of Cain. As late as the beginning of the nineteenth century, the legendary Afrikaner rebel Coenraad de Buys was married to a black wife, and a dark-skinned woman was the life companion of another opponent of the British rule, Frederik Bezuidenhout, eventually shot dead by British soldiers. Little racism, then; indeed any residua of nostalgia for the "old country," any consciousness of "Europeanness," faded completely from the memory of these sunburnt farmers and were replaced by a total identification with the "Black" continent and—before the diamonds and the gold—with the continent's indigenous people.

With the gold rush the sociology changed. The influx of vast masses of blacks into the teeming mining towns eventually came to be seen by the Afrikaners as a new threat. Since the threat was internal, and had an easily identifiable physiognomy, it unfortunately metamorphosed into institutionalized (as opposed to instinctual) racism. The nation's leaders gave it the seal of official policy at the precise moment when the external threat seemed to have been eliminated forever. After the election victory of the National Party in 1948, the Afrikaners, for the first time in their tortuous history, found themselves masters in their own house.

Only the house was hardly their exclusive property. There was the English-speaking minority—but they were white, and a sort of "equal but separate" development came as a natural way of life to these largely educated and apparently well-to-do people; besides, there were few objections to social mixing and intermarriage. A harder case were the Asiatics—but they represented a numerically weak segment and some, the Japanese for instance, came to be tolerated as a kind of honorary whites. That left the vast black—and not-so-black—cloud of the original Africans.

Brink believes that, in the absence of a truly free press, the writer is a rear guard of truth, not necessarily of something with a capital *T*, but of the veiled and metaphorized trickle of information about the human condition.
—Josef Skvorecky

By then, I suppose, though Brink does not dwell on this, the class divisions, more often than not, began to overlap with the color lines. A powerfully explosive social mixture emerged. It was made increasingly combustible by external outrage and internal radicalization of the oppressed, with the Communists adding their little drops of gasoline to the dangerous substance. After their well-known exploits elsewhere, the Communists put justifiable fright into the souls of the burghers, and also anxiety into those who trust that there cannot be much justice without political freedom. The old, also quite justifiable, fear of disunity reemerged and assumed the form of militant anticommunism, with its tragic tendency to see a Communist in everyone who speaks up for social feeling; that is, in the man who is serious about liberty.

The dissidents came to be seen as pinkos, as disrupters of the sacred unity in the face of danger, not as people who believe that it is in the interest of that very same national con-

cord to claim democracy for *all* citizens. "Afrikaners are so agonizingly aware what it means to be divided that dissidence in the present circumstance is viewed with . . . alarm and rage," writes Brink. Out of this "alarm and rage," the logical but ugly side effects of apartheid developed: the time-dishonored practices of censorship and a kind of "burghers democracy," an embarrassingly exact copy of the Communist police state, which is presented to the world under the rose-scented euphemism of "people's democracy."

It is censorship and the issues of artistic freedom that Brink's essays are mostly about. They do not dwell much on the physically inhuman aspects of apartheid—on jail deaths from the common cold that leave scars all over the deceased's body, or on the Nuremberg laws of Pretoria, which do not enforce the wearing of yellow stars only because the citizens to whom the laws apply are discernible without special accessories. Not that Brink would be insensitive to such sufferings—his novels prove that he is everything but indifferent to them—but he is a writer, and his pieces are articles of faith in the writer's mission in society. Brink believes that, in the absence of a truly free press, the writer is a rear guard of truth, not necessarily of something with a capital *T*, but of the veiled and metaphorized trickle of information about the human condition. His role in bringing about social change is indispensable—an opinion fully shared by the oppressors, otherwise they wouldn't bother to censor. Both Brink and Botha, of course, are right. The muzzling of the writers always comes in the wake of the gagging of the press, with the inevitable consequence that the only form of social change is an uprising, and the government's only solution is Jaruzelski.

But information—a simple, if perhaps complexly veiled, dispensing of the truths not to be found in the daily papers—is only one and, in the long run, less important, function of the novelist. With the characteristic tinge of a preacher that brings this man of the West close to the visionary voices of the East, Brink writes:

> By keeping alive the voice of reason and the search for meaning in a demented world [the writer] offers a safeguard to human dignity and an awareness of human values. If a writer falls silent, it becomes that much easier for society to sink back into the swamp of violence and hysteria . . . he knows only too agonizingly well that his vision may be defective, that some error may have entered into his analysis, that the meaning extrapolated from his probing may be distorted in the formulation of his findings. . . .

In the first part of this passage Brink sounds, to my ears at least, like Faulkner, perhaps the last American writer who knew that there is a dimension of mission in the writer's vocation, and who was not ashamed to let it show in his prose. The second part is a preventive defense against the gloomy voice of the ideological critic who confuses imagination with scholarly research. The concluding part of the diatribe, which follows, expresses Brink's diagnosis, which I fully share with him, of what constitutes health: "... but a healthy society can face this risk [i.e., the risk of artistic freedom]." A sick society, on the other hand, dreads "the vision of itself offered by an intrepid and impertinent individual."

In spite of abundant evidence of such dread in his country, perhaps because he is so well rooted in its history, Brink remains an optimist—a *rara avis* among people concerned with South Africa:

> If [the South African dilemma] *really* becomes a matter of survival, I believe Afrikaners will be prepared to adapt ... to drastic change.... They have survived for 300 years because ... they have learnt to contend with African realities.

Given my own experiences of a certain kind, I wish I could share this optimism.

But in fact even Brink, as the last essays reveal, has lately become less assured of a happy ending. Since he knows, unlike the majority of Western commentators, not only the present of his land but also its past, he sees the major threat to its future elsewhere than those who judge the unfortunate country from the safety of their lucky homes. The fear that makes many Afrikaners tacitly accept apartheid (and privately, I am sure, resent it)—the fear of an attack from abroad—has recently been considerably strengthened by a new external threat, more dangerous because more sophisticated and militarily powerful than the feeble efforts of the seventeenth-century Dutch governors or the nineteenth-century English imperialists. Brink is painfully aware of this most Orwellian of all neocolonialisms which, just like the early missionaries, teaches the illiterate to read only in order to be better able to manipulate their minds.

> A significant number of whites who would actively promote change are now held back for fear of another Hungary or Czechoslovakia. And many blacks in South Africa, too, may dread the simplistic exchange of one form of suppression for another.... The situation is complicated immeasurably by the presence of Russian and Cuban military power in Angola: a natural process of change may be inhibited by the fear that "the Russians are coming."

The explicit mentioning of my native country is not the only instance in *Writing in a State of Siege* that brought to my mind that corner of Europe where the "simplistic exchange" actually occurred when the Big Brother with the larger moustache replaced the one with the smaller moustache. Some opponents of right-wing totalitarianism grow red in the face when one brings up such similarities: when, for instance, one quotes from a rarely quoted speech of Dr. Goebbels, "Lenin Or Hitler?," which is a eulogy to the venerable introducer of institutionalized class justice whom only Faulkner, among the great American writers, had the guts to compare to the devil.

Not so Brink, who compares constantly; who in an essay entitled **"The Writer in a State of Siege"** (and elsewhere) invokes freely the names of Solzhenitsyn, Sinyavsky, Havel, or Grusa side by side with the sharers of their fate from Pinochet's Chile, or the colonels' Greece, and with his own friends from Africa, Jan Rabie, Etienne Leroux, Chris Barnard, Elsa Joubert, Breyten Breytenbach—a long line of them. And since the human mind is fed on associations, my mind, focused on the pages of *Writing in a State of Siege,* tirelessly traveled north, from unhappy Transvaal to the unhappy heart of Europe.

To be sure, there are differences. A black professor, Z.K. Matthew, could speak to the students of a white university and sow the seeds of doubt in the mind of a young Afrikaner called André Brink, whereas a brilliant professor of unswervingly socialist persuasion, Václav Cerný, could not sow any such seeds in my mind when I was a student at Charles University in Prague; no one would dream of letting him cross the threshold of that unswervingly Stalinist institution. Similarly, it is unthinkable that the signatories of Charter 77, once charged with the crime of having signed it, could be found innocent by a Czech court—even after a trial lasting five years—as the signatories of the Freedom Charter were by a South African court.

It is unthinkable, for that matter, that a political trial in Prague could last for five years: the courts over there are constantly setting world records in quick procedure. (Their only serious rival in that respect is Khomeini.) But such differences do not indicate any difference in the toughness of the two regimes. Why? Brink himself provides an explanation: "It would be most unwise at [this] particular juncture in history, for the South African government to alienate ... desperately needed allies by cracking down forcefully on writers." A small, nasty tyranny obviously needs allies much more urgently than the big nasty one and its colonies.

Yet even in these dissimilarities there is a nucleus of sameness. Brink's fine novel *A Dry White Season* and Nadine Gordimer's *Burger's Daughter* were "unbanned," *inter alia,* because they were found to be "so badly written as not to fool or offend anyone." Some two years ago, the spokesman for the Czechoslovak Cultural Ministry invoked similarly high aesthetic criteria for the opposite purpose when, in an interview in *The New York Times,* he explained why the recent novels by Milan Kundera had not been published in the author's homeland. As the chief arbiter of publishers' choices, he was "disappointed" in their artistic quality.

But not even the big bullies of international power play are entirely independent of the opinions of the public in the West. "Mutloatse's *Forced Landing* was unbanned," writes Brink,

> but Mutloatse [a black writer] was, at the time, a leading figure in the Soweto branch of PEN, with invaluable international connections: on the other hand, the moving and immensely important volume of short stories *Call Me Not a Man,* by Mtutuzeli Matshoba—who does not have such international contacts—remains banned.

The well-connected Czech writer Pavel Kohout, a recipient of the Austrian State Prize for Literature, had never been jailed, although he worked very hard toward that goal; eventually he was even permitted to accept a prestigious position at the Viennese Burgtheater, and then prevented from returning home. The remarkable poet Jiri Savrda, unconnected and prizeless, pines away in jail.

And so on. There are many—perhaps trifling—absurdities among the similarities. My name was deleted from a note of acknowledgement attached to an essay on the seventeenth-century Dutch painter Roland Savery in a scholarly journal published in Prague, in which the author, a colleague of mine at the University of Toronto, thanked me for the *ad hoc* translation of several Czech articles on the artist. Likewise, several writers banned at the moment in South Africa "may not be quoted in any manner." In Czechoslovakia, Hemingway's *A Farewell to Arms* had to be retranslated after the Soviet invasion, because the existing (and twice published) translation was contaminated by my authorship. When the new translator, a friend of mine, embarrassed by the commission, tried to present my re-typed translation as his own, he received a rebuke and a warning that his real version would be compared word by word, not with the English original, but with my rendition of it, and should any similarities be found . . .Whereupon my friend spent a year trying to discover a synonymous phrase for "he said" while staying faithful to Hemingway's predilection for the simplest word.

But there are also the not-so-trifling matters. In South Africa, due to the close watch on the stage, one can apparently see significant new plays only secretly in tents or abandoned warehouses, while state-subsidized theater, housed in "splendiferous buildings," equipped with the most sophisticated stage facilities, "is almost moribund," subsisting, I'd guess, on a diet of safely dead classics. In Prague, 1983 marked the one hundredth anniversary of the opening of the National Theatre. Under reconstruction for several years, the building was unveiled on that occasion, to reveal, finally, a wonderous new interior, resplendent with thousands of little red stars. However, while the theater had been opened one hundred years ago with a performance of a brand-new opera by the still living Bedrich Smetana (*Libuse,* 1881), last year the Byzantine building was reconsecrated with what must have been about the five thousandth production of an ancient operetta by J.K. Tyl, written in 1848. Václav Havel, whose name can be mentioned only in the West—as it was by Samuel Beckett in the dedication of his latest play—is produced only in what are called "living-room theaters" by groups of amateur enthusiasts who perform in private flats to an audience consisting of themselves, and sometimes joined by members of the secret police; that, however, invariably brings an intermission of indefinite duration. Kohout, while he still lived in Prague, directed *Macbeth* under such conditions, as people in the West have learnt from Tom Stoppard's *Kohout's Macbeth.*

"In a society like South Africa," says Brink, "the very threat of persecution may suggest to the writer that he is heading in the right direction." This insightful comment brings a jolly scene out of the gloom of my memories. That evening Milos Forman, freshly of International Festival fame, was accepting his State Prize from President Novotný for the recently pardoned *Loves of a Blond.* We, the laureate's friends, waited for him in a café in downtown Prague. Eventually he arrived, but not in the manner of the heroic entrances characteristic of Soviet drama. He pushed his lovely wife Vera before him as a shield and, guarding his face with one hand, he whimpered: "Please! Don't beat me! I'm innocent!"

Mostly, however, the similarities are no fun. In Prague as in South Africa, the 1970s, a decade of intensified suppression, were marked by the absence of any significant new authors, and by a considerable number of fresh graves in the form of banned old writers, banned books, and involuntary departures into exile. But worst of all, as Brink writes, ". . . the loss of creativity, the loss of larger *dimensions* in much of the writing . . . is one of the main arguments against the deliberate separation of cultures which leads not to development, but to stagnation." Perhaps this "loss of larger dimensions," resulting from all kinds of separations—of the races, of writers of the same national culture by an Iron Curtain and bans, of authors who respect the censorship from those who don't—is the ultimate insult to art. Some become silent, some turn into voices calling to the desert of foreign lands where nobody understands their languages. Some continue to publish at home. But these are like the hypothetical young Sam Clemens in the hypothetically totalitarian antebellum days, who, realizing that they would never be able to put an antislavery novel across plantation censorship, shifts his accents and comes up with a hilarious satire on Huck Finn's atrocious table manners. Hundreds of contemporary writers in societies like South Africa or Czechoslovakia produce such Huckleberries. Nat Nakasa, quoted by Brink, writes: ". . . the horrible truth [is]: most South Africans have simply never opened their eyes to . . . reality." The published writers in all kinds of Oceanias also never open—never *can* open, if they want to stay published—their eyes to the central, the burning, the all-important issues of their closely watched societies. So they embroider the eternal themes of love in the manner of eunuchs writing about sexual passion. They criticize the small imperfections of their communities in the spirit of Hasek's "mild progress within the boundaries of the Law." They enjoy the Ibsenian "smaller freedoms" of their countries that "know no freedom." Sometimes they do this with considerable technical skill and almost with the elaborateness of a Henry James. But under the syntactical mazes of James, as Graham Greene once observed, there always lurked his basic theme: the hatred of oppression in any form. That theme is taboo in the kingdoms of the kops.

John Sutherland (review date 18 May 1986)

SOURCE: Review of *The Ambassador,* in *Los Angeles Times Book Review,* May 18, 1986, p. 15.

[*In the following review, Sutherland, an American professor of Literature, looks at the elements of Brink's fictional commentary on South African politics and society in* The Ambassador.]

The Victorians liked to think of Charles Dickens as their "special correspondent to posterity." For the outside world and for posterity, South Africa's novelists currently serve the same function. Our durable impressions of the Republic are formed less by what "news" state censorship allows to escape, than by the fictions of Dan Jacobson, J.M. Coetzee, Alan Paton, Nadine Gordimer, Tom Sharpe and André Brink.

The list could be extended. And given the fact that its total white population is four million (rather less than the weekend readership of the *Los Angeles Times*), it is evident that in its last days as we know it, South Africa is enjoying a literary renaissance. Imminent destruction, it would seem usefully concentrates the novelist's mind as much as anybody else's.

Arguably, André Brink is the most South African of South African novelists. For one thing, he has remained in the country, where he now teaches Afrikaans and modern literature at Rhodes University. Others have fled, or have been harassed into exile, or have made a literary base abroad.

Brink himself was tempted in 1968 to move to Paris, a place which is congenial to him and which figures centrally in *The Ambassador.* But he decided to be a South African novelist in South Africa, on the courageous grounds that a writer must take full responsibility for what he writes; even if that means censorship and imprisonment.

Not only has Brink physically stayed put, he has increasingly drawn his literary energies from deep within his country's peculiarly divided traditions. Brink writes primarily in Afrikaans and has the distinction of being the first novelist in that language to suffer censorship for dealing with miscegenation, or as South African law oddly calls it, "morality." But Brink also translates his novels into English, in which they have their mass readership. I can't think of any other writer (with the possible exception of Isaac Bashevis Singer) who so heroically straddles the diversities of literary cultures. A cost is paid in the quality of Brink's English prose which often has the rather sapless feel of translation. But the price is small in proportion to the gulf which his novels bridge between the Boer and the Anglo Saxon mind.

> **Brink's fiction challenges what is called the "laager mentality"; the idea that South Africa and its (white) people can hunker down, and cut themselves off entirely from the rest of the human race in pure sectarian self-righteousness.**
> *—John Sutherland*

Although Summit Books presents *The Ambassador* as a new work, it was in fact written and published in Afrikaans in South Africa and in English in Britain 20 years ago. The story is set among the diplomatic corps of Paris. The plot is simple to the point of banality. A third secretary at the South African Embassy has an affair with a feather-brained Parisian stripper. She jilts him for the ambassador. In revenge, the underling informs Pretoria of his superior's sexual delinquency and for good measure seduces his wife. The ambassador, meanwhile, is in the grip of passions he thought long buried. His marriage and career fall apart, but he cannot end the affair which is destroying him and all he stands for. Meanwhile, on the diplomatic front delicate negotiations are under way with France for the sale of arms (which will be used for racial repression), and Johannesburg is in the grip of a black workers' strike.

The novel is narrated from the principals' abruptly shifting view-points, making up what Brink calls a "mosaic." The image is important. Mosaics are compositions formed of separate fragments. Embassies are sovereign fragments of foreign states implanted abroad. And, in the largest sense,

The Ambassador deals with the inevitable South African theme of apartheid. That is to say, separateness.

What Brink's novel asserts is the human impossibility of separate development, the ideology on which South Africa has pinned its hopes of salvation. The ambassador and the third secretary, even with the iron disciplines of diplomatic protocol and Dutch Calvinism, are sucked into Paris, and transformed by it. In spite of themselves, and with tragic consequences, they become decadents, lovers, Parisians. To the official South African eye they are traitors and immoralists. In reality they have been brought to a recognition of their common humanity. *The Ambassador* takes its portentous epigraph from Lawrence Durrell, "love is a form of metaphysical inquiry." But for Brink love is also a form of revolution. And destructive though the experience of love may be, it is preferable to the revolutionary blood bath which every day seems nearer in South Africa.

Brink's fiction challenges what is called the "laager mentality"; the idea that South Africa and its (white) people can hunker down, and cut themselves off entirely from the rest of the human race in pure sectarian self-righteousness. Brink's is a noble and in the national circumstances an almost heroic affirmation. And *The Ambassador* makes this affirmation more effectively for not being directly about black-white relationships, as the author's later fiction was to be. It is a fine novel, on a subject of enormous seriousness for the Western world.

George Stade (review date 29 June 1986)

SOURCE: "A Pipsqueak's Obsession," in *New York Times Book Review,* Vol.91, June 29, 1986, p. 21.

[*In the following review, novelist Stade explores the themes and imbroglios of* The Ambassador.]

"I was born on a bench in the Luxembourg Gardens in Paris, in the early spring of 1960," André Brink has written. He was in his mid-20's at the time. He was born again in 1968, during a second visit to Paris, when he was "caught up" in the student demonstrations. These Parisian rebirths, in Mr. Brink's own formulations, were political, literary, metaphysical and sexual, the outcome of a "romantic love-affair" with the city. When he first arrived in Paris, fresh from South Africa, he was comfortable with his Afrikaner convictions, stiffened by his religion and its puritanism; but then, as he puts it, he was transformed by "that great metropolis where every single thing I had taken for granted now had to be tested, explored, validated—or rejected."

His subsequent rejections, expressed publicly through a half-

dozen novels set in South Africa and Paris, got a number of his books banned at home, got him denounced as a traitor and pornographer, got him detained by the security police, his house searched, his typewriters confiscated. Mr. Brink is not, of course, a traitor or a pornographer. On the contrary, he has argued, it is the current South African establishment and its ideology of apartheid that have betrayed all that is best in the Afrikaner experience. As for the representations of sex in his novels, Mr. Brink believes that sexual liberation is the prototype and motive force of all liberations, that reading and writing are sexual activities, a kind of intercourse between writer and reader, for each of them a dying and rebirth of the self. He believes, in short, that sexual communication "is not only a biological function but the expression of a metaphysical inquiry."

In *The Ambassador,* the first point of view we get is that of Stephen Keyter, the 23-year-old third secretary in the South African Embassy in Paris. The personality we make out between the lines of his own words is not attractive: ambitious, driven, resentful, self-pitying, a sex-starved pip-squeak, a petty Nietzschean. He is the kind of person whose unconscious motives always defeat his conscious purposes. The more he pursues something, the more it eludes him. For 18 months he has been pursuing the elusive Nicolette, who for Keyter moves in the luminous haze of her own mythomania. He sees her as at once a liar and a touchstone, scheming and aimless, messy and fastidious, a prude and a tart—but always unobtainable, at least by him. For he has evidence that Nicolette is having an affair with the Ambassador himself, who is more than twice her age. He begins to spy on them, skulking in the shadows. "I had to make it my business to discover the whole truth." Convinced he has it, convinced of his own impeccable motives, he sends the Foreign Minister a report on the Ambassador's unprofessional conduct.

The ironies thicken during the narrative of Paul van Heerden, the Ambassador. He has not, for example, been having an affair with Nicolette. But he initiates one upon the arrival from Pretoria of a packet containing a copy of Keyter's report and an official demand for an explanation. The Ambassador's own motives remain obscure to him; so does Nicolette. He can think of her only as "a myth, a fairytale," as, above all, the embodiment of Paris, which is "a synthesis of all her elements." He does know that her greater if ungraspable reality forces him to question every single thing he has taken for granted: his career, his marriage, his Government, the whole prior regulated and dutiful course of his life. He does know that he has "been born again through her."

Nicolette's narrative is more down-to-earth. It is true that sometimes she sounds like Molly Bloom: thinking of the Ambassador, she says, "Dear God, forgive me for loving him, but it's like my father, and what we are doing is like the flowers he used to stick in my hair." And sometimes she sounds like Anna Livia Plurabelle: thinking of her father, her lover and the Seine, she says, "Let the stream take you away, slowly, very slowly drifting along, until you remember less and less, and care less and less, and feel death taking you, not in a hurry, but slowly, passing under all the bridges of the city, under the misty sky which grows darker and darker until you can see no more, a singing sound in your ears, singing everywhere, dying, dying splendidly, just like when there's someone inside you."

But mostly she sounds like that familiar yet unfathomable young woman who seems to have initiated every literary young man on the make in some great city. As evidence, there are all those novels written in chastened celebration of her damning and redeeming bitchery and bewitchery. Mr. Brink's job was to make us fall as hard for Nicolette as he seems to have fallen himself. He almost succeeds. Certainly he surprises and moves us, especially through her musings on Keyter, who becomes oddly likable. And certainly through Nicolette, Mr. Brink joins the last link to the first on a chain of themes that has been uncoiling throughout.

Nicollette is attracted to the Ambassador in part because "he's like Daddy," who ran out on her impossible mother. Similarly, the Ambassador tries to embrace his distant daughter in the person of Nicolette. He also relives through Nicolette an 18-month infatuation with a woman named Gillian, whose treatment of the Ambassador 25 years ago has pointed analogies with Nicolette's present treatment of Keyter. But Gillian through the Ambassador was getting revenge on her hated father. In betraying the Ambassador, Keyter also gets revenge on his own father, whom he hated, loved and wanted to impress. His brief fling with the Ambassador's wife is the working out of a "mother-fixation." He muffs his chances with her because he can see her only through his experiences of Nicolette. But then poor Keyter is always getting in his own way, in particular his way to the Ambassador, who sees in Keyter not only his younger self but also the son he never had. In summing up the metaphysics of his love for Nicolette, the Ambassador speaks for all the characters: "Through her I return to the past and call up all the possibilities left unfulfilled; through her I explore all my relations with those around me."

This theme is adroitly developed, as are a number of others: the will to create meaning, the compulsion to confess, "the terror of . . . freedom," the gratifications of guilt. And Mr. Brink plants his symbols with a deft hand—horoscopes, rain, couples embracing, headaches, suicide. He also juggles his multiple perspectives with Lawrence Durrell's dexterity, but without his pretensions. A few turns of phrase and we feel the ominous weight of the invisible Government in Pretoria. Mr. Brink even has an answer for the predictable

charge that his inventions and contentions are no longer news ("Was everything, essentially, no more than a melodramatic tale, told in clichés?").

For all that, "The Ambassador" is not entirely satisfying. The prose, although without cliché, is merely transparent. The idioms of the three narrators need to be more distinct, more shaped by the kinks in their personalities, more occluded by what they do not know about themselves. Above all, the novel needs humor, intimations of the bedroom farce that lies just beneath the melodrama, its darkening close, the characters bereft, all passion spent.

Philip Horne (review date 4 August 1988)

SOURCE: "Tunnel Visions," in *London Review of Books,* August 4, 1988, pp. 26-27.

[*In the following excerpt Horne closely examines the ideas developed in* States of Emergency *and critques the novel's premises and structure.*]

André Brink's **States of Emergency** [. . .] should perhaps be described as a would-be novel. Its subtitle is 'Notes towards a Love Story', and it represents—minimally fictionalises—an attempt by a South African writer, André Brink, to produce a 'love story' at a time of political crisis, in 1985, when the current State of Emergency was declared. There are generous impulses at work in it—to assert the value of love between men and women, to resist racial oppression, to be frank about authorial difficulties—but more than equally, there are distressing traces of uncomfortable self-consciousness about what one might call the apparent stupidity of fictional creation, uneasy reachings for the support of deconstructive authorities from Paris, gestures towards an imagined centre far from South Africa.

Brink's lovers are not like Gurnah's of differing race—his idea is that their liaison begin remote from political and racial reality and then be forced to recognise that its authenticity depends on political engagement—but while one is happy to grant him their whiteness, it is harder to take without irony his decision (after some deliberation) that they be a married professor of literary theory in his early fifties and his attractive blonde graduate student of 23 (who addresses him as 'prof'). There seems to be no significant satirical intention in this. The book's title refers to the actual situation which surrounds them in South Africa, to the inner troubles of the characters (the 'prof' and Melissa have 'an emergency within themselves'), and to the author's own crisis and dissatisfaction with 'this emergent story', which he is making up as he goes along. At the end, the lightly fictionalised André Brink decides, 'No, 'I don't think I shall be writing my book after all'—only for the real André Brink to go ahead and publish it.

That Philip Malan should be a professor of literary theory allows Brink to develop his leading idea, which to many will seem a duff one, that there is a fruitful analogy between old-fashioned structuralism, which he sees as imposing a rigid barrier between the text and the world, and South African apartheid, which imposes a rigid barrier between the comfortable lives of some citizens (including academics) and those of others less fortunate. Late in the work, in one of the passages of authorial reflection and name-dropping (apparently modelled on the sometimes charming tendentiousness of Roland Barthes), this flabby notion gets expounded in a characteristically portentous way: 'To keep things apart, distinct, separate (man and woman; life and death; beginning and end; the inside and the outside of a text; life and story), to define them in terms of their exclusivity rather than in terms of what they have in common, must end in schizophrenia, in the collapse of the mind which tries to keep the distinctions going. In this lies the failure of apartheid, and the failure, as I see it, of structuralism.' The evil of apartheid is not, though, evidence of the evil of making distinctions, only of the possible evil of false distinctions; and a true sense of relatedness is not the same as an acceptance of what he calls a moment later 'the fluid oneness of things'. It seems to me that the idiom of theory here leads Brink to an incredibly simple—and thus incredible—opposition. He depicts a too rigid orderliness failing to cope and then plunging into total collapse. The failure of 'André Brink' to write a novel tritely mimes the interference of life with text, the breaking-down of boundaries.

The love affair at the book's centre—its main 'text'—is set up to be initially an equivalent to structuralism and apartheid: it is a thing apart, secretive (because adulterous), and irresponsibly pleasurable. It is aligned, through a hefty apparatus of allusion, with various mythically transcendent loves, including those in Wagner, in a Zulu legend, and that of the invented Jane Ferguson, a young dead writer whose journal and unpublished novel have come into the hands of André Brink (who shows himself stealing inspiration from them). Eventually Philip and Melissa discover that their love is too intense to be kept apart from the rest of their lives— that is, both the political situation and the fact of Philip's marriage. In respect of the second of these concerns, we might contrast the achievement of another novelist who associated adultery in real life with adultery in grand opera— Flaubert in *Madame Bovary*—because of the vivid pathos of the betrayed spouse there, who is so treated as to become a substantial moral presence. Brink occasionally gestures towards giving Greta Malan her due, but finally makes her rage unsympathetically and unfairly and thus conform to the romantic convention of the cheated partner more sinning than sinned against. And this moral and aesthetic lapse in the

book's representations seems connected with the priority being given to the political end of the plot. Philip was in Paris in 1968, involved in thrilling demonstrations and a thrilling love with a non-white girl called Claire—but when it was over he chickened out, ditched Claire, forfeited his authenticity and returned to South Africa. Now he has his chance to expunge his liberal guilt, espouse radical action, and participate in the 'total exposure' of love by ecstatically holding hands with Melissa in the anti-apartheid demonstrations on the campus. 'In the simplicity of this singing all separateness is transcended.' And then:

> It is as if the events of the morning have torn open new depths inside them which must be plummeted immediately, urgently, passionately, triumphantly. Her orgasm is so violent that in a sudden rush of fear he wonders whether she's lost consciousness; he has to check that her heart has not stopped beating . . .This is what it was like in Paris, he thinks . . .When at last she gets up it is to kneel beside the record-player on the floor where she puts on a record, skipping a few cuts to find the groove she wants. Nana Mouskouri.

Brink is vitiatingly conscious that many of his lines track too worn a groove, but banks on the protection of 'Notes towards . . .', on disarming criticism by pre-emptive apology. But in the words of John Wayne, 'Sorry doesn't get it done.' Thus he writes, '(This really has the makings of a Mills & Boon)'—but lets it stand. He inserts a footnote in a scene between Philip and his rival for Melissa: 'It is difficult to render simultaneity in literature. If this were a film I would have used the dialogue as offscreen voices speaking over a collage of Melissa images as recalled by both men.' We may be grateful it is *not* a film. And there is another footnote: 'This scene, even more than some of the others, will require drastic revision if it is to be incorporated in a novel. The tit-for-tat confessions are too glib.' *States of Emergency* not only did but still does 'require drastic revision'. The 'novel' never emerges in any proper sense; it just comes out.

J. M. Coetzee (essay date Fall 1990)

SOURCE: "André Brink and the Censor," in *Research in African Literatures*, Vol. 21, No. 2, Fall 1990, pp. 59-74.

[*In the following essay, South African novelist Coetzee examines the role of the writer in a totalitarian state and the relationship between the state and the censored writer as expressed in Brink's essays. Coetzee points to Brink's view that "a state whose nature is repressive depends for its existence on something to repress."*]

The 1960s and 1970s saw the mounting and deployment of a comprehensive censorship apparatus in South Africa. In the forefront of opposition to this apparatus was the novelist André P. Brink. While he cannot be said to have stood alone, his position was in two senses exemplary: he exemplified the dissident Afrikaans intellectual, writing in a language spoken in only one country and therefore particularly vulnerable; and he took a stand that was consistent, principled and uncompromising in an exemplary way.

Since 1980 the grip of the official censors on "literature" has relaxed. Why this should have come about I prefer not to speculate on, since one purpose of this essay is to ask that question from Brink's point of view. It is undeniable, however, (a) that the authorities' attention has shifted away from books to newspapers and the electronic media, and (b) that under the state of emergency the police have taken over a proportion of the censors' work.

This essay falls into two halves. In the first half I discuss Brink's writings on censorship in what he calls the *strydperk,* the phase of more or less naked confrontation between dissident writers and censors. In the second I discuss Brink's position in the 1980s. I leave aside Brink's novels- –which have repeatedly been the object of the censors' attentions— confining myself to his two collections of essays.

1. Writer and state

When Brink reflects on the relationship between the writer and the state, it is not only the South African state he has in mind, and not even only the authoritarian state. In his writings of the 1970s he is clearly making an effort to align himself as a dissident writer with dissident writers elsewhere, particularly in Eastern Europe, and to see censorship, and in general the drive toward the control of dissidence, as inherent in the nature of state power. Nevertheless, so paradigmatic is the behavior of the South African state of the behavior of all authoritarian states in regard to censorship, in Brink's view, that we lose little by taking it that Brink is reflecting specifically on the writer vis-à-vis the South African state.

In an essay dating from 1970, Brink quotes from the poet N.P. van Wyk Louw a parable on the power of writing. On the eve of his execution, a condemned writer is visited in jail by the head of state. The tyrant promises him a reprieve if he will recant. Being certain that he will "win in the end," the writer refuses. How can he be so sure he will win, the tyrant asks? The writer gives two reasons: first, that the executioner will see him die; second, that the tyrant has found it necessary to visit him (MGT 56). [*Throughout Coetzee's essay, Brink's writings on censorship, collected in two volumes titled* **Mapmakers** *and* **Literatuur in die strydperk** *are abbreviated as follows:* from **Mapmakers** AS "After

Soweto" (1976); CL "Censorship and Literature"(1982); IN "Introduction" (1983); IR "Imagining the Real" (1980); IW "The Intellectual and his World" (1980); MGT "Mahatma Gandhi Today" (1970); MM "Mapmakers" (1978); WaS "Writing against Silence" (1980); WSS "The Writer in a State of Seige" (1979); from **Literatuur in die strydperk** AeO "Afrikaans en oorlewing" ("Afrikaans and Survival") (1982); BS "Die bedreighde skrywer" ("The threatened writer") (1979); DD "Denker en daa in Suid-Afrika" ("Thinker and action in South Africa") (1976); HH "Heerser en humanis 1984" ("Ruler and humanist 1984") (1984); KA "Die kuns is aanstootlik" ("Art is offensive") (1974); SLS "Skrywer en literatuur in die strydperk" ("Writer and literature in the time of struggle") (1976); STL "Samisjdat, tamisjdat, lamisjdat" ("Samisjdat, tamisjdat, lamisjdat") (1978); VW "Voorwoord" ("Foreword") (1985).]

Most of the elements of Brink's early model of the relation between writer and state are to be found in this parable. The relation is one of antagonism. The power of the writer is recognized and feared by the state: despite the apparent powerlessness of the writer, writer and state know that, in the deepest sense, they are on an equal footing. The ostensible powerlessness of the writer gives him a paradoxical potential for heroism in the face of persecution. And the writer triumphs in the end because his version of the truth will outlast his antagonist's. "Let this be a warning to *our* authorities," Brink writes in 1974 (in an essay whose thesis it is that "all great art is offensive"): "in the struggle between authority and artist it is always the artist, in the end, who wins. Because his voice continues to speak long after the members of the relevant government . . .have been laid to rest" (KA 64, 67).

In this model, the antagonism between writer and state is simple and undialectical. The writer tells his truth and the state stifles him; or the state puts forward its seductions to which, as in the Van Wyk Louw parable, the writer replies with his heroic, truth-affirming No. The exemplary figure here is Antigone, "the first rebel of Western tradition." "Antigone's key word is: NO! But it is a paradoxical thing, for she really means: YES!" (MGT 62).

Brink's later model of the relationship between writer and state is more complex and more dialectical. He returns to the figure of Antigone. Like Antigone, the writer affirms the higher authority of his own conscience. In the nature of things, this will give rise to a "relation of tension" (*spanningsverhouding*) with the state. In principle this situation remains "healthy," for "reasonable opposition by state and nation" compels the writer to examine his own conscience and refine his insight. However, interference from outside can reach a point where it affects the writer's ability to work. This is a point of crisis and also of paradox. The state appears to have the upper hand. But in fact, in trying to stifle the writer, the state endangers itself. (I will discuss later what Brink sees as the danger to the state in censorship).

How should the writer act, Brink asks, when this point of crisis is reached? He rejects the option of

> a direct answer on the same level . . . on which the authorities or the people (*volk*) issue their threats and ultimatums. The writer simply does not function, as writer, within the same dimension. . . . He should not even try to think in terms of immediate, practical consequences. A book cannot begin to fight against a sword on a battlefield. If the book does indeed in the end win, it is precisely because he refuses to take up the same weapons as his opponent. . . . The writer's answer lies in the first place in the quality of his work. He must not allow anything to affect this. . . . Even anger must be distilled to something lasting. (STL 115-117)

Thus in the later model the writer and the state, although necessarily claiming different mandates and starting from different positions, are not, in the wider view, doomed to be antagonists: there is a stage of "healthy" reciprocal criticism, a stage that benefits society in general, before a point is reached at which they become enemies and the earlier, simpler model is in effect re-entered. When Brink addresses this latter stage of conflict, his focus is now not on the existential duty of the writer but on the strategy of battle. The possibility he warns against is not of the victory of the state (for the word always triumphs) but of the self-defeat of the writer, who, perhaps out of (justified) anger, may betray his own calling.

The later model is elaborated more fully in an essay entitled "Censorship and Literature" (1982). Outlining an ideal dynamic between the writer who threatens the anarchy of "total freedom" and the state whose system of justice holds the potential for overriding all private interests, Brink postulates "an intricate system of checks and balances" to allow their co-existence.

What happens all too often in reality, however, says Brink, is that power seeks blindly to maintain itself, forcing the writer of conscience to react; or else that the writer threatens, or is felt to threaten, the interests of the state, which then reacts against him. "This is when taboo, which fulfils a creative and possibly indispensable function in primitive society, expresses itself in the form of censorship: what used to be constructive and wholesome now becomes destructive and a symptom of sickness."

The writer is in fact an organ developed by society to respond to its need for meaning. "His domain is that of mean-

ing, not of healing. But unless he performs his function and performs it well, and unless his diagnosis is heeded, healing will not be possible." A healthy society can face the writer's diagnosis, "but if it is sick it may dread the vision of itself offered by [the writer]. In this case a mortal sickness would remain undiagnosed." "The creative mind . . . guarantees growth and development and health in a community," whereas censorship "represents the protective mechanisms and processes of the social organism in a state of excessive, cancerous development" (CL 233-236, 248).

The picture of a creative state of tension as opposed to a destructive breakdown of tension into repression is extended in a 1984 essay:

> The totalitarian order depends for its very existence on a precarious equilibrium. Without the heretic, the rebel, the writer, the state crumbles [*gaan tot niet*]: but by tolerating him, the ruler equally well seals his fate. At least by implication, [in George Orwell's *1984*] Big Brother's mighty system disappears because he wanted to eradicate the dissident—but could not do without him. (HH 165)

That is to say, a state whose nature is repressive depends for its existence on something to repress (the shadow of Hegel's master-slave relationship falls over the state here).

Thus, whereas the metaphor underlying Brink's simpler model is one of battle, the metaphor underlying the second is one of disease. In this metaphor, a state can be imagined as a body which has developed a special organ whose function is diagnostic of the health of the whole. When the body is in reasonable health, it tolerates and benefits from the functioning of this organ. But in a condition of hypertrophic repression it will reject those of its own organs that cause it most disease, trying to kill the messenger who brings the bad tidings. Once this is done, however, the collapse of the state from unchecked disease is a foregone conclusion.

2. The contest

Thus far I have represented Brink's writings on censorship as an analytical account in which he as analyst occupies a position neutral between the contending parties. But in fact his position is more complex. As critic-essayist, therefore in some sense judge, he is outside the fray; as writer making a polemical intervention he is one of the parties to the fray. In occupying positions both of judicious distance and of commitment, he mirrors the doubled identity of the censor who responds to the writer's word both as offended citizen and as judge.

What is the polemical content of Brink's respective models?

The earlier model includes the following elements:

(i) The couples through whom Brink dramatizes the opposition between writer and state—condemned prisoner and tyrant, Antigone and Creon, Winston Smith and Big Brother—represent, on the one side, overwhelming power and deadly intent, on the other, heroic steadfastness despite powerlessness and isolation ("the artist prepared to risk everything [for] his little bit of truth" [KA 67]).

(ii) The contest itself is unequal and in fact anomalous in nature. "A book cannot enter the field of battle against a sword." "The writer simply does not function, as writer, within the same dimension [as the state]" (STL 116).

(iii) The contest is morally clearcut. The state upholds "the great Conspiracy of the Lie" (KA 67). But there will be no compromise with the lie (SLS 93). "Unless [the authorities] are prepared to change, . . .we shall go all the way . . .in making sure that their lies are exposed, . . .that truth will prevail" (WSS 194). For, like Antigone, the writer "affirm[s] a higher Order" (MGT 62).

(iv) The stakes are high. "Where the writer is allowed only the freedom to pronounce the letters from A to M, his word immediately acquires a peculiar weight if he risks not only his comfort but his personal security in choosing to say N, or V, or Z. Because of the risk involved, his word acquires a new resonance: it ceases, in fact, to be 'merely' a word and enters the world as an act in its own right" (MM 164-5).

(v) Victory for the writer is inevitable. This is the paradoxical other side of the anomalousness of the contest. "I will win in the end," says the prisoner to Van Wyk Louw's tyrant.

(vi) Confrontation is inescapable. This is so not only because the writer has to follow his conscience but because, being coupled to him in a master-slave relationship, the state cannot permit him to ignore it.

(vii) Finally, in this model the writer is never represented as taking the first confrontational step: he enters the fray always in *response* to outrages of the state, or else to efforts by the state to silence him.

In the case of the second model, the metaphoric opposition is between sickness and health. A society may become sick or cancerous, even mortally sick. Such sickness is, in its effects, no different from madness or "fatal folly" (WSS 194). The writer, in contrast, insofar as he is the diagnostic organ, is untouched by sickness and therefore stands on the side of health.

Why should the state be unable to coexist with its own best agencies? Here Brink quotes Orwell again: "The object of power is power" (HH 158). He proceeds: "Power . . .is narcissist by nature, striving constantly to perpetuate itself through cloning, approaching more and more a state of utter homogeneity by casting out whatever seems foreign or deviant" (WSS 173). Pointing to the closed character of language in Stalin's Russia, in which there is no distance between naming and judging, Brink defines one task of the writer as destroying simplistic polarities and opening up complexities (IW 202-3). Such an act angers, in particular, the modern heirs of rationalism "because they fear the harm it can do to their devastatingly logical systems and tyrannies" (IR 217). By its nature the state therefore gravitates toward homogeneity and impresses conformity on its citizens; the presence of a diagnostic organ within the body of the state contradicts its nature.

As social/historical analysis, this model of the relationship of writer and state is clearly full of gaps and loopholes. For instance, if the nature of power is to enforce homogeneity, and if society is in some sense a body generating its own organs, how does the critical intellectual ever emerge? How does it come about that the writer always stands on the side of health?

But it is not my purpose to interrogate Brink's Romantic organism in this way. Rather, I read his two models as polemical constructs, stages in the battle that they purport to analyze. For there is a very mundane sense in which the writer does indeed, as Brink says, always get the last word: the blow of the censor in banning the book can always be followed by the counter-blow of the writer holding up the censor to the public's gaze, usually to ridicule, never to admire. It may or may not be true that truth always triumphs; in South Africa, at least, it is almost always the case that the writer has the last word.

3. The writer's conscience

Brink refers repeatedly to Antigone as an emblem of what the writer should be. She is the citizen who rebels against the state in the name of "the truth," in the name of "a higher Order." She is prescribed to only by her own conscience (MGT 62; DD 98; STL 115-117).

But how does truth come to the writer? Brink describes the process as follows:

> Deep inside him [the writer] apprehends a welter
> and a whorl of truth, a great confounding darkness
> which he shapes into a word; surrounding him is
> the light of freedom into which his word is sent like
> a dove from the ark. In this way, through the act of

writing, truth and liberty communicate. (MM 163-4)

The writer is, then, if not the God of *Genesis* himself, at least the bearer of the divine *logos* (to be fair to Brink, he allows that the scientist and the philosopher have comparable access to the truth). To ignore his moments of illumination, to conceal the truth, is therefore a betrayal of the divine within him. The truth that he bears *demands* to be told: "When the conspiracy of lies surrounding me demands of me to silence the one word of truth given to me, *that word becomes the one word I wish to utter above all others*" (MM 165).

Is the writer always adequate as a vehicle for the truth entrusted to him? This is not a question that Brink dwells on. But he hints at two ways in which the writer can betray his mission. First, by subordinating his own aesthetic standards to the lust for battle: "Even anger must be distilled to something lasting" (STL 117). Second, by succumbing to the lure of uttering the forbidden simply because it is forbidden.

The prophetic role of the writer belongs to what I have called Brink's first model. In the second model, the connection between the writer and the truth is less absolute:

> Once the exploration has been undertaken, once the statement has been encoded in writing, it has to be published, "made public," in order to test its relevance within the context of communal life . . .[Truth] *has* to be private and individual to start with; but to become valid it must transcend the life of the individual. (WaS 210)

Truth is thus no longer simply a matter between the writer and his source of inspiration: it has to enter into a social dialectic to be tested for its social validity; and a precondition for such a test is the freedom of the writer to publish it. In the first model, the censor blocks the truth from reaching the people; in the second he merely blocks the possibility of truth.

4. The triumph of the truth

But why does the state abhor the truth? Brink, writing with South Africa and comparably tyrannous states in mind, does not have to answer the question in its general form. Founded on the lie, it is simply in the nature of tyranny to hate the truth:

> In the truth embedded in the writer's word lies that ineffable power feared so much by tyrants and tyrannies and other agents of death that they are prepared to stake everything they have against it. For they know only too well that no strategy or system can ever, finally, resist the word of truth. (WSS 195)

The tyrannic state hates the artist's truth and tries to obliterate it. Nevertheless, one way or another, "truth will out." As an instance of this dictum Brink recalls Osip Mandelstam, martyr to the truth, whose words had to be held in memory for thirty years by his wife before they could be published (MM 167). So let the South African authorities be warned. "It is always the artist, in the end, who wins. Because his voice continues to speak long after the members of the relevant government . . .have been laid to rest." The artist's work is lasting, the chatter (*gepeuter*) of the politician petty and transitory (SLS 93).

5. Madness and lies

"*Whom the gods wish to destroy . . . :* this must have been a spontaneous reflection in the minds of many as they saw the eruption of violence in Soweto in June, 1976," wrote Brink in 1976 (AS 128). *Mad* is a word Brink often applies to South African society; *sick* is another. The writer stands on the side of sanity and health, the state on the side of sickness and madness. We have already seen that the writer's role becomes that of diagnostician of society's sickness/madness. In the essays, the major diagnostic task is not undertaken. Instead, a catalogue of quick diagnoses passes before our eyes which might as well be terms of abuse. South Africa is "a demented world . . .[a] swamp of violence and hysteria" (AS 152) with "an insane structure" (IW 201), beset by "a sickness of the mind . . . a psychosis of fear" (WaS 205), "a psychosis about a 'state of emergency'" (SLS 91), a nation of "Gadarene swine" (AeO 150). The Afrikaner is "a political and cultural schizophrenic" (DD 95). The Publications Control Board itself is "[a] social organism in a state of excessive cancerous development," "the nucleus of a cancerous cell which divides and subdivides and multiplies rapidly to endanger the whole body" (CL 236, 249).

About accusations of madness in general I will note only one feature: that they aim to infirm the antagonist's response in advance by situating it outside the rational. To the extent that they close off the antagonist's entry into discourse, they predict and indeed invite his violence, which then in turn becomes a confirmation of their diagnostic truth.

Much the same can be said about accusations of lying when lying is presented as in the nature of the antagonist, and indeed in the nature of power ("We live in an age of the Lie": SLS 90). A lie is treated not as a dialectical strategy but as a manifestation of an evil essence. Again the antagonist's response is infirmed in advance as just another lie. "[For the Government and its agents and agencies] the lie has become established as the norm: truth is the real obscenity" (CL 247).

6. The 1980s

The polemical battle waged by Brink against the South African censors began to lose its urgency as the 1980s progressed, largely because of a relaxation of the censorship of works of literature. Brink's first comments on the thaw were cautious: the "puff-adder may only be *playing* dead." In his new situation he encountered the beginnings of an unfamiliar moral dilemma. For on the one hand it was clear that the State was using the new freedom it allowed to writers as window-dressing. ("Those of us who are today allowed more freedom in publishing than before are *indeed* being used.") "But is that a reason to fall silent, and thereby play even more neatly into the hands of the powers-that-be?" (CL 256). The game seemed to be moving into a new and subtler phase, whose rules Brink was not as yet sure he knew.

Could writers indeed be said to have won the first and more naked phase of the struggle, Brink ruminates? In many senses, undoubtedly so. But it might also be that the authorities had decided that naked battle was counterproductive, or that the security organs had become preoccupied with more pressing matters. It might even be that the government had decided that it had simply overestimated the importance of writers. This is the sobering thought with which concludes the 1985 preface to Brink's collection of essays on the *strydperk,* the period of struggle (FW 11-12).

7. The South African censor

How did the censors themselves see the situation? In 1980 a new chief censor (chairman of the Publications Appeal Board) was appointed: J.C.W. van Rooyen, Professor of Criminal Law at the University of Pretoria. Van Rooyen has written two books about the workings of the South African system. Reading Van Rooyen attentively, one can recover a submerged history of clashes of personality and compromises over standards within the corridors of the censorship bureaucracy. The watershed was clearly the banning of Etienne Leroux's novel *Magersfontein, O Magersfontein*! in 1978. In this *cause célèbre,* the Publications Appeal Board, under its then chairman Judge H.J. Snyman, adopted a highly confrontational posture toward those Afrikaans intellectuals who testified on behalf of the book:

> The point at issue is whether the position of the literary scholars [*letterkundiges*] regarding unsavoury language (however revolting [*vieslik*]) can really be justified.

> The law protects the morals of the entire public [*gemeenskap*]. The Appeal Board wishes to state expressly that, according to its assessment of the community view [*gemeenskapsopvatting*] of public morals, this approach of the literary scholars is at odds with the Publications Act . . .

> The general opinion of the literary scholars is that

the goal of the book is to satirize. . .our own age against the background of an heroic past.

> Nevertheless, the central question remains whether the public . . . is prepared to tolerate the manner in which this goal is attained. . . .

The Board concluded:

> The writer built into [his] novel excessive filthy language, excessive idle use of the Lord's name, vulgar references to excretion, masturbation, [etc.]. . .This novel is highly regarded by literary scholars. The broad public, however, as personified by the average man, regards the use [of such language] as an infringement of the dignity of the individual and an invasion of his respect for sexual privacy. (Van Rooyen, *Publikasiebeheer in Suid-Afrika,* 14-18)

In a double sense of the term, we see the Board here *deciding* for the public: both deciding in favor of the public seen as the antagonist of the intellectuals, and deciding on behalf of that public. The Board under Snyman acted as both champion of the public (a public whose feelings it assessed according to its own methods and embodied in its fiction "the average man") and arbiter between the public and the intellectuals in an aggressively emotional confrontation which it did as much as any other party to set up and stage-manage.

The banning of Leroux's novel, and the clear proof it gave that the censors were prepared to bow to ultra-conservative pressure, threatened to alienate even middle-of-the-road Afrikaans academics and intellectuals. One can cautiously surmise that this prospect was a factor in the appointment of Professor van Rooyen on the retirement of Judge Snyman in 1980. Van Rooyen's stated vision of the Publications Appeal Board (hereafter the PAB) is of a committee of technocrats in the field of morality and inter-group relations, their own personalities submerged in their work. Their attitude should be "not that of a persecutor [sic] but that of an arbiter who weighs all the relevant interests against each other." Even in the sensitive area of state security, their function "is not to restore order or to defend the country, but to strike a balance between the opposing interests" (*Censorship in South Africa,* 16, 51, 106).

Generally speaking, the Van Rooyen regime has been more rational, less confrontational than Snyman's. Under Snyman, the censor's touchstone had been the response of what was called "the reasonable reader," a concept with a clear ideological content. To Van Rooyen the touchstone became "the likely reader," a concept meant to be probabilistic, value-free.

Nevertheless, in persisting to claim the role of arbiter, Van Rooyen has kept alive the notion that there is a contest to arbitrate—or, in his own terms, that the interests of writers and the interests of the public are at odds. He is very clear about the matter: the amendment to the Publications Act that created advisory committees of experts gave recognition, he writes, to the "minority rights of literature, art and language." "I have described these as 'minority rights' since there is little doubt that, were a referendum to be held as to the value which should be given to these interests, majority opinion would deny them recognition" (*Censorship in South Africa,* 9).

Philosophically, Van Rooyen's position is much like that of Patrick Devlin, namely that to the extent that a shared morality is a cement that binds society together, society is within its rights to protect its moral system from subversion by whatever means are necessary.

Van Rooyen discreetly acknowledges that the censors played a partisan role in South African intellectual life in the 1960s and 1970s. "Tension between authors and a large section of the public reached a crisis point between 1960 and 1978," he writes. He implicitly blames this tension on the conservatism of South African public life, even on a conservative reaction. "In 1980, however, matters changed. The PAB, under the chairmanship of the acting chairman [i.e., Van Rooyen himself]," passed *Magersfontein.* A new policy allowing "strong protest" was adopted "based on the philosophy that it is often in the interests of state security to permit the expression of pent-up feelings and grievances" (*Censorship in South Africa,* 14-16). In practice this has meant that publications "with a sophisticated likely readership" have been passed "in spite of. . .material expressing hatred against the authorities. Such publications were regarded as useful safety-valves for pent-up feelings in a milieu where they would be understood not as a call to political violence but as a literary experience" (*Censorship in South Africa,* 115).

It was the possibility that the stringency of the censorship had been relaxed because the writer had been reassessed and found to pose no threat to the existing order after all, that writing had been recognized as nothing but a "useful safety-valve," that gave Brink cause to reflect, I believe, in his 1985 preface. Under the earlier dispensation he and numerous of his fellows had been diagnosed and treated as a subversive force, as a cancer in the social body. Under the new dispensation they were being dismissed as harmless dabblers. In the earlier case he had responded to the violence of the censor with an equivalent polemical violence. What would be the right response to this new and cunning insult? (If it seems paranoid to interpret Van Rooyen's remark as an insult, I should point out that paranoia is contagious.)

8. The dynamic of censorship

Brink's predicament is not unique. The presence of the censor in the field of writing creates a dynamic from which it takes more than a simple act of will to escape. What is this dynamic? An historical retrospect will help us to define it.

The sixteenth century in Europe, ushered in with the first preventive (pre-publication) censorship (instituted by Pope Alexander VI in 1501) is the great age of censorship. Not only were measures of extraordinary severity carried out against authors and printers: political censorship became, in the words of Annabel Patterson, "the central problem of consciousness and communication" among intellectuals. The reason is not far to seek. In the process of creating a market for its products the printing press called into being for the first time what we may properly call a *public,* however dispersed, in a way that was beyond the capacities of the early modern state to achieve. Propagating ideas through the press to this public—"his" public—the man of letters in effect converted mere ideas into what Elizabeth Eisenstein calls "*idées forces,*" ideas as social forces. Thus printing awoke in authority, or at least intensified dramatically, a paranoia characteristic of the modern state.

In the activity of disseminating writing, it is not self-evident that the originator of the text, the writer, should be regarded as the primary producer and the printer/publisher as a mere medium. The printer's colophon, after all, antedates the writer's signature on the book. When the authorities take action against books, it is their publishers who suffer the greatest material loss; printers rather than authors were the target of the great repressions of the sixteenth century. Nevertheless, printers and publishers have never put themselves forward as rivals to the authority of the state. That, significantly, is a role they have allowed their authors to play.

Why should the state, by conceiving the author as a rival for authority, grant him equivalence of status with itself? What is it in the author that the state is unable to ignore? It is, I suggest, a certain power exercised in the very medium of the law—words—to unlock and direct the desire of what the author calls a public and the state calls the people. Metonymically, through books signed with his name and adorned with his picture, he enters heart(h) and home, finding his way there not by force but by courtship. He has an art of commanding the heart of the public; he knows the secret of its desire. Designed for private and separate consumption, print builds upon a collusion of two intimacies: in hundreds or thousands of individual private acts, the author's intimate presence is projected into the reader's privacy.

What the state has envied and been puzzled by and not known how to imitate is the author's ability to woo a public for himself—a public whose desire it soon becomes to follow where he will take it. With apparently effortless ease authorship spreads its influence, its word, a word which is welcomed because it finds, unlocks and answers its readers' desire. When the state fantasizes about the spread of the rival word, it thinks of the spread of disease: it imagines the spread of the rival word or influence (It. *influenza*) as a plague on the land. If anything, it is of course the desire that welcomes infection that is self-destructive (i.e., irrational, mad), not the infection itself. But contagiousness is of the essence of the metonymic thinking of paranoia; madness as well as contagion itself—sickness—easily attach themselves to the word that answers to the public's desire.

Engrossed in the question of how the author commands the desire of the public, the censor directs his attention more and more exclusively upon those moments in the text where desire and the arousal of desire find representation. The object of his quest becomes desire itself, for whose textual manifestations he uses, in a gesture of denial, the blanket term "the undesirable." The censor desires the undesirable.

The author projects his works, marked as his by his signature and sometimes his picture, into the world in multiplied form. In the power given to him by printing he seems to overcome spatial and temporal boundaries. He sees himself "known all over the world," "outlasting death"; that is to say, he foresees fame and immortality.

Why is it, then, that this seemingly all-powerful author cannot ignore the state? What is there in authority that is *his* desire and envy?

In the self-sufficiency of authority that goes by the name *majesty,* the author sees the ultimate embodiment of *sway.* Majesty provides the model of a desire desiring only itself. The narcissism of majesty is a source of universal envy: the closer one approaches it, the stronger its attraction becomes. As desire at last independent of any object of desire, majesty performs the contradictory motion of commanding envy (a desire to be like it) while forbidding imitation under pain of death.

The type of all acts of censorship is the ban on lèse-majesté. Lèse-majesté, like blasphemy, is a symbolic (verbal) sacrilege, a touching of the sacred object, an infringement of ultimate authority. Since the abolition of kings the quintessentially forbidden verbal act has been contempt of court, infringement of the authority, the authorship of the law. When the court of law distances itself from authority and claims to stand outside the contestation of authority, the ban on contempt of court assumes the status of a meta-rule: a ban on contestation of its arbitration between rival authorities.

9. Paranoia

"No person shall insult, disparage or belittle any member of

the Publications Appeal Board, or do anything in relation to the Publications Appeal Board which if done in relation to a court would constitute contempt of court," writes Van Rooyen, quoting the statute that empowers him (*Censorship in South Africa,* 147). The entire South African censorship system is abstracted from interrogation of its authority and from the dynamic of blame. It is elided from rivalrous discourse in advance by means of the meta-rule of contempt: certain forms of blame, certain questionings of authority, are ruled inadmissible under penal sanction and form no part of the record. Even the present discourse, it is important to realize, in theory falls under this extraordinary ban. The central argument of Van Rooyen's 1987 book—that the PAB occupies a position of arbiter between contending interests—can be seen as an effort of persuasion, paralleling the effort of coercion, to situate the South African censorship outside contempt, outside insult, outside the paranoid dynamic of blaming.

The censor wishes to become invisible, or, in other terms, to be absorbed into the writer's unconscious. The ideal system of control, from the censor's point of view, is one in which the rules need neither be spelled out nor enforced, in which a tacit code is tacitly followed. Both Patterson, writing about Tudor England, and David Balmuth, writing about Tsarist Russia, confirm this.

The ultimate and all-pervasive *symptom* of the censor's paranoia lies in the mechanisms of denial, projection and displacement through which the censor—Van Rooyen, for instance—rationalizes his role. Offence, taking-offence, never belongs to the censor in his own person, always to someone else: to the man in the street, to the man in the street taking offence on behalf of someone else, woman or child, and so forth. When Freud draws up his table of the transformations of inadmissable impulses that paranoiacs perform, the projective transformation is the first.

The suspicion that the censor acts on the basis of unadmitted impulse belongs to the mode of paranoia. It is answered by the suspicion of the censor, also paranoid, that the call for the end of censorship in the name of free speech is part of a plot to subvert the state. Polemics around censorship soon fall into a paranoid mode in which each argument presented by the other is seen as a mask for a hostile intention. Once paranoid discourse is entered upon and its dynamic takes over, the intentions of the other cannot but be hostile since they are constituted by one's own projections.

The entry into paranoia is in fact an entry into an *automatism.* There can be no clearer illustration of this than the fact that, of all the pathologies, paranoia has been the most amenable to artificial simulation.

10. Brink

When Brink denounces the Publications Control Board as the nucleus of a cancerous cell, he mirrors the censor who denounces certain "undesirable" writings as the productions of sick minds (Van Rooyen, *Publikasiebeheer in Suid-Afrika*, 17, 18, 81). Both are caught in an escalating dynamic of paranoid rage. Not only does Brink's language become as excessive as the censor's: his very notion of the lone writer confronting the colossus of the state is excessive. [Elizabeth L.] Eisenstein reminds us how little attention has been given by literary scholarship to the rise of men of letters as a distinctive and powerful social group—"the Republic of Letters"—with its own values and loyalties. In his stand against the South African censors, Brink carried with him a considerable bloc of the intelligentsia, and some powerful voices in the national press. In claiming that "without the heretic, the rebel, the writer, the state crumbles," Brink is indeed pointing to the phenomenon of reciprocal definition by warring twins, but pointing to it polemically, from only one side of the mirror: one might equally say that, once caught up in the dynamic of blaming, the writer cannot do without the state and its denunciatory organ, the censorship.

It is not as though Brink is unaware of the dynamic: when he says that "a book cannot begin to fight against a sword," that "the writer simply does not function, as writer, within the same dimension" as the state, that the writer cannot give the state "a direct answer on the same level. . .on which the authorities. . .issue their threats," he sees the threat of the dynamic quite clearly. But awareness does not prove to be enough to liberate him from it. His metaphors do not stretch far enough. If the writer has his own dimension within which to function, how does he find his way to it? Can we be sure this dimension is not mythical? The paradox implied in Brink's major metaphor of the writer as the *diagnostic organ* of the body politic lays bare the problem even more cruelly. Is diagnosis carried out from inside or outside the body? Are Brink's essays on the censor written from inside or outside a warring relationship with him? If from inside, how does he escape contagion by the censor's paranoia (how does the diagnostic organ escape corruption by the sick body)? If from outside, how did the organ find its way out of the body? The problem is ultimately not one of knowing what to say about the censor, but of finding a position from which to say it. I would be the last to claim that the present essay locates such a position and speaks from it; but I would also be the last to deny that such an ingenuous abdication of discursive authority would be just the right rhetorical note on which to end, and just the move for the suspicious eye of the censor to detect as a disingenuous lie.

Randolph Vigne (review date January 1992)

SOURCE: "The Argument for Terrible Deeds," in *San Francisco Review of Books*, Vol. 17, No. 1, January 1992, p. 5.

[*The following review by Randolph Vigne, a South African activist of the 1960s, praises* An Act of Terror *for its depiction of South Africa on the threshold of social change.*]

This is a story told against three very different backgrounds: first, the political and social turmoil of South Africa and the imperatives that bring a young man like Brink's Thomas to act as he does; secondly, the specific place of his people, the white Afrikaners, whose rule has led to the conflict that claims him; and thirdly, the nature of the morality that both forbids and condones the taking of life.

Brink is a brilliant storyteller and his moments of pity and terror more than recompense the reader for occasional longueurs containing more background than story, little humor or irony, and—particularly in the last 200 pages or so of historical flashback—a heavy dose of cheap magazine fiction. But since he is seen by many to be so much more than a teller of tales, it is against these three backgrounds that we must judge Brink. Is his book, as the publicity blurb intones, "a profound meditation on the ethics of violence", and, in the marmoreal phrase of the London *Times,* "deeply honoring the profession of literature"? His interpretation of the South African scene is memorable, at times penetrating. Thomas, a young white press photographer, exhibits his pictures abroad, exposing the brutal oppression his people have inflicted on the racial underdogs, one of whom recruits him to their freedom movement. He is ordered, with others, to kill the head of state. The president escapes the bomb blast but six bystanders are killed. In the subsequent manhunt Thomas's lover is shot down by police. He takes up with another woman, while his comrades try to organize his escape. Betrayed by both his brother and the father of his second love, Thomas makes it to the border, where he shoots the young woman to save her from the security police. Minus one hand, Thomas ends up with the freedom movement in exile, asking, "Have I sacrificed all this—my life, many lives, your life—in vain?" He finds no answer except "It has to be remembered."

> **Afrikaners, in Brink's vision, have inflicted on the Africans an oppression and denial of humanity which far exceeds their own experience of British imperialism.**
> **—Randolph Vigne**

Tellingly, Brink juxtaposes the die-hard older men of apartheid with the sleek young Afrikaner business and professional community, both almost equally hostile to revolutionaries like Thomas and his two women-friends—children respectively of a school-master, a judge, and a minister of religion (three most honored position in old Afrikanerdom). Picturing a society that has fought its way from the disaster of defeat in the Anglo-Boer War in 1902, through poor-whiteism in the early 1930s to forty years of hegemony, he hides no warts in the portrayal of this final phase, taking place on the eve of Nelson Mandela's release from jail and the start of negotiations towards a democratic future. Afrikaners, in Brink's vision, have inflicted on the Africans an oppression and denial of humanity which far exceeds their own experience of British imperialism.

The gradual awakening of Thomas to the horrors of racial supremacy is powerfully conveyed, as is his disillusion at the mythical in his people's history. He writes off its center-piece, the Great Trek—that much-vaunted movement north during the late 1830s—as a chaotic flight from responsibility and the hardships of the frontier. He seeks out friends, even father figures, among the Africans, seen by most Afrikaners as their natural enemies. He carries his loyalty to a new South Africa (which knows no racial divisions) to the point of committing an act of terror against Afrikaner rule, taking the lives of six human beings. Yet, in a sense, Thomas remains firmly embedded in his Afrikaner culture, unceasingly conscious of the thirteen generations of his Boer forebears and still clinging to some myths of the past. Those final 200 pages chronicling the family history reveal that Thomas—and, perhaps, Brink—is hypnotized by an Afrikaner past peopled by a cast of supermen and super-women unparalleled since the Norse sagas.

Perhaps one should allow Brink his Days of the Giants fantasy, and be thankful that like Thomas, he has turned his back upon exclusivist, wounded-pride nationalism, and his people's greed and cruelty toward their black countrymen. But this is not the stuff of "profound meditation," nor does it "honor the profession of literature," except as a work of commitment in a time of literary nihilism and postmodernist self-indulgence. Thomas's explanation of his willingness to kill does not go much beyond a clumsily expressed claim that the end justifies the means. The whole argument is within the terms of the South African situation, and at times it seems that the heroic character of Sipho, Thomas's mentor in the freedom movement, and Sipho's martyred wife Noni, is all the argument Thomas needs for his terrible deed.

As one persuaded of the same arguments thirty years ago, this reviewer can tell André Brink that a more powerful case is needed to justify such force against one's government in an underground movement. He should know few driven to such measures escape bouts of cynicism, even callousness, that sometimes put them on the level of the state functionaries pitted against them. Yet the ethical argument rages continually within and self-doubt plagues all but the psychopathic.

If Brink, in a novel that succeeds on so many levels, fails in his narration of an act of terror and its aftermath, the fault lies in his omission of that other remorseless companion of such an act—fear. The gnawing, constant sickness of fear will be readily recalled by all who have undergone a remotely similar experience. Thomas appears to escape that. Rich, complex and well-crafted, the novel holds the attention despite its length and wide canvas. To students of South African society it tells much about the Afrikaners as they prepare to step down from their long dominance. But it hardly satisfies the blurbwriter's claim of defining the ethics of violence in the greater context of the human condition.

Paul Preuss (review date 15 March 1992)

SOURCE: "Digging Their Own Graves," in *Book World—The Washington Post*, Vol. XXII, No.11, March 15, 1992, pp. 4, 11.

[*In the following review of* An Act of Terror, *Preuss relates the structure and conflicts of the novel and its theme of "aletheia," or "truth as remembrance."*]

André Brink's new novel is touted as a political thriller, and it is a very effective one, but that is just part of the story. *An Act of Terror* is a modern parable and a highly mythologized history of southern Africa's oldest white tribe, a story that concerns black Africans only indirectly; its real subject is the self destruction of the Afrikaners.

"Today it's no longer black against white, we don't want to repeat the mistakes of the previous generations. It's democrats against racists," one black character tells the white protagonist, Thomas Landman, who at the time of this conversation is not yet a terrorist, not even an activist; he's a student, an amateur photographer only sentimentally attached to his art. When his first exhibit is shut down by university authorities, when the police come around to suggest he find new subject matter, and when the people he photographs begin turning up dead, Thomas gets serious about his work and the message it carries to the world.

> *An Act of Terror* **is a modern parable and a highly mythologized history of southern Africa's oldest white tribe, a story that concerns black Africans only indirectly; its real subject is the self destruction of the Afrikaners.**
>
> **—Paul Preuss**

A thin, intense young Afrikaner woman, Nina Jordan—the daughter of an infamous hanging judge and therefore, perhaps, intemperate in her passion for justice—finally tips the scales of Thomas's reticence to do violence. "Observing the two of them stroll hand in hand through the Cape that late summer's day . . . no one could have imagined, not even in an outrageous fantasy, that next day they would take part in a bomb attack."

What follows this sentence, the novel's first, is intricate storytelling, much of it in flashback, much of it stream-of-consciousness from many points of view, with frequent jumps into the future—glimpses of impending fate, which in the author's skillful hands heighten suspense instead of detracting from it.

The terrorist cell to which Thomas and Nina belong is an exemplary mix of races and classes and religions. We come to know their Afrikaner enemies better, only a few of whom are less bestial than they appear, for example, the hairy, guitar-and gun-loving trucker who helps Thomas and his companion on their way through the northern desert. Most are irredeemably evil. Thomas's own brother is a coward and bully who works as a weapons engineer, and who betrays Thomas even before knowing what he has done.

Nina's father, the judge, weighs in with a whining deposition in his own behalf (numbered paragraphs and all): "In a modest way I see my own work as a form of art; and the death penalty is my signature." Which reads more like satire than realism.

Brink's portrait of murderous Special Branch Brigadier Kat Bester is a little more convincing. Bester's musings about his pursuit of the terrorists are one extended metaphor: "Got to know your fish. Got to know your bait. . .Same thing in this job. Set about this bomb story as if *it was a* fishing trip." This threatens to grow tedious, until in a stunning passage Brink gives us a peek at Bester's nightmares: "A day so quiet the sea was like a lake. Then all of a sudden the whale. . .Like something from the Old Testament, leviathan . . . a single flick of the tail and you've had it." One knows very well why those "smooth dark bodies, moving like submarines" terrify the brigadier.

If the white villains of this piece are so bad one has to persuade oneself to believe in them, the black characters are, with minor exceptions, without weakness or rancor. True, necklacing—the practice of placing tires around the body of a suspected informer or collaborator and then setting the tires on fire—is alluded to and disapproved of. But Buthulezi's Inkatha party and its collusion with the government are never mentioned.

As matters come to a head, Thomas reflects upon his violent deeds and their human cost. "Had I known then what I do now, would I have chosen a different course?" Either to deny his acts or to justify them would be false, he concluded. "Perhaps the whole reason for the chronicle I have been driven for so long to write . . . is this very need to record, to thwart forgetfulness; to grasp at that truth which is not so much the opposite of the lie as of forgetting. *A-letheia.*"

And so, after the thriller reaches its bloody, surprising climax, author Brink attaches a long "supplement" that is the chronicle Thomas had felt driven to write—a chronicle of 13 generations of Landmans, beginning with the Dutch stowaway who reached Cape Town in the 1660s.

The Landman family Bible is stained with the blood of Thomas's great-great-grandfather Petrus, who was saved as an infant when the Bible deflected a Zulu spear. But Landman hearts circulate more than Boer blood, and Landman minds have been occupied by more than Calvinism. "How many of them have gone into the shaping of myself," Thomas wonders, "Hollander, French Huguenot, English, a wandering Jew, black African, Khoikhoin." (Not to mention a half-black, half-Dutch convert to Islam.) The family history recapitulates many mythologies, those of Greek tragedies as well as those of the Old Testament and the Great Trek.

The most realistic 600-page thriller and the often fantastic 200-page Landman chronicles entwine the theme of *aletheia*, truth as remembrance, with a different and more sinister theme. "There is an expression in Afrikaans, 'to see your own hole,'" Thomas tells us. "It was first used in the Anglo-Boer War with reference to traitors who had been forced to dig their own graves before being shot."

Black and white, good and evil, most of Brink's characters will have seen their own holes by story's end. Suspenseful and exciting, Brink's story would be a bit easier to believe if it were not so negatively Manichean, so inversely Zarathustran. But nothing in the news from South Africa suggests Brink has distorted the Afrikaner dilemma, which is ultimately the dilemma of all South Africans.

Lillian Hilja Andon-Milligan (essay date Fall 1992)

SOURCE: "André Brink's South Africa: A Quality of Light," in *Critique*, Vol. 34, No. 1, Fall, 1992, pp. 19-32.

[*Drawing on ideas from Vincent Van Gogh and Milan Kundera in the following essay, Andon-Milligan explores the aesthetics of Brink's work in which she sees a convergence of love and art and an ongoing attempt to tell love stories that can never be completed.*]

Exile, for artists like Milan Kundera, includes the "unbearable lightness of being." For others, exile means the obsessive hallucinations of a "Hottentot Room" (Christopher Hope) or the fetid rubbish left behind after Doris Lessing's "Good Terrorists" have swept past. Some of André Brink's exiles anticipate another outbreak of the Black Plague, the same plague that swept away Francesco Petrarca's Laura and much of Europe (*The Wall of the Plague*). Unfortunately, plagues do not spare artists: Van Gogh's personal plague left him mad and suicidal; Brink's plague drives him to declare a "State of Emergency" in the province of art. I want to focus on his crisis and the problems it poses for a South African artist who risks everything for a love story, for his art.

Writing from a similar catastrophe in the world of letters, Boris Pasternak reminds us that poetry flourishes in the wilderness and is a "laughable business if it is devoid of sacrifice." Even after sacrifice and exile, Milan Kundera finds art a laughable business: "Man thinks, God laughs" (*The Art of the Novel* 158). Kundera, the artist, defers to the "wisdom of the novel" but brings himself up short; he forgets that "God laughs when he sees [him] thinking" (165). And the novel is, above all, man thinking.

If we trace the development of André Brink's art, we notice that, over the years, his quixotic search for story, form, hero, action, and even for a theory of the novel ends in a state of aesthetic emergency. Nothing holds still long enough for him to get it down on paper; beginnings become entangled with ends, and middles turn chaotic when invaded by stories in search of an author, by journalists and diarists peddling their wares, by Security Police, or by literary theorists in search of a textual *bundu* (bush or wilderness) in which to poach. In Brink's *States of Emergency* the surrogate author throws up his hands in despair and exclaims, "No, I don't think I shall be writing my book after all" (243). Somehow, the story, in fact, does gather itself together. Words become flesh once again. But more of that later. The novelist's creative autonomy is no laughing matter.

In **"Censorship and Literature"** André Brink laments, "Language is unique as a medium of artistic expression, differing radically from, say, the marble of the sculptor, the paint used by the painter or the sounds employed by the composer" (*Mapmakers* 231). The writer trades in common currency:

> All I have is a word. I am weary to the bone. But I have no choice. In the beginning was the word; it is still with us. The only remaining sign, perhaps, of our dignity. We must tell stories because it is the stuff we're made on. And our little life, dear God, is rounded with Thokozile's sleep. (*States* 239)

A writer's tools—the mortar, the bricks, the beams—serve

politicians, popes, and prostitutes. Everyone gets along, more or less, with words; very few with marble.

The novelist picks up a used, badly chipped "brickword" and goes to work. In *Dry White Season* Brink's surrogate journalist-author sits with all the "litter of another man's life spread over [his] desk" and muses, "Why should [Ben Du Toit] pick on me to write his story?" (10). The story teller rages: he is past fifty, "no longer immortal." Faced with an imperative to write, he protests, "Politics isn't my line" (13). The imperative remains and rewards are unlikely. During a touching visit, Melanie's father advises Ben, "Never aspire to save the whole world. Your own soul and one or two others are more than enough" (189).

> **If we trace the development of André Brink's art, we notice that, over the years, his quixotic search for story, form, hero, action, and even for a theory of the novel ends in a state of aesthetic emergency.**
> **—Lillian Hilja Andon-Milligan**

Brink has not set out to save the whole world. He will settle for saving his life as an artist, for saving one or two other South African artists. If he also helps save Cape Province or even South Africa, so much the better.

No other Afrikaner writer devotes more attention to the architectonics of his novels and to examining the borderlines between theory, politics, history, journalism, and art. But in South Africa he also has run a very special kind of personal risk, the danger of losing that spirit of freedom: "the openness, the open-endedness, the endlessness—the silence as you call it—of a country for which the future is still possible, a love not yet circumscribed, a story not yet written" (*States* 244).

Brink risks losing his voice. Censorship also threatens the artist's spiritual and moral autonomy, both so essential if a writer is to say things "about our human condition (as it reveals itself in our century) that no social or political thought could ever tell us" (Kundera 117). Under repressive circumstances, according to Kundera, the artist stops listening to his own moral convictions and to

> the wisdom of the novel. Every true novelist listens for that supra personal wisdom, which explains why great novels are always a little more intelligent than their authors. Novelists who are more intelligent than their books should go into another line of work. (158)

Brink has another line of work; he is a professor of Afrikaans Literature (at Rhodes University in Grahamstown and now at the University of Cape Town). But he also has a supra personal love—writing novels.

The wisdom that grows out of such love may not survive long under siege. We can only hope that recent events in South Africa presage greater autonomy for all South African novelists.

Because societies continue to exile and censor artists, Milan Kundera calls for

> (1) a new art of *radical divestment* (which can encompass the complexity of existence in the modern world without losing architectonic clarity); (2) a new art of *novelistic counterpoint* (which can blend philosophy, narrative, and dream into one music); (3) a new art of the *specifically novelistic essay* (which does not claim to bear an apodictic message but remains hypothetical, playful or ironic). (65)

André Brink's latest novel *States of Emergency* (1989) is an anxious, elliptical experiment with the creation of just such an art, with that wisdom superior to philosophy, literary theory, sociology, history, and politics.

Brink discards other theorists for Kundera's quintessentially "novel" approach to truth. By the time he writes *States of Emergency* he has responded to Milan Kundera's call for a new art. Perhaps he also hears echoes of God laughing. So far, I think he has laughed back—the reckless laughter of the artist gone as far south as possible to find that clarity of light. With present developments in South Africa, perhaps he will abandon even Kundera's formula and listen to his own supra personal voice.

Brink has not set out to save the whole world. He will settle for saving his life as an artist, for saving one or two other South African artists. If he also helps save Cape Province or even South Africa, so much the better.
—Lillian Hilja Andon-Milligan

Let us look more closely at the special wisdom of novels that flourish in wildernesses created by censorship or exile. André Brink's art bumps up against "Walls of the Plague," "Looks on Darkness," suffers through "Dry White Season" and deconstructs under "States of Emergency." Not a hopeful trend.

II

Before examining *The Wall of the Plague,* we take a detour through Vincent Van Gogh's Province. In Brink's novel Van Gogh's room at the Priory Saint Paul of Mausole and his landscapes painted from the asylum window figure almost as centrally as do the Black Plague and Petrarca's "Ascent of Mont Ventoux."

Van Gogh once said that disease is necessary for man to realize he is not made of wood. Perhaps the twin plagues of censorship and exile remind the writer that stories are not made of "romantic evasion" and "non-existent utopias" (*Mapmakers* 168). André Brink warns—in **"Languages and Culture"**—that "We live among the ruins of not one but two utopian visions of the world," Christianity and Marxism (225).

Only the artist creates radically new worlds. The beginning of true artistic vision, according to Van Gogh, requires that the artist go south, to Province, to Arles and finally (sadly) to Saint-Rémy. To the young Emile Bernard he writes (*Letters* 3:512, 514), "The South will charm you and make a great artist out of you. Gauguin himself owes his superiority to the South. I myself have now seen the stronger sunlight here for months." He advises his young friend Bernard, "In the South one's senses get keener, one's hand becomes more agile, one's eyes more alert, one's brain clearer." For Van Gogh such clarity leads to madness.

The obsessed Van Gogh looks out of the barred windows of the asylum in Saint-Rémy at the landscape and notices a "certain quality of loftiness and nobility which can be found" around Saint-Rémy (518). His south positively vibrates with colors that he has never seen before—colors and a quality of light that have him begging Theo for enormous supplies of white and yellow pigments. He reminds Theo that in the south he has painted his lightest canvases: *Green Wheat Fields* and *Champ de blé au faucheur* (185).

Surely those Province landscapes vibrate with color, with light. But Van Gogh seeks more than light; he seeks a quality of representation. To Theo he writes, "When the thing represented is, in point of character, absolutely in agreement and one with the manner of representing it, isn't it just that which gives a work of art its quality?" (179). Between bouts of madness Van Gogh continues to seek the quality of light that enables him to represent so appositely even after he leaves Saint-Rémy. He never again finds it.

It is impossible to say how much of his illness came from the search, the sun, the pigments, or a sudden catastrophe in art. In his last letter to Theo, which is found in the dead artist's pocket, Vincent alludes to a crisis:

The other painters, whatever they think, instinctively keep themselves at a distance from discussions about the actual trade. Well, the truth is, we can only make our pictures speak. But yet, my dear brother, there is this that I have always told you, . . . I shall always consider you to be something more than a simple dealer in Corots, that through my mediation you have had your part in the actual production of some canvases, which will retain their calm even in the *catastrophe*. For this is what we have got to, and this is all or at least the main thing that I can have to tell you at a moment of *comparative crisis*. At a moment when things are very strained between dealers in pictures of dead artists, and living artists. Well, my own work, I am *risking my life for it and my reason has half foundered because of it* . . . (298) [Emphasis added.]

The crisis reflected in the letter, reflects on the artist. Van Gogh shoots himself, the ultimate exile from that certain quality of light he could only find briefly in the south.

André Brink experiences similar risks at another moment of comparative crisis.

III

In one of the many journeys represented in André Brink's **The Wall of the Plague,** Andrea Malgas, a Cape-Coloured, and Brian, her Afrikaner lover, escape persecution and find themselves very far north in Provence. But Andrea's journey with Brian gets mixed up with "so many journeys travelled on a single trip" (13, 446). Andrea travels alone from Paris to Provence to find locations for a film about the Black Plague that her present lover Paul plans to produce. Andrea also relives an earlier journey that spring with Paul to the same haunts. However, she conducts a more important journey from Paris to South Africa in a series of meditations inspired by Mandla.

On one level Andrea's personal journey takes her from Brian to Paul to Mandla to South Africa. On another level Mandla (whose name means freedom) journeys from South Africa to Mont Ventoux and, after a glimpse of his beloved Africa, dies.

However, on still another level, **The Wall of the Plague** represents the journey of an artist in a moment of personal crisis. Vincent Van Gogh makes a cameo appearance in Andrea's quest.

On that earlier trip, Brian wants to visit Van Gogh's room in the asylum at Saint-Rémy. He asks a nun to show them Van Gogh's bedroom. She shows them a room; however, Brian has read Van Gogh's letters and the room she shows them is not the room of his visions. The nun insists that a room is a room; Brian refuses to see it that way. Only one provided that certain kind of light that illuminated Van Gogh's art.

The two lovers go back to try again. After scurrying up a ladder to the second floor, Andrea searches all the rooms upstairs until the view of fields, enclosures and mountains matches Van Gogh's description and paintings.

When she climbs down, Brian asks her if it was worth the trouble. She admits she is not sure. It is as though when the artist finished with the paintings, he was

> so thoroughly through with it that only second-hand thoughts remained for others. . . . There ought to be something so worth while in itself that it will always stay worth while . . . so that you needn't go on trying to satisfy yourself with inferior imitations all the time . . . Something you will never ever lose again . . . something so important that you're prepared to *risk your whole life for it* because your whole history, everything you've ever been or can hope to be, is caught up in it . . . something which suddenly makes you see very clearly what you're doing and why you are here. (358) [Emphasis added.]

Van Gogh felt the same way about his painting of the bedroom at Arles. According to his last letter, Van Gogh sacrificed his sanity and ultimately his life for that clarity, that light. Mandla risks his life to raise money for resistance. Andrea risks her life to return to South Africa. Even Paul risks his career to write the story of South Africa that we read as **The Wall of the Plague.**

Significantly, Andrea does not return to Van Gogh's room on her journey with Mandla. The artist took what light there was out of the landscape, distilled it, and put it in his painting. Nothing but darkness remains. Like Andrea who names herself Nanna, a writer finds words, names for that darkness.

On the top of Mont Ventoux—not an inauspicious spot for visionary moments of Petrarchan kind—Andrea looks out to the thin line of the horizon that could be Africa. She explains (303), "I wanted to find out how far I could really see. For the first time in God knows how many years I was prepared to look at what I'd tried to forget for so long"—Africa.

Mandla dies. Andrea writes a letter to Paul who waits to hear whether she will marry him. She asks, "Do you understand, do you really understand, *why* I can see so clearly today? *Why* I've recognized this emptiness and this light the moment it occurred?" (400). She finds no "miracle" in Van Gogh's room (357). Instead, from Mont Ventoux, Andrea

Malgas, sea bird that she is, follows the light back to South Africa.

Petrarca found a special lightness of mind on Mont Ventoux; Vincent Van Gogh found the essence of his art in the light of Provence; Andrea sees a light shining out of Africa; Milan Kundera found that quality of light reflected in the works of Kafka, Boch, and Tolstoy and called it the "wisdom of the novel" (158). Vaclav Havel saw such a light, which he called "responsibility," while watching a flustered weatherwoman on television during a sudden sound failure (*Letters to Olga* 321 +). André Brink also returned to the south but he looks on darkness.

IV

In the novel *Looking on Darkness* André Brink uses eleven of Shakespeare's sonnets to provide the scaffolding on which Joseph Malan is hung. The formal structure of this novel (which deserves a study of its own) remains part of its greatness and presages the structural elegance of his later novels.

From prison Joseph Malan, an actor turned activist, writes his tragic story of furtive love and political persecution. He has been sentenced to death—confiscated, one might say, like the copy of *Michelangelo* impounded by customs—on his return from exile.

As surrogate, doomed author he feels impelled to clear up a few issues, shed some "'light on the subject'" in the manner of meditations by St. John of the Cross. He hopes to fight his way "through a web of syntactic certainties toward a final, possible glimpse of truth" (*Looking on Darkness* 8). He tells his story to "empty himself so that he can return to himself" (8).

In every sense of the word, writing is an emptying of the self in a much more profound way than painting or music. The self is words. Words pour out and dwell among us, are us, are all that really define both our certainties and our uncertainties, our moments of comparative crisis, out light and our darkness.

Art requires forced labor. John writes furiously in his cell but tears it all up and flushes his words down the toilet as fast as he can write them. The real story, its point of origin, lies safely embedded in Shakespeare's sonnets, which Joseph writes from memory while he really writes his story—between the lines so to speak. By destroying his words as he goes, he saves his story.

> It will remain my own, which is all that matters now. I'll fool them all the same. I know they're constantly spying on me through the peephole as I'm writing, those vultures, awaiting their prey. For them, especially, for them, on separate sheets, I'll write out and save ten or twelve or however many of Shakespeare's sonnets I can remember. (10)

Vultures wait to pounce on his words—a paradigm for the fate of stories under censorship. All that is left when Joseph dies is a tidy pile of sonnets from which his whole story is recoverable—but only by those who have the code or by those who scrounge around in latrines.

Shakespeare's sonnets and plays are Brink's hidden recitative. His title comes from the sonnet "Weary with toil, I haste to my bed." Joseph, dark poet, rewrites plays and memorizes sonnets in order to address the problems of South Africa, of art under siege. Joseph's theater is closed down, his players arrested or intimidated and he is forced into exile. He returns, falls in love, kills Jessica to keep her and kills his words to keep himself. The world and the word killeth. But the word also resurrects.

Art is a dangerous game. The writer, like the actor, gives "life to the words of others" and the only criteria is whether the artistry "has been more or less coherent and more or less convincing. A matter of technique. Some live and die better than others. The same darkness overtakes all" (389). Some artists survive intimidation, censorship, and exile better than others. André Brink switched from the "intimacy" of Afrikaans to English after the banning of *Looking on Darkness* (*Los Angeles Times* 17 April 1990: E 1, 5).

At Joseph's "last supper" held in his cell under a naked light bulb, he drinks red wine and eats brown bread. His last request: "I'd be glad if they'd put off my light, tonight, if you could arrange it" (390). There are some evils for which even writers require darkness. The light remains turned on but Joseph anticipates death, a more profound darkness and writes, "Yet I look upon the same darkness which the blind do see and find meaning and beauty in it. The night is a great redeemer" (392). Joseph's tragic story provides the most eloquent yet darkest moments in André Brink's art. Surely no God would laugh when he finds Brink, or one of his surrogate authors, thinking.

For that truth-seeking quality of light, the contemporary historian has been advised to go to the sociologist who has been told to consult the politician who has been told to consult the philosopher who has been ordered to refine his experiments. The historian has been taught to recognize his fictions. All of them have been referred to novelists like André Brink who promptly declare a "state of emergency."

V

By the time André Brink publishes *States of Emergency*, he

has succeeded in fulfilling the three revolutions in art suggested by Milan Kundera: radical divestment, novelistic counterpoint, and novelistic essay that is hypothetical, playful, ironic. This novel foregrounds art in the emergency ward suffering compound structural fractures, spiritual lesions, moral contusions, and profound political palpitations. Some artists in South Africa have abandoned their art entirely for the sake of what Nadine Gordimer (*The Essential Gesture* 276) calls *agitprop.* Brink continues his struggle with a wildly "hypothetical and ironic" novel that wanders in and out of reportage during moments of creative crisis.

It strikes me that Brink wrote ***States of Emergency*** while surrounded with the litter of the world's latest theoreticians who do little to advance the wisdom of novels or to lift his state of emergency. In such other works as ***Looking on Darkness, Rumors of Rain,*** and even in ***Chain of Voices,*** Brink represents the creative artist under siege and hints that most love stories written under censorship end up as a series of Sunday supplements to the *Roman de la Rose,* or *Tristan und Isolde.*

Brink blurs the boundaries between authors, surrogate authors, implied authors, embedded authors, precursors, and ghosts. His ghost-writer tries to start a novel "untarnished by politics" (13) or "uncluttered by the 'political dimension' demanded by. . .agents and publishers"—and theorists we might add (5). He pulls no punches, "what is at stake is the whole concept of writing, of Literature. The boundaries between 'text' and 'world,' the 'responsibility' of the writer" (5).

The ghost's profound sense of responsibility determines that he cannot begin to tell a story without recognizing a host of supplemental stories clamoring to be told. Jane's romantic novella forces its way into the novelist's story about Philip and Melissa, which gets tangled up with theories of the novel from de Saussure, Heidegger, Godamer, Barthes, and Kristeva to Lotman (Melissa's last name), Kermode, and Derrida. Jane's diary gets tangled with newspaper articles, novellas, and Melissa's romance.

But political and theoretical controversies do not tell the whole structural story because woven into it all we find Richard Wagner's *Tristan und Isolde.* Ultimately, the writer and his reader cannot disentangle Tristan and Isolde or Jane and Chris de Villiers from Philip and Melissa who are the apparent heroes of this novel. All three sets of fugitive lovers demand that Brink tell their story, which he pawns off on his ghost-writer who keeps interrupting their stories to report the tragedy of Milton and Thokozile Thaya. Or Carlos Fuentes enters the novel and announces, "That is what novels are about—a postponement of death" (205). Instead the beleaguered ghost-writer postpones his love story to report Milton's death.

Vincent Van Gogh made an observation that carries implications for modern writers of fiction—especially ones who need a ghostwriter in order to say anything at all. Van Gogh reminds Emile Bernard that "one can try to give an impression of anguish without aiming straight at the historic Garden of Gethsemane" (*Letters,* 3:524). In aiming at anguish, Brink resorts to allegories and allusions to novels, novelists, critics, and even to the Garden of Eden, *Roman de la Rose,* the Garden of Earthly Delight (*le jardin de déduit*), and Wagner's Cave of Lovers. They all get transformed into isolated, forsaken wildernesses belonging to a run-down hotel in the mountains near Bains Kloof fashioned out of a decaying old farm house seen somewhere near Franschhoek or Stellenbosch and transferred again to a farm in the Northern Transvaal portion of the Drakensberg Mountains. And onward.

Brink's lovers meet in a sandy and wet bower on the beach. Or they seek refuge in a hotel on the coast that they pretend is John Donne's island; mostly they just take their chances and hide away in an apartment with plenty of light and a balcony. Of course the Security Police lurk about in all these gardens so little has changed since Cornwall. Any gardens for the South African novelists, real or ghostly, exist in "a park garden of the imagination, a state of mind rather than a topographical reality" (49).

One of the epigraphs to ***States of Emergency*** comes from Athol Fugard who warns that, "The only safe place in the world is inside a story," but, if we are to believe André Brink's surrogate, stories are no longer safe places in which to hide, even for a ghost. They aren't even safe to construct. Nevertheless, we remind ourselves that art flourishes in such wildernesses.

The true emergency for writers like André Brink is a failure of the imagination because plagues attack the story and lead to a madness we ought not call political. Novels, bereft of imagination and vision, end up neither love stories nor politics.

André Brink's paradigm for modern writers centers on Wagner's impulse to stop composing his *Ring* cycle long enough to write *Tristan und Isolde.* Love cannot wait. Jane's novelette, her diary, Philip and Melissa's love story all happen in what Brink calls the

> Circle of fire. The ring of artifice, wrought in words; the verbal image of that basic sign: Woman: the Vulva. Novels have ends, stories run on in everlasting spirals, circles, rings. No, I don't think I shall be writing my book after all. (243)

The love story must wait. The ghost-writer abandons his lovers who founder in political crosscurrents.

Brink's surrogate insists, that "no one commits suicide over a manuscript turned down" (4). Instead, the novel self-destructs, deconstructs itself before our very eyes—a series of false starts, possible plots, interruptions, invasions by other stories, and only a vague sense of an ending followed by a desperate prayer for freedom and a ray of hope. The story never gets told. Or, to put it another way, instead of telling one story, the writer tells other stories demanding to use him as a Medium.

Most of André Brink's works are haunted by blindness, by a fear of being lost in fog, of being plunged into some sort of primeval chasm. Virtually all of André Brink's novels contain at least one such primal scene. To locate only a few: The *Ambassador*—Nicolette's room an early precursor; *Looking on Darkness*—several scenes in the Tulbagh Valley mountains where the children wander as helpless as "Brueghel's blind" (99) and several scenes at Bains Kloof (385-386); *An Instant in the Wind*—most of the novel set in scenes of primal beauty and terror; *Rumors of Rain*—Martin becomes lost and meets the circumciser/mystic/visionary in a narrow kloof (woods) near the farm in Ciskei. Martin listens to the tale of Momlambo; *A Dry White Season*—Ben's first "descent" into Soweto; *Chain of Voices*—Galant and Nicolaas are lost in the Tulbagh Mountains in the fog (215-235); *Wall of the Plague*—the ancient ruins of the wall built to ward off the Plague at Murs, France; *States of Emergency*—the farm for Jane and the hotel for Melissa and Philip where many primeval things of the mind turn up.

> **Most of André Brink's works are haunted by blindness, by a fear of being lost in fog, of being plunged into some sort of primeval chasm. Virtually all of André Brink's novels contain at least one such primal scene.**
> —*Lillian Hilja Andon-Milligan*

His pantheon of loving women try to close the gap between utopian ideals and the grim realities of life in South African wildernesses. Ma Rose, Elizabeth, Jessica, Melanie, Melissa, and Andrea all try to build human bridges across the chasms that separate people in much the same way as Nadine Gordimer's Liz, Ann, Maureen, Hillela, and Burger's daughter try to link hands across racial boundaries. All of their efforts fail. Love remains the only solution. Our world needs a love story.

VI

In *States of Emergency* André Brink tries to build his love story in the midst of political chaos. The prognosis is not good:

If ever we wander through that deserted garden again, in a dream perhaps—the cries of ghost peacocks, of hadidas, of Valkyries, of mountain eagles soaring over the cliffs . . . And what does the artist need to go on trying to find the truth? (243-244)

According to Brink, to write is to love (48). He continues to search for a world in which a love story can happen. So far he has not found it. Nor has he found a sense of an ending. Why not? The artist needs what Brink calls that "inner lucidity without which, even when one is in pain or rage, writing is impossible" (3).

Richard Rorty argues for the ideal of freedom, for "leaving people alone to dream and think and live as they please, so long as they do not hurt other people—and that idea provides as viscous a social glue as that of unconditional validity" ("Truth and Freedom" 635). André Brink's ghostly surrogate seeks that freedom, some peace and quiet and room to write a love story without feeling guilty about *all* those "great currents of history," without feeling threatened by *all* those powerful forces trying to drown out his voice with their own thunder (*States* 5). In the end he cannot write his love story.

Brink, however, still can in spite of overwhelming pressures—from both Afrikaner and anti-apartheid critics as well as from the great babel of theoretical, philosophical and political voices trying to supersede the novelist in his role as visionary and prophet.

When that certain quality of South African light so essential to art fails to illuminate, then politicians, sociologists, historians, and philosophers plunge into darkness along with the rest of us. We wander through the wilderness, "Hand in hand, as helpless as Brueghel's blind men"—heads upturned with empty eyesockets, we stumble, fall, link ourselves together with groping hands and wooden sticks (*Looking on Darkness* 99). We need new metaphors. New stories.

The worst exile we can fashion for a novelist involves depriving him of the freedom to pursue his story—*wherever* it might lead. The worst censorship comes from ideologues bent on drowning out his voice. Theorists who poach in the artist's provinces swarm around his work like angry gnats and cloud his vision. Too much exile, censorship, and theoretical poaching send the artist, limping and stumbling, after Brueghel's blind men.

We could do with a little less theory, less poaching, and a lot more love. To write is also to imagine love. We might be wise to put our faith in our novelists, in their sense of responsibility and above all in the quality of their light that enables us to see better in the dark.

Abdulrazak Gurnah (review date 26 February 1993)

SOURCE: "Prospero's Nightmare," in *Times Literary Supplement*, No. 4691, February 26, 1993, p. 21.

[*In the following review, Gurnah identifies the narrative sources of* The First Life of Adamastor. *Among these sources are: the Khoi myths of Creation; the Portuguese poet Camões; and French novelist Rabelais; and Gurnah examines how Brink uses these sources to deal with "moral and historical issues."*]

In his epic poem *The Lusiads* (1572), Luis de Camões celebrates the Portuguese national myth through Vasco da Gama's first journey from Lisbon to Calicut round the southern tip of Africa. In the seventy-two years between the poem's publication and the events it celebrates, the Portuguese had raided and traded (mostly raided) their way along the west and east African coasts, the Malabar coast of India, and as far as Siam and Macao. They had also landed on several points along the coast of southern Africa. In his account of Gama's first journey in 1500, Camões describes how, as the Portuguese approach the Cape of Good Hope, they are confronted by a huge and ugly figure in human shape. He pronounces terrible prophecies on the Portuguese before telling them his story. His name is Adamastor, a Titan who had fought against Zeus and his allies, and was transformed into the "mighty Cape occult and grand" in his defeat. He had lusted to distraction after Thetis, a nymph of the sea, whom he had seen bathing naked, but she rejected him because of his deformity and his great size. Thetis's mother, Doris, tricked Adamastor into believing that she had arranged a tryst for him with her daughter, and as the passionate Titan rushed at the figure of what he took to be the nymph, he found himself embracing a rock and he was transformed into the Cape. This is the starting-point of Brink's narrative.

Adamastor is an invention of Rabelais. He first appears in that list of Pantagruel's progenitures (in the opening chapter of *Pantagruel*), which parodies the "So-and-So begat So-and-So" of the Genesis chapter of the Bible. If Camões is the starting-point of Brink's story, it is Rabelais who provides the narrative model. Each chapter begins with a loud gloss on what is to follow. The narrator's voice is self-conscious, even at one point "absent". The prevailing tone is Rabelaisian, broad and bawdy humor whose targets are often solemn moral and historical issues.

Brink's narrator is a Khoi called T'kama, one of those who witnessed the first arrival of the Portuguese in southern Africa. The Khoi, who were called Hottentots by Europeans, were probably the oldest inhabitants of southern Africa, and were expected to die out speedily after their encounter with

civilization. There is obvious irony in having one of them narrate the arrival of southern Africa's newest people. Like Rabelais's Pantagruel, T'kama, too, is given a genealogy in the first chapter, some of whose ancestors bear a striking resemblance to Pantagruel's. The Portuguese who land from the ships are deliberately made composite and representative. Events which befell Bartholomeu Dias, Gama's predecessor in southern Africa, as well as Gama himself, are run together. The sites of two encounters, Mossel Bay and Algoa Bay, are compressed into one. The arrival of the ships, then, becomes archetypal of the encounter of Europe with primitive people, and is presented in familiar tropes of imperialism: the natives' innocent misunderstanding of the purposes of the invaders, the unequal nature of the trade—a handful of beads for a flock of sheep, the corruption of native people with alcohol and prostitution. The natives inevitably give away the secrets of the land. In this respect, the narrator's tone has an elegaic undercurrent, aware that matters will end badly. For it is soon clear that T'kama's story is an allegory of the coming-into-being of South Africa told by one of its silenced people. The Khoi are attacked and dispersed, and the Europeans have come to stay.

The attack on the Khoi is triggered by the presence of a European woman. Brink affirms the woman's metaphorical dimension by telling us that there is no known account which says that "Da Gama or Cam or Dias or d'Almeida or any other seafarer at the time took along women on their ships". In fact, Dias carried four "negresses" who were well-versed in Portuguese ways with him. They were to be put ashore where they could tell the locals about the greatness of the King of Portugal. The last one of them was put ashore at Algoa Bay in southern Africa, close to two women who were gathering shellfish. Nothing was ever found of any of these women, and they are also absent in Brink's account.

Brink's woman is clearly European, though, and her presence on the ship is magical, unheard of. T'kama is found stroking her after he had caught sight of her bathing naked. This not only recalls Adamastor, but sites the primal transgression in the story of the encounter between Europe and Africa in the unbearability of native "gaze" on European woman. It is Prospero's nightmare, the plantation owner's darkest fear. Brink's use of the woman figure in this way is problematic because of its brutality. Her presence in the narrative is necessary for the Adamastor parallel, but she also represents Europe as the irresistible nymph who provokes Africa's penetration but cannot bear it, for T'kama's uncontrollable love for her demonizes him. His penis is too big to penetrate her, and grows bigger and bigger every time he touches her. Thus Europe and Africa remain unjoined, and calamity befalls the people, while T'kama's lust remains unsated. A predictably "ribald" account is given of how union is achieved. Eventually, the woman has no place in the land and is taken away by the ships, while T'kama, like

Adamastor, is turned into rock and suffers the first of his repeated deaths.

Brink's text is a little too dependent on the allegorical framework it sets up. And if T'kama's narrative is delivered in "natural" metaphors and comparisons to suggest the pastoral condition of his intellect, and to contrast his account with the authoritative "grand narratives" of European discovery, it also has a folkloric quaintness which, at times, locks it into another stereotype. But the story Brink constructs out of Camões's myth of demonic love and suffering, and Khoi myths of Creation, and of battles between good and evil is complex and challenging, and satisfying in its narrative playfulness.

Mario Vargas Llosa (review date 25 July 1993)

SOURCE: "Love Finds a Way," in *New York Times Book Review*, July 25, 1993, pp. 1, 23, 24.

[*In the following review of* Cape of Storms: The First Life of Adamastor, *celebrated novelist Mario Vargas Llosa praises Brink's novel for its imagination and humor. Vargas Llosa interprets the allegorical features of the book in which he reads that "rapprochement between human beings of differing skins, languages and customs is impossible, for even with the best will on both sides it will inevitably be frustrated by cultural conditioning."*]

"There is no problem in the world that cannot be solved with a story." That is what a witch doctor of the Xhosa tribe tells the tormented narrator of *Cape of Storms,* a giant of the Khoikhoi people named T'kama, whose inordinately large penis, along with several other areas of incompatibility, prevents him from having a normal relationship with his European wife. In this case, the prescription does not work, for the tale told by the witch doctor to the enraptured superman illustrates the racist and apocalyptic conviction that those who break ethnic barriers for the sake of love are condemned to wretchedness and to bringing catastrophe down on their people.

The South African author André Brink has never been afraid to face this threat, in his life or in his literature. From the time of his earliest writings he has been in conflict with his country's Government, fighting against the segregation of people according to skin color. In his many essays, and in novels like *An Instant in the Wind,* and *A Chain of Voices,* he has described calamities and absurdities of the apartheid system with a cold lucidity that in no way interferes with high emotion and daring flights of the imagination.

Something of this moral independence—as well as a certain vocation for dampening the reader's spirits—can be observed in the elegant parable with which, in *Cape of Storms,* he evokes the first encounter of Europeans and Africans five centuries ago, when the ships of the Portuguese navigator Vasco da Gama sailed around the Cape of Good Hope. The tale, or fable, is told by a reincarnation of Adamastor, the "savage" or "untamed" giant alluded to by Rabelais in "Gargantua and Pantagruel" and developed by the Portuguese poet Camões in his *Lusiads.* He reappears here as the young chieftain of the Khoikhoi (whom the Dutch insultingly renamed "Hottentots"), a sentimental giant wounded by the arrows of Eros when he sees the first white woman to tread the sands of that corner of Africa. Blinded with love, he steals her, marries her and spends the rest of his life trying in vain to know her in the biblical as well as all other senses of the word.

This is not the first time that a work of fiction has attempted to reconstruct, from a native perspective, the historical and cultural trauma that the arrival of the "Bearded Men" from Europe signified for the indigenous peoples of Africa (or America, Asia and Oceania). The result of such inventions has almost always been disastrous: unconvincing texts in which imagination and prose are strangled by a guilty conscience and virtuous sentiments. But André Brink has managed to play this difficult hand with great success, thanks to humor: *Cape of Storms* is so entertaining that one reads it almost without noticing that it is also an extremely polemical allegory of the relationship between dissimilar races and cultures.

> **In his many essays, and in novels like *An Instant in the Wind,* and *A Chain of Voices,* he has described calamities and absurdities of the apartheid system with a cold lucidity that in no way interferes with high emotion and daring flights of the imagination.**
> **—*Mario Vargas Llosa***

If the story of T'kama's love for the white woman, whom he calls by the generic feminine name "Khois," is symbolic, it means that rapprochement between human beings of differing skins, languages and customs is impossible, for even with the best will on both sides it will inevitably be frustrated by cultural conditioning. On his wedding night, following the usage of his tribe, the groom smears his body with grease, bedecks himself with feathers and flowers and, in a gracious concession to Khois's people (so he thinks) covers his head with a Portuguese helmet captured in battle. What is the bride's reaction when she sees her new husband in this bizarre get-up? She bursts into convulsive, unmanning, interminable laughter that turns their wedding, night into a circus clown act.

Similar misunderstandings, although not always so amusing, appear throughout this impossible love story. After many more lunacies like that first one, the foreigner at last seems ready to break out of her isolation, to make an effort to join the tribe and behave like a true wife to T'kama. But in her ignorance she kills and cooks a hare, an untouchable animal that for the community represents, and causes, death. Everyone is terrified by what she has done, and the wizard Khamab has to summon all his magic to conjure away collective misfortune.

The woman's failure plunges her into total despair, and her transplanted European's lament, in the context of what is occurring four centuries later in South Africa, has rather sinister premonitory connotations: "I can't do anything right. I understand nothing about you or your people or this goddamned country. There's nowhere I can go to. My own people abandoned me long ago. Everything is impossible."

Rather than cooling his ardor, however, these clashes, and the very lack of communication that separates them keep the indigenous giant's rapturous love for the white woman alive and burning. Why has he been smitten with such overwhelming passion? He claims it is because she is so beautiful, and undoubtedly that is true. But by his own confession he clearly finds the exoticism of his kidnapped bride no less attractive than her beauty: that unbridgeable difference she occupies by virtue of her incomprehensible language and her inability to understand nature and life as the Khoikhoi do.

The greatest obstacle to their life as a couple is the monstrous size of T'kama's sexual member, which is at once the pride and misfortune of the narrator. Were its dimensions the same before she arrived on the shores of the Cape of Storms, or is this a cause-and-effect relationship between his condition as unicorn-man and the presence of that pale silhouette before which his virile frenzy swells like a purebred bull at the sight of a red flag?

The second proposition seems more likely. It goes without saying that his outsized proportions give rise to some of the funniest scenes in the novel; they are also the motive for the most tragic when, impelled by the desire to make love to his wife, T'kama submits to a magical mutilation that replaces his powerful natural cudgel with a modest and functional clay prosthesis.

The symbolism of this episode could not be more dismal: it seems to say that the price of understanding between human beings of different ancestry and culture is renouncing oneself and replacing one's own identity with a false one, because every interracial or intercultural relationship is an exercise in domination and power in which someone always wins, and someone always loses.

Is this true? Certainly it is a very old theory, made respectable by the fathers of cultural nationalism such as the philosophers Herder and Fichte in Germany; contemporary multiculturalists have revived it in the name of the right to survival of small, primitive cultures threatened by modernity. But if preserving the cultural identity of the weak demands that their exchanges with people from more powerful and advanced cultures be reduced to a minimum or eliminated altogether, since such contact is considered destructive, how will a world we view as discriminatory and unjust even change?

The rejection of integration and racial mixing in the name of the "identity" of exploited and marginalized peoples, preached in our day by certain systems of thought that are considered progressive, brings those systems dangerously close to the reactionary philosophies of Nazi Germany or apartheidist South Africa, which not too long ago called for the segregated development of cultures and races.

Naturally this does not apply to a writer who has given as many courageous demonstrations of his democratic convictions as André Brink, and perhaps it is excessive to make too many theoretical extrapolations from a text like *Cape of Storms,* which is not an anthropological essay but a wonderfully entertaining work of fiction. But, as Sartre said, "words are acts," and in the South African context, in the delicate transition that country is living through, nothing written about race and culture can be irrelevant to the current problematical situation. However much we enjoy reading the book, André Brink's beautiful mythological re-creation leaves us anguished over what appear to be its predictions regarding a society where, after a bloody past of injustice and institutionalized racism, different races and cultures are finally preparing to try co-existence under conditions of equality.

The story of T'kama and Khois is a migratory tale that unfolds to the rhythm of the tribe's perpetual pilgrimage through an elemental and mysterious geography that is inseparable from the rites, beliefs, fears and dreams of the Khoikhoi and is beautifully incorporated into the narrator's account in subtle, poetic strokes. One of the greatest successes of the book, in addition to its humor is the functioning of this landscape imbued with taboos and surprises. The human beings who, like the birds and the river, live at one with their environment, naturally project their ideas of the sacred and the transcendental onto the natural world that not only feeds them but also imposes a rhythm of life, a notion of time and a system of prohibitions and activities that establish a complementary, a common denominator between people and landscape. For a reader from an industrialized civilization, this involves a good deal of magical realism that awakens irresistible nostalgia for lost paradises.

Clarence Major (review date 29 August 1993)

SOURCE: "An Improbable Love," in *Los Angeles Times Book Review,* August 29, 1993, pp. 3, 8.

[*In the following review, Major draws parallels between some of the features in* Cape of Storms: the First Life of Adamastor *and several other tales and myths.*]

In André Brink's novella, **Cape of Storms,** one day near the end of the 16th Century, a young white woman is left on a South African coastal beach by sailors—probably Portuguese—who had to make a hasty getaway after cheating and offending a nomadic tribe temporarily stopped near the beach. Why the woman was left and why she was on the ship in the first place, these things we never find out.

But really, it doesn't matter. What does matter is that the young tribal chief, T'kama, falls in love with this "bird" from the sea and she with him—that is, once she overcomes her fear of this strange place and these strange people with customs she doesn't understand. The chief and his tribe quickly depart, taking the woman with them. Trusting their god, Tsui-Goab, they follow rain and such as they cross the desert in search of unspoiled places.

What evolves as they travel is a frustrated love story. Brink has given us this time around a fable of an improbable love that takes long to consummate because of a big, big difficulty. But more about that later.

What's really refreshing is that the story can be read in several different ways. I think it would be a mistake simply to read it as a narrative of the historical roots of black-white conflict at the heart of South African's present-day racial nightmare. It's much more than the story of the first white men to drift onto the shores of South Africa, more than an interracial romance, or an attempt on the part of white men to kill a black man over a white woman.

In a brief introduction, Brink talks about the Greek mythic models he had in mind for the book. Predictably, he meant T'kama to represent wildness, the untamed. By this I take Brink to mean he's trying to get at the unrestrained creative powers of nature as represented by these tribal people, and the way they live in rhythm with the weather and the land. Though Eurocentric in perspective—despite being told from the point of view of the tribal chief T'kama himself—this is not another *Heart of Darkness.*

Kols—the name T'kama gives the white woman—is based on the Greek sea-goddess, Thetis, one of the Nereids, daughter of Proteus and mother of Achilles. Thetis then must represent the sea, and by extension life. Not much in the story leads me to think she's meant to represent that embattled, greed-driven, process called "civilization" taking place at that time in Portugal—and the rest of Europe for that matter.

Actually, Kols may represent some of the significance of her father's relationship with Africa. Proteus, old man of the sea, is based on an island off the Nile delta. In any case, his daughter, the "Nymph and Princess of the Wave" (as represented by Kols), now land-bound, adjusts quickly to tribal life—where she spends much of her time with the other women and the children—and even tries to be a good wife, despite her homesickness.

But the big problem T'kama has to deal with is his penis. It's literally too big for Kols. And every time he thinks of consummating his relationship with her, it gets even bigger. At least in terms of his anatomy, we're dealing with gigantism. T'kama is a sort of comic giant in a reflexive text with chapter headings such as "A short chapter that may be skipped by readers who object to descriptions of sexual intercourse."

As the tribe wanders the desert, thirsty and hungry, T'kama seeks a solution to his problem. The wise elder of the tribe, Khamab, believes that the luck of the tribe will change once T'kama is able to mate with his strange wife.

Related in some ways to the tradition of the bawdy tale, **Cape of Storms** even has a moment of cuckoldry. In their wanderings, they come upon a tribe whose witch doctor vows to help T'kama. But the herbal solution with which he treats the problem only makes it bigger and causes a terrible burning. While T'kama weeps in pain the witch doctor seduces or attempts to seduce Kols. T'kama's penis now grows so long he has to wrap it around his body several times to keep it from dragging on the ground.

While, on this surface, this is comic and tragic, there is a profoundly relevant subtext. T'kama's problem is not simply a cruel trick nature has played to conspire against the relationship. In fact, his problem might be read as no problem at all. He can be seen as a fertility trickster figure, a kind of malevolent spirit.

Such a character requires a suspension of disbelief similar to the kind needed to believe in Swift's little people, the Lilliputians or Voltaire's Micromegas, or the Cyclops of the Odyssey or Rabelais' Gargantua, who starts out a giant and ends up a normal-size man. In ancient tribal myths fertility demons such as these abound. The ancient aboriginal people of North-east Australia, for example, believed in fertility demigods, called Quinkans, who were blessed with penises so long they could use them to pole vault for great distances across the land.

In T'kama's case, a crisis proves a paradoxical solution of sorts. Crazed with thirst, the tribe comes upon a river. Kols, the only one of the group who can swim, jumps in and is immediately chased by a crocodile. T'kama unwinds his penis and throws it like a rope to her rescue; she pulls herself to safety.

Without giving away too much of the outcome, I can say that this is a story for anyone who enjoys reading about troubled love or the classic plights of fabled giants.

And it's funny.

Mark Wormald (review date 3 September 1993)

SOURCE: "Images of Africa," in *Times Literary Supplement,* No. 4718, September 3, 1993, p. 23.

[*In the following review, Wormald explores the rich texture of the historical and imaginative world of Brink's* On the Contrary.]

On a solitary excursion at sunset, during the first of the three journeys into the dark heart of Africa that make up this extraordinary novel, André Brink's hero, Estienne Barbier, sees a unicorn. "It appears, heraldic, flat against the sun . . . its tall single horn rising like a scimitar from its forehead." Then, with a single shot from his gun, he kills it. Standing over the dead body, he is "stunned by the creature's beauty":

> It is a curious emotion that overwhelms me: not so much elation at having in one shot introduced a creature of myth into the domain of the possible, *voire* the real, as sorrow. I am standing at some desolate frontier, and no one can tell what lies beyond.

If this is not quite the story's definitive moment, then it is as close to one as Barbier's mercurial narrative comes. It also suggests the ambitiousness of the novelist's project in giving him a voice. For Barbier, a French adventurer from Orléans who found his way to the Cape of Good Hope in the 1730s, and proved an unlikely leader of rebel Afrikaner colonists in their struggle with the corrupt administration of the East India Company, is potentially a yet more problematic narrator. An outsider, he struggles with Dutch grammar, and has only unreliable Latin; the official journal he keeps of his first journey of exploration on behalf of the expedition's commander, the sordidly ambitious Lieutenant Allemann, hovers on "the limits of the sayable", and excludes the unspeakable actions they commit on the native Hottentots and animal life they encounter, for reasons of basic practicality as well as of political expediency.

Yet no such inhibitions confine the narrative we read. The novel takes the form of a letter, presented in over 300 variously fragmentary instalments, which immediately and showily deconstructs any pretence of its own accountability or coherence. Composed in the "Dark Hole of the Castle", at Cabo de Bonne-Espérance, where Barbier is awaiting execution and official dismemberment, and dated "*sine die*", the narrative confronts our expectations with a knowing challenge. "I am dead: you cannot read: this will (therefore) not have been a letter." In one of many acknowledgements, Brink reminds us that his hero is implausibly borrowing from Derrida; but the exuberance with which Barbier embraces the world of the unknown and the unverified, means that the reader needs no notes to share in the story's adventure.

Barbier's forays into the African interior, first for Monomotapa, "a city made of words", lurking just beyond the limits of each exploration he undertakes, then for Rosette, Allemann's enigmatically beautiful slave with whom he claims, on that first journey, to have seen another mythical creature, the hippogryph, and whom he subsequently helps to escape from (graphically realized) abuse at the hands of his fellow Europeans, involve a chain of equally vivid episodes. Each of its links extends the pattern established in that early encounter with the unicorn. Each, that is, presents a tantalizingly plausible image of the marvellous, of the willed extension of the possible, then translates that image into brutal physical and emotional realities. Exotic sexual encounters and opulent feasts alternate with, and utterly contradict, brutal examinations of the Hottentot tribes whom the Afrikaners trade with then betray. Lechery yields to treachery, and then—as the story advances—to Barbier's recognition of his own guilt in perpetrating both.

This reaction, this sense of being implicated in a luridly horrifying entertainment, constitutes the real significance of *On the Contrary.* It is a timeless, intensely metaphorical novel, but it is also urgently topical. Crouching beside the carcass of the unicorn he has just killed, Barbier confesses himself, on that "desolate frontier", to be "shot with a terror beyond anything the mind can imagine, delivered to whatever is preparing to avenge" the crime. By the book's end, prompted by the fantastic intervention of other imagined and imaginary companions—the voice of Jeanne d'Arc, his father's copy of *Don Quixote,* and his humbling experience of the land—Barbier is no closer, physically, to escaping the cycle of madness and injustice of life and politics on the Cape. Neither he nor Brink has found a solution to the problems that land still contains. But Barbier's experience does force his strange composite voice towards a resonant, helpless comment on southern Africa's many peoples, indigenous and colonizing. "They are not problems to be solved. They are here, that's all. They can be loved, I suppose."

Charles R. Larson (review date 5 September 1993)

SOURCE: "André Brink's Bawdy Romp," in *Tribune Books*, September 5, 1993, p. 3.

[*In the following review, Larson presents an appreciation of* Cape of Storms: The First Life of Adamastor *in which he sees "a comic masterpiece."*]

André Brink must have had great fun writing "Cape of Storms." There is nothing so rollicking in this South African novelist's earlier works (*A Dry White Season, Rumors of Rain,* etc.) nothing nearly as playful or as bawdy, nothing quite so terse, certainly nothing so parabolic. Only the matter of cultural interaction (or lack thereof) unites this mythic gem with Brink's bleak earlier accounts of man's inhumanity to his fellow man under what was—and what subsequently became officially sanctified—apartheid in South Africa.

In an introductory chapter beginning "Once upon a time there was and there wasn't," Brink explains the rationale behind his daring venture into the territory of myth. Harkening back to the Greeks, Rabelais' and the Portuguese epic poet Camoes' stories of Adamastor provide the context for the gigantic monster who was punished by Zeus and turned into "the jagged outcrop of the Cape Peninsula."

Then Brink asks, "Suppose there were an Adamastor, a model for the giant of Camoes' fanciful history; and suppose that original creature, spirit, or whatever he may have been, has survived through the centuries in a series of disparate successive avatars in order to continue watching over the Cape of Storms: how would *he* look back, from the perspective of the late twentieth century, on that original experience?"

That's a whopper of a question, but *Cape of Storms* is also a whopper—or at least about a whopper, for Brink keeps one part of his hero's anatomy gigantic, while shrinking the rest. T'kama, the Adamastor of Brink's story, has been given his name (which also means Big Bird) because of the size of his member. Because of his unnatural endowment, T'kama's stature among his people is equivalent to chief.

Whether Brink has bestowed this status upon him because of Eurocentric preoccupation with genital size never becomes quite clear, though the implication seems to be that Western societies would also choose their leaders somewhat differently if statistics about male organ size were made public.

The actual story, set during the time of Vasco da Gama's explorations, begins with the arrival of the first Europeans at what they would subsequently call Algoa Bay (Port Eliza-

beth). We have heard this story before, in many different contexts.

Strangers arrive who initially appear to be friendly. Gifts are exchanged, including fire water. The locals go wild for want of more of it. Then, suddenly, the scene turns ugly, as each side fails to understand the other.

Brink's original twist to the story is the sudden appearance of a white woman who has come ashore from the ship in order to bathe in fresh water. It is at that moment that T'Kama observes her and falls covetously in love with her.

The woman screams. T'Kama thinks that it is his clothing that frightens her, since she is swimming in a pool of water. What better way to ease her fears than to undress himself? He forgets that what she sees will frighten her even more.

Forget the sexual stereotyping (at least for the moment). After the fight that follows, once the Europeans realize that the woman has been discovered, T'kama and his people flee with their captive into the hinterlands, where they wander for many a moon. Khois (T'kama's name for woman) shortly loses her fear of her captor, even, in time, desires union with him; in the series of attempts that follow, though, things deteriorate.

The problem is that T'kama's member never gets any smaller. Rather, the opposite. A witch doctor tricks him into undergoing a painful rite to reduce the size of his organ, but the result backfires. Even worse, T'kama's people believe that their sorry fate—their aimless wanderings, even the drought in the Cape—has been brought upon them because T'Kama and Khois have never managed to consummate their ritualistic intercourse.

In time, a certain tenderness develops between the culture-crossed lovers. They even learn enough of each other's language to communicate with one another. But there's still that major obstacle. T'kama laments:

> "That bird in my loins continued to grow. For a
> while I kept it tied to my knee with a leather thong
> to keep it from swinging and slapping about; then
> to my calf, but still it went on growing until I was
> getting worried it would get trampled underfoot or
> trip me up while walking. So I made a loop and tied
> the end to my waist. And all for nothing a useless,
> in fact obnoxious, appendage."

Can things get worse than this? You bet. Our hero must be brought low, though rarely has a writer chosen a fate more painful than this. Rescuing the drowning woman from a pond, T'kama throws her the only thing available. Khois is saved, but a ferocious crocodile bites off T'kama's appendage, prompting him to remark, "I had lost the greater part of my body."

> **What makes *Cape of Storms* a comic masterpiece is not simply the pyrotechnics surrounding the cross-cultural seduction engaged in by Brink's lovers (and the deliberate play on sexual stereotyping) but the equally imaginative narrative form.**
> **—*Charles R. Larson***

Then things improve. In what must be considered the oldest organ implant recorded in history, T'kama is saved by his faithful shaman, brought down to the size of the average man and made whole again. What happens afterward isn't nearly as inevitable as it initially appears. Yes, T'kama and Khois are finally able to complete the act and it isn't much later before their son is born. But just as the reader anticipates a happy ending, the plot takes another twist that it would not be fair to divulge.

What makes *Cape of Storms* a comic masterpiece is not simply the pyrotechnics surrounding the cross-cultural seduction engaged in by Brink's lovers (and the deliberate play on sexual stereotyping) but the equally imaginative narrative form. There are footnotes that contradict facts within the text, hilarious epic similes and digressions, a narrative point of view that defies categorization, clever illustrations and even a map to lend credibility to the story.

As if that weren't enough, Brink adds to the fun a creation myth that has to be the wildest sub-story in the adventure. If this work has a flaw, it is its brevity. One wishes for more.

Peter S. Prescott (review date 14 August 1994)

SOURCE: "The Cape of Not Much Hope," in *New York Times Book Review,* August 14, 1994, pp. 7-8.

[*In the following review, Prescott examines* On the Contrary *in the context of a changing South Africa and commments on its picaresque qualities.*]

A newly democratic South Africa confronts its novelists with the same problem that the end of the cold war posed for the writers of spy stories: Is there any life left in the old conflict that I've spent my career defining? For years André Brink, at great risk to himself, wrote realistic novels exposing the cruelty of apartheid. Now, with the urgency of racial conflict diminished, he responds with more fanciful novels that look to his country's past, even to its myths: How

did this horror come about? Must interracial contact inevitably culminate in misunderstanding, violence and oppression? His answer appears to be yes—but with the proviso that as long as a flicker of good will endures, injustice need not be permanent.

His previous novel, *Cape of Storms* (1993), was a surreal fable about the first European encounter with Africans five centuries ago at what is now the Cape of Good Hope. ***On the Contrary: Being the Life of a Famous Rebel, Soldier, Traveller, Explorer, Reader, Builder, Scribe, Latinist, Lover and Liar*** is in some ways even odder. It is also set in the Cape Colony, but the time is the 18th century—as suggested by the florid subtitle, intended to remind us of picaresque novels like Defoe's *Colonel Jack* and Fielding's *Life and Death of Jonathan Wild the Great.*

The colony is very much a frontier territory. Although it is nominally governed by a committee in the Netherlands, real power resides with the corrupt and callous Dutch administrators in Cape Town, here called Cabo. The European interlopers have been around long enough for an indigenous white population—the Afrikaners—to achieve an identity of its own. Mr. Brink is quick to point out that even then the Afrikaners, of whom he is one, were a surly lot, distrusting the Dutch and, as they pressed their settlements into native territory, despising the people they called "Hottentots." Through his narrator, Mr. Brink provides an unforgettable image of the settlers: "Relying, it seems, almost exclusively on slaves and Hottentots for whatever work is to be done on their farms, they spend their time eating, drinking, breeding and bickering."

The narrator, Estienne Barbier, reveals the end of his story at its beginning. Condemned for high treason, he lies in a stinking dark hole awaiting his fate: "Bound to a cross . . . his right hand and his head severed from the body, subsequently to be drawn and quartered, the head and hand to be placed on a stake in the Roodezands Xloof, and the four remaining quarters to be displayed in four different places alongside the most frequented highways of the Settlement as prey to the air and the birds from heaven." An irresistible beginning—in those days they tried to make capital punishment a credible deterrent—but it promises a grand tale that is not to come.

From prison, Estienne casts his narrative as an imaginary letter directed to an escaped slave who cannot read. Arriving after a perilous voyage at Cabo in 1734—he claims his ship was saved only after its cargo of slaves was thrown overboard—Estienne, a Frenchman and a stowaway, poses as an inspector of fortifications. Conscripted into the army, he joins an expedition into the interior to see how the Dutch East India Company posts are faring; his assignment is to make the official record of the trip. The brutality he witnesses is appalling, and his determination to record it sets him at odds with the despots in Cabo.

To condense what follows: Estienne becomes an outlaw; he is jailed; he escapes; he hides on remote farms, sleeping with innumerable widows. He helps a slave escape; like Scheherezade, she is both a lover and a storyteller, and in South Africa then and until recently storytellers were on the wrong side of the law. In time, Estienne launches a rebellion, and a price is put on his head.

If this sounds simple enough, Mr. Brink makes sure that it isn't. *On the Contrary* isn't a bad novel; it's ambitious and imaginative, and it marked the important point that the Afrikaners' savagery toward blacks was based on fear. Nevertheless, the author struggles with a serious confusion of styles. He could easily have written a contemporary picaresque novel: Estienne fulfills the picaro's requirements as a man of loose morals who does menial work and moves around a lot. But from its early manifestation in *La Vida de Lazarillo de Tormes* in 1564, the picaresque novel has been noted for its laconic cynicism and irreverent wit. There's none of that here. Mr. Brink is a moralist and not, at least in this novel, inclined to humor. Estienne carries a copy of *Don Quixote* and reads it as many do the Bible. He dreams the impossible—the inarticulate—dream: 'The desire for the Beyond was as fierce as the lust of the flesh." "As long as you or I can name it it is not enough. What I want lies beyond. Even beyond nations." O.K., but basically what Estienne dreams of is finding Monomotape, the African El Dorado, the city of gold.

The other important baggage he brings from Europe is Joan of Arc. Being French, he calls her Jeanne; she sits somewhere inside his skull and prods him to do the sort of thing that brought her to the stake. Neither Mr. Brink nor Estienne thinks it funny when she says: "You cannot avoid trouble forever, Estienne. It's better to get involved from the beginning." Later Jeanne says, "Never trust the cunning of your enemy." What can she them? Never trust, or never underestimate, your enemy? Jeanne, we remember from Shaw's play, can be provocative, but here she's an astonishing bore. *La pucelle* remains calm while Estienne refers to women by a slang word for their genitals. But then Estienne lacks charm; he can be boring himself: "Love of parents, I know now, love of brothers and sisters, of family and friends and lovers, all this dies away: only the love of the earth remains." Scarlett O'Hara couldn't have said it better.

David Plott (review date 16 October 1994)

SOURCE: "African Realities," in *Tribune Books,* October 16, 1994, pp. 6, 7.

[In the following review, Plott outlines the story that makes up On the Contrary, *and explores the protagonist as relevant historical figure.]*

The work of Andre Brink, one of South Africa's finest writers, has always been linked to the struggle to satisfy the conscience in an unjust land. In such harrowing novels as *A Dry White Season* (1980) and *An Act of Terror* (1991), he has, like fellow South Africans Nadine Gordimer and J.M. Coetzee, made apartheid and its corrupting terrors a centerpiece of his fiction.

At the same time, Brink's work in recent years has shown an increasing and sophisticated preoccupation with the broader themes of myth, fable and history—in short, with the nature of storytelling itself. In his last novel, *Cape of Storms: The First Life of Adamastor* (1993), the mountains of the Cape, as in an ancient fable, literally tell the tale of the arrival of the first Europeans. While the future, disastrous clash of African and European civilizations is obliquely foretold, the emphasis is on the rendering of that clash as myth. And in *On the Contrary,* which takes its title from Henrik Ibsen's last words, Brink has produced what is perhaps his most ambitious effort to combine searing political drama with a meditation on the art of storytelling.

> The work of Andre Brink, one of South Africa's finest writers, has always been linked to the struggle to satisfy the conscience in an unjust land. . . . At the same time, Brink's work in recent years has shown an increasing and sophisticated preoccupation with the broader themes of myth, fable and history—in short, with the nature of storytelling itself.
> —*David Plott*

The novel is based loosely on the real life of an 18th Century French immigrant to South Africa, Estienne Barbier, who was executed by officers of the Dutch East India Company in 1739 for attempting to lead a rebellion against the Cape's colonial authorities. Barbier himself narrates the story in the form of a letter to an ex-slave, Rosette, whom he has helped escape and for whom he has been futilely searching. The letter, however, is never written; it is only imagined. Barbier, in prison awaiting execution and confined to a darkened cell, has neither pen nor paper. "I am dead: you cannot read: this will (therefore) not have been a letter," he says in the novel's opening sentence.

In part, it is the odd double freedom of composing a non-letter to a non-reader that unleashes Barbier's imagination. He can invent and reinvent the story of his life with impunity; and as an inveterate liar, it quickly becomes clear that he is not a reliable narrator. He is obsessed with Cervantes' *Don Quixote*—that preeminent tale of the imagined life—and throughout the novel carries on imaginary conversations with Jeanne d'Arc, whom he believes accompanies him wherever he goes. His story is filled with fables, fantastic creatures and events that never took place. "In this place," he says of Africa, "the imagination is more real than memory."

And yet, throughout the narrative, what is known of the real life of Barbier—as gleaned by Brink from available historical records—gradually unfolds as a powerful tale of the corrupt moral landscape of colonial South Africa. Soon after arriving, Barbier gains the favor of the Cape elite and is invited to join an expedition to the interior. He quickly runs afoul of the authorities, however, when as scribe for the expedition, he insists on recording the truth in the official journal. After several warnings from the expedition's leader, Lt. Allemann, he is fired for refusing "to plague the world with mutilated fact and historical fiction."

On returning to the Cape, however—in a move reminiscent of Brink's novels of modern South Africa under apartheid—Allemann promotes Barbier in an attempt to convince him that life would be more comfortable if he participated in, rather than subverted, the system. Barbier proves immune to the temptation and ultimately blows the whistle on Allemann's efforts to skim off funds meant for ordinary soldiers and a scheme to force Cape residents to buy wood from the military rather than from Afrikaner colonists.

To be sure, these offenses are not the material of great moral drama, but in Brink's hand, Barbier's defiance of Allemann and the system that sustains him emerges as a compelling indictment of the corrupt colonial authorities. The noose tightens around Barbier, who eventually faces trial for libel. Like many of Brink's characters, he believes he can find justice within the system and only elects to escape prison when he realizes he cannot.

His flight to join the Afrikaner farmers, however, only compounds his problems. On treks into the interior Barbier witnesses the brutal, senseless slaughter of Hottentots and other natives, and reaches this conclusion:

"I understood at last something of what I'd been living with those past months: this violence, this energy, this seeming exuberant cruelty, this need to subdue all adversaries real and imagined by brute force, this passion to destroy. All of it sprang not from exaggerated confidence, nor even from hate, but from terror: the fear of this vast land, of its spaces, of its unmerciful light, of what lay lurking in this light, of its dark people."

Barbier eventually leads a rebellion against the Cape elite, but the ability of the authorities to lure even the insolent and disgruntled Afrikaner farmers back into the system assures his abandonment. Designated an outlaw, he finally surrenders.

What he is left with in the end is his tortured conscience and his quest for the escaped slave, Rosette, to whom he has addressed his tale. It is at this point—near the close—that the novel soars to extraordinary poetic heights. Facing execution, he imagines a solitary trek into the interior of Africa to ask absolution for all that the white man has done: "This is my necessary purging on behalf of all of us who have invaded this space to subjugate it with our presumption and visit it with our devastation."

Michael Kerrigan (review date 9 February 1996)

SOURCE: "A Vision of Birds," in *Times Literary Supplement,* No. 4845, February 9, 1996, p. 22.

[*In the following review, Kerrigan focuses on the protagonist of* Imaginings of Sand *and examines the implications of this fictional creation.*]

History is in the making in South Africa, the elections of 1994 due to be held in just a few days, yet it is personal news that brings thirty-three-year-old Kristien Müller home from her London exile. An ANC supporter—and, before world-weariness set in, an activist—she has become disenchanted before her time.

Back in the Little Karoo, however, her grandmother retains the capacity to weave spells. Kristien sensed something amiss when Ouma Kristina appeared to her in a vision, riding on the back of a great bird. A phone call from her elder sister Anna, the next day, confirms it: Ouma's house has been firebombed by "terrorists", and Ouma left seriously injured. Kristien must go to her. "It is time", she tells herself, "to return to older kinds of knowing, to withdraw again to that desert where Ouma and her spirits have roamed and where they are now in danger of extinction." Only Kristien will do, she realizes: to Anna, Ouma's stories are so much eccentric maundering. The Martha to Kristien's Mary, stoic, stay-at-home Anna married an unreconstructed Boer farmer and has remained in the Little Karoo throughout, keeping some obscure sort of faith with a life of childbirth, violence and frustration. And sure enough, when Kristien arrives at the hospital where Ouma Kristina lies—surrounded by the birds which flock about her wherever she goes—she learns that her grandmother has willed her return. "You were away too long", says Ouma. "But I'll give you back your memory."

First, however, Ouma must be restored—much against the wishes of the hospital authorities and of Anna, who share the prevalent white paranoia about further terrorist outrages—to her now semi-derelict home, "The Bird Place". A veritable palace built on the back of the early-century ostrich-feather boom, the original plans were lost, and the house was put together piece-meal by Ouma's grandmother, Petronella. "Three storeys high, topped with turrets, minarets, flèches, campaniles, domes, what had started off as a High Victorian folly turned out as Boer Baroque." This rococo ruin provides the perfect setting for Ouma's astonishing "testament". "A whole virulent past made flesh", Ouma now works herself out in words, bequeathing to Kristien the stories of her female ancestors: women like Kamma/Maria, who in the eighteenth century became an intermediary between Boers and Koikhoi, her words interpreting, her body a bridge; and Lottie, who disappeared while seeking her shadow. There's the woman who lived as a man and married, and the woman (Kristina herself) who flew to Baghdad on a magic carpet with her young Jewish lover. Beside the solid stone monuments of the official, male past, these "imaginings of sand" seem shifting and insubstantial. Yet it is this rambling roundabout skein of stories, we understand, which comprises the true history of the Afrikaners, its conventional chronology mocked by incestuous relations and deceits between generations, its certainties called into question by a hundred hidden compromises, its purity informed against by centuries of secret miscegenation. Where the dead, sterile annals of white supremacism—so recently established, and so soon set aside—belong strictly and solely to the past, this living history, rooted as it is in "older kinds of knowing", has a present and a future too.

More sceptical readers will, of course, feel that the "older kinds of knowing" turned up by Kristien's quest in the end resemble nothing more antique than 1970s "herstory". Such cynics will find in Ouma Kristina's view that birds are the spirits of dead women nothing more moving than an echo of P.G. Wodehouse's Madeline Bassett. They may even wonder whether it is really so impressive, after all, that the old wise-woman should have carefully preserved a complete menarche-to-menopause set of her used sanitary towels—or whether there isn't, for all the laudable womanly defiance Kristien manages to find in the fact, something a shade narcissistic about the idea. Just what sort of femininity is it that *Imaginings of Sand* is affirming? There are more fundamental reasons for finding the novel unsatisfactory, however: Kristien herself, as narrator-protagonist, represents a major weakness, both moral and structural.

Unimpeachably feisty, excitingly sexy and intriguingly liberated (she has slept with black freedom fighters), she remains, none the less, deliciously vulnerable. How then does such a paragon come to hit it off so badly with her reader? Not because, as her intendedly disarming self-characteriza-

tion early in the novel would have it, she "can be nasty, prejudiced, petulant, vindictive, unreliable": this is just another of the promises on which the novel fails to deliver. Rather, it is because she has no imagination. A strange thing to say, perhaps, of a woman so admirably equipped for the reception of stories and the seeing of spirits, yet it is the most striking thing about her. Kristien may see the strangest visions, but she is quite unable to engage imaginatively, with her sister Anna, to sympathize with her experience or, from the lofty heights of her heroic radicalism, to comprehend her struggle. Such sisterly sympathy as Kristien has attained after a novel's worth of personal growth is achieved entirely in her own sophisticated terms of reference. Yet it is precisely the prosaic, fearful Annas of Afrikaner history (glimpsed only in passing here as we trace the meandering journey of Ouma Kristina's visionary company down the dreaming, healing centuries) whom the reader ends up wanting to have known better. Such people have no real place in Kristien's imagination: do they have any in André Brink's new South Africa?

Amanda Hopkinson (review date 23 February 1996)

SOURCE: "Hidden from History," in *New Statesman and Society,* February 23, 1996, p. 45, 46.

[*In the following review, Hopkinson discusses Brink's presentation of "a multiplicity of women's viewpoints" in* Imaginings of Sand.]

We've had a few centuries to accustom ourselves to women writing as men what they couldn't write as women. Curiously, though, while Richardson's *Clarissa* and *Pamela* served as prototypes both of the novel and of women's writing, later male authors have generally shunned female voices. Where men are active and women passive, for a man to adopt a female pseudonym would be as pointless as to make menstruation, childbearing and domestic violence—rather than their supposed counterparts of politics, lovers, independence—the proper subject of male literary creation.

Yet this is what the South African novelist André Brink has done in his fictitious family history as he alternates the choices made by two Afrikaner sisters, Anna and Kristien. It is, through the stories of their grandmother, the account of a female dynasty in which the men—drunk, violent or merely callously careless—are "best left out of it".

In a South Africa remarkably free from violent black-on-white recrimination, there still exists one critical backlash—white-on-white, against the Afrikaner. Brink is an Afrikaner writer, who has the ear and the talent to subvert stereotypical right-wing rhetoric. The characters in his novels stand out from their political and geographical context to carry the enterprise through convincingly.

Put like this, the scheme of *Imaginings of Sand* sounds simplistic. A white woman reaches inner maturity and autonomy and discovers she stands alone in the world; the new South Africa, ditto. It's a danger Brink forestalls by acknowledging the tendency to "melodrama" and, more importantly, by blending story and history, fantasy and actuality, through the figure of her dying grandmother.

Kristien is the book's protagonist, and the canny way-in for western readers: she got away as a student, worked for the ANC and became the lover of a (married) future minister. But Ouma, the reason for her return, is its heroine. Ouma starts by sitting on the tombstone of her ancestors and conversing with them. Kristien ends by sitting on Ouma's stone and reliving her origins, overturning her identity as one who runs away and who "believes the future is more important than the past".

Ouma comes accompanied by birds and announces that "Birds are the spirits of dead women". The family business involved ostrich farming; two of the wonderfully named mahems are regular companions; a starling crashes into the window as Kristien first visits her in hospital after the fire-bombing of her home; flights of birds circle as Ouma tells her stories. With her dying words, Ouma wonders at the cosmic joke: "If there is a God, why am I allergic to feathers?"

Ouma is the bearer of the word. Her story-spinning intermingles the intimacies of family romance with the intricacies of history. From the frontispiece (which quotes the Mexican poet Octavio Paz) onwards, creation myths loom large. Aztec culture re-cast Adam and Eve as Cortés and empress Malinche, begetters of a hybrid race. Azania's tradition gives us Kamma (or Maria or Eva), the bigamous, indigenous wife of the white settler at the laboured birth of a new nation. Brink's other stories draw directly on Susanna Smit's diaries of the Boer pioneers' Great Trek, but all reiterate the shadow-selves who are the true companions on life's journey. Kristien concludes that: "History is not an impersonal force that sweeps us along like a flood; it is as real and physical as this body, which so serenely enfolds its past selves."

In a South Africa remarkably free from violent black-on-white recrimination, there still exists one critical backlash—white-on-white, against the Afrikaner.
    —Amanda Hopkinson

Ultimately, what carries this—or any—good book is simply

the quality of its writing. Here, that is ambitiously varied and highly accomplished; never more so than in turning the familiar to novel advantage. From Kristien's sharp acknowledgement of her weaknesses ("I could do with a respite from my habitual casting of false pearls to real swine") to Ouma's conviction that through every contrary revision of her story "there's nothing wrong with my memory", there is always fresh material to ponder.

Via the alternation of history and legend, an ancient weight is lent to political arguments. Humorously, they are put into the mouths of each gender and race, as at a dinner-party confrontation about whether women have a legitimate right to power. Brink raises even familiar feminist issues in intelligent ways. The oddity is his determination to work from a multiplicity of women's viewpoints.

Presumably, there hovers the eye and (acknowledged) hand of Mrs Brink in many details. The rites-of-passage involved in secretively obtaining a first bra, or transforming the barrenness of menopause, have a ring of experience denied to men by definition. That all this rings so true cannot be entirely down to Brink's fine writing or sensitive soul.

Rule from the pillow? An *éminence grise*? Perhaps the debate comes not simply from dinner-party wranglings, but also from heart and hearth of their transmitter. In a book whose double culmination is the achievement of majority rule via the ballot box *and* a family massacre, the political is unarguably the personal.

John F. Baker (essay date 25 November 1996)

SOURCE: "André Brink: In Tune with His Times," in *Publisher's Weekly,* Vol. 243, No.48, November 25, 1996, pp. 50-51.

[*In the following interview/profile, Baker and Brink discuss the progress in Brink's work alongside developments in South African politics and society.*]

André Brink finds himself in an almost unbelievable position for a writer: one where he can see a profound kinship between his own work and the aspirations of his country—a newly minted South Africa free of the intolerable burden of apartheid under which it had labored for most of the author's life.

"There's just such an overwhelming amount of material to be used that sometimes you want, as an author, simply to take a breather from it," says Brink, whose latest novel, *Imaginings of Sand,* begins, very notably, to make use of such new material. It has just been published here by

Harcourt after winning stellar reviews in its Secker & Warburg London edition. "What was it the poet said?" Asks Brink, echoing Wordsworth. "'What bliss was it in that dawn to be alive!'"

A degree of comfort with his native land has been a long time coming to Brink, who, as an Afrikaner born into a conservative South African household 60 years ago, has improbably (for most of the vociferous opponents to apartheid came from the English-speaking side) spent most of his mature years at war with it.

Brink meets *PW* in a chic Chelsea Italian restaurant during one of his occasional visits to this country just before returning to his work as Professor of English at Capetown University. With his open-neck black shirt and leather jacket, dark curly hair tinged with gray, brooding eyes behind his glasses and rugged features, he looks not unlike what James Dean might have looked like had he lived to see 60.

And in fact, Brink has cut a rather romantic figure in his homeland, a rebel ever since he first began to write for publication. "I knew I would be a writer, whatever else I might be, since I was nine years old," he says in his distinctive South African twang that is like a strange cross between Australian and Merseyside. "That's when I published my first atrocious little poem. I wrote my first novel at 12, sent the first one to a publisher at 14. They turned it down as too erotic. I didn't even know what the word meant!" When he did start to publish, as a student at an Afrikaner university in the late 1950s, it was "very unimpressive stuff. The Afrikaner tradition then was all naturalistic." It was when he went to the Sorbonne in Paris for postgraduate studies in 1959 that Brink's life turned around.

"I saw this huge Picasso retrospective exhibition, and I was amazed; I thought if he could turn everything upside down like that, so could I as a writer." When he went home, it was to join with a handful of other young writers who became known as "The Sixties," and whose very experimental work aimed to question every kind of authority—political, religious and moral. The only work from that time that achieved any overseas circulation was *The Ambassador,* translated by Brink (who at that time wrote only in Afrikaans) as *File on a Diplomat* (1965).

But although the 1960s were an exciting decade, Brink also became increasingly uncomfortable in his rigidly conservative—and increasingly brutal—surroundings. "The massacre at Sharpeville [where, in 1960, dozens of demonstrating blacks were gunned down] really shook me up," he remembers. He went abroad again, back to Paris, in 1967. "I was sick and tired of South Africa and thought I'd settle abroad permanently." Then, next year, came the French student revolt and the whole "Year of Revolutions," which turned out to be a watershed for Brink. "It made me realize I couldn't just be a solitary agent as a writer. I had to be involved in society. So I went back, knowing it would be difficult but knowing too that I had to explore where I'd come from, where the whole country had come from and what was really happening there."

Brink's next book, *Looking on Darkness* (1973) was his first overtly political work, the story of a "Cape Colored" man (one of the many endless gradations of nonwhite in South Africa) who has a suicide pact with his white lover but is jailed for her murder and becomes aware of the torture of political prisoners in South African jails. It was promptly banned, the first book written in Afrikaans ever to suffer this fate and which, Brink asserts, "was devastating to me. It meant I'd lost my readership." From then on, he realized he would have to look for English-speaking readers overseas, because he could expect little circulation at home. *Looking on Darkness* was published a year later, in Brink's own English translation, by W.H. Allen in London and, another year later, in the U.S. by William Morrow, whose Larry Hughes became an admirer—a pattern that was to last for most of the next decade.

Because much of his audience was now in the U.K. and the U.S., Brink began writing not only in his native tongue but also in English. For 1977's *Instant in the Wind,* he says, "I started making notes in both languages, which is something I've done ever since as necessary. It was intended to establish in my own mind different attitudes towards the material."

Writing Under Surveillance

The banning of *Looking on Darkness* immediately drew the attention of the omnipresent South African state security apparatus, and from then until the 1994 triumph of the ANC, Brink was a watched man, at home and abroad. "My phone was tapped, my mail was opened in very obvious ways—they *wanted* you to know they were doing it. Then of course there were the anonymous phone calls, at all hours of the day and night, threatening to kill you and your family. Once a fire bomb was thrown at my house. There was an attempt to sabotage my car. I would be called in for interrogation, they would search my house, turning everything upside down. Once they even confiscated my typewriter, but I borrowed one from a friend, and it inspired me to work harder than ever."

Brink's *A Dry White Season* (1980), which studies the consequences of a white man's investigation into the prison death of a black acquaintance, became the best-known of his early books, partly as a result of an admirable movie version—incidentally, one of the earliest movies made by a black woman director, Euzhan Palcy. While acknowledging its virtues, Brink notes wryly that "It was vastly overshadowed by the big-budget *Cry Freedom,* which covered some of the same sort of ground."

The banning of *Looking on Darkness* immediately drew the attention of the omnipresent South African state security apparatus, and from then until the 1994 triumph of the ANC, Brink was a watched man, at home and abroad.
                                                —*John F. Baker*

Meanwhile, one of the indirect effects of the ban on his work in South Africa was to make him a sort of guiding figure for many unhappy Africans. "Since it was obvious I was dead against apartheid, they assumed I could help them, and I had an endless stream of people coming to me with their problems, asking for help. Some of them I was able to help, some not." But it all took its toll on his time, and for some years in the 1980s Brink found he had little time for writing.

When he came back, in 1988, it was with a peculiarly personal novel—one embracing the difficulties faced by a writer in his circumstances who wants to create work that is not essentially political: *States of Emergency,* he says, was set down in a rush. "Day after day, I worked at it, fitting together the pieces of a mosaic." Its publication also marked the end of a chapter in his American publishing life: Hughes retired at Morrow, and Brink (who, like most foreign writers with things worth saying, is represented here by agent Georges Borchardt) was taken up by Jim Silberman, then at Summit. There, and later at Little, Brown, Silberman remained Brink's publisher until the most recent book. "Jim was a splendid man to work with, and I don't think he has been well treated," notes Brink, who enjoys working with his new Harcourt editor Drenka Willan and hopes this too can be a long relationship.

After such recent books as *An Act of Terror* (Summit, 1991), an intense and disturbing examination of the lives and motives of anti-apartheid terrorists, and *On the Contrary* (Little, Brown, 1994), a quirky retelling of South African history as a series of picaresque legends done in the style of an 18th-century English novel, *Imaginings of Sand* is a bold departure in many ways. At once a starkly realistic picture of a country in the midst of major upheaval and a lyric relating of its past in a series of tales strongly laced with elements of magic, the book is infused with an intensely feminine perspective.

Brink thought long and hard before taking such a chance (in fact, one London reviewer lambasted him for trespassing on

feminist concerns). "For a long time, I couldn't be involved in anything but apartheid, it was all-pervasive," he muses. "Now I felt the silences of the past could be revisited. And one of the things I discovered was that the real enemy wasn't apartheid, it was the abuse and misuse of power, which is the enemy, in different forms, everywhere in the world. Previously I concentrated on racial aggression, but there are many other kinds—sexual, for instance—which went hand in hand with it. I felt it inevitable that I should explore the female side, and to do this I had to adopt a woman's voice."

The results are astonishingly successful. The story is told through the eyes of an attractively feisty, liberal white South African woman who returns home, after years of exile, to be at her ancient grandmother's deathbed. Issues of sisterhood, motherhood and crude male predation are in the contemporary forefront, and the history of grandmother Ouma's amazing ancestry is laid out in a series of dazzlingly vivid parables centered on the essential female ethos of procreation.

If the current turnaround in South Africa (one of the great scenes in *Imaginings of Sand* is a joyful pageant of the election day that brought Nelson Mandela to the presidency) has freed Brink to concentrate on concerns other than the political, it is not without its poignancies. "In the old days, we [meaning also anti-establishment writers like Nadine Gordimer, Athol Fugard and the late Alan Paton] had the opportunity to establish regular, active contacts with writers in like circumstances in Central Europe and Latin America. We got used to being seen as beacons in the struggle against demonic systems, and that gave us as writers a sense of importance we lack now. We tend to be absurdly nostalgic from time to time."

For the past five years, Brink, formerly at the secluded Rhodes University in Grahamstown, has taught half the year at Capetown, which has meant a much broader literary life: "I got to know J.M. Coetzee, the best writer South Africa has ever produced—if anyone can be said to really know him." And he tells the story of how the highly reclusive Coetzee, who had once unprecedentedly agreed to give a speech at the university, did so by getting up from his seat, turning on a tape recorder and sitting down again while the machine played his pre-recorded speech.

Brink is still hard at work, even if fiction at present, despite a multitude of ideas and themes, is on the back burner. He has just completed a book on the narrative language of the novel, and currently making the rounds ("Georges is peddling it, and I hope Drenka will take it") is *Reinventing a Continent: Essays on South African Writing & Politics,* for which, Brink is delighted to report, President Mandela has written a foreword. There are fine South African writers he would like to see better known overseas, and he mentions

Njabulo Ndebele and Joel Matlou, both short-story writers ("Black South Africans excel in shorter forms, for a good reason; they never had time or opportunity for anything longer") and a playwright, Zakes Mda.

And, surprisingly, Brink himself has theatrical ambitions. "I wrote some plays back in the '60s, but unless you had your own theater group, like Fugard, you had no chance of getting them mounted. But two months ago, at a conference in Salzburg with Ariel Dorfman and Arthur Miller, I found all my old passion being rekindled. I've written a new play, and it will be staged in South Africa. After that, who knows?"

He breathes the happy sigh of a writer for whom new material is no problem. "It's as if the whole nation is going to the shrink, and you're sitting there with your notebook," he exults. No 50-minute hour for Dr. Brink.

Theodore F. Sheckels Jr. (essay date 1996)

SOURCE: "Action," in *The Lion on the Freeway: A Thematic Introduction to Contemporary South African Literature in English*, Peter Lang Publishing, Inc., 1996, pp. 181-99.

[*In the following excerpt from Sheckels's book, the author examines Brink's* A Dry White Season *and Nadine Gordimer's* Burger's Daughter, *considering the development of the protagonists via the actions they engage in.*]

At the end of Coetzee's *Waiting for the Barbarians,* we leave the magistrate a guilt-ridden, but broken man. His guilt has led him to a futile act of rebellion and into an equally futile act of redemption. At the end of Fugard's "*Master Harold*" *. . . and the Boys,* we leave Hally a guilt-ridden and confused seventeen year-old boy/man. In the text, there is some hope that his guilt will lead to action; in the theatre, this hope can be strengthened or weakened, depending upon how the director and the actors choose to interpret the script. Only outside of the text and the theatre does hope truly blossom, for guilt over what he did when he was seventeen to his friend Sam led Athol Fugard to act, the writing and staging of the play being *the* particular act (with Fugard's oeuvre being the act on a larger scale).

In this chapter, we deal with two works, both written in 1979, where the action is *in* the text. Nadine Gordimer's *Burger's Daughter* is the more difficult of the two, for Gordimer takes us very much inside the mind of her central character, Rosa Burger. Rosa has lived in the shadow of her activist parents. Now, on her own, she must figure out, first, who she is, and, second, who she is *in relation to* her South African homeland. Andre Brink's *A Dry White Season* is the easier. Al-

though the novel's mode of narration is sophisticated, once the reader gets to the core of the story—the enlightenment of comfortably middle class Afrikaner school teacher Benjamin Du Toit, one is able to follow the plot as if the novel were a suspenseful thriller. The ferocity of Brink's indictment of *his* people and the philosophical depth of the novel's politics do not strike one until the story reaches its conclusion.

Action then is so much a part of Brink's novel that it dominates our mind *as* we read. The action in Gordimer's masterpiece is quieter; nonetheless, it is to what Rosa Burger ultimately *does* that the entire novel points. In both cases, the action is on behalf of the nation's oppressed people—on behalf of the lion; in both cases, the action is premised upon an awareness on the part of the central character of her or his complicity in the oppression.

Burger's Daughter

The bulk of Nadine Gordimer's *Burger's Daughter* is appropriately titled, for, until the very end of the novel, she has no clearly-defined identity of her own. Her father's life, in many ways (and in ways she resented) defined her own:

> My mother is dead and there is only me, there, for him. Only me. My studies, my work, my love affairs must fit in with the twice-monthly visits to the prison, for life, as long as he lives—if he had lived. My professors, my employers, my men must accept this overruling, I have no passport because I am my father's daughter. People who associate with me must be prepared to be suspect because I am my father's daughter. And there is more to it, more than you know—what I wanted was to take a law degree, but there was no point; too unlikely that, my father's daughter, I should be allowed to practise law, so I had to do something else instead, anything, something that would pass as politically innocuous, why not in the field of medicine, my father's daughter. (62-63)

The novel, in fact, is very much an account, told from five if not more narrative perspectives, of her struggle to find this separate identity. Although Gordimer has denied that she is a "feminist" writer, the novel will take us through three phases in this struggle and ultimately demonstrate—in line with a feminist ideology—that, for Rosa, personal and political *must* be connected. The novel will further demonstrate that body and mind (the sensual and the ideological) must be connected.

The novel has three parts. The long first part reviews, in a meandering manner, Rosa's life before and immediately after her father's death in prison. Her father, perhaps—as

Stephen Clingman has suggested in his 1986 *The Novels of Nadine Gordimer*—modeled on South Africa Communist Party leader Bram Fischer, was famous for the intense political debates that took place around his swimming pool. All, regardless of race, were welcomed to Dr. Burger's home and to these discussions, and all were treated as equals. Many of these "liberals" and "revolutionaries" brought their families along. When Rosa was growing up, she often played with the children, some white and some black. One in particular, a black boy she knew as "Baasie" (i.e., "little boss"), will prove significant later in Rosa's story. Back when they were children together, there was no awareness of his "otherness" because of either sex or race. Their relationship was a sensual one but not a sexual one. "He and Rosa had often shared a bed when they were as little as Tony . . ."; they "fought for the anchorage of wet hair on Lionel Burger's warm breast in the cold swimming pool" (55). Rosa's father was a surrogate father to the boy; Rosa's mother was a surrogate mother. When circumstances resulted in Baasie's being sent away, Rosa "forgot Baasie. It was easy" (71). But the person she forgot when she was young returns to her mind frequently when she matures. She recalls "a special, spreading warmth when Baasie had wet the bed in our sleep" and how "in the night [she] didn't know whether this warmth that took us back into the enveloping fluids of a host body came from him or [her]" (139-40). When, still later, she feels she has "lost connection" with the human dimension of politics, she re-recalls this "memory of childhood warmth" (172).

Rosa grew out of this asexual sensuality. Soon, politics was ideological and public, and she found herself expected to embrace her father's (and mother's) ideology and to be as comfortable in the public arena as they were. As a young girl, she never really questioned these expectations, but, after her parents' deaths, she did. Largely as a monologue addressed to her dropout friend Conrad, she does so, as she reviews her life thus far, in the novel's first part.

During this first part, politics has a sterile feel. It swirls around Rosa, occasionally occupying her mind. It does not, however, affect her body. But her body, we discover, is central to how Rosa expresses herself and, thereby, *is* herself:

> Rosa Burger's prim thighs closed at the bony outline of pubis in shrunken jeans, a long sunburned neck with the cup at the collarbones where—she sat so still; no nerves, she did not fidget—a pulse could be seen beating: Noel de Witt's girl; also the mistress of a Swede (at least; of those that were known) who had passed through, and some silent bearded blond fellow, not someone who belonged, not he, either. A body with the assurance of embraces, as cultivated intelligence forms a mind. Men would recognize it at a glance as the other can be recognized at a word. (121)

In just a few movements, one could discern how Rosa's being was wrapped in her body just as, in a few words, one can discern who is and who is not intellectually gifted. The most crucial event of that first part is tied to this sensuality. That event was not her father's death (which liberated her) but, rather, her meeting Marisa Kgosana, the activist wife of an imprisoned African leader. Marissa is dynamic and very sensual—so much so that Rina Leeuwenberg refers to her as "Mother Africa," a figure who, Richard I. Smyer argues, embodies the physicality, the wholeness, and the primal energy that Gordimer's heroines increasingly aspire to or exhibit. Rosa is *strongly* attracted to Marisa—more because of this over-powering sensuality than the "black consciousness" ideology she preaches.

Rosa's initial description stresses Marisa's "half-bare back," "the colour of her skin," "two rounded shoulder-blades," "proud backside jutting negligently at the angle of the weight-bearing hip," and "long legs" (134). Marisa's physical appearance has a powerful effect on Rosa:

> To touch in women's token embrace against the live, night cheek of Marisa, seeing huge for a second the lake-flash of her eye, the lilac-pink of her inner lip against transluscent-edged teeth, to enter for a moment the invisible magnetic field of the body of a beautiful creature and receive on oneself its imprint—breath misting and quickly fading on a glass pane—this was to immerse in another mode of perception. (134)

This kiss causes Rosa to speak of "a sensual redemption" into "a new brotherhood of flesh" (135). She connects the sensuality she feels in Marisa's presence with her earlier relationship with Baasie: "I felt it in Marisa's presence; the comfort of Baasie in the same bed when the dark made that house creak with threats" (135).

Unfortunately, as Leeuwenberg goes on to note, Rosa cannot be like Marisa in the patriarchal white society of South Africa which insists (albeit at times subtly) on female passivity. There is, Rosa thinks, no *place* for a white woman like Marisa. Since she wishes to become a white woman like Marisa, this means that there is no *place* for her. Furthermore, political South Africa, even though Lionel is dead, is still the place it was while he lived. This political place is not Rosa's *place* either; it's too public. So, Rosa, seeking a private place where she can be assertively sensual, leaves South Africa for France. Her linking of political with public leads her to set aside politics—for the time being.

The second part of *Burger's Daughter* is the French interlude. There, Rosa explores her sensuality fully. Perhaps, Rosa seems to be thinking in this section, which (according to Margot Heinemann) is addressed to her father's first wife

Katya, Rosa's lover Bernard, and Rosa herself, that France—Nice, in particular—can be her *place*. It certainly is a sensual place, for there she finds herself "[d]issolving in the wine and pleasure of scents, sights and sounds existing only in themselves, associated with nothing and nobody . . ." (222). The exterior space was "filled with the peppery-snuff scent of celery, weak sweet perfume of flowers and strawberries, cool salty secretions of sea-slippery fish, odours of cheeses, contracting the nasal membranes; the colours, shapes, shine, density, pattern, texture and feel of fruits and vegetables; the encounters and voices of people handling them" (244). A sensual feast! The interior space, the guestroom at Katya's villa, was "clear with different qualities of light," had "a long cane chair to read the poetry and elegant magazines in, a large low bed to bring a lover to," and was the perfect place for "[a] girl, a creature whose sense of existence would be in her nose buried in flowers, peach juice running down her chin, face tended at mirrors, mind dreamily diverted, body seeking pleasure" (229-30).

Bernard is a crucial figure in this second section of the novel: he alerts Rosa to pleasures and appetites that she never knew she had. As a result, it is clear, as Margot Heinemann suggests in *The Uses of Fiction* (1982), that she is very much *physically* in love with Bernard. Their initial lovemaking is described in terms that evoke Eden:

> They emerged for each other all at once: they had never seen each other on a beach. . . . He might never have been presented with a woman before, or she a man. Tremendous sweet possibilities of renewal surged between them; to explode in that familiar tender explosion all that has categorized sexuality, from chastity to taboo, illicit license to sexual freedom. In a drop of saliva there was a whole world. He turned the wet tip of his tongue round the whorl of the navel Didier had said was like that of an orange. (277-78)

And after that initial experience, there were many others. They yearned for the few times when they could forget the rest of the world and enjoy "the experience of being alone, a couple in the pure state," pure "because the night-and-day presence of the other, sensation and rhythm of breathing, smell, touch, voice, sight of, interpenetration with was total provision" and "becomes in itself one single unifying demand" (305).

And when he offers to set her up as his mistress in a stylish apartment in Paris, she finds the proposition very appealing. Perhaps this apartment can be her *place*.

I keep emphasizing "place" for a reason. As Lorraine Liscio has stressed in an article in *Modern Fiction Studies,* Gordimer precedes the novel *per se* with the following epigraph from Claude Levi-Strauss: "I am the place in which something has occurred." However, about halfway through the novel, Rosa talks about "A 'place'" as "somewhere to belong," as "something that establishes one's lot and sets aside much to which one doesn't belong" (149). This latter quotation suggests that Rosa is still looking for a literal place—a some*where;* a some*thing,* not realizing yet what Levi-Strauss' words suggest, that she *is* the place—by definition private and (especially now in France) sensual, but not yet political or ideological.

What completes her search is her encounter—in person and then by telephone—with her childhood playmate Baasie. Zwelinzima, as Baasie is now known, forces Rosa to see him (and, by extension, other blacks) as she really had never seen him before. As Clingman notes, Zwelinzima, by viciously attacking her father's legend and her comfortable liberalism, forces Rosa to see him as "other."

Zwelinzima had been offended earlier in the evening by the way people treated Rosa's father as noble (because he had gone to prison) and Rosa herself as noble (because her father had died in prison). Many black men, including his father, he reminds her, had gone to prison; and many blacks, including himself, had fathers who had died—had been murdered—in prison:

> There are dozens of our fathers sick and dying like dogs, kicked out of the locations where they can't work anymore. Getting old and dying in prison. Killed in prison. It's nothing. I know plenty blacks like Burger. It's nothing, it's us. . . . (320)

He had also been offended by Rosa's addressing him as "Baasie," "little boss," the unintentionally offensive nickname he had acquired in the Burger household, not the noble name his father had given him. This nickname encapsulated to Zwelinzima the shallowness of Burger's liberalism. He recalls his childhood in terms very unlike those used earlier by Rosa:

> . . . your parents took the little black kid into their home, not the backyard like other whites, right into the house. Eating at the table and sleeping in the bedroom, the same bed, their little black boss. And then the bastard was pushed off back to his mud huts and tin shanties. . . . One of Lionel Burger's best tame blacks sent scuttling like a bloody cockroach. . . . (320)

Seeing him this way—as someone patronized and then discarded by white liberalism—results in Rosa, for really the first time, seeing herself as white and all that entails. She realizes the truth in Zwelinzima's rhetorical question, "why do you think you should be different from all the other whites who've been shitting on us ever since they came?" (322) Her body literally revolts at the realization (which is reinforced for both of them when she first asks him if he wants money and then can't even pronounce his Xhosa name correctly):

> . . . she ran to the bathroom and fell to her knees at the lavatory bowl, vomiting. The wine, the bits of sausage—she laid her head, gasping between spasms, on the porcelain rim, slime dripping from her mouth with the tears of effort running from her nose. (323)

Shortly thereafter, she commits herself to doing whatever is necessary to obliterate the gap between black and white, between Zwelinzima and herself. The first step, she realizes, is to return to her native South Africa. There she lets her body, as Judie Newman has suggested in her 1988 *Nadine Gordimer,* reject the male genital-sexual definition of sensuality. Rose then replaces it with a more all-body-encompassing definition. Her body then leads her to work as a physiotherapist among black children. Poignantly, she notes that, after the Soweto massacre and riots, there are many black children in need of more than just physical therapy:

> In the second half of 1976 those who were born deformed were joined by those who had been shot. The school riots filled the hospital; the police who answered stones with machine-guns and patrolled Soweto firing revolvers at any street-corner group of people encountered, who raided High Schools and picked off the targets of youngsters escaping in the stampede, also wounded anyone else who happened to be within the random of their fire. (342)

In the hospital, she busied herself "[e]xtracting bullets from the matrix of flesh, picking out slivers of shattered bone, sewing, succouring, dripping back into arteries the vital fluids that flowed away in the streets with the liquor bottles smashed by children who despised their fathers' consolations . . ." (343). As she chooses this course of action, she also is choosing a political ideology. This ideology is not, however, one rooted in the abstract theorizing that occurred around her father's swimming pool but rather in the battered bodies of the black children of Soweto. As several commentators have noted, Rosa seems to be suggesting that, post-Soweto, her father's white liberalism is no longer going to be sufficient.

Once back in South Africa, it little matters where Rosa does her chosen work. The literal *place* is not important, for Rosa has found within herself a place that merges personal and political, private and public, body and mind, sensual and ideological. From this place, Rosa hopes that she can obliterate one more bipolar dualism, that between "white" and "other." Although Gordimer claims not to be a "feminist,"

she seems to suggest that the way to achieve this final dissolution is through the common bond as "other" shared with blacks by women.

Rosa, as she embraces *her* kind of political action in the novel's third and final section, proves to be her father's daughter, However, the course she has taken in the novel has led her to a kind of political action unlike her father's before her. That activism finally find her in prison. There, although physically separated from women of other colors, she finds ways through "tiny scrolled messages," through shared gifts, and through songs both religious and revolutionary, to unite the different groups:

> . . . the prison was so old that actual physical barriers against internal communication were ramshackle and the vigilance of the female warders . . . could not prevent messages, the small precious gifts of prison economy (cigarettes, a peach, a tube of handcream, a minute electric torch) from being exchanged between the races. Or songs. Early on, Marisa's penetrating, wobbly contralto announced her presence not far off, from her solitary confinement to Rosa's, and Clare's. She sang hymns, piously gliding in and out of the key of 'Abide with me' to ANC freedom songs in Xhosa, and occasionally bursting into Miriam Makeba's click song—this last to placate and seduce the wardresses, for whom it was a recognizable pop number. The voices of the other black women took up and harmonized whatever she sang, quickly following the changes in the repertoire. (355)

Marisa would later complain about a spinal ailment, and Rosa would be recruited to provide Marisa with twice weekly therapeutic massages. "Laughter escaped through the thick diamond-mesh and bars of Rosa's cell during these sessions" (355).

This prison *place* may seem to be the one Rosa finally finds, but its similarity to her father's last place should signal us that this literal place is a coincidence. Rosa *is* her own place, and, as Rosa Burger now, not Lionel Burger's daughter, she can address the novel's last section, where she *acts,* to her dead father. She is now acting on her own terms, acting as Rosa Burger, not Lionel Burger's daughter.

A Dry White Season

Rosa had to separate herself from her father's shadow in order to act; Benjamin Du Toit will have to separate himself from his entire family, from his entire Afrikaner people. He initially, however, is unaware of what the price of action will be.

Ben is slowly drawn into action. His black gardener, Gordon Ngubene, comes to Ben for help. Gordon's son had been arrested during the Soweto riots of June 1976. Gordon wants Ben to help him find out where his son is. When Ben discovers and tells Gordon that his son is dead, Gordon wants Ben to help him recover his son's body so that he may properly bury it. Refusing to accept the police's refusal to produce the body and believing that his son was *not* killed in the rioting but rather in police custody, Gordon begins making inquiries (to the extent a black man can). This investigating quickly lands him in prison, where he, under suspicious circumstances, dies.

Ben cannot rest until he finds out what happened to Gordon. Early on, he is fairly committed to this quest. After he sees Gordon's dead body and the marks of what the police did to Gordon while he was in custody, "[a] barely recognizable face, the left side distorted and discoloured, a blackish purple" (91), he becomes firmly—very firmly—committed:

> Now he had to believe it. Now he'd seen it with his own eyes. But it remained ungraspable. He had to force himself, even as he stood there looking down into the coffin, to accept that this was indeed Gordon. . . . (91)

Ben quickly discovers the costs of this commitment. He becomes the subject of police scrutiny. His home becomes the site of, first, security police searches and, later, security police counter-terrorist burglaries and bombings.

What makes Brink's *A Dry White Season* exceptional is its exploration of the pitfalls that a white liberal who commits to the black cause faces.
—*Theodore F. Sheckels Jr.*

Ben is becoming an embarrassment to the Afrikaner community he has long been a complacent, trusting member of. His church turns on him, so he rejects it. His compatriots at the school where he teaches reject him and malign him because of his "politics." His wife and his married daughters turn on him. His wife eventually leaves; one of his daughters, Suzette, cozies up to her father in order to find out where he is hiding the documents he and other friends of Gordon had been gathering to use against the security police in a court of law. She then tells the police. When Ben catches on and uses his awareness of her unconfessed complicity to outwit the police and mail the documents to a college friend who is now a writer, the police get angry and even. They arrange Ben's murder.

The story thus far is dramatic but superficial. What makes Brink's *A Dry White Season* exceptional is its exploration of the pitfalls that a white liberal who commits to the black cause faces.

Ben—any white liberal—faces at least five dangers. First, he faces losses—losses that will be personally wrenching:

> I was forced to draw up a balance sheet in my mind. On the one side, all the bits and pieces we'd assembled so far. Not an unimpressive list by any means—at first glance. But then the debit side. Isn't the price becoming too high? I'm not thinking of what I have to go through, worried and harassed and hounded day by day. But the *others*. Especially the others. Because, at least partly, it is through my involvement that they have to suffer. (236)

Ben then lists the others:

> The cleaner: "disappeared".
>
> Dr. Hassiem: banished to Pietersburg. Julius Nqakula: in jail.
>
> The nurse: detained.
>
> Richard Harrison: sentenced to jail—even though he's going to appeal.
>
> And who else? Who is next? Are the names written on some secret list, ready to be ticked off as our time comes? (236)

Then, he asks himself an especially scary question: was he, Ben, responsible for what happened to Gordon Ngubene?

> I wanted to "clean up" Gordon's name, as Emily had put it. But all I've done so far is to plunge other people into the abyss. Including Gordon? It's like a nightmare, when I wake up at night, wondering in a sweat: Suppose I'd never tried to intercede for him after they'd detained him—would he have survived then? Am I the leper spreading disease to whoever comes close enough? (236)

Second, he faces excessive ego involvement, an involvement that leads to his acting, not for the sake of the oppressed, but rather for the personal glory he feels he will gain—in his eyes and in the eyes of a few others. Although *we* disagree with much that Ben's racist wife Susan says, we grant that there is some truth when she tells Ben that "all that matters to you is Ben Du Toit. For a long time now it's had nothing to do with Gordon or with Jonathan or anybody else" (261).

Third, he faces over-optimism: believing that he can right all wrong, reveal the truth, restore justice. He needs to learn the wisdom in a remark offered him by a friend: "There are only two kinds of madness one should guard against Ben . . . . One is the belief that we can do everything. The other is the belief that we can do nothing" (244). Fourth, as this quoted advice suggests, he faces despair when he realizes that he cannot accomplish as much as he thought. This despair is exacerbated by the losses he has suffered.

Fifth and finally, he faces the fact that he is white and therefore privileged and, as a result, damned if he acts and damned if he doesn't act:

> Whether I like it or not, whether I feel like cursing my own condition or not—and that would only serve to confirm my impotence—*I am white*. This is the small, final, terrifying truth of my broken world. I am white. And because I'm white I am born into a state of privilege. Even if I fight the system that has reduced us to this I remain white, and favoured by the very circumstances I abhor. Even if I'm hated, and ostracised, and persecuted, and in the end destroyed, nothing can make me black. And so those who are cannot but remain suspicious of me. In their eyes my very efforts to identify myself with Gordon, with all the Gordons, would be obscene. Every gesture I make, every act I commit in my efforts to help them makes it more difficult for them to define their real needs and discover for themselves their integrity and affirm their own dignity. How else could we hope to arrive beyond predator and prey, helper and helped, white and black, and find redemption?

> On the other hand: what can I do but what I have done? I cannot choose not to intervene: that would be a denial and a mockery not only of everything I believe in, but of the hope that compassion may survive among men. By not acting as I did I would deny the very possibility of that gulf to be bridged.

> If I act, I cannot but lose. But if I do not act, it is a different kind of defeat, equally decisive and maybe worse. Because then I will not even have a conscience left. (304-05)

Ben faces these pitfalls throughout the bulk of the novel— especially in those sections that he narrates directly in the pages of his diary. To a large extent, he faces them alone. His son Johan provides moral support, but the rest of his family as well as his Afrikaner friends are certainly no help to Ben. He does, however, receive some help from a young journalist named Melanie Bruwer whom he meets at the in-

quest into Gordon Ngubene's death and from her father, a retired philosophy professor.

To overcome the first two pitfalls, Ben must put the personal aside. Melanie helps Ben do this by sharing with him how she has put the personal aside in her own work on behalf of the oppressed people of southern Africa. Melanie's story is a painful one for her to tell. She was once as idealistic and as naive as Ben is now. Then, on assignment in Mozambique, she was gang-raped by a platoon of black Frelimo soldiers: "One night on my way back to the hotel I was stopped by a group of drunken soldiers . . . . They dragged me off to an empty lot and raped me, the whole lot of them" (132).

Such a personal violation could easily have caused her to retreat from her very public life as an activist. It did not. Rather than flying home, she finished her newspaper assignment in Mozambique. Years later, she is able to "chuckle" (132) about it and to even claim the gang rape "even made things easier for [her]" in so far as it enabled her to "get out of myself. To free myself from my hangups" (133). She later explains what she means by getting out of herself when she differentiates between her body and her self. Before she was raped, the two were intertwined; now, she realizes that she is not her body and that, therefore, what happens to her body does not happen to *her*. Personal hardships, losses, and vile indignities are relevant to her body, but not to *her*. She can continue on with her important political work. Ben similarly must realize that the personal hardships, etc., that he suffers are relevant to the material Ben but not the moral-spiritual Ben. That latter Ben, the *real* Ben, can continue on with his important political work. If Melanie Bruwer can put aside what she had suffered, Ben can certainly put aside what he has.

Later, Melanie talks more about her personal losses—in particular her quickly approaching loss, as a thirty year-old woman, of the potential to bear children. She tells Ben, "This country doesn't allow me to indulge myself like that. It isn't possible to lead a private life if you want to live with your conscience" (246). Not only can she and Ben cast aside the personal, they *must*, given the situation in South Africa.

Events take care of over-optimism, the third pitfall. The fourth and the fifth are more troublesome. To overcome them, Ben must keep foremost in his mind the flesh-and-blood realities that abstractions and systems and even words can mute. Melanie and her father, in very different ways, help Ben focus on flesh-and-blood. This focus gets Ben past despair and past the dilemma he faces as a privileged white South African.

Professor Phil Bruwer, when we first meet him, is working in the earth of his garden. Both the scene and the earthy condition of his attire suggest his attachment to the natural:

At first sight I took him for a Coloured gardener, squatting on his haunches beside a flower bed, pulling out weeds. Soiled corduroy trousers, black beret sporting a guinea-fowl feather, khaki shirt, pipe in his mouth, and the filthiest pair of mud-caked shoes—worn without socks or laces—I'd ever seen . . . .

His wild white mane couldn't have been combed in months. Small goatee stained with tobacco juice. The skin of his face dark and tanned like old leather, like an old discarded shoe; and two twinkling dark brown eyes half-disappearing below the unkempt eyebrows . . . .

He grinned, exposing his uneven, yellow-stained teeth, many of them mere stumps. (185-86)

Ben and Professor Bruwer begin talking history teacher to philosophy professor, but, as soon as the discussion drifts into abstractions away from the natural, the earthy, the physical, Professor Bruwer launches into a lecture indicting abstractions. He prefaces it by talking about how "the more one gets involved in philosophy and stuff, in transcendental things, the more surely you're forced back to the earth" (186). Then, he talks about how the twentieth century is "living in the spell of the Abstract. Hitler, Apartheid, the Great American Dream, the lot" (186). The abstract leads some people to commit inhuman actions and other people to ignore inhuman actions. He saw it in the '30s when he was in Nazi Germany; he is seeing it now in apartheid South Africa.

The way to overcome the evil that abstractions lead to— "[t]his sickness of the Great Abstraction" (187)—is "to come back to the physical, to flesh and bone and earth" (187). "We're running after the *verbum,* forgetting about the flesh" (187), he tells Ben.

Once you've refocused on the flesh and blood, then it becomes impossible to tolerate the oppression of human beings that *is* South Africa under apartheid. The lesson Professor Bruwer offers then is really an extension of what Ben learned when he went to Soweto (for the first time in his life) to see Gordon's battered corpse. When you see the human flesh-and-blood reality of oppression, you know you must act, even if you also know how very little your actions can accomplish.

Ben requires more than just Professor Bruwer's eloquent words. He needs contact with flesh-and-blood as well as a lecture about it. Melanie decides to provide this flesh-and-blood contact by making love with Ben. How Brink presents their love-making is important. He emphasizes Ben's desperate state in the way he has Ben narrate the event; Ben

uses and then rejects various *words* in trying to explain things. Words, it seems, are inadequate to explain what is very much a matter of the body. And it is Melanie's body— and her gift of it to Ben—that Ben ends up emphasizing:

The candour of her body. Her presence was total, and overwhelming. I feel quite ridiculous trying to grasp it now with nothing but words. How paltry it sounds, almost offensive, reduced to description. But what else can I do? Silence would be denial.

Her hair undone, loose and heavy on her shoulders. Her breasts so incredibly small, mere swellings, with dark, elongated, erect nipples. The smooth belly with the exquisite little knot in its hollow. Below, the trim triangular thicket of black hair between her legs.

But it is not that. Nothing I can ennumerate or adequately name. What mattered was that in her nakedness she was making herself available to me. The incomprehensible gift of herself. (272)

Ben continues, delighting in the physical reality of Melanie's body in print as he delighted in it that night. He celebrates "[t]he full frank miracle of her body," "the unbelievable reality of her body," "the marvel and mystery of the flesh" (273). Like a priestess in a ritual of the flesh and blood, she leads him through an experience he describes as "[a] newness, as of birth" (272). In a sense then, Melanie is leading Ben to the rebirth within him of a necessary awareness of (in her father's words) "flesh and bone and earth" (187).

Unfortunately, Melanie and Ben's lovemaking, although it may help Ben maintain the necessary contact with flesh-and-blood and remain a revolutionary actor, leads to the final collapse of his personal Afrikaner world. The security police, spying on Ben and Melanie, take pictures of the couple having intercourse and send these picture to Ben's employer and Ben's wife. Work and family (except Ben's young son) turn on poor Ben DuToit. He does not, however, react as he might have earlier. Helped by Melanie to overcome the pitfalls of pride and despair, he accepts his losses and pursues his revolutionary action with undiminished determination.

Ben Du Toit ultimately fails in so far as he is killed. His failure to succeed does not, however, diminish the fact that he acted *and* he managed to reveal the truth to a wide public. Here, we need to discuss the manner in which the novel is narrated. We begin and end *A Dry White Season* with the voice of Ben's college roommate. We learn a great deal about this man: primarily, we learn that he has very complacently accepted his lot as a white South African. He clearly has literary talent, but, thus far, he has put it to little serious use. He has spent "half a lifetime devoted to writing romantic fiction" (9) and thereby achieved some fame—enough to be bothered by members of the public who want him to write their story and flattered by members of the opposite sex who want their (to borrow from Kenyan writer Ngugi wa Th'iongo) "moments of glory" in his bed. But, at the moment Ben reestablishes contact with him after a hiatus of several years, he is experiencing a creative drought, a "dry white season." As he faces the pile of papers, newspaper clippings, and photographs Ben posted to him days before Ben was killed, this writer finds his energy returning.

This unnamed writer (perhaps Brink's semi-satiric version of himself) manages to assemble and tell, from the third person point of view, Ben Du Toit's story. The pace quickens. Eventually, it seems as if this narrator no longer feels he has the leisure to assemble Ben's story, so he shifts from third person narration to the first person narration of Ben's journal. This shift also suggests that he has found the objective stance impossible to sustain and now must merge his voice with Ben's voice. Ben has, posthumously, converted his friend to the cause.

> **Brink is suggesting that South Africa is now facing a dry white season, the word "white" serving as a wicked pun. The season suggests a kind of death. Ben, before facing his literal death, avoids a moral one—by acting.**
> —*Theodore F. Sheckels Jr.*

When the writer's voice returns at the novel's end, he is clearly changed. He is feeling some of the same feelings that Ben felt—that he is being drawn into the swirling vortex of oppression just as Ben was; that he must do something, but he can't do much:

> Is everything really beginning anew with me? And if so: how far to go? . . . Is it really just a matter of going on, purely and simply? Prodded, possibly, by some dull, guilty feeling of responsibility towards something Ben might have believed in: something man is capable of being but which he isn't very often allowed to be?
>
> I don't know.
>
> Perhaps all one can really hope for, all I am entitled to, is no more than this: to write it down. To report what I know. So that it will not be possible for any man ever to say again: *I knew nothing about it.* (315-16)

The writer does, however, succeed in accomplishing two tasks. First, he gets the story out; second, he draws us, the readers, into that same swirling vortex.

As I've already suggested, the novel's title is relevant to the narrator's situation. But, of course, its relevance goes beyond that. Brink borrows the title from Mongane Wally Serote's poem "For Don M.—Banned," in which Serote links "a dry white season" to the pain of a time in the course of revolutionary action when nothing, either constructive nor destructive, seems to be happening. Brink, however, has Ben explain the novel's title in the agrarian terms of the Afrikaner as "[t]he drought that took everything from [Pa and me], leaving us alone and scorched among the white skeletons." Ben refers to that time when, as a young boy, he saw all the sheep die as a defining point in his life. Now, he says, "it seems to me I'm finding myself on the edge of yet another dry white season, perhaps worse than the one I knew as a child" (163).

Brink is suggesting that South Africa is now facing a dry white season, the word "white" serving as a wicked pun. The season suggests a kind of death. Ben, before facing his literal death, avoids a moral one—by acting. Similarly, the unnamed writer avoids a kind of death by acting. If we are pulled into the novel, we also—Brink hopes—can avoid a moral death by first knowing and then acting. Serote tells us that "seasons come to pass," suggesting that the dry white season *will* yield to another season. It could be bloody; it could be peaceful. Brink himself offers much the same suggestion in his earlier novel ***Rumours of Rain,*** in which we are never sure whether the rumored change in weather will be violently destructive or nourishing. Brink seems to hope that, through action on the part of the nation's white population, the more peaceful alternative will prove to be the future.

FURTHER READING

Criticism

Hassall, A. J. "The Making of a Colonial Myth: The Mrs. Fraser Story in Patrick White's *A Fringe of Leaves* and André Brink's *An Instant in the Wind.*" *Ariel* 13 (July 1987): 3-28.

> An informative discussion of the sources of the story for Brink's *An Instant in the Wind* and a close examination of the novel in relation to the use of the story by another author.

Peck, Richard. "Condemned to Choose, But What?: Existentialism in Selected Works by Fugard, Brink, and Gordimer." *Research in African Literatures* 23 (Fall 1992): 67-84.

A study of Brink and compatriots Nadine Gordimer and Athol Fugard in terms of a common influence and concerns.

Additional coverage of Brink's life and career is contained in the following source published by Gale: *Contemporary Authors New Revision Series*, Vol. 39.

Blaise Cendrars

1887-1961

(Given name Fréderic Louis Sauser-Hall) Swiss-born French poet, novelist, autobiographer, editor and essayist.

The following entry provides an overview of Cendrars's career. For further information on his life and works, see *CLC,* Volume 18.

INTRODUCTION

It is necessary to add the labels "traveler" and "adventurer" to the list of Cendrars's credits to begin to describe him, for they are as much a part of his life and work as the descriptions "poet" and "novelist." From the day he ran away from home at age fifteen until his confinement due to illness, his extensive travels were the source and subject of his work. A prolific writer, his collected works in the original French fill eight hefty volumes. His best known works in English translation are the long poems *Prose du transsibérien et de la petite Jehanne de France* (1913; *Prose of the Transsiberian with Little Jean of France*) and *Le Panama ou les aventures de mes sept oncles* (1918; *Panama or the Adventures of My Seven Uncles*) and the novels *L'Or* (1925; *Sutter's Gold*), which was filmed in 1936, and *Moravagine* (1926). Although there is considerable critical disagreement on the literary importance of Cendrars's writing, his influence on both his contemporaries and many subsequent writers is widely recognized.

Biographical Information

Cendrars was born in La Chaux-de-Fonds, Switzerland on September 1, 1887, to a Swiss father and Scottish mother. His father, an inventor-businessman, traveled extensively in pursuit of various business ventures; consequently, Cendrars spent his childhood in Alexandria, Naples, Brindisi, Neuchâtel, and other places. A rebellious child, Cendrars was expelled from numerous boarding schools. By his own accounts, at age fifteen he literally escaped his family by climbing out of a fifth story window (with the family silver) and began his own life of travel. Cendrars journeyed from St. Petersburg across Siberia to China, working a variety of jobs before returning to St. Petersburg, then briefly settling in Paris, which became his adopted home. There he married his first wife, Fela, and fathered two sons, Rémy and Odilon, both killed in World War II, and a daughter, Miriam.

Cendrars traveled to New York and there wrote his first major work, *Les Pâques à New York* (1912; *Easter in New York*), and adopted the name Blaise Cendrars. The poem was written in one long session, interrupted only by brief periods of exhausted sleep. Cendrars considered the poem an epiphany, a phoenix-like rebirth, and created the name "Blaise Cendrars" out of a loose anagram of the French words for fire (*braise*), cinders (*cendres*) and art (*ars*). He returned to Paris, where the work was published and he was acknowledged as a significant new writer; *Prose of the Transsiberian with Little Jean of France* was published the next year. When World War I broke out, Cendrars enlisted in the French Foreign Legion, the branch of the French army that accepted non-citizens. In September 1915, he was injured in battle and lost his right arm. He was despondent and enraged until he learned that on the same day of his injury, his idol Rémy de Gourmont had been killed in action. Cendrars returned to Paris, where his disability made it difficult to find work. For a while he was reduced to begging for alms. After traveling for a while with a group of gypsies, he returned to Paris and to writing, producing his third and final long poem, *Panama, or the Adventures of My Seven Uncles.*

In 1924 Cendrars went to Brazil. This was another major

turning point in his life. Cendrars was impressed by what he saw as a powerful cultural synthesis taking place in the country. For the next twenty years he traveled frequently between Europe and South America. Engaging in several business ventures, Cendrars made and lost several fortunes. It was also during this period that his writing career began to shift from poetry to prose. The pace of Cendrars's writing slowed in the late 1950s as his health failed, and he died in January of 1961.

Major Works

Cendrars's first major work was the long poem *Easter in New York.* Stylistically innovative, it was described by Sven Birkerts as "one of the first poems in the modernist canon" and by Richard Sieburth, referring to Allen Ginsberg's famous work, as "the *Howl* of its generation." It is a poem of dark, gnostic theology, mixing Christian imagery with the vulgar world of the lower East Side. Cendrars's second major poem, *Prose of the Transsiberian,* uses the extended image of a long train ride and the scenes outside the window to present a vision of the modern world. Cendrars's view of the world as being simultaneously larger and smaller as a result of the advances in transportation is further refined in his last long poem, *Panama, or the Adventures of My Seven Uncles.* The poem, in a style described as "fractured" and "without a direct narrative," tells the story of the narrator's far-flung relations, capturing the idea of dissolution of relationships within its style. His first (and most commercially successful) novel, *Sutter's Gold,* is the story of Johann Sutter, on whose California plantation gold was discovered in 1848, touching off the California Gold Rush. Although much of the narrative is historical fact, Cendrars changed certain major events to increase the dramatic effect of the story. The changing of history for effect is noted in the other biographies Cendrars wrote of historical figures, and created some suspicion among critics of the accuracy of events in his autobiographical novels, including *L'Homme foudroyé* (1945; *The Astonished Man, La Main coupée* (1946; *Lice*), and *Bourlinguer* (1948; *Planus.* The title character of the novel *Moravagine* would not be out of place in modern popular fiction. A psychotic genius with an obsession for disemboweling young women, Moravagine leaves a wake of death in his trans-world wanderings. The narrator of the story, Raymond La Science, is a psychiatrist who helped Moravagine escape from an asylum and accompanies him on his journeys. The doctor is motivated by his radical belief that sickness and health, both mental and physical, are ordinary phases in a life, and that it is therefore unnatural to punish them with confinement. The heroine of *Emmène-moi au bout du monde* (1956; *To the End of the World*) is Emmène, an octogenarian libertine who has been reduced to buying her sexual favors. Once a theatrical rival of Sarah Bernhardt, Emmène is enjoying a second chance on stage in an avant-garde production. Totally naked, she stands alone on stage reciting Villon's lament for vanished beauty, "Ballade des dames du temps jadis." Her revival is marred by a murder and the subsequent investigation. The book was described as a *roman à clef,* and there is some debate about the actual events to which it might refer.

Critical Reception

The works of Blaise Cendrars have elicited a broad range of critical response. At one end of the spectrum is Cendrars's friend and perhaps most ardent supporter, Henry Miller. Miller wrote, "Worshiping life and the truth of life, he comes closer than any author of our time to revealing the common source of word and deed." Near the other end, Frank McGuinness, in a review of *To the End of the World,* remarked, "As savagely contemptuous of bourgeois timidity and reserve as Henry Miller himself, Cendrars is of the school that believes it salutary to rub the reader's nose in dirt, outrage his susceptibilities at every turn and open his eyes to how much more dynamic life is in those insalubrious regions where the rate of copulation among the layabouts, pimps and bohemians far exceeds the Kinsey average and an atmosphere of amoral and stimulating vitality constantly prevails." The diversity of his critical reception may be in part related to the diversity of the man himself. Most critics find a common ground with the idea that Cendrars's life and work are mirrors of each other, each influencing the other, and that his work is at several levels a journal of his life. Birkerts noted, "the fact is that Cendrars cannot be considered apart from his biography. . . . The two are intimately interfused. The writings have to be read as a footnote to the life, as an interlinear, if you will. It is as if to make this process even more forbidding and complex that Cendrars chose to write poetry, novels, reportage, criticism, autobiography, film scripts, radio plays—apart from which he also anthologized and translated. He could not have set his gift at the heart of a labyrinth any more artfully had he tried." Of Cendrars's work, William Rose Bennett commented: "This poetry is the poetry of adventure, of the search for new lands and new skies; new sensations; of constantly moving about; ocular poetry, pictorial description, poetry bright with color and telegraphic in its presentation of impressions." Matthew Josephson favorably reviewed Cendrars, but added that "his poems seldom touch a great music which would hypnotize us into reading them over and over again. They compose rather the journal of a modern poet; they give us his nostalgias and his visions, often penetrating, violent, yet as bewildering and neutralizing in their total effect as prolonged sight-seeing from an observation car." Paul Zweig echoed that sentiment, adding an explanation: "Cendrars was not a great poet. He was too much of an innovator for that. He could never stop long enough on any ground to conquer it. After it was staked out, he moved on." Of his innovation, John Porter Houston said, "Cendrars abandoned symbolist free-verse patterns, with their many echoes of conventional metrics—'Prufrock' is an English ex-ample—for a more visual kind of effect: he was among the first to mingle type-faces, exploit non-horizontal word se-quences and, in general, to incorporate into poetry the var-ied lay-outs of advertising." The anti-heroes and nihilistic plots in some of Cendrars's novels, *Moravagine* and *To the End of the World,* for example, garnered praise from some critics and disapproval from others. Speaking of the death of the heroine Emmène at the conclusion of *To the End of the World,* Peter Sourian said, "That she dies almost as a pointless footnote may be part of the point. But if it's point-less on purpose, then the writer ought to be passionately pointed about the pointlessness. There is a flatness, a lack of remorse, a thinness of desire." Other critics saw the cruel, cold world of Cendrars's fiction as visionary. "Cendrars was one of the first to embrace 'the modern' in the full sense of the term. He saw clearly where the age was headed: toward speed, machinery, violence," observed Birkerts. John Harding, in an essay on the recurring themes shown in Cendrars's protagonists, stated, "the Cendrarsian hero is both a cosmopolitan and an outsider. His cosmopolitanism has two main stimuli, one being his desire to escape restriction, and the other being the sheer fascination of travel, with its influence on the development of the world. Both, when linked to his strong love/hate relationship with home, make him an eternal outsider in a world where conformity is ever the norm, and individuality is viewed with suspicion or hos-tility."

PRINCIPAL WORKS

Les Pâques à New York [*Easter in New York*] (poetry) 1912
Séquences (poetry) 1912
Prose du transsibérien et de la petite Jehanne de France [*Prose of the Transsiberian with Little Jean of France*] (poetry) 1913
Profond aujourd'hui (poetry) 1917
Le Panama ou les aventures de mes sept oncles [*Panama, or the Adventures of My Seven Uncles*] (poetry) 1918
Dix-neuf Poèmes élastiques [*Nineteen Elastic Poems*] (po-etry) 1919
L'Anthologie nègre [*Negro Anthology*] (poetry) 1921
*Kodak (poetry) 1924
L'Or [*Sutter's Gold*] (novel) 1925
Moravagine (novel) 1926
†*Le Plan de l'aiguille* [*Antarctic Fugue*] (novel) 1927
†*Les Confessions de Dan Yack* [*The Confessions of Dan Yack*] (novel) 1929
Rhum (novel) 1930
Hollywood, la mecque du cinéma [*Hollywood, Mecca of the Movies*] (journal) 1936
La Vie dangereuse [*The Dangerous Life*] (novel) 1938

L'Homme foudroyé [*The Astonished Man*] (autobiographi-cal novel) 1945
La Main coupée [*Lice*] (autobiographical novel) 1946
Bourlinguer [*Planus*] (autobiographical novel) 1948
Emmène-moi au bout du monde [*To the End of the World*] (novel) 1956

*This work is also known as *Documentaire.*
†These novels were published in a single-volume edition in 1946, which was translated and published as *Antarctic Fugue* in 1948.

CRITICISM

Faith Maris (review date 13 October 1926)

SOURCE: "California Gold," in *New Republic,* Vol. XLVIII, No. 619, October 13, 1926, p. 227.

[*In the following review, Maris provides some of the histori-cal background for Cendrars's novel* Sutter's Gold.]

In **Sutter's Gold** Blaise Cendrars has once more turned to America, a literary field that has kindled his imagination many times before, and to what was perhaps the most thrill-ing, as certainly it was the most convulsive, period the New World has known—the discovery of gold in California in 1848. Blaise Cendrars, like Valéry Larbaud, Paul Morand and Jean Giraudoux, possesses a cosmopolitan outlook and has done not a little to fructify French culture by introduc-ing France to some of her more and less remote neighbors. It is the more remote peoples that chiefly interest M. Cendrars. He is a world traveler and adventurer and is rarely observed in the haunts of Parisian writers, save when he re-appears, like a literary colporteur, from some far-away coun-try with the material for a new anthology of folk lore, or a volume of sketches or poems. His nostalgia for the primi-tive became evident with the appearance of his admirable **Anthologie Nègre,** of which a second volume is now in preparation. His love for the flora, fauna and human species of the tropics has given color, ardor and an exotic warmth to virtually everything that he has written.

Impudent poet and incorrigible romantic that he is, Blaise Cendrars is not without respect for historical records and documents when he chooses a theme with an historical ba-sis. **Sutter's Gold** is a sufficiently accurate account of the life and adventures of John Augustus Sutter, the Swiss emi-grant who sought his fortune in America, and who, after stir-ring adventures in various parts of the United States and the South Seas, became the founder of Sutter Fort and the owner of the agricultural colony of New Helvetia in the Sacramento Valley. The discovery of gold on his property brought the world to Sutter's gates; eager gold-seekers invaded his fields, trampled his vineyards, laid waste his crops, and left fire and destruction behind them. Ruined, the doughty pioneer sought restitution, and the famous Sutter suit against the United States government and the state of California was inaugurated. After years of heartbreaking litigation, a favorable verdict, indemnifying Sutter for his losses, was reached only to be quickly overthrown by political forces in Washington. Penniless, and now actuated by a religious passion for obtaining justice, the pitiful old man wandered from one bureau to another in a final effort to overcome official inertia and regain his rights; then came death in the protective fold of a religious brotherhood in Pennsylvania.

Such in brief are the facts upon which Blaise Cendrars has built his story. What matter if he has changed names and places, if he has added a fictive touch of color or of drama here and there? It is true that his description of life at Sutter Fort in the era of peace and plenty before the discovery of gold reads like life on the estate of some governor of a particularly rich Roman province. He fills it with a suavity and grace that is more south-European than Californian. Nevertheless, he manages to express the spirit and life of the country during that period of unparalleled expansion and exploitation with almost uniform fidelity. The tale is an epic of American life; and reviewing the career of Sutter, even in this romantic form, one comes to understand and even to go far toward forgiving the whole from-outcast-to-millionaire genre of fiction, for, after all, it has been rooted in reality.

John Dos Passos (review date 16 October 1926)

SOURCE: "Homer of the Transsiberian," in *The Saturday Review of Literature*, Vol. III, No. 12, October 16, 1926, pp. 202-22.

[*Below, novelist and poet Dos Passos offers an interpretive discussion of Cendrars's poetry.*]

At the Paris exposition of 1900—but perhaps this is all a dream, perhaps I heard someone tell about it; no it must have happened at the Paris Exposition Universelle of 1900— somewhere between the Eiffel tower and the Trocadero there was a long shed. In that shed was a brand new train of the Trans-Siberian Railroad, engine, tender, baggage coach, sleeping cars, restaurant car. The shed was dark, and girdered like a station. You walked up wooden steps into the huge dark varnished car. It was terrible. The train was going to start. As you followed the swish of dresses along the corridor the new smell gave you gooseflesh. The train smelt of fresh rubber, of just bought toys, of something huge and whirring and oily. The little beds were made up, there were mirrors, glittering washbasins, a bathtub. The engine whistled. No don't be afraid, look out of the window. We

are moving. No outside a picture is moving, houses slipping by, bluish-greenish hills. The Urals. Somebody says names in my car. Lake Baikal, Irkutsk, Siberia, Yanktse, Mongolia, pagodas, Peking. Rivers twisting into the bluish-greenish hills and the close electric smell of something varnished and whirring and oily, moving hugely, people in boats, junks, Yellow Sea, pagodas, Peking.

And the elevator boy said the trains in the Metro never stopped, you jumped on and off while they were going, and they showed magic lantern slides and cinematograph pictures in the Grande Roue and at the top of the Eiffel Towel ... but that must have been years later because I was afraid to go up.

I've often wondered about the others who had tickets taken for them on that immovable train of the Trans-Siberian in the first year of the century, whose childhood was also full of "Twenty Thousand Leagues" and Jules Verne's sportsmen and globetrottairs (if only the ice holds on Lake Baikal) and Chinese Gordon stuttering his last words over the telegraph at Khartoum; and Carlotta come back mad from Mexico setting fire to the palace at Terveuren full of Congolese curiosities, fetishes of human hair, ithiphallic idols with shells for teeth and arms akimbo, specimens of crude rubber in jars; and those magnates in panama hats shunted slowly in private cars reeking with mint and old Bourbon down new lines across the Rio Grande, shooting jackasses, prairie dogs, and an occasional greaser from the platform, and the Twentieth Century and Harvey lunchrooms and Buffalo Bill and the Indians holding up the stage and ocean greyhounds racing to Bishop's Rock and pictures of the world's leading locomotives on cigarette cards. O, Thos. Cook and Son, here's meat for your hopper. Uniformed employees meet all the leading trains. Now that Peary and Amundsen have sealed the world at the top and the bottom and there's an American bar in Baghdad and the Grand Llama of Thibet listens in on Paul Whiteman ragging the Blue Danube and the caterpillar Citroëns chug up and down the dusty streets of Timbuctoo, there's no place for the Rover Boys but the Statler hotels and the Dollar Line (sleep every night in your own brass bed) round the world cruises.

That stationary Trans-Siberian where the panorama unrolled Asia every hour was the last vestige of the Homeric age of railroading. Now's the time for the hymns and the catalogues of the ships. The railsplitting and the hacking and hewing, the great odysseys are over. The legendary names that stirred our childhood with their shadows and rumble are only stations in small print on a time table. And still... Or is it just the myth humming in our drowsy backward turned brains?

Does anything ever come of this constant dragging of a ruptured suitcase from dock to railway station and railway station to dock? All the sages say it's nonsense. In the countries of Islam they know you're mad.

In the countries of Islam they know you're mad, but they have a wistful respect for madness. Only today I was fed lunch, beef stewed in olives and sour oranges, couscous and cakes, seven glasses of tea and a pipe of kif, by the extremely ugly man with a cast in his eye and a face like a snapping turtle who hangs round the souks buying up fox skins, in the company of his friend the tailor, a merry and philosophic individual like a tailor in the Arabian Knights, all because I'd been to Baghdad, the burial place of our lord Sidi Abd el Kadr el Djilani (here you kiss your hand and murmur something about peace and God's blessing); for they feel that even a kaffir passing by the tomb may have brought away a faint whiff of the marabout's holiness. So a pilgrim has a certain importance in their eyes.

They may be right, but more likely this craze for transportation, steamboats, trains, motorbuses, mules, camels, is only a vicious and intricate form of kif, a bad habit contracted in infancy, fit only to delight a psychoanalyst cataloguing manias. Like all drugs you have to constantly increase the dose. One soothing thought; while our bodies are tortured in what Blaise Cendrars calls the squirrel cage of the meridians, maybe our childish souls sit quiet in that immovable train, in the dark-varnished new-smelling trans-Siberian watching the panorama of rivers and seas and mountains endlessly unroll.

Now's the time for the Homeric hymns of the railroads, Blaise Cendrars has written some of them already in salty French sonorous and direct as the rattle of the Grands Express Européens. Carl Sandburg has written one or two. I'm going to try to string along some hastily translated fragments of Cendrars **Prose du Trans-Siberien et de la Petite Jeanne de France.** It fits somehow in this hotel room with its varnished pine furniture and its blue slop-jar and its faded dust-eaten window curtains. Under the balcony are some trees I don't know the name of, the empty tracks of the narrow gauge, a road churned by motor trucks. It's raining. A toad is shrilling in the bushes. As the old earth-shaking engines are scrapped one by one, the myth-makers are at work. Eventually they will be all ranged like Homer's rambling gods in the rosy light of an orderly Olympus. Here's the hymn of the Trans-Siberian.

> I think I should not have known what to make of her performance, of her first number indeed, if I had never seen the pictures of Manet, Picasso, Cezanne and other moderns, far and near from us in time and place. I should have recognized of course the presence of design. But the language of this design would have been strange to me without the training of modern painting. . . . What she creates is never dependent on the music. . . . The completeness of Miss Enters's achievement consists in what very artist's achievement must consist in when it is successful: the whole translation of every element employed into her art.

In those days I was still a youngster
Only sixteen and already I couldn't remember my childhood
I was sixteen thousand leagues away from my birthplace
I was in Moscow, in the city of a thousand and three belfries and seven railroad stations
And the seven railroad stations and the thousand and three belfries were not enough for me
For my youth was then so flaming and so mad
That my heart sometimes burned like the temple of Ephesus, and sometimes like the Red Square at Moscow
At sunset.
And my eyes lit up the ancient ways.
And I was already such a bad poet
That I never knew how to get to the last word.
I spent my childhood in the hanging gardens of Babylon
Played hockey in railway stations in front of the trains that were going to leave
Now, all the trains have had to speed to keep up with me
Bale-Timbuctoo
I've played the races too at Auteuil and Longchamps
Paris-New York
Now, I've made all the trains run the whole length of my life
Madrid-Stockholm
And I've lost all my bets
And there's only Patagonia, Patagonia left for my enormous gloom, Patagonia and a trip in the South Seas.

I'm travelling
I've always been travelling
I'm travelling with little Jehanne of France
The train makes a perilous leap and lands on all its wheels
The train lands on its wheels.

"Say Blaise are we very far from Montmartre?"

We are far, Jeanne, seven days on the rails.
We are far from Montmartre, from the Butte that raised you, from the Sacred Heart you huddled against

Paris has vanished and its enormous flare in the
sky.
There's nothing left but continual cinders
Falling rain
Swelling clouds
And Siberia spinning
The rise of heavy banks of snow
The crazy sleighbells shivering like a last lust in
the blue air
The train throbbing to the heart of lead horizons
And your giggling grief. . . .

"Say Blaise are we very far from Montmartre?"
The worries
Forget the worries
All the cracked stations raticornered to the right of
way
The telegraph wires they hang by
The grimace of the poles that wave their arms and
strangle them
The earth stretches elongates and snaps back like
an accordion tortured by a sadic hand
In the rips in the sky insane locomotives
Take flight
In the gaps
Whirling wheels mouths voices
And the dogs of disaster howling at our heels. . . .

And so he goes on piling up memories of torn hurtling metal,
of trains of sixty locomotives at full steam disappearing in
the direction of Port Arthur, of hospitals and jewelry merchants, memories of the first great exploit of the Twentieth
Century seen through sooty panes, beaten into his brain by
the uneven rumble of the broad-gauge Trans-Siberian. Crows
in the sky, bodies of men in heaps along the tracks burning
hospitals, an embroidery unforeseen in that stately panorama
unfolding rivers and lakes and mountains in the greenish
dusk of the shed at the Exposition Universelle.

Then there's *Le Panama ou Les Aventures de Mes Septs
Oncles,* seven run-away uncles, dedicated to the last Frenchman in Panama, the barkeep at Matachine, the death place
of Chinamen where live oaks have grown up among the
abandoned locomotives, where every vestige of the [*de
Lesseps*] *attempt* is rotten and rusted and overgrown with li-
anas except a huge anchor in the middle of the forest
stamped with the arms of Louis XV.

It is about this time too, that I read the history of the earthquake at Lisbon.

But I think
The Panama panic is of a more universal impor-
tance
Because it turned my childhood topsyturvy.

I had a fine picture-book
And I was seeing for the first time
The whale
The big cloud
The walrus
The Sun
The great walrus
The bear the lion the chimpanzee the rattlesnake
and the fly
The fly
The terrible fly
"Mother, the flies, the flies and the trunks of
trees!"
"Go to sleep, child, go to sleep."
Ahasuerus is an idiot

It's the Panama panic that made me a poet!
Amazing
All these of my generation are like that
Youngsters
Victims of strange ricochets
We don't play any more with the furniture
We don't play any more with antiques
We're always and everywhere breaking crockery
We ship
Go whaling
Kill walrus
We're always afraid of the tse-tse fly
Because we're not very fond of sleep. . . .

Fantastic uncles they are; one of them was a butcher in
Galveston lost in the cyclone of '95, another washed gold
in the Klondike, another one turned Buddhist and was arrested trying to blow up the Britishers in Bombay, the fourth
was the valet of a general in the Boer War, the fifth was a
cordon bleu in palace hotels, number six disappeared in
Patagonia with a lot of electromagnetic instruments of precision; no one ever knew what happened to the seventh
uncle.

It was uncle number two who wrote verse modelled on
Musset and read in San Francisco the history of General
Sutor, the man who conquered California for the United
States and was ruined by the discovery of gold on his plantation. This uncle married the woman who made the best
bread in a thousand square kilometers and was found one
day with a rifle bullet through his head. Aunty disappeared.
Aunty married again. Aunty is now the wife of a rich jam
manufacturer.

And Blaise Cendrars has since written the history of General Johann August Sutor, *L'Or,* a narrative that traces the
swiftest leanest parabola of anything I've ever read, a narrative that cuts like a knife through the washy rubbish of
most French writing of the present time, with its lemon-col-

ored gloves and its rosewater and its holywater and its *policier-gentleman* cosmopolitan affectation. It's probably because he really is, what the Quai d'Orsai school pretended to be, an international vagabond, that Cendrars has managed to capture the grandiose rhythms of America of seventy-five years ago, the myths of which our generation is just beginning to create. (As if anybody *really was* anything. He's a good writer, leave it at that.) In *L'Or* he's packed the tragic and turbulent absurdity of '49 into a skyrocket. It's over so soon you have to read it again for fear you have missed something.

But the seven uncles. Here's some more of the hymn to transportation that runs through all his work, crystallizing the torture and delight of a train-mad, steamship-mad generation.

> I'm thirsty
> Damn it
> Goddamn it to hell
> I want to read the Feuille d'Avis of Neuchatel or the Pamplona Courrier
> In the middle of the Atlantic you're no more at home than in an editorial office
> I go round and round inside the meridians like a squirrel in a squirrel cage
> Wait there's a Russian looks like he might be worth talking to
> Where to go
> He doesn't know either where to deposit his baggage
> At Leopoldville or at the Sedjerah near Nasareth, with Mr. Junod or at the house of my old friend Perl
> In the Congo in Bessarabia on Samoa
> I know all the time tables
> All the trains and their connections
> The time they arrive the time they leave
> All the liners all the fares all the taxes
> It's all the same to me
> Live by grafting
> I'm on my way back from America on board the Volturno, for thirty-five francs from New York to Rotterdam.

Blaise Cendrars seems to have a special taste for the Americas, in the U.S. preferring the sappier Southern and Western sections to the bible-worn hills of New England. Here's poem about the Mississippi, for which Old Kentucky must have supplied the profusion of alligators, that still is an honorable addition to that superb set of old prints of sternwheel steamboats racing with a nigger or on the safety valve.

> At this place the stream is a wide lake
> Rolling yellow muddy waters between marshy banks.

> Water-plants merging into acres of cotton
> Here and there appear towns and villages carpeting the bottom of some little bay with their factories with their tall black chimneys with their long wharves jutting out their long wharves on piles jutting out very far into the water
> Staggering heat
> The bell on board rings for lunch
> The passengers are rigged up in checked suits howling cravats vests loud as the incendiary cocktails and the corrosive sauces
> We begin to see alligators
> Young ones alert and frisky
> Big fellows drifting with greenish moss on their backs
> Luxuriant vegetation announces the approach of the tropical zone
> Bamboos giant palms tulip-trees laurel cedars
> The river itself has doubled in width
> It is sown with floating islands from which at the approach of the boat water-birds start up in flocks
> Steamers sailboats barges all kinds of craft and immense rafts of logs
> A yellow vapor rises from the too warm water of the river

> It's hundreds now that the 'gators play round us
> You can hear the dry snap of their jaws and can make out very well their small fierce eyes
> The passengers pass the time shooting at them with rifles
> When a particularly good shot manages to kill or mortally wound one of the beasts
> Its fellows rush at it and tear it to pieces
> Ferociously
> With little cries rather like the wail of a new-born baby.

In *Kodak* there are poems about New York, Alaska, Florida, hunting wild turkey and duck in a country of birchtrees off in the direction of Winnipeg, a foggy night in Vancouver, a junk in a Pacific harbor unloading porcelain and swallows' nests, bamboo tips and ginger, the stars melting like sugar in the sky of some island passed to windward by Captain Cook, elephant hunting in the jungle roaring with torrents of rain; and at the end a list of menus featuring iguana and green turtle, Red River salmon and shark's fins, suckling pig with fried bananas, crayfish in pimento, bread-fruit, fried oysters, and guavas, dated en voyage 1887-1923. 1887 must be the date of his birth.

Dix-Neuf Poémes Elastiques. Paris. After all, Paris, whether we like it or not has been so far the center of unrest, of building up and the tearing down of this century. From Paris has spread in every direction a certain esperanto of the arts that has "modern" for its trademark. Blaise Cendrars is an itinerant Parisian well-versed in this as in many other dialects. He is a kind of medicine man trying to evoke the things that are our cruel and avenging gods. Turbines, triple-expansion engines, dynamite, high tension coils, navigation, speed, flight, annihilation. No medicine has been found yet strong enough to cope with them, but in cubist Paris they have invented some fetishes and grisgris that many are finding useful. Here's the confession of an *enfant du siêcle*, itinerant Parisian.

> I am the man who has no past.—Only the stump of
> my arm hurst,—
> I've rented a hotel room to be all alone with
> myself.
> I have a brand new wicker basket that's filling up
> with manuscript.
> I have neither books nor pictures, not a scrap of
> aesthetic bric-a-brac.
> There's an old newspaper on the table.
> I work in a bare room behind a dusty mirror,
> My feet bare on the red tiling, playing with some
> balloons and a little toy trumpet
> I'm working on THE END OF THE WORLD.

I started these notes on the little sunny balcony at Marrakesh with in front of me the tall cocoa-colored tower of the Koutoubia surmounted by three high balls banded with peacock-color, gilded each smaller than the other, and beyond the snowy ranges of the high Atlas; I'm finishing it in Mogador in a shut-in street of houses white as clabber where footsteps resound loud above the continual distant pound of the surf. It's the time of afternoon prayer and the voice of the meuzzin flashes like brace from the sky announcing that there is no god but God and that Mahomet is the prophet of God; and I'm leaving at six in the morning and there's nothing ahead but wheels and nothing behind but wheels. O, Thomas Cook and Son, who facilitate travel with their long ribbons of tickets held between covers by an elastic, what spells did you cast over the children of this century? The mischief in those names: Baghdad Bahn, Cape to Cairo, Transsiberian, Compagnie des Wagons Lits et des Grands Expresses Internationals, Christ of the Andes, the Panama Canal, mechanical toy that Messrs. Roosevelt and Goethals managed to make work when everyone else had failed; a lot of trouble for the inhabitants of the two Americas you have dammed up within your giant locks. The flags, the dollars, and Cook's tours marching round the world till they meet themselves coming back. Here in Morrocco you can see them hour by hour mining the minaret where the muezzin chants five times a day his superb defiance of the multiple universe.

If there weren't so many gods, tin gods, steel gods, gods of uranium and manganese, living gods—here's Mrs. Besant

rigging a new Jesus in Bombay, carefully educated at Oxford for the rôle—red gods of famine and revolution, old gods laid up in libraries, plaster divinities colored to imitate coral at Miami, spouting oil gods at Tulsa Okla., we too, might be able to sit on our prayer carpets in the white unchangeable sunshine of Islam. The sun of our generation has broken out in pimples, its shattered light flickers in streaks of uneasy color. Take the train, they're selling happiness in acre lots in Florida. So we must run across the continents always deafened by the grind of wheels, by the roar of aeroplane motors, wallow in all the seas with the smell of hot oil in our nostrils and the throb of the engines in our blood. Out of the Babel of city piled on city, continent on continent, the world squeezed small and pulled out long, bouncing like a new rubber ball, we get what? Certainly not peace. That is why in this age of giant machines and scuttleheaded men it is a good thing to have a little music. We need sons of Homer going about the world beating into some sort of human rhythm the shrieking hullaballo, making us less afraid.

M. R. Werner (review date 30 October 1926)

SOURCE: "The Irony of Life," in *The Saturday Review of Literature,* Vol. III, No. 14, October 30, 1926, p. 253.

[*In the following review, Werner provides some of the facts behind the fiction of* L'Or, *Cendrars's account of Johann Sutter's life.*]

The romantic mind of a French poet has conceived a superb book concerning the Swiss adventurer who was the first enthusiast for California, and who ended his days at Washington as a penniless petitioner for his rights. Blaise Cendrars's **L'Or,** carefully and intelligently translated by Henry Longan Stuart, is one of the most fascinating biographical studies that has been published since Lytton Strachey published his "Eminent Victorians."

The author of that extraordinary poem, "**Le Panama ou les Aventures des Mes Septs Oncles,**" has found a large outlet for his keen poetic imagination in the ironic story of Johann August Sutter. Unfortunately for the sense of the dramatic with which M. Cendrars is so powerfully endowed, the facts are sometimes somewhat different from those he presents concerning Captain Sutter, but the liberties he has taken for the sake of coloring are minor liberties. His scene in which Sutter's wife, after the perilous journey in 1848 from France to California via Panama, drops dramatically dead at the feet of her millionaire husband at the moment of her arrival at his hacienda is less stirring when one discovers from other accounts of Sutter that Madame Sutter lived to go to General Sutter's funeral. And the assurance with which Mr. Cendrars burns alive Sutter's sons in the fire that the mob started to destroy his property seems somewhat excessive when it is a fact that J.A. Sutter, Jr., for one, was for many years United States Consul at Acapulco, Mexico, and lived to produce many grandchildren, in whom the General is alleged by another biographer to have taken a great interest.

Johann August Sutter, who was born in the Grand-Duchy of Baden of Swiss parentage in 1803, left his wife and four children in Switzerland in 1834, managed to get to Paris without starving, where Cendrars has him forge a letter of credit with which to make his way from Havre to New York by the new steamer, *Esperance*.

In the New York of 1834 Sutter is alleged to have earned his living as a runner among immigrants for an innkeeper, messenger, packer, and bookkeeper for Hegelstroem, the inventor of Swedish matches, as draper's, druggist's, delicatessen keeper's assistant, as Rumanian peddler's partner, and as ringmaster in a circus, blacksmith, dentist, and taxidermist. Cendrars gives sundry other picturesque occupations too numerous to mention. But New York could not hold Sutter, for he had already heard of the opportunities in the great West, and he was soon afterwards a farmer on fertile land at the junction of the Missouri and Mississippi Rivers. But this was the terminus for all stories of the greater, farther West which were brought back by those few men who had seen or heard of its wonders, and Sutter sold his farm to join a company of traders who were going West.

Before he could reach California Sutter had to go to Vancouver and the Sandwich Islands, but he did not lose time, for his dream of dominion had already formed in his mind, and, being a practical man he made arrangements in Honolulu for shanghaiing bands of Kanakas, who were to labor on his lands.

The prosperity of the Franciscan missions of California was beginning to decline when Sutter arrived. He established himself in the valley of the Sacramento with his first shipment of Kanakas and nineteen well-armed white men. Governor Alvarado, the Mexican Governor of California, granted a temporary concession of all the land he required. Sutter's labor was efficient under his capable management, and California was amazingly fertile. He was able to manipulate his sympathies in such a way that he was friend of all the factions then fighting for control of California, and he received from the Mexicans additional grants of land, expressed in the picturesque, but fortunately indefinite phrase, "twelve hours square." His settlement was known as New Helvetia. Cendrars imagines this scene meeting the eye of Captain Fremont when he visited California:

Countless herds of pedigree cattle were at pasture

in the meadows. The orchards were loaded with fruit. In the truck gardens, vegetables of the Old World grew side by side with those of tropical countries. Wells and irrigation ditches were everywhere. The Kanaka villages were neat and orderly. Everyone was at work. Alleys of magnolias, palms, banana, and orange trees traversed the cultivated area, converging toward the settlement. The walls of the hacienda almost disappeared under climbing roses, geraniums, and bougainvilleas. The great door of the master's house was shaded by a curtain of sweet-smelling jasmine.

The table was splendidly set; *hors d'oeuvres*; trout and salmon from near-by brooks; ham, roasted *a l'ecossaise*; wood-pigeons; haunch of venison, bear's paws; smoked tongue; suckling-pig stuffed with mincemeat and powdered with tapioca; green vegetables, cabbage palms, and salads of crocodile pears; every variety of fruit, fresh and candied; mountains of pastry. The viands were washed down with Rhine wine and certain old bottles from noted French cellars which had been carried, with infinite precautions against breakage, from the other side of the world.

The guests were served by young women from the Sandwich Isles or half-caste Indian girls, who came and went with imperturbable gravity, carrying each course enveloped in linen napkins of dazzling whiteness. A Hawaiian orchestra played throughout the meal, rendering the "Berne March" with a drum accompaniment upon the skin of its guitars, or imitating the trumpet music of the "Marseillaise" by sonorous chords drawn upon their strings. The table was laid with ancient Spanish silver, massive, graceless, and stamped with the royal arms.

Sutter presided, surrounded by his partners. Among the guests was the governor, Alvarado.

Sutter was one of the richest men in America in 1847, and Cendrars imagines him sending for his three sons and his daughter, even for his wife, and also for a grand piano from Pleyel in Paris. Then James W. Marshall, one of Sutter's workmen, discovered gold on Sutter's land. Sutter knew what would happen, but he was powerless to stop the avalanche of fortune hunting that was going to wreck his own fortunes. Unlike Brigham Young, he could not keep his followers from digging for gold by promises of riches in the world to come and threats of damnation if they disobeyed. Presently, in Sutter's own sentence, "All were washing for gold, which they exchanged for liquor." This is the picture of Sutter's estate given by Colonel Masson, the new American governor, on July 3, 1848, six months after Marshall found the first nugget:

> On July 3d we arrived at Fort Sutter. The mills were standing idle. Immense droves of oxen and horses had broken through the fences and were eating the standing corn and maize. The barns were falling into ruin and the smell from them was very offensive. At the fort itself we observed much activity. Barges and pinnaces were discharging and taking on a great quantity of merchandise. Convoys of covered wagons were parked round the walls. Others were coming and going. For the smallest room one hundred dollars a month is paid. For a miserable cottage with one floor, five hundred dollars. Sutter's blacksmith, and farrier, who are still with him, earn fifty dollars a day. For five miles round, the sides of the hills are white with tents. The country swarms with people. All are busy washing for gold.

All of these people who were washing for gold were using Sutter's land, and all of Sutter's laborers were washing for gold. A Sutterville, Sutter's Creek, and Sutter County sprang up, but Sutter himself was ruined. His name became world famous, but it was no longer good for unlimited credits in Paris and London and New York. There was no law in California except that which told each man to grasp what he could get. However, Sutter decided to start his suit, "a lawsuit that stirred California to its depths and which even put the existence of the newly formed state in peril." Sutter claimed all the land in which the cities of San Francisco, Venicia, Sacramento, and Riovista are located. He estimated their value at $200,000,000. He also demanded damages from 17,221 individuals who had trampled on his property in their search for gold. He also asked $25,000,000 from the state of California for confiscating his property for roads, bridges, and other public works. He also demanded an indemnity of $50,000,000 from the federal government because it had failed to protect his rights and his royalties in the gold that had been minted already. And the inhabitants of San Francisco retaliated by burning down the offices of Sutter's son, Emile, where the deeds from Governors Alvarado and Michel-Torena were guarded. Then Captain Sutter was honored above all men by the same inhabitants at the celebration of the fifth anniversary of the founding of San Francisco. They even made him a general. The orator of the day, the Mayor, remarked in the peroration of his speech:

> In days to come, gentlemen, when the state that is our home has become one of the greatest and most powerful countries in the world, and when the historian of the future seeks to trace its origin and foundation back through the misery and privations of its early beginnings, and to recount the epic be-

ginnings of the fight for liberty in the great West, one name will outshine all others—the name of our distinguished guest—the immortal SUTTER! (Loud and prolonged applause.)

The following spring Judge Thompson of the highest court in the state decided that Sutter was the rightful owner of "the immense territories on which so many towns and villages have been built." And in answer to this decision the inhabitants of San Francisco decided that it was time to burn down The Hermitage, Sutter's home, and all his remaining workshops, saw-mills, and factories. They also hanged Sutter's Kanakas, Indians, and Chinese. . . .

[Sutter] was granted a pension of $3,000 a year by the state of California. He became a member of a German communist sect, the Herrenhutters, and he paid considerable attention to the Book of Revelations. This is Cendrars's image of Sutter's interpretation of that Book:

> The Great Harlot who was given birth upon the Sea is Christopher Columbus, discovering America.
>
> The Angels and the Stars of St. John are in the American flag. With California, a new star, the Star of Absinthe, has been added.
>
> Anti-Christ is Gold....

Johann August Sutter was seventy-three years old when he died in the city of Washington.

Matthew Josephson (review date 2 December 1931)

SOURCE: "A Neo-Romantic Poet," in *The Nation,* Vol. 133, No. 3465, December 2, 1931, pp. 616-17.

[*In the following review, Josephson summarizes Cendrars's work as lacking the long-term appeal of great poetry.*]

John Dos Passos has made a felicitous translation of a group of poems by Blaise Cendrars, at least one of which, the long Prosody of the Transsiberian, has been a famous example of modern poetry for almost a generation. Dos Passos has much in common with Cendrars; he has the same vibrant revolutionary spirit, the same overwhelming interest in the actual world with all its characteristic sores, the same love of travel, the same effect of speed in writing combined with indifference to musical perfection. Nevertheless, the appearance of Cendrars's poems in English tempts one to reconsider the whole twentieth-century school of poets with which the versatile Swiss Parisian is identified.

Cendrars is one of a number of writers and painters who used to gather about Guillaume Apollinaire in Paris and who absorbed much of that fertile man's instructions as well as his gift for pleasantries. Through Apollinaire, toward 1910, the cubist movement in painting grew articulate; in the reviews he founded, Blaise Cendrars, André Salmon, Max Jacob, and many others were launched or relaunched upon the public. Later the dadaists, or super-realists, such as Philippe Soupault and Louis Aragon, blossomed under Apollinaire's friendly offices. Even certain (recently deceased) Russian poets, such as Yessenine and Maiakovsky, hark back to the same source; while younger American poets have not escaped the influence of this school, received either at first or second hand. These various writers, though differing in personal accent and style, do exhibit a perceptibly common point of view upon the affairs of the twentieth century, and as a group oppose themselves to the literature of the neo-Catholics, or neo-classicists, whose philosophies, according to the foreword by Dos Passos, "are vaguely favorable to fascism, pederasty, and the snob-mysticism of dying religion."

Cendrars, who certainly shares some of Apollinaire's honors as a forerunner, reflects both the more adventurous artistic qualities and the weaknesses of his school. Broadly speaking, his poetry is "neo-romantic" in its feeling; and we perceive this best when we compare him to Valéry or the later T.S. Eliot. Like Apollinaire he found himself at odds with the mechanized and rather brutal society of the early twentieth century. He set about expressing his contempt, not too solemnly, and praying for the downfall of this society. (Later the dadaists would be hatching fantastic conspiracies to "demoralize all the bourgeois" through a propaganda of anarchy.) But Cendrars and Apollinaire before the World War, both feeling themselves outside society, had instinctively embraced a Bohemian tradition; Bohemianism seems to keep art alive in capitalist democracies. They were also deeply impressed by the revolutions in the plastic arts which followed the work of Cézanne and which they witnessed at close hand from the cafe tables of Montmartre. African sculpture had been discovered; the primitive Italians had been discovered. Their friends Picasso, Modigliani, Chagall had all become primitives. The poets too tried to develop a new palette of colors; they too sought the primitive note. Cendrars found it in an altered, Manchester-like Europe of factories and slums, a new Europe of trans-continental trains, revolutions, immigrant steamships. He looked for the primitive as far as Abyssinia (in the footsteps of Rimbaud), Siberia, and America. The world into which he was born had already lost its values; it had lost all the refinements of aristocratic society; its salient traits were instability and confusion. Hence there is bitterness in the laughter of Cendrars.

But the sense of life was strong in these new poets. They were more deeply prompted than the classicists to return to a fresh observation of the actual, vulgar world about them in process of transformation. They anticipated drastic changes in our arts and culture; they were ready to attempt new forms for the theater, the movies, the press; they courted the novel and the exotic as all romantics have done.

Cendrars was not a man to retire into the shuttered depths of a monastery. He was seized with the restlessness which was an effect of his age. He must be a globe-trotter, galloping about the world.

> Paris—New York
>
> Now I've made all the trains race the whole length
> of my life . . .
> I'm traveling
> I've always been traveling
> I'm traveling with little Jehanne of France
> The train makes a perilous leap and lands on all its
> wheels
> The train lands on its wheels
> The train always lands on all its wheels

These poems of eighteen years ago have the quality of motion pictures taken from a shaking express train, a quality which Cendrars tried for deliberately. Was he not cultivating the two hemispheres as his garden patch? His pages are peopled with allusions to, rather than pictures of, tropical seaports, Oriental deserts, locomotives, revolutions, skyscrapers, wars. Moreover, his poems date from a period in French literature when it was a fashionable affectation to use the names of outlandish places like Mississippi or Timbuktu, or foreign words like "cocktail" and "policeman." The effectiveness of such tricks sometimes disappears in translation; but the overwhelming effect of mobility, of breathless speed, is successfully captured.

"Forgive me for not knowing the antique game of verse," the poet says. *His* verse is to be free, discursive, profane. Or now it may be in the form of telegraphic jottings, or Whitmanesque catalogues of places and sights and people. But his poems seldom touch a great music which would hypnotize us into reading them over and over again. They compose rather the journal of a modern poet; they give us his nostalgias and his visions, often penetrating, violent, yet as bewildering and neutralizing in their total effect as prolonged sight-seeing from an observation car. Cendrars's deficiencies, I have always felt, result from his own poetic limitations. Apollinaire and Soupault, with much the same approach, have remained artists. The poems of Cendrars leave us but the notebook of a colorful and itinerant modern personality who has come to know all the trains by the sound of their wheels.

I've deciphered all the muddled texts of the
wheels
and collected a few elements of violent beauty . . .

He has looked for everything under the sun and has found fatigue. His last station is Paris: "Central terminal, transfer station of the will, crossroad of unrest."

William Rose Benet (review date 12 December 1931)

SOURCE: "Round about Parnassus," in *The Saturday Review of Literature,* Vol. VIII, No. XXI, December 12, 1931, pp. 378-9.

[*In the following excerpt, Benet favorably reviews John Dos Passos' translation of Cendrars's* Panama, or The Adventures of My Seven Uncles.]

The most living and original work before me this week is undoubtedly John Dos Passos's translation from the French of certain poems of Blaise Cendrars. The translator has also illustrated his book with twelve excellent drawings in color. While I cannot criticize this poetry in English by comparing it with the poetry in the original, I think it sufficient to quote Mr. Dos Passos in this connection. He says very sensibly, in part, "I think it has been worth while to attempt to turn these alive, informal, personal, everyday poems of Cendrars into English, in spite of the obvious fact that poetry by its very nature can't be lifted out of the language in which it was written. I only hope it will at least induce people to read the originals." Certainly Mr. Dos Passos's translation should do this, for *Panama, or The Adventures of My Seven Uncles* is brilliant and sensitive in the English version. It has been made into a most attractive large paperbound volume by Harper & Brothers. It contains "**Prosody of the Transsiberian and of Little Jeanne of France,**" "**Panama, etc.,**" "**Two Rivers,**" from *Kodak Documentaire,* "**Elephant Hunt,**" from *Kodak Documentaire,* and "**Notes on the Road: The SS. Formosa.**" Lewis Galantière, as I cannot, could explain to you the exact position Cendrars occupies in modern French poetry, but in the "Translator's Foreword" there is enough to give us a hint of this. It begins, "The poetry of Blaise Cendrars was part of the creative tidal wave that spread over the world from the Paris of before the last European war." And the translator cites such manifestations as the music of Stravinsky and Prokovieff, Diageleff's Ballet, the windows of Saks Fifth Avenue, skyscraper furniture, the Lenin Memorial in Moscow, and the paintings of Diego Rivera in Mexico as part of this same movement. In the America of today he feels that poetry has "subsided again into parlor entertainment for high

school English classes. The stuffed shirts have come out of their libraries everywhere and rule literary taste." There we take issue with him, though it is certain that American poetry is no longer, as a general phenomenon, in nearly so exciting or stimulating a condition as it was in 1914. Certainly the translation of Cendrars's "**Prosody of the Transsiberian**" gives us back some of that exhilaration of youthful observation, that contagious excitement at a world freshly perceived through all the senses. This poetry is the poetry of adventure, of the search for new lands and new skies; new sensations; of constantly moving about; ocular poetry, pictorial description, poetry bright with color and telegraphic in its presentation of impressions. Its manner is casual and colloquial and always autobiographical. One does not remember separate phrase or line, one reads it as one would listen to a brilliant narrator of an active life, who had accumulated myriad impressions and possessed the gift of words to make them vivid to the auditor. Cendrars begins by saying, "I was a youngster in those days, hardly sixteen," adds "I was a pretty poor poet, I never knew how to get to the end of things," and proceeds to tell how he left Moscow, on fire for adventure, "as assistant to a jewelry salesman who was going to Harbin."

> I was happy without a thought in the
> world,
> I thought I was playing brigands;
> We'd stolen Golconda's treasure
> And we were fleeing on the Trans-
> siberian to bury it on the other side
> of the world.

Next he dwells on his girl, Jeanne, "the poor poet's flower," who is always asking, "Say, Blaise, are we very far from Montmartre?" Somehow, in his descriptions of Jeanne, the vision of De Quincey arises,—no such traveller as Cendrars but with the same power over language, the same sensitive pity. Dos Passos, vivid poet himself, does well with the adaptation of the best passages of the poem. Here is one:

> I've seen the silent trains, the black trains
> coming back from the Far East that
> passed like haunts
> And my eye like the red light on the rear
> car still speeds behind those trains.
> At Talga one hundred thousand wounded
> dying for lack of care;
> I went through all the hospitals of Kras-
> noyarsk
> And at Khilok we passed a long hospital
> train full of soldiers that had gone
> mad;
>
> I saw the dressing stations the widening
> gashes of wounds bleeding at full

throb
And amputated limbs dance fly off into
the shrieking wind.
Conflagration flared in every face in every
heart,

Idiot fingers beat a tattoo on every win-
dowpane
And under the pressure of fear stares
burst like ulcers.
In every station they'd set the rollingstock
on fire,
And I've seen
I've seen trains of sixty locomotives fleeing at full steam cut off by howling
horizons with flocks of crows flying
desperately after
Disappear
In the direction of Port Arthur.

As we have said this is principally the poetry of "I have
seen." "**The Adventures of My Seven Uncles**" begins delightfully with Cendrars's memory of his mother telling him
as a child of the adventures of her seven brothers. Letters
from these marvellous, almost mythical, creatures, fed the
young Cendrars's romantic imagination. One uncle "disappeared in the cyclone of '95"; one, as a prospector in Alaska,
had three fingers frozen, and so on. Small wonder that the
schools and the college to which Cendrars was sent seemed
as nothing to the boy compared with that fascinating school
of the wide world in which he might learn all manner of dangerous and exciting things. Though a minor refrain of a few
lines is introduced at the end of all the uncles' communications;

Then there was something else too
Gloom
Homesickness.

The poet never saw but one of his uncles. He came home to
go crazy and to be shut up in an asylum. Another was a master chef whose "menu cards are the new prosody." This poem
has real fascination,—though just why a page pronouncement of the Denver Chamber of Commerce is introduced on
page 65 one may be given leave to wonder. One uncle, for
whom Cendrars waited a year in the tropics, went off with
an astronomical expedition to Patagonia and never did turn
up. Also "in the fjords of the Land of Fire On the fringes of
the world" he

fished out protozoic mosses drifting between
two tides in the glimmer of
electric fish
collected aeroliths of peroxide of iron.

One Sunday morning
You saw a mitered bishop rise up out of
the waters,
He had a tail like a fish and sprinkled you
with signs of the cross;
You ran off into the hills howling like a
wounded lemur.

What uncles to have! It is the vast fantasticality of the world
at large, as well as its beauty and drama and terror that the
poet celebrates. His attitude toward love is stated later, in a
poem entitled "**Thou Art Lovelier than the Sky and Sea,**"
and immediately perversely beginning

When you're in love you must get out
Leave your wife leave your children
Leave your boyfriend leave your girl-
friend
Leave the woman you love leave the
man you love
When you're in love you must get out.

Among the shorter poems, some of which become rather too
telegraphic toward the end of the volume, there is one superb description, in "**The Bubus,**" of French colonial negro
women. In general it is easy to see why the French poet has
attracted his American translator. He has the same painter's
eye and the same roving foot. Dos Passos has brought to the
translation a few of his own verbal peculiarities, but it is not
the worse for that. He has made the poet speak to us like a
man alive.

Morton Dauwen Zabel (essay date January 1932)

SOURCE: "Cendrars," in *Poetry,* Vol. XXXIX, No. IV, January, 1932, pp. 224-27.

[*In the essay below, Zabel discusses Dos Passos's translations of Cendrars and Cendrars's place in the evolution of
French literature.*]

The enthusiasm of Mr. Dos Passos' project is well warranted,
although his *Foreword* succeeds in being little more than an
exhibition of sore-headed commiseration to which its
sprinkle of misprints and historical lapses does little injustice. He has, at the outset, an inheritor's fitness to be
Cendrars's translator: the rapid verbal and imaginative impulse of *Les Pâques à New-York, La prose du
Transsibérien, Panama,* and *Kodak documentaire* is likewise the fever in the nerves of *Orient Express, Rosinante,*
and *Manhattan Transfer,* and it remains largely intact in
these lucid versions from three of Cendrars's books. Dos
Passos has also retained from the years of his own appren-

ticeship a keen memory of the ardor of discovery that ran through French and American writing twenty years ago. He has invested his English Cendrars with the tone and impudence, the sprawling arrogance and splendor, which bloomed on the pages of twentieth-century poetry in its first conscious rejection of foregoing conventions and, more specifically, of the formal and intellectual disciplines of Symbolism. The translation here may likewise count in its favor an actual experience as close to that of Cendrars's contemporaries as the post-war years are able to supply. Of the four American poets who have shown some ability in handling contemporary French verse (the task thus far remains inconceivable in an Englishman's hands), Dos Passos easily merits the honor of introducing Cendrars to American readers, because his own excursions and protests, like Cendrars's, have had their inception in the confusion of contemporary civilization.

> I go round and round inside the meridians like a
> squirrel in a squirrel cage.

As with Cendrars, this has been his lot, but out of confusion he has rescued the vitality and energy which a creative criticism demands if the resources of an excessive experience are to be extracted, and ultimately ordered, by the critical mind inside it.

Cendrars's work began in a gratuitous demolition of the order and method of his immediate forerunners. Among the first to signalize the exhaustion of material resources which Mallarmé's and Verlaine's successors encountered, he started by launching an ambitious explorative campaign and thus helped to instigate the French insurgence of 1910-14. By that time the symbolist technique which a half-century before had appeared purely arbitrary in its allegorical assumptions and impulsive in its technical canons, had become almost as rigorous a system of poetic ideas as the doctrinaire classicism which it had come to reject; the time was ready for another of those revitalizing conquests of the actual, or of the creatively adaptable, which have become habitual in French art. Other literatures pass through these periods of rehabilitation with gusto and fervor, but usually with a more or less complete aloofness from technical responsibilities. Of the French it may generally be said that the value of reform or experiment is implicit in the strength or weakness of the technical innovation required to express it; that innovation of matter, to be complete, requires a concurrent and corresponding innovation in form. In painting and sculpture as in poetry, from symbolism itself through *surréalisme*, the terminology of recent innovation is largely technical, and it is well to observe in the case of Cendrars and his contemporaries—Apollinaire, Salmon, Max Jacob, and later Cocteau, Mac-Orlan, Fargue, and Radiguet—that any novelty of conception or association was aimed at through some adequate refinement or revision of technical approach. Obviously the technique may be as suspect as the creative aim or material with which it coin-

cides: if these poets merely "*ecrivirent comme des médiums,*" in M. Porché's phrase, or "*s'ils ont manqués de clarté*" with results that have played havoc in the camps of *dadaisme* and *surréalisme,* their work might even now appear as little more than an overwrought episode in the life of wartime Europe. And with them it would pass not only the more remarkable elements in Picasso, Léger, Miro, Satie, and Antheil, but the more generally criticized—and unread— parts of Pound and Joyce.

These men, however, refuse to be dismissed. It is their dye that stains the sea of contemporary feeling and expression. The discipline that reaches its climax in pure form invariably reveals the sterility of purely intellectual processes in art. The intellectual process has seldom had as logical and as exhaustive a demonstration of its possibilities as in recent creative work, but running counter to the anesthetic and elegiac tendencies of recent intellectual pessimism has been an extraordinary inventive enthusiasm which may ultimately be our period's most important manifestation. This invention has followed various lines: socio-geographical canvases as in Apollinaire and Cendrars; historical analogues as in Chirico, Salmon, and Pound; detailed objective analysis as in Léger, Picasso, Eliot, and Miss Moore; the development of myth as in Lewis, Döblin, Joyce. Mr. Dos Passos praises in Cendrars "virility" and "meaning in everyday life." Had he seen these merely as the basis of the literature which Cendrars did much to instigate, he might, through greater appreciation for the work of Cendrars's followers, have spared himself much of the excited irritation with which his translation is launched. It is neither in mere "everyday life" nor in psychological delusion and trance that a permanent esthetic concept is wrought, but in a discipline which encompasses the vital elements of the two, and which, had he mastered it more fully, would have made Cendrars a greater poet.

Meanwhile, Mr. Dos Passos has given, in the right colloquial key and with the spontaneity of deep sympathy, his brilliant translations of some of Cendrars's best work, adding to the volume his lively designs in color. His work will remind current writers of an inheritance of which they might profitably be more conscious.

Blaise Cendrars with Michel Manoll (interview date 25 April 1950)

SOURCE: An interview in *American Poetry Review,* translated by Bertrand Mathieu, May/June 1980, pp. 40-44.

[In the following interview, originally broadcast on April 25, 1950, Cendrars ruminates on the artists and authors of his time.]

Blaise Cendrars (1887-1961) is one of the giants of modern literature. In addition to poetry, he wrote novels, travel books, biographies, autobiographies, film scenarios, letters, translations, essays, operas, and ballet choreographies. Yet hardly any of Cendrars's writings have been translated into English.

Bertrand Mathieu has already published a number of Cendrars's translations: his translations of Rimbaud's *Illuminations* and *A Season in Half* have been published by BOA Editions. He has also written a book on Henry Miller and a volume of his own poetry.

This interview was broadcast on April 25, 1950. The translation was completed in 1974.

[*Manoll:*] *Do you* really *believe that the poets are fifty years ahead of the painters?*

[Cendrars:] As far as the poets of today are concerned, there isn't a shred of doubt. The painters *still* haven't discovered Rimbaud. Do you know a single good illustrator of Rimbaud's *Illuminations*?

Rimbaud's genius seems to me absolutely one-of-a-kind.

So one-of-a-kind that all the commentaries that've been devoted to Rimbaud, from Claudel and Arthur Rimbaud's sister, Madame Paterne Berrichon, right down to the very latest of the zealots or bench-warmers, you know what I mean? are an appalling hodge-podge because Rimbaud himself took off and never said boo. Just look at him in that "table corner" by Fantin-Latour, that marvelous little hoodlum sitting there, leaning on his elbows and impatiently biting his fingernails with eagerness to shove off, to say to these Proper Gentlemen: SHIT! Now where do you think he was *living* at that period?

In Paris.

He was living at the Senate. He'd been taken in by Leconte de Lisle who was librarian at the Senate. You can understand his eagerness to buzz off, huh? Even Leon Bloy hadn't caught on to a thing, he kept putting down the little delinquent: "Rimbaud's just a brat who's pissing on the Himalayas!" Aside from "le pauvre Lelian" (Verlaine), all Paris had taken him for a young pervert, a faggot. It's unbelievable . . . !

You've said that your own coming-of-age dates from 1917 when you "understood that the poetry which was beginning to appear was basically a misunderstanding which was going to overrun the entire country and then spread throughout the world." What were you trying to say exactly? Why a misunderstanding?

I've told you already. In 1917, I left Paris determined not to come back after having nailed the manuscript of *At The Heart of the World* in a crate. Like a woman who wants to have a child, has it, then leaves the man and takes away her treasure to coddle it, to spoil it, make it smile and watch it grow up in solitude and keeps tough by devoting herself to it with a blind devotion and a limitless tenderness (it's a rare *thing*, but I've known some who've done it and who're happy), I was happy. I was in love. Love's exclusive.

"When you love you've got to leave . . ."

So I left Paris. I'd taken a break from Poetry. I was happy. I'd come out of the war alive and I wanted to live. I'm talking to you about poetry. About the misunderstanding of modern poetry. About the surrealists. There isn't a single one of those young mothers' sons who produced anything new. They're a flea market. Everything the surrealists have brought out since the jail-house of Dada you can find the sources of in *Les Soirees de Paris*, whose last number is dated August 1914. Personally, I've been waiting in vain for something from them, something original, something really *new* Like everybody else, I've always given the young credit. "Youth is a priesthood... But it's youth that *says* so," as Baudelaire puts it, that disillusioned man. The surrealists were supposed to start from scratch. They said so a hundred times. They were bursting with talent, the buggers. Nothing came of it. When that smiling old bogeyman Anatole France died, they spat on his corpse which was being paraded through the streets of Paris, and they were all carried away by their own daring because in addition to their talent, they had connections, these scions of families, and on the same day they threw themselves down on hands and knees to pay homage to André Gide, who was nothing but a *living* corpse. In fact, Gide's popularity really begins on that day. Devil take him . . .

That's a bit strong, Cendrars.

You think so? Well, that's the way I really feel.

You're exaggerating.

What *else* do you want me to tell you about the surrealists? I've never associated much with that crowd. At the start, they came to see me in my attic on the rue de Savoie: the sweet Phillippe Soupault, a very lovely guy, who was bashful and has become a trifler to put it mildly: a flincher. The high and mighty André Breton, who already had that Ubu-esque air of the great man from the provinces to whom, someday, the fatherland WOULD BE grateful, and who has never been able to rid himself of that tremendous burden of premortem glory. Louis Aragon, with whom I nearly became friends, by far the most intelligent of the three, the most sensitive, the smartest, but also the most fragile because I could hear the pulse of poetry beating just beneath his feverish words, a rebel who's tripped himself into hysteria. Soupault, who'd dragged the other two over to my place, wanted me to give a lecture to the *Dames de France*. I put him in touch with Guillaume Apollinaire, who he'd never heard of, and Apollinaire appeared delighted at the opportunity to show himself off and make a speech in his lieutenant's uniform before the lovely ladies of the world of big business and industry all tricked out as nurses. The whole thing was a farce. But how could you hold it against poor Guillaume, eh? Ever since his trepanning, his personality'd become unrecognizable and Apollinaire had become childishly vain. But when André Breton prides himself on having known Guillaume Apollinaire intimately and having "visited him regularly in 1917 and 1918" the way he allows them to put it in his latest biographical notice, in order to derive some glimmering of glory out of it, I laugh in his face and say he's lying . . .

Is that so?

Sure, and it's a *shame*! Anyway, the attitude of the surrealists disgusts me and I would never've permitted myself such a diatribe except that despite Apollinaire, Max Jacob, and many other dead poets who can't speak out, André Breton still insists on an absolute monopoly on Rimbaud and Lautrémont, and I keep asking myself how such a thing could've happened in a country like France where he's been allowed to dish out Passes and Fails in the free Republic of Letters? People put up with it. It's really side-splitting! We were much more free-wheeling at the *Soirées de Paris*. We'd shake up the coconut tree and there'd *always* be a few poets who'd make fun of everything, of one and all. Respect for officialdom didn't muzzle us, and nobody took himself as seriously as they all do today. We knew how to laugh . . .

And what do you think of Jean-Paul Sartre?

I've got no opinion on him, Sartre doesn't send me his books. As for existentialism . . . ? When it comes to philosophical doctrines, it's Schopenhauer who put me on guard against the professors of philosophy who, after getting the "official line," meditate, write, think, regurgitate, compose manifestos—and Sartre is a professor. Philosophical plays are a bore on the stage, and Sartre dramatizes his theses for the theater. Novels are either well or badly written, Sartre's are middling. I see some of the young people of today all the time since I've come back to Paris and I ask myself in what way they're existentialist, exactly? Is it because they disguise themselves every night to go to Saint-Germaindes-Prés the way their parents dressed up every night to slip in among society people or get past the door of a private club?? It's a fashion that'll pass, that's already passed... I don't understand this fuss about *display* all over the place. How *bored* people must be...! Movies, radio, television...? The

truth is few people know how to live and those who accept life as it is are even rarer...

I don't know what can be said about this epidemic of professors of literature, but one thing that's certain is that Jean-Paul Sartre's movement hasn't produced any poets. They didn't turn out poets. No poet managed to come out of that.

Your view's probably right. Among the surrealists, I'd make only one exception: Robert Desnos. Robert was a really nice guy with whom I had lots of good times and used to have a drink with in a bar where we'd meet, which I'd baptized *The Eye of Paris*, because it was located on the rue de Rivoli, under the arcades, a stone's throw from the Concorde and you could see all Paris passing by without budging from your stool, a place which Robert had maliciously nick-named *Madame Lots O'Eyes* because of the women who'd come in to go down to the toilet and come back out without so much as looking at us so as not to diminish their dignity as pissers, which used to make us burst out, since we were being ogled by the cherries dipped in brandy which we kept emptying from the glasses, spitting the pits at the backs of the anonymous furclad ladies swishing past us who'd just finished touching up their good looks with a little make-up. Youki had no cause to be jealous. Robert was a marvelous pal. We didn't talk about automatic writing, and the two or three times I tried to question him about that fatal gift they've tried to badger him with, he simply winked at me and smiled in a funny way, like someone who knows too much! That's why I've never believed in Desnos the Medium, any more than in Max Jacob the Mystic. Robert Desnos was a great *poet*. A real one. Read *Quartier Saint-Merri* again. It's in the same vein as Villon. One was from the quartier Saint-Jacques, the other from Saint-Martin. Left bank, right bank. Same difference. Drinking at the source. The little *bistros* of Paris...

And what do you have to say about the young people of 1950?

The young are desperate. They're now writing to me! When I was young, the young weren't writing to me—rightly, because I was young myself. The reason the young are writing to me today is that they take me for an old-timer, and that saddens me despite my age. But anyway, let's continue . . . I swear to you there's a whole generation of very young poets who haven't been published yet who write to me. I get three or four deliveries of poems a day and, every once in a while, a little book. Unknowns . . .

People with talent?

Like life. Some young people with talent, some young people without talent, some people with genius, some people without genius. It moves me deeply and I always answer them.

But if they're turning to me with the intention of choosing a master of their own, they've got the wrong address. I'm not the leader of a movement. I'm not *that* old . . . That's *senility* . . .

But even though you don't accept this role of master, you yourself have your own ancestors, there are writers who've been profoundly important to you, poets by whom you were influenced. Baudelaire is usually considered the father of modern poetry. From him two roads branched out, one which shaped artists of the Word such as Mallarmé and Valéry, the other poets that moved in the direction of an adventurous conquest of the modern world . . .

I'll *pass* on Mallarmé, but Paul Valéry, that epigone who received all the honors due to his master, even a state funeral! And the surrealists didn't even protest?! As for Baudelaire, certainly I was influenced by him. He's a very great poet, but he's especially a profoundly catholic spirit in his critique of modern life. As a critic he was even a *stunning* type, way ahead of his time and I'm convinced that for a long time to come, let's say until the end of the twenty-second century, he'll be an influence on young people through his criticism and his dandyism. His most beautiful poems *date* already. I place myself under the sign of François Villon.

Another one who seems to me to've left his mark on you—insofar as it's possible to leave a mark on a man like yourself, because you're not a man who's been influenced so much as a man who's influenced others, and many contemporary writers have been influenced by you . . .

That scares me to death!

There's nothing you can do about it. **"The Easter in New York"***, the* **"Transsiberian,"** *the* **"Panama,"** *the . . .*

How long've they been talking about'em, tell me?

. . . the **19 Elastic Poems** *. . . They've been talking about them, and they cite them, for the simple reason that those poems are the very* basis *of modern poetry, they're at the roots of modern lyric style . . .*

It's very nice of you, Manoll, to tell me such pleasant things . . .

But after all, you're famous*, Cendrars!*

Well, like the cuckolded husband, I'm the last one to *believe* it! No, no, not at all, I'm the basis of nothing at all. It's the modern world which is the basis, "immense and delicate" like the Middle Ages. And the root is Villon. If they ever publish the letters of Max Jacob, you'll discover all *kinds* of roots and bases and points of departure and arrival. Now

there's one who knew how to shake up the coconut tree and make the phoney geniuses and the real, the authentic and the inauthentic, fall out helter-skelter! And he had as sharp a tongue as you could wish for, and he wriggled like a devil in holy water.

What's that*? Even the good ones?*

He peels them up with a burst of laughter. You'll see! It's a riot.

I can hardly believe it.

Poets no longer have any *fun*. That's what frightens me most these days when I look around and see how *seriously* they take themselves.

It's true we don't know how to laugh, and very few things still actually amuse us. I hate to admit it, but my whole generation's like that: we don't laugh. But the reason for this is that there are obvious social problems, economic problems . . .

You think our life was a picnic in the old days?

Wasn't it?

My dear Manoll, in the Good Old Days writers of copy were paid a penny a line on the newspapers, and a man like Apollinaire had to wait for months and years before he could sign his own copy and count on a steady paying job. That's why he published erotic books, to earn a bite. You can't begin to imagine how the doors were closed to us. It's my impression that today they're much more hospitable, I meet young people everywhere, on the newspapers, in radio, at the movie studios. Before '14, those who were desperate enough showed up real early in line at the door, even at the entrance which was always kept locked. The others did their guzzling whenever they'd had the good fortune to get blood out of a stone, in the streets. We didn't give a fuck. We laughed. Paris girls are nice...

Our generation also *swallowed quite a bit . . . !*

Everybody's eaten some, that's the way it is with younger generations. It's a good thing the bloody stones exist and that they haven't started packing them in tin cans and exporting them like K-rations or corned-beef. They're saving them for the younger generation so that it'll remain a nice, resourceful generation. One word of advice: when you see an open door—newspaper, radio, theater, movie studio, bank—well, *stay out*! Otherwise you'll be gaga by the time you're thirty, because the laughter's always got to be checked at the door. That's been my experience. Poetry's out in the streets. It goes arm-in-arm with Laughter. It takes it out for a drink, at the source, in the neighborhood *bistros*, where the laughter of ordinary people is so tasty and the language that flows from their lips is so beautiful.

> *"The gift of the gab's gift of the streets..."*

Blaise, tell me a bit more about Guillaume Apollinaire.

Well, what *else* do you want me to tell you about poor Guillaume?

To begin with, why do you always call him "poor" Guillaume?

Because he's on the wrong side . . .

What do you mean by the "wrong side?"

The realm of the shades . . .

The realm of the dead . . .

No, what I said is the realm of the shades . . . That's why I don't like to talk about Guillaume Apollinaire . . .

Why not? Weren't you at his funeral?

That's the *reason*. I had such an experience at his funeral that after thirty-two years it's hard for me to believe he's dead . . .

What are you talking about, Cendrars?

Are you one of those people who *believe* in his death?

Well of course, unfortunately!

Then, Manoll, you've simply never read *The Decaying Spellbinder*.

The Decaying Spellbinder . . .?

Read it. It's the book that's the key to Apollinaire, the book that contains all the secrets of poor Guillaume . . .

What secrets?

The secrets of his genius, of his evocative power, of his double, his *triple* nature!

But what on earth happened to you at Apollinaire's funeral that you should suddenly be talking to me about him in that tone?

I'll tell you. The absolution had just been given, you see?

And through the portico of Saint Thomas Aquinas, out came Apollinaire's coffin which they placed in the hearse, draped with a flag, where Guillaume's lieutenant's *képi* on top of the Tricolor was visible among the wreaths and the flowers. The guard of honor, a halfsquad of troopers with weapons slung over their shoulders, was taking its place and the cortège was slowly getting under way, the family right behind the hearse, his mother, his wife, in their funeral veils, poor Jacqueline who'd just barely escaped the epidemic of Spanish influenza which'd now taken Guillaume, still convalescing and completely broken up, Apollinaire's closest friends, Prince Yaztrebzoff, Serge, his sister, Baroness von Oettingen, Max Jacob, Picasso, all of Guillaume's other friends, including Pierre-Albert Birot and his wife who'd broken their backs to stage *The Breasts of Tiresias* at the Théâtre Maubel, the whole of literary Paris, the arts and the press, but as soon as we turned the corner at the Boulevard-Saint-Germain, the cortège was suddenly besieged by the huge howling mobs that had broken loose from the crowds that were celebrating the Armistice, men and women, arm-in-arm, who were singing, dancing, hugging each other, and deliriously bawling out the refrain of the famous French war song:.

> *"No, you really shouldn't have gone Guillaume,*
> *No, you really shouldn't have gone!"*

It was unbelievably sad. And right behind me, I could overhear the tiresome glories of the dead-end of symbolism, all those immortal poets who're forgotten today, clucking and arguing among themselves about the future of Poetry, asking themselves what would become of the young poets now that Apollinaire was dead, and having a good time, as if they'd just won the battle of the Ancients and the Moderns. It was nightmarish. And I could feel anger, indignation, getting the better of me. So to avoid making a scene, I got out of the ranks at the intersection of Boul' Mich' and left the cortège, along with my wife Raymone and the painter Fernand Léger, to go drink a really hot toddy at the nearest *bistro*, to warm us up a bit and keep from catching influenza ourselves. After drinking the toddy standing up, we jumped into a taxi and as it turned out, when we arrived at Perè-Lachaise, the funeral, which had gone on foot, had made better time than we had, despite the congestion of the Armistice crowds which were demonstrating at every street corner, and the ceremony had already taken place at the cemetery and Apollinaire's friends had completely scattered. I asked Paul Fort where it had been and following his vague, *extremely* vague directions, we started groping among the grave-sites, Raymone, Fernand Léger and me. We bumped into two freshly dug graves. The gravediggers were shoveling in the dirt. We asked them which was the grave of Apollinaire? They didn't know. "You realize, with this influenza, with the war, they don't *tell* us the names of the dead we lower into the hole. There's too many. Try the management. We haven't got time. We're dead tired." "But he's a *lieutenant*," I said, "Lieutenant Apollinaire or Kostrowitsky. They must've fired a salvo on his grave!" "My poor fellow," the foreman said to me, "they fired two salvos. They're both lieutenants. We have no idea which one you're looking for. Look yourselves!" We leaned over the graves. They were half-filled. Nothing to identify them. The flowers, the bouquets, had already vanished, ripped off by the bargain-sellers who make new bouquets and sell the flowers from the Paris cemeteries, at night, in the métro. We were about to leave when I noticed a lump of earth with a little grass at the bottom of one of the graves. "Look," I said to Raymone and Fernand Léger, "look, it's incredible! It's just like the head of Apollinaire...!" The lump of solid earth fallen at the bottom of the hole had exactly the shape of Guillaume's head and the grass was planted like his hair was, when he was alive, around the scar of his trepanning. There was no *question* of gazing too long at that eerie look-alike. As usual when an inanimate object starts becoming radiant to the point of being about to take on, of *reassuming* life, the psychic charge which it emits is too intense, you can't believe your eyes. We beat a retreat, staggered. Raymone was crying. Fernand bit his lips. I waited till I was out of the cemetery, where already a glacial fog was smothering the shrubs and monuments, before I said: "It was him, all right. We've seen him. Apollinaire's not dead. Pretty soon, he's *bound* to show up. Remember what I've just told you . . ." And during our whole way back, I recited to Ramone and Fernand whole tatters of *The Decaying Spellbinder*, which were coming back to me in pieces, depending on the jolts and changes of speed of the bus that charged down from Ménilmontant the way Lord Blackguard's coach and horses used to come down from Courtille on a day of fiesta in times gone by! It was fantastic. Paris was celebrating a victory. Apollinaire had lost. I was in the dumps. It was absurd. I kept turning around, often, to examine the aisle of our bus. In what guise was Guillaume going to come aboard, along the way, to take part in the great Paris holiday? Fernand Léger had a date. Raymone was acting in a play at the theater in Belleville that evening. I prowled around until midnight on the rue de Belleville, the rue de Crimée, the Place des Fêtes, sticking close to people to see them better, then I went to plant myself in front of the stage-entrance at the far end of the dead-end. When Raymone came out, we went back home sneakily. Where was I living then? At the *Hôtel Mirabeau*, on rue de la Paix, and I stayed in Paris another eight days, in Apollinaire's place, to correct the proofs and prepare to bring out his *Loiterer on the Two Banks* which I was publishing at *Sirène*. And then I went to Nice where they were waiting for me to finish a film I was making. The wheel turns fast. Poor Guillaume. The following year, in 1919, I was still publishing him at the *Sirène*, the limited edition of *Bestiary*, or *The Cortège of Orpheus* with little woodcuts by Dufy. But what's *really* left me heartbroken is that I wasn't able to publish Guillaume Apollinaire's last book which we'd talked

about together for a long time, which he'd finally written and couldn't find a title for. It consisted—collected in a single volume, entirely revised, recast, corrected, linked up, organized and carefully tuned up and improved so as to form a continuous whole, rolling along like the current of a stream rushing headlong—of the prefaces, the notes, the biographical sketches he'd been able to publish hastily, even carelessly, in the collection *Masters of Love* of the *Bibliotheque des Curièux*, on the rue Furstenberg. It was a *prodigious* book, which went *way* beyond ordinary strangeness and erudition. It wasn't an erotic book but a poet's book. It was a book that dazzled me out of my mind, a book for which I'd found a title: *The Styx*; after the river in Hell, which flows around it seven times. That's what that book *was*: a dark river, full of tar and sulphur. It *still* hasn't been published, but it's hard for me to believe that the manuscript's never going to show up—I mean, show up for the people of today. It probably lost its way towards the rue de Condèe or the rue Furstenberg. Unless it's fallen into someone's hands, into the hands of someone who can't give good directions, which I doubt. Then there'd still be some hope. I'm on the lookout.

Henry Miller (essay date 1952)

SOURCE: "Blaise Cendrars," in *The Henry Miller Reader*, edited by Lawrence Durrell, New Directions Books, 1959, pp. 327-52.

[*Henry Miller (1891-1980) was an American novelist and critic. In the following essay, first published in 1952, he presents a warm and personal look at Cendrars's life and work.*]

[Miller's introduction, written for the 1959 collection:] *Against the advice of editor and publisher, I have insisted on the inclusion of this piece—as a substitution for passages on "Mona" of the* Tropics. *It was suggested that the essay called "Balzac and his Double" be used instead of this. But Balzac is long dead, and the halo which surrounds his name is still untarnished. Cendrars is still living, though gravely ill now and confined to a wheel-chair. Alive or dead, he is, to my mind, vastly more important to our generation than Balzac ever could be.*

For no contemporary author have I struggled harder to obtain a hearing than for Blaise Cendrars. And all my efforts have been in vain. I consider it a shame and a disgrace that no American publisher has shown the least interest in this undisputed giant of French letters. All we have of him, in translation, to my knowledge, are several poems, the novel called Sutter's Gold *(an early work), the African Anthology (a collection of African poems translated into French, by Cendrars) and the* Antarctic Fugue, *published in England, this being only part of a longer work,* Dan Yack.

Yes, this chapter from The Books in My Life *was written here in Big Sur and it was written from the heart. Cendrars is not easy reading—to an American like myself whose French is far from perfect. But he has been the most rewarding, to me, of all contemporary French writers. If, in the early stages of my career, it was Knut Hamsun whom I idolized, whom I most desired to imitate, in the latter stage it has been Cendrars. With the exception of John Cowper Powys, no writer I have come in contact with, gives more than he. He gives and he sends. He is inexhaustible. Among all living writers he is the one who has lived the most, lived the fullest. Beside him, for example, Ernest Hemingway is a Boy Scout.*

And this is the writer we have chosen to neglect and ignore. I don't understand it. I refuse to understand it. Those who criticize me for being too eulogistic have never read him—they have only dipped into him.

This is no commentary, this is an exordium. Read him! I say. Read him, even if at the age of sixty you have to begin to learn French. Read him in French, not in English. Read him before it is too late, for it is doubtful if France will ever again produce a Cendrars.

Cendrars was the first French writer to look me up, during my stay in Paris, and the last man I saw on leaving Paris. I had just a few minutes before catching the train for Rocamadour and I was having a last drink on the *terrasse* of my hotel near the Porte d'Orléans when Cendrars hove in sight. Nothing could have given me greater joy than this unexpected last-minute encounter. In a few words I told him of my intention to visit Greece. Then I sat back and drank in the music of his sonorous voice which to me always seemed to come from a sea organ. In those last few minutes Cendrars managed to convey a world of information, and with the same warmth and tenderness which he exudes in his books. Like the very ground under our feet, his thoughts were honeycombed with all manner of subterranean passages. I left him sitting there in shirt sleeves, never dreaming that years would elapse before hearing from him again, never dreaming that I was perhaps taking my last look at Paris.

I had read whatever was translated of Cendrars before arriving in France. That is to say, almost nothing. My first taste of him in his own language came at a time when my French was none too proficient. I began with *Moravagine,* a book by no means easy to read for one who knows little French. I read it slowly, with a dictionary by my side, shifting from one café to another. It was in the Café de la Liberté, corner of the Rue de la Gaieté and the Boulevard Edgar Quinet,

that I began it. I remember well the day. Should Cendrars ever read these lines he may be pleased, touched perhaps, to know that it was in that dingy hole I first opened his book.

Moravagine was probably the second or third book which I had attempted to read in French. Only the other day, after a lapse of about eighteen years, I reread it. What was my amazement to discover that whole passages were engraved in my memory! And I had thought my French was null! Here is one of the passages I remember as clearly as the day I first read it. It begins at the top of page 77 (Editions Grasset, 1926).

> I tell you of things that brought some relief at the start. There was also the water, gurgling at intervals, in the watercloset pipes... A boundless despair possessed me.

(Does this convey anything to you, my dear Cendrars?)

Immediately I think of two other passages, even more deeply engraved in my mind, from "**Une Nuit dans la Forêt**," which I read about three years later. I cite them not to brag of my powers of memory but to reveal an aspect of Cendrars which his English and American readers probably do not suspect the existence of.

> 1. I, the freest man that exists, recognize that there is always something that binds one: that liberty, independence do not exist, and I am full of contempt for, and at the same time take pleasure in, my helplessness.

> 2. More and more I realize that I have always led the contemplative life. I am a sort of Brahmin in reverse, meditating on himself amid the hurly-burly, who, with all his strength, disciplines himself and scorns existence. Or the boxer with his shadow, who, furiously, calmly, punching at emptiness, watches his form. What virtuosity, what science, what balance, the ease with which he accelerates! *Later, one must learn how to take punishment with equal imperturbability.* I, I know how to take punishment and with serenity I fructify and with serenity destroy myself: in short, work in the world not so much to enjoy as to make others enjoy (it's others' reflexes that give me pleasure, not my own). Only a soul full of despair can ever attain serenity and, to be in despair, you must have loved a good deal and *still love the world.*

These last two passages have probably been cited many times already and will no doubt be cited many times more as the years go by. They are memorable ones and thoroughly the author's own. Those who know only *Sutter's Gold,*

Panama and **On the Trans-siberian,** which are about all the American reader gets to know, may indeed wonder on reading the foregoing passages why this man has not been translated more fully. Long before I attempted to make Cendrars better known to the American public (and to the world at large, I may well add), John Dos Passos had translated and illustrated with water colors **Panama, or the adventures of my seven uncles.**

However, the primary thing to know about Blaise Cendrars is that he is a man of many parts. He is also a man of many books, many kinds of books, and by that I do not mean "good" and "bad" but books so different one from another that he gives the impression of evolving in all directions at once. An evolved man, truly. Certainly an evolved writer.

His life itself reads like the *Arabian Nights' Entertainment.* And this individual who has led a super-dimensional life is also a book-worm. The most gregarious of men and yet a solitary. ("*O mes solitudes!*") A man of deep intuition and invincible logic. The logic of life. Life first and foremost. Life always with a capital L. That's Cendrars.

To follow his career from the time he slips out of his parents' home in Neufchâtel, a boy fifteen or sixteen, to the days of the Occupation when he secrets himself in Aix-en-Provence and imposes on himself a long period of silence, is something to make one's head spin. The itinerary of his wanderings is more difficult to follow than Marco Polo's, whose trajectory, incidentally, he seems to have crossed and recrossed a number of times. One of the reasons for the great fascination he exerts over me is the resemblance between his voyages and adventures and those which I associate in memory with Sinbad the Sailor or Aladdin of the Wonderful Lamp. The amazing experiences which he attributes to the characters in his books, and which often as not he has shared, have all the qualities of legend as well as the authenticity of legend. Worshiping life and the truth of life, he comes closer than any author of our time to revealing the common source of word and deed. He restores to contemporary life the elements of the heroic, the imaginative and the fabulous. His adventures have led him to nearly every region of the globe, particularly those regarded as dangerous or inaccessible. (One must read his early life especially to appreciate the truth of this statement.) He has consorted with all types, including bandits, murderers, revolutionaries and other varieties of fanatic. He has tried at no less than thirty-six métiers, according to his own words, but, like Balzac, gives the impression of knowing every métier. He was once a juggler, for example—on the English music-hall stage—at the same time that Chaplin was making his debut there; he was a pearl merchant and a smuggler; he was a plantation owner in South America, where he made a fortune three times in succession and lost it even more rapidly

than he had made it. But read his life! There is more in it than meets the eye.

Yes, he is an explorer and investigator of the ways and doings of men. And he has made himself such by planting himself in the midst of life, by taking up his lot with his fellow creatures. What a superb, painstaking reporter he is, this man who would scorn the thought of being called "a student of life." He has the faculty of getting "his story" by a process of osmosis; he seems to seek nothing deliberately. Which is why, no doubt, his own story is always interwoven with the other man's. To be sure, he possesses the art of distillation, but what he is vitally interested in is the alchemical nature of all relationships. This eternal quest of the transmutative enables him to reveal men to themselves and to the world; it causes him to extol men's virtues, to reconcile us to their faults and weaknesses, to increase our knowledge and respect for what is essentially human, to deepen our love and understanding of the world. He is the "reporter" par excellence because he combines the faculties of poet, seer and prophet. An innovator and initiator, ever the first to give testimony, he has made known to us the real pioneers, the real adventurers, the real discoverers among our contemporaries. More than any writer I can think of he has made dear to us "*le bel aujourd'hui.*"

Whilst performing on all levels he always found time to read. On long voyages, in the depths of the Amazon, in the deserts (I imagine he knows them all, those of the earth, those of the spirit), in the jungle, on the broad pampas, on trains, tramps and ocean liners, in the great museums and libraries of Europe, Asia and Africa, he has buried himself in books, has ransacked whole archives, has photographed rare documents, and, for all I know, may have stolen invaluable books, scripts, documents of all kinds—why not, considering the enormity of his appetite for the rare, the curious, the forbidden?

He has told us in one of his recent books how the Germans (*les Boches*!) destroyed or carried off, I forget which, his precious library, precious to a man like Cendrars who loves to give the most precise data when referring to a passage from one of his favorite books. Thank God, his memory is alive and functions like a faithful machine. An incredible memory, as will testify those who have read his more recent books— **La Main Coupée, l'Homme Foudroyé, Bourlinguer, Le Lotissement du Ciel, La Banlieue de Paris.**

On the side—with Cendrars it seems as though almost everything of account has been done "on the side"—he has translated the works of other writers, notably the Portuguese author, Ferreira de Castro (*Forêt Vierge*) and our own Al Jennings, the great outlaw and bosom friend of O. Henry. What a wonderful translation is *Hors-la-loi* which in English is called *Through the Shadows with O. Henry*. It is a sort of secret collaboration between Cendrars and the innermost being of Al Jennings. At the time of writing it, Cendrars had not yet met Jennings nor even corresponded with him. (This is another book, I must say in passing, which our pocket-book editors have overlooked. There is a fortune in it, unless I am all wet, and it would be comforting to think that part of this fortune should find its way into Al Jennings' pocket.)

One of the most fascinating aspects of Cendrars's temperament is his ability and readiness to collaborate with a fellow artist. Picture him, shortly after the First World War, editing the publications of La Sirène! What an opportunity! To him we owe an edition of *Les Chants de Maldoror*, the first to appear since the original private publication by the author in 1868. In everything an innovator, always meticulous, scrupulous and exacting in his demands, whatever issued from the hands of Cendrars at La Sirène is now a valuable collector's item. Hand in hand with this capability for collaboration goes another quality—the ability, or grace, to make the first overtures. Whether it be a criminal, a saint, a man of genius, a tyro with promise, Cendrars is the first to look him up, the first to herald him, the first to aid him in the way the person most desires. I speak with justifiable warmth here. No writer ever paid me a more signal honor than dear Blaise Cendrars who, shortly after the publication of *Tropic of Cancer*, knocked at my door one day to extend the hand of friendship. Nor can I forget that first tender, eloquent review of the book which appeared under his signature in *Orbes* shortly thereafter. (Or perhaps it was *before* he appeared at the studio in the Villa Seurat.)

There were times when reading Cendrars—and this is something which happens to me rarely—that I put the book down in order to wring my hands with joy or despair, with anguish or with desperation. Cendrars has stopped me in my tracks again and again, just as implacably as a gunman pressing a rod against one's spine. Oh, yes, I am often carried away by exaltation in reading a man's work. But I am alluding now to something other than exaltation. I am talking of a sensation in which all one's emotions are blended and confused. I am talking of knockout blows. Cendrars has knocked me cold. Not once, but a number of times. And I am not exactly a ham, when it comes to taking it on the chin! Yes, *mon cher* Cendrars, you not only stopped *me*, you stopped the clock. It has taken me days, weeks, sometimes months, to recover from these bouts with you. Even years later, I can put my hand to the spot where I caught the blow and feel the old smart. You battered and bruised me; you left me scarred, dazed, punch-drunk. The curious thing is that the better I know you—through your books—the more susceptible I become. It is as if you had put the Indian sign on me. I come forward with chin outstretched—"to take it." *I am your meat*, as I have so often said. And it is because I believe I am not unique in this, because I wish others to enjoy

this uncommon experience, that I continue to put in my little word for you whenever, wherever, I can.

I incautiously said: "the better I know you." My dear Cendrars, I will never know you, not as I do other men, of that I am certain. No matter how thoroughly you reveal yourself I shall never get to the bottom of you. I doubt that anyone ever will, and it is not vanity which prompts me to put it this way. You are as inscrutable as a Buddha. You inspire, you reveal, but you never give yourself wholly away. Not that you withhold yourself! No, encountering you, whether in person or through the written word, you leave the impression of having given all there is to give. Indeed, you are one of the few men I know who, in their books as well as in person, give that "extra measure" which means everything to us. You give all that *can* be given. It is not your fault that the very core of you forbids scrutiny. It is the law of your being. No doubt there are men less inquisitive, less grasping, less clutching, for whom these remarks are meaningless. But you have so refined our sensitivity, so heightened our awareness, so deepened our love for men and women, for books, for nature, for a thousand and one things of life which only one of your own unending paragraphs could catalogue, that you awaken in us the desire to turn you inside out. When I read you or talk to you I am always aware of your inexhaustible awareness: you are not just sitting in a chair in a room in a city in a country, telling us what is on your mind or in your mind, you make the chair talk and the room vibrate with the tumult of the city whose life is sustained by the invisible outer throng of a whole nation whose history has become your history, whose life is your life and yours theirs, and as you talk or write all these elements, images, facts, creations enter into your thoughts and feelings, forming a web which the spider in you ceaselessly spins and which spreads in us, your listeners, until the whole of creation is involved, and we, you, them, it, everything, have lost identity and found new meaning, new life...

Before proceeding further, there are two books on Cendrars which I would like to recommend to all who are interested in knowing more about the man. Both are entitled *Blaise Cendrars*. One is by Jacques-Henry Levèsque (Editions de la Nouvelle Critique, Paris, 1947), the other by Louis Parrot (Editions Pierre Seghers, Paris, 1948), finished on the author's deathbed. Both contain bibliographies, excerpts from Cendrars's works, and a number of photographs taken at various periods of his life. Those who do not read French may glean a surprising knowledge of this enigmatic individual from the photographs alone. (It is amazing what spice and vitality French publishers lend their publications through the insertion of old photographs. Seghers has been particularly enterprising in this respect. In his series of little square books, called *Poètes d'Aujourd'hui*, he has given us a veritable gallery of contemporary and near contemporary figures.)

Yes, one can glean a lot about Cendrars just from studying his physiognomy. He has probably been photographed more than any contemporary writer. In addition, sketches and portraits of him have been made by any number of celebrated artists, including Modigliani, Apollinaire, Léger. Flip the pages of the two books I just mentioned—Levèsque's and Parrot's; take a good look at this *"gueule"* which Cendrars has presented to the world in a thousand different moods. Some will make you weep; some are almost hallucinating. There is one photo of him taken in uniform during the days of the Foreign Legion when he was a corporal. His left hand, holding a butt which is burning his fingers, protrudes from beneath the cape; it is a hand so expressive, so very eloquent, that if you do not know the story of his missing arm, this will convey it unerringly. It is with this powerful and sensitive left hand that he has written most of his books, signed his name to innumerable letters and post cards, shaved himself, washed himself, guided his speedy Alfa-Romeo through the most dangerous terrains; it is with this left hand that he has hacked his way through jungles, punched his way through brawls, defended himself, shot at men and beasts, clapped his *copains* on the back, greeted with a warm clasp a long-lost friend and caressed the women and animals he has loved. There is another photo of him taken in 1921 when he was working with Abel Gance on the film called *La Roue,* the eternal cigarette glued to his lips, a tooth missing, a huge checkered cap with an enormous peak hanging over one ear. The expression on his face is something out of Dostoievski. On the opposite page is a photo taken by Raymone in 1924, when he was working on ***l'Or (Sutter's Gold).*** Here he stands with legs spread apart, his left hand sliding into the pocket of his baggy pantaloons, a *mégot* to his lips, as always. In this photo he looks like a healthy, cocky young peasant of Slavic origin. There is a taunting gleam in his eye, a sort of frank, good-natured defiance. "Fuck you, Jack, I'm fine ... *and you*?" That's what it conveys, his look. Another, taken with Levèsque at Tremblay-sur-Maulne,1926, captures him square in the prime of life. Here he seems to be at his peak physically; he emanates health, joy, vitality. In 1928 we have the photo which has been reprinted by the thousands. It is Cendrars of the South American period, looking fit, sleek almost, well garbed, his conk crowned by a handsome fedora with its soft brim upturned. He has a burning, faraway look in the eyes, as if he had just come back from the Antarctic. (I believe it was in this period that he was writing, or had just finished, **Dan Yack,** the first half of which [**Le Plan de l'Aiguille**] has only recently been issued in translation by an English publisher.) But it is in 1944 that we catch a glimpse of *le vieux Légionnaire*—photo by Chardon, Cavaillon. Here he reminds one of Victor McLaglen in the title role of *The Informer.* This is the period of ***l'Homme Foudroyé,*** for me one of his major books. Here he is the fully developed earth man composed of many rich layers—roustabout, tramp, bum, panhandler, mixer, bruiser, adventurer, sailor, soldier, tough guy, the man of a thousand-and-one hard, bitter experiences who never went under but ripened, ripened, ripened. *Un homme, quoi!* There are two photos taken in 1946, at Aix-en-Provence, which yield us tender, moving images of him. One, in which he leans against a fence, shows him surrounded by the urchins of the neighborhood: he is teaching them a few sleight of hand tricks. The other catches him walking through a shadowed old street which curves endearingly. His look is meditative, if not *triste.* It is a beautiful photograph, redolent of the atmosphere of the Midi. One walks with him in his pensive mood, hushed by the unseizable thoughts which envelop him... I force myself to draw rein. I could go on forever about the "physiognomic" aspects of the man. His is a mug one can never forget. It's *human,* that's what. Human like Chinese faces, like Egyptian, Cretan, Etruscan ones.

Many are the things which have been said against this writer ... that his books are cinematic in style, that they are sensational, that he exaggerates and deforms *à outrance,* that he is prolix and verbose, that he lacks all sense of form, that he is too much the realist or else that his narratives are too much the infinitum. Taken altogether there is, to be sure, a grain of truth in these accusations, but let us remember— *only a grain*! They reflect the views of the paid critic, the academician, the frustrated novelist. But supposing, for a moment, we accepted them at face value. Will they hold water? Take his cinematic technique, for example. Well, are we not living in the age of the cinema? Is not this period of history more fantastic, more "incredible," than the simulacrum of it which we see unrolled on the silver screen? As for his sensationalism—have we forgotten Gilles de Rais, the Marquis de Sade, the *Memoirs* of Casanova? As for hyperbole, what of Pindar? As for prolixity and verbosity, what about Jules Romains or Marcel Proust? As for exaggeration and deformation, what of Rabelais, Swift, Céline, to mention an anomalous trinity? As for lack of form, that perennial jackass which is always kicking up its heels in the pages of literary reviews, have I not heard cultured Europeans rant about the "vegetal" aspect of Hindu temples, the façades of which are studded with a riot of human, animal and other forms? Have I not seen them twisting their lips in distaste when examining the efflorescences embodied in Tibetan scrolls? No taste, eh? No sense of proportion? No control? *C'est ça. De la mesure avant tout*! These cultured nobodies forget that their beloved exemplars, the Greeks, worked with Cyclopean blocks, created monstrosities as well as apotheoses of harmony, grace, form and spirit; they forget perhaps that the Cycladic sculpture of Greece surpassed in abstraction and simplification anything which Brancusi or his followers ever attempted. The very mythology of these worshipers of beauty, whose motto was "Nothing to the extreme," is a revelation of the "monstrous" aspect of their being.

Oui, Cendrars is full of excrescences. There are passages

which swell up out of the body of his text like rank tumors. There are detours, parentheses, asides, which are the embryonic pith and substance of books yet to come. There is a grand efflorescence and exfoliation, and there is also a grand wastage of material in his books. Cendrars neither cribs and cabins, nor does he drain himself completely. When the moment comes to let go, he lets go. When it is expedient or efficacious to be brief, he is brief and to the point—like a dagger. To me his books reflect his lack of fixed habits, or better yet, his ability to break a habit. (A sign of real emancipation!) In those swollen paragraphs, which are like *une mer houleuse* and which some readers, apparently, are unable to cope with, Cendrars reveals his oceanic spirit. We who vaunt dear Shakespeare's madness, his elemental outbursts, are we to fear these cosmic gusts? We who swallowed the *Pantagruel* and *Gargantua*, via Urquhart, are we to be daunted by catalogues of names, places, dates, events? We who produced the oddest writer in any tongue—Lewis Carroll—are we to shy away from the play of words, from the ridiculous, the grotesque, the unspeakable or the "utterly impossible"? It takes a *man* to hold his breath as Cendrars does when he is about to unleash one of his triple-page paragraphs without stop. *A man*? A deep-sea diver. A whale. A whale of a man, precisely.

What *is* remarkable is that this same man has also given us some of the shortest sentences ever written, particularly in his poems and prose poems. Here, in staccato rhythm—let us not forget that before he was a writer he was a musician!—he deploys a telegraphic style. (It might also be called "telesthetic.") One can read it as fast as Chinese, with whose written characters his vocables have a curious affinity, to my way of thinking. This particular technique of Cendrars's creates a kind of exorcism—a deliverance from the heavy weight of prose, from the impedimenta of grammar and syntax, from the illusory intelligibility of the merely communicative in speech. In "*l'Eubage,*" for example, we discover a sibylline quality of thought and utterance. It is one of his curious books. An extreme. Also a departure and an end. Cendrars is indeed difficult to classify, though why we should want to classify him I don't know. Sometimes I think of him as "a writer's writer," though he is definitely not that. But what I mean to say is that a writer has much to learn from Cendrars. In school, I remember, we were always being urged to take as models men like Macaulay, Coleridge, Ruskin, or Edmund Burke—even de Maupassant. Why they didn't say Shakespeare, Dante, Milton, I don't know. No professor ever believed, I dare say, that any of us brats would turn out to be writers one day. They were failures themselves, hence teachers. Cendrars has made it clear that the only teacher, the only model, is life itself. What a writer learns from Cendrars is to follow his nose, to obey life's commands, to worship no other god but life. Some interpreters will have it that Cendrars means "the dangerous life." I don't believe Cendrars would limit it thus. He means *life* pure and simple,

in all its aspects, all its ramifications, all its bypaths, temptations, hazards, what not. If he is an adventurer, he is an adventurer in all realms of life. What interests him is *every* phase of life. The subjects he has touched on, the themes he has pursued, are encyclopedic. Another sign of "emancipation," this all-inclusive absorption in life's myriad manifestations. It is often when he seems most "realistic," for example, that he tends to pull all the stops on his organ. The realist is a meager soul. He sees what is in front of him, like a horse with blinders. Cendrars's vision is perpetually open; it is almost as if he had an extra eye buried in his crown, a skylight open to all the cosmic rays. Such a man, you may be sure, will never complete his life's work, because life will always be a step ahead of him. Besides, life knows no completion, and Cendrars is one with life. An article by Pierre de Latil in *La Gazette des Lettres*, Paris, August 6, 1949, informs us that Cendrars has projected a dozen or more books to be written within the next few years. It is an astounding program, considering that Cendrars is now in his sixties, that he has no secretary, that he writes with his left hand, that he is restless underneath, always itching to sally forth and see more of the world, that he actually detests writing and looks upon his work as forced labor. He works on four or five books at a time. He will finish them all, I am certain. I only pray that I live to read the trilogy of "*les souvenirs humains*" called **Archives de ma tour d'ivoire,** which will consist of: *Hommes de lettres, Hommes d'affaires* and *Vie des hommes obscurs*. Particularly the last-named...

I have long pondered over Cendrars's confessed insomnia. He attributes it to his life in the trenches, if I remember rightly. True enough, no doubt, but I surmise there are deeper reasons for it. At any rate, what I wish to point out is that there seems to be a connection between his fecundity and his sleeplessness. For the ordinary individual sleep is *the* restorative. Exceptional individuals—holy men, gurus, inventors, leaders, men of affairs, or certain types of the insane—are able to do with very little sleep. They apparently have other means of replenishing their dynamic potential. Some men, merely by varying their pursuits, can go on working with almost no sleep. Others, like the yogi and the guru, in becoming more and more aware and therefore more alive, virtually emancipate themselves from the thrall of sleep. (Why sleep if the purpose of life is to enjoy creation to the fullest?) With Cendrars, I have the feeling that in switching from active life to writing, and vice versa, he replenishes himself. A pure supposition on my part. Otherwise I am at a loss to account for a man burning the candle at both ends and not consuming himself. Cendrars mentions somewhere that he is of a line of longlived antecedents. He has certainly squandered his hereditary patrimony regally. *But*—he shows no signs of cracking up. Indeed, he seems to have entered upon a period of second youth. He is confident that when he reaches the ripe age of seventy he will be ready to embark on new adventures. It will not surprise me in the least if he does; I can see him at ninety scaling the Himalayas or embarking in the first rocket to voyage to the moon.

But to come back to the relation between his writing and his sleeplessness... If one examines the dates given at the end of his books, indicating the time he spent on them, one is struck by the rapidity with which he executed them as well as by the speed with which (all good-sized books) they succeed one another. All this implies one thing, to my mind, and that is "obsession." To write one has to be possessed and obsessed. What is it that possesses and obsesses Cendrars? *Life*. He is a man in love with life—*et c'est tout*. No matter if he denies this at times, no matter if he vilifies the times or excoriates his contemporaries in the arts, no matter if he compares his own recent past with the present and finds the latter lacking, no matter if he deplores the trends, the tendencies, the philosophies and behavior of the men of our epoch, he is the one man of our time who has proclaimed and trumpeted the fact that *today* is profound and beautiful. And it is just because he has anchored himself in the midst of contemporary life, where, as if from a conning tower, he surveys all life, past, present and future, the life of the stars as well as the life of the ocean depths, life in miniscule as well as the life grandiose, that I seized upon him as a shining example of the right principle, the right attitude towards life. No one can steep himself in the splendors of the past more than Cendrars; no one can hail the future with greater zest; but it is the present, the eternal present, which he glorifies and with which he allies himself. It is such men, and only such men, who are in the tradition, who carry on. The others are backward lookers, idolaters, or else mere wraiths of hopefulness, *bonimenteurs*. With Cendrars you strike ore. And it is because he understands the present so profoundly, accepts it and is one with it, that he is able to predict the future so unerringly. Not that he sets himself up as a soothsayer! No, his prophetic remarks are made casually and discreetly; they are buried often in a maze of unrelated material. In this he often reminds me of the good physician. He knows how to take the pulse. In fact, he knows all the pulses, like the Chinese physicians of old. When he says of certain men that they are sick, or of certain artists that they are corrupt or fakes, or of politicians in general that they are crazy, or of military men that they are criminals, he knows whereof he speaks. It is the magister in him which is speaking.

He has, however, another way of speaking which is more endearing to me. He can speak with tenderness. Lawrence, it will be remembered, originally thought of calling the book known as *Lady Chatterley's Lover* by the title "Tenderness." I mention Lawrence's name because I remember vividly Cendrars's allusion to him on the occasion of his memorable visit to the Villa Seurat. "You must think a lot of Lawrence," he said questioningly. "I do," I replied. We exchanged a few

words and then I recall him asking me fair and square if I did not believe Lawrence to be overrated. It was the metaphysical side of Lawrence, I gathered, that was not to his liking, that was "suspect," I should say. (And it was just at this period that I was engrossed in this particular aspect of Lawrence) I am sure, at any rate, that my defense of Lawrence was weak and unsustained. To be truthful, I was much more interested in hearing Cendrars's view of the man than in justifying my own. Often, later, in reading Cendrars this word "tenderness" crossed my lips. It would escape involuntarily, rouse me from my reverie. Futile though it be, I would then indulge in endless speculation, comparing Lawrence's tenderness with Cendrars's. They are, I now think, of two distinct kinds. Lawrence's weakness is man, Cendrars's men. Lawrence longed to know men better; he wanted to work in common with them. It is in *Apocalypse* that he has some of the most moving passages—on the withering of the "societal" instinct. They create real anguish in us—for Lawrence. They make us realize the tortures he suffered in trying to be "a man among men." With Cendrars I detect no hint of such deprivation or mutilation. In the ocean of humanity Cendrars swims as blithely as a porpoise or a dolphin. In his narratives he is always together with men, one with them in deed, one with them in thought. If he is a solitary, he is nevertheless fully and completely a man. He is also the brother of all men. Never does he set himself up as superior to his fellow man. Lawrence thought himself superior, often, often—I think that is undeniable—and very often he was anything but. Very often it is a lesser man who "instructs" him. Or shames him. Lawrence had too great a love for "humanity" to understand or get along with his fellow man.

It is when we come to their respective fictional characters that we sense the rift between these two figures. With the exception of the self portraits, given in *Sons and Lovers, Kangaroo, Aaron's Rod* and such like, all Lawrence's characters are mouthpieces for his philosophy or the philosophy he wishes to depose. They are ideational creatures, moved about like chess pieces. They have blood in them all right, but it is the blood which Lawrence has pumped into them. Cendrars's characters issue from life and their activity stems from life's moving vortex. They too, of course, acquaint us with his philosophy of life, but obliquely, in the elliptic manner of art.

The tenderness of Cendrars exudes from all pores. He does not spare his characters; neither does he revile or castigate them. His harshest words, let me say parenthetically, are usually reserved for the poets and artists whose work he considers spurious. Aside from these diatribes, you will rarely find him passing judgment upon others. What you do find is that in laying bare the weaknesses or faults of his subjects he is unmasking, or endeavoring to unmask, their essential heroic nature. All the diverse figures—human, all too human—which crowd his books are glorified in their basic, intrinsic being. They may or may not have been heroic in the face of death; they may or may not have been heroic before the tribunal of justice; but they *are* heroic in the common struggle to assert and uphold their own primal being. I mentioned a while ago the book by Al Jennings which Cendrars so ably translated. The very choice of this book is indicative of my point. This mite of a man, this outlaw with an exaggerated sense of justice and honor who is "up for life" (but eventually pardoned by Theodore Roosevelt), this terror of the West who wells over with tenderness, is just the sort of man Cendrars *would* choose to tell the world about, just the sort of man he *would* uphold as being filled with the dignity of life. Ah, how I should like to have been there when Cendrars eventually caught up with him, in Hollywood of all places! Cendrars has written of this "brief encounter" and I heard of it myself from Al Jennings' own lips when I met him by chance a few years ago—in a bookshop there in Hollywood.

In the books written since the Occupation, Cendrars has much to say about the War—the First War, naturally, not only because it was less inhuman but because the future course of his life, I might say, was decided by it. He has also written about the Second War, particularly about the fall of Paris and the incredible exodus preceding it. Haunting pages, reminiscent of Revelation. Equaled in war literature only by St. Exupéry's *Flight to Arras*. (See the section of his book, **Le Lotissement du Ciel,** which first appeared in the *revue, Le Cheval de Troie,* entitled: **Un Nouveau Patron pour l'Aviation.**) In all these recent books Cendrars reveals himself more and more intimately. So penetrative, so naked, are these glimpses he permits us that one instinctively recoils. So sure, swift and deft are these revelations that it is like watching a safecracker at work. In these flashes stand revealed the whole swarm of intimates whose lives dovetail with his own. Exposed through the lurid searchlight of his Cyclopean eye they are caught in the flux and surveyed from every angle. Here there is "completion" of a sort. Nothing is omitted or altered for the sake of the narrative. With these books the "narrative" is stepped up, broadened out, the supports and buttresses battered away, in order that the book may become part of life, swim with life's currents, and remain forever identical with life. Here one comes to grips with the men Cendrars truly loves, the men he fought beside in the trenches and whom he saw wiped out like rats, the Gypsies of the Zone whom he consorted with in the good old days, the ranchers and other figures from the South American scene, the porters, concierges, tradesmen, truck drivers, and "people of no account" (as we say), and it is with the utmost sympathy and understanding that he treats these latter. What a gallery! Infinitely more exciting, in every sense of the word, than Balzac's gallery of "types." This is the real *Human Comedy*. No sociological studies, *à la* Zola. No satirical puppet show, *à la* Thackeray. No pan-humanity, *à la*

Jules Romains. Here in these latter books, though minus the aim and purpose of the great Russian, but perhaps with another aim which we will understand better later, at any rate, with equal amplitude, violence, humor, tenderness and religious—yes, religious—fervor, Cendrars gives us the French equivalent of Dostoievski's outpourings in such works as *The Idiot, The Possessed, The Brothers Karamazov.* A production which could only be realized, consummated, in the ripe middle years of life.

Everything now forthcoming has been digested a thousand times. Again and again Cendrars has pushed back—where? into what deep well?—the multiform story of his life. This heavy, molten mass of experience raw and refined, subtle and crude, digested and predigested, which had been lodging in his entrails like a torpid and amorphous dinosaur idly flapping its rudimentary wings, this cargo destined for eventual delivery at the exact time and the exact place, demanded a touch of dynamite to be set off. From June, 1940, to the 21st of August, 1943, Cendrars remained awesomely silent. *Il s'est tu. Chut! Motus!* What starts him writing again is a visit from his friend Edouard Peisson, as he relates in the opening pages of *l'Homme Foudroyé. En passant* he evokes the memory of a certain night in 1915, at the front—"*la plus terrible que jai vécue.*" There were other occasions, one suspects, before the critical visit of his friend Peisson, which might have served to detonate the charge. But perhaps on these occasions the fuse burned out too quickly or was damp or smothered under by the weight of world events. But let us drop these useless speculations. Let us dive into Section 17 of *Un Nouveau Patron Pour l'Aviation* . . .

This brief section begins with the recollection of a sentence of Rémy de Gourmont's: "And it shows great progress that, where women prayed before, cows now chew the cud . . ." In a few lines comes this from Cendrars's own mouth:

> Beginning on May 10th, Surrealism descended upon earth: not the works of absurd poets who pretend to be such and who, at most, are but sou-realistes since they preach the subconscious, but the work of Christ, the only poet of the sur-real...

> If ever I had faith, it was on that day that grace should have touched me . . .

Follow two paragraphs dealing in turbulent, compressed fury with the ever execrable condition of war. Like Goya, he repeats: "*J'ai vu.*" The second paragraph ends thus:

> The sun had stopped. The weather forecast announced an anti-cyclone lasting forty days. It couldn't be! For which reason everything went wrong: gear-wheels would not lock, machinery everywhere broke down: the dead-point of everything.

The next five lines will ever remain in my memory:

> No, on May 10th, humanity was far from adequate to the event. Lord! Above, the sky was like a backside with gleaming buttocks and the sun an inflamed anus. What else but shit could ever have issued from it? And modern man screamed with fear . . .

This man of August the 21st, 1943, who is exploding in all directions at once, had of course already delivered himself of a wad of books, not least among them, we shall probably discover one day, being the ten volumes of **Notre Pain Quotidien** which he composed intermittently over a period of ten years in a château outside Paris, to which manuscripts he never signed his name, confiding the chests containing this material to various safety vaults in different parts of South America and then throwing the keys away. ("*Je voudrais rester l'Anonyme*," he says.)

In the books begun at Aix-en-Provence are voluminous notes, placed at the ends of the various sections. I will quote just one, from **Bourlinguer** (the section on Genoa), which constitutes an everlasting tribute to the poet so dear to French men of letters:

> Dear Gerard de Nerval, man of the crowd, nightwalker, slang-ist, impenitent dreamer, neurasthenic lover of the Capital's small theatres and the vast necropoli of the East: architect of Solomon's Temple, translator of Faust, personal secretary to the Queen of Sheba, Druid of the 1st and 2nd class, sentimental vagabond of the Ile-de-France, last of the Valois, child of Paris, lips of gold, you hung yourself in the mouth of a sewer after shooting your poems up to the sky and now your shade swings ever before them, ever larger and larger, between Notre-Dame and Saint-Merry, and your fiery Chimaeras range this square of the heavens like six dishevelled and terrifying comets. By your appeal to the New Spirit you for ever disturbed our feeling today: and nowadays men could not go on living without this anxiety:

> 'The Eagle has already passed: the New Spirit calls me...' (Horus, str. III, v. 9)

On page 244, in the same body of notes, Cendrars states the following: "The other day I was sixty and it is only today, as I reach the end of the present tale, that I begin to believe in my vocation of writer . . ." Put that in your pipe and smoke it, you lads of twenty-five, thirty and forty years of age who are constantly bellyaching because you have not yet succeeded in establishing a reputation. Be glad that you are still alive, still *living* your life, still garnering experience, still enjoying the bitter fruits of isolation and neglect!

I would have liked to dwell on many singular passages in these recent books replete with the most astounding facts, incidents, literary and historic events, scientific and occult allusions, curiosa of literature, bizarre types of men and women, feasts, drunken bouts, humorous escapades, tender idylls, anecdotes concerning remote places, times, legends, extraordinary colloquies with extraordinary individuals, reminiscences of golden days, burlesques, fantasies, myths, inventions, introspections and eviscerations... I would have liked to speak at length of that singular author and even more singular man, Gustave Le Rouge, the author of three hundred and twelve books which the reader has most likely never heard of, the variety, nature, style and contents of which Cendrars dwells on *con amore*; I would like to have given the reader some little flavor of the closing section, "Vendetta," from **l'Homme Foudroyé,** which is direct from the lips of Sawo the Gypsy; I would like to have taken the reader to La Cornue, *chez* Paquita, or to that wonderful hideout in the South of France where, hoping to finish a book in peace and tranquility, Cendrars abandons the page which he had slipped into the typewriter after writing a line or two and never looks at it again but gives himself up to pleasure, idleness, reverie and drink; I would like to have given the reader at least an inkling of that hair-raising story of the "homunculi" which Cendrars recounts at length in **Bourlinguer** (the section called "Gènes"), but if I were to dip into these extravaganzas I should never be able to extricate myself.

I shall jump instead to the last book received from Cendrars, the one called **La Banlieue de Paris,** published by La Guilde du Livre, Lausanne. It is illustrated with one hundred and thirty photographs by Robert Doisneau, sincere, moving, unvarnished documents which eloquently supplement the text. *De nouveau une belle collaboration.* (*Vive les collaborateurs, les vrais*!) The text is fairly short—fifty large pages. But haunting pages, written *sur le vif.* (From the 15th of July to the 31st of August, 1949.) If there were nothing more noteworthy in these pages than Cendrars's description of a night at Saint-Denis on the eve of an aborted revolution this short text would be worth preserving. But there are other passages equally somber and arresting, or nostalgic, poignant, saturated with atmosphere, saturated with the pullulating effervescence of the sordid suburbs. Mention has often been made of Cendrars's rich vocabulary, of the poetic quality of his prose, of his ability to incorporate in his rhapsodic passages the monstrous jargon and terminology of science, industry, invention. This document, which is a sort of retrospective elegy, is an excellent example of his virtuosity. In memory he moves in on the suburbs from East, South, North, and West, and, as if armed with a magic wand, resuscitates the drama of hope, longing, failure, ennui, despair, frustration, misery and resentment which devours the denizens of this vast belt. In one compact paragraph, the second in the section called "*Nord*," Cendrars gives a graphic, physical summary of all that makes up the hideous suburban terrain. It is a bird's-eye view of the ravages which follow in the wake of industry. A little later he gives us a detailed description of the interior of one of England's war plants, "a shadow factory," which is in utter contrast to the foregoing. It is a masterful piece of reportage in which the cannon plays the role of vedette. But in paying his tribute to the factory, Cendrars makes it clear where he stands. It is the one kind of work he has no stomach for. "*Mieux vaut être un vagabond,*" is his dictum. In a few swift lines he volplanes over the eternal bloody war business and, with a cry of shame for the Hiroshima "experiment," he launches the staggering figures of the last war's havoc tabulated by a Swiss review for the use and the benefit of those who are preparing the coming carnival of death. They belong, these figures, just as the beautiful arsenals belong and the hideous *banlieue*. And finally, for he has had them in mind throughout, Cendrars asks: "What of the children? Who are they? Whence do they come? Where are they going?" Referring us back to the photos of Robert Doisneau, he evokes the figures of David and Goliath—to let us know what indeed the little ones may have in store for us.

No mere document, this book. It is something I should like to own in a breast-pocket edition, to carry with me should I ever wander forth again. Something to take one's bearings by . . .

It has been my lot to prowl the streets, by night as well as day, of these God-forsaken precincts of woe and misery, not only here in my own country but in Europe too. In their spirit of desolation they are all alike. Those which ring the proudest cities of the earth are the worst. They stink like chancres. When I look back on my past I can scarcely see anything else, smell anything else but these festering empty lots, these filthy, shrouded streets, these rubbish heaps of jerries indiscriminately mixed with the garbage and refuse, the forlorn, utterly senseless household objects, toys, broken gadgets, vases and pisspots abandoned by the poverty-stricken, hopeless, helpless creatures who make up the population of these districts. In moments of high fettle I have threaded my way amidst the bric-a-brac and shambles of these quarters and thought to myself: What a poem! What a documentary film! Often I recovered my sober senses only by cursing and gnashing my teeth, by flying into wild, futile rages, by picturing myself a benevolent dictator who would eventually "restore order, peace and justice." I have been obsessed for weeks and months on end by such experiences. But I have never succeeded in making music of it. (And to think that Erik Satie, whose domicile Robert Doisneau gives us in one of the photos, to think that this man also "made music" in that crazy building is something which makes my scalp itch.) No, I have never succeeded in making music of this insensate material. I have tried a number of times, but my spirit is still too young, too filled with re-

pulsion. I lack that ability to recede, to assimilate, to pound the mortar with a chemist's skill. But Cendrars *has* succeeded, and that is why I take my hat off to him. *Salut, cher* Blaise Cendrars! You are a musician. Salute! And glory be! We have need of the poets of night and desolation as well as the other sort. We have need of comforting words—and you give them—as well as vitriolic diatribes. When I say "we" I mean all of us. Ours is a thirst unquenchable for an eye such as yours, an eye which condemns without passing judgment, an eye which wounds by its naked glance and heals at the same time. Especially in America do "we" need your historic touch, your velvety backward sweep of the plume. Yes, we need it perhaps more than anything you have to offer us. History has passed over our scarred *terrains vagues* at a gallop. It has left us a few names, a few absurd monuments—and a veritable chaos of bric-a-brac. The one race which inhabited these shores and which did not mar the work of God was the redskins. Today they occupy the wastelands. For their "protection" we have organized a pious sort of concentration camp. It has no barbed wires, no instruments of torture, no armed guards. We simply leave them there to die out . . .

But I cannot end on this dolorous note, which is only the backfire of those secret rumblings which begin anew whenever the past crops up. There is always a rear view to be had from these crazy edifices which our minds inhabit so tenaciously. The view from Satie's back window is the kind I mean. Wherever in the "zone" there is a cluster of shabby buildings, there dwell the little people, the salt of the earth, as we say, for without them we would be left to starve, without them that crust which is thrown to the dogs and which we pounce on like wolves would have only the savor of death and revenge. Through those oblong windows from which the bedding hangs I can see my pallet in the corner where I have flopped for the night, to be rescued again in miraculous fashion the next sundown, always by a "nobody," which means, when we get to understand human speech, by an angel in disguise. What matter if with the coffee one swallows a mislaid emmenagogue? What matter if a stray roach clings to one's tattered garments? Looking at life from the rear window one can look down at one's past as into a still mirror in which the days of desperation merge with the days of joy, the days of peace, and the days of deepest friendship. Especially do I feel this way, think this way, when I look into my *French* backyard. There all the meaningless pieces of my life fall into a pattern. I see no waste motion. It is all as clear as "The Cracow Poem" to a chess fiend. The music it gives off is as simple as were the strains of "Sweet Alice Ben Bolt" to my childish ears. More, it is beautiful, for as Sir H. Rider Haggard says in his autobiography: "The naked truth is always beautiful, even when it tells of evil."

My dear Cendrars, you must at times have sensed a kind of

envy in me for all that you have lived through, digested, and vomited forth transformed, transmogrified, transubstantiated. As a child you played by Vergil's tomb; as a mere lad you tramped across Europe, Russia, Asia, to stoke the furnace in some forgotten hotel in Pekin; as a young man, in the bloody days of the Legion, you elected to remain a corporal, no more; as a war victim you begged for alms in your own dear Paris, and a little later you were on the bum in New York, Boston, New Orleans, Frisco . . . You have roamed far, you have idled the days away, you have burned the candle at both ends, you have made friends and enemies, you have dared to write the truth, you have known how to be silent, you have pursued every path to the end, and you are still in your prime, still building castles in the air, still breaking plans, habits, resolutions, because *to live* is your primary aim, and you *are* living and will continue to live both in the flesh and in the roster of the illustrious ones. How foolish, how absurd of me to think that I might be of help to *you*, that by putting in my little word for you here and there, as I said before, I would be advancing your cause. You have no need of *my* help or of anyone's. Just living your life as you do you automatically aid us, all of us, everywhere life is lived. Once again I doff my hat to you. I bow in reverence. I have not the right to salute you because I am not your peer. I prefer to remain your devotee, your loving disciple, your spiritual brother in *der Ewigkeit.*

You always close your greetings with *"ma main amie."* I grasp that warm left hand you proffer and I wring it with joy, with gratitude, and with an everlasting benediction on my lips.

Kenneth Rexroth (review date 9 October 1966)

SOURCE: "Cooey-Booey Cubist," in *The New York Times Book Review,* October 9, 1966, pp. 4, 20.

[*Rexroth is a poet, critic, and translator. In the following review, he presents a mixed opinion of Cendrars's poetic contribution.*]

The greatest poet of the Cubist epoch was Pierre Reverdy, because he had distinguished emotions. The next was Gertrude Stein, because she had none. Both had perfect ears and impeccable style. Blaise Cendrars, (1887-1961), like Max Jacob, was a professional personality of the same period, rather than an artist. Henry Miller, who writes a brief preface to this collection, has written about Cendrars extensively elsewhere and admires him greatly. They have a good deal in common.

Both Cendrars and Miller present themselves to the public as livers rather than artists, and both have a talent for engaging implausibility, which sometimes catches them short. Actually this sort of thing is just as literary as Walter Pater or Henry James. It's just a different pitch, and it depends for its effectiveness on its literary convincingness. Blaise Cendrars portrays himself in his poetry as a more picaresque and more robust and very French Whitman, a nonchalant knockabout who had been for to see and for to admire in all the most remote and exciting parts of the world.

It is interesting to go back and read some of the things that made him his reputation—the volume called *Kodak,* the poem **"Far West,"** most emphatically pronounced "Fahvest," as you discover on reading it. San Bernardino, Calif., is built in the center of a verdant valley, watered by a multitude of little brooks from the neighboring mountains. Trout pullulate in these brooks; innumerable herds graze in the fat fields and the shepherds stuff themselves with the local fruits, which include pineapples. Game abounds. The *lapin à queue de coton* called "cottontail" and the hare with long ears called "jackass," the *chat sauvage* and *le serpent à sonnette* "rattlesnake," but there aren't any more pumas nowadays. So it goes on. Hilaire Hiler used to read the whole poem, ad-libbing all sorts of French-pronounced Westernisms with hilarious effect on the select audience in the old Jockey on Boulevard Montparnasse.

As a cowboy poet, Cendrars is, I'm afraid, only a *cooey-booey.* As a poet of tourism, he is less convincing than Valery Larbaud and his world-wandering, world-weary billionaire, A. O. Barnabooth. Yet convincing he is, not for what he pretends to be, but for what he is. He is the poet of the *lumpen demimonde*, of the sword-swallowers, escape-artists and street-corner acrobats in the cheap hotels back of the Gaité, of the worn and innocent whores of the Passage du Départs with runs in their stockings and holes in their shoes. It's not just that he writes about them, although when he does he's very good indeed, but that he thinks like them and speaks in their very voices.

This is not true of other poets of the *métier*, who sublimate the idiom with their own sentiment. This is the sort of thing that translators seem unable to catch. The desperate insouciance that underlies the rhythms of Cendrars's verse and the twists of his syntax are inaccessible to American professors of French who get foundation grants.

Yet Cendrars was also intellectual and the introduction to these translations makes much of his writing on poetics. His ideas are pretty much the orthodoxy of the Cubist period and now have the musty smell of dead cafe conversation. Our principal emotion on reading Cendrars today is nostalgia for him and his friends and the beautiful epoch in which they came to maturity, and this is greatly reinforced by the fact that nostalgia is also close to being his own principal subject. Far away at the ends of the earth he meets a wandering tart on a transcontinental train and all the sordid purgatorial excitement of the streets of Paris lit with prostitutes floods back on him. The Far West or the Argentine pampas, which he probably never saw, are symbols of lost innocence and glamour.

One of Cendrars's most important contributions to French literature is his prosody. He began writing *vers libre* in Vielé-Griffin's sense, which is not to be translated "free verse," but which in Cendrars's case was a kind of rushing, sprung alexandrine or hexameter or hendecasyllable. In his first long poem, this approaches the impetuous rocking rhythm of Apollinaire's "Zone." Cendrars, although he always denied discipleship, was a very obvious continuator of one aspect of Apollinaire, as person, poet and prosodist. Soon he was writing free verse in the English sense, a little like the early, best poetry of Carl Sandburg or even more like the long swaying rhythms of Robinson Jeffers.

His translators do not manage to transmit these virtues. I think the reason is that poetry like Cendrars's, for all its surface blustery extroversion, is really very intimate. To translate him successfully, it would be necessary to have either shared his background and his attitude toward it or to be a consummate actor able to project oneself imaginatively into almost complete identification with his personality. However, this book contains the French texts on facing pages, and the English is usually not too far off to serve as a pony.

The youngest generation of American poets should find Cendrars stimulating. It's a long time since poetry like this, as good as this, has been written in America. Nothing less like the imitation Jacobean verse of the older Establishment and the Pound-Williams-Olson verse of the new Establishment could be imagined. People are trying to write like this again and Cendrars could be of help—although the world of the working-class Bohemia of the slums of Paris that gives his poetry its special quality is utterly vanished from the earth.

Frank McGuinness (review date February 1967)

SOURCE: A review of *To the End of the World*, in *London Magazine*, Vol. 6, No. 11, February, 1967, pp. 114-18.

[*In the following excerpt, McGuinness presents a negative review of the book.*]

On the evidence of *To the End of the World*, the first of his works to be translated into English, it would hardly seem that we have been deprived to any great extent by the continued neglect of the twenty odd other books written by Blaise Cendrars in the countless years he has been promi-

nent in French literary circles. As savagely contemptuous of bourgeois timidity and reserve as Henry Miller himself, Cendrars is of the school that believes it salutary to rub the reader's nose in dirt, outrage his susceptibilities at every turn and open his eyes to how much more dynamic life is in those insalubrious regions where the rate of copulation among the layabouts, pimps and bohemians far exceeds the Kinsey average and an atmosphere of amoral and stimulating vitality constantly prevails. In consequence, his book is loaded with the sort of crapulous incident that the *avant-garde* writer almost invariably serves up when he sets out to be shocking. Of course, this may well what the appetites of those doddering crusaders who still imagine that the publication of any lewd word is a further blow against the prurient and taboo-ridden conventions of a society that virtually crumbled away twenty years ago, the period in which the novel is set. They won't be disappointed. Nevertheless, authors and their publishers should get wise to the changing scene. At a time when even clerics flirt with adultery, and fornication at last shows signs of becoming old hat, we may be approaching the point where a successful novel will have to be something more than a string of erotic escapades involving characters whose only claim to our attention is their promiscuity. This is where *To the End of the World* flops. The blurb may pontificate about this legendary figure who, together with Apollinaire and Max Jacob, founded the modern movement in literature etc, but stripped of its titillating and scabrous trappings the book has little to offer.

Its bizarre and raddled heroine is Thérèsa Églantine, a garrulous ex-beauty with three husbands and innumerable lovers behind her, but now reduced to paying for her pleasure in the seamier quarters of Paris. Close on eighty but still as game as they come, the opening chapter finds her in bed with her latest pick-up, a drunken deserter from the Legion, much tatoo'd and homicidal. The author dwells on the scene at some length and it sets the tone of the book. Punctuating his labour with continual cries of 'Pox', the man takes her Turk-fashion, 'turning her this way and that, making her gyrate again and again on its axis as though she were impaled on a pivot' until she loses her false teeth with a blow from his naked heel and achieves an orgasm while he is content to vomit in her lap. Such is the bliss that at once binds her to him, offering everything she possesses and finally sealing the incongruous match in a blood-letting ceremony in a subterranean hideout thirty yards beneath *Radio-Télèvision Française*. But Thérèsa is more than a debauched and washed-up voluptuary. A one-time rival of Bernhardt, she has been rescued from obscurity by a percipient critic and now reigns as the uncrowned queen of the theatre, shortly to star in a play in which she will shake Paris to its foundations by appearing in all her wrinkled and sagging nudity to recite verses from Villon. Lavishly staged and dressed, it is to be a fitting vehicle for her farewell, a performance that will render her supreme and immortal. She herself when not actually naked will wear a spectacular gown studded with jewels borrowed from her closest friend, a legless woman who was once the pride of a harem only to be rescued by a legionary and exhibited in sideshows before being saved again, this time by a Colonel who left her a fortune. All this seems likely to come to nought when she is implicated in the sudden and violent death of a local barkeeper, and her half-crazed sister, incessantly plotting her downfall, denounces her to the police as the culprit. The situation looks grave but the way in which this bold and flamboyant old woman turns even this threat to her own advantage provides what little plot there is in a book that is sometimes funny, more often irritating and frequently tedious as the characters become increasingly grotesque and their behaviour more bewildering and capricious.

Paul Zweig (essay date November 1967)

SOURCE: "French Chronicle," in *Poetry,* Vol. 111, No. 2, November, 1967, pp. 124-28.

[*In the following excerpt, Zweig provides a mixed, but generally favorable, review of the volume* Blaise Cendrars, Selected Writings. *He is, however, critical of the quality of translation.*]

Blaise Cendrars was a monument. He spent his life crossing and recrossing the world as if it might collapse beneath him when he stopped, like those glossy insects that scoot endlessly over a pond, held up by "surface tension". Except that Cendrars drew the tension out of his own mind. In his preface to the New Directions volume, Henry Miller describes the man: "I see his slouch hat and battered mug beneath it. I see him 'revolutionizing' because there is nothing else to do . . . . He was not a rebel, he was an absolute traitor to the race, and as such I salute him. The salute is wasted of course, because Cendrars didn't give a damn whether you saluted him or not."

> **Cendrars was not a great poet. He was too much of an innovator for that. He could never stop long enough on any ground to conquer it.**
> —*Paul Zweig*

Words, jagged phrases, lists of objects leaping on each other's backs; the rhythm of railroad wheels, of boats, of feet tramping in Panama and in New York: these were his itineraries. They both were, and they recorded, the connection he spent his life making between places, images, and head-

lines. The face on the cover of the *Selected Writings* tells all that. It is a face eaten from inside by decades of imperfectly expended energy, with eyes that are like the cigarette in his mouth, still glowing but covered by a long, unshaken ash. Cendrars was not a great poet. He was too much of an innovator for that. He could never stop long enough on any ground to conquer it. After it was staked out, he moved on. Thus his fine poem "**Les Paques à New York**"—perhaps the best long poem he wrote, along with the "**Transsibérien**"—creates a mood which Apollinaire was able to learn from, especially in *Zones,* yet it is Apollinaire's poem which is by far the more memorable. The erratic and often violent associations of the early travel poems, the *Nineteen Elastic Poems* and others preceded and influenced the spirit of Dada and Surrealism. Yet Cendrars by the 1920's had moved beyond even this. He turned to publishing—we owe to his care the first re-edition of Lautréamont's *Les Chants de Maldoror*—, then to the cinema, and finally to endless globetrotting, novels, and autobiographic prose. Those who admire the wordy travel fantasies of Ginsberg and Kerouak would do well to read Cendrars, who should be a hero of today's Beat wanderers.

Unfortunately the New Directions volume does Cendrars something of a disservice. The translations are clumsy, turning Cendrars's already prosy line into a kind of sub-prose. One also wonders why the very long and boring poem *Panama or the Adventures of My Seven Uncles* is included, when its place could well have been taken by a more ample selection from Cendrars's interesting prose works. Still the volume is worthwhile, if only because it gives access to the French on facing pages, and is, I believe, the only Cendrars we have in print in America.

Peter Sourian (review date 4 August 1968)

SOURCE: "The Rage of Paris," in *The New York Times Book Review,* August 4, 1968, p. 28.

[*In the following review of* To the End of the World, *Sourian is of the opinion that the only saving grace of the novel is the poetic language of Cendrars's original French, which he feels was lost in the translation.*]

One of Blaise Cendrars's 20 books is called *Too Much Is Too Much,* and that might be said of this one, the first of his novels to be published in English. On the other hand it could also be said that too much does not amount to enough. There is a lot of adventure, yet not much happens; a regular tiger of color comes on ferocious but lies down flat. There are many exclamation points (over a dozen on some pages) but little in the way of feeling; much too much is bizarre and not enough is truly strange.

Cendrars, who died in 1961, six years after writing *To the End of the World* at the age of 68, had perhaps always overdone things. He'd climbed down the side of a building to run away from home at 15, and traveled the Orient as a jewel merchant; he'd lost an arm as a corporal in the Foreign Legion, and been a movie-maker, a loner and a family man, and a prolific member of the group of writers and painters who frequented the Lapin Agile in the early 1900's, including Picasso, Max Jacob and Modigliani. A French publishing house, in its biographical series, categorizes Cendrars as a *témoin*, along with Adenauer and Simone Weil, rather than as a *classique* with Claudel, Valéry and Malraux.

Some writers do seem more important as witnesses, figures or influences than as writers. Though Villiers de l'Isle Adam preferred writing to living and Proust preferred it to breathing, and Faulkner, while pretending otherwise, preferred it to moseying around, Hemingway may have preferred fighting to writing, Oscar Wilde liked to talk, and Norman Mailer has wanted to be President.

A pioneer of Whitmanesque freedom in French verse, Cendrars may be most important for having directly influenced Apollinaire. His dynamic long poem, *Easter in New York,* written in 1915, early claimed the modern industrial and urbanized world for art, taking the ritual of the mass by the hair and dragging it through 20th-century streets. Gaetan Picon says that in Cendrars telephone operators have replaced the goddesses of Olympus. Yet it is Apollinaire who has lasted as a poet, whose free-lined "Zone" is enough but not too much. Cendrars made a career out of writing poetry, without regard to rules, in a language whose genius demands them; a lot of it seems like automatic writing, set down in the belief that whatever comes to the poet's mind must automatically be good. Such an attitude, as an influence, was importantly liberating. As a credo, the reader may not wish to take Communion.

The strident, thinnish and mildly haunting book of an old man, *To the End of the World* rattles with careless bravado through the last bravura years in the life of a fantastically vigorous, amoral and clever old actress, Thérèse Eglantine, who at 80 becomes the rage of postwar Paris by exposing her aged, shrunken body on a stage nightly and nightly reciting Villon's lament for vanished beauty.

It quickmarches through her last love, for a tattooed deserter from the Legion who gives her black eyes. A minor character is murdered, and for a time the reader supposes he is reading a somewhat inept mystery, but the murder is never solved. The author's flailing hand, breaking charcoal all over the place, sketches a gallery of raffish Paris types: a beautiful quadruple amputee, a pimp bartender, an effeminate stage designer, a tongueless Negro, a police chief in love with a dumb ingenue, wealthy old gentlemen, critics, black marketeers. Then Thérèse dies.

That she dies almost as a pointless footnote may be part of the point. But if it's pointless on purpose, then the writer ought to be passionately pointed about the pointlessness. There is a flatness, a lack of remorse, a thinness of desire.

The bookjacket states that this is a *roman à clef*, and indeed we keep feeling that it is referring to something happening somewhere else, outside of the book. We are informed that people are madly in love, informed that a performance is great, informed that someone is beaten up. Characters don't talk to each other, they deliver long set speeches.

Some part of the difficulty also lies with the translation. Cendrars was a poet, and there is a nice slangy flavor to the writing in French, which is the novel's most pungent virtue, but which is hard to render in English.

Times Literary Supplement (review date 13 March 1969)

SOURCE: "Cendrars Revived," in *Times Literary Supplement,* No. 3498, March 13, 1969, p. 262.

[*The following is a brief review of Cendrars's novel* Moravagine.]

A certified lunatic leaps over a Swiss asylum wall to the car of the psychiatrist abetting his escape. In his hand there is a bloody knife. He has just disembowelled a girl. "Everywhere Moravagine left one or more female corpses behind him. Sometimes out of fun."

Moravagine's misogynic sense of humour takes him to Berlin, Moscow, the United States, South America and back to Europe to join in the fun of the First World War. Under the clinical observation of his fascinated psychiatrist rescuer he shows what you can do to upset the bourgeois applecart if you really try. He becomes Germany's own Jack the Ripper, Russian revolutionary and terrorist, music student, pilot, prospector, explorer, potential sacrifice of a tribe of Orinoco Indians and then their god—a cerebral superman and emotional Zombie: a monster who keeps his cool.

There is a strange paradox in the anarchic and headlong career of this Quixotic pair from continent to continent. They look for life in action, "the transvaluation of all social values and of life itself". Yet action, the only form of truth for Moravagine, invariably takes the form of destruction, murder, disembowelling—affirmation through nihilism. It is very tempting to gather up the titbits of Cendrars's philosophy that sugar the narrative in an attempt to put them into a general interpretation of this action idea, without regard to their basic implausibility. Cendrars is not an ideas man, a novelist philosopher. A good many of his intellectual generalizations, while entertaining, are embarrassing to read on a serious level.

Whatever the real or supposed conceptions that may lie beneath the narrative, they certainly make a good formula for rip-roaring fiction, imaginative adventuring on all planes of experience. Moreover, the long overdue translation loses as little as possible of the original. The lush descriptions of the Orinoco, the cool and involved medical digressions, the breathless enumerations and even the slightly stilted style of Cendrars's French are still there. Above all, however, it has not lost the real significance of the so-called philosophy of action, which lies not in any explicit and tangible interpretation, but in its overwhelming dynamism.

David Plante (review date 5 March 1970)

SOURCE: "Aztec Alphabet," in *The Listener,* March 5, 1970.

[*In the following excerpt, Plante provides a favorable summary of* The Astonished Man.]

The whole world seems to have belonged to Blaise Cendrars: the steppes of Russia, the jungles of South America, New York, artistic and intellectual Paris between the wars. He knew the best whore-houses in Peking, the opium dens in Marseilles, the richest Mexicans, the poorest fishermen; he directed movies, was a capitalist businessman, a jewel-peddler, a poet, a novelist. Even his losses were gains: though he lost an arm serving in the Foreign Legion during the First World War, he could add to his possessions the war itself and a host of legionaries, among them gypsies who later adopted him as one of their own. He must have thought he could, if not order, at least account for, the entire world in terms of places visited and people met.

The Astonished Man **is a kind of heightened memoir: its images, taken from his life, act as mysterious and evocative emblems.**
                                                                              —David Plante

---

The Astonished Man is a kind of heightened memoir: its images, taken from his life, act as mysterious and evocative emblems. There is the wealthy Mexican woman, Paquita, married five or six times, living just outside Paris in 'a château in splendid Louis XIV Baroque', with a 'gold and

ebony gondola that brought one to the main gate', who meticulously fashions small waxwork figures of characters from Flaubert and Dickens, teaches Cendrars the complex Aztec alphabet, and gives half her fortune to the Mexican Revolution. There is the beautiful, sharp-witted American virgin, Diana, whom Cendrars rescues when her Buick breaks down in North Africa. There is La Mère, the matriarch of a vast gypsy community, marked by infibulation, yet wife to 14 dispensable husbands. Long after the book has been read one goes on seeing details that are so vivid—a hoard of wild pigs chasing a car in the jungles of Paraguay, a defect in a gypsy's eye 'known in medical terms as a colomba, a defect in the iris in the shape of a keyhole'—that they seem like letters in a rich alphabet (like the letters in the Aztec alphabet) which Cendrars has fashioned to describe an astonishing world.

John Porter Houston (review date April 1970)

SOURCE: "Cendrars's Modernism," in *The Southern Review,* Vol. VI, No. 2, April, 1970, pp. 561-65.

[*Below, Houston reviews several of Cendrars's poems from the volume* Selected Writings of Blaise Cendrars.]

After a recent spate of good biographies and translations of Apollinaire, the English-speaking reader is now presented (in a bilingual text for the poems) with selected works of Blaise Cendrars, Apollinaire's contemporary in remaking French poetry. Cendrars was a minor poet, and not a very productive one at that, but he occupies a significant place in the development of a modernist poetic style on the eve of World War I.

The modernism of Cendrars involves both subject and form. His poems reject the old humanism in favor of celebrating an age of large-scale industry, of speed and consumption. **"Advertising=Poetry"** is the title of one of his occasional essays, and he felt life to be enhanced by the new sense of movement embodied in cinema, Cubist painting, tall buildings, and economic expansion. From the point of view of form, Cendrars's verse reflects the acute dilemma facing poets in the early decades of the century, essentially the problem of innovation confronted, to various degrees, by Whitman and Claudel, Pound and Williams. Feeling that poetry must reject metrics, if not rhythm, as well as traditional poetic vocabulary and syntax, they nonetheless wanted the resulting verse to have the peculiar stamp of poetry. Cendrars abandoned symbolist free-verse patterns, with their many echoes of conventional metrics—"Prufrock" is an English example—for a more visual kind of effect: he was among the first to mingle type-faces, exploit non-horizontal word sequences and, in general, to incorporate into poetry the varied lay-outs of advertising. The early theorist of this kind of modernism was Marinetti, the leader of the Italian Futurists, but in Cendrars's case, we must also remember that he frequented Cubist circles, where visual surprise was an important aesthetic principle.

Cendrars's most characteristic style is rich in juxtaposed images, the syntax tending to be loose and mostly paratactic:

> It's raining electric light bulbs
> Montrouge Gare de L'Est Metro North-South
> tourist-boats world
> All is shrouded in halos
> Impenetrable
> On the Rue de Buci they're hawking
> *L'Intransigeant and Paris-Sports*
> The celestial airport is now, in flames, a painting
> by Cimabue
> While in the foreground
> Men are
> Long
> Dark
> Sad
> And smoking, factory chimneys
>
> **("Contrasts")**

The laconic disposition of the words on the page succeeds in creating intensity while in no way suggesting the rhythm of prose. There is a chaste spareness in the lines that French metrical verse rarely attained. Unfortunately Cendrars did not always achieve such sharpness of outline; often the words and phrases isolated on the page do not seem worthy of such singling out. And in long poems there almost always occur passages in which inspiration flags and the typography seems merely a gimmick.

Nearly all of Cendrars's important poetry was produced between 1912 and 1914, and we know little of what prompted his vocation. He was born Frédéric-Louis Sauser in 1887 in Switzerland; after an eccentric early life with eccentric parents, he became something of an adventurer, traveling widely and trying his hand at various jobs. "**Easter in New York**" (1912), his first generally known poem, draws on liturgical tradition and has the rather monotonous movement of litany. More interesting is "**Prose of the Transsiberian and of Little Jeanne of France**" (1913), with which Cendrars reached his mature style. This long, uneven poem (the title-word "prose" is taken in the medieval Latin sense of a sequence of rhythmic lines) evokes a railway journey across Russia, which is at the same time a journey into the self:

> I was in Moscow, city of the one thousand and
> three bell
> towers and the seven stations

> And I was not satisfied with the seven stations and
> the one
> thousand and three bell towers
> Because my adolescence was so intense and so
> insane
> That my heart, in turn, burned like the temple at
> Ephesus
> or like the Red Square of Moscow
> When the sun is setting.

The poet is accompanied by a prostitute ("She is quite naked, has no body—she is too poor") who, by her name, Jeanne [d'Arc], suggests France. Actually she seems to represent the poet's stable moorings as she constantly asks, "Blaise, tell me, are we very far from Montmartre?" He consoles her by describing tropical paradises beneath and beyond Siberia: real geography assumes quite anagogical meanings in the poem.

The unifying images of "**Prose**" are those of movement, pain, and fire:

> If I were a painter I would spill great splashes of
> yellow
> and red over the end of this trip
> Because I am quite sure we were all a little mad
> And that a raging delirium was bloodying the
> lifeless faces
> of my traveling companions
> As we approached Mongolia
> Which roared like a bonfire.

Rather than on tropical islands, the journey ends at Harbin, "just as they set fire to the offices of the Red Cross."

Like certain poems of Apollinaire's which it closely resembles, "**Prose**" is shaped by a frankly autobiographical sequence, formal structuring elements (Jeanne's Montmartre refrain, for example, or "Still, I was a very bad poet"), and shifting moods and time planes. It concludes with an abrupt change to a present which is also a partial return to the past:

> I would like
> I would like never to have taken my trips
> This evening an intense love torments me
> And in spite of myself I think of little Jehanne of
> France
> It was on an evening filled with sadness that I
> wrote this poem in her honor
>
> ...
>
> Paris
>
> City of the incomparable Tower of the Rack and the Wheel

The Eiffel Tower (which also obsessed Cocteau and Apollinaire) serves as an end point to the horizontal journey across Russia, and the reader senses more acutely the metaphorical dimensions of Red Square and crossing Siberia. Paris is the figurative center of the world, and journeys from its nostalgia-filled reality become harrowing quests into a land of fire and spinning motion, of demonic violence. No illumination comes of the quest, however, and the poet finds himself back in the city, brooding on Jeanne, dead apparently like his youth in Russia, and contemplating the sinister image of the Tower, at once a point of stability and a reminiscence of the torturous journey. The various parts of "**Prose**" are ingeniously linked in a way which isolated quotations can but meagerly suggest.

After "**Prose of the Transsiberian**" Cendrars wrote, besides the *Nineteen Elastic Poems,* from which my first quote comes, one more long poem, "**Panama or the Adventures of My Seven Uncles**" (presented in this volume in John Dos Passos' spirited translation). "**Panama**" is even more diffuse than "**Prose,**" but it has a greater degree of colloquial verve and allusiveness:

> What the hell
> Aren't there any more good yarns?
> *The Lives of the Saints*
> *Das Nachtbuechlein von Schuman*
> *Cymballum mundi*
> *La Tariffa delle Puttane di Venegia...*

Despite splendid sections, however, the wanderings of the speaker's seven uncles fail to create a progression in theme or mood, and one also becomes unpleasantly aware of the facile exoticism which was Cendrars's most dangerous pitfall as a poet.

Cendrars's poetic gifts lasted only a brief season; by the end of World War I, in which he was wounded, his production of verse had dwindled off, never again to attain its first brilliance. Furthermore, literary life had begun to disgust him: the Surrealists, in particular, struck him as derivative rather than fresh. He continued to write, nonetheless, but now in prose: a great mass of essays, novels, and autobiographical works came forth, among which the latter are the last and most important. But Cendrars's prose is at best more curious than enduring. Samples of it are included in the present volume.

Walter Albert's introduction is perceptive and thorough; the translations from his hand (including "**Prose of the Transsiberian**," *Nineteen Elastic Poems,* and most of the prose works) are of a high order. Henry Miller's Preface is what one might expect of him.

Times Literary Supplement **(review date 14 April 1972)**

SOURCE: "Down to the Sea," in *Times Literary Supplement,* No. 3659, April 14, 1972, p. 408.

[*The following is a mixed review of the translation of* Planus, *providing some description of the structure of the novel.*]

An "edited" version of Blaise Cendrars such as this poses many problems. The original of *Planus* was *Bourlinguer,* the third volume of the four "autobiographies" which Cendrars—poet, adventurer, business man and marvellous writer—published between 1945 and 1949. *Bourlinguer* is the one that combines real or fantasied autobiography with travelogue. The titles of its eleven sections are all great sea or river-ports: Naples, Antwerp, Rotterdam, etc, and finally Paris—"Port-de-Mer." Nina Rootes's editing has, at her publishers' request, reduced *Bourlinguer* from the 440 pages of its French (paperback) edition to a mere 220 pages in English. Is this wise? Is it justified? In a frank and useful "Translator's Note" she tells us the principles on which she did this hatchet-job, apologizes to the ghost of Cendrars for tampering with his work, and hopes that "this shortened version will introduce many readers to the delights of his writing, who perhaps would have been deterred by a longer and more discursive book."

It is true that Cendrars did tend to go on and on, to diverge, to divagate, to meander, but this is part of his charm and our interest. Miss Rootes tells us that she has "tried to omit whole sections which are self-contained in the French original rather than nibble piecemeal at the text." In general, she has indeed omitted what might be considered the less interesting sections (though this means that "Venice," "Bordeaux," "Brest," "Toulon" and the original "Naples" are lost)—but she has also indulged in quite extensive nibbling. Two or three lines disappear here, odd parentheses there (particularly in "Hamburg"). Cendrars's grandfather is left out of the comic description of his relations (again: real or imagined—for how many of the seven uncles in *Panama ou la véritable histoire de mes sept oncles* ever saw the light of non-fiction?) We lose also the droll paragraphs about the Eiffel Tower which, Cendrars claimed, was so rotten that it was about to collapse on the Parisians at any moment. These brought him an indignant letter from La Société de la Tour Eiffel, in answer to which Cendrars wrote, in November 23, 1948:

> c'est bien l'aventure la plus incroyable qui pouvait m'arriver que de subir aujourd'hui les foudres de la Société de la Tour Eiffel ... moi, que les journaux de Paris ont surnommé depuis bientôt quarante ans "le poète de la Tour Eiffel."

In producing what amounts almost to a work of popularization, Miss Rootes has to a certain extent ironed out the boastful, lying, exaggerating, but immensely human, humorous and erudite Cendrars, and made his writing follow an atypically logical pattern. What we surely need is an English biography of Cendrars—Henry Miller's short, lyrical appreciation, published in 1951, is not nearly enough—and then perhaps the reading public here will be more than eager to accept him in his entirety.

In general Miss Rootes has succeeded extraordinarily well in the extraordinarily difficult task of translating Cendrars. She has reproduced his style much more exactly than she did in her translation of his *L'Homme foudroyé*, though there is still the odd phrase where French slang simply won't turn into English slang. There is the occasional enormity— a woman likened to a *truie informe* (a shapeless sow) turns into a "knowing sow"—but one or two such examples seem, without exception, to be inevitable in every translation. Miss Rootes fails with the poems, but her choice of title cannot be faulted. *Bourlinguer,* as she tells us, means "to knock about the world, to lead an adventurous life." She gives us *Planus.* Cendrars, on page forty-five of the present edition, tells us that, according to "the scholarly Canon Cristiani," Pliny uses the word in the sense of a buffoon, but it also means vagabond or adventurer. This is Cendrars *tout craché.*

Patrick Lindsay Bowles (review date 4 February 1983)

SOURCE: "Going West," in *Times Literary Supplement,* No. 4166, February 4, 1983, p. 116.

[*In the following review, Bowles praises Cendrars's* Gold.]

In the spring of 1834, Johann August Suter, a thirty-one-year-old bankrupt Swiss papermaker, deserted his wife and four children and set sail for America. Penniless and without prospects, his "professional contacts" were restricted to the fellow fugitives, swindlers and n'er-do-wells he was to meet on his journey. Through a combination of cunning or crooked business deals, prowess as an Indian fighter, indefatigable effort and extraordinary good luck, less than ten years later John Augustus Sutter had become America's first millionaire and multi-millionaire, the most prosperous landowner in the United States, and the founder of a new country which he patriotically christened New Helvetia. Coming to join her husband at last, Anne Sutter hears him described by strangers: "He is a king; he is an emperor. He rides on a white horse. The saddle is made of gold, the bit is gold, the stirrups, the spurs and even the horseshoes are of gold." By the time she arrives in Panama, one lock of her hair has turned white. John Sutter had been the poorest of men; he

is now among the richest. Frau Sutter dies, of exhaustion and amazement, on her husband's doorstep.

Well on his way to becoming "the richest man in the world", Sutter is ruined in January 1848, when an employee, James W. Marshall, discovers gold on Sutter's property. Within months, squatters from all over the world have come to his vast El Dorado to prospect. A few months more and New Helvetia has evaporated, Sutter's Garden of Eden has become the City of San Francisco. His house is burned down and his lands are taken over by mud-covered men with strange accents. One of his sons is murdered, another commits suicide. A pauper, Sutter will spend the next thirty years of his life vainly trying to obtain some kind of compensation from the federal government in Washington. Irony and rage kill him on June 17, 1880 at the age of seventy-eight.

The vertiginous extremes of Sutter's life-history place it squarely alongside a number of other "higher horror" stories: those, notably, of Job and Midas. But his is also a quintessentially American tragedy, and *Gold* itself is perhaps best regarded as an American novel. No other figure of the nineteenth century—not even Lincoln—and few others in American history, can have lived the American dream more literally or incarnated it more gloriously than did Sutter. The pathfinder and the pioneer, the rugged individualist, the self-made man and the natural aristocrat all come together in the person of this insignificant Swiss immigrant.

Certain details of the story—Sutter's Platonic self-image, his *Heimweh*, his demented Biblical exegeses, his membership of a wealthy communist religious sect at the end of his life— bear a superficial resemblance to the odyssey that has so often been traced by American royalty, from Jay Gatsby and Citizen Kane to Daniel K. Ludwig and Bob Dylan, whose absolute wealth and freedom have fuelled an already burning hatred of mere metaphorical existence and turned them towards religion and babyhood. Howard Hughes, subsisting at the end on a child's diet of ice cream and biscuits; Elvis Presley, who died wearing diamonds and nappies; H. L. Hunt (the model for *Dallas*'s J. R.), who, padding around his office on all fours, once confided to a reporter, "I'm crazy about crawling"—each is an exemplary American career.

But few individuals can have lived the American nightmare more pitifully than Sutter. He was left in the cold, a moral and material wreck. He died, like all poor people, wrong in the eyes of justice. His story is thus less like that of a Ford or a Rockefeller than a Lemuel Pitkin, whose dismantling Nathanael West recounts in *A Cool Million.* Indeed Sutter remains a major exhibit in what West called the American Museum of Hideosities.

No one could have been better suited to tell Sutter's story than his fellow-countryman and adventurer Blaise Cendrars, whose jeweller's eye was finely focused on all that glistens. (One of Cendrars's most compelling, if elusive dreams was "de rouler en Cadillac, d'avoir des poules à perlouzes et zibeline, et de boire des scotchs sans soda dans des boites de nuit à strip-tease.") The startling incongruity of the mock-naive tone in which Cendrars recounts this long, cruel joke is supremely effective. First published in 1925, or four years before American riches to rags stories were to become commonplace, Cendrars's first novel remains a minor masterpiece. This fine new translation should give it its rightful place on the golden periphery of American letters.

Sven Birkerts (essay date 1987)

SOURCE: "Blaise Cendrars," in *An Artificial Wilderness*, William Morrow and Company, New York, 1987, pp. 143-55.

[*In the essay below, Birkerts provides a detailed summary of Cendrars's life and major works.*]

In the last phase of his career, when he was already in his sixties, Blaise Cendrars wrote and published a series of autobiographical works that are as singular as anything in literature. Coming after a lifetime of publications, these books—available in England as **The Astonished Man** (1970), **Planus** (1972), and **Lice** (1973)—form a kind of entryway through which we pass to meet a rare, titan-scale individual. The life we encounter is as vast and variously textured as a composition by Stravinsky, and is as difficult to assimilate at first contact. Here is Cendrars in his full amplitude: wanderer, sailor, scholar, collector, entrepreneur, anarchist, soldier, pivotal figure in the Paris avant-garde, trickster, intimate of Picasso, Apollinaire, Stravinsky, Dos Passos (who translated him), Modigliani (who painted him), Duchamp (who probably played chess with him), Le Corbusier, Eisenstein, Satie, Chagall . . . The ellipses are rightfully suggestive. In these works we have him in many locales of his nomadic life: Africa, Russia, China, the Americas, the heartland of France, not to mention the great capital cities of the world. We have so much, and yet it feels like we are chasing quicksilver, or, better yet, like we are in the hands of a Scheherazade, a teller of tales with an ever-changing repertoire, a repertoire that will never be exhausted.

Cendrars is obscure. Few literate people will recognize the name. This is as unfortunate as it is comprehensible, for reputations flourish and wither in the hands of critics and litterateurs, and these types have always had a hard time with renegades. The situation is aggravated further by Cendrars's penchant for invention and exaggeration. Were it not that the life and writings are so intertwined—the two halves of a grand and mysterious destiny—this would not matter so much. But the fact is that Cendrars cannot be considered apart from his biography. To read anything that he wrote is to be implicated, present at the joining point of life and art. The two are intimately interfused. The writings have to be read as a footnote to the life, as an interlinear, if you will. It is as if to make this process even more forbidding and complex that Cendrars chose to write poetry, novels, reportage, criticism, autobiography, film scripts, radio plays—apart from which he also anthologized and translated. He could not have set his gift at the heart of a labyrinth any more artfully had he tried. And yet there will be those who will undertake to find their way in, for there is something in Cendrars that matters greatly and that is not to be found elsewhere. It is a vision fresh and authentic from a man who tunneled his way through considerable despair, who lived all aspects of life to the extreme, and who, for that reason alone, has more to tell us than the sort of academic epigone who seems to dominate the literature of our time.

> Cendrars: "No, no, no, no, not at all, you won't find me in it, I shall write a novel-novel, and I won't appear in it, because they don't see but one character in all my books: Cendrars: *L'Or* is Cendrars; *Moravagine* is Cendrars; *Dan Yack* is Cendrars— I'm annoyed with this Cendrars!"
>
> —*Paris Review* interview

In treating the life and writings of Cendrars, the main task is to establish the context of myth and self-creation. Some biography seems to flow more or less evenly from circumstance; in other cases, it is wrested forth with much turmoil, imagination, and daring, and this is the case with Cendrars.

"Blaise Cendrars" is a pseudonym for Frédéric Louis Sauser, who was born in 1883 in the Swiss canton of Neuchâtel. (Le Corbusier was born in the same little village just one month later.) The restlessness that would infect him lifelong was already present in the gene pool. His father, an inventor but also a man of many careers and aspirations, dragged the family from Switzerland to Egypt, then to Naples. It is no accident, especially in view of his late escapades, that Cendrars's poetic trademark became the listing of places—ports, cities, destinations.

Cendrars reports that his adolescence was wild, his character intractable. He was sent to one boarding school after another. In each he resisted, racked up absences. Then, when he was fifteen, he stole the family silver and made his escape out the window. For a time his career resembles that of Rimbaud. He wandered Europe, riding trains, hiking, finally ending up in St. Petersburg. There, the story goes, he met up with a jewel merchant named Rogovine, who took him into his employ. They rode the Trans-Siberian into Asia. In 1904—the testimony here, as everywhere, being as reliable as Cendrars—he worked stoking furnaces in Peking.

Two years later, by whatever circuitous route, he was back in St. Petersburg.

It is hard to avoid making all this picturesque. The settings are right, the movement is swift and dramatic. But we must not forget that Cendrars/Sauser is only in his teens. Present, too, are his fear, his loneliness, his homesickness. These elements, compressed and matured, will show up later in his two long poems: *Prose of the Trans-Siberian* and *Panama, or, The Adventures of My Seven Uncles.* He will write:

> And beyond, the Siberian plains the lowering sky
> and the tall shapes of the Silent Mountains that
> rise and fall
> I am curled up in a plaid shawl
> Motley
> Like my life
> And my life doesn't keep me any warmer than this
> Scotch
> Shawl
> And the whole of Europe seen through the
> windcutter of an
> Express racing ahead at full speed
> Is no richer than my life
> My poor life . . .
>   —*Prose of the Trans-Siberian*

There are more imponderable events. In St. Petersburg Cendrars falls in love with a young woman. She dies in a hotel fire. Nothing further is known of this. Cendrars, heartbroken, moves to Paris. The chronology is vague. Forty years later, writing in *Planus,* he states that his anguish and rage drove him to Finland, that he spent a summer manufacturing bombs for terrorists. A cryptic passage with much left unexplained, but the facts do correlate, at least imaginatively, with events in his doomsday novel *Moravagine.*

It is in Paris, in 1907, that Sauser rebaptizes himself Blaise Cendrars. He makes a compact with himself that he will henceforth be a writer, a poet. (He has produced a few fledgling pieces while in St. Petersburg.) But the wanderlust is undimmed. In the next four years he moves from Paris to Bern (where he takes up medicine for a year), then to St. Petersburg again. In 1911 he is in New York City, on the bum, starving. In one delirious night he writes *Les Pâques à New York* (*Easter in New York*), one of the first poems in the modernist canon, a work distinguished by its intensity and urban torsions. With this explosion his stay in New York ends. He returns to Paris via cattle boat and throws himself into the artistic life of the city.

Les Pâques foreshadows the *Trans-Siberian* and *Panama,* both of which were written in 1913. By that time Cendrars was already at the spearpoint of the avant-garde, consorting with Léger, Stravinsky, Apollinaire, Picasso, appearing in public attired in a demolished chair, or one of his painted suits. (Roger Shattuck gives a fascinating portrait of this era in *The Banquet Years.*) Cendrars was one of the first to embrace "the modern" in the full sense of the term. He saw clearly where the age was headed: toward speed, machinery, violence. The basis of human relationships was changing, and this change called for a new way of writing poetry. He responded. He wanted to do for poetry what the cubists were doing for painting. But where they worked spatially, looking for means by which to transmit all visual aspects of an object, Cendrars was concerned with time and events: he was after simultaneity, situations registered from all geographic and temporal perspectives.

Prose of the Trans-Siberian sent out shock waves when it first appeared. The poem made use of salad techniques: very long lines punctuated with lines of one or two words, abrupt transitions, shifting tenses, and imagery that anticipated the surrealists. By setting the narrative on a moving train, Cendrars was able to explore nuances of sound and tempo. This he did with the skilled ear of a jazz musician. The poem was, in fact, dedicated to "the musicians." (Cendrars had studied music, and he claims somewhere in his writings that he very nearly became a composer instead of a poet.) The format of the poem was unprecedented: it was printed on a single sheet seven feet long, folded up like a railroad timetable. Sonia Delaunay painted an abstract accompaniment on the left-hand side of the sheet. Cendrars then announced that the full first edition of the poem, unfolded, laid end to end, would match exactly the height of the Eiffel Tower. If "the modern" was a religion in Paris, then the Eiffel Tower was its altar.

There was some controversy in academic circles as to whether Cendrars or Apollinaire was the first to write the modernist poem. No settlement was ever reached, though publication dates are in Cendrars's favor. There is no real point in arguing one way or the other. From a book like Shattuck's we get a clear picture of the cross-pollination that went on from one end of Paris to the other. Cendrars later professed indifference to the whole question of precedence. The war years were to bring decisive changes in his outlook.

> The war saved me by dragging me away and throwing me amongst the people in arms, one anonymous number amongst millions of others. No. 1529. What intoxication!... It takes a long experience of life, and many a tot of rotgut in the low dives Zola wrote about, amongst the common people, to relearn how to love your fellow man as a brother.

In 1914, calling upon his fellow poets to follow him, Cendrars rushed off to join the fighting. After many months in the trenches at the front lines, in September of 1915—a decisive date in his personal chronology—he was wounded by a mortar shell. His right arm had to be amputated. The injury threw him into despair. There are accounts of Cendrars refusing his prosthesis, pounding the walls of the hospital with his stump. It was not until he learned that his idol Rémy de Gourmont had died that same day that he was able to interpret his loss as a symbolic figure in his destiny. He will refer to this conjunction of events time and again.

The injury was to become a major turning point for Cendrars. Practically, it made it difficult for him to find work when he returned to Paris. For a period he begged alms in the streets, but that was not to be endured, and he fled the city. (Before the war, Cendrars had made a hasty marriage, a mistake. His wife, Fela, had borne him two sons, Rémy and Odilon. He left the family behind—an episode about which little is known.) In Cendrars's mythology this move was of great consequence. He was breaking with the past, leaving behind all literary and artistic circles, all family responsibilities. Henceforth he was to identify himself as a solitary, a member of no school, a man whose true home was among the poor and oppressed. He spent a part of the next year living and traveling with a band of gypsies, an experience that would later supply him with much of the narrative for *The Astonished Man.*

Cendrars was never one to occupy a place or a life-pattern for very long. In the epoch following the war he went through a number of careers. The personal changes, the motives, are only partially illuminated by his writings—once again the specific gravity of the man is hard to calculate. In 1917, for example, he announces that he is through with poetry. Two years later he reverses himself and issues the collection *Dix-neuf Poèmes Elastiques.* He has taken his techniques to new extremes—the lines are now short, the imagery sharp, concrete, the leaps rapid-fire and unpredictable. But Cendrars is right in one respect: poetry is no longer to be his major avocation. Five years later, with the appearance of *Kodak* and *Feuilles de Route,* his poetic vector reaches its terminus. *Kodak* is by far the more innovative. Cendrars pointed out, after publication, that every line in every poem had been lifted from a novel by Gustave Le Rouge.

During this period the poetic energies were deployed along other fronts. Cendrars was working as editor of Editions de la Sirène, publishing, among other things, a reissue of Lautréamont's *Les Chants de Maldoror,* a work that had been inaccessible for many years, and that was soon to generate a powerful influence on the surrealists. He also published his own *Anthologie Nègre,* a compilation and translation of African tales. But this was just one of his activities. In 1921 Cendrars was working with the film director Abel Gance on *The Wheel,* and was directly responsible for the montage sequences (which were said to influence Eisenstein). Afterward, continuing his involvement with film—which he celebrated as the modern art form *par excellence*—Cendrars

went to Italy and formed his own film company, a venture that made him a fortune. The fortune disappeared shortly afterward in an international banking scandal. His last escapade in cinema was to be in 1924, the year that he went to Africa to film elephants. He would later spend time in Hollywood in a different capacity, supervising the work on the film version of his novel *Sutter's Gold.*

The next major epoch—if we can so divide a life (Cendrars himself spoke in terms of personal epochs)—came in 1924 with his first trip to Brazil. He discovered an immediate affinity with the South American geography, and for the next twenty years was to travel constantly between Europe and Brazil. During this long period Cendrars was conducting a number of highly mysterious business transactions, involving the import of motor fuel. He was also buying and operating a plantation in Brazil, and writing, but novels, not poetry. The publications continue: *L'Or* in 1925, *Moravagine* in 1926, *Le Plan de l'Aiguille* and *Les Confessions de Dan Yack* in 1929, as well as nearly a dozen volumes of reportage, translation, and anthology. Of the lot, *L'Or,* translated as *Sutter's Gold* (1926), scored the greatest popular success.

Sutter's Gold is the easiest of Cendrars's novels to assimilate. It deals in a compressed, minimalist prose with the epic downfall of his countryman August Sutter, the man who made the mistake of discovering gold on his property. The message of the book is as old as language itself: what shall it profit a man, if he gain the whole world . . . ? The tempo and simplicity of the work gained it a wide audience in many languages.

Moravagine, which did not appear in English until 1969, presents a wholly different side of Cendrars. Where *Sutter's Gold* is trim, concise, a parable, *Moravagine* represents inversion, excess—it is clearly the product of a tormented, even sadistic temperament.

Moravagine stakes out human extremity as its subject matter. The language is pained, exacerbated. Long, telescopic sentences carry us through revolution, terror, a zone of sexual and moral nihilism. To call the book depraved is to soft-pedal the issue. Nothing on that order, excepting Lautréamont, had appeared before. Moravagine seeks damnation and extinction with a glee unequaled in literature. The only parallels that come to mind are with Céline and Beckett. We can imagine an energized Molloy with limbs that function and a bomb in his pocket. Not a drop of sentimentality is to be found. Moravagine is projected as human nature stripped of culture and civilization—pessimistic, yes, but in view of the atrocities that Cendrars had witnessed (and of which he writes so well in *Lice*) not pure fabrication.

Le Plan de l'Aiguille and *Les Confessions de Dan Yack*

both appeared in 1929. The former was published in English as *Antarctic Fugue* in 1948 and is unobtainable. The two were intended as consecutive novels, the latter meant to explain and fulfill the former—an effect never achieved in English since *Dan Yack* was never translated. Taken together, or separately, they are probably the least successful of Cendrars's writings. They represent an all too private working out of obsession. The settings and symbol constructions are fantastic—fascinating as well—but are not calculated to reach any but the most loyal partisans.

In the character of Dan Yack (the "hero" of both books), Cendrars gives us the polarities of his own nature: Yack is torn between his solitude and mysticism and his love of the world and activity among men, his self-sufficiency and his romantic will, his intellect and his senses. His realizations, accompanied by catastrophe and pain, come to him in the desolate silence of the Antarctic. In the course of the narrative he comes to terms with his past, his many selves, his loves, and, in an action of supreme self-transcendence, listens in to the way of the world. The message is not unlike Wittgenstein's "The world is everything that is the case." Yack has come to grips with renunciation and assent. The resolution, after so much of the fantastic, is his acceptance of the recognized proportions of things.

Cendrars did not find his ideal expression in the novel. The fact is that Cendrars was at his best when he worked either in loose associative verse forms, as in *Trans-Siberian* or *Panama,* both of which stand up as virtuoso performances; or when he worked in the autobiographical vein. The shorter poems, those of *Kodak* and *Dix-neuf Poèmes Elastiques,* strike us with their quickness and modernity, but hardly comprise a major testament.

In 1940, after a year or so as a war correspondent for the French press, disgusted by the reaction of his countrymen to the world situation, Cendrars withdraw to Aix-en-Provence and stopped writing. He once again drew the curtain on his literary career. What did he do, think? No one knows. Reports from friends and visitors had him meditating in an unheated kitchen. It was a period of sorrow for Cendrars. He was to learn from two separate telegrams that his sons, Rémy and Odilon, had been killed. Though his marriage had been brief and long since dissolved, Cendrars had felt close, at least spiritually, to the two boys.

The career does not end here, however. As before, Cendrars's pronouncements that he is "through" are reversed. After three years of silence his picks up his pen once again, this time to deliver a series of autobiographical chronicles. They are to be his major achievement. In a footnote to one of the volumes, *Bourlinguer,* translated as *Planus,* he writes: "The other day was my sixtieth birthday, and it is only today, as I draw towards the end of the present work, that I begin to believe in my vocation as a writer. . . ." Says Henry Miller, in his essay on Cendrars, "Put that in your pipe and smoke it, you lads of twenty-five, thirty and forty years of age . . . ."

What was it that detonated the man? Cendrars supplies one kind of answer in a dedication to his friend Edouard Peisson, who had come to visit him in his seclusion:

> If, in my desire to share that burden of responsibility, I ask myself how it is that your brief visit this morning triggered something in me so forcibly that I immediately started writing. . . . I am not too sure how to answer. What you told me about your experience last night, the sky, the moon, the landscape and the silence must have rekindled similar reminiscences in me, stirred as I was by the reverberations of the war which seemed to echo through the bitter thoughts you had. . . . Or do you not believe, quite simply, that sailors, like poets, are too sensitive to the magic of moonlight and to the destiny that seems to come down to us from the stars, on sea, on land, or between the pages of a book when at last we lower our eyes from the heavens, you the sailor and I the poet, and that when you and I write, we are prey to an obsession or victims of the distortions of our vocation?

> Today I am sixty years old, and the gymnastics and juggling I once indulged in to beguile the ship's boy, I now perform in front of a typewriter, to keep my body in training and my spirits lively, for it is years now since I went out; I no longer move, no longer travel, no longer see anyone, sliding my life under the roller of my typewriter, like a sheet of carbon between two sheets of white paper, and I type and type, recto and verso, and re-read like a somnambulist, intercalating the direct image with the reflection, which can only be deciphered in reverse, mirror-wise; I am master of my life, dominating time, for I have succeeded in dislocating and disarticulating it, sliding relativity into my sentences like a substratum, using it as the very mainspring of my writing.... It may be the literary novelty of the 20th century, the skill and art of applying the analytic procedures and mathematical deductions of an Einstein to the essence, the structure, the propagation of light in the technique of the novel!

> —*Planus*

Cendrars's return to literature at the age of sixty, his subsequent productivity, and the excellence and singularity of the works are matters for rejoicing. The three volumes, *The Astonished Man, Lice,* and *Planus,* originally *L'Homme Foudroyé* (published in French in 1945), *La Main Coupée*

(1946), and **Bourlinguer** (1948), are not diminished by mention of Rousseau or Montaigne, though in their savor and energy they might more aptly be compared with Villon or Rabelais.

Diffusion is probably the major obstacle to Cendrars, but it is also a mark of his genius.
                    —*Sven Birkerts*

The content of these three works is at first glance diffuse. The diffusion is probably the major obstacle to Cendrars, but it is also a mark of his genius. The works *are* Cendrars, to the limit of the meaning of such a pronouncement. Adventure and reflection interpenetrate. Chapters, even paragraphs, even single sentences, zigzag back and forth through time. Nor are the sequences made any more accessible by Cendrars's penchant for rambling anecdotes, lengthy asides, footnotes, and the like. It is the content that excuses all the confusion. Familiarity with the voice and its owner provoke fascination. And as the reader submits to this fascination, the chronological jumble takes on a different aspect. He starts to experience the narrative with the acuity of one following a thread through a labyrinth. The time sense, the demand for sequence, are cast aside. The narrative, like the life, like *any* life, reveals that its true character is referential. A memory from childhood interlocks with an episode from later life—only a writer who has penetrated to the core of his being can offer us experience at this level.

Cendrars's life, I will not tire of repeating, was epic, the appetites gargantuan. **The Astonished Man** is a perfect title, for at the heart of this network is the figure of Cendrars—stripping himself of myth, layering himself with myth, we are never sure which—the astonishment of being alive always in his voice.

Miller again: "There were times when reading Cendrars—and this is something which happens to me rarely—that I put the book down to wring my hands with joy or despair. . . ."

The content? Cendrars's life. The volumes can be read in any order. They are simply tales, events, and encounters that Cendrars saw fit to put on paper. Reading them, picking up hints at every turn of stories and events not related, we wish there were more, but we find ourselves grateful, too, for what he has given.

There is no point in trying to invent a summary. What matters is not the content, but the man, our sense of his spirit and its amplitude. The spirit of the narrative voice is what alters a set of casually narrated tales into literature. Our sense

of this spirit grows as we read and remains with us after we are finished. The reader who has persevered may find that Cendrars has become a taste, and, past that, an emblem for a whole way of looking at the world.

Cendrars was in his early sixties when the last of the chronicles was completed. In 1950 he returned to Paris from Aix. He was once again a married man; the rejuvenation he had experienced led him to cement a relationship that had been going on for some thirty years. This was with Raymone, the one true love to whom he alludes ever so discreetly in his works.

For the next ten years Cendrars was mainly active in radio work. His literary output diminished, consisting mainly of interviews and occasional pieces. One last novel, **Emmène-moi au Bout du Monde,** was published in 1956. It was translated into English as **To the End of the World** (1966). While it does not represent a major literary event, it was controversial upon publication—Cendrars took some well-aimed shots at Parisian society figures.

The last five years of his life were not happy. A deteriorative disease stopped his wanderings, confined him to a wheelchair. The writing stopped. In January 1961, three days after being awarded his only literary prize, Cendrars died. Had he been able to script it, he would probably have chosen a more dramatic exit. Perhaps something in the matter of Lord Mountbatten. Otherwise, though, he had less to regret than most. The life was rich. His testament is there for anyone who wants to find it.

Postscript: There is one major mystery yet to be solved. Cendrars stated many times that he had consigned a large number of manuscripts, unsigned, to various strongboxes in South American banks. He may have been exaggeration-prone, but he was not a liar. To date none of these manuscripts has been found.

Don Kennison (review date Fall 1991)

SOURCE: A review of *Moravagine,* in *Review of Contemporary Fiction,* Vol. II, No. 3, Fall, 1991, pp. 278-79.

[*Below, Kennison presents an emphatically positive review of* Moravagine.]

Moravagine is that rare novel that sticks in your soul like a new gospel, written in blood in the last days, lost to us till now after having echoed only secretly through the last millennium to us here in the New World. It stabs the heart with grace, traces the paths of our lives bowing down before our demon selves in order to reveal the flesh worth redeeming. It believes what it tells us.

Moravagine is one of the many wounds of road trod by the legendary Blaise Cendrars in a life as extraordinary as any novel. Cendrars leaped out of his bedroom window in Switzerland at the age of fifteen and never looked back. He was a poet even before he lost his right arm in World War I. Like Céline and Apollinaire, he caught himself up in the Great War and it became a battleground for his life and art until he died in 1961.

Cendrars's narrator in his novel **Moravagine**—as in all his work, a man in many ways not unlike himself—is a physician in a Swiss asylum who befriends a terminal patient named Moravagine, and finds him to be a human specimen of exceptional constitution. They fall in as fellow outsiders and escape together to wander the world, encountering the depth of human function on a planet temporarily called home. They leave a violently scintillating and spirit-crushing trail from Paris to Berlin to the Russian steppes and the washes of the Amazon in a series of adventures as extravagant and unpredictable as a biblical epic.

Too, theirs is a story of friendship, a friendship from sickness through pain and betrayal to questionable redemption. A necessary travail. As a doctor of mental health, the narrator informs his reader from the start: "Diseases are a transitory, intermediary, future state of health. It may be that they are health itself. . . . What convention calls health is, after all, no more than this or that passing aspect of a morbid condition, frozen into an abstraction, a special case already experienced, recognized, defined, finite, extracted and generalized for everybody's use." Moravagine, a human vessel of extraordinary presumptions, is the disease made manifest. It is this physician's task, he states unequivocally, to see Moravagine, "this human wild animal," into the wide world once more and convince all skeptics—victims and executioners both—that he is indeed Life itself in all its guises, contradictory and immutable. A truer tale of devotion (if not persuasion) has rarely been told.

Cendrars's prose leaps off the page like live jewels. His is a poetry of a breathing variety, bred in the world before it reaches the page. **Moravagine** is great fun to read. Its idea and images and insights are so numerous that it merits at least several readings. My last desire would be to read the book in its original French. In the meantime, I am grateful for this new edition of a classic of modern lit—as alive in the nineties as we imagine it must've been in the twenties, when it was originally published.

Giles Foden (essay date 26 August 1994)

SOURCE: "The Burning Phoenix," in *Times Literary Supplement*, No. 4769, August 26, 1994, pp. 9-10.

[*Below, Foden gives a comprehensive review of Cendrars's body of poetry.*]

Fighting in the First World War as a Swiss national in "la Marocaine", the original Foreign Legion, Blaise Cendrars lost an arm during the assault on the Navarin Farm in Champagne on September 28, 1915. It was his writing arm that went, "planté dans l'herbe comme une grande fleur épanouie, un lys rouge, un bras humain tout ruisselant de sang, un bras droit sectionné au-dessus du coude et dont la main encore vivant fouissait le sol des doigts comme pour y prendre racine . . ." (**La Main coupée**).

Cendrars himself never took root. Right from the start, travel was his subject and the making of him; it gave him the opportunity to "make" his own sprawling biography (itinerant poet, novelist-adventurer, "style" journalist, bohemian business schemer), sometimes in the spirit of fictional invention, sometimes as a charming but down-right lie. So it is hard to answer his own question: "à qui était cette main, ce bras droit, ce sang qui coulait comme la sève?"

Born Frédéric Louis Sauser in the same year and place as Le Corbusier (La Chaux-de-Fonds, Switzerland, 1887), Cendrars used to say he was born at the Hôtel des Etrangers on the Left Bank, the building where the *Roman de la Rose* was written. He may have been in Egypt as a child; we know that his family (his father was a dealer in clocks and timepieces) was in Naples by the time he was eight. He left his parents in his early teens (fleeing them, in his embroidered version, by climbing down from a fifth-floor balcony), journeying across Germany and Russia, where he ended up in St. Petersburg. There—probably, in fact, by his father's intervention—he worked for H.A. Leuba, a Swiss watch merchant, from 1904 to 1907, during which time, Jay Bochner writes in his excellent introduction to Ron Padgett's translation of the **Complete Poems,** he established "a lifelong pattern of alternating travel with long sessions in libraries".

Cendrars certainly ventured to Russia, Germany, Poland, Britain, the United States and Brazil. His poems and memoirs imply that he traveled even more widely. On the way, he worked. He claimed, as Barbara Wright wrote in a review of a translation of his novel **L'Homme foudroyé** (*TLS*, February 26, 1971), "to have fait 36 métiers, including those of farm worker, tractor driver, big-game hunter, prospector, juggler, smuggler . . . . In his bread-and-butter activities during the 1920s he seems to have been some sort of business agent, making and losing (or spending) fortunes with the greatest nonchalance."

For all his own capitalist activity, in his Russian period

Cendrars forged a lifelong attachment to anarchism (there are some Poundian attacks on usury in the poems). Meanwhile, he gathered material for his most famous novel, *Moravagine* (published in 1926 but set against the background of pre-revolutionary insurrections in St. Petersburg), and the long railway poem, *The Prose of the Trans-Siberian and of Little Jeanne of France* (published in Paris in 1913 and printed as a 2-metre-high, multi-inked, multi-typefaced "simultaneous" *objet* along with his friend Sonia Delaunay's abstract silk-screen painting). "A projected 150 copies were advertised as equaling", says Bochner, "at two metres a copy, the height of the Eiffel Tower, which is invoked in the last line of the poem and at the very bottom of the painting."

During his early travels, as a (half-serious) medical student at Berne University, Cendrars met Féla Poznanska, the Polish student who was to become his first wife and the mother of Miriam Cendrars. (The latter it is who has produced *Blaise Cendrars*, a substantial and comprehensive, if slightly eccentric, biography-memoir, which, as one would expect, is full of fascinating material. Even Miriam's tendency to mimic her father's direct, quasi-imagist, "telegraphic" style, and her propensity for flashbacks and "flash-forwards," grow on you after a while. Given the personal connection, this was always, after all, going to be an idiosyncratic book, though it is scholarly too, with a useful bibliography.)

Between October 1910 and March 1911, Cendrars was in Paris with Féla. The following year he produced his first great poem, *Easter in New York,* the fruit of a six-month, poverty-stricken stay in the city, from where Féla, staying with her sister, had sent him a ticket. It was in New York (where the young modernist found himself "desperate to find a way past" the retrograde European neo-symbolism that was wowing the American avant-garde at the time) that Freddy Sauser took on the name of Blaise Cendrars. This burning phoenix rose, Bochner tells us—by way of Saint Blaise, *braise, cendres* and the Latin *ars*—out of "a few smouldering lines" of Nietzsche: "And everything of mine turns to mere cinders / What I love and what I do".

Back in Paris by the middle of 1912, Cendrars was introduced into the more exciting European avant-garde—literary and artistic—by Apollinaire, to whom he had sent a manuscript copy of *Easter in New York,* which is supposed by some critics to have had a dramatic effect on the senior poet's style in "Zone". For all that, Cendrars's relationship with other artists was never solely professional; the idea of "the career artist" was, anyway, anathema to him. As well as the Delaunays and Apollinaire, he knew Chagall, Braque, Léger, Modigliani (one of his closest friends, who painted his portrait several times), Picabia, Soutine, Arthur Cravan (Oscar Wilde's nephew, a poet and boxer), Max Jacob, Pierre Reverdy, Arthur Honegger, Poulenc, Satie, Cocteau and the

film-maker Abel Gance. They must have been heady, as well as hard, times: with Cravan and the Delaunays, Cendrars would go to "Bal Bullier dances in 'modern' attire dipped in painters' colours". And then there were more worshipful attachments, like that to Remy de Gourmont, his literary hero and friend, who died, Cendrars was upset to hear, on the day he lost his arm. Gourmont's beautiful version of Venantius Fortunatus' *Pange lingua* (part of the medieval Latin liturgy) provides the epigraph to *Easter in New York,* which is also addressed to Christ on the cross, though in a more problematic, socialized and splintered way. This is the Gourmont extract, in Padgett's translation:

> Bend your branches, tall tree, relax your
> deep tension
> And let your natural hardness give way,
> Don't tear off the arms of the highest King. . . .

And here is Cendrars below:

> Lord, the poor masses for whom you made
> the Sacrifice
> Are here, penned in, heaped up, like cattle,
> in poorhouses.
>
> Huge dark ships come in around the clock
> And dump them off, pell-mell, onto the dock . . .
>
> Lord, I'm in the neighborhood of vagrants,
> Good thieves, bums and fences.
>
> I think of the two thieves who shared your
> torture.
> I know you deign to smile on their misfortune,
>
> Lord, one wants a rope with a noose on the end,
> But they aren't free, ropes, they cost a couple
> of cents.
>
> This old robber talked like a philosopher.
> I gave him some opium so he'd get to heaven
> faster.
>
> I think also of the street singers.
> The blind violinist, the one-armed organ-grinder,
>
> The straw-hat, paper-rose singer; surely
> These are the ones who sing throughout eternity.
>   (*Easter in New York,* 1912)

By 1916, Cendrars was turning his own remaining hand, with which he had had to learn to write again, more and more to prose, producing some of the *bouleversant* surrealist pieces assembled in *Modernities and Other Writings,* in translations by Esther Allen. By 1920, he had dabbled in publishing (with Cocteau) and film-making (with Gance); in 1923, he collaborated on a ballet, *La Création du Monde,* with Léger and Darius Milhaud. By 1924, he had almost stopped writing poetry altogether. Over the next six years, starting his long journeys again, he combined five trips to South America with the production of his three greatest novels: *Sutter's Gold, Moravagine* and the two-part *Dan Yack.* From then, through the Second World War (during which, until the fall of France, he was correspondent with the British forces) until his death in 1961, he produced a steady but diminishing stream of volumes: of reportage (on the underworlds of Paris and Marseille, on Al Capone), travel-writing (*Hollywood*), a four-volume, phantasmagoric, fictionalized memoir (*L'Homme foudroyé,* 1945, *La Main coupée,* 1946, *Bourlinguer,* 1948, *Le Lotissement du ciel,* 1949), and sporadic fiction.

Even in death, in his own sepulchral ode, the geographical theme resurfaces—sparkling,too, where Pound's and Yeats's equivalent poems ("Pour l'élection de son sépulchre" and section six of "Under Ben Bulben") are full of bile and world-weariness respectively:

> *Là-bas git*
> Blaise Cendrars
> Par latitude zéro
> Deux ou trois dixièmes sud
> Une deux, trois douzaines de degrés
> Longitude ouest
> Dans le ventre d'un cachalot
> Dans un grand cuveau d'indigo.

Altogether, Cendrars's was a very considerable body of work that was to earn him, in those last years (though his fame was much eclipsed and came rather late in the day), a number of prizes from his adoptive country. There is something rather pathetic about the idea of André Malraux visiting, in 1958, the apartment of the paralysed Cendrars (who had suffered two strokes) to give him the award of Commander of the Légion d'Honneur, as if those formative lines of Nietzsche had been realized.

Looking at the poetry more closely, though, you wouldn't think so. Elastic (his first collection proper was actually called *Nineteen Elastic Poems*), resisting abstraction, grounded on the quotidian and on the conversational tones of their imagined speaker, full of "found, cubist, assemblage and collage techniques" (Bochner) and—what is rare in this type of avant-garde formalism—full of colour and lived experience, Cendrars's poems are anything but burnt out. Just as most of his prose is concerned with the life of the adventurous male, so the verse (straightforwardly rendered by Padgett, with an appendix of the French texts), eschewing the interior life, is about, and goes out into, the physical world. The "Prose" in *The Prose of the Trans-Siberian,*

Cendrars explained, springs from the low Latin *prosa*—projection, or speaking forth.

Fulfilling a bridging role between different poetic traditions, Cendrars now seems a very contemporary poet; it is, for example, worth comparing the lines from *Easter in New York* above with Geoffrey Hill's "Crucified Lord, you swim upon your cross / And never move"; or *The Trans-Siberian* with Amy Clampitt's "Babel Aboard The Hellas International Express"; or Cendrars's Tonga-talk poem **"Mee Too Buggi"** with Craig Raine's "Gauguin." Cendrars did, after all, always make much "of the mania of being so self-possessed and up-to-date", as one critic has put it.

But the tradition, mainly American, in which he is most at home—that of the longish-lined, expansive but quirky poem of everyday life, rhetorical but streetwise, sometimes street-talking—as articulated by, say, Frank O'Hara or John Ashbery—was one extant in his own life-time, and one that he sought out. Whitman's *Leaves of Grass,* translated into French in 1909, had a tremendous effect on French poets of the time. Cendrars, Miriam tell us, characteristically "fait à Guillaume [Apollinaire] un fantastique récit des funerailles de Whitman, qu'il tient, dit-il, d'un témoin qui a assisté à la cérémonie. Avec ses trois mille cinq cents participants, et *les pédérastes qui étaient venus en foule*, et la claironnante fanfare, et l'orgie qui ensuivit, ce fut un mémorable enterrement. . ."

Yet the most attractive poems are not the great long poems of 1912-14—*Easter in New York, The Trans-Siberian* and *Panama,* a tale of seven uncles dispersed across the globe, narrated by the nephew—so much as those in the later volumes and batches that represent Cendrars's "documentary" phase: the *Black African Poems* published in magazines in 1922, *Kodak* and *Travel Notes* (both published in 1924). Exotic, sexy, mixing a quiet lyricism with "modern"—trains, ships, radios, the laboratory—and "primitive" subject-matter (Cendrars was instrumental in bringing the fetish for African fetishes to Paris and Picasso), dandyish in the spirit of Valery Larbaud's Barnabooth, these "snapshots" or "ocean letters" belie their own lightness; by making less of the poem as an art object (so different to the monumentalism of that early project with Delaunay), they achieve their own artistic substance in the act of recording, as in **"The Thousand Islands"** from *Kodak:*

> The sun disappears on the horizon of Lake
> Ontario
> The clouds bathe their folds in vats of purple
> violet scarlet and orange
> What a beautiful evening murmur Andrea and
> Frederika seated on the
> terrace of a medieval castle
> And the ten thousand motorboats reply to
> their ecstasy.

Other poems in *Kodak* show how taxonomy drives Cendrars's documentary technique: "The California quail / The rabbit known as the jackass / The prairie hen the turtle-dove the partridge / The wild duck and wild goose / The antelope / It's true you still see wildcats and rattlesnakes / But there aren't pumas anymore." If zoology and scientific examination in general is one of his methods of proceeding, or appearing to proceed—remembering Zola in a skewed, rebellious sort of way (as did his concern for the poor and abused)-another is plain, or, in the case of **"Menus"**, sumptuous and weird presentation:

> Pickled shark fins
> Stillborn dog in honey
> Rice wine with violets
> Cream of silkworm cocoon
> Salted earthworms and Kava liqueur
> Seaweed jam....

But this is not, as with Zola, a case of the artist trying to give an objective, "measured" picture of the world; indeed, most of the "fact" in *Kodak* was lifted from *Le Mystérieux Docteur Cornélius*, a second-rate contemporary popular novel by one Gustave Le Rouge, to be transmuted by Cendrars into seemingly ingenuous poems with their own "real" fabric. One assumes that Cendrars planned the discovery of this, five years after he died, by writing twenty years earlier in a memoir of how he had shown Le Rouge a volume of poems "scissor-and-pasted out of the latter's adventure novels". *Travel Notes,* on the other hand, says Bochner, is "definitely Cendrars's own trip, the journal of his first voyage to South America".

One of the two keynotes, in all this, is production, of one sort or another; there are manufacturing city poems as well as luxuriant island poems, internal combustion poems as well as landscape poems, lists of goods as well as animals. Behind every line you hear, if not cicadas in some tropical scene, the rattling of machines. ("In the years 1910 and 1911", says Cendrars, "Robert Delaunay and I were perhaps the only people in Paris who were talking about machines and art and who were vaguely conscious of the great transformations of the modern world.")

The other note, almost the note not struck, is of a pastoral latency that puts interpretation at its ease; of an image, immediate but strangely inert, which the poet presents without comment or formal pressure, as if to say "there is this other life too", beyond machines, beyond machine-poems. As it would be with the driver of a coach in Tampa, "asleep with his mouth open"; or with old Jupiter, at a sign from his master, bringing out "a little lacquered stand / A bottle of sherry / An ice bucket / Some lemons / And a box of Havana cigars/... No one spoke / The sweat was streaming down their faces". These, production and latency, are the twin poles of

Cendrars's art as a whole. The sheer, diverse fact of the burgeoning physical world, the crowd of images alone, is sufficient for him; the reader must supply the unifying idea if he wants to, or just take it "as read".

Some—like John Dos Passos, who translated *Panama,* hailing Cendrars as "the Homer of the Transsiberian", and Henry Miller, who also championed him—were able to. Others, like the English poet F. S. Flint (one of the contributors to *Des Imagistes*, the first Imagist anthology, published under Pound's editorship in 1914), reviewing *Nineteen Elastic Poems* in the *TLS* in 1919 under the headline "A New Decadence", were not:

> M. Cendrars is as sensitive to impressions and as clever as any minor poet; but ... he now pretends to look out with one eye half-opened on a world for which it is really not worth while finding a definite form and expression .... There never was any other unity than that made by the artists, and you are not creating new art by allowing the spectacle of modern life to pour pell-mell through you without selection or arrangement. ... We are not afraid of audacities, but we do want composition. Mallarmé is said to have left out the first half of the comparison; but the composition was there, and it was clear, if you had wit enough to divine the missing half. M. Cendrars leaves out indifferently the first or the second half, or both, and he does not trouble to compose, so that you are left wondering whether he has any intentions at all—except to pull your leg.

What this suggests is how much the old modernists would abhor today's postmodernists. The wild, brilliant texts collected by Monique Chefdor in *Modernities and Other Writings*—including *Profound Today, I Have Killed, In Praise of the Dangerous Life* and *The End of the World Filmed by the Angel of Notre Dame*—certainly bear out her view that Cendrars was "at once on a par with his contemporaries and far ahead of them, anticipating the present postmodern moment".

These "other writings"—as distinct from the *Modernités* proper, a more journalistic though no less strange and unrestrained series on the painters of the day—may represent a more lasting achievement than many of the poems. They take the form, mostly, of staccato, gnomic utterances on such subjects as war, the camera, crowds, apocalypse, chemistry, biology, commercial iconography and techno-sexual mania. Velocity (of machines, of social life, of travel, of trade) is one significant concept in these intense, associative, high-focus pictures chronicling the "altered state" of emergent modern society; another is perspective, an adjusted perspective ready to look at new types of social and physical space and render that vision formally. To get any sense of what

Cendrars is about in these pieces (because their fragmentariness works by cumulative total effect rather than, as with most of the poems, through the projection of a series of more discrete images), you have to quote at length. The difference, remembering Pound's *phanopoeia*—"a casting of images upon the visual imagination"—as well as Cendrars's role in the development of the cinema through his relationship with Gance is akin to that between photography and cinematography:

> The terrible blast of a whistle furrows the continent. Here is Egypt on camelback. Choose Engadine for winter sports. Read Golf's *Hotels* under the palm trees. Think of four hundred windows flashing in the sun. You unfold the horizon of a timetable and dream of southern islands. . . . Watches set themselves. From every direction ocean liners move towards their connection. Then the semaphore signals. A blue eye opens. The red one closes. Soon there is nothing but colour. Interpenetration. Disk, Rhythm, Dance. Orange and violet hues devour each other. Checkerboard of the port . . . . Barrels of fire. Cinnamon. European women are like subaqueous flowers confronting the stern labouring longshoremen and the dark red apotheosis of machines. A tram slams into your back. A trap door opens under your feet. There's a tunnel in your eye. You're pulled by the hair to the fifteenth floor. Smoking a pipe, your hands at the faucets—cold water, hot water—you think of the captain's wife, whose knee you will soon surreptitiously caress. The golden denture of her smile, her charming accent. And you let yourself slip down to dinner. The tongues are stuffed. Everyone must grimace to be understood. Gesticulate and laugh loudly. Madame wipes her mouth with her loincloth of a napkin. Boeuf Zephir. Cafe Euréka. Pimodan or Pamodan. Seated in my rocking chair I'm like a Negro fetish, angular beneath the heraldic electricity. The orchestra plays *Louise*. To amuse myself, I riddle the fat body of an old windbag that is floating at the level of my eyes with pinpricks. A deep-sea diver, submerged in the smoke from my cigar, alone I listen to the dying music of sentimentality that resonates in my helmet. The lead soles of my boots keep me upright and I move forward, slow, grotesque, stiffnecked, and bend with difficulty over the swamp life of the women. Your eye, seahorse, vibrates, marks a comma, and passes.
>
> (***Profound Today***, 19)

Though their sensibilities were totally different from that of Cendrars (he celebrated the dissociation, diversity and transmutation, the change in the old order that they bemoan), and their aesthetics more complex, the Anglo-American modernists certainly traversed his route. Considering Cendrars's role within modernism as a poet and a novelist (and, indeed, as a grand fibber), one is driven back to some other remarks of Pound's in "How to Read" (collected in his *Literary Essays*, edited by Eliot) where, making a distinction between "charged" poetry and "cumulative" prose, he argues that some poets are still able to get a prose-like effect "by a greater heaping up of factual data; imagined fact if you will, but nevertheless expressed in factual manner". To some degree, this distinction mirrors what have been seen to be Cendrars's own structures, formal and material, in the poetry itself, their being in between "production" and "latency".

Was a similar kind of in-betweenness suffered personally by Cendrars through the loss of his arm—a charged sense of the missing portion *being there* but not really being there, not being able to function authentically? The vision contiguous to that personal disability certainly bespoke the times, it reflected the climate of thought, all the more so because the vision was there prior to the injury. "We are the amputees of space", as Cendrars put it in the ***Trans-Siberian***—proleptically, two years before he lost his arm—in a phrase that has lots of resonance for modernist preoccupations and formal practice.

For all that, Blaise Cendrars's preoccupations were adventurous rather than introspective; certainly not the type, anyway, in Yeats's disdainful but self-knowing phrase in "The Scholars", to cough in ink or wear the carpet with his shoes.

John L. Brown (review date Spring 1996)

SOURCE: A review of *Correspondance 1934-1979; 45 ans d'amitié*, in *World Literature Today*, Vol. 70, No. 2, Spring, 1996, p. 359.

[*In the following review, Brown praises the compilation and editing of the correspondence between the Cendrars and American author Henry Miller.*]

A group of three collaborators prepared this scrupulously edited and richly documented correspondence between Blaise Cendrars and Henry Miller [entitled *Correspondance 1934-1979; 45 ans d'amitié*]. Cendrars's daughter Miriam supervised the edition and contributed a preface. Frédéric-Jacques Temple, who knew both correspondents, wrote an account of their friendship and their many contacts with the international avant-garde. Detailed notes on each letter (sometimes longer than the letters themselves) were prepared by Jay Bochner.

A chronological listing reveals that the correspondence was somewhat one-sided. Miller's letters are numerous, detailed, often three to four pages in length. Cendrars's correspondence, in comparison, seems laconic, almost telegraphic. The numerous photographs are also copiously annotated. The "annexes" include Cendrars's text on Miller's poem "Alraure," presented on French radio in 1952; Miller's preface to *L'homme foudroyé;* the English originals of Miller's letters to Cendrars, Miriam, and others; a chronological listing of the letters; and a résumé of the biographies of both correspondents. An impressive (and indeed a somewhat intimidating!) documentation, which occupies almost as much space as the letters themselves.

Miller first writes to Cendrars (in English) on 26 November 1934 from the Villa Seurat, enclosing a copy of *Tropic of Cancer* ("the first book of a young author of nearly 50") as "a slight recompense for the pleasure I have had in reading your books." (He mentions particularly *Moravagine.*) Several pages of notes, including a letter from Anaïs Nin, follow the brief communication. Miller (25 December 1934) thanks "Dear Mr. Cendrars" for his visit to the Villa Seurat. He excuses himself for not having written sooner, but he "is in a terribly despondent mood" following his divorce from "June," his second wife. A third letter (13 January 1935), mailed from New York, brands Manhattan as "a detestable place," "une grande sauvagerie babylonienne." Miller never stops denouncing "his native land"! He is looking for a publisher for *Black Spring* and hopes to return to Europe soon, for "that's where I really belong." Significantly, during the many years of their correspondence, the exchanges remained quite formal in tone: Cendrars always wrote to "Mon cher Henry Miller"; Miller addressed his mentor and model as "Mon cher Cendrars." Although Miller wrote often and expansively, Cendrars's replies, frequently just a few lines, never exceeded a page. But Miller did not reproach his laconic friend: "Je sais que les lettres ne sont pas votre fort." (They never employ "tu.")

Unlike many of their distinguished contemporaries—a Gide, a Martin du Gard—Cendrars and Miller devoted little discussion to literature but rather (especially Miller) dwelled on literary "business": finding a publisher, arranging for translations, seeking coverage in the press. Neither had a favorable opinion of publishers. For Miller, they were "putains," just whores. Cendrars agreed, but in more polite terms: "Publishers are a writer's greatest enemies." Writing to Duell, Sloane, and Pearce, Miller urges them to publish Cendrars, "one of the great figures of our time." Miller, more frequently than Cendrars, makes brief comments on contemporary writers: "The American public doesn't like expatriates and even Hemingway is out of favor." Both Cendrars and Miller admire Dos Passos, who had a chapter on Cendrars in *Orient Express* and provided illustrations and an introduction for *Panama.* Among the nineteenth-century giants mentioned are Balzac ("Balzac and His Double" figured as a chapter in *The Wisdom of the Heart*) and

Dostoevsky: "Blaise Cendrars is the French equivalent of Dostoevsky." Both friends admired Rimbaud and published essays about him. Cendrars immediately appreciated Miller, writing the first important article to appear about him in French, "Un écrivain américain nous est né"; and Miller is fervid in his cult of Blaise Cendrars, for him "a universal man," a man "aux stratifications innombrables," whom he literally adores. "At the end of each letter, you extend to me your friendly hand. I grasp it with joy and gratitude."

Following the death of Cendrars, Miller was invited to speak at the memorial service. He declined: "I have thought about Blaise Cendrars almost every day since we met. I have lived with him as a disciple lives with his master." And he desired to continue to live in silence with the man he adored.

Ellen Lampert-Gréaux (review date May 1996)

SOURCE: A review of *Hollywood, Mecca of the Movies,* in *The French Review,* Vol. 69, No. 6, May, 1996, pp. 1033-34.

[*In the following review, Lampert-Greaux finds Cendrars's journal of his trip to Hollywood still relevant sixty years later.*]

Hollywood has always held a fascination for the French, much to the dismay of French filmmakers who shake their berets at the supremacy of American movies in their cinemas. Blaise Cendrars's journal, *Hollywood: Mecca of the Movies,* proves that as early as 1936 there was already a healthy appetite in France for news of the American movie capital.

A popular French poet, novelist, essayist, and sometime newspaper man, Cendrars spent two weeks in Hollywood in 1936, installed in the luxury of the Roosevelt Hotel. On assignment for the daily newspaper *Paris-Soir,* Cendrars filed lively dispatches describing the activity along the palm-lined boulevards, and at the gates to the great studios. While circling the lives of the rich and famous, Cendrars proved to be a perceptive reporter, and his brief chronicle of Hollywood captured both the essence of the city and the imagination of his readers. Serialized in the newspaper as *The Secrets of Hollywood,* Cendrars's collected reports were published in France by Grasset in August 1936.

The University of California edition of *Hollywood: Mecca of the Movies* has been translated by Garrett White, a writer who contributes to *The Los Angeles Times* and *Premiere* magazine. Browsing in the stacks of the UCLA library in 1988, White came across an original copy of Cendrars's book, visibly neglected and forgotten. This first English-language edition is an attractive volume which reproduces 29 light-hearted pen and ink drawings by illustrator Jean Guérin, a portraitist and part of the French colony in California in the 1930s.

It was not just serendipity that sent Cendrars to Hollywood. He had written enthusiastically about the early filmmakers in France and the United States. He also had been associated with such French pioneers as Abel Gance and Jean Vigo, having written the scripts and worked on the production of several films, and published *The ABC's of Cinema* in 1926. One of Cendrars's novels, *Sutter's Gold,* was even made into a Hollywood film. Directed by James Cruze for Universal, the film was released in 1936 just as Cendrars hit Hollywood, but met with little success. The experience did, however, give Cendrars his own taste of the excitement and disappointment of the American mecca for dreams that may or may not come true.

Taking the train across the America continent, Cendrars treats his readers to a landscape of a United States in the aftermath of the great depression and of a country in a deep transition. Stepping off of the train into the brilliant sunshine of Southern California, Cendrars discovers Hollywood at its heyday, and he quickly made it the subject of his inquisitive style and piercing pen. Cendrars wrote in a casual, conversational tone, appropriate for an accomplished man of letters writing home to the large, appreciative audience of *Paris-Soir*.

Whether taking his readers with him along the sunny boulevards or into dressing rooms and hot jazz clubs, or bringing them along on interviews or long waits at the impenetrable studio gates, Cendrars joyously shares his two-week foray into the Hollywood he was able to see. Since his brief stay allowed him only limited access to the real stars, his colorful accounts are perhaps more interesting than if he had been the toast of the town. His perception of the movie capital could almost have been written last year, rather than almost 60 years ago. In just two weeks, Cendrars felt the pulse of a magical, mythical place whose axis spun around the movie makers and their stars.

Six decades later, Hollywood is still spinning as fast as it can to create new heroes and new stars, and the French are still avidly devouring the product of this myth factory. Cendrars's *Hollywood: Mecca of the Movies* confirms the author's own fascination with the movies, and provides a charming insight into the Hollywood of 1936.

Richard Sieburth (essay date 1996)

SOURCE: "One Hand Clapping," in *Parnassus: Poetry in Review,* Vol. 21, Nos. 1 & 2, 1996, pp. 78-89.

[*In the following essay, Sieburth offers an overview of Cendrars's writings and their translations.*]

After you have taken in the battered old boxer's mug and the inevitable Gauloise glued to the lower lip, the thing you most notice about Blaise Cendrars in the old photos is his missing hand. The left hand writes, smokes, drinks, eats; but from above the elbow down, the right arm just hangs there, all sleeve.

Cendrars lost his right hand to a mortar shell at the Ferme Navarin in 1915. As he would later describe it, part of him lay there by his side, "planted in the grass like a great spreading flower, a red lily, a human arm streaming with blood, a right arm severed above the elbow, its hand, still alive, digging its fingers into the soil as if to take root." From the killing fields of the Marne, the hand then rose up into the sky to become the constellation Orion:

> It's my star
> It's in the form of a hand
> It's my hand gone up into the sky
> During the entire war I saw Orion through a
> lookout slit
> When the zeppelins came to bomb Paris they
> always came from
> Orion
> I have it above my head today
> The main mast pierces the palm of that hand
> which must hurt
> As my amputated hand hurts me pierced as it is by
> a continual
> stabbing pain

This is one of the *Travel Notes* Cendrars jotted down as he crossed the Equator en route to Sao Paulo in 1924—and it reads just as flatly in the original French as it does in Ron Padgett's English. The zeppelins over Paris and the dazed camera eye of the *poilu* looking out of the aperture of his loophole are, by the early twenties, fairly standard-issue modernism. But the mythopoeia at work in these lines might be Dante's: A pilgrim poet looks to the heavens and sees the entire cosmos transformed into a vast projection of the martyred body of Jesus. The vision telescopes the carnage of war, the mast-pierced palm of the warrior Orion, and his own missing hand, a sidereal Christ nailed to the firmament like a pulse-star of pain.

In an uncanny coincidence, Cendrars's hand was blown off the very day Remy de Gourmont died. Influential editor of the *Mercure de France*, polymath novelist, poet, and critic, Gourmont was the Roland Barthes of the prewar avant-garde, a figure whom Cendrars so idolized that he actually signed some of his own early manuscripts with the master's name. With his spiritual father now gone, Cendrars-the-son, orphaned, maimed to the core, also undergoes a symbolic death. Switching from the right hand to the left, having literally to learn to write all over again, he will compose almost no more poetry after 1915—indeed, if we are to believe his own carefully forged hagiography, he will abandon Literature altogether, choosing instead the career of a latter-day Rimbaud or Dada saint. Though he will continue to publish enormously over the following half century (his collected works come to eight hefty tomes in the standard French edition), what he writes with his left hand no longer strictly matters: After the mortar shell, all his works are posthumous, ghostwritten by a phantom limb. One of his last poems runs: "Je suis l'homme qui n'a plus de passé.—Seul mon moignon me fait mal." I'm the man who no longer has a past. Only my stump aches.

The ache is already there in Cendrars's very first poem, **Les Pâques à New-York,** published in 1912—the same year as Apollinaire's *Zone.* Compared to Apollinaire's exuberant, kaleidoscopic collage of modernity, Cendrars's poem, inspired by the incantatory cadences of Gourmont's *Latin mystique,* scans more like the coarse gougings of a medieval woodcut, its blocky alexandrines thudding down the page. Padgett's translation catches the rhythm beautifully:

> The apartment windows are filled with blood
> And the women behind them are like flowers of
> blood,
>
> Orchids, strange, bad, withered blooms,
> Chalices inverted underneath your wounds.
>
> They never drank of your blood collected there.
> They have red on their lips, and lacy underwear.

The violent juxtaposition of the Savior's sacrificial blood with the menstrual effluvia of the modern world is typical of the poem's rather lurid expressionistic effects. Whereas *Zone* is closer to the futurist experiments of a Boccioni, Severini, or Balla, Cendrars's agonistic litany of Easter in New York—down to the very frontispiece he designed for it, which depicts a man bent over, holding his crotch—is pure Kollwitz, Kokoschka, or Schiele.

Cendrars's residences in Russia and his bilingual Bernese background make him one of the few intermediaries between the modernisms of Mitteleuropa (notably, the Blaue Reiter school) and the Parisian avantgarde; **Easter in New York,** significantly enough, was first published in a Franco-German anarchist review printed in Paris. He is, for example, probably the only French poet of his period to know all of Rilke's work by heart in the original. A key image from the latter's *Malte Laurids Brigge,* published in 1911, is adapted by Cendrars to express the utter facelessness of New York:

> Lord, make my face, buried in my hands,
> Leave there its agonizing mask.
>
> Lord, don't let my two hands, pressed here
> Against my lips, lick the foam of wild despair.

In an inspired feat of translation, Padgett manages to capture Cendrars's expressionistic *Menschheitsdämmerung* by transposing it into the more familiar idiom of the early Eliot:

> In the night the street is like a gash
> Filled with gold and blood, fire and trash.

Or this couplet, which reads like something Pound might have slashed from the manuscript of *The Waste Land:*

> Lord, the humble women who were with you at
> Golgotha
> Are hidden, in filthy backrooms, on obscene sofas.

Unreal city, indeed.

Easter in New York was the *Howl* of its generation. Written while Cendrars was down and out in New York, living the life of a dharma bum, its hallucinatory catalogue of Lower East Side immigrants, skid row drunks, and assorted spiritual and sexual cripples is one slow scream of pain. The theology of the poem (a further link to the German expressionists and the American Beats) is darkly gnostic, dismissing as it does the entire incarnate world as an obscene, female simulacrum of the Creation. If there is redemption, it lies only in the suffering body of the crucified Christ—a body, however, that is no longer (or not yet) ready to rise:

> Lord, cold as a shroud the dawn slipped away
> And left the skyscrapers naked in the day.

Easter in New York concludes with a vision of failed resurrection in the New World; the harrowing night of the soul it records, however, at least allowed its author to be reborn. Sloughing off his previous identity as the Swiss Freddy Sauser, the poet for the first time signs his work "Blaise Cendrars"—a man on fire (*braise*), determined to reduce the world to cinders (*cendres*) through the flame of his art (*ars*).

Nineteen thirteen is Cendrars's annus mirabilis. Returning to Paris, he is quickly caught up in the vortex of the avantgarde. He meets Apollinaire and Jacob, but his closest imaginative commerce is with painters: Léger, Chagall, Modigliani, Soutine, Robert and Sonia Delaunay. With the last, he collaborates on his first great *simultanéiste* work, **Prose du Transsibérien,** an object half-painting, half-book: Cendrars's poem runs down the right hand of the two-meter sheet, while Sonia Delaunay's swirls of color occupy the left, now and then spilling over into the typographical indentions of the text. One hundred and fifty copies were printed; folded like a pleated map, the sheets came to the size of an average paperback—stood end to end, however, they equaled the height of the Eiffel Tower. Modern editions of the text, of course, cannot convey the full optic and semiotic complexity of this publishing event. Following in the footsteps of Mallarmés' "Un coup de dés" and anticipating the experiments of Apollinaire's *Calligrammes*, Cendrars scores the page, using a range of typefaces and blocks of print to syncopate his epic (and purely imaginary) journey through Russia on the Transsiberian Express. A similar attention to the graphic lie of print on page informs his other great poem of 1913, *Panama* (not published until 1918). Designed by Cendrars and executed by Raoul Dufy, the book's folded format imitates a steamship schedule or railway timetable, its cover emblazoned with a logo that parodies the trademark emblem of the Union Pacific Railroad. The stanza breaks within the body of the poem are in turn filled with maps of train routes in the American West—vectors of verse visually rhymed with the branching trunk lines of modern transportation.

Despite their cinematographic appeal to the reader's eye, these are also very much poems about new ways of hearing. Nineteen thirteen is, after all, the year of Stravinsky's *Rite of Spring* and **The Prose of the Transsiberian** is accordingly "dedicated to musicians" (later, in the early twenties, Cendrars will work with Darius Milhaud on his jazzy *Création du monde*). The very "Prose" of the title gestures toward music—specifically the Latin *prosa* of medieval Gregorian chant that Cendrars (like Pound) discovered in the elastic rhythmic units of Gourmont's *Latin mystique*, a prose both colloquial and liturgical, a cadence to be at once spoken and droned. This particular fusion of the hieratic and the vernacular is perhaps the most difficult thing to translate—and for the most part it eludes Padgett's ear, attuned as it is to the deadpan diction of the New York School. Here are the opening lines of his **Prose of the Transsiberian:**

> Back then I was still young
> I was barely sixteen but my childhood memories
> were gone
> I was 48,000 miles away from where I was born

Compare Dos Passos' version: "I was a youngster in those days," where, right off the bat, we feel ourselves in the presence of a great spinner of yarns; "Hardly sixteen and already I couldn't remember my childhood," which retains the original's clunky copula, smoothed out by Padgett's adversative "but," and "I was sixteen thousand leagues away from the place I was born," whose register is appropriately epic, involving distances measured in mythical leagues, not in Padgett's American miles.

Translating the **Transsibérian** and **Panama** in 1931, Dos

Passos of course came to his task with certain advantages: Cendrars was a personal acquaintance whose poetics of montage had already influenced the jump cuts of his own *Orient Express* and the "Newsreel" and "Camera Eye" sections of *The 42nd Parallel*. Although his versions are often slapdash and their slang now somewhat dated—their lexicon includes words like "flappers," "hornswaggled," "jack" (for money), and "on the bum"—they at least manage to register something of Cendrars's characteristic voice: "J'ai été libertin et je me suis permis toutes les privautés avec le monde." With his trained novelist's ear, Dos Passos catches the precise inflection of wounded swagger: "I've done what I damn pleased I've taken all sorts of liberties with the world." Padgett, by contrast, chooses to remain more literal, but in the process misreads the French "libertin" as a false friend of the English "libertine," producing the awkward repetition of "I've been a libertine and have taken every liberty with the world"—a line one cannot imagine anyone possibly *saying*. Or take this famous phrase from **Panama:** "Je tourne dans la cage des méridiens comme un écureuil dans la sienne"—where the subtle internal off-rhyme established at the median caesura ("méridiens" / "sienne") reproduces the futile rotation of a mind trapped on its own treadmill. Padgett merely sight-reads the original, giving us the stunted line: "I go round in the cage of meridians like a squirrel in his," whereas Dos Passos conveys the frenzy of immobility: "I go round and round inside the meridians like a squirrel in a squirrelcage."

If Dos Passos' ear is almost always superior to Padgett's, it is because he has actually experienced the acoustic universe of the great international express trains:

> Women brushing past
> Hiss of steam
> And the eternal rack of crazy wheels in the ruts of
> the sky.

Padgett is more bloated:

> Swishing of women
> And the whistle blowing
> And the eternal sound of wheels wildly rolling
> along ruts in the sky.

A veteran of the Great War like Cendrars, Dos Passos also knows the precise shadings of military jargon. His Captain Dreyfus, for example, is "reduced to the ranks before the army," whereas Padgett's, "stripped in front of the army," is actually forced to publicly unclothe. Furthermore, Dos Passos has lived through the dawn of aviation: When, toward the end of **Panama,** Cendrars dreams of participating in a "rallye aérien," he perfectly renders the period feel with "Air Circus" (as opposed to Padgett's blander "airplane races"). The original French is deceptively simple:

La voie lactée autour du cou
Les deux hémisphères sur les yeux
A toute vitesse
Il n'y a plus de pannes

Padgett's version is entirely correct, but, as usual, overcautious:

The Milky Way around my neck
The two hemispheres on my eyes
At top speed
There are no more breakdowns

Dos Passos gives the last two lines as "Full speed ahead / Never stall again," at least capturing something about the flight of early airplanes. And his first two lines miraculously improve upon the original, sharpening the image of the pilot as an astral Icarus, transmogrified by ascension:

With the Milky Way around my neck
And the two hemispheres for goggles

The Prose of the Transsibérian is a narrative about the disintegration of narratives, a modernist *Childe Harold's Pilgrimage* whose fast-forward imagery culminates in a vision of holocaust at Port Arthur before looping back (somewhat cornily) to the Eiffel Tower and the arms of Jeanne, the brave little Paris whore. *Panama, or The Adventures of My Seven Uncles* in turn deploys a dazzling array of plots and location shots—less to map the modern world in all its photogenic variety than to erase it, to denounce it as a Big Lie. (Despite his advanced poetic techniques, Cendrars remains very much the fin-de-siècle student of Schopenhauer, Nietzsche, and Mallarmé.) Leaving these experiments with cinematographic epic behind, he now turns, in late 1913 and 1914, to the dismantling of lyric in a series of texts later collected as *19 Elastic Poems.*

Padgett on the whole does very well with this collection, perhaps because it so explicitly anticipates the repertoire of the New York School, particularly the knowing in-jokes about the art world ("The Weather Bureau is forecasting bad weather / There is no futurism"; "Art criticism is as idiotic as Esperanto"; "Simultaneism is old hat"). The language of these texts, originally published in such avant-garde magazines as *Les Soirées de Paris, Dèr Sturm, De Stijl, Cabaret Voltaire*, and *Littérature*, reads like a cross between the culled snippets of Apollinaire's "conversation poems" and the cut-ups of Tzara. Cendrars himself referred to them as "poèmes de circonstance," underscoring the deliberate casualness of their occasion—browsing through a newspaper, having a drink in a café, chatting with a fellow poet, looking out a window, having one's portrait painted. Their idiom is supple enough to explore the smallest, most prosaic incidents of daily life and then to compact these anecdotes into

a private, often gnomic shorthand. Though they still gesture toward narrative, most of these poems take the form of lists—as in this stroboscopic record of a visit to Chagall's studio, dated October 1913:

Cossacks Christ a shattered sun
Roofs
Sleepwalkers goats
A lycanthrope
Pétrus Borel
Madness winter
A genius split like a peach
Lautréamont
Chagall
Poor kid next to my wife
Morose delectation
The shoes are down at heel
An old jar full of chocolate
A lamp that's split in two
And my drunkenness when I go see him

The "I" who makes his appearance here is no longer, strictly speaking, a lyric subject. Recording his drunkenness as he would any other random stimulus or association, he has become an impersonal seismograph of the self (Rimbaud's "Je est un autre"). His job, in short, is no longer to express the world but merely to document it, to inventory it, to place it within quotations, as in the following **"News Flash"**:

OKLAHOMA, January 20, 1914
Three convicts get hold of revolvers
They kill their guard and grab the prison keys
They come running out of their cells and kill four
guards in the
yard
Then they grab the young prison secretary
And get into a carriage waiting for them at the gate
They leave at top speed
While guards fire their revolvers in the direction
of the fugitives

This rapid-fire narrative reads like the shooting script for one of Mack Sennett's manic two-reelers. Cendrars copied it out of the morning newspaper. It is said to be the first found poem in French, the literary equivalent of the ready-mades Duchamp had exhibited at the Armory Show the previous year. Well before Dada, Cendrars is trying to find a way out of Poetry once and for all.

Although he continues to compose a few scattered poems after his amputation, the ***Elastic Poems*** of 1913-1914 announces Cendrars's crossover into left-handed prose, or a genre that might be best labeled anti- or post-poetry. After a hiatus of ten years, he returns to the lineations of verse in a series of texts jotted down over the course of 1924 and published in book form under the titles **Kodak** and **Feuilles de route;** under the threat of a trademark infringement suit from the Eastman Company, however, the title of the former was changed to **Documentaires.** This legal contretemps, co-incidentally enough, underscores the (postmodernist) strategies of reappropriation at work throughout the volume. As its title suggests, **Kodak** displays the world in the age of mechanical reproduction as a snapshot album or a medley of souvenir postcards. As it moves out from Manhattan into the great American vastness, the camera pans down the Mississippi, up to Canada and Alaska, then across the Pacific into Asia and Africa—an entirely imaginary tracking shot, for Cendrars never visited any of the landscapes he photographically documents with such precision. Nor can he really be said to be the owner or originator of the texts gathered in the volume, for virtually every word has been cut and pasted from the adventure stories of the minor French popular novelist Gustave Le Rouge (bearing out T.S. Eliot's dictum that bad poets borrow but good poets steal). Cendrars's samplings from Le Rouge's novels are exactly contemporary with the archival montage techniques of Pound's "Malatesta Cantos," but whereas Pound, working as a historian, still believes in the recoverable truth inherent in fact, Cendrars's documentary footage functions more ironically, reminding us that the world is mere representation (Schopenhauer again), that all reality has now become as virtual as his missing hand.

Padgett's translations of **Kodak** and **Travel Notes** are among his finest achievements. Far more relaxed than Monique Chefdor's previous renderings of these same texts, Padgett's versions actually manage to invent Cendrars as a plausible twentieth-century American poet. We hear hints of Hart Crane, for example, in this Florida landscape:

> On these stinking waters in the poisonous muck
> Flowers bloom with a stunning scent a heady and
> persistent smell
> Burst of blue and purple
> Chrome leaves
> Everywhere

Or this, a possible outtake from an early Williams poem, lensed through the precisionist eye of Charles Sheeler:

> A six-cylinder and two Fords out in the field
> All around and as far as you can see the slightly
> tilted sheaves form
> a checkerboard of wavering rhomboids
> Not a tree
> From the north the chugging and clatter of the
> thresher and hay
> wagon
> And from the south the twelve empty trains
> coming to load the
> wheat

Or this, from Gary Snyder's poems of the Northwest:

> Strings of wood doves red-legged partridge
> Wild peacock
> Wild turkey
> And even a big reddish-brown and white eagle
> brought down from
> the clouds

Or this, an objectivist Cid Corman noting the specifics of a Japanese home:

> Bamboo stalks
> Thin boards
> Paper stretched across frames
> There is no real heating system

Kodak presents us with a world drained of all affect and exotic glamour. Though he knows its landscapes to be mere simulacra, mere images, mere quotations, Cendrars arrives at an almost Zen-like acceptance of their lovely, illusory prose. He is, as he reports in his **Travel Notes,** content to be simply here—that is, as always, elsewhere:

> Today I am perhaps the happiest man in the world
> I have everything I don't want

FURTHER READING

Criticism

Bickel, Beatrice. "African Folk-Lore." *The Nation* 115, No. 2990 (25 October 1922): 442-43.
    Brief background on the African folklore in Cendrars's *Anthologie Nègre.*

Chefdor, Monique. "Blaise Cendrars's Americas: From World to Text, From Text to World." *Proceedings of the Xth Congress of the International Comparative Literature Association.* New York: Garland Publishing, 1985, pp. 216-26.
    Traces the geographical connections in Cendrars's work.

Harding, John. "The Cendrarsian Hero-Cosmopolitan Outsider." *Swiss French Studies* III, No. 2 (November 1982): 6-23.
    Offers a perspective on the common qualities of the central characters of Cendrars's fiction.

Kellerman, Steven G. "Blaise Cendrars's *L'OR* as Cinematic Novel." *Post Script* 4, No. 3 (Spring/Summer 1985): 16-28.
    Analysis of the cinematic structure of *L'Or* in light of its adaptation as the film *Sutter's Gold.*

Miller, Henry. "Reading Blaise Cendrars." *Mademoiselle* 77, No. 6 (October 1977): 58, 62.

> Personal account in which Miller discusses the impact he felt from Cendrars's writing.

Stenhouse, Charles. "Cinema Literature." *Close-Up* VII, No. 5 (November 1930): 335-40.

> Discusses the influence of Cendrars on French cinematographer Abel Gance.

Additional coverage of Cendrars's life and career is contained in the following sources published by Gale: *Contemporary Authors,* Vol. 102; *Contemporary Authors New Revision Series,* Vols. 36 and 62; and *Major Twentieth Century Writers.*

Pier Paolo Pasolini

1922-1975

Italian poet, novelist, essayist, playwright, critic, editor, short story writer, screenplay writer, film director, and actor.

The following entry presents criticism of Pasolini's work through 1997. For further information on his life and career, see *CLC*, Volumes 20 and 37.

INTRODUCTION

Although recognized outside his country primarily as a filmmaker, Pasolini was well known in Italy for the strong and controversial views on Marxism and religion he presented in his poetry, novels, and essays. Over the course of his career, his observations on Catholicism, communism, and the existing social order alternately pleased and angered conservatives and leftists alike. Central to Pasolini's life and works were his despair over Italy's impoverished conditions and his anger over the indifference of the materialistic bourgeoisie. Joseph P. Consoli, writing in *Gay & Lesbian Literature,* observes, "Without a doubt, the author's homosexuality, or as the Italians call it, *inversion,* contributed to Pasolini's predilection to view his subject matter from nonconforming, contrary, yet innovative, perspectives."

Biographical Information

Pasolini was born March 5, 1922, in Bologna, Italy. His father was a career army officer, a fact which forced political awareness upon the boy at an early age. His childhood and early adult experiences in the poverty-stricken village of Casarsa, located in the province of Friuli, inspired his lifelong identification with the poor. Pasolini was called to military duty in September 1943 but escaped after just a week and returned to Casarsa, where he was strongly influenced by the ideas of Karl Marx and Antonio Gramsci, the leading theoretician of Italian communism. Pasolini took a teaching position in a public school while engaging in frenetic intellectual and artistic pursuits, writing and publishing poetry in the Friulian dialect; these activities became his forms of resistance against Nazism and Fascism. In 1949, Pasolini was arrested and accused of "the corruption of minors and committing obscene acts in a public place." The charges were eventually dropped, but the ensuing scandal—Pasolini lost his teaching position and was expelled from the Italian Communist Party—forced him and his mother to move to Rome, where he became immersed in the slum life of that city.

Pasolini was murdered the night of November 1-2, 1975; his

death is considered an ironic end to a life spent absorbed in and concerned with the violent nature of contemporary society. Reports of his death often conflict, but most sources agree that the young man convicted of the crime struck Pasolini with a board and then ran over him with his own car. What is still debated is the killer's motive: some say he was an innocent boy who panicked when Pasolini propositioned him; other reports indicate that he was a street hustler who was picked up by Pasolini and then killed him, while still others theorize that the killer was an assassin sent by one or more of Pasolini's political enemies to murder him under embarrassing circumstances.

Major Works

Pasolini has been called one of the most notable poets to have emerged during post-World War II Italy. He wrote his earliest poetry in the northern Italian peasantry's native Friulian language in the hope of creating a literature accessible to the poor. Pasolini rejected the official Italian language, believing it had been created by and for the bourgeoisie. These early poems appear in his first booklet of verse, *Poesie a Casarsa* (1942), and in an expanded and revised version, *La meglio gioventu* (1954). These works center on his renunciation of Catholicism and his endorsement of Marxism. Other early poems, along with some experiments in the tradition of religious poetry, are collected in his second volume, *L'usignolo della Chiesa Cattolica* (1958). The poetry of *Le ceneri di Gramsci* (1957; *The Ashes of Gramsci*) and *La religione del mio tempo* (1961; *The Religion of My Time*) reflects, among other beliefs, Gramsci's idea of a "popular national literature." Pasolini's later poetry, *Poesia in forma di rosa* (1964) and *Poesie* (1970; *Poems*), is more autobiographical and confessional, yet the political concerns central to the majority of his works are still evident.

Pasolini's experiences in the Roman slums and his impressions of urban poverty inspired two novels: *Ragazzi di vita* (1955; *The Ragazzi*) and *Una vita violenta* (1959; *A Violent Life*). These highly controversial novels were largely responsible for Pasolini's notoriety. Here again, Pasolini rejected formal, official language in favor of dialect, in this case "a harsh, often crude and obscene, minimized Roman street vocabulary," Consoli explains. *The Ragazzi* centers on a group of youths whose poverty has led them to a life of violence, crime, and indiscriminate sex. Rejecting the official language of the bourgeoisie, Pasolini liberally utilizes Roman dialect and slang. Though free of authorial intrusion, the work is considered an indirect attack on the Italian establishment; its depiction of Italian young people was particularly shocking. Harshly realistic in its explicit language and political implications, *The Ragazzi* angered many factions of the community and resulted in Pasolini's prosecution for obscenity, of which he was acquitted. *A Violent Life* is the second book of his unfinished trilogy on street life. Similar in theme and milieu to *The Ragazzi, A Violent Life* was praised abroad for its realism and the characterization of its protagonist. After his death, two previously unpublished autobiographical novels, *Amado mio* and *Atti impuri,* were published under the title *Amado mio* in 1983. These works explore Pasolini's homosexuality and his emotional torment over what he saw as the disintegration of Italian society.

During the last fifteen years of his life, Pasolini made films in which he sought to combine his socialist sensibilities with a profound, nondenominational spirituality. His films were often anti-Catholic in their implications and controversial for their explicit sexual subject matter. Among his best-known films are *Accattone* (1961), adapted from *Una vita violenta*; *Il vangelo secondo Matteo* (1964; *The Gospel According to Saint Matthew*); *Teorema* (1968; *Theorem*); and *Salò o le 120 giornate di Sodoma* (1975; *Salò: 120 Days of Sodom*). Pasolini films traverse a constantly changing range of styles and contents, and his handling of the medium was at times coarse and graphic. He used nonprofessional actors and avoided many standards of the industry, choosing his subject matter from classical legends, tragedies, political diatribes, and other unconventional sources.

Critical Reception

Critical reaction to Pasolini's work generally extends beyond its value as literature or film, considering also its implications for political and religious thought. "Pasolini was first a thinker, and then an artist," Consoli remarks, relating a comment from Stefano Casi, who said that despite the many genres in which he worked, "In reality only one definition can render with precision the area of cultural diligence attended to by Pasolini: intellectual." Critics tend to look for meanings and messages beyond the actual storylines of Pasolini's work, often interpreting them as evidence of his stance for or against a particular theory, practice, or governing body. The often conflicting messages of his various works led many to define him as indefinable: Edmund White described Pasolini as "a sort of Marxist and, off and on, a Communist, but his politics were too personal, too shifting and too adversarial to fit into any orthodoxy." Also common in critical discussion of Pasolini's work is the subject of obscenity: the graphic nature of much of his work is seen by some as crucial to its message and by others as gratuitous. Some critics have linked this issue with Pasolini's tendency toward impassive recording of events. Robert Crichton found "an almost perverse misplacement of emphasis" in *The Ragazzi,* noting that "pages are devoted to stealing six or eight cauliflowers and a paragraph or two to burning a boy at the stake." These critical themes followed Pasolini when he began to explore filmmaking, a transition which brought new complaints as well. Critics were divided over condemning Pasolini for his lack of technical skill or seeing his directorial style as brilliant in its simplicity. John Bragin wrote, "In contrast to most first films *Accattone* is completely free of technical experiment. It evokes the same tone of sanctity as much of Pasolini's poetry by its direct, frontal presentation of events and characters." Pasolini's third film, *The Gospel According to Saint Matthew,* won the approval of the International Catholic Office of the Cinema (OCIC), which awarded the film its Grand Prix in 1965, "thus making it clear," Maryvonne Butcher stated, "that they considered this picture to be, of all pictures produced in the year, the one which contributed most to the development of spiritual and human values, as well as being outstanding for its technical and artistic standards."

PRINCIPAL WORKS

Poesie a Casarsa (poetry) 1942
Poesie (poetry) 1945
Suite furlan (poetry) 1947

Poesie dialettale del Novecento [with Mario dell'Arco] (essays) 1952

Le ceneri di Gramsci [*The Ashes of Gramsci*] (poetry) 1954

Ragazzi di vita [*The Ragazzi*] (novel) 1955

L'usignolo della Chiesa Cattolica (poetry) 1958

Una vita violenta [*A Violent Life*] (novel) 1959

Passione e ideologia (1948-1958) (poetry) 1960

La religione del mio tempo (poetry) 1961

Accattone [*Beggar*] (screenplay) 1961

Il sogno di una cosa [*A Dream of Something*] (novel) 1962

L'odore dell'India [*The Scent of India*] (travel journal) 1962

Mamma Roma (screenplay) 1962

Il Vangelo secondo Matteo [*The Gospel According to Matthew;* edited by Giacomo Gambetti] (screenplay) 1964

Poesia in forma di rosa (poetry) 1964

Poesie dimenticate (poetry) 1965

Potentissima signora [with Laura Betti] (poetry) 1965

Ali dagli occhi azzurri [*Roman Nights and Other Stories*] (short stories) 1965

Uccellacci e uccellini [*The Hawks and the Sparrows*] (screenplay) 1966

Edipo re [*Oedipus Rex;* edited by Gambetti] (screenplay) 1967

Teorema (novel and film adaptation) 1968

Medea (screenplay) 1970

Poesie (poetry) 1970

Trasumanar e organizzar (poetry) 1971

Empirismo eretico [*Heretical Empiricism*] (essays) 1972

Calderon (play) 1973

Tal cour di un frut: Nel cuore di un fanciullo (poetry) 1974

La nuovo gioventù: Poesie friulane, 1941-1974 (poetry) 1975

Trilogia della vita [*Trilogy of Life*] (*Il Decameron, I racconti di Canterbury* [*Canterbury Tales*], *Il fiore delle Mille e una notte* [*Arabian Nights*]) (screenplays) 1975

Scritti corsari (essays) 1975

Le poesie (poetry) 1975

Petrolio (unfinished novel) 1992

CRITICISM

Maryvonne Butcher (review date Fall 1965)

SOURCE: "Greatest Story Ever Told . . . by a Communist," in *Film Comment,* Vol. 3, No. 4, Fall, 1965, pp. 22-24.

[*In the following review, Butcher asserts that* "The Gospel According to St. Matthew *is incomparably the most effective picture ever made on a scriptural theme."*]

Almost from the beginning of the commercial cinema, it was discovered that the religious film, preferably a religious epic or spectacular, was one of the most foolproof formulas for box-office success. From the earliest *Quo Vadis* or *Ben Hur,* the religious picture has packed them in and even in this materialistic age still does.

Those interested in religion, and even those interested in the cinema, have become increasingly despondent about this. It was not, we felt, Cecil B. DeMille's ingredients of sex and scripture that were really going to fire people with the love of God. Indeed, most of the really good religious films have not been found among the great religious epics, though the most recent *Ben Hur* was pretty good of its kind. There have been pictures like *Monsieur Vincent* which, by the marvellous acting of Pierre Fresnay as St. Vincent de Paul and the solid worth of its presentation, really did make one feel that it was possible to recognise a saint when one met him. Or they have been raw, angry pictures like *Cielo Sulla Palude,* whose portrayal of St. Maria Goretti's ordeal was so realistic that it got itself banned from Ireland, simply for telling the facts of that most savage of stories. Or they have been challenging, provocative movies like *Leon Morin, Priest,* which brought into contemporary terms the problem of the priesthood in the modern world.

Recently, two major films have been made on the gospel story itself. It was perhaps hardly fair to *The Greatest Story Ever Told* that we saw it after we had seen (at the London Film Festival) Pier Paolo Pasolini's incomparably better ***The Gospel According to St. Matthew.*** The great ponderous American epic had a far less chance to shine beside the Italian work than had there been nothing but the disastrous *King of Kings* with which to compare it.

The two films—the one made in America by George Stevens at enormous cost and on an enormous scale with a vast cast of famous names, the other made in Italy at a fraction of the cost and on a scale which can almost be described as domestic—provide almost every contrast that one might care to make. And to my mind, excellent through the intentions of the Hollywood film undeniably are, there is absolutely no doubt that the Italian is not only a much better film, artistically and technically, but also certainly the more authentically religious work, *for all that its director is an Italian communist!* [author's italics]

That this judgment is not entirely personal prejudice is demonstrated by the fact that not only did the International Catholic Office of the Cinema (OCIC) award its prize to Pasolini's film, but the assembled officers of OCIC, gathered from all over the world in Assisi for their general annual meeting, gave it the Grand Prix, thus making it clear that they considered this picture to be, of all pictures produced in the year, the one which contributed most to the development of spiritual and human values, as well as being outstanding for its technical and artistic standards. Remarkable, you may well feel, that a specifically Catholic organization, meeting in Italy of all countries, felt strongly enough about a picture to make so controversial an award. But once you have seen the film, you understand exactly why this revolutionary step was taken.

The commercial cinema has been making scriptural spectaculars for something like fifty years. While we were told in advance that *The Greatest Story Ever Told* was going to be different, except for the skilful use of modern techniques like Panavision, Cinerama and Technicolor, it is hardly any advance on the earlier pictures. The opening sequences of the Magi and the stable are really nothing like so good as the opening sequences in *Ben Hur;* while the camel caravan in the desert with the Christmas card star above it is unbelievably tasteless. Dedicated moviegoers may have found themselves wondering, as I did, whether the heavily symbolic line of crucified corpses on the road taken by Mary and Joseph could have been borrowed from the final shots of *Spartacus.* It must be agreed that some of the most valid sequences of this very, very long film were unashamedly borrowed, and borrowed from a category of film in which American directors hardly ever put a foot wrong—the western. So we smiled, but appreciatively, when the Roman soldiers were lined up in silhouette along a bluff, in the fashion of countless Indian marauders; and the murderous charge of Herod's troops upon the Innocents at play could have been duplicated from almost any Civil War film; and both these loans were at once effective and beautiful. Which is not what one could say about the vast blown-up buildings which housed Herod or Pilate or the Ark of the Covenant—they seemed to have been lifted from the architectural excesses which loaded the second (and inferior) half of *Cleopatra.*

> **The Gospel According to St. Matthew is incomparably the most effective picture ever made on a scriptural theme.**
> —*Maryvonne Butcher*

Pasolini's film, on the other hand, came again and again with a salutary shock of surprise, starting with the very first sequence. *Gospel* was shot in a series of episodes in which the scale was clearly deliberately reduced. With neither the money nor the facilities to embark on farflung locations, Pasolini made his picture in the rock country of his own southern Italy, as bare and as austere as Stevens's American desert, but far more intimately related to the scale of men working for their living in an unkind land. Pasolini employs no stars. His Christ is a young Spanish student with a thin, stern face, wind-blown hair and a rare, sweet smile, but his performance is *allowed* to be more significant than the great Swedish actor von Sydow in the American epic. Pasolini

has—quite naturally, considering his own background—treated the gospel more as a divinely-inspired document of social revolution than as a great panorama of historical events—the blind see, the lame walk and, above all, the poor have the gospel preached to them.

When we come to what Stevens made into great set-pieces—the entry into Jerusalem or the Last Supper—Pasolini makes them as domestic as he can. I have never seen any representation of the Last Supper which made one feel so immediately "This is how it must have been"—a gathering of tired men who love each other sit down to a meal in a humble room and, suddenly, become aware that this is something quite different from anything that has ever happened before.

And this, surely, is the true aim of a religious picture—that it should disconcert and dislocate the comfortable preconceptions of the believer and, at the same time, make the unbeliever feel that after all there is something valid and important in a story that he has dismissed as a pious convention. It was not for nothing that this intelligent and sensitive Italian Marxist dedicated his picture to "the memory of good Pope John" who achieved very much the same kind of breakthrough to the world, making even the most cynical acknowledge the tremendous power of sheer goodness and charity.

In my opinion, *The Gospel According to St. Matthew* is incomparably the most effective picture ever made on a scriptural theme, and it reduces the grandiose *Greatest Story Ever Told,* however good its intentions may have been, to the proportions of a conventional "holy picture."

Pier Paolo Pasolini with James Blue (interview date Fall 1965)

SOURCE: "Pier Paolo Pasolini: An Interview with James Blue," in *Film Comment,* Vol. 3, No. 4, Fall, 1965, pp. 25-32.

[*In the following interview, Pasolini discusses how he approached his film* The Gospel According to St. Matthew *and explains his use of non-professional actors.*]

[*BLUE:*] *I have been wondering what I should ask you. Often I ask questions of directors that seem a little stupid, you see, but I don't want to avoid those, for finally the stupid questions are the ones to which I most want reply. I know that it will be difficult—I don't think I would be able to answer very well concerning my own films—but I hope that your replies help me to arrive at certain conclusions later. Have you understood?*

[PASOLINI:] Yes, I understand.

You know I'm compiling a book on the directing of the non-actor. I am meeting many directors. The book is primarily a way for me to organize my own thinking and to take advantage of the experiences of other directors in order to see how I may be able to create more completely a kind of human existence in front of the camera, without the use of professional actors, and without falling into cinema conventions. The ideas I'm looking for have been discreetly developing for twenty years. So that's why I'm writing this book, to clarify my ideas. Have you understood?

Yes, very well.

Let me start with a question that may seem stupid—how do you create? Are you aware—even vaguely—of certain recurring processes? What helps you? What pushes you to create? When you want to work, what steps do you take to get started?

What is it that urges me to create. As far as film is concerned, there is no difference between film and literature and poetry—there is this same feeling that I have never gone into deeply. I began to write poetry when I was seven years old, and what it was that made me write poetry at the age of seven I have never understood. Perhaps it was the urge to express oneself and the urge to bear witness of the world and to partake in or to create an action in which we are involved, to engage oneself in that act.

Putting the question in that manner forces me to give you a vaguely spiritualistic answer . . . a bit irrational. It makes me feel a bit on the defensive.

Some artists collect information on a subject, like journalists. Do you do this?

Yes, there is this aspect, the documentary element. A naturalistic writer documents himself through his production. Because my writing, as Roland Barthe would say, contains naturalistic elements, it is evident therefore that it contains a great interest in living and documentary *events*. In my writing there are deliberate elements of a naturalistic type of realism and therefore the love for real things . . . a fusion of traditional academic elements and of contemporary literary movements.

What bought you to **The Gospel According to St. Matthew,** *and once you had the idea, how did you start work on it? Why did you want to do it?*

I recognized the desire to make **The Gospel** from a feeling I had. I opened the Bible by chance and began to read the first pages, the first lines of St. Matthew's Gospel, and the idea of making a film of it came to me. It's evident that this is a feeling, an impulse that is not clearly definable. Mulling over this feeling, this impulse, this irrational movement or experience, all my story began to become clear to me as well as my entire literary career.

Once you had this feeling, what did you look for to give it form, to make the feeling concrete?

I discovered first of all that there is an old latent religious streak in my poetry. I remember lines of poetry I wrote when I was eighteen or nineteen years old, and they were of a religious nature. I realized, too, that much of my Marxism has a foundation that is irrational and mystical and religious. But the sum total of my psychological constitution tends to make me see things—not from the lyrical-documentary point of view—but rather from an epic point of view. There is something epic in my view of the world. And I suddenly had the idea of doing **The Gospel,** which would be a tale that can be defined metrically as Epic-lyric.

Although St. Matthew wrote without metrics, he would have the rhythm of epic and lyric production. And for this reason, I have renounced in the film any kind of realistic and naturalistic reconstruction. I completely abandoned any kind of archaeology and philology, which nevertheless interest me in themselves. I didn't want to make an historical reconstruction. I preferred to leave things in their religious state, that is, their mythical state. Epic-mythic.

Not desiring to reconstruct settings that were not philosophically exact—reconstructed on a sound stage by scene designers and technicians—and furthermore not wanting to reconstruct the ancient Jews, I was obliged to find everything—the characters and the ambiance—in reality. And so the rule that dominated the making of the film was the rule of *analogy.* That is, I found settings that were not reconstructions but that were analogous to ancient Palestine. The characters, too—I didn't reconstruct characters but tried to find individuals who were analogous. I was obliged to scour southern Italy, because I realized that the pre-industrial agricultural world, the still feudal area of southern Italy, was the historical setting analogous to ancient Palestine. One by one I found the settings that I needed for **The Gospel.** I took these Italian settings and used them to represent the originals. I took the city of Matera, and without changing it in any way, I used it to represent the ancient city of Jerusalem. Or the little caverns of the village between Lucania and Puglia are used exactly as they were, without any modifications, to represent Bethelehem. And I did the same thing for the characters. The chorus of background characters I chose from the faces of the peasants of Lucania and Puglia and Calabria.

How did you work with these non-actors to integrate them

into a story that was not their own, although analogous to their own?

I didn't do anything. I didn't tell them anything. In fact, I didn't even tell them precisely what characters they were playing. Because I never chose an actor *as an interpreter.* I always chose an actor *for what he is.* That is, I never asked anyone to transform himself into anything other than what he is.

Naturally, things were a little more difficult with regard to the main actors. For example, the fellow who played Christ was a student from Barcelona. Except for telling him that he was playing the part of Christ, that's all I said. I never gave him any kind of preliminary speech. I never told him to transform himself into something else, to interpret, to feel that he was Christ. I always told him to be just what he was. I chose him because he was what he was, and I never for one moment wanted him to be anyone else other than what he was—that's why I chose him.

But to make your Spanish student move, breathe, speak, perform necessary actions—how did you obtain what you wished without telling him something?

Let me explain. It happened that in making **The Gospel,** the footage of the characters told me almost always the truth in a very dramatic fashion—that is, I had to cut a lot of scenes from **The Gospel** because I couldn't "mystify" them. They rang false. I don't know what it is, but the eye of the camera always manages to express the interior of a character. This interior essence can be masked through the ability of a professional actor, or it can be "mystified" through the ability of the director by means of cutting and divers tricks. In **The Gospel** I was never able to do this. What I mean to say is that the photogram or the image on the film filters through what that man is—in his true reality, as he is in life.

> Being a "non-professional" director I've always had to "invent" a technique that consists of shooting only a very brief bit at one time. Always in little bits—I never shoot a scene continuously. And so even if I'm using a non-actor lacking the technique of an actor, he's able to sustain the part—the illusion—because the takes are so brief.
> —*Pier Paolo Pasolini*

It is possible at times in movies that a man who is devious and shady can play the part of one who is naive and ingenuous. For example, I could have taken a professional and given him the part of one of the three magi—an unimpor-

tant part—and by the way it is clear that there is a deep candor in the souls of the three magi. But I didn't use professionals, and therefore I couldn't have their ability to transform themselves into others. I used real human beings, and so I made a mistake and misjudged a man psychologically. My error was immediately evident in the photographed image. There is another rather unpleasant example that has sprung to mind—for the two actors who played those possessed by the Devil,—I chose actors from the Centro Sperimentale film school in Rome. I chose them in a hurry. Later, I had to cut the scene because it was obvious that they were two actors from the Centro Sperimentale.

In reality, my method consists simply of being sincere, honest, penetrating, precise in choosing men whose psychological essence is real and genuine. Once I've chosen them, then my work is immensely simplified. I don't have to do with them what I have to do with professional actors: tell them what they have to do and what they haven't to do and the sort of people they are supposed to represent and so forth. I simply tell them to say these words in a certain frame of mind and that's all. And they say them.

To get back to Christ, once I had chosen the person whose essence or interior was more or less that needed to play the part of Christ, I never obliged him to do any specific things. My suggestions were made one by one, instance by instance, moment by moment, scene by scene, action by action. I said to him "do this" and "get angry." I didn't even tell him how. I simply said "you're getting angry" and he got angry in the way he usually got angry and I didn't intervene in any way.

My work is facilitated by the fact that I never shoot entire scenes. Being a "non-professional" director I've always had to "invent" a technique that consists of shooting only a very brief bit at one time. Always in little bits—I never shoot a scene continuously. And so even if I'm using a non-actor lacking the technique of an actor, he's able to sustain the part—the illusion—because the takes are so brief. And if he doesn't have the technical ability of an actor, at least he doesn't get lost, he doesn't freeze up.

Although I was able to find characters analogous to the wise men or to an angel or to Saint Joseph, it was extremely difficult to find a character analogous to Jesus Christ. And so I had to be content with finding someone who at least came close to resembling Christ externally and interiorly, but actually I had to construct Christ in the cutting room.

Although other directors make tests, I never make them. I had to make one for Christ, though—not for myself—but for the producer who wanted a certain guarantee. When I choose actors, instinctively I choose someone who knows how to act. It's a kind of instinct that so far hasn't betrayed me except in very minor and very special cases. So far I've chosen Franco Citti for *Accattone* and Ettore Garofolo for the boy in *Mamma Roma.* In *La Ricotta,* a young boy from the slums of Rome. I've always guessed right, that from the very moment in which I chose the face that seemed to me exact for the character, instinctively he reveals himself a potential actor. When I choose non-actors, I choose potential actors.

Naturally, Christ was a more difficult thing for me than Franco Citti because Franco, after all, was to play a part that was more or less himself. First of all, this young Spanish student at the beginning was inhibited about playing the part of Christ—he wasn't even a believer. And so the first problem was that I had playing Christ a fellow who didn't even believe in Christ. Naturally this caused inhibitions. This young student wasn't an extrovert or a simple, normal type of person. He was psychologically very complex, and for this reason it was difficult the first few days to get him to win out over his timidity, his restraint, his inhibitions, while for the other actors I didn't have this problem. The very minute I put them in front of the camera, they acted the way I wanted them to.

What did you do with your Spanish non-believing non-actor to get the results you wanted?

Nothing really. I simply appealed to his good will. He was a very intelligent and a very cultured young man who became bound to me by the friendship that grew up between us in those few days—however, he had the basis of an ideological background and a rather strong desire to be useful to me. It was by this means that he succeeded in overcoming his timidity.

As far as the rest goes, I had him perform in very small segments, one at a time, without even preparing them first. I would suggest the expressions while he acted. Inasmuch as we were shooting without sound, I could talk to an actor while he was performing. It was a little bit like a sculptor who makes a sculpture with little improvised blows of the chisel. While the actor was acting, I said to him "Look here"—and I told him each expression, one by one, and he followed them almost mechanically. I shot everything that way. He had the speech memorized more or less, and he began to say it. He had to—for example—take ten steps forward, or move, or look at someone. I never told him beforehand, except in a very vague way, what it was all about, and gradually as he performed, I said "now look at me . . . now look down there with an angry expression . . . now your expression softens . . . look toward me and soften your expression slowly, very slowly. Now look at me!" And so while the camera rolled, I told him these things. I prepared the action beforehand, in a very vague way, so that he would know more or less what he was supposed to do and where he was supposed to go. Whatever the nuances,

the little movements, I suggested to him one by one. Prior to the shot, I gave him general movements and told him more or less what he was supposed to do. Then I explained these things more precisely while we shot. Once in a while I would surprise him—I would say to him "Now look at me with a sweet expression on your face." And while he did this I would say suddenly "Now get angry!" And he obeyed me.

Didn't this request make him attempt to imitate the way an actor he had seen got angry?

No. Actors would be tempted to do this, but one who is not an actor—for example, those whom I chose—would never do this. It's not possible, because they have never confronted themselves with the technical problems of an actor—that is, he doesn't have a technical idea of "anger," he has a natural and genuine idea of anger.

I've done this rather often in other films. For example, I would have the person say a line that was not what it was supposed to be in the text. If he was supposed to say "I hate you," I would have him say "Good Morning," and then when I dubbed I would put in "I hate you." Normally, I should have said to him, "All right now, say 'I hate you' as if you were saying 'good morning.'" But this is pretty complicated reasoning for a person who is not an actor. So I simply tell him to say "Good morning," and then in the dubbing I put in his mouth "I hate you."

For dubbing, do you use non-actors or professionals?

I do both. That is, I take non-actors who generally reveal themselves to be splendid dubbers. For Christ I was obliged to use a professional actor, so it depends on the circumstances. More than anything else, I try to balance everything out between the professional and non-professional performances. For instance, the boy in *Mamma Roma* did his own dubbing. But Franco Citti could not do his own dubbing, for even though he was *bravissimo* his voice was rather unpleasant. So I had him dub another character.

If you don't give the non-actor much explanation of character, do you at least tell him the story?

Yes, I do, in two words. Just out of curiosity. But I never go into a serious discussion with him. If he has any doubts . . . if he says to me "what do I have to do here," I try to explain to him. But always point by point, particular by particular, never the whole thing.

Do you add expressive gestures, which are not normally a part of the non-actor's personal comportment?

No, I never have him do gestures that are not his. I always let him use the gestures that are natural to him. I tell him what he has to do—for example, slap someone or pick up a glass—but I let him do this with the gestures that are natural to him. I never intervene regarding his gestures.

If I want to underline some act, I do so with my own means, with technical means—with the camera, with the shot, with editing. I don't have him emphasize it. Actually, I am very careful not to indicate to him the "intention," because these "intentions" are the phony part of the actor.

Do you trick at all, in order to produce emotional responses?

Up to now it has never happened. If it were necessary, I'd do it. It's never happened to me because my actors do not have petit-bourgeois inhibitions. They don't care. They do what I tell them, generously. Franco Citti, Ettore Garofolo, the protagonist of *La Ricotta,* and my Christ as well—they gave of themselves completely, blindly. They don't have that conventionality or false modesty of hypocrites, so I've never had to do this. However, if I had to trick, I'd do it.

Do you see a way of directing the bourgeois-class person who is a non-actor?

I was faced with this problem filming **The Gospel.** Whereas in my other films my characters were all "of the people," for **The Gospel** I had some characters who were not. The Apostles, for example, belonged to the ruling classes of their time, and so obeying my usual rule of analogy, I was obliged to take members of the present-day ruling class. Because the Apostles were people who were definitely out of the ordinary, I chose intellectuals—from the bourgeoisie, yes—but intellectuals.

Although these non-actors as Apostles were intellectuals, the fact that they had to play intellectuals removed, not instinctively but consciously, the inhibition of which you spoke. However, in the case of one's having to use bourgeois actors who are not intellectuals, I think that you can get what you want from them, too. All you have to do is love them.

How did you work with the intellectuals to rid them of their inhibitions?

The process was identical with that for the lower-class performers. With the former naturally, I used a language that was on a more elevated level. But my methods were the same.

Do you feel the need of knowing your people a long time before shooting, to make friends with them, to learn their natural gestures in order to use them later?

I had known Franco Citti for years, because he was the

brother of a friend. I knew his character more or less. On the other hand, Ettore Garofolo of **Mamma Roma**—I saw him once in a bar where he was working as a waiter. I wrote my whole script around him without speaking to him further. Because I preferred not to know him. I took him and began to shoot after having seen him for just that one minute. I don't like to make an organized and calculated effort to know someone. If you can intuit a person, you know him already.

Generally I have very precisely in mind what I'm going to do. Because I've written the script myself, I've already organized the scene in a given way. I see the scene not only as a director but also with the different eyes of the scriptwriter. In addition, I choose the settings. I go to these places and make an adjustment of what I've written in my script to fit the place where we are going to shoot. And so when I go to shoot, I more or less know already how the scene is going to go.

> **Generally I have very precisely in mind what I'm going to do. Because I've written the script myself, I've already organized the scene in a given way. I see the scene not only as a director but also with the different eyes of the scriptwriter.**
> —*Pier Paolo Pasolini*

I did this for every film except **The Gospel.** With **The Gospel,** the thing was so delicate that it would have been easy to fall into the ridiculous and the banal and the typical costume film genre. The dangers were so many that it wasn't possible to foresee them all. And it being so difficult, we had to shoot three or four times more material than necessary. In effect, most of the scenes I created in the cutting room. I shot the whole **Gospel** with two cameras. I shot every scene from two or three angles, amassing three or four times more material than necessary. It was as if I had done a documentary on the life of Christ. By chance. With the moviola, I constructed the scene.

Did you seek a particular style in the framing, and was this possible with two cameras going?

Yes, I always have a rather clear idea of the shot I want, a kind of shot that is almost natural to me. But with **The Gospel** I wanted to break away from this technique because of a very complicated problem. In two words it's this: I had a very precise style or technique with which I had experimented in **Accattone,** in **Mamma Roma** and in the preceding films, a style which is, as I said before, fundamentally religious and epic by its very nature. And so I thought that my style—possessing naturally these qualities of sacredness and epicness—would go well with *The Gospel* also. But in practice, that was not the case. Because in *The Gospel* this sacredness and epic quality became a prison, false and insincere, and so I had to reconstruct my whole technique and forget everything I knew, everything that I had learned with *Accattone* and *Mamma Roma,* and begin from the beginning. I relied on chance, on confusion, and so forth.

All this was due to the fact that I am not a believer. In *Accattone,* I myself could tell a story in the first-person because I was the author and I believed in that story, but I could not tell the story of Christ—making him the son of God—with myself as the author of this story, because I'm not a believer. So I didn't work as an author. And so this forced me to tell the story of Christ indirectly, as seen through the eyes of one who does believe. And as always when one tells something indirectly, the style changes. While the style of a story told *directly* has certain characteristics, the style of a story told *indirectly* has other characteristics. That is, if in literature I am describing Rome in my own words, I describe it in one style. But if I describe Rome—using the words of some Roman character—the result is a completely different style because of the dialect, the popular language, and so forth. The style of my preceding films was a simple style—almost straightforward, almost hieratic—while the style of *The Gospel* is chaotic, complex, disordered. Despite this difference in style, I shot all my films in little pieces all the same. Except the frame, the point of view, the movement of the extras were changed.

I have read that you have said that you have trouble with actors. Why is that?

I wouldn't like people to take this too literally, not in a dogmatic way. In *La Ricotta* I used Orson Welles and I got along beautifully with him. In the film I'm making now I'm going to use Totò, a popular Italian comic, and I'm sure everything will work out fine. When I say I don't work well with actors I'm uttering a *relative* truth—I want to be sure that this is clear. My difficulty lies in the fact that I'm not a professional director, and so I haven't learned the cinematographic techniques. And that which I have learned least of all is what they call the "technique of the actor." I don't know what kind of language to use to express myself to the actor. And in this sense, I'm not capable of working with actors.

After your directing experiences with Anna Magnani in **Mamma Roma** *and Orson Welles in* **La Ricotta,** *what have you learned about using professional actors as distinct from non-actors?*

The principal difference is that the actor has an art of his own. He has his own way of expressing himself, his own technique which seeks to add itself to mine—and I cannot succeed in amalgamating the two. Being an author, I could

not conceive of writing a book together with someone else, and so the presence of an actor is like the presence of another author in the film.

With Welles, how did you get a result you felt was fruitful?

For two reasons—first of all in **La Ricotta** Welles did not play another character. He played himself. What he really did was a caricature of himself. And also because Welles, in addition to being an actor, is also an intellectual—so in reality, I used him as an intellectual director rather than as an actor. Because he's an extremely intelligent man, he understood this right away and there was no problem. He brought it off well. It was a very brief and simple part, with no great complications. I told him my intention and I let him do as he pleased. He understood what I wanted immediately and did it in a manner that was completely satisfying to me.

With Magnani, it was much more difficult. Because she is an actress in the true sense of the word. She has a whole baggage of technical and expressive notions into which I was unable to enter, because it was the first time I had any kind of contact with an actor. At present, I've had a little bit of experience and at least can face the problem—but at that time, I couldn't even face it.

Now that you have experience, have you thought how you may overcome this acting "baggage" of the professional performer? You said you are using Totò in your next film—have you reflected upon your way of directing him?

> **My difficulty lies in the fact that I'm not a professional director, and so I haven't learned the cinematographic techniques. And that which I have learned least of all is what they call the "technique of the actor." I don't know what kind of language to use to express myself to the actor. And in this sense, I'm not capable of working with actors.**
> —*Pier Paolo Pasolini*

Yes, I think the way to get around this problem is to *use* the fact that they are actors. Just as with a non-actor I use a whole series of things unexpected and unforeseen—leaving them to their own vital confusion (for example, when I tell them to say "Good morning" instead of "I hate you"), leaving them to the ambiguousness of their *being*—so I must use the actor *specifically* for his actor's baggage. If I try to use an actor as if he were not an actor, I would be wrong. Because in the cinema—at least in my cinema—the truth always comes out sooner or later. On the other hand, if I use an actor *knowing* that he is an actor, and therefore using him for that which he *is* and not for that which he is not, I hope to succeed. Naturally, the character whom he interprets must be adapted to this idea.

It just happens that the characters in my new film are all ambiguous characters who have something real, human, profound about them, and at the same time something invented, absurd, clownish and fable-like. The double nature of the actor, Totò-man and Totò-Clown, this double nature can be used by me for my character. In Totò himself this double nature—man and clown, or man and actor—functions because it corresponds to the double nature of the character in the film.

Do you plan to explain to Totò this double nature you've outlined?

Yes, of course. As soon as I met him I explained that I needed a character just like himself. I needed a Neapolitan. Someone profoundly human, who has at the same time this art that is clownish and abstract. Yes, I told him right away.

Are you not afraid that now that he knows, Totò will try to play both the clown and the human being?

No, I told him to make him feel freer. Because I saw that he would worry about it. It's the first time that he has worked on a film that has this kind of ideological content. Of course, he has made several good films, but they were always on an artistic level, without political commitment. So probably he was a little worried. In order to leave him completely free, I told him—so that he could go on doing what he had always done, so he won't have to do anything different.

Do you rehearse a lot or do you shoot immediately?

I never rehearse. I shoot right away.

Does this impose simple camera work?

My camera movements are very simple. For **The Gospel,** I used camera movements that were a little more complicated, but I never use a dolly, for example. I've always shot in pieces. Shot by shot. A few pans and very simple tracking shots but nothing more.

What are your observations about the aesthetic and technical characteristics of film as you have gained experience?

My lack of professional experience has not encouraged me to invent. Rather it has urged me to "re-invent." For instance, I never studied at the Centro Sperimentale or any other school, and so when the time came for me to shoot a panoramic shot, for me it was like the first time in the history of cinema that a panorama was shot. And so I re-invented the panoramic.

Only a person with a great deal of professional experience is capable of inventing technically. As far as technical inventions go, I have never made any. I may have invented a given style—in fact, my films are recognizable for a particular style—but style does not always imply technical inventions. Godard is full of technical inventions. In *Alphaville* there are four or five things that are completely invented—for example those shots printed in negative. Certain technical rule-breakings of Godard are the result of a pains-taking personal study.

> **Only a person with a great deal of professional experience is capable of inventing technically. As far as technical inventions go, I have never made any. I may have invented a given style—in fact, my films are recognizable for a particular style—but style does not always imply technical inventions.**
> **—*Pier Paolo Pasolini***

As for me, I never dared to try experiments of this kind, because I have no technical background. And so my first step was to simplify the technique. This is contradictory, because as a writer I tend to be extremely complicated—that is, my written page is technically very complex. While I was writing **Una Vita Violenta**—technically very complex—I was shooting **Accattone,** which was technically very simple. This is the principal limitation of my cinematic career, because I believe that an author must have complete knowledge of all his technical instruments. A partial knowledge is a limitation. Therefore, at this particular moment, I believe that the first period of my cinematic work is about to close. And the second period is about to start, in which I will be a professional director also as far as technique in concerned.

But what have you discovered about film in an aesthetic sense?

Well, to tell the truth, the only thing I discovered is the pleasure of discovery.

You're talking like Godard now.

I answered like Godard because the question is impossible to answer. Look, if I believed in a teleology of the cinema, in a teleology of development, if I believed in an end-goal of development, in progress as improvement . . . but I don't believe in a "bettering," an improvement. I think that one *grows,* but one does not *improve.* "Improving" seems to me an hypocritical alibi. Now, believing in the pure growth of each one of us, I see the development of my style as a continuous modification about which I can say nothing.

How do you conceive the structure of your films, what makes them move from one end to another?

It's too demanding a question. For the moment it's impossible to answer. But I would like for you to read in *Cahiers* an article I wrote. This question implies not only an examination of my films and my conscience, it brings up the question of my Marxism and my whole cultural struggle during the 1950's. The question is too vast. It's impossible.

But let me say this now in a very schematic fashion. At this point, the cinema is dividing itself into really two large trunks, and these two different types of films correspond to what we already have in literature: that is, one type on a high level and another type on a low level. While cinema production until now has given us films of both a high and low level, the distribution apparatus has been the same for both. But now the organization or structure of the cinema industry is starting to differentiate . . . the *cinéma d'essai* is becoming more important and will soon represent a channel for distribution through which certain films will be distributed, whereas the remainder of the distribution will take place normally. This will bring about the birth of two completely different cinemas. The high level of cinema—that is, the *cinéma d'essai*—will cater to a selected public and will have its own history. And the other level will have its own story.

In this important change, the selection of non-actors will be one of the most important structural aspects. Probably the structure of this high level cinema will be modified by the fact that no longer will there be an industrial organization hanging over it. And so all kinds of experiments will be possible, including that of using non-actors, and this will transform the cinema even stylistically.

In Cahiers, *do you speak of aesthetic structure?*

The structure of cinema has a special unity. If the structuralist critic were to describe the structural characteristics of the cinema, he would not distinguish a story cinema from a non-story cinema. I don't believe that this story distinction affects the structure of cinema; rather it affects the superstructure—I mean the style. The lack or the presence of a story is not a structural factor. I know that some of the French structuralists have attempted to analyse the cinema, but I don't believe that they have succeeded in making these distinctions.

Literature is unique, it has unity. Literary structures are unique and include both prose and poetry. Nevertheless,

there is a language of prose and a language of poetry, although the literary structure is *one*. In the same way, the cinema will have these distinctions. Obviously, the structure of cinema is *one*. The structural laws regarding any film are more or less the same. A banal western or a film by Godard have structures that are fundamentally the same. A certain rapport with the spectator, a certain way of photographing and framing are the identical elements of all films.

The difference is this: the film of Godard is written according to the typical characteristics of poetic language; whereas the common cinema is written according to the typical characteristics of prose language. For example, the lack of story is simply the prevalence of poetic language over prose language. It isn't true that there isn't a story; there is a story, but instead of being narrated in its *integrality,* it is narrated *elliptically,* with spurts of imagination, fantasy, allusion. It is narrated in a distorted way—however, there is a story.

Fundamentally, the distinction to be made is between a cinema of prose and a cinema of poetry. However, the cinema of poetry is not necessarily poetic. Often one may adopt the tenets and canons of the cinema of poetry and yet make a bad and pretentious film. Another director may adopt the tenets and canons of the prose film—that is, he could narrate a story—and yet he creates poetry.

Robert Crichton (review date 10 November 1968)

SOURCE: "Ragazzi Will Be Ragazzi, and Sometimes They'll Be Scugnizzi," in *The New York Times Book Review,* November 10, 1968, pp. 4, 44.

[*In the following review, Crichton criticizes* The Ragazzi, *asserting that "there is a sensation of the writing being fashioned because the style is fashionable, that it is an artifice, not an art, a stylization and not a style."*]

Thirteen years ago, when this book was published in Italy, it set off a storm of controversy. There were those who wished to do to the author what was done to Mussolini: up by the heels in some vacant lot in the shabby outskirts of town, Pasolini country. American readers today will be puzzled about the reasons for the uproar. By present standards **The Ragazzi** conceivably could be merchandised as one of those hip "young adult" novels coming into vogue.

There isn't much to be puzzled about. As Luigi Barzini has documented, the Italians have perfected the ability to deceive themselves about the reality of life around them to a form of art. Someone else has pointed out (me, in fact) that if the mass of Italian peasants ever allowed themselves to face what the future held in store for them there would be lines of people outside graveyards demanding to be buried.

Because of this need for self-deception, the first condition imposed on Italian writers is that they make life bearable and acceptable. To his credit, Pasolini chose not to do this. He wrote, instead, about the *ragazzi,* the street urchins of Rome, specifically the ones who came to age in the disjointed and disillusioning years after the war, the way they were. Pasolini's *ragazzi* lie and steal. They are cruel and cynical; they despise authority, mock the church, experience sexual intercourse while still in short pants. Worst of all, they actually use all those words that everyone in Italy hears them use every hour of the day.

So the roof fell in. Pasolini had broken the code. In fairness to critics the use of the title word was partly to blame. *Ragazzi* actually means "kids," and the term thus implies that the book is a picture of all Italian youth. Pasolini is actually writing about a sub-breed—the deserted, desperate, homeless waifs of Italy known as *scugnizzi.* The word derives from the verb *scugnare,* which means "to gyrate, to spin around like a top," which is marvelously descriptive.

Pasolini, then, deserves credit for courage, but a nagging question remains: Does his book have any value or meaning for Americans today? The answer is, not very much. Part of the reason for this lies in the form of the book, and part in the author's approach.

> **Pasolini's *ragazzi* lie and steal. They are cruel and cynical; they despise authority, mock the church, experience sexual intercourse while still in short pants. Worst of all, they actually use all those words that everyone in Italy hears them use every hour of the day. So the roof fell in. Pasolini had broken the code.**
> **—*Robert Crichton***

This is not a novel, but a loosely connected series of sketches, verbal pictures, unresolved short stories and fragments of life, sometimes revolving around a boy named Riccetto, sometimes around his friends and sometimes around no one in particular. There is no effort to transfigure experience or to make any of it meaningful, even that which is meaningless. The result is an imbalanced mass of behavioristic description, whose intent is not to re-create a human being or a life, but to expose a condition of life.

This in itself needn't have been fatal if the approach had been different. Pasolini seems to be saying that one can't question, one can't reflect, probe, comment; one can only

record. While reading his book, I had the distinct image of the author trailing his subject through the weeds of the vacant lots where most of the scenes take place—hand-held camera whirring quietly, recording, recording, but always only the surface of things, life as seen through a strip of film darkly. It came as no surprise to learn that the publisher compares his work with the neo-realist films (*Shoeshine, The Bicycle Thief*) that came out of Italy just after the war, or that Pasolini has spent the major part of his energies in film making during the last ten years.

Pasolini's book, "the non-committed" novel, represents a kind of writing that continues to have an effect on American writers and intellectuals, is generally considered "serious" (it rarely contains any humor) and is rewarded with a highly inflated respect. Because the author is really a camera, because the writing is really notes for a future producer, the prose often lacks energy, becomes secondary. To cover this lapse of literary imagination, however, writers have discovered the winning effect of what used to be thought of as "existential" prose. More recently, it has come to be known as a sort of "white style," where everything is impersonal, dry, devoid of emotion, not abstract in the way of Kafka, but transparent in the way of film.

There is always the sensation of a lens between the matter and the beholder. The effect, worked at, is one of flatness. The tone is down, everything down, always down, very fashionably down—and that is ultimately, the word for the style, fashionable.

Years ago, I ended a short story this way: "They told him she was dead. He went out into the hall. It was bright in the hall. He noticed one of the bulbs was out. Someone would have to fix that bulb. Outside it was cold. It hadn't been cold before but now it was cold. He noticed the leaves were falling. Someone was going to have to rake those leaves." Down, man! Bulbs going out, repetitive words, leaves falling. As much attention paid to a blank bulb as a human death. The writing is what I term "ostentatious simplicity."

There is almost a perverse misplacement of emphasis in this fashionable writing. In **The Ragazzi,** pages are devoted to stealing six or eight cauliflowers and a paragraph or two to burning a boy at the stake.

There are a few writers who use these techniques in a legitimate way. I think of Cesare Pavese and Tomasso Landolfi, both simple and quiet, almost as if in protest to their loquacious countrymen. For some reason their writing is genuine, there is the hint of genius operating and the simplicity of the prose strikes one as stemming from compressed intelligence.

But for the others—and for this novel—there is a sensation

of the writing being fashioned because the style is fashionable, that it is an artifice, not an art, a stylization and not a style. Here is the end of Pasolini's book. It's about as bad as the end of my short story:

"There wasn't even a car going by, or one of the old buses that ran through that section. In the enormous silence, all you could hear was a tank, lost somewhere beyond the playing fields in Ponte Mammolo, plowing up the horizon with its roar."

Some silence! Some tank! Some book!

Olga Ragusa (essay date 1969)

SOURCE: "Gadda, Pasolini, and Experimentalism: Form or Ideology?" in *From* Verismo *to Experimentalism: Essays on the Modern Italian Novel,* edited by Sergio Pacifici, Indiana University Press, 1969, pp. 246-69.

[*In the following excerpt, Ragusa compares the works of Pasolini and Carlo Emilio Gadda and explores each writer's relationship with experimentalism.*]

The subject of this essay is threefold—threefold precisely in the sense which the title implies of simply juxtaposing the names of two writers and a concept rather than relating them more closely at a deeper level. To do full justice to the complex development of Carlo Emilio Gadda, to the equally complex but entirely different development of Pier Paolo Pasolini, and to the multiple aspects of linguistic and structural experimentation in Italian literature, three distinct and quite extensive studies would be required.

The connection between Gadda and Pasolini is not genetic. Although to the hasty reader the two are united by their rejection of the traditional literary language and their tapping of the dialect resources of Italy, it cannot truly be maintained that the older writer is a necessary premise for the younger, as Virgil was for Dante, Mallarmé for Valéry, or Shakespeare for Manzoni. Pasolini's work, which ranges from lyric to philosophical poetry, from political to literary journalism, from travel reports to film scenarios, is not patterned on the example—the Italians would say "the lesson"—of Gadda, who made his debut in 1926 in the pages of the review *Solaria* with literary essays and narrative fragments that owe much to the hermeticism of that time.

But though the connection is not a genetic one, it exists. And it exists primarily by virtue of the concept of experimentalism. The term was first used by the Romance philologist Gianfranco Contini in his studies of early Italian literature. It was then chosen by Pasolini to describe an important, and

to him determining, aspect of the poetic production of the Fifties. And finally it was adopted by the new avant-garde, the so-called *Gruppo 63*. This group of writers—this "new literary generation," as their mentor Luciano Anceschi called them—first gathered together in 1963 at a noisy literary congress in Palermo which reminded many of the participants of the fuss and fanfare raised half a century earlier by the futurists. The writers of *Gruppo 63* were convinced that, as one of their exponents put it, the literature of the future would be marked by experimentation with form and not with subject matter, that is, by a new use of the means of expression rather than by raising to literary dignity—as was done in naturalism, for instance—subjects that had formerly been avoided. Angelo Guglielmi, one of the theoreticians of the group wrote:

> Up to now language has tried to reflect reality as in a mirror. Henceforth language must take its place at the very heart of reality and instead of being a mirror must become a faithful recording machine. Or, as a second solution, language must remain outside and look in at reality as through a filter, so that objects will appear in distorted, surrealistic, or hallucinatory images and forms, and thus once again be capable of revealing their hidden meanings.

In the new literature, then, and in the experimental novel, as it was soon to be called, language would no longer state and describe, but mimic and express. Pasolini made a similar distinction in the 1956 article **"Il neo-sperimentalismo"** referred to above, when he opposed the "stylistic syndrome of the new 'committed' writers" to "pathological, expressionistic neo-experimentalism." But while both uses of language, the mimetic and the expressionistic, appear true and revolutionary innovations with respect to its conventional use in narrative to reflect the chronology of events in terms of logical discourse, only the second, the expressionistic, actually represents a total subversion of the accepted social and psychological structures. Only the expressionistic use of language, in the words of another critic, concerns itself with "the perceptual level, with the way in which time and space are conceived, how objects are seen, how feelings are recognized and designated, how syntax is articulated." Or to return to the connection between Gadda and Pasolini, only Gadda—for reasons that I hope will become clear in the course of this essay—is recognized by the new avant-garde, whether it thinks of itself as politically committed or uncommitted, as a true and authentic forerunner.

There are certain obvious differences between Gadda and Pasolini, a consideration of which will, I believe, place the discussion of their work in a better perspective. The first— and it is no mean one—concerns the generation to which each belongs. Gadda was born in 1893; Pasolini, in 1922. Both, upon reaching manhood, found themselves on the threshold of war. But though some historians like to link the two World Wars, seeing in the second merely a continuation of the first, they were in fact quite dissimilar, both in the manner of fighting and in the changes which each brought to the social environment. Gadda fought in the First World War; he was captured and spent a long time in a prison camp made famous in the history of Italian literature because he had as barracks mates Ugo Betti, destined to become Italy's most important playwright after Pirandello, and Bonaventura Tecchi, who became a writer and scholar of repute and held the chair of German literature at the University of Rome until his death in 1968. During his early years Gadda witnessed and lived through that collapse of old and well-established values which characterizes the transition period between the nineteenth and early twentieth centuries. The world that is reflected in most of his works is that of the stable *fin de siècle* bourgeoisie, specifically of the Milanese upper classes—whose children were taken to play in the park of the Castello; who were concerned with keeping their houses in immaculate order; who built summer villas among the hills of the Brianza, the gentle countryside north of Milan immortalized by Manzoni; and whose family memories included the still vivid recollections of Hapsburg rule, felt not so much finished and done with as simply removed in time.

> **There seems to be something eternally young in Pasolini, and this impression is borne out by his restless seeking for always new avenues of expression: from poetry to militant journalism, from the novel to cinema.**
>
> —*Olga Ragusa*

Pasolini, instead, spent his childhood following his army officer father from one military post in northern Italy to another. In 1943 while he was studying at the University of Bologna, he was evacuated, as were thousands of other civilians all over Europe. He was sent to Casarsa, the village in the Friuli from which his mother came. There, in that northeastern corner of Italy close to the Yugoslav border, he watched the Partisan warfare, which was as distinctive of the later years of the Second World War in occupied Europe as trench warfare had been of the First. Pasolini's earliest works were poems in Friulian, inspired by his love for the simple, instinctive peasant life of a rural region that progress had bypassed, the same region that a century earlier served as the setting for Nievo's wonderful *contes champêtres*. But Pasolini's interest in dialect poetry was not limited to his practice of it. A number of essays attest to his broader view, and in 1955 he published an important anthology of Italian dialect poetry, *Canzoniere italiano*. Its long introductory essay combines scholarly competence with a Marxian inter-

pretation of the relationship of folk and art poetry, dwelling on the reasons for the progressive disappearance of folk poetry in the awakening class consciousness of the backward peasant populations on their way to urban proletariat status. Marxism, of course, is a doctrine that played no role in the formation of Gadda, whose whole orientation was away from the political and economic problems of society and toward those of the individual and collective psyche. Indeed, in the figures of Freud and Marx, we have as good symbols as any to epitomize the historico-cultural differences in the situation we have been discussing.

The second difference between Gadda and Pasolini concerns their temperaments. There seems to be something eternally young in Pasolini, and this impression is borne out by his restless seeking for always new avenues of expression: from poetry to militant journalism, from the novel to cinema. Gadda, by contrast, was born old, old and weary, with a tendency to pessimism, to bitter humor, to foreseeing catastrophes and therefore treading lightly. In the self-portrait which Pasolini contributed in 1960 to a volume of autobiographies by contemporary Italian writers, he speaks of his daily routine, and especially of his tireless wanderings through Rome, the city to which he moved in 1950:

> I spend the greater part of my life beyond the edges of the city, or as a bad neo-realist poet imitating the hermetics would say, beyond the city's end-stations. I love life with such violence and such intensity that no good can come of it. I am speaking of the physical side of life: the sun, the grass, youth. It is an addiction more terrible than cocaine. It doesn't cost anything, and it is available in boundless quantities. I devour it ravenously.... How it will all end, I don't know....

In his contribution to the same volume, Gadda wrote:

> By temperament I am rather inclined to solitude, incapable as I am of chattering vivaciously, uninterested in mundane social life. I approach my fellow-men and associate with them with a certain amount of difficulty and hesitation; the hesitation and difficulty increase, the more virtuous they are. In the presence of another human being I feel like a student at an examination. Instead, in my leisure hours I take pleasure in clarifying some "algebra" to myself. This tires me less than a drawing-room conversation where I am forced to appear witty and intelligent without being either.

The juxtaposition of the two passages suggests that we are dealing with two personalities that would have manifested opposite characteristics even if the external circumstances of their lives had been identical. Gadda and Pasolini were not only born into different historical times; they were born as two completely different psychological types. The two facts that psychoanalytically inclined critics would pounce on and magnify—that Gadda and Pasolini both lost a dearly loved and not easily forgotten older brother through war, and that each had a typically ambivalent relation to his parents—turn out to be insignificant and nondetermining in the light of the broad attitudes toward life which make the one man a misanthrope and the other—if I may be permitted to give the word its etymological meaning—a philanthrope. This divergence in basic personality traits is of necessity reflected in the manner in which each faces his task as a writer.

During a recent trip to the United States, the novelist Italo Calvino told of a radio talk on the building industry which Gadda was once asked to give. It seems that he spoke first, with scientific precision, of houses built of reinforced concrete and how it is impossible to insulate them against noise. He then went on to the physiological effects of noise on the nervous system. And finally in a display of verbal fireworks he burst forth against the noises of city life themselves. A similar mounting progression is recalled by Gadda in the self-portrait from which I quoted earlier. He speaks there of the many "philosophical meditations," all written in excellent prose (i.e., conventional style), which he has stored away at home and which are survivals of a time when he had not yet devoted himself to narrative writing. He then mentions the effects the experience of the war had on him: how because of it he turned from philosophy to the vicissitudes of human life and found himself torn between a strong predisposition to give expression exclusively to his lyric and satirical veins and an equally strong desire to understand his fellowmen by "noting down events." Finally he acknowledges that for him writing is often a means of "seeking vengeance" for the injuries inflicted on men by fate: "So that my storytelling often manifests the resentful tone of the person who speaks while holding back his wrath, his indignation." The anecdote and the self-analysis reveal that Gadda did not choose the narrative style which is most closely associated with his name because he was incapable of expressing himself in any other way. Rather he chose it—or it chose him, a formulation closer, as we shall see, to his view of the polarization of tensions which determines the relationship between the writer and his subject—because it alone could give shape to the noumenal reality, that "algebra" of the universe, which he pursues. On this last point, it might be fruitful to consider carefully the answer Gadda gave when in 1950 he was asked for his opinion on the then triumphant school of neorealism. He voiced his lack of sympathy for its basic assumptions in these terms:

> It is all well and good to tell me that a volley of machine gun fire is reality. But what I expect from the novel is that behind those seven ounces of lead there be some tragic tension, some consecution at

work, a mystery, perhaps the reason for the fact, or the absence of reasons. . . . The fact by itself, the object by itself, is but the dead body of reality, the—pardon the expression—fecal residue of history. I would therefore want the poetics of neo-realism to be extended to include a nouminous dimension.

The search for the nouminous dimension is what gives its peculiar form to *Eros e Priapo* (*Da furore a cenene*), 1967 [Eros and Priapus (From Frenzy to Ashes)], Gadda's most recently published work. In spite of what the jacket blurb claims, this is not an antinovel—except if we are ready to make of this expression a catchall for everything that we cannot define otherwise; nor is it a piece of historical writing, history being the complement to fiction as a narrative mode. *Eros e Priapo,* an indictment of the Fascist era, might be called a psychoanalysis of history, conceived as a scientific research problem with theorems and propositions, but conducted with a virulence and an emotional involvement which allow for no other conclusion than the one already implied in the premise. Specifically, it is an *exposé* of the pathology of exhibitionistic narcissism and its effects on an audience (in this case the Italian people under fascism), seen with the devastating clarity and single-mindedness of an individual who could never be a consenting and participating member of that audience. Early in the book Gadda states that his purpose in writing it is to induce self-knowledge, for "only an act of knowledge can bring about the resurrection of the Italian people, if indeed resurrection can even be attempted from so horrendous a ruin."

The two novels of Gadda's I am about to discuss also deal with knowledge. The first is a detective novel *manqué,* which means that the quest for the specific knowledge which is its objective is eventually foiled. The second proclaims by its very title that knowledge is its subject, and it is in fact a *meditation* on anguish and not the dramatization of that feeling through a story. Both novels can also be said to deal with ruin, "frenzy and ashes." In the first, crime upsets the social order and allows all the baseness and vileness that usually lies hidden under the mantle of convention to rise to the surface. In the second, it is mental disease, *il male oscuro* (the dark evil), which muddies the waters and breaches that moral order which appeases the savage drives in man and makes civilized living possible. In neither novel do we reach the stage of "resurrection," that is, of catharsis. They are both unfinished, perhaps unfinishable. . . .

For all its being rooted in historical and geographical reality, *Quer pasticciaccio* is a novel that has left naturalism behind. Not that Gadda's imagination is not nature-bound, as is attested by his strongly concrete and sensual vocabulary. As a matter of fact, he seems to take contact with the world almost exclusively through the senses. His verbal ingenuity, his creative facility, remind one often of the physical pleasure of "mouthing" words, an extension of the joys of the palate, of his self-confessed gluttony. There is a magnificent passage to be mentioned in this connection, an unforgettable episode in *La cognizione del dolore* which shows the principal character gorging himself on an enormous lobster. It is carried off with such Rabelaisean gusto that it reveals the hand of the man both attracted and repelled, but essentially fascinated, by "oral" excess. Excess of this kind leads inevitably to deformation, and the world Gadda writes about is deformed by his singular, eccentric—I am tempted to say, in this connection, artistic as opposed to moralistic—vision. In this sense Gadda has gone well beyond naturalism in its literary-historical definition. Like the expressionists in the very years when he began to write, he must have felt at one time that it was senseless to set about "reproducing" the world as it is, that it is indeed impossible to do so, given the absence of any permanent rapport between the individual and reality.

Much of what we have said about *Quer pasticciaccio* also holds true for *La cognizione,* but generally to a more concentrated degree. *Quer pasticciaccio* is an unfinished work; *La cognizione* is not only unfinished but also fragmentary. In *Quer pasticciaccio* the creation of suspense inherent in the detective story is constantly undercut by the author's pursuit of the verbal and other associations that come his way. In *La cognizione* the story line at one point breaks down completely. (It is taken up again in Part Two, both parts of the book dealing with the same subject matter in a manner somewhat reminiscent of Faulkner's *The Sound and the Fury.*) *Quer pasticciaccio* goes deep into the amalgam of petty crime, violence, and unspoken wrongs; *La cognizione* adds to these the horror of unresolved guilt. In *Quer pasticciaccio* the setting is not only recognizable as Rome, it actually is Rome; in *La cognizione* the setting is recognizable as Lombardy, but is actually, within the fiction of the book, the imaginary South American country of Maradagàl. In *Quer pasticciaccio* the principal character, who is searching for the nouminous reality of life, is a stand-in for the author; in *La cognizione* the principal character is even closer to being the author himself (he is a war veteran, has lost a brother in the war, and suffers from a mysterious malady which renders life bitter and unendurable), although he hides under the fictional identity of Gonzalo Pirobutirro d'Eltino, hidalgo and engineer of Maradagàl. *La cognizione* has one quality which *Quer pasticciaccio* lacks: it is a book about suffering, and its vehemence is therefore frequently softened to elegy. It is a more human book built around a truly tragic if monstrous character.

More even than *Quer pasticciaccio* it is a book for connoisseurs, with hardly a word in it that is not intended to call to mind another word, to refer to some cultural or literary experience of Italian history. While the ordinary reader can approach the Rome of *Quer pasticciaccio,* find his way in

it, and move among familiar monuments, only a learned and sophisticated reader will be able to identify in the landscape of Maradagàl not merely the landscape of the Brianza, but the landscape of the Brianza as seen in Manzoni's *I promessi sposi.* Failure to note connections such as this one would seriously impede not only the comprehension but the enjoyment of the book. It is essential, for instance, that in the passage which describes the mountain Serruchòn the reader be able to detect beneath Gadda's words the counterpoint of Manzoni's description of the same—or is it another?—mountain, the Resegone. Gadda plants an open clue by referring to the Resegone by name; but it is not sufficient to recognize the source intellectually, it must also be savored esthetically by "close" and expert reading. *La cognizione del dolore* is a book that clamors for an annotated edition, to make explicit its wonderful richness of references, its extraordinary abundance. The English translator of *Quer pasticciaccio,* William Weaver, has done something of this in his edition of *That Awful Mess.* Unfortunately, his explanatory notes are limited almost exclusively to historical and political references, thus magnifying the element of anti-Fascist satire which is present in the book, but which by this treatment receives undue emphasis at the expense of the subtler, more literary aspects of the work of this most literary, most idiosyncratic and socially alienated of contemporary Italian writers.

In reviewing *Quer pasticciaccio* in 1958, Pasolini recognized in it a stylistic versatility which, he said, would make a critic like Spitzer as exhilarated—and the comparison is his—as a mouse in a chunk of cheese. Pasolini analyzed briefly four basically different uses of dialect in the book; pointed to the extraordinary range of its syntactical forms, even coining the word *hypertaxis* to place beside the more usual *parataxis* and *hypotaxis* for describing Gadda's "monstrous syntactical jungle"; and compared Manzoni's and Gadda's use of tenses as a key to their respective narrative techniques. As can be seen, his is a most competent and expert approach, a far cry from the run-of-the-mill practice of journalistic reviewing, which looks for little more than a novel's relationship to everyday reality. As a reader of Gadda, Pasolini certainly ranks with the best. In an earlier review of a collection of Gadda short stories, *Novelle dal Ducato in fiamme,* 1953 (*Stories from the Duchy Aflame*), he had surveyed, again with economy and concentration, the nineteenth and twentieth century literary precedents to which Gadda owes aspects of his style: the "art prose" movement of the Twenties, which treated prose as though it were poetry and against which specifically the neorealists reacted; Verga's "narrated interior monologue"; Manzoni's continuing orientation to the Lombard components of his culture, even under the surface aspiration to national unity; the social satire and irony of the Roman dialect poet Belli; and the post-Romantic avant-garde movement of the Piedmontese and Lombard *scapigliati,* whose truly revolutionary experimentation with linguistic and literary forms is barely beginning to be studied. In view of the breadth and depth of Pasolini's understanding of Gadda and of his admiration for what he calls "that very great mind and heart," it is all the more interesting to note his formulation of the latter's shortcomings. I pass here from the context of esthetics and literary craftsmanship to that of ideology and from the novelist Gadda to the novelist Pasolini.

Speaking of Pasolini earlier, I referred briefly to the role played by the partisan movement in the formation of his basic sympathies and convictions. The struggle for liberation from fascism during the later stages of the War was felt by the more idealistic and committed of its exponents as the beginning of a new era in Italian history, the harbinger of a social revolution which would finally wipe out all class and regional inequalities. This feeling of buoyancy persisted in spite of many disappointments and delays until roughly the time of the Hungarian uprising, an event which seriously shook confidence in the Communist solution to Italy's problems. Pasolini's political optimism, nurtured in the successful defeat of fascism, combined with his personal responsiveness to others and his acceptance of Marxism as a unifying ideological structure for judging progress, enabled him to focus on what he sees as the reactionary side of Gadda's position. [In a review of *Quer pasticciaccio,*] Pasolini presents Gadda as simultaneously accepting and rejecting the social reality of Italy as created by the middle classes in the wake of the *Risorgimento*. The resultant ambivalence caused that feeling of despondent anguish and that "tragically mixed and obsessive style" which are the marks of Gadda's helpless and ever renewed fury at finding institutions which are potentially good turned into organizations which are actually bad. "Gadda belongs to an historical time," Pasolini concludes, "when it was impossible to see the world—this magma of disorder, corruption, hypocrisy, stupidity, and injustice—in a perspective of hope."

The full significance of this statement becomes apparent when we examine Pasolini's two novels, ***Ragazzi di vita*** . . . and ***Una vita violenta.*** . . . In both Pasolini would like to see the world "in a perspective of hope" but both of them fall short of being true documents, the first of the "magma of disorder . . . and injustice" which must be destroyed, the second of the awakening of the social consciousness through which this destruction will be effected.

Ragazzi di vita is a novel because it deals with a group of fictional characters, the course of whose life we follow during a determined period of time. But it could just as easily be conceived of as a series of vignettes or episodes only loosely related to one another, whose main function is the representation of a milieu rather than the construction and revelation of a character. ***Ragazzi di vita*** came out at the height of the neorealistic vogue and was read at first as a document of the desperate conditions of the Roman

subproletariat in the disconsolate slums springing up with unbelievable rapidity on the outskirts of the city.

The documentary aspect of the book appeared to be underlined by the glossary of dialect terms and underworld jargon which Pasolini provides at the end. To some readers the list seems incomplete and insufficient, although it is true, as Pasolini claims in his covering note, that comprehension of the story or of any one episode of it is not really impeded by the inability to translate into standard Italian every one of the rude, vulgar, obscene expressions which occur in the speech of its protagonists. Pasolini feels that no reader coming upon these words for the first time could fail to grasp their meaning through intuition of the context in which they are used. And indeed the dialogue which makes up so much of the book is little more than a string of curses, cries, expletives, urgings, exclamations—the typical "conversational" exchanges which occur when people do not *speak* to one another but simply, almost by the accident of propinquity, share common experiences.

Dialogue in novels has often been used to discuss important philosophical problems or to introduce the author's personal convictions. Nothing could be further from Pasolini's practice. His message is never entrusted to the words of his characters. Rather it is implicit in his representation of selected conditions, or, in some rare cases, in his own narrated third-person comment on what he is telling. Thus, for instance, there is an episode toward the end of *Ragazzi di vita* in which one of the protagonists returns to the factory area which had figured in the opening pages. Almost everything is changed: the buildings and grounds are now shining with cleanliness and order, and a new, unbroken wire fence surrounds them. Only the watchman's hut is still the same: it continues to be used as an abusive public latrine. "That was the only spot that Riccetto found familiar," Pasolini unobtrusively comments, "exactly as it was when the war had just ended."

The time span covered by ***Ragazzi di vita*** goes from the liberation of Rome in 1944 to the early Fifties. Riccetto, who might be considered the principal character if for no other reason than that he is most frequently on stage, lives through the years of his adolescence: he is eleven and receiving his first communion when the story begins, eighteen and having served a three-year term in jail when it ends. In noting with precision the exact limits of the historical situation which serves as background, Pasolini is fulfilling one of the desiderata of the esthetics of neorealism, which calls for the concrete rooting of fiction in a definite and verifiable reality. But ***Ragazzi di vita*** is in no sense an historical novel. It has nothing of Pratolini's *Metello* where historical events are made part of the plot. Nor do historical events shape its story as they do, in however muted a manner, in Verga's *I Malavoglia,* for instance. ***Ragazzi di vita*** gives back the "color" of a time only in an episodic, allusive manner. Thus we have in the early pages of the book the description of the pilfering of food and other necessities characteristic of day-to-day existence in occupied Rome. There is reference to the emergency housing of the homeless and the destitute— as a matter of fact, Riccetto's mother is killed in the collapse of an old school building which had been turned to this use. And there is an endless stream of "things," objects of all sorts from sewer lids to automobile tires to articles of furniture, which at one time or another fetched a good price on the market of stolen goods. We have, in other words, the landscape made familiar by films such as *Bicycle Thief,* but without the underlying ethic of that film which dealt with a man's effort to make good, to find his place in society through his work. The protagonists of *Ragazzi di vita* do, from time to time, work. They sometimes have money, not necessarily honestly come by. And that money quickly slips out of their fingers again, for they do not consider it as a means of insuring security, of building a place for themselves in society—witness the amusing episode at Ostia, where the fifty-thousand lire that Riccetto had just stolen from swindlers for whom he was working are with a Boccacioesque twist in turn stolen from him.

The truth of the matter is that Riccetto and his friends are outsiders, typical juvenile delinquents unable and unwilling to make the compromises necessary to find their way into a social order, and that it is therefore difficult to consider their stories as representative of a socio-historical condition. Though *Ragazzi di vita* can be read as a Marxist indictment of the capitalist society which makes lives such as it describes possible, it is in no way an example of socialist realism, for it sets up no exemplary hero who through his awareness of the dynamics of social change can become the potential founder of a new order. *Ragazzi di vita* is the representation of a nether world no less absolute than that of *Quer pasticciaccio.* No broad and happy roads leads out of this world, toward that triumph of reason which Marxist writers, mindful of their Enlightenment origins, like to prognosticate.

But if the vision of the road leading to the transformed society is missing in *Ragazzi di vita,* it is not because Pasolini, as we have seen in his review of *Quer pasticciaccio,* does not consciously believe in its existence. It is simply that he has lost sight of it while telling his story, while exploring with loving attention the teeming life of the Roman underworld. For that underworld has a vitality for him, a gay insouciance, a forceful optimistic *élan,* a *joie de vivre,* that obscures its horror. As one of the gang exults, referring to the company that finds itself associated in petty crime one epic night at the Villa Borghese: "Two from Tiburtino, one from Acqua Bullicante, two from Primaville, one deserter, and Picchio here from Valle dell'Inferno: why, we could band together and found the League of the Suburbs of

Rome!" One hears echoes of the exploits of the Three Musketeers, of the Chevaliers de la Table Ronde of ballad fame, of all the merry bands that have roamed the face of the earth, recklessly following where adventure called. . . .

The first reviewers of *Ragazzi di vita* singled out its social nihilism and its literary esthet"icism for special criticism. Pasolini's insistence on a monotonous and unrepresentative segment of the Roman subproletariat seemed to them a deformation and a stylization of reality which went counter to the fundamental documentary intention of neorealism. Moreover, an episode such as the one in which the thoughts of a couple of mongrel dogs during a fight are recorded as though spoken in the same dialect used by the human protagonists of the book was cited as a clamorous instance of that flight from naturalistic objectivity to decadent self-indulgence which was also underlined by the picaresque aspects of the novel.

In an essay on Italian dialect poetry which he had written some years earlier, Pasolini had already implicitly defended his narrative approach in *Ragazzi di vita.* In speaking of the Roman poet, Gioacchino Belli, the nineteenth century interpreter of the feelings and opinions of the city's unruly populace, he emphasized, as many other observers had done, the uniqueness of the Roman citizenry, those descendants of the *plebs* of antiquity, who in the midst of splendid testimonials of their past have always lived and continue to live outside of history, that is, outside the awareness and the dynamics of change. To the ideal of progress conceived in terms of social betterment, these people substitute the excitement of life lived exclusively for the moment, the happy-go-lucky acceptance of whatever opportunities, however slight and brief, chance offers them. To represent this "aristocratic Roman proletariat"—the expression is Pasolini's— in their saga of roguish adventure is thus, Pasolini claimed, to reflect the "real" Rome, the Rome that rebels against the political and economic structures of bourgeois society *not* by taking a conscious position against them but by simply ignoring them. And to use the Roman dialect to record the inner content of the fictional lives of these people (dialect is used only in the dialogue parts of the book and in some rare cases of stream of consciousness) is to apply the general rule later formulated by Pasolini in his answer to a questionnaire on the novel sponsored by the periodical *Nuovi argomenti:* "If the character and milieu chosen by the novelist are proletariat, let him use dialect in part or wholly; if they are middle-class, let him use the *koiné.* In this way he cannot go wrong." By *koiné* Pasolini means the uniform, nondialect Italian usage of the petite bourgeoisie as formed by the unification of Italy, or, to use Gramsci's description, the language of the bureaucrats who effectively united the new state at the administrative level but left the Italy of regions and city districts virtually untouched. *Ragazzi di vita,* it should be remembered, was written and is set in the period immediately preceding the new levelling and cohesive forces of Italy's "economic miracle," which were to do so much to destroy the nation's compartmentalized subcultures and to turn large segments of its proletariat into a middle class—without, however, the contributions of Marxism.

Pasolini's second novel, *Una vita violenta* is in part an answer to the more justified objections raised against *Ragazzi di vita.* Pasolini, a convinced and avowed Marxist, was especially sensitive to the critics who took him to task for ideological inadequacy, for having escaped into the private world of a kind of eternal adolescence and primitiveness instead of attempting to represent the awakening social consciousness of the masses on their way to claim their place in the sun. Thus Tommaso Puzzilli, the protagonist of *Una vita violenta,* is seen as more fully rounded than [*Ragazzi di vita's*] Riccetto and is made to undergo a political education which changes his initial heedless spontaneity into a sense of responsibility toward others. Whether the book for all its orthodox intentions is as successful as its predecessor is questionable. My own feeling is that the first part of *Una vita violenta* is more effective than the second and that the episodes most strongly reminiscent of *Ragazzi di vita* are what saves it from being a completely pedestrian and unimaginative illustration of a thesis.

Tommaso is at the beginning just another Riccetto. He too lives in a Hooverville on the outskirts of Rome. He too is involved with the other boys of his district in a number of wild exploits, such as stealing a car and holding up a hapless gas station attendant one night. He too meets a girl to whom he becomes engaged and with whom he plays the role of the proper young fiancé: the descriptions of their Sunday outings are peculiarly and unexpectedly condescending, but I believe unwittingly so. There are other episodes in the first part of the book which mark a departure from *Ragazzi di vita:* Tommasino's participation in a "rumble" staged by a group of Fascist sympathizers, and the revolt of the women of Pietralata against the police, who are rounding up their suspect husbands and sons. But the most striking innovation has to do with technique. It is in a flashback at the beginning of Part Two that we are told of the Puzzillis' coming to Rome as refugees during the war, of how they were forced to leave the country, where their land and animals and the father's job as caretaker in the public schools had permitted them to live quite comfortably, much better than they now live in Rome. Still, in the long run they turn out to be more fortunate then many of their new neighbors, for they are assigned an apartment in the complex of public housing being built in the no-man's-land of Pietralata. It is to this apartment that Tommaso returns after his stint in jail for having stabbed a heckler during a street fight, and it is at this point that the thrust of the narrative changes.

Tommaso appears to have left his adolescence behind him.

He finds work and becomes a respectable member of society—so much so that he averts his eyes when he happens upon an ex-companion who has not succeeded as he has, but has become a crippled beggar huddling on a street in Rome. At the beginning of this turning point, however, Pasolini introduces the theme of death. First there is the brief report of the sudden death of Tommasino's two baby brothers, an episode which makes a strong appeal for sympathy from the reader by bringing into view the injustices and deprivations which reduce human life to the level of animal, or even insect, life. Then there are the first symptoms of Tommasino's tuberculosis, which eventually leads him to a long stay in a city hospital. There he meets and learns to admire and respect a group of Communists who are organizing and supporting the hospital attendants in a strike. Tommasino joins the party upon his release. But the story is now rapidly approaching the end. Tommasino dies in a new tubercular attack, brought on by his trying to save a prostitute during a flood.

As can be seen, Pasolini's intention in *Una vita violenta* was to write a novel which would follow the classical pattern by being the complete and exemplary story of a central character. In this respect *Una vita violenta* is not different from the social novels of the nineteenth century, from Zola, for instance. But while Pasolini is excellent at catching the "feeling" of the life of his protagonists, he is less successful with the concreteness of historical background. He leaves the reader with strong sense impressions: unpleasant odors, rough and dirty textures, deformed limbs, blemished skins, rotting clothing, mud, heaps of garbage. But there is little or nothing in the book which will help a future reader to reconstruct the complexity of an epoch. Pasolini's talent is lyrical and sentimental, not narrative and historical. That is why the episode of the "talking" dogs, tucked away in the flow of euphoric slang, is the real clue to the quality of his art. . . .

Now, while for Gadda one could certainly speak of *vision autre,* the deformation and excess of a disordered psyche which gives his expression such virulence, there can be no question that for neither Gadda nor Pasolini has writing a novel ever been equivalent to constructing a game. They are both fundamentally earnest and moralistic in their approach to art. They have a message to transmit, easily recognizable in Pasolini, less so in Gadda. The themes they treat undoubtedly present only divergences if we examine them in the context of one another's work. But when we look at Gadda and Pasolini from a certain distance, from the perspective of the new new experimentalism, for instance, we can only conclude that the themes they treat are the old ones—crime, guilt, death—and that the feeling of revulsion for the fault in nature that both writers' experience derives from the traditional, classic view of man in his relation to other men and to the world about him.

John Bragin (essay date January 1969)

SOURCE: "Pier Paolo Pasolini: Poetry as a Compensation," in *Film Society Review,* Vol. 4, No. 5, January, 1969, pp. 12-18.

[*In the following essay, Bragin discusses examples of Pasolini's work in the genres of the novel, film, and poetry.*]

Pier Paolo Pasolini was born in Bologna in 1922. His father was a government official and Pasolini travelled constantly as a boy, mastering many of the Northern Italian dialects. He attended the University of Bologna until the war forced him to flee to his mother's home in Casarsa, where he remained until 1949, writing his first fiction. In 1949 he moved to Rome, where he taught literature. Because of his poor financial status he was forced to live in the *borgata,* slum suburbs, which became the major source of subject matter for his writings and films.

Since that time he has continued writing both poetry and prose, as well as literary criticism and linguistic analysis. He wrote a column for the Italian Communist Party's popular weekly magazine *Vie Nuove* in which he answered questions from readers about his work, and about art and politics in general.

Before making his directorial debut in 1961 with *Accattone* (the word is Roman slang for scrounger) Pasolini had collaborated on scripts and conceived ideas for Federico Fellini, Mauro Bolognini and several other directors. With his first film it was immediately apparent that Pasolini was not just a fine writer turned dilettante film director, his succeeding work has established him as a major figure in contemporary film-making.

Up until 1961 Pasolini was one of many Italian artists firmly devoted to the causes and organization of the Italian Communist Party. Since then, he has become gradually estranged from their ranks, but without the spiritual crisis which led his forerunner Cesare Pavese to commit suicide. (Pasolini's own crisis of 1961 is discussed later in this article.) The creative expression of these men is deeply rooted in a tradition which stretches back to the ancient Etruscan civilization—a period of almost uninterrupted activity longer than in any other country of the Western world. This sense of artistic tradition is one of the main reasons why Italian artists of the Left have not fallen prey to the deadly style of Socialist Realism which has encumbered so many American and Soviet artists. Even the post-War Italian cinema was not Realist, per se, but Neo-Realist. That is, it treated the social and economic chaos of Italian society from a fragmented, lyric point of view which was neither doctrinaire nor exploitive of the physical and spiritual squalor.

This sense of history has contributed to the development of the Party and its members by modifying and softening doctrinaire Marxism and producing Italy's peculiar brand of modern Communism. (A Communism that flourishes in the Italian sun, and which is far different from the Communism of the snows of Moscow and the Asian desolations to the east.)

Besides the sense of artistic continuity in Italy there is the all-pervasive influence of the Catholic Church. Even professed atheists like Pasolini have a firmly indoctrinated past of religious mystery and of Christ as man's sole salvation. For most Italian artists—of the Right or Left—the structure of the Church in Italy and its dogma influence their work. The metaphysical doctrines of the Catholic Church have been a compelling force for almost 2000 years.

The tendency toward dependence on religious mystery has been greater for Pasolini than for most other members of the artistic Left. In Pasolini's spiritual and political crisis, exemplified by *Accattone* made in 1961, this aspect of Pasolini came forward more strongly than in any of his previous writings. His swing from rationality to mystery to rationality can be traced through his novels, poetry and films from 1959 to 1965.

Pasolini's novel *Una Vita Violenta* deals with the same subject matter as his first two films: the slum suburbs of Rome and the young men who inhabit them, pimps, thieves, scroungers and deadbeats. They are a modern breed pre-occupied with all the modern as well as traditional pleasures which they indulge in without the conventional financial means to do so. The gap between the squalor and hopelessness of their lives in the *borgata* and the growing economic miracle within the city aggravates their plight. The consciousness of a better life only worsens their state of mind and, combined with a pagan sense of Christian morality, produces strange codes of behavior often ending in violence, brutality and death.

When one of the group becomes separated from his fellows it is a sure sign that a crisis is growing for him. Whether it is the crisis which causes the separation, or the separation the crisis is hard to say. The exact dividing line is blurred so that social, personal and ultimately spiritual causes intermix to determine the fate and destiny of the character. At the point when the character comes fully into view, out from under social and individual games, Pasolini is faced with a naked soul who has only two possible roads confronting him: salvation or death.

In the novel Tommaso finds salvation through the Communist Party. For Pasolini the Hungarian uprising was an indication of the falling away of the Moscow-centered Stalinist strangle-hold over satellite parties, and the beginning of the end of Stalinism within the parties themselves. It represented the growing self-sufficiency of these parties, their organic re-birth into individual groups tailored to deal with the specific problems of their own cultures. Pasolini viewed the PCI (Italian Communist Party) as the most advanced of these, and the vehicle for Tommaso's climb out of an oblivion of poverty and squalor. Tommaso leaves the chaotic world of the slum sub-proletariat to join the ranks of the Party as a member of the working class. From there he will undoubtedly rise to higher echelons within the Party, and greater positive influence within the society as a whole.

Accattone never makes it. He tries to work, but cannot stand the physical strain. In the end he dies in a motorcycle crash, pursued by the police for being a thief. Pasolini describes the story of Tommaso as "drama," the story of Accattone as a "tragedy." What was to happen to Pasolini in two years (between 1959 and 1961) and why this sealed the tragic fate of Accattone will be presented after a brief review of Pasolini's poetry.

> **Pasolini is not primarily interested in socio-historic context as an explanation or justification for the thoughts and actions in his work. Even when a poem deals directly with a contemporary event in which Pasolini is a highly partisan actor, he approaches it poetically on an artistically instinctive level which, although it may not render exact answers on how to act in a particular situation, provides in Pasolini's words "poetry as a compensation."**
> *—John Bragin*

Pasolini's three main collections of poetry are *Le Ceneri Di Gramsci* (*The Ashes of Gramsci*), *La Religione del Mio Tempo* and *Poesia in Forma di Rosa.* The first deals with the passing of the period in Italian history dominated by the highly respected, fiery leader of the PCI, Antonio Gramsci. Gramsci was not only a major figure in the Italian underground during World War II, but also a major literary critic as well. He was an important influence on Pasolini both politically and artistically. Gramsci was a much more militant advocate of international Marxist-Leninism than his successor Palmiro Togliatti, and Pasolini's book looks with nostalgia, tempered with the realization of the need for change, at the passing of the period dominated by Gramsci. Today, Party head Luigi Longo seems to be in the same relation to Togliatti that Togliatti was to Gramsci, so much so that one Italian film critic called Pasolini's fourth feature, *Uccellacci E Uccellini* (released in the U.S. as *The Hawks and The Sparrows*), "The Ashes of Togliatti!"

In his next two collections Pasolini works with several ideas. He deals with the theory of ideology, and the practical effects of ideologies on the sub-proletarian culture of his novels and films. One of the most virulent examples of this is the first poem in *Poesia in Forma di Rosa,* a harsh and ironic treatment of the cliché of Italian-style motherhood. Influenced strongly by the crystaline images of Godard's film, *Contempt,* Pasolini opens another poem in the collection (**"Una Disperata Vitalita," "A Desperate Vitality"**) with verses comparing his surrealistic thoughts and feelings to Godard's images. The fragility of the pictures evoked in the poem express the contingent nature of life which exists for the upper classes who live on "the highways of Latin neo-capitalism." A more brittle, but no less terminal malady than that suffered by the world of Accattone.

In general these poems crystalize and magnify incidents, emotions and ideas which occur in his novels. Pasolini isolates them, dealing with them intensely and in depth. The result marks an important aspect in Pasolini's artistic and spiritual development, and strongly affects his particular use of the film medium.

In dealing specifically and at length with one or a few facets of his longer works Pasolini lifts each subject from its context and works it with a near-religious love, putting it directly, forcefully and frontally to the reader. His poetry evokes universal, religious and ritualistic feelings. The bits of concrete realism (usually of sub-proletarian life) are infused with an aura of reverence by the very nature of poetic expression. But more importantly Pasolini is not primarily interested in socio-historic context as an explanation or justification for the thoughts and actions in his work. Even when a poem deals directly with a contemporary event in which Pasolini is a highly partisan actor, he approaches it poetically on an artistically instinctive level which, although it may not render exact answers on how to act in a particular situation, provides in Pasolini's words "poetry as a compensation."

Pasolini writes in a fresh, direct style so that even those emotions or ideas which might at first appear pedantic, transient or clichéd are presented with moving force and conviction. It is this quality which dominates Pasolini's first film.

When Pasolini began work on this film he was a complete neophyte in film technique. Although he knew nothing about the craft of film-making, not even the terminology, he had a feeling for the film image from his earlier script collaborations. Because the directors he had worked with had only partially realized his ideas, he decided to try his own hand at film-making.

When confronted with the actual task of direction he decided to limit himself technically in order to gain control of the medium. He attempted to do this by using only two focal length lenses (one for full shots and one for closeups), several limited variations on tracking shots and slow, smooth pans; and direct simple staging and composition. In contrast to most first films *Accattone* is completely free of technical experiment. It evokes the same tone of sanctity as much of Pasolini's poetry by its direct, frontal presentation of events and characters.

The overall structure of the film, its editing, the balance between scenes and sequences, and Pasolini's control of the development and movement of the film with a sense for the organic whole is missing. The film tends to sprawl all over. It is not Pasolini's masterful handling of the film medium, as with Orson Welles on *Citizen Kane,* but his attitude towards the subject matter, his deep love and understanding of the characters and their plight, which is the binding force on the film.

Pasolini was faced with a deep political and spiritual crisis at this time in his life. So much so that no solution within the context of the life of Accattone seemed possible. No such internal, contextual solution as the Communist Party was for Tommaso. Pasolini describes the crisis of the summer of 1961 and the Tambroni government:

> Everything in my country, in those months, seemed to have fallen back into its everlasting, uniform greyness, of superstition, of servileness and of useless vitality.

He described the life of the sub-proletariat in

> its material and moral misery, its ferocious and useless irony, its scattered, demonic anxiety, its contemptuous laziness, its idealized sensuality, and, together with all of this its atavistic, superstitious, pagan Catholicism. That's why he [Accattone] dreams of dying and going to Paradise.

In the film Pasolini does not even remotely concern himself with political, economic, or social ideologies. No one, not even the director, offers Accattone the alternative of either the Party or any other system of reform. The only redemption is found in the external factor of the director's guiding hand. Through his love, Pasolini reaffirms the humanity and very existence of Accattone and the other characters. (The external imposition of Bach's music on the sound track, which at first may seem trite, works because of Pasolini's honesty, and his direct use of the music to comment on the characters and mold our reactions to them. The music is the director's own 'narrating voice.')

In 1961 Pasolini had hit bottom ideologically, but his will to tackle a new medium, to come to grips with it and have it speak his mind and convey his deepest feelings, created a directness and strength that has not been paralleled in his film work since then. Pasolini quotes from Dante in the titles to *Accattone:*

> The Angel of God took me and Satan cried out, "Why do you rob me? You take for yourself the eternal part of him for one little tear which takes him from me. . . ."

The poet in relation to his film is analogous to God in relation to his creation.

Pasolini's self-imposed technical limitations were not consciously done to obtain this sanctifying stylistic effect through which the director finally, though externally, redeems Accattone. Pasolini felt the need to control a medium which could be all too complex for a neophyte, and was influenced in his visual style by the painter Masaccio and Carl Dreyer's *Passion de Jeanne D'Arc.* It was Italian film critics who first commented on what Pasolini had fully accomplished. For once they put aside their ideological demands and came up with illuminating statements which, as is a principle function of criticism lead the viewer to a closer understanding of how a work expresses its creator's ideas and feelings. This affected Pasolini deeply, for he saw its truth and realized that this quality was one which had dominated much of his writing as well.

Pasolini's realization of this aspect of his work, and his growing familiarity with the techniques of film-making are the two most important factors in his next three films: *Mamma Roma, La Ricotta* (*The Milk-Cheese*), and *Il Vangelo Secondo Matteo* (*The Gospel According to St. Matthew*).

The prime fault with *Mamma Roma* is that Pasolini, in his continuing ideological crisis, self-consciously and awkwardly applied the style of *Accattone* in an attempt to redeem his next main character as well, Richard Roud wrote:

> What impressed in last year's *Accattone* was the exciting feeling of directness, of a story that was bursting to be told, and of a tragedy that was inherent in the social environment and psychology of the characters. *Mamma Roma* is burdened with a complicated and melodramatic plot: an ex-whore is forced to abandon her vegetable barrow because her ex-pimp, needing more money than his new wife can provide, threatens to reveal to Mamma Roma's illegitimate son that his mother has been a whore, etc. Thus Mamma Roma's cry of protest, "Whose fault is it?" is seriously weakened by the contingent nature of the drama. When a story is so dependent on chance complications, tragedy and social com-

ment go out the window, and one is left with Anna Magnani up to her old tricks . . . There are some telling moments—Magnani teaching her son to dance the tango, the boy's "crucifixion" and death—but the promise of *Accattone* has not been fulfilled.

The last scenes of the boy strapped to a table and foreshortened by a wide angle lens, recreating Mantegna's *Cristo Morto* (*Dead Christ*), is not a "telling moment" in the sense Roud means. It is a telling example of Pasolini's failure in this film. The boy, contrary to Roud's statement, does not die in the film. He is seen intercut with his mother, Magnani, about to commit suicide herself. Each time we return to the boy he is becoming more and more like a mad dog. There is no relief for him, not even the release of death as there was for Accattone.

Pasolini pushed and forced all the stylistic elements of *Accattone* into his desperate struggle to redeem the boy. He conscientiously applied his slow pans, few lenses, sacred music (Vivaldi), and recreations of religious paintings to create an atmosphere of mystic redemption. But he lost control. The stylistic devices do not grow from the story, but are enforced on it.

In the few scenes of the film such as the wedding at the beginning and the dancing lesson, where Pasolini is most interested in a finely drawn portrait of the characters and situations, he succeeds as well as, if not better than, in *Accattone.* There is the same kind of simplicity here that keynotes Ermanno Olmi's work, notably the opening dance hall sequence in his film *I Fidanzati* (*The Fiancés*). Pasolini creates a joy and love that is neither morbid nor frustrated by social or psychological circumstances.

T. O'Neill (review date March 1969)

SOURCE: "Pier Paolo Pasolini: *Biciclettone,*" in *Modern Languages,* March, 1969, pp. 11-3.

[*In the following review, O'Neill discusses Pasolini's* Biciclettone *as an introduction to the themes and style found in his other novels.*]

One of the most interesting and original personalities of postwar Italian literature is Pier Paolo Pasolini, poet, film director and critic, and novelist.

Such is the complexity and development of the spiritual and intellectual capacities of Pasolini, such is the difficulty of language in his novels, written to a great extent not in Italian but in the Romanesco 'gangster' dialect of the capital's slums, that it is not easy for the philologically untrained

reader of Italian literature to appreciate them as much as they deserve to be. Despite these difficulties, Pasolini's *novella Biciclettone* should be read, not only as a good example of that *genre* in which Italy has always been so strong, but also as an excellent introduction to the more complex novels of Pasolini, for in this *novella* we have *in nuce* all the thematic and stylistic material which will find development in the novels.

The short story is essentially a description of the meeting of the Narrator with the young boy Nando, and of the sympathetic and spontaneous friendship that develops between them because he, the Narrator, has shown this young boy from the slums of Rome a kindness which is all the more poignant because, given his personal situation—he is unemployed—he is unable to do anything of a more concrete nature.

> **Such is the complexity and development of the spiritual and intellectual capacities of Pasolini, such is the difficulty of language in his novels, written to a great extent not in Italian but in the Romanesco 'gangster' dialect of the capital's slums, that it is not easy for the philologically untrained reader of Italian literature to appreciate them as much as they deserve to be.**
> **—T. O'Neill**

Perhaps the most important point is the obvious sympathy Pasolini has for this young lad, a sympathy which mirrors a deep vein of humanity in the author. This comes across in the actions and general attitude of the Narrator who, although obviously not to be confused with Pasolini himself, has this in common with him. For example, the Narrator goes out of his way to please Nando and though he is not a good diver: 'Feci un qualsiasi mediocre caposotto'; on being requested for a running dive he complies willingly: 'Non l'avevo mai fatto, ma per accontentarlo mi ci provai'. Or again when Nando offers him the magazine *Europeo*, he takes it 'per fargli piacere'. This sympathy, although evident in the attitude of the Narrator, is even more marked in his presentation of the make up of Nando, both physical and spiritual. He is first of all described to us physically. Note the forceful evocative adjectives used: 'Magro' (lack of food?); 'storcinatello' (from illness—lack of medical care?); 'faccina' (perhaps wasted away—emphasised by 'stenta' and later on by the 'ghiandola in suppurazione'). Note also the affectionate use of the diminutive 'ragazzino' and the neat descriptive detail: 'con un ciuffo biondo' and 'una grande bocca sorrideva senza sosta'. Later on he again returns to the physical facts: 'Aveva le spalle scottate, come se fosse la febbre ad arrosarle, invece del sole'. Note also how he describes his arms: 'braccini'—that is, pitiful little arms. The thought of the slum where Nando lives also touches him very deeply: '. . . e pensai alla baracca dove viveva. Gli tolsi la cuffia carezzando gli il ciuffo . . .' The sympathy of the Narrator for Nando comes out across the simple narration of the facts.

We are given a wonderful picture of this young lad. Hesitant at the beginning: 'Egli mi guardava obliquamente', wanting to be asked—his joy at being pushed on the swing—his opening up and his overcoming of his inhibitions: '. . . e questa volta non si limitò a guardarmi'. The presentation of this rather self-conscious, shy young lad: 'incerto, ridendo e facendosi rosso', is very natural.

But perhaps the most important feature of Nando is his resignation to his state of life:

> 'Quant'è bella—disse, mettendosela in testa.—Noi siamo poveri, mia se fossimo ricchi mia mamma me la comprerebbe, la cuffia.
>
> —Siete poveri?—gli chiesi.
>
> —Sí, abitiamo nelle baracche di via Casilina.'

It would seem that Nando bears his poverty with a philosophical patience due undoubtedly to his youth. It is a poverty which as yet has not corrupted him. Yet this seemingly philosophical resignation of Nando; this lack of bitterness on his part is not only due to his age but also and especially to his peculiar situation with regard to 'society'. There is no bitterness or corruption in Nando because these come from society, and he lives outside society—on the margins of society. According to Pasolini, and the idea came to him through Antonio Gramsci, a founder of the Italian Communist Party in 1921 and 'lately recognised as one of the most important Marxist theoreticians of the twentieth century', society consists of three classes: aristocracy, *bourgeoisie,* working class—all people who, living in society, have a consciousness of their historical existence and therefore are capable of a moral and intellectual development, which will, of course, vary in degree depending on the class and on the individual. In addition to these classes, however, there is also the 'sottoproletariato'—the subproletarian strata, those who live on the margins of society, who have no consciousness of their historical existence and who are incapable of moral and intellectual development. What we have in this case is a strata that lives its life at the level of pure instinct. What we have from Pasolini in the case of Nando is a depiction of this pure existence and a great admiration for it. It is a modern version of the Romantic concept of the noble savage, with instinct the equivalent to purity. In the novels this instinctive living will be seen mainly through its explosion into violence, and in the mind of Pasolini the violence will be rendered the equivalent of purity.

If one considers the style of the *novella,* one word at once springs to mind—Neorealism. With Pasolini, as with Pavese (and with Pavese we think of the great influence of the Americans in post-1945 Italian prose writings), what we have is not the smooth flowing style of the 'bello scrivere' of the Fascist period—the writing for writing's sake of the *Prosa d'Arte*—but bare essential prose with short sentences, brief annotations, light brush strokes. The events are merely recounted as they happen; there is no attempt to embellish them. The *novella* consists of a series of little scenes with one thing happening after another as in a film.

Along with this bare essential style there is also, predominant in the *novella,* the use of dialogue. This, of course, is another feature of Neorealism but one that is handled extremely well by Pasolini. The whole tone of the exchange between Nando and the Narrator is very convincing and realistic. Kept down to a minimum, it is little more than a series of questions and answers, and yet it puts across to the reader a whole range of emotions from amazement to disappointment in a way that is completely natural.

Another feature, not so much in evidence here as in the novels, is the use of dialect. This again goes back to the Gramscian concept of a national-popular literature. According to Pasolini, if a literature is to be popular it must be written to a great extent in the language of the people. How, he asks, can one possibly claim adherence to reality in the depiction of the character if the transcription of that character is in terms of a literary language whose usage is restricted to a social and cultured minority? Pasolini, however, does not restrict his use of dialect to the transcription of dialogue but also, following on from Verga, (the Verga of *Vita dei Campi* and *I Malavoglia*) tends to describe through his characters' minds, a use, *suo modo,* of the 'discorso libero indiretto' of the great Sicilian writer. Thus, scenic impressions and descriptions are to a great extent contaminated by dialect although written in a highly literary language.

In a country like Italy, struggling as it still is with the vexed *Questione della Lingua,* the linguistic innovations of Pasolini have caused no small degree of controversy. In his enthusiasm Pasolini has perhaps gone to an extreme, and people have rightly pointed out the limitations of such an overwhelming use of dialect. What he does with his use of Romanesco is to transfer the restriction of the language from one social group to another. Instead of widening the horizons of the language through a careful and positive use of dialect, he has, if anything, restricted them through an arbitrary and in many ways negative use of it. In the novels, for example, his use of dialect is not popular, not of the people, but is rather the 'gergo' or slang of the Roman 'malavita', an element which of its nature is ever changing and hence incapable of any linguistic permanency or stability.

And yet in spite of these restrictions, the linguistic balance sheet of Pasolini is far from being 'in the red'. Even critics who deny all else cannot deny his highly original and literary style. Who, for example, can fail to recognise his poetic ability (and Pasolini stands high as a poet in his own right) to clothe a word with richly complex symbolic meanings? Who can fail to appreciate the imagery and comparison that he draws from the animal kingdom? Thus, for example, in **Biciclettone:** 'In mezzora lo spiazzo di sabbia tra il muraglione e il galleggiante fu un verminaio' where 'verminaio' not only conveys to us that the strip of sand was crawling with people but also through its link with 'verme' tells us something about these people—viz. that they come from a very low social strata. So too in **Biciclettone** we have the affectionate use of 'cagnolino' which comes up again and again like a *leit-motif* and which gives us the picture of the little boy trotting behind the Narrator just like a little dog.

But all this imagery is of little importance compared with Pasolini's ability (and again the name of Verga springs to mind) to convey his deeply felt sympathy through a prose style, bare and brilliant. And the sympathy strikes us all the more because it remains under control.

Even in the last paragraph, where the impersonality of the Narrator is completely abandoned, the sympathy does not flow out in a rhetorical torrent of cheap sentimentalism, but remains simple, and in its simplicity all the more moving.

Times Literary Supplement (review date 21 July 1972)

SOURCE: "Not Forgetting the Artist," in *Times Literary Supplement,* No. 3673, July 21, 1972, p. 833.

[*In the following review, the critic states that Pasolini's* "Empirismo eretico *is the record of the intellectual activity of an individual struggling with a protean culture which changed form just as he seemed to be about to comprehend it.*"]

Pier Paolo Pasolini is best known internationally as a film director, but he is also a novelist and poet of considerable talent and a notorious publicist and intellectual provocateur. Much of his non-fictional writing is devoted to the task of explaining and theorizing his artistic activity proper. Thus he has written at length about the language question, still a live issue in Italy, about literature and about the semiology of the cinema.

But there is in this and in his other writing a secondary aspect also, not simply a justification by the author for doing what he does, but a more personal justification for being who he is. This aspect of Signor Pasolini's public demeanour can be, and has been, dismissed as mere narcissism. Why for example does he insist on casting himself in the role of "The Artist" in his film of the **Decameron?** And why does he have to insert passages of infantile sexual autobiography in an essay on language whose prevailing tone is scientific and pseudo-objective?

Taken as a whole, however, these recurrent interventions by the author in a work, whether a film or a poem or an essay, which he has produced and, so to speak, rendered external to himself, can be seen to have an aesthetic purpose. They are a reminder that a work of art, or even of science, is not merely an object, but is an act of expression by an author who does not cease to exist and to be himself once the act is completed. And at the same time, because the author in question is Signor Pasolini and not someone else, the interventions are structured to represent a challenge to the cultural orthodoxy, including the Marxist counter-orthodoxy, judged by Signor Pasolini to have grown impersonal and desiccated and therefore moribund.

Empirismo eretico brings together the corpus of Signor Pasolini's nonfictional writing over the past ten years. Taken singly, few of the essays in the book stand out as being of independent importance. The essays on the cinema, which employ semiological techniques in defence of a curious theory of ultra-realism ("the written language of reality") form a section on their own. There is also a brilliant interpretation of the Vanni Fucci episode in Dante's *Inferno* and an ingenious attempt to categorize the literary style of contemporary writers in relation to what Signor Pasolini aptly calls the *koinè,* the featureless standard language approved by grammarians and diffused by radio announcers. But most of the writings on language, which seemed so prophetic when they first came out, have lost their force with the failure of neocapitalism to attain the cultural hegemony which Pasolini prematurely attributed to it in the mid-1960s. What survives in these essays is the personal aspect, the cry of pain for the loss of the maternal world embodied in the peasantry and the lumpenproletariat, submerged under the weight of patriarchal technocracy.

That the personal, the social and the would-be scientific can be so jumbled together within the confines of a single essay is a notable achievement. More remarkable still, however, is the way the pieces in ***Empirismo eretico*** actually cohere to form a book. ***Empirismo eretico*** is the record of the intellectual activity of an individual struggling with a protean culture which changed form just as he seemed to be about to comprehend it. Failure, in this context, is often as significant as success, and it is to Signor Pasolini's credit that he has even dared to republish the atrocious poem **"The Communist Party to Youth"** which he wrote on the occasion of a battle between student demonstrators and police in 1968. The "apologia" for the poem, half critical and half justification, which he appends to the new edition, is unfortunately totally unconvincing and disingenuous. But perhaps for that very reason, as Sartre suggested of Baudelaire, it is most authentically Pasolini.

Andrew Sarris (essay date 17 November 1975)

SOURCE: "Pasolini Leaves a Literary Legacy," in *Village Voice*, Vol. XX, No. 46, November 17, 1975, p. 127.

[*In the following essay, Sarris discusses Pasolini's career and gruesome death.*]

Pier Paolo Pasolini, the 53-year-old film director, was murdered last week near Rome. His confessed killer, 17-year-old Giuseppe Pelosi, says that he rejected Mr. Pasolini's sexual advances, beat him unconscious with a piece of wooden fencing, and then ran over him in Pasolini's own sportscar.

The gruesome murder of Pier Paolo Pasolini was more violent and more senseless than anything he had ever conceived in his films. He died on the edge of an abyss he had attempted to explore in *Accattone* back in 1961. The eponymous protagonist of *Accattone* was no mere middle-class "vitellone" with time on his hands. Pasolini's characters, unlike Fellini's, were hopelessly mired in the lower depths. Indeed, Accattone might have been the cinematic prototype of 17-year-old Giuseppe Pelosi, the alleged real-life murderer of Pasolini. The *Times* quoted Michelangelo Antonioni to this effect: "In the end, he (Pasolini) was the victim of his own characters—a perfect tragedy foreseen in its different aspects—without knowing that one day it would end up overcoming him."

I was struck also by a quotation in the *Times* from Pasolini's October 18 column (a regular feature) in the Milan daily *Corriere della Sera* in which he blamed television for "having ended the era of compassion and initiated the era of hedonism." In this context, Giuseppe Pelosi may turn out to be less an underprivileged Accattone of the '70s than a child of television. It may be suggested also that Pasolini was fatally attracted to the amoral dealers in "rough trade". Pasolini would have been the last person to sentimentalize or even rationalize his own restless homosexuality. As a Marxist theoretician, he might have derived some dark humor from his belonging to a relatively privileged class of exploiter as he cruised in his silver Alfa Romeo, never suspecting what a murderous metaphor for the class struggle this vehicle

would turn out to be. But to live at all in these times is to live dangerously. Hence, on the last night of his life Pasolini spoke at dinner with friends of the violence and criminality engulfing Rome. A premonition or a persistent refrain? We shall never know. When I read of Pasolini's death I felt as if a whole chain of senseless murders (and one, particularly, of a child of dear friends) represented a global plague which our civilization would never survive. It had simply become a race between the unruly crazies and the uniformed bullies to see which form of fearsome tyranny would do us in first: anarchy or totalitarianism.

Back in 1967 I wrote of Pasolini in "Interviews with Film Directors": "Pier Paolo Pasolini comes to the cinema from literature, and his films tend to follow a literary schema. Nonetheless, Pasolini has emerged as one of the most articulate and erudite theoreticians of the cinema. Consciously a classicist and a humanist, Pasolini is nonetheless sensitive to the achievements of the formalists in the cinema. His career thus far demonstrates the path a literary artist can follow in the cinema. In addition, Pasolini has evolved a unique blend of Marxist historical consciousness and Christian compassion."

The word "compassion" came very easily when one thought of Pasolini. On the few occasions I met him he struck me as a gentle, thoughtful, unsuspicious soul. I was dazzled by his lucid lecture on semiotics at the Pesaro Film Festival in 1964 or 1965, and by his appraisal of Godard, Antonioni, and Bertolucci on that occasion. I am not qualified to evaluate his ultimate significance as a poet, novelist, and journalist. As a film-maker, he generally seemed too theoretical for my taste. His films were too often amalgams of painting and literature rather than authentic cinema in their own right. Hence, his images were often as segmented as the flight of Zeno's arrow.

Pasolini fully understood the problem. "We might say that the selection of actors, of expressions, of clothing, of place, of lighting—all these are the various components of the overall vocabulary; they are, so to speak, the nouns, the verbs, the adjectives, the adverbs, while the choice of camera movements, of framing, etc., is the syntax itself, the rhythmical arrangement of the various components into one complete sentence. In speaking or writing, this can be done with extreme rapidity—the words and the syntax, or the meter, spring forward almost simultaneously. But in cinematic expression, a kind of interruption takes place, a pause. The 'words' pile up in front of you unmercifully, almost brutally, then wait there to be formed into a complete 'sentence' by the mind behind the camera that sets up the particular shot (syntax)."

There should be a Pasolini retrospective as soon as possible so that we may reappraise *Accattone, Mama Roma,*

RoGoPaG, The Gospel According to St. Matthew, The Hawks and the Sparrows, Teorema, The Arabian Nights, The Decameron, Oedipus Rex, Medea, The Canterbury Tales, and the recently completed *The 120 Days of Sodoma.* It would not bring him back, but it would help keep his spirit alive. I, personally, shall miss the presence of Pasolini's elegant mind on this planet.

T. O'Neill (essay date December 1975)

SOURCE: "Pier Paolo Pasolini's Dialect Poetry," in *Forum Italicum,* Vol. IX, No. 4, December, 1975, pp. 343-67.

[In the following essay, O'Neill traces the influences, themes, and stylistic devices of Pasolini's dialect poetry.]

Perhaps the best synthesis of the world of Pasolini's dialect poetry is that given, unconsciously, by the author himself in the important 1952 essay on *La poesia dialettale del Novecento,* talking of the Triestine poet, Giotti:

> Una povera storia, infinitamente più nuda e deserta che nei crepuscolari, poiché nella sua angoscia non c'è compiacimento o ripensamento da favola decadente, ma come un interno terrore, una nozione della morte e del disfacimento del mondo, delle cose care e degli affetti, che ha quasi un remoto accento leopardiano.

The "mondo" of which Pasolini speaks is that of Friuli, specifically Casarsa, the birthplace of his mother, to where his family had been evacuated in 1943, and where he remained until 1949, when, he moved, definitively, to Rome. But the Casarsa of Pasolini is not a precise, well-defined geographical location; it is not, in a word, realistically described and recognisable as such, like, say, the Tuscany or Umbria of Luzi: rather it has become, to adopt an expression of Silone's, the poet's *paese dell'anima.* Casarsa is not part of the geographical world, but rather the symbol of a world complete in itself, an absolute (and therefore perfect) idyllic world of youth and innocence: in the words of the poet himself, it is the world of "coloro che egli amava con dolcezza e violenza, torbidamente e candidamente," a "vita rustica, resa epica da una carica accorante di nostalgia"—"il calore puro e accecante dell'adolescenza." In this respect the *dedica* speaks clearly:

> Fontana di aga dal me país.
> A no è aga pí fres-cia che tal me país.
> Fontana di rustic amòur.

> (Fontana d'acqua del mio paese. Non c'è acqua più fresca che nel mio paese. Fontana di rustico amore).

His poetry will be a celebration of the "país" in the absolute sense to which we have alluded, and the "fontana di rustic amòur," with its "aga fres-cia"—a recurring motif in the early poetry, perhaps of Machadian derivation—the concrete symbol of a world of innocence and purity, untrammeled by complications.

So too, just as Casarsa is his *paese dell'anima,* its young inhabitants—given in the infinite and evocative variations of the dialects: *nini* (fanciullo), *fì* (ragazzo), *zòvin* (giovane), *soranèl* (ragazzetto), *fantassùt* (giovinetto), *donzel* (giovinetto), *frut* (fanciullo)—are also simply, to use Eliot's term, objective correlatives of the poet himself, loaded with the emotion that is his, deriving from the consciousness he has of the fleeting nature of the world and its inhabitants which he contemplates. In this sense, the diminutive "fantassùt," used vocatively at the beginning of *Ploja tai cunfins* (Pioggia sui confini), can legitimately be compared to the "corpo fanciulletto" of Foscolo's *A Zacinto,* and, perhaps more so, to the "fanciullo mio" of Leopardi's *Il sabato del villaggio,* both of which perform the same poetic function as Pasolini's "fantassùt"—that is to say, they are persons representing a state of innocence, of unawareness, and are attractive precisely because of these qualities, but at the same time they are poetically intensified by the awareness, as we shall see shortly, of a different reality on the part of the poet.

This nostalgic, memorial evocation of an idyllic, perfect world of youth and innocence, such as permeates Pasolini's early dialect poetry, is, of course, more than understandable in the climate of the early forties in Italy. Pasolini, to an extent, explains it himself in the concluding pages of *La poesia dialettale del Novecento,* where, talking of the regress from language to dialect in his own poetry, he says it was:

> causato da ragioni più complesse, sia all'interno che all'esterno: compiersi da una lingua (l'italiano) a un'altra lingua (il friulano) divenuta oggetto di accorata nostalgia, sensuale in origine (in tutta l'estensione e la profondità dell'attributo) ma coincidente poi con la nostalgia di chi viva—e lo sappia—in una civiltà giunta a una sua crisi linguistica, al desolato, e violento, *"je ne sais plus parler"* rimbaudiano.

The civilisation in linguistic crisis which, given the strong link in Pasolini between language and society, indicates a civilisation in crisis *tout court,* was, of course, that of fascism which, thanks to Mussolini's tactics, starting with the anti-Semitic legislation of the summer of 1938, and continuing with the Rome-Berlin pact of the following year, was gradually drawing closer in form and outlook to Hitler's Germany. Pasolini's withdrawal into the Casarsa of his youth is, in its way, a withdrawal from the unacceptable reality of fascist Italy, a rejection of history. It too is part of that "evasività," which he attributes to Solmi, "che coincide, in parte, con quella ermetica dell'anteguerra."

Nor, besides this evident political cause, is his choice of subject matter strange in the light of the vogue in Italy at that period of two masterpieces in the literature of adolescence, Alain-Fournier's *Le grand Meaulnes* and Raymond Radiguet's *Le diable au corps.* Nor, as we shall discuss later, is there to be excluded the possible influence of the Spanish poet, Antonio Machado, whose memorial evocation of the Castille of his youth—*Mi juventud, veinte años en tierra de Castilla*—is not dissimilar in intention, and, on occasions, in style and vocabulary, to the Casarsa of Pasolini.

In the last analysis, however, neither political cause nor literary affinity completely explain Pasolini's choice of subject matter. His evocation of an adolescent world would seem to have deeper, perhaps more psychological roots, for, on examination, it can be seen to be a constant in his works. The *ragazzi di vita* of the 'Roman' novels, in fact, although influenced by the Neapolitan Russo, and particularly by the Roman Belli, are still basically the *frutin* who populate his early poetry. It would seem to us that Pasolini himself wished to stress the constant importance the world of adolescence had for him, when, in reprinting his dialect poems in 1954, he chose as their title **La meglio gioventù,** stressing thereby his belief in it—youth—as the best period of one's life, conscious as he was then that, alas, it was—in the words of the *canto popolare* he was citing—"soto tera."

If the early dialect poetry of Pasolini, however, were simply a highly lyrical, descriptive evocation of youth, it is doubtful whether it would be able to hold our attention as it does. In fact, the world of youth and innocence evoked by the poet is, in many respects, only the framework of the collection, its "povera storia," to use his own expression. As we have already indicated, the various youths who pass through his poetry are the objective correlatives of the poet himself. The objective world of Casarsa is simply one side of the coin. On the other side there stands the poet himself, remembering and endowing that world with a richness, complexity and ambiguity that is his. The "carica accorante di nostalgia" is counterbalanced by the consciousness or awareness of reality that he has. The awareness of what he is (reality), compared with what they are (nostalgia), brings in the consciousness of change, and, ultimately, of death. What we have, in effect, is a repetition of a well-known Leopardian situation, typical of the *grandi idilli:* namely, the nostalgic evocation of a situation, which nostalgic evocation contains within itself the consciousness of its being no more. From this nostalgia, which is not an escape from reality but rather a sublimation of it, there derives that "nozione della morte e del disfacimento del mondo, delle cose care e degli affetti"

that Pasolini sees in Giotti, and which we believe mirrors accurately his own poetry.

An examination of the opening poems from his first collection will illustrate this situation of nostalgia-consciousness. It is well illustrated in the volume's first poem following the *dedica,* **"Il nini muart"** (Il fanciullo morto):

> Sera imbarlumida, tal fossál
> a cres l'aga, na fèmina plena
> a ciamina pel ciamp.
>
> Jo ti recuardi, Narcìs, ti vèvis il colòur
> de la sera, quand li ciampanis
> a sùnin di muart.
>
> (Sera luminosa, nel fosso cresce l'acqua, una donna incinta cammina per il campo. Io ti ricordo, Narciso, avevi il colore della sera, quando le campane suonano a morto.).

The poem is divided into two tercets. The first one presents us with a simple scene, evoked with a few impressionistic strokes, reminiscent of Pascoli's *Myricae,* against which there stands out the "fèmina plena," symbol, like the water running in the ditch, of life. What at first sight may seem a simple, descriptive piece, takes on its full significance in the light of the second tercet, for there the poet's memory, through the unifying element of the "colòur / de la sera," leads to his awareness that that life, mirrored in the first tercet, cannot be separated from its necessary counterpart, death, and it is the awareness of death, inherent in that incipient life, that takes the first tercet (and the complete poem) beyond the bounds of a merely descriptive piece, and makes it, instead, a poetic vehicle for the intense emotion of the poet.

A similar situation is to be found in the poem immediately following, **"Ploja tai cunfins"** (Pioggia sui confini):

> Fantassùt, al plòuf il Sèil
> tai spolèrs dal to paìs,
> tal to vis de rosa e mèil
> pluvisìn al nas il mèis.
>
> Il soreli scur di fun
> sot li branchis dai moràrs
> al ti brusa e sui cunfins
> tu i ti ciantis, sòul, i muàrs.
>
> Fantassùt, al rit il Sèil
> tai barcòns dal to paìs,
> tal to vis di sanc e fièl
> serenàt al mòur il mèis.

(Giovinetto, piove il Cielo sui focolari del tuo
paese, sul tuo viso di rosa e miele, nuvoloso nasce
il mese. Il sole scuro di fumo, sotto i rami del
gelseto, ti brucia e sui confini, tu solo, canti i morti.
Giovinetto, ride il Cielo sui balconi del tuo paese,
sul tuo viso di sangue e fiele, rasserenato muore il
mese.)

In this poem, with its three quatrains of *ottonari* rhyming
ABAB, CDCD, ABAB, the reader is once again confronted
with the presence of life in the form of the "vis di rosa e
mèil," standing out in contrast with the natural scene, the dismal, raining first day of the month, and here also, as in **"Il
nini muart,"** with its "sera imbarlumida" as a mirror of
death, the nascent month already contains within itself, in
the adjective "pluvisìn," underscored in the "soreli scur di
fun" of the second quatrain, a premonition of what is to
come. And so, with the inevitable passing of time, the life
of the *fantassùt* wastes away, the initial "vis di rosa e mèil"
becomes, with a neat assonance between "mèil" and "fièl,"
its opposite, "vis di sanc e fièl," contrasting with the
"serenàt" of the month in the same way it had in the opening quatrain.

As a final example, let us examine the next poem, **"Dili"**:

Ti jos, Dili, ta li cassis
a plòuf. I cians si scunìssin
pal plan verdùt.

Ti jos, nini, tai nustris cuàrps,
la fres-cia rosada
dal timp pierdùt.

(Vedi, Dilio, sulle acacie piove. I cani si sfiatano
per il piano verdino. Vedi, fanciullo, sui nostri corpi
la fresca rugiada del tempo perduto.)

Here too we have the same procedure as in **"Il nini muart"**:
the evocation of the scene in the first tercet through a few
impressionistic strokes, and the completion of that initial
scene by the awareness of the poet in the second tercet, with
its beautiful image of the "fres-cia rosada," of the fleeting
nature of that scene and everything in it, including himself
and Dilio, underlined by the rhyme between "verdùt" of the
first tercet—the greenness and freshness of youth—and the
truncated "pierdut" of the last line of the poem.

These opening poems, with their nostalgia-cum-conscious-
ness situation centred on a life-death cycle, are exemplary
in that they clearly delineate, right from the outset, what will
be one of the constants in Pasolini's work. Usually reflected
against a backcloth of seasonal change, the inevitable passing of time occurs again and again in *Poesie a Casarsa.* If
one were to sum up the predominant sentiment present in

these poems, one could do no better than cite—perhaps
ironically—Pasolini himself, who, talking of Luzi's *Onore
del vero,* said that the Florentine poet—and the judgment describes perfectly his own early poetry:

si trova in possesso di una grande ricchezza, di un
capitale inesauribile: la coscienza della morte.
Profondamente originale e profondamente ovvio, il
suo messaggio poetico non è che un "memento
mori."

This consciousness of life being a "memento mori" has two
results. On the one hand, the perfect, innocent world of
youth, the "calore puro e accecante dell'adolescenza" evoked
with the "carica accorante di nostalgia," subject as it is to
the laws of time, will gradually be subjected to maturity, that
is to say, to the imperfect, the impure, the corrupt which in-
filtrate it. This was already to be seen in *Ploja tai cunfins,*
in the change from the "vis di rosa e mèil" to the "vis di
sanc e fiel." More than a direct mutation from one state to
another, however, more often than not there is a state of co-
existence, indicative perhaps of the unwillingness of the author, although only too aware of the reality of the situation,
to abandon the intensely loved world of his youth. Thus in
"O me donzel" (O me giovinetto), the poet can define himself as a "lontàn frut peciadòur" (lontano fanciullo
peccatore), where the first adjective and the noun are the attributes of innocent youth (or of nostalgia), whereas the second adjective is that of corrupt maturity (or reality). To this
same category belong the "ridi scunfuartàt" (riso sconsolato)
of the same poem—taken up in the "ridi pens" (grave riso)
of **"David"**—and the autodefinition of the poet in **"Vilota"**
as an "antìc soranel" (antico ragazzetto). This coexistence
of youth-maturity, innocence-corruption, adumbrated in the
poetry in dialect, will be developed fully in the Italian poems of *L'Usignolo della Chiesa Cattolica.*

On the other hand, even if there is present a consciousness
of progression towards maturity and corruption, and even if
this progression is only reluctantly accepted by the poet, who
would prefer that his chosen world remain unchanged in its
youthful innocence, there is also an increasing awareness on
the poet's part that so to wish is to deny the march of history, of progress. The deliverance from maturity is at the
same time a condemnation to a stunted existence. This dilemma, which will never really be resolved and which will
appear constantly in all Pasolini's works, is present already
in his *Poesie a Casarsa.*

Symptomatic of this is the poem **"Tornant al pais"**
(Tornando al paese), constructed on a dialogue between the
poet and a *fantassuta* in the town to which he now returns:

Fantassuta, se i fatu
sblanciada dongia il fòuc,

coma una plantuta
svampida tal tramònt?
'Jo i impiji vecius stecs
e il fun al svuala scur
disìnt che tal me mond
il vivi al è sigùr.'
Ma a chel fòuc ch'al nulìs
a mi mancia il rispìr,
e i vorès essi il vint
ch'al mòur tal país. (I)

. . . .

A fiesta a bat a glons
il me país misdì.
Ma pai pras se silensi
ch'a puarta la ciampana!
Sempre chè tu ti sos,
ciampana, e cun passiòn
jo i torni a la to vòus.
'Il timp a no'l si mòuf:
jot il ridi dai paris,
coma tai rams la ploja,
tai vuj dai so frutíns.' (III)

(Giovinetta, cosa fai sbiancata presso il fuoco, come
una pianticina che sfuma al tramonto? 'Io accendo
vecchi sterpi, e il fumo vola oscuro, a dire che nel
mio mondo il vivere è sicuro.' Ma a quel fuoco che
profuma mi manca il respiro, e vorrei essere il vento
che muore nel paese. . . Festoso nel mio paese
rintocca il mezzogiorno. Ma sui prati che silenzio
porta la campana! Sempre la stessa tu sei, campana,
e con sgomento ritorno alla tua voce. 'Il tempo non
si muove; guarda il riso dei padri, come nei rami la
pioggia, negli occhi dei fanciulli.')

Here, in the opening stanza, we have the first sign of the
awareness on the poet's part of the stunted existence of his
beloved Casarsa in the contrast between the affectionately
evoked "fantassuta" lighting the "vecius stecs" to indicate
that "il vivi al è sigùr," and the poet who, although attracted
by the fire, by its perfume, is also choked by its smoke. This
awareness is heightened in the third stanza where the
realisation that the bell ringing out across the town and the
fields is that same bell of many years ago, brings home to
the poet the fact that time has stood still for the folk of
Casarsa. This realisation, however, is no longer a source of
joy but rather a source of "passiòn" (sgomento), because the
poet realises, in the words of the young girl, that "nualtris
si vif, / a si vif quiès e muàrs" (noi si vive, si vive quieti e
morti), where the adjective to be stressed is not so much
"quiès" as "muàrs."

This awareness of condemnation inherent in the perfect, un-

changing world of the Friuli, already hinted at in the poems
of the first collection, will become progressively deeper in
the volumes following. In **"La not di maj"** (La notte di
maggio), for example, of *Suite furlana,* the sense of time
precipitating has become much more intense, and as a result of this the elegiac world of the first poems, "clar e fer"
(chiaro e fermo), lightly covered with "la fres-cia rosada /
dal timp pierdùt," is now reflected in the "rèit / di rujs
insanganadis" (rete / di rughe sanguinose) of the young boy
grown old as "ains scurìs / e nos dismintiadis / e passiòns
soteradis" (anni oscuri / e notti dimenticate / e passioni
sepolte), in a word, "Vita senza distìn, puartada via cu'l
cuarp" (Vita senza destino, portato via col corpo).

The dilemma is perhaps presented in its clearest terms in the
poem **"Mostru o pavea"** (mostro o farfalla), with its two
series of contrasting terms. On the one hand, there is the butterfly, "pavea di serèn" (farfalla di sereno), symbol of youthful innocence—"Pavea selesta sensa ombrenis" (Farfalla
celeste senza ombre) which "A pausa viola ta li me violis /
tal grin da li vualvis oris" (Si posa viola tra le mie viole,
nel grembo delle ore uguali). On the other hand, the same
butterfly is seen as a "mostru di seren" (mostro di sereno)
which "mi cres / coma una nula" (mi cresce come una nube)
and which "va cuntra di dut, fòut di dut, / al sporcia i flòurs
di me frut" (va contro di tutto, fuori di tutto, sporca i fiori
di me fanciullo). But perhaps the most telling lines of the
poem are the final ones:

No, al è un mostru di speransa
tal vagu disperàt di Ciasarsa:
al mi fai no essi un omp cu'l nut
suspièt di no vej mai vivùt.

(No, è un mostro di speranza nel vuoto disperato
di Ciasarsa: mi fa non essere un uomo col nudo
sospetto di non aver mai vissuto.)

Here there is quite evidently the awareness of the harsh reality of the situation (vagu disperàt di Ciasarsa), and, along
with this realisation, the consciousness of the stunted nature
of a childhood not allowed to develop to maturity (nut /
suspièt di no vej mai vivùt), but also, in spite of this, the
inability of the poet to accept that reality, resulting in that
sineciosi—"mostru di speransa"—that we have already seen
to be a constant in his poetry.

The awareness of the existence of a different world from that
of his youthful Friuli, a world of movement reflecting not
only the cycle of life but also that of progress, and which
therefore puts his Friuli in a completely different light, however contrasted it may be, as we have seen, does nevertheless exist. And if proof were needed, it could be gleaned
from the faint but noticeable insertion into his early poetry—
of its nature essentially and highly lyrical: a poetry of mood,

for the most part fragmentary and impressionistic—of a certain narrative tendency—in, for example, **"Pastorela di Narcis"** (Pastorella di Narciso)—and, along with this a certain linguistic realism such as we find, for example, in the third stanza of **"Il diaul cu la mari"** (Il diavolo con la madre):

> Bessòul al pompa l'aga, al glutàr
> di aga ch'a cola cun un amàr
> sunsàr tal giàtu; e al pissa
> sot li stelis de la not lissa.

> (Solo, pompa l'acqua, una sorsata d'acqua che cade
> con un amaro strepito nel rigagnolo; e piscia sotto
> le stelle della notte liscia.)

The tendency towards a narrative discourse, influenced no doubt by the poetry of Pavese and by the polemical, strongly realistic programmes of the numerous and, for the most part, ephemeral *riviste di poesia* of the post-war period, particularly *La strada,* was continued in the poems of *Romancero.* The poetry from being, as we have seen, prevalently fragmentary and impressionistic, tends now to the longer, narrative structure, rendered frequently, rhythmically, by a popular movement based to a great extent on repetition, exclamation, invocation, such as in *Spiritual.* This tendency towards a narrative structure is accompanied by a much clearer tendency towards objectivity in which the protagonists of the poems exist in their own right and not simply as projections of the poet himself. Along with this, the dichotomy innocence-maturity, which we have seen on occasions of awareness configured as exclusion-inclusion in society in progress, is now, frequently, seen in a polemical note of poor-rich, whether it be in the anguished questions posed in **"Fiesta"**:

> Aleluja aleluja aleluja!
> Cui sìntia la vòus dai Anzuj?
> Cui sàia la possiòn di un puòr?
> Cui sìntia il ciant dai Anzuj?
> E cui sàia il me nòn: Chin Cianòr?
> Cui ghi cròdia ai Anzuj?

> (Aleluja aleluja aleluja! Chi sente la voce degli
> angeli? E chi sa il tormento di un povero? Chi sente
> il canto degli Angeli? E chi sa il mio nome: Chino
> Canòr? Chi crede negli Angeli?)

or, perhaps more clearly, in the contrast between Chino Canòr and the others, the "siòrs" (signori), emphasized polemically through repetition, in the concluding lines of the same poem:

> Aleluja aleluja aleluja!
> Li ciampanis a sunin pai siòrs,

> jo i sint altris ciampanis:
> ciampanis vissinis pai siòrs,
> par me ciampanis lontanis
>
> > coma i siòrs.

> (Aleluja aleluja aleluja! Le campane suonano per i
> ricchi, io sento altre campane: campane vicine per
> i ricchi, per me campane lontane come i ricchi.)

And, as a result of this, the "dis perdut" become "dis robat" (giorni rubati) where, in the poem of that title, beauty, innocence and youth are now seen not as eternal but rather as an all too fleeting prelude to the harsh reality of maturity:

> Nos ch'i sin puòrs i vin puòc timp
> de zoventùt e de belessa:
> mond, te pòus stà sensa de nos.

> Sclafs da la nàssita i sin nos!
> Pavèjs ch'a no àn mai vut belessa
> muartis ta la galeta dal timp.

> (Noi che siamo poveri abbiamo poco tempo di
> gioventù, e di bellezza: mondo, tu puoi stare senza
> di noi. Schiavi della nascita siamo noi! Farfalle che
> non hanno mai avuto bellezza, morte nel bozzolo
> del tempo.)

This tragic note, accompanied by a polemical anti-bourgeois tone, is best expressed in the naked realism, contrasting with the unfulfilled dreams, of **"Vegnerà el vero Cristo"**:

> No gò corajo de ver sogni:
> il blù e l'onto de la tuta,
> no altro tal me cuòr de operajo.

> Mort par quatro franchi, operajo,
> il cuòr, ti te gà odià la tuta
> e pers i to più veri sogni.

> El jera un fiol ch'el veva sogni,
> un fiol blù come la tuta.
> Vegnerà el vero Cristo, operajo.

> a insegnarte a ver veri sogni.

> (Non ho coraggio di avere sogni: il blu e l'unto della
> tuta, non altro nel mio cuore di operaio. Morto per
> due soldi, operaio, il cuore, hai odiato la tuta e perso
> i tuoi più veri sogni. Era un ragazzo che aveva
> sogni, un ragazzo blu con la tuta. Verrà il vero
> Cristo, operaio, a insegnarti ad avere veri sogni.)

This tendency to an ever-increasing awareness of a reality outside of himself, alternating between acceptance and rejection, accompanied, stylistically, by a movement from the lyricism of the early Friulan *villotta* to the larger, epico-narrative dimension in the later poems, culminating in the novel *Il sogno di una cosa* of 1949-50, is undoubtedly a reflection (or result) of the increasing ideological concern in Pasolini—the discovery of Marx and Gramsci in 1949—as well as a reflection of the study in those same years of dialect and popular literature, leading to the publication of *La poesia dialettale del Novecento* in 1952, and *La poesia popolare italiana* in 1955.

This thematic, stylistic development, which we have tried to document in the dialect poems from the early *Poesie a Casarsa* to those written in Rome in the early fifties—coeval, as we have seen, with his fundamental critical studies of those years, and also, in part, it may be added, with the first 'Roman' novel, *Ragazzi di vita*—is accompanied by a similar development in Pasolini's use of dialect and his attitude towards it to which we should now like briefly to direct our attention.

Pasolini himself has briefly but succinctly described the evolution of his use of dialect in two documents which, taken together, provide the reader with all the necessary details. These documents are the already cited autobiographical pages at the conclusion of *La poesia dialettale del Novecento,* and the *nota* added to the various volumes of dialect poetry gathered together and reprinted in 1954 with the collective title of *La meglio gioventù.*

We already examined some years ago the importance given by Pasolini to dialect in his novels—how, briefly, its adoption was an attempt, a conscious attempt to resolve the linguistic impasse in which the literary language found itself in the immediate post-war period. In this respect, his claim that his regress to dialect was "coincidente . . . con la nostalgia di chi viva—e lo sappia—in una civiltà giunta a una sua crisi linguistica" is wholly acceptable. In addition to his novels, the 1953 poems of *Romancero* should also be included in this category, for there too the dialect is undoubtedly used, to adopt the poet's own expression, "nella intera sua istituzionalità." In many respects, however, these poems are the least interesting, the fruit of his research into dialect and popular literature rather than of his lyrical inspiration. What interests us more particularly here is his use of dialect not in these later poems where, under the ideological impetus of Gramsci and his concept of a "letteratura nazionale-popolare," Pasolini is already in the process of developing those ideas on language which will permeate his critical work in the fifties and have their practical fruits in the two 'Roman' novels, but rather his use of it in the early *Poesie a Casarsa.* When Pasolini states in the cited *nota* that "là—in the first edition, that is to say—la 'violenza' linguistica (cui accennavo in una noticina) tendeva a fare del parlato casarsese insieme una koinè friulana e una specie di

linguaggio assoluto, inesistente in natura, mentre qui il casarsese è riadottato nella intera sua istituzionalità," what he says of his use of dialect in the first edition may be true, but what he says of it in the second, namely that it is "riadottato nella intera sua istituzionalità" is, I feel, resultant on hindsight rather than on a radical change in the function of the casarsese dialect used. What, then, if not "nella intera sua istituzionalità," is the way Pasolini uses dialect in these first poems, and why is it so?

Why he uses it, of course, is easily explained. To the absolute and perfect idyllic world of youth and innocence there corresponds the absolute and perfect expression of dialect. The private, unchanging world of the poet requires a private, immutable language in order to adequately reflect the poet's chosen world of youth and innocence. In this respect the regress "da un parlante—the poet—a un parlante presumibilmente *più puro, più felice*" (italics mine) is quite understandable.

More important than why he uses it, however, is *how* he uses it, and, here again, the poet, perhaps, as I have suggested, with hindsight, lucidly accounts for his use of it. This, he recognises, was "sensuale in origine (in tutta l'estensione e la profondità dell'attributo)" and as such had implicit in it both "un eccesso di ingenuità" and—undoubtedly more important—"un eccesso di squisitezza" with, later on, "qualche prevedibile involuzione verso più pericolose zone letterarie (per es. Mallarmé e gli Spagnuoli)." It was undoubtedly this sensual, exquisite use of dialect by him that made it, as he says in the *nota,* "una specie di linguaggio assoluto, inesistente in natura," if one likes, Pasolini's equivalent of what Pascoli in *Addio* calls a "lingua di gitane, / una lingua che più non si sa." This absolute, inexistent, if one likes, ideal rather than real nature of the dialect is evidenced by the second paragraph of the original *noticina,* where the poet calls upon the non-Friulan reader to pay particular attention to certain words, which, he says, "nel testo italiano, ho variamente tradotti, ma che, in realtà, restano intraducibili."

If further confirmation of the sensual, exquisite nature of the dialect were required, it would be sufficient to note how Pasolini does not really, as he says, move from dialect in its sensual, exquisite aspects to dialect "nella intera sua istituzionalità," that is to say, from its hermetic, allusive qualities to its more realistic aspects in the period 1947-49, but rather how he deepens or extends the sensual, exquisite element by multiplying the choice of dialects. Thus, to the original *friulano di Casarsa,* which was itself, as he admitted in the original *noticina,* not "quello genuino, ma quello dolcemente intriso di veneto che si parla nella sponda destra del Tagliamento," there are added the Friulan of Valvasone, of Cordenons, of Cordovado, of Gleris and Bannia, as well as the Venetian dialects of Pordenone and Caorle, all used in the poems of 1947-49, and published in the 1949 edition,

Dov'è la mia patria by the Academiuta at Casarsa. I also feel that his adoption of popular poetic forms, such as the Friulan *villotta* in the earlier poems, and, later on, the Piedmontese epico-lyrical *canzoni,* comes into the same category, that is to say, it is dictated by purely aesthetic considerations rather than a desire to adhere more closely to reality.

The sensual, exquisite, evocative musical qualities of the dialect and the poet's treatment of it (". . . non poche sono le violenze che gli ho usato per costringerlo ad un metro e a una dizione poetica") reveal close affinities both with the Symbolists and the Parnassians, a concern with heightened language and form, in a word, an adherence to *littèrature.* As such Pasolini would clearly enter into that category of Italian literature, which, taking up a note of Gramsci, he defines as "una letteratura d'*élites* intellettuali, la cui storia stilistica è una storia d'individui protetti, nell'*inventio,* da una *koinè* già 'per letteratura,' da una parte, e dall'altra da una condizione sociale preservante l'io nella sua passione estetica a coltivare o le abnormità di tipo religioso o intimistico o l'*otium* classicheggiante o squisito." In other words, Pasolini too, at least at the outset of his literary career, belongs to "la torre d'avorio ermetica, implicante un'orgogliosa e in fondo condiscente religione delle lettere."

That this is so can be confirmed by the numerous influences which can be traced in his early poetry—corresponding, it may be said, to the main stages of the development of contemporary Italian poetry outlined by Luciano Anceschi in his *Le poetiche del Novecento in Italia*—and which range from Pascoli, through the *crepuscolari,* to Ungaretti and Montale, through Quasimodo and the Hermetics, to external literary influences, in the case of his early poetry, especially, I would suggest, that of Antonio Machado.

The all-pervading influence is, of course, that of Pascoli. Pasolini's interest in the poet of San Mauro and the influence of his poetry on him started early and can be quite clearly documented. From his *tesi di laurea* to the article in *Convivium* in 1947, and again in the opening number of **Officina** in 1955, Pascoli forms a constant obbligato in the critical writings of Pasolini and remains just as strongly an influence in **Le ceneri di Gramsci** as in the early poetry.

In his early poetry, of course, in addition to certain metrical borrowings, it is easy to see the link between Pasolini's world of youth and innocence and Pascoli's *poetica del fanciullino.* It is undoubtedly from this theory—and its practical results in poetry—that Pasolini's early verse derives its rich, detailed, impressionistic mixture of sound and colour that is so common in Pascoli's *Myricae.*

However, Pasolini's poetry is much more than a simple mimesis, much more, that is, than a simple external repetition

of Pascolian stylistic features. Rather it is a conscious adoption of one of those features, what he calls "il particolare," which merits examination in some detail since it confirms, while stressing its Pascolian origin, what I individuated in the opening pages of this paper as Pasolini's use of the objective correlative. The source of Pasolini's theorization of this aspect of Pascoli's *poiesis* is his 1947 *Convivium* article **"Pascoli e Montale."** This essay, which is one of his earliest, is, perhaps because of its dating, almost as penetrating and acute as his slightly later one on Ungaretti, since both are singularly free from the strait jacket of ideology which was to characterize to a great extent his later essays of the fifties. Starting, as his mentor, Contini, would have done, from the individual word—in this case, the distinctly Pascolian vocabulary, *frullo, volo, grembo,* adopted in Montale's poem, *In limine:* "Il frullo che tu senti non è un volo / ma il commuoversi dell'eterno grembo"—Pasolini moves out to examine Pascoli's limited, because unconscious, use of "il particolare," especially its visual qualities, in the *Myricae* and the better poems of the *Canti di Castelvecchio;* and then goes on to examine how Montale, in the wake of the lesson of Symbolism, develops consciously what Pascoli had used unconsciously. He then illustrates how the "stupendo" in Pascoli, which was to all intents and purposes simply one of the aspects of the *poetica del fanciullino,* is, for the most part, innovative merely in language and not in substance, and how it is only in the better of his poems, that is in those "legati a un particolare visivo o, insomma, fisico, in cui si innesta una 'metafisica' tutta di parole," that he manages to do what Montale will later consciously and constantly do. In the second half of this essay, centered on a telling comparison between Pascoli's *Vischio* and Montale's *Casa dei doganieri,* he defines the "metafisica" of the "particolare" as:

> . . . lo scaturire improvviso nella coscienza di un pensiero, che era stato elaborato nel subconsciente, al contatto di un "riflesso condizionato," scelto e riconosciuto tra i simboli del mondo esteso; è il substrato emotivo che viene tratto alla luce secondo un canone puramente estetico.

I feel it is quite evident from this definition, from what he later individuates in both Pascoli and Montale as "la distensione del loro attimo lirico nella memoria, uno storicizzarsi della loro emozione," the similarity with the objectified, emotive, memorial movement which I have already analysed in some of Pasolini's own early poems.

Pascoli, in addition to providing the source of the Montalian element in Pasolini's poetry, is also the ultimate source of his crepuscular element, to wit, his sense of death. Starting from "Il giorno dei morti" of the *Myricae,* to the "estate fredda dei morti" of *Novembre,* and "il vanire e lo sfiorire, / e i crisantemi, il fiore della morte" of *I gattici,* Pascoli's poetry is continually permeated with a sense of death, of time inexorably passing, perhaps best summed up in the final lines of *Il ritardo:*

> Oh! tardi! Il nido ch'è due nidi al cuore,
> la fame in mezzo a tante cose morte;
> e l'anno è morto, ed anche il giorno muore,
> e il tuono muglia, e il vento urla più forte,
> e l'acqua fruscia, ed è già notte oscura,
> e quello ch'era non sarà mai più.

It is precisely this "interno terrore," this "nozione della morte e del disfacimento del mondo"—to use the poet's own terms from his essay on Giotti—, deriving from Pascoli, that Pasolini has in common not only with the poet of San Mauro but also with the *crepuscolari,* especially, I would say, with Corazzini; and which, as I have indicated earlier, is an indispensable complement to the world of adolescence evoked in the early poems.

The influence of Pascoli, and, through him, of the *crepuscolari* and Montale, can, as I would hope to have demonstrated, be fairly well substantiated from the text themselves, and is, as in the essays, the predominant influence. The influence of Ungaretti, and of Quasimodo and the strictly Hermetic line, is, although present, much more evanescent, and, consequently, more difficult to pin down with precision.

In general terms I would say that if the highly lyrical, fragmentary and impressionistic poetry of the early years, completely lacking in any narrative structure, is, in the final analysis, also derivative from Pascoli, where with the *Myricae* there was initiated that process of disintegration of the poetic form which was to characterize Italian poetry in the late nineteenth and early twentieth century, it is also, in no small part, a reflection of the hermetic, allusive nature of poetry in the thirties and forties, and as such, along with his choice of subject-matter (adolescence) and language (dialect), is a reaction against the incursions of the fascist régime on the autonomy of art.

More specifically the Hermetic influence is to be seen in specific images, consciously or unconsciously derivative from the Hermetic poets, and also, on occasions, in a daring use of language, again typical of the early Hermetics.

In the first category, that of the derivative image, one could include, for example, the first two stanzas of **"Aleluja"** where, in the first, the dying goldfinch echoes Ungaretti's "Ma non morire di lamento / come un cardellino accecato" of *Agonia,* while, in the second, the image of the "fanciullo di luce" (frut di lus) would seem to be a direct borrowing from the opening lines of the 57 poem of Onofri's *Vincere il drago!:* "Con un'arancia in mano, abita il prato / un

fanciullo di luce e d'aria tenue." **"La Domenica Uliva,"** the final poem of the first volume, although prefaced in its first edition with the opening lines of Ungaretti's *La madre,* would in its dialogue between mother and son seem modelled rather on Quasimodo's *Laude 29 aprile 1945.* Similarly, in the next volume, **Suite furlana,** the introduction of a realistic note in, for example, **Ciants di un muart** (Canti di un morto), with its precise date, "vuei XIII Zenar MCMXLIV" (oggi XIII gennaio MCMXLIV), would seem modelled on a similar technique used by Quasimodo in that same period in *Giorno dopo giorno:* in, for example, the titles of such poems as *19 gennaio 1944, Milano, agosto 1943, Anno Domini MCMXLVII.*

In the second category, that of a daring use of language, individual combinations of adjective and noun as, for example, in "colòur smarit" (colore smarrito) of **"Ciant da li ciampanis"** (Canto delle campane) belong to that typically Hermetic combination one frequently finds in Luzi's *Avvento notturno,* such as, for example, the "vie pensierose" of *Passi,* and the "albero increscioso" of *Periodo;* as do poems such as the *Lengas dai frus di sera* (Linguaggi dei fanciulli di sera) and, especially I would say, the complete section of *Lieder.*

What, finally, of the influence of the contemporary Spanish poets, especially, I would suggest, Machado? That he was familiar with the Spanish poets in general is clear from that autobiographical-critical page I have already quoted, where he talks about "qualche prevedibile involuzione verso più pericolose zone letterarie (per es. Mallarmè e gli Spagnoli)"; that he was familiar, perhaps more especially, with Machado we can gather from the direct quotation from the Spanish poet's *Retrato* which prefaced **Suite furlana.** To be more specific, however, is somewhat hazardous. To be sure, in Pasolini's early poems the time of day that recurs most frequently is the evening, and this is very similar to the *tarde* of Machado. The very description of the evening given by Pasolini in **"Il nini muart":** "Sera imbarlumida" (Sera luminosa) may even be a direct calque of Machado's "!Oh tarde luminosa!," the opening line of Poem LXXVI. Similarly the frequent recurrence of the fountain as a leit-motif in his early poetry—the "fontana di aga dal me pais" of the **Dedica**—may betray a Machadian influence as may the equally frequent recurrence of bells, although, in this latter case, their frequent presence in both Corazzini and, needless to say, Pascoli, makes any precise location of sources very difficult. The great wealth of visual detail that one finds in Machado's poetry and which is also evident in Pasolini's turns up frequently in Pascoli, so that it may not be inappropriate to say that Pasolini is attracted to and influenced by Machado precisely because of the Pascolian qualities of the Spanish poet's verse. In addition to this—and in more general terms—it may simply be that he is attracted to a poet who, regardless of differences that undoubtedly exist in detail, is, in his general development, very close to him: both poets' early work is, in many respects, based on a contrast between a past happiness and a present bitterness, centered around a memorial evocation of youthful innocence, mirrored or identified with a precise geographical location: in Pasolini, Friuli with its "vita rustica, resa epica da una carica accorante di nostalgia;" in Machado, the province of Soria:

> En la desesperanza y en la melancolía
> de tu recuerdo, Soria, mi corazón se abreva,
> Tierra de alma, toda, hacia la tierra mía,
> por los floridos valles, mi corazón te lleva.

And just as Pasolini was to move, if ever so slightly, from an evocative, memorial poetry to verse in a more realistic vein as a result of the effect upon him of the Resistance, so too Machado, as a result of the Spanish Civil War, moved towards a more *engagé* poetry.

Perhaps, in conclusion, the best summation of *Poesie a Casarsa,* thematically and stylistically, is provided by the concluding lines of Maria Luisa Spaziani's *Sera di vento:*

> Vorrei cogliervi tutte, o mie nel tempo
> ebbre, sfogliate voci lungo l'arida
> corona dell'inverno,
> e ricomporvi in musica, parole
> sopra uno stelo eterno.

—that is to say, the voices of youthful innocence, recollected in the winter of maturity, and translated and rescued from the laws of time in the style and form of poetry.

Teresa de Lauretis (essay date Fall/Winter 1980-81)

SOURCE: "Re-Reading Pasolini's Essays on Cinema," in *Italian Quarterly,* Vol. XXI and XXII, No. 82-3, Fall/Winter, 1980-81, pp. 159-66.

[*In the following essay, de Lauretis asserts that "for Pasolini cinema is precisely writing in images, not to describe (portray) reality or fantasy, but to inscribe them as representations."*]

That Pier Paolo Pasolini was a man of contradiction, and a figure in excess of its cultural ground, is worth repeating. Time and again the "scandal of contradiction" has been found to mar his politics and his poetics, his personal and public life—though not, ironically, his death. For tragic irony composes and resolves all contradictions, recasting them in the terms of narrativization, of dialectical opposition, of a final coherence of discourse which then allows itself the

privilege of excess as an esthetic plus, a something more. Yet, is it not that very scandal, and the possible truth of contradiction, that draws us to Pasolini? Contradiction as—precisely—excessive, irreducible to the dominant ideological scenarios.

Some said he could not be a theorist because he was an artist, and there may be truth in that, though we would much prefer to think one could be both. He was a homosexual but could not be claimed as fellow by gay liberation; nor was his communism acceptable to the Italian Communist Party. As a poet and a writer of literature, his use of language and dialect strove, it has been said, toward a form of "representation which goes beyond the word, beyond the page," exceeding language and "obeying rules that are heteronomous to literature." What he intended as realism in his (early) films was not really realism, it was argued, due to his "wilful disregard of the constructive nature of the editing process," or to his obsessive, even regressive preoccupation with reality, physicality, corporality, narcissistic sensuality. But most of all—and on this nearly everyone agrees—Pasolini was not a semiologist. Here again, it seems, reality got in the way. Nevertheless he was deeply interested in semiology, for a time, and that interest, concurrent as it was with cinema, prompted his interventions on questions of film theory which are still very much at issue today. Thus I would disagree with the assessment (made in 1974; however) that "Pasolini's theoretical writings on cinema are of little or no use for the development of a scientific semiology of the cinema, nor for film theory and/or film criticism." Or rather, I would disagree with the latter part of the statement, since "the development of a *scientific* semiology of the cinema," which never was Pasolini's concern, is no longer a concern at all: it is a moot case. But the value of some of his views on the relation of cinema to reality and to what he called human action (I will call it social practice), the value of his observations for *current* theoretical work in and on cinema is what I will address myself to in this paper.

A growing concern of film theory, in the past decade, has been to understand the working of the cinematic apparatus as a social technology, a relation of the technical and the social. If film as a textual system and cinema as a language were the theoretical objects of classical semiology in the sixties, during the early to mid-seventies, in response to the feminist critique of representation and other political issues, these hypotheses were displaced and film theory began to address questions of sexuality, identification, subjectivity, spectatorship, and the effectivity of various practices of cinema in that respect. Psychoanalysis, with its attention to the signifier and its articulation of subject processes across the imaginary and the symbolic registers, provided an important theoretical framework, a discourse which addressed those questions, albeit in its own specificity. What is necessary for film theory, at the present moment, is an understanding of the interrelations or mediations between the systems of determinations embedded in cinema as a social technology (systems of pre-construction of meaning, codes, technical availability and access), its institutional orders of coherence (the various discourses on cinema), and practices—social practices as well as practices of cinema. Such understanding requires an exploration of the conditions of possibility of those practices and discourses, in and against those systems of determinations. An understanding, then, of the contradictions, the breaking points, the areas of rupture and excess, the limits of those systems. Central to this project is the question of cinematic signification: on the one hand, the articulation of meaning to image, language and sound (Pasolini's insistence on the "audio-visuality" of cinema: "cinema is not the image, it is an audio-visual technique in which the word and the sound have the same importance as the image"); on the other hand, the question of cinema's productive relations, of representation as "the process of the engagement of subjectivity in meaning" and of the ideological as "the constant political institution of the productive terms of representation." These questions may be usefully posed, initially, by retracing something of the history of semiotics from the debate on cinematic articulation which took place during the mid-sixties around the Mostra del Nuovo Cinema in Pesaro; and by re-reading some of Pasolini's unorthodox, "naive" or "idealist" statements, as they were called, in light of later developments in semiotics, as well as the current concerns of film theory.

The debate on articulation in the early years of semiology seemed to crystallize an opposition between linguistic and iconic signs, between verbal language and visual images, their difference being thought of as inherent in two irreducible modes of perception, signification and communication: mediated, coded, symbolic—the former, verbal language; while the latter, iconism, appeared to be immediate, natural, directly linked to reality. On the possibility of determining an articulation (preferably a double articulation) for the cinematic signs hinged cinema's status as a semiotic system, a language. Although a narrow linguistic notion of articulation has proved to be something of a theoretical liability and is no longer adequate to the concerns of film theory, it may be useful to revisit the terms of the argument and its development over the years. For the question "what is cinematic articulation, how is cinema articulated, what does it articulate?" is still very much at issue.

According to Metz's first paper on the topic, "Le cinéma: langue ou langage?" a position which he later revised, cinema could only be described as a language without a code, lacking altogether the second articulation, at the phonemic level; in the cinematic image, wrote Metz, "meaning is naturally derived from the signifier as a whole, without resorting to a code." Pasolini, on the other hand, in his now famous paper **"La lingua seritta della realtà,"** reprinted with all

his other writings on cinema in ***Empirismo eretico,*** argued that cinema was a language with a double articulation, though unlike verbal language, in fact more like written language, in which the minimal units were the various objects in the frame or shot (*inquadratura*); these he called "*cinèmi,*" by analogy with *fonemi,* phonemes. The *cinèmi* combine into larger units, the shots, which are the basic significant units of cinema, corresponding to the morphemes of verbal language. In this way, for Pasolini, cinema articulates reality precisely by means of its second articulation: the selection and combination of real, profilmic objects or events (faces, landscapes, gestures, etc.) in a shot; and it is these profilmic and pre-filmic objects or events ("oggetti, forme o atti della realtà"), which are already *cultural* objects, that constitute the paradigm of cinema, its storehouse of significant images, of image-signs (*im-segni*).

> I cinèmi hanno questa stessa caratteristica di obbligatorietà: non possiamo che scegliere che i cinèmi che ci sono, ossia gli oggetti, le forme e gli atti della realtà che noi cogliamo coi sensi. A differenza di fonemi, però, che sono pochi, i cinèmi sono infiniti, o almeno innumerevoli.

Yet, contended Eco, another participant in the debate, the objects in the frame do not have the same status as the phonemes of verbal language. Even leaving aside the problem of the qualitative difference between objects and their photographic image (a difference central to semiotics, for the real object, the referent, is neither the signified nor the signifier but "the material precondition of any coding process," as Garroni put it), the objects in the frame are already meaningful units, thus more like morphemes. In fact, within the idea of cinema as a system of signs—an idea that Eco himself rightfully suspected of metaphysical complicity—the "code of cinema" could be better described as having not two, nor one, but three articulations (which he designated as semes, iconic signs, and *figurae*).

However, the notion of a triple articulation of the image does not account for the "phenomenon" cinema. For the "phenomenon," the events of cinema are not the photogram, the still image, but at the very least the shot (again, Pasolini's emphasis on *inquadratura*), images in motion which construct not only linear movement but also a depth, an accumulation of time and space that is essential to the meaning, the reading of the image(s). And this spatiotemporal relation is what Pasolini tentatively called "*ritmema*" in a short paper of 1971 entitled **"Teoria delle giunte"** ("A theory of splicing," i.e. of montage). At the conclusion of this phase of the debate, summarized in *La struttura assente,* Eco admitted that, even though cinema as a language could be said to possess a triple articulation, film as discourse is constructed on, and puts into play, many other codes—verbal, iconographic, stylistic, perceptual, narrative . . .

With the shift from the notion of language to the notion of discourse began to appear the limitations, theoretical and ideological, of the semiological analysis. First, the determination of an articulated code (single, double, triple or whatever), even if possible, would offer neither an ontological nor an epistemological guarantee of the event, of what cinema is—to cite the title of a famous book. For indeed one never encounters "cinema" or "language," but practices of language, practices of cinema, which is what Pasolini was talking about: cinema-as-signifying-practice, not cinema-as-system. Secondly, that notion of articulation, concerned as it was with the homogeneity of the theoretical object, and "vitiated [in Pasolini's phrase] by the linguistic mould," was predicated on an imaginary if not "metaphysical" unity of cinema as system, independent, that is, of a viewing situation. Thus it tended to hide or make non-pertinent the other components of the signifying process; for example, to hide the fact that cinematic signification and signification in general are not systemic but rather discursive processes, that they not only engage and overlay multiple codes but also involve distinct communicative situations, particular conditions of reception, enunciation and address, and thus, crucially, the notion of spectatorship—the positioning of spectators in and by the film, in and by cinema. In this sense, for example, Claire Johnston writes, "feminist film practice can no longer be seen simply in terms of the effectivity of a system of representation, but rather as a production of and by subjects already in social practices which always involve heterogeneous and often contradictory positions in ideologies . . . Real readers are subjects in history rather than mere subjects of a single text." In short, spectators are not, as it were, *either* in the film-text *or* simply *outside* the film-text; rather, we might say, they intersect the film, as they are intersected by cinema.

Semiotics, too, has moved along these lines, to some extent, toward the analysis of reading processes and text pragmatics. Eco's own critique of iconism, by displacing the notion of articulation, as well as the classical notion of sign, to a much less central position in his *Theory of Semiotics,* argues that there is no such thing as an iconic sign; there are only visual texts, whose pertinent features are established—if at all—by the context. And it is a code that "decides on what level of complexity it will single out its own pertinent features."

Let me go back from these recent semiotic positions to some of Pasolini's statements, perhaps too easily dismissed as unsemiotic, scientifically improper, because—as he ironically put it—"so extravagantly interdisciplinary." His often quoted slogan, "cinema is the language of reality," was in part provocatively outrageous, in part very earnestly asserted. To be exact, the words he used (it is the title of his 1966 essay) are the following: cinema is "the written language of reality," "la lingua scritta della realtà;" by which he meant that,

as the invention of the alphabet and the technology of writing revolutionized society by "revealing" language to men (men, this is the word he used, I will not revise), making them conscious of spoken language *and thus instituting a cultural consciousness of thought as representation* (while earlier thought and speech must have appeared as natural), cinema is a kind of "writing" (*scrittura*) of reality, that is to say, *the conscious representation of human action,* hence "the *written* language of action." For Pasolini human action, human intervention in the real is the first and foremost expression of men, their primary "language," primary not (or not just) in the sense of originary or pre-historic, but primary to the extent that it encompasses all other "languages"—verbal, gestual, iconic, musical, etc. In this sense he says, what Lenin has left us—the transformation of social structures and their cultural consequences—is "a great poem of action." But

> From Lenin's great action poem to the short pages of action prose of a Fiat worker or a petty government official, life is undoubtedly moving away from the classical humanistic ideals and is becoming lost in pragma. *Cinema* (with the other audio-visual techniques) *seems to be the written language of this pragma.* But this may be its salvation, precisely *because it expresses it* from within: being produced out of this pragma [cinema] reproduces it.

Another statement: cinema, like poetry (he means poetic writing, again, poetry as a practice of language) is "translinguistic." It encodes human action in a grammar, a set of conventions, a vehicle; but as soon as it is perceived, heard, received by a reader-spectator, the convention is discarded and action (reality) is "recreated as a dynamics of feelings, affects, passions, ideas" in that reader-spectator. Thus in living, in practical existence, in our actions, "we represent ourselves, we perform ourselves, and watch others representing-performing-enacting themselves [*rappresentare* in Italian conveys all of these]. Human reality is this double representation in which we are at once actors and spectators: a gigantic happening, if you will." Cinema, then, is "but the 'written' [recorded, stored] moment of a natural and total language, which is our action in the real."

It is easy to see why Pasolini's arguments could have been so easily dismissed. He himself, only half-jokingly, asked: "What horrible sins are crouching in my philosophy?" and named the "monstrous" juxtaposition of irrationalism and pragmatism, religion and action, and other "fascist" aspects of our civilization. I should like to suggest, however, that an unconventional, less literal or narrow reading of Pasolini's pronouncements (for such they undoubtedly were), one that would accept his provocations and work on the contradictions of his heretical empiricism, could be very helpful to resist, if not to counter, the more subtle seduction of a logico-semiotic humanism.

This is not the place, nor is there time, for an extensive reading of essays, articles, screenplay notations, interventions and interviews spanning nearly a decade; or to consider the originality of his insights with regard to, for example, the function of montage as "negative duration" in the construction of a "physio-psychological" continuity for the spectator; or the qualities of "physicality" (*fisicità*) and *oniricità,* the dreamlike state film induces in the spectator—insights which he tried to couch in the terms of the theoretical discourse of semiology (and they didn't fit) but which several years later, recast in psychoanalytic terms, were to become central to films theory's concern with visual pleasure, spectatorship, and the complex nexus of imaging and meaning that Metz was to locate in "the imaginary signifier." That relation of image and language in cinema, wrote Pasolini in 1965, is *in* the film and *before* the film: "*un complesso mondo di immagini significative*—sia quelle mimiche o ambientali che corredano i linsegni, sia quelle dei ricordi e dei sogni—*che prefigura e si propone come fondamento 'strumentale' della comunicazione cinematografica,*" a complex nexus of *significant images* (imaginary signifiers?) which *pre-figures* cinematic communication *as its instrumental foundation.* What Pasolini touches upon here is possibly one of the most important and most difficult problems confronting cinematic theory and iconic, as well as verbal, signification: the question of inner speech, of forms of "imagist, sensual, pre-logical thinking" already posed by Eikhenbaum and Eisenstein in the twenties about the relation of language to sensory perception, of what Freud called word-presentation and thing-presentation in the interplay of primary and secondary processes. A question that, clearly, could not be answered by semiology—but through no fault, no limitation, of Pasolini's.

I will take up just a few other points. First, Pasolini imagines *cinema as the conscious representation of social practice* (he calls it action, reality—reality as human practice). This is exactly, and explicitly, what many independent filmmakers are in fact doing or trying to do today. Pasolini, of course, speaks as a filmmaker—*en poète,* as he said; he is concerned with film as expression, with the practice of cinema as the occasion of a direct encounter with reality, not merely personal and yet subjective; he is not specifically taking on, as they are, cinema as institution, as a social technology which produces or reproduces meanings, values and images *for* the spectators. But he is keenly aware, nevertheless, in the passages I quoted and elsewhere, that cinema's writing, its representation of human action, institutes "a cultural consciousness" of that encounter with reality. Which is why he says, and this is my second point, cinema, like poetry, is *trans*linguistic: it exceeds the moment of the inscription, the technical apparatus, to become "a dynamics of

feelings, affects, passions, ideas" in the moment of reception. Cinema and poetry, that is, are not languages (grammars, articulatory mechanisms) but discourses and practices of language, modes of representing—signifyingpractices, we would say; he said "the written language of pragma." The emphasis on the subjective in three of the four terms, "feelings, affects, passions, ideas," cannot be construed as an emphasis on the merely 'personal,' that is to say, an individual's existential or idiosyncratic response to the film; on the contrary, it points to the current notion of spectatorship as a site of productive relations, of the engagement of subjectivity in meaning, values and imaging, and therefore suggests that the subjective processes which cinema instigates are "culturally conscious," that cinema's binding of fantasy to images institutes, *for* the spectator, forms of subjectivity which are themselves, unequivocally, social.

I could go on recontextualizing, intertextualizing, overtextualizingPasolini's extravagant statements. But I shall instead conclude going back to semiotics, where it all started—not only my reading of Pasolini's text but also the theoretical discourse on cinema through which I have been reading it. Pasolini's use of semiology, aberrant as it might have seemed, was in fact prophetic. The notion of *im-segno* proposed in the 1965 essays **"Il cinema di poesia"** and **"La sceneggiatura come 'struttura che vuol essere altra struttura'"** is much closer to Eco's notion of sign-function than anyone would have suspected, way back then. And so is Pasolini's attempt to define the "reader's collaboration" in the *sceno-testo,* the screenplay as text-in-movement, as diachronic structure or structure-in-process—another of his scandalous contradictions, yet no longer so if we compare it with Eco's recent reformulation of the notion of open text. As for the question of cinematic articulation and iconism, the *context* of cinema, as Pasolini outlines it, the context which makes certain "features" pertinent and thus produces meaning and subjectivity, is not only a discursive context or a textual co-text (linguistic or iconic); it is the context of social practice, that human action which cinematic representation articulates and inscribes from both sides of the screen, so to speak, for both filmmakers and spectators as subjects in history. And therefore cinema's iconicity, its complex overlay of visual, aural, linguistic and other coding processes, does remain an issue for semiotics and for film theory; it should not be too quickly cast aside as irrelevant, false or superseded. For at least two reasons. On one front, it is important to pursue the question of iconic representation and of its productive terms in the relations of meaning, as a sort of theoretical resistance: to oppose the trend toward an increasing grammatization of discursive and textual operations, toward, that is, logico-mathematical formalization. On another front, it continues to be necessary to reclaim iconicity (including above all visual pleasure and the attendant questions of identification and subjectivity) not so much *from* the domain of the natural or *from* an immediacy of referential reality, but *for* the ideological; to wrench the visual from its vision, as it were—***Salò,*** the film one simply *can not* see, or cannot *simply* see: one must decide, choose, will oneself to see it, to look at it, to listen to it, to stay in one's chair, not to get up and leave. No spell binds us to such a film; the questioning of vision, in its most literal terms, and the violence with which such questioning imposes itself on the spectator, belie the comfortable belief in an innocence of images that would make them "allegory and literality, but no symbol, metaphor or interpretation . . . Fantasy can only be written (says Barthes, speaking of Sade), not portrayed." But for Pasolini cinema is precisely writing in images, not to describe (portray) reality or fantasy, but to inscribe them as representations; to reclaim the imaginary of the image for the symbolic of cinema (as Metz might say). In that essay of 1966 Pasolini insisted, "bisogna ideologizzare." Ideologize, he said. Fourteen years later, we still need to.

Norman MacAfee (essay date Fall/Winter 1980-81)

SOURCE: "'I Am a Free Man': Pasolini's Poetry in America," in *Italian Quarterly,* Vol. XXI and XXII, No. 82-83, Fall/Winter, 1980-81, pp. 99-105.

[*In the following essay, MacAfee discusses the relationship between Pasolini's poetry and American culture and art.*]

Pasolini's Italian poems were made as civil poems, in bright contrast to the then still dominant mode of poetic discourse, hermeticism—whose style was, I think, a function of its poets living under the growth and success of fascism. Pasolini's Italian poems, from 1954 to his death, are discourse appropriate to a post-fascist society, and fully use a climate of freer speech. Pasolini's long civil poems link him to Whitman and Pound and Ginsberg, but he is a real original—and just as the films of this film-poet have had roughest going in America, of all the non-Communist world, the poems will also upset some ideas about what a poem can't be—but I think the soil is already prepared by the three aforementioned American poets, and that Pasolini's poetry and career will have a deep effect on American poetry, and thus on American life.

American poetry 1980 is at a point of particular opportunity. For at least ten years a network of poetry queries and magazines has been in the process of organizing itself. The outlets are there for publishing good and great work, as well as the usual vast amount of mediocre writings. But hermeticisms of all kinds abound, and an unworkable hermetic esthetic has hold of most of the organs that publish poetry. The poet is still at the outskirts of the society, however. And Pasolini's example of gaining and maintaining a

central place as poet in the society will I hope be noted by all poets.

I think his poetry will in fact have an effect on ours similar to its impact on Italian poetry, because American poetry takes its cues largely from master poets who are hermetics (Whitman, Pound, and Ginsberg excepted) rather than civil poets. Though Pound supported fascism and Pasolini his own form of "never-orthodox" Marxism, it was special versions of each, and both poets share many qualities—most importantly, they included politics in their poetry, and they were tireless in promoting the well-being of culture.

In 1968 Pasolini interviewed Pound for Italian television. Excerpts of the interview have been published in *Ezra Pound in Italy.* Pasolini's aunt has told me Pasolini drew a sketch of Pound while they talked. Giuseppe Zigaina, a painter and great friend of Pasolini, tells me there may be three such sketches. Alas they seem to have been lost or mislaid perhaps in some book in some trunk in Venice or Casarsa. But what a document in modern poetry and art they would be!

Pasolini begins the interview by quoting Pound's early poem "A Pact"—"I make a pact with you, Walt Whitman— / I have detested you long enough. / I come to you as a grown child / Who has had a pigheaded father; / I am old enough now to make friends. / It was you that broke the new wood, / Now is a time for carving. / We have one sap and one root— / Let there be commerce between us." Pasolini is offering a peace between the never-orthodox Marxist and the former sympathizer with fascism, between generational and other differences (heterosexual, homosexual, American, Italian), in other words, building quite a bridge. Pound replies, over the decades, and by using Latin, for all to hear who have ears to hear, for the centuries: "All right—Friends! Pax tibi. Pax mundi." Pasolini quotes from Canto 67 "Woe to them that conquer with armies and whose only right is their power." Then asks: "These are pacifist verses. Would you like to participate in one of the demonstrations that are taking place in America to help the world remain at peace?" Pound: "I think the intentions are good, but I don't think these demonstrations are the right answer. I see things from another angle. As I wrote in a draft for a recent Canto: 'When one's friends hate one another / how can there be peace in the world.'"

The editor's synopsis of the interview concludes: "On Pasolini's asking was Pound thinking of himself when he wrote: 'The young Dumas weeps because the young Dumas has tears'—he replied: 'No, by the "young Dumas" I was not thinking of myself. In the Pisan Cantos I wrote: "Tard, très tard, je t'ai connue, la tristesse / I have been hard as youth sixty years."'"

Pound writes in the book's introduction: "It was my first talk with Pasolini—enjoyable if a bit one-sided because of me. I would like to meet him in an atmosphere less bristling with question marks." I doubt if they met again, since Pound's famous silence was then in progress—a decade-long silence that ended with his death in 1972, in Venice. But beneath the surface testiness, it was a fruitful, noble encounter.

Seven years after it, in 1975, Pasolini, in *Salò*'s final bloody minutes, quotes Pound's Canto 99 as though it were being played over fascist radio (even though it was written in 1949—Pasolini knew this; genius makes its own rules): "The whole tribe is from one man's body / The father's word is compassion / The son's filiality." Meanwhile on the screen, enraged father-torturers rape, mutilate, and murder their young victims. It is a particularly rich and plentiful moment in one of cinema's truly revolutionary works. It is a moment of splendid poetry (thesis) and terrible images (antithesis) that are memory's images of terrible times, the last days of fascism. Thesis and antithesis with no synthesis is a typical Pasolini situation. Question marks and questions end long poems and long films. The reference to "compassion" as the father's word is an echo of Pound's own self-criticism in the interview: "I have been hard as youth sixty years." The reference is as well a hommage: the lines are indeed splendid.

Salò is the ultimate post-hermetic poem. Pasolini said to his publisher that if it were shown, there would be no more censorship. Although its distributor withheld it for two years from American audiences, it finally was released in 1977 and continues to be shown with regularity in the repertory houses. As for censorship in general, perhaps *Salò* is the last major case; I haven't heard of another one. (In fact, another, more insidious kind of censorship is and has been practiced in the last ten years in the United States and that is the self-censorship by such corporations as United Artists, which withheld *Salò* for two years without giving any valid reason. United Artists is owned by the giant Transmerica Corporation, and most of its releases start with the motto "Entertainment from Transmerica" but not *Salò*). The film has had a strange life here and has not been reviewed by most of the weekly and monthly middlebrow critics who have helped create an audience of semiserious filmgoers (Sarris, Kael) and has been dismissed by most of the daily reviewers here (and has thus been subjected to the press's self-censorship: turn away whenever anything serious approaches), but serious pieces have appeared in art, film, literary, and political journals: *The New York Arts Journal, Cineaste, Film Comment, Boss,* and the latest issue of *October.*

More than anything else, what sets it and most of Pasolini's work apart from ways of thinking that collide with Power, the power of the superpowers, for example, is the element of homosexuality. Much of the critical antipathy to Pasolini's films here has been because of this. I am sure several of the critics who so hate Pasolini are closet homosexuals, but the

great majority of them are heterosexuals. Pasolini made an effort to be honest about his homosexuality, if for no other reason than to avoid the blackmail inevitable to those who have something to hide. The boys and young men he was attracted to had mythic status for him; as he writes in a late poem, "A boy in his first loves is none other than the fecundity of the world." Two subproletarian boys spark the long poem **"The Religion of My Time"** from 1959 which is one of the great visions of Italy and the world at that time. His relations with peasant and sub-proletarian males were completely in line with his politics. His behavior as lover of them and memorializer of them in film and poem causes a whole group hitherto almost unseen in art to be brought forward. I would like to read a rather long excerpt from the long poem, **"A Desperate Vitality,"** written in 1963, which illustrates the method well: the poet has been interviewed by a newspaper reporter. The poem is filled with cinematic touches, with references to Godard's film *Contempt* (based on a story by Alberto Moravia then being filmed in Rome; one of the first lines is: "As in a film by Godard"): the reporter asks "What's the function of the Marxist?" The poet answers and the politics and homosexuality are brought together.

> nibbling her ballpoint—"What's
> the function of the Marxist?" And she gets ready
> to take notes.
>
> "With . . . the delicacy of the bacteriologist . . . I'd
> say [I stammer,
>   seized by impulses of death]
> to move masses such as Napoleonic, Stalinist
> armies . . .
>   with billions of annexings . . .
>   so that . . .
>   the masses that call themselves conservative [of
>   the Past] lose it, while
>   the revolutionary masses acquire it,
>   rebuilding it in the act of defeating it . . .
>   It is because of the Instinct of Conservation
>   that I'm a communist!
>
>   A move
>   on which depends life and death, through the
>   centuries
>   forever and ever
>
>   To do it little by little, as when
>   an army engineer unscrews
>   the safety catch of an unexploded bomb, and,
>   for a moment, can remain in the world
>   (with its modern city blocks, all around him, in the
>   sunlight)
>   or be erased from it forever:
>   an inconceivable distance

between the two horns!
A move
to be made bit by bit, stretching the neck,
stooping, wrinkling the belly,
biting one's lips or squinting
like a bocce player
who, twisting his body, seeks to dominate
the course of his throw, to rectify it
toward a solution
that will map out life through the centuries."

V

Life through the centuries . . .
This then is what was being
hinted at—last evening . . .
stunned in the brief segment of its wailing—
by that distant train . . .

That train that was wailing,
disconsolate, as though astonished to exist
(and, at the same time, resigned—because every
act
of life is a segment already marked in a line
that is life itself, clear only in dreams)

that train was wailing, and the act of wailing
—unthinkably distant, beyond the Appian Ways
and Centocelles of the world—
was joining another act: chance union,
monstrous, bizarre
and so private
that behind the line of my eyes,
which were perhaps closed, it is possible to know
of it . . .

My act is love, but lost in the misery
of a body granted miraculously in
the stress of hiding, gasping
alongside a gloomy railroad track, stalking
a muddy countryside farmed by giants . . .

Life through the centuries . . .
like a star falling
beyond the sky of gigantic ruins,
beyond the properties of the Caetanis or Torlonias,
beyond the Tuscolanas and Capannellas of the
world—
this mechanical wail was saying:
life through the centuries . . .

And my senses were there to listen to it.

I was stroking a disheveled dusty head,
blond, as life would have it,

of the shape that destiny desires,
the agile tender body of a colt, the rough
material of garments that have known a mother's
care:
I was performing an act of love,
but my senses were there, listening:

life through the centuries . . .

Then the blond head of destiny disappeared
through a hole,
and the hole filled with the white sky of night,
until against the strip of sky appeared
another head of hair, another nape,
black, perhaps, or brown; and I,
in a cave lost in the heart of the estates
of the Caetanis or Torlonias
among ruins built by 17th-century giants
in the immense days of the carnival, I
was there with my senses to listen . . .

life through the centuries . . .

Over and over in the hole,
as the pale night dispersed
beyond the Casilinas of the world,
disappeared and reappeared the head of destiny,
with the sweetness now of the southern mother,
now of the alcoholic father, always the same
dear little head, disheveled and dusty or already
combed up by the vanity of a working-class youth:
and I,
I was there with my senses to listen

to the voice of another love
—life through the centuries—
which was rising most pure into the sky.

VI

(*A fascist victory*)

She looks at me pityingly
And . . . but, then you . . . [worldly smile, greedy,
conscious of its greed and its captivating
ostentation—eyes and teeth sparkling
and with a slight hesitating infantile contempt
toward herself]—then you, you're very unhappy!"

"Ah (I must admit)
I'm in a state of confusion, signorina."

There are two loves, then: of the boy ("a boy in his first loves
is none other than the fecundity of the world"—that is, the

future) and "another love: life through the centuries"—which is the same as the "fecundity of the world."

In another 1963 poem, **"Plan of Future Works,"** Pasolini expressed the need for an alliance of minorities, and, as a homosexual and outsider, his solidarity with other outcast groups—such as blacks and Jews. Since Pasolini was an outsider, and grew more and more self-reliant, his relationship with homosexuality in Italy was different from what it might be here today. The drawing of homosexuals into a political and social group is part self-protection. Pasolini didn't have this kind of group situation in his Italy till late in his life, and by then he was such an opposer it is doubtful he would have joined for long. In America this tension between individual and group is usually tilted toward the individual, which makes organizing homosexuals difficult. But the less regulated homosexual life in Italy is fraught with the dangers of having a sexual life outside the homosexual circle. He seems to have been most attracted to young heterosexuals. This linked him to the general life in Italy—the point at which young men have left their parents and have not yet become parents, but will, as their mark of virility. His killer's reason for the murder is that he didn't want to be sodomized. Pelosi's refusal and subsequent crime and lenient punishment dovetail nicely. Sexually conventional or at least hypocritical society nods its head understandingly and gives the killer nine years.

I have seemed to stray far away from the original starting point, which was Pasolini's departure from hermeticism, and his celebration of free speech. But a true coming out from hermeticism entailed this other, homosexual, coming out.

I can only guess how Pasolini's poems will affect American poetry and culture, since only a few of the poems have appeared in magazines; only once our selection is published—next fall—will we really be able to talk about effects.

I will conclude with a few general thoughts on the poems.

Pasolini tends to concentrate not on things, as many moderns have—from Rilke to William Carlos Williams to Charles Simic—but rather on a general portrayal of the world—or at least an Italy not misrepresentative of the world in its conflicts and ideologies. And on a world full of people, whether the handsome teenagers maturing into mediocrity in **"Reality"** or the vulgar interviewer in **"A Desperate Vitality."**

Cinema as a mass art has affected all the other arts—the novel, the still photograph—and poetry has not been immune. Hart, Crane, Pound, Williams are early examples. Pasolini is the child not just of poetry but also of film. He wrote his first poem at seven and came into contact with both arts earlier than that. The films have outbursts of poetry—often verbal, as in *Porcilè,* when Julian reveals his manias,

in verse: and visual, in a directness that isn't documentary, in a subjectivity (the handheld camera). In the poems we have not only the obvious references of a film director in **"A Desperate Vitality"** but also the cinematic techniques in that poem's jump cuts, in the quick breathtaking shots of landscapes in **"The Ashes of Gramsci"** and the whole section of landscape writing in **"The Tears of the Excavator"** of 1956—a section that would be perhaps better filmed than written.

Pasolini, as word poet and film poet, dragged poetry further out of the cloister than any other great poet this century. In the poem **"Reality,"** he defines the title word as the "practical end of my poetry" and later in a 1968 interview talks of his coming to film as an "explosion of my love for reality." In a sense his film poetry was the "practical end" of his verse poetry. His poetry will bring some shibboleths into American poetry: "reality," for one; another: "class struggle." The 3-decade-long debate he had with Marxism humanized the poetry. This type of debate has been almost impossible in American poetry because of the bias against ideas—especially Marxist ideas—in poetry and in society at large, which most poetry merely reflects.

A further link between Pasolini and Americans is their common effort at creating roots. His earliest published poems were in the dialect of Friuli; he founded an Institute of Friulian Language to further the regional culture in 1946, he later edited anthologies of regional folk songs.

The structure of the long poems is astounding. A poem like the 30-page **"Religion of My Time"** holds together amazingly well. Perhaps only in his last two films—*Arabian Nights* and *Salò*—are the structural feats as astonishing.

I would like to conclude my reading from **"Reality,"** another major poem from 1963, the poem from which the line "I am a free man" comes—but the poem is too long to be read in its entirety—it takes at least 20 minutes—and yet too cohesive to be excerpted. I will only say that three pages after the line "I am a free man," there is this line, which should be taken much more as a simple description of the toll taken on one who is free than as a prophecy: "Free with a freedom that's massacred me."

Wallace P. Sillanpoa (essay date January 1981)

SOURCE: "Pasolini's Gramsci," in *Modern Language Notes,* Vol. 96, No. 1, January, 1981, pp. 120-37.

[*In the following essay, Sillanpoa analyzes the relationship between Pasolini and the writings of Antonio Gramsci.*]

When discussing those who perhaps most influenced the thought of the late Pier Paolo Pasolini, poet, novelist, critic and filmmaker, one critic recently spoke of 'il *suo* Gramsci.'' Implied in this possessive is the highly personal interpretation that Pasolini attached to the example and writings of Antonio Gramsci, revolutionary political theorist whose famous notebooks survived their author's death in 1937 after eleven years of Fascist imprisonment. What follows attempts to qualify this implication through a survey of Pasolini's writings directly linked to a reading of Gramsci. Demonstration should emerge to bolster those claims of a subjective interpretation whose ultimate complexity can best be described generally as a curious admixture of confraternity and contradiction.

The closing section of *L'usignolo della Chiesa Cattolica,* containing verse composed between 1943 and 1949, carries the subtitle, *La scoperta di Marx.* War and the Italian Partisan response had transformed Pasolini, leading him to the conviction that life demands "qualcos'altro che amore / per il proprio destino." For the young Pasolini, that "something other" prompted a probe into an alternative world view, grounded in reason, synthesized in Marx, and calling for a commitment to popular political struggle. Within a short period of time, this newly explored world view began to intrude upon the sentimental universe of the poet's earlier verse, linguistically and thematically circumscribed by his maternal Friuli.

Pasolini's idiolect thus evolved into the idiom of a wider historical and class perspective, but without ever causing the poet to dismiss his previous experience. Pasolini's topocentric perspective widened, that is, and allowed the peasant world of Friuli, a world of primitive innocence and religious fatality, to assume even greater mythic proportions in the course of this investigation of a Marxist rationalism. During these years, first as a witness to Partisan struggles, and then as a sympathizer to the uprisings of Friulan day laborers, Pasolini participated in the local politics of the Italian Communist Party. But also in these years, he helped found, together with other young Friulans, the *Academiuta de lengua furlana,* a small circle dedicated to the philological study and social diffusion of Friulan language and culture. Thus Pasolini's early formation joined a sentimental attachment to the linguistic and cultural environment of his adolescence to an examination of Marxist rationalism and political ideology.

Pasolini says his introduction to Marx took place early: "In Friuli ho letto Gramsci e Marx." This particular pairing suggests, however, that his introduction was only nominally Marxist. Paolo Volponi reports, in fact, that Pasolini himself once confessed: "Sono un marxista che ha letto poco Marx. Ho letto di più Gramsci." Moreover, the Gramsci read during this period in Friuli must have been the Gramsci of

the *Lettere dal carcere,* for, with the sole exception of *Il materialismo storico e la filosofia di Benedetto Croce,* it wasn't until 1949 (when Pasolini had already been in Rome for a year) that the first of the other major texts of the *Quaderni del carcere* began appearing in print. This observation contends that this Marxist formation was really a Gramscian one, and it underscores the special character of the Gramsci first encountered by Pasolini. To a great degree this Gramsci was, and essentially continued to be, the pathetic hero of the prison letters, only in part counterbalanced by the figure of the revolutionary theorist of political and cultural praxis.

Nevertheless, in 1948 Pasolini was forced to abandon his region and his people under personal and political circumstances that left deep scars. Amid the disinherited of Rome's shantytowns (*borgate*), he felt painfully torn from the world of his youth. That emotional and ethical energy previously nourished through his contact with Friuli was thus diverted to these emarginated urban poor who, lured by the promises of postwar industrial reconstruction, were leaving behind their Southern agrarian communities to find themselves amid the wretched conditions of those inhabiting the periphery of many large Italian cities. The poet's myth of an a-temporal and a-rational Friuli was hence transferred to the neo-primitive and socially incohesive topography of Rome's dispossessed. Pasolini's presence among these poor of the Roman *borgate,* his passion for their dialect and street-wise slang, his fascination with their desperate vitalism and what he considered their pre-political rebelliousness, supplanted his poeticized concept of Friuli. *Ragazzi di vita,* Pasolini's celebrated novel begun in 1950 and published in 1955, emerged from this newly uncovered social and linguistic reality.

At the same time, some of the verse Pasolini composed while in Rome marked the survival of his passionate attachment to the *locus amoenus* of his youth, through memories populated by farm hands and shepherd boys at ease in the fields, mountains and wind-washed village squares of his mythic Friuli. Once removed from his native setting and confronted with the back-street humanity of Rome's periphery, however, Pasolini found it difficult to reconcile the poetic concepts of his earlier work to the expressive demands of his present writings. While Friuli quite often appeared in his verse as a natural utopia, by contrast, the Roman borgate of his novels *Ragazzi di vita* and *Una vita violenta* seem an inferno of degradation and disassociation. In his esthetic treatment of the socially downtrodden, Pasolini nonetheless tempered this hellish world with residues of primitive purity and adolescent innocence present beneath the coarse language and brutal(ized) faces of its inhabitants. In the end, death triumphs over the instinctual guile and bruised grace of these *ragazzi di vita,* as the novelist underscores the social and political pathos of this cast-off race and class. But, as just stated, Pasolini never dismissed the primordial virtues of a simpler world, and so it is in Rome during the early 1950's that he came to believe his primitive innocents the victims of a Neocapitalism that he claimed would eventually destroy the very humanity of these people as it swept away time-honored linguistic and social patterns.

In truth, that afore-mentioned rupture in Pasolini's poetry had already manifested itself to some extent at the time of his "discovery of Marx." One such example can be found in **"Testament Coran,"** a part of the verse in dialect written between 1947 and 1952. Here Pasolini depicts a young peasant in Friuli who joins the Partisans and is then captured and hung by the Nazis. While dying, the boy-soldier commits his image to the conscience of the rich, as he sadly salutes the courage, pain, and innocence of the poor.

Similarly, the underlying evangelism of **Poesie a Casarsa** gradually replaced a traditional peasant demand for an avenging afterlife with a here-and-now vindication. In one poem, now part of **La meglio gioventù** containing all of Pasolini's verse in dialect, the peasants' figure of Christ crucified, index of a future retribution, takes on the workclothes and identity of a laborer who promises more than an atonement to come.

To repeat, the passage of Pasolini's rhapsodized race from a natural-religious state to an historical-political one was greatly influenced by the catalytic intrusion of external events. The esthetic and sensual aura of a poeticized Friuli gave way to the cruel incandescence of the War and Resistance and stirred the poet's ethical consciousness. The Resistance, above all, deeply affected Pasolini (as it did an entire generation), modifying his poetic sensibility. In 1957, when censuring what he considered the political quietism of many writers during Fascism, Pasolini remarked:

> La Resistenza ha soprattutto insegnato a credere nuovamente nella storia, dopo le introversioni evasive ed estetizzanti di un ventennio di poesia.

One must then see this 'historical lesson' in conjunction with the poet's turn to Gramsci, for throughout the 1950's, the example of the Sardinian revolutionary played an important role in defining Pasolini's pronounced conflict between the pull of a visceral and esthetic passion and a call to rational, ideological exactitude. It was precisely this conflict that became the ferment of much of Pasolini's later works.

Although the volume's title poem was actually composed in 1954, **Le ceneri di Gramsci** was published in 1957. These poems, written in Italian (and not in dialect) occupy a special place in postwar Italian literature, for they signal a significant departure from pre- (and post-) war Hermeticism.

Contesting the Hermetics' mystique of the word, Pasolini models his verse on a rejuvenation of certain traditional stylistic modes (*e.g.,* adjectivization; the *terzina,* reminiscent of post-Dantean didactic and satirical verse; the *poemetto,* evoking the Romantic-patriotic poetry of the *Risorgimento*), motivated by the desire for a return to a 'civil' poetry that might effectively challenge the Hermetic postulates of absolute self-expression and pure lyricism. At the same time, Pasolini's 'civil' poetry shares little with various strains of postwar prose *à thèse,* nor does it confuse reportage with poetic expression. Instead, his verse proceeds from a conflict experienced between public commitment and poetic predilection—instinct and reason. Within a context based on seemingly irreconcilable antitheses Gramsci represents a world of reason and ideological precision both guiding and goading the poet. This world clashes with Pasolini's visceral-irrational feelings that ultimately precede his ideology. Thus, **Le ceneri di Gramsci** records a struggle between reason (Gramsci) and passion (Pasolini).

A note to the text establishes Rome as the location of the collection's title poem: specifically, the Testaccio (working-class) quarter; the English cemetery; Gramsci's grave. It is an "autunnale / maggio" in the mid-1950's, a decade once anticipated with hope by the Resistance: "la fine del decennio in cui ci appare / tra la macerie finito il profondo / e ingenuo sforzo di rifare la vita." The poet, "capitato / per caso" into Rome's cemetery for non-Catholics, finds there a "mortale / pace" that shuts out the industrious clatter of the nearby proletarian neighborhood, providing a proper situation for his colloquy with Gramsci. This setting lends an immediate air of elegy that reduces all color and contour to an achromatic grey in a meeting of the living dead: "e noi morti ugualmente, con te, nell'umido / giardino."

From the beginning, then, the poem's metaphoric progression rests on a series of contrasts. The juxtaposition of the cemetery's quiet to the frenzy of the surrounding neighborhood is the first in succeeding analogical contrasts that culminate in the poet's self-reflexion and refraction in his hero—who is simultaneously his antagonist. Attraction and repulsion result from Pasolini's thirst for vitalistic passion and Gramsci's somber reminder of the need for rational articulation:

> con la tua magra mano
> delineavi l'ideale che illumina
> (. . .)
>   questo silenzio.
> (. . .)
> Lo scandalo del contraddirmi, dell'essere
> con te e contro te; con te nel cuore,
> in luce, contro te nelle buie viscere;
> del mio paterno stato traditore

  —nel pensiero, in un'ombra di azione—
mi so ad esso attaccato nel calore

  degli istinti, dell'estetica passione

For Pasolini, Gramsci's "rigore" denoting the antithesis of his own "violento / e ingenuo amore sensuale," has "scisso / (. . .) il mondo" into opposing poles. Nonetheless, it soon becomes clear that despite the poet's insistence on living "nel non volere / del tramontato dopoguerra," of surviving through a refusal to choose between passion and reason ("sussisto / perché non scelgo"), a decision has really already been made:

  Mi chiederai tu, morto disadorno
  d'abbandonare questa disperata
  passione di essere nel mondo?

Elegy renders Pasolini's evocation of Gramsci the commemoration of a lost ideal, for Gramsci, as person and precept, undergoes a figurative transformation. The force of **"Le ceneri di Gramsci"** is discharged through an extension of personal conflict ("con te nel cuore, / in luce, contro te nelle buie viscere") to a general, and generational, crisis ("e noi / morti ugualmente, con te"). In bemoaning the loss of the hopes and ideals of the Resistance, Pasolini indirectly censures the *pis-aller* of the 1950's, while implying that the 'committed' poet and critic of his times must paradoxically operate within and without conventional political structures. Gramsci, meanwhile, must necessarily remain a luminary ("in luce"), iconically remote and ideally distant from the poet's inner torment: "Lì tu stai, bandito e con dura eleganza / non cattolica, elencato tra estranei / morti: Le ceneri di Gramsci." Thus Pasolini's Gramsci lives only insofar as he is 'ashes'; insofar as his presence is experienced emblematically and at a defining distance. Without this figure, Pasolini's visceral passion would have no ballast. Gramsci is thus made to assume the role of an ideological counterpoise, keeping in check the grip of the poet's "calore / degli istinti" and "estetica passione."

As for the torment that lies outside, Pasolini identifies with the humble poor:

  Come i poveri povero, mi attacco
  come loro a umilianti speranze
  come loro per vivere mi batto
  ogni giorno.

But the poet's poor are the poor of a pre-proletarian state championed for their inbred and sacred vitalism: "come / d'un popolo di animali, nel cui arcano / orgasmo non ci sia altra passione / che per l'operare quotidiano." Hence, again addressing Gramsci, Pasolini declares himself:

  attratto da una vita proletaria
  a te anteriore, è per me religione

  la sua allegria, non la millenaria
  sua lotta: la sua natura, non la sua
  coscienza

Moreover, Pasolini's apostrophe here is to a "giovane," . . . "non padre, ma umile / fratello." One should note that in an article of 1957, the year of the publication of *Le ceneri di Gramsci,* Pasolini called the Sardinian a "maestro." But here the emphasis on Gramsci's 'youth', his evocation as 'brother', and the strange erotic attraction that takes hold of the poet at graveside ("ebbra simbiosi / d'adolescente di sesso con la morte") suggest a commutation of Pasolini's emblem. In effect, it appears that the poet is impressing on Gramsci the figure and force of his own dead brother, tragic youthful martyr to the Resistance. This commutation gives rise to a fundamental ambiguity surrounding the image of Gramsci as master and luminary and as shadow of the poet's dead young brother. Meanwhile, it should be observed that the one clear bibliographical allusion to Gramsci focuses on the latter's presumed stoic character:

       sento quale torto
  —qui nella quiete delle tombe—e insieme
  quale ragione—nell'inquieta sorte
  nostra—tu avessi stilando le supreme
  pagine nei giorni del tuo assassinio.

From the above it appears that pathos insures Gramsci's longevity. In fact, in yet another essay published the same year as the poem, Pasolini asserted that:

  (. . .) su qualsiasi altro, domina nella nostra vita politica lo spirito di Gramsci: del Gramsci 'carcerato', tanto più libero quanto più segregato dal mondo, fuori dal mondo, in una situazione suo malgrado leopardiana, ridotto a puro ed eroico pensiero.

Here, as in the poem, Pasolini elevates Gramsci to a symbolic, and hence metahistorical, plane. What he terms a reduction to "puro ed eroico pensiero" is really a dilation of the human and historical Gramsci (political revolutionary, jailed party leader, and philosopher of praxis) to an ideal interlocutor and rational censor. Pasolini's search to construct a 'civil' poetry requires this sort of Gramsci responding to the poet's existential and cognitive needs for such an ideal and exacting interlocutor, by necessity remote and at odds with his own inner feelings.

At the same time, however, Pasolini's 'sanctified' Gramsci shared little with official hagiographies, such as those of Togliatti and other PCI ideologues of the 1950's. Pasolini's 'saint' is to be debated, even cursed, with no intent of making his "puro ed eroico pensiero" conform to the immediate dictates of party tactics. In addition, when reflecting on the extra-literary dimension of the Gramsci-Pasolini relationship, one should consider what the Sardinian revolutionary must have meant to the young poet. When expelled from his beloved region to find himself practically friendless amidst the depressing reality of the Roman *borgate,* that is, Pasolini must have seen Gramsci—the jailed Gramsci, suspected by party leaders in the 1930's for his polemically unorthodox views and scorned even by fellow Communist inmates for his refusal to adhere uncritically to Togliatti's official line— as a kindred spirit, as well as a beacon to his banishment and bewilderment ("con te nel cuore / in luce").

Together with his central presence to this collection of poetry, Gramsci likewise appears later throughout Pasolini's critical writings. He is cited frequently in the essays of *Passione e ideologia* (1948-1958) and *Empirismo eretico* (1964-1971), while his influence can be felt in many of the polemics of *Scritti corsari* (1973-1975).

A look at Pasolini's literary and cultural criticism calls for a distinction, nevertheless, between what Gramsci continues to represent, and how extracts from the latter's writings serve as supports or counterpoints to Pasolini's analysis. Without such a distinction, a reading of Pasolini's treatment of Gramsci could result in the annotation of contradictions, on the surface devoid of any internal connection or (ideo-) logic.

"Non posso accettare nulla del mondo dove vivo," Pasolini once claimed in a newspaper interview. This held true for all cultural and literary, as well as social and political, questions. The one constant in Pasolini's criticism is its refusal to adhere for any length of time to solicited or self-imposed canons. As Dario Bellezza notes: "La sua voglia di contraddire e contraddirsi era l'unica sua folle coerenza." And Gianni Scalia, who collaborated with Pasolini during the years of the review, "Officina," often referred to him as an "intellettuale disorganico,"—in contrast to Gramsci's celebrated notion of the "intellettuale organico"—, while dubbing him a "poeta civile, etico-politico, in contraddizione perenne (. . .) tra irrazionalità esistenziale e razionalità storica, impegno e autonomia, cuore e critica."

As for Gramsci's influence, Pasolini's essays provide ample testimony of a constantly shifting critical attitude that never abandons, however, an appeal to the lessons of the "maestro." When not discussing specific authors and works, *Passione e ideologia* (the title itself evinces a continuation of the conflict expressed poetically in **"Le ceneri di Gramsci"**) studies the problem of language (dialect and standard Italian), the 'questione della lingua' in Italian literature, and a whole area of sociolinguistics. Working from a methodological framework at times defined as

"gramscismo-stilistico," Pasolini, almost alone among contemporary critics, staunchly defended spoken and literary dialect against the assaults of an imposed national idiom that he believed came more and more to serve the ends of Neocapitalism. Those assaults, he contended, were masked as the needs for a progressive national unity to be forged through modern technological and social channels (*e.g.,* compulsory education; the mass media; etc.).

In *Passione e ideologia's* **"Un secolo di studi sulla poesia popolare"** (a part of his acclaimed philological anthology, **"La poesia popolare italiana"**), Pasolini often summons Gramsci's *Letteratura e vita nazionale* from the *Quaderni del carcere,* while nevertheless declaring foreign to his own linguistic and poetic beliefs the Gramscian notion of a national-popular literature. That is, although he basically agrees with Gramsci's demand for a popular literature, Pasolini cannot reconcile that Sardinian's analytical model with his own ideas on literature. Gramsci's examination of feuilletons, popular melodrama, detective and adventure stories, etc., says Pasolini, corresponds to what "oggi si definisce 'cultura di massa'," which he in turn excoriates as consumer society's manipulation of taste to the detriment of authentic popular (*i.e.,* dialect) culture. For want of adequate means of research, and despite his "passione e chiarezza innovativa," Gramsci "sfiora appena" the problem of popular-dialectical poetry. Thus, to no small degree, Gramsci is to be held responsible for the "inopia di studi marxisti postgramsciani sull'argomento," Pasolini concludes.

In **"La confusione degli stili,"** Pasolini maintains that Gramsci "non spiega quale dovrebbe essere la ricerca di uno scrittore che volesse celare in un'opera l'ideale nazional-popolare." Addressing himself to the problem of literature's language, he raises the point after having asked how it is ever possible to think that "le concrezioni letterarie del concetto di 'nazional-popolare' si debbano realizzare in una simile lingua, creazione appunto della borghesia conservatrice." But in addition to all this, he does concede that all of *Letteratura e vita nazionale* hinges positively on the axiom that every time the language question arises, in one way or another, a whole spectrum of other problems are about to surface.

This paraphrase of Gramsci seems exactly the issue that distinguishes Gramsci's position from that of Pasolini. The Sardinian's argument is motivated by a holistic (*i.e.,* political) overview since problems of language, literature, etc., are studied and analyzed as integral parts of a complex of socio-political factors and functions. Pasolini, on the other hand, regards socio-political and cultural problems as reflections of the gradual surrender of that mythicized social and linguistic universe that he desires to defend. Gramsci sees socio-cultural problems through politics; his analysis is of the cultural institutions and structures 'materially' at work in Western industrial civilization, and how these can be used politically to promote a revolutionary new cultural hegemony. For Pasolini, (Neo-) capitalist society is a moral category—a *malum*—to be rejected *tout court* in the name of a purer (pre-industrial) one threatened with extinction.

Just the same, Pasolini is not given to simple nostalgia. In later writings, his attachment to a pre-proletarian cosmos evolved into a complex longing nourished on the trenchant criticism that his particular brand of 'Marxism' elicited: "Rimpiango l'immenso universo contadino e operaio prima dello Sviluppo: universo transnazionale nella cultura, internazionale nella scelta marxista." Despite admitting the difficulty in defining this new and corrupting power that has "manipolato e radicalmente (antropologicamente) cambiato le grandi masse contadine e proletarie italiane," Pasolini's scorn for contemporary reality ("io considero peggiore il totalitarismo del capitalismo del consumo che il totalitarismo del vecchio potere") is never presented as a politically scientific measure: "L'ordine in cui elenco questi mondi riguarda l'importanza della mia esperienza personale, non la loro importanza oggettiva."

For Gramsci, meanwhile, the intellectual who 'goes to the people' seeking contact and inspiration for a new literature to emerge from the "humus della cultura popolare così come è, coi suoi gusti, le sue tendenze ecc., col suo mondo morale e intellettuale sia pure arretrato e convenzionale," does so with the aim of articulating moral and intellectual needs for an eventual emancipation of the masses from just such a "humus." Hence, over all, Gramsci appears to advocate education, while Pasolini seems to demand a 'preservation' of the subaltern classes.

Pasolini is operating, nevertheless, in an artistic and cultural climate very different from that of Gramsci. His defense of a waning popular-dialectical culture is thus a polemical response to both contemporary mass culture and the elitism he considered inherent in present-day literary avant-gardes. In **"La libertà stilistica,"** he examined his own poetic which a year earlier, on the pages of "Officina," he had defined as "neo-sperimentalismo." His position, he maintained, stood midway between an adulation of tradition and an untempered celebration of novelty, animated by a "spirito filologico (. . .) strumento di una diversa cultura (. . .) che non può accettare nessuna forma storica e pratica di ideologia" in the spirit of the imprisoned Gramsci, "tanto più libero quanto più segregato dal mondo (. . .), ridotto a puro ed eroico pensiero." Pasolini then advances his "neo-sperimentalismo" as the stylistic and thematic countertype to the "poetare (. . .) mistico, irrazionale e squisito" of 'pure poetry', as well as to an opposing tendency which he claims lowers all expressive language to the "*livello della prosa,* ossia del razionale, del logico, dello storico."

In terms of stylistic appraisal, Pasolini appears correct in his

critique of the literary (but also, politico-cultural) shortcomings of any rigid 'hermeticism' or codified 'neorealism'. But as regards the political role assigned by Gramsci to the intellectual, he seems to bypass the significance of a proposed interaction bent on destroying 'una tradizione di casta, che non è mai stata rotta da un forte movimento politico o nazionale dal basso." Gramsci's comprehensive definition of 'political' suggests that this 'coming from below' be concerned primarily with the genesis and destination of any literary-cultural reform, and how such might foster an active co-participation, while Pasolini appears to treat the writer-public relationship in a conventionally vertical manner. Although Pasolini would agree with Gramsci that a 'new art' cannot be created "dall'esterno (pretendendo un'arte didascalica, a tesi, moralistica), ma dall'intimo, perché si modifica tutto l'uomo in quanto si modificano i suoi sentimenti, le sue concezioni e i rapporti di cui l'uomo è l'espressione necessaria," he presents an excessively internalized premise for the realization of any 'new culture' that might give rise to a 'new art':

> Oggi una nuova cultura, ossia una nuova interpretazione intera della realtà, esiste, e non certamente nei nostri estremi tentativi di borghesi d'avanguardia (. . .) esiste, in potenza, nel pensiero marxista; in potenza ché l'attuazione è da prospettare nei giorni in cui il pensiero marxista sarà (se è questo il destino) prassi marxista (. . .). Ma benché in forma potenziale, esiste, agisce, già oggi, se quel pensiero marxista determina, nei nostri paesi occidentali, una lotta politica e quindi una crisi nella società e nell'individuo: esiste dentro di noi, sia che aderiamo, sia che la neghiamo; e proprio in questo nostro impotente aderirvi, e in questo nostro impotente negarla.

Pasolini's preference for a methodology based on antitheses—an extension of the passion-ideology dichotomy—is manifest in the essays of **Empirismo eretico.** Here Pasolini stresses the incompatibility of Neocapitalism's "linguaggio tecnocratico" with its attendant "prevalere del fine comunicativo sul fine espressivo," and the poetic demands of literary expression. Chances for a possible "lingua nazionale attraverso operazioni letterarie" have been undermined by a politico-linguistic levelling to the degree that, at present, shaping language is not "letteratura, ma la tecnica." The sweeping power of technological and consumer society, says Pasolini, is actually affecting "mutazioni antropologiche" threatening to flatten Italian linguistic and social civilization into a sterile conformity. For him, "la cultura tecnocratica-tecnologica (. . .) contesta e si accinge a mettere fuori gioco, tutto il passato classico e classicistico dell'uomo: ossia l'umanesimo." Marxism, while exploiting certain positive contributions of Neocapitalism's neo-language, "come 'parte' specializzata e ellittica (. . .) contiene in sé evidentemente un futuro umanistico e espressivo." To define Marxism in terms of a poetic prolepsis and simultaneous guardianship of popular speech and culture appears to underscore further Pasolini's mythic conception of a preindustrial artist/public relationship.

Then again using Gramsci as theoretical support, Pasolini argues the necessity of bringing together in harmony two contrasting linguistic modes: "irrazionalismo contadino piccolo-borghese del Terzo mondo (ivi compreso il Sud italiano) e razionalismo capitalistico liberale." He advances this notion as the possible cure for a current anomaly whereby "il discorso di un comunista, in quanto espressione di una profonda e vasta spinta dal basso, e in quanto improntato da uno spirito fondamentalmente scientifico, tende a una sintesi dell'italiano, e si pone come fondamentalmente comunicativo." According to this critique, today's Italian Marxists function more as technical 'administrators' than as popular 'humanists.'

For the Marxist writer, instead, a genuine linguistic synthesis should thus be realized by applying to literature the Gramscian notion of the national-popular; *i.e.,* the concomitance of two linguistic ways of being in the world: that of the committed intellectual, and that of the 'common man', in a "'contaminatio' di 'stile sublime' e di 'stile umile'." One is led to wonder to what degree Pasolini would endorse Gramsci's idea of the national-popular as only the first step towards an ultimate emancipation from conventional linguistic and cultural hierarchies. At the same time, one must again admit that the situation from which Gramsci's analysis proceeds differs greatly from the one that Pasolini contests. Gramsci was interested in the entry of the Italian agricultural and proletarian masses into the mainstream of Western thought and culture: in a radical democratization of culture. Pasolini, instead, champions a refusal by these same masses of a society grounded in the false values of consumerism and conformity *qua* liberation. After, in the mid and late 1960's, Pasolini took stock of the actual situation of his chosen people and realized to what an extent those "anthropological mutations" so long prophesized had taken place. The result of his awareness was a bitter anguish, an intensified attack on all causes of such "mutations," and a turn to the Third World as final possible repository for his mythic primitive purity.

"Dal laboratorio," meanwhile, deals almost exclusively with the question of oral and written expression in Gramsci. For Pasolini, Gramsci's language underwent a profound transformation in "falsa liberazione" (*i.e.,* from a native Sardinian) in the slow acquisition of an Italian passing from an initial "enfasi espressivo-umanitaria," through a "fase francesizzante" in Turin, and arriving at true maturity at the time of the "Ordine Nuovo." Such a transformation was due to a "lungo e quasi religioso tirocinio di razionalità." "Tutte

le pagine giovanili di Gramsci sono scritte in un brutto italiano," charges Pasolini. And even after Gramsci's acquisition of a mature and exact rational prose, maintains Pasolini in a contradictory manner, such language, "analizzata freddamente (. . .) può apparire ancora (. . .) 'brutta': cioè umiliata dal grigiore manualistico, dal gergo politico, dalla lingua delle traduzioni, da un incancellabile fondo professionale e francesizzante. Ma tutto ciò è reso irrilevante dalla sua funzionalià che la rende, in qualche modo, assoluta."

Then Pasolini passes to a (hypothetical?) discussion of Gramsci's oral expression. He points to the three fundamental characteristics of Gramsci's pronunciation (*i.e.,* Sardinian-dialectical, Piedmontese-dialectical, and bureacratic-professional petty bourgeoise) as "tutti elementi immensamente inferiori di livello alla 'lingua scritta'." For this reason, "l'incertezza, la povertà, la miseria, la genericità della lingua orale di Gramsci (. . .) non è proporzionata alla sicurezza, alla richezza, all'assolutezza di molte sue pagine scritte."

In truth, it is impossible to pinpoint with any great accuracy the linguistic criteria guiding Pasolini's contradictory critique of Gramsci. Nonetheless, it would appear that behind his observations stand those antithetical poles of expressive *versus* communicative language found throughout the essays of **Empirismo eretico.** If this be the case, then Pasolini errs through excess in regard to Gramsci whose sole aim was notional (self-) clarification, and not connotational, or polysemous, (self-) expression.

In fact, these two contrasting voices in Gramsci: one a determined and self-conscious appropriation of rational-scientific discourse; the other, an ever-present, however submerged, irrational (or better, pre-rational) dialectical expressiveness, are reconciled *in extremis,* claims Pasolini, through a syncretic correlation that unites Gramsci's two linguistic and experiential situations:

> Solo nelle lettere dal carcere, verso la fine della sua vita, egli riesce a far coincidere irrazionalismo e esercizio della ragione: ma non si tratta però dell'irrazionalismo che alona o segue, come per impeto sentimentale o rabbia polemica, la ragione del pensiero politico. (. . .) Si tratta, piuttosto, verso la fine della sua vita, di dar voce di racconto o evocazione anche a fatti più umili e casuali della vita, a quel tanto di misterioso e di irrazionale che ogni vita ha in abbondanza, e che è la 'poeticità naturale' della vita. Allora l'abitudine razionalistica che ha dominato la lingua (. . .) a contatto con quell'elemento irrazionale dominato (. . .) si colora di una pateticità (. . .)

This passage could lead to the observation that though every poet be an ideologue despite claims to the contrary, the opposite is not necessarily true. It does, in any event, substantiate the initially made contention that the Gramsci of Pasolini remained first and foremost the pathetic hero of the prison letters. Complexity arises, however, from the fact that, in effect, this Gramsci functioned as an emblematic composite: Gramsci victim and hero of the *Lettere dal carcere* merging with Gramsci the author of the *Quaderni,* iconic symbol of reason urging the poet's self-proclaimed "ossessivo bisogno di tornare al marxismo—ossia all'unica ideologia che mi protegga dalla perdita della realtà." And these two aspects of Pasolini's Gramsci coincide with the poet's problematic inner conflict of reason with passion.

Thus, in his tireless attack on Neocapitalism's damage to popular speech and culture, together with his diffidence for what he considered the verbal pyrotechnics of much of the 1960's neo-avantgarde, Pasolini deliberately planted his criticism in contradiction and controversy. Throughout, Gramsci remained a preferential point of confrontation between the demands of a visceral estheticism and objectively formulated dissent. Pasolini's unorthodox interpretation of Gramsci, based on a positive heresy, has nonetheless guaranteed the revolutionary theorist of praxis a place in contemporary Italian culture beyond the schematic exegesis of many official tacticians. Since his death, moreover, that culture is in want of a poet-polemicist as uniquely uncompromising and authentically ambivalent as was Pasolini.

Edmund White (review date 27 June 1982)

SOURCE: "Movies and Poems," in *The New York Times Book Review,* June 27, 1982, pp. 8-9, 14.

[*In the following review, White discusses Enzo Siciliano's biography of Pasolini, Pasolini's work, and Pasolini's similarities to Japanese novelist Yukio Mishima.*]

Pier Paolo Pasolini was violently murdered near Rome on Nov. 2, 1975. He was only 54 years old, but he had managed to produce a lifetime of work in several genres. The publication of a translation of the first biography of him, by Enzo Siciliano, and a volume of translations by Norman MacAfee of Pasolini's best poems remind us what an extraordinary man he was.

He had gained fame first as a poet in the dialect of his native region, Friuli—the area north of Venice that extends into Yugoslavia. Soon he switched to Italian, in which he went on to publish more than 40 volumes of poetry, fiction, travel notes and cultural and political criticism.

But it was as a film maker that he won international fame.

His first feature, *Accattone,* was released in 1961. Three years later he made his spare, smoldering *Gospel According to Saint Matthew.* His biggest successes at the box office (at least in Europe) comprised *The Trilogy of Life,* of which the best was the innocent, spontaneous and delectable *Arabian Nights.* His last film, *Salò or the 120 Days of Sodom,* was surely his masterpiece, an appalling study of sadism in the last days of Italian Fascist rule. No film has come closer to genuine Satanism; *Salò* seems as much a transgression against decency as a condemnation of evil.

> [Pasolini's] last film, *Salò or the 120 Days of Sodom,* was surely his masterpiece, an appalling study of sadism in the last days of Italian Fascist rule. No film has come closer to genuine Satanism; *Salò* seems as much a transgression against decency as a condemnation of evil.
>
> —*Edmund White*

The man behind this work was an enigma. Pasolini led an exemplary life in the sense that he embodied most of the contradictions troubling modern Italy. He was a sort of Marxist and, off and on, a Communist, but his politics were too personal, too shifting and too adversarial to fit into any orthodoxy. He was an atheist, but two of his films (*The Gospel According to Saint Matthew* and *Teorema*) received awards from Catholic organizations. Moreover, he had a devout respect for what he considered "divine" in human beings (youth, the body, spontaneity). He was a big-city sophisticate and moved easily in international film circles but, like his exact contemporary, the Japanese novelist Yukio Mishima (also a globetrotting cosmopolite), Pasolini rejected the glossy consumer culture that had made him famous in favor of the standards of an earlier, more rigid and more traditional society.

The greatest social change in the industrial world since World War II has been a shift away from conservation to consumption and, in the consumers themselves, a corresponding movement away from an ethic of self-sacrifice to a hedonistic code of self-fulfillment. Both Pasolini and Mishima opposed this fitful, always painful and disruptive process. Both of them had a utopian vision of an earlier, more honorable, more disciplined time. Thus Pasolini argued against the liberalization of the abortion law on the grounds that sacrificing procreation to pleasure is a way of "Americanizing" sex, making it into a diversion. More broadly, Pasolini bitterly ridiculed the "economic miracle" that quadrupled Italian income in the 1960's but also polluted the nation's shores and countryside, led to wholesale migrations of workers out of southern Italy and created a tacky mass culture. Similarly, Mishima scorned the industrialization (Westernization) of Japan.

To be sure, most political theorists would say that Pasolini was on the left and Mishima on the right. Pasolini felt that the Italian Communist Party was the only decent, uncorrupted, longsighted and humane political organization in the country. Indeed, he was from a poor family, and his own early years of deprivation made him champion the poor everywhere, not only in Italy but also throughout the third world (he wrote a book about India and another about Africa). By contrast, Mishima was from an upper-class family, and he committed seppuku (ritual suicide by disembowelment) in the name of emperor worship and a return to a feudal code (he even had a private army).

In short, Mishima was a fascist and Pasolini a communist. But underneath that ambiguous distinction one can detect strong affinities between them. Both were powerhouses who almost hysterically produced works in many genres: Mishima wrote plays, novels and poems and practiced body building and martial arts. Pasolini was tireless throughout his adulthood, typically tossing off a novel while shooting a film. Both men were homosexuals who were remarkably well integrated into heterosexual social circles and who worked overtime in order to transcend the isolation imposed on them by their sexual identity. Mishima was married, though he was quite public about his homosexuality; Pasolini's great friendships were with the actress Laura Betti, the singer Maria Callas and the novelists Elsa Morante and Alberto Moravia, all of them heterosexual.

Given the cult of *machismo* in Italy, Pasolini's candor was a tribute to his feistiness. He had been hounded out of Friuli (and out of the Communist Party) on charges of corrupting the morals of three teen-age boys. He and his mother fled to Rome, where over the years he was subjected to other legal actions. But none of these efforts to repress him silenced Pasolini; he referred quite openly to his homosexuality in his regular newspaper columns and employed it as a theme in many of his films. But my point is that though both Pasolini and Mishima were frankly, even scandalously, homosexual (Mishima's first book is the semiautobiographical *Confessions of a Mask*), neither man withdrew from the world into the gay subculture of Tokyo or Rome. Both were determined to be dominant figures of their national artistic and intellectual life, and both succeeded publicly, although neither could ever overcome private feelings of alienation.

Finally, one should point out that both men died violent deaths—Mishima by his own hand, Pasolini in a ghastly encounter with a young Roman hustler who beat him and then ran over his body with an automobile. The facts of Pasolini's murder remain cloudy. At the time, Communists insisted that several Fascists had killed him for political motives and then covered up the crime (and discredited Pasolini) by staging the event as a sordid encounter with a prostitute. Those who didn't interpret his death politically interpreted it morally as though the excesses of *Salò* had invited just such violence. Surrendering to paranoia or blaming the victim seem to be the only possible responses to what probably (and more horribly) was merely random violence.

Was Pasolini a great artist? His ***Gospel According to Saint Matthew*** is a radical and original reimagining of the Christ story in the terms of peasant culture, filmed in a corresponding visual style of poverty. *Salò* is great for its unforgettable assault on the senses and sensibilities of the viewer. Of his copious writings, his poems seem the most likely to endure. In the United States we have become used to a poetry that is subjective, dreamlike, mysterious, obvious only in its agitated or exalted state of emotion. Pasolini wrote poems of a very different sort. His poems, which have been translated now with clarity, ingenuity and fidelity by Norman MacAfee, are chatty letters to the world, by turns confessional and polemical.

Of the confessional poems, the most convincing is **"The Tears of the Excavator,"** in which Pasolini recalls his years as a poor schoolteacher when he lived in a shantytown outside Rome. Of the polemical poems, **"A Desperate Vitality"** will shock Americans with its explicit references to names and political jargon: "as in a film by Godard—rediscovery / of romanticism in the seat of / neocapitalistic cynicism and cruelty." This is not the vatic tone of American lyricism. Indeed, an American who reads Enzo Siciliano's biography of Pasolini is struck by how much Pasolini was immersed in ideology. To us, a writer is political only peripherally, when he or she makes political pronouncements. But Pasolini worked in a milieu where an artist was supposed to situate each of his works in an ideological context and to have a ready opinion on every occasion about Freud, Marx and Lévi-Strauss.

Mr. Siciliano himself is the same sort of intellectual. At times the American reader feels daunted when encountering such a sentence as "The conflict, in essence, was between a residue of traditional humanism to be revitalized through Marxist historicism and neopositivist sociological thinking imbued with existential inhibitions." No matter. Mr. Siciliano tells the fascinating facts clearly enough and with sympathy (he was a friend of Pasolini's); the story is steadily absorbing.

Alexander Stille (review date 24-31 July 1982)

SOURCE: "Poet, Martyr, Myth," in *The Nation,* Vol. 235, No. 3, July 24-31, 1982, pp. 86-8.

[*In the following review, Stille analyzes Pasolini's relationship with Italian society and politics.*]

Pier Paolo Pasolini, probably the most famous writer of postwar Italy, is best known in America for his lurid X-rated movies *Arabian Nights* and *'Salo,' the 120 Days of Sodom.* An immensely gifted poet, novelist, film director, literary critic and social commentator, Pasolini was a tangle of contradictions—Communist and Catholic, artist and ideologue, celebrity and outcast, homosexual and rigid traditionalist.

No single work can convey his importance in Italy as a public figure and a national myth: the bête noire of the right (and sometimes of the left) and, for millions of young people, a cult figure whose actions and opinions were the subject of great controversy. Pasolini's murder in 1975, apparently by a teen-age male prostitute, divided the country. For the right it was a fitting end for a man with pernicious habits and violent ideas. For the left it was a martyrdom, perhaps even a political assassination.

Both detractors and admirers agree on one point: Pasolini's death was the moral of a story of deep national significance. He, more than anyone else, embodied the enormous contrasts and dislocations of postwar Italy, a backward peasant nation lurching into the twentieth century, a democracy with a historical memory formed by Fascism.

It is appropriate that Enzo Siciliano's biography *Pasolini* should be published simultaneously with the first Italian-English edition of Pasolini's poetry. The biography is not merely an aid to understanding the poetry; indeed, it is more likely that the poems will serve as an aid to the biography, for Pasolini's most important artistic creation was his life. A longtime friend and follower, Siciliano has written a book that is more of a contribution to the Pasolini myth than a dispassionate analysis of it. However, he has collected a wealth of material from many sources, including Pasolini's unpublished letters and papers. Despite his worshipful tone, Siciliano does let the material speak for itself, and it is fascinating.

This most political of artists began his career as a lyric poet. Born in 1922 (the year Mussolini took power), Pasolini came of age during World War II. When his father, a Fascist army officer, was taken prisoner, the family moved to his mother's village in the remote region of Friuli near the Yugoslav border. Young Pasolini was fascinated by the ancient peasant civilization and by its dialect: "It was possible in ten minutes by bicycle to pass from one linguistic area to another more archaic by fifty or a hundred years." Influenced by Rimbaud and the decadent poets, he saw the Friulian dialect as a "language of pure poetry"; because of its unfamiliarity to most Italians, it would "prolong the lag between sound and meaning." Some critics believe that Pasolini's

early lyrics, published in 1942, are his highest poetic achievement.

Poems omits this early verse. While the Friulian dialect would arguably lose too much in translation to make inclusion worthwhile, one misses a selection from his second book, *The Nightingale of the Catholic Church,* which was written in standard Italian. Instead, *Poems* concentrates on the mature "public verse" that Pasolini wrote after moving to Rome in 1949. This is a curious mixture of political and personal confession, of ideological speechifying shot through with flashes of brilliance, with, every now and then, moments of equilibrium when political and personal passions coincide with great force. His first major success, **"The Ashes of Gramsci,"** presents his paradoxical public persona:

> The scandal of contradicting myself,
> of being
> with you and against you; with you
> in my heart,
> in light, but against you in the dark
> viscera . . .

At his best, Pasolini created an outrageous synthesis of Christian imagery, Marxism and private despair. The suffering of Italy was transformed into his own personal Calvary:

> For one crucified to his tormenting
> rationality,
> butchered by puritanism, nothing
> makes sense anymore
> but an aristocratic and alas
> unpopular opposition.
>
> The revolution is now just a
> sentiment.
>
> **("Plan of Future Works")**

Pasolini did not live up to his potential as a poet, and clearly he knew it. "Oh practical end of my poetry!" he wrote. "To this I'm reduced: when I write / poetry, it's to defend myself, to fight, / compromising myself, renouncing / all my ancient dignity; thus / my defenseless elegiac heart comes / to shame me . . ." (**"Reality"**). But his early lyric inspiration never entirely left his poetry and redeems even his harsher polemics.

In 1949 Pasolini was forced to flee in disgrace from Friuli. He had been accused of corrupting minors and was expelled from the Communist Party. In Rome, he transferred his fascination with Friulian civilization to the violent and gregarious world of the subproletariat in which he lived during his first desperately poor years there. Pasolini's life among the new rootless underclass of Southern peasants was central to his career. With the ear of a linguist and the sensitivity of an anthropologist, he observed the mingling of the cutthroat ethics of the street with the naïve, easygoing ways of the country. Here he found sexual freedom, friendship, material for much of his work and a laboratory in which he watched Italy's social changes played out before him.

His shocking novel about this world, *Ragazzi di Vita,* made Pasolini famous overnight. Outraged, the government tried to suppress the book, as it would his first movie, *Accattone.* The move to Rome also put Pasolini into the mainstream of Italian culture. During the 1950s, he became friends with the best writers of his generation: Alberto Moravia, Elsa Morante, Giorgio Bassani and Italo Calvino.

The beginning of Pasolini's career coincides with the end of Italian neo-Realism—the films of Rossellini, De Sica and the early Fellini (Pasolini wrote the dialogue in Roman dialect for Fellini's *Nights of Cabiria*). But there is a tough, gritty, unsentimental quality that distinguishes Pasolini from the neo-Realists. Fellini's Cabiria was a whore with a heart of gold; Pasolini's *Accattone,* the story of an opportunistic, cynical pimp, neither justifies nor condemns its subject.

With Pasolini's growing celebrity in the 1960s, both his work and his life became a source of scandal. The openings of his films were followed by obscenity trials, and their showings disrupted by gangs of neofascist thugs. He was indicted (falsely) for robbery. All this exacerbated his persecution complex, his sense, as a homosexual, of being a pariah; but it also gratified his narcissism and stimulated his need to provoke the public. "By now," writes Siciliano, "Pier Paolo's sense of being alive was inextricably bound up with his provocatory relationship with the public. Irresistibly he ended up coinciding with his public image."

His literary production dropped off; he never completed a novel after 1960. He grew apart from many of his literary friends. His movies were increasingly dominated by his sexual and political obsessions. By the early 1970s he was in a state of crisis. His artistic inspiration was drying up, and he was convinced that everything he loved in Italian life was being destroyed. His one steady lover had left him, and there was a new psychopathic brutality in the life of the Roman slums. He was badly beaten up several times.

Out of this despair, Pasolini forged a second career as a polemicist, writing front-page articles for Italy's largest newspaper, *Il Corriere della Sera.* With his genius for capturing in a phrase an entire mood or situation, Pasolini, perhaps more than any other intellectual, defined the political vocabulary of the New Left in Italy.

He became the spokesman for Italy's new marginal groups—an entire generation of jobless university graduates, the masses of displaced peasants who crowded the factory towns

of the north—a dangerous class, unassimilated by society, which formed the extraparliamentary left. Unlike the perpetually optimistic Communists, Pasolini foresaw that the victory of consumer capitalism and the destruction of traditional Italian culture were inevitable. He also appealed to a conservative nostalgia for agrarian life and old values. He offered rebellion, "pure opposition," rather than social revolution: "I can no longer believe in revolution, but I can't help being on the side of the young people who are fighting for it." He was particularly sensitive to the linguistic, cultural and behavioral shifts that to him were signals of "the new barbarism," and he cleverly pointed out the ways in which fascist cultural and rhetorical patterns had been subtly transformed in the postwar period. In the first years after World War II, "the values which counted were the same as under fascism": church, country, family, obedience, order and morality. The profound changes took place during the economic boom of the 1960s, which he described in a beautiful article, **"The Disappearance of the Fireflies."**

Consumer society was, according to Pasolini, a new and more insidious form of fascism which had succeeded, where Mussolini's fascism had failed, in unifying Italy for the first time in history. Mass communication and mass consumption were quickly leveling the wide cultural and linguistic differences between the various regions: "No country has possessed like ours such a quantity of 'particular and real cultures,' such a quantity of 'little homelands'—no country, that is, in which there was later such an overwhelming 'development.'" For Pasolini, the new consumer society was characterized by self-indulgence, materialism, sexual license, drugs, conformism and violence, values he termed "cultural genocide."

Pasolini's equation of fascism with the corrupt and inefficient Christian Democratic rule became the stock in trade of the extraparliamentary left. Indeed, Pasolini's Swiftian suggestion that the leadership of the Christian Democrats be placed on trial for cultural genocide was literally carried out by the Red Brigades, with the kidnapping of Aldo Moro. (The Red Brigades skipped the line in which Pasolini wrote that the trial of the Christian Democrats "is only a metaphor.") Much of the ideology of the far-left group Autonomia, with its anti-industrial orientation and its support for "spontaneous" rebellion, also drew on Pasolini's antiprogressive rhetoric.

Such groups overlooked Pasolini's equally sharp criticism of the left, particularly of the student movement. Believing that the students had little to do with the proletariat they claimed to represent, Pasolini insisted that they behaved with the dogmatism, intolerance and hatred of the Fascist *Squadri:* "So many Catholics, in becoming Communists, bring with them Faith and Hope, while neglecting, without realizing it, Charity. This is how fascism of the left is born."

Pasolini's articles on "fascism of the left" and on the horrifying spread of violence among the young seem uncannily prophetic in light of the prevalence of terrorism in Italy today and in light of his own gruesome murder at the hands of one of the *ragazzi di vita* he had described so often. Pasolini was brilliant diagnostician ·of Italian diseases because he himself suffered from them: a critic of the far left, he was its unwitting prophet. While he condemned the violence of the Roman subproletariat, he was erotically attracted to it. He was one of those "unconscious Christians" of the left, whose apocalyptic vision could be resolved only through the crucifixion that was his murder.

Gary Steele (review date 25 July 1982)

SOURCE: "Pasolini: Complex Life, Bloody Death," in *The Los Angeles Times Book Review,* July 25, 1982, p. 7.

[*In the following review, Steele considers a biography of Pasolini written by Enzo Siciliano and a collection of Pasolini's poetry, asserting that understanding Pasolini's work "is a possible, difficult and liberating task."*]

In November, 1975, Pier Paolo Pasolini's savagely maimed body was found near a shantytown outside Rome. Giuseppe Pelosi, a 17-year-old male prostitute, was quickly arrested, tried and convicted of the brutal murder. Yet a multitude of evidence suggests that Pelosi did not act alone: Pasolini's friends and his biographer assume that he was assassinated by the Italian ultra-right, to whom his life, work and influence were anathema. Thus in death as in life, the scandal and controversy surrounding Pasolini threaten to obscure his extraordinary and multifaceted accomplishments.

Indeed, politically motivated threats and turmoil marked Pasolini's career. At 27, he faced a legal charge of "corrupting minors"; public rumor aroused the interest of the police. Within days, he was both expelled from the Communist Party and dismissed from his teaching position. The charges eventually were dropped, but he had long since, in his own words, "escaped to Rome with my mother, as in a novel." In Rome he produced more than 50 books and directed nearly 20 feature films, as well as issuing a flood of critical journalism of the highest quality, ranging from fashion to philology to politics. He was a liberating force in Italian literature and film, as an artist and as a (usually) successful defendant in court against persistent charges of obscenity and blasphemy.

Biographer Siciliano has performed a heroic labor in portraying this complex figure. Two major obstacles, however, present themselves. One is the writing itself, a frenetic, convoluted, didactic prose that sometimes seems more interested in thematically unifying the meaning of Pasolini's life than

in the life itself. Siciliano is better at describing the works, although their vast bulk and scope sometimes dictate an overview too insubstantial for the interpretive load that accompanies it.

The other obstacle is the common one among biographers—assuming homosexual orientation to be a deformative, rather than formative, influence. That first scandal propelled Pasolini into the center of Italian politics and culture, where he was long overdue. Once in Rome, the lives and rhythms of the Roman underclass youths to whom he was so drawn were central to his poetic and film achievements. In these and many other ways, homosexuality seems to have been the underlying drive powering, even unifying his personal and political temperaments. Siciliano depicts all this but is unwilling or unable to draw the logical inferences.

Given these caveats, there is a great compensation: Random House simultaneously presents a selection of Pasolini's poetry. Here is the unmediated voice, full of discouragement, sensual joy, unhappiness, idealism. The poetry vaults past interpretation into a life of its own. The artist/politician knew what life and death for him were: "Death is not in not being able to communicate but in no longer being able to be understood." Understanding the life may be beyond us. Understanding the work, fortunately, is a possible, difficult and liberating task; both books help.

N. S. Thompson (review date 8 October 1982)

SOURCE: "Poet into Man," in *Times Literary Supplement,* No. 4149, October 8, 1982, p. 1105.

[*In the following review, Thompson discusses Pasolini's Poems and Enzo Siciliano's biography of the poet and filmmaker.*]

As a poet, Pier Paolo Pasolini was an arch-traditionalist; as a man, a "politikon zoon", he was a radical romantic whom disillusion drove to despair. The man frustrated the poet and forced him, first, to relinquish his traditional means in favour of a freer approach to poetry, and later, to abandon his poetry—ostensibly, at least—for the cinema.

The present volume of ***Poems,*** as the translators state, represents about a sixth of Pasolini's published work in Italian and none of his early lyrics in the Friulan dialect. It is based on a selection Pasolini himself made for an edition in 1970, and includes his introduction to this volume as an appendix. Certainly, making a first, rigorous choice from among the works of such a wide-ranging poet is an exceedingly difficult task, and, while this selection is inclusive, showing the move from rational public poet to tortured private man, the picture it presents is inevitably incomplete. Quite rightly, the long title poems of his first two collections, **"The Ashes of Gramsci"** and **"The Religion of My Time"** have been included, but the translators have preferred the agonized **"A Desperate Vitality"** from *Poesia in forma di rosa,* rather than that poem itself, and some shorter poems from his last volume *Trasumanar e organizzar.*

What kind of a poet emerges? As may be expected of a writer who also painted, and later turned to film, a very visual one; the two long poems in *terza rima* are intense metaphysical meditations, but firmly located in time and place. A visit to the grave of Antonio Gramsci in the Protestant Cemetery in Rome is the setting for a scrupulously honest self-examination in the course of which the rational Communist finds that he does not want his beloved working class to change, to lose its traditional vital qualities; "Two days of fever" give rise to a scrutiny of his concepts of religion and love, where he remembers his earlier Catholicism, contrasting it with his present Marxism. In both poems, descriptions of his environment amplify and extend his state of mind. But, unlike the *ermetici,* Pasolini is not locked inside himself; the problems he examines, albeit from a personal, even private point of view, are universal: society, religion, social change. As most critics agree, Pasolini's great contribution was the creation of "una poesia civile", the rational argument of a civilized mind. But the adjective also carries the meaning of "civil": his is a public poetry, even if there is no consensus of acceptance by the public. After the strenuous effort to arrive at these well-reasoned, balanced poems of the 1950s, he changed direction, turning inwards to become a "kinetic poet": his subjective reactions are given first place, making for an engaging warmth, until they become the agony of his later years. However, in both modes, Pasolini was a skilled prosodist—especially in his resurrection of Dante's *terza rima*—who twisted and broke the rules to great effect. Naturally, this causes problems for the translator and MacAfee, while his versions are "correct", ignores this important aspect of a "civil (ized) poem".

Reviewing Pasolini's first small book, of dialect poetry in the *Corriere di Lugarno* in 1943, Gianfranco Contini, then a young professor, hit a prophetic note in remarking on the "scandal" which it introduced into the "annals of dialect literature". The scandal was in trying to use dialect for the expression of honest, personal sentiment rather than as a medium for folk tales.

Contini's review is noted by Enzo Siciliano in his excellent biography, which, while giving a sensitive appreciation of his literary and cinematographic production, amply chronicles Pasolini's own personal struggles. These centred on his homosexuality, which caused scandal enough in the 1940s and 50s. In 1950, when he was twenty-eight, it led to his being expelled from his posts as schoolteacher and lo-

cal Communist Party secretary in Friuli, and with his mother he fled to Rome. There he sought work as a teacher until scriptwriting in the burgeoning film industry enabled him to concentrate on writing. His two novels, *Ragazzi di vita* and *Una vita violenta,* brought him fame, and more scandal, mainly because of their use of obscenity, but also because of his accurate descriptions of living conditions in the *borgate,* the shanty towns around Rome, which the reading public was either unaware of or refused to acknowledge. Given the opportunities of the day and the contacts he had already established in Cinecittà, it seemed a simple step to make a film himself, and *Accattone,* the story of a young pimp who can find no place in the world, was actually set in these desolate outskirts. It was the first of many films in which a young man is stigmatized or martyred, whether it be Oedipus or Christ or Ettore (*Mamma Roma*). In the polemics of his last years, which were confined to the Italian political scene, Pasolini appeared to offer himself up in the same way as his heroes.

According to Dario Bellezza, Pasolini's one-time literary secretary and friend (and himself a poet), Pasolini's last scandal was in "choosing" his death. In *Morte di Pasolini* Bellezza examines the prefigurations of it in his poetry, especially in the *Poesia in forma di rosa* volume, where the poet leaves his earlier rationality behind; the poetry becomes a cry *de profundis* and the figure of a "poeta martirizzato" constantly appears. In his biography, Siciliano presents the detailed evidence and hypotheses surrounding Pasolini's death (he was found beaten and crushed to death in Ostia in 1975), and casts doubt on the court's final decision. Though not ignoring the doubts or the contradictory evidence, Bellezza is more concerned to present a picture of a man who was looking for death; a man who, well into middle age, should have been reaching some stasis, but who was more than ever tormented by his sexual instincts and who felt betrayed by the new liberality and the embourgeoisification of the proletarian youths he desired. It is a very convincing portrait.

David Robey (review date 7 January 1983)

SOURCE: "Boys in Their Mystery," in *Times Literary Supplement,* No. 4162, January 7, 1983, p. 23.

[*In the following review, Robey discusses two of Pasolini's novels,* Amado mio *and* Atti impuri, *that were published posthumously and asserts that "The two texts are very close in style and subject-matter . . . and quite different from the author's later work."*]

At his death Pasolini left two unpublished novels among his papers, both of them dating from the late 1940s, when he lived in Friuli. *Amado mio*—scarcely more than a long no-vella—is the shorter and more polished of the two. Pasolini seems to have continued working on it after he moved to Rome in 1950, and to have contemplated publishing it in the early 1970s; the version edited in this volume by Concetta D'Angeli is the most recent of four successive drafts. *Atti impuri,* which is also published here for the first time, is con-siderably longer. It exists in only one manuscript, probably written before the move to Rome, and left in a far from fin-ished state. It contains a number of inconsistencies and con-tradictions, some of which, notably the oscillation between first and third-person narrative, have been ironed out by the editor, while others have been allowed to stand.

The two texts are very close in style and subject-matter—Pasolini also left a common preface for them among his pa-pers—and quite different from the author's later work. They are written in a conventional narrative form far removed from the dazzling, disruptive impasto of literary Italian and dialect or slang in the subsequent Roman novels; at this early stage Pasolini reserved dialect for his lyric poetry alone. They are both about homosexual love, more exactly a young man's love for adolescent boys. And they are both substan-tially autobiographical, indeed confessional—particularly *Atti impuri,* which in the manuscript was written mainly in the first person, is partially in diary form, incorporates large sections of Pasolini's own diaries and has a protagonist in almost every respect indistinguishable from Pasolini himself. In the later novels, in contrast, homosexuality is a very mi-nor theme, and the tone is predominantly objective. Nowhere else, in fact, either in writing or on film, did the author ex-pose his private inclinations and feelings as much as they are exposed in this book.

Nevertheless the book's interest is not purely documentary, nor indeed is it pornographic. Each novel centres on the se-duction, after initial resistance, of a Friulan country boy, but scabrous though this subject may sound, the focus is defi-nitely emotional rather than erotic. The protagonists' homo-sexual feelings are described with a relentless, compelling analytical thoroughness, a thoroughness that sometimes verges on irony, especially in *Amado mio,* where the narra-tive is in the third person, the pace is more rapid and the tone more cynical. They are obsessive, tortured feelings, though on account of their ferocity, not on account of a sense of guilt. They oscillate between violent extremes of vindic-tiveness and affection, and lead repeatedly to humiliation and despair, quite unlike the self-contained hedonism of Gide, whom Pasolini seems to have had particularly in mind as he wrote.

The novels are therefore far from being an apology for ho-mosexual love, even though they contain no explicit criti-cism of it. Moreover while the potential sexual attractions of adolescent boys are expressed with considerable lyrical

force, they appear to be such as to guarantee the frustration of the lover's desires. What excites Pasolini's protagonists is precisely what is lost through seduction: the boys' inno-cence and naturalness, and also their "mystery", as he calls it, their absorption in a closed adolescent world inaccessible to an older man, especially, perhaps, to an intellectual. One can understand easily enough why in each novel the object of desire seems always to elude the lover's grasp, condemn-ing him to the constant, compulsive repetition of the same vain attempt at satisfaction.

The innocence, naturalness and "mystery" of adolescents is also a central theme of Pasolini's three later novels, *Ragazzi di vita, Una vita violenta* and *Il sogno di una cosa.* There, however, they are the subject of a more detached, much less egotistical kind of celebration, rather than the target of a character's desire; art seems to have been distanced from life, acquiring in the process a far more original and revelatory character. Interesting and powerful though the two early nov-els are, it is thus not hard to imagine why Pasolini never pub-lished them.

Judith L. Greenberg (review date Spring 1983)

SOURCE: A review of *Les dernières parole d'un impie: Entre-tiens avec Jean Duflot,* in *World Literature Today,* Vol. 57, No. 2, Spring, 1983, p. 267.

[*In the following review, Greenberg states that Pasolini's* Les dernières parole d'un impie *"is part autobiography, part analysis, part remembrance, part explanation, part (self-) justification."*]

As Duflot remarks, this series of interviews with Pasolini (in-cluding several just prior to his death) is not only in a sense a political and spiritual (and artistic or, better, poetic) last will and testament. *Les dernières paroles d'un impie* is also an exegesis, by the best possible exegete, of the Passion of Pasolini (1922-75).

The book is part autobiography, part analysis, part remem-brance, part explanation, part (self-)justification. Pasolini felt himself to be—and was, as were all his characters—an out-sider, an *exclus;* allergic to most of modern civilization, feel-ing himself hated "racially," he was obsessed with exclusion, marginality. His *Dernières paroles* goes a long way toward showing how much of this role of pariah was self-induced and espoused due to deliberate provocation, and how much to the incomprehension and fear of others.

The book covers a lot of ground—from the Friulian soil of his early poems to (nearly) the beach at Ostia where he met his death. All is fertile ground, showing the continuity he believes to underlie evolution: nothing in man or in history is ever completely destroyed; each step goes beyond its predecessor, but the present is superimposed on the past; man is the sum of his parts and his pasts. The sacred is juxtaposed with the desacralized—multi-leveled, as is his work.

Pasolini discusses his fascination with language, with languages, with varied modes of communication, and offers in each case detailed reasonings to explain his sense of semiology and his own semiology of the cinema. He returns always, of course, to the cinema—as "poetry," as the written language of action, of the living, of reality—and to myth, its other face. In doing a film, he says, he fixes on an object, a face, a landscape, as though within it the sacred were about to explode. One might treat this book in the same manner.

C. Fantazzi (review date Summer 1983)

SOURCE: A review of *Amado mio,* in *World Literature Today,* Vol. 57, No. 3, Summer, 1983, p. 443.

[*In the following review, Fantazzi discusses Pasolini's early novels,* Amado mio *and* Atti impuri.]

Preceding the completed novella **Amado mio** is another slightly longer piece, **Atti impuri,** which lay in more fragmentary state among the writer's papers. It is fitting that they appear together, for Pier Paolo Pasolini had written a single preface for both of them, which is published in an appendix. The tone of these notes by the author is very hesitant and apologetic, pleading for comprehension of the "abnormal" love presented. In the incomplete pages of the first early reminiscences the author vacillates between the first and third persons in the various drafts, but the editor chooses to use only the first person in a diaristic fashion. The tale is one of ephebic love, idyllic afternoon frolics in the cornfields or along the banks of a river in Friuli. Among the playmates of the protagonist are a priapic shepherd named Bruno, a lad with the very peasant name of Nisiuti and a girl named Dina, who tries in vain to deliver him from his "diversity."

Amado mio, which takes its title from the hit song of the 1950s film *Gilda,* starring Rita Hayworth, is a more polished work with almost a mythical quality even in the names of the lovers: Desiderio (or Desi) and Iasìs. It has some good moments of lyricism, bathed in an aura of innocence. At one point Pasolini quotes Foscolo: "Guilt is purified by the ardor of passion and shame embellishes the admission of lust." Such ingenuous outpourings are not for all tastes.

Naomi Greene (essay date Spring 1984)

SOURCE: "Reading Pasolini Today," in *Quarterly Review of Film Studies,* Vol. 9, No. 2, Spring, 1984, pp. 143-8.

[*In the following essay, Greene discusses Enzo Siciliano's* Pasolini: A Biography, *Paul Willeman's* Pier Paolo Pasolini, *Beverly Allen's* Pier Paolo Pasolini: The Poetics of Heresy, *and Pasolini's* Poems *translated by Norman MacAfee.*]

Poet, novelist, critic, essayist, political polemicist, Pasolini was virtually unique among contemporary filmmakers in the variety of his activities. Fortunately, the publication of these recent volumes begins to give the English-speaking world a glimpse into the range of his interests and a context within which to place his films. At first, the very disparate approaches represented here (critical articles by and about him, a biography, translations of his poems) would seem to preclude any general remarks. And then, one begins to sense that to some extent at least, and of course with certain exceptions, the approaches correspond to national preoccupations. Most striking of all is probably the way Italian writers are drawn, again and again, to the character of Pasolini himself and to the vital role that he played in Italian culture and politics (and in Italy, the two are closely linked) for nearly thirty years. But even here, approaches vary greatly, ranging from Andrea Zanzotto's highly theoretical piece entitled "Pedagogy" (in *The Poetics of Heresy*) to the fairly sensationalist biography by the writer, and former friend of Pasolini, Enzo Siciliano. Siciliano sets the tone of his book in its opening chapter which delves—exhaustively—into the horrible manner in which Pasolini met his death in 1976. (Although Pasolini apparently died at the hands of a young homosexual pickup, Siciliano, like others, questions whether this death was the result of some kind of conspiracy.) By opening his book in such a manner, Siciliano immediately calls to mind the way the Italian press played upon Pasolini's gruesome death and, in so doing, he raises one of the very issues that came to haunt Pasolini in the 1970s: the role played by the media in modern consumer society. Discussing this issue, Andrea Zanzotto writes: "What happened later . . . just after his death, on his body mistaken for a pile of refuse by the woman who saw it first, demonstrates once again, if demonstrations ever were necessary, the degree to which the media are most of all—or perhaps exclusively— violence . . . Pasolini was killed once again by the deprivation of silence, by the vile din surrounding his death, by a monstrous, slavering turbidity of, 'information-by redundance.'"

But Pasolini's death, as Siciliano is eager to make clear, was only the last in a series of scandals the director provoked as much by the way he lived (his open homosexuality) as by what he wrote and filmed. (It was rare indeed that a Pasolini film didn't encounter censorship difficulties.) Siciliano's detailed explorations of these scandals, his relentless probing into Pasolini's sexual proclivities (he is unaccountably fascinated by Pasolini's friendship with women), his need to "explain" and in some sense defend Pasolini's homosexuality lend what must surely be an inadvertent anti-gay tone to the book. Yet one must ask whether Siciliano is totally to blame for the tone of scandal-mongering and gossip one finds in his book. For wasn't Pasolini, torn as he was by contradictions, both a fierce opponent of the debasement provoked by a consumer society that would feed on everything and, at the same time, a man who chose to play out his life upon that stage that was Rome, subject to its gossip, fearful lest he lose the public eye? Didn't his need to be the "victim" of society extend to a willingness to be the victim of a sensationalist press? And if the early "scandals" he experienced (which began when he lost his teaching post in Friuli and was virtually forced to flee to Rome in 1947) were traumatic and by no means his own doing, by the 1970s it seemed that he needed to take unpopular positions for reasons that were psychological (his need to be a victim and to remain in the public eye) as well as ideological (he was always to maintain that any position taken by the majority, even the left-wing majority, had to be questioned).

Nonetheless, even those readers who might be disturbed by the tone and emphasis of Siciliano's book should, I think, be grateful for the wealth of details it offers us concerning both Pasolini's life and the various cultural/political contexts in which he found himself: the postwar years in Friuli, his ins and outs with the Communist Party, his position in the literary and cinematic circles of Rome. Without a knowledge of much of the material presented by Siciliano it would be hard to fully understand, for example, Zanzotto's more abstract reading, or decoding, of Pasolini's life which, for him, revolves about a pedagogical drive: not only did Pasolini begin as a teacher, but in his writings he assumed the role of the public "praeceptor." Even a film like *Salò,* in Zanzotto's words, "gravitates . . . around the problem of a 'genealogy of morals.'" And, finally, Zanzotto gives a pedagogical reading of Pasolini's death, remarking that: "But this death has burned every halo of guilt (real or imaginary) that surrounded Pasolini. Stripped of everything, made a victim and nothing but a victim, even he, in the most barbarically 'distracted,' or most barbarically cynical way, even he appears to us in the horrible showdown to which he would have wished to summon people so that they could confront themselves. In his death there existed a situation in which all are obliged to 'know,' and also to recognize themselves; there was pedagogy: true pedagogy, which is always an event and not a word." And if this reading seems too symbolic, just as that of Siciliano seems too preoccupied with the theme of conspiracy, it may be because both men, like so many who admired or loved Pasolini, feel pressed by the desire to make this death mean something: otherwise, its existential absurdity is too overwhelming.

If, for the most part, Italian critics are inexorably drawn towards Pasolini the man, and the role he played in Italian life, foreign critics, understandably more removed from these concerns, tend to focus on his films and on some of the principal theoretical and political issues raised by his work. This is true, by and large, of the British critics (represented in the BFI booklet on Pasolini) who seem particularly concerned with the political and semiological issues raised by Pasolini's films and writings. Given Pasolini's urge to attack majority opinion at the cost of taking extreme positions, it hardly comes as a surprise that many of the political positions he took—especially in the late 1960s and 1970s—were deeply problematical. Hence, in those years, when leftist ideology had, in some sense, become "official" in Italy, when the economic boom of the 1960s had changed the face of the country, his rejection of modern consumer society and his hatred of neocapitalism made him turn toward the Third World, toward the peasantry, toward mythic and archaic civilizations. Just when others ardently embraced political filmmaking, Pasolini turned his back on the contemporary world in films like *Teorema, Medea, Porcile* and *Edipo Re.* Not surprisingly, he became the target of leftists who labeled his behavior "nostalgic" and "regressive." And this is the view shared by at least half of the British critics who qualify Pasolini's attitude with terms such as "right-wing anarchism," "anachronistic" and "regressive fixations."

However tempting and somehow justified such terms may be, I do not think they provide an adequate measure of the complexity of Pasolini's thought. To begin with, they ignore, or gloss over the fact that no one was more aware of such problems, of his own inner contradictions, than Pasolini himself: again and again, he was to describe the pull within him between what he called "reason" (rational thought, history, Marxism) and "passion" (a visceral attraction to myth, to archaic or peasant civilizations, to the irrational). Nor do they acknowledge that the extreme positions he struck often had the salutary function of questioning accepted modes of thought, on the left as well as on the right. Certainly, his despair at contemporary civilization, his conviction that real change was impossible in a world dominated by technology and mass consumerism, are far more widely shared today than in the political climate of the late 1960s. And his deep distrust of any "power" or "ideology" has become one of the dominant themes in the work of another great iconoclast, Michel Foucault. Lastly, as Zanzotto remarks, can we even take all the attitudes he struck at face value: "Absurd to think of a Pasolini dreaming of the return to a peasant civilization taken as a block, or even taken as a preeminent indication; much further back than any antiquity was that which he 'remembered' via peasant or third-world civilization, a 'then' that was enough to justify his idea of a 'revolutionary force which is in the past' (an idea misunderstood, as were other of his themes outside the manuals in fashion, as being reactionary). It was a simple matter of a past understood as a metaphor for the first dawn. Infinitely far back and always in the future."

Equally as provocative as his politics were Pasolini's theoretical writings on cinema in which, again and again, in opposition to Metz and other semiologists, he voiced his conviction that cinema was not, as they claimed, a linguistic system but rather, the "language of reality." This attitude, too, has let him in for several severe remarks on the part of some of the critics in the BFI booklet: one calls his essentially anti-semiological stance the "latest incarnation of his regressive series of subversions of the institution of language." To be fair, some of the critics do point out that Pasolini's attempt somehow to capture reality through both verbal language and cinema must be seen as a poet's attempt to embrace a desperately loved reality. (In this respect, Pasolini was very close to the Rimbaud he so loved in his youth, the Rimbaud who wrote ecstatically "J'ai embrassé l'aube.") But above and beyond his personal needs, it also seems that as semiology has given way to and/or incorporated the multiple readings of a Derrida or the psychoanalysis of a Lacan, Pasolini's investigation and espousal of the poetic, oneric quality of cinema appears that much more interesting and less easily dismissable.

The essays in the BFI booklet are at their best, I think, not when they somehow judge, or seek to disprove, the extreme stands taken by Pasolini, but when they analyze—at times with acute sensitivity—the films themselves or Pasolini's cinematic style. One reads with pleasure Geoffrey Nowell-Smith's analysis of the ways in which Pasolini breaks with what could be called "classical" narrative or Noel Purdon's analysis of how geometric structures and color operate within Pasolini's films. Of great polemical interest are the opposing positions taken by Nowell-Smith and Richard Dyer on the images of homosexuality within Pasolini's films. While Nowell-Smith feels that Pasolini's films are radically different from most cinema in that "there is no privileged role attributed to the male heterosexual vision," Richard Dyer argues that the erotic depiction of attractive young men is essentially a self-oppressive view of gayness which "reinforces the image of male-sexuality-as-activity, just as relentlessly as the standard images of women enforce the concept of female-sexuality-as-passivity."

Whereas the BFI essays are devoted essentially to Pasolini's films, the essays found in the more recent volume, published after Pasolini's death, entitled *The Poetics of Heresy* (edited by Beverly Allen who has also done a number of the translations) range over the whole of Pasolini's work and, for the most part, are informed by current theoretical preoccupations inspired by Derrida, Lacan, narratology, etc. This often means that many of the most problematical issues raised by Pasolini's work are given radically new readings. This is the case, for example, of Pasolini's desire—given such short

shrift by the British critics—to create a poetics, and later a cinema, able to encompass reality. Here, in a piece entitled "The Word Beside itself," Stefano Agosti analyzes the way this desire informs Pasolini's poetics. Beginning with the dialectic, if you will, between the Subject and Discourse, he notes that the desire to encompass reality meant that Pasolini ranged over the "utmost range of contents (*niveau de l'énoncé*)" as well as "the full involvement of the Subject in its own discourse (*niveau de l'énonciation*)." And, in addition to the "plurality of the contents expressed and of the discursive typologies employed," his efforts to capture reality as much as possible led Pasolini to "processes of homologation (of mimesis) between discourse structures and the structures of reality" through, for example, "mimesis of temporal duration and of spatial continuity (viewing time)." Although Agosti's analysis of these mimetic structures principally bears upon Pasolini's poetry, a number of his remarks concerning Pasolini's cinema are highly suggestive and certainly offer a way out of the narrow arena of semiotics which, for Pasolini, can constitute only a dead end.

Probably the greatest percentage of articles in this anthology (some of them written by Italian men of letters such as Italo Calvino and Leonardo Scasia) attempt to come to terms with Pasolini's last film, *Salò* (based on Sade's *120 Days in Sodom*) whose cold-blooded scenes of cruelty and horror distressed many of Pasolini's most ardent admirers. One of the most disturbing aspects of the film was probably, as Calvino puts it, the explicit analogy between Sadian sadism and the historical phenomenon of Italian Fascism. (The film takes place in Salò, the last stronghold of Italian Fascism, while its frightful torturers are clearly Fascists.) In Calvino's eyes, the horror of Fascism was so great, and is still so vivid in the minds of those who lived it, that "it cannot serve as background to a symbolic and imaginary horror constantly outside the probable such as is present in Sade's work." Roland Barthes agrees with this, but goes even further, objecting to Pasolini's mimetic depiction of Fascism (he believes that "Fascism is a coercive object [which] forces us to think it accurately, analytically, philosophically" and, as such, should be treated in a Brechtian manner) and to his literal transcription of Sade. This last objection is hardly surprising given the fact that much of Barthes' own work on Sade revolves about his passionate conviction that the only reality for Sade was "écriture"; hence, any depiction of his libertinage, which is essentially a "fact of language," can only betray it.

The most complex reading of this film is probably that of Leo Bersani and Ulysse Dutoit who limit themselves to the film, excluding both historical factors as well as extra-textual ones (i.e., the relationship between Sade's text and Pasolini's film). In their effort to see how violence works within the textual system, they begin by examining the relationship between representation and sadism ("Sexual excite-

ment must be represented before it can be felt; or, more exactly, it *is* the representation of an alienated commotion")
and then proceed to analyze the relationship between sadism
and narration asserting that Sade's "calculation, preparation
and control of climaxes" is also a narrative strategy in that
"the climactic significances of narrative are made possible
by a rigidly hierarchical organization of people and events
into major and minor roles." But whereas most narrative
tends to "sequester" violence, a sequestration which endows
it with fascination at the same time that it allows us to reject it, Pasolini refuses such strategies with the result that
he "deprives us of the narrative luxury of isolating the obscene or violent act and rejecting it." And here they come
to the crux of the unease created in the spectator by the film,
for once violence is no longer sequestered, but rather,
theatricalized and surrounded by verbal narratives, it becomes an entertaining spectacle, such that a complicity is
established between the viewer and the Fascist libertines. At
this point, it would seem that the spectator is right to feel
uneasy. But Bersani and Dutoit do not let matters rest here:
proceeding with their complex argument, they seem to conclude that, paradoxically, "the morality of the scene consists
in our having been compelled to see the nonmoral nature of
our interest in violence." Subtle and intricate as their argument is, I'm not sure that their conclusion is entirely borne
out by the reactions of most spectators who, appalled by the
violence of the film they are viewing, are not likely to question their own interest in violence.

Whether or not one agrees with the piece by Bersani and
Dutoit, like most of the articles in *The Poetics of Heresy*
(which also contains a good bibliography), it is highly intelligent—brilliant at times—intent on seeing Pasolini in a
new critical light, removed from the arena of moralistic judgments which have plagued his work from the beginning. And
the challenge of the critical pieces in this anthology is
matched by a number of Pasolini's own articles made accessible here for the first time in English. *The Poetics of
Heresy* opens, in fact, with an essay entitled **"The End of
the Avant-Garde"** which shows Pasolini at his maddening
best, making us re-think assumptions taken for granted. Here
is Pasolini, in 1966 and hence at the heyday of Structuralism, taking on both Lucien Goldmann and Roland Barthes
for being essentially content-oriented in their notion of literary structure; here, too, at a time when the left-wing avant-
garde lionized Brecht and eschewed realism, is Pasolini
arguing paradoxically that the avant-garde really represented
a new Classicism ("from an avant-garde text I learn nothing
of the author who composed it, except precisely, that he is
an author. And this is how Italian literature's ancient, incur-
able classicism is perpetuated") and that its "terror" of naturalism was really a "terror, taboo and obsession for reality."
But perhaps the most provocative part of this essay, which
characteristically interweaves literature, culture, and politics,
resides in the way he groups together some very disparate

forces which, in his eyes, contradict "both Marxist rationalism and bourgeois rationalism." For here, he includes not
only the growing revolt within the bosom of the bourgeoisie (and here, as so often, he was prophetic since this revolt
was to erupt two years later), the presence of the Third
World, *but* also "the uninterrupted presence of Nazism as
the only true bourgeois ideology (for instance, rural America,
Dallas, etc. etc.)."

The provocations in this essay of the 1960s have a force, a
vitality which contrasts—a bit sadly, I think—with the more
disillusioned and bitter tone of his writings of the 1970s.
Having lost all belief—for both personal and political reasons—in the possibility of real change, he seemed to feel it
necessary to question those measures of reform which the
left hailed as a victory. Two of his most important "interventions" of the 1970s—which voice his reactions to the passage, first, of a political bill granting divorce and to a later
one allowing abortion—are included in *The Poetics of Heresy.* Although he based his objections on ideological
grounds—for him, the passage of the divorce bill indicated
a new consensus of power as clerical and paleo-industrial
Italy gave way before the "hedonistic ideology of consumerism," while the bill granting abortion suggested a "false
tolerance" which still did not permit sexual diversity—one
wonders if his ire didn't stem as much from his need to hold
the spotlight as from his conviction that all these liberalized
laws were made by, and for, the heterosexual world from
which he was forever excluded.

Although the tone of these pieces seems bitter, Pasolini's
most personal despair is reserved for his poems. And it is
in his poems—those interspersed throughout the volume of
The Poetics of Heresy, as well as those selected and translated by Norman MacAfee, that Pasolini's most intimate
voice is found. But—as befits his pre-romantic conception
of the poet as a public figure—Pasolini's intimacy is deeply
embedded in a web of political and social allusions; like his
"interventions," many of the poems were written in response
to precise events. Happily, the notes provided by Norman
MacAfee clarify many of these allusions which would otherwise remain mysterious for the Anglo-Saxon reader. Lastly,
as one who knows firsthand the immense difficulty of translating Pasolini's poetry, I have nothing but admiration for
the high literary quality of the translations in these two collections. Together with his other writings, they constitute a
valuable addition to the corpus of Pasolini's work now available in English.

N. S. Thompson (review date 25 May 1984)

SOURCE: "Consumerism Rampant," in *Times Literary
Supplement,* No. 4234, May 25, 1984, p. 596.

[In the following review, Thompson discusses the themes present in Pasolini's Lutheran Letters *which he states focuses on the moral state of Italy since Mussolini.]*

Lutheran Letters is a posthumous collection of the provocative articles which Pasolini started writing for the *Corriere della sera* in March, 1975; a series which spread to the weekly *Il Mondo* and which he continued up to the time of his death. The last piece in the collection is the address Pasolini was to have delivered at a Radical Party Congress in Florence two days after his body was found at Ostia: his appearance would have marked a return to the party political sphere from which he had been absent for over twenty-five years.

He was also planning the publication of his "Lutheran Letters" at the time of his death: the title is his and among his papers were found sketches for further articles rounding out the proposed collection. As the title would suggest, Pasolini is concerned with the moral state of the nation, examining the cultural and political changes that have occurred in Italy since Mussolini and the immediate post-war period, and, as he sees it, the loss of values which occurred in the neo-capitalist 1950s and 60s. From being almost a traditional peasant society in 1945, Italy underwent not so much an Industrial, as a Consumer Revolution, which, according to Pasolini's individualistic Marxist analysis, brought about the loss of traditional values among the lower classes and a homogenization of the middle strata, based on bourgeois self-interest. He launches a bitter attack against the crime wave among the young, linking it to the overwhelming pressure exerted on them to be good middle-class consumers: they either overreach in their urge for acquisition or drop out into the underworld of drugs in a search for an alternative.

Pasolini has two striking "modest proposals" to stop the rot: the suspension of obligatory secondary education and of television until a satisfactory effort is made to reverse the cultural regression. The collection also contains an essay which calls for the whole Government to be put on trial for corruption. Apart from its political interest, ***Lutheran Letters*** is also the record of a sensitive artist's reaction to the consequences of profound social change and many of the themes in his prose, poetry and films are here treated in a very different manner.

John Ahern (review date Spring/Summer 1984)

SOURCE: "Pasolini: His Poems, His Body," in *Parnassus,* Vol. 11, No. 2, Spring/Summer, 1984, pp. 103-26.

[In the following review, Ahern provides an overview of Pasolini's life and poetry.]

It is easy to forget that Pier Paolo Pasolini is a major poet. Between 1950 and his death in 1975 he published four volumes of vigorous criticism—social, political, cultural, linguistic, and literary. Some of these pieces, just a few years after newspaper publication, have already found their way into anthologies. He wrote or directed over two dozen compelling, highly personal movies. He translated Aeschylus and Plautus, and wrote four plays of his own. He edited two anthologies of poetry in Italian dialects. He produced two linguistically remarkable novels. Given the bulk of his work and the notoriety of his life and death, it is easy to overlook his five volumes of Italian verse and his single volume in the *Friulano* dialect. The two-decade time lag between Italian and American culture puts us at a further disadvantage. Montale's essays, for example, appeared here only two years ago. It will probably take as long before we have Pasolini's or Calvino's essays in English. Now, at last, nine years after his murder, we have Norman MacAfee's able translation of a sixth of the Italian poetry, fourteen important long poems, a hundred pages of translation, and another hundred of Italian text. Previously we relied on versions scattered in specialized journals or in *The New Italian Poetry*. At the same time we have been given Enzo Siciliano's exemplary biography which allows us to recreate the context in which these poems were born. Most of the information about Pasolini's life which follows derives from this splendid book.

Pasolini was the adored son of an adored mother. His tolerated, absent father was a career military man, a patriot and enthusiastic Fascist. In his childhood the family moved every two or three years, spending summers in Friuli, his mother's region, a pastoral oasis in northeastern Italy between Venice and Udine. Just before the Second World War he studied at the University of Bologna with Roberto Longhi, the art historian, and various eminent philologists. A curious, enterprising student and a born organizer, had he followed the course of least resistance—something this courageous man rarely chose—he would have become a great poet-philologist like Poliziano, Leopardi, Carducci, or Pascoli. He spent the war in Friuli where he set up a private school at home. His students wrote poems in *Friulano,* learned the Latin names of plants, memorized the witty didactic verses he composed for them, and listened to him read Verga, Chekhov, Black Spirituals, and *The Spoon River Anthology.* He bicycled through the countryside, scientifically collecting its speech, which changed every few kilometers, as if his mother's mother tongue were the primal language and Friuli Eden. Summers he swam with other boys in the Tagliamento and sometimes made love to them on the white stones of the river bed. Winters were for remorse. Much later he would recall the "terrible, anxious sweetness that took my guts and consumed them from my sixteenth to my thirtieth year." He practised an aesthete's liturgical, uninstitutional Catholicism. Friends noticed an innate puritanism. His younger brother, after fighting with the partisans, was traitorously murdered by rival Communist partisans. Like young intellectuals all over the peninsula, Pasolini joined the Communist Party soon after the war. He turned out brilliant propaganda posters for it in Italian and *Friulano,* became its local secretary, secured a regular job in a state high school, organized a lively film club. Then a priest blackmailed him: either resign the party or his love affairs with boys would be revealed. He ignored the threat. The police were informed. Newsboys hawked the story on the piazza. The Party expelled him as "morally and politically untrustworthy." He lost his teaching job. He and his family faced despair and hysteria. One bleak winter dawn in 1949 the twenty-seven-year-old ex-school teacher escaped to Rome with his mother.

In these years he wrote many poems in various *Friulano* dialects—a choice Americans unfamiliar with Italy might find quixotic. When Italy attained national unity in 1870 eighty percent of its population spoke a dialect as the mother tongue, and sometimes, but not always, Italian as a second language. These dialects are as old as Italian and like it derive from Latin. They are not ignorant, fallen forms of Italian, but regional languages, sometimes with literatures of their own, which larger linguistic groups term "dialects." The Fascists repressed the dialects in favor of Italian more vigorously than even the first national governments. Poets and writers found themselves in a bind. Before the twentieth century, Italian was primarily a written language of Tuscan origin, static and insulated from daily life, a literary language in the worst sense. In the nineteenth century many writers, such as Manzoni and Verga, mastered Italian after childhood. The *milanesi,* for example, snickered at Verga's peculiar, heavily accented Italian, literally translated from Sicilian. Patriotism and the desire for large audiences led most writers to choose Italian, but they still found it difficult to create a living literature in a language few readers did their living in. For Pasolini, whose mother tongue was in fact Italian, the publication of poetry in *Friulano* between 1942 and 1954 was a polemical gesture. To convey some idea of these poems (MacAfee includes no dialect poetry) here are three:

> Sera imbarlumida, tal fossàl
> a cres l'aga, na fèmina plena
> a ciamina pal ciamb.
>
> Jo it recuardi, Narcís, it vèvis il colòur
> da la sera, quand li ciampanis
> a súnin di muàrt.

> ("Il nini muàrt")

Luminous evening, in the ditch
the water rises, a pregnant woman
walks through the field.

I remember you, Narcissus, you had the color

of evening, when the bells
toll death.

> ("The Dead Lad")

> Xe Domenega! Mi son so'o
> in una barcheta sul Lemene.
> El Burín el xè de veudo.
>
> Tuti i fa festa e mi so'o
> meso nuo sul cuòr del Lemene
> scaldo i me strassi al solo de veudo.
>
> No go un scheo, son paron so'o
> dei mei cavei de oro sul Lemene
> pien de pissígoe de veudo.
>
> El xe pien de pecai el me cuòr so'o.

> ("El cuòr su l'aqua")

It is Sunday! I am alone
in a small boat on the Lemene.
The Borino seems velvet.

Everyone is celebrating and I alone,
half-naked in the heart of the Lemene,
warm my rags in the velvet sun.

I don't have a cent. I own only
my golden hair on the Lemene
full of little velvet fish.

Full of sins is my solitary heart.

> ("The Heart on the Water")

> Vuei a è Domènia,
> doman a is mòur,
> vuei mi vistís
> di seda e di amòur.
>
> Vuei a è Domènia,
> pai pras com frescs piès
> a sàltin frutíns
> lizèirs lai scarpès.
>
> Ciantànt al me spieli
> ciantànt mi petèni.
> Al rit tal me vuli
> il Diàul peciadòur.
>
> Sunàit, mes ciampanis,
> paràilu indavòur!
> "Sunàn, ma se i vuàrditu

ciantànt tai to pras?"

I vitardi il soreli
di muartis estàs,
i vuardi la ploja
li fuèjs, i gris.

I vuardi il me cuàrp
di quan' ch'i eri frut,
li tristia Domèniis,
il vivi pierdùt.

"Vuei it vistíssin
la seda e l'amòur,
vuei a è Domènia
domàn a is mòur."

("Li letanis dal biel fi," III)

Today is Sunday,
tomorrow you die,
today I dress
in silk and love.

Today is Sunday,
through the fields with cool feet
young boys are jumping
light in their shoes.

Singing to my mirror,
singing, I comb my hair.
The sinning Devil
laughs in my eye.

Ring, my bells,
drive him back!
"We are ringing, but what are you looking at
as you sing in your meadows?"

I am looking at the sun
of dead summers.
I am looking at rain,
leaves, crickets.

I am looking at my body
when I was a young boy,
the sad Sunday,
the living that is lost.

"Today they shall dress you
with silk and love.
Today is Sunday,
tomorrow you die."

**("The Litanies of
the Beautiful Boy," III)**

Pasolini chose dialect not to get a better grip on reality, but as an absolutely pure language, not found in nature, "which no one knows any more." His choice was neither provincial nor folkloric. He worried *Friulano* into a delicious music similar to that of the Parnassians and Symbolists. The spectre of Giovanni Pascoli's equally artificial but less decadent lyrics haunt these poems. Their ideal public could never have consisted of Friulano peasants. The enormous range of literary references, the rhyme schemes drawn from literatures far removed in time and space, the falsely ingenuous sensibility are simply too alien. To be savored fully these poems demand the most refined literary palate. Their ideal reader would register the pervasive influence of Antonio Machado's lyrical evocation of Castile, and hear behind "*O sera imbarlumida*" in **"Il nini muàrt"** (which Pasolini renders in Italian as "*O sera luminosa*") Machado's "*O tarde luminosa!*" (Poem LXXVII). The bodies of doomed *kouroi* dominate all these precious anthems. At the heart of this timeless, fatherless world lies a Friulan Adonis—a *fantassút,* a *fanciullino,* Osiris, Narcissus, Jesus, and the adolescent poet himself—whose mother's rapt attention (the true ideal audience?) will modulate into mourning at the inevitable death of her sterile, parthogenetic son. His obscurely necessary sacrifice does not renew the world.

Rome, mediterranean, pagan, and urban, had little in common with sub-Alpine, Christian, and rural Friuli. A hot, hard, restless, invigorating city. Pasolini faced desperate poverty with courage and energy. His middle-class mother worked as a maid, while he took a modest teaching job in a distant shanty town. He declaimed Ungaretti and Dante to dirt-poor, thirteen-year-old sub-proletarians. He threw himself into furious literary activity, making friendships with Bassani, Gadda, Morante, and Moravia. He vied with the poet Sandro Penna in compiling lists of his conquests. Rome was a "muscular city of virile egotism" with no room for humility or forgiveness. Endless, willing, dialect-speaking boys could be had for a few *lire*. To buy them he sold his patiently acquired library of Greek and Latin authors. He transformed texts into life, and life back into texts. Fanatic linguist that he was, preternaturally sensitive to the most ephemeral permutations of Roman dialect, he stalked his boy informants, notebook in hand, lured by their language and their bodies. He worked as an extra at Cinecittà, quit teaching, became a script-writer, moved to a decent *petit bourgeois* apartment with his mother. His redundant, world-hating father joined them in 1952. Six years later he had drunk himself to death. Pasolini became a notorious public figure. He won prizes, was tried for obscenity, pornography, and offending religion. It was the happiest, most fertile period of his life. He was, he thought, inventing a new poetic language, rooted in history and part of its slow rush towards revolution. Expelled from Eden into time, his happy fall brought him to Rome in a moment of national crisis, whose witness and protagonist he chose to become.

After the war Italy suffered an intellectual and an economic upheaval. The rapid industrialization of an agricultural society produced the Boom or Economic Miracle. Intellectuals threw off the idealism and liberalism of Benedetto Croce for Antonio Gramsci's very original, very Italian Marxism. Mussolini had kept Gramsci, a founder of the Italian Communist Party, in prison from 1926 to 1933. The post-war publication of the noble letters which he wrote in prison established him as the supreme materialist intellectual, deeply committed to bringing Marxist revolution to the peninsula and martyred in the attempt. In prison he also filled dozens of notebooks with powerful essays on many topics, especially Italian history and culture since 1870. Most intellectuals, Communist or not, accepted the substance of this massive revision of the Italian past. Gramsci argued that in Italy the party should first attain cultural hegemony and only then attempt to implement the revolution. The post-war Communist Party accepted this argument, and bestowed great prominence on intellectuals. At the same time, however, great material prosperity and the logic of Cold War politics made the dream of revolution recede further into the future, provoking a malaise in even the most committed intellectuals. Their recently discovered prophet had not foreseen this economic counter-revolution.

Narcissus woke to find himself a revolutionary intellectual. In 1957 he printed his elegy for Gramsci, **"The Ashes of Gramsci,"** which he had composed two years before. It sold out immediately, and has since been rarely out of print. The preceding generation of poets, Montale, Ungaretti, and the Hermeticists, adopted a diffident, marginal stance before the world. They scrutinized the text of nature, not civilization: clouds, waves, the play of light and wind on water. Pasolini broke with all that. He took history and society as his texts. He composed his non-transcendental graveyard poem in the *terza rima* of Dante, Pascoli, and the civic poets of the Risorgimento, replacing full rhyme with assonance and eye-rhyme. He fashioned a tense, broken, adjective-laden narrative in violation of the abstemious Hermetic precepts, mixing the exquisite with the ordinary. He assumed the persona of a national poet measuring his private passions against a dead heroic thinker who represents perfect historical consciousness.

The scene: nightfall in the English Cemetery in Rome where Gramsci is buried with others whom Italian society excluded. Shelley, who is also buried there, is invoked as representing high, non-revolutionary nineteenth-century culture. Surrounding the cemetery is the teeming, sub-proletarian, historically unconscious neighborhood of Testaccio. The poem is a meditation on passion and ideology, pleasure and praxis: it neither embraces nor challenges Marxism. The poet establishes a permanent tension between the movements of history and individual desire. Marxism is one term in his oxymoron, he is the other. He enriches the vocabulary and syntax of contemporary spoken Italian with the lexica of bible, church, and historical materialism. At times divergent semantic charges converge powerfully in single words. *Coscienza* denotes historical and class consciousness, ethical and religious conscience, and consciousness broadly understood. **"Le ceneri di Gramsci"** is a prosaic, gnomic, memorable dialogue between light and dark, heart and guts (*viscere*).

> Ed ecco qui me stesso . . . povero, vestito
> dei panni che i poveri adocchiano in vetrine
>
> dal rozzo splendore, e che ba sbiadito
> la sporcizia delle più sperdute strade,
> delle panche dei tram, da cui stranito
>
> è il mio giorno: mentre sempre più rade
> bo di queste vacanze, nel tormento
> del mantenermi in vita: e se mi accade
>
> di amare il mondo non è che per violento
> e ingenuo amore sensuale
> così come, confuso adolescente, un tempo
>
> l'odiai, se in esso mi feriva il male
> borghese di me borghese: e ora, scisso
> —con te—il mondo, oggetto non appare
>
> di rancore e quasi di mistico
> disprezzo, la parte che ne ha il potere?
> Eppure senza il tuo rigore, sussisto
>
> perché non scelgo. Vivo nel non volere
> del tramontato dopoguerra: amando
> il mondo che odio—nella sua miseria
>
> sprezzante e perso—per un oscuro scandalo
> della coscienza. . . .
>
> **("Le ceneri di Gramsci," III)**

And here am I . . . poor, dressed in
clothes that the poor admire in store

windows for their crude splendors
and that filthy back streets and tram
benches (which daze my day)

have faded; while, less and less often, these
moments come to me to interrupt my torment
of staying alive; and if I happen

to love the world, it's a naive
violent sensual love, just as I
hated it when I was a confused

adolescent and its bourgeois evils
wounded my bourgeois self; and now, divided—
with you—doesn't the world—or at least

that part which holds power—seem worthy only
of rancor and an almost mystical contempt?
Yet without your rigor I survive because

I do not choose. I live in the non-will
of the dead post-war years: loving
the world I hate, scorning it, lost

in its wretchedness—in an obscure scandal
of consciousness. . . .

(According to Siciliano, Pasolini in this period took three
trams to reach his distant school and dressed like the poor
boys he pursued. Narcissus traded in velvet for glad rags.)
The poet annexes the cultural and economic crises of the
nation to the pulsating tension of his own moral and intellectual conflicts, and then expresses these contrary forces in
breathless, seemingly artless discourse which is barely saved
from rant by Latinate precision ("*senza il tuo rigore
sussisto*"—'without your rigor I survive') in the midst of
willfully banal fixed phrases ("*le più sperdute strade*"—'the
most out of the way streets') and by the ghost of broken
hypermetric hendecasyllables which haunts his prose into
poetry. If his awesome self-dramatization succeeds, it is because we finally accept the outrageous language. Nor has he
forgotten the lyricism of the *Friulano* verse. In the poem's
famed apophatic opening he politicizes the chaste silence,
subtle coloring, and luscious epithets of the Decadents and
Hermeticists, while abandoning their terseness for manic
wordiness.

Non è di maggio questa impura aria
che il buio giardino straniero
fa ancora più buio, o l'abbaglia

con cieche schiarite . . . questo cielo
di bave sopra gli attici giallini
che in semicerchi immensi fanno velo

alle curve del Tevere, ai turchini
monti del Lazio . . . Spande una mortale
pace, disamorata come i nostri destini,

tra le vecchie muraglie l'autunnale
maggio. In esso c'è il grigiore del mondo
la fine del decennio in cui ci appare

tra le macerie finito il profondo
e ingenuo sforzo di rifare la vita;
il silenzio, fradicio e infecondo . . .

("Le ceneri di Gramsci," I)

It isn't May-like, this impure air
which darkens the foreigners' dark
garden still more, then dazzles it

with blinding sunlight . . . this foam-
streaked sky above the ocher roof
terraces which in vast semicircles veil

Tiber's curves and Latium's cobalt
mountains. . . . Inside the ancient walls
the autumnal May diffuses a deathly

peace, disquieting like our destinies,
and holds the whole world's dismay,
the finish of the decade that saw

the profound naive struggle to make
life over collapse in ruins;
silence, humid, fruitless . . .

Pasolini moved from script-writing to directing. His first fea-
ture-length movie, *Accattone,* caused a scandal when it appeared in 1961. Moving pictures brought him far larger
audiences and incomes than printed words. He continued to
write poems. He collected the early poems in Italian in *The
Nightingale of the Catholic Church. The Religion of My
Time* carried on the enterprise begun in *The Ashes of
Gramsci.* Now that he was a filmmaker, he could not easily
play the national poet with a rare, albeit Marxist, sensibility. In *Poems in the Shape of a Rose* he included a poem
in the form of a filmscript of an interview with a French journalist, the Cobra, a cautionary fictionalization of the reader
as well brought up, middle-class ignoramus. The poem is "*in
cursus*"—the rhetorical name for solemn rhythmical medieval Latin prose—a phrase which MacAfee incorrectly renders as "in progress." He also mistranslates "*clausola,*" in
the poem's final section in accountant-like terms as "end of
statement." In the art of *cursus,* a *clausola* is a sentence's
concluding cadence. The translator misses the deliberate
mixture of ancient and cinematic rhetorics.

(Senza dissolvenza, a stacco netto, mi rappresento
in un atto—privo di precedenti storici—di
"industria culturale.")

Io volontariamente martirizzato . . . e,
lei di fronte, sul divano:
campo e contracampo, a rapidi flash,
"Lei—so che pensa, guardandomi,
in più domestica-italica M.F.
sempre alla Godard—lei, specie di Tennessee!",
il cobra col golfino di lana
                    (col cobra subordinato
che screma in silenzio magnesio).
Poi forte: "Mi dice che cosa sta scrivendo?"

"Versi, versi, scrivo! versi!
(maledetta cretina,
versi che lei non capisce priva com'è
di cognizioni metriche! Versi!)
VERSI NON PIÙ IN TERZINE!

Capisce?

Questo è quello che importa: non più in terzine!
Sono tornato tout court al magma!
Il Neo-capitalismo ha vinto, sono
sul marciapiede
come poeta, ah [singhiozzo]
e come cittadino [altro singhiozzo]."

E il cobra con il biro:
"Il titolo della Sua opera?" "Non so . . .
[Egli parla ora sommesso come intimidito,
rivestendo
la parte che il colloquio, accettato, gli impone di
fare: come sta poco
a stingere
la sua grinta
in un muso di mammarolo condannato a morte]
. . .

(from **"Una disperata vitalità,"** III)

(Without a dissolve, in a sharp cut, I portray
myself in an act—without historical precedents—
of "cultural industry.")

I, voluntarily martyred . . . and
she in front of me, on the couch:
shot and countershot in rapid flashes,

"You"—I know what she's thinking, looking at
me,
a more domestic-Italian *Masculine-Feminine,*
always à la Godard—"you, sort of a Tennessee!"
the cobra in the light wool sweater
                    (and the subordinate cobra
                    gliding in magnesium silence).
Then aloud: "Tell me what you're writing?"

"Poems, poems, I'm writing! Poems!
(stupid idiot,
poems she wouldn't understand, lacking as she is
in metric knowledge! Poems!)
POEMS NO LONGER IN TERCETS!

Do you understand?
This is what's important: no longer in tercets!
I have gone back, plain and simple, to the magma!
Neocapitalism won, I've

been kicked out on the street
as a poet [boo-hoo]
and citizen [another boo-hoo]."
And the cobra with the ballpoint:
"The title of your work?" "I don't know . . .
[He speaks softly now, as though intimidated,
assuming
the role the interview, once accepted, imposes
on him: how little it takes
for his sinister mug
to fade into
the face of a mama's boy condemned to death] . . .

(from **"A Desperate Vitality,"** III)

This poem, a self-deprecating apology for abandoning *terza rima,* written partially in *terza rima,* attempts to exorcise the poet's bad conscience at abandoning full-time dedication to writing and poetry to become a movie director and media personality. The usual systematic contamination of styles and media (*singhiozzo, singhiozzo,* sob, sob, is comic strip language) does not produce a convincing poem. The merciless self-portrait ("sinister mug," thinning hair) and self-revelation (masturbation until he bled) do not efface the disingenuousness in characterizing himself as success's "voluntary martyr on a couch."

MacAfee's otherwise strong plain translation suffers from occasional errors. The *Cinquecento* is the sixteenth rather than the fourteenth century. *Deludere* means to disappoint or deceive, not to undeceive. *Treni* refers to threnodies, such as the Lamentations of Jeremiah; MacAfee confuses it with its homonym, which means "trains." The traditional English equivalent of the liturgical formula *nei secoli dei secoli* is "world without end" not "through the centuries forever and ever." *Crisma* is "chrism," oil used in various church ceremonies, not "baptism."

MacAfee also garbles allusions to Dante's poetry or allows them to slip by unnoticed. Pasolini identified with Dante as prophet, poet, outsider, and fearless confounder of styles and genres. To use the famous distinction of Gianfranco Contini, which he loved to cite, he wanted to be a plurilinguistic poet like Dante, rather than a monolinguistic one like Petrarch. When Pasolini refers to the Bourgeois "*il cui pane certo non sa di sale,*" 'whose bread certainly does not taste salty,' he is remembering a prophecy which Dante put in the *Comedy* that in exile he would no longer eat the unsalted bread of Florence. MacAfee mistranslates the line as "The Bourgeois for whom no salt tears pour" and provides no note. Nor does he indicate that "*libito far licito,*" 'making lust licit' occurs in *Inferno* 5, 56, where it describes how Queen Semiramis legalized incest, and so prefigured the lustful Francesca. Pasolini's application of these words to himself constitutes a criticism of Dante's Christianity as well as an uneasy self-condemnation. "Legitimating my desire" is a misleading translation because it suggests that lust can be made legitimate. Dante's words suggest just the opposite. Likewise, when the poet applies to himself a famous description of Dante's Virgil, *"fioco per lungo silenzio,"* many American readers need a note to point this out. In **"The Poetry of Tradition,"** the last poem which MacAfee translates, Pasolini criticizes the generation of 1968 as ignorant of the poetry of tradition (like the Cobra), and so capable of creating only bureaucracy and organization: *"Che organizzar significar per verba non si porìa,"* 'Because organization cannot be signified in words.' Here the allusion is to *". . . transumanar per verba / non si porìa,"* whose first word, a famous neologism, meaning "passing beyond humanity," he replaces with the quasi-bureaucratic, quasi-Marxist *"organizzar."* Because this poem appears in a volume whose title is **Transumanar e organizzar,** the reader who knows the poetry of tradition can hardly miss the allusion. The title must be read as the usual oxymoron joining Catholic transcendence and Marxist praxis. MacAfee gives the American reader (who cannot be counted upon to know the poetry of *Italian* tradition) no help. He destroys the tension of the title by suppressing the crucial conjunction. His translation, **To Transfigure, To Organize,** suggests that these two operations are equivalents rather than possible contraries. In general, however, this is a sound, accurate translation. I hope that MacAfee one day will provide us with a much-needed second volume, twice as long as this one, with extensive selections from **The Nightingale of the Catholic Church,** **"L'Appennino," "L'umile Italia," "La rabbia,"** the splendid epigrams in **The Religion of My Time, "The Sonnet Hobby,"** and the elegy for Robert Kennedy. We also need a separate, complete version of all the poems in *Friulano* as they appear in the disturbing, double version called **La nuova gioventù.**

In the Sixties Pasolini became rich and almost happy. He and his mother moved to better lodgings. He met the love of his life, Ninetto Davoli, a fifteen-year-old Calabrian from a Roman slum. The curly-haired, hoarse-voiced, wise-cracking, joyous boy spoke an odd amalgamation of dialects which delighted him. Ninetto's shout the first time he saw snow, "Hè-eh, Hè-eh, Heeeeeeeh," seemed to him proto-Greek, a pure Adamic tongue. That same year Pasolini, the atheist Catholic, who thought Christ divine but not the Son of God, shot the **Gospel of St. Matthew,** using non-professional actors. Enzo Siciliano played Simon, Ninetto an innocent child ("of such is the Kingdom of Heaven"), and his mother was Mary. The Catholics gave him prizes. Others questioned whether Pasolini's humanist, socialist Christ with a permanent slow burn takes away the sins of the world when he sheds his blood.

One night in 1966 in a Roman *trattoria* Pasolini collapsed in a pool of his own blood when an undetected stomach ul-

cer hemorrhaged. His body showed signs of aging and softening. After convalescence he toughened it in workouts, and dressed it in levis, sleeveless T-shirts and desert boots. 1968 was the year of crisis. In a verse pamphlet to the students who revolted that May, he sided with the Police (the sons of the poor) against the students (the sons of the Bourgeois). His new film, *Teorema,* received poor notices. In it a Ninetto-like *anghelos*-herald (Terence Stamp) carnally seduced an entire middle-class Milanese household—a cool allegory of how the Sacred, in the form of an erotically irresistible young male, bursts into the stultified life of the Bourgeoisie.

Pasolini feared that his domination over cultural life was waning. In Palermo in 1963 an "avant-garde" of university professors had attempted to unseat Italy's leading writers, including Pasolini and Calvino. They drew unflattering comparisons between the truly "experimental" poetry of Ezra Pound and that of Pasolini. In this period he worked on a Dantean pastiche, **The Divine Mimesis** (posthumously published in unfinished form in 1975), whose manuscript he claimed had been found on the corpse of a poet "beaten to death with a stick in Palermo in 1963." At the Venice premier of *Teorema* in 1968 he contrived to interview an ailing Ezra Pound in a bold attempt to win his public support. The two poets shared a love of Italy's landscape and literature, as well as eccentric political beliefs, a knack for cultural organization, and a tendency to rant. No interchange occurred. Chastened, humble, courteous, Pound left his *tempus tacendi* long enough to affirm the failure and incoherence of a life dedicated to poetry. This was exactly what Pasolini feared most, and would have none of it. Shortly before his own death seven years later he would repudiate a large part, if not all, of his work.

His love for Ninetto deepened and eventually excluded sex. Never did he interrupt his nightly hunt for boys. Fear of separation haunts his single happy love poem:

> . . . prendo con paura
> l'aereo per un luogo lontano. Della nostra vita
> sono insaziabile,
> perché una cosa unica al mondo non può essere
> mai esaurita.

> (from **"Uno dei tanti epiloghi"**)

> . . . I fearfully take
> the plane for a distant place. I'm insatiable for our
> life,
> because something unique in all the world can
> never be exhausted.

> (from **"One of Many Epilogs"**)

His literary life was also moving toward a crisis. His final, slack book of verse, *Transumanar e organizzar,* received few and poor notices. His own review of it conceded its "falsity, insincerity and awkwardness," but not its "unreality." He observed that "an Oedipal terror of coming to know and admit determines the strange unhappy fortune of this book and probably of all Pasolini's work." Oedipal jealousy probably led him to attack Montale's Satura, which had received far more favorable reviews that year. For Pasolini's generation Montale had been the supreme poet. His brother Guido joined the Resistance with Montale's poems in his pocket. In that same period, Pasolini's contemporary, Italo Calvino, had committed poem after poem from Ossi di seppia to memory, as did so many others. Now Pasolini accused Satura of being an "anti-Marxist tract . . . based wholly on the naturalness of power"—an odd charge from someone who had never really read Marx and had recently announced he no longer believed in revolution. Pasolini also hinted that Montale was a coward. Montale replied in two bitter epigrams which addressed Pasolini as Malvolio, the dour puritan hypocrite of Twelfth Night. Did Montale know, one wonders, that William Savage Landor had dispatched a similar epigram to Wordsworth, addressing him too as Malvolio?

> Con quale agilità rimescolari
> materialismo storico e pauperismo evangelico,
> pornografia e riscatto, nausea per l'odore
> di trifola, il denaro che ti giungeva.

> (from Eugenio Montale,
> "Lettera a Malvolio")

> With what ease you stirred together
> historic materialism and evangelical poverty,
> pornography and redemption, nausea at the smell
> of truffles, the money that came to you.

Montale spoke for many of Pasolini's critics when he blamed on him "the conceptual phocomelia" of the recent past. Pasolini's was the hour, he said, when "honor and indecency, joined in a single pact, founded the permanent oxymoron."

In his late forties the decline of sexual desire tormented him. He continued working out but in his films took delight in showing the full age of his body in walk-on parts as Giotto and Chaucer. In Spring 1971 he went to Romania for Gerovital anti-aging treatments, accompanied by Alberto Moravia and Ninetto, now twenty-four and girl-crazy. There he completed the second film in *The Trilogy of Life, The Canterbury Tales.* The *Trilogy,* a box office success and critical failure, made him richer still. Its ostensible theme was the destruction of stagnant middle-class values by angelic, child-like subproletarians from the Third World or a storybook past. When he shot the *Canterbury Tales* in Bath, Ninetto played the Chaplinesque Perkin, a charming thief of

brides from grooms and food from babies. Ninetto's announcement of his marriage broke Pasolini's heart. His black despair exasperated his closest friends. In a Shakespearean sonnet sequence, **"The Sonnet Hobby,"** he called his faithless beloved his "Lord," and made him a "her," accused of "vile betrayal" after eight years of love. He was inconsolable.

Siciliano says that in this period Pasolini engaged in "severely masochistic practices," and argued that artistic creation was essentially sadomasochistic. Grave doubts about the revolutionary power of sex crept into the *Trilogy's* last film, *The Arabian Nights.* Aziz (played by the recently married Ninetto) breaks the heart of his girlfriend Aziza and causes her death when he nonchalantly abandons her. He soon finds a crazy new girlfriend and betrays her as well. When she tries to kill him, he remembers some magic words which Aziza had taught him. They so placate the new girlfriend that she merely ties a string around his testicles and rips them off. Several times in this final film homosexuality is presented as a terrifying phenomenon. Its covert themes subvert the overt themes of the entire trilogy. The criminal selfishness of beautiful young men continued to obsess Pasolini. In June 1975, a few months after finishing the *Trilogy of Life* and a few months before his death, he repudiated it and, by implication, much earlier work, in words of astonishing ferocity:

> Sincerity and necessity drove me to represent bodies and their culminating symbol, the sex organ. . . . I now hate bodies and sex organs. . . . The young people and boys of the Roman subproletariat . . . if they are now human garbage were already such before. . . .

Hatred consumed him: hatred for himself, his boys, his utopian political visions. He revised many poems in *Friulano* and published them with the originals in *La nuova gioventù* (*The New Youth*) in Spring 1975. More than savage palinodes, they are an assault on the corpus of his verse. In the poem that follows—original first, then revision—his village's mulberry plantation (silkworms feed on mulberry leaves) has been covered with asphalt, people live in new apartment houses, no smoke rises from the hearths of the old houses. The poet, now just the 'spirit' of a boy rather than a real boy, hates his ancestors instead of singing them, and befouls his face: shit instead of roses, piss instead of blood. Sadism now touched the securest part of his literary corpus, as it did his actual body.

> Fantassút, al plòuf il Sèil
> tai spolers dal to país,
> tal to vis di rosa e mèil
> pluvisín al nas il mèis.

Il soreli scur di fun
sot li branchis dai moràrs
al it brusa e sui confíns
tu i il ciantis, sòul, i muars.

Fantassút, al rit il Sèil
tai barcòns dal to país,
tal to vis di sanc e fièl
serenàl al mòur il mèis.

(**"Ploja tai cunfíns"**)

Lad, Heaven rains
on the hearths of your town,
on your face of rose and honey
in drizzle the month is born.

The sun, dark with smoke,
beneath the mulberry branches
burns you, and on all the borders
you alone sing the dead.

Lad, Heaven smiles
on the balconies of your town,
on your face of blood and gall,
the month dies clear and bright.

(**"Rain on the Borders"**)

Spirt di frut, al plòuf il Sèil
tai spolers di un muàrt país,
tal to vis di merda e mèil
pluvisin a nas un mèis.

Il soreli blanc e lustri
sora asfàlt e ciasis novis
al it introna, e fòur di dut
non i it às pí amòur pai muàrs.

Spirt di frut, al rit il Sèil
ta un país sensa pí fun,
tal to vis di pis e fèil,
mai nassút, al mòur un mèis.

(**"Ploja fòur di dut"**)

Spirit of a boy, Heaven rains
on the hearths of a dead town,
on your face of shit and honey
in drizzle the month is born.

The sun, white and glistening,
over the asphalt and new houses,
stuns you, and you, outside of everything,
have no more love for the dead.

Spirit of a boy, Heaven smiles
on a town with no more smoke:
in your face of piss and gall,
the month, never born, dies.

(**"Rain Outside of Everything"**)

After 1968 when he said he would "throw his body into the struggle," the poet in him began to die. His greatest work, the Friulan poems, *The Ashes of Gramsci* and *The Nightingale of the Catholic Church,* was behind him. Filmmaking, journalism, and his lonely, prophetic politics took all his energy. Never had he seen his poems as making up a body of work exempt from the mortality of his actual body. Rather he looked upon them as extensions of that body and filled them with images of recently or soon-to-be-slaughtered bodies, all of which were eventually his. He had decided to be the "lamb slain from the foundation of the world." He appears really to have believed that the death of his body could make a difference in the world which no poem could ever hope to. Who dare criticize him for choosing physical courage over the humility of the poet's craft?

He felt that he was on the verge of some radical change. His voice took on a vehement, prophetic, conservative tone. As Eros failed him, fidelity and social order became urgent concerns. In his last two or three years he tried to be St. Paul and Luther, flogging the world for its degradation. His dazzling, scandalous, unconvincing jeremiads appeared on the front pages of the *Corriere della sera* and other newspapers. Under Neo-Capitalism Italy had suffered an anthropological transformation, he said. Sexual permissiveness, abortion, television, and obligatory school (both of which he proposed outlawing) had murdered the Sacred. The only form of contraception he recommended wholeheartedly was homosexuality. Kidnappings, petty crime, and *terrorism* made life unbearable. "The night," he said, "is as deserted and sinister as in the blackest centuries of the past." He now found the poor Roman boys he had once courted so fraternally to be violent and calculating thieves. He underestimated the barriers which his age and wealth created. A lack of Gramscian rigor had undermined his work and was pushing it toward incoherence. His poetic and political vision was finally based on his body's experience. He played awakening Bourgeois Italy, while his subproletarian boys were messengers of liberation from a mythic, pre-conscious world. The incompatibility of this vision with any kind of Marxism never troubled him. Nor had he meditated deeply enough on Eros to understand why no artist dare denigrate it and hope to continue creating.

In the winter and spring of 1975 he filmed a version of De Sade's *120 Days of Sodom* set in the last days of the Fascist Republic of Salò. Four libertines incarcerate, torture, and finally murder a group of attractive, acquiescent young people. Shot in a dead frigid light, their bodies take on a dreadful gray pallor. The libertines ban heterosexuality in favor of homosexuality—the most "mortal" and "ambiguous" gesture which the human race can make, according to characters in the film. In the disquieting final scene, as the young people go to their deaths, one of them shouts Christ's words on the cross, "My God, my God, why have you forsaken me?" Two young Fascist soldiers, out of uniform, but in all respects similar to the victims, dance an indifferent fox trot together, while discussing their girlfriends. The repudiation of the young as "human garbage" has passed from prose to film. Ben Lawton traces an evolving rejection of homosexuality and the proletariat in the *Trilogy of Life* and *Salò*. Pasolini expounded but never fully accepted such ideas. His desire to break with old habits, Siciliano tells us, did not succeed. That fall he was assaulted more than once during his late-night forays. In October he had himself photographed at home, naked, in various poses remarkable for their ordinariness. He wanted the pictures of his slender, strong body to illustrate his long, unfinished, still-unpublished novel, *Vas*. Two weeks later *Salò* premiered to the consternation of many friends and supporters. The subtle Sicilian novelist Leonardo Sciascia feared it might drive some viewers to the nunnery. Barthes called it "absolutely unredeemable."

On the night of All Souls, November 2, which in Italy is the Feast of the Dead, he picked up a hustler named Pino the Frog at the train station, and drove him to a garbage-strewn field in a shanty town north of Rome, near the sea. The boy hit Pasolini's head with a plank until it opened and brain matter spattered the plank. The beating almost detached an ear from the head. He kicked the scrotum hard, then drove over the body. Pasolini died of internal and external hemorrhages. Some people believe that groups opposed to Pasolini's politics hired the boy to entrap and murder him. The audience of his poems, novels, essays, and films knew this scene and this event before they read about it in the newspapers. The very condignity of Pasolini's death and works raised suspicions. Ninetto identified the body for the police. Early the next morning reporters waited outside his house until his almost-senile mother let out a high wail of grief on being given the news—Isis mourning Osiris, Mary mourning Jesus. Life validated Art.

Pasolini's death conferred on his poetry a retroactive coherence that almost nullified the retroactive meaninglessness of his **"Repudiation of the *Trilogy of Life*"** five months earlier. The closure which his death provided his texts resembles that given to the Hebrew Scriptures by Jesus' death—it cries out for and resists interpretation. Sciascia said that the Catholic elements in it annihilate the anarchic ones. Does he mean, one wonders, that Pasolini's death was a sacrifice like Jesus'? These lines from an early poem in *The Nightingale of the Catholic Church* will not be read today as they were

first read over thirty years ago. In them Christ looks upon his crucifiers as would a sexually excited homosexual masochist:

> Cristo, il tuo corpo
> di giovinetta
> è crocefisso
> da due stranieri.
> Sono due vivi
> ragazzi e rosse
> hanno le spalle,
> l'occhio celeste.
> Battono i chiodi
> e il drappo trema
> sopra il Tuo rentre . . .

                         (from **"La passione"**)

> Christ, your young
> girl's body
> is crucified
> by two foreigners.
> They are two living
> boys and have
> red shoulders,
> blue eyes.
> They hammer in the nails
> and the cloth quivers
> over Thy belly . . .

There are those who argue that the linguistic sign is by origin and forever sacrificial. The word "stands for" what it represents as a sacrificial victim "stands for" the people. Following this line of thought, poetry, as the highest form of language, is *ipso facto* its most violent manifestation. Thus Pasolini's death was more than just thematically implicit in his poetry. His whole poetic career can be seen as a doomed struggle with the violence of poetic language. Hence his attempt to transform Friulano into an ahistoric Adamic tongue, and his fascination with Ninetto's joyous howl on first seeing snow. Acoustic signifiers with no assignable signifieds imply a non-violent because non-signifying language. Unfallen tongues bespeak no bloodshed. Pasolini's tragedy was never to have found an untragic language. Yet whatever relations one posits between language and violence, Pasolini's violent death does not redeem his poetry, even though it seals forever its union with his life. His poems, films, essays, novels, articles, and interviews are microtexts which together constitute a single *persona,* or macrotext. As the central man of the central decades of this century in Italy, he compels us to read his poems. Could they be detached from his life (and it is exactly this that his death will not allow), to be read only for themselves, we would find them less compelling. Nothing, not even a poet's blood, quite replaces craft.

Anne Rice (review date 3 November 1985)

SOURCE: A review of *A Violent Life,* in *The New York Times Books Review,* November 3, 1985, p. 38.

[*In the following review, Rice states that Pasolini's Marxism is evident in his novel* A Violent Life, *but asserts that in addition to the political overtones, "Tommaso's story has its own profound and cumulative power; his world boils with life created by Pasolini's relentless use of dialogue and vivid detail."*]

It begins as a guided tour of hell. Tommaso, the protagonist of *A Violent Life,* grows up in a stinking shantytown on the outskirts of Rome shortly after World War II. Half-starved children play in sand littered with human excrement beside a river fouly polluted, their everyday speech a litany of curses, taunts and threats. As a young man Tommaso becomes a thief, a bully and a sometime hustler, a homosexual prostitute. He and his vicious companions rob at random, sometimes beating their victims, their goal being to get no more than a few thousand lire with which to buy food, drink or the company of a woman. They are without talent, ambition or hope.

Even when Tommaso courts a respectable young woman, he seethes with resentment and hatred as he makes his crude advances in the darkness of a cheap movie house—the same hatred he feels for the "queens" or "faggots" he tries to hustle, or for his companions who remain unimpressed with him no matter what he does. He is in fact a pathetically ordinary young man who elicits little or no interest from anyone save his mother and his lackluster girlfriend, and the indifference he endures is emphasized by the author almost as much as the hunger and poverty he suffers all of his life.

But halfway through this gritty, dark and absorbing narrative, Tommaso is changed by unexpected good fortune. After serving time in prison for murder, he returns home to find his family living not in a stinking hovel but in a Government-financed house. A new optimism is born in him, a new tolerance for respectability; he gets a job and contemplates marriage to his girlfriend.

Then a strike in the Government hospital to which he is confined for treatment of tuberculosis brings him in contact with political activists. He is forced into displaying courage and then praised for it; it is perhaps the first real recognition he has ever known. And courage will later lead him to genuine altruism and his eventual death at the novel's end.

The political overtones are blatant. One doesn't have to know that Pier Paolo Pasolini, who was as celebrated during his lifetime for his politics as for his films, fiction and poetry, was a Marxist to see the statement being made here.

Tommaso is not unredeemable. What he might have become, if he had been given half a chance, will never be known.

But this novel is a great deal more than the sum of its political ideas. It is not devitalized by or dependent on Marxist philosophy. Tommaso's story has its own profound and cumulative power; his world boils with life created by Pasolini's relentless use of dialogue and vivid detail.

Nothing is asserted that is not proven. You see and hear these people as they drink, quarrel and make love. And in the novel's larger moments—the brutal police raids on the shantytown and the Government hospital—his attention to detail invariably enlivens the grand scheme.

One doesn't come to like Tommaso. But a finer, more interesting feeling is evoked. When he faces his last moments with the same toughness that he has displayed all along, there is more than a touch of tragedy. It very nearly takes the breath away.

The novel raises two questions, however. The first has to do with the inevitable problems met in translations. The narrative, echoing the voice of its characters, is sprinkled with phrases like "good as gold" and "on the ball" and "it was no joke." And I can not help but wonder, are these English clichés really the equivalent of the original Italian? Or has freshness been sacrificed for words an English or American reader will more easily understand? Whatever the case, these tired expressions do not detract much from the impact of the book.

My second question has more to do with the artistic validity of the book. *A Violent Life* is about illiterate and inarticulate people and it purports to show them as they see themselves. Does it represent an informed and truly realistic insight into the nature of these people? Or is it a grossly exaggerated view of their brutality created by one who was never a part of them, a view that might be as romantic in its excess as a cloying sentimental approach? On the basis of the text alone I would say the question is impossible to answer, at least for this American reader. The milieu is simply too foreign, the poverty too oppressive, the minds of the characters too different from our own. Yet the question is of enormous importance, surely, even if all political considerations are put aside.

What can be said with certainty is that the novel not only works as a novel, it overwhelms. In fact, I found the effect of *A Violent Life* so strong that I have little desire to be reserved with my praise. Not since Hubert Selby's *Last Exit to Brooklyn* have I read a work so muscular and sublimely ugly, one that elicited so much revulsion and compassion at the same time. The endless violence of its petty characters transcends time and place and becomes a symphony of human struggle similar in impact to Martin Scorsese's masterly film, *Raging Bull.*

It probably should be mentioned here that Pasolini was murdered in 1975 at the age of 53 by a young man who some say was much like the young men described in this book.

Peter Brunette (review date 30 November 1986)

SOURCE: "Focused on the Body," in *The New York Times Book Review,* November 30, 1986, p. 12.

[*In the following review, Brunette lauds John Shepley's translation of Pasolini's* Arabian Nights and Other Stories.]

Pier Paolo Pasolini was much more than an avant-garde film director who enjoyed thumbing his nose at middle-class audiences. A theorist of culture and a poet both in standard Italian and in his native Friulian dialect, he was also a writer of powerful and disturbing fiction. His talents in this last field are brilliantly demonstrated in ***Arabian Nights***. The language of these five stories, all published between 1950 and 1965, is lush and overripe, like the images of his films. Always focused on the body, these stories are nevertheless dense with thought. Even his intensely physical descriptions of characters are curiously abstract as well, as though they were being recorded by a camera, from the outside. Plot disappears and time is shuffled like a deck of cards, made spatial and affective. Precisely evoked emotion and sensation organize these tales more than chronology or narrative thrust.

Several of the stories are so strong, so raw in their homoeroticism, that one is dumbfounded to discover that the earliest was written more than 35 years ago. Pasolini's characteristic style is a kind of supercharged realism. In some stories it becomes surrealistic; in others the realism is so stylized that every detail of the terrain seems, as in a Dürer engraving, filled with meaning beyond its brute existence. His principal subject is the articulation of a landscape, usually a Roman slum, and though his humans sometimes seem accidental features, his vision is always a moral one.

At times Pasolini is the ironic, detached observer as in **"Studies on the Life of Testaccio,"** a superb sketch of a working-class gang in a Roman suburb, filled with psychological insight into the calculating cruelty that motivates the warped lives of the gang members. At other times he inserts himself as the "author" in search of sexual fulfillment; here his restless prose seems almost mad with desire, paralleling Pasolini's own relentless sexuality and the charged aimlessness of the young boys he describes. The final story, **"Rital and Raton,"** shows the author overtly rejecting both the demands of a shocked bourgeoisie and those of the moralistic

Communist Party to which he belonged—to the party's great embarrassment—for many years. Suggesting an early Jean-Luc Godard film in prose, the story is a montage of fact, fiction, quotes from Roland Barthes, political polemic, an appearance by Mr. Godard himself and autobiographical rumination. It constitutes a powerful meditation on language, marginality, racism, and sex, and their interrelationships. Though written more than 20 years ago, it is a nearly paradigmatic postmodern text.

John Shepley's translation of these stories is a triumph. Rendered into a dense, visceral English, it is startlingly true to the lushness of the Italian original.

Patrick McCarthy (review date 17 April 1987)

SOURCE: "Between Sin and Scandal," in *Times Literary Supplement,* No. 4385, April 17, 1987, p. 408.

[*In the following review, McCarthy discusses what Pasolini's* Lettere 1940-1954 *reveals about the themes found in his work.*]

This first volume of Pasolini's collected letters covers the period from his undergraduate years, and recounts the apprenticeship, persecution and tribulations of a writer who continues to hypnotize Italian intellectuals. In his *Cronologia* Nico Naldini has filled in some of the gaps in Enzo Siciliano's biography. Although Siciliano's judgments on Pasolini's life were generally correct, his book lacked detail. Drawing on Pasolini's unpublished diaries, the *Quaderni rossi,* Naldini provides much information on the Friulan years and in particular on Pasolini's homosexuality.

The volume opens in June 1940, and the Bologna period, 1940-43, reveals a young writer who was reaching maturity during the last years of Fascism. Pasolini's father was an army officer and an admirer of Mussolini, while Pasolini, who was born in 1922, had known nothing but Fascist rule. The first signs of his revolt were cultural. He and his friends admired artists who were distrusted by the régime: J. M. Synge, the American novelists from Melville to Erskine Caldwell, and French film directors like Jean Renoir. The Bologna painter Giorgio Morandi was the model of an artist who paid no attention to Fascist aesthetics. But most of all Pasolini, who had been writing poetry since he was seven, read Ungaretti and Montale.

Many of these early letters deal with the magazine *Il Setaccio,* which Pasolini helped to edit in 1942-43. Whereas the mainstream intellectuals of what historians call "second-generation" or "left-wing" Fascism—such as Elio Vittorini or Renato Guttuso—were calling for a committed culture,

Pasolini seems to take a non-political stance. But in fact he too was groping for some sort of populism, as he demonstrates when he argues that Ungaretti is not just the poet of an élite but offers broad ethical lessons. Meanwhile the pessimistic tone of *Il Setaccio* reflected the view that the war was lost, that Fascism was bankrupt and that there would be no "second generation".

A political awareness which was frustrated under Mussolini could grow after the Duce was overthrown in July 1943. By now Pasolini's father was in an Allied prisoner-of-war camp and the family had retreated to his mother's home in Casarsa, which lies on the Tagliamento river in Friuli. Pasolini, whose first poems in the Friulan dialect, **Poesie a Casarsa,** had appeared in 1942, found teaching jobs and scoured the countryside studying the various brands of dialect that the peasants used. From his letters it emerges that he rejected the conservative notion of a fixed Friulan language, stressing instead that newcomers like himself could re-invent the language and raise dialect poetry to the level of avant-garde writing. He also saw the Friulan language as the culture of an oppressed peasantry which could be politically awakened if its language were re-emphasized. This led Pasolini to join the Partito Comunista Italiano (PCI) in 1947 and to become the secretary of his cell.

Behind his decision there lay a riddle that this volume does nothing to resolve. Pasolini's brother, Guido, who had joined the non-Communist partisans, was killed in February 1945 by a Communist unit. While historians agree that the reasons for the Porzùs massacre were complex, there was no doubt in Guido's mind that the Communists wanted to destroy his unit because it was resisting not merely the Nazis but Yugoslav penetration into Friuli. A letter which he wrote to Pier Paolo, and which is published in the *Cronologia,* describes what Guido perceived as a PCI concession to Tito. Whatever Pasolini's admiration for the PCI as the voice of the peasantry in the land struggles of the post-war years, it seems surprising that he should have set aside this letter.

In 1943 Pasolini had his first homosexual experience. In the Bologna letters there are many references to girls but after brief courtships Pasolini pulls back. *The Quaderni rossi* explain why: a powerful erotic attraction to boys, which was a source of ecstasy, guilt and frustration. It provided the energy for the entire Friulan adventure, guiding Pasolini to reject conventional ideas about beauty, language and the social order. To say this is not, of course, to reduce his achievements to a series of sublimations. His dialect poetry is good, according to critics like Gianfranco Contini. But Pasolini's identity was caught up with his homosexuality: he notes that even the act of writing poetry confirmed him in his sense of being "abnormal".

In 1949 he was arrested and accused of interfering with mi-

nors. Christian Democrat newspapers exploited the case, Pasolini lost his teaching post, Friuli turned against him and he was expelled from the PCI. "I remain and shall remain a Communist", he replied and for the rest of his life he sought ties with the PCI, which is a further puzzle. His father, who had returned from the war as a paranoid alcoholic, made home life so intolerable that in January 1950 Pasolini and his mother fled to Rome.

He spent the next years in poverty, eking out a living by teaching and journalism. Yet, while one does not wish to belittle his hardships, one cannot helping feeling—as he himself writes—that Rome was a further liberation. He could now live somewhat more openly, while the boys of the Rome subproletariat offered him experiences that were sexually and sometimes emotionally rich.

Once more his homoerotic urge led him to literary and political discoveries, **Ragazzi di vita** is not a conventional realistic novel that describes the Rome slums; instead it reconstructs the world as the slum-dwellers see it. It was also a political statement in that the subproletariat was an affront both to Christian Democrat notions of progress and to the Communist myth of a rational working class. Pasolini was castigated by both sides and brought to trial for obscenity.

This volume of letters ends on a misleadingly calm note. By 1954 Pasolini was on the brink of success and yet his life was not really changing. The reason for this lies in his homosexuality. After the Friulan disgrace he writes that "I have never accepted my sin, I have never come to terms with my nature". Italian advocates of gay rights sometimes criticize Pasolini because he is of scant use to them in their campaign to present homosexuality as a normal and happy form of human behaviour, but the special interest of his case is that he lived his homosexuality as a necessary sin—"I was obliged to sin", he writes.

His religious sense, which surprised some of his admirers when it found objective expression in the film *The Gospel According to Matthew,* had its origins in his predicament. Unable to deny or to accept his homosexuality, he sought refuge in Christian notions that the man who is scorned by his fellows is especially dear to God, that suffering redeems both the sufferer and others and that the bearer of scandal is playing his part in a divine plan.

Whether this is sound theology or a private mythology, it led Pasolini into headlong confrontations with Italian society. It also explains why it is misleading to present him merely as a victim who was persecuted and destroyed by prejudice. But Pasolini did not passively acquiesce in his own destruction. By his books, his films and most of all his public persona he challenged Italian society, and whenever it showed signs of tolerance, he challenged the tolerance in order to reveal the oppression that lay beneath. Pasolini did not want us to forgive or accept him; he wanted us to keep worrying about ourselves and about what constitutes our normality.

George Armstrong (review date 23 March 1997)

SOURCE: "Double Trouble," in *The Los Angeles Times Book Review,* March 23, 1997, p. 9.

[*In the following review, Armstrong calls Pasolini's* Petrolio *"maddeningly incoherent and self-contradictory."*]

Pier Paolo Pasolini was murdered in 1975 by a 17-year-old male hooker. This book—written between 1972 and 1974—was not published in Italy until 1992. Had the author lived longer than his 53 years, *Petrolio* would never have been published anywhere. It is the first draft of a book that, as Pasolini said in a letter to his pal, the widely read novelist Alberto Moravia, he hoped would eventually be issued in only a limited edition. This sprawling draft of what might have developed into a novel culls "documentation" from the overheated Italian press relating to the nefarious doings of Italy's political bosses, the Christian Democrats and the fascists in particular. The dark nature of the material also raised questions concerning his death.

Pasolini's killer did not convince the film director's friends and admirers that he acted alone. *Ergo,* fascist thugs had followed the Marxist Pasolini and the youth to a deserted place outside Rome and they may have done the actual killing. (The argument was that Pasolini was too smart and too athletic to be subdued by a kid armed with a wooden plank.) The aura of mystery surrounding his death probably convinced the Italian publishers to give this very botchy draft a try.

But publishing it has proved a disservice to all. It is maddeningly incoherent and self-contradictory. The time-frame is not linear, which would not have been a problem if, at the end, the pieces fell into place. Alas, they never do.

Pasolini's letter to Moravia, which was never mailed and is included in the book, reveals some of his high ambitions for this unfinished work. He mentions planning to insert quotes from the classic Greek texts (for example, the "beginning lines from the Oresteia"). He also envisioned his work as a "monumental work, a modern Satyricon."

Carlo, the principal character, is a "Catholic of the left wing" with a top position in the state-owned oil refinery company. Another Carlo in the novel is the same man but with a different personality. Oh, good, the reader may think: What we have here is another "Dr. Jekyll and Mr. Hyde" leitmotif! Pasolini says that he will call them Carlo I and Carlo II. Later on, he opts for Carlo and Karl. Pasolini soon forgets to distinguish between the two, and the reader is left adrift and, in my particular case, angry. For the sake of this review, I will give the two Carlos their numbers.

Carlo I, "a wealthy cultivated engineer" of 35, starts off, interestingly enough, by seducing and having sex with his mother; he then goes on to expose himself to her servant girls. His hand is seldom far from his crotch. Carlo II lives in the slums of Rome. He is unwashed and seeks out cheap female whores.

We follow Carlo I to a literary salon where Pasolini gives us a neat sketch of Moravia and himself, though not identified as such: "Timid, and so more aggressive, an aggressiveness mixed with natural sweetness. . . . He did not seem to feel at all at ease; if anything, he seemed to feel he had been placed there by his success and his stormy reputation."

Is there any chance that, with the alleged collapse of Communism in the Western world, no one will ever again dismiss his or her adversary as being "bourgeois"? Pasolini, a purer Marxist than most members of the Italian Communist Party, writes of "stairs smelling of bourgeois wax" and of a worker who "was clearly distinguishable *by his physical presence alone,* from a bourgeois, as a mechanic from a student, a left-wing intellectual from one of the right, an academic from a writer. Confusion was not possible."

At one moment, Carlo I looks in a mirror and realizes that he has two large breasts and that his penis has vanished. On the next page, Carlo II goes to a dump heap outside Rome where someone has set up 20 working-class boys for him to sexually service. The first five or six encounters are described in vivid detail. This is hard-core stuff. And how does the reader know if this is No. 1 or No. 2 out there amid the garbage? Pasolini offers one clue: One of the boys compliments Carlo on his servicing by saying "Bravo!" Had it been Carlo I, with those breasts and that vulva, it would have been "Brava!"

Apparently, the reader is expected to understand that Carlo I's painless and almost instantaneous sex change takes place when his alter-ego is being possessed by the 20 boys. Later, he looks in that mirror again and still sees the breasts, but when he is importuned by a handsome Sicilian restaurant worker in Rome (Pasolini suggests that Carlo I is in the pay of the fascists and that blackmail is the motive for this sexual liaison), he manages to sexually satisfy the youth as an anatomical male. The youth then vanishes forever from these pages. In reflection, Carlo I muses: "If boys of the people were supposed to have penises bigger and more powerful than those of their masters, who are farther from nature, then that penis (his one-night-stand's) confirmed a common and current conviction." This is certainly in keeping with Pasolini's own view of Marxism.

When the young Pasolini applied for his Communist Party card, he put down "intellectual" on the line asking for his occupation. Fair enough, in a country where even journalists are classified in that category. He was a screenwriter once for Fellini; he wrote a series of intelligent, coherent political columns for the once staid Milan paper, *Il Corriere della Sera*. He directed numerous films, but I would consider only two low-budget ones worthy: *The Hawks and the Sparrows* and *The Gospel According to St. Matthew,* perhaps the best film about Jesus ever made and the one least likely to become dated. Pasolini's last film, completed a few days before his murder, was *Salo—the 120 Days of Sodom.* It was about the last-ditch stand of depraved Italian fascists in the last days of the German occupation.

Translator Ann Goldstein was heroic, in her herculean undertaking. But twice she has a character smelling the scent of "lime" trees. As once the owner of Italy's only lime tree (imported from Los Angeles) I think she meant "linden" (*Tilia europea*).

Fernanda Eberstadt (review date 23 March 1997)

SOURCE: "Courting Contradiction," in *The New York Times Book Review,* March 23, 1997.

[*In the following review of* Petrolio, *Eberstadt asserts that "all of Pasolini's most passionate opinions—from the sanctity of poverty to the vileness of heterosexual couples—have been folded together in this messy, harsh austerely intelligent phantasmagoria-cum-political treatise* [Petrolio].*"*]

In 1975, Pier Paolo Pasolini—philologist, film maker, poet, novelist and political essayist—was murdered on a wintry beach near Rome by a teen-age hustler with unknown accomplices. Throughout his fervidly productive career, Pasolini had courted contradiction. He was an open homosexual who deplored sexual permissiveness, divorce and the legalization of abortion; a radical who despised the student protesters of 1968; a Marxist who elegized rural tradition and believed that "internationalism" equaled cultural genocide; a professed nonbeliever who—in films like *Teorema* and *The Gospel According to St. Matthew*—produced very powerful religious art. At the time of his still unsolved murder, Pasolini was under siege from both left and right as a gadfly, a self-deluded messiah.

Pasolini has aged better than his critics. Today he is acknowledged as one of the great firebrand prophets of 20th-cen-

tury European culture. International festivals are devoted to his movies; his analysis of the rottenness of Italian politics and the resurgence of Fascism in Europe appears ever more prescient; even his demands that the Christian Democrats, among others in Italy, be put in the dock have been realized. In 1993 Giulio Andreotti (the former Prime Minister, now on trial for consorting with the Mafia) confessed, as a *Corriere della Sera* headline put it: "Pasolini was right!"

Pasolini's life was stamped with the same obstinate originality as his work. Born in Bologna in 1922, the son of a Fascist army officer and a Friulian schoolteacher, at 20 Pasolini published his first book of poems in a Friulian dialect very much of his own concoction. After two decades of the Fascist project of "Italianization," this young poet's decision to launch his career in dialect stood as a provocatively countercultural profession of faith. Having made his name as a poet and scholar of "regionalism," Pasolini—now transplanted to Rome—won overnight fame for his novels and films of the 1960's; they documented in street dialect the forgotten, violent underworld of prostitutes, pimps and petty pickpockets living in Rome's outlying projects. It is part of Pasolini's humanistic mission that much as he reworked the Christian Gospels and Greek tragedies in contemporary Calabria, Tanzania or Yemen—landscapes where ancient rites were still intact—so in his novels and in films like *Mamma Roma* and *Accattone,* he sought to show Jesus or Mary Magdalen in the faces of broken hoodlums.

Pasolini's late work is altogether less tender in its intonations, less redemptive in its import. By the early 70's, he had become convinced that Italy's distinctive peasant cultures— "the great world of Masses and tabernacles, of sacred woods and slavery, of poverty and the return of the seasons," whose urban remnants his art had celebrated—were being systematically annihilated. Supplanting them was the new ideology of what he called "consumeristic hedonism," which had transmuted the country's once proud working classes into a homogeneous generation of "gray, fearful neurotics," unmanned by false freedoms, sedated by prosperity. In apocalyptic newspaper columns, Pasolini condemned Italy's politicians, who had substituted "the penitentiary of consumerism" for traditional values, and who were using terrorism to shore up their rule.

Power—specifically, Italy's amoral interlacing of state, business and party politics—is the subject of his posthumous novel, *Petrolio,* now making its first appearance in English. *Petrolio,* which Pasolini also named "Vas" or "Vessel," is a roughly 500-page "preamble" to a novel, a dense complex of notes left unfinished at his death.

Set in Italy in the politically violent early 70's, it features a man and his double. Carlo 1, a left-wing Roman Catholic from Turin's upper bourgeoisie, is an engineer employed in the higher reaches of ENI, Italy's gas and oil company. To hasten his professional ascent, Carlo 1 makes a strategic alliance with the Mafia and the Neo-Fascists. Carlo 2 is the engineer's lower-class "twin." If Carlo 1—flabby, colorless—represents power in all its portentous mediocrity, Carlo 2 embodies a sexual vocation so consuming that in Pasolini's vocabulary it amounts to a martyrdom. While Carlo 1 tours the Persian Gulf on an ENI delegation, attends a Roman literary salon or dines with Mafia members of Parliament, Carlo 2 seduces his own mother, his grandmother, three sisters and, having assumed female form, has sex with 20 boys in a field. When Carlo 2 disappears, Carlo 1—unmoored by the loss of his erotic Mr. Hyde—abjures careerism, castrates himself, joins Eastern mystery cults and becomes a holy man.

> *Petrolio* reveals its author as the grateful possessor of a Mediterranean culture stretching from Homer through Apollonius of Tyana and Petronius, and on to Dante and Leopardi—a salty humanistic tradition to which Pasolini, chaser of slum boys, lover of flashy sports cars, castigator of the powerful, was the fitting heir.
> —*Fernanda Eberstadt*

Petrolio for the most part renounces the novel's formal consolations and sleights of hand: flesh-and-blood characters, an overarching structure, "the wonderful illusion of a story that unfolds on its own," as Pasolini puts it in an accompanying letter to the novelist Alberto Moravia. But despite its refusal to ingratiate, *Petrolio* is full of raw beauty and an otherworldly strangeness.

All of Pasolini's most passionate opinions—from the sanctity of poverty to the vileness of heterosexual couples—have been folded together in this messy, harsh, austerely intelligent phantasmagoria-cum-political treatise. There are terrorist bombings, C.I.A. plots, Decameron-style fables told in a time of plague, allegorical interventions from angels and devils with names like "Pragma," "Porsche," "the Take," "Fridge." There is a resetting of "Medea" in contemporary Iran: Jason and the Argonauts are oilmen drilling for the modern-day "Golden Fleece" and the chorus consists of bored diplomats' wives gossiping around the swimming pool of the Teheran Hilton. There is a mini-epic devoted to ENI's chief executives, delineating in Homeric style their hometowns, genealogies, hobbies and a tax-evading web of "subsidiaries." (It is a tribute to Pasolini's worldliness that 20 years after his death, the financial misdeeds and illegal government alliances of ENI detailed in this novel were making front-page news in Italy.)

This is a book in which the mundane is shown as diaboli-

cal, and the atrocious is made lovely: in the orgy that Carlo 2, after becoming female, stages with 20 youths, each of the 20 sets of male genitals is catalogued with elegance, spirit and tender appreciation. For readers unfamiliar with Pasolini, this half-finished anti-novel—scatological, hectoring, frequently obscure—makes a forbidding introduction. For those who persevere, *Petrolio* offers a trove of searingly beautiful apercus and images, a caustic compendium of this modern-day Jeremiah's last thoughts on class, anthropology, sex, psychoanalysis and male hairstyles. *Petrolio* reveals its author as the grateful possessor of a Mediterranean culture stretching from Homer through Apollonius of Tyana and Petronius, and on to Dante and Leopardi—a salty humanistic tradition to which Pasolini, chaser of slum boys, lover of flashy sports cars, castigator of the powerful, was the fitting heir.

FURTHER READING

Biography

Consoli, Joseph P. Essay on Pasolini in *Gay & Lesbian Literature,* St. James Press, 19, pp. 291-94.

> Presents an overview of Pasolini's life and career, including consideration of his homosexuality and its impact on his work.

Criticism

Bongie, Chris. "A Postscript to Transgression: The Exotic Legacy of Pier Paolo Pasolini." In his *Exotic Memories: Literature, Colonialism, and the Fin de Siècle,* pp. 188-228. Stanford, CA: Stanford University Press, 1991.

> Analyzes Pasolini's relationship with the Third World in his work.

Capozzi, Frank. "Pier Paolo Pasolini: An Introduction to the Translations." *Canadian Journal of Italian Studies* 5, No. 1-2 (Fall/Winter 1981-82): 109-13.

> Provides a brief overview of Pasolini's life and career.

Casarino, Cesare. "Oedipus Exploded: Pasolini and the Myth of Modernization." *October,* No. 59 (Winter 1992): 27-47.

> States that "Pasolini in *Edipo Re,* rather than rewriting the myth of Oedipus, writes a myth of the myth of Oedipus: the focus shifts from Oedipus to the myth itself as a narrative practice."

Michalczyk, John J. "Pier Paolo Pasolini: The Epical-Religious Cinema of Political Sexuality." In his *The Italian Political Filmmakers,* pp. 64-107. Rutherford, NJ: Fairleigh Dickinson University Press, 1986.

> Discusses Pasolini's aesthetic and personal evolution and the provocative nature of his work.

Pivato, Joseph. "Cultural Differences." *Canadian Literature,*
No. 138/139 (Fall/Winter 1993): pp. 146-47.
    Favorably reviews Antonio Mazza's translation of some
    of Pasolini's selected poetry.

Additional coverage of Pasolini's life and career is contained in the following sources published by Gale Research: *Dictionary of Literary Biography,* **Vol. 128, and** *Major Twentieth-Century Writers.*

Alan Paton
1903-1988

South African novelist, nonfiction writer, short story writer, autobiographer, biographer, dramatist, essayist, and poet.

The following entry presents criticism of Paton's work through 1989. For further information on his life and career, see *CLC,* Volumes 4, 10, 25, and 55.

INTRODUCTION

One of the earliest proponents of racial equality in his native South Africa, Paton made considerable practical contributions to political life there. His place in the literature of social protest rests primarily on the novels *Cry, the Beloved Country* (1948) and *Too Late the Phalarope* (1953), both of which made him South Africa's most celebrated writer. In both his fiction and political writings Paton confronted the horrors of South African apartheid. His works have been admired particularly for their perceptive and sympathetic treatment of the exploitation of nonwhites by the elite ruling class and its tragic effects on both the exploited and South African society as a whole. John Romano has observed that Paton's "steady devotion to the ideal of the empathetic imagination in fiction . . . is an example of Paton's characteristic method. Individual human dilemmas are never swallowed up or diminished by the overarching political context of the story he is telling. Paton is relentless in his faith in the moral meaning of individual human experience."

Biographical Information

Born January 11, 1903, in Pietermaritzburg, Natal, South Africa, Paton attended Maritzburg College and Natal University College, where he prepared for a career in teaching and began writing dramas and poetry, much of the latter comprising the collection *Songs of Africa* (1995). After graduating in 1922 with a B.S. degree and teacher's certificate, he returned to teach at Maritzburg College until 1935, when he was appointed principal of Diepkloof Reformatory for young African delinquents by Jan Hofmeyer, Paton's hero and subject of the biography *Hofmeyr* (1964). Within weeks he had changed the administration's principles from force, rebellion, and disorder to respect, trust, and internal commitment, which prompted him to write *Freedom as a Reformatory Instrument* (1948). Versions of the troubled youths appear in some of Paton's stories and in his play *Sponono* (1965). While touring prisons and reformatories in Europe and the United States in 1947, Paton wrote *Cry, the Beloved Country,* which brought him fame, financial security, and the

Anisfield-Wolf Award for 1948. However, the novel was published in the same year that Prime Minister Daniel François Malan came to power and instituted apartheid; consequently Paton resigned from Diepkloof and devoted his life to writing and social action. In the early 1950s he was a founding member of the Liberal Party of South Africa, of which he later became president until the party was outlawed by the government in 1968. His moral commitment to opposing racism increased while working in the Anglican Church with Bishop Geoffrey Clayton, the subject of the biography *Apartheid and the Archbishop* (1973). After the publication of *Too Late the Phalarope,* Paton concentrated on completing several nonfiction books about contemporary South African politics and its problems, most notably *The Land and People of South Africa* (1955). In 1961 he issued the collection of short stories *Tales from a Troubled Land,* followed by several more nonfiction books. When his wife, Debbie, died in 1967, Paton wrote a tribute to her, *For You Departed* (1969). His humanitarian and literary efforts garnered Paton the 1960 Freedom House award and the 1977 International League for Human Rights prize, as well as several honorary doctorates from prestigious universities around the world. Paton's last novel, *Ah, But Your Land Is Beautiful* (1981), followed the publication of the first installment of his autobiography, *Towards the Mountain* (1980). Paton died of throat cancer on April 12, 1988, at his home near Durban, just three weeks after he had completed the second part of his autobiography, *Journey Continued* (1988).

Major Works

The bulk of Paton's writings are nonfiction works about political and social conditions in South Africa, and this theme also appears in much of his fiction, though always as background for his art. *Cry, the Beloved Country* is an episodic portrayal of racially-divided South Africa concerning the fate of Absalom Kumalo, a young African who, while committing a robbery, murders Arthur Jarvis, a wealthy, white social activist. The novel opens with Kumalo's father, a humble Zulu country pastor, who journeys to Johannesburg to search for his delinquent and missing son. When he finds his son, Steven Kumalo learns that Absalom has confessed to the murder and will be put to death. Meanwhile Arthur Jarvis Sr. reads his dead son's papers and speeches and acquires knowledge of both the hostile, squalid living conditions of most of South Africa's native peoples and his son's ideas about changing the apartheid system. Finally, after Absalom has been executed, both fathers meet and share mutual comprehension of each other's loss. *Too Late the Phalarope* relates the story of Pieter van Vlaanderen, a promising Afrikaner police lieutenant. When he is discovered violating the South African Immorality Act of 1927 by engaging in sexual intercourse with an African woman, Stephanie, he is imprisoned and shunned by his well-established and conservative family. According to South African social mores at the time, his shame spells the downfall of his family as well. Most of the stories in *Tales from a Troubled Land* relate sometimes tragic, sometimes comic episodes involving the inmates and staff at the Diepkloof reformatory. *Ah, But Your Land Is Beautiful* recounts in the form of a pastiche-memoir the Defiance Campaign and the Liberal Party in the 1950s. The narrative comprises letters, reflections, character sketches, bits of dialogue, the transcripts of a trial, a summary of newspaper accounts and scraps of official documents juxtaposed or sewn together by a narrator who seems himself the possessor of a long, patient, irresistible historical vision. The story begins with the arrest of an Indian girl, Prem, for deliberately using a white library in violation of the color bar. When Prem defies the authorities, her struggle ignites the sudden imposition of new, strict apartheid measures and increasingly severe persecution of anti-apartheid forces. The novel concludes with the election to Prime Minister of a character who represents Dr. Henrik Verwoerk, which marks the beginning of the most bitter period in South African history. *Towards the Mountain* describes Paton's early years as an educator and his conversion from the white racist paternalism up to the publication of *Cry, the Beloved Country;*

Journey Continued picks up from that point and focuses on his involvement with the Liberal Party through 1968, including a brief epilogue on the two decades preceding his death.

Critical Reception

Paton's works generally have received little critical attention despite the widely favorable reviews of his first two novels. Still, *Cry, the Beloved Country* has continued to attract readers around the world, achieving an almost legendary status. Paton's other works have assumed their niche in the English literary canon as well, but rarely have attracted much commentary. Since the 1980s, however, a number of critical assessments have appeared, focusing on such aspects of Paton's works as the thematic universality of *Too Late the Phalarope;* environmental, liturgical, and spiritual influences in Paton's art; and the classical, epic, psychological, and religious dimensions of *Cry, the Beloved Country*. Most critics have tended to agree with Harold C. Gardiner, who has summarized an often-repeated critical commentary on *Cry:* "Its subject matter is as explosive as any that can be handled in today's fiction—the tensions between Negroes and whites—and yet there is not the faintest whisper of shrill propaganda; it deals plainly with the lusts of the flesh, and yet there is not the slightest suggestiveness; it plumbs deep into human suffering and punishment without a hint of moralizing or of maudlin sentimentality. It is a fine, indeed a great book." Others, however, have objected to the politics, or rather the absence of political responsibility, of *Cry.* A. A. Moyne has noted that Paton "believes like his chief character, Rev. Kumalo, that love is the solution to the problems of the oppressed blacks. It is doubtful how love would work, when fear rules the lives of both races in South Africa." Nevertheless, William Minter has concluded that Paton "will be remembered not for that fear, but for his cry for justice that continues to echo today."

PRINCIPAL WORKS

Meditation for a Young Boy Confirmed (short stories) 1944
Cry, the Beloved Country (novel) 1948
Freedom as a Reformatory Instrument (nonfiction) 1948
Christian Unity: A South African View (nonfiction) 1951
South Africa Today (nonfiction) 1951
Too Late the Phalarope (novel) 1953
The Land and People of South Africa (nonfiction) 1955; also published as *South Africa and her People,* 1957; revised editions, 1965, 1972
South Africa in Transition [with Dan Weiner] (nonfiction) 1956
Hope for South Africa (nonfiction) 1959
Tales from a Troubled Land (short stories) 1961; also published as *Debbie Go Home: Stories,* 1961

Hofmeyr (biography) 1964; abridged edition as *South African Tragedy: The Life and Times of Jan Hofmeyr,* 1965

Sponono [with Krishna Shah] (drama) 1965

Civil Rights and Present Wrongs (nonfiction) 1968

Instrument of Thy Peace: The Prayer of St. Francis (nonfiction) 1968; revised edition, 1982

The Long View (nonfiction) 1968

For You Departed (memoir) 1969; also published as *Kontakion for You Departed,* 1969

Apartheid and the Archbishop: The Life and Times of Geoffrey Clayton, Archbishop of Cape Town (biography) 1973

Knocking on the Door: Shorter Writings (essays) 1975

Towards the Mountain (autobiography) 1980

Ah, But Your Land Is Beautiful (novel) 1981

Journey Continued (autobiography) 1988

Songs of Africa: The Collected Poems of Alan Paton (poetry) 1995

CRITICISM

Harold C. Gardiner (essay date 13 March 1948)

SOURCE: "On Saying 'Boo!' to Geese," in his *In All Conscience: Reflections on Books and Culture,* Hanover House, 1959, pp. 108-12.

[*In the following essay, first printed in 1948 in* America *magazine, Gardiner commends Paton's artistic treatment of racial tensions in* Cry, the Beloved Country, *especially in comparison to contemporary trends in fiction.*]

At the risk, perhaps, of sounding like a proper Bostonian, I want to raise a standard to which I think all critics ought to be willing and eager to repair. I'd like to start a movement or found an organization for the Cessation of Adulation Heaped on Authors (generally Young Authors) Because They Write in a Bizarre, Shocking, Grotesque, and Violent Style of Bizarre, Shocking, Grotesque, and Violent Things. Will my fellow critics, of both the secular and the religious press, care to come in?

If they do join, they will find themselves in good company. They will meet, for example, Mr. Edwin Waugh remarking: "Exaggeration, violence, and vulgarity are [literature's] deadliest banes; reticence, modesty, and shy beauty are its infallible qualities." Or they will hear more famous S. H. Butcher, in his *Aristotle's Theory of Poetry and the Fine Arts,* proclaiming: "The esthetic pleasure produced by any ideal imitation must be a sane and wholesome pleasure, which would approve itself to the better portion of the community." Or even still better-known Arnold Bennett would tell them (in

his *Literary Taste*): "The pleasure derived from a classic is never a violent pleasure; it is subtle—it will wax in intensity. . . .The artistic pleasures of an uncultivated mind are generally violent. . . . The pleasure of a classic does not at all knock you down—rather, it steals over you."

These are but three of a veritable chorus of critics who have affirmed, down through the history of our literature, that it is the common, universal human values, and not the shock techniques, which have been the touchstone of excellence. The persistence of this critical tradition is not invalidated by the undoubted fact that there are recognized masterpieces of macabre writing—Edgar Allan Poe's, for instance—but I doubt that anyone would deny that such work is automatically relegated to a lesser sphere of literary blessedness, perhaps almost to a limbo of letters.

And it is equally true that there are classics with violent and even distasteful themes—we have some of the great Russians and an Oedipus. But it will be found, I think, that these apparent exceptions but prove the rule; they are not violent for the sake of the violence, for beneath their fury and their immediate repulsion lies the common and universal human struggle, the all-pervading and supporting atmosphere of human morality.

However far afield a consideration of other literatures might lead us, I think it is demonstrably evident that in very much current American fiction the frenzied striving for the unusual, the shocking, the grotesque is dehumanizing the writing, stultifying the authors, and, it is to be feared, debauching the reader. And the evil, far from being checked, is not even noted by critics who award to neurotic exhibitionism the accolade of "genius" or "virtuosity."

This mild animadversion is prompted because I have just finished a magnificent story. Its subject matter is as explosive as any that can be handled in today's fiction—the tensions between Negroes and whites—and yet there is not the faintest whisper of shrill propaganda; it deals plainly with the lusts of the flesh, and yet there is not the slightest suggestiveness; it plumbs deep into human suffering and punishment without a hint of moralizing or of maudlin sentimentality. It is a fine, indeed a great book.

It is *Cry, the Beloved Country,* by Alan Paton. The scene is South Africa, the main character a magnificently conceived native Anglican minister, the theme a twofold one: the struggle of the natives, attracted from the land and their tribes to the huge mining towns like Johannesburg, for tolerable living and working conditions; and the decline of tribal life and customs, fostered by the white man who had nothing to give the natives in return. All this is superbly told in a rather stately style, which is presumably a fairly literal transcription of the Zulu idiom and which gives the poignant tale a somewhat Biblically patriarchal tone.

Kumalo, the hero, is summoned from his little church among his tribe to go down to the frightening big city to help his sister, who has fallen on evil ways, and to find his son, from whom his parents have not heard since he left to work in the mines. The boy runs away from a reform school and becomes involved in a killing, the victim being the son of the white farmer whose lands lie near Kumalo's church; the son himself had sacrificed a career of great promise to work for the betterment of the natives. The pastor's sister agrees to return home with him but runs off at the last minute, leaving the crushed and, he thinks, disgraced man to go back to his tribe with his sister's child and the pregnant young wife of his condemned son. Drought and poor farming are threatening the life of his tribe when no one else steps in to assist them but the father of the murdered son, who does it in remembrance of his own son's devotion to the natives.

But the story is pre-eminently one of individuals. There are no sweeping and grandiose statements about "the race problem." Jarvis, the white father, and Kumalo, the black one, are two men sorrowing for their sons, and the reader soon realizes that it matters not a tinker's dam what the color of their respective skins is. It is the human (and divine) values by which the two men live, the human dignity both portray, the sublimation of human suffering they achieve, which puts the black man and the white man shoulder to shoulder in the book and suggests by implication that the black and the white populations of South Africa and indeed of all the world can work shoulder to shoulder as well, if only every person will stop looking at the "race question" and start looking at the individual soul. This thought the book presents superbly. Though its very theme is race tension, in the inner workings and motivation of the characters the book shows utter unconsciousness of "race."

I wish there were space to quote many of the deeply moving passages of this most truly compassionate book. There is the scene in which Kumalo tells Jarvis that it was his son who had killed the white man's, or the scene in which Kumalo says farewell to his son, awaiting execution, or that which depicts the old pastor, back with his parish, leading prayers for his condemned son. But as I want to draw the comparison suggested at the start of this discussion, I must leave you to read these for yourself. I must remark, in passing from this truly noble novel, that there is one defect in it. It is marred by a page or so of some very shallow remarks on what law is and whence it derives its authority. . . .

The loud and the startling things are not always the significant things in life; they are rarely the important things in a novel. *Cry, the Beloved Country* is an Everest in the flat wastes of modern fiction precisely because it is not shrill

about the riots, the broken heads, the sullen hatreds of race tensions, but rather delves deeply into the serenity of love, compassion, consideration, and devotion that can alone solve race tensions.

The literature of exaggeration may be inescapable today. We live in an age of exaggeration—millions of slave laborers in Russia, sky-blanketing fleets of war planes, supersonic flight. Who knows when we will return to the human level again and leave the apocalyptic? Literature can, I think, help in its relatively small way to lead us back, but it will first have to rediscover the truth about life as well as about itself—the truth that "the Lord is not in the wind, and after the wind an earthquake: the Lord is not in the earthquake. And after the earthquake a fire: the Lord is not in the fire, and after the fire a whistling of a gentle air."

And the Lord—of literature as of life—was and is in the gentle air.

Harvey Breit (essay date 20 November 1949)

SOURCE: "Alan Paton," in his *The Writer Observed,* World Publishing Company, 1956, pp. 89-93.

[*In the following essay, originally printed in 1949 in* The New York Times Review *as regular feature interviews, Breit asks Paton about the differences between South African and American blacks, his career preoccupations, and his literary influences and methods.*]

This reporter saw Alan Paton on the eve of his leaving for England to receive a special literary award from *The London Times* for his distinguished novel, **Cry, the Beloved Country.** In New York he had seen the "musical tragedy" version of his novel; in London he will put the finishing touches to the screen version of it for Alexander Korda.

About the award Mr. Paton said: "The *Times* gives a literary prize for the best and most important book of the year. The prize went to Winston Churchill's *The Gathering Storm.* In any year, any book Mr. Churchill writes—especially given the topic on which he was writing—must be the best and most important book of the year." The *Times,* apparently feeling they'd like to do something for Mr. Paton's novel, created a special prize.

Mr. Paton, in his middle forties, the son of a Presbyterian Scotsman, was born in South Africa, where he grew up and where he did everything (from pedagogy to penology) but write. It was after the war that he got started, and in a faraway country. He held the manuscript for a time after finishing it, it was a private matter, and not for publication. But a friend gave him wise counsel. Now Mr. Paton's life is changed. "I am in a dilemma," he says (pronouncing it *digh-lemma*). The reader, however, need not concern himself with Mr. Paton's dilemma. Mr. Paton, small and wiry and with a lean and hungry look, is an impressive gentleman. His mind is lucid and tough, his speech is precise, unembellished and neutral, yet nevertheless touched as though with a bitter memory. The over-all sense of him is of iron—iron-minded, iron-willed and iron-muscled. If the impression Mr. Paton inevitably gives is roughly accurate, dilemmas will get resolved in double time.

When he was asked if he would talk about the South African Negro and the American Negro, Mr. Paton nodded affirmatively, thought for a few moments, then spoke in an exact, nearly formal platform manner.

> "The first great class of Negroes in South Africa one might still call tribal," he said. "Even so, they don't lead a life completely untouched by Europeans. From a tribal life they go to the mines and industry—mainly the mines. They, as a rule, are the most primitive of South Africans.

> "You have a second great class, those who live on the white farms in the country. The great tendency, however, is for the most intelligent of them to drift away from the farms and go to the cities and then you get the third great class—already broken from the tribal and rural life and become somewhat urbanized. They are much more in touch with the ideas of the world.

> "Already there is emerging a fourth group, also preponderantly urban—teachers, ministers, doctors, business men. Oh, they form what may be called an African intelligentsia. They read books and newspapers. They know a great deal of what is going on in the world. They provide the political leadership. On the whole, they tend to become embittered and to feel frustrated. And already there is a tendency among them to look to themselves for their own salvation and even to scorn cooperation with those white people who have always devoted themselves to the cause of their advancement."

What percentage of the population did the Negro make up? Mr. Paton nodded agreeably.

> "About 75 per cent," he said, "and it is for that reason that the white man fears his advancement. And it is this fear which is responsible for much of the legislation. I think it should be made clear that our parliament and senate are entirely white.

> "The American Negro, for his numbers, has produced a far greater proportion of eminent and distinguished men. The reason for this is, of course, that there are not so many barriers toward his advancement as in South Africa; and the reason for that is, of course, that they constitute a much smaller percentage of the population, and that therefore the white American is less afraid of according him these privileges. At the same time I do not underestimate the great power of the American conscience. I do not suppose for a moment that it is just a matter of statistics. We in South Africa also have a conscience. But our fears are so great that the conscience is not so clearly apparent."

What was Mr. Paton going to do next? "My book," he said, "has had such a terrific backwash that I have not had time to sit down to do more work." What was Mr. Paton going to do about that? (It was here that Mr. Paton faced a certain *digh*-lemma.) "I haven't yet discovered whether I would write more if I went back to affairs, to a life of active participation in society. It just might be that I'm not the sort of person who can withdraw to some secluded spot and write books. I haven't yet found an answer to that question. But my mind is full of ideas and I should like nothing better than to be left alone to work some of them out."

I should like to write books about South Africa which would really stab people in the conscience. I don't see any point in writing provocatively for the sake of being provocative, or antagonizingly for the sake of being antagonizing. But I do believe there is a level at which one can write where it is no longer a question of provoking or antagonizing, but simply a question of stating an overwhelming truth that a man just cannot deny.
—Alan Paton

He paused, a barely ironic pause. "However," he continued, "I am now expected to lend support to innumerable causes to which people suppose—and rightly suppose—I'm sympathetic. One cannot withdraw entirely from such participation, and so I still find myself going through an extremely difficult stage of adaptation and adjustment."

What sort of literature, Mr. Paton's interlocutor asked, moved him? "If you asked me," Mr. Paton replied, "what kind of topics appealed to me in writing, I would have to confess to you that I couldn't bring myself to write any book which would increase the amount of depression and dejection that exists in so many people already."

But how would it be known whether a book would depress and deject? There was proof everywhere that depressing material did not need to depress. There was the idea of the catharsis. "Ah, yes," Mr. Paton said, "that's a different thing where writing tragedy brings out a catharsis. My objection isn't to tragedy, because I believe tragedy and human life are inseparable. I believe that human life is meaningful and purposeful, and just to write a story of human corruption— I think I could write it as horribly as anyone [from out the stern face there issued, surprisingly, a brief, loud laugh]. I don't find corruption a fascinating or rich theme to write about.

"I should like to write books about South Africa which would really stab people in the conscience. I don't see any point in writing provocatively for the sake of being provocative, or antagonizingly for the sake of being antagonizing. But I do believe there is a level at which one can write where it is no longer a question of provoking or antagonizing, but simply a question of stating an overwhelming truth that a man just cannot deny. He may still be angry with you for having presented the truth, but he is not angry with you for the way in which you've presented it. After he has confronted the truth in that fashion, he is not the same man again."

Mr. Paton stared sternly at his interviewer. Was it the end, was Mr. Paton finished? No, Mr. Paton was not finished. "One rather good critic," he said, "entitled his review of my book, 'A Gentle Protest.' But I believe the book is not so gentle as it looked. What looks gentle is often far more powerful than all the ranting and raving in the world. And it is my hope to go on touching the conscience of South Africa in this fashion. But I haven't purely a moral purpose. I also believe in the task of trying to interpret South Africa to the South Africans so that they can see themselves without illusions. It is a very fascinating and exciting task."

That, it was suggested, ended the talk rather nicely. "Let us end it," Mr. Paton said, "while there is an end."

Orville Prescott (essay date 1952)

SOURCE: "Four Great Novels," in his *In My Opinion: An Inquiry into the Contemporary Novel,* Bobbs-Merrill Company, 1952, pp. 235-48.

[*In the following excerpt, Prescott opines that* Cry, the Beloved Country *is among the "great novels," praising Paton's artistic treatment of the story's themes.*]

The second modern novel which I dare call great is the finest I have ever read about the tragic plight of black-skinned people in a white man's world, *Cry, The Beloved Country*

by Alan Paton. Without any of the blind rage which has led so many writers on similar themes into bitterness and dogmatism, without any of the customary oversimplification and exaggerated melodrama, Mr. Paton wrote a beautiful and profoundly moving story, a story steeped in sadness and grief but radiant with hope and compassion. He contrived for it a special prose of his own which is both richly poetic and intensely emotional. Anyone who admires creative fiction of a high order, anyone who cares to see how a thesis novel can be written without sacrificing artistic integrity, should not miss this notable book.

Alan Paton is a South African and his novel is about that beautiful and unhappy land. For many years he was the principal of the Diepkloof Reformatory, a Johannesburg institution for delinquent African boys. He has lectured and written on the South African race problem, but this is his first book. He brought to it a rare technical skill as well as the contagion of his love for Africa and her tormented people. He is a man who can see evil and greed and cruelty and tragedy and not sink into despair. He knows that simple human goodness can still be found in a weary world.

Cry, The Beloved Country is the story of the progress of a Christian in whose path many lions stood. The Reverend Stephen Kumalo was an *umfundisi,* or parson, of St. Mark's Church at Ndotsheni high in the hills of Natal. He was an elderly Zulu, quite unacquainted with the dangers which lay in wait for his people when they left their hungry, eroded country for the great city of Johannesburg on the Witwatersrand. There segregation, poverty, a fantastic housing shortage, temptation and vice destroyed hordes of young men who sought a living in the gold mines. Their tribal society with its ancient laws and customs and moral traditions had been destroyed by the white people. And it had not been replaced by anything else save police and courts and jails.

Kumalo went to Johannesburg to hunt for his sister and his son who had disappeared there. His search was a tragic one. He found his sister first, and she had become a prostitute. He found traces of his son. As he plodded from address to address, finding graver news at each, Kumalo realized that Absalom, his son, had descended into a bottomless pit. So when the good white man who crusaded for native rights was murdered, Kumalo was appalled but not surprised to learn that Absalom was the murderer.

Kumalo's pitiful martyrdom was not all bitterness. His friend, Msimangu, a fellow preacher, proved to be an almost saintly man. The young white man from the reformatory where Absalom had been confined was hot-tempered, but earnest and kind. The white man who was the father of the murdered man was the source of unexpected comfort. The meeting of the two grief-stricken fathers, the proud, silent, conventional Englishman and the humble Zulu, is the high point of *Cry, The Beloved Country.* Then all the complicated social and personal threads of Mr. Paton's story meet and are entwined together in a powerful and extraordinarily touching climax.

Cry, The Beloved Country consists of an amazingly deft fusion of realistic detail and symbolical synthesis of various points of view and emotional reactions. As a picture of the fear and suspicion and hatred which haunt all South Africans, black or white, it is brilliant. The whites, who are so few, are frightened by the blacks, who are so many. Education, public health, social advancements of all kinds are dreaded for their capacity to make the Negroes more insistent in their demands and more conscious of their power. A minority of the disinterested and farsighted whites—and Mr. Paton pays them full tribute—are fighting for social justice. But they themselves are doubtful if they can persuade the whites to love soon enough—before the blacks learn to hate too well.

In conveying his message Mr. Paton never once damages his story, never once mounts a soapbox to orate at the expense of his novel as a work of fiction. His men and women are intensely real and sympathetic persons. Their conversations and their inner monologues are warm with the breath of life, in spite of the cadenced, lyrical quality which distinguishes them. Perhaps people don't really think or talk with such simple nobility of expression; but they never spoke in Shakespearean blank verse either. It is the truth of the spirit that counts, not stenographic reporting.

Current fiction, while often competent, interesting and provocative, rarely discusses an important and controversial subject with both creative artistry and generosity of mind. Because *Cry, The Beloved Country* is both so skillful and so generous it seems to me a great novel.

Myron Matlaw (essay date 1975)

SOURCE: "Alan Paton's *Cry, the Beloved Country* and Maxwell Anderson's/Kurt Weill's *Lost in the Stars:* A Consideration of Genres," in *Arcadia*, Vol. 10, No. 3, 1975, pp. 260-72.

[*In the essay below, Matlaw compares the generic methods of* Cry, the Beloved Country *to Maxwell Anderson's* Lost in the Stars *(1949), a stage adaptation of Paton's novel, demonstrating how each work uses such formal strategies as narrative, stylistic devices, and characterization that achieve "very similar effects."*]

Drama, if it is not stillborn, is the joint creation of writer, producer, director, actors, stage technicians, musicians, and others. It comes to life only if and when performed in theatres before groups of people (audiences), who respond positively, negatively, or apathetically. Their response, whatever it is, at least to some extent affects the character and quality of the performance, i.e., the character and quality of the play. For this and other reasons inherent in the very nature of live performances, no production can ever be exactly the same as any other one of the same play, even in the same run and with the identical cast. Furthermore, if a production is to survive, audiences must be entertained. Entertainment in the theatre appeals first of all to the senses and the emotions. Of primary importance and meaning, therefore, are the means by which the various senses of audiences are assaulted: spectacle, sounds, actions, movements, gestures, facial expressions—all of which are usually not even noted and are but rarely stressed in the published play. The dialogue—which constitutes virtually the whole of the published play—is often of secondary importance in performance, for spoken words are elusive and difficult to assimilate.

In sum, drama does not aim to engage the intellect primarily—if at all. Rather, it appeals primarily to somatic responses, to passions, to feelings, and to sentiments. To be understood and responded to immediately, as drama must be if it is to be viable, it can not be hedged by subtlety. Action and dialogue must be clear, direct, and simple. And reading a play, if it is to be meaningful, must therefore necessarily be most imaginative: the whole theatre—setting, actors, sounds, movements, spectacle, and yes, even audience responses—must be constantly evoked in the reader's mind, as it always is and as it has to be in the mind of the playwright. For example, Bertolt Brecht, who like many playwrights was deeply involved in the staging of his plays, kept the model of a theatre within view as he worked, to remind himself of his purpose, and of the trappings of the live theatre for which he wrote. Reading a play thus is analogous to reading a musical score: the reader must continuously translate (i.e., imagine or recreate) the written symbols into their total objective realities (the produced play, the performed musical composition), for the reading of scripts and scores is significant only if it is accompanied by the evocation of live performances. At the same time, reading scripts and scores can be the most rewarding possible experience of such works: it enables the conjuring up, at any imaginative reader's convenience and pleasure, performances which are ideal, perfect, flawless.

Fiction, on the other hand, is the product of one individual creator (for a story or a novel may exist as a completed work of art even in unpublished form). Fiction is written solely for other individual—not groups of—readers, who customarily peruse it in solitude, and at a pace wholly determined by each individual reader. A reader may stop and mull over single phrases or sentences or whole paragraphs, skip others, and return from time to time to reread passages or, for that matter, the whole work. Unlike the play, whose production is a juggernaut that proceeds on its preordained route without concern for individuals in the audience group, the novel lends itself to varying individual manipulations and responses, emotional as well as intellectual. Unless the aim is for a popular best seller—a product marketed for relatively unsophisticated and shallow minds—a novelist may therefore shape the language, ideas, and form of the work without any concern whatever with the need for simplicity, directness, and instant clarity. Subtlety, length, difficulty, neologistic experimentation and syntactical or semantic obfuscation (as in the novels of James Joyce), serpentine sentences (as in the works of William Faulkner), convoluted diction and loaded pronouns (such as those of Henry James), projections of dense and symbolic subjectivity (as in Marcel Proust's octad)—all these, which require careful exegesis for an understanding of even the surface meaning of the narrative, rather than being flaws, when artistically wrought may even enhance a novel. The same characteristics destroy a play.

These perhaps obvious but all-too-often forgotten generic distinctions must be borne in mind in any comparison of particular works of drama and fiction, even if their plots and characters be the same. If the comparison is that of a novel with a musical play, the generic distinction is even greater and more interesting. A case in point is Maxwell Anderson's *Lost in the Stars* (1949), a dramatization of Alan Paton's *Cry, the Beloved Country* (1948).

Paton's novel, it may be recalled, is an episodical portrayal of racially-divided South Africa. The sufferings of Kumalo, a Zulu country pastor who visits Johannesburg, epitomize the sufferings of the blacks—just as the tragedy befalling Jarvis, Kumalo's wealthy white neighbor, universalizes the tragedy of racial strife. With the help of a Johannesburg minister and others, Kumalo finds his brother John, a successful merchant and politician whose oratorical skills arouse the blacks and alarm the police, and his sister, who has become a prostitute and neglects her child. Most painful of all is Kumalo's discovery that his son, Absalom, had become a delinquent, been sentenced to a reformatory, and is now missing. Absalom participates in a notorious Johannesburg murder—that of Jarvis' son, a fervent civil rights advocate. At the trial, Absalom confesses his part in the crime, and is condemned to death. The heart-broken Kumalo returns to his village, where crop failures are causing starvation. Unable to help, he is urged by his superior to leave his congregation. The slain man's little boy unwittingly saves the blacks by describing their plight to his grandfather. Jarvis, who in his grief has tried to understand his murdered son's social views, ultimately provides the villagers with the desperately needed help. Coming to terms with the murder and the racial gulf between them, the two bereaved fathers are able, however painfully, to communicate and understand each

other's sorrow even as Kumalo, on the dawn of his son's scheduled execution, goes up the mountain and weeps in solitude.

Though the play, with its haunting musical score by Kurt Weill, has been criticized as a feeble replica of a powerful novel ("A strong novel can make a weak book", the Washington *Daily News* of February 21, 1972, headlined its review of a recent revival), both works are deeply moving. But they accomplish their very similar effects in quite different ways, each in a manner befitting its own genre.

The emotional impact of *Cry, the Beloved Country* is achieved, first of all and most consistently, by Paton's stylistic understatement, by his use and reuse of a few simple, almost stilted, formal phrases. *Is it heavy?* Jarvis asks Stephen Kumalo when the latter haltingly and painfully reveals his identity as the father of the murderer of Jarvis' son. Kumalo's reply echoes and reechoes the adjective: *It is very heavy, umnumzana. It is the heaviest thing of all my years . . . This thing that is the heaviest thing of all my years, is the heaviest thing of all your years also.* Another example occurs early in the novel; after Kumalo commends Msimangu's kindness, the latter's demurrer, *I am not kind, I am a selfish and sinful man, but God put his hands on me, that is all,* is echoed by him and by Jarvis at the end of the novel in his last meeting with Kumalo, when the white man fiercely interrupts the black pastor's praise by disclaiming any great personal virtue:

> —I am no saintly man, said Jarvis fiercely.
> —Of that I cannot speak, but God put His hands on you.
> And Jarvis said, That may be, that may be . . .

Similarly Mrs. Lithebe, whenever she is praised for her great generosity, repeatedly responds with a question that becomes something of a litany: *Why else were we born?*

In their stark simplicity, these and other phrases often suggest the biblical. Like the scripture readings (Chapter 13) and the errant son's name (Absalom), they sometimes even echo the Bible directly, as in this passage: Kumalo's *heart went out in great compassion for the boy that must die, who promised now, when there was no more mercy, to sin no more.* Such phrases are so effective because their very understatement heightens the impact of what is clearly implied. They achieve yet greater power because they appear at climactic moments, such as the ones just cited, and they are repeated periodically. Thus their effect also resembles that of the incremental repetition of folk ballads.

Paton's selection of episodes and his narration and descriptions follow a similar stylistic manner. In these, too, understatement and repetition predominate, thus contributing to the desired effect. Almost conspicuously Paton eschews depicting—instead he merely alludes to or presents in the form of newspaper accounts—externally dramatic situations. This is true not only of the most consequential event of the novel—the murder itself—but also of such inherently dramatic situations as the abortive miners' strike or the confrontations between the novel's four sets of fathers and sons: the Kumalos, the Jarvises, the Harrisons, and the Johannesburg Kumalos (John and his son, who represent a different kind of opposition to apartheid).

Instead of depicting violent scenes, Paton interweaves into the narrative events seemingly tangential to the main story line. These events are made interesting in themselves as history, but they are also made immediately pertinent to and revealing of the novel's action and characters. Thus the portrayal of the natives' boycott of the buses (Chapter 8) juxtaposes a vivid picture of this historical event with old Kumalo's search for his son, with Dubula's type of black leadership, and with Msimangu and Kumalo's reactions of some whites' incredible and courageous kindness to the blacks. (Yet another contrast is of course implied in the portrayal of the other black leaders, especially with Kumalo's brother, discussed below.) Similarly, the vignettes of Chapter 9, like John Dos Passos' *U.S.A.* vignettes of the American milieu of the early part of the century, depict the desperate natives' housing shortage and their misery and corruption which accompany the erection of Shanty Town. These vignettes appear as Kumalo prepares to visit his son and the girl in that very Shanty Town, an environment which has already predetermined those young people's wretched existences. In a comparable manner, the discovery of gold in Odendaalsrust (Chapter 23) occurs at the time of Absalom's trial, and it is tied in with the socio-economic realities that, like the treatment of the native miners, have brought and (unless ways are changed) will continue to bring tragedy to blacks and whites alike.

Striking in these descriptions are Paton's changing tone and point of view. Much of the story is seen through the eyes of an omniscient author whose tone ranges from reportorial objectivity to editorial evangelism. Parts of the story, however, are presented through the eyes of one or another of the characters, though this apparently limited point of view is controlled by the author to convey specific effects. Whatever the viewpoint, there are constant yet subtle shifts in tone, ranging from sympathy and hope through bewilderment, grief, and indignation.

The lyrical first paragraph of the brief opening chapter of Book I is identical, word for word, with the opening of Book II: *There is a lovely road that runs from Ixopo into the hills . . .* which *are lovely beyond any singing of it. . . .* Both openings describe the panoramic beauty and the lush vegetation of the hills. This is the home of Jarvis, and the opening description of Book II, which focuses on Jarvis, stops with the hills. The opening chapter of Book I, which focuses on Kumalo, continues with another and in all respects contrasting description, that of land that is barren and desolate, the valley in which Kumalo and the other blacks live. *The titihoya does not cry here any more,* for here there is insufficient food to attract even a bird. The tone becomes indignant as the green fecundity of the hills is contrasted with the red barrenness of the valley: *Stand shod upon it, for it is coarse and sharp, and the stones cut under the feet. It is not kept, or guarded, or cared for. . . .* Finally, as we are shown the sterile land in which only the aged are left, the tone becomes elegiac: *. . . the young men and the girls are away. The soil cannot keep them any more.*

Even more explicitly 'editorial' are the sections that follow newspaper accounts and such other apparently journalistic digressions as the vignettes on the erection of Shanty Town, the panoramic view of Johannesburg's fear after the murder, and the descriptions of the discovery of gold and the miners' strike. In these chapters' terminal sections, the attitudes implied in the apparently objective narrative are made explicit. After the newspaper report of the murder is read aloud by Father Vincent, for example, his listeners remain silent. But the author editorializes: *Sadness and fear and hate, how they well up in the heart and mind, whenever one opens the pages of these messengers of doom. Cry for the broken tribe, for the law and the custom that is gone. Aye, and cry aloud for the man who is dead, for the woman and children bereaved. Cry, the beloved country, these things are not yet at an end. The sun pours down on the earth, on the lovely land that man cannot enjoy. He knows only the fear of his heart.* The chapter immediately following (Chapter 12) presents numerous vignettes (paralleling the vignettes of the misery of Shanty Town in Chapter 9) vivifying the *fear in the land* and the *fear in the heart* that preclude enjoyment of life and the beauty of nature: scenes at a suburban meeting in which are expressed demands for greater police protection, proposals for the amelioration of the natives' poverty and despair, debates on the efficacy (and expense) of educating the blacks, and arguments about enforcing the pass laws; ladies chatting in a country club about various proposals that are unfeasible because they would inconvenience or threaten the whites and are therefore discarded (*Oh, it's too hot to argue. Get your racquet, my dear, they're calling us. . . ;* and other such settings and discussions. At the conclusion, the author once more editorializes: *Cry, the beloved country, for the unborn child that is the inheritor of our fear. . . .*

Understatement, deceptive simplicity, repetition, selectivity of narrative, episode, and setting, as well as the emotional charge of Paton's style—all these are manifested also in Paton's characterizations.

The novel's major character, the Reverend Stephen Kumalo, has evoked its readers' greatest compassion. Throughout his sufferings he remains an apparently humble, affectionate, kindly, simple, pious, God-fearing old man. Yet far from being simple or simply virtuous, he is portrayed in depth, as a flawed human being. Heroic in his ability to bear terrible private afflictions and tragedy, he is also able to continue to lead his parishioners out of communal suffering and tragedy. At the same time he is subject, too, to anger that manifests itself even in cruelty: to prove her *depravity,* Kumalo viciously tricks his son's mistress into admitting that she *could be willing* to become his own mistress; and he frightens his brother by lying, by falsely asserting that John is being observed by spies. Kumalo is guilty even of the most heinous of all Christian sins, despair, a sin against which both Msimangu and the kindly English pastor, Father Vincent, sternly caution him on different occasions. Kumalo is marred, too, by such lesser human flaws as jealousy (when he learns about the salary of the agricultural demonstrator), vanity (his boastful behavior toward fellow blacks in the train to Johannesburg), and pride (in being the brother of a man who enjoys material luxuries); and there is an allusion to an earlier episode that had nearly culminated in adultery with one of his parishioners. Finally, though he is well aware of its futility, Kumalo cannot resist repeatedly nagging his already contrite and doomed son with recriminations and unanswerable or futile questions. All these attributes of Kumalo are shown rather than stated, and their manifestations are narrated with striking verbal economy and deceptive simplicity.

Jarvis, Kumalo's white pendant, is more elusively characterized. Seen only after tragedy has struck, Jarvis is never actually shown in his opposition to his son's socio-political beliefs and practices. A single brief speech, however, makes clear that the unportrayed relationship between Jarvis and his son was identical to that of the Harrisons, his daughter-in-law's brother and father. One of their functions in the novel is, precisely, to suggest—without actually depicting—the affectionate yet antagonistic relationship that had existed between Jarvis and his son, Arthur. *My son and I didn't see eye to eye on the native question,* Jarvis tells the younger Harrison; *in fact, he and I got quite heated about it on more than one occasion.* But the novel itself depicts only Jarvis' painfully going through his dead son's belongings, agonizing over them, and finally coming to terms not merely with his son's murder (ironically by one of the very natives whose cause he had so fervently championed and whose love he had so widely enjoyed) but with the whole 'native question' and, indeed, with the central 'question' of South Africa—and of universal human brotherhood. His last gesture on that sad visit to Johannesburg is to leave young Harrison a large check with instructions to *do all the things you and Arthur wanted to do.*

Even some of the minor characters are portrayed in three-dimensional terms. The almost saintly Msimangu, as he himself says in his already quoted remark, is not flawless; though he later apologizes for his bitter, sarcastic comments to Kumalo about Absalom's girl and her unborn child, these comments deeply wounded the already stricken father, as Msimangu knew they were bound to do. His white counterpart, the sympathetic young reformatory worker (who in part personifies Paton himself), later apologizes for his similarly harsh outburst, which also was caused by such frustration, anger, and grief.

Though less subtle, the characterization of Kumalo's brother is striking. Both John's private and his public actions (especially in Chapter 26, which shows him on the speaker's platform, mesmerizing even his brother and worrying the white constabulary) help to develop his portrayal as a very great orator with the voice of a bull (and other bullish attributes) who could rally the natives to revolution in order to assert their human rights. But he stops short of the decisive step because he is a cowardly opportunist out only to get what he can in a society structured to keep him enslaved, and he is too amoral and—above all—too fearful of jeopardizing his personal comfort and success. *There is no applause in prison,* the omniscient author wryly observes, and Msimangu expresses his relief at John's corruption, *for if he were not corrupt, he could plunge this country into bloodshed. He is corrupted by his possessions, and he fears their loss, and the loss of the power he already has.* How right Msimangu is in this assessment is clearly shown in the brief description of John's immediate panicky reaction to his brother's suggestion that he might be arrested: *The big bull man wiped the sweat from his brow.* His deficient leadership is thus explicitly contrasted with that of Dubula and Tomlinson, especially as depicted in Dubula's participation in the bus boycott scene (Chapter 8).

In a comparable manner, their sister, Gertrude, another minor character, is also presented meaningfully. She is believable as a decent woman driven to brassy whoredom and shabby motherhood by apartheid and its effects. But she strives for decency, however unsuccessfully, escaping her tormenting fleshly temptations only by joining a nunnery. In contrast, Absalom's mistress, despite a similar past, fits into Kumalo's pious life style as soon as she enters Mrs. Lithebe's house. *The girl is not like Gertrude. She is openly glad to be in this house,* the narrator says, and Mrs. Lithebe does not need to chide her as she must chide Gertrude. Such carefully and subtly and symmetrically wrought contrasts are achieved in the portrayals of these women just as they are in the portrayals of the Kumalo brothers, of Jarvis, and of Harrison—all members of the conflicting old order as well as fathers in conflict with their sons, proponents of differing new moral as well as new social orders.

All such subtleties as well as the earlier noted understatements and modulations in viewpoint are not practicable in the theatre. Here, as been suggested before, speech and action, taking the place of the written word, must move more rapidly, simply, and clearly. Yet even within the limits imposed by the medium of the stage, Anderson in *Lost in the Stars* strove not only to dramatize Paton's story but also to communicate Paton's attitudes, to recreate the effects Paton had sought, and to evoke comparable responses.

The most immediately striking changes in the stage adaptation are the additions, the various types of ensemble and choral 'numbers' that are obligatory in the musical theatre: comedy (the honky-tonk law court spoof of I 6 as well as Alex' playful song and game of II 5), sex (Linda's *Who'll Buy?* song in I 6), romance (Irina's *Trouble Man* and *Stay Well* of I 7 and II 2), and sentimentality (winsome children—Alex, and to a lesser degree Edward—and Kumalo's *Thousands of Miles* and *The Little Grey House* songs in I 1 and I 5). Though fashioned for Broadway audiences, these numbers are well integrated in the plot and they do not distort or detract from Paton's story. Some of them, particularly Kumalo's songs, even enhance it. *Thousands of Miles,* as will be seen, transcends the sentimental and provides an effective musical equivalent to Paton's final narrative in the novel. *Lost in the Stars,* the first-act curtain song, movingly dramatizes the old pastor's temporary religious doubts—perhaps not quite as *sinful* as his despair, but certainly as effective in the theatre as Msimangu's and Father Vincent's castigations are in the novel. Similarly, Kumalo's agonizing over Absalom's dilemma in *The Soliloquy* (*Must be tell a lie and live—* / *Or speak truth and die?* II 1), while it adds a doubt not entertained by Kumalo in the novel, prepares for his appeal to Jarvis for a mercy plea in the next scene, and conveys his impotence in helping his son as powerfully as does his futile nagging in the novel.

These musical additions have the same effect as Paton's novelistic understatements: they heighten the emotional impact. Kurt Weill's characteristic 'song play' score, though it lacks the Brechtian bite of his most famous works, articulates Anderson's stark if sometimes sentimental lyrics which explicitly articulate Paton's implications. Matching these lyrics, Weill's swelling, operatic music and his jazz idiom permeate his score for *Lost in the Stars*—his last score for Broadway and the one Lotte Lenya thought superior to all his others except for *Die Dreigroschenoper* and *Mahagonny.*

Almost as obvious a change as the addition of music is the simplification of the novel's plot. It is reduced to but a few highlights, for on the stage Paton's story necessarily had to be cut all the more because of the added 'numbers'. Anderson sacrificed many of the novel's subtleties and omitted many of its episodes entirely. The omissions constitute substantial elements of the novel: Kumalo's extensive associa-

tions with Msimangu, Father Vincent, Mrs. Lithebe, and others (none of whom appear in the play); fictionalized treatments of historical events (the bus boycott, the discovery of gold at Odendaalsrust, and the miners' strike); Kumalo's reunion and subsequent relations with Gertrude (who does not appear in the play either); most of the episodes dealing with Jarvis and with John Kumalo and, of course, everything relating to their associates; and virtually the novel's entire denouement.

Such substantive cuts necessitated changes in plot and character, and additions of new episodes to clarify and speed the action along. Thus Kumalo's extended and eventful search for Absalom, constituting much of the novel's Book I, is telescoped into a single scene (I 4), the dread as Kumalo hurries alone from address to address being conveyed effectively by the chorus. His two visits to Absalom's Shanty Town shack (Chapters 10 and 16) are fused in I 7, where the pregnant girl, Irina (she is nameless in the novel), sings tenderly about her love for her *Trouble Man.* In place of Msimangu and others who in the novel share Kumalo's experiences, thoughts, and discussions, Anderson expands the role of Gertrude's boy, Alex. It is he who has a long talk with Jarvis' grandson (not Kumalo, who in Chapters 31 and 33 has three different encounters with the white boy). And Alex also appears prominently in various episodes invented by Anderson, such as the one in which Kumalo sings to him about their home in Ndotsheni (I 5).

The portrayal of the murder, which in the novel is revealed indirectly and only gradually, through rumors and in the cross examination (Chapter 22), is acted out on the stage in a brief but tense and violent scene (I 8). The ensuing communal fear (described in the various episodes of the novel's twelfth chapter) is dramatized by a chorus of blacks and whites on a Shanty Town street (I 10). On the stage, both fathers are seen aware of the murder immediately: there is no dramatization of Chapters 18-21, for example, which portray Jarvis' learning of and attempting to come to terms with his son's death; or of Chapters 11 and 13, in which Kumalo has premonitions that associate Absalom with the latest reported murder. Necessarily such expediting of the plot sacrifices suspense as well as subtlety of characterization.

Anderson's most radical change of the story line is in the denouement. Paton's ending fuses Kumalo's acceptance of divine will and an understanding and mutual compassion between Kumalo and Jarvis as men and as fathers as well as members of different races, within the social and economic context of apartheid. The complexity and implications of that context, so sensitively structured in the novel's last five chapters, are deleted from the play. Anderson's simplification not only does away with the perhaps undramatizable descriptions of Kumalo's feelings and thoughts during the solitary vigil on the mountain. It substitutes for them

Kumalo's and Jarvis' exclamations of brotherhood—*I have a friend*—as the white man puts his arm around the black man and the clock strikes the fatal hour. This simplistic resolution is undeniably sentimental as well as meretricious.

As these changes suggest, much of the novel's subtlety and suspense are sacrificed. Characterization in the play too is simplified, both in variety and depth. Not only are Msimangu, Father Vincent, Mrs. Lithebe, Gertrude, as well as the various Jarvis in-laws and friends and many others, black and white, completely eliminated in the play. The major characters themselves are diminished as characters.

Kumalo remains a simple, humble, affectionate, kindly, pious and God-fearing old man—but the 'negative' qualities that make him believably human are missing. Instead of being shown in sinful despair he is shown in abject misery. And he has none of the flaws he exhibits in the novel: jealousy, vanity, pride, and fleshly temptations. Omitted, too, are his futile nagging of the contrite Absalom. There is only a single manifestation of his anger (Kumalo's tricking Irina into agreeing to become his mistress, Chapter 16 // I 7, its sexual suggestiveness perhaps making it irresistible for a Broadway musical.

Jarvis, instead of being Kumalo's white pendant—a major and well-rounded character who helps to universalize the meaning of the novel's plot—here is a villainous but a minor character. In Anderson's dramatization of the racial themes, Jarvis is a stereotyped bigot who at the very end 'reforms', suddenly and totally. In an early scene (I 2), for example, the arguments between Jarvis and his son, merely hinted at in the novel, are portrayed in an explosive outburst of paternal fury when Arthur, in violation of South African custom, crosses racial lines to greet Kumalo. The novel's muted portrayal of Jarvis' feelings after the murder (Chapters 18-21) is similarly changed: instead of Paton's descriptions of Jarvis' reactions of shock, grief, and concern for his wife, Anderson has Jarvis merely rail contemptuously at all blacks (I 9). The identical effect is achieved in the complete alteration of the post-murder meeting between the two fathers: instead of the painfully allusive few words following their accidental confrontation (Chapter 25), Anderson has Kumalo seek Jarvis' intercession for mercy for Absalom, thus eliciting yet another of Jarvis' bitter racial tirades (II 1).

The character of Kumalo's brother, John, is similarly diminished and altered. In the play he is simply a sleazy operator and a gross human being. His summoning letter to Kumalo (Anderson's substitute for Msimangu's letter in the novel) foreshadows his actual appearance in the play in the letter's opening words (*Dear Stephen, you old faker in Christ . . .*) and in the blunt report of their sister's flagrant promiscuity (not even mentioned in the original letter by Msimangu)

which, he complains, is ruining his business (I 1). The substitution of two bland Zulu or Bantu political lieutenants for the novel's black leadership group of which he is a powerful and shrewd member further diminishes his significance in the play. These and other simplifications of plot and characterization seem to destroy a complex, moving, and believable story. Nonetheless, Anderson and Weill's generic conversion of this story is essentially faithful to and communicates much of the effect of Paton's work.

For what is most felicitously theatricalized is what is central to the novel, the narrative and the perspective. As has been suggested above, Paton's authorial intrusions and shifting viewpoint are not only integral to the story line. Rather, it is they that give the story much of its meaning and power. And while the story and the characters are indeed considerably simplified in the play, these fundamental elements of narrative intrusion and point of view are effectively and pervasively adapted into dramatic terms.

In place of the novel's narrator and author, a chorus of 'singers' and a 'Leader' articulate the narrative and the viewpoint of the action on the stage. Commenting on individual episodes and participating in them, the chorus and Leader are the most prominent characters on the stage—visually, aurally, and kinetically. Throughout the play, they sit, stand, and move about on flights of steps that lead from the orchestra pit up to the center and the sides of the stage. Thus the chorus and the Leader are invested with the fluidity and flexibility to translate the shifting narrative tone of the novel into quite theatrical terms. The lyrical introduction of the novel (*There is a lovely road that runs from Ixopo into the hills . . .*), for example, is sung by the Leader in the opening number of the play, the contrast between the hill and the valley stressed by the spoken interpolations of a straight man (the 'Answerer'). *The Wild Justice* song that starts the second act does not (as does the novel's opening of Book II) repeat these words. However, it conveys a similar theme: the injustice of men, who punish crime by committing further crimes—in contrast to *wild* (or nature's) justice which, as a series of images suggests, is divine and ineffable. (The injustice of man is the subject again in the brief lyrical choral interpolations during the trial in II 3.)

Paton's angry compassion is expressed by the chorus in its principal numbers. Immediately after Absalom's conviction, the chorus sings *Cry, the Beloved Country* (II 4), a lament for the human waste, rapacity, destruction, and fear that will pass on to the next generation. The chorus' reprise following Absalom and Irina's marriage in prison explicitly incorporates this thought into the general lament: *Cry, the unborn son, / fatherless, / . . . / Cry, the beloved country!* Echoing the novel's narrator, the chorus, constituting Kumalo's congregation at his resignation, prays for divine guidance as it reviews man's brief *earthly pilgrimage* in the *A Bird of Passage* song (II 5).

Here and elsewhere the chorus not only comments on but also itself participates in and becomes a part of the action. As a group of Zulus bidding farewell to a companion at the village railroad station (I 2), it intersperses its singing with the thrice reiterated lines suggested in the novel (Chapter 2) by Kumalo and his wife, that while

> *White man go to Johannesburg—*
> *He come back, he come back.*
> *Black man go to Johannesburg—*
> *Never come back, never come back!*

To accentuate the frantic father's search for his son in Johannesburg (I 4), the chorus is used imaginatively and effectively to recite the various addresses he is given, to comment on the tearful omens (*A boding song, / Searing like flame*), and to articulate Kumalo's humiliation when he hears that his son has been in jail (*In prison cells they give you a number, / Tag your clothes with it, / Print your shame!*). Reporting the crime, the chorus in the *Murder in Parkwold* song (I 8) conveys the frenzy as it repeats the simple title phrase, adding descriptive phrases spoken (not sung) by individual members of the chorus who represent various townspeople: *Nobody knows why or by whom! . . . He* [the victim] *went to help the servant!* etc. In a song that constitutes the whole of I 10, a chorus of black and white singers articulates various forms of the *Fear of the few for the many, / Fear of the many for the few!* that pervades the land following this latest crime. In the play's final scene, the chorus dramatizes and heightens the apprehensive suspense as Kumalo awaits the hour of his son's execution by the repeated chanting of the ominous words *Four o'clock, it will soon be four.*

The play's curtain is the choral reprise of Kumalo's *Thousands of Miles* song, his first song in the play:

> *Each lives alone in a world of dark,*
> *Crossing the skies in a lonely arc,*
> *Save when love leaps out like a leaping spark*
> *Over thousands, thousands of miles!*

These words are the peroration of the paean to familial love with which Kumalo had consoled his wife in the play's modification of the couple's painful recriminations during the letter episode (Chapter 2 // I 1). Coming here, right after the Kumalo-Jarvis 'brotherhood' scene and at the very end of the play, the choral reprise constitutes an effective equivalent to Paton's narrative section that ends the novel: his confidence, however tentatively formulated, that South Africa will some day become emancipated from racism, hatred, and fear. Though in manifestly different ways, the endings of both the novel and the play communicate similar feelings

with equally great intensity. But each does so with complete appropriateness and consistency to its particular genre.

Weill's music and Anderson's lyrics as well as his selectivity and reshaping of the novel's episodes—all these translate Paton's novel into theatrical terms. As does any translation, of course, this one too presents many problems, some of them insoluble. Necessarily something of the original is lost, as is always the case. At the same time (as is true particularly of poetry), effective translating can be done only by reshaping the original in accord with the translator's own and very different language. The result is a new work that may be as good as or even better than the original. Though *Lost in the Stars* may not be 'better' than **Cry, the Beloved Country,** or perhaps is not even 'as good', it conveys the essentials of the original work in a powerful manner. Both in artistic and in commercial terms, it successfully transposed Paton's novel from the printed page to the living theatre, employing the different means necessary to portray similar characters and actions, to express similar attitudes, and to convey similar effects.

J. B. Thompson (essay date March 1981)

SOURCE: "Poetic Truth in 'Too Late the Phalarope,'" in *English Studies in Africa,* Vol. 24, No. 1, March, 1981, pp. 37-44.

[*Below, Thompson explains how* Too Late the Phalarope *manifests universality despite the contemporary relevance of the novel's historical aspects.*]

Instead of entitling this essay as I have done, I might simply have said an 'interpretation' of the novel, or more confidently (and, probably, more honestly) 'its meaning' or 'its value for us'. But what I wanted to stress were the limitations of focusing on the mere 'historic truth' of the novel. By historic truth I mean of course something much broader than what Aristotle had in mind in his *Poetics* and what historiographers aim at. Any novel offers itself not as fact but as fiction, but it is nevertheless possible to limit its significance to a particular time and place, to the social situation it purports to describe, or the one out of which it grew. (The two are of course the same in the case of **Too Late the Phalarope.**) This circumscription of literature happens not only when one adopts an explicitly historical approach, but also when one places too much emphasis on its historical aspects, or for that matter on its anthropological, sociological, economic or political aspects. The immediate relevance of a novel may in fact obscure its universality.

Too Late the Phalarope is, no less than Turgenev's *Fathers and Sons,* a great classic that will be read long after the Immorality Act has been blotted from the statute book as completely as Pieter's name was from the Van Vlaanderen family bible; long after apartheid has *really* 'died' and the Afrikaner has taken his rightful place in our society. But Alan Paton's fame as a champion of liberalism and the current world preoccupation with racialism in South Africa may well result in excessive emphasis being given to the novel's political or sociological aspects.

It certainly is a bitter attack on the Immorality Act, the "iron law" of "a people of rock and stone in a land of rock and stone" and the ferocity of it is brought home by the case of Smith, "an ordinary man, quiet and inoffensive" as his name implies and "a religious man after his own fashion" who is driven so far as to drown his partner in crime, chop off her head and bury it and sink her body in the river with weights. Similarly when Pieter's guilt is made public, it is realized immediately by Kappie, the captain and his aunt that he might very well be driven to suicide. But it would be absurd to say that the novel was about "Act 5 of 1927" or even about the mores of the community which imposes a "sentence for life" on people who contravene it.

> **One must indeed pay tribute to Alan Paton's integrity as an artist, his refusal to indulge in mere 'finger-pointing', his deep sense of the delicacy and complexity of human relationships.**
> **—J. B. Thompson**

Had this sort of propaganda been the author's purpose, he would surely have adopted a very different strategy. He might for instance have shown how ordinary members of the police force—and good Christians too—are compelled by the Act to become professional voyeurs: I remember a case of a policeman climbing a tree outside a bedroom in a Johannesburg suburb (armed with binoculars, I think) for a purpose as obscene as May's when she climbs the tree in Chaucer's *Merchant's Tale*. More important, however, than the sort of ammunition the author neglected to use is the sort of material he does use, the quality of the relationship with which he confronts us. To bring home the iniquity of the act and the sickness of the mentality behind it, he would surely have depicted a decent, upright man like Pieter falling foul of the tyrannical law, as a result of a noble passion for a soul mate whose skin pigmentation happened to be black; a case of "mind-forged manacles", imposed, in the name of a highly selective, arbitrary and hypocritical morality, upon true love (the sort of thing I read of as having happened once in Beaufort West which is perhaps the Cape equivalent of Venterspan as far as cultural deprivation is concerned, where a Brown middle-aged Anglican priest fell in love with the White spinster who was the village librarian and they were subjected

to the indignity of a court-appearance). But Stephanie is no soul mate of Pieter's and not even a 'playmate', but is joylessly used by him as a sexual object for sinister psychological purposes of his own, and certainly not in a spirit of heroic defiance of a law that would fetter love.

It seems to be a proof of the author's integrity or honesty that he presents this sort of relationship, which, given the stratification or compartmentalization of our society, could probably be proved, statistically, to be typical of contraventions of the Act. I feel, however, that it is typical only in a negative way, that is as regards the absence of 'true-love' or a meaningful relationship. Pieter's complex motivation is, surely, far from representative (in a sociological sense, at any rate). His desire for Stephanie—one hesitates to call it sexual—is condemned by him as a "sin" and he clear-sightedly diagnoses it as a "mad sickness" and as "some mad desire of a sick and twisted soul". He is pained and perplexed to find himself tempted by something "unspeakable . . . that [brings] no joy" and that he hates. Not that he hates Stephanie herself: all he feels for her, apart from his temptation, is the sort of benevolence he feels towards all members of "the black nation".

The nature of this "mad sickness" which he himself cannot understand is, I feel, the crux of the novel, the question of universal significance that it raises. What makes him do it? The narrator's description of him as being "denied" and her image of the "man who is robbed of a jewel and goes seeking it amongst the dross and filth" refers of course to his wife's sexual reticence. Here one must indeed pay tribute to Alan Paton's integrity as an artist, his refusal to indulge in mere 'finger-pointing', his deep sense of the delicacy and complexity of human relationships. Nella is certainly not portrayed as frigid or unloving, though Pieter's mother perhaps goes too far when she declares in her charity: "she has no blame". Timid country-girl though she is, she was the one who, during the courtship that was so "long and shy and protracted" took the initiative that led to their marriage, and we are given two vivid and moving scenes in which their "joy" of their love is "complete" and in which she takes the initiative. The first is after the new dominee's sermon, when Pieter is self-conscious and hesitant on sensing her nervousness about any love he shows her, and the second is on her return from their temporary separation when she, not he, makes up a bed for them in front of the symbolic fire. We are left in no doubt that such generosity in love would make Pieter safe but we are also left in no doubt that these experiences are the exception, not the rule, that what is safe for him is seen by her as dangerous, for she very soon starts "withdrawing, to some safer ground, to some world where she was safe and sure". As her husband explains it, her idea of love, one that is "good and true but twisted in some small place" is that, "the love of the body, though good and true, was apart from the love of the soul, and had a place where it stayed and had to be called from, and when it was called and done, then it went back to its place and stayed till it was called again, according to some rule and custom". No wonder he has to ask her "to love [him] more often". Here again the author's integrity is apparent, in that we do not have to take the word of one of the parties involved: the shortcomings of her basic attitude to sex are cogently and impartially dramatized by the letter she writes from her parents' farm. In his letter, he has explained that it is not just 'sex' that he is after: "my love of you is a love of everything about you, and not just a love of your body" and "my love of your body is part of my love of you yourself" and on this basis has made a delicate and tactful appeal. Hurt by his implied criticism, she defends herself in terms that lend support to his accusation. Talking, for instance, of her loneliness without her husband, she concedes that she does "have the children" with her but adds that "that is not quite the same". This suggests a serious underestimation of the importance of sex in marriage. And her sarcastic rejoinder "Do you think that Frikkie and Greta came straight from heaven?" proves nothing more than that they have had sexual intercourse twice—in how many years?—and leaves one wondering about the spirit of her participation, if that is the word. And as for the way she feels towards it, the most she thinks of claiming in arguing the normality of her attitude is that she "accept[s]" the kind of love he writes about. Acceptance is usually a response to something unwelcome or unpleasant, a resignation to a necessary evil. And this impression that she generally puts up with love-making for his sake or to be 'kind' is confirmed by her subsequent affirmation that "a woman's nature is different from a man's" and that "for a happy marriage each must give up something, which I try to do". No wonder he reads her letter "with a face of stone".

Pieter's relationship with his wife is far from ideal, but Paton makes it clear that his problem goes much deeper than sexual frustration as a result of his wife's somewhat puritanical attitude. The very fact that he needs her love to make him "safe" suggests dangers whose origin lies elsewhere. What brings home most dramatically that his sickness does not stem in the last analysis from marital difficulties is the strategic placing of his fall in the narrative chain of the novel: it comes immediately after he has been picked up by his cousin Anna, and has enjoyed a drinking session with her at the local hotel. Here, one would think, would be the perfect opportunity for someone suffering from sexual deprivation. Anna is, after all, the one "who wears the yellow trousers" and "talk[s] in English"—both pointing to moral laxity of course. She adores Pieter and declares quite openly that he is the reason why she never married. She is thoroughly bored with her holiday in Venterspan (her parents would not trust her in Durban and regarded her proposed trip there in the light of a journey to the devil), his wife is away, he has been confiding in Anna, and they are in the precarious situation of having drunk too much. But Pieter

does not commit adultery with her and more important is not even tempted, and their outing ends with her "lean[ing] over the gate" and chastely kissing him. This gate, I might mention, is, like the many doors in the novel, a symbol of a barrier between people, this time one that is not being broken down. And, if I may digress a moment, I might mention here the subtlety with which these and other related details of body language are consistently handled by Alan Paton in a manner reminiscent of Dickens and even of Conrad at his best. Immediately after this, for instance, we see Pieter "bump . . . against the iron standard at the corner of the fence" as if in anticipation of his crime, and, within a page, he is depicted symbolically taking off his uniform, carefully refraining from looking at the beds of his wife and children, "lock[ing] the front door after him" and standing "a moment" at his own gate, before disappearing into the still darkness.

It is not, then, a simple "desire of the flesh". He lusts after someone with very few personal charms, who is a member of a generally despised race and of an inferior social class, who is not only dull and destitute but is also an habitual criminal (Stephanie is forced to brew and sell liquor illegally and is in and out of jail). If his aim were to bring the maximum disgrace upon his family, he could not have made a better choice, and that, I feel, is precisely the point. It is a sort of blind irrational retaliation. His father, he realizes, has never really loved him and has, in fact, been ashamed of "the woman" in him, his tenderness and gentleness and his fondness for books and flowers. No wonder Pieter implies to Kappie that the "trouble" started when he was born. Hurt by this rejection, the sensitive child "armour[s] himself against hurts and the world" by withdrawing into himself. But he was always "eager to please" and later speculates that his trouble might be that he had "perhaps been too obedient as a boy, too anxious to please and win approval, so that [he] learned to show outwardly what [he] was not within" and that "perhaps when you were too obedient, and did not do openly what others did, and were quiet in the church and hard-working at school, that [*sic*] some unknown rebellion brewed in you, doing harm to you". Or again "Had I had too great a hunger for praise so that I turned in on myself, and hid all my weaknesses?" The consequence is an eruption of defiance that is tantamount to saying: "Since you cannot accept me for what I am, I'll give you good reason to reject me." His friend Japie the social welfare officer who "tinkered in his merry way with this problem and that, and saw nothing of the greatest problem of them all", unwittingly puts his finger on the root cause of his friend's problem when he declares rather pompously in the "university words": "We begin to think that lack of affection is one of the greatest causes of juvenile delinquency in a child".

Pieter's deprivation of paternal love is not merely asserted by the narrator in the abstract but is vigorously dramatized in concrete detail. For instance, Jakob never once smoked the pipe his son chose for him for a birthday present, and, before this, imposed on his sensitive son the unimaginative and severe penalty of forbidding him to go on with his stamps just because he once failed to come top of his class. The difference between his wife's understanding and compassion and his "unsmiling" and unloving justice is effortlessly established in two brief lines. "The boy wasn't well, said my sister . . . I said put them away, he said". Nor is this just a case of excessive sharpness on his part: one senses here a resentment of a part of his son's nature and an attempt to obliterate it. Later, when a professor at Stellenbosch pays his son a glowing tribute, he does not even bother to tell him. Worse, the DSO he won in the war is contemptuously dismissed as "*uitheemse kaf*".

The constraint in the relationship on both sides, even when overtures of friendship are being made, is neatly and unobtrusively conveyed. Pieter's response to his aunt's anxious reminder: "you won't forget his birthday" is "As if I would dare", and when Jakob and Pieter happen to meet in Kappie's store, he approaches his own son "*determined* to be friendly". The sequel is that Pieter is "caught" and starts like the guilty child his father still treats him as. The psychological and moral complexity of this scene, where the existence of a barrier is brought home to the reader by means of a well-meant attempt to break it down, points to the same sort of authorial integrity as was manifest in the portrait of the wife. The father is no mere villain or tyrant: in fact he has all the virtues except, unfortunately, the one that matters most of all. And in the period covered by the narrative he is frequently seen reaching out to his son, the pattern culminating in his buying for his son a set of special stamps, of all things. His delight in the book so carefully chosen by his son for his birthday strengthens the sort of impulse that made him determined to be friendly in the shop, so much so that he actually proposes an outing or picnic with his son, ostensibly to prove the book wrong about phalaropes being restricted to coastal areas. In fact he is "looking for no phalarope, but for something he had lost, twenty, thirty years ago". He cannot, however, propose an outing with his son "carelessly and naturally", despite or rather because of the earnestness of his effort, and so "the unusual words that his wife had never thought to hear spoken, but which she had prayed to hear these many years", "cry themselves out aloud in the room".

The overture has come 'too late'. Pieter has not yet broken the law but he is already deeply compromised with Stephanie and the insidious and relentless advance of his "mad sickness" to this stage has been forcefully dramatized. At the fall we remember—and this setting seems highly appropriate after the powerful evocation of the Eden-like "freshness of the day . . . the cleanness of the grass country [and] the purity of the great bowl of the sky"—while the two of them are alone, there is a moment of intimate physical contact, at first

accidental but deliberately indulged and prolonged. And we are given a subtle hint of his own evaluation of this seemingly trivial incident when, just afterwards, he sees young Vorster "jump[ing] like a cat, softly and easily" and observes wistfully, "I could do that once", as if he has lost his youthful exuberance. The next step, placed just after it transpires that the book interests and delights his father (such scenes evoking hope are skilfully interposed between the steps of his downfall, for an effect of tragic inevitability) is when she calls at his father's house to ask him to "tell the government" that she has found a job. When he asks why she has come to him and not to the social welfare officer, she replies: "because the baas would do it for me". He fails to dismiss her suggestion of intimacy as he could so easily by saying "in a voice of every day": "how can you know such a thing?" or "do not be foolish" but confirms it by saying "quiet and trembling, how did you know?" At this juncture they are interrupted and she puts up a poor pretence of discussing police matters; but what is most significant is that he is "angry and afraid too", "not so much because of the boldness of the look as of the poor pretence that followed it". Like Macbeth he is worried not so much by his sin as by the chance of its being found out. The next step is even more drastic: she calls at his house in his wife's absence and suddenly comes past him into the kitchen. And, momentously, he "shut[s] the door". Throughout the novel doors are invested with great symbolic significance and the closing of this one acknowledges and increases the intimacy between them at the same time as it reduces the chance of discovery. And when she offers to let him know about the job, he replies rather irresolutely, "do not come any more to this house", thereby leaving open the possibility of meetings elsewhere. This is how she takes it and in telling him "when I am working I go home at eight o'clock past the place where the baas saw me running" she has arranged a tryst. Instead of his closing the door on her, she herself opens it and lets herself out. His doom is thus virtually sealed before the picnic is arranged.

On the outing itself, Jakob is "more gentle" and seems to lavish on Pieter's son some of the tenderness that Pieter himself had so desperately needed. When the phalarope appears, Jakob "rest[s] his arm on his son's shoulder to point" and so unprecedented is even this degree of tenderness that Pieter is "moved in some deep place within and something welled up within him that, if not mastered, could have burst out of his throat and mouth, making him a girl or child". But the intimacy associated with the father's discovery of the phalarope has come after Pieter has broken the law a second time "of his own will and choice". And it is a subtle touch, not always fully appreciated, that it should be the phalarope of all birds to bring father and son together, temporarily at least, for its distinctive feature is that it is the male which hatches the eggs and cares for the young, and shows, in general, the sort of tenderness for them that is associated with women. Thus we feel the full force of the narrator's observation at the beginning that her nephew had "something of the woman in him" but "the father none at all until it was too late".

Closely related to this theme of love and complete acceptance is that of compassion and forgiveness, as embodied ideally in Pieter's mother as against her patriarchal husband's stern, cruel, eye-for-an-eye type of justice, the fundamental contrast between them being succinctly established by Pieter's observation that his father he "could never have openly disobeyed" and his mother he "could never knowingly have hurt". And inseparable from all these is the Conradian idea of human interdependence, of our essential reliance on our neighbours for moral support.

Throughout his temptation and trial, Pieter feels a desperate longing "to tell one human soul of the misery of my life". A wise and loving father would be the obvious person but it is this very lack that has caused the whole problem. Nor can he confide in his wife though he does try to. But bearing in mind her idea of the coarseness of men's sexuality and her unforgiving attitude to Dick's "chasing" a Black girl—one remembers the bitter irony of this woman's not even wanting Dick in their lounge—he realizes she is hardly likely to understand and might well "fly away". He seriously contemplates confiding in the young dominee for whom rugby is "almost a religion"—he studied at Stellenbosch—but when he is called "the Lion of the North" and is accorded the adulation that is owing to a potential Springbok when he desperately needs help as a struggling Christian, his pride gets the better of him and he "[draws] back from the very edge of his salvation" or in the words of his aunt, "held [his] peace that was no peace at all". The same happens with his "true and faithful" friend, Kappie, who "understood the ways of the world and did not judge". He actually knocks on Kappie's door but when he enters he finds he lacks the resolution to open the doors of his soul. His other friend, Japie, is of course too flippant and superficial even to be considered as a confidant.

What finally provokes Pieter to broach the subject with a fellow human being is, appropriately, a gesture of tenderness from someone who might be seen as a surrogate father. At the time of the smallpox epidemic, the captain, noticing Pieter's exhaustion, calls him by his first name and puts his hand tenderly on his shoulder "as some fathers touch their grown sons and as some do not". Pieter is "moved in some deep place within", as he will be on the picnic, and momentously declares: "There's something I ought to tell you, sir." But he is silenced by the captain's "authority" and dismissed with a well-meant but disastrous "farewell salute". His aunt continually reproaches herself for not forcing him to confide in her, but on the day of the birthday party it is made clear that she could have done nothing. His startling declaration that he wishes he had not been born gives her

an opening which she too eagerly seizes. Realizing that "he had opened the door of his soul and now repented it" she tries to force her way in before he shuts it again and literally shuts the pantry door on the two of them—as Stephanie will later—but realizes immediately that she had not "shut [herself] in" but "out". And on the picnic she receives a similar rebuff. This forcing of a confidence is seen to work in the case of young Vorster who has been having sleepless nights, like Pieter's, over a trivial debt, and this makes one wonder whether Kappie might not have saved him had he been less self-effacing and less in awe of Pieter. But this was not to be. And in the end, Pieter's craving for sympathetic understanding finds its only outlet in the keeping of a diary.

Kappie provides the crucial link between the different aspects of the theme of love in that, although he fails to elicit the confession that would have saved Pieter, he extends to him the understanding and love that give him the courage to go on living after his fall. This is graphically portrayed by Kappie's sitting down "beside him" at the side of the deserted rugby field with "his arm about him". His father by this stage has in his hurt pride (and let us not forget that this was, after all, Pieter's purpose) shut the doors of his house and withdrawn completely into himself. After his death, however, his wife opens the front door and has the blinds rolled up "so that something [can] go out of [the] house" and it is the sustaining love of people like her and her sister and Kappie and the captain that leaves us with "some kind of peace" and with some "comfort in desolation".

These, surely, are no mere "African truths".

Irma Ned Stevens (essay date Winter 1981)

SOURCE: "Paton's Narrator Sophie: Justice and Mercy in *Too Late the Phalarope*," in *The International Review*, Vol. 8, No. 1, Winter, 1981, pp. 68-70.

[*In the following essay, Stevens examines Sophie's function and position as narrator in* Too Late the Phalarope *in terms of the novel's concerns with the natures of obedience and love.*]

On its publication in 1953, **Too Late the Phalarope,** Alan Paton's second novel, was greeted with praise. With increasing focus on civil rights, not only in the Union of South Africa but also in the United States, the novel has become even more timely than when it was originally published. Further, Paton's continuing participation in politics and harassment by his own government have focused public attention on his works as social documents. Certainly, his novels are reflections of social injustice. Their importance as social criticism, however, should not blind us to their worth as literature.

While traditional standards of literary criticism have been applied to *Cry, the Beloved Country, Too Late the Phalarope* has been especially neglected since the publication reviews.

Like *Cry, the Beloved Country,* Paton's second novel reveals a skillful use of traditional techniques of fiction, including point of view. In *Cry, the Beloved Country,* the first-person narrator in the first and third sections is Stephen Kumalo, a Zulu minister who leaves his rural Ixopo to search for his lost son in Johannesburg. In the intervening second section, the narrator is James Jarvis, a wealthy European farmer who is Kumalo's neighbor and whose son Kumalo's son has killed. This double point of view serves to emphasize the two men's parallel spiritual growth, their movement through suffering to self-knowledge and knowledge about their nation. In *Too Late the Phalarope,* Paton also uses a first-person narrator, Sophie, the beloved maiden aunt of the main character, Pieter van Vlaanderen. The novel is composed of Sophie's reflections about her family as she reads sections of a diary Pieter has left her while he is in prison. The novel concerns both the nature of obedience, questioning the morality of a nation's requiring obedience to man-made laws which conflict with God's laws, and also the nature of love, recognizing the unity of body and spirit. Throughout the novel the mercy-justice dichotomy, as it affects obedience and love, is repeatedly dramatized in the action or examined in commentary by either Sophie herself, Pieter's diary, or the young dominee's sermons.

Paton suggests in several ways that the narrator's view is the standard by which to judge the characters' concepts of obedience and love. The first clue to Sophie's importance is her name, for her view is indeed that of "wisdom." She describes herself as an observer rather than a participant in life, and she is loved and respected by all the characters. Sophie's position of wisdom is a middle way between two extremes symbolized by Pieter's father, Jakob, whom Pieter recalls as "strict and stern," and his mother, "tender and loving." Allegorically, the parents seem to represent the stern justice of the Old-Testament God, as opposed to the loving mercy of the New-Testament God, with Pieter as an Everyman searching for the right way. Sophie's position is closer to that of Pieter's mother than his father, but in Sophie we see more strength and questioning than in his mother. Several times Sophie condemns traditional concepts of love and obedience as she recognizes how man's laws can wrongly conflict with God's. About Nella, Pieter's childlike wife, Sophie thinks, "For the mean and the cruel were not destroyed, only the kind and gentle. And God forgive me that I should write such words, which seem to doubt His Providence, but I will be obedient even when the words seem disobedient, and will obey the voice that says to me, what thou seest, write it in a book." And later, "But may God forgive me if what I write is wrong, and against His Laws; for I believe His laws are made in love, and though one does not understand, one should be obedient. And it is because I am obedient that I write these words." Sophie recognizes then the superiority of individual conscience over church dogma or state law.

Unlike Nella, Sophie also understands the nature of love. Nella, reared in the Dutch Reformed Church of the Afrikaner, accepts the Puritan belief in the evil of the body, but Sophie knows that mortal love must include the physical: "Ah, how great is God's gift of love, that love which is of body and mind and soul, and what should she who had it, not understand, and why should I understand who never had it?"

Sophie's wisdom becomes especially apparent where her commentary on a scene follows her reading of sections in Pieter's diary which dramatize that scene. Paton frequently juxtaposes Sophie's view as an observer with Pieter's feelings as they appear to Sophie as she watches him; then in turn Paton juxtaposes Pieter's apparent emotions with Sophie's later understanding of Pieter's actual emotions. Thus, although Paton does not employ two separate narrators as in his first novel, he achieves in this second novel a similar irony or recognition of discrepancies between appearance and reality by juxtaposing two characters' views of the same event. For example, the reader hears through Sophie the young Dominee Vos's two sermons about mercy and obedience. Then the reader sees through her eyes Pieter's response to the sermon and reexperiences with her Pieter's self-hate as she reads his diary. Similarly, at the birthday party for Jakob, the reader learns first in Pieter's diary of the visit of Stephanie, Pieter's black lover, and then reads Sophie's commentary as she recognizes that Stephanie is the cause of Pieter's suffering. In another illustration of the dual view, Sophie describes her pride at watching Pieter play rugby and her lack of understanding of Pieter's suspicious actions. In a succeeding section, the reader learns with Sophie of Pieter's fear that the young recruit Vorster knows of Pieter's liaison with Stephanie. In all three examples, the juxtaposition of sections of Pieter's diary with Sophie's commentary is effective because it allows the reader to learn with Sophie of Pieter's increasing agony, and it thus emphasizes the contrast between appearance and reality in Pieter's life.

Paton's placing Sophie between Pieter and the reader, just as his placing Pieter's philosophy between that of his parents, is an effective method of achieving aesthetic distance, which he achieves in *Cry, the Beloved Country* by expressing his own views through the manuscript of Arthur Jarvis or by dramatizing his views through Stephen Kumalo's odyssey. What then can we conclude about Paton's own opinion of the South-African conflicts between mercy and justice and between obedience and love? He condemns those laws and mores which inculcate hard justice without tempering it with love. That Captain Massingham and Sophie must go outside legal and familial restriction to show their love for Pieter suggests that acts of mercy or compassion must be committed outside the law or social approval. Does Paton suggest in this novel that there is hope for positive change? Despite Pieter's imprisonment for breaking the morality act, Paton seems to suggest some hope; Pieter's mother and Sophie reopen the family home after his father's death. Perhaps love and mercy will one day prevail.

Studying the narrator's position shows us the value of the novel as a work of psychological as well as sociological truth. As Pieter's dilemma and his anguish are recorded and examined by Sophie with a poignant sensitivity without sentimentality, the characters are seen as not only South African but human.

John Romano (review date 4 April 1982)

SOURCE: "A Novel of Hope and Realism," in *The New York Times Book Review,* April 4, 1982, p. 7.

[*In the review below, Romano celebrates the classical emphasis on human truths and values of* Ah, But Your Land Is Beautiful.]

Alan Paton's first novel, *Cry, the Beloved Country,* is one of the few works by a contemporary writer one would risk calling a classic; in the case of that novel, published in 1948, the word has a rather specific meaning. The idea of a classic is historically bound up with the view, powerfully embodied in Paton's book, that there are certain perdurable human truths and values, immune from geographical or historical vitiation. The classical view, with its Judeo-Christian modifications, acknowledges that we are flawed, but not therefore ignoble; the classical view is famously realistic about our limitations, but celebrates our sense of possibility and the idea of hope. Indeed, the one ignoble thing, from the classical perspective, is despair.

Paton has spent his long life—he will be 80 next year—in circumstances in which despair might long since have seemed reasonable. As a white man in his native South Africa, he has written nearly a dozen books in support of the struggle for racial equality there. He taught school in the outlying districts, managed reformatories, was a founder of the Liberal Party and saw it suppressed by the Government. And yet *Ah, But Your Land Is Beautiful* shows no slackening of either his hope or his realism. This novel is as vigorously and as exquisitely written as anything he has produced. It has the eloquence, the special commingling of sweetness and anger, the Orwellian force and lucidity, familiar to readers of *Too Late the Phalarope* (1953), his second novel, and several other volumes since. Its tone is quietly anguished.

Its classical appeal is based on a direct and simple confidence that the facts of his country's moral disaster will move all men and women, all at once, in the same direction.

Ah, But Your Land Is Beautiful is a novel in the form of a pastiche-memoir of the Defiance Campaign and the Liberal Party in the 1950's. The narrative is made up of letters, reflections, character sketches, bits of dialogue, the transcripts of a trial, a summary of newspaper accounts and scraps of official documents juxtaposed or sewn together by a narrator who seems himself the possessor of a long, patient, irresistible historical vision. It begins with the arrest of an Indian girl, Prem, a lovingly drawn character, for deliberately using a white library in violation of the color bar. (American readers will be interested in the multi-racial character of the rights struggle in South Africa; it's not simply a matter of blacks and whites.) Prem's story recurs throughout the novel and includes her love affair with a white student activist, the son of a prominent Government official. The novel also traces the careers of several white leaders of the new Liberal Party, in particular Robert Mansfield, a respectable upper-middle-class headmaster and former soccer star, who is ultimately driven to emigrate to Australia by the fierce hatred his espousal of the cause of equality arouses. There are glimpses, too—and these are among the most telling moments in the novel-into the minds of some South Africans who are opposed to racial equality: an Afrikaner civil servant whose letters to his aunt defend the new apartheid policies, a spinsterish character who writes hate letters signed "Proud Christian White Woman" and whose letters reek of diseased fascination/abhorrence of interracial sex. The episodic threads are brought together by the sudden imposition of new and strict apartheid measures in 1958, as the Afrikaner Nationalist Party comes to power. The persecution of anti-apartheid forces grows quickly more severe: newspapers are suppressed and 150 black and white activists and politicians are arrested. In the novel's final darkest pages a character who is transparently Dr. Henrik Verwoerk has become Prime Minister, and the bitterest and most hopeless period in the South African struggle for equality—a period which extends to the present—has begun.

> **Alan Paton's considerable practical contributions to political life in South Africa aside, his place in the literature of social protest has been secured by the his steady devotion to the ideal of the empathetic imagination in fiction.**
> **—*John Romano***

The cumulative anecdotal force of *Ah, But Your Land Is Beautiful* is difficult to convey. Considering its abundant violence, the passion of its advocacy, and the hatred it matter-of-factly reports, the book is remarkably gentle. Something of its anomalous calm, and one hopes its effectiveness, can be found in the following passage, an elegy to Sophiatown, a "blackspot" within the white quarter of Johannesburg that was physically broken up by the Government in 1955. Father Trevor Huddleston, a white Anglican priest, and a real historical figure, spent long years working in the vice-ridden slum.

> Sophiatown had become to him the home of all things lovely. It was the place where old men and women came into the great church of Christ the King on their hands and knees. The humility and faith of it smote him in the inward parts. It was the place where small black children ran out from the houses to hold the hand of the father. It was the place where he and Sister Dorothy Maud could walk safe at any hour of the day or night.

> "—Father
> "—Yes
> "—I have killed a man.
> "—When?
> "—Now now. In Sithole's yard.
> "—You were gambling.
> "—Yes.
> "—You promised me.
> "—I promised you, Father, but I broke it.
> "—What happened?
> "—This man played a card that was not in his hand. I said, That card was not in your hand. So he pulled out his knife.
> "—And you pulled out yours?
> "—Yes, Father.
> "—Which you promised not to carry.
> "—I repent, Father.
> "—Go on.
> "—He would have killed me, but I struck first. In a minute he was dead.
> "—And everyone saw it?
> "—Yes, Father.
> "—Let us pray, Michael, then we shall go to the police.
> "—Let us pray then.

This quietly forceful exchange—unprepared for and never alluded to again—emerges abruptly in the text. It is an example of Paton's characteristic method. Individual human dilemmas are never swallowed up or diminished by the overarching political context of the story he is telling. Paton is relentless in his faith in the moral meaning of individual human experience. The incident is an ugly one; but Michael's confession restores to him the dignity of which he has nearly robbed himself. Paton's faith is not a religious one, but a faith in the function, the usefulness of personal sympathy.

We can ameliorate any situation we can describe in language; communication and empathy are the truly revolutionary forces in this novel, where people are converted to causes not by argument but by, as one of them puts it, "a lump in the throat."

Alan Paton's considerable practical contributions to political life in South Africa aside, his place in the literature of social protest has been secured by the his steady devotion to the ideal of the empathetic imagination in fiction.

Rose Moss (essay date Spring 1983)

SOURCE: "Alan Paton: Bringing a Sense of the Sacred," in *World Literature Today,* Vol. 57, No. 2, Spring, 1983, pp. 233-37.

[*In the following essay, Moss traces environmental, liturgical, and spiritual influences in Paton's art.*]

There is a country its writers do not name. Not all, or not in all works. But time after time, and more frequently during the last decade, we read the country's name into a negative space where, in works from another country, we would find a name. Or we read a circumlocution. Or we read an invented name and geography through whose features we recognize known eyes.

There may be many reasons its writers do not name this country. For some, no name presents the country as their own. Their intimate experience of the place, its land, its people and its voices may be so different from anything evoked by the common political title that they veer away. Perhaps they feel like members of a family who do not use the world's formal titles for each other. For some, the name threatens the intimacy of their warmth, because the name means something hateful, but the land is one they love. For some, to use the name would imply political recognition, which they refuse to grant. For some, the country is so doomed one can no longer employ the name it used to have; but the doom is not completed yet, and what will come in place of the doomed name remains unimaginable. They write of people, of birds, of places, but not of the whole under one name.

Whether as the creator of a tradition or as the prophet of a powerful imaginative prohibition, Alan Paton (b. 1903) was the first to use a circumlocution for the place alluded to ambiguously by Karel Schoeman as "the promised land" and by J. M. Coetzee as a "duskland," macrocosm of the microcosm in Athol Fugard's "Island," masked as the Republic of Sarmeda by Dan Jacobson, enduring nameless war in Barney Simon's "Our War," entering into the aftermath in

Nadine Gordimer's *July's People* and, in Coetzee's masterpiece, *Waiting for the Barbarians,* fused with the United States and other political, historical and spiritual powers and principalities as "the Empire."

Whatever tragic doubts about its identity which this country imposes on its writers, in Paton the circumlocution suited much else in his style: a taste for the general over the particular, the moral over the physical, meaning over sense. The lyrical, homesick evocation of one of the fairest valleys of Africa, where the titihoya used to cry, an evocation which moved the world in 1948, comes to our attention as a sacred, biblical place. The lovely road from Ixopo to the hills takes us to a sensuously present Carisbrook, from where you look down; there is grass and bracken about you, you hear the crying of the titihoya. Perhaps one may see the valley of the Umzimkulu below. However, the river's journey from the Drakensberg to the sea and the mountains of Ingeli and East Griqualand behind the visible hills are present only to the mind's eye.

Carisbrook is a liturgical location: "The grass is rich and matted, you cannot see the soil. . . . Stand unshod upon it for the ground is holy, being even as it came from the Creator. . . . Destroy it and man is destroyed." Paton does not care for the prosy density of things that smell so and weigh so and taste so, whose meaning is in themselves. His physical world is translucent with significance—mental, moral and liturgical. Things do not speak of themselves; they testify to the presence or absence of the Creator.

In *Too Late the Phalarope* (1953) Pieter van Vlaanderen gives his father, who reads only one Book, a book of color plates titled *The Birds of South Africa.* At the evening prayer that night his father reads a passage from the Book of Job wherein Job has protested that his sufferings are undeserved and has been challenged by the voice from the whirlwind: "Who is this that darkeneth counsel by words without knowledge? . . . Where wast thou when I laid the foundations of the earth? . . . Hast thou entered into the treasures of the snow? or hast thou seen the treasures of the hail? . . . Gavest thou goodly wings unto the peacocks? . . . Hast thou given the horse strength? . . . Canst thou draw out Leviathan with an hook?" Job (and Pieter's father), overwhelmed by the magnificence of creation and the Creator it implies, confesses, "I have heard of thee by the hearing of the ear; but now mine eye seeth thee." For Paton, as for his character, the meaning of natural beauty is that it reveals its maker. The meaning of human life is similar, and the way it reveals is not by physical beauty but by moral righteousness. It is Paton's work as a writer to show that righteousness and to bring us, through what he shows, to a sense of the sacred or, in an irreligious age, of the significant. As a writer, Paton does not intervene to change or repair or prevent the imminent doom his stories portend. He does instruct on how to respond: cry.

Paton's liturgical style and its clear connections with the Bible and Christian practice offer a way to connect individual virtue with the virtue and sufferings of others.

                   —*Rose Moss*

The instruction to lament may be as prophetic as Paton's hesitation to name the beloved country. More than twenty years later Coetzee's magistrate uses images of birds and the original untainted garden that echo Paton's to begin an account of how the people of an outpost spent their last year composing their souls as they waited for the barbarians.

> No one who paid a visit to this oasis failed to be struck by the charm of life here. We lived in the time of the seasons, of the harvests, of the migrations of the waterbirds. We lived with nothing between us and the stars. We would have made any concession, had we only known what, to go on living here. This was paradise on earth.

The cadences of mourning are the dominants in contemporary South African literature as more and more writers see and imagine the impasse Paton foresaw in 1948. Given the political hopelessness of peaceful change that would fundamentally reorder the beloved country and allow justice and peace, contemporary writers turn, as Paton did, to individuals. Perhaps in the scope of a single life one may see an image of meaning or decency one dare not look for in the society.

Paton's liturgical style and its clear connections with the Bible and Christian practice offer a way to connect individual virtue with the virtue and sufferings of others, with the history and hopes of devout people in other times and places and, finally, with the story of Christ, whose suffering and death demonstrate that the end of the story is not despair but hope. To most contemporary writers, Paton's faith and the literary means that connect present experience with larger, enduring myths of resurrection no longer have power. But, although such writers cannot share Paton's answer to the common dilemma, they often take a similar stance, perhaps the only stance from which the story can be told. It is the stance of an observer, a chorus, one who knows and feels what happens but cannot prevent it or alter it.

In *Cry, the Beloved Country* (1948) we adopt this stance of liturgical participation as we follow the way of Kumalo's cross, his journey from Ixopo to Johannesburg, his search for his son and the discovery that the youth has lived in what Kumalo calls sin with a woman, the discovery that his son has murdered. As for the son himself, we know him as "son" and "boy" rather than by any name of his own. When the action is not mediated through Kumalo, we learn of what happened through Jarvis. Here too, the actions happen off-stage, often in the past.

The movement of the book, then, is not in the actions of central characters but rather in the understanding and feeling of Kumalo and Jarvis. It drives toward resolutions that are symbolically significant. A dam is built. Kumalo waits for a dawn; it is the dawn of his son's execution, but it offers hope of the dawn of another day, the day when justice will light the earth: "But when that dawn will come, of our emancipation, from the fear of bondage and the bondage of fear, why, that is a secret." Paton's fusion of the longing for a day of political and social justice in his country, like numerous other prophetic elements in his early fiction, prefigures many contemporary South African writers who turn to images of a final judgment and a new order in heaven and earth.

In *Too Late the Phalarope,* Paton's second and finest novel, we stand again at a remove. We learn of the action from the spinster aunt of Pieter van Vlaanderen, usually called "the lieutenant." She recounts and interprets the story, but she is powerless to act. What she tells us is finished, done. When she tried to intervene, her nephew "shut the door of his soul" on her. She laments that she never spoke the words that might have saved him and "us all."

The action from which they are not saved is foreshadowed at the beginning of the novel when the lieutenant arrests a white boy who has been pursuing a Coloured woman to break the "Immorality Law" with her. We infer Pieter's own punishment when he warns, "It's a thing that's never forgiven, never forgotten. The court may give you a year, two years. But outside it's a sentence for life." As the action unfolds step by step, we recognize inevitability rather than feel suspense.

In the center of the book the quality of the narrative changes for a while. We come close enough to feel as well as observe the shock of the note on the door that says "I SAW YOU," the church bells that record black hours, the coldness of Pieter's subordinate and, the "most frightening thing of all," old Geyer's response to the lieutenant's greeting: Geyer "did not answer him with any word. He took the pipe from his mouth and spat with anger and contempt. Then he turned his back to the lieutenant and walked up the path to his house." We do not know, any more than Pieter, that these signs are ironically not related to his crime. We do know that when he feels relief to discover himself reprieved, something will happen to bring sentence down on him after all. We en-

ter again into the numbness of one who knows what has happened and what cannot be undone.

Paton's liturgy contemplates tragedy in a world where spiritual power lacks material strength and is overcome by complex but unintelligent, undirected forces. The murder in *Cry, the Beloved Country* is not premeditated or malicious. It comes about almost by accident, in a state of confusion. The immorality in *Too Late the Phalarope* comes from Pieter's yielding to depression because his wife is confused about sex and inarticulately frigid, not from anything he—or Paton—recognizes as rage or evil intent. Paton does concede malice to Sergeant Steyn. Who contrives to accuse Pieter because he resents one rebuke made in anger, but we see Steyn's malice peripherally. The focus of the story is on the lieutenant and his yielding to temptation, not on the drama of one man's lust to destroy another.

Just as the patient, unflinching grief of *Too Late the Phalarope* conveys a sense of strength and endurance that become like hope and compassion and epitomize Paton's power to give a sense of universal dignity to suffering, what the author does not pay attention to in the book reveals the limitations of his imagination. Steyn's malice is significant. So also is the way we see Pieter van Vlaanderen's undoing but pay little attention to the woman who is the occasion of his sin. Her passion to remain with her child is supposed to motivate her complicity in betraying van Vlaanderen, although it is not clear what she stands to gain. We may guess at her anguish, but we do not see her with her child or know what happens to her after she has betrayed van Vlaanderen. Neither she nor anyone else in the book attacks the pharisaical self-righteousness of the women who know that they are better than she, that they are Afrikaners and are entitled to take her child from her. In the novel we accept their right, as we accept van Vlaanderen's potential to be a great man, although his happiest destiny would have been to lead, without question, the people, his own people, who define his sin and crime as "a thing never forgiven."

We accept Pieter van Vlaanderen as a good man because he is good in his private life. In all Paton's work, personal decency weighs strongly against political opinions Paton knows to be destructive, and personal cowardice or narrowness outweighs liberal theory. We know his good characters by their deeds and by what they endure to remain good—losses of comfort, wealth, community respectability, security and safety. They show compassion, generosity and tolerance even when the world threatens them. They often come into conflict with South Africa's laws because they obey higher laws. We do not know much about what distinguishes them in taste, appearance, humor, cadence of speech or characteristic turn of mind. We do know that they would choose peace if they could. With the passage of time and the increasing ferocity of South Africa's racism, conflict between Paton's good characters and those who support apartheid has become more open and more inevitable. Kumalo was a victim, but he still believed so much in white benevolence that some called him—and meek, devout men like him—"a white man's dog." In Paton's latest novel, *Ah, But Your Land Is Beautiful* (1981), central protagonists begin lives of protest in the Defiance Campaign of the early 1950s. Paton has never consented to the rhetoric of revolutionary violence.

The split in Paton's imagination between spiritual and physical, which underlies his lack of interest in sensuous qualities and unique characters, shows up in political terms as a belief in a somewhat disembodied spiritual virtue as opposed to material power. Describing the nature and ground of modern-day Christian hope in 1974, he quotes Isaiah and Revelations as inspirations to look to a time of peace that transcends anything we can expect in historical time. The vision of dazzling sweetness, forgiveness and harmony that sustains Paton's hope has little specific, local vindication. He knows that the New Jerusalem, where all tears will be wiped from our eyes, looks like pie in the sky. He makes the claim of faith that it is also pie on earth.

The validity of Paton's vision was affirmed by two early and immense successes. After a life-threatening illness in his early thirties, Paton sought work with young criminals. Thanks to Jan Hofmeyer, then Administrator of Transvaal Province, who was to become Paton's hero and subject of a biography, Paton was appointed to run the Diepkloof reformatory for black boys. Within weeks he had changed the principles of governance from force, rebellion and disorder to respect, trust and internal commitment. One by one he unlocked the gates of the reformatory and left them open. Under the honor system fewer boys escaped for good than under the rule of iron. Versions of the troubling recalcitrant incorrigibles appear in some of Paton's stories and in his play *Sponono* (1965). For the most part, Diepkloof demonstrated the transforming power of faith, care and trust—and did so in a country deeply hostile to Paton's implicit respect and concern for his charges. When the Nationalists came into power in 1948, they rapidly changed the way Diepkloof was run and showed another way to treat lawbreakers and blacks.

Homesick on his first trip abroad, an expedition to learn about prisons and penal reform in Europe and the United States, Paton wrote the novel that brought his country's beauty and sad destiny to the attention of millions. The instant success of *Cry, the Beloved Country,* his first book, brought Paton fame and the financial security to devote his life to writing.

Soon Paton was drawn to realize his vision again in social action as well as in writing. He worked in the Anglican Church with Bishop Clayton, another hero and subject of a biography. When the Nationalists arrested more than 250 people on trumped-up charges of treason, Paton helped establish a fund for the defense and aid of political prisoners. The fund is now outlawed. Paton also became leader of the Liberal Party of South Africa, which advocated universal adult suffrage. The party never sent a member to Parliament and was outlawed by government legislation that prohibited racially mixed political parties. Through speeches and writing at home and (when he was allowed a passport) abroad, Paton worked to spread the vision of peace through trust that had seemed so efficacious at Diepkloof.

Paton has never acknowledged that racism and other kinds of evil might be as spiritual as the goodness he presents for us to see, revere and emulate. In a recent interview (1982) he talked of "the Afrikaner with his strong belief in God, but his real trust in the tank and the gun. As a matter of fact, it has always been." Deliberate, clear, chosen adult malice, Paton seems to believe, does not exist. In his most recent novel he presents a pitiful caricature of evil in a crazed writer of poison-pen letters. When she realizes that she is about to die, she repents. She says of the viciousness she recognizes, "Sometimes it seemed as though the Devil got into me," but we do not believe in the Devil and do not hold her fully responsible.

In history as in fiction, Paton does not imagine that evil can be practiced as an outcome of choice by competent adults who understand fairly clearly what they are doing or whose refusal to understand is itself a choice. Those who seem evil must be mistaken, misled or unfree. In Paton's writing, political monsters of our century seem anemic, hollow men. Paton mourns them in a tone that resembles his lament for Ixopo's lost beauty. Writing of the grand architect of apartheid, Verwoerd, he says, "That there is an element of cruelty in baaskap apartheid and in separate development seems to me incontrovertible." Then he wonders whether Verwoerd knew some of apartheid's implemented cruelties. Could Verwoerd, or anyone, know and relish cruelty?

Verwoerd admired and supported Hitler. He protested the admission of Jews to South Africa in the 1930s. He made Nazi propaganda during the 1940s and was found guilty in a court of law for siding with South Africa's enemy during World War II. He designed the main principles of apartheid still in place today and implemented them. He instituted Bantu education to teach blacks that "the green pastures reserved for whites are not for them." During a passive-resistance protest police opened fire, killing more than eighty people and wounding more than 200. Both the scene and the victims' hospital were sealed off from the press and other communication. When an international out-cry followed the publication of news and photographs, Verwoerd declared a state of emergency and had thousands arrested between evening and dawn. He appointed as Minister of Prisons and Justice a man who had been interned during the 1940s for supporting Nazi action in South Africa, and he passed laws that permitted arrest without warrant or charge and allowed indefinite confinement in solitary. Some of the arrested went mad. Some suffered accidents: they fell down stairs and died, or they fell from the tenth floor of the police building where political prisoners are questioned. Those events were known to Verwoerd. So were the conditions of life the political prisoners protested: fathers arrested when they came to cities to look for their children, wives who petitioned for permission to visit their husbands for seventy-two hours for "purposes of procreation," black/white wage ratios of one to fourteen. Paton knew what Verwoerd knew. On Verwoerd's death he wrote, "I cannot help reflecting that had Dr. Verwoerd been born into a wider world, where his gifts could have been used for the wider benefit of mankind, he might have achieved more than this limited greatness. . . . He could have been great under different stars, but he was born into a society whose definition of greatness is not accepted anywhere else, except in those societies and those minds dedicated to the same ideals of white security, white survival, and, inescapably, white supremacy, by whatever grand name they may be called." Paton recoils from a vision of evil and from a Christianity that accepts Dante's moral ferocity or Blake's observation that "He who loves his enemies betrays his friends, / That, surely, is not what Jesus intends."

Like his hero Jan Hofmeyer, Paton went from a pious childhood to adult life as a Christian without an intervening period of sophomoric skepticism at college to inoculate him with the doubt that marks much twentieth-century thinking. Paton's great move was from his Christadelphian home, through Methodism to the Anglican Church. The great intellectual influences on his life have come predominantly through personal relationships and, until he was in his forties, predominantly with white men. His thinking shows some effects of his distance from intellectual centers. Although the fame of *Cry, the Beloved Country* took Paton's vision to the world, it has not been easy for the world to enter Paton's vision. He mentions Hitler and World War II in biographies, but his imagination seems not to lead him to mention Auschwitz, Dresden or Hiroshima. He mentions a visit by Hofmeyer to India but says nothing of the country. He seems hardly to know of the change from colonial rule that marked so much of Africa and the rest of the world. Speaking to Harvard alumni in 1971, he did not mention Vietnam. He did say that some in South Africa at that time took America's "tribulations" to be "due to your policies of racial integration." Kent State? Watergate? Cambodia? In the same speech Paton approved of American companies that invest in South Africa, because they "improve dramatically the salaries and other benefits of non-white employees." His trust is not in the direct economic effect of these policies, which have affected fewer than ½% of South Africa's black workers. His trust is in the "moral pressure" they exert on South African employers "to do the same."

A few years ago Paton published *Towards the Mountain* (1980), the first volume of a three-part autobiography. The themes of his fiction and other writing remain, but a new element enters his written voice, a directness and a renunciation of liturgical weight. There is revealed here a dry, quiet humor that must have been part of the person hidden in earlier writing. The work is remarkable for its lack of anger and bitterness and for the quiet, honest light it shines on childish stupidity and adult weakness. Paton does not spare himself and does not castigate himself. He accepts the fact that life is complicated and that even good people do not act as they would have thought they should. It is rare to read an autobiography so unassuming, unpretending and undeceived.

Paton turns eighty this year, and the world has now heard other writers from his country. What he did not see and would not say are clear. It is clear too that he has disdained the literary objectives of many other distinguished writers of the century. In current South African politics he has little place. In the tides of literary fashion his reputation is ebbing. But what enabled Paton's cry to find resonance in the hearts of millions of readers has not passed. What Paton calls faith, interviewers tend to call optimism. Paton rejects the word. He has never been an optimist. The prophetic imperative he spoke in 1948 remains the imperative. Now other voices have joined his to cry the beloved country.

Paton's images for what he mourns transcend his country. Some of them draw from universal, mythic wells of feeling: the lost paradise of earth, fertile as a garden received straight from the Creator's hand; the birds who sing there; the human life that is destroyed when its precious place is destroyed. What Paton cherishes also draws loyalty: the firmness of people who act from principle and not for show, the strength of those who endure suffering, the sweet dignity of daily acts performed for the sake of another, the goodness of water treated like wine. Paton's remains a voice to hear, a vision to regard.

Nicholas H. Z. Watts (essay date June 1984)

SOURCE: "A Study of Alan Paton's *Too Late the Phalarope*," in *Durham University Journal*, Vol. LXXVI, No. 2, June, 1984, pp. 249-54.

[*Below, Watts discusses the classical, epic, psychological, and religious dimensions of* Too Late the Phalarope.]

The role of the White South African novelist is often assumed by outsiders to be primarily that of keeper of the national conscience. We may be surprised at the number of important writers—André Brink, Athol Fugard, Nadine

Gordimer, Alan Paton and Laurens van der Post come quickly to mind—who have been nurtured in that beautiful and troubled land, but we expect their work to be, as it often is, a vehicle for social protest: fiction is one doorway to truth not yet quite closed in the blank wall of censorship.

Alan Paton's best known novel, the unforgettably compassionate *Cry, the Beloved Country,* is such a book. Published in 1948, its protest at the iniquities of apartheid has lasted well: it moves us still, sixteen years after the political party headed by its author was forced to disband rather than comply with the apartheid laws. Paton's latest novel, *Ah, But Your Land is Beautiful* also tells a story of the interwoven struggle of South African men and women to assert the dignity of the individual. It has an intensity of purpose that suggests the author has begun to despair of change. *Too Late the Phalarope,* another early work that was first published in 1955, is also a novel of protest. It matches the elegiac beauty and power of the earlier novel and the intensity of Paton's most recent one and deserves greater recognition than it has yet received.

The story is a simple one. The van Vlaanderens are a well established and conservative family in a small town deep in the heartland of the Afrikaaners. They are sober and religious, and the hopes of the family rest with the son Pieter. He is a promising police officer of considerable charm and presence, with an enviable war record behind him. His ability and the family connections should ensure his success. In the meantime he is achieving the pinnacle of fame in South Africa: he plays rugby for the Springboks. People say he will captain them. To complete the picture, he is married to the shy Nella and has two children whom he adores. This tranquil picture is shattered when Pieter becomes obsessed, against his will it seems, with a black girl, Stephanie. He is seen with her by a jealous subordinate, informed upon, arrested, tried and sent to prison. In that conservative environment, his shame spells the downfall of his family as well.

The nature of Pieter's downfall may be in doubt, but its inevitability is not, for the book opens with the words: "Perhaps I could have saved him . . . Perhaps I could have saved us all". Once Paton has assured us of the hero's ultimate fate he is free to concentrate on the cause of it and this is at the heart of the novel.

At first glance Pieter seems to have committed two wrongs. The first one is a moral wrong; he commits adultery with Stephanie in spite of the mutual love which he and Nella share. The second is a legal wrong: he breaks the fundamental rule of South African law and crosses the racial barrier. In the conservative religious environment that the book describes, either action appears sufficient to cause his destruction. But Paton appears not to think so. If the theme of the book is "a wife wronged", Nella plays a curiously remote part. Although they love each other, there is a distance between them which seems caused in part because Nella cannot easily keep pace with Pieter's development; "For he was the one that was like a god, not she". There is also a strong suggestion of sexual incompatibility:

> She was frightened of Johannesburg, and of the evil things that men and women do, even of staying in an hotel. She was frightened even of the laughter that came out of the Royal Bar, where men like her father and brothers were jesting a little coarse and rough. Therefore when he in his extremity asked for more of her love, she shrank from him, thinking it was the coarseness of a man.

Later, when Nella goes to the coast with the children to visit her father, she exchanges letters with Pieter and he is more explicit:

> And perhaps one day when you are convinced, and know that my love of your body is part of my love of you yourself, and when you are no longer afraid of it . . . I believe too that you would give me more sweetly of your body (I mean more sweetly than you do, which is almost enough already) not because you wished to be kind or suffer me, but because you too would wish to do so.

Nella's reply is loving but constrained, and "he sat and read her letter with a face of stone".

On the other hand, the story strongly suggests (even to someone unfamiliar with Paton's political viewpoint) that the colour bar is too arbitrary a law to justify the tragic tone of the book. The nature of the Afrikaaner who made the laws and of the Dutch Reformed Church which supported them are expressed in the character of Pieter's father, Jacob, and his attitudes are frequently contrasted unfavourably to those of Pieter, his mother and the narrative judgments of Tante Sophie. Moreover, this is not a story of someone who crosses the colour bar at the urging of an irresistible love, a Romeo pursuing his Capulet Juliet, but of Pieter drawn against his will into a furtive and unfulfilling relationship. Pieter is a victim, not a martyr.

Paton also takes pains to show that he is not concerned with a moral wrong. Very early in the book, Pieter apprehends a young rugby-playing friend running suspiciously after Stephanie in a dark side street. When he speaks to Dick later he is concerned only with the power of the law and the unforgiving nature of public opinion: "whether you're a Cabinet Minister or a predikant or a headmaster or a tramp, if you touch a black woman and you're discovered nothing'll save you . . . The court may give you a year, two years. But outside it's a sentence for life". This unmoralistic approach to the law on interracial relationships is explored further in the report of the farmer Smith who makes one of his servants pregnant and kills her to conceal the fact. His act is contrasted with the morality of the black race, ". . . who would have gone shamefaced to her father, to confess and make reparation as was their custom", and the climax of the story is not a moral judgment by Tante Sophie, who admits to confusion but an emphasis on the "great machinery of the law . . . this sudden manifestation of the certitude and majesty of the white man's law". This law, and the morality that created it, is summarized at the end of the novel in an exchange between the police Captain and Nella's father, who exclaims: "I would shoot him like a dog . . . he has offended against the race". The Captain replies: "as a policeman I know an offence against the law, and as a Christian I know an offence against God; but I do not know an offence against the race".

Paton uses the effects of the apartheid laws to explore issues of universal significance and he emphasises this universality by using both a dramatic structure and language that transcend the setting of the story. The novel carries very significant echoes of Greek tragic form and the language has the simplicity and repetitive devices of epic poetry or the phrases of the Bible. These emphasise that Pieter is threatened by some powerful and destructive inner force. Tante Sophie says he "shut the door of his soul [and] behind was a man in danger". The nature of this danger is the heart of the novel.

There are four elements that echo classical Greek tragedy. First, the classical authors wrote on well-known themes. Since the audience knew from the start what tragedy would unfold, they were free to concentrate on the dramatic skills and interpretative glosses of the playwright. Paton takes a contemporary and unknown theme but moves at once to reach the starting point of his classical counterpart: the inevitability of the tragic fall. He sustains dramatic tension from that notable first sentence, "Perhaps I could have saved him, with only a word, two words, out of my mouth"; by withholding the exact nature of the tragedy, adding touches of explanatory colour rather as an artist might sketch the outlines of his picture before he starts to paint.

Secondly, the book also enjoys in large measure the classical unities of time, place and action, for it is a retrospective novel set in a small Boer township. It is written (except for the final page) in the past tense to underscore the inevitability (though not the finality) of the destruction. The story is related by Pieter's aunt, Tante Sophie, so that the main vehicle of the plot is the narrative of an onlooker: this sense of the onlooker who sees what others fail to notice, but who is powerless to change the course of events, helps build the claustrophobic atmosphere within which Pieter feels himself trapped.

The role of Tante Sophie is the third echo of classical form. She is an elderly woman, and her deformity of a harelip means that she has never married. She thus has a sexless quality which is reminiscent of the old and hermaphrodite prophet, Teiresias. Her perception is intuitive. Of Teiresias it is said: "In your heart, if not with the eye, you see our city's condition". Tante Sophie says:

> Yet because I am apart, being disfigured, and not like other women, yet because in my heart I am like any other woman, and because I am part, so living apart and watching I have learned to know the meaning of unnoticed things.

She does not know what is the matter with Pieter until the moment when she encounters him in the kitchen with Stephanie and then her knowledge is intuitive: "for now suddenly, and it unwanted, I found what I had searched for all these years". It is clear from the context that she sees beyond the dangerous but technical illegality of a relationship between black and white. Instead, she sees the unconscious forces that push relentlessly against the shores of Pieter's conscious world and, though broken again and again by habit and discipline, build into new and more dangerous waves. Like Teiresias, Tante Sophie has the inner intuitive vision but, also like him, she is rejected by those who fear the implications of her knowledge.

Finally, Pieter is also a classical figure; one of heroic proportions. He is highly talented and seems to those around him to have a classical balance and proportion. He is loving but austere; passionate but aloof; able but modest; strict but compassionate and just. Paton develops these qualities so that he seems uniformly excellent except for his one flaw and the black mood, the *swartgalligheid,* which assails him. His heroic stamp is enhanced by the language used in the last days before his fall. He has indeed been selected as captain of the Springboks—a position of God-like authority to the Boers—and, as Agamemnon was "sacker of Troy", so Pieter is "the Lion of the North".

If we look for a classical antecedent, however, it is not to be found in the story of Antigone, although there appears to be a parallel in her struggle to reconcile personal honour with the unbending rule of the State. The true parallel is with the *Bacchae* of Euripides which explores the influence of the unconscious personified in the form of Dionysus (the god who can inspire a person but from whose rejection springs madness).

Before examining the way in which Paton develops this study of the unconscious mind, we should first establish how he came to choose such an unusual title for the book. Why select the phalarope, a bird which is only rarely seen ashore in South Africa on its migratory passage? At one level, the answer is straightforward. Pieter has boldly given his father a book about South African birds—boldly because his father "read only the One, and the newspapers". Jacob is delighted by the present despite the unpromising fact that the author is an Englishman and not an Afrikaaner, and he is especially pleased when he discovers an apparent error in it. To prove it, he promises a picnic near the coast to show Pieter the phalarope. At the picnic, Jacob sees the bird and

> because the son could not see, the father went and stood behind him, rested his arm on the son's shoulder, and pointed at the bird. But the son could see no bird, for he was again moved in some deep place within, and something welled up within him that if not mastered could have burst out of his throat and mouth, making him a girl or a child.

The phalarope is one of the very few birds in which the traditional roles of male and female are reversed. Once the female has laid the eggs they are incubated by the male who rears the young. The female is, unusually, the more colourful of the pair and determines their territory. The bird is therefore a vivid image of the development of characteristics predominantly associated with the instinctive behaviour patterns of the opposite sex. Furthermore, the bird is associated with the shore and its movement between sea and land symbolises the movement of ideas between the conscious mind and the subconscious, for which the sea is an enduring symbol.

So the title prepares us for a novel that examines the polarities of human existence within the framework of a Jungian psychology. It is a book about the importance of a man respecting and developing the "feminine" qualities within himself, such as the emotions, intuition and imagination (and, similarly, for a woman, her masculine qualities such as reason, control and discipline). Tante Sophie seems to realise that this is the heart of the issue on the first page of the book when she observes that:

> His father was a giant of a man, and the boy grew as tall and broad as he; but the boy Pieter had something of the woman in him, and the father none at all until it was too late.

Paton characteristically enters a quiet warning against taking the book as an excessively simplistic argument in favour of living out all one's subconscious desires. Pieter has been attracted by Stephanie for some time before he breaks the law by having a sexual relationship with her. When he does, it is after an evening when he has been drinking (most unusually) with his cousin Anna and when he "knew that he had drunk too much. But he did not care, for the world was good and happy, and the black mood of the day seemed foolishness, and he was full of power".

The language has a lapidary quality, but also a warmth, that makes this a book for the ear as well as for the eye. The language constantly mirrors the structure of the novel and throws back light on to the development of the plot. A striking feature is the use of repetition. It is used in three ways.

First, repetition is used to give emphasis to a word. The most effective example of this is when Sophie sets the scene and explains why she is telling the story. She writes with a determined purpose:

> . . . it is not only that [these events] trouble my mind . . . nor is it only that men may have more knowledge of compassion. For I remember the voice that came to John in Patmos . . . Therefore I set aside my fears and am obedient.

She cannot understand God's ways: "small strength, small weakness, that I understand; but why a man should have great strength and weakness I do not understand . . ." She expresses this perplexity by a constant repetition of the word "strange". This word is used casually in everyday English, and at first glance it seems that this repetitious use of the word reflects the narrow imagination of a woman who probably received no formal education. But the repetition—seven times in the opening three pages—gives the word a prominence that demands a more forceful meaning. Given the classical awareness which the structure of the novel seems to demonstrate, the word may be used with some of the force which its Greek counterpart, *deinos,* held. The earlier uses of *deinos* carry the meanings of "fearful" and "powerful" (either for good or ill). It is the characteristic adjective for Dionysus, who inspires men but from whose rejection springs madness. Tante Sophie's language suggests that the power that Pieter had over her from childhood, and her inability to speak out to avert disaster, were more than curiosities of behaviour: they were the strange manifestations of unconscious forces which had been denied their natural, untrammelled expression. At the same time, almost with an ironic awareness of her language, she uses the word in its most casual sense, but in a context that reveals how fully she understands the nuances of English as well as her native Afrikaans:

> Strange is it that one could run crying to the house of a man that one loved, to save him from danger . . . And strange it is that one should withdraw, silent and shamed . . . and because of the power he held over me, I held, in the strange words of the English, I held my peace . . . There were strange things in the boy's mind that none of us knew or understood . . . One could not tell whether [Pieter's father] were proud and pleased or angry, for the truth was that he had fathered a strange son, who had his father's will and strength and could ride and

outshoot them all, yet had all the gentleness of a girl, and strange unusual thoughts in his mind . . . and [of his mother] the black moods and the coldness, the gentleness and the tenderness, the shooting and the riding and the books, the strange authority, she pondered them all in her heart . . .

Repetition is also used in the manner of epic poetry to emphasise key characteristics and to give a sense of universality. Thus, Pieter is first described as "the bravest and gentlest of them all" and these words, separately or more often together, are frequently used to describe him. His father is often described as a lion. On his birthday, when his daughter kissed him, "he growled like a lion", and at the picnic "we packed him in with rugs, for he was still weak from the influenza . . . and it was like packing a lion into the car, for he growled and threw his head about just as a lion does".

Paton uses repetition in a third way: to express the way a person's mind can be obsessed by a single idea. When Pieter acknowledges the attraction that Stephanie holds for him, and has made love to her, he is filled with guilt and fear of discovery and the narrative tells us again and again how he "vowed and prayed" that he might resist her in future, and escape discovery.

The author uses a simple symbolism that is more accessible than that of the title to develop further the universality of the tragedy. Tante Sophie recalls the end of the picnic:

> So we drove back to Venterspan when the sun was almost down, and the world was filled with beauty and terror. And darkness came down over the grass country, and over the continent of Africa, and over man's home and the earth, and over us all. And the sun went down, and never rose again.

Finally, the language is full of biblical echoes, as befits a story told by a woman for whom the Bible was almost her only reading and attendance at church a major occupation (she calculates that she had heard "three thousand sermons, and could have heard five thousand, except that at Buitenverwagting we had to travel far, and went to church only in the mornings").

The book is thus structured around three parallel dynamics. Classical form underlies the more flexible form of the novel; an epic universality underlies the small-town particulars; and the unconscious mind underlies and influences the conscious mind. Each of these dynamics sheds light upon the tensions that underlie Boer society and make it so resistant to change and progress.

There is another dynamic that is central to Paton's theme: religion. Jacob's is legalistic in form and is essentially a non-redemptive creed. It is "a matter for obedience and not for tears". He reads mainly from the Old Testament, using it as a touchstone for his judgement. He uses the Bible as the ledger where all family events of consequence are entered. As we have seen, he scores out Pieter's name as though that act alone can confirm the legitimacy of his rejection. In the end, however, his narrow faith cannot support him and he dies "bowed over the Book of Job".

Tante Sophie's faith is more generous and her references are more often to the New Testament. She writes "and I too, having lived this story in grief and passion, close it in some kind of peace, remembering God's mercy, Who gave us all such friends". Earlier on, she cannot accept the retributive attitude of the whole community towards the wretched Smith. She compares the words of Christ to other writings urging obedience to the law and although she admits to some confusion she concludes on a note of compassion: "yet I grieved for the man in my heart, that did such evil because he was in terror". This, as well as her inability to condemn Pieter, is in sharp contrast to her brother who read about Smith's case "with a face of anger and revulsion".

Pieter's mother represents a yet further move beyond the constraints of the Dutch Reformed Church and this is made clear early in the book by the unmistakable echo of St. Luke's gospel as she watches her son's different moods and the strange authority: "she pondered them all in her heart . . .". She also works fearlessly, with her son, among the black people during a smallpox epidemic. She appears only rarely in the book and at first she appears a minor character. Yet it is her standards against which most of the actions in the book are assayed. We never learn her name, so that she is both Pieter's mother and a representative of a universal feminine nature. Whereas at the end of the book Jacob dies defeated, the others survive, "borne on the deep river of this woman's love, that sustained us all".

Within this framework that compares two strong faiths, one grounded in the Old and one in the New Testament, Paton explores the relationship between Pieter and Tante Sophie. It has been a complex one since he was a child. Sophie refers to it on the opening page of the novel and later describes it in terms which convey an astonishing relationship between a young child and a mature woman:

> I took him in my arms, with all the passion of a hungry woman that would have had this child if God had given her one . . . Then he stiffened in my arms and looked away from me, as though there was something of which he was ashamed. And the passion went out of me and I was afraid . . . And from that day he had the power over me.

The importance of this passage is reinforced by the moment

when she recalls it; when Pieter for an instant "opened the door of his soul". His power lies in his dark gift for self control, the withholding of himself, which quenches her passion (the word is typically thrust into prominence in this key paragraph by repetition). He is unable to respond to her love and expresses it in behavioural terms by looking away from her. This is an early demonstration of the deep similarities between Pieter and his father, similarities we tend to overlook because of the emphatic differences between them. But Sophie had asserted on the opening page of the book that "he and his father both had the power over me". Later we learn of Jacob that "that was a habit of his, to start to leave a room, and then to stop and to talk with his back turned". Nowhere is this unwillingness to see the true meaning in the eyes of others more obvious than when, after Pieter's arrest, his mother says that she must go to him. Jacob stopped "and without turning he said to her 'you must do what you wish, but if you once go out of this house you shall not enter it again'."

The corrosive effect on Pieter of being unable to respond, of being unable to free his unconscious urges from the twin shackles of society and his own consciousness, is revealed in the intense guilt he feels when he sees the note left by his friend Japie as a joke: "I saw you". This phrase, in its present tense, is the traditional greeting amongst the Zulus, one of the main black races subjected to apartheid, and it is a greeting that acknowledges and respects the identity of the other. Pieter's reaction is a measure of how far apart he has drifted from those around him. He is unable to see the real love of those around him; instead he feels slighted by his father and sees the possessiveness of Sophie's love and the shortcomings of Nella's shy offering rather than the warmth and commitment that underlie them all, albeit so deeply in the case of his father that it is almost hidden. He is also unable to see himself as others do and is conscious only of the "black mood" and the desperate acts to which it drives him.

There is no suggestion in Pieter's relationship with Stephanie that they meet on any conscious level at all; his conscious efforts indeed are spent on resisting her. He seeks a fulfilment that cannot be found there. The social constraints make their meetings furtive and guilt-ridden. The imagery reflects this: they meet in darkness, upon waste ground amongst the rank smell of the Kakiebos weed. The several voices of his reason, his faith and his social code tell him that his search will never end in these secretive encounters. It is as though he acts despite these warnings because it is the only course left open to him and it is thus a measure of his despair.

In these meetings there is the same layering of meaning which pervades the whole book; the meeting of white and black; of the conscious mind with the unconscious; the altruistic giver who gives everything except himself and the

instinctive sharer who gives herself, having nothing else to give. The blackness is the dark of the night, of his own fear, and of the Afrikaaners' suppression (transposed on to the black races) of the dark forces that they cannot so easily quell in the apartheid of their own souls. Only once does Tante Sophie uncharacteristically misjudge Pieter, when she sees him as a man who "could now afford to come out from his armour, it being complete", but she chooses a military metaphor that is so clearly absurd that it highlights the falseness of her premise. Pieter's armour can never be a complete protection, for it guards him against the wrong threat. He will not be safe until he can hold the feminine qualities within him in balance with his own masculine characteristics and those of the culture in which he lives.

Much of the tragedy centres on the fact that, while he might be able to reach this balance in different surroundings, (for he respects the dichotomy in himself,) the society he lives in prevents it. His attraction to Stephanie is rooted in his admiration for the fierce, instinctive pride of motherhood which she shows towards her child and which is in sharp contrast to Jacob who can dismiss his son from his heart with that single, ritualistic and highly conscious act: striking Pieter's name from the flyleaf of the great Bible.

Paton's message in *Cry, the Beloved Country* was concerned primarily with the suffering inflicted by apartheid on the Black people of South Africa. The emphasis in *Too Late the Phalarope* is different. Stephanie is the only black character, and she does indeed suffer; she is imprisoned and deprived of her child because she brews illicit liquor to support her mother whom no one else would help. But it is the suffering of the white Afrikaaners on which Paton concentrates. He argues that Pieter's weakness is inseparably bound up with the repression of the spirit which is inherent in the rigid codes of apartheid. By dominating the Black races, the Afrikaaners are repressing vital forces in their own souls and they thus destroy not the blacks, but themselves. If even the "bravest and the gentlest" can be struck down, how can there be any hope for the proponents of the system, such as Jacob?

At the end of the book, Pieter is in prison while his mother, Nella and Sophie wait for his release and the limited hopes of a new start. Pieter's younger brother Frans now lives in the family home with his wife. Their son, Koos, had always admired Pieter and on the final page Sophie hints that the pattern of repression may be about to repeat itself: "The boy Koos is tall and dark, and seems to have some special mark of solitariness". And the pattern is already being repeated in other families: "Yet my grief can still come back when I read of some tragic man who has broken the iron law".

Despite these two warnings, the last pages are written with a clear sense of hopefulness. Jacob dies, and after the funeral his wife reads the diary in which Pieter has recorded his version of events. Then, as Tante Sophie wonders about the future, she writes for the first time in the present tense, giving the reader a powerful sense that at last the mould of inevitability has been broken. That hope is very fragile. Pieter and Nella will have to go abroad to rebuild their lives and nothing has changed in South Africa to make life easier for the solitary Koos. The hope is confined to the hearts of the main actors of this tragedy. They have been brought face to face with the logical conclusion of the "old" ways: the Old Testament religion, the iron law, the social pattern that exemplifies the inner determination to subdue the feminine spirit. Through the suffering that Pieter brings on his family, and through the lead given by his mother, they have some hope of finding more balanced lives. Tragically late though it is, they have seen the phalarope.

This, Paton's finest novel, thus operates with great success on several levels. It is a convincing story of crime and punishment. It is a strong study of individuals who, despite their pronounced characteristics, are always more than stereotypes. As a psychological novel, it is a powerful depiction of the corrosive effect of guilt and the destructive power of a repressed subconscious and it provides a lively model of Jung's understanding of the human spirit. In this respect it uses South Africa as an allegory for the path of western culture. And it turns out to be what we perhaps first expected: a devastating critique of apartheid and the spirit that underlies it. Paton's commitment to social justice and compassion, which rise so movingly from the pages of *Cry, the Beloved Country* here find such unity of composition, such austerity of expression, such integrity of faith and such universal meaning that *Too Late the Phalarope* stands as an exceptional book both in comparison with Paton's distinguished peers and within the wider context of recent literature.

William Minter (review date 20 November 1988)

SOURCE: "Moderate to a Fault?," in *The New York Times Book Review,* November 20, 1988, p. 36.

[*In the review below, Minter outlines the major events of Paton's life covered in* Journey Continued.]

For four decades, Alan Paton's novel *Cry, the Beloved Country* has given millions their first glimpses of the human tragedy of South African racism. Its simple eloquence leaves few unmoved. Appropriately, it forms the hinge between the two volumes of Paton's autobiography.

Towards the Mountain, which was published in 1980, recounted Paton's conversion from the white racist paternalism he had accepted until his mid-30's. Between 1941 and 1943 he sat on an Anglican commission on South African

society that consisted of 31 whites and two blacks. From his fellow commissioners and others associated with the liberal Institute of Race Relations, Paton gained a vision. "I was no longer a white person but a member of the human race."

On leave from his position as director of a reformatory for African boys, Paton was inspired to write *Cry, the Beloved Country.* Its publication in 1948 transformed him overnight into South Africa's most celebrated writer. He was then 45 years old. *Journey Continued* takes up his story at this point, with his reactions to fame and to the election that year of the Afrikaner-based National Party, which advocated an intensification of the country's system of white racial dominance, using as a slogan, "apartheid" ("apartness").

Journey Continued maintains the clear writing style, the attention to detail and the candor of Paton's earlier works. It discusses South African politics, as well as his family, friends and life as a writer. Yet there is no strong theme comparable to the first volume's vision of a journey toward the holy mountain of justice.

Paton carries the narrative to 1968, with a brief epilogue on the two decades before his death on April 12 this year. One major topic is his leading role in the Liberal Party, which from 1953 to 1968 worked within the white electoral system for racial equality.

His principal literary project during this period was the biography of Jan Hofmeyr, the moderate Afrikaner politician who died in 1948, shortly after his party lost to the hardline Nationalists.

Paton's participation in the Liberal Party, he makes clear, came from moral duty, not from any expectation that the majority of whites would respond. Duty also motivated his decision to testify for political prisoners in the 1950's, even though he rejected the politics of the African National Congress as too radical. He also never participated in the nonviolent resistance campaigns of the time. His vision of change was "to persuade white South Africa to share its power, for reasons of justice and survival."

His heroes were all white: men like Hofmeyr and Archbishop Geoffrey Clayton, whose biography Paton published in 1973. Like Paton, Clayton was eventually impelled to denounce racial injustice, but often seemed as disturbed by intemperate protest as by the system itself.

One of the most revealing passages in *Journey Continued* deals with the young members of the Liberal Party who, in the tumult of the 1960's, joined a clumsy sabotage campaign against the Government, causing the accidental death of a 77-year-old white woman. Paton's deep revulsion at this act contrasts strikingly with his description of the 1960

Sharpeville massacre, which verges on an apologia for the policemen who killed 69 black protesters.

Such glimpses make some sense of Paton's otherwise puzzling political stance of later years, when he found it easier to praise President P. W. Botha's willingness to reform than to accept Bishop Desmond Tutu's call for economic pressures against the apartheid regime. Although Paton refers several times to the mellowing of his outrage against apartheid, his political views probably changed little from his initial conversion in the 1940's.

In *Cry, the Beloved Country,* the black pastor expresses the fear that "when they turn to loving they will find we are turned to hating." Paton, it seems, found it impossible to listen with openness instead of fear to the new black voices of the 1960's, 70's or 80's. In the end, nevertheless, he will be remembered not for that fear, but for his cry for justice that continues to echo today.

Myrtle Hooper (essay date 1989)

SOURCE: "Paton and the Silence of Stephanie," in *English Studies Africa,* Vol. 32, No. 1, 1989, pp. 53-63.

[*In the following essay, Hooper investigates the function and effects of Stephanie's "silence" in* Too Late the Phalarope.]

> In every story there is a silence, some sight concealed, some word unspoken, I believe.
> [J. M. Coetzee, *Foe*]

I think it might be safe to describe the affiliations of Alan Paton as liberal and humanist, and his endeavour as a writer of fiction as realist and didactic. Certainly in *Too Late the Phalarope* his concern is to investigate the implications of an "iron law" for the lives of individual people, and to demonstrate its destructive effect. Yet, in the voicelessness of Stephanie, the story contains a "silence", the functioning and effects of which I would like to investigate.

In *Too Late the Phalarope* Paton sets up a narrative frame behind which his own position may be veiled: he has Sophie—and less importantly the captain—to speak for him. Sophie's character is quite carefully developed. She is physically deformed, hence has never married, hence remains something of an outsider even within the socially important and emotionally close-knit Afrikaner family to which she belongs. She says of herself,

> Yet because I am apart, being disfigured, and not like other women, yet because in my heart I am like any other woman, and because I am apart, so liv-

ing apart and watching I have learned to know the meaning of unnoticed things, of a pulse that beats suddenly, and a glance that moves from here to there because it wishes to rest on some quite other place.

She has quite definite opinions about matters such as the Smith case, but these are moderated by a perspective on human nature which is sympathetic and accommodating to experiences such as that of Maria Duvenage. She is able to draw connections that do not isolate or condemn, and in general she avoids making judgements. Yet her attachment to her nephew is excessive, as he knows; in his terms, she desires to "possess him". If the novel is a tragic one, the tragedy is hers as it is Pieter's: it is her life that is "at the turn", and it is she who is deprived of the peace she anticipates with age. So her act of narration is an attempt to regain that peace, as well as an attempt to render the interiority of Pieter to those who would judge and condemn him. She says . . . ,

> And if I write it down, maybe it will cease to trouble my mind. And if I write it down, people may know that he was two men, and that one was brave and gentle; and they may know, when they judge and condemn, that this one struggled with himself in darkness and alone, calling on his God and on the Lord Jesus Christ to have mercy on him.

Yet Sophie fairly frequently steps into her narrative to comment on the action and events she is describing. She acts in the role that Robyn Warhol has termed an "engaging narrator":

> Using narrative interventions that are almost always spoken in earnest, such a narrator addresses a 'you' that is intended to evoke recognition and identification in the person who holds the book and reads, even if the 'you' in the text resembles that person only slightly or not at all.

A case in point is her description, with its built-in judgement, of the consummation of the relationship between Pieter and Sophie. She says, "And there, God forgive him, he possessed her". Another instance occurs . . . when, in making her disclaimers about judgement, Sophie foregrounds the act of judging: if she claims the characters cannot be judged she indicates at least that larger social units must be. At points like these the veil slips, and the writer behind the narrator steps forward to speak to his readers.

Although the narrative is predominantly Sophie's, Pieter is allowed to speak for himself through the diaries to which she gains access, and out of which she recreates the course of events. He is given, in other words, a voice. The first time we hear this voice is in the comment he makes in Afrikaans after his encounter with Dick, "*O God wees hom genadig.*

Here Jesus wees hom genadig", and *"O God wees my genadig, Here Jesus wees my genadig"*. These words anticipate and predict the confessional nature of the diary entries. Significantly, the first of these entries is given immediately after his encounter with Stephanie in the kloof. If Sophie is endeavouring, as I claimed earlier, to render the interiority of Pieter to those who would judge and condemn him, then giving his reaction at this point is clearly crucial.

I think it might be safe to describe the affiliations of Alan Paton as liberal and humanist, and his endeavour as a writer of fiction as realist and didactic.
—*Myrtle Hooper*

To serve her function in the plot Stephanie is equipped with certain attributes. In contrast to Pieter she is uneducated, hence illiterate, hence keeps no diary. Besides the 'black woman's burden' of two indigent relatives whom she supports single handed and with unquestioned acceptance, she has no family, as Pieter has, to sustain or morally circumscribe her. Her father and her mother are unknown, as is the father of her child. She has "a good deal of lightness in her colour", and, caught as she is in a cycle of unemployment, poverty and 'crime', her social contacts seem to be limited to random sexual encounters. Sophie says of her, "It's a lost creature . . . that will go with any man that comes. . .". Yet her evident amorality is qualified by a powerful 'maternal imperative'. Sophie remarks how "she has a passion for that child", and says later, "I saw that she was like a tigress for the child". This attachment is the key to her integrity, and to her relationship with Pieter. It is also the key to her 'career' which includes collisions with the law and, ultimately, with Japie and the Women's Welfare. (It is harshly ironic that in passing her "gentle sentence" on Stephanie, Pieter's mother effectively passes sentence on her son.)

Perhaps Stephanie's most significant quality, however, is knowledge. It is this that sets her in contrast with Pieter's wife Nella, who is shocked into knowledge "by the hard hand of Fate . . . only after we had been destroyed". Pieter's question to Stephanie when she comes to ask him "to tell the Government" she has found work is, "how did you know [I would do it for you]?" Soon after, when she comes to his house:

> . . . *she smiled at me, and the mad sickness that I hate and fear came over me, and she knew it, it being one of the things that she understands* . . .

If she has knowledge it is not such as to take away her innocence, however. Her habitual expression is a combination of smile and frown, and Sophie says of her, "she had a queer look of innocence also, though she was no stranger to those things which are supposed to put an end to innocence".

I said above that Stephanie is equipped with these attributes so as to serve her function in the plot. What is this function? I would like to identify it indirectly by assessing her impact on Pieter: by comparing Pieter as he is at the start of the novel with Pieter as he is at the end, and by considering his reactions to the relationship as it develops.

Pieter is described as a boy by Sophie as

> a strange son, who had all his father's will and strength, and could outride and outshoot them all, yet had all the gentleness of a girl . . . Had he been one or the other, I think his father would have understood him better, but he was both.

And growing out of this, he becomes "two men":

> The one was the soldier of the war, with all the English ribbons that his father hated; the lieutenant in the police, second only to the captain; the great rugby player hero of thousands of boys and men. The other was the dark and silent man, hiding from all men his secret knowledge of himself, with that hardness and coldness that made men afraid of him, afraid even to speak to him.

Other critics have examined Pieter's relationship with his father as more and less significant for his relationship with Stephanie. For my purposes, his motives in entering into this relationship are less important than the effect it has upon him, which is to strengthen, not to trigger, the tendency in his nature towards schism. Hence I must, in passing, take issue with Ian Glenn's claim, that

> All of Tante Sophie's portentous division of the selves of Pieter boils down, it seems, to the description of a man whose marriage is sexually unfulfilling in the most obvious physical way.

After his arrest, Pieter's mother provides confirmation that Pieter's conflicts predate both marriage and acquaintance with Stephanie: ". . . from the years of childhood she had feared for him, and had known that he was hiding away, in some deep place within, things that no man might safely conceal".

. . . [After] seeing (and touching) Stephanie in the kloof, Pieter writes as follows:

> *If it shocked me to see myself, it shocked me no less to see my danger. It was like a kind of shadow of myself, that moved with me constantly, but always*

apart from me; I knew it was there, but I had known it so long that it did not trouble me, so long as it stayed apart. But when the mad sickness came on me, it would suddenly move nearer to me, and I knew it would strike me down if it could, and I did not care.

This archetypal formulation is interesting, as John Cooke has pointed out. Desire for Stephanie is "mad sickness"; but "mad sickness" is not what threatens him. What threatens is his "danger", which has been with him over a long period of time, and which thus predates Stephanie. This danger is like "a shadow" of himself which moves closer when he succumbs to desire for Stephanie and threatens to strike him down. This perception should be enough to dismiss as misplaced Pieter's quest for safety in his wife's love. The "danger" is a part of himself, suppressed, projected outwards, and associated with desire for Stephanie. Yet, as my students have pointed out to me, "Pieter is looking for something he doesn't get, even from Stephanie. Stephanie is not an object of desire because she doesn't satisfy him."

His comment after their first sexual encounter is thus illuminating.

> *In those twelve hours the whole world had changed, because of one insensate act. And what madness made a man pursue something so unspeakable, deaf to the cries of wife and children and mother and friends and blind to their danger, to grasp one unspeakable pleasure that brought no joy, ten thousand of which pleasures were not worth one of the hairs of their heads? Such desire could not surely be a desire of the flesh, but some mad desire of a sick and twisted soul. And why should I have it? And where did it come from? And how did one cure it? But I had no answers to these questions.*

He cannot expect to, because his pleasure is "unspeakable"—in more than one sense. In his earlier interrogation of Dick, Pieter asked four times why he "did it". Dick could only answer "I don't know". Pieter, likewise, cannot verbalise his desire for Stephanie in terms other than those his society supplies: and these are imprecise and extremely hostile.

What he is able to predict, and with some accuracy, is the effect that discovery would have on him.

> *It would seem to me that every act, every word, every gesture, would fit only and could fit only into the pattern of my offence; that every reasonable man would see it, and I being also reasonable could not deny it.*

And if I denied what they could see to be the truth, then something within me would be broken, and I would cry out, or break down and weep, or something within me would break, so that they, knowing that I had never been so before, would know beyond doubt that I lied.

He acknowledges how tenuous is his hold on secrecy. If once a minute piece of evidence leads to his exposure then the pattern of events will reveal itself as the only reasonable explanation. It is 'their' discovery of his actions that he foresees leading to the breakdown of "something within" him.

After his final encounter with Stephanie, "he bathed himself from head to foot, trembling with the secret knowledge of the abject creature that was himself". This knowledge is distinguished from his earlier "knowledge of himself" in bringing humility and gentleness to his dealings with his wife, his aunt, and his children.

> Then he sat alone by the fire, and the thought, the hope, came to him that this strange mood of humility and gentleness might be some turning point, and that this perhaps might be the finding of that which was sought, and the opening of the door that was knocked on.

As I see it, this is precisely what it is: he finds what he sought, the door is opened. After the exposure he has foreseen, he is rescued from suicide by Kappie, and once in Kappie's house he breaks down. Sophie and the captain arrive to overhear him,

> . . . saying that he was cleansed, once and for ever, and that this blow that had struck him down had cleansed him for ever, but why must a man be struck down to be cleansed, and why could not the man who had struck him down have warned him, for by this very warning he would have been cleansed for ever, and why could not God have warned him, and why must God strike him down so utterly, and why must the innocent also be struck down, and why and why and why.

His protest contains a moving if indirect indictment of the system which has brought him to tragedy. Yet his questions are surely rhetorical. He has in fact been "warned"—three times if one counts the examples of Dick and of Smith. and Japie's note saying "I saw you". He has at least once broken the law "of his own will and choice". He has known all along the consequences of his actions, and predicted his own response to them, as I have shown. His rhetorical questions underline how in fact "a man must be struck down to be cleansed", if by "a man" he refers to himself. His formulation is still couched in the terms available to him: if he has been suffering from a "mad sickness" he has now been "cleansed", and the catharsis which has "cleansed" him is his exposure.

For Sophie his outcry confirms that he has "been destroyed". But the last word must surely be that of the other voice which veils and at times reveals Paton's. The captain comments as follows on Sophie's reluctance to give the diaries to Nella:

> You surely don't think, *mejuffrou,* that some other woman could save him? And if you are thinking, *she couldn't help before,* don't you see this is quite another man?

From the two men whom he was Pieter has become one man, "quite another man". The transformation is effected by his relationship with Stephanie, and by its public exposure.

I have noted above that, if anyone's, the novel is Sophie's and Pieter's. Yet I would like to examine in more detail the narrative treatment Stephanie receives, because, as outlined, her defining characteristics are largely given by her function in the plot, and because, in contrast to Pieter, these defining characteristics act to prevent a sense of interiority. Her social and moral isolation, her knowledge and innocence, her smiling and frowning, make her an enigmatic figure: and the enigma she presents to Pieter generates a response on his part that is morally ambiguous and inadequate. As a prominent and respected member of his community, as a policeman, is he not simply exploiting someone weaker than himself, disadvantaged, and voiceless? If it is Stephanie who is manipulating him then is he not collaborating in this abuse, instead of carrying out his "duty"? If he does 'love' her, then why does he not care for her, or even get to know her better than he does?

In the kloof this interchange takes place:

> —I'm here, called the lieutenant, the girl's here too.
>
> —*Baas.*
>
> —Yes.
>
> —Can I see the child before I go?
>
> —Yes.

The smile of irresponsibility left her face, changing it and surprising him.

> —*Dis my enigste kind,* it's my only child, she said.

She was filled with some hurt pride of possession, so that he, knowing her life, wondered at it.

> —It's my only child, she said, and looked down at the ground again, waiting hopelessly. He, feeling pity for her, was suddenly purged of the sickness of his mind, and stood up and put on his cap.

Paton treats with sympathetic humour the power of her sexual effect on him and its implications for his official position. Earlier, "he, shaking with shame, went and sat on a stone, and took off his cap and wiped his brow, hot and cold and trembling". Yet what Pieter's gestures underline, significantly, is how pity for her as a mother is able to vanquish desire for her as a woman. In pitying her he is "purged of the sickness of his mind". Because the terms of his perception of her are socially prescribed for him he does not see or respond to her whole. The money he gives her later seems less a payment for services rendered than a vague benevolence to someone suffering hardship, as is the loan he makes to young Vorster. Yet (again as my students have pointed out) "if she is his mistress he doesn't look after her very well". Perhaps it is such a disjunction in expectations that leads Stephanie finally to pass "sentence" on him and become involved in his entrapment. But her motives are left unclear, since even here Paton refrains from passing judgement on her. Her words are quoted to Pieter at his arrest but the details of her collaboration with Sergeant Steyn are not revealed, and she is effectively removed from the action after Pieter's last contact with her. This narrative protection from judgement serves to prevent a sense of her interiority.

There are, however, three points at which Stephanie seems to me to transcend the closure of her character. After the first court case we witness, at which she learns she may lose her child if she continues to brew liquor, she surprises Sophie into empathy and a sense of maternal community.

> She did not smile any more. She left the dock and followed the policeman to the door, but half way there she halted, as though she would not go, as though something must be done or be said, as though it were unbelievable that her offences, for which she had been willing to pay without complaint, should suddenly threaten her with such a consequence. She turned and looked at me and my nephew as though she would say something to us, but she knew that she could not do such a thing in a court.
>
> So then she went out.
>
> —It's a lost creature, I said, that will go with any man that comes, but she has a passion for that child . . .
>
> —Perhaps even as your mother and I had a passion for a child.

Of course, even this event is functional in revealing Sophie's relative enlightenment. Yet her speculations and interpretations here are for once able to convey something of Stephanie's inner feelings.

The last time Pieter goes to Stephanie it is to give her the money she has requested "to make a case". Of course, we have just had Sophie observe her leaving the court "not like one on whom sentence is passed, but like one who passes it". Of course, it is this encounter which entraps Pieter, despite the relief and optimism which her ironic "this other case will also be for the child" inspires in him. These things he cannot know; yet he does recognise in her a sense of intention. He comments afterwards,

> *And it was my purpose, made in prayer, to keep the law. And it was her purpose, for what reason I did not know, to break the law. And I carried out her purpose, and not my own which was made in prayer.*

Alerted as we have been, we are conscious here of Stephanie exerting her will to shape the course of events.

In analysing Paton's use of landscape, John Cooke has observed how Paton gives to Pieter's encounter with Stephanie in the kloof a pastoral and lyric force, and how this animates his memories of childhood. He observes,

> Prior to his first confrontation with her, Pieter is clearly attempting to recapture a childhood world in which separation from such qualities [feminineness, gentleness] was not demanded.

Pieter's own description goes further.

> . . . and why and why, why no one knew, it was the nature of man and of creation, that some sound, long remembered from the days of innocence before the world's corruption, could open the door of the soul, flooding it with a sudden knowledge of the sadness and terror and beauty of man's home and the earth.

His associations are with Eden, with the lost world of innocence before the fall, before the door to the soul was shut and knowledge excluded. Given this, his encounter with Stephanie carries the added weight of biblical allusion, and makes her flight from him an act of enticement and temptation as well as one of escape.

> But seemingly she did not want to ride, for suddenly she had fled by a little path at the side of the fall, that came to another, with no way up except over the rocks of the fall itself, green and slippery. He

followed her at leisure, and came to where she was standing.

—Why did you do that, he asked.

She made him no answer, except to smile in her strange and secret way. Then she heard the sound of the men above, and drew back. And as she drew back, she touched him. And he did not move.

He did not move, neither forward nor back, nor did she. It was all silent but for the sounds of the men above, and for his breathing and the racing of his heart. Then she turned round and smiled at him again, briefly, and moved forward an inch or two, standing still with her eyes on the ground; while he, shaking with shame, went and sat on a stone, and took off his cap and wiped his brow, hot and cold and trembling.

She runs from Pieter so that he may pursue her. She initiates physical contact; she breaks it off. She retains her composure. Pieter does not: his response to her leaves him trembling and perspiring. Sophie's description of the consummation this looks forward to is, "he possessed her". It is inaccurate. Pieter may 'possess' Stephanie physically, he may 'know' her biblically: but never longer than transiently. Stephanie may be allowed to 'transcend' her character at points such as these, but ultimately Pieter cannot reach her because she is closed to him as she is to the reader of her story.

> The true story will not be heard till by art we have found a means of giving voice to Friday.

So says Susan Barton in J. M. Coetzee's *Foe*. In this novel, consciousness is located within the character, and the attempt made by the character's self is to reach outside its consciousness. Susan Barton says,

> The story of Friday's tongue is a story unable to be told, or unable to be told by me. That is to say, many stories can be told of Friday's tongue, but the true story is buried within Friday, who is mute. The true story will not be heard till by art we have found a means of giving voice to Friday.

In his paper on the novel, Paul Williams asks, "How then are Susan and Foe going to get Friday's story? By making him speak or by speaking on his behalf?" Friday cannot be made to speak because his tongue has been cut out and the world he inhabits is one of silence. And neither Susan nor Foe is willing to speak on his behalf.

In contrast to Friday Stephanie has a tongue; yet she has no voice. Paton neither makes Stephanie speak, nor speaks, to any great extent, on her behalf. This could be because he is not aware of her silence. Yet in ***Cry, the Beloved Country*** he does attempt to give voice to a black character. It could be because her voice would interfere with his didactic purpose, which is focused on Pieter and Sophie and the community to which they belong. Thus in contrast to Coetzee's, Paton's endeavour is not one that allows consciousness to be problematised in a dominating or alienating way. Yet it seems to me there is something more. With all the attributes she is given, with the narrative restraint from judgement upon her, Stephanie's silence remains, ultimately, closed to 'penetration'. Her elusion of Pieter in the Edenlike setting of the kloof is metaphoric for her elusion of both author and reader.

FURTHER READING

Criticism

Davies, Horton. "Pilgrims, Not Strangers." In his *A Mirror of the Ministry in Modern Novels,* pp. 113-36. New York: Oxford University Press, 1959.

> Studies the characters of Reverend Stephen Kumalo and Father Vincent in *Cry, the Beloved Country,* focusing on the relationship of Protestant missionaries to the interracial complexities of South Africa.

Hogan, Patrick Colm. "Paternalism, Ideology, and Ideological Critique: Teaching *Cry, the Beloved Country.*" *College English* 19, No. 3 (October 1992-February 1993): 206-10.

> Espouses an ideological approach to teaching *Cry, the Beloved Country,* deconstructing the racist and sexist thinking that structures the novel.

Paton, Alan. "A Patriot's Dilemma: Why I Stay in South Africa." *Commonweal* CV, No. 22 (10 November 1978): 714-17.

> Discusses the pros and cons of exile and the effects of Western investment strategies in South Africa.

May Swenson
1919(?)-1989

American poet, translator, author of children's books, dramatist, and critic.

The following entry presents an overview of Swenson's career through 1996. For further information on Swenson's life and works, see *CLC,* Volumes 4, 14, and 61.

INTRODUCTION

Respected for her colorful and perceptive observations of natural phenomena and human and animal behavior, Swenson playfully experimented with poetic language, form, and sound, making extensive use of such devices as metaphor, alliteration, assonance, and dissonance. Critics often compare Swenson's poetic style with those of Marianne Moore, Elizabeth Bishop, and e e cummings; like Moore and Bishop, Swenson used richly evocative language and exacting detail in descriptions of the complexities of nature, and, like cummings, she displayed a penchant for wordplay. Swenson's poems are typically related in an objective, detached voice that approaches everyday human concerns, scientific topics, and nature with a sense of curiosity and wonder. Dennis Sampson described Swenson as "mischievous, inquisitive in the extreme, totally given over to the task of witnessing the physical world."

Biographical Information

Swenson was born May 28, 1919 (although some sources say she was born in 1913), in Logan, Utah, the oldest child in a devoutly Mormon family of ten children. She attended Utah State University and upon graduation worked as a reporter in Salt Lake City. Moving to New York in 1949, she held various jobs before becoming an editor for New Directions Press in 1959. She resigned the position seven years later in order to devote her time to writing and subsequently served as poet-in-residence at several colleges, including Purdue University, the University of North Carolina at Greensboro, and the University of California at Riverside. She spent the last two decades of her life with her companion, R. R. Knudson, and died on December 4, 1989, in Delaware.

Major Works

Many of the poems in Swenson's first three volumes, *Another Animal* (1954), *A Cage of Spines* (1958), and *To Mix with Time: New and Selected Poems* (1963), are carefully structured in sound patterns and treat various themes, includ-

ing human and animal behavior and features of life and death. Swenson examined the worlds of nature and science in *Half Sun Half Sleep* (1967) and *Iconographs* (1970). The latter title is the word Swenson used to describe typographically distinct pieces, including her "shape poems," which are rendered in visual form and syntactical structures associated with the subjects or objects being discussed. For example, the poem "Stone Gullets" is divided into three sections by vertically curving lines, providing a visual image to accompany words that describe the ebb and flow of water in a rocky seascape. Visual and aural elements of language are prominent concerns in *New and Selected Things Taking Place* (1978) and *In Other Words* (1988), which collect many poems originally published in periodicals, including Swenson's frequent contributions to *The New Yorker.* The subject matter of these poems ranges from such ordinary activities as going to the dentist to contemplations of animals, trees, and landscapes. Swenson's continuing interest in science is reflected in poems about an eclipse and the passing of Halley's comet; the five-part "Shuttles" discusses the launches of these spaceships and concludes with ruminations on the *Challenger* shuttle disaster of 1986. Since the time of her death in 1989, four volumes of Swenson's poetry have been published, most of which are comprised of both poems previously published and poems published for the first time. *The Love Poems of May Swenson* (1991) contains poems that address romantic and erotic subjects, and *The Complete Poems to Solve* (1993) contains poems for children, some of which appeared in *Poems to Solve* (1966). In *Nature: Poems Old and New* (1994), the poems examine various aspects of the environment, while in *May Out West* (1996) the focus is specifically on poems centered in the American West.

Critical Reception

Critics have praised Swenson's verbal ingenuity, clear images, and skillful use of internal rhyme, all of which contribute a fresh perspective on human and animal characteristics, death, sexuality, and the art of poetry. Sven Birkerts commented upon Swenson's early work: "The complexities of animal life and natural form are eagerly seized upon, while the intricacies of the social order and the human emotions are not so much overlooked as proscribed. It is as if the greater part of Swenson's psychic endowment has been channeled into the sense organs, which then become capable of the most precise registrations." While several critics have maintained that Swenson adopted a more introspective, self-conscious voice in her later work that lessened the exuberance of her experiments with poetic form and language, and others commented on the lack of emotion and social consciousness throughout her writings, she has been generally praised for her technical abilities and explorations of the challenges and possibilities of language. Mary Jo Salter commented: "Swenson provides comedy in two senses: marrying her words off in one happy ending after another, she makes us laugh as she does so. But whether she writes in jest or earnest, she belongs to that rare company of poets who convert the arbitrary correspondences among the sounds of words into what seems a preexisting order."

PRINCIPAL WORKS

Another Animal (poetry) 1954
A Cage of Spines (poetry) 1958
To Mix with Time: New and Selected Poems (poetry) 1963
Poems to Solve (juvenilia) 1966
Half Sun Half Sleep (poetry) 1967
Iconographs (poetry) 1970
More Poems to Solve (juvenilia) 1971
The Guess and Spell Coloring Book (juvenilia) 1976
New and Selected Things Taking Place (poetry) 1978
In Other Words (poetry) 1988
The Love Poems of May Swenson (poetry) 1991
The Complete Poems to Solve (juvenilia) 1993
Nature: Poems Old and New (poetry) 1994

May Out West (poetry) 1996

CRITICISM

John Berryman (review date 1956)

SOURCE: "The Long Way to MacDiarmid," in *Poetry*, Vol. 88, 1956, pp. 52-61.

[*In the following excerpt, Berryman provides a primarily positive review of* Another Animal.]

[May Swenson is described] on the jacket [of *Another Animal*] as having come from Utah "to New York City where she holds an active job." One looks to the next sentence to hear what this may be. No: "Her poems have appeared" etc. It is hard to know whether to be pleased that she holds an active job, or sorry, for an inactive job is surely better for a poet. The difficulties in communication with which modern poetry is charged have reached the jackets. The energy of her versemaking, though, suggests that the job can hardly be too active for her; her first selection is as long as Harry Duncan's and Murray Noss's together, and franker, and more experimental, and vervier. She splits her eighty pages into four sections. With the first and the fourth let us dispense, and she might have done; although the first, which consists of descriptive poems, contains one good description, a fair pastiche of Miss [Marianne] Moore (**"Sketch for a Landscape"** and **"Horse and Swan Feeding"** these are), and the least dramatic account of a lion's private parts that I have seen for some time. Nor is this an exceptional passage, and one hesitates to attribute it to the influence of her general master, Cummings, because other young poets have been doing the same sort of thing—I suppose, to prove that they are not squeamish, for no real use is made of these passages which import perfectly valid but obviously difficult material. A poet is to prove that he is not squeamish, as a poet (his private attitude being nothing), by being absolutely responsible for his material and its psychological or spiritual employment, while technically he is absolutely independent of both; flourishes will not do at all; Baudelaire is our best locus here for both success and failure, unless the reader can call up a better one, and I concede that Rochester at his level gives a sharper black-and-white. The details of pain and humiliation fall under all this along with the various obscene areas; and the subject is of importance, not so much because of Joyce's celebrated admirable, nervous, limited, and driven explorations, as for other reasons: first, the broad squeamishness of American writers as Americans, and second, the supreme exception, in the greatest poem yet written on this continent, "Song of Myself."

Miss Swenson shows that she is probably not squeamish in

the love-poems of her second section and in the poems about death in her third section. There are some chat-poems, like those James Laughlin used to write (maybe he still does), such as **"The Key to Everything"**; and sometimes she lets the last line do the work. Both these bad kinds of poems are pleasant. But she uses both Cummings's cursory and organ styles (**"Evolution"; "Why We Die"; "Organelle"; "To Confirm a Thing"**) and these poems are her best; besides, she writes about her own death as if she had it in mind. It will be interesting to see what she does next. Miss Adrienne Cecile Rich is more accomplished, of course, so far, but I don't know that anyone else is. It is not the least of Miss Swenson's signs that she is livelier at sonal organization over a paragraph or passage than in a phrase or line, though she can make a line ("Yield to the wizard's piercing kiss"). She probably does not revise enough. Who does?

Barbara Gibbs (review date 1959)

SOURCE: A review of *A Cage of Spines,* in *Poetry,* Vol. 94, 1959, pp. 189-91, 193-94.

[*In the following excerpt from a review of poetry collections by five different authors, Gibbs characterizes* A Cage of Spines *as the best of the five volumes, but notes that Swenson could have been "less cautious" in presenting more than superficial topics in her poems.*]

Here are five books of poetry [Swenson's *A Cage of Spines,* Donald Hall's *The Dark Houses,* Richard Lyons's *One Squeaking Straw,* Jon Silkin's *The Two Freedoms,* and John Heath-Stubbs's *The Triumph of the Muse*], one by a woman, four by men, two by British writers, three by American—beyond these banal facts there is very little to say about them as a group. The writers seem not to have been influenced by one another, and, in fact, to have widely different conceptions of what poetry is and what makes a good or successful poem. Far from being a novel situation, I believe that this is the one facing most reviewers of poetry today, as the single review of a single book becomes a rarer and rarer thing, and as the appearance, on the horizons of poetry, of a new savior, leader, teacher, or amalgamator, is longer and longer delayed. It is not always natural or easy for one mind to assume in turn a number of different postures, and yet I suppose one is bound to approach a book of poetry by doing one's best to view it from where the author stands, at least provisionally. My only program for this review will be to make this attempt for each book in turn (reserving the right to make any comment I like, but only *after* having tried the first exercise), and while I don't hope to succeed perfectly—or even very well—I do hope to stretch my awareness and that of any reader who feels like making the trip with me. To make everything as impartial as I can, I've written the

poets' names on slips of paper, and in whatever order they come out, I will discuss them.

The first name to come out of the hat is Miss Swenson's. The question is, how, on the basis of the poems in *A Cage of Spines,* would I, as a particular critic—not speaking at all for Miss Swenson, but putting myself as nearly as possible in the poems' posture—describe the view of poetry herein represented? Several questions that I might ask myself occur to me: (1) Does the poem have a subject, other than itself? (2) If it has such a recognizable subject, then in what relation to same does the poem stand (setting to jewel, pattern to thread, identity, *jeu d'esprit* to occasion, or some other that I cannot now think of)? (3) Or, another way of inquiring about what may well be the same thing, how seriously does the poem take, or commit itself to, its subject? Then (4) What is its language like, not in its personal and particular flavor, but as regards formality or lack thereof, crispness or sloppiness, tightness or looseness—these being the lines of division today? These four will do to start, and I may as well begin by saying that the answer to number one (*does the poem have a subject other than itself?*) will be yes in all cases here under consideration, so that question number one may be eliminated from further discussion. As for number two (*if it has such a recognizable subject, then in what relation to same does the poem stand?*), for *A Cage of Spines* I would answer that the figure of "pattern to thread" comes closest, since the subjects are most often clusters of observation about a single conceit, like fire/lion, or hand/starfish, and the poem is finished when all the small conceits adhering to the central one have been stated. Thus there is no decoration of the subject, but neither is there complete identity between poem and subject, as it is quite easy to imagine there having been one less small conceit in the cluster. This, I believe, points the answer to number three (*how seriously does the poem take, or commit itself to, its subject?*): neither frivolously, nor yet with utter seriousness of commitment, but rather as though one were to play an exquisite game for the sake of the game, and either because of some code of manners, or through fear of the passion's becoming self-destructive, keep oneself partly aloof. In other words, poetry is either an exercise in which manners are important, or else it is a dangerous exercise. And question number four (*what is its language like?*): this is, of course, the hardest to answer, since language must be used to describe language, but I'll do my best. It is *not* a rhetorically heightened language—rather on the plain side, likewise as to vocabulary. It *is* fairly tightly worked as to sound, with rhyme and assonance occurring subtly, irregularly, and often. It is a language without waste—or to avoid the pejorative word—without slack, taken up to the full by its subject. Now, I will make one, perhaps unjustifiable, assumption, namely that a connection exists between a poet's critical position and/or taste, and the poems he writes, and acting on this assumption—with the proviso that it may be wrong—I will hazard these remarks about what Miss Swenson might consider a good poem: it will have a subject, it will not have a merely decorative relation to that subject, it will take its subject seriously, perhaps with a limitation of good manners, and its language will be plain, well-wrought, close-fitting, and addressed to the ear in some fashion. . . .

If I were to rank the five [books reviewed here] according to my sense of their value as poetry, Miss Swenson's would probably come first. However, I would say of *A Cage of Spines* that, just as it chooses its own tradition by the laws of self and idiosyncrasy, it submits to a self-imposed limitation, that of the surface, or mere existence, of things. This can be a prison, and I think in some of her poems one has a sense of too little ventured, while in the book as a whole the riddles and the miraculously apt descriptions tend to cancel one another, in effect. You begin to see, by the end of the book, that if Miss Swenson can do it once—and she certainly can—then there's nothing to prevent her doing it over and over *ad infinitum.* A somewhat depressing thought. Even granting, as I do, that since she is a gifted poet in this way, each time she does it, it is a new creation, full of marvelous and sparking revelations. I should probably not have brought up this point at all, were it not for the fact that in a few poems it is gainsaid and something entirely different happens and one is suddenly face to face with an emotion rather than a jubilant play of sense. Poems in which this happens are, for me, **"Frontispiece," "The Tide at Long Point," "The Even Sea,"** and some others. I wish there were more like these (not fewer of the others). Why should someone of Miss Swenson's gifts settle for less than the whole business of poetry? Let her be less cautious, I say, less nice. A more hazardous game and chance of greater winnings, as well as greater losses.

Jean Gould (essay date 1984)

SOURCE: "May Swenson," in *Modern American Women Poets,* Dodd, Mead, and Company, 1984, pp. 75-96.

[*In the following excerpt from her* Modern American Women Poets, *Gould provides an overview of Swenson's life and career.*]

It has been said that some people are born disillusioned—in the best sense of the word—and May Swenson might be considered one of the few. The eldest child in a brood of ten children whose Swedish parents had left the faith of their fathers to become ardent Mormons, May, born in 1913, on the twenty-eighth day of the month for which she was named, in Logan, Utah, was indoctrinated into Mormonism at the age of eight; but five years later, when at thirteen, she was teaching Sunday school, she began to regard the fundamentalism of Bible stories as fables or myths. Her viewpoint would have shocked her parents, particularly her father, whose heart and soul was bound up in his religion.

Daniel Arthur Swenson had come to the United States from his native Sweden as a young seeker of the religious truth he found in all he had heard about Mormonism. He worked his way across country, on the railroad, as a cowhand, till he reached the Mormon Center in Utah. A hard worker of high intelligence, he educated himself, took a Bachelor's degree in agriculture and then a Master's in mechanical engineering and wood building. At the age of twenty-one, he was "called" on a mission, sent back to Sweden to spread the word of Mormonism. During his years there he converted and fell in love with a very young girl, Margaret Elizabeth Helborg, but they could not be married until she had been formally indoctrinated into the Mormon church in Utah, in the beautiful Temple or Tabernacle in Salt Lake City. The couple settled in the little town of Logan, and immediately began to beget and raise a large family. One of the cardinal precepts of their chosen religion was the reproduction of the human race, no matter what social changes were wrought by the mechanization of the means of livelihood, or the possibility of a future population explosion. Procreation was—and is—a prime precept, one with which the future poet could not agree, perhaps because as the oldest she had to help most with the babies as they came along, but more because from early childhood she was a thinker, interested in books. Many years later, she related that she had always liked to observe and think things out for herself. "Your own perceptions and senses come first," she said. "Then perhaps you can look at others'."

She expressed little of her feelings to her parents. They were strict in a way, but quiet, never quarreled audibly—or inwardly, as far as May could see—since they were of one accord in their beliefs and actions. With their Scandinavian heritage they were hardworking, thrifty, always occupied with useful and spiritual pursuits. Her father's woodworking skill enabled him to design and build much of the furniture in their house. As the children became of school age, they all were given house-hold duties to perform and they worked together as a family. They all went to church and to Sunday school as a matter of course. And all but May and her youngest brother, Paul, who became a journalist and publishes a magazine in Utah, accepted the Mormon precepts without question. However, she kept her own counsel, out of respect and love for her parents, as well as sheer common sense, of which May Swenson has full measure; it told her that open rebellion would only bring sorrowful rebuke from her parents and concerned alarm for the safety of her soul in the "hereafter." (Two evenings a week her mother went to sit with the church circle that prayed for the conversion of the souls of her ancestors who died without benefit of Mormonism.)

Her childhood, moreover, was not overburdened with religious rigour; like most children with an ounce of imagination, and May had more than enough to balance her common sense, she was able to create her own fantasy world, particularly in outdoor pastimes during the long golden days of summer. Her poem, **"The Centaur,"** in the early volume, *A Cage of Spines,* is one of the delights of Swenson readers in its description of her make-believe and real world. "The summer that I was ten" begins the first of twenty three-line stanzas and one final four-line revealing a little tomboy's solitary joy of living-playing. She is "the centaur": we learn in the first six stanzas how the transformation takes place as she goes each day to choose a fresh horse from her stable, "which was a willow grove / down by the old canal. / I'd go on my two bare feet." But when, with her brother's jack-knife, she had cut and peeled a willow wand and "cinched her brother's belt around the thick knob of her horse's head"; she would "trot along in the lovely dust," her head and her neck were hers, "yet they were shaped like a horse." Drawing a graphic picture, she shows a horse who "shied and skittered and reared, . . . pawed at the ground and quivered," an accurate, action-filled picture: "I was the horse and the rider," she proclaims, "and the leather I slapped to his rump / spanked my own behind."

After several more striking strophes, the girl-centaur suddenly becomes two separate creatures as they drew up to the porch of the Swensons' house. Reality returns, but not entirely. "I tethered him to a paling. / Dismounting, I smoothed my skirt / and entered the dusky hall. / My feet on the clean linoleum / left ghostly toes in the hall." The last three stanzas form a masterly rendition of parent-child relationship and the merging of two worlds through the medium of a mature poet:

> Where have you been? *said my mother.*
> Been riding, *I said from the sink,*
> *and filled me a glass of water.*
>
> What's that in your pocket? *she said.*
> Just my knife. *It weighted my pocket*
> *and stretched my dress awry.*
>
> Go tie back your hair, *said my mother,*
> *and* Why is your mouth all green?
> Rob Roy, he pulled me some clover
> as we crossed the field, *I told her.*

Here is an encapsulated account of May Swenson's childhood in a small western town. Although her parents' partiality for Mormonism had some influence on her early life, it did not smother her capacity for "thinking things out," as in her querying poem, **"The Universe,"** ("What / is it about, / the universe / the universe about us stretching out?") which is set in a visual pattern suggesting a puzzle and puzzled

mind seeking an answer. (One must read the poem to figure out the full significance of the pattern; for example, the key words "think" and "about" and "universe" are repeated in the same place—"think" at the end of six consecutive lines— to form half-hidden columns vertically within the horizontal lines.) Perhaps this makes too much of a game of poetry, but in this, and the poem, **"God,"** which follows it in a different pattern, the device is so skillfully done that it is an integral part of the inner meaning of the metaphysical poems in the volume, *To Mix With Time.* Such mental creativity, sometimes profound, sometimes merely dextrous, was the result of Swenson's Swedish-American-Mormon upbringing.

Her father's reverence for religion was exceeded only by his respect for education; and May, working summers to help pay for tuition in addition to scholarships she received, attended Utah State Agricultural College (now a state university), graduating at the age of twenty-one, with a B.A. degree in English. She worked on the *Desert* and on the Logan *Herald* newspapers as a regular reporter for three years. She kept abreast of all that was going on in the literary world, and realized that the East was the center of artistic activity, and that New York was the publishing center of the country. When she heard that a cousin of hers was going East to Jacob's Pillow for the summer in 1937, and would like to have May accompany her, she made up her mind to leave Logan and live in New York City, but again, she said nothing to her parents. Her plan would depend on her ability to find a job in New York. If there was none to be had, she would be coming home anyway, so there was no need to make an issue of the matter. Yet she had the feeling that she would not be going back to Logan. The lure of New York was too strong: She had read about the American Place Gallery, made famous by Georgia O'Keeffe and the artists in all fields photographed by Steiglitz, who ran the gallery; e.e. cummings, whose poetry May admired, and Marianne Moore, one of May's early idols, who was to become her friend. So after Jacob's Pillow, she headed for New York.

Her first job, which she got "through *The New York Times,*" was as an "amanuensis to an author"; it sounded grand to a budding poet-journalist. After one interview she got the job, which paid more than her post on the Logan *Herald.* She wrote her family that she had found a well-paying job and thought she would stay in New York for a while. They offered no objection; May was over twenty-one; she had been more or less on her own ever since she started working. She soon discovered that *The New York Times* ad had neglected entirely to mention that her employer was a *would-be* author, who expected more than secretarial assistance from an amanuensis. In fact, he seemed more interested in seducing May, a round-faced young blond with a pert, retroussé nose and sharp blue eyes that should have warned him the daily chase around the davenport was futile. If May was astonished at this interpretation of her title, she was no less equal to meeting the situation with resolution.

In relating the story, her wry humor came to the fore. "I had doubted the Word of my religion," she said, "but believed implicitly every word of *The New York Times*." When she saw that the would-be author was hardly discouraged, and that she was expected to welcome instead of ward off his clumsy advances, she left him and tried another, a *published* author this time. However, although her second employer took some interest in perfecting his manuscripts, he was almost as eager for sex as her first. She finally "left the field," as she said, and became an office secretary-typist, at which she "made out better."

All this time she was writing poetry, sending out her poems with persistent regularity and, finally, had two poems accepted by the then *Saturday Review of Literature*. It was her big break-through, bringing her name to the attention of the quality publishing houses. By 1952, as a result of her appearance in such periodicals as *Poetry, The Nation, Hudson Review, Partisan Review,* and *Contact,* she was on the staff at New Directions Press, working from nine until 3:00 P.M., hours which gave her time for her own writing, but still were too confining for the number of hours she needed to accumulate enough poems to make up a volume. Then one day a letter came in the mail informing her that she, May Swenson, had been selected by the Rockefeller Foundation to receive a grant of two thousand dollars. With the confidence she felt from the unexpected award, she applied and received a residence period at Yaddo. New Directions, which had included May Swenson in their *Poets of Today* series with a small collection entitled, **Another Animal: Poems,** in 1949, gave her a leave of absence so she could complete a volume to be published individually. After her residence at Yaddo was over, she received a fellowship to the MacDowell Colony, where she spent the summer.

At about this time she met a young woman who seemed ideally suited to be her roommate: Pearl Schwartz was a hearty, down-to-earth person with a good sense of humor and a deep appreciation of the arts. She and May were a congenial pair at once, and while May was at the MacDowell Colony Pearl visited her, staying at a nearby inn. She met the artists in residence with whom May had become friends and everyone agreed that she was a fine foil for the poet's makeup, physically and emotionally. Pearl's brunette coloring, her olive skin and dark curly hair, her snapping dark eyes and ready laughter bespoke a warm, outgoing nature in contrast to May's blond, Nordic physical features and reserved, inward searching psyche. They complemented each other and understood each other's needs and desires.

Soon after the MacDowell residency ended, the two found a place in Greenwich Village which had the advantage of a

balcony at the back overlooking the garden of St. John's church, which ran the length of the block between the two streets (Eleventh and Perry), a hidden oasis that became the subject of a poem, one of Swenson's early works suggesting its substance by the diagonal, wall-like structure of its stanzas. Titled simply, **"The Garden at St. John's,"** this is no mere description of an unexpected beauty spot in the half-sordid, half-splendid city, but a keen combination of skepticism and compassion that is the hallmark of May Swenson's religion in poetry. It begins, "Behind the wall of St. John's in the city"; but it is as much, if not more concerned with the rector's wife, holding her new-and-first-born baby in her arms "like a basket of tenderest fruit" than the sheltered garden in which she walks, accompanied by a frisky, little white dog. The reader is aware of the poet on the balcony looking down on the scene and interpreting the thoughts of the novice mother, who "thinks as she fondles,"

> the nape of the infant its sweat is like dew
> like dew and its hair is as soft as soft
> as down as the down in the wingpits of angels. . . .

After an interlude depicting the little dog as he "scoots in the paths of the garden's meander / behind the wall of St. John's in the city," the poet takes up the interpretive meditation again: "She walks where the wrinkling tinkling fountain / laps at the granite head of a monk"; and continues:

> A miracle surely the young wife thinks
> from such a hard husband a tender child
> and thinks of his black sleeves on the hymnbook
> inside the wall of St. John's in the city
> the Ah of his stiff mouth intoning Amen
> while the organ prolongs its harmonious snore.

(The "hard husband" was the late Father Graf, an eminent clergyman in the Episcopal hierarchy; but as administrator of the church property, which included the row of brownstones on Perry Street where the poet and her friend lived, he was as hard a man of business as any landlord. Privately the girls called him Father "Graft.") The final stanza states the more obvious contrast: "A miracle surely this child and this garden / Of succulent green in the broil of the city," and brings in the sound from "under the wall of St. John's in the city" with accurate imagery, through the mind of her subject,

> the rectal rush and belch of the subway
> roiling the corrugate bowels of the city
> and sees in the sky the surgical gleam
> of an airplane stitching its way to the West
> above the wall of St. John's in the city
> ripping its way through the denim air.

The above conclusions of "the garden at St. John's," (seen

from behind, inside, below, and above the wall) are significant whether they represent the rector's young wife or the poet's projected feelings about her surroundings. Landlord relations aside, May and Pearl enjoyed their apartment, and at a little ceremony witnessed by a few friends, during which they exchanged Indian silver fidelity rings (worn on the third finger), they pledged a lasting alliance and set up a smooth-running household, which in due course included a cat, who in turn was included in a poem.

Weather permitting, many a poem was conceived and created on that balcony-porch, and many a friend enjoyed the view of the garden from that vantage point. At parties, it was indispensable for an overflow of guests, or if someone had to be revived with a little fresh air, winter or summer. It was not long before the household at 23 Perry Street was well known for its genial atmosphere, its lively talk, literary and otherwise, and the general charm of the place. Like many brownstone apartments, it had old-fashioned fireplaces in both the ample living room and bedroom. On the mantle in the latter was a pipe rack holding four small white clay pipes, which May and her friend smoked when they wished to cut down on cigarettes. Somehow those small neat white pipes personified the bachelor air of the well-organized menage. Both roommates were meticulous in their housekeeping, down to the budgeting of incomes. Pearl kept a daily log of the marketing expenses, setting down in a hardcover lined notebook the cost of each item in the daily list of their individual tastes. "'Swen' likes more fruit than I do," she said once, "and I eat more eggs,"—a remark which might have triggered one of May's *Riddling Poems,* **"At Breakfast,"** again an amazingly accurate view of her subject in depicting both the physical and metaphysical aspects of the egg, without naming it once.

Pearl worked in an office and was studying for a college degree at night, so May had the place to herself for her poetry writing after her hours at New Directions until dinnertime, and several evenings a week. (Meals were cooked together or alternately by one or the other; occasionally there would be a guest or two, usually on weekends.) In spite of their busy schedule, the two found time not only to entertain but to help their friends in various ways; but let anyone take advantage of their concern, as one writer did by making more and more demands on their time, and the friendship was severed abruptly, with a finality that left no room for reconciliation. There were those who criticized the action, but May was adamant. When the demands of a friendship interfered with her writing schedule it was not possible to continue the relationship. (Subsequently her expedience proved just, for others had a similar experience with the same writer.)

The second big breakthrough for the poet from Utah came in 1954, when she was "discovered" by Scribner's through the good offices of [the late] John Hall Wheelock, who had been commissioned by the publishing house (with whom he kept his connection, though he had retired from editorship some years before) to uncover new and promising talent. Swenson was informed that Scribner's would like to publish a volume of her poetry as soon as she had one prepared which met the approval of the editorial board. Years later, toward the end of the sixties, Wheelock said, "May was the first of the six young poets I discovered for Scribner's—and she was the best."

It was a cause for celebration, and a fine celebration there was at 23 Perry Street. Poets and writers in all fields, painters, composers, all the people May had made friends with at the various colonies, and more she had met through them showed up for the event. To one early arrival, Pearl confided, "Howard Moss is coming!" her inflection implying another possible break-through for May: Moss had been poetry editor of *The New Yorker* for a number of years at that point, and was the target then already of every poet aiming for publication in the magazine. He arrived at the party along with John Hall Wheelock, who, though nearing seventy, looked like a man in his early fifties; he regarded May as his prodigy, his gaze resting on her occasionally with pride and satisfaction. His tall, lean figure could be seen moving among the guests, as he conversed with the ease, graciousness and good humor that had won Sara Teasdale's heart more than thirty years before.

Those two innovators of electronic music, Otto Luening and Vladimir Ussachevsky, were on hand to toast the poet and her future success. Luening had set May's poem, **"Night Wind,"** to his experimental music, turning into an extended, weird whistling sound the cadence of the poet's lines. As the crowd increased, the decibel of high talk and laughter rose in direct ratio. The noted artist, Beaufort Delaney, then just about to leave for Paris where he gained recognition for his striking abstract expressionism, added to the level of happy din as he beat out rhythms on a bongo drum he had brought along. A ring of admiring listeners stood around him, either clapping hands in time or, if they held glasses of wine, stamping their feet to the beat. Several clamored to try out their skill and begged Beaufort to show them the correct way to handle the drum.

The occasion was memorable in many ways. It marked the beginning of May Swenson's association with Scribner's and Wheelock, who proved her friend and adviser as he had to so many young poets. And soon after the party, May received her first acceptance from *The New Yorker* for one of her poetic riddles which she called, **"By Morning,"** a delicate description of a snowfall with a philosophic finale containing a biblical reference tinged with Swensonian skepticism. Some of the images are particularly telling:

> Streets will be   fields

cars be   fumbling sheep

A deep bright harvest will be seeded
in a night

By morning we'll be   children
feeding on manna

a new loaf on every doorsill

As sophisticated as *The New Yorker* is, the editors felt that the title was too subtle. It was preceded by the explanatory word, "Snow," when the poem appeared in the magazine. May was distressed; she had protested the addition to no avail, and since she did not want to jeopardize this or future publication, she let it stand. But when she prepared her second book, *A Cage of Spines,* she restored the original brief, enigmatic, two-word title, and placed this second in a section called, "Riddling Poems," which led off with **"At Breakfast."** As things turned out, Scribner's did not want to publish this volume, though Wheelock assured her they were still interested and would probably take the next. It was a disappointment, but May found another publisher.

In her poetry, May Swenson plays a different game—one of shapes, startling images, and mystery in her metaphors.
— *Jean Gould*

In the summer of 1957, she received a Robert Frost Fellowship to the Breadloaf Conference at Middlebury, Vermont, where she met William Rainey, editor at Holt & Rinehart (Winston had not yet been added to the company), Robert Frost's publishers. As a "fellow," May was entitled to a reading by "the great man," as she put it. He gave an informal lecture to all the participants at the beginning of the conference, followed by informal discussion. Afterward May went up to him with her portfolio, which he took, telling her to come back the next morning and meet him there at Treman Hall. She showed up on time, in fear and trembling for his verdict. As she approached the table where he was sitting, on the top of which lay her manuscript, he stood up, reaching for the portfolio. Handing it back to her, he said, "It *reeks* of poetry!" and walked away without further comment, or giving her a chance to thank him or question him, leaving her nonplussed, utterly bewildered as to whether he was condemning or complimenting her work.

If she had known Frost better, she probably would have realized that his verdict contained both approval and disapproval. Frost was too keen a craftsman himself not to recognize poetry when he saw it, but hers was not the kind he cottoned to. He was famous for his remark that he would

"as soon play tennis with the net down" as write poetry without meter, whether it was iambic pentameter, tetrameter, or hexameter; and though he himself took liberties with form, seeing how far he could go and still stay within the guidelines—he called it "riding easy in harness"—only made the game more interesting. In her poetry, May Swenson plays a different game—one of shapes, startling images, and mystery in her metaphors. The philosophic content, though not foremost, is always present, sometimes as an afterthought or an ironic twist, as in **"Southbound on the Freeway,"** when a "tourist from Orbitville, parked in the air," observes that "the creatures of this star / are made of metal and glass." After nine two-line stanzas the Orbitvillian asks: "Those soft shapes, / shadowy inside / the hard bodies—are they / their guts or their brains?" Whether Frost agreed with her technique or not, he obviously realized that this was an original poet, for Holt published *A Cage of Spines* in 1958. William Rainey became her editor there and could have had something to do with the decision to publish, but it is quite likely that the Board asked Frost's opinion, and that he gave his recommendation without ever mentioning it, just as he had in the case of Babette Deutsch. May should have made the connection but she did not, and his remark remained a conundrum to her for almost twenty years. She kept it to herself all that time and only in 1976, when she was a counsellor at Breadloaf, did she have the courage and the confidence to tell the anecdote to the aspiring poets. And a little later, in September, talking with someone who suggested the above, did she realize, with relief, that Frost's succinct critique was not scathing or entirely negative.

A Cage of Spines, moreover, received such good notices that Scribner's decided the time had come to fulfill its promise of publication. Swenson's third volume, *To Mix With Time,* was the first to appear under the imprint of that house and was followed by at least half a dozen more. As the title implies, in the collection which came out in 1963, this poet, like many of her colleagues, is concerned with the passage of time, the inevitability of death; but her outlook is objective, even optimistic. The title itself is contained in a poem that exemplifies Swenson's wit and calm approach to age, to the usually terrifying aging process. **"How To Be Old,"** written in straight stanza form, is one of the poems of a group Swenson made during a journey through France, Italy, and Spain while on an Amy Lowell Travelling Scholarship, which she received in 1961.

"It is easy to be young," this poem starts. "(Everybody is / at first.) It is not easy / to be old. It takes time./ Youth is given; age is achieved. / One must work a magic to mix with time / in order to become old." In the second stanza the poet likens youth to a doll that is given but must be put away in a closet, to be played with "only on holidays." She gives the formula for preserving the doll, adoring it, remembering it in the dark on ordinary days, "and every day congratulate one's aging face in the mirror." The closing stanza summarizes the results of the prescribed "magic":

> In time one will be very old.
> In time, one's life will be accomplished.
> And in time, in time, the doll—
> like new, though ancient—may be found.

The scholarship, intended for one person, was not large but Pearl, who had never seen Europe, was longing to go, and with the savings she and May had managed to put away, they decided to make the funds do for two. New Directions, where May was still on the same schedule, gave her a leave as they had before, and Pearl took off from her job. Though both were in their forties, they planned to stay in youth hostels whenever possible, hire a car so they could drive wherever they pleased, and provided themselves with sleeping bags, so they could sleep on the ground if necessary or the weather permitted. It was a frugal but fruitful safarilike grand tour, yielding all the poems in section two of *To Mix With Time*. And though the subjects might be old as the hills they travelled—one poem, **"Instead of the Camargue,"** where they "hoped to find wild bulls and flamingos," narrates the experiences of a motor trip through Cezanne and Van Gogh country—the treatment was brand-new. Elizabeth Bishop wrote of Swenson's unique style, "If you have thought that no one could ever again react as originally, and, above all, simply, as though she were the first tourist to see the Pantheon, say, or the Arno—you should buy and read this book." Robert Lowell was of the opinion that "Miss Swenson's quick-eyed poems should be hung with permanent fresh paint signs." Her technique of designing visual typography is especially effective in **"Fountains of Aix,"** where the reader sees a stream of "water" running diagonally down the page. The word, repeated fifteen times, forming the ends of fifteen lines but separated from the rest of the words in each by a single-spaced gap, gives the impression of a constant flow from fountains placed at intervals down the terraced land.

Back in New York, May returned to her post at New Directions, which always seemed to be open to her when she needed it, but was not binding when funds came her way. In 1959 she had received a Guggenheim Fellowship, and in 1960, an award from the National Institute of Arts and Letters. She had also begun to go on reading tours, which were more of an interruption than an inspiration for her creativity, but they provided a few weeks' income and kept her name before the literary public.

The flexible relationship with New Directions was maintained until 1965 or 1966, when May Swenson became poet in residence at Purdue University, and the leave of absence (which started in 1965 at her departure for Purdue) became permanent. By then, Scribner's was eager to have her name

on their roster of regular authors and, in 1966, brought out *Poems to Solve*, a collection of the riddling poems for a younger audience. A year later *Half-Sun, Half-Sleep*, a slim volume of her most recent work, appeared (1967), and in 1970 the controversial *Iconographs* came out. May coined the title word, chose the typography, and designed the cover in black and red, signifying a typewriter ribbon. The controversy arose over the makeup of the book, and the fact that the majority of the poems were set in varying shapes or "graphs" suggesting the image employed in the content (hence May's new-minted word).

Some found this graphic poetry a stunning innovation; to others it seemed stilted on one hand because of the typescript, and on the other too diffuse because of the varying shapes, which were a distraction. For example, **"The Lowering,"** a memorial poem concerned with the military funeral honoring Robert Kennedy, a powerful denunciation in ironic terms, decrying the falseness of pomp and ceremony, was first published in *The New Yorker* in straight stanzas. The lines offering a folded flag to members of Kennedy's family instead of the dear one they had lost, and to the "Nation, instead of a leader, to take / this folded flag" had tremendous impact. But in *Iconographs* the poem appeared in graphic shape, intended to depict folding and burial of the flag, thereby heightening the drama. However, some of the power was lost in the figured presentation since the reader was occupied with puzzling out the shape. When asked during an interview why she changed the framework of this poem, and indeed, devised so many typographical tricks, she answered slowly, as if trying to puzzle it out for herself: "I can't tell you why exactly. I guess it was instinctive. About halfway through the preparation, as I began to type the manuscript, I suddenly felt that this was the way to offer these poems, and I had to do it."

At the back of the book is a rather ambivalent explanation of both title and technique, in which Swenson says in part: "To cause an instant object-to-eye encounter with each poem even before it is read word—after—word. To have simultaneity as well as sequence. To make an existence in space, as well as in time, for the poem. These have been, I suppose, the impulses behind the typed shapes and frames invented for this collection." Then, after an explanation of the derivations of the title (quite obvious to anyone with a rudimentary knowledge of language), she resumes, "I suppose these were my aims. But I come to definition and direction only *afterwards*. . . . I have not meant the poems to depend upon, or depend from, their shapes or their frames; these were thought of only after the whole language structure and behavior was complete in each instance. What the poems say or show, their way of doing it with *language*, is the main thing." (The italicized words are the poet's.) The discussion seesaws between justification and negation of her method in this volume, and the "Note" concludes: "The first instrument to make contact, it seems to me, and the quickest to report it, is the eye. The poems in *Iconographs,* with their profiles, or space patterns, or other graphic emphases, signal that they are to be seen, as well as read and heard, I suppose."

The final phrase indicates the tentative attitude Swenson herself took toward the experimental volume, which was so uneven in its appeal and achievement. The hymnlike lyric, **"Black Tuesday,"** praising the heroic martyrdom of Martin Luther King, with the dedicatory line at the end bearing his name and the date, April 4, 1968, is much more successful than **"The Lowering,"** which follows it on the opposite page. Here one sees at a glance that the poet is holding a flag aloft for the murdered black leader. The title, **"Black Tuesday,"** repeated six times and running vertically alongside the lines, forms the pole. And the lyric beginning, "Blessèd is the man of color / for his blood is rich with / the nuclear sap of the sun," a series of stanzas set in straight sequence, suggests a flag flung out against the infinite sky. The word "blessèd" is repeated as each aspect of the man of color is brought out; and the whole has the Biblical tone of a Negro spiritual. The visual frame of the flag adds to the tribute paid. Swenson did not seem perturbed that some readers found her technique, though successful in poems like **"Black Tuesday,"** (or the early **"Fountains of Aix"**) often failed, or detracted from the deeper meaning of others. Instead of taking offense, she was interested in the various reactions, negative as well as positive.

One might assume from the examples given so far that May Swenson's poetry is entirely cerebral, but it is balanced by an earthy eroticism that is present in all her descriptions of the bodies of the human and other animals. Breasts and buttocks are noted in her lines with a tactile sense, along with hips and thighs and genitals. Of a lion, his "unused malehood" swaying idly as he paces in his cage; or a young gondolier, his testicles bulging like a limp frog beneath his tight trousers; "big-hipped nature bursts forth . . . / from pelvic heave of mountains / On swollen-breasted clouds he fattens and feeds"; and "fireflies throw / love winks / to their kind / on the dark." The effect is sensual as well as sexual. Even a poem with the innocuous title, **"One Morning in New Hampshire,"** has its appeal to the senses with sexual overtones: "we are ripe / as fruits ourselves, enjoyed / by lips of wind our burnished slopes" and "rapt bumble-eyes of susans are deployed / as if to suck our honey-hides. Ants nip / tasting us all over / with tickling pincers. / We are a landscape to daddy-long-legs / whose ovoid hub on stilts climbs us like a lover, / trying our dazzle, our warm sap."

As she became known, May's contact with her colleagues increased, and she found new friends among those whose poetry she admired. One of these was Elizabeth Bishop, as her poem, **"Dear Elizabeth"** (A Reply to Elizabeth Bishop

in Brazil), clearly indicates. It opens, "Yes, I'd like a pair of 'Bicos de Lacre'—meaning beaks of 'lacquer'. . ."; and in the fourth stanza she plans, "on the back porch on Perry St.; here, I'd / build them a little Brazil. / . . . I can see them as I write—on their perch on my porch." The poem first appeared in *The New Yorker* in 1964, then in the volume, ***Half-Sun, Half-Sleep;*** but it was not included in *Iconographs,* nor in ***New & Selected Things Taking Place,*** Swenson's latest collection (1979). At a poetry reading by Elizabeth Bishop and Howard Moss at the YMHA in New York City in 1976, it was Swenson who was asked to introduce Bishop, and in her remarks one heard her high esteem for her colleague and friend.

Shortly before *Iconographs* appeared, May met a young woman of Scandinavian background—Roxana Knudsen, a buxom, blond teacher and author of children's books—and she was so taken with her new friend's well-rounded person, intellectually and physically, that the close ties with Pearl began to weaken. The latter had begun to write poetry, which might have put a strain on their relationship. In any case, those who had always known them together were more than startled when Swenson decided to move from Perry Street to the home Knudsen owned in a seacoast suburb. The news that May and Pearl were separating after so many years caused a great commotion among their long associates in the literary world. No one could understand why the alliance was breaking up. Speculation ran high among their mutual friends. Babette Deutsch, meeting one of these on the Fifth Avenue bus, began discussing the situation. On hearing that Pearl had been writing poetry, she nodded her head sagely. "That could be cause for divorce," she said.

Whether it was or not, the two parted amicably, and May Swenson has lived on the Atlantic seaboard and in Southern California for at least ten years, writing, appearing in poetry readings, observing and enjoying a new kind of life. Several poems in *Iconographs,* such as, **"A Trellis for R.,"** seem to refer to her companion, whose name she soon shortened to "Zana." Roxana had no objection, and "Zana" she has remained.

In the early seventies, May was commissioned by the University of Pittsburgh to translate the poems of Tomas Transtömer, a Swedish contemporary poet. It was a challenge she could not resist. She had spoken Swedish at home until she was six years old and, though she had lost most of it, the effort of translation brought it all back. However, her grammar was "shaky," so she was given an assistant, Leif Sjoberg, with whom she worked for over a year. He would do a "word-for-word" translation, and so would she; and then she would make poems of them. Transtömer later came to the United States, after the University of Pittsburgh published the volume of translations, and the two poets gave readings of them together, in Swedish and English.

For several years, Swenson had not been satisfied with her publishers, and her latest volume, **New and Selected Things Taking Place,** was brought out by Atlantic/Little, Brown. In 1979, with many honors and awards to her credit, Swenson, still the skeptic, designated her work as "things taking place" rather than poems. Anne Stevenson, an American poet living in England, was of the opinion (in *The New York Times Book Review*) that they took place "in a number of shapes and a few too many tricks" for the critic's taste, but she praised the overall effect of the book for its keen wit, sophistication, and the accuracy of Swenson's descriptive powers in drawing word-pictures of birds and landscapes. She concedes that "there is no doubt that underneath the verbal fireworks lies a sophisticated seriousness" and that Swenson "has a heart but keeps it strictly under the discipline of her brain." Unfortunately Stevenson reviewed the volume along with the superlatively laudatory estimate of Muriel Rukeyser's *Collected Poems,* which detracted from the praise she bestowed on Swenson. Her opening sentence, "It would be difficult to conceive of a greater contrast to the spiritual and moral commitments of Muriel Rukeyser than the clever, skeptical poems of May Swenson," unwarrantedly puts one on guard against mistaking brilliant technique for genuine poetic genius. And though the critic follows her statement with the acknowledgment of Swenson's heartfelt—if controlled—emotions, and goes so far as to admit, with validity, that the poems about May's parents, their lives and deaths, are moving in their objective yet tender view, the reader cannot help feeling that Swenson's art lacks the depth of Rukeyser's.

Another reviewer, in the *Christian Science Monitor,* spoke of Swenson's poems as "sparkling jewels," but perhaps gems that had been polished too highly: the glitter outshone the substance in many instances, he felt. Yet, in spite of occasional objections to her dazzling technique, May Swenson's **New and Selected Things Taking Place** was received with critical enthusiasm and admiration. Stevenson ended her appraisal by linking Swenson to Rukeyser and another of her peers, Elizabeth Bishop; citing the qualities they have in common despite their differences, she observed, "They are all survivors, and they are all wise." The review closed, "It is good to read these collections, in which Ms. Swenson and Ms. Rukeyser, in their different ways, celebrate so much without any trace of sentimental ignorance."

Swenson's volume, her eighth, was nominated for the 1979 National Book Award, and the Academy of American Poets awarded her its 1979 Fellowship of ten thousand dollars for "distinguished poetic achievement." Her career as poet has shown a steady rise in stature, the kind of growth that stems from a directness of purpose marking the dedicated poet. Nowhere is this attitude more clearly illustrated than in the series of seven meditative poems under the title, **"October,"** published first in *The New Yorker* in 1978. Here is

the early autumn of the artist's life, her recollections of her father, his skilled hand marred by a scarred nailles thumb that was "nipped by a saw," peeling a pear while her mother boiled the bottles for "putting up." Part of these meditations take place as the poet sits in the barber chair, her "round head a newel poked out of the . . . sheet."

To a stranger, May Swenson's round head, her round Swedish face, her hair worn in a straight cut with a line of bangs across her forehead, makes her seem at first meeting a stolid, even stern person; but her playful wit soon comes to the fore when one talks with her. She will make a comic remark, keeping a straight face, and not until she smiles, when the lines around her eyes crinkle with silent laughter does one realize that she is full of mischievous humor. Life to her is a game, earnestly played, as much of her poetry is a game. And nowhere is this contrast in mood to the meditations of **"October"** more apparent than in the semisatiric, punning fantasy piece, **"The Pure Suit of Happiness,"** a first-line title, followed by, " / not yet invented. How I long / to climb into its legs," the poem continues, and goes on to the second of the seven three-line stanzas: "fit into its sleeves, and zip / it up, pull the hood / over my head." She gives other features of the sought after suit: "It's / not too heavy, not too / light. It's my right. / It has its own weather, /

> which is youth's breeze,
> equilibrated by the ideal
> thermostat of maturity,
>
> and built in, to begin with,
> fluoroscopic goggles of
> age. I'd see through
>
> everything, yet be happy.
> I'd be suited for life. I'd
> always look good to myself.

Contrived? Too clever? Perhaps. However, the poem catches the essence of May Swenson's personality as well as her outlook on life—skeptical, but often playful, gently satiric, imaginative, perceptive, and subtly serious.

Thomas M. Disch (review date 22 May 1988)

SOURCE: "Rhyme and Reason: Reading Poetry for Pleasure," in *The Washington Post Book World,* Vol. XVIII, No. 21, May 22, 1988, pp. 1, 14.

[*In the following excerpt from a review of five books of poetry, Disch offers praise for* In Other Words, *noting especially Swenson's flair for writing poetry that deals with minutiae.*]

We pick the poets we read (supposing we read poetry at all) as we pick our friends, for a disposition, sensibility and sense of humor that complement our own. This simple fact of readerly life is often a source of distress to particular poets and their partisans, who feel that esthetic merit should be commendation enough. They live in that fantasy world created at the universities, the Republic of Letters, where every two or three decades constitutes an Age with its own roster of canonical Authors. Almost all the teapot tempests of the world of poetry revolve about questions of admission into the short-list of candidates of canonical status in our own, as-yet-unnamed Age, to become one of the poets destined to be discussed for an hour on PBS, poets we are supposed to read, as we take medicines, whether we like the taste or not.

The five poets here under review are all of a competence and (relative to their ages) recognized stature sufficient to qualify them as canonical contenders, yet I cannot imagine a single reader of so catholic a taste as to relish all five. Here it is not only safe, but true, to say that admirers of X will be delighted with X's new book. If X = May Swenson, they will be delighted with *In Other Words,* which James Merrill praises on the back jacket with undisguised equivocation: "Wonderful May Swenson. . . . Without her to write them, who could have imagined these poems?" Well, Marianne Moore for one, and Moore's protegé Elizabeth Bishop for another, nor can I imagine Swenson taking umbrage at having Merrill's question answered so, for her poems are clearly in that line of descent.

Readers who love to see the curious and lovely objects of the world, its flora and fauna and choicer collectibles, catalogued and anatomized will admire Swenson's skills at such tasks much as they would Moore's or Bishop's. She is a magpie of rare proper nouns: "palo verde, teddybear cholla, ocotillo, bristlebush, and organpipe" are strung together in one catalogue. Words are her Tinkertoys: "The roldengod and the soneyhuckle / the sack eyed blusan and the wistle theed" is the beginning of the relentlessly playful **"A Nosty Fright."** She commemorates all of life's smallest occasions just as she collects string, as witness the first stanzas from **"A Thank-You Letter"**:

> Dear Clifford: It took me half an hour to undo the
> cradle of string in which your package from
> Denmark came.
>
> The several knots tied under, over and
> athwart each other—tightly tied and
> looped
> and tied again—proved so perplexing.
> When,
>
> finally, the last knot loosened, letting

the string—really a soft cord—fall free
the sense of triumph was delicious.

> I now have this wonderful cord 174"
> long
> although your package is only 13 x 10
> x 2. . .

Swenson can be spinsterish in larger-spirited, less cozy ways than this, but "spinsterish" is the operative adjective throughout, and readers who do not wish to adopt a maiden aunt into their imagination's extended family won't get on with her. It's their loss.

Sven Birkerts (essay date 1989)

SOURCE: "May Swenson," in *The Electric Life: Essays on Modern Poetry,* William Morrow and Company, Inc., 1989, pp. 197-215.

[*In the following essay taken from his volume,* The Electric Life, *Birkerts explores Swenson's progression during her career from an emphasis on presenting detached, technically adroit poems treating outside objects to an emphasis on more introspective poems expressing an inner voice and treating themes such as the role of the self in the scheme of life. Birkerts concludes by asserting his contention that Swenson did not always utilize her full capacity as a writer in her poetry.*]

Reverse chronology appears to be enjoying a vogue among publishers of collections of poetry. I can't see the logic of it myself. If the poet in question has improved over the years, shedding bad habits, widening the reach, then we are apt to get increasingly demoralized as we turn the pages. If, on the other hand, the poet has declined, then the arrangement scarcely serves his or her best interests—though, admittedly, when that's the case any policy other than self-censorship is a bad one. And if the poet has not so much progressed or declined, has simply changed? Well, then the result can be quaint, like watching the dog running backward over the lawn while the ball arcs back into the hand; or, provided our study is motion and change, instructive.

May Swenson's *New & Selected Things Taking Place* has been put together in just such a fashion. I read it, as I'd been trained, in the Christian manner—proceeding from left to right, top to bottom, front to back—and after a time I realized that I was participating in a most curious event: an eclipse of personality. Section by section, I felt voice and expressiveness yielding ground to formal precision. Subject matter was increasingly framed and distanced. I was disappointed, not because I couldn't enjoy the poems themselves, but because I'd missed the experience of the real process behind the career. Where I should have felt some of the exalting sensations of struggle and self-liberation, I traced only diminution. Any transposition I make now is intellectual and *a posteriori*.

Not every reader, I suspect, will agree that the changes in Swenson's poetry represent positive growth. Those with a bias toward strict form might argue that her poems have declined from purity. The early work has a structural self-containment largely absent from recent offerings; artifice is prized. Those who value poetry as a vehicle for personal expression, on the other hand, will want to praise the human event: Here is a poet who has, with patience and determination, made her way from a detached fascination with otherness to an increasingly subjective recognition of the self as an agent in the chaotic here and now. The inevitable question arises: What do we cherish more, technical excellence or voice? In Swenson's poetry the latter has been achieved to some extent at the price of the former.

The transformation I would chart is a gradual one, and there are exceptions to the pattern everywhere. I can locate freespoken lines in *Another Animal,* the earliest included section, and formal austerities in *Things Taking Place,* the latest. But the overall steady displacement of aesthetic distance by personal involvement seems incontestable. A few sample poems might make my distinction clearer. Here, from *Another Animal,* is **"Horse and Swan Feeding"**:

> Half a swan a horse is
> how he slants his muzzle to the clover
> forehead dips in a leaf-lake
> as she the sweet worm sips
> spading the velvet mud-moss with her beak
> His chin like another hoof he plants
> to preen the feathered green
> Up now is tossed her brow from the water-mask
> With airy muscles black and sleek
> his neck is raised curried with dew
> He shudders to the tail delicately
> sways his mane wind-hurried
> Shall he sail or stay?
> Her kingly neck on her male
> imperturbable white steed-like body
> rides stately away

Note the control. In almost every line the natural flow of the language is subverted, either syntactically, through subject-predicate reversal, or through the clided pronoun ("forehead dips in a leaf-lake"). Persistent artifice, grafted upon the mythic conceit, gives the poem an autonomous character; it is something fashioned *out of* language, not discovered *in* it. The horse has been seen with astonishing accuracy, and the diction expertly serves its ends ("His chin like another

hoof he plants" or "Up now is tossed her brow from the water-mask"), but its animal life is passed to us through a mesh woven, at least in part, of the cadences and imaginings of Marianne Moore. Compare it with the first stanza of Moore's "No Swan So Fine":

> "No water so still as the
> dead fountains of Versailles." No swan,
> with swart blind look askance
> and gondoliering legs, so fine
> as the chintz china one with fawn-
> brown eyes and toothed gold
> collar on to show whose bird it was.

Moore announces her aestheticism, struts it; Swenson is less flamboyant. But in both poems the attention is less focused upon the intrinsic merits of subject, more upon the delays and revelations possible through careful clause manipulation.

Now, from the front of the book, from *Things Taking Place* (and we might remark the two respective titles, the one— *Another Animal*—signaling modest detachment, the other a more embracing sense of activity), here is a poem called **"The Willets"**:

> One stood still, looking stupid. The other
> beak open, streaming a thin sound,
> held wings out, took sideways steps,
> stamping the salt marsh. It looked threatening.
> The other still stood wooden, a decoy.
>
> He stamp-danced closer, his wings arose,
> their hinges straightened,
> from the wedge-wide beak the thin sound
> streaming agony-high—
> in fear she wouldn't stand? She stood.
>
> Her back to him pretended—
> was it welcome, or only dazed
> admission of their fate?
> Lifting, he streamed a warning
> from his beak, and lit
>
> upon her, trod upon her
> back, both careful feet.
> The wings held off his weight.
> His tail pressed down, slipped off. She
> Animated. And both went back to fishing.

That Swenson's diction has loosened is obvious immediately. The lines, still tensed, are now open to the event, and the literary nimbus has been blown off. A word like "curried" would be as out of place in this poem as "stupid" would be in its predecessor. But the most fundamental change is of vision. Though both poems belong to the same genre—nature observed—they are as unlike as can be. In **"Horse and Swan Feeding,"** nature has been entirely appropriated by art. **"The Willets,"** while it acknowledges the poet's projections ("in fear she wouldn't stand?"), does not varnish or transform the real event. What's more, it embodies a wisdom, a note of mature reconciliation, that the earlier poem does not. The limitations of language are implicit—we can reflect upon the world around us, but we cannot penetrate its strangeness. What a difference between "white steed-like body / rides stately away" and "She / Animated. And both went back to fishing." Diction is the least of it. The conceptual gulf is as wide as that between Tennyson and Auden.

> **Swenson's aesthetic has always been exclusionary. We sense, especially in the early poems, that every choice of subject also involves the deliberate avoidance of other subjects.**
> **—*Sven Birkerts***

Swenson's aesthetic has always been exclusionary. We sense, especially in the early poems, that every choice of subject also involves the deliberate avoidance of other subjects. And in this, I think, her debt to Marianne Moore and the early Elizabeth Bishop is most conspicuous. (One cannot but wonder in what ways aesthetic reticence is bound up with the privacies of sexual preference, whether the line between private and public is not differently drawn.) The complexities of animal life and natural form are eagerly seized upon, while the intricacies of the social order and the human emotions are not so much overlooked as proscribed. Perception sustained; feeling overruled. It is as if the greater part of Swenson's psychic endowment has been channeled into the sense organs, which then become capable of the most precise registrations. The early sections are filled with *tour de force* lines and images, and playful imaginings that are in no way held by the gravitational field of the emotions. In the poem **"At East River,"** for instance, Swenson artfully turns floating gulls into "ballet slippers, dirty-white," points out how a plane "Turns on its elegant heel: / a spark, a click / of steel on blue," and concludes by describing Brooklyn as "a shelf of old shoes / needing repair."

These early poems, outward looking though they might be, are not all of a kind. Self-exempted from the hazards of voicing emotion, Swenson is free to try on different styles. (Or is this a polite way of saying that she has not yet forged her own distinctive idiom?) In the opening lines of **"Two-Part Pear Able"** (from *A Cage of Spines*), we see her making use of a lucent, Williams-like diction:

> In a country where
> every tree is a pear tree

> it is a shock to see
> one tree
> (a pear tree undoubtedly
> for its leaves are the leaves
> of a pear)
> that shows no pears

> It is a fairly tall tree
> sturdy
> capable looking
> its limbs strong its leaves glossy
> its posture in fact exceptionally
> pleasing

The play of long *ee* sounds against sharply articulated consonants leaves a vivid impression of etched branches. The very same section, however, also finds her using these clotted lines to characterize a squirrel:

> Furry paunch, birchbark-snowy, pinecone-brown
> back,
> a jacket with sleeves to the digits.
> Sat put, pert, neat, in his suit and his seat, for a
> minute,
> a frown between snub ears—bulb-eyed head
> toward me sideways, chewed.

> —from **"News from the Cabin"**

Which would we say is the definitive Swenson? Or should we look instead to the shaped quickness of **"Fountain Piece"**?:

> A bird
>   is perched
>   upon a wing

>   The wing
>   is stone
>   The bird
> is real

This is where the perspectives of hindsight turn out to be useful. If we read from the vantage of Swenson's later *Iconographs* phase, then **"Fountain Piece"** is the more prophetic. If, on the other hand, our ear is more attuned to the most recent work, then the cadences, as well as the relaxed presence of the first-person pronoun, of a poem like **"Waiting for *It*"** will seem to be the truest heralds:

> My cat jumps to the windowsill
> and sits there still as a jug.
> He's waiting for me, but I cannot be
> coming, for I am in the room.

His snout, a gloomy V of patience,
pokes out into the sun.
The funnels of his ears expect
to be poured full of my footsteps.

The lines are vigilant and precise, hovering at the edge of humor. The language is transparent, stripped of excess vowels and consonants; the living creature fills the space exactly. Swenson may have tossed human nature out with a pitchfork, but it has found a way in through the back window. The nonhuman order vibrates at a frequency very near that of the human. A charming domesticity results.

The natural world in Swenson's early poetry is delicately perceived, and its hierarchies are carefully set out. If the household cat reigns over the near end of the spectrum, its counterpart roars at the other:

In the bend of your mouth soft murder
in the flints of your eyes
the sun-stained openings of caves

—from **"Lion"**

In the intervals between we come upon pigeons, owls, butterflies, horses, and monkeys, to name a few. Here, though, is one way in which Swenson differs from Moore. Moore would pounce upon the peculiarities of nature, allowing her observations to coax her language to the idiosyncratic extreme. Swenson is more intent upon charting the distance between creature and human; peculiarity is merely a by-product. Thus, the cat is in intimate alliance ("He's waiting for me"), while the squirrel occupies a middle ground—in nature, but wearing "a jacket with sleeves to the digits"—and the lion is emphatically other: "in the flints of your eyes / the sun-stained openings of caves."

The animal kingdom is just one part of Swenson's subject. Geographical and geological environments are of nearly equal importance. Her poetry moves freely among the different kinds of urban habitat, but it annexes just as avidly the less tenanted places—mountains, plains, shores, and waters. She finds poetic material wherever the eye can discover movement or form. And, I might add, the nuances that she fastens upon are predominantly visual; the delicate measuring tool of the ear works to underscore the masses and details of the seen world. One could put together quite an anthology of kinds of settings, moving from city:

From an airplane, all
that rigid splatter of the Bronx
becomes organic, logical
as web or beehive. Chunks

of decayed cars in junkyards,

garbage scows (nimble roaches
on the Harlem), herds of stalled
manure-yellow boxes on twisting reaches

of rails, are punched clean and sharp
as ingots in the ignition of the sun.

—from **"Distance and a Certain Light"**

to garden:

You've put out
new nooses since
yesterday.

With a hook and
a hook and a hook
you took territory

—from **"A City Garden in April,"** *The Vine*

to lakes:

The hazel waves slip toward me,
the far arcade
honed by the sunset; nothing tears
the transparent skin that water
and sky and, between them,
the undulant horizon wears.

—from **"A Lake Scene"**

to the sea (and note here the remarkable interiorization of the imagery):

Slowly a floor rises, almost becomes a wall.
Gently a ceiling slips down, nearly becomes a floor.
A floor with spots that stretch, as on a breathing animal's hide. It rises again with a soft lurch.

—from **"A Hurricane at Sea"**

Nor is Swenson content to observe the limits of the terrestrial. There are poems that survey landscape from the air, poems that observe clouds from the windows of a plane, and then, with increasing frequency, poems about the sun, the moon, the galaxies. In more recent work the landing of the Apollo astronauts becomes a topic of some fascination. Swenson delights in rendering the technological penetration of the unearthly in terms of the most archaic human images:

A nipple, our parachute
covers the capsule: an
aureole, on a darker aureole

like the convex spiral of
a mollusc, on a great breast:

—from **"'So Long' to the Moon
from the Men of Apollo"**

The more adventurously Swenson ranges among the outer
universe of images in these poems, the more conspicuous is
her rejection of the human subject. So successful is she at
keeping her gaze trained outward that one begins to wonder if she is not is some way using the whole natural world
as a correlative for the psyche and its processes. Indeed,
couldn't we argue that the psyche is bound to represent itself, its repressed contents, in whatever images it selects,
whatever rhythms it convokes? Or is the dissociation of self
a better explanation? Eliot, of course, maintained that the
progress of the artist was a "continual extinction of personality." But then Eliot did not foresee that posterity would
read his poetry with a watchful eye on the individual conspicuously positioned behind the arras of his words. I am
not going to debate here whether dissociation or psychic determinism is the key to interpretation. But Swenson's work,
as we shall see, makes the question a live one.

In her contribution to a volume entitled *The Contemporary
Poet as Artist and Critic* (1964), in her discussion of fellow
formalist Richard Wilbur, Swenson wrote: "The modern lyric
is autonomous, a separate mobile, having its own private
design and performance. It may be little on the page, yet
project a long and versatile dance in the mind. Its total form
and gesture is not a relative, it is an absolute, an enclosed
construct." This would have been written at about the time
that Swenson published ***To Mix with Time: New and Selected Poems*** (1963). Her description is striking, for it joins
together the precise fixities of something constructed and the
fluidity of dance—form and freedom. Certainly she had her
own work in mind. As it happens—and as the phrase "a
separate mobile" suggests—Swenson was beginning to
develop an interest in the semantic possibilities of a
poem's appearance. A number of poems in that collection
explore the relationship between the look of a poem and
its meaning. Some even put the visual and phonic elements on an equal footing, trusting that the disjunction
between the seeing and hearing would set up an unexpected propulsion of parts:

They said there was a	Thing
that could not	Change
They could not	Find
it so they	Named
it	God
They had to	Search
so then it must be	There

—from **"God"**

To my mind, any attempt to subvert the aural foundation of
poetry is doomed to failure. Not only is the natural integrity of the genre compromised—for no effective oral performance is possible—but our own allegiances are strained.
A poem like this asks us to admire its concept even more
than its verbal reality. It is, in a sense, the ultimate attempt
to pry poetry loose from the spoken idiom. To make of words
"an enclosed construct" is to follow the formalist impulse
for its own sake; and pure form, as Hans Castorp discovered on the Magic Mountain, is death.

Swenson continued for a time to move in this direction.
Some time after the 1963 collection came ***Iconographs***, in
which, as is obvious from the title, the visual aspects of the
poems were dominant. Some of the artifacts, typographically
too complex to be reproduced here, were clearly to be considered as artistic shapes in their own right. Poem and world,
form and idiom, were set into opposition.

If we were to draw a figure (how apropos) representing
Swenson's poetic development, ***Iconographs*** would mark—
according to bias—either an apogee or a nadir. By insisting
that the poem function visually, she drew the elastic to its
limit. Since that time, obedient perhaps to the laws of elas-
ticity (otherwise known as dialectics), she has been moving
decisively in the opposite direction, toward a poetry of natural diction. The change in orientation could not be more
complete. I will not presume to theorize about the deeper
causes of this change, but a closer look at the shape of some
of the ***Iconographs*** poems might give us some idea about
the tensions involved.

Let us accept, for argument's sake, that poetry—indeed, any
mode of expression—is entirely determined by the forces of
the unconscious. We could agree, then, that both the linguistic and the visual choices in these poems were responses to
specific psychic pressures—in which case, the iconographic
features would be most telling. Now, even a glance at the
poems in this collection will reveal that a great number of
them are in some way fissured or fractured, that their lay-
out strains against the unity implicit in our conception of
poetry. Here are just two examples:

Stop bleeding said the knife.
I would if I could said the cut.
Stop bleeding you make me messy with this
blood.
I'm sorry said the cut.
Stop or I will sink in farther said the knife.

Don't said the cut.

—from **"Bleeding"**

What does love look like?   We know the shape of death
Death is a cloud, immense   and awesome, At first a
lid is lifted from the   eye of light. There is a
clap of sound. A white   blossom belches from the
jaw of fright.

—from **"The Shape of Death"**

Of course, not all of the poems are iconographically split—some essay other effects—but the tendency is pronounced enough to give pause. There is, as I see it, a fundamental contradiction at the heart of the matter. The dominant impulse sponsoring the visual construction is a formal one; it is a desire for aesthetic wholeness and self-containment. Swenson certainly described her lyric ideal unambiguously enough in the sentences I quoted. How is it then that the artifacts themselves are so often emblems of rupture? Does it seem too farfetched to say that the tension between form-making and form-destroying forces determines this phase of Swenson's career? Or that the obvious movement away from "enclosed construct[s]" in the subsequent poetry marks a victory for the deeper—repressed—demands of the self? The poems in *Things Taking Place* are, with few exceptions, repudiations of the credo cited above. It is almost as if *Iconographs* allowed Swenson to discharge her own imperatives once and for all, as if the artifacts self-destructed out of their own inner necessity, freeing her to move in a new direction.

Things Taking Place, comprising mainly work from the 1970's, is an uneven collection. In some ways it is like a first book, exhibiting that on-off quality that often accompanies a new poet's search for voice. But with this important difference: that the poems that do achieve that expressive synthesis of subject and tone are unquestionably the work of a mature and sophisticated artist. Though there is a paradox here, it shouldn't be too perplexing. For in one very important sense this is a debut. In a long lifetime of writing, Swenson has never before tried to bring her own self forward.

The change is conspicuous, but not dramatic. Readers familiar with Swenson will find many of her customary subjects—there are poems on landscape, animals, the moon landing, and even a few more formal exercises that hearken back to earlier work. But then, alongside this archive of the known, Swenson has included a dozen or so longer pieces that are different from anything she has done before. Not only does she take her own experience as a central subject, but she allows a stubborn and distinctive personal voice to emerge. Restraint has not vanished—hers is not a declamatory "I"—but the ideal of a pure and autonomous poetry has been left behind.

The austerities of observation, once central, are now placed in the service of the voice. Swenson uses the first-person pronoun without coyness or artifice; formerly this could not have happened. Here is a section from an earlier poem called **"Riding the 'A'"**:

I ride
the 'A' train
and feel
like a ball-
bearing in a roller skate.
I have on a gray
rain-
coat. The hollow
of the car
is gray.

The "I" is a situating device, utterly opaque. Compare this with the opening lines of the recent **"Staying at Ed's Place"**:

I like being in your apartment, and not disturbing
anything.
As in the woods I wouldn't want to move a tree,
or change the play of sun and shadow on the
ground.
The yellow kitchen stool belongs right there
against white plaster. I haven't used your purple
towel
because I like the accidental cleft of shade you left
in it.

Measured against the best work of a generation of autobiographical poets, this sort of expression does not command special attention. When compared to Swenson's previous work, however, the departure is quite startling.

Swenson begins *Things Taking Place* with a series of poems about travels in the American West. (As she was born in Utah, this could be interpreted as a gesture of homecoming.) Her description of spaces, mountains, and natural detail is calm and loving. Though their subjectivity is tentative, the poems diverge from previous efforts in that the perceptions are not rendered out of omniscient objectivity, but are controlled by the vantage of the speaker:

Great dark bodies, the mountains.
Between them wriggling the canyon road,
little car, bug-eyed, beaming, goes
past ticking and snicking of August insects,
smell of sage and cedar, to a summit of stars.
Sky glints like fluorescent rock.
Cloth igloo erected, we huff up our bed,
listen to the quaking of leaf-hearts
that, myriad, shadow our sleep.

—from **"The North Rim"**

The lines have a casual, intimate fall. I would even say that they stray over into cuteness—with the punning "bug-eyed, beaming," and the oddball pairing of "ticking and snicking." Nature is not so much the fierce and fabulous architect as a friendly—though still bewitching—presence. The poet herself, as part of the "we," has moved forward into the middle distance. She is not exactly confessional, but she is *there.*

Throughout **Things Taking Place,** we feel Swenson looking for a comfortable way to lodge herself in her settings. Her most successful mode, and the one that she resorts to most often, is both personable and precise. She gives us the human element, but her incessant detailing keeps us at arm's length from intimacy, even when the situation is relatively "unbuttoned":

> When, squint-eyed from the flashing river,
> we climbed into farmyard shade, I spied
> the squeaking door of a little privy
> of new pine board, among trees beyond
> where the blond horse crops. The bright
> hook worked like silk. One seat, and no wasps,
> it was all mine. An almanac, the pages Bible-thin,
> hung by a string through a hole made with an awl.
> Outside, steady silence, and in
> the slit-moon-window, high up, a fragrant
> tassel of pine. Alone, at peace, the journey done,
> I sat. Feet planted on dependable planks, I sat.
> Engrossed by the beauty of the knothole panel
> before me,
> I sat a nice long time.

> —from **"The Beauty of the Head"**

Earlier parts of the poem have set up the relentless swaying of the boat; the square solidity of the privy comes to seem like the very image of heaven—or haven. The delicacy of the description ("The bright / hook worked like silk" and "An almanac, the pages Bible-thin, / hung by a string through a hole made with an awl") yields beautifully to the flat, emphatic repetitions of "I sat." My delirious ear hears "satisfaction" and "satiety"; my Swiftian self bids I add "shat."

Emotion is still problematic for Swenson. While she has begun to address herself and her fellows as subjects, protocols of reserve are studiously observed. When she does allow her gaze to settle on another person, it is generally from a distance, either literal, as in this painterly composition:

> I see Captain Holm
> in yellow slicker,
> right hand behind him
> on the stick of the tiller,
> feet in the well
> of his orange Sailfish:

> like a butterfly's
> single wing, it slants
> upright over the bay.

> —from **"Captain Holm"**

or, as in this poem on the death of her mother, through the scrim of a conceit:

> Mother's work before she died was self-purification,
> a regimen of near-starvation, to be worthy to go
> to Our Father, Whom she confused (or, more aptly,
> fused)
> with our father, in Heaven long since. She
> believed
> in evacuation, an often and fierce purgation,
> meant to teach the body to be hollow, that the soul
> may wax plump. At the moment of her death, the
> wind
> rushed out from all her pipes at once. Throat and
> rectum
> sang together, a galvanic spasm, hiss of ecstacy.

> —from **"That the Soul May Wax Plump"**

This conflation of the spiritual and profane senses of *pneuma* is not my idea of an emotional farewell. It achieves a note of liberation, but precisely because it bypasses the expected pieties. Swenson's extreme detachment keeps her hovering between the exacerbated directness of Villon and the nervous tittering of Monty Python.

In **"Poet to Tiger,"** Swenson attempts a good-humored love poem. But even here, she cannot free herself for apostrophe before she has turned the object of her affections into a hyperbolic dream-creature:

> Or else you wake me every hour with sudden
> growled I-love-yous
> trapping my face between those plushy
> shoulders. All my float-dreams turn spins
> and never finish. I'm thinner
> now. My watch keeps running fast.
> But best is when we're riding pillion
> my hips within your lap. You let me steer.
> Your hand and arm go clear
> around my ribs your moist
> dream teeth fastened on my nape.

Still, this is a less restrained Swenson than we're used to seeing. The active pressure of the lines—not to mention their content—shows a woman's determination to assert herself more vigorously. The to-and-fro modulations between dream and wakefulness make it clear that the contest is, at least in some sense, between the unconscious and conscious parts of the self.

Much as I approve Swenson's effort to present more of herself in her poetry, I do not find that she has fully mastered her new voice. For one thing, there are a number of instances—like the mother poem—where she cannot align her address with her subject. She is skillful when the narration is centered upon material surfaces, but often irritating and unconvincing when she tries her techniques on popular or topical subjects:

> Sent aloft by a leather toe,
> a rugged leather baby
> dropped from the sky and slammed
>
> into the sling of your arms.
> Oh, the feel of that leather bundle.
> Oh, what a blooper and fumbler
> you are, that you couldn't nest it

—from **"Watching the Jets Lose to Buffalo at Shea"**

> Like, everyone wants to look black
> in New York these days.
> Faces with black lenses, black
> frames around the eyes,
> faces framed in black
> beards. Afros on all the blacks—
> beautiful. But like,
> *everyone* looks puff-headed.

—from **"Fashion in the 70's"**

This brings me to the heart of my complaint about Swenson. She is a poet of obvious gifts, among them a lively imagination and a most delicate sensory apparatus. But I rarely find her gifts working on behalf of her full sensibility. The material has always been thought through or imagined through; it has seldom been felt through. The eye does work that the heart should be doing. I cannot speak for everyone, naturally, but I find that poetry not fundamentally rooted in the tears of things is quickly forgotten and seldom, if ever, returned to. Entirely too many of these pieces are of this stamp.

To be fair, though, there are several praiseworthy exceptions; poems, indeed, that distinguish themselves by striking a balance between the inner claim and the external detail. And, as it happens, they tend to be the very poems that take aging and death as their subject. Swenson's reticence and her way with natural images stand her in good stead. In "October," for instance, one of the finest lyrics in the book, she

allows the images to hew to the track of the unstated emotion. The yield is an unaffected and clear-sighted eloquence:

> Now and then, a red leaf riding
> the slow flow of gray water.
> From the bridge, see far into
> the woods, now that limbs are bare,
> ground thick-littered. See,
> along the scarcely gliding stream,
> the blanched, diminished, ragged
> swamp and woods the sun still
> spills into. Stand still, stare
> hard into bramble and tangle,
> past leaning broken trunks,
> sprawled roots exposed. Will
> something move?—some vision
> come to outline? Yes, there—
> deep in—a dark bird hangs
> in the thicket, stretches a wing.
> Reversing his perch, he says one
> "Chuck." His shoulder-patch
> that should be red looks gray.
> This old redwing has decided to
> stay, this year, not join the
> strenuous migration. Better here,
> in the familiar, to fade.

The clean observation, always a feature of Swenson's poetry, is no longer serving strictly aesthetic ends. The images, carried by a steady voice, take their place naturally in a procession that is simultaneously outward and inward. We do not have to be told that the landscape is itself *and* the correlative for the past as it presents itself to memory. The hard-won calm that suffuses the lines could never have been manufactured; the daring of that single "Chuck" certifies that we are in the hands of a genuine poet. I have but one quarrel: that the poem itself belies the final adjuration. Its strength and its grasp of the surrounding world point less to fading than to that singing that comes with the tatters of the mortal dress. Passionate proclamation may yet be in the cards.

Richard Bernstein (essay date 5 December 1989)

SOURCE: "May Swenson, a Humorous Poet of Cerebral Verse, Is Dead at 76," in *The New York Times,* December 5, 1989, p. D24.

[*In the following obituary, Bernstein surveys Swenson's life and career.*]

May Swenson, a poet known for her cerebral, playful verse, and a recipient two years ago of a MacArthur Foundation

Fellowship, died yesterday in Ocean View, Del. She was 76 years old and had been suffering from chronic asthma.

Miss Swenson, who came to New York half a century ago from her birthplace, Logan, Utah, published her first collection of poems, *Another Animal,* in 1954. That book led the critic John Ciardi to declare: "May Swenson is not a promise, but a fact. She has daring, a true feeling for the structure of the whole poem, precision of phrase, and a magic eye for the exact image."

In all, Miss Swenson published nine volumes of poems, many of which first appeared in *The New Yorker.* Unlike many of her counterparts, she did not treat poetry as a tragic expression, a mode of despair. She was associated instead with a more joyful, clever, often lighthearted sensibility. In her poem **"Analysis of Baseball,"** she wrote:

> It's done
> on a diamond,
> and for fun.
> it's about
> home, and it's
> about run.

She transformed her daily experiences—a walk in fresh snow, a view of the surface of water, the observation of a bee sipping nectar from a yellow rose—into objects of art. She was able, as one critic wrote, to make her readers see what they had only glanced at before.

In 1979, when her collection *New and Selected Things Taking Place* was published, a reviewer in *The New York Times* spoke of Miss Swenson's "refreshing delight in the metaphysically absurd." The poet and critic Anne Stevenson called Miss Swenson "a dazzling technician and manifestly an intelligent and sympathetic woman."

May Swenson is not a promise, but a fact. She has daring, a true feeling for the structure of the whole poem, precision of phrase, and a magic eye for the exact image.
—John Ciardi

The idea of the 1979 volume was not so much to write poems but, in the words of the title, to describe "things taking place." Miss Swenson concerned herself with the observations her eyes made, as in this line from a poem entitled **"Colors Without Objects"**:

> I wait for a few
> iridium specks of idea to thrive

in the culture of my eye.

Reflecting poetically on the relationship between observation and intellect, vision and thought, Miss Swenson in 1963 closed a poem entitled **"Cabal"** this way:

> Eye light and mind light,
> lightning taming leather
> I will turn, and be
> a swiftness on the dark.

Miss Swenson, who lived for the last two decades of her life with her companion, R.R. Knudson, in Sea Cliff, L.I., graduated from Utah State Agricultural College. She worked for a year on a Salt Lake City newspaper before coming to New York in the late 1930's. She worked for several years as a stenographer and then as an editor for New Directions, writing poems all the time.

With recognition came awards, including Rockefeller, Guggenheim, and Ford foundation grants, the Brandeis University Creative Arts Award and, in 1981, the Bollingen Prize in Poetry from Yale University. Two years ago, she received a $130,000 Fellowship from the MacArthur Foundation.

Miss Swenson is survived by eight brothers and sisters, all of Utah.

Mona Van Duyn (essay date 1990)

SOURCE: "Important Witness to the World," in *Parnassus,* Vol. 16, No. 1, 1990, pp. 154-56.

[In the following essay, Van Duyn, who was a friend of Swenson, offers a tribute to Swenson, reflecting on both Swenson's personal attributes and on her poetry.]

May Swenson twice warmly introduced me from the reading platform, but I never had the privilege of introducing her. When I was invited to write a "blurb" for her last book, my eager pen moved on and on, writing, I knew, too long a response to be useful; passages were, however, taken from that tribute and printed on the book, along with praise from some of her many other admirers. I will begin by repeating those relatively condensed feelings of mine about her work, with the already printed parts indicated by quotation marks:

> "May Swenson's is an art that comes as close as I know to what I like to think must have been the serious fun, the gorgeous mix of play and purpose of Creation itself. One almost feels that nothing has gone before it; no visions of earlier perfections impinge on its originality; it is a First Thing."

Under the spell of her work, poems of more apparent high finish seem false—their glaze would not have let show the grainy, the gritty detail; the big and little pits; the funny, the quirky, the cranky; the gratuitous streakings of the earth itself out of which the poems were shaped. Focussed almost always on a reality outside herself, her camera records it for our viewing, and, in **"Double Exposure"** like that produced by the human lovers who simultaneously snap pictures of each other in her poem of that name, her ground in return has pictured for us the poet's face at camera. "Drawn up into" her own absolutely unmistakable "squint," her lens of hardheaded affectionate wonder is aimed *into* the light by a mind that has always taken its own advice to "make your own moves."

"What would the rest of us who truly love the world, but whose self-absorption will not usually permit so clear a sight of it, do without her poetry?"

And now we must do without any more of it than we already have.

I first met May, whose poetry I loved, so many years ago that I cannot guess at the date, when, in the early days of readings, she was invited to Washington University (St. Louis). In those bygone days the poet was put up in the guest room of someone congenial (ours, almost always) and fed by that host; the payment was a pittance. May had given few readings (I none, I think), and the rows of chairs in the reading room were arranged in a semi-circle which curved round behind the podium. I sat on one of the ends, front row, and could see May's knees shaking so wildly all during her performance that I wondered how they could hold her upright. Her voice was, throughout, courageously and amazingly controlled, as if the knees were living a terrified life of their own which had nothing to do with the mind, face, and voice. How I admired her! Later, of course, along with the rest of us, she became a calm performer.

At home with us, she and my husband (Jarvis Thurston) discovered a warm connection which kept them excitedly chattering for hours. They had both grown up in Mormon families in Utah, May in Logan, Jarvis in Ogden; May came from a large family of eight or nine children, my husband had only one sister by a mother who was his father's fifth wife (the wives were not simultaneous—each of them had died before a remarriage), but he lived in a small community filled with his grown-up half-brothers and half-sisters. Both he and May had "escaped" from Mormonism, physically and emotionally. While she rested before returning, May read a book of my poems and enthusiastically praised it. When she left St. Louis, Jarvis and I knew we had found a friend, one whom we did not often see in person, but who had permanently lodged herself in our affections.

Still, we did meet from time to time, at Bread Loaf, New York, or St. Louis, and kept in erratic touch by mail. For one reason or another, Jarvis and I never got out to the Sea Cliff house with the inadequate or nonexistent heating system which there was never enough money to repair. May was one of the most unmaterialistic people I know. Nunlike, she warmed and fed herself primarily with writing. A croissant, a paté, the goodies I bought for her lunch when she came to see us in a borrowed apartment in Manhattan, seemed gustatory wonders to her. Some genius in the mysterious awardmaking machine of the MacArthur Foundation gave her a MacArthur in time for her and Zan to go to New Zealand, feel its warmth, and see its animals. The first taste of travel pleasures came in the nick of time.

Her poems were often playful, as Marianne Moore's were often playful—in rhyming, in tone, in shape. Different as they are from each other, unique as is each poet's voice, it is as if the most minute detail of the visible world flowered for both of them with a brightness that lit up the dark personal feelings; or that the rich, exciting passage of discovery through external Creation continually brought to them both "good tidings of comfort and joy." Zan tells me that May particularly loved my poem "Letters from a Father," which contains a litany of birds, seen toward the morose and self-hating end of the father's life with the kind of love with which May saw them (and all nonhuman creatures) *all* her life. In my poem "the world," through the birds which come to a new bird feeder, slowly "woos its children back for an evening kiss."

That round, lined face, framed by an undeviating Dutch bob, its characteristic expression seeming to say, "I am precisely who I am; take me or leave me," will stay with us as long as we can keep our own memories. She was a wonderful woman, a wonderful poet.

Michael Collier (essay date Summer 1991)

SOURCE: "Poetic Voices," in *Partisan Review,* Vol. LVIII, No. 3, Summer, 1991, pp. 566-67.

[*In the following excerpt, Collier applauds* In Other Words: New Poems, *asserting that the volume presents what he terms Swenson's "vision of incredible integrity."*]

The familiar voice in May Swenson's *In Other Words: New Poems* speaks with a naturalist's love for the variety and particularity of the world. In poems that take great delight in discovering the shapes and associations hidden in the natural world, Swenson pays homage to Marianne Moore and Elizabeth Bishop, yet her poems are quirkier, more playful and more celebratory than her two precursors. In **"Three White Vases,"** Swenson suggests that the act of making a metaphor precedes the act of description so that the three white egrets she sees "On a lonely, reedy patch / of sand" are first vases, "each differently shaped." By such perceptions Swenson leads us from the surprises inherent in the world back to the world itself. In an elegy for Elizabeth Bishop, Swenson writes, "A life is little as a dropped feather. Or split shell / tossed ashore, lost under sand. . . . But vision lives! / Vision, potent, regenerative, lives in bodies of words." May Swenson's "bodies" are not metaphorical or symbolic but corporeal, shaped and formed in our mouths as we speak. These bodies make the vision which provides continuity to the human world. Swenson continues her elegy for Bishop, ". . . vision multiplies / is magnified in the bodies of words. / Not vanished, your vision lives from eye to eye, / your words from lip to lip perpetuated."

Although May Swenson often writes about nature and geographies, she is not a poet of place. Instead she is a steadfast and faithful visitor who masks her restlessness with a clear-eyed optimism and curiosity. As a result she searches with patience for ". . . the scene beyond the apron of the eye / about to shift," as she writes in **"From a Daybook."** Sometimes we may feel that a poem has missed this subtle 'shift.' When this happens Swenson's poems can be too purely descriptive. But even when this occurs, as it does in **"Teddy Bears"** and **"Shuttles,"** the writing is always full of exuberance as the poet looks for ways to praise and enjoy the world.

In a section of the book titled "Comics," Swenson plays with the shape of stanzas (one of her long-standing trademarks), mimics songs and advertisements, and includes a parody of a *New Yorker* poem. Her humor and wit are not limited to parody and comedy however. In the poem **"Strawberrying,"** from the book's first section, she writes an optimist's reply to Sylvia Plath's "Blackberrying." Her poem ends with an audacious pun, "—I rise / and stretch. I eat one more big ripe lopped / head. Red-handed, I leave the field." This leads us delightfully back to the poem's opening line, "My hands are murder-red."

In Other Words is spacious book. It is May Swenson's seventh volume of poetry and unfortunately her last. (She died in 1989.) Appearing more than two years ago, it has received scant attention yet it is a book that deserves to be read widely, for it contains a vision of incredible integrity, a vision that "lives in bodies of words."

Richard Wilbur (essay date Winter 1992)

SOURCE: "May Swenson: A Memorial Tribute," in *Gettysburg Review,* Vol. 5, No. 1, Winter, 1992, pp. 81-5.

[*In the following essay, Wilbur commemorates Swenson's contributions to poetry, providing an overview of her life and career.*]

May Swenson was not much given to self-absorption or self-portraiture, but in one of her later poems we find her looking at herself and seeing the lineaments of her mother and father. "I look at my hand," she says—

> I look at my hand and see
> it is also his and hers;
> the pads of the fingers his,
>
> the wrists and knuckles hers.
> In the mirror my pugnacious eye
> and ear of an elf, his;
>
> my tamer mouth and slant
> cheekbones hers.

That gives us a glimpse of May Swenson, though I should like to qualify it; she did indeed inherit a brow and set of eyes which were capable of pugnacity, but what I mostly saw in her blue eyes was forthrightness, independence, good nature, and a great power of attention. She had an appealing and sociable Swedish face, with fair hair cut in a Dutch bob across the forehead.

> **Miss Swenson's quick-eyed poems should be hung with permanent fresh-paint signs.**
> **—Robert Lowell**

May's parents came over from Sweden and settled in Logan, Utah, were converted to Mormonism, and had ten children of whom she was the eldest. After her graduation from the college where her father taught mechanical engineering, and after a spell of journalism in Utah, she came east and lived, for most of her writing life, in the New York area. Nevertheless, she remained Western in many ways. She had a great relish for wild nature and a knowing sympathy with wild creatures; her poems are full of tents and cabins and the out-of-doors; when an Amy Lowell Poetry Travelling Scholarship took her to Europe for the first time, at the age of forty-one, she and a companion "bought a small French car and tenting equipment" and, in their travels through France, Spain, and Italy, spent most of their nights under canvas. Effete Easterners do not make the grand tour in that fashion. The poems are Western, too, in their openness of tone and diction; even at their trickiest, they are made out of plain American words. The breezy spontaneity of their technique—the lineation and spacing, the playful random rhyming—makes sometimes for a lack of finish, but more usually seems in perfect accord with the swift vigor of her spirit.

One thing she did not bring east was Mormonism, or any other kind of church religion. This did not result in any sense of loss or any want of scope. What May put in the place of any supernatural view was a truly knowledgeable awareness, rare among poets of our time, of the world as perceived and probed by contemporary science. An initial reaction to the mention of science, in connection with May's poetry, might be to think of her famous descriptive power, her ability to make us see objects sharply and in new ways. It was this talent that led Robert Lowell to say, "Miss Swenson's quick-eyed poems should be hung with permanent fresh-paint signs." When we talk about Marianne Moore or Elizabeth Bishop, we soon find ourselves quoting their brilliant captures and sightings of things, and so it is with May Swenson, who admired them both; one thinks of how, in a poem of May's, young skunk cabbages rise up out of a swamp like "Thumbs of old / gloves, the nails / poked through // and curled." Or one remembers the lines in which she conveys the shape, motion, and wake of an East River tugboat: "A large shoe / shuffles the floor of water, / leaving a bright scrape."

But this power to observe things keenly is not all that May Swenson shares with the scientist, as may be learned from an essay which she wrote for the Voice of America in the sixties, and entitled **"The Experience of Poetry in a Scientific Age."** What is central in that essay is its acceptance, as a model for poetry, of our cognitive situation as described by the atomic physicist, for whom the swarming particles that constitute the cosmos are not knowable in themselves, but are inevitably altered by our instruments of perception. If that is the way we know the universe, then the unit of reality is not an objective recording of data, or an imposition of order, but an occasion of interplay or dialogue between perceiver and world—what Whitehead called a "prehension." May's poetry is full of such moments of interplay—perceptual games and experiments in seeing that are grounded in a serious theory of knowledge. Her little poem **"Forest,"** for example, begins this way:

> The pines, aggressive as erect tails of cats,
> bob their tips when the wind freshens.

It then proceeds to depict the pine forest entirely in the key of cat—discovering a feline character in its brindled colors, its humped and springy floor, its lashed and winking boughs, and the purring sound of the wind going through them. This might seem merely a fanciful imposition, a virtuoso feat, were it not for the fact that the poet's accurate metaphors realize the forest more vividly than any botanist's language could do—so that the poet in her turn is acted upon, and the

revealed strangeness of the scene creates in her a mood of forest-fear, of panic. The poem thus ends with these lines:

> My neck-hairs rise. The feline forest grins
>
> behind me. Is it about to follow?
> Which way out through all these whiskered
> yawns?

At the beginning of the essay to which I referred, May Swenson says this about the poetic experience: "I see it based in a craving to get through the curtains of things as they *appear,* to things as they *are,* and then into the larger, wilder space of things as they are *becoming.*" That sentence contains the whole drama of May Swenson's poetry, the passion that underlies her playfulness. Though she knows that the senses can deceive us, it is through the alert, surprising use of those instruments that she seeks to break through to reality, refusing (as she says) "to take given designations for granted" or "to accept without a second look the name or category of a thing for the thing itself." Her poetry is, in fact, at war with names and designations, insofar as they can occlude our vision or foreclose our curiosity. *God,* she tells us in one of her poems, is a name that men have given to the idea of changelessness, and such a name is delusive in a world where everything moves and alters, where all is "breathing change." As for lesser names—such as *stream, flower,* or *roller coaster*—it is a special and frequent strategy of hers to withhold them, so that the poem may look more closely, naively, and inquiringly at the things to which they refer.

The riddle is an ancient poetic form in which an object is darkly described and its name withheld. May wrote a good many fine riddles about such objects as *egg* and *fire* and *butterfly*—enough so that a selection could be made "for young readers" and published in 1966 under the title of **Poems to Solve**. We are foolishly inclined nowadays to look at such poems as kid stuff, but to see May Swenson's riddles as part of her whole poetic enterprise is to rediscover the dignity of the form. Richard Howard was right to say that, in this aspect of her work, May wrote "a poetry that goes back to Orpheus." A riddle is at first a concealment, the withholding of a name; but as and when we solve its dark metaphor, the riddle is a revelation, giving us not only a name, but an object freed from clichés of perception and seen with wonder as if for the first time. Most of May's poems, of course, are not riddles, yet again and again they make use of riddling strategy to produce their revelations and to enforce an intense participation by the reader. In a poem called **"Motherhood,"** we seem at first to be looking at an unusually ugly naked woman, who is holding a skinny, louse-ridden child to her breast; yet by the end of the poem, when the mother is proudly swinging from bar to bar with the infant clinging to her armpit hair, we have somehow been led to see her as beautiful. One reason for the success of the piece is that no-where in title or text are we given such words as *ape* or *zoo* or *cage*—words that would allow us to relax into precon-ceptions. The poem is by no means obscure; one begins rather early to know the "answer"; and yet this withholding of a few clinching words prompts one to look hard at the object, be limber in one's response to it, and rejoice at last in another creature's splendid life.

That is what May meant by *getting through,* a process in which the poet transforms the object by some imaginative approach, draws closer to it by repeated acts of attention, and is at last, herself, transformed by the object. We have this pattern at its simplest in a poem called **"While Seated on a Plane."** There, the poet looks out of window and sees the cloudscape as a great parlor full of soft chairs and couches. She dreams of walking out to make herself com-fortable in that "celestial furniture," but is perplexed by its vast, turbulent changes of form. She solves the problem through a further act of imagination, in which she forsakes her own shape and substance and conceives herself as per-petually "deformed / and reformed." "One must be a cloud," as the poem says, "to occupy a house of cloud." Playful and charming as the poem is, it is like many another poem of May's in its passionate wish to cancel the distinction between subject and object and to be at one with the portion of real-ity described. That is the impulse behind the "shaped po-ems," of which she wrote so many, and of which my favorite is a study of wave behavior called **"How Everything Hap-pens."** These creations, which dispose their words on the page to suggest the form or motion of the subject, represent not only pictorial wit but the desire of the poem to become what it is about.

Like Emily Dickinson, who much influenced her, May lived in the universe. No poet of our day has said and conjectured so much about stars and space. But whereas Dickinson's soul could expand to the limits of space and beyond, May's uni-verse is ultimately that of the astronomer and physicist—a storm of galaxies and particles still uncharted by the mind, in which the mind itself may seem anomalous and lonely. Such a reality can be frightening, and May's poems have their moments of Pascalian dread; but her prevalent mood is one of delight. That needs no explaining, I think; when art is morose, we want to know why, but joy requires no rea-sons. It is clear, however, that she trusted her craving to get beyond the self and her rapture in making imaginative fu-sions with the other. In consequence, her poems find the erotic in all forms of natural energy and, whether they speak of nebulae or horses or human love, are full of a wonder-fully straightforward and ebullient sexuality. As for death, she approaches it often in a spirit of Whitmanian merging. Here are the opening lines of a sprightly late poem called **"Ending"**:

> Maybe there *is* a Me inside of me
> and, when I lie dying, he
> will crawl out. Through my toe.
> Green on the green rug, and then
> white on the wall, and then
> over the windowsill, up the trunk
> of the apple tree, he
> will turn brown and rough and warty
> to match the bark. . . .

She is poking fun at conventional notions of the soul, but there is no missing the fact that blessedness, for her, would be a state of perfect transparency. I do not know where May is now, but her poems continue to mix with time, and to be part of the vitality of the world.

Edward Hirsch (review date 19 January 1992)

SOURCE: "'Turned Back to the Wild by Love,'" in *The New York Times Book Review,* January 19, 1992.

[*In the following review, Hirsch offers a highly laudatory assessment of* The Love Poems of May Swenson.]

"Listen, there's just one 'Don't,' one 'Keep Off,' / one 'Keep Away From,'" May Swenson advised the graduating class in her 1982 Harvard Phi Beta Kappa Poem, **"Some Quad-rangles"**: "*Don't be a clone.*" Whatever you do, she en-joined them, "make *your own* / moves. Go opposite, or upside down, or Odd." As a poet May Swenson, who died in 1989 at the age of 76, certainly took her own advice. She was an American original, and her poems—with their aston-ishing formal variety, their quirky visual shapes and incan-tatory rhythms, and their refreshingly odd, insightful observations about the natural world—stand by themselves in the ever-changing landscape of contemporary poetry. No one else could have created them.

The Love Poems of May Swenson is a sexy book. It is also a useful, even necessary addition to the 10 volumes of po-ems that Swenson published in her lifetime. "In love are we made visible," she wrote, and indeed these 55 poems—13 of which are previously unpublished—help make visible an aspect of her work that has been obscure but nonetheless present all along. Rereading her work by the open light of the love poems, tracking the main themes from her first book, *Another Animal* (1954), to the last one published in her lifetime, *In Other Words* (1987), paying particular at-tention to the emblematic *Iconographs* (1970) and the two volumes of selected poems, *To Mix With Time* (1963) and *New and Selected Things Taking Place* (1978), it becomes increasingly evident that a large number of Swenson's radiant nature poems are also love poems. Her shaped verses, elaborately designed spacing and quasi-mathematical forms are love letters to Creation itself, and she continually invests the physical world (and the verbal world) with Eros, celebrating its mysteries and discovering a ravenous erotic drive in all natural processes and transfigurations. The sexual energy that flows through her work is defined as both human and natural.

One of the pleasures in reading Swenson's love poems is the way she discovers appropriate sexual metaphors, resonances and overtones almost anywhere at all, but particularly in observed—inspected—nature.

—Edward Hirsch

There is an injunction in all of Swenson's work to "look closely." She was a riddling Dickinsonian poet of Being whose initiating impulse was to describe, and whose many poems (she published 450 out of the 800 she wrote) celebrate the external world in all its bewildering variety. Swenson owes her greatest poetic debt to Marianne Moore and Elizabeth Bishop, the two writers who most firmly set the formal terms and moral values—studious observation, visual accuracy, verbal clarity—by which she would proceed as a lyric poet. Much as she owes to the descriptive mode, however, these love poems reveal that there is a sexual ebullience and emotional candor that distinguish Swenson from her poetic models.

Swenson's poems are more high-spirited and unruly, emotionally riskier and more exposed. Her finely shaped surfaces may appear to be reticent and cool, but, in fact, these love poems show her to be anything but reserved. They are filled with moral pangs and surges, with passionate and sometimes awkward desires, with sweet embraces and eager declarations, with fiery invitations and witty promises. The poem **"Untitled"** is characteristic:

> I will be earth you be the flower
> You have found my root you are the rain
> I will be boat and you the rower
> You rock you toss me you are the sea
> How be steady earth that's now a flood
> The root's the oar's afloat where's blown our bud
> We will be desert pure salt the seed
> Burn radiant sex born scorpion need

One of the pleasures in reading Swenson's love poems is the way she discovers appropriate sexual metaphors, resonances and overtones almost anywhere at all, but particularly in observed—inspected—nature. The birds and especially the

bees have never been so slyly deployed. Thus she calls dark wild honey that her lover brings home "the sweet that burns." She declares, "I'm a flower breathing / bare, laid open to / your bees' warm stare." She speaks of a splendid day in summer when "the honey in our veins burned deep / We are stored with sweetness / Our breasts are golden hives." I know of no other contemporary poet who has spoken more convincingly of being "unloosed, unharnessed, turned back to the wild by love," or who has more boldly described being in the storm-tossed throes of sexual passion. Here was a late-modern poet willing to risk sentimentality in trying to get at one of the oldest and most traditional poetic subjects—the pure and elemental amazements of love.

In the final poem in this volume, **"Equilibrist,"** Swenson speaks of her body as a "sharpened dart / of longing / coming toward you always." The undertow in these poems sets in when that longing is not reciprocated, isolating and unmooring the lover, leaving her free-floating. In Swenson's highly charged physical world, love alone wakens the self and makes its conscious existence possible. Human connection is all. How firmly she asserts: "No one / can be sure / by himself / of his own being." The beloved is a necessary twin, a mirror to make the self possible. This is less explicit than it might be because of Swenson's ambiguous use of pronouns. "He" is always rhetorical (there are no physical beings who are men here), employed in poems structured like parables. The passionate love poems leave gender unspecified. But when this poet looks in the mirror of the beloved the reflection is female.

There is a compelling reverse spin on Cartesianism in many of Swenson's finest lyrics. Instead of Des cartes's *cogito,* we get a plaintive call to the beloved. In **"Symmetrical Companion,"** she writes, "Come release me / Without you I do not yet exist." "Because you believe I exist I exist," she assures her lover in the poem **"You Are."** "Am I?" she asks, and then answers her own question: "yes / and never was / until you made me."

Because I dwell in you, her poetic syllogism runs, I know I am. Because you enfold me, *we know* you are. Therefore, she exclaims happily, "It is proven and the universe exists!" The lovers "prove" each other's reality, confirming their own existence, confirming the existence of all things. They also liberate each other from the enclosures of mind, from the isolated cell of the self. Thus, according to the poem **"In Love Made Visible"**:

> In love are we set free
> Objective bone
> and flesh no longer insulate us
> to ourselves alone
> We are released
> and flow into each other's cup

Our two frail vials pierced
drink each other up

The Love Poems of May Swenson is a culled, declarative, magnificent book. Part of the splendor of these poems comes from the way they turn not only to the beloved but to the natural world—to the teeming, fluid, emerging, unnamed physical world. These affectionate and intimate poems remind us that May Swenson was that rarest of literary creatures in our century, an authentic poet of celebration and praise, an Orpheus fulfilled. As she wrote in **"Evolution,"** the first poem in her first book:

beautiful each Shape
to see
wonderful each Thing
to name

Doris Earnshaw (review date Winter 1993)

SOURCE: A review of *The Love Poems of May Swenson,* in *World Literature Today,* Vol. 67, No. 1, Winter, 1993, p. 185.

[*In the following review, Earnshaw praises* The Love Poems of May Swenson.]

The posthumous publication of May Swenson's poems celebrating Eros adds luster to the reputation of a major American poet. Swenson (1913-89) came from Logan, Utah, to enter the world of honors, awards, and fellowships as her poetry became known. She writes a language rich in sensual texture, rich in rhyme, and strong in rhythm. Still, however enchanting her wordplay or music, what strikes the reader more deeply in these poems is the intelligence of her understanding. Love, as she tells us about it, has little of the narrative or dramatic interest we might expect. Instead, she exposes the nature of attraction with the precision of a physics text revealing nature's laws. Love for her is akin to Martin Buber's definition of God: a power to be found, from time to time, "between me and thee." Dialectical relationships of all kinds arrest her eyes: tree to tree, bee to flower, human male-female lovers, but also human to self, mind to heart, even a human to his shadow. She feels, and makes us feel, the dialectical form of our most vital moments.

Since love runs as a current between two poles, her symbols and images express connections and meeting places: horizons, balances, arrivals, partings, edges, rims, the season's turnings. In **"He That None Could Capture"** we meet a circus high-wire acrobat who "swims the color-stippled height" and who leaves the light to become (in

dream?) her lover. The final poem, **"Equilibrist,"** suggests that the poet herself is walking the high wire, "instep on the quivering wire" coming toward her lover, who remains "behind the bars of distance / where merge sea and sky." Her power of enfolding extends to a dream in which she dreams. **"The Pregnant Dream"** is a rare poem of dialogue in which the conversation in the dream about the dream is repeated in a time of now. The contraries of love—dryness and water—in two poems about love's bittersweet nature, **"Wild Water"** and **"Stone or Flame,"** recall the compression of Catullus' "Odi et Amo."

Erotic appeal addressed to the ear, eye, and mind together makes Swenson's most powerful poems memorable. This is a sophisticated poetry in its use of line length, refrains, typography, and tone. The short, one- or two-word line of **"A Couple"** brings us like a zoom lens into the mating of a bee and flower. A delicious feeling of a rondo is created in the irregular repeat of the title line in **"All That Time,"** enacting the meaning of the poem in the form. The intricate beauty of love matches between the sentence and the line, as in the virtuoso **"Four-Word Lines,"** indicates a familiarity with the traditions of Western love poetry. The talking tone of a very erotic poem such as **"In Love Made Visible"** reminds one of the way Anna Akhmatova speaks coolly of intimate things. This tone unites the physical and spiritual dimensions of love. For Swenson, the very truth of our identity remains with the lover, as she says in **"You Are"**: "no one / can be sure / by himself / of his own being."

Appropriately, pairs of poems have been arranged on facing pages to speak to one another. A mating scene of water birds in **"The Willets"** is similar to the nonchalant, impersonal bonding of two people in **"Holding the Towel."** Love and death are juxtaposed in both **"Satanic Form"** and **"Night Before the Journey."** In the first, artifacts of civilization (clocks, metal boxes, glass bricks) are overcome by "the intricate body of man without rivet or nail" and other natural forms "not cursed with symmetry." In the second, love asserts its power to enchant and bless as the world ends. Single lines, of course, come to dwell in the reader's imagination. Swenson's words about fear impress me: "Empty of fear and therefore without weight," "our very skin— / a sheath to keep us pure of fear," and the lilting "O love the juice in the green stem growing."

Several poems taken from the volume *Iconography* have undergone changes in line lengths, spacing, and vowel markings. About half the poems may be found in *New and Selected Things Taking Place* (1978). The thirteen previously unpublished poems are listed by title in the front matter.

Alfred Corn (essay date February 1993)

SOURCE: A review of *The Love Poems of May Swenson,* in *Poetry,* Vol. CLXI, No. 5, February, 1993, pp. 295-98.

[In the following review, Corn applauds the poems in The Love Poems of May Swenson, *which he asserts are, except one, all erotic in nature.]*

Maybe I had too high expectations for this collection when it was first announced. A new book by May Swenson is always welcome, and this time normal anticipation was heightened by the possibility that her estate had decided to publish work that shyness or prudence had prevented her from making available during her lifetime. Hopes slipped a notch when the credits page stated that only thirteen of the poems were previously unpublished; five have before now appeared in magazines, but the remaining thirty-seven can be found in earlier volumes of her poetry.

The title isn't quite accurate. For "love" we should substitute "erotic." In a quite good poem called **"Café Tableau,"** the eroticism involved is not even the author's but high-voltage description of the visible attraction between a white woman and a black waiter. Only in the poem **"Year of the Double Spring"** (one of the poems already collected) is the poet's beloved portrayed in non-erotic contexts so as to emerge as specific and individual—one result being that painful currents of feeling are allowed to appear as they inevitably must when love beyond pure eroticism is dealt with realistically. Partly for that reason **"Year of the Double Spring"** is the poem I liked best in the volume:

> I'm thinking of how I leaned on you, you leaning
> in the stone underpass striped with shadows of tracks
> and ties, and I said, "Give me a kiss, A.D.,
> even if you are tranquilized," and I'm thinking
> of the Day of the Kingfisher, the Indigo Day of the Bunting,
> of the Catfish Night I locked the keys in the car
> and you tried to jimmy in, but couldn't with a clothes hanger.

We later see A.D. at a juke joint, pretending to "flake out on the bench," still later, "riffling *Playboy.*" Perfect accessibility, perfect unity is not being described: this is a believable love.

Here, as in all the other poems in this volume, the beloved is addressed as "you," never as "she." Agreed, second-person address is more intimate than the third-person, and it removes an obstacle (minor or enormous, depending on the reader) that stands in the way of entire identification with the poet. At a time when we are witnessing the emergence of a new lesbian poetry, it is also a lost opportunity—not just at the level of bare fact or politics, either. When the poet

composes with a built-in hindrance, other kinds of unconscious hindrances are likely to operate as well. Not every feeling will be within reach, a loss for the poet and for the audience, unless the audience belongs to those (including, alas, Elizabeth Bishop) who "wish they would just keep it to themselves." The sex of the beloved could, of course, be made explicit even in poems addressed to "you," but this happens glancingly in only a couple of instances where the poet mentions, "our breasts." Otherwise we have to "guess," as the jeans ad tells to, peering intently through the gorgeous beaded curtain of this poet's language where we believe we can see two women, and not the nude male-female couple of the pretty cover photograph. No one who did not come of age as a lesbian in the 1940s, though, has the right to judge Swenson's (or Bishop's) choices, so I will shut up.

The women glimpsed in these poems are in any case very fulfilled. To find physical pleasure rendered as ecstatically as this, you'd have to go to the Bible—*The Song of Songs*—or friezes of Hindu temples. It's as though the poet were paraphrasing Whitman, saying, "There's a lot of us and all so luscious."

> In the sun's heart we are ripe
> as fruits ourselves, enjoyed
> by lips of wind our burnished slopes.
> All round us dark, rapt
> bumble-eyes of susans are deployed
> as if to suck our honey-hides. Ants nip,
> tasting us all over
> with tickling pincers. We are a landscape
> to daddy-long-legs, whose ovoid
> hub on stilts climbs us like a lover,
> trying our dazzle, our warm sap.
>   **[—"One Morning in New Hampshire"]**

It's true that, reading this and some of the other more rapturous poems, I had to contend with feeling like a third wheel or some irrelevant daddy-long-legs, enjoying borrowed glory. It may also be true that the storehouse of traditional metaphoric terms for sex is pretty quickly used up: sex is like a dip in the ocean, the visit of a honeybee to a flower, it is like daring to eat a peach or being turned into pure gold. Uninterrupted delight produces a strangely solemn effect in any lyric longer than eight lines, which will always need at least a minimal plot beyond the very familiar one of tingle-to-ecstasy.

On the other hand, when the comic narrative of a poem like **"Wednesday at the Waldorf"** seems to invite the laughter of an audience in on the joke, almost everyone will cheerfully go along with it:

> Two white whales have been installed at
> the Waldorf. They are tumbling slowly

above the tables, butting the chandeliers,
submerging, and taking soft bites
out of the red-vested waiters in the
Peacock Room. They are poking *fleurs-de-lys*
tails into the long pockets on the
waiters' thighs. They are stealing
breakfast strawberries from two eccentric
guests—one, skunk-cabbage green with
dark peepers—the other, wild rose and
milkweed, barelegged, in Lafayette loafers.

The buoyant anarchists somehow follow Swenson's two guests up the elevator to their rooms, where, presumably, Lafayette loafers are kicked off before the pair get in bed and allow the no doubt female Mobys to inspire them to still greater heights. This poem has to be added to the growing literature about one of old New York's classic hotels, the best known example up to now Steven's "Arrival at the Waldorf," for him a hotel "Where the wild poem is a substitute / For the woman one loves or ought to love. . . ."

There are actually an impressive number of other memorable poems in this collection, **"Swimmers," "Early Morning: Cape Cod," "Each Day of Summer," "Organs," "The School of Desire,"** and **"Dark Wild Honey,"** for example. But I will conclude by quoting **"Our Forward Shadows,"** which is suggestive in metaphysical as well as physical ways. Swenson seems to sense that she is on the brink of something for which sex is, apart from being fun, also a metaphor, a metaphor we might understand as describing a future tradition Swenson's poetry is helping to found:

> we are dressed
> each in the other's kisses
>
> our shadows reach
> to teach us our parts
>
> the enchanted prelude starts

Forward, shadows!

The Horn Book Magazine (review date May/June 1993)

SOURCE: A review of *The Complete Poems to Solve,* in *The Horn Book Magazine,* Vol. LXIX, No. 3, May/June, 1993, p. 341.

[*The following review offers a highly favorable assessment of* The Complete Poems to Solve.]

Included in this volume are seventy-two poems for young

readers, many of which appeared in *Poems to Solve*. In addition to several riddle poems, the collection contains a variety of verses that are evidence of the scope of Swenson's imaginative powers and verbal skills. Examples of her shaped poems, in which the placement of the words on the page suggests the subject, are represented by **"Of Rounds"** and **"How Everything Happens (Based on a Study of the Wave),"** two of her more accessible and most frequently anthologized works. This gifted poet asks much of her young readers. As she says in her introduction, "The identity or significance of what's inside [a poem] may be concealed or camouflaged by the dimensions or shape of its 'box.'" For the perceptive reader, however, the joys of revealed meaning can be intense and personal. Swenson's unique vision can bring an egg, a stick afloat in the ocean, or a dandelion into fresh perspective. There is humor in **"Analysis of Baseball,"** clever word play in **"To Make a Play,"** and unexpected, dazzling imagery everywhere. Swenson's reputation has grown since her death in 1989, and for good reason.

Sue Russell (essay date Summer 1994)

SOURCE: "A Mysterious and Lavish Power: How Things Continue to Take Place in the Work of May Swenson," in *Kenyon Review,* Vol. XVI, No. 3, Summer, 1994, pp. 128-39.

[*In the following essay, Russell examines Swenson's poetry, focusing on the author's approach to and treatment of lesbian themes.*]

May Swenson, who died in 1989 at the age of seventy-six, was a lover of riddles. She liked to write them as well as to solve them—the harder the better. Like the riddle poems she assembled in two books for young readers, all her poems have the capacity to tease and delight. "A poem is a thing," Swenson tells us in her introduction to one of these collections, *More Poems to Solve* (1972). Often based on intricate mechanisms that are not easily replicated, Swenson's poems seem more to have been constructed than composed. Excerpting them is an extreme disservice, as it limits the reader's perspective of the overall design. The poems often take up space in every direction on the page, asserting their identity quite literally at every turn. Individual poems have the kinetic ability to spill over diagonally into stanzaic receptacles, embody the shape and spirit of paintings by De Chirico, and spin like a top around a still center. Although Swenson was clearly engaged in the experimental enterprise to a degree that would charm any scientist, her poetic experimentation was more a means than an end. A language poet before the phrase was coined, she surely would have disdained the label, for her poems are clearly "about" more than the words themselves.

If, like Dickinson, Swenson "tells it slant," that slantwise logic is as much a part of her identity as any political or aesthetic affiliation. Riddling, like role playing, is made up of art and craft, and the critic or biographer must rise to the challenge. The poem, **"Her Early Work,"** with its overt reference to Elizabeth Bishop's 1933 poem, "A Word with You," anticipates the biographer's task:

> Talked to cats and dogs,
> to trees, and to strangers.
> To one loved, talked through
> layers of masks.
> To this day we can't know
> who was addressed,
> or ever undressed.
> Because of the wraparounds,
> overlaps and gauzes,
> kept between words and skin,
> we notice nakedness.
> Wild and heathen scents
> of shame or sin
> hovered since childhood,
> when the delicious was always
> forbidden. "A Word with You"
> had to be whispered,
> spoken at the zoo,
> not to be overheard
> by eavesdropping ape or cockatoo.

(***In Other Words***)

The "eavesdropping ape or cockatoo" is imported directly from Bishop. The sense of "delicious sin" is more typically Swenson. Bishop had a formative impact on Swenson's poetry, as the two met at Yaddo when Swenson was producing her own "early work." That literary kinship implies a verbal give-and-take which stretches the boundaries of time and corporeality. "A Word with You" is, in fact, a very early poem for Bishop. Its completion date of 1933 places it long before the publication of Bishop's first book, *North and South,* in 1946. **"Her Early Work"** is from the last book published in Swenson's lifetime, ***In Other Words*** (1987). These "early and late" historical markers are bookends for a literary era. Swenson's book title suggests an act of interpretation which translates the whispered "word with you" into her own terms. The fact that Swenson would choose to look back at this particular Bishop poem implies a personal connection, since the poem is seldom mentioned in other critical or biographical sources on Bishop. Of course the Bishop reference is more far-reaching than any one poem. One instance in which Bishop might be said to have "talked to dogs" is in the poem "Pink Dog," which is among her final work, having been published in 1979, the year of Bishop's death. This particular dog—"naked and pink, with-

out a single hair"—is emblematic of the female condition at its most exposed.

The poem **"Her Early Work"** thus presupposes the sorting and filing of a poetic enterprise that generally happens after death, or that can feel, to the living writer, like death in life. It has the cumulative effect of drawing us back to the body of Swenson's work and to the work of others by whom she was influenced. In addition, the poem anticipates the possibility of Swenson's own literary influence to poets of future generations. Since Bishop is included in this gesture, the circle of influence would also extend to Bishop's own poetic mentor, Marianne Moore. The critic Sven Birkerts has noted as well the influence of Moore on Swenson's early work in ***Another Animal*** (1954), citing similarities between Swenson's **"Horse and Swan Feeding"** and Moore's **"No Swan So Fine"**. Interestingly, Birkerts makes the point that Swenson seems to have grown beyond the influence of Moore and Bishop to establish an individual voice in her own later work, which for him, includes the new poems in ***Things Taking Place*** (1978).

All three poets shared a lifelong fascination with animals and their habits. Each in her own way used observations of animals in natural or man-made environments to suggest elements of the human drama. The zoo setting generates mental images of the famous photograph of Marianne Moore in front of the elephant cage or of a young Bishop and an older Moore on their first public outing to the Ringling Brothers Barnum and Bailey circus in 1934.

Another Swenson poem, **"Zambesi and Ranee,"** from her second book, ***A Cage of Spines*** (1958), describes a lioness and tigress caged together at the Bronx Zoo. An epigraph from the plaque on their cage attests to the fact that the animals had been "'reared together by hand from early infancy'" because their mothers refused to nurse them. The poet's stance as observer outside the cage stirs a sense memory which Swenson brings home in the poem's penultimate stanza: "The life these ladies lead / upon their stage, repeats itself behind the walls / of many city streets."

In **"Her Early Work,"** Swenson makes a broad gesture to include other poems which document "The life these ladies lead." With the title's assumption of the third-person feminine pronoun, Swenson as tour guide points us in the direction of other poets of her own gender who might be said to have "talked through / layers of masks." For contemporary readers, prominent among them would be Muriel Rukeyser, whose epigrammatic proclamation in "The Poem as Mask" became the title of one of the early feminist anthologies, *No More Masks,* a volume in which a selection of Swenson's poems was also included. Venturing further back in time, she might direct us to certain poems by Emily Dickinson, particularly since the lack of historical documentation precludes any irrefutable knowledge of "who was addressed / or ever undressed." Swenson, herself a close reader of Dickinson, raises these very questions in her essay on the poet, **"'Big My Secret, But It's Bandaged'"** (1984), which takes its title from poem #1737 in Thomas Johnson's edition of Dickinson's *Complete Poems.* In Swenson's poem, **"Daffodildo,"** published posthumously, the poet makes the ritual gesture of laying a daffodil from the Dickinson homestead beside Emily's headstone and taking another for herself "threaded / through my buttonhole." The flower becomes a receptacle for the poet's essence, "a yellow small decanter / of her perfume, hermit-wild / and without a stopper," suggesting the physical infusion of one poet's language into another. The poem continues with embedded quotations and complex interlocking rhymes which seem to reinforce the implicit transgenerational connection.

All of these voices are reflected in eulogy, as if the poet had dropped down on her own funeral Tom Sawyer-like, heard these words, and recorded them for the inquiring minds of future generations. Although the speaker may seem to be apologizing for a lack of candor in "her early work," there is also a cautionary note to the reader who is apt to get it wrong, to mistake "her" for the eccentric "spinster" poet talking to "cats and dogs." The continued presence of "that damned ape," as Bishop calls him, mandates secrecy. "Wraparounds, / overlaps and gauzes" are a paradoxical attempt at protection against discovery in a most vulnerable state. With or without them, we are left with the nakedness of body on body, the native ritual with its "wild and heathen scents." The gauzy veil is evidence of the sin of Eve. The child, who would run naked in the street, has parents to rein her in. The poem's closing quatrain rhymes "whispered" with "overheard" and "zoo" with "cockatoo," clashing hard consonants with open vowels for sonorous effect. Another rhyme, "taboo," hovers in the white space.

We do not have to look very far or deep to discern the nature of the taboo. While Swenson did not go out of her way to disclose her lesbianism, neither did she go out of her way to hide it. Relatively late in her life, she expressed her pleasure at the possibility of having certain poems understood in their proper context, but she was apparently less happy about the implication of being a "lesbian poet," with "lesbian" as the modifier or defining term. Swenson's poem, **"To Confirm a Thing,"** dated 1957, appeared in Joan Larkin and Elly Bulkin's anthology, *Amazon Poetry,* the first major collection of its kind, which came out in 1975. Swenson accepted the editors' invitation to include a sample of her work and suggested this particular poem, which after its appearance in *To Mix with Time* (1963), according to Swenson, "has never been paid any particular attention that I know of." She notes as well in her reply to Larkin: "To me the statement it makes doesn't seem at all obscure, but perhaps the

metaphors constitute a thicker veil than I expected" (letter 2 Sept. 1975).

Elly Bulkin calls attention to the poem **"To Confirm a Thing"** in her introduction to *Lesbian Poetry,* focusing particularly on these lines: "We are Children incorrigible and perverse / who hold their obstinate seats / on heaven's carousel." It is important as well to examine the formal elements which are indicative of Swenson's larger design. The upper case *C* of children is a characteristic Swenson device. Particularly in her early work, she often used capitalization in a manner which might be equated with Dickinson's use of the dash—to guide the reader in hearing the rhythm as she herself heard it. In addition, and also like Dickinson, she played with the distinction between common and "proper" nouns, sometimes creating her own heretical orthography. In this and in other ways, Swenson proved herself to be a formalist outside of that historically feminine tradition of what Carolyn Kizer has called "toast-and-teasdales." As a poet, Swenson is more architect than sylph, more athlete than Barrett Browningesque invalid. It would be possible to read right through that word "perverse" but for such devices. The collective pronoun, the first "We" in the poem, forces our attention. The father here is not simply a genetic forebear but Zeus himself. On "heaven's carousel," then, the speaker is horse and rider, who "snort[s] at death." Although there are no gender identities clearly revealed in this poem, and words like *gay* or *lesbian* or even *homosexual* seem distant, the weight of the poem's design is balanced on the word "perverse." We are not sure exactly what "thing" the poem "confirms," but the spirit of vigorous rebellion seems almost to suggest the more contemporary usage of "queer."

The correspondence between Larkin and Swenson also provides a revealing illustration of the care Swenson typically devoted to the technical aspects of poetic construction:

> I found no errors in the text on the Galley [*sic*] of my poem. But the typesetter has not followed the arrangement as shown on the manuscript. Note that the righthand margin of the whole poem, on manuscript, is justified—that is, set straight in same way as the left-hand margin is, whereas your typesetter has left it jagged. I enclose a printed copy to help him see how to set. There is one line in the poem that's not indented either to the left or right side, and this determines the width of the poem. I've marked it with Xs. There are 47 *typed* characters in this line (spaces between words included)—and on my Ms. copy you would find that each two lines, as indented, take up the same number of spaces—47—because letters and spaces on typewriter are all of equal width. But, in *print* this is not the case—that's why the setting of this poem is tricky . . . (28 Oct. 1975).

These instructions illustrate an engineer's precision upon the typewriter's possibilities. In this and in other ways, Swenson seems to be applying the "womanly" skill of typing to arrive at her "manly" poetic blueprint. I imagine that she would have been happy to get her hands dirty in the printshop if it would have helped to assure the accuracy of the final product. The fact that Swenson herself typed the shaped poems which appear in *Iconographs* attests to the artisan-like physicality of her poetic temperament.

Several years after the publication of *Amazon Poetry,* Bulkin and Larkin approached Swenson and the other poets who appeared in this volume for permission to include their work in a more comprehensive anthology, *Lesbian Poetry.* Swenson withdrew her permission, citing the use of the word "lesbian" in the title as problematic for her. She wrote to Larkin: "I have not sent you any poems for inclusion in the proposed anthology—nor would I do so—anymore than I would submit any writing to a book titled, for instance, "The Heterosexual Women's Poetry Anthology" (30 July 1980). In a longer letter following Larkin's response to this decision, she explained her reasoning:

> It strikes me as a label placed on a collection simply in order to arouse attention, and I believe it invites misunderstanding. It is not a *subject* that gives merit (or subtracts it) from poetry; the sole criterian [*sic*] for choosing poems to go into an anthology with that label as title will look as though it was 1. written by Lesbians, 2. about Lesbianism. People attracted to such a title would not, I think, be looking principally for first rate poetry (19 Aug. 1980).

She wrote that she would have been happier with the title "Amazon Poetry II," as she found the title of the earlier anthology to be "suggestive" but "not inviting the charge of being crude."

Although she seldom wrote explicitly of feminist issues (the poem "Women" is an important exception), Swenson, like Elizabeth Bishop, was part of a transitional generation from the older wave of feminism, with its heartfelt insistence on equality.
—Sue Russell

Swenson's sensitivity to the new book's title, though potentially disappointing to contemporary readers in search of the "gay positive," does make sense in historical context and in the context of her work. The act of naming, as Richard Howard has pointed out, takes on a significance for Swenson that is, if not conventionally religious, at least pantheistic.

The capacity to name a thing is a sign of mythic understanding. On the other hand, as Alicia Ostriker notes, Swenson would not want her readers to be trapped in "the folly of mistaking names for things." Swenson had a seemingly encyclopedic knowledge of the names of exotic birds, flowers, and moons, and she used them frequently in her work to great effect. One poem, **"If I Had Children"** (***In Other Words***, 1987), continues from the "if" clause of the title, "I might name them astrometeorological names: Meridian, a girl. Zenith, a boy. / Eclipse a pretty name for either one." It seems likely that Swenson's image of herself as a "nonbreeder" must have brought with it the iconoclastic power to choose from a larger pool of names than those in the conventional baby book. Still, to be categorized, to be collected under a subject heading, must have carried with it a patronizing air. "Amazon" has the metaphorical resonance of the woman warrior, but "lesbian," in spite of its classical origins, is a demographic instrument, a way of putting people, or women, or poets, in their places. And it seems to have been Swenson's nature to resist any assumption of what now might be called political correctness.

Although she seldom wrote explicitly of feminist issues (the poem **"Women"** is an important exception), Swenson, like Elizabeth Bishop, was part of a transitional generation from the older wave of feminism, with its heartfelt insistence on equality. This sympathy is likely to have been enhanced by experience with the male critical establishment. In a 1977 interview with George Starbuck, Elizabeth Bishop notes, "Most of my life I've been lucky about reviews. But at the very end they often say, 'The best poetry by a woman in this decade, or year, or month.' Well, what's that worth?" Even Bishop's close friend Robert Lowell referred to two of her poems as "the best . . . that I know of written *by a woman* [author's italics] in this century." It is not surprising that Bishop refused the invitations from women-only anthologies that Swenson accepted. Whether the designation came from a woman editor or a male critic, Bishop was not one to call attention to her gender. Goldensohn points out that it was not until the feminist resurgence of the 1970s that Bishop was able to talk with some degree of openness about her own experience *as a woman,* as the Starbuck interview indicates. Where contemporary feminists express concern over the misrepresentation of female experience through the assumption of universal maleness, Bishop and Swenson are likely to have been concerned with the possibility that segregation by gender would diminish the impact of their artistic contribution. Separate, by this definition, could not possibly be equal. Guilt by association is a related concern.

Swenson and Bishop are also likely to have been influenced by the tenets of formalist criticism, as they achieved recognition in the era of its prominence. In this case it would be natural, and perhaps socially desirable, to see art as gender-free. If the poem is an artifact with objective existence apart from historical or social context, the gender of the poet is extratextual information. Our backward-looking lens may reject this prescriptive stance from the Old Boys of the New Criticism, but it is not possible to dismiss the impact of their work.

On a continuum of belief, however, Swenson was more willing to show some allegiance to feminist causes and perhaps less concerned with what poet Honor Moore has called "male approval desire." In the year before she died, several of her poems were included by permission in Larkin and Morse's *Gay and Lesbian Poetry in Our Time.* It is difficult to speculate about why she accepted the later invitation and not the earlier one, but we can certainly be grateful for the presence of her poems alongside those of Muriel Rukeyser, Audre Lorde, Adrienne Rich, and many of her gay male peers. In one of the two Swenson poems the editors include, **"Poet to Tiger"** (*Things Taking Place*, 1978), the veil seems to be lifted, and she writes with startling openness of the sensual daily interactions between two women. The poetic sleuth will note the presence of the anatomically correct "three-cornered pelt" embedded in this symmetrical stanza:

> You get into the tub holding *The Naked Ape*
>   in your teeth. You wet that blond
>   three-cornered pelt lie back wide
>   chest afloat. You're reading
>   in the rising steam and I'm
>   drinking coffee from your tiger cup.
>   You say you dreamed
>   I had your baby book
>   and it was pink and blue.
>   I pointed to a page and there
>   was your face with a cub grin.

The notion of the "pink and blue" baby book plays tenderly with the subtleties of gender roles in a nontraditional relationship.

"Poet to Tiger," also featured in the posthumously collected *Love Poems* (1991), is one among many poems which communicate the nuances of domestic life in women's long-term partnering with more clarity than perhaps any other poet has done before or since. These are poems in which women not only sleep together, they also buy beds (or talk about doing so), build shelves, and admire each other's handiwork. There are also poems in this collection which document the double lives of working women from those pre-Stonewall years. One small love lyric, **"To F.,"** an early poem published in *The Formalist* but not included in later book-length collections, reflects the familiar daily experience of not being able to kiss one's lover good-bye. In the absence of that gesture, hands manage to join and speak:

> Your bus will stop at Christopher
> Mine at Abingdon Square
> Your hand . . . "Good luck" and mine "So long"
> The taxi trumpets blare

In addition to these largely undocumented details of domestic life, Swenson's close concentration on observable phenomena activates a level of metaphor in which the natural world radiates with sensuality. The poem **"Little Lion Face"** (*In Other Words*, 1987), excerpted below, is one of many examples of this tender attention:

> Little lion face
> I stooped to pick
>
> among the mass of thick
> succulent blooms, the twice
>
> streaked flanges of your silk
> sunwheel relaxed in wide
> dilation, I brought inside. Milk
>
> of your shaggy stem
> sticky on my fingers, and
> your barbs hooked to my hand,
> sudden stings from them
>
> were sweet. Now I'm bold
> to touch your swollen neck,
> put careful lips to slick
> petals, snuff up gold
>
> pollen in your navel cup.
> Still fresh before night
> I leave you, dawn's appetite
> to renew our glide and suck. . .

In a reverse of this metaphorical relationship, **"A Trellis for R."** (formerly titled **"Blue"**) functions as a lesbian "Song of Songs," with each of the lover's features appreciated in turn as individual roses in the lattice frame of human touch: "Glinting hairs / shoot back of your ears' Rose / that tongue likes to feel / the maze of . . . (*Love Poems*). The downward flow of the enjambed lines is openly sexual and distinctly female.

It is easy to see why the poet Mona Van Duyn called this collection "simply . . . the most moving book of love poems I have ever read" (jacket copy). The book lets us fall in love with love, but in this case it is "the love that dares not speak its name" finally given voice. Even the poems that show evidence of the "gauzes and overlays" of "her early work" take on a clarity in this context which is particularly poignant.

In the long run, it would seem more appropriate to focus on

what Swenson was willing to make public than on what she wished not to disclose. The oldest child of ten born to Swedish immigrant parents who settled in Utah, she was raised with a rigid set of expectations of how boys and girls should behave. Having grown up in a family of practicing Mormons, it is certainly not surprising that Swenson would show an overactive attention to "delicious sin." The theme of the recalcitrant child is a strong presence throughout her work in poems like **"The Centaur."** Indeed, the word "tomboy" seems to have been created with Swenson in mind. Her boyish, close-cropped hair is a constant on the dust jacket of each new book. This healthy resistance to authority, however, did not stand in the way of her filial loyalty. From the stringencies of her family of origin to the self-made family of women implied in such poems as **"The Beauty of the Head,"** Swenson seems to have negotiated the boundaries of her various worlds with remarkable grace.

Swenson's eight surviving siblings attended her memorial tribute, given in March 1991 by the Academy of American Poets, for whom Swenson had served as chancellor from 1980 until her death in 1989, replacing Elizabeth Bishop in that post. Swenson's sister, Margaret Swenson Woodbury, one of her younger siblings, was among the presenters who offered reminiscences and read selected poems from the body of Swenson's work. Woodbury read the poem **"I Look at My Hand"** (*Iconographs*, 1970), in which the physical inheritance from parents is literally traced down to the fingertips. In another poem, **"Night Visits with the Family"** (*Things Taking Place,* 1978), variant dreams are attributed to a multitude of family members all identified by first name, including May and Margaret.

The collective presence of the family group takes on added significance in the poem **"Feel Me"** (*Iconographs,* 1970), in which, through a combination of apparent autobiography and linguistic analysis, Swenson/the speaker recalls "our father's" last words and puzzles through several possible interpretations:

> "Feel me to do right," our father said on his
> deathbed.
> We did not quite know—in fact, not at all—what
> he meant.
> His last whisper was spent as through a slot on a
> wall.
> He left us a key, but how did it fit?. . .

The microscopic attention to a small syntactic unit here stands in for the larger emotional work of grief, as if to say, in the absence of any clear message, we fix on the little we have. One possible interpretation to which the speaker does not allude is that, instead of (or in addition to) addressing the family members in his presence, the father might be offering a prayer for God's grace. The implicit "you," in this

case, would be God. "Feel me to [have done] right" (with my life) would then be the sense of his words. This seemingly intentional misreading reflects a narrowing perspective which sidesteps the extremity of the situation. If the father is talking to someone other than "us," "we" lose the exercise which gives meaning to "our" grief. Given Swenson's background, it seems likely that she assumes an implicit dialogue between "our father" on his deathbed and "Our Father," the heavenly maker, to whom the earthbound family members are denied access. In another family poem, **"That the Soul May Wax Plump,"** Swenson writes: "Mother's work before she died was self-purification / a regimen of near starvation, to be worthy to go / to Our Father, Whom she confused (or, more aptly, fused) / with our father, in Heaven long since. . ." (*Things Taking Place,* 1978).

The internal dialogue was a useful strategy for Swenson in grappling with the important questions of her own life. In the previously unpublished poem, **"Manyone Flying,"** she returns to a favorite visual format—the symmetrical arrangement of lines built around a narrow column of white space. In this instance, the structure suggests both the visual formation of birds in flight and the verbal precipice over which the speaker is poised. Swenson's notation on this poem tells us that she started it on a plane flight to Utah for a family visit. It is not surprising that this situation would evoke a soliloquy which traces the speaker's role as both loner and member of the flock, perpetually flying from one life to another and wondering at the need for such flight:

> Out on the ragged   edge flying lonely
> Not all alone   not that brave
> or foolish or   self-sufficient
> or self-believing   In the middle

In other poems, Swenson tackles metaphysical questions with an ironic spin that is gently irreverent. Just as **"Feel Me"** begins with a key that does not seem to fit in any known door, an earlier poem, **"The Key to Everything"** (*Another Animal,* 1954), looks at the hopeless task of the eternal seeker for answers. Here, Swenson uses breathless, unpunctuated verse paragraphs to characterize such an individual, "waiting for / the right person the doctor or / the mother or / the person with the name you keep / mumbling in your sleep. . . ." This is the kind of poem one would love to thrust in the face of New Age friends, particularly for the impact of its final lines: ". . . no once you'd / get there you'd / remember and love me / of course I'd / be gone by then I'd / be far away" (*New and Selected*).

The first two poems in *To Mix with Time* (1963) are entitled **"The Universe"** and **"God."** As Alicia Ostriker has pointed out, there may be no other poet with the audacity to use such titles, and it may be the quality Anthony Hecht refers to as "calculated naiveté" which allows Swenson to pull off the gesture. But Swenson is a child here in Blake's sense of wonderment before the infinite. And, like Whitman, her first poetic impulse is to celebrate. Her early short story, **"Appearances"** (one of two she published in her lifetime), sets up a dialogue between a physician and a visual artist that embodies Swenson's continuing stance. "'After all,'" the story opens in the tired, paternalistic voice of the doctor, "'we are no longer children.'" The artist, that callow youth, responds, "'On the contrary, I believe that we are all still children.'" The artist then refines his position, exalting the role of the senses in coming to terms with "'a mysterious and lavish power veining everything in nature, spilling free and raw from every stone and leaf'" (*New Directions,* 1951).

Peter Pan, both ageless and androgynous, remains the essential archetype, with nature a positive force that cannot be denied. It is that persistent spirit which leads me to resist a reading of Swenson's work and life that belabors the idea of internalized homophobia or self-hatred. Her absolute willingness to confound gender expectations for subject matter, genre, and style far outweighs her apparent ambivalence about being politically "out."

The first Swenson book I purchased was *To Mix with Time*, and this was long before I called myself a lesbian or saw her work collected in *Amazon Poetry*. I remember standing in the bookstore, transfixed by these lines from **"Out of My Head"**:

> If I could get
> out   of my
> head   and
> into   the
> world.
>
> What am I saying?
> Out   of my
> head?   Isn't my
> head
> in   the
> world?

That immediate move to stand the question itself "on its head," the refusal to separate "head" from "world," the enactment of this separation by means of a continental divide of white space—these are qualities that disarmed me then and now. As a teenager with a hyperactive intelligence and a bent toward poetry, I sensed in Swenson's work the possibilities of a future I did not yet have the words to imagine—one in which I could be "in my head" and "in the world" at the same time and in equal measure. This lesson, of course, is the opposite of what parents and teachers had to say to smart girls—that experience was something we had to go out there and "get" if we wanted to fulfill ourselves as women. Swenson's work and life palpably contradict the voice of

authority. Somehow, finding out that she was a lesbian simply confirmed what I already knew. Swenson had an innate distrust for the separation of thinking and feeling states. What she recognized, instead, was the seductive energy of words and ideas, the sensual allure of exploration and discovery, the sexiness of a machine's (or a poem's) working parts. It is the word made flesh and the flesh made word— that moment of union protracted in a body of work. For these reasons, Swenson's readers tend to offer an unqualified admiration that is closer to love. We love the poet who brings us closest to our own true nature—who shows us, through her example, what it means to be truly alive.

Grace Schulman   (essay date September/October 1994)

SOURCE: "Life's Miracles: The Poetry of May Swenson," in *American Poetry Review,* Vol. 23, No. 5, September/October, 1994, pp. 9-13.

[*In the following essay, Schulman explores Swenson's treatment of the themes of life, love, and death in her poetry.*]

The voice of May Swenson combines the directness of intimate speech and the urgency of prayer:

> Body my house
> my horse my hound
> what will I do
> when you are fallen
>
> Where will I sleep
> How will I ride
> What will I hunt
>
> Where can I go
> without my mount. . .

The magic of that lament, **"Question,"** from *Another Animal* (1954), is in its contrasts: while the details are specific, the central situation is a mystery that terrifies with each new speculation. Here as elsewhere in her poems, Swenson dwells on the living body with an immediacy that heightens the dread of its loss. Other gestures that recur in Swenson's poetry are the insistent, unanswerable questions, "what will I do," "How will I ride," "What will I hunt," "Where can I go," all of them precise, all ironic, because futile. Here they are enhanced by obsessive rhyme ("house," "horse," "hound," "hunt," "mount"). Their futility is emphasized by the absence of punctuation, and again by its sudden presence, in the final line. They are meditations. Admirable too, is the voice that is neither androgynous nor gendered, but one that encompasses both sexes in its fluid boundaries and essentially human dimension: "What will I hunt," the male speaker's question, modulates here, with no abrupt tonal change, to a woman's query, "With cloud for shift / how will I hide?"

Questions are the wellsprings of May Swenson's art. She inquires about simple things, such as "What is the worm doing / making its hole," and about principles such as "What / is it about, / the universe, / the universe about us stretching out?" or, considering the moon landing, "Dare we land upon a dream?" In her speculations and her close observations, she fulfills Marianne Moore's formula for the working artist: "Curiosity, observation, and a great deal of joy in the thing." In subject matter a poet who, like Donne, takes all of knowledge as her province, she is as comfortable with animals and flowers as she is with anti-matter, electronic sound, and DNA. Some of her chosen forms incorporate questions, such as her ballad, **"The Centaur"**: *"Where have you been?" "Been riding."* Another is the ancient riddle, a form that enables her to concentrate on the object without naming it. **"The Surface,"** for example, has affinities to Dickinson's riddles, and to her wit: "First I saw the surface, / then I saw it flow, / then I saw the underneath," the poet begins, and gradually unravels the answer, the image of an eye. Swenson riddles in a quest to find a higher reality obscured by conventional names, and to fathom what is deepest within the self. By rejecting ready-made definitions—those designations that enlighten—Swenson sees in the dark. She derides the ordinary labeling of things with its consequent reduction of greatness:

They said there was a	Thing
that could not	Change
They could not	Find
it so they	Named
it	God. . .

("**God**")

The poet's unnaming allows her to rename, in an effort to see things outside the context of common parlance. Continually the search is for a deeper meaning, the essence of the thing observed. In **"Evolution,"** the first poem of her first book, she exclaims:

> beautiful each Shape
>   to see
> wonderful each Thing
>   to name
>   here a stone
>   there a tree
>   here a river
>   there a Flame. . .

May Swenson was born in 1913 in Logan, Utah, of a Mormon family, and educated at Utah State University. She was a New Yorker from 1936, and lived in Sea Cliff, New York, for twenty-three years before her death in Ocean View, Delaware, in 1989. In her lifetime, she published eleven books over three decades, nine of them poetry collections, from *Another Animal* (1954) to *In Other Words* (1987). Honored as she was during her lifetime, her books included only four hundred and fifty of the nine hundred poems she composed. Since her death, as new poems and new books continue to appear, it becomes apparent not only that he output is larger than readers have supposed, but that her stature is major.

> **Swenson's tone embraces the full human drama. Her metaphors often are male, or animal, or flower. Nevertheless, the sexual love she dramatizes so brilliantly is Sapphic.**
> **—*Grace Schulman***

Nature (1994), the newest of the posthumous books, contains some early poems, hitherto unpublished, whose dominant tone is awe: "Remain aghast at life," the poet resolves in **"Earth Your Dancing Place,"** composed as early as 1936:

> Enter each day
> as upon a stage
> lighted and waiting
> for your step. . .

Wonder prevails in **"Manyone Flying"** (1975), another of the poems that appear posthumously in *Nature.* Here, the poet, in the guise of a high flying bird, considers the divisions between the individual and humanity:

	Out on the edge,
my maneuverings,	my wings, think
they are free.	Flock, where do we
fly? Are we Ones?	Or One, only?
if only One, not lonely	. . . being Manyone. . .
but Who	are We? And Why?

The liveliest of the posthumous books, *The Love Poems of May Swenson* (1991), contains poems that illuminate the work as a whole. Here, the poet who continually questions existence finds love at the source of the quest: existence depends on the other. The bridge between self and other is basic to the polarities, found throughout her work, of life and death wildness and restraint, past and present, sun and moon, stone and flame. Although out of the fifty-five poems, *The Love Poems* contains only thirteen hitherto unpublished, as well as some familiar poems in altered forms, their publication—as well as their arrangement here—reveal the force of that important theme. And as the love poems occupy the full span of her career, having been composed between 1938 and 1987, so does the theme.

Before elaborating on that large concern, I want to comment on the poetry's marvelous erotic power. Heightened sensations recall the Song of Songs: "thy breasts shall be as clusters of the vine" (King James Version 7:8). All the more credible for risking sentimentality without approaching it, Swenson conveys physical intimacies and shares sensual delights, as, for example, the "dark wild honey,"

> Thick transparent amber
> you brought home,
> the sweet that burns.

The poet cries out in passion: "Burn radiant sex born scorpion need." She writes of joy: "A rain of diamonds virgule in the mind (**"Love Is"**); of pain: "Now heart, take up your desert; virgule this spring is cursed" (**"Wild Water,"** 1938); and of yearning: "my body is a sharpened dart / of longing / coming toward you always," in **"The Equilibrist,"** composed in the forties. As for her lustiness, I cannot describe it better than did Edward Hirsch, who wrote in a review of *Love Poems*: "The birds, and especially the bees, have never been so slyly deployed."

Vivid, moving, the love poems take in the intricacies of human nature, the natural world, geography, and invention. They are poems of intense love between women, written at a time when that genre was rare in poetry. I say love between women with qualifications, because of the poetry's aesthetic complexity. Swenson's tone embraces the full human drama. Her metaphors often are male, or animal, or flower. Nevertheless, the sexual love she dramatizes so brilliantly is Sapphic. This is subtly and beautifully apparent in the imagery of four poems that did not appear during Swenson's lifetime:

> I exist in your verdant garden
>
> I unfurled in your rich soil
>
>   (**"You Are"**)
>
> We are released
> and flow into each other's cup
> Our two frail vials pierced
> drink each other up
>
>   (**"In Love Made Visible,"** 1946)
>
> To feel your breast

> rise with my sigh
> To hold you mirrored
> in my eye
>
> Neither wanting more
> Neither asking why
>
>   (**"Neither Wanting More,"** 1944)
>
> I open to your dew,
> beginning in the spring again. . .
>
>   (**"Annual,"** 1959).

Sexy poems dominate this book, either by shining out in their own light or by illuminating others. In *Love Poems*, many titles are familiar to Swenson's readers, such as **"August Night"** and **"Another Animal."** Those familiar poems are strengthened by the context of the newly-published pieces. For example, **"The School of Desire"** (from *A Cage of Spines*, 1958) is a symphonic reiteration—the theme stated in full force—of the wildness and freedom that are more reflective in the more recently surfaced poems such as **"In Love Made Visible."** In a biography published in 1993, *The Wonderful Pen of May Swenson*, R.R. Knudson observed, "For May, power was fear pushed back." So, too, many of the love poems, like primitive chants, derive their power from the expression of inner wildness as well as the immense effort to order it. **"The School of Desire"** captures the poet's energies at their strongest:

> Unloosed, unharnessed, turned back to the wild by love,
> the ring you cantered round with forelock curled,
> the geometric music of this world
> dissolved and in its place,
> alien as snow to tropic tigers, amphitheatric space
> you will know the desert's freedom, wind and sun
> rough-currying your mane, the plenitude
> of strong caresses on your body nude.

And yet, while the poems capture the physical ecstasy of consummated love, they also evoke the elusiveness of a world beyond the physical. In the grand design of an Elizabethan sonneteer, she writes of mutability: desire changes, the moment it is given form, to flame up and die. Love, a reaction against the process of temporal decay, can enable flesh-bound companions at least to intuit spiritual value.

> In love are we set free
> Objective bone
> and flesh no longer insulate us
> to ourselves alone. . .
>
>   (**"In Love Made Visible"**)

As I've said, *The Love Poems* highlights Swenson's manner of incessant inquiry. Early and late, her intellectual probing is accompanied by passionate identification with objects, with technology, and, especially, with nature: the lion's yearning, the lamb's way, the deer's eye; recumbent stones, thighs of trees, horses whose colors are "like leaves or stones / or wealthy textures / liquors of light."

On the other hand, when human love is at stake, human sensibility replaces the unity with animals, as in the poem **"Evolution"**:

> an Evolution strange
> two Tongues touch
> exchange
> a Feast unknown
> to stone
> or tree or beast. . .

In the love poems, particularly those that appeared recently, the persistent questions of Swenson's world are put aside as the lover lies content without searching for data: "Because I don't know you / I love you," admits the speaker of an early poem. Fulfillment is

> To hold you mirrored
> in my eye
>
> Neither wanting more
> Neither asking why. . .

Although the love poems do not question overtly, they exhibit a more essential phase of the poet's constant quest. Swenson's earliest efforts on any theme probe the reality of being, and the utter dependence of being upon its opposite is dominant here, especially in the early, posthumously-published work: "As you are Sun to me / O I am moon to you," cries the lover in **"Facing."** "They are like flame and ice / the elemental You and Me," begins **"The Indivisible Incompatibles,"** a poem written in the 1940s. The lovers are "Not twin / but opposite / as my two hands are opposite," according to **"Symmetrical Companion,"** another early poem, from 1948, that has for an ending, "Come release me / Without you I do not yet exist." Even more directly, the lover asserts:

> I dwell
> *in* you
> and so
> I know
> I am
>
> no one
> can be sure
> by himself

of his own being. . .

And, more firmly, "because you believe I exist I exist" (**"You Are"**).

Here the passion is metaphorical, though the details are concrete. The lovers of her poems, steamy though they are, represent parts of a divided self. Their union, that blessed state in which opposites are conjoined, reveals essential being. Mooring in one's otherness allays unanswerable queries about life and death. Furthermore, the process of finding a hidden part of the self reveals a remote world beyond the tangible: "In love are we made visible. . . In love are we set free."

The title of her 1967 volume, **Half Sun Half Sleep,** announces that division of what May Swenson once called, "the primitive bipolar suspension in which my poems often begin to form." Her theme of division is conveyed by many of her shaped poems, or those which contain visual as well as textual metaphors.

Actually, the poet's primary effects are her cadences. The impact of her poems lies in their urgent speech and incantatory rhythms, their music of charms, spells, curses, ritual dances. Never does the typography, however intricate, supersede the cadence. As in primitive poetry, word and appearance are fused for a total effect.

As if to demonstrate subtly that the shaped poems have an auditory life of their own, May Swenson chose to read aloud many of her typographical poems in 1976 on a Caedmon recording, which could not, of course, exhibit the visual pattern to her listeners. One of the poems she read was **"The Lightning,"** which she referred to as a pivotal poem in *Half Sun Half Sleep.* Of its typographical device, the visual metaphor, she commented: "As seen on the page, there is a streak of white space that runs diagonally through the body of the poem and this even splits some of the words." The poem celebrates speech, and the white streak creates meditative pauses in lines, indicating the gap between word and event, between experience and its realization in the poem:

> **"The Lightning"**
>
> The lightning waked me. It slid unde   r
> my eyelid. A black book flipped ope   n
> to an illuminated page. Then insta   ntly
> shut. Words of destiny were being   ut-
> tered in the distance. If only I   could
> make them out!. . . Next day, as I   lay
> in the sun, a symbol for concei   ving the
> universe was scratched on my e   yeball.
> But quickly its point eclipse   d, and
> softened, in the scabbard of   my brain.

My cat speaks one word: Fo   ur vowels
and a consonant. He rece   ives with the
hairs of his body the wh   ispers of the
stars. The kinglet spe   aks by flashing
into view a ruby feath   er on his head.
He is held by a threa   d to the eye of
the sun and cannot   fall into error.
Any flower is a per   fect ear, or else it
is a thousand lips   . . . When will I grope
clear of the entr   ails of intellect?

Swenson spoke, too, of a poem whose title is, antithetically, **"Untitled,"** commenting on an earlier version she read on the recording. She described the visual metaphor created by the typographical appearance on the page, noting that "two black crooked lines pass through the text as if to x it out. The bipolar words 'you,' 'me,' are in the center as if entangled where the two black lines cross." Here, the spaces are between words, and they designate a meditative, almost painful effort at speech. "I will be earth you be the flower. . .," the poem begins, and the voice rises in passionate intensity as the lovers flail, boat and sea, earth and flood, desert and salt.

Utterance is the theme, too, of **"Fountains of Aix,"** a poem from the 1963 collection, *To Mix With Time*. In it, the word "water" is split fifteen times from its lines, and poured, in effect, down the side of one stanza:

A goddess is driving a chariot through water.
Her reins and whips are tight white   water.
Bronze hoofs of horses wrangle with   water.

The streak of space separates the fountain's sculptures from the water spouting from their mouths. Here are dolphins and lions and bulls, and "faces with mossy lips unlocked," all uttering water, "their eyes mad / or patient or blind or astonished." She builds a metaphor of the fluidity of utterance, and thence of poetry. Swenson's pauses emphasize her wonder: In **"Fire Island,"** from *Iconographs* (1970), the poet contemplates the miracle of beholding light and dark—milky foam, black sky—of solitude and the group—walkers on the beach and "other watchers"—while the two ends of the narrow island are splayed out in type above and below, creating pauses between the letters of the words "Fire" and "sight."

Typographical pauses appear throughout Swenson's writing career. Some are part of an intricate pattern, as in **"The Fountains of Aix"** and **"The Lightning."** Many occur in poems of two columns, and of those, some are read down the page, some across the page and still others across *and* down. Early and late, those patterned spaces between the words indicate opposites, ironies, reversals, paradoxes, ambiguities. For example, in a poem whose title conveys a mo-

ment in time, **"While Sitting in the Tuileries and Facing the Slanting Sun,"** the poet ironically associates, and then divides by space, a swaddled infant in Giotto's fresco, **"Birth of the Virgin,"** and a mummy in the Vatican Museum:

There is a   Person
of flesh that is a rocking   Box
There is a   Box
of wood that is a painted   Person. . .

In **"Bleeding,"** from *Iconographs*, a space through the center is a jagged, running wound, effecting caesuras of hesitation in a dialogue between the knife and the cut. The force grows along with the grim realization that bleeding is precisely feeling, in this devastating relationship:

I feel I have to bleed to   feel I   think   said the cut.
I don't I don't have to   feel said   the knife drying now
becoming shiny.

Like the polarized images found throughout Swenson's work, the contrasts created by her typographical separations have their roots in the love poems. There are the two columns of **"Evolution"** and **"Facing"** (both to be read down the page, rather than across), each indicating another animal, the lover who is an aspect of the self. Like all the love poems, these two praise opposite beings—flame and ice, sun and moon—who move forward to their destiny.

> [Swenson's] love poems, with their high energy and "desert freedom," contain, as do the poems of Shakespeare and Sir Philip Sidney, the irony that vitality can emphasize its very opposite, the certainty of life's decline.
> —*Grace Schulman*

The love poems, with their high energy and "desert freedom," contain, as do the poems of Shakespeare and Sir Philip Sidney, the irony that vitality can emphasize its very opposite, the certainty of life's decline. From early on, May Swenson sings of life in death's shadow, as in **"Question,"** quoted above, and in poems that have the word "Death" in their titles: **"Deaths," "Death Invited," "The Shape of Death."**

Did Swenson suffer great personal loss? Her biographer, R.R. Knudson, writes that the death of a beloved grandfather prompted May, as a child, to question the finality of loss. Then, as a teenager, May questioned Mormonism, and, in fact, normative religions with their conventional notions of God. It seems that later she was deeply saddened by the atrocities of World War II. Young May's lover, the Czech poet, Anca Vrboska, lost her family to the Nazi death camps. While Vrboska wrote of Auschwitz directly, Swenson internalized, objectified, searched, as always, for the essence of death:

> I will lie down in Autumn
> let birds be flying
>
> swept into a hollow
> by the wind
> I'll wait for dying
>
> I will lie inert unseen
> my hair same-colored
> with grass and leaves. . .

(**"I Will Lie Down"**)

Later still, in those poems whose titles say "death," Swenson plays on the Elizabethan paradox that tragic implications are perceived in the midst of life's personal, intimate experience. All are poems that embody contrasts, either in their divided shape on the page, or in their imagery, or both. A fascinating early example is **"Death, Great Smoothener"**:

Death,
great smoothener,
maker of order,
arrester, unraveler, sifter and changer
death, great hoarder;
student, stranger, drifter, traveler,
flyer and nester all caught at your border;
death,
great halter;
blackener and frightener,
reducer, dissolver,
seizer and welder of younger with elder,
waker with sleeper
death, great keeper
of all that must alter;
death,
great heightener,
leaper, evolver,
greater smoothener,
great whitener!

The poem's sheer energy cries of life even as it speaks to death. It has the sound of a pagan incantation, with its frightening direct address presented in clusters of heavy stresses. Swenson achieves her falling rhythm here, as in **"Question,"** with reversed iambs, and depicts death in lists of epithets, enforced by rhyme: "order," "hoarder," "border." In contrast to the chant rhythm, the typographical shape on the page is that of an ornate Christian cross. The resonant epithets echo,

for me, Caedmon's hymn, the legendary first song of our first English poet, a song of thanksgiving:

Nu sculon herigean	heofonrices weard
metodes meahte	and his modgethanc
weorc wuldorcedur	swa he wundra gehwœs
now shall we praise	heaven's keeper
the maker's might	and his mind thought
father of the world	as of all wonder. . .

Poetically, their techniques are alike: to sing of God. Caedmon takes epithets for the Anglo-Saxon warlords, such as ruler and father, and qualifies them with Christian adjectives such as . . . "eternal." Swenson chants death in life, and engraves a pagan rhythm in a Christian cross.

The poetry of May Swenson celebrates life's miracles even with death in view: the wonder of speech (**"Fountains of Aix"**); the grandeur of God (**"God"**); the radiance of sight (**"Fire Island"**). In each of these three poems, typographical divisions—white streaks down the middle of the text, make for breath-catching pauses that enhance the excited tone. The ambiguities and paradoxes of Swenson's poetry result from basic contradiction between our illusion of permanence and an underlying certainty of fatality. This contradiction is articulated explicitly in one of the love poems, **"The Shape of Death,"** as it was printed, in *Iconographs*, with a white streak down the middle of the text:

What does love look like?	We know the shape of death.
Death is a cloud, immense	and awesome. At first a
lid is lifted from the	eye of light. There is a
clap of sound. A white	blossom belches from the
jaw of fright.	

Then, in sharp contrast to those positive assertions about death, love is presented in a series of questions: "What is its / color and its alchemy?" "Can it be sown and harvested?" The resounding theme of Swenson's poems is there, in her concluding statement. Like life, love, though fatally transient, is "not alien—it is near—our very skin, a sheath to keep us pure of fear."

Susan E. Gunter (review date Fall 1996)

SOURCE: A review of *May Out West* and *Nature: Old and New*, in *Western American Literature*, Vol. 31, Fall, 1996, p. 270.

[*In the following review, Gunter praises* May Out West *and* Nature: Old and New, *commending both Swenson's poetic voice and her technical mastery.*]

The latest two books released by the late Utah poet May Swenson remind us of the scope and the precision of her gift. They are treasures for the Swenson enthusiast as well as for the general reader.

May Out West would be a starting place for readers new to Swenson's work. A carefully selected and beautifully presented edition of thirty-four poems, it contains two previously unpublished: **"The Seed of My Father"** and **"White Moon."** This book is not just for Westerners, though they will relish the portrait of our landscape it offers: it is for all who value their connection with the earth that sustains us. Reading through these poems, one is struck by the vastness of her poetic project, her deeply-felt and clearly expressed attachment with the world. She does not just admire nature, she becomes an integral part of it in a Whitmanesque integration of self and world. In **"The Seed of My Father,"** the poet's father gives her the moon, a peach tree, the sun, and seeds, and they become the essence of her art. In **"White Moon,"** the narrator's thoughts are not *like* snow, they *are* snow. Nature's very richness was for her an inexhaustible source: the cumulus clouds, the willow sticks that became her horses, the western tanager above Bear Lake, the varied saguaros, all are grist for her magical mill.

Nature, larger and even more varied, reveals that Swenson is not just a regional poet, but a universal one. This collection contains ten previously unpublished poems, dated from 1952 to 1984. It is arranged in graceful thematic units and has a useful index, containing dates for the poems. Of the new poems, **"Incantation,"** written in 1952, reveals the power of a mature poet with Gerard Manley Hopkins's command of words and sprung rhythms, particularly the penultimate stanza:

> Burning snow spin me so with black sea
> to braided be In green sleep eons leap
> from gray slime past thought and time
> to pith and power to bathe in the immortal hour
> to breathe from another pulsing flower

Occasionally her world seems almost too perfect: in **"Camping in Madera Canyon,"** for example, we wish for an occasional mosquito.

This is a book of surprises. Of all the fine twentieth-century western writers, it is Swenson who has most clearly moved from region to eternity. In the tradition of Emerson, Whitman, Dickinson, and Bishop, she merges the human with the physical world in almost seamless fashion. Here is a baroque world, sometimes more visually than aurally successful. Her poems arranged for the page, as **"How Everything Happens (Based on the Study of a Wave),"** while clever, are perhaps not as successful as her more lyrical, musical poems, like **"Still Turning."**

But the reader must take her slowly, poem by poem, as there will be something to please every taste in this all-encompassing collection. One, **"Water Picture,"** is almost perfect in its conflation of art and nature as Swenson takes a Monet-like view of the pond in the park, where "all things are doubled" and the swan, kissing herself, makes the scene troubled: "water-windows splinter, / tree-limbs tangle, the bridge / folds like a fan."

FURTHER READING

Biographies

Knudson, R. R. *The Wonderful Pen of May Swenson.* New York: Macmillan, 1993, 112 p.
    Book-length biography of Swenson by her companion, R. R. Knudson, that contains excerpts from Swenson's poetry and photographs from her personal collection.

Bibliographies

Gadomski, Kenneth E. "May Swenson: A Bibliography of Primary and Secondary Sources." *Bulletin of Bibliography* 44, No. 4 (December 1987): 255-80.
    Bibliography of works by and about Swenson.

Criticism

Clarence, Judy. Review of *Nature: Poems Old and New,* by May Swenson. *Library Journal* 119, No. 11 (15 June 1994): 72.
    A brief but highly laudatory review of *Nature: Poems Old and New.*

George, Diana Hume. "'Who Is the Double Ghost Whose Head Is Smoke?': Women Poets On Aging." In *Memory and Desire: Aging—Literature—Psychoanalysis,* edited by Kathleen Woodward and Murray M. Schwartz, pp. 134-53, Bloomington: Indiana University Press, 1986.
    An essay examining the treatment of the topic of aging by Swenson and other women poets.

Howard, Richard. "Elizabeth Bishop—May Swenson Correspondence." *Paris Review* 36 (Summer 1994): 171-86.
    A compilation of excerpts from letters exchanged by Swenson and Elizabeth Bishop concerning Swenson's poem "Dear Elizabeth" and, as Howard termed it, "other literary matters of interest to both poets at the time (1963-1965)."

Additional coverage of Swenson's life and career is contained in the following sources published by Gale: *Contemporary Authors,* First Revision, Vols. 5-8; *Contemporary Authors,* Vol. 130; *Contemporary Authors New Revision Series,* Vol. 36; *DISCovering Authors; DISCovering Authors: British; DISCovering Authors: Canadian; DISCovering Authors Modules: Most-Studied and Poets; Dictionary of Literary Biography,* Vol. 5; *Major Twentieth-Century Writers; Poetry Criticism,* Vol. 14; and *Something about the Author,* Vol. 15.

Andrew Vachss

1942-

American novelist, short story writer, poet, essayist, and non-fiction writer.

The following entry presents criticism of Vachss's work through 1997.

INTRODUCTION

Drawing upon more than twenty years of experience in the field of child welfare, Vachss (pronounced "vax") writes novels that address the issues of child abuse and exploitation. Most of these novels revolve around the character known only as Burke, a self-styled private investigator who employs violence when dealing with "freaks"—people who perpetrate crimes against children.

Biographical Information

Born in 1942, Vachss grew up on the Lower West Side of Manhattan. After graduating from Western Reserve University in 1965, he held a series of public service positions with organizations such as the U.S. Public Health Service in Ohio, the Department of Social Services in New York City, and the Medfield-Norfolk Prison Project in Massachusetts. In 1972, he became director of ANDROS II, a maximum-security juvenile facility near Boston. During this time, Vachss resumed his education, earning his J.D. from the New England School of Law in 1975. In 1976, Vachss established his juvenile-defense law practice, devoting his time exclusively to child welfare issues. Because the children he defends lack the resources to pay him, Vachss began writing fiction to supplement his income. In 1983, Vachss started writing bits of plot, dialogue, and character sketches on index cards, collecting them in a box; the result was his first novel, *Flood* (1985). In addition to numerous "Burke" novels, Vachss has produced a collection of essays and prose poems and has worked with Dark Horse comics to produce graphic adaptations of his short stories. Vachss also maintains a homepage on the World Wide Web, entitled "The Zero," containing information and resources on his work and the topics covered in his novels (see www.vachss.com). Vachss and his wife, Alice, also an attorney, live in New York.

Major Works

Though he had published *The Life-Style Violent Juvenile: The Secure Treatment Approach* (1979) six years earlier, Vachss first drew critical attention with the publication of

Flood, the novel that introduces his favorite protagonist, Burke. Rather than subscribe to the standard conventions of the detective novel protagonist, Vachss has created in Burke the atypical hero, described by David Morrell as "a con-man, a survivor, a cynic, a repressed romantic and a very dangerous guy." Burke is an ex-convict who makes his living selling fake identification, doing "dirty work" for wealthy clients, and, on occasion, serving as a private investigator on cases dealing with the abuse and exploitation of children. The perpetrators of these crimes against children usually meet with a violent end, courtesy of Burke. Some critics have argued that Burke's vigilante justice is a form of "wish fulfillment" for Vachss, allowing him to achieve retribution that is unavailable through legal means. To this Vachss has responded, "I've never considered that. . . . I've tried to keep my books tight within the realm of what actually can happen."

Critical Reception

Vachss's novels have met with popular appeal, but critical reviews of his work are mixed. David Morrell of the *Wash-*

ington Post praises Vachss's style, saying that "the words leap off the page. . ., and the style is as clean as haiku." Others have credited him for the creation of an original protagonist and an intriguing supporting cast. Some reviewers, however, have criticized Vachss for redundant plot elements and a lack of character development through the course of the Burke series. The harshest criticism of his work has come from those who claim that Vachss himself is guilty of exploiting children by making them the focus of his novels. To these critics, Vachss has responded, "I'm curious to know how you could bring about social change without acknowledging the existence of that you wish to change."

PRINCIPAL WORKS

The Life-Style Violent Juvenile: The Secure Treatment Approach (nonfiction) 1979
Flood (novel) 1985
Strega (novel) 1987
Blue Belle (novel) 1988
Hard Candy (novel) 1989
Blossom (novel) 1990
Sacrifice (novel) 1991
Hard Looks (graphic novel series) 1992
Another Chance to Get It Right (essays) 1993
Shella (novel) 1993
Down in the Zero (novel) 1994
Batman: The Ultimate Evil (novel) 1995
Footsteps of the Hawk (novel) 1995
False Allegations (novel) 1996

CRITICISM

Michael Dirda (review date 15 September 1985)

SOURCE: "Down and Dirty," in *Washington Post Book World,* Vol. XV, No. 37, September 15, 1985, p. 6.

[*In the following review, Dirda provides a brief overview of* Flood.]

Andrew H. Vachss has written quite an extraordinary thriller in *Flood.* Imagine a New York where the streets are worse than mean, they're positively depraved. The hero Burke is a private detective (sort of) with an engineer's approach to survival. He lives with a huge mongrel named Pansy in an apartment fortified like a bank vault; he drives a $40,000 Plymouth loaded with more gadgetry than James Bond's Aston Martin. His friends include a transvestite prostitute,

a mute Tibetan fighting machine named Max, a panhandler called the Prof (short for Professor or Prophet, no one's sure which), an electronic wizard who lives underground beneath a pile of junked cars, and a doctor who doubles as the secret leader of an Hispanic revolutionary group.

In his first case, Burke takes on a client named Flood, a martial arts expert, searching for the man who raped and killed a little girl. Together they make quite a team, something like Modesty Blaise and Willie Garvin in a novel by Celine. For this is a very violent book, and Vachss never flinches from the horror: he includes a sickening description of a snuff movie, chilling (yet comic) portraits of would-be soldiers of fortune, and a convincing look at the underworld of child pornography. Indeed, he veers close to the didactic in some of his rants about the slime who prey on little kids—but who can blame him? Vachss himself is an expert on child abuse and juvenile delinquency. His is not a pretty world, and he has no use for conventional pieties to excuse atrocity.

Virtually every survivalist fantasy of urban life finds its place here—Burke the vigilante, with his superhero comrades; the city as concrete jungle; civilization constantly assaulted by fiends in human form. Vachss' language is wry, Chandleresque, and laced with authentic details about the methodology and gadgetry of crime.

> "I sell a lot of identification, mostly to clowns who want the option to disappear but never will. The stuff looks pretty good—all you need are some genuine state blanks, like for drivers' licenses, and the right typewriter. IBM makes a special typing element. . . . They call it an OCR element and you can't buy it over the counter but this is something less than a significant deterrent to people who steal for a living. I have a complete set in the office."

Flood's only fault—assuming, of course, one is not dismayed by its draconian social views—may be its length: it sacrifices a tight artistry for a rambling panorama of damned souls. In the end, though, Burke does find the child-killer, and Flood fights for her life in ritual combat.

Newgate Callendar (review date 31 May 1987)

SOURCE: A review of *Strega,* in *The New York Times Book Review,* May 31, 1987, p. 45.

[*In the following brief review, Callendar calls* Strega *"unbelievable and slick, but fun."*]

Want a tough New York crime novel? Try *Strega* by Andrew Vachss. It features Burke, a private investigator, a former convict, a man who gets things done and never mind the letter of the law. In *Strega* (meaning "witch" in Italian) Burke is hired by a woman to find a pornographic photo of a boy. He was forced into sex acts by a pornographic ring and is now all but a mental case. The woman—the Strega of the story—thinks if she tears up the photo in front of the boy, all will be well. His anxieties will go away.

In this book New York is a jungle, and Burke is a very big cat prowling at night. He has some friends to help him, notably a lethal Oriental instrument named Max, who is to Burke what Hawk is to Spenser in the Robert Parker series. When Burke and Max swing into action, they are fearful to behold. They make Mickey Spillane's exploits read like the minutes of a Harvard alumni meeting, class of 1920. *Strega* is unbelievable and slick, but fun.

Bill Brashler (review date 4 September 1988)

SOURCE: "Burke's Law: A Vivid Quest for Vengeance," in *Tribune Books,* September 4, 1988, p. 5.

[*In the following review, Brashler provides a brief summary of* Blue Belle.]

A sleuth who lives not just on society's edge, but on its underbelly. An Amazon of a heroine whose thoughts never assume the proportions of her body. A city full of mercenaries, psychopaths and deviates. An unsmiling author with an open collar and an eye patch.

Such is *Blue Belle,* the third episode in the sullen existence of Burke, the outlaw private eye created by Andrew Vachss. It is a book so ferocious, with characters so venal and action so breakneck, that you dare not get in the way.

Burke, just Burke, is an ex-con, no-b.s. operative who pretty much detests the small stuff of life. Things such as taxes, Social Security numbers, driver's licenses and bills. He avoids most of them and doesn't even own a telephone—you want him, you call Mama Wong's Chinese restaurant and Burke just might call back.

His friends are similarly shadowy. Max is a martial arts expert. Mole is a mechanic who can rig any device. Prof is a hustler. Michele is a pre-op transsexual. Pansy, Burke's dog, is a lethal mastiff who lays down when Burke says, "Jump."

Life is this way, the premise holds, in order for Burke to get things done. He only takes on a gumshoe job, however, for big money, which he then spreads among his friends, or to avenge situations he finds repulsive, such as cases involving child abuse. In *Blue Belle* he is commissioned by a Man-

hattan pimp to get rid of the "Ghost Van," a nasty RV whose occupants kidnap and murder teenage prostitutes.

All of this is strong, gritty, gut-bucket stuff, so unsparing and vivid that it makes you wince. Vachss knows the turf and writes with a sneering bravado. In Burke's world guys have "cement mixer eyes," and "everybody's lying but you and me." Burke prowls the city with a seething, angry, almost psychotic voice appropriate to the devils he deals with.

But hold on. Just when you think you have come up with a companion to your Elmore Leonard collection, Burke meets Belle. And Belle is a disaster. She is a backwoods behemoth—there are enough descriptions of her chest and hind quarters to fill a butcher's manual—with more excess emotional baggage than Sybil. Worst of all, Belle complains, nags, clings and whines incessantly.

In so doing, she turns Burke, who, we must charitably assume, is addled by her gravity-defying body, into a dimestore shrink. In scene after scene he is a tedious, know-it-all with a pat answer for Belle's every psychological glitch, misgiving and whine. Beneath his two-day stubble and street-smarts, Burke becomes a Dr. Joyce Brothers in conversations that end with, "Tears spilled down her face."

Finally the ghost van beckons, and Burke gets back on the case. With Belle not central to the operation, every nasty, frightening element falls into place, and nothing disappoints.

Vachss is good, his Burke books first-rate. Find a new date, Belle.

David Nicholson (review date 4 September 1988)

SOURCE: "Lord of the Asphalt Jungle," in *Washington Post Book World,* Vol. XVIII, No. 36, September 4, 1988, p. 7.

[*In the following review, Nicholson compliments Vachss for the entertainment value his work provides, but criticizes him for a lack of character development and utilizing formulaic plots.*]

Reading Andrew Vachss is a sordid pleasure, like eating a tub of greasy, buttered popcorn while watching a double feature of kung-fu movies. Afterwards, bloated and bleary-eyed, most adults of reasonable intelligence will feel a little guilty at having wasted so much time, for Vachss' novels—*Flood, Strega,* and his latest, *Blue Belle*—are examples of the novel as comic book, the novel as television. Taken together, they remind one of the comment made by the producer of a television action show starring Lee Majors. During a story conference, a new writer asked about the motivation of the character Majors played.

"Motivation?" said the producer. "What motivation? The show's about a 14-year-old kid and his two buddies who are 13 and how they all go about having adventures." Which just about sums it up. Consider the following:

Vachss' hero, Burke, is an ex-con with a soft spot for abused children. He lives with a large and dangerous dog named Pansy. Unlike most New Yorkers, the two live rent-free (Burke once "did a favor" for the landlord), in rooms booby-trapped against unauthorized entry. Burke makes some of his money running scams involving phony Social Security numbers, unauthorized government checks and advertisements recruiting mercenaries. In terms of the genre and for convenience's sake we might call him a private eye or an investigator, except that he has no license and no listing in the telephone book. Burke drives a primer-gray Plymouth with (need it be said?) an exceedingly powerful engine and a 40-gallon gas tank. The Plymouth too is booby trapped.

Reading Andrew Vachss is a sordid pleasure, like eating a tub of greasy, buttered popcorn while watching a double feature of kung-fu movies.
—David Nicholson

One of Burke's sidekicks is Max, a mute Mongolian martial arts expert. Another is Michelle, a transvestite prostitute saving to have a sex-change operation. The third is Mole (Vachss seems to like M's), a Zionist electronics genius who lives beneath a junkyard populated by dozens of rusting cars and packs of wild dogs. Mole makes many of the booby traps, including lighters that look like ordinary butane lighters but are filled with napalm.

The plot of a Vachss novel goes something like this: A beautiful woman seeks Burke's assistance in finding someone who abuses and/or murders children. Burke and the woman join forces to go after the child abuser. The beautiful woman, spirited and independent, has trouble doing what Burke tells her to do. She and Burke argue. She and Burke make love. Burke calls on his buddies—Max, Michelle and Mole—for help in tracking down the child abuser. Burke gets beaten up (sometimes by the beautiful and spirited woman). Burke finds the child abuser. Burke kills the child abuser. The beautiful woman dies or goes somewhere Burke cannot follow; either way, Burke loses her.

In *Blue Belle,* the beautiful woman is named Belle, and the child abuser drives a van around New York, shooting teen prostitutes through the back door. Belle and Burke argue.

Belle and Burke make love. Burke calls on his buddies—Max, Michelle and Mole—for help in tracking down the child abuser. Burke gets beaten up. Burke . . . well, surely you get the point.

Vachss deals, as do many television shows, in broad strokes. And as on most big-city, urban crime shows, blacks exist as either pimps or prostitutes. In *Blue Belle,* the pimp is Marques (those M's again), who recruits Belle to hire Burke to find the killer. The killers' victims are young white girls, but there are several, unnamed, black prostitutes Burke encounters as he proceeds with his investigation. Racial epithets are freely tossed around. Their use does not, however, add to the depiction of a gritty twilight world; instead, they come off as a cheap way of authenticating the atmosphere in which the characters move.

Those characters, Burke, Max, Mole, Michelle, are less characters than types or collections of traits; Max, for example, is literally the strong, silent type. And the plot of the novel is less a series of incidents flowing organically from the interaction of particular, realized human beings than a string of events that must happen if Vachss is to keep the story going. That he does and does well, for there is an undeniable raw power to *Blue Belle* that keeps the reader turning the pages.

But sheer narrative drive is only part of what has kept readers coming back for more. The key to the attraction of the novels lies in Burke's role as fantasy figure. He is a hero of our times, a kind of urban Tarzan, lord of the asphalt jungle. Like other tough-guy, private investigator heroes, Burke lives by his own moral code in an amoral world. But to an unprecedented extent, he lives in the twilight between the legal and the illegal. He strives to be his own man, knowing he is not truly part of the system, and knowing too that he can never escape it. Burke's solution, then, is to devise ways to make the system work for him.

Some of this is occasionally moving, as when Burke reminisces about his stints in prison and the reasons for his choices. These have a ring of authenticity. Much of the novel, however, reads like the fantasies of a fed-up New Yorker: Burke never comes home to find a notice that the telephone company is going to cut off his telephone; he's managed to tap into the line used by his upstairs neighbors. He owns nothing in his own name (something he reminds us of constantly), so nothing can be taken from him. With a booby-trapped apartment—poison darts, explosives and an attack dog—he never has to worry about burglars. Burke just may be the ultimate urban paranoid—you can't call him, and when he calls you, it's from a phone booth Mole has rigged up to relay the call several times so that it can't be tapped.

All this technology, like so much else in *Blue Belle* and

Vachss' other novels, while possible, just isn't credible. The effect of Vachss' exaggeration, for this reader at least, is the opposite of what he intends: His characters are larger than life, but it is distortion, not mythmaking, and **Blue Belle,** like its predecessors, isn't about people we can recognize in situations that, no matter how fantastic, compel our belief.

Despite Burke's moral stance against child abuse and exploitation, despite Vachss' energetic rendering of the sensational, there is, in the end, little to engage the reader in **Blue Belle.** At a time when a substantial case can be made that the mystery (or, if you prefer, crime novel or thriller) ought to be promoted from the strait jacket of genre fiction, Vachss has expanded the genre's conventions without testing their limits. Burke remains the same from novel to novel, which is comforting for those who dislike surprises, but disappointing for those readers who believe that even the characters of a mere detective story should show some evidence of the human capability to react and change.

Andrew Abrahams (essay date 19 September 1988)

SOURCE: "On the Subject of Child Abuse, Andrew Vachss is One Tough Lawyer Plus One Tough Author," in *People Weekly,* Vol. 30, No. 12, September, 1988, pp. 78-80.

[*In the following essay, Abrahams provides a brief biographical profile of Vachss.*]

> *Max grabbed the freak's fingertips, stretching the hand out for me. I raised the butcher knife high above my head . . .*

The man with the knife is a private eye known only as Burke. He is a fictional character, but his feelings about child molesters—freaks, as he calls them—are real. They are the feelings of his creator, Andrew Vachss.

A Manhattan attorney who represents victims of child abuse, Vachss (rhymes with "fox") has worked 13 years in an insidious world where kids are bought and sold as objects of desire. He has also sued groups like the venerable Fresh Air Fund, which, he charged, had unwittingly sent some children to homes where they were abused. These experiences have left him with plenty to say about this shame of our society, and he says it in detective novels.

"I get incest cases, kiddie porn and torture of one kind or another. I get cases from doctors or psychiatrists," says Vachss, 45. "Perpetrators call looking for me to defend them because I'd be good. And I would be. I just won't. I've turned people down who then say, 'Well, how much do you want?' Someone who knows children are for sale wouldn't be shocked to think lawyers are too, now would they?"

Vachss has taken his own anger and turned the flame up higher to create Burke, the central character in all of his books. An orphan raised by the state and an ex-con, Burke has parlayed his knowledge of criminal life into a shady private-eye business. He has a staff working for him, which includes Max, a mute who is a sweet, sensitive guy, when he's not beating a tattoo on the ribs of some freak.

Vachss's raw prose has hit home with critics almost as hard as one of Max's karate chops. "The words leap off the page, the principal character is original, and the style is as clean as a haiku," wrote David Morrell in the *Washington Post.* This month Vachss, as tough and blunt as his fictional voice, will have his third book, **Blue Belle,** published. His first, **Flood,** has sold more than 250,000 copies in hardcover and paperback; **Strega** (published in paperback last spring) has already sold twice as many, and Vachss is mulling over film offers for both **Strega** and **Blue Belle.**

When the movies are cast, Vachss might be considered for the principal role. Handsome, with a taut, angular face, the author wears a patch over his right eye as the result of an incident he says he can't recall—though he does remember it was a chain that did the damage. When he describes some of the countless atrocities that have been inflicted upon children, some as young as 3 months old, his good eye fixes on the listener as if to burn the image of each infuriating act deep into the visitor's brain.

Surprisingly, Vachss denies that his books are autobiographical, and he insists the graphic violence that permeates them is not meant to titillate but to evoke the gamy reality of the streets. "I'm not selling vigilantism," he maintains.
—*Andrew Abrahams*

Though they use different means to achieve their ends, Vachss and Burke have much in common. Burke's pet is an attack-trained 140-lb. mastiff; Vachss happens to own a 140-lb. mastiff as well. In **Strega,** Burke falls for a character named Eva Wolfe, a special prosecutor for New York City's "Citywide Special Victims Bureau." Vachss's wife, Alice, 37, is an assistant district attorney who runs the Special Victims Bureau in the Queens district attorney's office, which prosecutes, among others, cases of child abuse.

Surprisingly, Vachss denies that his books are autobiographical, and he insists the graphic violence that permeates them is not meant to titillate but to evoke the gamy reality of the streets. "I'm not selling vigilantism," he maintains. "The parts of the books that have survived from my life are the moralities, the principles and some of the situations, not the characters."

Vachss started writing fiction four years ago to supplement his meager income as a lawyer; the children he defends, of course, have no financial resources, while their parents may be the ones charged with abuse. He also hopes to educate the public. "I want to make people think, and I want them to get angry," he says. He spends much of his time searching the seamiest parts of New York, hoping to wrest an innocent child from the pimps and the kiddie-porn merchants. "A kid getting off a bus at Times Square is a piece of raw meat being thrown into a shark tank," says Vachss. "Whoever gets there first gets it." If he succeeds in intercepting a runaway, Vachss attempts to get the child into foster care or place him or her in a juvenile facility.

The son of a shipping manager who played semipro football, Vachss grew up amid the teeming tenements of Manhattan's pregentrified Lower West Side, where he learned the rough-and-tumble rules of the street. According to his brother, Woody, young Andrew became familiar early on with the gritty side of urban life. "Andy was always off on his own," says Woody, 43, a probation officer in New Hampshire. "He had a group of friends that I remember as being kind of weird." Woody also recognizes a few of the characters in his older brother's books. "Max existed. So did the Mole [an unsavory character who lives in a junkyard and hunts Nazis]. He may have borrowed a little from one guy and folded it into another, but those guys were real."

> I don't fancy myself a *writer*. I've only got but one story to tell.
> —*Andrew Vachss*

Andrew Vachss became acquainted with all the dismal details of child abuse when, after graduating from Western Reserve University in 1965, he tracked the spread of syphilis for the U.S. Public Health Service in Ohio. "I saw kids who were horribly abused," he recalls. "If you're going to follow syphilis to its end, you're going to find incest. I wasn't shocked at people being shot or stabbed when I was growing up, but I was real shocked that people would do these things to their own kids." From 1971 to 1975, he held a string of jobs, most of them dealing with the rehabilitation of juvenile offenders.

In 1972 Vachss jumped at the chance to run ANDROS II, a maximum-security juvenile facility near Boston, and he is proud of having turned it around. "The place was below a jungle when I got there," he says. "I learned that you can run a jail without letting the inmates run the show." There he met Alice, then a law student, who was writing a history of the institution. "He was extremely intense, and he was also effective," says Alice. "There were three rules in that place: no sex, no violence and no drugs. They were enforced, and that was the first time the kids ever had that." She and Vachss married a few years later—both profess not to remember exactly when. "I think it's our 10th anniversary this year, but we're not very sentimental about those things," says Alice.

Both are intensely devoted to their work and jealous of their privacy. They live in a one-bedroom brick Queens house protected by guard dogs and a number of security devices since each has been threatened many times by criminals they have opposed in court. Because of their commitment to their jobs, they say, and not because of the wretchedness they have seen in the world, the Vachsses have chosen not to have children. Andrew Vachss's writing is not a release from that commitment, he insists, but an extension of it. "I don't fancy myself a *writer*," he says, leaning back in a creaky chair and speaking in a gravelly voice Burke would be proud of. "I've only got but one story to tell."

Richard Gehr (review date 29 November 1988)

SOURCE: "Righteous Brother," in *Village Voice,* Vol. XXXIII, No. 48, November 29, 1988, p. 66.

[*In the following review, Gehr criticizes Vachss for "redundancy, if not hypocrisy."*]

Having now struck thrice, it's time for popular and once-promising crimester Andrew Vachss to be called out on grounds of redundancy, if not hypocrisy. In *Blue Belle,* the most recent in his series of novels featuring Burke, a stone-hard sociopath, Vachss lazily follows the pattern familiar to readers of his *Flood* and *Strega.*

In all three books the titular women enlist this quintessential underground man to seek out and destroy various "freaks" involved in some form of child abuse. Burke gladly complies, using prison-yard instincts, con games, survivalist wiles, justified violence ("'Damn their souls to hell.' 'I don't do souls,'" Burke replies, "'Just bodies'"), and his ongoing retinue of post-Runyon cohorts. These include a golden-hearted former hooker saving up for a sex change, an inscrutable deaf-mute martial-arts expert, and a Puerto Rican liberation group. Along the way, he gets it on with the invariably strong-willed title character, and in *Blue Belle,* this is where my Vachss problem begins.

The novel opens with Burke earning a bundle at the expense of some Wall Street creeps while whining about lower

Manhattan's new gentry, "who get preorgasmic when you whisper 'investment banking.'" He lives like a paranoid war criminal in a heavily fortified bunker along with a vicious yet lovable Neapolitan mastiff named Pansy—not all that different from the newcomers he despises. A loner among loners, he has a father complex on account of his institutional upbringing; Vachss reads savviest in scenes involving supercynical Burke with the police, attorneys, and family agencies.

This stems from Vachss's impeccable credentials as a lawyer in the fields of juvenile justice and child abuse (he still lectures and trains on the subject). His indignation at pedophiles, pimps, and pornographers is righteous as hell and has grown over the course of the books. Now Burke's personal torments seem secondary to the children's crusade he has undertaken ("I was going to be a scam artist. But I kept running into kids. And they keep pulling me into what I didn't want to be"). What's good for the world is bad for Vachss's fans; Burke's scams are much more intriguing than his social services. In **Blue Belle,** the "kids" are menaced by the Ghost Van, which appears out of nowhere to torment New York's underage girl hookers, who are either offed on the spot or sped to a Times Square porn palace to star in snuff films.

The dead pros may be white, but the perps are Hispanic: "Word is he uses blood the way some freaks use Vaseline. . . . The Spanish guy, he don't want nothing to do with nothing that ain't white. No Puerto Ricans, no Chinese . . . nothing that's out there but white meat." The total weirdness to be found in New York always seems to surprise the good guys, who repeatedly gasp things like, "Who does this . . . What kind of freaks?"

Yet the city's inherent freakiness appears to have rubbed off on Vachss/Burke. Belle, the novel's lust interest, is a strapping 29-year-old blond stripper endowed with inordinate t&a; she appears much younger, however, speaks in a "little-girl" voice, and is herself an incest child. The surly kiddie defender wastes no time falling for this big baby, whose predilections run toward spanking and buggery ("If I try to sit on your face again, you going to give me another smack?"). But since all good things must end for Burke, the former swamp sister falls in the line of duty. Vachss might consider giving Burke a rest, too. The line between virtue and vice is always problematic, and with Burke's secret proclivities now uncovered, he should probably be kept off the streets for a while.

Gary Dretzka (review date 11 June 1989)

SOURCE: "Disturbed Avenger," in *Chicago Tribune,* June 11, 1989, p. 5.

[In the following review, Dretzka provides a brief summary of Hard Candy *and praises Vachss for his exploration into the darker side of human nature.]*

Andrew Vachss' crime novels—all of which feature Burke, an unlicensed Manhattan P.I. and scam artist who doubles as an avenging angel—are as unsettling a collection of books as one is likely to find.

His novels, as cleverly scripted as any currently in the genre, are less about solving crimes than they are about forcing readers to come to grips with the evil around them. Like Jim Thompson in such works as *The Killer Inside Me,* Vachss puts that evil under a microscope, revealing aspects of the human character that most of us gladly choose to ignore.

Using their brains more often than their brawn, Burke and his motley band of urban guerrillas do battle against the most vile kind of sociopaths: child abusers, rapists and pedophiles. When perpetrators ignore pointed warnings, Burke's, "crew" administers the brand of street justice to which one is compelled only when a close friend, a relative or a young child is violated. We applaud from our easy chairs, but not without experiencing a palpable degree of queasiness.

In **Flood, Strega** and **Blue Belle,** Vachss turned the crime genre upside down by portraying his P.I. not as a modern-day cowboy hero or hardboiled Knight of the Round Table but as a paranoid, and increasingly morose, vigilante. Burke is a crafty ex-con, and his turf is the dark underbelly of Manhattan. His "street family" army consists of a deaf-mute Mongolian warrior, a jive-talking black street hustler, a transsexual prostitute, a mole-like electronics genius, a teenager rescued from a life of sexual abuse, and a monstrous dog. His enemies, usually martial-arts experts, possess superhuman skills.

Vachss' fans will find in **Hard Candy** a tight summation of the emotional tension that has built within Burke like a volcano through the earlier books, then an explosively cathartic resolution. It begins with a particularly troubling example of frontier justice—a settling of scores left over from **Blue Belle**—when Burke confronts the fear and anxiety that have paralyzed him since the shootout that unnecessarily claimed his lover in that book.

"Down here, we have rules," Burke says, explaining his call to action. "We made them ourselves. Feeling dead inside me—that was a feeling. It wouldn't bring Belle back to me—wouldn't get me closer. But making somebody dead . . . that was a debt."

He subsequently is hired by Candy, a kinky call-girl and acquaintance from his twisted childhood, to rescue her daughter from a cult leader called Train. Simple enough, but he manages at the same time to cross paths with a spooky freelance assassin named Wesley—another blast from Burke's past—who thinks that Burke is cutting into his business. And, for their part, certain NYPD detectives are none too pleased that he double crossed them in a Times Square sting operation in *Blue Belle.*

Through Candy and Wesley, Vachss exposes many of Burke's early roots and sets him on a course that either will rid New York of some of its most carnivorous perverts, mobsters and religious charlatans or put him in a straitjacket. Harkening back to earlier books, the author calls in Burke's haunting, red-haired nemesis, Strega, and the memory of his beloved Flood, now in faraway Japan.

Because of all this emotional and textual baggage, *Hard Candy* might be a difficult spot for newcomers to jump into Vachss' repertoire. The series, with its many continuing characters and themes, should be read in order; and so many loose ends are tied together in *Hard Candy* that it might be tough to appreciate Burke's motivations without having already read *Blue Belle,* at least.

Vachss, an attorney specializing in child-abuse cases, has placed on Burke's shoulders the weight of America's frustrations over courtroom failures, its collective desire for retribution and the weakness of its people in the face of true evil. But the solutions to society's greatest ills aren't simple, and it's obvious in *Hard Candy* that Burke doesn't always make the right decisions and that knowing this is throwing him off-balance.

"Driving home [from an encounter with Strega], my black and white eyes were still working, but the images were reversed. Inside out. Inverted. For me, playing it safe wasn't playing—it was my life. I couldn't find the controls—nothing was where it had been. Terror said it was my partner, but I didn't have my old pal Fear to keep the nerve endings sharp. . . . Liars gave me their word, sociopaths gave me their trust."

Burke isn't for everyone—certainly the horrible violence, explicit sex and unspeakably ugly crimes of his books won't appeal to those who read mysteries each night to ease their journey into Dreamland—but he fills a void in a cluttered, too often unchallenging genre. With his soiled white hat, this Lone Ranger of the '90s asks difficult questions of readers, while also shining light into the darkest recesses of their souls. It wouldn't hurt for more people to pay attention.

Carol Anshaw (review date 8 July 1990)

SOURCE: "Doing Evil Unto Evil," in *Tribune Books,* July 8, 1990, pp. 3, 11.

[*In the following review, Anshaw claims that Vachss's work makes her "morally queasy" and criticizes the "feel-good roll of hate" created by the atmosphere of his novels.*]

By the traditions of fiction, the private eye is the conscience of the underside. No choirboy himself, his weariness of evil and its doers comes from close acquaintance. He stands in the same shadows they do, just a bit off to the side, staking out his sorry corner of society from behind a glowing cigarette ember.

A problem for modern writers is dragging this anti-hero into a present where evil no longer stays put in a bad neighborhood, no longer plays itself out within a circumscribed society of crooks and hoods and dolls who drink each other's rye (neat), frequent each other's gambling backrooms and plug each other with .38s. Today, crime can be a quick climb through a left-open window of opportunity, a not entirely unreasonable career choice for those extremely low on options. Anybody can turn out to be a player.

Andrew Vachss' way of updating the gumshoe to fit current crimestyles is to drop the figure's dispassionate pose and turn him from society's conscience into its avenger. The result is both dead-earnest and often inadvertently hilarious. In his worst patches, such as the following urban ode, Vachss sounds like the winner of a literary parody contest:

"Gut-grinding poverty. Sandpaper for the soul. Pigeons overhead, circling in flocks. Hawks on the ground. Make enough wrong turns and you're on a no-way street."

The going gets even rougher when Vachss' protagonist—the ex-con detective Burke—begins rhapsodizing on his favorite subject, himself:

> "A legless man pulled himself along the floor of the train, his hands covered with tattered mittens. The upper half of his body sat on a flat wooden disc, separated from the cart by a foot-high column. So you could see he wasn't faking it. He rattled the change in his cup, not saying a word. Humans buried their faces in newspapers, I tapped his shoulders as he rolled by. Stuffed a ten-dollar bill in his cup. He pulled it out, looked it over. Locked my eyes.
>
> "'Thank you, my brother,' he said. Strong, clear voice.
>
> "We always know each other, those of us with missing parts."

Burke's main missing part seems to be a sense of personal ironic detachment. He takes himself more seriously than even your average ultra-macho private eye. Although no one seems to be after him, Burke lives in a maximum-security apartment presided over by a killer attack-dog. Though he doesn't seem to get an undue number of calls, he has all his messages elaborately screened through the phone at Mama Wong's Chinese restaurant.

Basically a loner, he nonetheless clears a little space on the ground where he stands, so women can worship there. His basic attitude toward the female gender puts him somewhere in the company of Andrew Dice Clay. Burke's idea of a witty personals ad is: "Woman wanted. Disease-free. Self-lubricating. Short attention span."

Blossom is Burke's fifth appearance between covers. This time he leaves his Manhattan turf behind and heads for Merrillville, Ind., where an old jail-cell buddy has family troubles. His young cousin has been charged with a grim stack of serial killings—shootings of necking couples in parked cars. Burke quickly (operating on tough-guy instinct) decides the kid didn't do it. Who really did is sure to be some filthy sicko scum because these are the bad guys in society, as Vachss constructs it.

Burke (operating on tough-guy psychological acumen) figures this particular sicko's sickness is that he can't stand to see normal red-blooded guys and gals groping each other. Killing them is his way of having sex. Then (using tough-guy deductive reasoning) Burke figures out this means the killer must have been an abused child the court returned to his horrorshow family.

Not that this profound understanding of the criminal mind leads Burke to any wimp sympathy for it. When Blossom (the book's title character and typical female—diner waitress/doctor/wearer of stockings with garters) suggests the killer might be mentally ill, Burke says,

> "It felt like I was being baited. Goaded into something.
>
> "'You think he needs a psychiatrist?,' I asked her.
>
> "'Don't you?'
>
> "'No.'"

Burke has sterner measures in mind for this "filth," "freak," "greasy human," "thing," whom he tracks down through the roster of a rural neo-Nazi group.

When he's not writing, Vachss is a New York attorney specializing in juvenile justice and child abuse. Surely this has brought him up against the uglier side of humanity and probably accounts for the virulent hatred implicit in his fiction.

The Joel Steinbergs of the world bring vigilante blood to at least a simmer in most of us. But it's an impulse of unilateral judgment and one that civilization requires we resist. Vachss doesn't bother. *Blossom* gets on a feel-good roll of hate that doesn't brake for compassion.

Vachss draws his villains as right-wing paramilitary nutcases, making his story a perfect circle of violence and loathing. The good guys want to get rid of the filth and scum whose intent it is to get rid of the filth and scum. In a world like this the only difference in belief systems is one's definition of filth and one's choice of clean-up method.

That Vachss' books are popular scares me a little. I don't like thinking I'm the only reader made morally queasy inside his airless, closed loop.

Christopher Lehmann-Haupt (review date 12 July 1990)

SOURCE: "A Hard-Boiled Detective, and One Beyond That," in *The New York Times*, July 12, 1990, p. C20.

[*In the following excerpt, Lehmann-Haupt criticizes* Blossom *for a number of problematic plot elements.*]

Blossom is Andrew Vachss's fifth crime novel, after *Flood, Strega, Blue Belle* and *Hard Candy*. Mr. Vachss (pronounced VAX) is a lawyer in private practice specializing in juvenile justice and child abuse cases, so it's understandable that his tough-guy hero, Burke, concentrates on fighting people who prey on the lives of children.

But in *Blossom,* Mr. Vachss seems so eager to show off his specialty that much of his plot is gratuitous. While busy impressing the reader with the squalor and sordidness of juvenile life on the streets of New York City, Burke gets a call from Virgil, a former prison mate of Burke's who now lives in Indiana.

It seems that Virgil's young nephew, Lloyd, has been implicated in the sniper shooting of some teen-age lovers, and he's just disturbed enough about sex to be a plausible suspect. Could Burke come and check Lloyd out and maybe help him out of his jam? Burke could indeed: "Virgil had called at the right time. New York was always hard, but now," thanks to a newspaper personal ad suggesting pedophilia that Burke has just read, "it was ugly."

In fact Burke will not only convince himself of Lloyd's innocence, by palpating the boy's battered libido as only he can do, but he will also prove that Lloyd is guiltless by catching the real sniper. Three problems, however, now afflict Mr. Vachss's plot.

First, certain members of the police also become convinced of Lloyd's innocence, thereby weakening the urgency of the actual perpetrator's capture. Second, Burke begins to hound the real sniper by means that depend too strongly on instinct. One understands that there's little to distinguish the criminal mind from the policeman's; but in Mr. Vachss's handling of this truism there are a few too many lines about Burke's knowing freaks as nobody else does.

"You're scaring me," Burke's lover, Blossom, tells him long after the reader has grasped the idea. "Your voice. Like you're . . . him. Like you see what he saw."

Finally, the climax of **Blossom** is about what you expect it to be. True, there's one small twist, but it obscures more problems than it solves. Otherwise, what happens is precisely what you expect. Since you've been imagining it for a hundred pages or so, it is bound to seem disappointing.

Mr. Vachss is full of good ideas and a keen appreciation of human depravity, particularly as it affects children. But in **Blossom,** at least, his expertise seems two-dimensional. He paints the human soul gray, and that grayness suggests nothing so much as fog.

Charles Champlin (review date 9 June 1991)

SOURCE: A review of *Sacrifice,* in *Los Angeles Times Book Review,* June 9, 1991, p. 13.

[*In the following excerpt, Champlin states that despite its "combination of pulpish devices and empurpled rhetoric,"* Sacrifice *is "mesmerizing in its intensity."*]

Andrew Vachss is just about the toughest of contemporary crime novelists, a New York lawyer specializing in juvenile justice cases, who exposes his knowledge of the world's darkest side, and his rage at it, in novels that are not so much narratives as fragments of a mosaic of evil. (The present book has 195 fragments, some only a sentence long.) *Sacrifice* is Vachss' sixth tale of the horrors wrought upon children. This time his ex-con protagonist Burke is trying to help a child so badly abused that he has taken temporary refuge in a second, murderous personality who, or which, has murdered a baby but has no memory of it.

Burke has a circle of helpers that somewhat resembles the gangs who used to abet Doc Savage and the Shadow, including a deaf and speechless Chinese of enormous speed and stealth, a chap called The Prof who speaks in rap, a woman

who runs a Chinese restaurant and hates all customers except Burke and his pals, assorted Jamaicans and others. He is haunted by all the friends, including many women, he has lost violently in earlier books.

> **Vachss waves a powerful light across a city landscape that few writers go near, and none portray so convincingly. It is unpleasant, but it is also mesmerizing in its intensity.**
> —*Charles Champlin*

The combination of pulpish devices and empurpled rhetoric occasionally comes close to defeating Vachss intentions. "This isn't a city. It's a halfway house without a roof. Stressed to critical mass . . . Fear rules. Politicians promise the people an army of blue-coated street-sweepers for a jungle no chemical could defoliate. . . . The walls of some buildings still tremble with the molecular memory of baby-bashing violence and incestuous terror."

Yet despite the stressful writing, Vachss waves a powerful light across a city landscape that few writers go near, and none portray so convincingly. It is unpleasant, but it is also mesmerizing in its intensity.

George Stade (review date 23 May 1993)

SOURCE: "Looking for Her in All the Wrong Places," in *The New York Times Book Review,* May 23, 1993.

[*In the following review, Stade criticizes Vachss's novel* Shella *as having a "preposterous" plot and "dialogue unlike anyone has ever said, anywhere."*]

Ghost, the hero and narrator of Andrew Vachss's seventh *roman noir,* has just been released from prison. He is looking for his old flame Shella, as she calls herself (a social worker once told her she needed to "come out of her shell"), with whom Ghost used to work the badger game. But when Ghost killed a john who got his kicks by beating prostitutes, Shella fled the scene, leaving Ghost to face the music and serve serious time in jail. Now on parole, which he immediately violates, Ghost travels from city to city, casing the strip joints, Shella's old haunts, which are described by Mr. Vachss with prurient indignation.

He finances his quest with the odd job, for Ghost is by trade an assassin. A half-dozen or so of his killings are described in **Shella,** a dozen or so-more alluded to. His specialty is to break his victims' necks: Ghost, like Grendel, has a mighty grip. In fact, he is the best in the business, given his steady hands; his patience, his know-how, his invisibility ("Nobody sees me"), his ability to be physically and emotionally anesthetized, his absence of inner conflict, his single-mindedness. Ghost isn't much of a reader, doesn't know how to shake hands or smile; he is fairly indifferent to sex, eschews drugs and alcohol, can't understand why people put up pictures on their walls. But he does love his Shella—or maybe he hates her. With a man like Ghost, the difference hardly counts.

Getting nowhere, Ghost searches out a gangster named Monroe, who has many sources of information, and offers a trade: Ghost will do a guy for Monroe; Monroe will locate Shella. Ghost does the guy and even throws in a freebie, also a nasty character—but then all of Ghost's victims are nasty characters, usually sexual "freaks," for Mr. Vachss wants us to admire his hero. Unfortunately, Monroe welshes on his part of the deal and sends a hit man after Ghost. But this poor fellow fails, fatally.

Things begin to look up when Ghost is approached by an Indian, name of Wolf, who knows a soul mate when he sees one: "You and me, we're the same. Brothers in the blood," says Wolf, who belongs to a "pack" of Indian professional assassins. Their problem is that they can't get close to the man their client wants taken out, the leader of a neo-Nazi cult. If Ghost will do the job, the client, a mad computer genius, will locate Shella, guaranteed.

The second half of Mr. Vachss's novel is devoted to Ghost's adventures among the cult members, figures out of tabloid television, as he moves from the outer to the inner circle. Along the way, he easily passes his initiation test, which is to kill a black man; but because he selects a pimp who "works *little* girls," we aren't expected to hold it against him.

Does Ghost break the leader's neck? Does he find Shella? My lips are sealed. It can be said, though, that the plot is preposterous, the characters based on rumor, paranoia and light literature, the dialogue unlike anything anyone has ever said, anywhere. In this respect *Shella* is like Mr. Vachss's other novels, whose hero and narrator is Burke, another psychopath with whom his creator is in love. In *Shella* there is the same self-pity and self-congratulation as in the Burke novels, even the butterfly symbolism and sentimentality about dogs.

When it comes to style, however, *Shella* is an improvement over its predecessors. Burke tells his stories in a style that is both laconic and garrulous; the sentences are short or fragmentary, but there are pages of them given over to fulminations against urban-depravity and sexual predation, especially of children. Ghost, on the other hand, is laconic and affectless; in *Shella,* the righteous indignation is expressed through particulars, rather than by tone or outright assertion.

Ghost's character and Shella's gradually revealed savagery, as it turns out, are explained (and excused) by backgrounds of childhood neglect and abuse. These are serious matters, but as Mr. Vachss uses them they feel like moral blackmail, pretexts for murder and fantasies of revenge. It is no use, of course, knocking the other guy's fantasy fiction: the genre's function is to allow in the imagination what we deny ourselves in the flesh, and it is just as likely to siphon off dangerous emotions as to encourage them. If you are boiling over with vengeful fury upon which you cannot act, Mr. Vachss may be the man for you—now that Mickey Spillane is out of style.

Phil Baker (review date 26 November 1993)

SOURCE: A review of *Shella,* in *Times Literary Supplement,* No. 4730, November 26, 1993, p. 22.

[*In the following review, Baker criticizes Vachss for presenting his characters in a "heavy-handed" manner.*]

"The first time I killed someone, I was scared", confesses the narrator of Andrew Vachss's *Shella.* "Shella told me it was like that for her the first time she had sex. I was fifteen that first time. Shella was nine." The equation of sex and violence in this opening passage is to govern the book.

Our narrator is a contract killer who is nameless even to his girlfriends, although some people call him "Ghost". Ghost shacks up with a stripper who has the generic *nom de porn* of Candy, but her self-chosen name is Shella, suggesting a carapace: "Some social worker in one of the shelters told her she had to come out of her shell." Ghost and Shella make a living at "Badger", where she picks up marks and Ghost robs them. After killing one person too many, Ghost does time in prison, and when he comes out he starts searching for the vanished Shella.

He falls in with a group of American Indian criminals who want to assassinate a neo-Nazi leader. He infiltrates the Nazis, and it says something about the novel that the most sympathetic characters in it are to be found among these caricature white-trash losers. After Ghost kills the Nazi, the honest Indians keep their side of the bargain by tracing Shella. She has been working as a dominatrix, and the book's picturesque excursions into formal sadomasochism are only the logical extension of its first premisses. Shella has been going too far and murdering her clients, in a belated revenge on her father who sexually abused her. She has also, for reasons best known to Andrew Vachss, been drinking their blood, and it is this which has led to her slow death from AIDS. Ghost's final favour is as predictable as its simile; her neck snaps "like a dry twig".

Shella slips by in bite-sized chunks, the product of a culture with a short attention span. It is an exercise in style and ambience, in almost parodic masculine hardness ("Cancer don't *look* tough either", one character warns another about Ghost), against a background of deeply trawled contemporary sleaze. Underlying it is Vachss's picture of the effect of American prisons and juvenile detention centres, psychopath factories, where gang rape is routine (and consequently becoming commonplace in "new emetic" American crime fiction): Ghost began his lethal career by pulping the head of a sleeping rapist with a radio battery swung in a sock.

Vachss's presentation of damaged and ruined identities—people whose minds are "all scar tissue", as Ghost's is said to be—can be heavy-handed, and the emotional inarticulacy of his characters sometimes approaches the posturing pseudo-poetry of Bruce Springsteen lyrics. The book is narrated in three sections; clubs, diamonds and spades. There are no hearts in it. Like so much else in the book, the stylization and veiled sentimentality with which this point is made recalls the aesthetics of the tattoo parlour.

Wes Lukowsky (review date July 1994)

SOURCE: A review of *Born Bad* and *Down in the Zero,* in *Booklist,* Vol. 90, No. 21, July, 1994.

[*In the following review, Lukowsky calls* Born Bad *a "compelling view of the psychotic personality," but argues that in* Down in the Zero, *Vachss has abandoned "all pretense of character development."*]

Vachss, an attorney specializing in juvenile justice and child abuse, is the author of a series of very successful crime novels, most starring the unconventional detective Burke. His fiction, including this story collection and a new Burke novel, explores the recurring themes of his nonliterary professional life—incest, child abuse, violence to women—but does so from a distinctly nonestablishment, belly-of-the-beast perspective.

> **The Burke series once seemed innovative and utterly original. Now, with all pretense of character development abandoned, it's tough to distinguish one Burke novel from another.**
> —*Wes Lukowsky*

Born Bad comprises 44 short pieces—including a three-act play—that look inside the heads of a collection of serial killers, child abusers, and other violent criminals. Vachss' indignation is both his strength and his weakness. His zeal provides the power behind his largely unadorned prose, creating unrelenting pressure but ultimately threatening to jade readers. Still, these snapshots offer a compelling view of the psychotic personality. One story—a vignette, actually—consists of the eerily apologetic monologue a serial killer delivers to his victim; another offers a killer explaining why environment was not the cause of his aberration. By the time one encounters the tenth psycho killer, though, they all begin to sound the same.

In *Down in the Zero,* Burke, the dark, brooding street angel and avenger of children and exploited women, is critically depressed if not suicidal. On his last case, he was forced to kill a child, and the grief is eating him alive. When Randy, a youth from the wealthy suburbs and son of an old Burke flame, asks for help, Burke hesitates. It is only when Burke learns Randy's peers are committing suicide that he intervenes. The usual Burke potpourri of sexual perversion, incest, greed, and child abuse results. There are a few new spins: this time the evil emanates not from sleazy crime barons but from an ostensibly legitimate business, and the suburban locale provides Burke a forum to critique modern shopping-mall youth, which he does with gusto. Finally, though, it's still the same old Burke. He's a one-trick pony, a revenge machine who has no faith in the system and usually commits a criminal act to bring the bad guys down. Is Vachss using Burke to work out his own frustrations as a lawyer who must work within the system? Maybe so, but the demon-purging process is taking its toll. The Burke series once seemed innovative and utterly original. Now, with all pretense of character development abandoned, it's tough to distinguish one Burke novel from another.

Thomas Adcock (review date 20 November 1994)

SOURCE: "Some Are Born Violent, Others Achieve Violence...," in *The New York Times Book Review,* November 20, 1994, p. 45.

[*In the following review, Adcock argues that while* Down in the Zero *addresses issues more complex than in previous Vachss novels, it reverts to a "mundane plod" due to its failure to explore those issues more deeply.*]

Not so long ago, depravity was discussed only after the fact, in confessionals and related whispery venues of holy shame. This was back when such things as pedophilia, bestiality, transvestism, S & M, wife-swapping, incest, necrophilia and other lusty recreations held shock value.

Heaven knows, now anything goes.

Take note of the common stuff of contemporary American culture and you might well conclude that sexual depravity has been thoroughly democratized. No doubt this is why the abundant eroticism of Andrew Vachss's new novel, *Down in the Zero,* seems so quaint. Consider this bit of pillow talk:

> "'She's ready for you now, master,' she said to me.
>
> "I stepped behind Charm, put one hand on the small of her back. My right hand flashed.
>
> "'Aaaargh!' It was a scream of rage."

I cannot recall such flaccidity in the previous novels by Mr. Vachss starring Burke, the urban survivalist of one name, several sorrows and no excuses. In past offerings like *Flood, Strega* and *Hard Candy,* Mr. Vachss's readers have come to expect the sort of predatory sex that can cause some of them to run off and be sick, the natural-born violence of characters with lives as rough as plowed concrete, the bullet-riddled prose style. Mr. Vachss's leather and acid literary reputation was well deserved—then. Perhaps the great malling of depravity has caused Mr. Vachss to explore more complex (and potentially more timely) terrain than usual with *Down in the Zero,* set amid the moneyed squalor of suburban Connecticut and dealing with the abyss of adolescent suicide and with the guiltiest recesses of Burke's haunted soul.

Unfortunately, this meatier territory is much too briefly trodden. We are left, instead, with a mundane plod through most of this tale. Burke gets a telephone call out of the blue from a Connecticut lad named Randy, who fears he's the next probable victim in a rash of suspicious teen-age deaths. Randy is the son of an acquaintance of Burke's, a lesbian scamp to whom he is indebted for past favors; Burke reluctantly charges to the rescue, thereby booking up with a suburban kinky crowd, largely in the persons of two cutely named sisters, Fancy and Charm. Mucking up the enterprise are fatuous passages about smugglers, espionage and computers.

There are some finely sour riffs along the way: "Out here, they whip their kids with words. Cuts just as deep." "For the privileged, life is a karaoke machine—even if they can't sing, the background's always there for support." "People say you can't heal until you can forgive. . . . A beast steals your soul, you don't get it back by making peace with him. You make peace with yourself." But these hardly provide *Down in the Zero* the vital organs it needs.

Nor do the bons mots begin to address a worthy pair of social questions that somehow manage to limp through the thicket of an unremarkable plot: familial cruelty disguised as love, and our national habit of ignoring dead-eyed kids.

Mr. Vachss is a man with a sweet and angry heart, which has led him to specialize in juvenile justice and child abuse as a lawyer. His novels are, in a sense, an extension of the battle to protect children. Previously, his righteous heart has bled well in the cause of literature as in law. But this time, regrettably, the pulse of Mr. Vachss the novelist has very nearly struck zero.

Jack Womack (review date 24 December 1995)

SOURCE: "Children's Crusaders," in *Washington Post Book World,* Vol. XXV, No. 52, December 24, 1995, pp. 5, 10.

[*In the following review, Womack criticizes Vachss's work, likening* Footsteps of the Hawk *to drinking "near-beer," and faulting* Batman: The Ultimate Evil *for its comic-book style conventions.*]

Andrew Vachss has good intentions, surely. For years he has devoted himself to the defense of children against adults who would wreak physical and sexual harm upon them. In his fiction, Vachss's men and women—solitary, suspicious, stoic—tend to bear the scars of such abuse. Depicting the convoluted ways in which their childhood traumas haunt them in adult life often enables him to introduce into his plots an emotional resonance otherwise undeserved. Often; not always.

In *Footsteps of the Hawk,* Burke, Vachss's ex-con protagonist from his earlier *Down in the Zero,* finds himself squeezed by two New York cops as he tries to ascertain which one is a serial killer. Is it short-fused, ball-bearing-eyed Morales? "A thick, violent vein pulsed in his neck." Is it marble-thighed, pouty-voiced Belinda? Watching her climb stairs, Burke finds it "hard not to admire those fine flesh-gears meshing." He knows one thing: "I was a blind leech in muddy swampwater, searching for a pulse."

> **If Vachss never approaches James Ellroy in portraying a palpably evil or even believable world, rarely does he flounder into Mickey Spillane terrain—more's the pity.**
>
> —*Thomas Adcock*

In the past, Burke has suffered familial abuse and long-term stints in state facilities, but his allusions to these events are so perfunctory that he might be recalling someone else's recovered memories. Still, with impeccable timing, his reveries arise whenever the plot takes especially recherche twists. Burke doesn't much like his city ("New York may be a woman, the way some writers say. If she is, she's a low-class evil bitch"), yet he is keenly perceptive of her raffish byways, where "feral dogs fear the feral children, and even the STOP signs are bullet-pocked." He mimes the role of Chandlerian mean-street moralist with approximate panache: "Time and people passed, at about the same speed. I know about that—in my life, I've killed some of both. I learned something too—killing time is harder."

Vachss burdens Burke with roguish associates. There's Mama, whose Chinatown restaurant is the hub of a vast, shadowy operation whose miscreants manage to serve Burke's most petty needs; Max, his "warrior," i.e., goon; Fortunato, a mob lawyer who clips his cigars with a small silver guillotine; tawny-thighed hooker Mojo Mary, "half-Cajun, half-Lao;" and an entourage of Tyson-sized palookas, one of whom, regrettably, speaks in rhyme: "It don't take no rocket scientist to be a ho', bro—all you need is the lips and the hips." Burke also owns a Neapolitan mastiff named Pansy. He shouldn't.

If Vachss never approaches James Ellroy in portraying a palpably evil or even believable world, rarely does he flounder into Mickey Spillane terrain—more's the pity. But savor such delights as "'Liar!' she hissed" when you find them, and as for the episode of Burke being strapped naked into an electric chair while—no, see for yourself. For those who crave that bitter aftertaste, the frothy head on *Footstep*'s near-beer should momentarily slake their thirst.

Onward, downward. The inherent difficulty with transferring a popular-culture hero of an earlier era (e.g., Tarzan, James Bond) into the context of the contemporary world is that the retrofitted hero invariably becomes more two-dimensional. It pleases us to see Sherlock Holmes apply deductive reasoning sitting in a hansom cab on Baker Street; seeing him similarly ratiocinating, standing atop the grassy knoll in Dealey Plaza, evokes a different response. Believably recreating, in writing, a hero taken from a predominantly visual medium is even harder. Few writers try. In **Batman: The Ultimate Evil,** Vachss tries. Appended to the end of the novel is a heartbreaking article detailing the scope of child exploitation in Southeast Asia, notably Thailand. It's not fiction. Gotham, we have a problem.

The fondly remembered Caped Crusader no longer tilts at the likes of Guest Windmill Tallulah Bankhead to the accompaniment of "Wam-O!" and "Splurp!" In keeping with the Zeitgeist, he has of late been transmogrified into the moody, broody, gloom-'n'-doomy Night-Rider, as Vachss tags him (thankfully, no subtle homage to earlier masked

avengers seems intended). But in Vachss's mitts, noir becomes bete noire, and Batman battles pedophiles.

The reader is initially lulled into hoping the hazards ahead will not be so unfamiliar, as our hero busies himself of an evening snapping thuggish arms "like twigs," moving at the speed of "a turbo-charged mongoose" and listening contentedly to that "crackle-crunch sound that always foretells a fractured skull." The Batmobile is described lovingly, yet gnomically, as if a *Motor Trend* reviewer had been translated into Slovakian by someone more familiar with Czech. Its wheels, we are told, are guided by "massive iridium screws," probably in the manner of dilithium crystals. The Night-Rider may uphold the laws of Gotham City, but he remains blissfully oblivious to those of inertia, momentum, gravity.

In mufti, Batman encounters orange-eyed Debra Kane, a child protection services case-worker. ("'An albino woman,' Bruce Wayne thought. 'And a proud one too.'") As he isn't much of a raconteur and his unadorned face is no more than "a fleshy mask of blandness," when Kane meets Wayne she is forced to break the ice by telling him about child abuse; he's shocked. They go to a housing project, the sight of which nearly does him in. The reader slowly comprehends why Gotham's crime rate never seems to go down.

Then, having spent half the book striving to situate Batman in a city so reminiscent of New York that one seedy quarter is called, by happenstance, "The Bowery," Vachss proceeds in the second half to loose his Night-Rider upon a Satanic child-procuring cabal in—the projects? Thailand? No, in the land of "Udon Khai," where the leading industry is providing well-heeled tourists with sex with children aboard a ship called, truly, the Lollypop.

Be charitable—try. Imagine Vachss on the afternoon he wrote this book. *Two-thirty: time to send Batman to Thailand. My God . . . no.* His flesh-gears mesh uncontrollably as, horrified, he suddenly perceives the problem he has thus far managed to ignore: The broad shoulders of the Night-Rider will snap like twigs beneath the weight of this particular reality. *What to do? That's it . . .*

So, quickly: En route to Udon Khai, Batman encounters Evil in all its forms—a "portly man dressed in a white suit," possibly Sydney Greenstreet; a "muscular woman in a black Mohawk" who walks a snow leopard on a leash; cabal kingpin William X. Malady, who keeps his left hand close to "a giant globe on which a map of the world had been painted"; and countless Uzi-blasting extras shipped over as a job lot from a soft-porn version of "Terry and the Pirates." Good wins. Bad loses.

Batman: The Ultimate Evil is as satisfying—aesthetically, ethically, morally—as a pulse-pounding yarn in which pulp-fiction hero Doc Savage ransacks the shantytowns of South America in a terribly successful search for Doc Mengele.

Ryan Bishop and Lillian S. Robinson (review date 29 January 1996)

SOURCE: "Batman Goes to Bangkok," in *The Nation,* Vol. 262, No. 4, January 29, 1996, pp. 34-35.

[*In the following review of* Batman: The Ultimate Evil, *Bishop and Robinson discuss Vachss's use of Batman as a vehicle in his fight against child abuse.*]

Pow! What? Batman has taken on child prostitution in Thailand? No, we are not making this up. Zowie! Child abuse, whether at home in Gotham or over in exotic "Udon Khai," is at once the source and the reflection of the ultimate evil? And Batman, of all super heroes, despite his camp associations and (Holy Hypocrisy!) his historic relationship with Robin, enlists to combat commercial pedophilia? That struggle was (Wham!) his late mother's mission, the real reason his parents were murdered? You say the boss (Splat!), the ultimate kingpin of the ultimate evil, is named Malady? And the goal—not of the mythic Batman but of the story we're reading—is (Zap!) to destabilize the Thai government? Uh-uh, we are not making any of it up.

In fact, our only problem with the extraordinary new Batman project is that author Andrew Vachss simultaneously is and is not making it up. Vachss's new Warner novel, *Batman: The Ultimate Evil,* has also been adapted (Dynamic Dual Distribution!) as a two-part DC Comic. In both formats, Batman learns about the hideous child abuse perpetrated in his own grim Gotham and then follows the horror to mysterious Udon Khai, where he destroys a tourist industry founded on the sexual enslavement of children. Since Udon Khai, like Batman, exists only in fantasy, both novel and comic book include an appendix—journalist David Hechler's article describing actual child sex tourism in Thailand—along with a list of organizations working against it. One of these, Vachss's own Don't! Buy! Thai! (we are not making up those multiple, comic book-style exclamation points, either), is coordinating an international boycott of Thai exports in which Vachss hopes to engage his readers.

For Vachss, child prostitution and international pedophile tourism dwarf any revelations about Batman's past, as the superhero's fame becomes a vehicle for the author's larger project. In a recent interview, Vachss told us that "Batman is a story and Thailand is not enough of a story." In fact, even Thailand, a major but by no means solitary offender in this area, takes a back seat to the issue of child abuse writ large. Any apparent anomaly is resolved by Vachss's assertion that "child protection and crime prevention are the same thing." Hitherto, Batman has merely been "fighting criminals, not crime"; he can now trace his brooding dissatisfaction with his life's work to his inability to recognize this distinction. By linking child abuse, social ills and criminal activity, Vachss uses Batman in much the same way the comic-book hero uses his Batmobile: as a crime-fighting instrument. Vachss enlists Batman in his laudable thirty-year fight against child abuse of all sorts; he hopes that the superhero will take the cause to a super-big audience.

The contractual restrictions that Vachss accepted in order to enroll the Caped Crusader in this particular crusade require a clear disjunction between fiction (Batman and Udon Khai) and reality (the child prostitutes of Thailand). In the text, Vachss effects the transition with a signed statement, as the tone shifts from the mythic ("'In their name!' the Batman cried deep within himself as he swung through the open window to face the ultimate evil") to the reportorial ("Child sex tourism is not new"). Does the invented narrative support the real one? On the most basic level, of course it does. The fiction tells a story about child abuse and sexual slavery and the reportage exposes Batman's mass readership to facts about sex tourism in Thailand that arguably would reach them in no other way. But Batman's fictional adventures in fictitious Udon Khai may make it harder to appreciate the true story meant to mobilize readers to action.

Batman: The Ultimate Evil is a techno-thriller. The original Batman possessed no superpowers. Instead of extraterrestrial strength, flight or X-ray vision, he had an exquisitely trained body and loads of fancy equipment. Vachss builds on this history: Batman's workout is now so intense that the cool-down alone takes ninety minutes, and the Batmobile's new gadgetry makes the car a lot smarter than you are. He also has access to the latest weaponry—Batman supplies the Udon Khai guerrillas with an arsenal worth two-and-a-half pages of description—and computers loaded with all knowable information. To free the children of Udon Khai, Batman, himself a finely tuned machine getting in touch with its inner child, need only deploy the various mechanisms along the trail illuminated by the data—and Zap!

By contrast, the reader who joins the real-world struggle is assigned a much less glamorous task with far fewer visible results: simply refusing to buy products made in Thailand. It's not a role for which the political economy of mythical Udon Khai offers much preparation. Udon Khai's is a one-industry economy, based on specialized, pedophiliac sex tourism at astronomical prices and with long waiting lists, controlled by a single resident foreigner, the vicious William X. Malady. Thailand's real sex industry is part of an international development strategy favoring mass tourism, the attraction being cheap, abundant sex with teenage and adult prostitutes, as well as children. If there's a "kingpin"—and we're not sure it's that simple—it's the World Bank, and the malady is global capitalism. That and the international AIDS epidemic. . . .

Aware that he's writing for "an audience with an attention span of X," where X = minimal, Vachss intentionally narrows the focus of his novel to make his point more dramatic. But he also wants to motivate this attention-X audience to social action. Now, while they may indeed buy many of the products manufactured in Thailand (e.g., athletic shoes and action-hero figurines), Batman's principal audience, young males who read comic books, may not be the most likely source of international consumer activism, especially in these apolitical times. More worrisome is the efficacy of a boycott in this situation. Most people in Thailand who sell themselves or their children into sex work do so because they lack other options. Outside the sex trade, the labor market offers work—at a fraction of a prostitute's earnings—as domestics and production workers in the very sweatshops that produce athletic shoes and action-hero figurines. So a general boycott may result in even fewer choices for children and parents. Moreover, the Chuan government, which was publicly committed to ending child prostitution, has recently been replaced by a coalition of old-time politicos who favor a business-as-usual stance. Vachss may have the right idea, but action directed against the sex industry itself may be a more effective strategy.

FURTHER READING

Criticism

Bryant, Edward. A review of *A Flash of White. Locus,* September, 1993, p. 69.
> Brief review of a chapbook of material by and about Vachss.

Elliott, Steve. "Andrew Vachss Uses Printed Page, World Wide Web to Lobby for Young Victims." *The Fresno Bee,* August 4, 1997.
> Discusses Vachss's use of novels and the World Wide Web as tools for combating child abuse.

Additional coverage of Vachss's life and career is contained in the following sources published by Gale: *Contemporary Authors,* **Vol. 118, and** *Contemporary Authors New Revision Series,* **Vol. 44.**

☐ Contemporary Literary Criticism

Indexes

Literary Criticism Series
Cumulative Author Index
Cumulative Topic Index
Cumulative Nationality Index
Title Index, Volume 106

How to Use This Index

The main references

Camus, Albert
    1913-1960 . . . . **CLC 1, 2, 4, 9, 11, 14,
32, 69; DA; DAB; DAC; DAM DRAM,
MST, NOV; DC2; SSC 9; WLC**

---

list all author entries in the following Gale Literary Criticism series:

BLC = *Black Literature Criticism*
CLC = *Contemporary Literary Criticism*
CLR = *Children's Literature Review*
CMLC = *Classical and Medieval Literature Criticism*
DA = *DISCovering Authors*
DAB = *DISCovering Authors: British*
DAC = *DISCovering Authors: Canadian*
DAM = *DISCovering Authors Modules*
  DRAM = *dramatists;* *MST* = *most-studied
  authors;* *MULT* = *multicultural authors;* *NOV* =
  novelists; *POET* = *poets;* *POP* = *popular/genre
  writers;* *DC* = *Drama Criticism*
HLC = *Hispanic Literature Criticism*
LC = *Literature Criticism from 1400 to 1800*
NCLC = *Nineteenth-Century Literature Criticism*
PC = *Poetry Criticism*
SSC = *Short Story Criticism*
TCLC = *Twentieth-Century Literary Criticism*
WLC = *World Literature Criticism, 1500 to the Present*
WLCS = *World Literature Criticism Supplement*

The cross-references

See also CA 89-92; DLB 72; MTCW

---

list all author entries in the following Gale biographical and literary sources:

AAYA = *Authors & Artists for Young Adults*
AITN = *Authors in the News*
BEST = *Bestsellers*
BW = *Black Writers*
CA = *Contemporary Authors*
CAAS = *Contemporary Authors Autobiography
Series*
CABS = *Contemporary Authors Bibliographical
Series*
CANR = *Contemporary Authors New Revision
Series*
CAP = *Contemporary Authors Permanent Series*
CDALB = *Concise Dictionary of American Literary
Biography*
CDBLB = *Concise Dictionary of British Literary
Biography*

DLB = *Dictionary of Literary Biography*
DLBD = *Dictionary of Literary Biography
Documentary Series*
DLBY = *Dictionary of Literary Biography
Yearbook*
HW = *Hispanic Writers*
JRDA = *Junior DISCovering Authors*
MAICYA = *Major Authors and Illustrators for
Children and Young Adults*
MTCW = *Major 20th-Century Writers*
NNAL = *Native North American Literature*
SAAS = *Something about the Author Autobiography
Series*
SATA = *Something about the Author*
YABC = *Yesterday's Authors of Books for Children*

Literary Criticism Series
Cumulative Author Index

Abasiyanik, Sait Faik 1906-1954
See Sait Faik
See also CA 123
Abbey, Edward 1927-1989 .... **CLC 36, 59**
See also CA 45-48; 128; CANR 2, 41
Abbott, Lee K(ittredge) 1947- .... **CLC 48**
See also CA 124; CANR 51; DLB 130
Abe, Kobo 1924-1993**CLC 8, 22, 53, 81; DAM NOV**
See also CA 65-68; 140; CANR 24, 60; DLB 182; MTCW
Abelard, Peter c. 1079-c. 1142 ...... **CMLC 11**
See also DLB 115
Abell, Kjeld 1901-1961 .... **CLC 15**
See also CA 111
Abish, Walter 1931- .... **CLC 22**
See also CA 101; CANR 37; DLB 130
Abrahams, Peter (Henry) 1919- ....**CLC 4**
See also BW 1; CA 57-60; CANR 26; DLB 117; MTCW
Abrams, M(eyer) H(oward) 1912- ... **CLC 24**
See also CA 57-60; CANR 13, 33; DLB 67
Abse, Dannie 1923-..**CLC 7, 29; DAB; DAM POET**
See also CA 53-56; CAAS 1; CANR 4, 46; DLB 27
Achebe, (Albert) Chinua(lumogu) 1930-**C L C 1, 3, 5, 7, 11, 26, 51, 75; BLC; DA; DAB; DAC; DAM MST, MULT, NOV; WLC**
See also AAYA 15; BW 2; CA 1-4R; CANR 6, 26, 47; CLR 20; DLB 117; MAICYA; MTCW; SATA 40; SATA-Brief 38
Acker, Kathy 1948-.......................... **CLC 45**
See also CA 117; 122; CANR 55
Ackroyd, Peter 1949- .... **CLC 34, 52**
See also CA 123; 127; CANR 51; DLB 155; INT 127
Acorn, Milton 1923- ....**CLC 15; DAC**
See also CA 103; DLB 53; INT 103
Adamov, Arthur 1908-1970**CLC 4, 25; DAM DRAM**
See also CA 17-18; 25-28R; CAP 2; MTCW
Adams, Alice (Boyd) 1926-**CLC 6, 13, 46; SSC 24**
See also CA 81-84; CANR 26, 53; DLBY 86; INT CANR-26; MTCW
Adams, Andy 1859-1935 .... **TCLC 56**
See also YABC 1
Adams, Douglas (Noel) 1952- .... **CLC 27, 60; DAM POP**
See also AAYA 4; BEST 89:3; CA 106; CANR 34; DLBY 83; JRDA
Adams, Francis 1862-1893 .... **NCLC 33**
Adams, Henry (Brooks) 1838-1918 **TCLC 4, 52; DA; DAB; DAC; DAM MST**
See also CA 104; 133; DLB 12, 47
Adams, Richard (George) 1920-**CLC 4, 5, 18; DAM NOV**
See also AAYA 16; AITN 1, 2; CA 49-52; CANR 3, 35; CLR 20; JRDA; MAICYA; MTCW; SATA 7, 69
Adamson, Joy(-Friederike Victoria) 1910-1980 **CLC 17**
See also CA 69-72; 93-96; CANR 22; MTCW;

SATA 11; SATA-Obit 22
Adcock, Fleur 1934- .... **CLC 41**
See also CA 25-28R; CAAS 23; CANR 11, 34; DLB 40
Addams, Charles (Samuel) 1912-1988**CLC 30**
See also CA 61-64; 126; CANR 12
Addams, Jane 1860-1935 .... **TCLC 76**
Addison, Joseph 1672-1719 .... **LC 18**
See also CDBLB 1660-1789; DLB 101
Adler, Alfred (F.) 1870-1937 .... **TCLC 61**
See also CA 119; 159
Adler, C(arole) S(chwerdtfeger) 1932-..**C L C 35**
See also AAYA 4; CA 89-92; CANR 19, 40; JRDA; MAICYA; SAAS 15; SATA 26, 63
Adler, Renata 1938-...................... **CLC 8, 31**
See also CA 49-52; CANR 5, 22, 52; MTCW
Ady, Endre 1877-1919 .... **TCLC 11**
See also CA 107
A.E. 1867-1935 .... **TCLC 3, 10**
See also Russell, George William
Aeschylus 525B.C.-456B.C. ..**CMLC 11; DA; DAB; DAC; DAM DRAM, MST; DC 8; WLCS**
See also DLB 176
Africa, Ben
See Bosman, Herman Charles
Afton, Effie
See Harper, Frances Ellen Watkins
Agapida, Fray Antonio
See Irving, Washington
Agee, James (Rufus) 1909-1955 **TCLC 1, 19; DAM NOV**
See also AITN 1; CA 108; 148; CDALB 1941-1968; DLB 2, 26, 152
Aghill, Gordon
See Silverberg, Robert
Agnon, S(hmuel) Y(osef Halevi) 1888-1970 **CLC 4, 8, 14; SSC 30**
See also CA 17-18; 25-28R; CANR 60; CAP 2; MTCW
Agrippa von Nettesheim, Henry Cornelius 1486-1535 .... **LC 27**
Aherne, Owen
See Cassill, R(onald) V(erlin)
Ai 1947- .... **CLC 4, 14, 69**
See also CA 85-88; CAAS 13; DLB 120
Aickman, Robert (Fordyce) 1914-1981 . **C L C 57**
See also CA 5-8R; CANR 3
Aiken, Conrad (Potter) 1889-1973**CLC 1, 3, 5, 10, 52; DAM NOV, POET; SSC 9**
See also CA 5-8R; 45-48; CANR 4, 60; CDALB 1929-1941; DLB 9, 45, 102; MTCW; SATA 3, 30
Aiken, Joan (Delano) 1924- .... **CLC 35**
See also AAYA 1; CA 9-12R; CANR 4, 23, 34; CLR 1, 19; DLB 161; JRDA; MAICYA; MTCW; SAAS 1; SATA 2, 30, 73
Ainsworth, William Harrison 1805-1882 **NCLC 13**
See also DLB 21; SATA 24
Aitmatov, Chingiz (Torekulovich) 1928-**C L C 71**

See also CA 103; CANR 38; MTCW; SATA 56
Akers, Floyd
See Baum, L(yman) Frank
Akhmadulina, Bella Akhatovna 1937-**CLC 53; DAM POET**
See also CA 65-68
Akhmatova, Anna 1888-1966**CLC 11, 25, 64; DAM POET; PC 2**
See also CA 19-20; 25-28R; CANR 35; CAP 1; MTCW
Aksakov, Sergei Timofeyvich 1791-1859 **NCLC 2**
Aksenov, Vassily
See Aksyonov, Vassily (Pavlovich)
Aksyonov, Vassily (Pavlovich) 1932-**CLC 22, 37, 101**
See also CA 53-56; CANR 12, 48
Akutagawa, Ryunosuke 1892-1927 **TCLC 16**
See also CA 117; 154
Alain 1868-1951 .... **TCLC 41**
Alain-Fournier .... **TCLC 6**
See also Fournier, Henri Alban
See also DLB 65
Alarcon, Pedro Antonio de 1833-1891**NCLC 1**
Alas (y Urena), Leopoldo (Enrique Garcia) 1852-1901 .... **TCLC 29**
See also CA 113; 131; HW
Albee, Edward (Franklin III) 1928-**CLC 1, 2, 3, 5, 9, 11, 13, 25, 53, 86; DA; DAB; DAC; DAM DRAM, MST; WLC**
See also AITN 1; CA 5-8R; CABS 3; CANR 8, 54; CDALB 1941-1968; DLB 7; INT CANR-8; MTCW
Alberti, Rafael 1902- .... **CLC 7**
See also CA 85-88; DLB 108
Albert the Great 1200(?)-1280 ...... **CMLC 16**
See also DLB 115
Alcala-Galiano, Juan Valera y
See Valera y Alcala-Galiano, Juan
Alcott, Amos Bronson 1799-1888 ....**NCLC 1**
See also DLB 1
Alcott, Louisa May 1832-1888 . **NCLC 6, 58; DA; DAB; DAC; DAM MST, NOV; SSC 27; WLC**
See also AAYA 20; CDALB 1865-1917; CLR 1, 38; DLB 1, 42, 79; DLBD 14; JRDA; MAICYA; YABC 1
Aldanov, M. A.
See Aldanov, Mark (Alexandrovich)
Aldanov, Mark (Alexandrovich) 1886(?)-1957 **TCLC 23**
See also CA 118
Aldington, Richard 1892-1962 .... **CLC 49**
See also CA 85-88; CANR 45; DLB 20, 36, 100, 149
Aldiss, Brian W(ilson) 1925- . **CLC 5, 14, 40; DAM NOV**
See also CA 5-8R; CAAS 2; CANR 5, 28; DLB 14; MTCW; SATA 34
Alegria, Claribel 1924-**CLC 75; DAM MULT**
See also CA 131; CAAS 15; DLB 145; HW
Alegria, Fernando 1918-....................**CLC 57**
See also CA 9-12R; CANR 5, 32; HW
Aleichem, Sholom .... **TCLC 1, 35**

See also Rabinovitch, Sholem
Aleixandre, Vicente 1898-1984 ... **CLC 9, 36;**
   DAM POET; PC 15
   See also CA 85-88; 114; CANR 26; DLB 108;
   HW; MTCW
Alepoudelis, Odysseus
   See Elytis, Odysseus
Aleshkovsky, Joseph 1929-
   See Aleshkovsky, Yuz
   See also CA 121; 128
Aleshkovsky, Yuz .... **CLC 44**
   See also Aleshkovsky, Joseph
Alexander, Lloyd (Chudley) 1924- .. **CLC 35**
   See also AAYA 1; CA 1-4R; CANR 1, 24, 38,
   55; CLR 1, 5, 48; DLB 52; JRDA; MAICYA;
   MTCW; SAAS 19; SATA 3, 49, 81
Alexie, Sherman (Joseph, Jr.) 1966- **CLC 96;**
   DAM MULT
   See also CA 138; DLB 175; NNAL
Alfau, Felipe 1902- .... **CLC 66**
   See also CA 137
Alger, Horatio, Jr. 1832-1899 .... **NCLC 8**
   See also DLB 42; SATA 16
Algren, Nelson 1909-1981 .... **CLC 4, 10, 33**
   See also CA 13-16R; 103; CANR 20, 61;
   CDALB 1941-1968; DLB 9; DLBY 81, 82;
   MTCW
Ali, Ahmed 1910- .... **CLC 69**
   See also CA 25-28R; CANR 15, 34
Alighieri, Dante 1265-1321 ...... **CMLC 3, 18;**
   WLCS
Allan, John B.
   See Westlake, Donald E(dwin)
Allan, Sidney
   See Hartmann, Sadakichi
Allan, Sydney
   See Hartmann, Sadakichi
Allen, Edward 1948- .... **CLC 59**
Allen, Paula Gunn 1939- .... **CLC 84; DAM**
   MULT
   See also CA 112; 143; DLB 175; NNAL
Allen, Roland
   See Ayckbourn, Alan
Allen, Sarah A.
   See Hopkins, Pauline Elizabeth
Allen, Sidney H.
   See Hartmann, Sadakichi
Allen, Woody 1935- **CLC 16, 52; DAM POP**
   See also AAYA 10; CA 33-36R; CANR 27, 38;
   DLB 44; MTCW
Allende, Isabel 1942-. **CLC 39, 57, 97; DAM**
   MULT, NOV; HLC; WLCS
   See also AAYA 18; CA 125; 130; CANR 51;
   DLB 145; HW; INT 130; MTCW
Alleyn, Ellen
   See Rossetti, Christina (Georgina)
Allingham, Margery (Louise) 1904-1966 **C L C**
   19
   See also CA 5-8R; 25-28R; CANR 4, 58; DLB
   77; MTCW
Allingham, William 1824-1889 ...... **NCLC 25**
   See also DLB 35
Allison, Dorothy E. 1949- .... **CLC 78**
   See also CA 140
Allston, Washington 1779-1843 .... **NCLC 2**
   See also DLB 1
Almedingen, E. M. .... **CLC 12**
   See also Almedingen, Martha Edith von
   See also SATA 3
Almedingen, Martha Edith von 1898-1971
   See Almedingen, E. M.
   See also CA 1-4R; CANR 1
Almqvist, Carl Jonas Love 1793-1866 **N C L C**

42
Alonso, Damaso 1898-1990 .... **CLC 14**
   See also CA 110; 131; 130; DLB 108; HW
Alov
   See Gogol, Nikolai (Vasilyevich)
Alta 1942- .... **CLC 19**
   See also CA 57-60
Alter, Robert B(ernard) 1935- .... **CLC 34**
   See also CA 49-52; CANR 1, 47
Alther, Lisa 1944- .... **CLC 7, 41**
   See also CA 65-68; CANR 12, 30, 51; MTCW
Althusser, L.
   See Althusser, Louis
Althusser, Louis 1918-1990 .... **CLC 106**
   See also CA 131; 132
Altman, Robert 1925- .... **CLC 16**
   See also CA 73-76; CANR 43
Alvarez, A(lfred) 1929- .... **CLC 5, 13**
   See also CA 1-4R; CANR 3, 33; DLB 14, 40
Alvarez, Alejandro Rodriguez 1903-1965
   See Casona, Alejandro
   See also CA 131; 93-96; HW
Alvarez, Julia 1950- .... **CLC 93**
   See also CA 147
Alvaro, Corrado 1896-1956 .... **TCLC 60**
Amado, Jorge 1912- **CLC 13, 40, 106; DAM**
   MULT, NOV; HLC
   See also CA 77-80; CANR 35; DLB 113;
   MTCW
Ambler, Eric 1909- .... **CLC 4, 6, 9**
   See also CA 9-12R; CANR 7, 38; DLB 77;
   MTCW
Amichai, Yehuda 1924- .... **CLC 9, 22, 57**
   See also CA 85-88; CANR 46, 60; MTCW
Amichai, Yehudah
   See Amichai, Yehuda
Amiel, Henri Frederic 1821-1881 .... **NCLC 4**
Amis, Kingsley (William) 1922-1995 **CLC 1, 2,**
   3, 5, 8, 13, 40, 44; DA; DAB; DAC; DAM
   MST, NOV
   See also AITN 2; CA 9-12R; 150; CANR 8, 28,
   54; CDBLB 1945-1960; DLB 15, 27, 100,
   139; DLBY 96; INT CANR-8; MTCW
Amis, Martin (Louis) 1949- **CLC 4, 9, 38, 62,**
   101
   See also BEST 90:3; CA 65-68; CANR 8, 27,
   54; DLB 14; INT CANR-27
Ammons, A(rchie) R(andolph) 1926-**CLC 2, 3,**
   5, 8, 9, 25, 57; DAM POET; PC 16
   See also AITN 1; CA 9-12R; CANR 6, 36, 51;
   DLB 5, 165; MTCW
Amo, Tauraatua i
   See Adams, Henry (Brooks)
Anand, Mulk Raj 1905- .. **CLC 23, 93; DAM**
   NOV
   See also CA 65-68; CANR 32; MTCW
Anatol
   See Schnitzler, Arthur
Anaximander c. 610B.C.-c. 546B.C.**CMLC 22**
Anaya, Rudolfo A(lfonso) 1937- ..... **CLC 23;**
   DAM MULT, NOV; HLC
   See also AAYA 20; CA 45-48; CAAS 4; CANR
   1, 32, 51; DLB 82; HW 1; MTCW
Andersen, Hans Christian 1805-1875**NCLC 7;**
   DA; DAB; DAC; DAM MST, POP; SSC
   6; WLC
   See also CLR 6; MAICYA; YABC 1
Anderson, C. Farley
   See Mencken, H(enry) L(ouis); Nathan, George
   Jean
Anderson, Jessica (Margaret) Queale 1916-
   CLC 37
   See also CA 9-12R; CANR 4, 62

Anderson, Jon (Victor) 1940-.. **CLC 9; DAM**
   POET
   See also CA 25-28R; CANR 20
Anderson, Lindsay (Gordon) 1923-1994**C L C**
   20
   See also CA 125; 128; 146
Anderson, Maxwell 1888-1959**TCLC 2; DAM**
   DRAM
   See also CA 105; 152; DLB 7
Anderson, Poul (William) 1926- ...... **CLC 15**
   See also AAYA 5; CA 1-4R; CAAS 2; CANR
   2, 15, 34; DLB 8; INT CANR-15; MTCW;
   SATA 90; SATA-Brief 39
Anderson, Robert (Woodruff) 1917-**CLC 23;**
   DAM DRAM
   See also AITN 1; CA 21-24R; CANR 32; DLB
   7
Anderson, Sherwood 1876-1941 **TCLC 1, 10,**
   24; DA; DAB; DAC; DAM MST, NOV;
   SSC 1; WLC
   See also CA 104; 121; CANR 61; CDALB
   1917-1929; DLB 4, 9, 86; DLBD 1; MTCW
Andier, Pierre
   See Desnos, Robert
Andouard
   See Giraudoux, (Hippolyte) Jean
Andrade, Carlos Drummond de .... **CLC 18**
   See also Drummond de Andrade, Carlos
Andrade, Mario de 1893-1945 .... **TCLC 43**
Andreae, Johann V(alentin) 1586-1654**LC 32**
   See also DLB 164
Andreas-Salome, Lou 1861-1937 ... **TCLC 56**
   See also DLB 66
Andress, Lesley
   See Sanders, Lawrence
Andrewes, Lancelot 1555-1626 .... **LC 5**
   See also DLB 151, 172
Andrews, Cicily Fairfield
   See West, Rebecca
Andrews, Elton V.
   See Pohl, Frederik
Andreyev, Leonid (Nikolaevich) 1871-1919
   TCLC 3
   See also CA 104
Andric, Ivo 1892-1975 .... **CLC 8**
   See also CA 81-84; 57-60; CANR 43, 60; DLB
   147; MTCW
Androvar
   See Prado (Calvo), Pedro
Angelique, Pierre
   See Bataille, Georges
Angell, Roger 1920- .... **CLC 26**
   See also CA 57-60; CANR 13, 44; DLB 171
Angelou, Maya 1928-**CLC 12, 35, 64, 77; BLC;**
   DA; DAB; DAC; DAM MST, MULT,
   POET, POP; WLCS
   See also AAYA 7, 20; BW 2; CA 65-68; CANR
   19, 42; DLB 38; MTCW; SATA 49
Annensky, Innokenty (Fyodorovich) 1856-1909
   TCLC 14
   See also CA 110; 155
Annunzio, Gabriele d'
   See D'Annunzio, Gabriele
Anodos
   See Coleridge, Mary E(lizabeth)
Anon, Charles Robert
   See Pessoa, Fernando (Antonio Nogueira)
Anouilh, Jean (Marie Lucien Pierre) 1910-1987
   CLC 1, 3, 8, 13, 40, 50; DAM DRAM; DC
   8
   See also CA 17-20R; 123; CANR 32; MTCW
Anthony, Florence
   See Ai

Anthony, John
See Ciardi, John (Anthony)
Anthony, Peter
See Shaffer, Anthony (Joshua); Shaffer, Peter (Levin)
Anthony, Piers 1934- ..... **CLC 35; DAM POP**
See also AAYA 11; CA 21-24R; CANR 28, 56; DLB 8; MTCW; SAAS 22; SATA 84
Antoine, Marc
See Proust, (Valentin-Louis-George-Eugene-) Marcel
Antoninus, Brother
See Everson, William (Oliver)
Antonioni, Michelangelo 1912- .... **CLC 20**
See also CA 73-76; CANR 45
Antschel, Paul 1920-1970
See Celan, Paul
See also CA 85-88; CANR 33, 61; MTCW
Anwar, Chairil 1922-1949 .... **TCLC 22**
See also CA 121
Apollinaire, Guillaume 1880-1918**TCLC 3, 8, 51; DAM POET; PC 7**
See also Kostrowitzki, Wilhelm Apollinaris de
See also CA 152
Appelfeld, Aharon 1932- .... **CLC 23, 47**
See also CA 112; 133
Apple, Max (Isaac) 1941-.............. **CLC 9, 33**
See also CA 81-84; CANR 19, 54; DLB 130
Appleman, Philip (Dean) 1926-........ **CLC 51**
See also CA 13-16R; CAAS 18; CANR 6, 29, 56
Appleton, Lawrence
See Lovecraft, H(oward) P(hillips)
Apteryx
See Eliot, T(homas) S(tearns)
Apuleius, (Lucius Madaurensis) 125(?)-175(?) **CMLC 1**
Aquin, Hubert 1929-1977 .... **CLC 15**
See also CA 105; DLB 53
Aragon, Louis 1897-1982 ..**CLC 3, 22; DAM NOV, POET**
See also CA 69-72; 108; CANR 28; DLB 72; MTCW
Arany, Janos 1817-1882.................**NCLC 34**
Arbuthnot, John 1667-1735 .... **LC 1**
See also DLB 101
Archer, Herbert Winslow
See Mencken, H(enry) L(ouis)
Archer, Jeffrey (Howard) 1940- ..... **CLC 28; DAM POP**
See also AAYA 16; BEST 89:3; CA 77-80; CANR 22, 52; INT CANR-22
Archer, Jules 1915-............................ **CLC 12**
See also CA 9-12R; CANR 6; SAAS 5; SATA 4, 85
Archer, Lee
See Ellison, Harlan (Jay)
Arden, John 1930-**CLC 6, 13, 15; DAM DRAM**
See also CA 13-16R; CAAS 4; CANR 31; DLB 13; MTCW
Arenas, Reinaldo 1943-1990 . **CLC 41; DAM MULT; HLC**
See also CA 124; 128; 133; DLB 145; HW
Arendt, Hannah 1906-1975 .... **CLC 66, 98**
See also CA 17-20R; 61-64; CANR 26, 60; MTCW
Aretino, Pietro 1492-1556 .... **LC 12**
Arghezi, Tudor .... **CLC 80**
See also Theodorescu, Ion N.
Arguedas, Jose Maria 1911-1969 **CLC 10, 18**
See also CA 89-92; DLB 113; HW
Argueta, Manlio 1936-...................... **CLC 31**
See also CA 131; DLB 145; HW

Ariosto, Ludovico 1474-1533 .... **LC 6**
Aristides
See Epstein, Joseph
Aristophanes 450B.C.-385B.C.**CMLC 4; DA; DAB; DAC; DAM DRAM, MST; DC 2; WLCS**
See also DLB 176
Arlt, Roberto (Godofredo Christophersen) 1900-1942**TCLC 29; DAM MULT; HLC**
See also CA 123; 131; HW
Armah, Ayi Kwei 1939-**CLC 5, 33; BLC; DAM MULT, POET**
See also BW 1; CA 61-64; CANR 21; DLB 117; MTCW
Armatrading, Joan 1950- .... **CLC 17**
See also CA 114
Arnette, Robert
See Silverberg, Robert
Arnim, Achim von (Ludwig Joachim von Arnim) 1781-1831 ...... **NCLC 5; SSC 29**
See also DLB 90
Arnim, Bettina von 1785-1859 .... **NCLC 38**
See also DLB 90
Arnold, Matthew 1822-1888**NCLC 6, 29; DA; DAB; DAC; DAM MST, POET; PC 5; WLC**
See also CDBLB 1832-1890; DLB 32, 57
Arnold, Thomas 1795-1842 ....**NCLC 18**
See also DLB 55
Arnow, Harriette (Louisa) Simpson 1908-1986 **CLC 2, 7, 18**
See also CA 9-12R; 118; CANR 14; DLB 6; MTCW; SATA 42; SATA-Obit 47
Arp, Hans
See Arp, Jean
Arp, Jean 1887-1966 ....**CLC 5**
See also CA 81-84; 25-28R; CANR 42
Arrabal
See Arrabal, Fernando
Arrabal, Fernando 1932-.... **CLC 2, 9, 18, 58**
See also CA 9-12R; CANR 15
Arrick, Fran ....**CLC 30**
See also Gaberman, Judie Angell
Artaud, Antonin (Marie Joseph) 1896-1948 **TCLC 3, 36; DAM DRAM**
See also CA 104; 149
Arthur, Ruth M(abel) 1905-1979 ...... **CLC 12**
See also CA 9-12R; 85-88; CANR 4; SATA 7, 26
Artsybashev, Mikhail (Petrovich) 1878-1927 **TCLC 31**
Arundel, Honor (Morfydd) 1919-1973**CLC 17**
See also CA 21-22; 41-44R; CAP 2; CLR 35; SATA 4; SATA-Obit 24
Arzner, Dorothy 1897-1979 ....**CLC 98**
Asch, Sholem 1880-1957 .... **TCLC 3**
See also CA 105
Ash, Shalom
See Asch, Sholem
Ashbery, John (Lawrence) 1927-**CLC 2, 3, 4, 6, 9, 13, 15, 25, 41, 77; DAM POET**
See also CA 5-8R; CANR 9, 37; DLB 5, 165; DLBY 81; INT CANR-9; MTCW
Ashdown, Clifford
See Freeman, R(ichard) Austin
Ashe, Gordon
See Creasey, John
Ashton-Warner, Sylvia (Constance) 1908-1984 **CLC 19**
See also CA 69-72; 112; CANR 29; MTCW
Asimov, Isaac 1920-1992 **CLC 1, 3, 9, 19, 26, 76, 92; DAM POP**
See also AAYA 13; BEST 90:2; CA 1-4R; 137;

CANR 2, 19, 36, 60; CLR 12; DLB 8; DLBY 92; INT CANR-19; JRDA; MAICYA; MTCW; SATA 1, 26, 74
Assis, Joaquim Maria Machado de
See Machado de Assis, Joaquim Maria
Astley, Thea (Beatrice May) 1925- ...**CLC 41**
See also CA 65-68; CANR 11, 43
Aston, James
See White, T(erence) H(anbury)
Asturias, Miguel Angel 1899-1974 **CLC 3, 8, 13; DAM MULT, NOV; HLC**
See also CA 25-28; 49-52; CANR 32; CAP 2; DLB 113; HW; MTCW
Atares, Carlos Saura
See Saura (Atares), Carlos
Atheling, William
See Pound, Ezra (Weston Loomis)
Atheling, William, Jr.
See Blish, James (Benjamin)
Atherton, Gertrude (Franklin Horn) 1857-1948 **TCLC 2**
See also CA 104; 155; DLB 9, 78, 186
Atherton, Lucius
See Masters, Edgar Lee
Atkins, Jack
See Harris, Mark
Atkinson, Kate ....**CLC 99**
Attaway, William (Alexander) 1911-1986 **CLC 92; BLC; DAM MULT**
See also BW 2; CA 143; DLB 76
Atticus
See Fleming, Ian (Lancaster)
Atwood, Margaret (Eleanor) 1939-**CLC 2, 3, 4, 8, 13, 15, 25, 44, 84; DA; DAB; DAC; DAM MST, NOV, POET; PC 8; SSC 2; WLC**
See also AAYA 12; BEST 89:2; CA 49-52; CANR 3, 24, 33, 59; DLB 53; INT CANR-24; MTCW; SATA 50
Aubigny, Pierre d'
See Mencken, H(enry) L(ouis)
Aubin, Penelope 1685-1731(?)...............**LC 9**
See also DLB 39
Auchincloss, Louis (Stanton) 1917-**CLC 4, 6, 9, 18, 45; DAM NOV; SSC 22**
See also CA 1-4R; CANR 6, 29, 55; DLB 2; DLBY 80; INT CANR-29; MTCW
Auden, W(ystan) H(ugh) 1907-1973**CLC 1, 2, 3, 4, 6, 9, 11, 14, 43; DA; DAB; DAC; DAM DRAM, MST, POET; PC 1; WLC**
See also AAYA 18; CA 9-12R; 45-48; CANR 5, 61; CDBLB 1914-1945; DLB 10, 20; MTCW
Audiberti, Jacques 1900-1965**CLC 38; DAM DRAM**
See also CA 25-28R
Audubon, John James 1785-1851 ..**NCLC 47**
Auel, Jean M(arie) 1936-**CLC 31; DAM POP**
See also AAYA 7; BEST 90:4; CA 103; CANR 21; INT CANR-21; SATA 91
Auerbach, Erich 1892-1957 ....**TCLC 43**
See also CA 118; 155
Augier, Emile 1820-1889 ....**NCLC 31**
August, John
See De Voto, Bernard (Augustine)
Augustine, St. 354-430 .... **CMLC 6; DAB**
Aurelius
See Bourne, Randolph S(illiman)
Aurobindo, Sri 1872-1950 ....**TCLC 63**
Austen, Jane 1775-1817 **NCLC 1, 13, 19, 33, 51; DA; DAB; DAC; DAM MST, NOV; WLC**
See also AAYA 19; CDBLB 1789-1832; DLB

116

Auster, Paul 1947- .... CLC 47
See also CA 69-72; CANR 23, 52
Austin, Frank
See Faust, Frederick (Schiller)
Austin, Mary (Hunter) 1868-1934 . TCLC 25
See also CA 109; DLB 9, 78
Autran Dourado, Waldomiro
See Dourado, (Waldomiro Freitas) Autran
Averroes 1126-1198 .... CMLC 7
See also DLB 115
Avicenna 980-1037 .... CMLC 16
See also DLB 115
Avison, Margaret 1918- CLC 2, 4, 97; DAC;
DAM POET
See also CA 17-20R; DLB 53; MTCW
Axton, David
See Koontz, Dean R(ay)
Ayckbourn, Alan 1939- CLC 5, 8, 18, 33, 74;
DAB; DAM DRAM
See also CA 21-24R; CANR 31, 59; DLB 13;
MTCW
Aydy, Catherine
See Tennant, Emma (Christina)
Ayme, Marcel (Andre) 1902-1967 ..... CLC 11
See also CA 89-92; CLR 25; DLB 72; SATA 91
Ayrton, Michael 1921-1975 .... CLC 7
See also CA 5-8R; 61-64; CANR 9, 21
Azorin .... CLC 11
See also Martinez Ruiz, Jose
Azuela, Mariano 1873-1952 . TCLC 3; DAM
MULT; HLC
See also CA 104; 131; HW; MTCW
Baastad, Babbis Friis
See Friis-Baastad, Babbis Ellinor
Bab
See Gilbert, W(illiam) S(chwenck)
Babbis, Eleanor
See Friis-Baastad, Babbis Ellinor
Babel, Isaac
See Babel, Isaak (Emmanuilovich)
Babel, Isaak (Emmanuilovich) 1894-1941(?)
TCLC 2, 13; SSC 16
See also CA 104; 155
Babits, Mihaly 1883-1941 .... TCLC 14
See also CA 114
Babur 1483-1530 .... LC 18
Bacchelli, Riccardo 1891-1985 .... CLC 19
See also CA 29-32R; 117
Bach, Richard (David) 1936- CLC 14; DAM
NOV, POP
See also AITN 1; BEST 89:2; CA 9-12R; CANR
18; MTCW; SATA 13
Bachman, Richard
See King, Stephen (Edwin)
Bachmann, Ingeborg 1926-1973 ...... CLC 69
See also CA 93-96; 45-48; DLB 85
Bacon, Francis 1561-1626 .... LC 18, 32
See also CDBLB Before 1660; DLB 151
Bacon, Roger 1214(?)-1292 .... CMLC 14
See also DLB 115
Bacovia, George .... TCLC 24
See also Vasiliu, Gheorghe
Badanes, Jerome 1937- .... CLC 59
Bagehot, Walter 1826-1877 .... NCLC 10
See also DLB 55
Bagnold, Enid 1889-1981 ...... CLC 25; DAM
DRAM
See also CA 5-8R; 103; CANR 5, 40; DLB 13,
160; MAICYA; SATA 1, 25
Bagritsky, Eduard 1895-1934 .... TCLC 60
Bagrjana, Elisaveta
See Belcheva, Elisaveta

Bagryana, Elisaveta .... CLC 10
See also Belcheva, Elisaveta
See also DLB 147
Bailey, Paul 1937- .... CLC 45
See also CA 21-24R; CANR 16, 62; DLB 14
Baillie, Joanna 1762-1851 .... NCLC 2
See also DLB 93
Bainbridge, Beryl (Margaret) 1933-CLC 4, 5,
8, 10, 14, 18, 22, 62; DAM NOV
See also CA 21-24R; CANR 24, 55; DLB 14;
MTCW
Baker, Elliott 1922- .... CLC 8
See also CA 45-48; CANR 2
Baker, Jean H. .... TCLC 3, 10
See also Russell, George William
Baker, Nicholson 1957- . CLC 61; DAM POP
See also CA 135
Baker, Ray Stannard 1870-1946 .... TCLC 47
See also CA 118
Baker, Russell (Wayne) 1925- .... CLC 31
See also BEST 89:4; CA 57-60; CANR 11, 41,
59; MTCW
Bakhtin, M.
See Bakhtin, Mikhail Mikhailovich
Bakhtin, M. M.
See Bakhtin, Mikhail Mikhailovich
Bakhtin, Mikhail
See Bakhtin, Mikhail Mikhailovich
Bakhtin, Mikhail Mikhailovich 1895-1975
CLC 83
See also CA 128; 113
Bakshi, Ralph 1938(?)- .... CLC 26
See also CA 112; 138
Bakunin, Mikhail (Alexandrovich) 1814-1876
NCLC 25, 58
Baldwin, James (Arthur) 1924-1987CLC 1, 2,
3, 4, 5, 8, 13, 15, 17, 42, 50, 67, 90; BLC;
DA; DAB; DAC; DAM MST, MULT, NOV,
POP; DC 1; SSC 10; WLC
See also AAYA 4; BW 1; CA 1-4R; 124; CABS
1; CANR 3, 24; CDALB 1941-1968; DLB
2, 7, 33; DLBY 87; MTCW; SATA 9; SATA-
Obit 54
Ballard, J(ames) G(raham) 1930-CLC 3, 6, 14,
36; DAM NOV, POP; SSC 1
See also AAYA 3; CA 5-8R; CANR 15, 39; DLB
14; MTCW; SATA 93
Balmont, Konstantin (Dmitriyevich) 1867-1943
TCLC 11
See also CA 109; 155
Balzac, Honore de 1799-1850NCLC 5, 35, 53;
DA; DAB; DAC; DAM MST, NOV; SSC
5; WLC
See also DLB 119
Bambara, Toni Cade 1939-1995 CLC 19, 88;
BLC; DA; DAC; DAM MST, MULT;
WLCS
See also AAYA 5; BW 2; CA 29-32R; 150;
CANR 24, 49; DLB 38; MTCW
Bamdad, A.
See Shamlu, Ahmad
Banat, D. R.
See Bradbury, Ray (Douglas)
Bancroft, Laura
See Baum, L(yman) Frank
Banim, John 1798-1842 .... NCLC 13
See also DLB 116, 158, 159
Banim, Michael 1796-1874 .... NCLC 13
See also DLB 158, 159
Banjo, The
See Paterson, A(ndrew) B(arton)
Banks, Iain
See Banks, Iain M(enzies)

Banks, Iain M(enzies) 1954- .... CLC 34
See also CA 123; 128; CANR 61; INT 128
Banks, Lynne Reid .... CLC 23
See also Reid Banks, Lynne
See also AAYA 6
Banks, Russell 1940- .... CLC 37, 72
See also CA 65-68; CAAS 15; CANR 19, 52;
DLB 130
Banville, John 1945- .... CLC 46
See also CA 117; 128; DLB 14; INT 128
Banville, Theodore (Faullain) de 1832-1891
NCLC 9
Baraka, Amiri 1934-CLC 1, 2, 3, 5, 10, 14, 33;
BLC; DA; DAC; DAM MST, MULT,
POET, POP; DC 6; PC 4; WLCS
See also Jones, LeRoi
See also BW 2; CA 21-24R; CABS 3; CANR
27, 38, 61; CDALB 1941-1968; DLB 5, 7,
16, 38; DLBD 8; MTCW
Barbauld, Anna Laetitia 1743-1825NCLC 50
See also DLB 107, 109, 142, 158
Barbellion, W. N. P. .... TCLC 24
See also Cummings, Bruce F(rederick)
Barbera, Jack (Vincent) 1945- .... CLC 44
See also CA 110; CANR 45
Barbey d'Aurevilly, Jules Amedee 1808-1889
NCLC 1; SSC 17
See also DLB 119
Barbusse, Henri 1873-1935 .... TCLC 5
See also CA 105; 154; DLB 65
Barclay, Bill
See Moorcock, Michael (John)
Barclay, William Ewert
See Moorcock, Michael (John)
Barea, Arturo 1897-1957 .... TCLC 14
See also CA 111
Barfoot, Joan 1946- .... CLC 18
See also CA 105
Baring, Maurice 1874-1945 .... TCLC 8
See also CA 105; DLB 34
Barker, Clive 1952- .... CLC 52; DAM POP
See also AAYA 10; BEST 90:3; CA 121; 129;
INT 129; MTCW
Barker, George Granville 1913-1991 CLC 8,
48; DAM POET
See also CA 9-12R; 135; CANR 7, 38; DLB
20; MTCW
Barker, Harley Granville
See Granville-Barker, Harley
See also DLB 10
Barker, Howard 1946- .... CLC 37
See also CA 102; DLB 13
Barker, Pat(ricia) 1943- .... CLC 32, 94
See also CA 117; 122; CANR 50; INT 122
Barlow, Joel 1754-1812 .... NCLC 23
See also DLB 37
Barnard, Mary (Ethel) 1909- .... CLC 48
See also CA 21-22; CAP 2
Barnes, Djuna 1892-1982CLC 3, 4, 8, 11, 29;
SSC 3
See also CA 9-12R; 107; CANR 16, 55; DLB
4, 9, 45; MTCW
Barnes, Julian (Patrick) 1946- CLC 42; DAB
See also CA 102; CANR 19, 54; DLBY 93
Barnes, Peter 1931- .... CLC 5, 56
See also CA 65-68; CAAS 12; CANR 33, 34;
DLB 13; MTCW
Baroja (y Nessi), Pio 1872-1956TCLC 8; HLC
See also CA 104
Baron, David
See Pinter, Harold
Baron Corvo
See Rolfe, Frederick (William Serafino Austin

Lewis Mary)
Barondess, Sue K(aufman) 1926-1977 **CLC 8**
See also Kaufman, Sue
See also CA 1-4R; 69-72; CANR 1
Baron de Teive
See Pessoa, Fernando (Antonio Nogueira)
Barres, Maurice 1862-1923 .... **TCLC 47**
See also DLB 123
Barreto, Afonso Henrique de Lima
See Lima Barreto, Afonso Henrique de
Barrett, (Roger) Syd 1946- .... **CLC 35**
Barrett, William (Christopher) 1913-1992
CLC 27
See also CA 13-16R; 139; CANR 11; INT
CANR-11
Barrie, J(ames) M(atthew) 1860-1937 **T C L C**
2; DAB; DAM DRAM
See also CA 104; 136; CDBLB 1890-1914;
CLR 16; DLB 10, 141, 156; MAICYA;
YABC 1
Barrington, Michael
See Moorcock, Michael (John)
Barrol, Grady
See Bograd, Larry
Barry, Mike
See Malzberg, Barry N(athaniel)
Barry, Philip 1896-1949 .... **TCLC 11**
See also CA 109; DLB 7
Bart, Andre Schwarz
See Schwarz-Bart, Andre
Barth, John (Simmons) 1930-**CLC 1, 2, 3, 5, 7,**
9, 10, 14, 27, 51, 89; DAM NOV; SSC 10
See also AITN 1, 2; CA 1-4R; CABS 1; CANR
5, 23, 49; DLB 2; MTCW
Barthelme, Donald 1931-1989**CLC 1, 2, 3, 5, 6,**
8, 13, 23, 46, 59; DAM NOV; SSC 2
See also CA 21-24R; 129; CANR 20, 58; DLB
2; DLBY 80, 89; MTCW; SATA 7; SATA-
Obit 62
Barthelme, Frederick 1943- .... **CLC 36**
See also CA 114; 122; DLBY 85; INT 122
Barthes, Roland (Gerard) 1915-1980**CLC 24,**
83
See also CA 130; 97-100; MTCW
Barzun, Jacques (Martin) 1907- ...... **CLC 51**
See also CA 61-64; CANR 22
Bashevis, Isaac
See Singer, Isaac Bashevis
Bashkirtseff, Marie 1859-1884 .... **NCLC 27**
Basho
See Matsuo Basho
Bass, Kingsley B., Jr.
See Bullins, Ed
Bass, Rick 1958-................................ **CLC 79**
See also CA 126; CANR 53
Bassani, Giorgio 1916-......................... **CLC 9**
See also CA 65-68; CANR 33; DLB 128, 177;
MTCW
Bastos, Augusto (Antonio) Roa
See Roa Bastos, Augusto (Antonio)
Bataille, Georges 1897-1962............. **CLC 29**
See also CA 101; 89-92
Bates, H(erbert) E(rnest) 1905-1974**CLC 46;**
DAB; DAM POP; SSC 10
See also CA 93-96; 45-48; CANR 34; DLB 162;
MTCW
Bauchart
See Camus, Albert
Baudelaire, Charles 1821-1867 **NCLC 6, 29,**
55; DA; DAB; DAC; DAM MST, POET;
PC 1; SSC 18; WLC
Baudrillard, Jean 1929-.................... **CLC 60**
Baum, L(yman) Frank 1856-1919 ... **TCLC 7**

See also CA 108; 133; CLR 15; DLB 22; JRDA;
MAICYA; MTCW; SATA 18
Baum, Louis F.
See Baum, L(yman) Frank
Baumbach, Jonathan 1933-.......... **CLC 6, 23**
See also CA 13-16R; CAAS 5; CANR 12;
DLBY 80; INT CANR-12; MTCW
Bausch, Richard (Carl) 1945- .... **CLC 51**
See also CA 101; CAAS 14; CANR 43, 61; DLB
130
Baxter, Charles 1947-**CLC 45, 78; DAM POP**
See also CA 57-60; CANR 40; DLB 130
Baxter, George Owen
See Faust, Frederick (Schiller)
Baxter, James K(eir) 1926-1972 .... **CLC 14**
See also CA 77-80
Baxter, John
See Hunt, E(verette) Howard, (Jr.)
Bayer, Sylvia
See Glassco, John
Baynton, Barbara 1857-1929 .... **TCLC 57**
Beagle, Peter S(oyer) 1939- .... **CLC 7, 104**
See also CA 9-12R; CANR 4, 51; DLBY 80;
INT CANR-4; SATA 60
Bean, Normal
See Burroughs, Edgar Rice
Beard, Charles A(ustin) 1874-1948 **TCLC 15**
See also CA 115; DLB 17; SATA 18
Beardsley, Aubrey 1872-1898 .... **NCLC 6**
Beattie, Ann 1947-**CLC 8, 13, 18, 40, 63; DAM**
NOV, POP; SSC 11
See also BEST 90:2; CA 81-84; CANR 53;
DLBY 82; MTCW
Beattie, James 1735-1803 .... **NCLC 25**
See also DLB 109
Beauchamp, Kathleen Mansfield 1888-1923
See Mansfield, Katherine
See also CA 104; 134; DA; DAC; DAM MST
Beaumarchais, Pierre-Augustin Caron de 1732-
1799 .... **DC 4**
See also DAM DRAM
Beaumont, Francis 1584(?)-1616**LC 33; DC 6**
See also CDBLB Before 1660; DLB 58, 121
Beauvoir, Simone (Lucie Ernestine Marie
Bertrand) de 1908-1986**CLC 1, 2, 4, 8, 14,**
31, 44, 50, 71; DA; DAB; DAC; DAM MST,
NOV; WLC
See also CA 9-12R; 118; CANR 28, 61; DLB
72; DLBY 86; MTCW
Becker, Carl (Lotus) 1873-1945 ..... **TCLC 63**
See also CA 157; DLB 17
Becker, Jurek 1937-1997 .... **CLC 7, 19**
See also CA 85-88; 157; CANR 60; DLB 75
Becker, Walter 1950-....................... **CLC 26**
Beckett, Samuel (Barclay) 1906-1989 **CLC 1,**
2, 3, 4, 6, 9, 10, 11, 14, 18, 29, 57, 59, 83;
DA; DAB; DAC; DAM DRAM, MST,
NOV; SSC 16; WLC
See also CA 5-8R; 130; CANR 33, 61; CDBLB
1945-1960; DLB 13, 15; DLBY 90; MTCW
Beckford, William 1760-1844 .... **NCLC 16**
See also DLB 39
Beckman, Gunnel 1910-..................... **CLC 26**
See also CA 33-36R; CANR 15; CLR 25;
MAICYA; SAAS 9; SATA 6
Becque, Henri 1837-1899 .... **NCLC 3**
Beddoes, Thomas Lovell 1803-1849 **NCLC 3**
See also DLB 96
Bede c. 673-735 .... **CMLC 20**
See also DLB 146
Bedford, Donald F.
See Fearing, Kenneth (Flexner)
Beecher, Catharine Esther 1800-1878 **N C L C**

30
See also DLB 1
Beecher, John 1904-1980 .... **CLC 6**
See also AITN 1; CA 5-8R; 105; CANR 8
Beer, Johann 1655-1700 .... **LC 5**
See also DLB 168
Beer, Patricia 1924-............................ **CLC 58**
See also CA 61-64; CANR 13, 46; DLB 40
Beerbohm, Max
See Beerbohm, (Henry) Max(imilian)
Beerbohm, (Henry) Max(imilian) 1872-1956
TCLC 1, 24
See also CA 104; 154; DLB 34, 100
Beer-Hofmann, Richard 1866-1945**TCLC 60**
See also CA 160; DLB 81
Begiebing, Robert J(ohn) 1946- .... **CLC 70**
See also CA 122; CANR 40
Behan, Brendan 1923-1964 **CLC 1, 8, 11, 15,**
79; DAM DRAM
See also CA 73-76; CANR 33; CDBLB 1945-
1960; DLB 13; MTCW
Behn, Aphra 1640(?)-1689**LC 1, 30; DA; DAB;**
DAC; DAM DRAM, MST, NOV, POET;
DC 4; PC 13; WLC
See also DLB 39, 80, 131
Behrman, S(amuel) N(athaniel) 1893-1973
CLC 40
See also CA 13-16; 45-48; CAP 1; DLB 7, 44
Belasco, David 1853-1931 .... **TCLC 3**
See also CA 104; DLB 7
Belcheva, Elisaveta 1893- .... **CLC 10**
See also Bagryana, Elisaveta
Beldone, Phil "Cheech"
See Ellison, Harlan (Jay)
Beleno
See Azuela, Mariano
Belinski, Vissarion Grigoryevich 1811-1848
NCLC 5
Belitt, Ben 1911- .... **CLC 22**
See also CA 13-16R; CAAS 4; CANR 7; DLB
5
Bell, Gertrude 1868-1926 .... **TCLC 67**
See also DLB 174
Bell, James Madison 1826-1902 ... **TCLC 43;**
BLC; DAM MULT
See also BW 1; CA 122; 124; DLB 50
Bell, Madison Smartt 1957-........ **CLC 41, 102**
See also CA 111; CANR 28, 54
Bell, Marvin (Hartley) 1937-**CLC 8, 31; DAM**
POET
See also CA 21-24R; CAAS 14; CANR 59; DLB
5; MTCW
Bell, W. L. D.
See Mencken, H(enry) L(ouis)
Bellamy, Atwood C.
See Mencken, H(enry) L(ouis)
Bellamy, Edward 1850-1898 .... **NCLC 4**
See also DLB 12
Bellin, Edward J.
See Kuttner, Henry
Belloc, (Joseph) Hilaire (Pierre Sebastien Rene
Swanton) 1870-1953 **TCLC 7, 18; DAM**
POET
See also CA 106; 152; DLB 19, 100, 141, 174;
YABC 1
Belloc, Joseph Peter Rene Hilaire
See Belloc, (Joseph) Hilaire (Pierre Sebastien
Rene Swanton)
Belloc, Joseph Pierre Hilaire
See Belloc, (Joseph) Hilaire (Pierre Sebastien
Rene Swanton)
Belloc, M. A.
See Lowndes, Marie Adelaide (Belloc)

Bellow, Saul 1915-CLC 1, 2, 3, 6, 8, 10, 13, 15, 25, 33, 34, 63, 79; DA; DAB; DAC; DAM MST, NOV, POP; SSC 14; WLC
See also AITN 2; BEST 89:3; CA 5-8R; CABS 1; CANR 29, 53; CDALB 1941-1968; DLB 2, 28; DLBD 3; DLBY 82; MTCW
Belser, Reimond Karel Maria de 1929-
See Ruyslinck, Ward
See also CA 152
Bely, Andrey .... TCLC 7; PC 11
See also Bugayev, Boris Nikolayevich
Benary, Margot
See Benary-Isbert, Margot
Benary-Isbert, Margot 1889-1979 ... CLC 12
See also CA 5-8R; 89-92; CANR 4; CLR 12; MAICYA; SATA 2; SATA-Obit 21
Benavente (y Martinez), Jacinto 1866-1954 TCLC 3; DAM DRAM, MULT
See also CA 106; 131; HW; MTCW
Benchley, Peter (Bradford) 1940-. CLC 4, 8; DAM NOV, POP
See also AAYA 14; AITN 2; CA 17-20R; CANR 12, 35; MTCW; SATA 3, 89
Benchley, Robert (Charles) 1889-1945 T C L C 1, 55
See also CA 105; 153; DLB 11
Benda, Julien 1867-1956 .... TCLC 60
See also CA 120; 154
Benedict, Ruth (Fulton) 1887-1948 TCLC 60
See also CA 158
Benedikt, Michael 1935- .... CLC 4, 14
See also CA 13-16R; CANR 7; DLB 5
Benet, Juan 1927- .... CLC 28
See also CA 143
Benet, Stephen Vincent 1898-1943 . TCLC 7; DAM POET; SSC 10
See also CA 104; 152; DLB 4, 48, 102; YABC 1
Benet, William Rose 1886-1950 ... TCLC 28; DAM POET
See also CA 118; 152; DLB 45
Benford, Gregory (Albert) 1941- ..... CLC 52
See also CA 69-72; CAAS 27; CANR 12, 24, 49; DLBY 82
Bengtsson, Frans (Gunnar) 1894-1954 T C L C 48
Benjamin, David
See Slavitt, David R(ytman)
Benjamin, Lois
See Gould, Lois
Benjamin, Walter 1892-1940 .... TCLC 39
Benn, Gottfried 1886-1956 .... TCLC 3
See also CA 106; 153; DLB 56
Bennett, Alan 1934-CLC 45, 77; DAB; DAM MST
See also CA 103; CANR 35, 55; MTCW
Bennett, (Enoch) Arnold 1867-1931 TCLC 5, 20
See also CA 106; 155; CDBLB 1890-1914; DLB 10, 34, 98, 135
Bennett, Elizabeth
See Mitchell, Margaret (Munnerlyn)
Bennett, George Harold 1930-
See Bennett, Hal
See also BW 1; CA 97-100
Bennett, Hal .... CLC 5
See also Bennett, George Harold
See also DLB 33
Bennett, Jay 1912- .... CLC 35
See also AAYA 10; CA 69-72; CANR 11, 42; JRDA; SAAS 4; SATA 41, 87; SATA-Brief 27
Bennett, Louise (Simone) 1919-CLC 28; BLC;

DAM MULT
See also BW 2; CA 151; DLB 117
Benson, E(dward) F(rederic) 1867-1940 TCLC 27
See also CA 114; 157; DLB 135, 153
Benson, Jackson J. 1930- .... CLC 34
See also CA 25-28R; DLB 111
Benson, Sally 1900-1972 .... CLC 17
See also CA 19-20; 37-40R; CAP 1; SATA 1, 35; SATA-Obit 27
Benson, Stella 1892-1933 .... TCLC 17
See also CA 117; 155; DLB 36, 162
Bentham, Jeremy 1748-1832 .... NCLC 38
See also DLB 107, 158
Bentley, E(dmund) C(lerihew) 1875-1956 TCLC 12
See also CA 108; DLB 70
Bentley, Eric (Russell) 1916- .... CLC 24
See also CA 5-8R; CANR 6; INT CANR-6
Beranger, Pierre Jean de 1780-1857NCLC 34
Berdyaev, Nicolas
See Berdyaev, Nikolai (Aleksandrovich)
Berdyaev, Nikolai (Aleksandrovich) 1874-1948 TCLC 67
See also CA 120; 157
Berdyayev, Nikolai (Aleksandrovich)
See Berdyaev, Nikolai (Aleksandrovich)
Berendt, John (Lawrence) 1939- ...... CLC 86
See also CA 146
Berger, Colonel
See Malraux, (Georges-)Andre
Berger, John (Peter) 1926- .... CLC 2, 19
See also CA 81-84; CANR 51; DLB 14
Berger, Melvin H. 1927- .... CLC 12
See also CA 5-8R; CANR 4; CLR 32; SAAS 2; SATA 5, 88
Berger, Thomas (Louis) 1924-CLC 3, 5, 8, 11, 18, 38; DAM NOV
See also CA 1-4R; CANR 5, 28, 51; DLB 2; DLBY 80; INT CANR-28; MTCW
Bergman, (Ernst) Ingmar 1918- CLC 16, 72
See also CA 81-84; CANR 33
Bergson, Henri 1859-1941 .... TCLC 32
Bergstein, Eleanor 1938- .... CLC 4
See also CA 53-56; CANR 5
Berkoff, Steven 1937- .... CLC 56
See also CA 104
Bermant, Chaim (Icyk) 1929- .... CLC 40
See also CA 57-60; CANR 6, 31, 57
Bern, Victoria
See Fisher, M(ary) F(rances) K(ennedy)
Bernanos, (Paul Louis) Georges 1888-1948 TCLC 3
See also CA 104; 130; DLB 72
Bernard, April 1956- .... CLC 59
See also CA 131
Berne, Victoria
See Fisher, M(ary) F(rances) K(ennedy)
Bernhard, Thomas 1931-1989 CLC 3, 32, 61
See also CA 85-88; 127; CANR 32, 57; DLB 85, 124; MTCW
Bernhardt, Sarah (Henriette Rosine) 1844-1923 TCLC 75
See also CA 157
Berriault, Gina 1926- .... CLC 54
See also CA 116; 129; DLB 130
Berrigan, Daniel 1921- .... CLC 4
See also CA 33-36R; CAAS 1; CANR 11, 43; DLB 5
Berrigan, Edmund Joseph Michael, Jr. 1934-1983
See Berrigan, Ted
See also CA 61-64; 110; CANR 14

Berrigan, Ted .... CLC 37
See also Berrigan, Edmund Joseph Michael, Jr.
See also DLB 5, 169
Berry, Charles Edward Anderson 1931-
See Berry, Chuck
See also CA 115
Berry, Chuck .... CLC 17
See also Berry, Charles Edward Anderson
Berry, Jonas
See Ashbery, John (Lawrence)
Berry, Wendell (Erdman) 1934- CLC 4, 6, 8, 27, 46; DAM POET
See also AITN 1; CA 73-76; CANR 50; DLB 5, 6
Berryman, John 1914-1972CLC 1, 2, 3, 4, 6, 8, 10, 13, 25, 62; DAM POET
See also CA 13-16; 33-36R; CABS 2; CANR 35; CAP 1; CDALB 1941-1968; DLB 48; MTCW
Bertolucci, Bernardo 1940- .... CLC 16
See also CA 106
Berton, Pierre (Francis De Marigny) 1920-CLC 104
See also CA 1-4R; CANR 2, 56; DLB 68
Bertrand, Aloysius 1807-1841 .... NCLC 31
Bertran de Born c. 1140-1215 .... CMLC 5
Besant, Annie (Wood) 1847-1933 ..... TCLC 9
See also CA 105
Bessie, Alvah 1904-1985 .... CLC 23
See also CA 5-8R; 116; CANR 2; DLB 26
Bethlen, T. D.
See Silverberg, Robert
Beti, Mongo ...... CLC 27; BLC; DAM MULT
See also Biyidi, Alexandre
Betjeman, John 1906-1984 CLC 2, 6, 10, 34, 43; DAB; DAM MST, POET
See also CA 9-12R; 112; CANR 33, 56; CDBLB 1945-1960; DLB 20; DLBY 84; MTCW
Bettelheim, Bruno 1903-1990 .... CLC 79
See also CA 81-84; 131; CANR 23, 61; MTCW
Betti, Ugo 1892-1953 .... TCLC 5
See also CA 104; 155
Betts, Doris (Waugh) 1932- ...... CLC 3, 6, 28
See also CA 13-16R; CANR 9; DLBY 82; INT CANR-9
Bevan, Alistair
See Roberts, Keith (John Kingston)
Bialik, Chaim Nachman 1873-1934 TCLC 25
Bickerstaff, Isaac
See Swift, Jonathan
Bidart, Frank 1939- .... CLC 33
See also CA 140
Bienek, Horst 1930- .... CLC 7, 11
See also CA 73-76; DLB 75
Bierce, Ambrose (Gwinett) 1842-1914(?) TCLC 1, 7, 44; DA; DAC; DAM MST; SSC 9; WLC
See also CA 104; 139; CDALB 1865-1917; DLB 11, 12, 23, 71, 74, 186
Biggers, Earl Derr 1884-1933 .... TCLC 65
See also CA 108; 153
Billings, Josh
See Shaw, Henry Wheeler
Billington, (Lady) Rachel (Mary) 1942- C L C 43
See also AITN 2; CA 33-36R; CANR 44
Binyon, T(imothy) J(ohn) 1936- ...... CLC 34
See also CA 111; CANR 28
Bioy Casares, Adolfo 1914-CLC 4, 8, 13, 88; DAM MULT; HLC; SSC 17
See also CA 29-32R; CANR 19, 43; DLB 113; HW; MTCW
Bird, Cordwainer

See Ellison, Harlan (Jay)

Bird, Robert Montgomery 1806-1854 NCLC 1

Birney, (Alfred) Earle 1904- **CLC 1, 4, 6, 11; DAC; DAM MST, POET**
  See also CA 1-4R; CANR 5, 20; DLB 88; MTCW

Bishop, Elizabeth 1911-1979 **CLC 1, 4, 9, 13, 15, 32; DA; DAC; DAM MST, POET; PC 3**
  See also CA 5-8R; 89-92; CABS 2; CANR 26, 61; CDALB 1968-1988; DLB 5, 169; MTCW; SATA-Obit 24

Bishop, John 1935- .... **CLC 10**
  See also CA 105

Bissett, Bill 1939- .... **CLC 18; PC 14**
  See also CA 69-72; CAAS 19; CANR 15; DLB 53; MTCW

Bitov, Andrei (Georgievich) 1937- ... **CLC 57**
  See also CA 142

Biyidi, Alexandre 1932-
  See Beti, Mongo
  See also BW 1; CA 114; 124; MTCW

Bjarme, Brynjolf
  See Ibsen, Henrik (Johan)

Bjornson, Bjornstjerne (Martinius) 1832-1910 **TCLC 7, 37**
  See also CA 104

Black, Robert
  See Holdstock, Robert P.

Blackburn, Paul 1926-1971 .... **CLC 9, 43**
  See also CA 81-84; 33-36R; CANR 34; DLB 16; DLBY 81

Black Elk 1863-1950 **TCLC 33; DAM MULT**
  See also CA 144; NNAL

Black Hobart
  See Sanders, (James) Ed(ward)

Blacklin, Malcolm
  See Chambers, Aidan

Blackmore, R(ichard) D(oddridge) 1825-1900 **TCLC 27**
  See also CA 120; DLB 18

Blackmur, R(ichard) P(almer) 1904-1965 **CLC 2, 24**
  See also CA 11-12; 25-28R; CAP 1; DLB 63

Black Tarantula
  See Acker, Kathy

Blackwood, Algernon (Henry) 1869-1951 **TCLC 5**
  See also CA 105; 150; DLB 153, 156, 178

Blackwood, Caroline 1931-1996 **CLC 6, 9, 100**
  See also CA 85-88; 151; CANR 32, 61; DLB 14; MTCW

Blade, Alexander
  See Hamilton, Edmond; Silverberg, Robert

Blaga, Lucian 1895-1961 .... **CLC 75**

Blair, Eric (Arthur) 1903-1950
  See Orwell, George
  See also CA 104; 132; DA; DAB; DAC; DAM MST, NOV; MTCW; SATA 29

Blais, Marie-Claire 1939- **CLC 2, 4, 6, 13, 22; DAC; DAM MST**
  See also CA 21-24R; CAAS 4; CANR 38; DLB 53; MTCW

Blaise, Clark 1940- .... **CLC 29**
  See also AITN 2; CA 53-56; CAAS 3; CANR 5; DLB 53

Blake, Fairley
  See De Voto, Bernard (Augustine)

Blake, Nicholas
  See Day Lewis, C(ecil)
  See also DLB 77

Blake, William 1757-1827 . **NCLC 13, 37, 57; DA; DAB; DAC; DAM MST, POET; PC**

12; WLC
  See also CDBLB 1789-1832; DLB 93, 163; MAICYA; SATA 30

Blasco Ibanez, Vicente 1867-1928 **TCLC 12; DAM NOV**
  See also CA 110; 131; HW; MTCW

Blatty, William Peter 1928- **CLC 2; DAM POP**
  See also CA 5-8R; CANR 9

Bleeck, Oliver
  See Thomas, Ross (Elmore)

Blessing, Lee 1949- .... **CLC 54**

Blish, James (Benjamin) 1921-1975 . **CLC 14**
  See also CA 1-4R; 57-60; CANR 3; DLB 8; MTCW; SATA 66

Bliss, Reginald
  See Wells, H(erbert) G(eorge)

Blixen, Karen (Christentze Dinesen) 1885-1962
  See Dinesen, Isak
  See also CA 25-28; CANR 22, 50; CAP 2; MTCW; SATA 44

Bloch, Robert (Albert) 1917-1994 .... **CLC 33**
  See also CA 5-8R; 146; CAAS 20; CANR 5; DLB 44; INT CANR-5; SATA 12; SATA-Obit 82

Blok, Alexander (Alexandrovich) 1880-1921 **TCLC 5**
  See also CA 104

Blom, Jan
  See Breytenbach, Breyten

Bloom, Harold 1930- .... **CLC 24, 103**
  See also CA 13-16R; CANR 39; DLB 67

Bloomfield, Aurelius
  See Bourne, Randolph S(illiman)

Blount, Roy (Alton), Jr. 1941- .... **CLC 38**
  See also CA 53-56; CANR 10, 28, 61; INT CANR-28; MTCW

Bloy, Leon 1846-1917 .... **TCLC 22**
  See also CA 121; DLB 123

Blume, Judy (Sussman) 1938- ... **CLC 12, 30; DAM NOV, POP**
  See also AAYA 3; CA 29-32R; CANR 13, 37; CLR 2, 15; DLB 52; JRDA; MAICYA; MTCW; SATA 2, 31, 79

Blunden, Edmund (Charles) 1896-1974 **CLC 2, 56**
  See also CA 17-18; 45-48; CANR 54; CAP 2; DLB 20, 100, 155; MTCW

Bly, Robert (Elwood) 1926- **CLC 1, 2, 5, 10, 15, 38; DAM POET**
  See also CA 5-8R; CANR 41; DLB 5; MTCW

Boas, Franz 1858-1942 .... **TCLC 56**
  See also CA 115

Bobette
  See Simenon, Georges (Jacques Christian)

Boccaccio, Giovanni 1313-1375 .. **CMLC 13; SSC 10**

Bochco, Steven 1943- .... **CLC 35**
  See also AAYA 11; CA 124; 138

Bodenheim, Maxwell 1892-1954 .... **TCLC 44**
  See also CA 110; DLB 9, 45

Bodker, Cecil 1927- .... **CLC 21**
  See also CA 73-76; CANR 13, 44; CLR 23; MAICYA; SATA 14

Boell, Heinrich (Theodor) 1917-1985 **CLC 2, 3, 6, 9, 11, 15, 27, 32, 72; DA; DAB; DAC; DAM MST, NOV; SSC 23; WLC**
  See also CA 21-24R; 116; CANR 24; DLB 69; DLBY 85; MTCW

Boerne, Alfred
  See Doeblin, Alfred

Boethius 480(?)-524(?) .... **CMLC 15**
  See also DLB 115

Bogan, Louise 1897-1970 . **CLC 4, 39, 46, 93;**

DAM POET; PC 12
  See also CA 73-76; 25-28R; CANR 33; DLB 45, 169; MTCW

Bogarde, Dirk .... **CLC 19**
  See also Van Den Bogarde, Derek Jules Gaspard Ulric Niven
  See also DLB 14

Bogosian, Eric 1953- .... **CLC 45**
  See also CA 138

Bograd, Larry 1953- .... **CLC 35**
  See also CA 93-96; CANR 57; SAAS 21; SATA 33, 89

Boiardo, Matteo Maria 1441-1494 .... **LC 6**

Boileau-Despreaux, Nicolas 1636-1711 **LC 3**

Bojer, Johan 1872-1959 .... **TCLC 64**

Boland, Eavan (Aisling) 1944- .. **CLC 40, 67; DAM POET**
  See also CA 143; CANR 61; DLB 40

Bolt, Lee
  See Faust, Frederick (Schiller)

Bolt, Robert (Oxton) 1924-1995 ..... **CLC 14; DAM DRAM**
  See also CA 17-20R; 147; CANR 35; DLB 13; MTCW

Bombet, Louis-Alexandre-Cesar
  See Stendhal

Bomkauf
  See Kaufman, Bob (Garnell)

Bonaventura .... **NCLC 35**
  See also DLB 90

Bond, Edward 1934- **CLC 4, 6, 13, 23; DAM DRAM**
  See also CA 25-28R; CANR 38; DLB 13; MTCW

Bonham, Frank 1914-1989 .... **CLC 12**
  See also AAYA 1; CA 9-12R; CANR 4, 36; JRDA; MAICYA; SAAS 3; SATA 1, 49; SATA-Obit 62

Bonnefoy, Yves 1923- .. **CLC 9, 15, 58; DAM MST, POET**
  See also CA 85-88; CANR 33; MTCW

Bontemps, Arna(ud Wendell) 1902-1973 **CLC 1, 18; BLC; DAM MULT, NOV, POET**
  See also BW 1; CA 1-4R; 41-44R; CANR 4, 35; CLR 6; DLB 48, 51; JRDA; MAICYA; MTCW; SATA 2, 44; SATA-Obit 24

Booth, Martin 1944- .... **CLC 13**
  See also CA 93-96; CAAS 2

Booth, Philip 1925- .... **CLC 23**
  See also CA 5-8R; CANR 5; DLBY 82

Booth, Wayne C(layson) 1921- .... **CLC 24**
  See also CA 1-4R; CAAS 5; CANR 3, 43; DLB 67

Borchert, Wolfgang 1921-1947 .... **TCLC 5**
  See also CA 104; DLB 69, 124

Borel, Petrus 1809-1859 .... **NCLC 41**

Borges, Jorge Luis 1899-1986 **CLC 1, 2, 3, 4, 6, 8, 9, 10, 13, 19, 44, 48, 83; DA; DAB; DAC; DAM MST, MULT; HLC; SSC 4; WLC**
  See also AAYA 19; CA 21-24R; CANR 19, 33; DLB 113; DLBY 86; HW; MTCW

Borowski, Tadeusz 1922-1951 .... **TCLC 9**
  See also CA 106; 154

Borrow, George (Henry) 1803-1881 **NCLC 9**
  See also DLB 21, 55, 166

Bosman, Herman Charles 1905-1951 . **TCLC 49**
  See also Malan, Herman
  See also CA 160

Bosschere, Jean de 1878(?)-1953 ... **TCLC 19**
  See also CA 115

Boswell, James 1740-1795 . **LC 4; DA; DAB; DAC; DAM MST; WLC**

See also CDBLB 1660-1789; DLB 104, 142
Bottoms, David 1949- .... **CLC 53**
See also CA 105; CANR 22; DLB 120; DLBY 83
Boucicault, Dion 1820-1890 .... **NCLC 41**
Boucolon, Maryse 1937(?)-
See Conde, Maryse
See also CA 110; CANR 30, 53
Bourget, Paul (Charles Joseph) 1852-1935
TCLC 12
See also CA 107; DLB 123
Bourjaily, Vance (Nye) 1922- .... **CLC 8, 62**
See also CA 1-4R; CAAS 1; CANR 2; DLB 2, 143
Bourne, Randolph S(illiman) 1886-1918
TCLC 16
See also CA 117; 155; DLB 63
Bova, Ben(jamin William) 1932- ..... **CLC 45**
See also AAYA 16; CA 5-8R; CAAS 18; CANR 11, 56; CLR 3; DLBY 81; INT CANR-11; MAICYA; MTCW; SATA 6, 68
Bowen, Elizabeth (Dorothea Cole) 1899-1973
CLC 1, 3, 6, 11, 15, 22; DAM NOV; SSC 3, 28
See also CA 17-18; 41-44R; CANR 35; CAP 2; CDBLB 1945-1960; DLB 15, 162; MTCW
Bowering, George 1935- .... **CLC 15, 47**
See also CA 21-24R; CAAS 16; CANR 10; DLB 53
Bowering, Marilyn R(uthe) 1949- ... **CLC 32**
See also CA 101; CANR 49
Bowers, Edgar 1924- .... **CLC 9**
See also CA 5-8R; CANR 24; DLB 5
Bowie, David .... **CLC 17**
See also Jones, David Robert
Bowles, Jane (Sydney) 1917-1973 **CLC 3, 68**
See also CA 19-20; 41-44R; CAP 2
Bowles, Paul (Frederick) 1910- **CLC 1, 2, 19, 53; SSC 3**
See also CA 1-4R; CAAS 1; CANR 1, 19, 50; DLB 5, 6; MTCW
Box, Edgar
See Vidal, Gore
Boyd, Nancy
See Millay, Edna St. Vincent
Boyd, William 1952- .... **CLC 28, 53, 70**
See also CA 114; 120; CANR 51
Boyle, Kay 1902-1992 **CLC 1, 5, 19, 58; SSC 5**
See also CA 13-16R; 140; CAAS 1; CANR 29, 61; DLB 4, 9, 48, 86; DLBY 93; MTCW
Boyle, Mark
See Kienzle, William X(avier)
Boyle, Patrick 1905-1982 .... **CLC 19**
See also CA 127
Boyle, T. C. 1948-
See Boyle, T(homas) Coraghessan
Boyle, T(homas) Coraghessan 1948- **CLC 36, 55, 90; DAM POP; SSC 16**
See also BEST 90:4; CA 120; CANR 44; DLBY 86
Boz
See Dickens, Charles (John Huffam)
Brackenridge, Hugh Henry 1748-1816 **NCLC 7**
See also DLB 11, 37
Bradbury, Edward P.
See Moorcock, Michael (John)
Bradbury, Malcolm (Stanley) 1932- **CLC 32, 61; DAM NOV**
See also CA 1-4R; CANR 1, 33; DLB 14; MTCW
Bradbury, Ray (Douglas) 1920- **CLC 1, 3, 10, 15, 42, 98; DA; DAB; DAC; DAM MST,**

NOV, POP; SSC 29; WLC
See also AAYA 15; AITN 1, 2; CA 1-4R; CANR 2, 30; CDALB 1968-1988; DLB 2, 8; MTCW; SATA 11, 64
Bradford, Gamaliel 1863-1932 ...... **TCLC 36**
See also CA 160; DLB 17
Bradley, David (Henry, Jr.) 1950- .. **CLC 23; BLC; DAM MULT**
See also BW 1; CA 104; CANR 26; DLB 33
Bradley, John Ed(mund, Jr.) 1958- .. **CLC 55**
See also CA 139
Bradley, Marion Zimmer 1930- **CLC 30; DAM POP**
See also AAYA 9; CA 57-60; CAAS 10; CANR 7, 31, 51; DLB 8; MTCW; SATA 90
Bradstreet, Anne 1612(?)-1672 **LC 4, 30; DA; DAC; DAM MST, POET; PC 10**
See also CDALB 1640-1865; DLB 24
Brady, Joan 1939- .... **CLC 86**
See also CA 141
Bragg, Melvyn 1939- .... **CLC 10**
See also BEST 89:3; CA 57-60; CANR 10, 48; DLB 14
Braine, John (Gerard) 1922-1986 **CLC 1, 3, 41**
See also CA 1-4R; 120; CANR 1, 33; CDBLB 1945-1960; DLB 15; DLBY 86; MTCW
Bramah, Ernest 1868-1942 .... **TCLC 72**
See also CA 156; DLB 70
Brammer, William 1930(?)-1978 .... **CLC 31**
See also CA 77-80
Brancati, Vitaliano 1907-1954 .... **TCLC 12**
See also CA 109
Brancato, Robin F(idler) 1936- .... **CLC 35**
See also AAYA 9; CA 69-72; CANR 11, 45; CLR 32; JRDA; SAAS 9; SATA 23
Brand, Max
See Faust, Frederick (Schiller)
Brand, Millen 1906-1980 .... **CLC 7**
See also CA 21-24R; 97-100
Branden, Barbara .... **CLC 44**
See also CA 148
Brandes, Georg (Morris Cohen) 1842-1927
TCLC 10
See also CA 105
Brandys, Kazimierz 1916- .... **CLC 62**
Branley, Franklyn M(ansfield) 1915- **CLC 21**
See also CA 33-36R; CANR 14, 39; CLR 13; MAICYA; SAAS 16; SATA 4, 68
Brathwaite, Edward Kamau 1930- **CLC 11; DAM POET**
See also BW 2; CA 25-28R; CANR 11, 26, 47; DLB 125
Brautigan, Richard (Gary) 1935-1984 **CLC 1, 3, 5, 9, 12, 34, 42; DAM NOV**
See also CA 53-56; 113; CANR 34; DLB 2, 5; DLBY 80, 84; MTCW; SATA 56
Brave Bird, Mary 1953-
See Crow Dog, Mary (Ellen)
See also NNAL
Braverman, Kate 1950- .... **CLC 67**
See also CA 89-92
Brecht, (Eugen) Bertolt (Friedrich) 1898-1956
TCLC 1, 6, 13, 35; DA; DAB; DAC; DAM DRAM, MST; DC 3; WLC
See also CA 104; 133; CANR 62; DLB 56, 124; MTCW
Brecht, Eugen Berthold Friedrich
See Brecht, (Eugen) Bertolt (Friedrich)
Bremer, Fredrika 1801-1865 .... **NCLC 11**
Brennan, Christopher John 1870-1932 **TCLC 17**
See also CA 117
Brennan, Maeve 1917- .... **CLC 5**

See also CA 81-84
Brentano, Clemens (Maria) 1778-1842 **NCLC 1**
See also DLB 90
Brent of Bin Bin
See Franklin, (Stella Maraia Sarah) Miles
Brenton, Howard 1942- .... **CLC 31**
See also CA 69-72; CANR 33; DLB 13; MTCW
Breslin, James 1930-
See Breslin, Jimmy
See also CA 73-76; CANR 31; DAM NOV; MTCW
Breslin, Jimmy .... **CLC 4, 43**
See also Breslin, James
See also AITN 1
Bresson, Robert 1901- .... **CLC 16**
See also CA 110; CANR 49
Breton, Andre 1896-1966 **CLC 2, 9, 15, 54; PC 15**
See also CA 19-20; 25-28R; CANR 40, 60; CAP 2; DLB 65; MTCW
Breytenbach, Breyten 1939(?)- . **CLC 23, 37; DAM POET**
See also CA 113; 129; CANR 61
Bridgers, Sue Ellen 1942- .... **CLC 26**
See also AAYA 8; CA 65-68; CANR 11, 36; CLR 18; DLB 52; JRDA; MAICYA; SAAS 1; SATA 22, 90
Bridges, Robert (Seymour) 1844-1930 **TCLC 1; DAM POET**
See also CA 104; 152; CDBLB 1890-1914; DLB 19, 98
Bridie, James .... **TCLC 3**
See also Mavor, Osborne Henry
See also DLB 10
Brin, David 1950- .... **CLC 34**
See also AAYA 21; CA 102; CANR 24; INT CANR-24; SATA 65
Brink, Andre (Philippus) 1935- **CLC 18, 36, 106**
See also CA 104; CANR 39, 62; INT 103; MTCW
Brinsmead, H(esba) F(ay) 1922- ...... **CLC 21**
See also CA 21-24R; CANR 10; CLR 47; MAICYA; SAAS 5; SATA 18, 78
Brittain, Vera (Mary) 1893(?)-1970 **CLC 23**
See also CA 13-16; 25-28R; CANR 58; CAP 1; MTCW
Broch, Hermann 1886-1951 .... **TCLC 20**
See also CA 117; DLB 85, 124
Brock, Rose
See Hansen, Joseph
Brodkey, Harold (Roy) 1930-1996 ... **CLC 56**
See also CA 111; 151; DLB 130
Brodsky, Iosif Alexandrovich 1940-1996
See Brodsky, Joseph
See also AITN 1; CA 41-44R; 151; CANR 37; DAM POET; MTCW
Brodsky, Joseph 1940-1996 **CLC 4, 6, 13, 36, 100; PC 9**
See also Brodsky, Iosif Alexandrovich
Brodsky, Michael (Mark) 1948- .... **CLC 19**
See also CA 102; CANR 18, 41, 58
Bromell, Henry 1947- .... **CLC 5**
See also CA 53-56; CANR 9
Bromfield, Louis (Brucker) 1896-1956 **TCLC 11**
See also CA 107; 155; DLB 4, 9, 86
Broner, E(sther) M(asserman) 1930- **CLC 19**
See also CA 17-20R; CANR 8, 25; DLB 28
Bronk, William 1918- .... **CLC 10**
See also CA 89-92; CANR 23; DLB 165
Bronstein, Lev Davidovich

See Trotsky, Leon

Bronte, Anne 1820-1849 .... **NCLC 4**
See also DLB 21

Bronte, Charlotte 1816-1855 **NCLC 3, 8, 33, 58; DA; DAB; DAC; DAM MST, NOV; WLC**
See also AAYA 17; CDBLB 1832-1890; DLB 21, 159

Bronte, Emily (Jane) 1818-1848**NCLC 16, 35; DA; DAB; DAC; DAM MST, NOV, POET; PC 8; WLC**
See also AAYA 17; CDBLB 1832-1890; DLB 21, 32

Brooke, Frances 1724-1789 .... **LC 6**
See also DLB 39, 99

Brooke, Henry 1703(?)-1783 .... **LC 1**
See also DLB 39

Brooke, Rupert (Chawner) 1887-1915 **T C L C 2, 7; DA; DAB; DAC; DAM MST, POET; WLC**
See also CA 104; 132; CANR 61; CDBLB 1914-1945; DLB 19; MTCW

Brooke-Haven, P.
See Wodehouse, P(elham) G(renville)

Brooke-Rose, Christine 1926(?)- ...... **CLC 40**
See also CA 13-16R; CANR 58; DLB 14

Brookner, Anita 1928-**CLC 32, 34, 51; DAB; DAM POP**
See also CA 114; 120; CANR 37, 56; DLBY 87; MTCW

Brooks, Cleanth 1906-1994 .... **CLC 24, 86**
See also CA 17-20R; 145; CANR 33, 35; DLB 63; DLBY 94; INT CANR-35; MTCW

Brooks, George
See Baum, L(yman) Frank

Brooks, Gwendolyn 1917- **CLC 1, 2, 4, 5, 15, 49; BLC; DA; DAC; DAM MST, MULT, POET; PC 7; WLC**
See also AAYA 20; AITN 1; BW 2; CA 1-4R; CANR 1, 27, 52; CDALB 1941-1968; CLR 27; DLB 5, 76, 165; MTCW; SATA 6

Brooks, Mel .... **CLC 12**
See also Kaminsky, Melvin
See also AAYA 13; DLB 26

Brooks, Peter 1938- .... **CLC 34**
See also CA 45-48; CANR 1

Brooks, Van Wyck 1886-1963 .... **CLC 29**
See also CA 1-4R; CANR 6; DLB 45, 63, 103

Brophy, Brigid (Antonia) 1929-1995 **. CLC 6, 11, 29, 105**
See also CA 5-8R; 149; CAAS 4; CANR 25, 53; DLB 14; MTCW

Brosman, Catharine Savage 1934- ..... **CLC 9**
See also CA 61-64; CANR 21, 46

Brother Antoninus
See Everson, William (Oliver)

Broughton, T(homas) Alan 1936- .... **CLC 19**
See also CA 45-48; CANR 2, 23, 48

Broumas, Olga 1949- .... **CLC 10, 73**
See also CA 85-88; CANR 20

Brown, Alan 1951- .... **CLC 99**

Brown, Charles Brockden 1771-1810 **N C L C 22**
See also CDALB 1640-1865; DLB 37, 59, 73

Brown, Christy 1932-1981 .... **CLC 63**
See also CA 105; 104; DLB 14

Brown, Claude 1937- .. **CLC 30; BLC; DAM MULT**
See also AAYA 7; BW 1; CA 73-76

Brown, Dee (Alexander) 1908- .. **CLC 18, 47; DAM POP**
See also CA 13-16R; CAAS 6; CANR 11, 45, 60; DLBY 80; MTCW; SATA 5

Brown, George
See Wertmueller, Lina

Brown, George Douglas 1869-1902 **TCLC 28**

Brown, George Mackay 1921-1996**CLC 5, 48, 100**
See also CA 21-24R; 151; CAAS 6; CANR 12, 37, 62; DLB 14, 27, 139; MTCW; SATA 35

Brown, (William) Larry 1951- .... **CLC 73**
See also CA 130; 134; INT 133

Brown, Moses
See Barrett, William (Christopher)

Brown, Rita Mae 1944-**CLC 18, 43, 79; DAM NOV, POP**
See also CA 45-48; CANR 2, 11, 35, 62; INT CANR-11; MTCW

Brown, Roderick (Langmere) Haig-
See Haig-Brown, Roderick (Langmere)

Brown, Rosellen 1939- ....**CLC 32**
See also CA 77-80; CAAS 10; CANR 14, 44

Brown, Sterling Allen 1901-1989 **CLC 1, 23, 59; BLC; DAM MULT, POET**
See also BW 1; CA 85-88; 127; CANR 26; DLB 48, 51, 63; MTCW

Brown, Will
See Ainsworth, William Harrison

Brown, William Wells 1813-1884 .. **NCLC 2; BLC; DAM MULT; DC 1**
See also DLB 3, 50

Browne, (Clyde) Jackson 1948(?)- .... **CLC 21**
See also CA 120

Browning, Elizabeth Barrett 1806-1861 **NCLC 1, 16, 61, 66; DA; DAB; DAC; DAM MST, POET; PC 6; WLC**
See also CDBLB 1832-1890; DLB 32

Browning, Robert 1812-1889 **NCLC 19; DA; DAB; DAC; DAM MST, POET; PC 2; WLCS**
See also CDBLB 1832-1890; DLB 32, 163; YABC 1

Browning, Tod 1882-1962.................. **CLC 16**
See also CA 141; 117

Brownson, Orestes (Augustus) 1803-1876 **NCLC 50**

Bruccoli, Matthew J(oseph) 1931-....**CLC 34**
See also CA 9-12R; CANR 7; DLB 103

Bruce, Lenny ....**CLC 21**
See also Schneider, Leonard Alfred

Bruin, John
See Brutus, Dennis

Brulard, Henri
See Stendhal

Brulls, Christian
See Simenon, Georges (Jacques Christian)

Brunner, John (Kilian Houston) 1934-1995 **CLC 8, 10; DAM POP**
See also CA 1-4R; 149; CAAS 8; CANR 2, 37; MTCW

Bruno, Giordano 1548-1600 .... **LC 27**

Brutus, Dennis 1924- ... **CLC 43; BLC; DAM MULT, POET**
See also BW 2; CA 49-52; CAAS 14; CANR 2, 27, 42; DLB 117

Bryan, C(ourtlandt) D(ixon) B(arnes) 1936- **CLC 29**
See also CA 73-76; CANR 13; INT CANR-13

Bryan, Michael
See Moore, Brian

Bryant, William Cullen 1794-1878 . **NCLC 6, 46; DA; DAB; DAC; DAM MST, POET; PC 20**
See also CDALB 1640-1865; DLB 3, 43, 59

Bryusov, Valery Yakovlevich 1873-1924 **TCLC 10**

See also CA 107; 155

Buchan, John 1875-1940 .... **TCLC 41; DAB; DAM POP**
See also CA 108; 145; DLB 34, 70, 156; YABC 2

Buchanan, George 1506-1582 .... **LC 4**

Buchheim, Lothar-Guenther 1918- ....**CLC 6**
See also CA 85-88

Buchner, (Karl) Georg 1813-1837 .**NCLC 26**

Buchwald, Art(hur) 1925- ....**CLC 33**
See also AITN 1; CA 5-8R; CANR 21; MTCW; SATA 10

Buck, Pearl S(ydenstricker) 1892-1973**CLC 7, 11, 18; DA; DAB; DAC; DAM MST, NOV**
See also AITN 1; CA 1-4R; 41-44R; CANR 1, 34; DLB 9, 102; MTCW; SATA 1, 25

Buckler, Ernest 1908-1984 .... **CLC 13; DAC; DAM MST**
See also CA 11-12; 114; CAP 1; DLB 68; SATA 47

Buckley, Vincent (Thomas) 1925-1988**CLC 57**
See also CA 101

Buckley, William F(rank), Jr. 1925-**CLC 7, 18, 37; DAM POP**
See also AITN 1; CA 1-4R; CANR 1, 24, 53; DLB 137; DLBY 80; INT CANR-24; MTCW

Buechner, (Carl) Frederick 1926-**CLC 2, 4, 6, 9; DAM NOV**
See also CA 13-16R; CANR 11, 39; DLBY 80; INT CANR-11; MTCW

Buell, John (Edward) 1927- ....**CLC 10**
See also CA 1-4R; DLB 53

Buero Vallejo, Antonio 1916- ..... **CLC 15, 46**
See also CA 106; CANR 24, 49; HW; MTCW

Bufalino, Gesualdo 1920(?)- ....**CLC 74**

Bugayev, Boris Nikolayevich 1880-1934
See Bely, Andrey
See also CA 104

Bukowski, Charles 1920-1994**CLC 2, 5, 9, 41, 82; DAM NOV, POET; PC 18**
See also CA 17-20R; 144; CANR 40, 62; DLB 5, 130, 169; MTCW

Bulgakov, Mikhail (Afanas'evich) 1891-1940 **TCLC 2, 16; DAM DRAM, NOV; SSC 18**
See also CA 105; 152

Bulgya, Alexander Alexandrovich 1901-1956 **TCLC 53**
See Fadeyev, Alexander
See also CA 117

Bullins, Ed 1935- ... **CLC 1, 5, 7; BLC; DAM DRAM, MULT; DC 6**
See also BW 2; CA 49-52; CAAS 16; CANR 24, 46; DLB 7, 38; MTCW

Bulwer-Lytton, Edward (George Earle Lytton) 1803-1873 ....**NCLC 1, 45**
See also DLB 21

Bunin, Ivan Alexeyevich 1870-1953 **TCLC 6; SSC 5**
See also CA 104

Bunting, Basil 1900-1985 ..... **CLC 10, 39, 47; DAM POET**
See also CA 53-56; 115; CANR 7; DLB 20

Bunuel, Luis 1900-1983 .. **CLC 16, 80; DAM MULT; HLC**
See also CA 101; 110; CANR 32; HW

Bunyan, John 1628-1688 ... **LC 4; DA; DAB; DAC; DAM MST; WLC**
See also CDBLB 1660-1789; DLB 39

Burckhardt, Jacob (Christoph) 1818-1897 **NCLC 49**

Burford, Eleanor
See Hibbert, Eleanor Alice Burford

Burgess, AnthonyCLC 1, 2, 4, 5, 8, 10, 13, 15,

22, 40, 62, 81, 94; DAB
See also Wilson, John (Anthony) Burgess
See also AITN 1; CDBLB 1960 to Present; DLB 14

Burke, Edmund 1729(?)-1797 **LC 7, 36; DA; DAB; DAC; DAM MST; WLC**
See also DLB 104

Burke, Kenneth (Duva) 1897-1993 CLC **2, 24**
See also CA 5-8R; 143; CANR 39; DLB 45, 63; MTCW

Burke, Leda
See Garnett, David

Burke, Ralph
See Silverberg, Robert

Burke, Thomas 1886-1945 .... **TCLC 63**
See also CA 113; 155

Burney, Fanny 1752-1840 .... **NCLC 12, 54**
See also DLB 39

Burns, Robert 1759-1796 .... **PC 6**
See also CDBLB 1789-1832; DA; DAB; DAC; DAM MST, POET; DLB 109; WLC

Burns, Tex
See L'Amour, Louis (Dearborn)

Burnshaw, Stanley 1906- .... **CLC 3, 13, 44**
See also CA 9-12R; DLB 48

Burr, Anne 1937- .... **CLC 6**
See also CA 25-28R

Burroughs, Edgar Rice 1875-1950 . **TCLC 2, 32; DAM NOV**
See also AAYA 11; CA 104; 132; DLB 8; MTCW; SATA 41

Burroughs, William S(eward) 1914-1997 CLC **1, 2, 5, 15, 22, 42, 75; DA; DAB; DAC; DAM MST, NOV, POP; WLC**
See also AITN 2; CA 9-12R; 160; CANR 20, 52; DLB 2, 8, 16, 152; DLBY 81; MTCW

Burton, Richard F. 1821-1890 .... **NCLC 42**
See also DLB 55, 184

Busch, Frederick 1941- ..... **CLC 7, 10, 18, 47**
See also CA 33-36R; CAAS 1; CANR 45; DLB 6

Bush, Ronald 1946- .... **CLC 34**
See also CA 136

Bustos, F(rancisco)
See Borges, Jorge Luis

Bustos Domecq, H(onorio)
See Bioy Casares, Adolfo; Borges, Jorge Luis

Butler, Octavia E(stelle) 1947- CLC **38; DAM MULT, POP**
See also AAYA 18; BW 2; CA 73-76; CANR 12, 24, 38; DLB 33; MTCW; SATA 84

Butler, Robert Olen (Jr.) 1945- CLC **81; DAM POP**
See also CA 112; DLB 173; INT 112

Butler, Samuel 1612-1680 .... **LC 16**
See also DLB 101, 126

Butler, Samuel 1835-1902 . **TCLC 1, 33; DA; DAB; DAC; DAM MST, NOV; WLC**
See also CA 143; CDBLB 1890-1914; DLB 18, 57, 174

Butler, Walter C.
See Faust, Frederick (Schiller)

Butor, Michel (Marie Francois) 1926- CLC **1, 3, 8, 11, 15**
See also CA 9-12R; CANR 33; DLB 83; MTCW

Buzo, Alexander (John) 1944- .... **CLC 61**
See also CA 97-100; CANR 17, 39

Buzzati, Dino 1906-1972 .... **CLC 36**
See also CA 160; 33-36R; DLB 177

Byars, Betsy (Cromer) 1928- .... **CLC 35**
See also AAYA 19; CA 33-36R; CANR 18, 36, 57; CLR 1, 16; DLB 52; INT CANR-18; JRDA; MAICYA; MTCW; SAAS 1; SATA

4, 46, 80

Byatt, A(ntonia) S(usan Drabble) 1936- C L C **19, 65; DAM NOV, POP**
See also CA 13-16R; CANR 13, 33, 50; DLB 14; MTCW

Byrne, David 1952- .... **CLC 26**
See also CA 127

Byrne, John Keyes 1926-
See Leonard, Hugh
See also CA 102; INT 102

Byron, George Gordon (Noel) 1788-1824 **NCLC 2, 12; DA; DAB; DAC; DAM MST, POET; PC 16; WLC**
See also CDBLB 1789-1832; DLB 96, 110

Byron, Robert 1905-1941 .... **TCLC 67**
See also CA 160

C. 3. 3.
See Wilde, Oscar (Fingal O'Flahertie Wills)

Caballero, Fernan 1796-1877 .... **NCLC 10**

Cabell, Branch
See Cabell, James Branch

Cabell, James Branch 1879-1958 .... **TCLC 6**
See also CA 105; 152; DLB 9, 78

Cable, George Washington 1844-1925 T C L C **4; SSC 4**
See also CA 104; 155; DLB 12, 74; DLBD 13

Cabral de Melo Neto, Joao 1920- ... **CLC 76; DAM MULT**
See also CA 151

Cabrera Infante, G(uillermo) 1929- CLC **5, 25, 45; DAM MULT; HLC**
See also CA 85-88; CANR 29; DLB 113; HW; MTCW

Cade, Toni
See Bambara, Toni Cade

Cadmus and Harmonia
See Buchan, John

Caedmon fl. 658-680 .... **CMLC 7**
See also DLB 146

Caeiro, Alberto
See Pessoa, Fernando (Antonio Nogueira)

Cage, John (Milton, Jr.) 1912- .... **CLC 41**
See also CA 13-16R; CANR 9; INT CANR-9

Cahan, Abraham 1860-1951 .... **TCLC 71**
See also CA 108; 154; DLB 9, 25, 28

Cain, G.
See Cabrera Infante, G(uillermo)

Cain, Guillermo
See Cabrera Infante, G(uillermo)

Cain, James M(allahan) 1892-1977 CLC **3, 11, 28**
See also AITN 1; CA 17-20R; 73-76; CANR 8, 34, 61; MTCW

Caine, Mark
See Raphael, Frederic (Michael)

Calasso, Roberto 1941- .... **CLC 81**
See also CA 143

Calderon de la Barca, Pedro 1600-1681 .. L C **23; DC 3**

Caldwell, Erskine (Preston) 1903-1987 CLC **1, 8, 14, 50, 60; DAM NOV; SSC 19**
See also AITN 1; CA 1-4R; 121; CAAS 1; CANR 2, 33; DLB 9, 86; MTCW

Caldwell, (Janet Miriam) Taylor (Holland) 1900-1985 CLC **2, 28, 39; DAM NOV, POP**
See also CA 5-8R; 116; CANR 5

Calhoun, John Caldwell 1782-1850 NCLC **15**
See also DLB 3

Calisher, Hortense 1911- CLC **2, 4, 8, 38; DAM NOV; SSC 15**
See also CA 1-4R; CANR 1, 22; DLB 2; INT CANR-22; MTCW

Callaghan, Morley Edward 1903-1990 CLC **3,**

14, 41, 65; DAC; DAM MST
See also CA 9-12R; 132; CANR 33; DLB 68; MTCW

Callimachus c. 305B.C.-c. 240B.C. **CMLC 18**
See also DLB 176

Calvin, John 1509-1564 .... **LC 37**

Calvino, Italo 1923-1985 CLC **5, 8, 11, 22, 33, 39, 73; DAM NOV; SSC 3**
See also CA 85-88; 116; CANR 23, 61; MTCW

Cameron, Carey 1952- .... **CLC 59**
See also CA 135

Cameron, Peter 1959- .... **CLC 44**
See also CA 125; CANR 50

Campana, Dino 1885-1932 .... **TCLC 20**
See also CA 117; DLB 114

Campanella, Tommaso 1568-1639 ...... **LC 32**

Campbell, John W(ood, Jr.) 1910-1971 **C L C 32**
See also CA 21-22; 29-32R; CANR 34; CAP 2; DLB 8; MTCW

Campbell, Joseph 1904-1987 .... **CLC 69**
See also AAYA 3; BEST 89:2; CA 1-4R; 124; CANR 3, 28, 61; MTCW

Campbell, Maria 1940- .... CLC **85; DAC**
See also CA 102; CANR 54; NNAL

Campbell, (John) Ramsey 1946- CLC **42; SSC 19**
See also CA 57-60; CANR 7; INT CANR-7

Campbell, (Ignatius) Roy (Dunnachie) 1901-1957 .... **TCLC 5**
See also CA 104; 155; DLB 20

Campbell, Thomas 1777-1844 .... **NCLC 19**
See also DLB 93; 144

Campbell, Wilfred .... **TCLC 9**
See Campbell, William

Campbell, William 1858(?)-1918
See Campbell, Wilfred
See also CA 106; DLB 92

Campion, Jane .... **CLC 95**
See also CA 138

Campos, Alvaro de
See Pessoa, Fernando (Antonio Nogueira)

Camus, Albert 1913-1960 CLC **1, 2, 4, 9, 11, 14, 32, 63, 69; DA; DAB; DAC; DAM DRAM, MST, NOV; DC 2; SSC 9; WLC**
See also CA 89-92; DLB 72; MTCW

Canby, Vincent 1924- .... **CLC 13**
See also CA 81-84

Cancale
See Desnos, Robert

Canetti, Elias 1905-1994 CLC **3, 14, 25, 75, 86**
See also CA 21-24R; 146; CANR 23, 61; DLB 85, 124; MTCW

Canin, Ethan 1960- .... **CLC 55**
See also CA 131; 135

Cannon, Curt
See Hunter, Evan

Cape, Judith
See Page, P(atricia) K(athleen)

Capek, Karel 1890-1938 ... **TCLC 6, 37; DA; DAB; DAC; DAM DRAM, MST, NOV; DC 1; WLC**
See also CA 104; 140

Capote, Truman 1924-1984 CLC **1, 3, 8, 13, 19, 34, 38, 58; DA; DAB; DAC; DAM MST, NOV, POP; SSC 2; WLC**
See also CA 5-8R; 113; CANR 18, 62; CDALB 1941-1968; DLB 2; DLBY 80, 84; MTCW; SATA 91

Capra, Frank 1897-1991 .... **CLC 16**
See also CA 61-64; 135

Caputo, Philip 1941- .... **CLC 32**
See also CA 73-76; CANR 40

Caragiale, Ion Luca 1852-1912 ...... **TCLC 76**
See also CA 157

Card, Orson Scott 1951- **CLC 44, 47, 50; DAM POP**
See also AAYA 11; CA 102; CANR 27, 47; INT CANR-27; MTCW; SATA 83

Cardenal, Ernesto 1925- .... **CLC 31; DAM MULT, POET; HLC**
See also CA 49-52; CANR 2, 32; HW; MTCW

Cardozo, Benjamin N(athan) 1870-1938 **TCLC 65**
See also CA 117

Carducci, Giosue 1835-1907 .... **TCLC 32**

Carew, Thomas 1595(?)-1640 .... **LC 13**
See also DLB 126

Carey, Ernestine Gilbreth 1908- ...... **CLC 17**
See also CA 5-8R; SATA 2

Carey, Peter 1943- .... **CLC 40, 55, 96**
See also CA 123; 127; CANR 53; INT 127; MTCW; SATA 94

Carleton, William 1794-1869 .... **NCLC 3**
See also DLB 159

Carlisle, Henry (Coffin) 1926- .... **CLC 33**
See also CA 13-16R; CANR 15

Carlsen, Chris
See Holdstock, Robert P.

Carlson, Ron(ald F.) 1947- .... **CLC 54**
See also CA 105; CANR 27

Carlyle, Thomas 1795-1881 .. **NCLC 22; DA; DAB; DAC; DAM MST**
See also CDBLB 1789-1832; DLB 55; 144

Carman, (William) Bliss 1861-1929 **TCLC 7; DAC**
See also CA 104; 152; DLB 92

Carnegie, Dale 1888-1955 .... **TCLC 53**

Carossa, Hans 1878-1956 .... **TCLC 48**
See also DLB 66

Carpenter, Don(ald Richard) 1931-1995 **C L C 41**
See also CA 45-48; 149; CANR 1

Carpentier (y Valmont), Alejo 1904-1980 **CLC 8, 11, 38; DAM MULT; HLC**
See also CA 65-68; 97-100; CANR 11; DLB 113; HW

Carr, Caleb 1955(?)- .... **CLC 86**
See also CA 147

Carr, Emily 1871-1945 .... **TCLC 32**
See also CA 159; DLB 68

Carr, John Dickson 1906-1977 .... **CLC 3**
See also Fairbairn, Roger
See also CA 49-52; 69-72; CANR 3, 33, 60; MTCW

Carr, Philippa
See Hibbert, Eleanor Alice Burford

Carr, Virginia Spencer 1929- .... **CLC 34**
See also CA 61-64; DLB 111

Carrere, Emmanuel 1957- .... **CLC 89**

Carrier, Roch 1937- **CLC 13, 78; DAC; DAM MST**
See also CA 130; CANR 61; DLB 53

Carroll, James P. 1943(?)- .... **CLC 38**
See also CA 81-84

Carroll, Jim 1951- .... **CLC 35**
See also AAYA 17; CA 45-48; CANR 42

Carroll, Lewis ...... **NCLC 2, 53; PC 18; WLC**
See also Dodgson, Charles Lutwidge
See also CDBLB 1832-1890; CLR 2, 18; DLB 18, 163, 178; JRDA

Carroll, Paul Vincent 1900-1968 ..... **CLC 10**
See also CA 9-12R; 25-28R; DLB 10

Carruth, Hayden 1921- **CLC 4, 7, 10, 18, 84; PC 10**
See also CA 9-12R; CANR 4, 38, 59; DLB 5,

165; INT CANR-4; MTCW; SATA 47

Carson, Rachel Louise 1907-1964 .. **CLC 71; DAM POP**
See also CA 77-80; CANR 35; MTCW; SATA 23

Carter, Angela (Olive) 1940-1992 **CLC 5, 41, 76; SSC 13**
See also CA 53-56; 136; CANR 12, 36, 61; DLB 14; MTCW; SATA 66; SATA-Obit 70

Carter, Nick
See Smith, Martin Cruz

Carver, Raymond 1938-1988 **CLC 22, 36, 53, 55; DAM NOV; SSC 8**
See also CA 33-36R; 126; CANR 17, 34, 61; DLB 130; DLBY 84, 88; MTCW

Cary, Elizabeth, Lady Falkland 1585-1639 **LC 30**

Cary, (Arthur) Joyce (Lunel) 1888-1957 **TCLC 1, 29**
See also CA 104; CDBLB 1914-1945; DLB 15, 100

Casanova de Seingalt, Giovanni Jacopo 1725-1798 .... **LC 13**

Casares, Adolfo Bioy
See Bioy Casares, Adolfo

Casely-Hayford, J(oseph) E(phraim) 1866-1930 **TCLC 24; BLC; DAM MULT**
See also BW 2; CA 123; 152

Casey, John (Dudley) 1939- .... **CLC 59**
See also BEST 90:2; CA 69-72; CANR 23

Casey, Michael 1947- .... **CLC 2**
See also CA 65-68; DLB 5

Casey, Patrick
See Thurman, Wallace (Henry)

Casey, Warren (Peter) 1935-1988 ..... **CLC 12**
See also CA 101; 127; INT 101

Casona, Alejandro .... **CLC 49**
See also Alvarez, Alejandro Rodriguez

Cassavetes, John 1929-1989 .... **CLC 20**
See also CA 85-88; 127

Cassian, Nina 1924- .... **PC 17**

Cassill, R(onald) V(erlin) 1919- ... **CLC 4, 23**
See also CA 9-12R; CAAS 1; CANR 7, 45; DLB 6

Cassirer, Ernst 1874-1945 .... **TCLC 61**
See also CA 157

Cassity, (Allen) Turner 1929- .... **CLC 6, 42**
See also CA 17-20R; CAAS 8; CANR 11; DLB 105

Castaneda, Carlos 1931(?)- .... **CLC 12**
See also CA 25-28R; CANR 32; HW; MTCW

Castedo, Elena 1937- .... **CLC 65**
See also CA 132

Castedo-Ellerman, Elena
See Castedo, Elena

Castellanos, Rosario 1925-1974 **CLC 66; DAM MULT; HLC**
See also CA 131; 53-56; CANR 58; DLB 113; HW

Castelvetro, Lodovico 1505-1571 .... **LC 12**

Castiglione, Baldassare 1478-1529 ..... **LC 12**

Castle, Robert
See Hamilton, Edmond

Castro, Guillen de 1569-1631 .... **LC 19**

Castro, Rosalia de 1837-1885 **NCLC 3; DAM MULT**

Cather, Willa
See Cather, Willa Sibert

Cather, Willa Sibert 1873-1947 **TCLC 1, 11, 31; DA; DAB; DAC; DAM MST, NOV; SSC 2; WLC**
See also CA 104; 128; CDALB 1865-1917; DLB 9, 54, 78; DLBD 1; MTCW; SATA 30

Cato, Marcus Porcius 234B.C.-149B.C. **CMLC 21**

Catton, (Charles) Bruce 1899-1978 .. **CLC 35**
See also AITN 1; CA 5-8R; 81-84; CANR 7; DLB 17; SATA 2; SATA-Obit 24

Catullus c. 84B.C.-c. 54B.C. .... **CMLC 18**

Cauldwell, Frank
See King, Francis (Henry)

Caunitz, William J. 1933-1996 .... **CLC 34**
See also BEST 89:3; CA 125; 130; 152; INT 130

Causley, Charles (Stanley) 1917- .... **CLC 7**
See also CA 9-12R; CANR 5, 35; CLR 30; DLB 27; MTCW; SATA 3, 66

Caute, David 1936- .... **CLC 29; DAM NOV**
See also CA 1-4R; CAAS 4; CANR 1, 33; DLB 14

Cavafy, C(onstantine) P(eter) 1863-1933 **TCLC 2, 7; DAM POET**
See also Kavafis, Konstantinos Petrou
See also CA 148

Cavallo, Evelyn
See Spark, Muriel (Sarah)

Cavanna, Betty .... **CLC 12**
See also Harrison, Elizabeth Cavanna
See also JRDA; MAICYA; SAAS 4; SATA 1, 30

Cavendish, Margaret Lucas 1623-1673 **LC 30**
See also DLB 131

Caxton, William 1421(?)-1491(?) .... **LC 17**
See also DLB 170

Cayrol, Jean 1911- .... **CLC 11**
See also CA 89-92; DLB 83

Cela, Camilo Jose 1916- **CLC 4, 13, 59; DAM MULT; HLC**
See also BEST 90:2; CA 21-24R; CAAS 10; CANR 21, 32; DLBY 89; HW; MTCW

Celan, Paul .... **CLC 10, 19, 53, 82; PC 10**
See also Antschel, Paul
See also DLB 69

Celine, Louis-Ferdinand **CLC 1, 3, 4, 7, 9, 15, 47**
See also Destouches, Louis-Ferdinand
See also DLB 72

Cellini, Benvenuto 1500-1571 .... **LC 7**

Cendrars, Blaise 1887-1961 ..... **CLC 18, 106**
See also Sauser-Hall, Frederic

Cernuda (y Bidon), Luis 1902-1963 **CLC 54; DAM POET**
See also CA 131; 89-92; DLB 134; HW

Cervantes (Saavedra), Miguel de 1547-1616 **LC 6, 23; DA; DAB; DAC; DAM MST, NOV; SSC 12; WLC**

Cesaire, Aime (Fernand) 1913- . **CLC 19, 32; BLC; DAM MULT, POET**
See also BW 2; CA 65-68; CANR 24, 43; MTCW

Chabon, Michael 1963- .... **CLC 55**
See also CA 139; CANR 57

Chabrol, Claude 1930- .... **CLC 16**
See also CA 110

Challans, Mary 1905-1983
See Renault, Mary
See also CA 81-84; 111; SATA 23; SATA-Obit 36

Challis, George
See Faust, Frederick (Schiller)

Chambers, Aidan 1934- .... **CLC 35**
See also CA 25-28R; CANR 12, 31, 58; JRDA; MAICYA; SAAS 12; SATA 1, 69

Chambers, James 1948-
See Cliff, Jimmy
See also CA 124

Chambers, Jessie
See Lawrence, D(avid) H(erbert Richards)
Chambers, Robert W. 1865-1933 ... **TCLC 41**
Chandler, Raymond (Thornton) 1888-1959
   TCLC 1, 7; SSC 23
See also CA 104; 129; CANR 60; CDALB
1929-1941; DLBD 6; MTCW
Chang, Eileen 1921- .... **SSC 28**
Chang, Jung 1952- .... **CLC 71**
See also CA 142
Channing, William Ellery 1780-1842 . **N C L C**
17
See also DLB 1, 59
Chaplin, Charles Spencer 1889-1977 **CLC 16**
See also Chaplin, Charlie
See also CA 81-84; 73-76
Chaplin, Charlie
See Chaplin, Charles Spencer
See also DLB 44
Chapman, George 1559(?)-1634 **LC 22; DAM**
   DRAM
See also DLB 62, 121
Chapman, Graham 1941-1989 .... **CLC 21**
See also Monty Python
See also CA 116; 129; CANR 35
Chapman, John Jay 1862-1933 .... **TCLC 7**
See also CA 104
Chapman, Lee
See Bradley, Marion Zimmer
Chapman, Walker
See Silverberg, Robert
Chappell, Fred (Davis) 1936- ..... **CLC 40, 78**
See also CA 5-8R; CAAS 4; CANR 8, 33; DLB
6, 105
Char, Rene(-Emile) 1907-1988 **CLC 9, 11, 14,**
   55; DAM POET
See also CA 13-16R; 124; CANR 32; MTCW
Charby, Jay
See Ellison, Harlan (Jay)
Chardin, Pierre Teilhard de
See Teilhard de Chardin, (Marie Joseph) Pierre
Charles I 1600-1649 .... **LC 13**
Charriere, Isabelle de 1740-1805 ... **NCLC 66**
Charyn, Jerome 1937- .... **CLC 5, 8, 18**
See also CA 5-8R; CAAS 1; CANR 7, 61;
DLBY 83; MTCW
Chase, Mary (Coyle) 1907-1981 .... **DC 1**
See also CA 77-80; 105; SATA 17; SATA-Obit
29
Chase, Mary Ellen 1887-1973 .... **CLC 2**
See also CA 13-16; 41-44R; CAP 1; SATA 10
Chase, Nicholas
See Hyde, Anthony
Chateaubriand, Francois Rene de 1768-1848
   NCLC 3
See also DLB 119
Chatterje, Sarat Chandra 1876-1936(?)
See Chatterji, Saratchandra
See also CA 109
Chatterji, Bankim Chandra 1838-1894 **NCLC**
19
Chatterji, Saratchandra .... **TCLC 13**
See also Chatterje, Sarat Chandra
Chatterton, Thomas 1752-1770 . **LC 3; DAM**
   POET
See also DLB 109
Chatwin, (Charles) Bruce 1940-1989 **CLC 28,**
   57, 59; DAM POP
See also AAYA 4; BEST 90:1; CA 85-88; 127
Chaucer, Daniel
See Ford, Ford Madox
Chaucer, Geoffrey 1340(?)-1400 **LC 17; DA;**
   DAB; DAC; DAM MST, POET; PC 19;

WLCS
See also CDBLB Before 1660; DLB 146
Chaviaras, Strates 1935-
See Haviaras, Stratis
See also CA 105
Chayefsky, Paddy .... **CLC 23**
See also Chayefsky, Sidney
See also DLB 7, 44; DLBY 81
Chayefsky, Sidney 1923-1981
See Chayefsky, Paddy
See also CA 9-12R; 104; CANR 18; DAM
DRAM
Chedid, Andree 1920- .... **CLC 47**
See also CA 145
Cheever, John 1912-1982 **CLC 3, 7, 8, 11, 15,**
   25, 64; DA; DAB; DAC; DAM MST, NOV,
   POP; SSC 1; WLC
See also CA 5-8R; 106; CABS 1; CANR 5, 27;
CDALB 1941-1968; DLB 2, 102; DLBY 80,
82; INT CANR-5; MTCW
Cheever, Susan 1943- .... **CLC 18, 48**
See also CA 103; CANR 27, 51; DLBY 82; INT
CANR-27
Chekhonte, Antosha
See Chekhov, Anton (Pavlovich)
Chekhov, Anton (Pavlovich) 1860-1904 **TCLC**
   3, 10, 31, 55; DA; DAB; DAC; DAM
   DRAM, MST; SSC 2, 28; WLC
See also CA 104; 124; SATA 90
Chernyshevsky, Nikolay Gavrilovich 1828-1889
   NCLC 1
Cherry, Carolyn Janice 1942-
See Cherryh, C. J.
See also CA 65-68; CANR 10
Cherryh, C. J. .... **CLC 35**
See also Cherry, Carolyn Janice
See also DLBY 80; SATA 93
Chesnutt, Charles W(addell) 1858-1932
   TCLC 5, 39; BLC; DAM MULT; SSC 7
See also BW 1; CA 106; 125; DLB 12, 50, 78;
MTCW
Chester, Alfred 1929(?)-1971 .... **CLC 49**
See also CA 33-36R; DLB 130
Chesterton, G(ilbert) K(eith) 1874-1936
   TCLC 1, 6, 64; DAM NOV, POET; SSC 1
See also CA 104; 132; CDBLB 1914-1945;
DLB 10, 19, 34, 70, 98, 149, 178; MTCW;
SATA 27
Chiang Pin-chin 1904-1986
See Ding Ling
See also CA 118
Ch'ien Chung-shu 1910- .... **CLC 22**
See also CA 130; MTCW
Child, L. Maria
See Child, Lydia Maria
Child, Lydia Maria 1802-1880 .... **NCLC 6**
See also DLB 1, 74; SATA 67
Child, Mrs.
See Child, Lydia Maria
Child, Philip 1898-1978 .... **CLC 19, 68**
See also CA 13-14; CAP 1; SATA 47
Childers, (Robert) Erskine 1870-1922 **T C L C**
65
See also CA 113; 153; DLB 70
Childress, Alice 1920-1994 **CLC 12, 15, 86, 96;**
   BLC; DAM DRAM, MULT, NOV; DC 4
See also AAYA 8; BW 2; CA 45-48; 146; CANR
3, 27, 50; CLR 14; DLB 7, 38; JRDA;
MAICYA; MTCW; SATA 7, 48, 81
Chin, Frank (Chew, Jr.) 1940- .... **DC 7**
See also CA 33-36R; DAM MULT
Chislett, (Margaret) Anne 1943- .... **CLC 34**
See also CA 151

Chitty, Thomas Willes 1926- .... **CLC 11**
See also Hinde, Thomas
See also CA 5-8R
Chivers, Thomas Holley 1809-1858 **NCLC 49**
See also DLB 3
Chomette, Rene Lucien 1898-1981
See Clair, Rene
See also CA 103
Chopin, Kate TCLC 5, 14; DA; DAB; SSC 8;
   WLCS
See also Chopin, Katherine
See also CDALB 1865-1917; DLB 12, 78
Chopin, Katherine 1851-1904
See Chopin, Kate
See also CA 104; 122; DAC; DAM MST, NOV
Chretien de Troyes c. 12th cent. - .. **CMLC 10**
Christie
See Ichikawa, Kon
Christie, Agatha (Mary Clarissa) 1890-1976
   CLC 1, 6, 8, 12, 39, 48; DAB; DAC; DAM
   NOV
See also AAYA 9; AITN 1, 2; CA 17-20R; 61-
64; CANR 10, 37; CDBLB 1914-1945; DLB
13, 77; MTCW; SATA 36
Christie, (Ann) Philippa
See Pearce, Philippa
See also CA 5-8R; CANR 4
Christine de Pizan 1365(?)-1431(?) ...... **LC 9**
Chubb, Elmer
See Masters, Edgar Lee
Chulkov, Mikhail Dmitrievich 1743-1792 **LC 2**
See also DLB 150
Churchill, Caryl 1938- ..... **CLC 31, 55; DC 5**
See also CA 102; CANR 22, 46; DLB 13;
MTCW
Churchill, Charles 1731-1764 .... **LC 3**
See also DLB 109
Chute, Carolyn 1947- .... **CLC 39**
See also CA 123
Ciardi, John (Anthony) 1916-1986 . **CLC 10,**
   40, 44; DAM POET
See also CA 5-8R; 118; CAAS 2; CANR 5, 33;
CLR 19; DLB 5; DLBY 86; INT CANR-5;
MAICYA; MTCW; SATA 1, 65; SATA-Obit
46
Cicero, Marcus Tullius 106B.C.-43B.C.
   CMLC 3
Cimino, Michael 1943- .... **CLC 16**
See also CA 105
Cioran, E(mil) M. 1911-1995 .... **CLC 64**
See also CA 25-28R; 149
Cisneros, Sandra 1954- **CLC 69; DAM MULT;**
   HLC
See also AAYA 9; CA 131; DLB 122, 152; HW
Cixous, Helene 1937- .... **CLC 92**
See also CA 126; CANR 55; DLB 83; MTCW
Clair, Rene .... **CLC 20**
See also Chomette, Rene Lucien
Clampitt, Amy 1920-1994 ..... **CLC 32; PC 19**
See also CA 110; 146; CANR 29; DLB 105
Clancy, Thomas L., Jr. 1947-
See Clancy, Tom
See also CA 125; 131; CANR 62; INT 131;
MTCW
Clancy, Tom .... **CLC 45; DAM NOV, POP**
See also Clancy, Thomas L., Jr.
See also AAYA 9; BEST 89:1, 90:1
Clare, John 1793-1864 **NCLC 9; DAB; DAM**
   POET
See also DLB 55, 96
Clarin
See Alas (y Urena), Leopoldo (Enrique Garcia)
Clark, Al C.

See Goines, Donald

Clark, (Robert) Brian 1932- .... **CLC 29**
See also CA 41-44R

Clark, Curt
See Westlake, Donald E(dwin)

Clark, Eleanor 1913-1996 .... **CLC 5, 19**
See also CA 9-12R; 151; CANR 41; DLB 6

Clark, J. P.
See Clark, John Pepper
See also DLB 117

Clark, John Pepper 1935-...... **CLC 38; BLC; DAM DRAM, MULT; DC 5**
See also Clark, J. P.
See also BW 1; CA 65-68; CANR 16

Clark, M. R.
See Clark, Mavis Thorpe

Clark, Mavis Thorpe 1909- .... **CLC 12**
See also CA 57-60; CANR 8, 37; CLR 30; MAICYA; SAAS 5; SATA 8, 74

Clark, Walter Van Tilburg 1909-1971**CLC 28**
See also CA 9-12R; 33-36R; DLB 9; SATA 8

Clarke, Arthur C(harles) 1917-**CLC 1, 4, 13, 18, 35; DAM POP; SSC 3**
See also AAYA 4; CA 1-4R; CANR 2, 28, 55; JRDA; MAICYA; MTCW; SATA 13, 70

Clarke, Austin 1896-1974 .... **CLC 6, 9; DAM POET**
See also CA 29-32; 49-52; CAP 2; DLB 10, 20

Clarke, Austin C(hesterfield) 1934-**CLC 8, 53; BLC; DAC; DAM MULT**
See also BW 1; CA 25-28R; CAAS 16; CANR 14, 32; DLB 53, 125

Clarke, Gillian 1937-....................... **CLC 61**
See also CA 106; DLB 40

Clarke, Marcus (Andrew Hislop) 1846-1881 **NCLC 19**

Clarke, Shirley 1925- .... **CLC 16**

Clash, The
See Headon, (Nicky) Topper; Jones, Mick; Simonon, Paul; Strummer, Joe

Claudel, Paul (Louis Charles Marie) 1868-1955 **TCLC 2, 10**
See also CA 104

Clavell, James (duMaresq) 1925-1994**CLC 6, 25, 87; DAM NOV, POP**
See also CA 25-28R; 146; CANR 26, 48; MTCW

Cleaver, (Leroy) Eldridge 1935- ..... **CLC 30; BLC; DAM MULT**
See also BW 1; CA 21-24R; CANR 16

Cleese, John (Marwood) 1939- .... **CLC 21**
See also Monty Python
See also CA 112; 116; CANR 35; MTCW

Cleishbotham, Jebediah
See Scott, Walter

Cleland, John 1710-1789 .... **LC 2**
See also DLB 39

Clemens, Samuel Langhorne 1835-1910
See Twain, Mark
See also CA 104; 135; CDALB 1865-1917; DA; DAB; DAC; DAM MST, NOV; DLB 11, 12, 23, 64, 74, 186; JRDA; MAICYA; YABC 2

Cleophil
See Congreve, William

Clerihew, E.
See Bentley, E(dmund) C(lerihew)

Clerk, N. W.
See Lewis, C(live) S(taples)

Cliff, Jimmy .... **CLC 21**
See also Chambers, James

Clifton, (Thelma) Lucille 1936- **CLC 19, 66; BLC; DAM MULT, POET; PC 17**
See also BW 2; CA 49-52; CANR 2, 24, 42;

CLR 5; DLB 5, 41; MAICYA; MTCW; SATA 20, 69

Clinton, Dirk
See Silverberg, Robert

Clough, Arthur Hugh 1819-1861 ... **NCLC 27**
See also DLB 32

Clutha, Janet Paterson Frame 1924-
See Frame, Janet
See also CA 1-4R; CANR 2, 36; MTCW

Clyne, Terence
See Blatty, William Peter

Cobalt, Martin
See Mayne, William (James Carter)

Cobbett, William 1763-1835 .... **NCLC 49**
See also DLB 43, 107, 158

Coburn, D(onald) L(ee) 1938- .... **CLC 10**
See also CA 89-92

Cocteau, Jean (Maurice Eugene Clement) 1889-1963**CLC 1, 8, 15, 16, 43; DA; DAB; DAC; DAM DRAM, MST, NOV; WLC**
See also CA 25-28; CANR 40; CAP 2; DLB 65; MTCW

Codrescu, Andrei 1946-**CLC 46; DAM POET**
See also CA 33-36R; CAAS 19; CANR 13, 34, 53

Coe, Max
See Bourne, Randolph S(illiman)

Coe, Tucker
See Westlake, Donald E(dwin)

Coetzee, J(ohn) M(ichael) 1940- **CLC 23, 33, 66; DAM NOV**
See also CA 77-80; CANR 41, 54; MTCW

Coffey, Brian
See Koontz, Dean R(ay)

Cohan, George M(ichael) 1878-1942**TCLC 60**
See also CA 157

Cohen, Arthur A(llen) 1928-1986 **CLC 7, 31**
See also CA 1-4R; 120; CANR 1, 17, 42; DLB 28

Cohen, Leonard (Norman) 1934- **CLC 3, 38; DAC; DAM MST**
See also CA 21-24R; CANR 14; DLB 53; MTCW

Cohen, Matt 1942- .... **CLC 19; DAC**
See also CA 61-64; CAAS 18; CANR 40; DLB 53

Cohen-Solal, Annie 19(?)- .... **CLC 50**

Colegate, Isabel 1931- .... **CLC 36**
See also CA 17-20R; CANR 8, 22; DLB 14; INT CANR-22; MTCW

Coleman, Emmett
See Reed, Ishmael

Coleridge, M. E.
See Coleridge, Mary E(lizabeth)

Coleridge, Mary E(lizabeth) 1861-1907**TCLC 73**
See also CA 116; DLB 19, 98

Coleridge, Samuel Taylor 1772-1834**NCLC 9, 54; DA; DAB; DAC; DAM MST, POET; PC 11; WLC**
See also CDBLB 1789-1832; DLB 93, 107

Coleridge, Sara 1802-1852 .... **NCLC 31**

Coles, Don 1928- .... **CLC 46**
See also CA 115; CANR 38

Colette, (Sidonie-Gabrielle) 1873-1954**T C L C 1, 5, 16; DAM NOV; SSC 10**
See also CA 104; 131; DLB 65; MTCW

Collett, (Jacobine) Camilla (Wergeland) 1813-1895 .... **NCLC 22**

Collier, Christopher 1930- .... **CLC 30**
See also AAYA 13; CA 33-36R; CANR 13, 33; JRDA; MAICYA; SATA 16, 70

Collier, James L(incoln) 1928-**CLC 30; DAM POP**
See also AAYA 13; CA 9-12R; CANR 4, 33, 60; CLR 3; JRDA; MAICYA; SAAS 21; SATA 8, 70

Collier, Jeremy 1650-1726 .... **LC 6**

Collier, John 1901-1980 .... **SSC 19**
See also CA 65-68; 97-100; CANR 10; DLB 77

Collingwood, R(obin) G(eorge) 1889(?)-1943 **TCLC 67**
See also CA 117; 155

Collins, Hunt
See Hunter, Evan

Collins, Linda 1931- .... **CLC 44**
See also CA 125

Collins, (William) Wilkie 1824-1889**NCLC 1, 18**
See also CDBLB 1832-1890; DLB 18, 70, 159

Collins, William 1721-1759 . **LC 4, 40; DAM POET**
See also DLB 109

Collodi, Carlo 1826-1890 .... **NCLC 54**
See also Lorenzini, Carlo
See also CLR 5

Colman, George
See Glassco, John

Colt, Winchester Remington
See Hubbard, L(afayette) Ron(ald)

Colter, Cyrus 1910- .... **CLC 58**
See also BW 1; CA 65-68; CANR 10; DLB 33

Colton, James
See Hansen, Joseph

Colum, Padraic 1881-1972 .... **CLC 28**
See also CA 73-76; 33-36R; CANR 35; CLR 36; MAICYA; MTCW; SATA 15

Colvin, James
See Moorcock, Michael (John)

Colwin, Laurie (E.) 1944-1992**CLC 5, 13, 23, 84**
See also CA 89-92; 139; CANR 20, 46; DLBY 80; MTCW

Comfort, Alex(ander) 1920-**CLC 7; DAM POP**
See also CA 1-4R; CANR 1, 45

Comfort, Montgomery
See Campbell, (John) Ramsey

Compton-Burnett, I(vy) 1884(?)-1969**CLC 1, 3, 10, 15, 34; DAM NOV**
See also CA 1-4R; 25-28R; CANR 4; DLB 36; MTCW

Comstock, Anthony 1844-1915 ...... **TCLC 13**
See also CA 110

Comte, Auguste 1798-1857 .... **NCLC 54**

Conan Doyle, Arthur
See Doyle, Arthur Conan

Conde, Maryse 1937- ...... **CLC 52, 92; DAM MULT**
See also Boucolon, Maryse
See also BW 2

Condillac, Etienne Bonnot de 1714-1780 **L C 26**

Condon, Richard (Thomas) 1915-1996**CLC 4, 6, 8, 10, 45, 100; DAM NOV**
See also BEST 90:3; CA 1-4R; 151; CAAS 1; CANR 2, 23; INT CANR-23; MTCW

Confucius 551B.C.-479B.C.. **CMLC 19; DA; DAB; DAC; DAM MST; WLCS**

Congreve, William 1670-1729 **LC 5, 21; DA; DAB; DAC; DAM DRAM, MST, POET; DC 2; WLC**
See also CDBLB 1660-1789; DLB 39, 84

Connell, Evan S(helby), Jr. 1924-**CLC 4, 6, 45; DAM NOV**
See also AAYA 7; CA 1-4R; CAAS 2; CANR

2, 39; DLB 2; DLBY 81; MTCW

Connelly, Marc(us Cook) 1890-1980 .. **CLC 7**
See also CA 85-88; 102; CANR 30; DLB 7;
DLBY 80; SATA-Obit 25

Connor, Ralph .... **TCLC 31**
See also Gordon, Charles William
See also DLB 92

Conrad, Joseph 1857-1924 **TCLC 1, 6, 13, 25,
43, 57; DA; DAB; DAC; DAM MST, NOV;
SSC 9; WLC**
See also CA 104; 131; CANR 60; CDBLB
1890-1914; DLB 10, 34, 98, 156; MTCW;
SATA 27

Conrad, Robert Arnold
See Hart, Moss

Conroy, Donald Pat(rick) 1945- **CLC 30, 74;
DAM NOV, POP**
See also AAYA 8; AITN 1; CA 85-88; CANR
24, 53; DLB 6; MTCW

Constant (de Rebecque), (Henri) Benjamin
1767-1830 .... **NCLC 6**
See also DLB 119

Conybeare, Charles Augustus
See Eliot, T(homas) S(tearns)

Cook, Michael 1933- .... **CLC 58**
See also CA 93-96; DLB 53

Cook, Robin 1940- .... **CLC 14; DAM POP**
See also BEST 90:2; CA 108; 111; CANR 41;
INT 111

Cook, Roy
See Silverberg, Robert

Cooke, Elizabeth 1948- .... **CLC 55**
See also CA 129

Cooke, John Esten 1830-1886 .... **NCLC 5**
See also DLB 3

Cooke, John Estes
See Baum, L(yman) Frank

Cooke, M. E.
See Creasey, John

Cooke, Margaret
See Creasey, John

Cook-Lynn, Elizabeth 1930-.. **CLC 93; DAM
MULT**
See also CA 133; DLB 175; NNAL

Cooney, Ray .... **CLC 62**

Cooper, Douglas 1960- .... **CLC 86**

Cooper, Henry St. John
See Creasey, John

Cooper, J(oan) California .... **CLC 56; DAM
MULT**
See also AAYA 12; BW 1; CA 125; CANR 55

Cooper, James Fenimore 1789-1851 **NCLC 1,
27, 54**
See also AAYA 22; CDALB 1640-1865; DLB
3; SATA 19

Coover, Robert (Lowell) 1932- **CLC 3, 7, 15,
32, 46, 87; DAM NOV; SSC 15**
See also CA 45-48; CANR 3, 37, 58; DLB 2;
DLBY 81; MTCW

Copeland, Stewart (Armstrong) 1952-**CLC 26**

Coppard, A(lfred) E(dgar) 1878-1957 **TCLC
5; SSC 21**
See also CA 114; DLB 162; YABC 1

Coppee, Francois 1842-1908 .... **TCLC 25**

Coppola, Francis Ford 1939- .... **CLC 16**
See also CA 77-80; CANR 40; DLB 44

Corbiere, Tristan 1845-1875 .... **NCLC 43**

Corcoran, Barbara 1911- .... **CLC 17**
See also AAYA 14; CA 21-24R; CAAS 2;
CANR 11, 28, 48; DLB 52; JRDA; SAAS
20; SATA 3, 77

Cordelier, Maurice
See Giraudoux, (Hippolyte) Jean

Corelli, Marie 1855-1924 .... **TCLC 51**
See also Mackay, Mary
See also DLB 34, 156

Corman, Cid .... **CLC 9**
See also Corman, Sidney
See also CAAS 2; DLB 5

Corman, Sidney 1924-
See Corman, Cid
See also CA 85-88; CANR 44; DAM POET

Cormier, Robert (Edmund) 1925-**CLC 12, 30;
DA; DAB; DAC; DAM MST, NOV**
See also AAYA 3, 19; CA 1-4R; CANR 5, 23;
CDALB 1968-1988; CLR 12; DLB 52; INT
CANR-23; JRDA; MAICYA; MTCW; SATA
10, 45, 83

Corn, Alfred (DeWitt III) 1943- .... **CLC 33**
See also CA 104; CAAS 25; CANR 44; DLB
120; DLBY 80

Corneille, Pierre 1606-1684 .... **LC 28; DAB;
DAM MST**

Cornwell, David (John Moore) 1931-**CLC 9,
15; DAM POP**
See also le Carre, John
See also CA 5-8R; CANR 13, 33, 59; MTCW

Corso, (Nunzio) Gregory 1930- .... **CLC 1, 11**
See also CA 5-8R; CANR 41; DLB 5, 16;
MTCW

Cortazar, Julio 1914-1984**CLC 2, 3, 5, 10, 13,
15, 33, 34, 92; DAM MULT, NOV; HLC;
SSC 7**
See also CA 21-24R; CANR 12, 32; DLB 113;
HW; MTCW

Cortes, Hernan 1484-1547 .... **LC 31**

Corwin, Cecil
See Kornbluth, C(yril) M.

Cosic, Dobrica 1921- .... **CLC 14**
See also CA 122; 138; DLB 181

Costain, Thomas B(ertram) 1885-1965 . **C L C
30**
See also CA 5-8R; 25-28R; DLB 9

Costantini, Humberto 1924(?)-1987 . **CLC 49**
See also CA 131; 122; HW

Costello, Elvis 1955- .... **CLC 21**

Cotes, Cecil V.
See Duncan, Sara Jeannette

Cotter, Joseph Seamon Sr. 1861-1949 **T C L C
28; BLC; DAM MULT**
See also BW 1; CA 124; DLB 50

Couch, Arthur Thomas Quiller
See Quiller-Couch, Arthur Thomas

Coulton, James
See Hansen, Joseph

Couperus, Louis (Marie Anne) 1863-1923
TCLC 15
See also CA 115

Coupland, Douglas 1961-**CLC 85; DAC; DAM
POP**
See also CA 142; CANR 57

Court, Wesli
See Turco, Lewis (Putnam)

Courtenay, Bryce 1933- .... **CLC 59**
See also CA 138

Courtney, Robert
See Ellison, Harlan (Jay)

Cousteau, Jacques-Yves 1910-1997 .. **CLC 30**
See also CA 65-68; 159; CANR 15; MTCW;
SATA 38

Cowan, Peter (Walkinshaw) 1914- .... **SSC 28**
See also CA 21-24R; CANR 9, 25, 50

Coward, Noel (Peirce) 1899-1973**CLC 1, 9, 29,
51; DAM DRAM**
See also AITN 1; CA 17-18; 41-44R; CANR
35; CAP 2; CDBLB 1914-1945; DLB 10;

MTCW

Cowley, Malcolm 1898-1989 .... **CLC 39**
See also CA 5-8R; 128; CANR 3, 55; DLB 4,
48; DLBY 81, 89; MTCW

Cowper, William 1731-1800 . **NCLC 8; DAM
POET**
See also DLB 104, 109

Cox, William Trevor 1928- .... **CLC 9, 14, 71;
DAM NOV**
See also Trevor, William
See also CA 9-12R; CANR 4, 37, 55; DLB 14;
INT CANR-37; MTCW

Coyne, P. J.
See Masters, Hilary

Cozzens, James Gould 1903-1978**CLC 1, 4, 11,
92**
See also CA 9-12R; 81-84; CANR 19; CDALB
1941-1968; DLB 9; DLBD 2; DLBY 84;
MTCW

Crabbe, George 1754-1832 .... **NCLC 26**
See also DLB 93

Craddock, Charles Egbert
See Murfree, Mary Noailles

Craig, A. A.
See Anderson, Poul (William)

Craik, Dinah Maria (Mulock) 1826-1887
NCLC 38
See also DLB 35, 163; MAICYA; SATA 34

Cram, Ralph Adams 1863-1942 ..... **TCLC 45**
See also CA 160

Crane, (Harold) Hart 1899-1932 **TCLC 2, 5;
DA; DAB; DAC; DAM MST, POET; PC
3; WLC**
See also CA 104; 127; CDALB 1917-1929;
DLB 4, 48; MTCW

Crane, R(onald) S(almon) 1886-1967**CLC 27**
See also CA 85-88; DLB 63

Crane, Stephen (Townley) 1871-1900 **T C L C
11, 17, 32; DA; DAB; DAC; DAM MST,
NOV, POET; SSC 7; WLC**
See also AAYA 21; CA 109; 140; CDALB 1865-
1917; DLB 12, 54, 78; YABC 2

Crase, Douglas 1944- .... **CLC 58**
See also CA 106

Crashaw, Richard 1612(?)-1649 .... **LC 24**
See also DLB 126

Craven, Margaret 1901-1980 . **CLC 17; DAC**
See also CA 103

Crawford, F(rancis) Marion 1854-1909**TCLC
10**
See also CA 107; DLB 71

Crawford, Isabella Valancy 1850-1887**N C L C
12**
See also DLB 92

Crayon, Geoffrey
See Irving, Washington

Creasey, John 1908-1973 .... **CLC 11**
See also CA 5-8R; 41-44R; CANR 8, 59; DLB
77; MTCW

Crebillon, Claude Prosper Jolyot de (fils) 1707-
1777 .... **LC 28**

Credo
See Creasey, John

Credo, Alvaro J. de
See Prado (Calvo), Pedro

Creeley, Robert (White) 1926-**CLC 1, 2, 4, 8,
11, 15, 36, 78; DAM POET**
See also CA 1-4R; CAAS 10; CANR 23, 43;
DLB 5, 16, 169; MTCW

Crews, Harry (Eugene) 1935- **CLC 6, 23, 49**
See also AITN 1; CA 25-28R; CANR 20, 57;
DLB 6, 143; MTCW

Crichton, (John) Michael 1942-**CLC 2, 6, 54,**

90; DAM NOV, POP
See also AAYA 10; AITN 2; CA 25-28R; CANR 13, 40, 54; DLBY 81; INT CANR-13; JRDA; MTCW; SATA 9, 88

Crispin, Edmund .... **CLC 22**
See also Montgomery, (Robert) Bruce
See also DLB 87

Cristofer, Michael 1945(?)-....**CLC 28; DAM DRAM**
See also CA 110; 152; DLB 7

Croce, Benedetto 1866-1952 .... **TCLC 37**
See also CA 120; 155

Crockett, David 1786-1836 .... **NCLC 8**
See also DLB 3, 11

Crockett, Davy
See Crockett, David

Crofts, Freeman Wills 1879-1957 .. **TCLC 55**
See also CA 115; DLB 77

Croker, John Wilson 1780-1857 ..... **NCLC 10**
See also DLB 110

Crommelynck, Fernand 1885-1970 . **CLC 75**
See also CA 89-92

Cronin, A(rchibald) J(oseph) 1896-1981**C L C 32**
See also CA 1-4R; 102; CANR 5; SATA 47; SATA-Obit 25

Cross, Amanda
See Heilbrun, Carolyn G(old)

Crothers, Rachel 1878(?)-1958 ...... **TCLC 19**
See also CA 113; DLB 7

Croves, Hal
See Traven, B.

Crow Dog, Mary (Ellen) (?)- .... **CLC 93**
See also Brave Bird, Mary
See also CA 154

Crowfield, Christopher
See Stowe, Harriet (Elizabeth) Beecher

Crowley, Aleister .... **TCLC 7**
See also Crowley, Edward Alexander

Crowley, Edward Alexander 1875-1947
See Crowley, Aleister
See also CA 104

Crowley, John 1942- .... **CLC 57**
See also CA 61-64; CANR 43; DLBY 82; SATA 65

Crud
See Crumb, R(obert)

Crumarums
See Crumb, R(obert)

Crumb, R(obert) 1943- .... **CLC 17**
See also CA 106

Crumbum
See Crumb, R(obert)

Crumski
See Crumb, R(obert)

Crum the Bum
See Crumb, R(obert)

Crunk
See Crumb, R(obert)

Crustt
See Crumb, R(obert)

Cryer, Gretchen (Kiger) 1935- .... **CLC 21**
See also CA 114; 123

Csath, Geza 1887-1919 .... **TCLC 13**
See also CA 111

Cudlip, David 1933- .... **CLC 34**

Cullen, Countee 1903-1946**TCLC 4, 37; BLC; DA; DAC; DAM MST, MULT, POET; PC 20; WLCS**
See also BW 1; CA 108; 124; CDALB 1917-1929; DLB 4, 48, 51; MTCW; SATA 18

Cum, R.
See Crumb, R(obert)

Cummings, Bruce F(rederick) 1889-1919
See Barbellion, W. N. P.
See also CA 123

Cummings, E(dward) E(stlin) 1894-1962**CLC 1, 3, 8, 12, 15, 68; DA; DAB; DAC; DAM MST, POET; PC 5; WLC 2**
See also CA 73-76; CANR 31; CDALB 1929-1941; DLB 4, 48; MTCW

Cunha, Euclides (Rodrigues Pimenta) da 1866-1909 .... **TCLC 24**
See also CA 123

Cunningham, E. V.
See Fast, Howard (Melvin)

Cunningham, J(ames) V(incent) 1911-1985 **CLC 3, 31**
See also CA 1-4R; 115; CANR 1; DLB 5

Cunningham, Julia (Woolfolk) 1916-**CLC 12**
See also CA 9-12R; CANR 4, 19, 36; JRDA; MAICYA; SAAS 2; SATA 1, 26

Cunningham, Michael 1952- .... **CLC 34**
See also CA 136

Cunninghame Graham, R(obert) B(ontine) 1852-1936 .... **TCLC 19**
See also Graham, R(obert) B(ontine) Cunninghame
See also CA 119; DLB 98

Currie, Ellen 19(?)- .... **CLC 44**

Curtin, Philip
See Lowndes, Marie Adelaide (Belloc)

Curtis, Price
See Ellison, Harlan (Jay)

Cutrate, Joe
See Spiegelman, Art

Cynewulf c. 770-c. 840 .... **CMLC 23**

Czaczkes, Shmuel Yosef
See Agnon, S(hmuel) Y(osef Halevi)

Dabrowska, Maria (Szumska) 1889-1965**CLC 15**
See also CA 106

Dabydeen, David 1955- .... **CLC 34**
See also BW 1; CA 125; CANR 56

Dacey, Philip 1939-............................**CLC 51**
See also CA 37-40R; CAAS 17; CANR 14, 32; DLB 105

Dagerman, Stig (Halvard) 1923-1954 **T C L C 17**
See also CA 117; 155

Dahl, Roald 1916-1990**CLC 1, 6, 18, 79; DAB; DAC; DAM MST, NOV, POP**
See also AAYA 15; CA 1-4R; 133; CANR 6, 32, 37, 62; CLR 1, 7, 41; DLB 139; JRDA; MAICYA; MTCW; SATA 1, 26, 73; SATA-Obit 65

Dahlberg, Edward 1900-1977 .. **CLC 1, 7, 14**
See also CA 9-12R; 69-72; CANR 31, 62; DLB 48; MTCW

Daitch, Susan 1954- .... **CLC 103**
See also CA 161

Dale, Colin .... **TCLC 18**
See also Lawrence, T(homas) E(dward)

Dale, George E.
See Asimov, Isaac

Daly, Elizabeth 1878-1967 ....**CLC 52**
See also CA 23-24; 25-28R; CANR 60; CAP 2

Daly, Maureen 1921-........................**CLC 17**
See also AAYA 5; CANR 37; JRDA; MAICYA; SAAS 1; SATA 2

Damas, Leon-Gontran 1912-1978 .....**CLC 84**
See also BW 1; CA 125; 73-76

Dana, Richard Henry Sr. 1787-1879**NCLC 53**

Daniel, Samuel 1562(?)-1619 .... **LC 24**
See also DLB 62

Daniels, Brett

See Adler, Renata

Dannay, Frederic 1905-1982 . **CLC 11; DAM POP**
See also Queen, Ellery
See also CA 1-4R; 107; CANR 1, 39; DLB 137; MTCW

D'Annunzio, Gabriele 1863-1938**TCLC 6, 40**
See also CA 104; 155

Danois, N. le
See Gourmont, Remy (-Marie-Charles) de

d'Antibes, Germain
See Simenon, Georges (Jacques Christian)

Danticat, Edwidge 1969- ....**CLC 94**
See also CA 152

Danvers, Dennis 1947- ....**CLC 70**

Danziger, Paula 1944- ....**CLC 21**
See also AAYA 4; CA 112; 115; CANR 37; CLR 20; JRDA; MAICYA; SATA 36, 63; SATA-Brief 30

Da Ponte, Lorenzo 1749-1838 .... **NCLC 50**

Dario, Ruben 1867-1916 .... **TCLC 4; DAM MULT; HLC; PC 15**
See also CA 131; HW; MTCW

Darley, George 1795-1846 .... **NCLC 2**
See also DLB 96

Darwin, Charles 1809-1882 .... **NCLC 57**
See also DLB 57, 166

Daryush, Elizabeth 1887-1977 ..... **CLC 6, 19**
See also CA 49-52; CANR 3; DLB 20

Dashwood, Edmee Elizabeth Monica de la Pas-ture 1890-1943
See Delafield, E. M.
See also CA 119; 154

Daudet, (Louis Marie) Alphonse 1840-1897 **NCLC 1**
See also DLB 123

Daumal, Rene 1908-1944 .... **TCLC 14**
See also CA 114

Davenport, Guy (Mattison, Jr.) 1927-**CLC 6, 14, 38; SSC 16**
See also CA 33-36R; CANR 23; DLB 130

Davidson, Avram 1923-
See Queen, Ellery
See also CA 101; CANR 26; DLB 8

Davidson, Donald (Grady) 1893-1968**CLC 2, 13, 19**
See also CA 5-8R; 25-28R; CANR 4; DLB 45

Davidson, Hugh
See Hamilton, Edmond

Davidson, John 1857-1909 .... **TCLC 24**
See also CA 118; DLB 19

Davidson, Sara 1943- ....**CLC 9**
See also CA 81-84; CANR 44

Davie, Donald (Alfred) 1922-1995 **CLC 5, 8, 10, 31**
See also CA 1-4R; 149; CAAS 3; CANR 1, 44; DLB 27; MTCW

Davies, Ray(mond Douglas) 1944-....**CLC 21**
See also CA 116; 146

Davies, Rhys 1903-1978 .... **CLC 23**
See also CA 9-12R; 81-84; CANR 4; DLB 139

Davies, (William) Robertson 1913-1995 **C L C 2, 7, 13, 25, 42, 75, 91; DA; DAB; DAC; DAM MST, NOV, POP; WLC**
See also BEST 89:2; CA 33-36R; 150; CANR 17, 42; DLB 68; INT CANR-17; MTCW

Davies, W(illiam) H(enry) 1871-1940**TCLC 5**
See also CA 104; DLB 19, 174

Davies, Walter C.
See Kornbluth, C(yril) M.

Davis, Angela (Yvonne) 1944-**CLC 77; DAM MULT**
See also BW 2; CA 57-60; CANR 10

Davis, B. Lynch
See Bioy Casares, Adolfo; Borges, Jorge Luis

Davis, Gordon
See Hunt, E(verette) Howard, (Jr.)

Davis, Harold Lenoir 1896-1960 ..... **CLC 49**
See also CA 89-92; DLB 9

Davis, Rebecca (Blaine) Harding 1831-1910
TCLC 6
See also CA 104; DLB 74

Davis, Richard Harding 1864-1916 **TCLC 24**
See also CA 114; DLB 12, 23, 78, 79; DLBD 13

Davison, Frank Dalby 1893-1970 .... **CLC 15**
See also CA 116

Davison, Lawrence H.
See Lawrence, D(avid) H(erbert Richards)

Davison, Peter (Hubert) 1928- .... **CLC 28**
See also CA 9-12R; CAAS 4; CANR 3, 43; DLB 5

Davys, Mary 1674-1732 .... **LC 1**
See also DLB 39

Dawson, Fielding 1930- ....**CLC 6**
See also CA 85-88; DLB 130

Dawson, Peter
See Faust, Frederick (Schiller)

Day, Clarence (Shepard, Jr.) 1874-1935
TCLC 25
See also CA 108; DLB 11

Day, Thomas 1748-1789 .... **LC 1**
See also DLB 39; YABC 1

Day Lewis, C(ecil) 1904-1972 .. **CLC 1, 6, 10;
DAM POET; PC 11**
See also Blake, Nicholas
See also CA 13-16; 33-36R; CANR 34; CAP 1;
DLB 15, 20; MTCW

Dazai, Osamu .... **TCLC 11**
See also Tsushima, Shuji
See also DLB 182

de Andrade, Carlos Drummond
See Drummond de Andrade, Carlos

Deane, Norman
See Creasey, John

**de Beauvoir, Simone (Lucie Ernestine Marie
Bertrand)**
See Beauvoir, Simone (Lucie Ernestine Marie
Bertrand) de

de Beer, P.
See Bosman, Herman Charles

de Brissac, Malcolm
See Dickinson, Peter (Malcolm)

de Chardin, Pierre Teilhard
See Teilhard de Chardin, (Marie Joseph) Pierre

Dee, John 1527-1608 .... **LC 20**

Deer, Sandra 1940- .... **CLC 45**

De Ferrari, Gabriella 1941- .... **CLC 65**
See also CA 146

Defoe, Daniel 1660(?)-1731 **LC 1; DA; DAB;
DAC; DAM MST, NOV; WLC**
See also CDBLB 1660-1789; DLB 39, 95, 101;
JRDA; MAICYA; SATA 22

de Gourmont, Remy(-Marie-Charles)
See Gourmont, Remy (-Marie-Charles) de

de Hartog, Jan 1914- .... **CLC 19**
See also CA 1-4R; CANR 1

de Hostos, E. M.
See Hostos (y Bonilla), Eugenio Maria de

de Hostos, Eugenio M.
See Hostos (y Bonilla), Eugenio Maria de

Deighton, Len .... **CLC 4, 7, 22, 46**
See also Deighton, Leonard Cyril
See also AAYA 6; BEST 89:2; CDBLB 1960 to
Present; DLB 87

Deighton, Leonard Cyril 1929-
See Deighton, Len
See also CA 9-12R; CANR 19, 33; DAM NOV,
POP; MTCW

Dekker, Thomas 1572(?)-1632 .. **LC 22; DAM
DRAM**
See also CDBLB Before 1660; DLB 62, 172

Delafield, E. M. 1890-1943 .... **TCLC 61**
See also Dashwood, Edmee Elizabeth Monica
de la Pasture
See also DLB 34

de la Mare, Walter (John) 1873-1956 **TCLC 4,
53; DAB; DAC; DAM MST, POET; SSC
14; WLC**
See also CDBLB 1914-1945; CLR 23; DLB
162; SATA 16

Delaney, Franey
See O'Hara, John (Henry)

Delaney, Shelagh 1939- **CLC 29; DAM DRAM**
See also CA 17-20R; CANR 30; CDBLB 1960
to Present; DLB 13; MTCW

Delany, Mary (Granville Pendarves) 1700-1788
LC 12

Delany, Samuel R(ay, Jr.) 1942- **CLC 8, 14, 38;
BLC; DAM MULT**
See also BW 2; CA 81-84; CANR 27, 43; DLB
8, 33; MTCW

De La Ramee, (Marie) Louise 1839-1908
See Ouida
See also SATA 20

de la Roche, Mazo 1879-1961 .... **CLC 14**
See also CA 85-88; CANR 30; DLB 68; SATA
64

De La Salle, Innocent
See Hartmann, Sadakichi

Delbanco, Nicholas (Franklin) 1942- **CLC 6,
13**
See also CA 17-20R; CAAS 2; CANR 29, 55;
DLB 6

del Castillo, Michel 1933- .... **CLC 38**
See also CA 109

Deledda, Grazia (Cosima) 1875(?)-1936
TCLC 23
See also CA 123

Delibes, Miguel .... **CLC 8, 18**
See also Delibes Setien, Miguel

Delibes Setien, Miguel 1920-
See Delibes, Miguel
See also CA 45-48; CANR 1, 32; HW; MTCW

DeLillo, Don 1936- **CLC 8, 10, 13, 27, 39, 54,
76; DAM NOV, POP**
See also BEST 89:1; CA 81-84; CANR 21; DLB
6, 173; MTCW

de Lisser, H. G.
See De Lisser, H(erbert) G(eorge)
See also DLB 117

De Lisser, H(erbert) G(eorge) 1878-1944
TCLC 12
See also de Lisser, H. G.
See also BW 2; CA 109; 152

Deloria, Vine (Victor), Jr. 1933- ..... **CLC 21;
DAM MULT**
See also CA 53-56; CANR 5, 20, 48; DLB 175;
MTCW; NNAL; SATA 21

Del Vecchio, John M(ichael) 1947- ... **CLC 29**
See also CA 110; DLBD 9

de Man, Paul (Adolph Michel) 1919-1983
CLC 55
See also CA 128; 111; CANR 61; DLB 67;
MTCW

De Marinis, Rick 1934- .... **CLC 54**
See also CA 57-60; CAAS 24; CANR 9, 25, 50

Dembry, R. Emmet
See Murfree, Mary Noailles

Demby, William 1922- . **CLC 53; BLC; DAM
MULT**
See also BW 1; CA 81-84; DLB 33

de Menton, Francisco
See Chin, Frank (Chew, Jr.)

Demijohn, Thom
See Disch, Thomas M(ichael)

de Montherlant, Henry (Milon)
See Montherlant, Henry (Milon) de

Demosthenes 384B.C.-322B.C. ...... **CMLC 13**
See also DLB 176

de Natale, Francine
See Malzberg, Barry N(athaniel)

Denby, Edwin (Orr) 1903-1983 .... **CLC 48**
See also CA 138; 110

Denis, Julio
See Cortazar, Julio

Denmark, Harrison
See Zelazny, Roger (Joseph)

Dennis, John 1658-1734 .... **LC 11**
See also DLB 101

Dennis, Nigel (Forbes) 1912-1989 .... **CLC 8**
See also CA 25-28R; 129; DLB 13, 15; MTCW

Dent, Lester 1904(?)-1959 .... **TCLC 72**
See also CA 112; 161

De Palma, Brian (Russell) 1940- ...... **CLC 20**
See also CA 109

De Quincey, Thomas 1785-1859 .... **NCLC 4**
See also CDBLB 1789-1832; DLB 110; 144

Deren, Eleanora 1908(?)-1961
See Deren, Maya
See also CA 111

Deren, Maya 1917-1961 .... **CLC 16, 102**
See also Deren, Eleanora

Derleth, August (William) 1909-1971 **CLC 31**
See also CA 1-4R; 29-32R; CANR 4; DLB 9;
SATA 5

Der Nister 1884-1950 .... **TCLC 56**

de Routisie, Albert
See Aragon, Louis

Derrida, Jacques 1930- .... **CLC 24, 87**
See also CA 124; 127

Derry Down Derry
See Lear, Edward

Dersonnes, Jacques
See Simenon, Georges (Jacques Christian)

Desai, Anita 1937- **CLC 19, 37, 97; DAB; DAM
NOV**
See also CA 81-84; CANR 33, 53; MTCW;
SATA 63

de Saint-Luc, Jean
See Glassco, John

de Saint Roman, Arnaud
See Aragon, Louis

Descartes, Rene 1596-1650 .... **LC 20, 35**

De Sica, Vittorio 1901(?)-1974 .... **CLC 20**
See also CA 117

Desnos, Robert 1900-1945 .... **TCLC 22**
See also CA 121; 151

Destouches, Louis-Ferdinand 1894-1961 **C L C
9, 15**
See also Celine, Louis-Ferdinand
See also CA 85-88; CANR 28; MTCW

de Tolignac, Gaston
See Griffith, D(avid Lewelyn) W(ark)

Deutsch, Babette 1895-1982 .... **CLC 18**
See also CA 1-4R; 108; CANR 4; DLB 45;
SATA 1; SATA-Obit 33

Devenant, William 1606-1649 .... **LC 13**

Devkota, Laxmiprasad 1909-1959 . **TCLC 23**
See also CA 123

De Voto, Bernard (Augustine) 1897-1955
TCLC 29

See also CA 113; 160; DLB 9

De Vries, Peter 1910-1993 **CLC 1, 2, 3, 7, 10, 28, 46; DAM NOV**
See also CA 17-20R; 142; CANR 41; DLB 6; DLBY 82; MTCW

Dexter, John
See Bradley, Marion Zimmer

Dexter, Martin
See Faust, Frederick (Schiller)

Dexter, Pete 1943- ... **CLC 34, 55; DAM POP**
See also BEST 89:2; CA 127; 131; INT 131; MTCW

Diamano, Silmang
See Senghor, Leopold Sedar

Diamond, Neil 1941- .... **CLC 30**
See also CA 108

Diaz del Castillo, Bernal 1496-1584 ... **LC 31**

di Bassetto, Corno
See Shaw, George Bernard

Dick, Philip K(indred) 1928-1982 **CLC 10, 30, 72; DAM NOV, POP**
See also CA 49-52; 106; CANR 2, 16; DLB 8; MTCW

Dickens, Charles (John Huffam) 1812-1870 **NCLC 3, 8, 18, 26, 37, 50; DA; DAB; DAC; DAM MST, NOV; SSC 17; WLC**
See also CDBLB 1832-1890; DLB 21, 55, 70, 159, 166; JRDA; MAICYA; SATA 15

Dickey, James (Lafayette) 1923-1997 **CLC 1, 2, 4, 7, 10, 15, 47; DAM NOV, POET, POP**
See also AITN 1, 2; CA 9-12R; 156; CABS 2; CANR 10, 48, 61; CDALB 1968-1988; DLB 5; DLBD 7; DLBY 82, 93, 96; INT CANR-10; MTCW

Dickey, William 1928-1994 .... **CLC 3, 28**
See also CA 9-12R; 145; CANR 24; DLB 5

Dickinson, Charles 1951- .... **CLC 49**
See also CA 128

Dickinson, Emily (Elizabeth) 1830-1886 **NCLC 21; DA; DAB; DAC; DAM MST, POET; PC 1; WLC**
See also AAYA 22; CDALB 1865-1917; DLB 1; SATA 29

Dickinson, Peter (Malcolm) 1927- **CLC 12, 35**
See also AAYA 9; CA 41-44R; CANR 31, 58; CLR 29; DLB 87, 161; JRDA; MAICYA; SATA 5, 62, 95

Dickson, Carr
See Carr, John Dickson

Dickson, Carter
See Carr, John Dickson

Diderot, Denis 1713-1784 .... **LC 26**

Didion, Joan 1934- **CLC 1, 3, 8, 14, 32; DAM NOV**
See also AITN 1; CA 5-8R; CANR 14, 52; CDALB 1968-1988; DLB 2, 173; DLBY 81, 86; MTCW

Dietrich, Robert
See Hunt, E(verette) Howard, (Jr.)

Dillard, Annie 1945- . **CLC 9, 60; DAM NOV**
See also AAYA 6; CA 49-52; CANR 3, 43, 62; DLBY 80; MTCW; SATA 10

Dillard, R(ichard) H(enry) W(ilde) 1937- **CLC 5**
See also CA 21-24R; CAAS 7; CANR 10; DLB 5

Dillon, Eilis 1920-1994 .... **CLC 17**
See also CA 9-12R; 147; CAAS 3; CANR 4, 38; CLR 26; MAICYA; SATA 2, 74; SATA-Obit 83

Dimont, Penelope
See Mortimer, Penelope (Ruth)

Dinesen, Isak .... **CLC 10, 29, 95; SSC 7**

See also Blixen, Karen (Christentze Dinesen)

Ding Ling .... **CLC 68**
See also Chiang Pin-chin

Disch, Thomas M(ichael) 1940- ... **CLC 7, 36**
See also AAYA 17; CA 21-24R; CAAS 4; CANR 17, 36, 54; CLR 18; DLB 8; MAICYA; MTCW; SAAS 15; SATA 92

Disch, Tom
See Disch, Thomas M(ichael)

d'Isly, Georges
See Simenon, Georges (Jacques Christian)

Disraeli, Benjamin 1804-1881 .... **NCLC 2, 39**
See also DLB 21, 55

Ditcum, Steve
See Crumb, R(obert)

Dixon, Paige
See Corcoran, Barbara

Dixon, Stephen 1936- .... **CLC 52; SSC 16**
See also CA 89-92; CANR 17, 40, 54; DLB 130

Doak, Annie
See Dillard, Annie

Dobell, Sydney Thompson 1824-1874 **N C L C 43**
See also DLB 32

Doblin, Alfred .... **TCLC 13**
See also Doeblin, Alfred

Dobrolyubov, Nikolai Alexandrovich 1836-1861 **NCLC 5**

Dobyns, Stephen 1941- .... **CLC 37**
See also CA 45-48; CANR 2, 18

Doctorow, E(dgar) L(aurence) 1931- **CLC 6, 11, 15, 18, 37, 44, 65; DAM NOV, POP**
See also AAYA 22; AITN 2; BEST 89:3; CA 45-48; CANR 2, 33, 51; CDALB 1968-1988; DLB 2, 28, 173; DLBY 80; MTCW

Dodgson, Charles Lutwidge 1832-1898
See Carroll, Lewis
See also CLR 2; DA; DAB; DAC; DAM MST, NOV, POET; MAICYA; YABC 2

Dodson, Owen (Vincent) 1914-1983 **CLC 79; BLC; DAM MULT**
See also BW 1; CA 65-68; 110; CANR 24; DLB 76

Doeblin, Alfred 1878-1957 .... **TCLC 13**
See also Doblin, Alfred
See also CA 110; 141; DLB 66

Doerr, Harriet 1910- .... **CLC 34**
See also CA 117; 122; CANR 47; INT 122

Domecq, H(onorio) Bustos
See Bioy Casares, Adolfo; Borges, Jorge Luis

Domini, Rey
See Lorde, Audre (Geraldine)

Dominique
See Proust, (Valentin-Louis-George-Eugene-) Marcel

Don, A
See Stephen, Leslie

Donaldson, Stephen R. 1947- **CLC 46; DAM POP**
See also CA 89-92; CANR 13, 55; INT CANR-13

Donleavy, J(ames) P(atrick) 1926- **CLC 1, 4, 6, 10, 45**
See also AITN 2; CA 9-12R; CANR 24, 49, 62; DLB 6, 173; INT CANR-24; MTCW

Donne, John 1572-1631 **LC 10, 24; DA; DAB; DAC; DAM MST, POET; PC 1**
See also CDBLB Before 1660; DLB 121, 151

Donnell, David 1939(?)- .... **CLC 34**

Donoghue, P. S.
See Hunt, E(verette) Howard, (Jr.)

Donoso (Yanez), Jose 1924-1996 **CLC 4, 8, 11, 32, 99; DAM MULT; HLC**

See also CA 81-84; 155; CANR 32; DLB 113; HW; MTCW

Donovan, John 1928-1992 .... **CLC 35**
See also AAYA 20; CA 97-100; 137; CLR 3; MAICYA; SATA 72; SATA-Brief 29

Don Roberto
See Cunninghame Graham, R(obert) B(ontine)

Doolittle, Hilda 1886-1961 **CLC 3, 8, 14, 31, 34, 73; DA; DAC; DAM MST, POET; PC 5; WLC**
See also H. D.
See also CA 97-100; CANR 35; DLB 4, 45; MTCW

Dorfman, Ariel 1942- ...... **CLC 48, 77; DAM MULT; HLC**
See also CA 124; 130; HW; INT 130

Dorn, Edward (Merton) 1929- ... **CLC 10, 18**
See also CA 93-96; CANR 42; DLB 5; INT 93-96

Dorsan, Luc
See Simenon, Georges (Jacques Christian)

Dorsange, Jean
See Simenon, Georges (Jacques Christian)

Dos Passos, John (Roderigo) 1896-1970 **C L C 1, 4, 8, 11, 15, 25, 34, 82; DA; DAB; DAC; DAM MST, NOV; WLC**
See also CA 1-4R; 29-32R; CANR 3; CDALB 1929-1941; DLB 4, 9; DLBD 1, 15; DLBY 96; MTCW

Dossage, Jean
See Simenon, Georges (Jacques Christian)

Dostoevsky, Fedor Mikhailovich 1821-1881 **NCLC 2, 7, 21, 33, 43; DA; DAB; DAC; DAM MST, NOV; SSC 2; WLC**

Doughty, Charles M(ontagu) 1843-1926 **TCLC 27**
See also CA 115; DLB 19, 57, 174

Douglas, Ellen .... **CLC 73**
See also Haxton, Josephine Ayres; Williamson, Ellen Douglas

Douglas, Gavin 1475(?)-1522 .... **LC 20**

Douglas, Keith (Castellain) 1920-1944 **T C L C 40**
See also CA 160; DLB 27

Douglas, Leonard
See Bradbury, Ray (Douglas)

Douglas, Michael
See Crichton, (John) Michael

Douglas, Norman 1868-1952 .... **TCLC 68**

Douglass, Frederick 1817(?)-1895 **NCLC 7, 55; BLC; DA; DAC; DAM MST, MULT; WLC**
See also CDALB 1640-1865; DLB 1, 43, 50, 79; SATA 29

Dourado, (Waldomiro Freitas) Autran 1926- **CLC 23, 60**
See also CA 25-28R; CANR 34

Dourado, Waldomiro Autran
See Dourado, (Waldomiro Freitas) Autran

Dove, Rita (Frances) 1952- **CLC 50, 81; DAM MULT, POET; PC 6**
See also BW 2; CA 109; CAAS 19; CANR 27, 42; DLB 120

Dowell, Coleman 1925-1985 .... **CLC 60**
See also CA 25-28R; 117; CANR 10; DLB 130

Dowson, Ernest (Christopher) 1867-1900 **TCLC 4**
See also CA 105; 150; DLB 19, 135

Doyle, A. Conan
See Doyle, Arthur Conan

Doyle, Arthur Conan 1859-1930 **TCLC 7; DA; DAB; DAC; DAM MST, NOV; SSC 12; WLC**
See also AAYA 14; CA 104; 122; CDBLB 1890-

1914; DLB 18, 70, 156, 178; MTCW; SATA 24

Doyle, Conan
See Doyle, Arthur Conan

Doyle, John
See Graves, Robert (von Ranke)

Doyle, Roddy 1958(?)- .... **CLC 81**
See also AAYA 14; CA 143

Doyle, Sir A. Conan
See Doyle, Arthur Conan

Doyle, Sir Arthur Conan
See Doyle, Arthur Conan

Dr. A
See Asimov, Isaac; Silverstein, Alvin

Drabble, Margaret 1939-**CLC 2, 3, 5, 8, 10, 22, 53; DAB; DAC; DAM MST, NOV, POP**
See also CA 13-16R; CANR 18, 35; CDBLB 1960 to Present; DLB 14, 155; MTCW; SATA 48

Drapier, M. B.
See Swift, Jonathan

Drayham, James
See Mencken, H(enry) L(ouis)

Drayton, Michael 1563-1631 .... **LC 8**

Dreadstone, Carl
See Campbell, (John) Ramsey

Dreiser, Theodore (Herman Albert) 1871-1945 **TCLC 10, 18, 35; DA; DAC; DAM MST, NOV; WLC**
See also CA 106; 132; CDALB 1865-1917; DLB 9, 12, 102, 137; DLBD 1; MTCW

Drexler, Rosalyn 1926- .... **CLC 2, 6**
See also CA 81-84

Dreyer, Carl Theodor 1889-1968 ..... **CLC 16**
See also CA 116

Drieu la Rochelle, Pierre(-Eugene) 1893-1945 **TCLC 21**
See also CA 117; DLB 72

Drinkwater, John 1882-1937 .... **TCLC 57**
See also CA 109; 149; DLB 10, 19, 149

Drop Shot
See Cable, George Washington

Droste-Hulshoff, Annette Freiin von 1797-1848 **NCLC 3**
See also DLB 133

Drummond, Walter
See Silverberg, Robert

Drummond, William Henry 1854-1907**T C L C 25**
See also CA 160; DLB 92

Drummond de Andrade, Carlos 1902-1987 **CLC 18**
See also Andrade, Carlos Drummond de
See also CA 132; 123

Drury, Allen (Stuart) 1918- .... **CLC 37**
See also CA 57-60; CANR 18, 52; INT CANR-18

Dryden, John 1631-1700**LC 3, 21; DA; DAB; DAC; DAM DRAM, MST, POET; DC 3; WLC**
See also CDBLB 1660-1789; DLB 80, 101, 131

Duberman, Martin 1930-....................**CLC 8**
See also CA 1-4R; CANR 2

Dubie, Norman (Evans) 1945- .... **CLC 36**
See also CA 69-72; CANR 12; DLB 120

Du Bois, W(illiam) E(dward) B(urghardt) 1868-1963**CLC 1, 2, 13, 64, 96; BLC; DA; DAC; DAM MST, MULT, NOV; WLC**
See also BW 1; CA 85-88; CANR 34; CDALB 1865-1917; DLB 47, 50, 91; MTCW; SATA 42

Dubus, Andre 1936- **CLC 13, 36, 97; SSC 15**
See also CA 21-24R; CANR 17; DLB 130; INT

CANR-17

Duca Minimo
See D'Annunzio, Gabriele

Ducharme, Rejean 1941- .... **CLC 74**
See also DLB 60

Duclos, Charles Pinot 1704-1772 .... **LC 1**

Dudek, Louis 1918- ....**CLC 11, 19**
See also CA 45-48; CAAS 14; CANR 1; DLB 88

Duerrenmatt, Friedrich 1921-1990 **CLC 1, 4, 8, 11, 15, 43, 102; DAM DRAM**
See also CA 17-20R; CANR 33; DLB 69, 124; MTCW

Duffy, Bruce (?)- .... **CLC 50**

Duffy, Maureen 1933- .... **CLC 37**
See also CA 25-28R; CANR 33; DLB 14; MTCW

Dugan, Alan 1923-.......................... **CLC 2, 6**
See also CA 81-84; DLB 5

du Gard, Roger Martin
See Martin du Gard, Roger

Duhamel, Georges 1884-1966 ....**CLC 8**
See also CA 81-84; 25-28R; CANR 35; DLB 65; MTCW

Dujardin, Edouard (Emile Louis) 1861-1949 **TCLC 13**
See also CA 109; DLB 123

Dulles, John Foster 1888-1959 .... **TCLC 72**
See also CA 115; 149

Dumas, Alexandre (Davy de la Pailleterie) 1802-1870 ... **NCLC 11; DA; DAB; DAC; DAM MST, NOV; WLC**
See also DLB 119; SATA 18

Dumas, Alexandre 1824-1895 **NCLC 9; DC 1**
See also AAYA 22

Dumas, Claudine
See Malzberg, Barry N(athaniel)

Dumas, Henry L. 1934-1968......... **CLC 6, 62**
See also BW 1; CA 85-88; DLB 41

du Maurier, Daphne 1907-1989**CLC 6, 11, 59; DAB; DAC; DAM MST, POP; SSC 18**
See also CA 5-8R; 128; CANR 6, 55; MTCW; SATA 27; SATA-Obit 60

Dunbar, Paul Laurence 1872-1906 . **TCLC 2, 12; BLC; DA; DAC; DAM MST, MULT, POET; PC 5; SSC 8; WLC**
See also BW 1; CA 104; 124; CDALB 1865-1917; DLB 50, 54, 78; SATA 34

Dunbar, William 1460(?)-1530(?) .... **LC 20**
See also DLB 132, 146

Duncan, Dora Angela
See Duncan, Isadora

Duncan, Isadora 1877(?)-1927 .... **TCLC 68**
See also CA 118; 149

Duncan, Lois 1934-...........................**CLC 26**
See also AAYA 4; CA 1-4R; CANR 2, 23, 36; CLR 29; JRDA; MAICYA; SAAS 2; SATA 1, 36, 75

Duncan, Robert (Edward) 1919-1988**CLC 1, 2, 4, 7, 15, 41, 55; DAM POET; PC 2**
See also CA 9-12R; 124; CANR 28, 62; DLB 5, 16; MTCW

Duncan, Sara Jeannette 1861-1922 **TCLC 60**
See also CA 157; DLB 92

Dunlap, William 1766-1839 .... **NCLC 2**
See also DLB 30, 37, 59

Dunn, Douglas (Eaglesham) 1942- **CLC 6, 40**
See also CA 45-48; CANR 2, 33; DLB 40; MTCW

Dunn, Katherine (Karen) 1945- .... **CLC 71**
See also CA 33-36R

Dunn, Stephen 1939- .... **CLC 36**
See also CA 33-36R; CANR 12, 48, 53; DLB 105

Dunne, Finley Peter 1867-1936 ...... **TCLC 28**
See also CA 108; DLB 11, 23

Dunne, John Gregory 1932- .... **CLC 28**
See also CA 25-28R; CANR 14, 50; DLBY 80

Dunsany, Edward John Moreton Drax Plunkett 1878-1957
See Dunsany, Lord
See also CA 104; 148; DLB 10

Dunsany, Lord .... **TCLC 2, 59**
See also Dunsany, Edward John Moreton Drax Plunkett
See also DLB 77, 153, 156

du Perry, Jean
See Simenon, Georges (Jacques Christian)

Durang, Christopher (Ferdinand) 1949-**C L C 27, 38**
See also CA 105; CANR 50

Duras, Marguerite 1914-1996**CLC 3, 6, 11, 20, 34, 40, 68, 100**
See also CA 25-28R; 151; CANR 50; DLB 83; MTCW

Durban, (Rosa) Pam 1947- .... **CLC 39**
See also CA 123

Durcan, Paul 1944-**CLC 43, 70; DAM POET**
See also CA 134

Durkheim, Emile 1858-1917 .... **TCLC 55**

Durrell, Lawrence (George) 1912-1990 **C L C 1, 4, 6, 8, 13, 27, 41; DAM NOV**
See also CA 9-12R; 132; CANR 40; CDBLB 1945-1960; DLB 15, 27; DLBY 90; MTCW

Durrenmatt, Friedrich
See Duerrenmatt, Friedrich

Dutt, Toru 1856-1877 .... **NCLC 29**

Dwight, Timothy 1752-1817 .... **NCLC 13**
See also DLB 37

Dworkin, Andrea 1946- .... **CLC 43**
See also CA 77-80; CAAS 21; CANR 16, 39; INT CANR-16; MTCW

Dwyer, Deanna
See Koontz, Dean R(ay)

Dwyer, K. R.
See Koontz, Dean R(ay)

Dye, Richard
See De Voto, Bernard (Augustine)

Dylan, Bob 1941- .... **CLC 3, 4, 6, 12, 77**
See also CA 41-44R; DLB 16

Eagleton, Terence (Francis) 1943-
See Eagleton, Terry
See also CA 57-60; CANR 7, 23; MTCW

Eagleton, Terry .... **CLC 63**
See also Eagleton, Terence (Francis)

Early, Jack
See Scoppettone, Sandra

East, Michael
See West, Morris L(anglo)

Eastaway, Edward
See Thomas, (Philip) Edward

Eastlake, William (Derry) 1917-1997 . **CLC 8**
See also CA 5-8R; 158; CAAS 1; CANR 5; DLB 6; INT CANR-5

Eastman, Charles A(lexander) 1858-1939 **TCLC 55; DAM MULT**
See also DLB 175; NNAL; YABC 1

Eberhart, Richard (Ghormley) 1904-**CLC 3, 11, 19, 56; DAM POET**
See also CA 1-4R; CANR 2; CDALB 1941-1968; DLB 48; MTCW

Eberstadt, Fernanda 1960-............... **CLC 39**
See also CA 136

Echegaray (y Eizaguirre), Jose (Maria Waldo) 1832-1916...
TCLC 4

See also CA 104; CANR 32; HW; MTCW

Echeverria, (Jose) Esteban (Antonino) 1805-1851 ....**NCLC 18**

Echo
See Proust, (Valentin-Louis-George-Eugene-) Marcel

Eckert, Allan W. 1931- ....**CLC 17**
See also AAYA 18; CA 13-16R; CANR 14, 45; INT CANR-14; SAAS 21; SATA 29, 91; SATA-Brief 27

Eckhart, Meister 1260(?)-1328(?) ...**CMLC 9**
See also DLB 115

Eckmar, F. R.
See de Hartog, Jan

Eco, Umberto 1932-**CLC 28, 60; DAM NOV, POP**
See also BEST 90:1; CA 77-80; CANR 12, 33, 55; MTCW

Eddison, E(ric) R(ucker) 1882-1945**TCLC 15**
See also CA 109; 156

Eddy, Mary (Morse) Baker 1821-1910**T C L C 71**
See also CA 113

Edel, (Joseph) Leon 1907-1997 .. **CLC 29, 34**
See also CA 1-4R; 161; CANR 1, 22; DLB 103; INT CANR-22

Eden, Emily 1797-1869 ....**NCLC 10**

Edgar, David 1948-... **CLC 42; DAM DRAM**
See also CA 57-60; CANR 12, 61; DLB 13; MTCW

Edgerton, Clyde (Carlyle) 1944- .....**CLC 39**
See also AAYA 17; CA 118; 134; INT 134

Edgeworth, Maria 1768-1849 ....**NCLC 1, 51**
See also DLB 116, 159, 163; SATA 21

Edmonds, Paul
See Kuttner, Henry

Edmonds, Walter D(umaux) 1903- .. **CLC 35**
See also CA 5-8R; CANR 2; DLB 9; MAICYA; SAAS 4; SATA 1, 27

Edmondson, Wallace
See Ellison, Harlan (Jay)

Edson, Russell ....**CLC 13**
See also CA 33-36R

Edwards, Bronwen Elizabeth
See Rose, Wendy

Edwards, G(erald) B(asil) 1899-1976**CLC 25**
See also CA 110

Edwards, Gus 1939- ....**CLC 43**
See also CA 108; INT 108

Edwards, Jonathan 1703-1758.....**LC 7; DA; DAC; DAM MST**
See also DLB 24

Efron, Marina Ivanovna Tsvetaeva
See Tsvetaeva (Efron), Marina (Ivanovna)

Ehle, John (Marsden, Jr.) 1925- ......**CLC 27**
See also CA 9-12R

Ehrenbourg, Ilya (Grigoryevich)
See Ehrenburg, Ilya (Grigoryevich)

Ehrenburg, Ilya (Grigoryevich) 1891-1967 **CLC 18, 34, 62**
See also CA 102; 25-28R

Ehrenburg, Ilyo (Grigoryevich)
See Ehrenburg, Ilya (Grigoryevich)

Eich, Guenter 1907-1972 ....**CLC 15**
See also CA 111; 93-96; DLB 69, 124

Eichendorff, Joseph Freiherr von 1788-1857 **NCLC 8**
See also DLB 90

Eigner, Larry ....**CLC 9**
See also Eigner, Laurence (Joel)
See also CAAS 23; DLB 5

Eigner, Laurence (Joel) 1927-1996
See Eigner, Larry

See also CA 9-12R; 151; CANR 6

Einstein, Albert 1879-1955 ....**TCLC 65**
See also CA 121; 133; MTCW

Eiseley, Loren Corey 1907-1977 ....**CLC 7**
See also AAYA 5; CA 1-4R; 73-76; CANR 6

Eisenstadt, Jill 1963- ....**CLC 50**
See also CA 140

Eisenstein, Sergei (Mikhailovich) 1898-1948 **TCLC 57**
See also CA 114; 149

Eisner, Simon
See Kornbluth, C(yril) M.

Ekeloef, (Bengt) Gunnar 1907-1968 **CLC 27; DAM POET**
See also CA 123; 25-28R

Ekelof, (Bengt) Gunnar
See Ekeloef, (Bengt) Gunnar

Ekelund, Vilhelm 1880-1949 ....**TCLC 75**

Ekwensi, C. O. D.
See Ekwensi, Cyprian (Odiatu Duaka)

Ekwensi, Cyprian (Odiatu Duaka) 1921-**CLC 4; BLC; DAM MULT**
See also BW 2; CA 29-32R; CANR 18, 42; DLB 117; MTCW; SATA 66

Elaine ....**TCLC 18**
See also Leverson, Ada

El Crummo
See Crumb, R(obert)

Elder, Lonne III 1931-1996 ....**DC 8**
See also BLC; BW 1; CA 81-84; 152; CANR 25; DAM MULT; DLB 7, 38, 44

Elia
See Lamb, Charles

Eliade, Mircea 1907-1986 ....**CLC 19**
See also CA 65-68; 119; CANR 30, 62; MTCW

Eliot, A. D.
See Jewett, (Theodora) Sarah Orne

Eliot, Alice
See Jewett, (Theodora) Sarah Orne

Eliot, Dan
See Silverberg, Robert

Eliot, George 1819-1880 **NCLC 4, 13, 23, 41, 49; DA; DAB; DAC; DAM MST, NOV; PC 20; WLC**
See also CDBLB 1832-1890; DLB 21, 35, 55

Eliot, John 1604-1690 ....**LC 5**
See also DLB 24

Eliot, T(homas) S(tearns) 1888-1965**CLC 1, 2, 3, 6, 9, 10, 13, 15, 24, 34, 41, 55, 57; DA; DAB; DAC; DAM DRAM, MST, POET; PC 5; WLC 2**
See also CA 5-8R; 25-28R; CANR 41; CDALB 1929-1941; DLB 7, 10, 45, 63; DLBY 88; MTCW

Elizabeth 1866-1941 ....**TCLC 41**

Elkin, Stanley L(awrence) 1930-1995 **CLC 4, 6, 9, 14, 27, 51, 91; DAM NOV, POP; SSC 12**
See also CA 9-12R; 148; CANR 8, 46; DLB 2, 28; DLBY 80; INT CANR-8; MTCW

Elledge, Scott ....**CLC 34**

Elliot, Don
See Silverberg, Robert

Elliott, Don
See Silverberg, Robert

Elliott, George P(aul) 1918-1980 ....**CLC 2**
See also CA 1-4R; 97-100; CANR 2

Elliott, Janice 1931- ....**CLC 47**
See also CA 13-16R; CANR 8, 29; DLB 14

Elliott, Sumner Locke 1917-1991 .....**CLC 38**
See also CA 5-8R; 134; CANR 2, 21

Elliott, William
See Bradbury, Ray (Douglas)

Ellis, A. E. ....**CLC 7**

Ellis, Alice Thomas ....**CLC 40**
See also Haycraft, Anna

Ellis, Bret Easton 1964- .. **CLC 39, 71; DAM POP**
See also AAYA 2; CA 118; 123; CANR 51; INT 123

Ellis, (Henry) Havelock 1859-1939 **TCLC 14**
See also CA 109

Ellis, Landon
See Ellison, Harlan (Jay)

Ellis, Trey 1962- ....**CLC 55**
See also CA 146

Ellison, Harlan (Jay) 1934- ... **CLC 1, 13, 42; DAM POP; SSC 14**
See also CA 5-8R; CANR 5, 46; DLB 8; INT CANR-5; MTCW

Ellison, Ralph (Waldo) 1914-1994 **CLC 1, 3, 11, 54, 86; BLC; DA; DAB; DAC; DAM MST, MULT, NOV; SSC 26; WLC**
See also AAYA 19; BW 1; CA 9-12R; 145; CANR 24, 53; CDALB 1941-1968; DLB 2, 76; DLBY 94; MTCW

Ellmann, Lucy (Elizabeth) 1956- ......**CLC 61**
See also CA 128

Ellmann, Richard (David) 1918-1987**CLC 50**
See also BEST 89:2; CA 1-4R; 122; CANR 2, 28, 61; DLB 103; DLBY 87; MTCW

Elman, Richard 1934- ....**CLC 19**
See also CA 17-20R; CAAS 3; CANR 47

Elron
See Hubbard, L(afayette) Ron(ald)

Eluard, Paul ....**TCLC 7, 41**
See also Grindel, Eugene

Elyot, Sir Thomas 1490(?)-1546 ....**LC 11**

Elytis, Odysseus 1911-1996 **CLC 15, 49, 100; DAM POET**
See also CA 102; 151; MTCW

Emecheta, (Florence Onye) Buchi 1944-**C L C 14, 48; BLC; DAM MULT**
See also BW 2; CA 81-84; CANR 27; DLB 117; MTCW; SATA 66

Emerson, Mary Moody 1774-1863 **NCLC 66**

Emerson, Ralph Waldo 1803-1882 .**NCLC 1, 38; DA; DAB; DAC; DAM MST, POET; PC 18; WLC**
See also CDALB 1640-1865; DLB 1, 59, 73

Eminescu, Mihail 1850-1889 ....**NCLC 33**

Empson, William 1906-1984**CLC 3, 8, 19, 33, 34**
See also CA 17-20R; 112; CANR 31, 61; DLB 20; MTCW

Enchi Fumiko (Ueda) 1905-1986 ......**CLC 31**
See also CA 129; 121

Ende, Michael (Andreas Helmuth) 1929-1995 **CLC 31**
See also CA 118; 124; 149; CANR 36; CLR 14; DLB 75; MAICYA; SATA 61; SATA-Brief 42; SATA-Obit 86

Endo, Shusaku 1923-1996 **CLC 7, 14, 19, 54, 99; DAM NOV**
See also CA 29-32R; 153; CANR 21, 54; DLB 182; MTCW

Engel, Marian 1933-1985 ....**CLC 36**
See also CA 25-28R; CANR 12; DLB 53; INT CANR-12

Engelhardt, Frederick
See Hubbard, L(afayette) Ron(ald)

Enright, D(ennis) J(oseph) 1920-**CLC 4, 8, 31**
See also CA 1-4R; CANR 1, 42; DLB 27; SATA 25

Enzensberger, Hans Magnus 1929- ..**CLC 43**
See also CA 116; 119

Ephron, Nora 1941- .... **CLC 17, 31**
See also AITN 2; CA 65-68; CANR 12, 39
Epicurus 341B.C.-270B.C. .... **CMLC 21**
See also DLB 176
Epsilon
See Betjeman, John
Epstein, Daniel Mark 1948- ....**CLC 7**
See also CA 49-52; CANR 2, 53
Epstein, Jacob 1956- .... **CLC 19**
See also CA 114
Epstein, Joseph 1937- .... **CLC 39**
See also CA 112; 119; CANR 50
Epstein, Leslie 1938- .... **CLC 27**
See also CA 73-76; CAAS 12; CANR 23
Equiano, Olaudah 1745(?)-1797**LC 16; BLC;
DAM MULT**
See also DLB 37, 50
ER...................................... **TCLC 33**
See also CA 160; DLB 85
Erasmus, Desiderius 1469(?)-1536...... **LC 16**
Erdman, Paul E(mil) 1932- .... **CLC 25**
See also AITN 1; CA 61-64; CANR 13, 43
Erdrich, Louise 1954- ..... **CLC 39, 54; DAM
MULT, NOV, POP**
See also AAYA 10; BEST 89:1; CA 114; CANR
41, 62; DLB 152, 175; MTCW; NNAL;
SATA 94
Erenburg, Ilya (Grigoryevich)
See Ehrenburg, Ilya (Grigoryevich)
Erickson, Stephen Michael 1950-
See Erickson, Steve
See also CA 129
Erickson, Steve 1950- .... **CLC 64**
See also Erickson, Stephen Michael
See also CANR 60
Ericson, Walter
See Fast, Howard (Melvin)
Eriksson, Buntel
See Bergman, (Ernst) Ingmar
Ernaux, Annie 1940- .... **CLC 88**
See also CA 147
Eschenbach, Wolfram von
See Wolfram von Eschenbach
Eseki, Bruno
See Mphahlele, Ezekiel
Esenin, Sergei (Alexandrovich) 1895-1925
TCLC 4
See also CA 104
Eshleman, Clayton 1935- ....**CLC 7**
See also CA 33-36R; CAAS 6; DLB 5
Espriella, Don Manuel Alvarez
See Southey, Robert
Espriu, Salvador 1913-1985 .... **CLC 9**
See also CA 154; 115; DLB 134
Espronceda, Jose de 1808-1842 ..... **NCLC 39**
Esse, James
See Stephens, James
Esterbrook, Tom
See Hubbard, L(afayette) Ron(ald)
Estleman, Loren D. 1952-**CLC 48; DAM NOV,
POP**
See also CA 85-88; CANR 27; INT CANR-27;
MTCW
Eugenides, Jeffrey 1960(?)- .... **CLC 81**
See also CA 144
Euripides c. 485B.C.-406B.C.**CMLC 23; DA;
DAB; DAC; DAM DRAM, MST; DC 4;
WLCS**
See also DLB 176
Evan, Evin
See Faust, Frederick (Schiller)
Evans, Evan
See Faust, Frederick (Schiller)

Evans, Marian
See Eliot, George
Evans, Mary Ann
See Eliot, George
Evarts, Esther
See Benson, Sally
Everett, Percival L. 1956- .... **CLC 57**
See also BW 2; CA 129
Everson, R(onald) G(ilmour) 1903-.. **CLC 27**
See also CA 17-20R; DLB 88
Everson, William (Oliver) 1912-1994 **CLC 1,
5, 14**
See also CA 9-12R; 145; CANR 20; DLB 5,
16; MTCW
Evtushenko, Evgenii Aleksandrovich
See Yevtushenko, Yevgeny (Alexandrovich)
Ewart, Gavin (Buchanan) 1916-1995**CLC 13,
46**
See also CA 89-92; 150; CANR 17, 46; DLB
40; MTCW
Ewers, Hanns Heinz 1871-1943 ..... **TCLC 12**
See also CA 109; 149
Ewing, Frederick R.
See Sturgeon, Theodore (Hamilton)
Exley, Frederick (Earl) 1929-1992 **CLC 6, 11**
See also AITN 2; CA 81-84; 138; DLB 143;
DLBY 81
Eynhardt, Guillermo
See Quiroga, Horacio (Sylvestre)
Ezekiel, Nissim 1924- .... **CLC 61**
See also CA 61-64
Ezekiel, Tish O'Dowd 1943- .... **CLC 34**
See also CA 129
Fadeyev, A.
See Bulgya, Alexander Alexandrovich
Fadeyev, Alexander .... **TCLC 53**
See also Bulgya, Alexander Alexandrovich
Fagen, Donald 1948- .... **CLC 26**
Fainzilberg, Ilya Arnoldovich 1897-1937
See Ilf, Ilya
See also CA 120
Fair, Ronald L. 1932- .... **CLC 18**
See also BW 1; CA 69-72; CANR 25; DLB 33
Fairbairn, Roger
See Carr, John Dickson
Fairbairns, Zoe (Ann) 1948- .... **CLC 32**
See also CA 103; CANR 21
Falco, Gian
See Papini, Giovanni
Falconer, James
See Kirkup, James
Falconer, Kenneth
See Kornbluth, C(yril) M.
Falkland, Samuel
See Heijermans, Herman
Fallaci, Oriana 1930- .... **CLC 11**
See also CA 77-80; CANR 15, 58; MTCW
Faludy, George 1913- .... **CLC 42**
See also CA 21-24R
Faludy, Gyoergy
See Faludy, George
Fanon, Frantz 1925-1961**CLC 74; BLC; DAM
MULT**
See also BW 1; CA 116; 89-92
Fanshawe, Ann 1625-1680 .... **LC 11**
Fante, John (Thomas) 1911-1983 ..... **CLC 60**
See also CA 69-72; 109; CANR 23; DLB 130;
DLBY 83
Farah, Nuruddin 1945- **CLC 53; BLC; DAM
MULT**
See also BW 2; CA 106; DLB 125
Fargue, Leon-Paul 1876(?)-1947 ... **TCLC 11**
See also CA 109

Farigoule, Louis
See Romains, Jules
Farina, Richard 1936(?)-1966 .... **CLC 9**
See also CA 81-84; 25-28R
Farley, Walter (Lorimer) 1915-1989 **CLC 17**
See also CA 17-20R; CANR 8, 29; DLB 22;
JRDA; MAICYA; SATA 2, 43
Farmer, Philip Jose 1918- .... **CLC 1, 19**
See also CA 1-4R; CANR 4, 35; DLB 8;
MTCW; SATA 93
Farquhar, George 1677-1707 ...**LC 21; DAM
DRAM**
See also DLB 84
Farrell, J(ames) G(ordon) 1935-1979 **CLC 6**
See also CA 73-76; 89-92; CANR 36; DLB 14;
MTCW
Farrell, James T(homas) 1904-1979**CLC 1, 4,
8, 11, 66; SSC 28**
See also CA 5-8R; 89-92; CANR 9, 61; DLB 4,
9, 86; DLBD 2; MTCW
Farren, Richard J.
See Betjeman, John
Farren, Richard M.
See Betjeman, John
Fassbinder, Rainer Werner 1946-1982**CLC 20**
See also CA 93-96; 106; CANR 31
Fast, Howard (Melvin) 1914- **CLC 23; DAM
NOV**
See also AAYA 16; CA 1-4R; CAAS 18; CANR
1, 33, 54; DLB 9; INT CANR-33; SATA 7
Faulcon, Robert
See Holdstock, Robert P.
Faulkner, William (Cuthbert) 1897-1962**CLC
1, 3, 6, 8, 9, 11, 14, 18, 28, 52, 68; DA; DAB;
DAC; DAM MST, NOV; SSC 1; WLC**
See also AAYA 7; CA 81-84; CANR 33;
CDALB 1929-1941; DLB 9, 11, 44, 102;
DLBD 2; DLBY 86; MTCW
Fauset, Jessie Redmon 1884(?)-1961**CLC 19,
54; BLC; DAM MULT**
See also BW 1; CA 109; DLB 51
Faust, Frederick (Schiller) 1892-1944(?)
TCLC 49; DAM POP
See also CA 108; 152
Faust, Irvin 1924- ....**CLC 8**
See also CA 33-36R; CANR 28; DLB 2, 28;
DLBY 80
Fawkes, Guy
See Benchley, Robert (Charles)
Fearing, Kenneth (Flexner) 1902-1961 .**CLC
51**
See also CA 93-96; CANR 59; DLB 9
Fecamps, Elise
See Creasey, John
Federman, Raymond 1928- .... **CLC 6, 47**
See also CA 17-20R; CAAS 8; CANR 10, 43;
DLBY 80
Federspiel, J(uerg) F. 1931- .... **CLC 42**
See also CA 146
Feiffer, Jules (Ralph) 1929- ..... **CLC 2, 8, 64;
DAM DRAM**
See also AAYA 3; CA 17-20R; CANR 30, 59;
DLB 7, 44; INT CANR-30; MTCW; SATA
8, 61
Feige, Hermann Albert Otto Maximilian
See Traven, B.
Feinberg, David B. 1956-1994 .... **CLC 59**
See also CA 135; 147
Feinstein, Elaine 1930- .... **CLC 36**
See also CA 69-72; CAAS 1; CANR 31; DLB
14, 40; MTCW
Feldman, Irving (Mordecai) 1928- .....**CLC 7**
See also CA 1-4R; CANR 1; DLB 169

Felix-Tchicaya, Gerald
See Tchicaya, Gerald Felix
Fellini, Federico 1920-1993 .... **CLC 16, 85**
See also CA 65-68; 143; CANR 33
Felsen, Henry Gregor 1916- .... **CLC 17**
See also CA 1-4R; CANR 1; SAAS 2; SATA 1
Fenton, James Martin 1949- .... **CLC 32**
See also CA 102; DLB 40
Ferber, Edna 1887-1968 .... **CLC 18, 93**
See also AITN 1; CA 5-8R; 25-28R; DLB 9,
28, 86; MTCW; SATA 7
Ferguson, Helen
See Kavan, Anna
Ferguson, Samuel 1810-1886 .... **NCLC 33**
See also DLB 32
Fergusson, Robert 1750-1774 .... **LC 29**
See also DLB 109
Ferling, Lawrence
See Ferlinghetti, Lawrence (Monsanto)
Ferlinghetti, Lawrence (Monsanto) 1919(?)-
CLC 2, 6, 10, 27; DAM POET; PC 1
See also CA 5-8R; CANR 3, 41; CDALB 1941-
1968; DLB 5, 16; MTCW
Fernandez, Vicente Garcia Huidobro
See Huidobro Fernandez, Vicente Garcia
Ferrer, Gabriel (Francisco Victor) Miro
See Miro (Ferrer), Gabriel (Francisco Victor)
Ferrier, Susan (Edmonstone) 1782-1854
NCLC 8
See also DLB 116
Ferrigno, Robert 1948(?)- .... **CLC 65**
See also CA 140
Ferron, Jacques 1921-1985 ....**CLC 94; DAC**
See also CA 117; 129; DLB 60
Feuchtwanger, Lion 1884-1958 .... **TCLC 3**
See also CA 104; DLB 66
Feuillet, Octave 1821-1890 .... **NCLC 45**
Feydeau, Georges (Leon Jules Marie) 1862-
1921 .... **TCLC 22; DAM DRAM**
See also CA 113; 152
Fichte, Johann Gottlieb 1762-1814 **NCLC 62**
See also DLB 90
Ficino, Marsilio 1433-1499 .... **LC 12**
Fiedeler, Hans
See Doeblin, Alfred
Fiedler, Leslie A(aron) 1917-.. **CLC 4, 13, 24**
See also CA 9-12R; CANR 7; DLB 28, 67;
MTCW
Field, Andrew 1938- .... **CLC 44**
See also CA 97-100; CANR 25
Field, Eugene 1850-1895 .... **NCLC 3**
See also DLB 23, 42, 140; DLBD 13; MAICYA;
SATA 16
Field, Gans T.
See Wellman, Manly Wade
Field, Michael .... **TCLC 43**
Field, Peter
See Hobson, Laura Z(ametkin)
Fielding, Henry 1707-1754 **LC 1; DA; DAB;**
DAC; DAM DRAM, MST, NOV; WLC
See also CDBLB 1660-1789; DLB 39, 84, 101
Fielding, Sarah 1710-1768 .... **LC 1**
See also DLB 39
Fierstein, Harvey (Forbes) 1954-.... **CLC 33;**
DAM DRAM, POP
See also CA 123; 129
Figes, Eva 1932- .... **CLC 31**
See also CA 53-56; CANR 4, 44; DLB 14
Finch, Robert (Duer Claydon) 1900-**CLC 18**
See also CA 57-60; CANR 9, 24, 49; DLB 88
Findley, Timothy 1930-. **CLC 27, 102; DAC;**
DAM MST
See also CA 25-28R; CANR 12, 42; DLB 53

Fink, William
See Mencken, H(enry) L(ouis)
Firbank, Louis 1942-
See Reed, Lou
See also CA 117
Firbank, (Arthur Annesley) Ronald 1886-1926
TCLC 1
See also CA 104; DLB 36
Fisher, M(ary) F(rances) K(ennedy) 1908-1992
CLC 76, 87
See also CA 77-80; 138; CANR 44
Fisher, Roy 1930- .... **CLC 25**
See also CA 81-84; CAAS 10; CANR 16; DLB
40
Fisher, Rudolph 1897-1934 . **TCLC 11; BLC;**
DAM MULT; SSC 25
See also BW 1; CA 107; 124; DLB 51, 102
Fisher, Vardis (Alvero) 1895-1968 ...... **CLC 7**
See also CA 5-8R; 25-28R; DLB 9
Fiske, Tarleton
See Bloch, Robert (Albert)
Fitch, Clarke
See Sinclair, Upton (Beall)
Fitch, John IV
See Cormier, Robert (Edmund)
Fitzgerald, Captain Hugh
See Baum, L(yman) Frank
FitzGerald, Edward 1809-1883 .... **NCLC 9**
See also DLB 32
Fitzgerald, F(rancis) Scott (Key) 1896-1940
TCLC 1, 6, 14, 28, 55; DA; DAB; DAC;
DAM MST, NOV; SSC 6; WLC
See also AITN 1; CA 110; 123; CDALB 1917-
1929; DLB 4, 9, 86; DLBD 1, 15, 16; DLBY
81, 96; MTCW
Fitzgerald, Penelope 1916- ... **CLC 19, 51, 61**
See also CA 85-88; CAAS 10; CANR 56; DLB
14
Fitzgerald, Robert (Stuart) 1910-1985**CLC 39**
See also CA 1-4R; 114; CANR 1; DLBY 80
FitzGerald, Robert D(avid) 1902-1987**CLC 19**
See also CA 17-20R
Fitzgerald, Zelda (Sayre) 1900-1948**TCLC 52**
See also CA 117; 126; DLBY 84
Flanagan, Thomas (James Bonner) 1923-
CLC 25, 52
See also CA 108; CANR 55; DLBY 80; INT
108; MTCW
Flaubert, Gustave 1821-1880**NCLC 2, 10, 19,**
62, 66; DA; DAB; DAC; DAM MST, NOV;
SSC 11; WLC
See also DLB 119
Flecker, Herman Elroy
See Flecker, (Herman) James Elroy
Flecker, (Herman) James Elroy 1884-1915
TCLC 43
See also CA 109; 150; DLB 10, 19
Fleming, Ian (Lancaster) 1908-1964 . **CLC 3,**
30; DAM POP
See also CA 5-8R; CANR 59; CDBLB 1945-
1960; DLB 87; MTCW; SATA 9
Fleming, Thomas (James) 1927- .... **CLC 37**
See also CA 5-8R; CANR 10; INT CANR-10;
SATA 8
Fletcher, John 1579-1625 .... **LC 33; DC 6**
See also CDBLB Before 1660; DLB 58
Fletcher, John Gould 1886-1950 .... **TCLC 35**
See also CA 107; DLB 4, 45
Fleur, Paul
See Pohl, Frederik
Flooglebuckle, Al
See Spiegelman, Art
Flying Officer X

See Bates, H(erbert) E(rnest)
Fo, Dario 1926- .... **CLC 32; DAM DRAM**
See also CA 116; 128; MTCW
Fogarty, Jonathan Titulescu Esq.
See Farrell, James T(homas)
Folke, Will
See Bloch, Robert (Albert)
Follett, Ken(neth Martin) 1949- ..... **CLC 18;**
DAM NOV, POP
See also AAYA 6; BEST 89:4; CA 81-84; CANR
13, 33, 54; DLB 87; DLBY 81; INT CANR-
33; MTCW
Fontane, Theodor 1819-1898 .... **NCLC 26**
See also DLB 129
Foote, Horton 1916-**CLC 51, 91; DAM DRAM**
See also CA 73-76; CANR 34, 51; DLB 26; INT
CANR-34
Foote, Shelby 1916-**CLC 75; DAM NOV, POP**
See also CA 5-8R; CANR 3, 45; DLB 2, 17
Forbes, Esther 1891-1967 .... **CLC 12**
See also AAYA 17; CA 13-14; 25-28R; CAP 1;
CLR 27; DLB 22; JRDA; MAICYA; SATA 2
Forche, Carolyn (Louise) 1950- **CLC 25, 83,**
86; DAM POET; PC 10
See also CA 109; 117; CANR 50; DLB 5; INT
117
Ford, Elbur
See Hibbert, Eleanor Alice Burford
Ford, Ford Madox 1873-1939**TCLC 1, 15, 39,**
57; DAM NOV
See also CA 104; 132; CDBLB 1914-1945;
DLB 162; MTCW
Ford, Henry 1863-1947 .... **TCLC 73**
See also CA 115; 148
Ford, John 1586-(?) .... **DC 8**
See also CDBLB Before 1660; DAM DRAM;
DLB 58
Ford, John 1895-1973 .... **CLC 16**
See also CA 45-48
Ford, Richard .... **CLC 99**
Ford, Richard 1944- .... **CLC 46**
See also CA 69-72; CANR 11, 47
Ford, Webster
See Masters, Edgar Lee
Foreman, Richard 1937- .... **CLC 50**
See also CA 65-68; CANR 32
Forester, C(ecil) S(cott) 1899-1966 ... **CLC 35**
See also CA 73-76; 25-28R; SATA 13
Forez
See Mauriac, Francois (Charles)
Forman, James Douglas 1932- .... **CLC 21**
See also AAYA 17; CA 9-12R; CANR 4, 19,
42; JRDA; MAICYA; SATA 8, 70
Fornes, Maria Irene 1930- .... **CLC 39, 61**
See also CA 25-28R; CANR 28; DLB 7; HW;
INT CANR-28; MTCW
Forrest, Leon 1937- .... **CLC 4**
See also BW 2; CA 89-92; CAAS 7; CANR 25,
52; DLB 33
Forster, E(dward) M(organ) 1879-1970 **C L C**
1, 2, 3, 4, 9, 10, 13, 15, 22, 45, 77; DA; DAB;
DAC; DAM MST, NOV; SSC 27; WLC
See also AAYA 2; CA 13-14; 25-28R; CANR
45; CAP 1; CDBLB 1914-1945; DLB 34, 98,
162, 178; DLBD 10; MTCW; SATA 57
Forster, John 1812-1876 .... **NCLC 11**
See also DLB 144, 184
Forsyth, Frederick 1938-**CLC 2, 5, 36; DAM**
NOV, POP
See also BEST 89:4; CA 85-88; CANR 38, 62;
DLB 87; MTCW
Forten, Charlotte L. .... **TCLC 16; BLC**
See also Grimke, Charlotte L(ottie) Forten

See also DLB 50

Foscolo, Ugo 1778-1827 .... NCLC 8

Fosse, Bob .... CLC 20
See also Fosse, Robert Louis

Fosse, Robert Louis 1927-1987
See Fosse, Bob
See also CA 110; 123

Foster, Stephen Collins 1826-1864 . NCLC 26

Foucault, Michel 1926-1984 . CLC 31, 34, 69
See also CA 105; 113; CANR 34; MTCW

Fouque, Friedrich (Heinrich Karl) de la Motte
1777-1843 .... NCLC 2
See also DLB 90

Fourier, Charles 1772-1837 .... NCLC 51

Fournier, Henri Alban 1886-1914
See Alain-Fournier
See also CA 104

Fournier, Pierre 1916- .... CLC 11
See also Gascar, Pierre
See also CA 89-92; CANR 16, 40

Fowles, John 1926-CLC 1, 2, 3, 4, 6, 9, 10, 15,
33, 87; DAB; DAC; DAM MST
See also CA 5-8R; CANR 25; CDBLB 1960 to
Present; DLB 14, 139; MTCW; SATA 22

Fox, Paula 1923- .... CLC 2, 8
See also AAYA 3; CA 73-76; CANR 20, 36,
62; CLR 1, 44; DLB 52; JRDA; MAICYA;
MTCW; SATA 17, 60

Fox, William Price (Jr.) 1926- .... CLC 22
See also CA 17-20R; CAAS 19; CANR 11; DLB
2; DLBY 81

Foxe, John 1516(?)-1587 .... LC 14

Frame, Janet 1924-CLC 2, 3, 6, 22, 66, 96; SSC
29
See also Clutha, Janet Paterson Frame

France, Anatole .... TCLC 9
See also Thibault, Jacques Anatole Francois
See also DLB 123

Francis, Claude 19(?)- .... CLC 50

Francis, Dick 1920-CLC 2, 22, 42, 102; DAM
POP
See also AAYA 5, 21; BEST 89:3; CA 5-8R;
CANR 9, 42; CDBLB 1960 to Present; DLB
87; INT CANR-9; MTCW

Francis, Robert (Churchill) 1901-1987 . C L C
15
See also CA 1-4R; 123; CANR 1

Frank, Anne(lies Marie) 1929-1945TCLC 17;
DA; DAB; DAC; DAM MST; WLC
See also AAYA 12; CA 113; 133; MTCW; SATA
87; SATA-Brief 42

Frank, Elizabeth 1945- .... CLC 39
See also CA 121; 126; INT 126

Frankl, Viktor E(mil) 1905-1997 ..... CLC 93
See also CA 65-68; 161

Franklin, Benjamin
See Hasek, Jaroslav (Matej Frantisek)

Franklin, Benjamin 1706-1790 .. LC 25; DA;
DAB; DAC; DAM MST; WLCS
See also CDALB 1640-1865; DLB 24, 43, 73

Franklin, (Stella Maraia Sarah) Miles 1879-
1954 .... TCLC 7
See also CA 104

Fraser, (Lady) Antonia (Pakenham) 1932-
CLC 32
See also CA 85-88; CANR 44; MTCW; SATA-
Brief 32

Fraser, George MacDonald 1925- ...... CLC 7
See also CA 45-48; CANR 2, 48

Fraser, Sylvia 1935- .... CLC 64
See also CA 45-48; CANR 1, 16, 60

Frayn, Michael 1933-CLC 3, 7, 31, 47; DAM
DRAM, NOV

See also CA 5-8R; CANR 30; DLB 13, 14;
MTCW

Fraze, Candida (Merrill) 1945- .... CLC 50
See also CA 126

Frazer, J(ames) G(eorge) 1854-1941TCLC 32
See also CA 118

Frazer, Robert Caine
See Creasey, John

Frazer, Sir James George
See Frazer, J(ames) G(eorge)

Frazier, Ian 1951- .... CLC 46
See also CA 130; CANR 54

Frederic, Harold 1856-1898 .... NCLC 10
See also DLB 12, 23; DLBD 13

Frederick, John
See Faust, Frederick (Schiller)

Frederick the Great 1712-1786 .... LC 14

Fredro, Aleksander 1793-1876 .... NCLC 8

Freeling, Nicolas 1927- .... CLC 38
See also CA 49-52; CAAS 12; CANR 1, 17,
50; DLB 87

Freeman, Douglas Southall 1886-1953T C L C
11
See also CA 109; DLB 17

Freeman, Judith 1946- .... CLC 55
See also CA 148

Freeman, Mary Eleanor Wilkins 1852-1930
TCLC 9; SSC 1
See also CA 106; DLB 12, 78

Freeman, R(ichard) Austin 1862-1943 T C L C
21
See also CA 113; DLB 70

French, Albert 1943- .... CLC 86

French, Marilyn 1929-CLC 10, 18, 60; DAM
DRAM, NOV, POP
See also CA 69-72; CANR 3, 31; INT CANR-
31; MTCW

French, Paul
See Asimov, Isaac

Freneau, Philip Morin 1752-1832 ... NCLC 1
See also DLB 37, 43

Freud, Sigmund 1856-1939 .... TCLC 52
See also CA 115; 133; MTCW

Friedan, Betty (Naomi) 1921- .... CLC 74
See also CA 65-68; CANR 18, 45; MTCW

Friedlander, Saul 1932- .... CLC 90
See also CA 117; 130

Friedman, B(ernard) H(arper) 1926- . CLC 7
See also CA 1-4R; CANR 3, 48

Friedman, Bruce Jay 1930- ...... CLC 3, 5, 56
See also CA 9-12R; CANR 25, 52; DLB 2, 28;
INT CANR-25

Friel, Brian 1929- .... CLC 5, 42, 59; DC 8
See also CA 21-24R; CANR 33; DLB 13;
MTCW

Friis-Baastad, Babbis Ellinor 1921-1970C L C
12
See also CA 17-20R; 134; SATA 7

Frisch, Max (Rudolf) 1911-1991CLC 3, 9, 14,
18, 32, 44; DAM DRAM, NOV
See also CA 85-88; 134; CANR 32; DLB 69,
124; MTCW

Fromentin, Eugene (Samuel Auguste) 1820-
1876 .... NCLC 10
See also DLB 123

Frost, Frederick
See Faust, Frederick (Schiller)

Frost, Robert (Lee) 1874-1963CLC 1, 3, 4, 9,
10, 13, 15, 26, 34, 44; DA; DAB; DAC;
DAM MST, POET; PC 1; WLC
See also AAYA 21; CA 89-92; CANR 33;
CDALB 1917-1929; DLB 54; DLBD 7;
MTCW; SATA 14

Froude, James Anthony 1818-1894NCLC 43
See also DLB 18, 57, 144

Froy, Herald
See Waterhouse, Keith (Spencer)

Fry, Christopher 1907- CLC 2, 10, 14; DAM
DRAM
See also CA 17-20R; CAAS 23; CANR 9, 30;
DLB 13; MTCW; SATA 66

Frye, (Herman) Northrop 1912-1991CLC 24,
70
See also CA 5-8R; 133; CANR 8, 37; DLB 67,
68; MTCW

Fuchs, Daniel 1909-1993 .... CLC 8, 22
See also CA 81-84; 142; CAAS 5; CANR 40;
DLB 9, 26, 28; DLBY 93

Fuchs, Daniel 1934- .... CLC 34
See also CA 37-40R; CANR 14, 48

Fuentes, Carlos 1928-CLC 3, 8, 10, 13, 22, 41,
60; DA; DAB; DAC; DAM MST, MULT,
NOV; HLC; SSC 24; WLC
See also AAYA 4; AITN 2; CA 69-72; CANR
10, 32; DLB 113; HW; MTCW

Fuentes, Gregorio Lopez y
See Lopez y Fuentes, Gregorio

Fugard, (Harold) Athol 1932-CLC 5, 9, 14, 25,
40, 80; DAM DRAM; DC 3
See also AAYA 17; CA 85-88; CANR 32, 54;
MTCW

Fugard, Sheila 1932- .... CLC 48
See also CA 125

Fuller, Charles (H., Jr.) 1939-CLC 25; BLC;
DAM DRAM, MULT; DC 1
See also BW 2; CA 108; 112; DLB 38; INT 112;
MTCW

Fuller, John (Leopold) 1937- .... CLC 62
See also CA 21-24R; CANR 9, 44; DLB 40

Fuller, Margaret .... NCLC 5, 50
See also Ossoli, Sarah Margaret (Fuller
marchesa d')

Fuller, Roy (Broadbent) 1912-1991CLC 4, 28
See also CA 5-8R; 135; CAAS 10; CANR 53;
DLB 15, 20; SATA 87

Fulton, Alice 1952- .... CLC 52
See also CA 116; CANR 57

Furphy, Joseph 1843-1912 .... TCLC 25

Fussell, Paul 1924- .... CLC 74
See also BEST 90:1; CA 17-20R; CANR 8, 21,
35; INT CANR-21; MTCW

Futabatei, Shimei 1864-1909 .... TCLC 44
See also DLB 180

Futrelle, Jacques 1875-1912 .... TCLC 19
See also CA 113; 155

Gaboriau, Emile 1835-1873 .... NCLC 14

Gadda, Carlo Emilio 1893-1973 .... CLC 11
See also CA 89-92; DLB 177

Gaddis, William 1922- CLC 1, 3, 6, 8, 10, 19,
43, 86
See also CA 17-20R; CANR 21, 48; DLB 2;
MTCW

Gage, Walter
See Inge, William (Motter)

Gaines, Ernest J(ames) 1933- CLC 3, 11, 18,
86; BLC; DAM MULT
See also AAYA 18; AITN 1; BW 2; CA 9-12R;
CANR 6, 24, 42; CDALB 1968-1988; DLB
2, 33, 152; DLBY 80; MTCW; SATA 86

Gaitskill, Mary 1954- .... CLC 69
See also CA 128; CANR 61

Galdos, Benito Perez
See Perez Galdos, Benito

Gale, Zona 1874-1938TCLC 7; DAM DRAM
See also CA 105; 153; DLB 9, 78

Galeano, Eduardo (Hughes) 1940- .. CLC 72

See also CA 29-32R; CANR 13, 32; HW
Galiano, Juan Valera y Alcala
  See Valera y Alcala-Galiano, Juan
Gallagher, Tess 1943- ...... **CLC 18, 63; DAM POET; PC 9**
  See also CA 106; DLB 120
Gallant, Mavis 1922- ... **CLC 7, 18, 38; DAC; DAM MST; SSC 5**
  See also CA 69-72; CANR 29; DLB 53; MTCW
Gallant, Roy A(rthur) 1924- .... **CLC 17**
  See also CA 5-8R; CANR 4, 29, 54; CLR 30; MAICYA; SATA 4, 68
Gallico, Paul (William) 1897-1976 .....**CLC 2**
  See also AITN 1; CA 5-8R; 69-72; CANR 23; DLB 9, 171; MAICYA; SATA 13
Gallo, Max Louis 1932- .... **CLC 95**
  See also CA 85-88
Gallois, Lucien
  See Desnos, Robert
Gallup, Ralph
  See Whitemore, Hugh (John)
Galsworthy, John 1867-1933TCLC 1, 45; DA; DAB; DAC; DAM DRAM, MST, NOV; SSC 22; WLC 2
  See also CA 104; 141; CDBLB 1890-1914; DLB 10, 34, 98, 162; DLBD 16
Galt, John 1779-1839 .... **NCLC 1**
  See also DLB 99, 116, 159
Galvin, James 1951- .... **CLC 38**
  See also CA 108; CANR 26
Gamboa, Federico 1864-1939 .... **TCLC 36**
Gandhi, M. K.
  See Gandhi, Mohandas Karamchand
Gandhi, Mahatma
  See Gandhi, Mohandas Karamchand
Gandhi, Mohandas Karamchand 1869-1948 **TCLC 59; DAM MULT**
  See also CA 121; 132; MTCW
Gann, Ernest Kellogg 1910-1991 ..... **CLC 23**
  See also AITN 1; CA 1-4R; 136; CANR 1
Garcia, Cristina 1958- .... **CLC 76**
  See also CA 141
Garcia Lorca, Federico 1898-1936TCLC 1, 7, 49; DA; DAB; DAC; DAM DRAM, MST, MULT, POET; DC 2; HLC; PC 3; WLC
  See also CA 104; 131; DLB 108; HW; MTCW
Garcia Marquez, Gabriel (Jose) 1928-CLC 2, 3, 8, 10, 15, 27, 47, 55, 68; DA; DAB; DAC; DAM MST, MULT, NOV, POP; HLC; SSC 8; WLC
  See also AAYA 3; BEST 89:1, 90:4; CA 33-36R; CANR 10, 28, 50; DLB 113; HW; MTCW
Gard, Janice
  See Latham, Jean Lee
Gard, Roger Martin du
  See Martin du Gard, Roger
Gardam, Jane 1928- .... **CLC 43**
  See also CA 49-52; CANR 2, 18, 33, 54; CLR 12; DLB 14, 161; MAICYA; MTCW; SAAS 9; SATA 39, 76; SATA-Brief 28
Gardner, Herb(ert) 1934- .... **CLC 44**
  See also CA 149
Gardner, John (Champlin), Jr. 1933-1982 **CLC 2, 3, 5, 7, 8, 10, 18, 28, 34; DAM NOV, POP; SSC 7**
  See also AITN 1; CA 65-68; 107; CANR 33; DLB 2; DLBY 82; MTCW; SATA 40; SATA-Obit 31
Gardner, John (Edmund) 1926-CLC 30; DAM POP
  See also CA 103; CANR 15; MTCW
Gardner, Miriam

See Bradley, Marion Zimmer
Gardner, Noel
  See Kuttner, Henry
Gardons, S. S.
  See Snodgrass, W(illiam) D(e Witt)
Garfield, Leon 1921-1996 ....**CLC 12**
  See also AAYA 8; CA 17-20R; 152; CANR 38, 41; CLR 21; DLB 161; JRDA; MAICYA; SATA 1, 32, 76; SATA-Obit 90
Garland, (Hannibal) Hamlin 1860-1940 **TCLC 3; SSC 18**
  See also CA 104; DLB 12, 71, 78
Garneau, (Hector de) Saint-Denys 1912-1943 **TCLC 13**
  See also CA 111; DLB 88
Garner, Alan 1934-CLC 17; DAB; DAM POP
  See also AAYA 18; CA 73-76; CANR 15; CLR 20; DLB 161; MAICYA; MTCW; SATA 18, 69
Garner, Hugh 1913-1979 ....**CLC 13**
  See also CA 69-72; CANR 31; DLB 68
Garnett, David 1892-1981 ....**CLC 3**
  See also CA 5-8R; 103; CANR 17; DLB 34
Garos, Stephanie
  See Katz, Steve
Garrett, George (Palmer) 1929-CLC 3, 11, 51
  See also CA 1-4R; CAAS 5; CANR 1, 42; DLB 2, 5, 130, 152; DLBY 83
Garrick, David 1717-1779 ....**LC 15; DAM DRAM**
  See also DLB 84
Garrigue, Jean 1914-1972 ....**CLC 2, 8**
  See also CA 5-8R; 37-40R; CANR 20
Garrison, Frederick
  See Sinclair, Upton (Beall)
Garth, Will
  See Hamilton, Edmond; Kuttner, Henry
Garvey, Marcus (Moziah, Jr.) 1887-1940 **TCLC 41; BLC; DAM MULT**
  See also BW 1; CA 120; 124
Gary, Romain ....**CLC 25**
  See also Kacew, Romain
  See also DLB 83
Gascar, Pierre ....**CLC 11**
  See also Fournier, Pierre
Gascoyne, David (Emery) 1916- ....**CLC 45**
  See also CA 65-68; CANR 10, 28, 54; DLB 20; MTCW
Gaskell, Elizabeth Cleghorn 1810-1865NCLC 5; DAB; DAM MST; SSC 25
  See also CDBLB 1832-1890; DLB 21, 144, 159
Gass, William H(oward) 1924-CLC 1, 2, 8, 11, 15, 39; SSC 12
  See also CA 17-20R; CANR 30; DLB 2; MTCW
Gasset, Jose Ortega y
  See Ortega y Gasset, Jose
Gates, Henry Louis, Jr. 1950- CLC 65; DAM MULT
  See also BW 2; CA 109; CANR 25, 53; DLB 67
Gautier, Theophile 1811-1872 .. **NCLC 1, 59; DAM POET; PC 18; SSC 20**
  See also DLB 119
Gawsworth, John
  See Bates, H(erbert) E(rnest)
Gay, Oliver
  See Gogarty, Oliver St. John
Gaye, Marvin (Penze) 1939-1984 .....**CLC 26**
  See also CA 112
Gebler, Carlo (Ernest) 1954- ....**CLC 39**
  See also CA 119; 133
Gee, Maggie (Mary) 1948- ....**CLC 57**
  See also CA 130

Gee, Maurice (Gough) 1931- ....**CLC 29**
  See also CA 97-100; SATA 46
Gelbart, Larry (Simon) 1923- .... **CLC 21, 61**
  See also CA 73-76; CANR 45
Gelber, Jack 1932- .... **CLC 1, 6, 14, 79**
  See also CA 1-4R; CANR 2; DLB 7
Gellhorn, Martha (Ellis) 1908- .. **CLC 14, 60**
  See also CA 77-80; CANR 44; DLBY 82
Genet, Jean 1910-1986CLC 1, 2, 5, 10, 14, 44, 46; DAM DRAM
  See also CA 13-16R; CANR 18; DLB 72; DLBY 86; MTCW
Gent, Peter 1942- ....**CLC 29**
  See also AITN 1; CA 89-92; DLBY 82
Gentlewoman in New England, A
  See Bradstreet, Anne
Gentlewoman in Those Parts, A
  See Bradstreet, Anne
George, Jean Craighead 1919- ....**CLC 35**
  See also AAYA 8; CA 5-8R; CANR 25; CLR 1; DLB 52; JRDA; MAICYA; SATA 2, 68
George, Stefan (Anton) 1868-1933TCLC 2, 14
  See also CA 104
Georges, Georges Martin
  See Simenon, Georges (Jacques Christian)
Gerhardi, William Alexander
  See Gerhardie, William Alexander
Gerhardie, William Alexander 1895-1977 **CLC 5**
  See also CA 25-28R; 73-76; CANR 18; DLB 36
Gerstler, Amy 1956- ....**CLC 70**
  See also CA 146
Gertler, T. ....**CLC 34**
  See also CA 116; 121; INT 121
Ghalib ....**NCLC 39**
  See also Ghalib, Hsadullah Khan
Ghalib, Hsadullah Khan 1797-1869
  See Ghalib
  See also DAM POET
Ghelderode, Michel de 1898-1962CLC 6, 11; DAM DRAM
  See also CA 85-88; CANR 40
Ghiselin, Brewster 1903- ....**CLC 23**
  See also CA 13-16R; CAAS 10; CANR 13
Ghose, Zulfikar 1935- ....**CLC 42**
  See also CA 65-68
Ghosh, Amitav 1956- ....**CLC 44**
  See also CA 147
Giacosa, Giuseppe 1847-1906 ....**TCLC 7**
  See also CA 104
Gibb, Lee
  See Waterhouse, Keith (Spencer)
Gibbon, Lewis Grassic ....**TCLC 4**
  See also Mitchell, James Leslie
Gibbons, Kaye 1960-CLC 50, 88; DAM POP
  See also CA 151
Gibran, Kahlil 1883-1931 . **TCLC 1, 9; DAM POET, POP; PC 9**
  See also CA 104; 150
Gibran, Khalil
  See Gibran, Kahlil
Gibson, William 1914- .. **CLC 23; DA; DAB; DAC; DAM DRAM, MST**
  See also CA 9-12R; CANR 9, 42; DLB 7; SATA 66
Gibson, William (Ford) 1948- ... **CLC 39, 63; DAM POP**
  See also AAYA 12; CA 126; 133; CANR 52
Gide, Andre (Paul Guillaume) 1869-1951 **TCLC 5, 12, 36; DA; DAB; DAC; DAM MST, NOV; SSC 13; WLC**
  See also CA 104; 124; DLB 65; MTCW

Gifford, Barry (Colby) 1946- .... **CLC 34**
    See also CA 65-68; CANR 9, 30, 40
Gilbert, Frank
    See De Voto, Bernard (Augustine)
Gilbert, W(illiam) S(chwenck) 1836-1911
    TCLC 3; DAM DRAM, POET
    See also CA 104; SATA 36
Gilbreth, Frank B., Jr. 1911- .... **CLC 17**
    See also CA 9-12R; SATA 2
Gilchrist, Ellen 1935-**CLC 34, 48; DAM POP;**
    SSC 14
    See also CA 113; 116; CANR 41, 61; DLB 130;
    MTCW
Giles, Molly 1942- .... **CLC 39**
    See also CA 126
Gill, Patrick
    See Creasey, John
Gilliam, Terry (Vance) 1940- .... **CLC 21**
    See also Monty Python
    See also AAYA 19; CA 108; 113; CANR 35;
    INT 113
Gillian, Jerry
    See Gilliam, Terry (Vance)
Gilliatt, Penelope (Ann Douglass) 1932-1993
    CLC 2, 10, 13, 53
    See also AITN 2; CA 13-16R; 141; CANR 49;
    DLB 14
Gilman, Charlotte (Anna) Perkins (Stetson)
    1860-1935 .... **TCLC 9, 37; SSC 13**
    See also CA 106; 150
Gilmour, David 1949- .... **CLC 35**
    See also CA 138, 147
Gilpin, William 1724-1804 .... **NCLC 30**
Gilray, J. D.
    See Mencken, H(enry) L(ouis)
Gilroy, Frank D(aniel) 1925- .... **CLC 2**
    See also CA 81-84; CANR 32; DLB 7
Gilstrap, John 1957(?)- .... **CLC 99**
    See also CA 160
Ginsberg, Allen 1926-1997**CLC 1, 2, 3, 4, 6, 13,**
    36, 69; DA; DAB; DAC; DAM MST,
    POET; PC 4; WLC 3
    See also AITN 1; CA 1-4R; 157; CANR 2, 41;
    CDALB 1941-1968; DLB 5, 16, 169; MTCW
Ginzburg, Natalia 1916-1991**CLC 5, 11, 54, 70**
    See also CA 85-88; 135; CANR 33; DLB 177;
    MTCW
Giono, Jean 1895-1970 .... **CLC 4, 11**
    See also CA 45-48; 29-32R; CANR 2, 35; DLB
    72; MTCW
Giovanni, Nikki 1943-**CLC 2, 4, 19, 64; BLC;**
    DA; DAB; DAC; DAM MST, MULT,
    POET; PC 19; WLCS
    See also AAYA 22; AITN 1; BW 2; CA 29-32R;
    CAAS 6; CANR 18, 41, 60; CLR 6; DLB 5,
    41; INT CANR-18; MAICYA; MTCW; SATA
    24
Giovene, Andrea 1904- .... **CLC 7**
    See also CA 85-88
Gippius, Zinaida (Nikolayevna) 1869-1945
    See Hippius, Zinaida
    See also CA 106
Giraudoux, (Hippolyte) Jean 1882-1944
    TCLC 2, 7; DAM DRAM
    See also CA 104; DLB 65
Gironella, Jose Maria 1917-.............. **CLC 11**
    See also CA 101
Gissing, George (Robert) 1857-1903**TCLC 3,**
    24, 47
    See also CA 105; DLB 18, 135, 184
Giurlani, Aldo
    See Palazzeschi, Aldo
Gladkov, Fyodor (Vasilyevich) 1883-1958

TCLC 27
Glanville, Brian (Lester) 1931- .... **CLC 6**
    See also CA 5-8R; CAAS 9; CANR 3; DLB 15,
    139; SATA 42
Glasgow, Ellen (Anderson Gholson) 1873(?)-
    1945 .... **TCLC 2, 7**
    See also CA 104; DLB 9, 12
Glaspell, Susan 1882(?)-1948 .... **TCLC 55**
    See also CA 110; 154; DLB 7, 9, 78; YABC 2
Glassco, John 1909-1981 .... **CLC 9**
    See also CA 13-16R; 102; CANR 15; DLB 68
Glasscock, Amnesia
    See Steinbeck, John (Ernst)
Glasser, Ronald J. 1940(?)- .... **CLC 37**
Glassman, Joyce
    See Johnson, Joyce
Glendinning, Victoria 1937-.............. **CLC 50**
    See also CA 120; 127; CANR 59; DLB 155
Glissant, Edouard 1928-. **CLC 10, 68; DAM**
    MULT
    See also CA 153
Gloag, Julian 1930- .... **CLC 40**
    See also AITN 1; CA 65-68; CANR 10
Glowacki, Aleksander
    See Prus, Boleslaw
Gluck, Louise (Elisabeth) 1943-**CLC 7, 22, 44,**
    81; DAM POET; PC 16
    See also CA 33-36R; CANR 40; DLB 5
Glyn, Elinor 1864-1943 .... **TCLC 72**
    See also DLB 153
Gobineau, Joseph Arthur (Comte) de 1816-
    1882 .... **NCLC 17**
    See also DLB 123
Godard, Jean-Luc 1930- .... **CLC 20**
    See also CA 93-96
Godden, (Margaret) Rumer 1907-.... **CLC 53**
    See also AAYA 6; CA 5-8R; CANR 4, 27, 36,
    55; CLR 20; DLB 161; MAICYA; SAAS 12;
    SATA 3, 36
Godoy Alcayaga, Lucila 1889-1957
    See Mistral, Gabriela
    See also BW 2; CA 104; 131; DAM MULT;
    HW; MTCW
Godwin, Gail (Kathleen) 1937- **CLC 5, 8, 22,**
    31, 69; DAM POP
    See also CA 29-32R; CANR 15, 43; DLB 6;
    INT CANR-15; MTCW
Godwin, William 1756-1836 .... **NCLC 14**
    See also CDBLB 1789-1832; DLB 39, 104, 142,
    158, 163
Goebbels, Josef
    See Goebbels, (Paul) Joseph
Goebbels, (Paul) Joseph 1897-1945**TCLC 68**
    See also CA 115; 148
Goebbels, Joseph Paul
    See Goebbels, (Paul) Joseph
Goethe, Johann Wolfgang von 1749-1832
    NCLC 4, 22, 34; DA; DAB; DAC; DAM
    DRAM, MST, POET; PC 5; WLC 3
    See also DLB 94
Gogarty, Oliver St. John 1878-1957**TCLC 15**
    See also CA 109; 150; DLB 15, 19
Gogol, Nikolai (Vasilyevich) 1809-1852**NCLC**
    5, 15, 31; DA; DAB; DAC; DAM DRAM,
    MST; DC 1; SSC 4, 29; WLC
Goines, Donald 1937(?)-1974 **CLC 80; BLC;**
    DAM MULT, POP
    See also AITN 1; BW 1; CA 124; 114; DLB 33
Gold, Herbert 1924- .... **CLC 4, 7, 14, 42**
    See also CA 9-12R; CANR 17, 45; DLB 2;
    DLBY 81
Goldbarth, Albert 1948- .... **CLC 5, 38**
    See also CA 53-56; CANR 6, 40; DLB 120

Goldberg, Anatol 1910-1982 .... **CLC 34**
    See also CA 131; 117
Goldemberg, Isaac 1945- .... **CLC 52**
    See also CA 69-72; CAAS 12; CANR 11, 32;
    HW
Golding, William (Gerald) 1911-1993**CLC 1,**
    2, 3, 8, 10, 17, 27, 58, 81; DA; DAB; DAC;
    DAM MST, NOV; WLC
    See also AAYA 5; CA 5-8R; 141; CANR 13,
    33, 54; CDBLB 1945-1960; DLB 15, 100;
    MTCW
Goldman, Emma 1869-1940 .... **TCLC 13**
    See also CA 110; 150
Goldman, Francisco 1955- .... **CLC 76**
Goldman, William (W.) 1931- ...... **CLC 1, 48**
    See also CA 9-12R; CANR 29; DLB 44
Goldmann, Lucien 1913-1970 .... **CLC 24**
    See also CA 25-28; CAP 2
Goldoni, Carlo 1707-1793**LC 4; DAM DRAM**
Goldsberry, Steven 1949- .... **CLC 34**
    See also CA 131
Goldsmith, Oliver 1728-1774**LC 2; DA; DAB;**
    DAC; DAM DRAM, MST, NOV, POET;
    DC 8; WLC
    See also CDBLB 1660-1789; DLB 39, 89, 104,
    109, 142; SATA 26
Goldsmith, Peter
    See Priestley, J(ohn) B(oynton)
Gombrowicz, Witold 1904-1969**CLC 4, 7, 11,**
    49; DAM DRAM
    See also CA 19-20; 25-28R; CAP 2
Gomez de la Serna, Ramon 1888-1963**CLC 9**
    See also CA 153; 116; HW
Goncharov, Ivan Alexandrovich 1812-1891
    NCLC 1, 63
Goncourt, Edmond (Louis Antoine Huot) de
    1822-1896 .... **NCLC 7**
    See also DLB 123
Goncourt, Jules (Alfred Huot) de 1830-1870
    NCLC 7
    See also DLB 123
Gontier, Fernande 19(?)- .... **CLC 50**
Gonzalez Martinez, Enrique 1871-1952
    TCLC 72
    See also HW
Goodman, Paul 1911-1972 ...... **CLC 1, 2, 4, 7**
    See also CA 19-20; 37-40R; CANR 34; CAP 2;
    DLB 130; MTCW
Gordimer, Nadine 1923-**CLC 3, 5, 7, 10, 18, 33,**
    51, 70; DA; DAB; DAC; DAM MST, NOV;
    SSC 17; WLCS
    See also CA 5-8R; CANR 3, 28, 56; INT CANR-
    28; MTCW
Gordon, Adam Lindsay 1833-1870 **NCLC 21**
Gordon, Caroline 1895-1981**CLC 6, 13, 29, 83;**
    SSC 15
    See also CA 11-12; 103; CANR 36; CAP 1;
    DLB 4, 9, 102; DLBY 81; MTCW
Gordon, Charles William 1860-1937
    See Connor, Ralph
    See also CA 109
Gordon, Mary (Catherine) 1949-**CLC 13, 22**
    See also CA 102; CANR 44; DLB 6; DLBY
    81; INT 102; MTCW
Gordon, N. J.
    See Bosman, Herman Charles
Gordon, Sol 1923- .... **CLC 26**
    See also CA 53-56; CANR 4; SATA 11
Gordone, Charles 1925-1995**CLC 1, 4; DAM**
    DRAM; DC 8
    See also BW 1; CA 93-96; 150; CANR 55; DLB
    7; INT 93-96; MTCW
Gore, Catherine 1800-1861 .... **NCLC 65**

See also DLB 116

Gorenko, Anna Andreevna
See Akhmatova, Anna

Gorky, Maxim 1868-1936**TCLC 8; DAB; SSC 28; WLC**
See also Peshkov, Alexei Maximovich

Goryan, Sirak
See Saroyan, William

Gosse, Edmund (William) 1849-1928**TCLC 28**
See also CA 117; DLB 57, 144, 184

Gotlieb, Phyllis Fay (Bloom) 1926- . **CLC 18**
See also CA 13-16R; CANR 7; DLB 88

Gottesman, S. D.
See Kornbluth, C(yril) M.; Pohl, Frederik

Gottfried von Strassburg fl. c. 1210-. **CMLC 10**
See also DLB 138

Gould, Lois .... **CLC 4, 10**
See also CA 77-80; CANR 29; MTCW

Gourmont, Remy (-Marie-Charles) de 1858-1915 .... **TCLC 17**
See also CA 109; 150

Govier, Katherine 1948- .... **CLC 51**
See also CA 101; CANR 18, 40

Goyen, (Charles) William 1915-1983**CLC 5, 8, 14, 40**
See also AITN 2; CA 5-8R; 110; CANR 6; DLB 2; DLBY 83; INT CANR-6

Goytisolo, Juan 1931- . **CLC 5, 10, 23; DAM MULT; HLC**
See also CA 85-88; CANR 32, 61; HW; MTCW

Gozzano, Guido 1883-1916 .... **PC 10**
See also CA 154; DLB 114

Gozzi, (Conte) Carlo 1720-1806 .... **NCLC 23**

Grabbe, Christian Dietrich 1801-1836**NCLC 2**
See also DLB 133

Grace, Patricia 1937- .... **CLC 56**

Gracian y Morales, Baltasar 1601-1658**LC 15**

Gracq, Julien ....**CLC 11, 48**
See also Poirier, Louis
See also DLB 83

Grade, Chaim 1910-1982 .... **CLC 10**
See also CA 93-96; 107

Graduate of Oxford, A
See Ruskin, John

Grafton, Garth
See Duncan, Sara Jeannette

Graham, John
See Phillips, David Graham

Graham, Jorie 1951- .... **CLC 48**
See also CA 111; DLB 120

Graham, R(obert) B(ontine) Cunninghame
See Cunninghame Graham, R(obert) B(ontine)
See also DLB 98, 135, 174

Graham, Robert
See Haldeman, Joe (William)

Graham, Tom
See Lewis, (Harry) Sinclair

Graham, W(illiam) S(ydney) 1918-1986**CLC 29**
See also CA 73-76; 118; DLB 20

Graham, Winston (Mawdsley) 1910- **CLC 23**
See also CA 49-52; CANR 2, 22, 45; DLB 77

Grahame, Kenneth 1859-1932**TCLC 64; DAB**
See also CA 108; 136; CLR 5; DLB 34, 141, 178; MAICYA; YABC 1

Grant, Skeeter
See Spiegelman, Art

Granville-Barker, Harley 1877-1946**TCLC 2; DAM DRAM**
See also Barker, Harley Granville
See also CA 104

Grass, Guenter (Wilhelm) 1927-**CLC 1, 2, 4, 6, 11, 15, 22, 32, 49, 88; DA; DAB; DAC; DAM MST, NOV; WLC**
See also CA 13-16R; CANR 20; DLB 75, 124; MTCW

Gratton, Thomas
See Hulme, T(homas) E(rnest)

Grau, Shirley Ann 1929- ..**CLC 4, 9; SSC 15**
See also CA 89-92; CANR 22; DLB 2; INT CANR-22; MTCW

Gravel, Fern
See Hall, James Norman

Graver, Elizabeth 1964- .... **CLC 70**
See also CA 135

Graves, Richard Perceval 1945- .... **CLC 44**
See also CA 65-68; CANR 9, 26, 51

Graves, Robert (von Ranke) 1895-1985 **CLC 1, 2, 6, 11, 39, 44, 45; DAB; DAC; DAM MST, POET; PC 6**
See also CA 5-8R; 117; CANR 5, 36; CDBLB 1914-1945; DLB 20, 100; DLBY 85; MTCW; SATA 45

Graves, Valerie
See Bradley, Marion Zimmer

Gray, Alasdair (James) 1934- .... **CLC 41**
See also CA 126; CANR 47; INT 126; MTCW

Gray, Amlin 1946- .... **CLC 29**
See also CA 138

Gray, Francine du Plessix 1930- ..... **CLC 22; DAM NOV**
See also BEST 90:3; CA 61-64; CAAS 2; CANR 11, 33; INT CANR-11; MTCW

Gray, John (Henry) 1866-1934 ...... **TCLC 19**
See also CA 119

Gray, Simon (James Holliday) 1936- **CLC 9, 14, 36**
See also AITN 1; CA 21-24R; CAAS 3; CANR 32; DLB 13; MTCW

Gray, Spalding 1941-**CLC 49; DAM POP; DC 7**
See also CA 128

Gray, Thomas 1716-1771**LC 4, 40; DA; DAB; DAC; DAM MST; PC 2; WLC**
See also CDBLB 1660-1789; DLB 109

Grayson, David
See Baker, Ray Stannard

Grayson, Richard (A.) 1951- .... **CLC 38**
See also CA 85-88; CANR 14, 31, 57

Greeley, Andrew M(oran) 1928- ..... **CLC 28; DAM POP**
See also CA 5-8R; CAAS 7; CANR 7, 43; MTCW

Green, Anna Katharine 1846-1935 **TCLC 63**
See also CA 112; 159

Green, Brian
See Card, Orson Scott

Green, Hannah
See Greenberg, Joanne (Goldenberg)

Green, Hannah 1927(?)-1996 .... **CLC 3**
See also CA 73-76; CANR 59

Green, Henry 1905-1973 .... **CLC 2, 13, 97**
See also Yorke, Henry Vincent
See also DLB 15

Green, Julian (Hartridge) 1900-
See Green, Julien
See also CA 21-24R; CANR 33; DLB 4, 72; MTCW

Green, Julien .... **CLC 3, 11, 77**
See also Green, Julian (Hartridge)

Green, Paul (Eliot) 1894-1981**CLC 25; DAM DRAM**
See also AITN 1; CA 5-8R; 103; CANR 3; DLB 7, 9; DLBY 81

Greenberg, Ivan 1908-1973
See Rahv, Philip
See also CA 85-88

Greenberg, Joanne (Goldenberg) 1932- **CLC 7, 30**
See also AAYA 12; CA 5-8R; CANR 14, 32; SATA 25

Greenberg, Richard 1959(?)- .... **CLC 57**
See also CA 138

Greene, Bette 1934- .... **CLC 30**
See also AAYA 7; CA 53-56; CANR 4; CLR 2; JRDA; MAICYA; SAAS 16; SATA 8

Greene, Gael .... **CLC 8**
See also CA 13-16R; CANR 10

Greene, Graham (Henry) 1904-1991**CLC 1, 3, 6, 9, 14, 18, 27, 37, 70, 72; DA; DAB; DAC; DAM MST, NOV; SSC 29; WLC**
See also AITN 2; CA 13-16R; 133; CANR 35, 61; CDBLB 1945-1960; DLB 13, 15, 77, 100, 162; DLBY 91; MTCW; SATA 20

Greer, Richard
See Silverberg, Robert

Gregor, Arthur 1923- .... **CLC 9**
See also CA 25-28R; CAAS 10; CANR 11; SATA 36

Gregor, Lee
See Pohl, Frederik

Gregory, Isabella Augusta (Persse) 1852-1932 **TCLC 1**
See also CA 104; DLB 10

Gregory, J. Dennis
See Williams, John A(lfred)

Grendon, Stephen
See Derleth, August (William)

Grenville, Kate 1950- .... **CLC 61**
See also CA 118; CANR 53

Grenville, Pelham
See Wodehouse, P(elham) G(renville)

Greve, Felix Paul (Berthold Friedrich) 1879-1948
See Grove, Frederick Philip
See also CA 104; 141; DAC; DAM MST

Grey, Zane 1872-1939 .. **TCLC 6; DAM POP**
See also CA 104; 132; DLB 9; MTCW

Grieg, (Johan) Nordahl (Brun) 1902-1943 **TCLC 10**
See also CA 107

Grieve, C(hristopher) M(urray) 1892-1978 **CLC 11, 19; DAM POET**
See also MacDiarmid, Hugh; Pteleon
See also CA 5-8R; 85-88; CANR 33; MTCW

Griffin, Gerald 1803-1840 .... **NCLC 7**
See also DLB 159

Griffin, John Howard 1920-1980 ..... **CLC 68**
See also AITN 1; CA 1-4R; 101; CANR 2

Griffin, Peter 1942- .... **CLC 39**
See also CA 136

Griffith, D(avid Lewelyn) W(ark) 1875(?)-1948 **TCLC 68**
See also CA 119; 150

Griffith, Lawrence
See Griffith, D(avid Lewelyn) W(ark)

Griffiths, Trevor 1935- .... **CLC 13, 52**
See also CA 97-100; CANR 45; DLB 13

Grigson, Geoffrey (Edward Harvey) 1905-1985 **CLC 7, 39**
See also CA 25-28R; 118; CANR 20, 33; DLB 27; MTCW

Grillparzer, Franz 1791-1872 .... **NCLC 1**
See also DLB 133

Grimble, Reverend Charles James
See Eliot, T(homas) S(tearns)

Grimke, Charlotte L(ottie) Forten 1837(?)-1914

See Forten, Charlotte L.
See also BW 1; CA 117; 124; DAM MULT,
POET

Grimm, Jacob Ludwig Karl 1785-1863**NCLC
3**
See also DLB 90; MAICYA; SATA 22

Grimm, Wilhelm Karl 1786-1859 .... **NCLC 3**
See also DLB 90; MAICYA; SATA 22

Grimmelshausen, Johann Jakob Christoffel von
1621-1676 .... **LC 6**
See also DLB 168

Grindel, Eugene 1895-1952
See Eluard, Paul
See also CA 104

Grisham, John 1955- ..... **CLC 84; DAM POP**
See also AAYA 14; CA 138; CANR 47

Grossman, David 1954- .... **CLC 67**
See also CA 138

Grossman, Vasily (Semenovich) 1905-1964
CLC 41
See also CA 124; 130; MTCW

Grove, Frederick Philip .... **TCLC 4**
See also Greve, Felix Paul (Berthold Friedrich)
See also DLB 92

Grubb
See Crumb, R(obert)

Grumbach, Doris (Isaac) 1918-**CLC 13, 22, 64**
See also CA 5-8R; CAAS 2; CANR 9, 42; INT
CANR-9

Grundtvig, Nicolai Frederik Severin 1783-1872
NCLC 1

Grunge
See Crumb, R(obert)

Grunwald, Lisa 1959- .... **CLC 44**
See also CA 120

Guare, John 1938- . **CLC 8, 14, 29, 67; DAM
DRAM**
See also CA 73-76; CANR 21; DLB 7; MTCW

Gudjonsson, Halldor Kiljan 1902-
See Laxness, Halldor
See also CA 103

Guenter, Erich
See Eich, Guenter

Guest, Barbara 1920- .... **CLC 34**
See also CA 25-28R; CANR 11, 44; DLB 5

Guest, Judith (Ann) 1936- .**CLC 8, 30; DAM
NOV, POP**
See also AAYA 7; CA 77-80; CANR 15; INT
CANR-15; MTCW

Guevara, Che .... **CLC 87; HLC**
See also Guevara (Serna), Ernesto

Guevara (Serna), Ernesto 1928-1967
See Guevara, Che
See also CA 127; 111; CANR 56; DAM MULT;
HW

Guild, Nicholas M. 1944- .... **CLC 33**
See also CA 93-96

Guillemin, Jacques
See Sartre, Jean-Paul

Guillen, Jorge 1893-1984 .... **CLC 11; DAM
MULT, POET**
See also CA 89-92; 112; DLB 108; HW

Guillen, Nicolas (Cristobal) 1902-1989 . **C L C
48, 79; BLC; DAM MST, MULT, POET;
HLC**
See also BW 2; CA 116; 125; 129; HW

Guillevic, (Eugene) 1907- .... **CLC 33**
See also CA 93-96

Guillois
See Desnos, Robert

Guillois, Valentin
See Desnos, Robert

Guiney, Louise Imogen 1861-1920 **TCLC 41**

See also CA 160; DLB 54

Guiraldes, Ricardo (Guillermo) 1886-1927
TCLC 39
See also CA 131; HW; MTCW

Gumilev, Nikolai Stephanovich 1886-1921
TCLC 60

Gunesekera, Romesh 1954- .... **CLC 91**
See also CA 159

Gunn, Bill .... **CLC 5**
See also Gunn, William Harrison
See also DLB 38

Gunn, Thom(son William) 1929-**CLC 3, 6, 18,
32, 81; DAM POET**
See also CA 17-20R; CANR 9, 33; CDBLB
1960 to Present; DLB 27; INT CANR-33;
MTCW

Gunn, William Harrison 1934(?)-1989
See Gunn, Bill
See also AITN 1; BW 1; CA 13-16R; 128;
CANR 12, 25

Gunnars, Kristjana 1948- .... **CLC 69**
See also CA 113; DLB 60

Gurdjieff, G(eorgei) I(vanovich) 1877(?)-1949
TCLC 71
See also CA 157

Gurganus, Allan 1947- .. **CLC 70; DAM POP**
See also BEST 90:1; CA 135

Gurney, A(lbert) R(amsdell), Jr. 1930- . **C L C
32, 50, 54; DAM DRAM**
See also CA 77-80; CANR 32

Gurney, Ivor (Bertie) 1890-1937 ... **TCLC 33**

Gurney, Peter
See Gurney, A(lbert) R(amsdell), Jr.

Guro, Elena 1877-1913 .... **TCLC 56**

Gustafson, James M(oody) 1925- .. **CLC 100**
See also CA 25-28R; CANR 37

Gustafson, Ralph (Barker) 1909- ..... **CLC 36**
See also CA 21-24R; CANR 8, 45; DLB 88

Gut, Gom
See Simenon, Georges (Jacques Christian)

Guterson, David 1956- .... **CLC 91**
See also CA 132

Guthrie, A(lfred) B(ertram), Jr. 1901-1991
CLC 23
See also CA 57-60; 134; CANR 24; DLB 6;
SATA 62; SATA-Obit 67

Guthrie, Isobel
See Grieve, C(hristopher) M(urray)

Guthrie, Woodrow Wilson 1912-1967
See Guthrie, Woody
See also CA 113; 93-96

Guthrie, Woody .... **CLC 35**
See also Guthrie, Woodrow Wilson

Guy, Rosa (Cuthbert) 1928- .... **CLC 26**
See also AAYA 4; BW 2; CA 17-20R; CANR
14, 34; CLR 13; DLB 33; JRDA; MAICYA;
SATA 14, 62

Gwendolyn
See Bennett, (Enoch) Arnold

H. D. .... **CLC 3, 8, 14, 31, 34, 73; PC 5**
See also Doolittle, Hilda

H. de V.
See Buchan, John

Haavikko, Paavo Juhani 1931- .. **CLC 18, 34**
See also CA 106

Habbema, Koos
See Heijermans, Herman

Habermas, Juergen 1929- .... **CLC 104**
See also CA 109

Habermas, Jurgen
See Habermas, Juergen

Hacker, Marilyn 1942- .**CLC 5, 9, 23, 72, 91;
DAM POET**

See also CA 77-80; DLB 120

Haggard, H(enry) Rider 1856-1925**TCLC 11**
See also CA 108; 148; DLB 70, 156, 174, 178;
SATA 16

Hagiosy, L.
See Larbaud, Valery (Nicolas)

Hagiwara Sakutaro 1886-1942**TCLC 60; PC
18**

Haig, Fenil
See Ford, Ford Madox

Haig-Brown, Roderick (Langmere) 1908-1976
CLC 21
See also CA 5-8R; 69-72; CANR 4, 38; CLR
31; DLB 88; MAICYA; SATA 12

Hailey, Arthur 1920-**CLC 5; DAM NOV, POP**
See also AITN 2; BEST 90:3; CA 1-4R; CANR
2, 36; DLB 88; DLBY 82; MTCW

Hailey, Elizabeth Forsythe 1938- .... **CLC 40**
See also CA 93-96; CAAS 1; CANR 15, 48;
INT CANR-15

Haines, John (Meade) 1924- .... **CLC 58**
See also CA 17-20R; CANR 13, 34; DLB 5

Hakluyt, Richard 1552-1616 .... **LC 31**

Haldeman, Joe (William) 1943- .... **CLC 61**
See also CA 53-56; CAAS 25; CANR 6; DLB
8; INT CANR-6

Haley, Alex(ander Murray Palmer) 1921-1992
**CLC 8, 12, 76; BLC; DA; DAB; DAC;
DAM MST, MULT, POP**
See also BW 2; CA 77-80; 136; CANR 61; DLB
38; MTCW

Haliburton, Thomas Chandler 1796-1865
NCLC 15
See also DLB 11, 99

Hall, Donald (Andrew, Jr.) 1928- **CLC 1, 13,
37, 59; DAM POET**
See also CA 5-8R; CAAS 7; CANR 2, 44; DLB
5; SATA 23

Hall, Frederic Sauser
See Sauser-Hall, Frederic

Hall, James
See Kuttner, Henry

Hall, James Norman 1887-1951 ..... **TCLC 23**
See also CA 123; SATA 21

Hall, (Marguerite) Radclyffe 1886-1943
TCLC 12
See also CA 110; 150

Hall, Rodney 1935- .... **CLC 51**
See also CA 109

Halleck, Fitz-Greene 1790-1867 .... **NCLC 47**
See also DLB 3

Halliday, Michael
See Creasey, John

Halpern, Daniel 1945- .... **CLC 14**
See also CA 33-36R

Hamburger, Michael (Peter Leopold) 1924-
CLC 5, 14
See also CA 5-8R; CAAS 4; CANR 2, 47; DLB
27

Hamill, Pete 1935- .... **CLC 10**
See also CA 25-28R; CANR 18

Hamilton, Alexander 1755(?)-1804 **NCLC 49**
See also DLB 37

Hamilton, Clive
See Lewis, C(live) S(taples)

Hamilton, Edmond 1904-1977 .... **CLC 1**
See also CA 1-4R; CANR 3; DLB 8

Hamilton, Eugene (Jacob) Lee
See Lee-Hamilton, Eugene (Jacob)

Hamilton, Franklin
See Silverberg, Robert

Hamilton, Gail
See Corcoran, Barbara

Hamilton, Mollie
See Kaye, M(ary) M(argaret)
Hamilton, (Anthony Walter) Patrick 1904-1962
CLC 51
See also CA 113; DLB 10
Hamilton, Virginia 1936- .... **CLC 26; DAM MULT**
See also AAYA 2, 21; BW 2; CA 25-28R; CANR 20, 37; CLR 1, 11, 40; DLB 33, 52; INT CANR-20; JRDA; MAICYA; MTCW; SATA 4, 56, 79
Hammett, (Samuel) Dashiell 1894-1961 **C L C 3, 5, 10, 19, 47; SSC 17**
See also AITN 1; CA 81-84; CANR 42; CDALB 1929-1941; DLBD 6; DLBY 96; MTCW
Hammon, Jupiter 1711(?)-1800(?) . **NCLC 5; BLC; DAM MULT, POET; PC 16**
See also DLB 31, 50
Hammond, Keith
See Kuttner, Henry
Hamner, Earl (Henry), Jr. 1923- ...... **CLC 12**
See also AITN 2; CA 73-76; DLB 6
Hampton, Christopher (James) 1946- **CLC 4**
See also CA 25-28R; DLB 13; MTCW
Hamsun, Knut .... **TCLC 2, 14, 49**
See also Pedersen, Knut
Handke, Peter 1942- **CLC 5, 8, 10, 15, 38; DAM DRAM, NOV**
See also CA 77-80; CANR 33; DLB 85, 124; MTCW
Hanley, James 1901-1985 ..... **CLC 3, 5, 8, 13**
See also CA 73-76; 117; CANR 36; MTCW
Hannah, Barry 1942- .... **CLC 23, 38, 90**
See also CA 108; 110; CANR 43; DLB 6; INT 110; MTCW
Hannon, Ezra
See Hunter, Evan
Hansberry, Lorraine (Vivian) 1930-1965 **CLC 17, 62; BLC; DA; DAB; DAC; DAM DRAM, MST, MULT; DC 2**
See also BW 1; CA 109; 25-28R; CABS 3; CANR 58; CDALB 1941-1968; DLB 7, 38; MTCW
Hansen, Joseph 1923- .... **CLC 38**
See also CA 29-32R; CAAS 17; CANR 16, 44; INT CANR-16
Hansen, Martin A. 1909-1955 .... **TCLC 32**
Hanson, Kenneth O(stlin) 1922- ...... **CLC 13**
See also CA 53-56; CANR 7
Hardwick, Elizabeth 1916- .... **CLC 13; DAM NOV**
See also CA 5-8R; CANR 3, 32; DLB 6; MTCW
Hardy, Thomas 1840-1928 **TCLC 4, 10, 18, 32, 48, 53, 72; DA; DAB; DAC; DAM MST, NOV, POET; PC 8; SSC 2; WLC**
See also CA 104; 123; CDBLB 1890-1914; DLB 18, 19, 135; MTCW
Hare, David 1947- .... **CLC 29, 58**
See also CA 97-100; CANR 39; DLB 13; MTCW
Harewood, John
See Van Druten, John (William)
Harford, Henry
See Hudson, W(illiam) H(enry)
Hargrave, Leonie
See Disch, Thomas M(ichael)
Harjo, Joy 1951- .... **CLC 83; DAM MULT**
See also CA 114; CANR 35; DLB 120, 175; NNAL
Harlan, Louis R(udolph) 1922- .... **CLC 34**
See also CA 21-24R; CANR 25, 55
Harling, Robert 1951(?)- .... **CLC 53**
See also CA 147

Harmon, William (Ruth) 1938- .... **CLC 38**
See also CA 33-36R; CANR 14, 32, 35; SATA 65
Harper, F. E. W.
See Harper, Frances Ellen Watkins
Harper, Frances E. W.
See Harper, Frances Ellen Watkins
Harper, Frances E. Watkins
See Harper, Frances Ellen Watkins
Harper, Frances Ellen
See Harper, Frances Ellen Watkins
Harper, Frances Ellen Watkins 1825-1911
TCLC 14; BLC; DAM MULT, POET
See also BW 1; CA 111; 125; DLB 50
Harper, Michael S(teven) 1938- ... **CLC 7, 22**
See also BW 1; CA 33-36R; CANR 24; DLB 41
Harper, Mrs. F. E. W.
See Harper, Frances Ellen Watkins
Harris, Christie (Lucy) Irwin 1907- . **CLC 12**
See also CA 5-8R; CANR 6; CLR 47; DLB 88; JRDA; MAICYA; SAAS 10; SATA 6, 74
Harris, Frank 1856-1931 .... **TCLC 24**
See also CA 109; 150; DLB 156
Harris, George Washington 1814-1869 **NCLC 23**
See also DLB 3, 11
Harris, Joel Chandler 1848-1908 ... **TCLC 2; SSC 19**
See also CA 104; 137; DLB 11, 23, 42, 78, 91; MAICYA; YABC 1
Harris, John (Wyndham Parkes Lucas) Beynon 1903-1969
See Wyndham, John
See also CA 102; 89-92
Harris, MacDonald .... **CLC 9**
See also Heiney, Donald (William)
Harris, Mark 1922- .... **CLC 19**
See also CA 5-8R; CAAS 3; CANR 2, 55; DLB 2; DLBY 80
Harris, (Theodore) Wilson 1921- ...... **CLC 25**
See also BW 2; CA 65-68; CAAS 16; CANR 11, 27; DLB 117; MTCW
Harrison, Elizabeth Cavanna 1909-
See Cavanna, Betty
See also CA 9-12R; CANR 6, 27
Harrison, Harry (Max) 1925- .... **CLC 42**
See also CA 1-4R; CANR 5, 21; DLB 8; SATA 4
Harrison, James (Thomas) 1937- **CLC 6, 14, 33, 66; SSC 19**
See also CA 13-16R; CANR 8, 51; DLBY 82; INT CANR-8
Harrison, Jim
See Harrison, James (Thomas)
Harrison, Kathryn 1961- .... **CLC 70**
See also CA 144
Harrison, Tony 1937- .... **CLC 43**
See also CA 65-68; CANR 44; DLB 40; MTCW
Harriss, Will(ard Irvin) 1922- .... **CLC 34**
See also CA 111
Harson, Sley
See Ellison, Harlan (Jay)
Hart, Ellis
See Ellison, Harlan (Jay)
Hart, Josephine 1942(?)- **CLC 70; DAM POP**
See also CA 138
Hart, Moss 1904-1961 **CLC 66; DAM DRAM**
See also CA 109; 89-92; DLB 7
Harte, (Francis) Bret(t) 1836(?)-1902 **TCLC 1, 25; DA; DAC; DAM MST; SSC 8; WLC**
See also CA 104; 140; CDALB 1865-1917; DLB 12, 64, 74, 79; SATA 26

Hartley, L(eslie) P(oles) 1895-1972 **CLC 2, 22**
See also CA 45-48; 37-40R; CANR 33; DLB 15, 139; MTCW
Hartman, Geoffrey H. 1929- .... **CLC 27**
See also CA 117; 125; DLB 67
Hartmann, Sadakichi 1867-1944 ... **TCLC 73**
See also CA 157; DLB 54
Hartmann von Aue c. 1160-c. 1205 **CMLC 15**
See also DLB 138
Hartmann von Aue 1170-1210 ...... **CMLC 15**
Haruf, Kent 1943- .... **CLC 34**
See also CA 149
Harwood, Ronald 1934- .... **CLC 32; DAM DRAM, MST**
See also CA 1-4R; CANR 4, 55; DLB 13
Hasek, Jaroslav (Matej Frantisek) 1883-1923
TCLC 4
See also CA 104; 129; MTCW
Hass, Robert 1941- ... **CLC 18, 39, 99; PC 16**
See also CA 111; CANR 30, 50; DLB 105; SATA 94
Hastings, Hudson
See Kuttner, Henry
Hastings, Selina .... **CLC 44**
Hathorne, John 1641-1717 .... **LC 38**
Hatteras, Amelia
See Mencken, H(enry) L(ouis)
Hatteras, Owen .... **TCLC 18**
See also Mencken, H(enry) L(ouis); Nathan, George Jean
Hauptmann, Gerhart (Johann Robert) 1862-1946 .... **TCLC 4; DAM DRAM**
See also CA 104; 153; DLB 66, 118
Havel, Vaclav 1936- ... **CLC 25, 58, 65; DAM DRAM; DC 6**
See also CA 104; CANR 36; MTCW
Haviaras, Stratis .... **CLC 33**
See also Chaviaras, Strates
Hawes, Stephen 1475(?)-1523(?) .... **LC 17**
Hawkes, John (Clendennin Burne, Jr.) 1925-
CLC 1, 2, 3, 4, 7, 9, 14, 15, 27, 49
See also CA 1-4R; CANR 2, 47; DLB 2, 7; DLBY 80; MTCW
Hawking, S. W.
See Hawking, Stephen W(illiam)
Hawking, Stephen W(illiam) 1942- **CLC 63, 105**
See also AAYA 13; BEST 89:1; CA 126; 129; CANR 48
Hawthorne, Julian 1846-1934 .... **TCLC 25**
Hawthorne, Nathaniel 1804-1864 **NCLC 39; DA; DAB; DAC; DAM MST, NOV; SSC 29; WLC**
See also AAYA 18; CDALB 1640-1865; DLB 1, 74; YABC 2
Haxton, Josephine Ayres 1921-
See Douglas, Ellen
See also CA 115; CANR 41
Hayaseca y Eizaguirre, Jorge
See Echegaray (y Eizaguirre), Jose (Maria Waldo)
Hayashi Fumiko 1904-1951 .... **TCLC 27**
See also CA 161; DLB 180
Haycraft, Anna
See Ellis, Alice Thomas
See also CA 122
Hayden, Robert E(arl) 1913-1980 **CLC 5, 9, 14, 37; BLC; DA; DAC; DAM MST, MULT, POET; PC 6**
See also BW 1; CA 69-72; 97-100; CABS 2; CANR 24; CDALB 1941-1968; DLB 5, 76; MTCW; SATA 19; SATA-Obit 26
Hayford, J(oseph) E(phraim) Casely

See Casely-Hayford, J(oseph) E(phraim)
Hayman, Ronald 1932- .... **CLC 44**
    See also CA 25-28R; CANR 18, 50; DLB 155
Haywood, Eliza (Fowler) 1693(?)-1756 **LC 1**
Hazlitt, William 1778-1830 .... **NCLC 29**
    See also DLB 110, 158
Hazzard, Shirley 1931- .... **CLC 18**
    See also CA 9-12R; CANR 4; DLBY 82;
    MTCW
Head, Bessie 1937-1986 .. **CLC 25, 67; BLC;**
    DAM MULT
    See also BW 2; CA 29-32R; 119; CANR 25;
    DLB 117; MTCW
Headon, (Nicky) Topper 1956(?)- .... **CLC 30**
Heaney, Seamus (Justin) 1939- **CLC 5, 7, 14,**
    25, 37, 74, 91; DAB; DAM POET; PC 18;
    WLCS
    See also CA 85-88; CANR 25, 48; CDBLB
    1960 to Present; DLB 40; DLBY 95; MTCW
Hearn, (Patricio) Lafcadio (Tessima Carlos)
    1850-1904 .... **TCLC 9**
    See also CA 105; DLB 12, 78
Hearne, Vicki 1946- .... **CLC 56**
    See also CA 139
Hearon, Shelby 1931- .... **CLC 63**
    See also AITN 2; CA 25-28R; CANR 18, 48
Heat-Moon, William Least .... **CLC 29**
    See also Trogdon, William (Lewis)
    See also AAYA 9
Hebbel, Friedrich 1813-1863**NCLC 43; DAM**
    DRAM
    See also DLB 129
Hebert, Anne 1916-**CLC 4, 13, 29; DAC; DAM**
    MST, POET
    See also CA 85-88; DLB 68; MTCW
Hecht, Anthony (Evan) 1923- **CLC 8, 13, 19;**
    DAM POET
    See also CA 9-12R; CANR 6; DLB 5, 169
Hecht, Ben 1894-1964 .... **CLC 8**
    See also CA 85-88; DLB 7, 9, 25, 26, 28, 86
Hedayat, Sadeq 1903-1951 .... **TCLC 21**
    See also CA 120
Hegel, Georg Wilhelm Friedrich 1770-1831
    NCLC 46
    See also DLB 90
Heidegger, Martin 1889-1976 .... **CLC 24**
    See also CA 81-84; 65-68; CANR 34; MTCW
Heidenstam, (Carl Gustaf) Verner von 1859-
    1940 .... **TCLC 5**
    See also CA 104
Heifner, Jack 1946- .... **CLC 11**
    See also CA 105; CANR 47
Heijermans, Herman 1864-1924 .... **TCLC 24**
    See also CA 123
Heilbrun, Carolyn G(old) 1926- ...... **CLC 25**
    See also CA 45-48; CANR 1, 28, 58
Heine, Heinrich 1797-1856 ....**NCLC 4, 54**
    See also DLB 90
Heinemann, Larry (Curtiss) 1944- .. **CLC 50**
    See also CA 110; CAAS 21; CANR 31; DLBD
    9; INT CANR-31
Heiney, Donald (William) 1921-1993
    See Harris, MacDonald
    See also CA 1-4R; 142; CANR 3, 58
Heinlein, Robert A(nson) 1907-1988**CLC 1, 3,**
    8, 14, 26, 55; DAM POP
    See also AAYA 17; CA 1-4R; 125; CANR 1,
    20, 53; DLB 8; JRDA; MAICYA; MTCW;
    SATA 9, 69; SATA-Obit 56
Helforth, John
    See Doolittle, Hilda
Hellenhofferu, Vojtech Kapristian z
    See Hasek, Jaroslav (Matej Frantisek)

Heller, Joseph 1923-**CLC 1, 3, 5, 8, 11, 36, 63;**
    DA; DAB; DAC; DAM MST, NOV, POP;
    WLC
    See also AITN 1; CA 5-8R; CABS 1; CANR 8,
    42; DLB 2, 28; DLBY 80; INT CANR-8;
    MTCW
Hellman, Lillian (Florence) 1906-1984**CLC 2,**
    4, 8, 14, 18, 34, 44, 52; DAM DRAM; DC 1
    See also AITN 1, 2; CA 13-16R; 112; CANR
    33; DLB 7; DLBY 84; MTCW
Helprin, Mark 1947-**CLC 7, 10, 22, 32; DAM**
    NOV, POP
    See also CA 81-84; CANR 47; DLBY 85;
    MTCW
Helvetius, Claude-Adrien 1715-1771 . **LC 26**
Helyar, Jane Penelope Josephine 1933-
    See Poole, Josephine
    See also CA 21-24R; CANR 10, 26; SATA 82
Hemans, Felicia 1793-1835 .... **NCLC 29**
    See also DLB 96
Hemingway, Ernest (Miller) 1899-1961 **C L C**
    1, 3, 6, 8, 10, 13, 19, 30, 34, 39, 41, 44, 50,
    61, 80; DA; DAB; DAC; DAM MST, NOV;
    SSC 25; WLC
    See also AAYA 19; CA 77-80; CANR 34;
    CDALB 1917-1929; DLB 4, 9, 102; DLBD
    1, 15, 16; DLBY 81, 87, 96; MTCW
Hempel, Amy 1951- .... **CLC 39**
    See also CA 118; 137
Henderson, F. C.
    See Mencken, H(enry) L(ouis)
Henderson, Sylvia
    See Ashton-Warner, Sylvia (Constance)
Henderson, Zenna (Chlarson) 1917-1983**S S C**
    29
    See also CA 1-4R; 133; CANR 1; DLB 8; SATA
    5
Henley, Beth .... **CLC 23; DC 6**
    See also Henley, Elizabeth Becker
    See also CABS 3; DLBY 86
Henley, Elizabeth Becker 1952-
    See Henley, Beth
    See also CA 107; CANR 32; DAM DRAM,
    MST; MTCW
Henley, William Ernest 1849-1903 .. **TCLC 8**
    See also CA 105; DLB 19
Hennissart, Martha
    See Lathen, Emma
    See also CA 85-88
Henry, O. .... **TCLC 1, 19; SSC 5; WLC**
    See also Porter, William Sydney
Henry, Patrick 1736-1799 .... **LC 25**
Henryson, Robert 1430(?)-1506(?) ..... **LC 20**
    See also DLB 146
Henry VIII 1491-1547 .... **LC 10**
Henschke, Alfred
    See Klabund
Hentoff, Nat(han Irving) 1925- .... **CLC 26**
    See also AAYA 4; CA 1-4R; CAAS 6; CANR
    5, 25; CLR 1; INT CANR-25; JRDA;
    MAICYA; SATA 42, 69; SATA-Brief 27
Heppenstall, (John) Rayner 1911-1981 . **C L C**
    10
    See also CA 1-4R; 103; CANR 29
Heraclitus c. 540B.C.-c. 450B.C. .... **CMLC 22**
    See also DLB 176
Herbert, Frank (Patrick) 1920-1986 **CLC 12,**
    23, 35, 44, 85; DAM POP
    See also AAYA 21; CA 53-56; 118; CANR 5,
    43; DLB 8; INT CANR-5; MTCW; SATA 9,
    37; SATA-Obit 47
Herbert, George 1593-1633 ..... **LC 24; DAB;**
    DAM POET; PC 4

See also CDBLB Before 1660; DLB 126
Herbert, Zbigniew 1924- ...**CLC 9, 43; DAM**
    POET
    See also CA 89-92; CANR 36; MTCW
Herbst, Josephine (Frey) 1897-1969 **CLC 34**
    See also CA 5-8R; 25-28R; DLB 9
Hergesheimer, Joseph 1880-1954 ... **TCLC 11**
    See also CA 109; DLB 102, 9
Herlihy, James Leo 1927-1993 ....**CLC 6**
    See also CA 1-4R; 143; CANR 2
Hermogenes fl. c. 175- .... **CMLC 6**
Hernandez, Jose 1834-1886 .... **NCLC 17**
Herodotus c. 484B.C.-429B.C. .... **CMLC 17**
    See also DLB 176
Herrick, Robert 1591-1674**LC 13; DA; DAB;**
    DAC; DAM MST, POP; PC 9
    See also DLB 126
Herring, Guilles
    See Somerville, Edith
Herriot, James 1916-1995**CLC 12; DAM POP**
    See also Wight, James Alfred
    See also AAYA 1; CA 148; CANR 40; SATA
    86
Herrmann, Dorothy 1941- .... **CLC 44**
    See also CA 107
Herrmann, Taffy
    See Herrmann, Dorothy
Hersey, John (Richard) 1914-1993**CLC 1, 2, 7,**
    9, 40, 81, 97; DAM POP
    See also CA 17-20R; 140; CANR 33; DLB 6;
    MTCW; SATA 25; SATA-Obit 76
Herzen, Aleksandr Ivanovich 1812-1870
    NCLC 10, 61
Herzl, Theodor 1860-1904 .... **TCLC 36**
Herzog, Werner 1942- .... **CLC 16**
    See also CA 89-92
Hesiod c. 8th cent. B.C.- .... **CMLC 5**
    See also DLB 176
Hesse, Hermann 1877-1962**CLC 1, 2, 3, 6, 11,**
    17, 25, 69; DA; DAB; DAC; DAM MST,
    NOV; SSC 9; WLC
    See also CA 17-18; CAP 2; DLB 66; MTCW;
    SATA 50
Hewes, Cady
    See De Voto, Bernard (Augustine)
Heyen, William 1940- .... **CLC 13, 18**
    See also CA 33-36R; CAAS 9; DLB 5
Heyerdahl, Thor 1914- .... **CLC 26**
    See also CA 5-8R; CANR 5, 22; MTCW; SATA
    2, 52
Heym, Georg (Theodor Franz Arthur) 1887-
    1912 .... **TCLC 9**
    See also CA 106
Heym, Stefan 1913- .... **CLC 41**
    See also CA 9-12R; CANR 4; DLB 69
Heyse, Paul (Johann Ludwig von) 1830-1914
    TCLC 8
    See also CA 104; DLB 129
Heyward, (Edwin) DuBose 1885-1940 **T C L C**
    59
    See also CA 108; 157; DLB 7, 9, 45; SATA 21
Hibbert, Eleanor Alice Burford 1906-1993
    CLC 7; DAM POP
    See also BEST 90:4; CA 17-20R; 140; CANR
    9, 28, 59; SATA 2; SATA-Obit 74
Hichens, Robert S. 1864-1950 .... **TCLC 64**
    See also DLB 153
Higgins, George V(incent) 1939-**CLC 4, 7, 10,**
    18
    See also CA 77-80; CAAS 5; CANR 17, 51;
    DLB 2; DLBY 81; INT CANR-17; MTCW
Higginson, Thomas Wentworth 1823-1911
    TCLC 36

See also DLB 1, 64

Highet, Helen
See MacInnes, Helen (Clark)

Highsmith, (Mary) Patricia 1921-1995 **CLC 2, 4, 14, 42, 102; DAM NOV, POP**
See also CA 1-4R; 147; CANR 1, 20, 48, 62; MTCW

Highwater, Jamake (Mamake) 1942(?)- **C L C 12**
See also AAYA 7; CA 65-68; CAAS 7; CANR 10, 34; CLR 17; DLB 52; DLBY 85; JRDA; MAICYA; SATA 32, 69; SATA-Brief 30

Highway, Tomson 1951- **CLC 92; DAC; DAM MULT**
See also CA 151; NNAL

Higuchi, Ichiyo 1872-1896 .... **NCLC 49**

Hijuelos, Oscar 1951- **CLC 65; DAM MULT, POP; HLC**
See also BEST 90:1; CA 123; CANR 50; DLB 145; HW

Hikmet, Nazim 1902(?)-1963 .... **CLC 40**
See also CA 141; 93-96

Hildegard von Bingen 1098-1179 . **CMLC 20**
See also DLB 148

Hildesheimer, Wolfgang 1916-1991 . **CLC 49**
See also CA 101; 135; DLB 69, 124

Hill, Geoffrey (William) 1932- **CLC 5, 8, 18, 45; DAM POET**
See also CA 81-84; CANR 21; CDBLB 1960 to Present; DLB 40; MTCW

Hill, George Roy 1921- .... **CLC 26**
See also CA 110; 122

Hill, John
See Koontz, Dean R(ay)

Hill, Susan (Elizabeth) 1942- . **CLC 4; DAB; DAM MST, NOV**
See also CA 33-36R; CANR 29; DLB 14, 139; MTCW

Hillerman, Tony 1925- .. **CLC 62; DAM POP**
See also AAYA 6; BEST 89:1; CA 29-32R; CANR 21, 42; SATA 6

Hillesum, Etty 1914-1943 .... **TCLC 49**
See also CA 137

Hilliard, Noel (Harvey) 1929- .... **CLC 15**
See also CA 9-12R; CANR 7

Hillis, Rick 1956- .... **CLC 66**
See also CA 134

Hilton, James 1900-1954 .... **TCLC 21**
See also CA 108; DLB 34, 77; SATA 34

Himes, Chester (Bomar) 1909-1984 **CLC 2, 4, 7, 18, 58; BLC; DAM MULT**
See also BW 2; CA 25-28R; 114; CANR 22; DLB 2, 76, 143; MTCW

Hinde, Thomas .... **CLC 6, 11**
See also Chitty, Thomas Willes

Hindin, Nathan
See Bloch, Robert (Albert)

Hine, (William) Daryl 1936- .... **CLC 15**
See also CA 1-4R; CAAS 15; CANR 1, 20; DLB 60

Hinkson, Katharine Tynan
See Tynan, Katharine

Hinton, S(usan) E(loise) 1950- **CLC 30; DA; DAB; DAC; DAM MST, NOV**
See also AAYA 2; CA 81-84; CANR 32, 62; CLR 3, 23; JRDA; MAICYA; MTCW; SATA 19, 58

Hippius, Zinaida .... **TCLC 9**
See also Gippius, Zinaida (Nikolayevna)

Hiraoka, Kimitake 1925-1970
See Mishima, Yukio
See also CA 97-100; 29-32R; DAM DRAM; MTCW

Hirsch, E(ric) D(onald), Jr. 1928- ..... **CLC 79**
See also CA 25-28R; CANR 27, 51; DLB 67; INT CANR-27; MTCW

Hirsch, Edward 1950- .... **CLC 31, 50**
See also CA 104; CANR 20, 42; DLB 120

Hitchcock, Alfred (Joseph) 1899-1980 **CLC 16**
See also AAYA 22; CA 159; 97-100; SATA 27; SATA-Obit 24

Hitler, Adolf 1889-1945 .... **TCLC 53**
See also CA 117; 147

Hoagland, Edward 1932- .... **CLC 28**
See also CA 1-4R; CANR 2, 31, 57; DLB 6; SATA 51

Hoban, Russell (Conwell) 1925- . **CLC 7, 25; DAM NOV**
See also CA 5-8R; CANR 23, 37; CLR 3; DLB 52; MAICYA; MTCW; SATA 1, 40, 78

Hobbes, Thomas 1588-1679 .... **LC 36**
See also DLB 151

Hobbs, Perry
See Blackmur, R(ichard) P(almer)

Hobson, Laura Z(ametkin) 1900-1986 **CLC 7, 25**
See also CA 17-20R; 118; CANR 55; DLB 28; SATA 52

Hochhuth, Rolf 1931- ... **CLC 4, 11, 18; DAM DRAM**
See also CA 5-8R; CANR 33; DLB 124; MTCW

Hochman, Sandra 1936- .... **CLC 3, 8**
See also CA 5-8R; DLB 5

Hochwaelder, Fritz 1911-1986 **CLC 36; DAM DRAM**
See also CA 29-32R; 120; CANR 42; MTCW

Hochwalder, Fritz
See Hochwaelder, Fritz

Hocking, Mary (Eunice) 1921- .... **CLC 13**
See also CA 101; CANR 18, 40

Hodgins, Jack 1938- .... **CLC 23**
See also CA 93-96; DLB 60

Hodgson, William Hope 1877(?)-1918 **T C L C 13**
See also CA 111; DLB 70, 153, 156, 178

Hoeg, Peter 1957- .... **CLC 95**
See also CA 151

Hoffman, Alice 1952- ... **CLC 51; DAM NOV**
See also CA 77-80; CANR 34; MTCW

Hoffman, Daniel (Gerard) 1923- **CLC 6, 13, 23**
See also CA 1-4R; CANR 4; DLB 5

Hoffman, Stanley 1944- .... **CLC 5**
See also CA 77-80

Hoffman, William M(oses) 1939- ...... **CLC 40**
See also CA 57-60; CANR 11

Hoffmann, E(rnst) T(heodor) A(madeus) 1776-1822 .... **NCLC 2; SSC 13**
See also DLB 90; SATA 27

Hofmann, Gert 1931- .... **CLC 54**
See also CA 128

Hofmannsthal, Hugo von 1874-1929 **TCLC 11; DAM DRAM; DC 4**
See also CA 106; 153; DLB 81, 118

Hogan, Linda 1947- ... **CLC 73; DAM MULT**
See also CA 120; CANR 45; DLB 175; NNAL

Hogarth, Charles
See Creasey, John

Hogarth, Emmett
See Polonsky, Abraham (Lincoln)

Hogg, James 1770-1835 .... **NCLC 4**
See also DLB 93, 116, 159

Holbach, Paul Henri Thiry Baron 1723-1789 **LC 14**

Holberg, Ludvig 1684-1754 .... **LC 6**

Holden, Ursula 1921- .... **CLC 18**
See also CA 101; CAAS 8; CANR 22

Holderlin, (Johann Christian) Friedrich 1770-1843 .... **NCLC 16; PC 4**

Holdstock, Robert
See Holdstock, Robert P.

Holdstock, Robert P. 1948- .... **CLC 39**
See also CA 131

Holland, Isabelle 1920- .... **CLC 21**
See also AAYA 11; CA 21-24R; CANR 10, 25, 47; JRDA; MAICYA; SATA 8, 70

Holland, Marcus
See Caldwell, (Janet Miriam) Taylor (Holland)

Hollander, John 1929- .... **CLC 2, 5, 8, 14**
See also CA 1-4R; CANR 1, 52; DLB 5; SATA 13

Hollander, Paul
See Silverberg, Robert

Holleran, Andrew 1943(?)- .... **CLC 38**
See also CA 144

Hollinghurst, Alan 1954- .... **CLC 55, 91**
See also CA 114

Hollis, Jim
See Summers, Hollis (Spurgeon, Jr.)

Holly, Buddy 1936-1959 .... **TCLC 65**

Holmes, Gordon
See Shiel, M(atthew) P(hipps)

Holmes, John
See Souster, (Holmes) Raymond

Holmes, John Clellon 1926-1988 ...... **CLC 56**
See also CA 9-12R; 125; CANR 4; DLB 16

Holmes, Oliver Wendell 1809-1894 **NCLC 14**
See also CDALB 1640-1865; DLB 1; SATA 34

Holmes, Raymond
See Souster, (Holmes) Raymond

Holt, Victoria
See Hibbert, Eleanor Alice Burford

Holub, Miroslav 1923- .... **CLC 4**
See also CA 21-24R; CANR 10

Homer c. 8th cent. B.C.- ... **CMLC 1, 16; DA; DAB; DAC; DAM MST, POET; WLCS**
See also DLB 176

Honig, Edwin 1919- .... **CLC 33**
See also CA 5-8R; CAAS 8; CANR 4, 45; DLB 5

Hood, Hugh (John Blagdon) 1928- **CLC 15, 28**
See also CA 49-52; CAAS 17; CANR 1, 33; DLB 53

Hood, Thomas 1799-1845 .... **NCLC 16**
See also DLB 96

Hooker, (Peter) Jeremy 1941- .... **CLC 43**
See also CA 77-80; CANR 22; DLB 40

hooks, bell .... **CLC 94**
See also Watkins, Gloria

Hope, A(lec) D(erwent) 1907- ...... **CLC 3, 51**
See also CA 21-24R; CANR 33; MTCW

Hope, Brian
See Creasey, John

Hope, Christopher (David Tully) 1944- **C L C 52**
See also CA 106; CANR 47; SATA 62

Hopkins, Gerard Manley 1844-1889 .. **N C L C 17; DA; DAB; DAC; DAM MST, POET; PC 15; WLC**
See also CDBLB 1890-1914; DLB 35, 57

Hopkins, John (Richard) 1931- .... **CLC 4**
See also CA 85-88

Hopkins, Pauline Elizabeth 1859-1930 **T C L C 28; BLC; DAM MULT**
See also BW 2; CA 141; DLB 50

Hopkinson, Francis 1737-1791 .... **LC 25**
See also DLB 31

Hopley-Woolrich, Cornell George 1903-1968
See Woolrich, Cornell
See also CA 13-14; CANR 58; CAP 1

Horatio
See Proust, (Valentin-Louis-George-Eugene-) Marcel

Horgan, Paul (George Vincent O'Shaughnessy) 1903-1995 .... **CLC 9, 53; DAM NOV**
See also CA 13-16R; 147; CANR 9, 35; DLB 102; DLBY 85; INT CANR-9; MTCW; SATA 13; SATA-Obit 84

Horn, Peter
See Kuttner, Henry

Hornem, Horace Esq.
See Byron, George Gordon (Noel)

Horney, Karen (Clementine Theodore Danielsen) 1885-1952 .... **TCLC 71**
See also CA 114

Hornung, E(rnest) W(illiam) 1866-1921 **TCLC 59**
See also CA 108; 160; DLB 70

Horovitz, Israel (Arthur) 1939-**CLC 56; DAM DRAM**
See also CA 33-36R; CANR 46, 59; DLB 7

Horvath, Odon von
See Horvath, Oedoen von
See also DLB 85, 124

Horvath, Oedoen von 1901-1938 ... **TCLC 45**
See also Horvath, Odon von
See also CA 118

Horwitz, Julius 1920-1986 .... **CLC 14**
See also CA 9-12R; 119; CANR 12

Hospital, Janette Turner 1942- .... **CLC 42**
See also CA 108; CANR 48

Hostos, E. M. de
See Hostos (y Bonilla), Eugenio Maria de

Hostos, Eugenio M. de
See Hostos (y Bonilla), Eugenio Maria de

Hostos, Eugenio Maria
See Hostos (y Bonilla), Eugenio Maria de

Hostos (y Bonilla), Eugenio Maria de 1839-1903 .... **TCLC 24**
See also CA 123; 131; HW

Houdini
See Lovecraft, H(oward) P(hillips)

Hougan, Carolyn 1943- .... **CLC 34**
See also CA 139

Household, Geoffrey (Edward West) 1900-1988 **CLC 11**
See also CA 77-80; 126; CANR 58; DLB 87; SATA 14; SATA-Obit 59

Housman, A(lfred) E(dward) 1859-1936 **TCLC 1, 10; DA; DAB; DAC; DAM MST, POET; PC 2; WLCS**
See also CA 104; 125; DLB 19; MTCW

Housman, Laurence 1865-1959 .... **TCLC 7**
See also CA 106; 155; DLB 10; SATA 25

Howard, Elizabeth Jane 1923- ..... **CLC 7, 29**
See also CA 5-8R; CANR 8, 62

Howard, Maureen 1930- .... **CLC 5, 14, 46**
See also CA 53-56; CANR 31; DLBY 83; INT CANR-31; MTCW

Howard, Richard 1929- .... **CLC 7, 10, 47**
See also AITN 1; CA 85-88; CANR 25; DLB 5; INT CANR-25

Howard, Robert E(rvin) 1906-1936 **TCLC 8**
See also CA 105; 157

Howard, Warren F.
See Pohl, Frederik

Howe, Fanny 1940- .... **CLC 47**
See also CA 117; CAAS 27; SATA-Brief 52

Howe, Irving 1920-1993 .... **CLC 85**
See also CA 9-12R; 141; CANR 21, 50; DLB 67; MTCW

Howe, Julia Ward 1819-1910 .... **TCLC 21**
See also CA 117; DLB 1

Howe, Susan 1937- .... **CLC 72**
See also CA 160; DLB 120

Howe, Tina 1937- .... **CLC 48**
See also CA 109

Howell, James 1594(?)-1666 .... **LC 13**
See also DLB 151

Howells, W. D.
See Howells, William Dean

Howells, William D.
See Howells, William Dean

Howells, William Dean 1837-1920**TCLC 7, 17, 41**
See also CA 104; 134; CDALB 1865-1917; DLB 12, 64, 74, 79

Howes, Barbara 1914-1996 .... **CLC 15**
See also CA 9-12R; 151; CAAS 3; CANR 53; SATA 5

Hrabal, Bohumil 1914-1997 .... **CLC 13, 67**
See also CA 106; 156; CAAS 12; CANR 57

Hsun, Lu
See Lu Hsun

Hubbard, L(afayette) Ron(ald) 1911-1986 **CLC 43; DAM POP**
See also CA 77-80; 118; CANR 52

Huch, Ricarda (Octavia) 1864-1947**TCLC 13**
See also CA 111; DLB 66

Huddle, David 1942- .... **CLC 49**
See also CA 57-60; CAAS 20; DLB 130

Hudson, Jeffrey
See Crichton, (John) Michael

Hudson, W(illiam) H(enry) 1841-1922**TCLC 29**
See also CA 115; DLB 98, 153, 174; SATA 35

Hueffer, Ford Madox
See Ford, Ford Madox

Hughart, Barry 1934- .... **CLC 39**
See also CA 137

Hughes, Colin
See Creasey, John

Hughes, David (John) 1930- .... **CLC 48**
See also CA 116; 129; DLB 14

Hughes, Edward James
See Hughes, Ted
See also DAM MST, POET

Hughes, (James) Langston 1902-1967**CLC 1, 5, 10, 15, 35, 44; BLC; DA; DAB; DAC; DAM DRAM, MST, MULT, POET; DC 3; PC 1; SSC 6; WLC**
See also AAYA 12; BW 1; CA 1-4R; 25-28R; CANR 1, 34; CDALB 1929-1941; CLR 17; DLB 4, 7, 48, 51, 86; JRDA; MAICYA; MTCW; SATA 4, 33

Hughes, Richard (Arthur Warren) 1900-1976 **CLC 1, 11; DAM NOV**
See also CA 5-8R; 65-68; CANR 4; DLB 15, 161; MTCW; SATA 8; SATA-Obit 25

Hughes, Ted 1930- **CLC 2, 4, 9, 14, 37; DAB; DAC; PC 7**
See also Hughes, Edward James
See also CA 1-4R; CANR 1, 33; CLR 3; DLB 40, 161; MAICYA; MTCW; SATA 49; SATA-Brief 27

Hugo, Richard F(ranklin) 1923-1982 **CLC 6, 18, 32; DAM POET**
See also CA 49-52; 108; CANR 3; DLB 5

Hugo, Victor (Marie) 1802-1885**NCLC 3, 10, 21; DA; DAB; DAC; DAM DRAM, MST, NOV, POET; PC 17; WLC**
See also DLB 119; SATA 47

Huidobro, Vicente
See Huidobro Fernandez, Vicente Garcia

Huidobro Fernandez, Vicente Garcia 1893-1948 .... **TCLC 31**

See also CA 131; HW

Hulme, Keri 1947- .... **CLC 39**
See also CA 125; INT 125

Hulme, T(homas) E(rnest) 1883-1917 **TCLC 21**
See also CA 117; DLB 19

Hume, David 1711-1776 .... **LC 7**
See also DLB 104

Humphrey, William 1924-1997 .... **CLC 45**
See also CA 77-80; 160; DLB 6

Humphreys, Emyr Owen 1919- .... **CLC 47**
See also CA 5-8R; CANR 3, 24; DLB 15

Humphreys, Josephine 1945- ..... **CLC 34, 57**
See also CA 121; 127; INT 127

Huneker, James Gibbons 1857-1921**TCLC 65**
See also DLB 71

Hungerford, Pixie
See Brinsmead, H(esba) F(ay)

Hunt, E(verette) Howard, (Jr.) 1918- . **CLC 3**
See also AITN 1; CA 45-48; CANR 2, 47

Hunt, Kyle
See Creasey, John

Hunt, (James Henry) Leigh 1784-1859**NCLC 1; DAM POET**

Hunt, Marsha 1946- .... **CLC 70**
See also BW 2; CA 143

Hunt, Violet 1866-1942 .... **TCLC 53**
See also DLB 162

Hunter, E. Waldo
See Sturgeon, Theodore (Hamilton)

Hunter, Evan 1926- . **CLC 11, 31; DAM POP**
See also CA 5-8R; CANR 5, 38, 62; DLBY 82; INT CANR-5; MTCW; SATA 25

Hunter, Kristin (Eggleston) 1931- ... **CLC 35**
See also AITN 1; BW 1; CA 13-16R; CANR 13; CLR 3; DLB 33; INT CANR-13; MAICYA; SAAS 10; SATA 12

Hunter, Mollie 1922- .... **CLC 21**
See also McIlwraith, Maureen Mollie Hunter
See also AAYA 13; CANR 37; CLR 25; DLB 161; JRDA; MAICYA; SAAS 7; SATA 54

Hunter, Robert (?)-1734 .... **LC 7**

Hurston, Zora Neale 1903-1960**CLC 7, 30, 61; BLC; DA; DAC; DAM MST, MULT, NOV; SSC 4; WLCS**
See also AAYA 15; BW 1; CA 85-88; CANR 61; DLB 51, 86; MTCW

Huston, John (Marcellus) 1906-1987 **CLC 20**
See also CA 73-76; 123; CANR 34; DLB 26

Hustvedt, Siri 1955- .... **CLC 76**
See also CA 137

Hutten, Ulrich von 1488-1523 .... **LC 16**
See also DLB 179

Huxley, Aldous (Leonard) 1894-1963 **CLC 1, 3, 4, 5, 8, 11, 18, 35, 79; DA; DAB; DAC; DAM MST, NOV; WLC**
See also AAYA 11; CA 85-88; CANR 44; CDBLB 1914-1945; DLB 36, 100, 162; MTCW; SATA 63

Huysmans, Charles Marie Georges 1848-1907
See Huysmans, Joris-Karl
See also CA 104

Huysmans, Joris-Karl .... **TCLC 7, 69**
See also Huysmans, Charles Marie Georges
See also DLB 123

Hwang, David Henry 1957-...**CLC 55; DAM DRAM; DC 4**
See also CA 127; 132; INT 132

Hyde, Anthony 1946- .... **CLC 42**
See also CA 136

Hyde, Margaret O(ldroyd) 1917- .... **CLC 21**
See also CA 1-4R; CANR 1, 36; CLR 23; JRDA; MAICYA; SAAS 8; SATA 1, 42, 76

Hynes, James 1956(?)- .... **CLC 65**

Ian, Janis 1951- .... **CLC 21**
See also CA 105

Ibanez, Vicente Blasco
See Blasco Ibanez, Vicente

Ibarguengoitia, Jorge 1928-1983 ..... **CLC 37**
See also CA 124; 113; HW

Ibsen, Henrik (Johan) 1828-1906 **TCLC 2, 8, 16, 37, 52; DA; DAB; DAC; DAM DRAM, MST; DC 2; WLC**
See also CA 104; 141

Ibuse Masuji 1898-1993 .... **CLC 22**
See also CA 127; 141; DLB 180

Ichikawa, Kon 1915- .... **CLC 20**
See also CA 121

Idle, Eric 1943- .... **CLC 21**
See also Monty Python
See also CA 116; CANR 35

Ignatow, David 1914- .... **CLC 4, 7, 14, 40**
See also CA 9-12R; CAAS 3; CANR 31, 57; DLB 5

Ihimaera, Witi 1944- .... **CLC 46**
See also CA 77-80

Ilf, Ilya .... **TCLC 21**
See also Fainzilberg, Ilya Arnoldovich

Illyes, Gyula 1902-1983 .... **PC 16**
See also CA 114; 109

Immermann, Karl (Lebrecht) 1796-1840 **NCLC 4, 49**
See also DLB 133

Inchbald, Elizabeth 1753-1821 ...... **NCLC 62**
See also DLB 39, 89

Inclan, Ramon (Maria) del Valle
See Valle-Inclan, Ramon (Maria) del

Infante, G(uillermo) Cabrera
See Cabrera Infante, G(uillermo)

Ingalls, Rachel (Holmes) 1940- .... **CLC 42**
See also CA 123; 127

Ingamells, Rex 1913-1955 .... **TCLC 35**

Inge, William (Motter) 1913-1973 **CLC 1, 8, 19; DAM DRAM**
See also CA 9-12R; CDALB 1941-1968; DLB 7; MTCW

Ingelow, Jean 1820-1897 .... **NCLC 39**
See also DLB 35, 163; SATA 33

Ingram, Willis J.
See Harris, Mark

Innaurato, Albert (F.) 1948(?)- .. **CLC 21, 60**
See also CA 115; 122; INT 122

Innes, Michael
See Stewart, J(ohn) I(nnes) M(ackintosh)

Ionesco, Eugene 1909-1994 **CLC 1, 4, 6, 9, 11, 15, 41, 86; DA; DAB; DAC; DAM DRAM, MST; WLC**
See also CA 9-12R; 144; CANR 55; MTCW; SATA 7; SATA-Obit 79

Iqbal, Muhammad 1873-1938 .... **TCLC 28**

Ireland, Patrick
See O'Doherty, Brian

Iron, Ralph
See Schreiner, Olive (Emilie Albertina)

Irving, John (Winslow) 1942- **CLC 13, 23, 38; DAM NOV, POP**
See also AAYA 8; BEST 89:3; CA 25-28R; CANR 28; DLB 6; DLBY 82; MTCW

Irving, Washington 1783-1859 . **NCLC 2, 19; DA; DAB; DAM MST; SSC 2; WLC**
See also CDALB 1640-1865; DLB 3, 11, 30, 59, 73, 74; YABC 2

Irwin, P. K.
See Page, P(atricia) K(athleen)

Isaacs, Susan 1943- .... **CLC 32; DAM POP**
See also BEST 89:1; CA 89-92; CANR 20, 41;

INT CANR-20; MTCW

Isherwood, Christopher (William Bradshaw) 1904-1986 .... **CLC 1, 9, 11, 14, 44; DAM DRAM, NOV**
See also CA 13-16R; 117; CANR 35; DLB 15; DLBY 86; MTCW

Ishiguro, Kazuo 1954- **CLC 27, 56, 59; DAM NOV**
See also BEST 90:2; CA 120; CANR 49; MTCW

Ishikawa, Hakuhin
See Ishikawa, Takuboku

Ishikawa, Takuboku 1886(?)-1912 **TCLC 15; DAM POET; PC 10**
See also CA 113; 153

Iskander, Fazil 1929- .... **CLC 47**
See also CA 102

Isler, Alan (David) 1934- .... **CLC 91**
See also CA 156

Ivan IV 1530-1584 .... **LC 17**

Ivanov, Vyacheslav Ivanovich 1866-1949 **TCLC 33**
See also CA 122

Ivask, Ivar Vidrik 1927-1992 .... **CLC 14**
See also CA 37-40R; 139; CANR 24

Ives, Morgan
See Bradley, Marion Zimmer

J. R. S.
See Gogarty, Oliver St. John

Jabran, Kahlil
See Gibran, Kahlil

Jabran, Khalil
See Gibran, Kahlil

Jackson, Daniel
See Wingrove, David (John)

Jackson, Jesse 1908-1983 .... **CLC 12**
See also BW 1; CA 25-28R; 109; CANR 27; CLR 28; MAICYA; SATA 2, 29; SATA-Obit 48

Jackson, Laura (Riding) 1901-1991
See Riding, Laura
See also CA 65-68; 135; CANR 28; DLB 48

Jackson, Sam
See Trumbo, Dalton

Jackson, Sara
See Wingrove, David (John)

Jackson, Shirley 1919-1965 . **CLC 11, 60, 87; DA; DAC; DAM MST; SSC 9; WLC**
See also AAYA 9; CA 1-4R; 25-28R; CANR 4, 52; CDALB 1941-1968; DLB 6; SATA 2

Jacob, (Cyprien-)Max 1876-1944 .... **TCLC 6**
See also CA 104

Jacobs, Jim 1942- .... **CLC 12**
See also CA 97-100; INT 97-100

Jacobs, W(illiam) W(ymark) 1863-1943 **TCLC 22**
See also CA 121; DLB 135

Jacobsen, Jens Peter 1847-1885 ..... **NCLC 34**

Jacobsen, Josephine 1908- .... **CLC 48, 102**
See also CA 33-36R; CAAS 18; CANR 23, 48

Jacobson, Dan 1929- .... **CLC 4, 14**
See also CA 1-4R; CANR 2, 25; DLB 14; MTCW

Jacqueline
See Carpentier (y Valmont), Alejo

Jagger, Mick 1944- .... **CLC 17**

Jakes, John (William) 1932- .. **CLC 29; DAM NOV, POP**
See also BEST 89:4; CA 57-60; CANR 10, 43; DLBY 83; INT CANR-10; MTCW; SATA 62

James, Andrew
See Kirkup, James

James, C(yril) L(ionel) R(obert) 1901-1989

CLC 33
See also BW 2; CA 117; 125; 128; CANR 62; DLB 125; MTCW

James, Daniel (Lewis) 1911-1988
See Santiago, Danny
See also CA 125

James, Dynely
See Mayne, William (James Carter)

James, Henry Sr. 1811-1882 .... **NCLC 53**

James, Henry 1843-1916 **TCLC 2, 11, 24, 40, 47, 64; DA; DAB; DAC; DAM MST, NOV; SSC 8; WLC**
See also CA 104; 132; CDALB 1865-1917; DLB 12, 71, 74; DLBD 13; MTCW

James, M. R.
See James, Montague (Rhodes)
See also DLB 156

James, Montague (Rhodes) 1862-1936 **TCLC 6; SSC 16**
See also CA 104

James, P. D. .... **CLC 18, 46**
See also White, Phyllis Dorothy James
See also BEST 90:2; CDBLB 1960 to Present; DLB 87

James, Philip
See Moorcock, Michael (John)

James, William 1842-1910 .... **TCLC 15, 32**
See also CA 109

James I 1394-1437 .... **LC 20**

Jameson, Anna 1794-1860 .... **NCLC 43**
See also DLB 99, 166

Jami, Nur al-Din 'Abd al-Rahman 1414-1492 **LC 9**

Jammes, Francis 1868-1938 .... **TCLC 75**

Jandl, Ernst 1925- .... **CLC 34**

Janowitz, Tama 1957- ... **CLC 43; DAM POP**
See also CA 106; CANR 52

Japrisot, Sebastien 1931- .... **CLC 90**

Jarrell, Randall 1914-1965 **CLC 1, 2, 6, 9, 13, 49; DAM POET**
See also CA 5-8R; 25-28R; CABS 2; CANR 6, 34; CDALB 1941-1968; CLR 6; DLB 48, 52; MAICYA; MTCW; SATA 7

Jarry, Alfred 1873-1907 . **TCLC 2, 14; DAM DRAM; SSC 20**
See also CA 104; 153

Jarvis, E. K.
See Bloch, Robert (Albert); Ellison, Harlan (Jay); Silverberg, Robert

Jeake, Samuel, Jr.
See Aiken, Conrad (Potter)

Jean Paul 1763-1825 .... **NCLC 7**

Jefferies, (John) Richard 1848-1887 **NCLC 47**
See also DLB 98, 141; SATA 16

Jeffers, (John) Robinson 1887-1962 **CLC 2, 3, 11, 15, 54; DA; DAC; DAM MST, POET; PC 17; WLC**
See also CA 85-88; CANR 35; CDALB 1917-1929; DLB 45; MTCW

Jefferson, Janet
See Mencken, H(enry) L(ouis)

Jefferson, Thomas 1743-1826 .... **NCLC 11**
See also CDALB 1640-1865; DLB 31

Jeffrey, Francis 1773-1850 .... **NCLC 33**
See also DLB 107

Jelakowitch, Ivan
See Heijermans, Herman

Jellicoe, (Patricia) Ann 1927- .... **CLC 27**
See also CA 85-88; DLB 13

Jen, Gish .... **CLC 70**
See also Jen, Lillian

Jen, Lillian 1956(?)-
See Jen, Gish

See also CA 135
Jenkins, (John) Robin 1912- .... **CLC 52**
　See also CA 1-4R; CANR 1; DLB 14
Jennings, Elizabeth (Joan) 1926-. **CLC 5, 14**
　See also CA 61-64; CAAS 5; CANR 8, 39; DLB
　27; MTCW; SATA 66
Jennings, Waylon 1937-.................. **CLC 21**
Jensen, Johannes V. 1873-1950 ...... **TCLC 41**
Jensen, Laura (Linnea) 1948- .... **CLC 37**
　See also CA 103
Jerome, Jerome K(lapka) 1859-1927**TCLC 23**
　See also CA 119; DLB 10, 34, 135
Jerrold, Douglas William 1803-1857**NCLC 2**
　See also DLB 158, 159
Jewett, (Theodora) Sarah Orne 1849-1909
　　TCLC 1, 22; SSC 6
　See also CA 108; 127; DLB 12, 74; SATA 15
Jewsbury, Geraldine (Endsor) 1812-1880
　　NCLC 22
　See also DLB 21
Jhabvala, Ruth Prawer 1927-**CLC 4, 8, 29, 94;**
　　DAB; DAM NOV
　See also CA 1-4R; CANR 2, 29, 51; DLB 139;
　　INT CANR-29; MTCW
Jibran, Kahlil
　See Gibran, Kahlil
Jibran, Khalil
　See Gibran, Kahlil
Jiles, Paulette 1943- .... **CLC 13, 58**
　See also CA 101
Jimenez (Mantecon), Juan Ramon 1881-1958
　　**TCLC 4; DAM MULT, POET; HLC; PC
　　7**
　See also CA 104; 131; DLB 134; HW; MTCW
Jimenez, Ramon
　See Jimenez (Mantecon), Juan Ramon
Jimenez Mantecon, Juan
　See Jimenez (Mantecon), Juan Ramon
Joel, Billy .... **CLC 26**
　See also Joel, William Martin
Joel, William Martin 1949-
　See Joel, Billy
　See also CA 108
John of the Cross, St. 1542-1591 .... **LC 18**
Johnson, B(ryan) S(tanley William) 1933-1973
　　CLC 6, 9
　See also CA 9-12R; 53-56; CANR 9; DLB 14,
　40
Johnson, Benj. F. of Boo
　See Riley, James Whitcomb
Johnson, Benjamin F. of Boo
　See Riley, James Whitcomb
Johnson, Charles (Richard) 1948-**CLC 7, 51,
　　65; BLC; DAM MULT**
　See also BW 2; CA 116; CAAS 18; CANR 42;
　　DLB 33
Johnson, Denis 1949- .... **CLC 52**
　See also CA 117; 121; DLB 120
Johnson, Diane 1934- .... **CLC 5, 13, 48**
　See also CA 41-44R; CANR 17, 40, 62; DLBY
　80; INT CANR-17; MTCW
Johnson, Eyvind (Olof Verner) 1900-1976
　　CLC 14
　See also CA 73-76; 69-72; CANR 34
Johnson, J. R.
　See James, C(yril) L(ionel) R(obert)
Johnson, James Weldon 1871-1938 **TCLC 3,
　　19; BLC; DAM MULT, POET**
　See also BW 1; CA 104; 125; CDALB 1917-
　1929; CLR 32; DLB 51; MTCW; SATA 31
Johnson, Joyce 1935- .... **CLC 58**
　See also CA 125; 129
Johnson, Lionel (Pigot) 1867-1902 **TCLC 19**

See also CA 117; DLB 19
Johnson, Mel
　See Malzberg, Barry N(athaniel)
Johnson, Pamela Hansford 1912-1981**CLC 1,
　　7, 27**
　See also CA 1-4R; 104; CANR 2, 28; DLB 15;
　　MTCW
Johnson, Robert 1911(?)-1938 .... **TCLC 69**
Johnson, Samuel 1709-1784**LC 15; DA; DAB;
　　DAC; DAM MST; WLC**
　See also CDBLB 1660-1789; DLB 39, 95, 104,
　　142
Johnson, Uwe 1934-1984 .. **CLC 5, 10, 15, 40**
　See also CA 1-4R; 112; CANR 1, 39; DLB 75;
　　MTCW
Johnston, George (Benson) 1913-..... **CLC 51**
　See also CA 1-4R; CANR 5, 20; DLB 88
Johnston, Jennifer 1930- .... **CLC 7**
　See also CA 85-88; DLB 14
Jolley, (Monica) Elizabeth 1923-**CLC 46; SSC
　　19**
　See also CA 127; CAAS 13; CANR 59
Jones, Arthur Llewellyn 1863-1947
　See Machen, Arthur
　See also CA 104
Jones, D(ouglas) G(ordon) 1929- ......**CLC 10**
　See also CA 29-32R; CANR 13; DLB 53
Jones, David (Michael) 1895-1974**CLC 2, 4, 7,
　　13, 42**
　See also CA 9-12R; 53-56; CANR 28; CDBLB
　　1945-1960; DLB 20, 100; MTCW
Jones, David Robert 1947-
　See Bowie, David
　See also CA 103
Jones, Diana Wynne 1934- ....**CLC 26**
　See also AAYA 12; CA 49-52; CANR 4, 26,
　　56; CLR 23; DLB 161; JRDA; MAICYA;
　　SAAS 7; SATA 9, 70
Jones, Edward P. 1950-.....................**CLC 76**
　See also BW 2; CA 142
Jones, Gayl 1949- ...... **CLC 6, 9; BLC; DAM
　　MULT**
　See also BW 2; CA 77-80; CANR 27; DLB 33;
　　MTCW
Jones, James 1921-1977 ...... **CLC 1, 3, 10, 39**
　See also AITN 1, 2; CA 1-4R; 69-72; CANR 6;
　　DLB 2, 143; MTCW
Jones, John J.
　See Lovecraft, H(oward) P(hillips)
Jones, LeRoi .... **CLC 1, 2, 3, 5, 10, 14**
　See also Baraka, Amiri
Jones, Louis B. .... **CLC 65**
　See also CA 141
Jones, Madison (Percy, Jr.) 1925- ....**CLC 4**
　See also CA 13-16R; CAAS 11; CANR 7, 54;
　　DLB 152
Jones, Mervyn 1922- .... **CLC 10, 52**
　See also CA 45-48; CAAS 5; CANR 1; MTCW
Jones, Mick 1956(?)- .... **CLC 30**
Jones, Nettie (Pearl) 1941- .... **CLC 34**
　See also BW 2; CA 137; CAAS 20
Jones, Preston 1936-1979 ....**CLC 10**
　See also CA 73-76; 89-92; DLB 7
Jones, Robert F(rancis) 1934-.............**CLC 7**
　See also CA 49-52; CANR 2, 61
Jones, Rod 1953-................................**CLC 50**
　See also CA 128
Jones, Terence Graham Parry 1942- **CLC 21**
　See also Jones, Terry; Monty Python
　See also CA 112; 116; CANR 35; INT 116
Jones, Terry
　See Jones, Terence Graham Parry
　See also SATA 67; SATA-Brief 51

Jones, Thom 1945(?)- .... **CLC 81**
　See also CA 157
Jong, Erica 1942- **CLC 4, 6, 8, 18, 83; DAM
　　NOV, POP**
　See also AITN 1; BEST 90:2; CA 73-76; CANR
　　26, 52; DLB 2, 5, 28, 152; INT CANR-26;
　　MTCW
Jonson, Ben(jamin) 1572(?)-1637 .. **LC 6, 33;
　　DA; DAB; DAC; DAM DRAM, MST,
　　POET; DC 4; PC 17; WLC**
　See also CDBLB Before 1660; DLB 62, 121
Jordan, June 1936- .... **CLC 5, 11, 23; DAM
　　MULT, POET**
　See also AAYA 2; BW 2; CA 33-36R; CANR
　　25; CLR 10; DLB 38; MAICYA; MTCW;
　　SATA 4
Jordan, Pat(rick M.) 1941- .... **CLC 37**
　See also CA 33-36R
Jorgensen, Ivar
　See Ellison, Harlan (Jay)
Jorgenson, Ivar
　See Silverberg, Robert
Josephus, Flavius c. 37-100 .... **CMLC 13**
Josipovici, Gabriel 1940- .... **CLC 6, 43**
　See also CA 37-40R; CAAS 8; CANR 47; DLB
　　14
Joubert, Joseph 1754-1824 .... **NCLC 9**
Jouve, Pierre Jean 1887-1976 .... **CLC 47**
　See also CA 65-68
Joyce, James (Augustine Aloysius) 1882-1941
　　**TCLC 3, 8, 16, 35, 52; DA; DAB; DAC;
　　DAM MST, NOV, POET; SSC 26; WLC**
　See also CA 104; 126; CDBLB 1914-1945;
　　DLB 10, 19, 36, 162; MTCW
Jozsef, Attila 1905-1937 .... **TCLC 22**
　See also CA 116
Juana Ines de la Cruz 1651(?)-1695 ..... **LC 5**
Judd, Cyril
　See Kornbluth, C(yril) M.; Pohl, Frederik
Julian of Norwich 1342(?)-1416(?) .... **LC 6**
　See also DLB 146
Juniper, Alex
　See Hospital, Janette Turner
Junius
　See Luxemburg, Rosa
Just, Ward (Swift) 1935- .... **CLC 4, 27**
　See also CA 25-28R; CANR 32; INT CANR-
　　32
Justice, Donald (Rodney) 1925- .. **CLC 6, 19,
　　102; DAM POET**
　See also CA 5-8R; CANR 26, 54; DLBY 83;
　　INT CANR-26
Juvenal c. 55-c. 127 .... **CMLC 8**
Juvenis
　See Bourne, Randolph S(illiman)
Kacew, Romain 1914-1980
　See Gary, Romain
　See also CA 108; 102
Kadare, Ismail 1936- .... **CLC 52**
　See also CA 161
Kadohata, Cynthia .... **CLC 59**
　See also CA 140
Kafka, Franz 1883-1924**TCLC 2, 6, 13, 29, 47,
　　53; DA; DAB; DAC; DAM MST, NOV;
　　SSC 29; WLC**
　See also CA 105; 126; DLB 81; MTCW
Kahanovitsch, Pinkhes
　See Der Nister
Kahn, Roger 1927- .... **CLC 30**
　See also CA 25-28R; CANR 44; DLB 171;
　　SATA 37
Kain, Saul
　See Sassoon, Siegfried (Lorraine)

Kaiser, Georg 1878-1945 .... **TCLC 9**
  See also CA 106; DLB 124
Kaletski, Alexander 1946- .... **CLC 39**
  See also CA 118; 143
Kalidasa fl. c. 400- .... **CMLC 9**
Kallman, Chester (Simon) 1921-1975 **CLC 2**
  See also CA 45-48; 53-56; CANR 3
Kaminsky, Melvin 1926-
  See Brooks, Mel
  See also CA 65-68; CANR 16
Kaminsky, Stuart M(elvin) 1934- .... **CLC 59**
  See also CA 73-76; CANR 29, 53
Kane, Francis
  See Robbins, Harold
Kane, Paul
  See Simon, Paul (Frederick)
Kane, Wilson
  See Bloch, Robert (Albert)
Kanin, Garson 1912- .... **CLC 22**
  See also AITN 1; CA 5-8R; CANR 7; DLB 7
Kaniuk, Yoram 1930- .... **CLC 19**
  See also CA 134
Kant, Immanuel 1724-1804 .... **NCLC 27**
  See also DLB 94
Kantor, MacKinlay 1904-1977 .... **CLC 7**
  See also CA 61-64; 73-76; CANR 60; DLB 9, 102
Kaplan, David Michael 1946- .... **CLC 50**
Kaplan, James 1951- .... **CLC 59**
  See also CA 135
Karageorge, Michael
  See Anderson, Poul (William)
Karamzin, Nikolai Mikhailovich 1766-1826
    NCLC 3
  See also DLB 150
Karapanou, Margarita 1946-........... **CLC 13**
  See also CA 101
Karinthy, Frigyes 1887-1938 .... **TCLC 47**
Karl, Frederick R(obert) 1927-........ **CLC 34**
  See also CA 5-8R; CANR 3, 44
Kastel, Warren
  See Silverberg, Robert
Kataev, Evgeny Petrovich 1903-1942
  See Petrov, Evgeny
  See also CA 120
Kataphusin
  See Ruskin, John
Katz, Steve 1935- .... **CLC 47**
  See also CA 25-28R; CAAS 14; CANR 12; DLBY 83
Kauffman, Janet 1945- .... **CLC 42**
  See also CA 117; CANR 43; DLBY 86
Kaufman, Bob (Garnell) 1925-1986 **CLC 49**
  See also BW 1; CA 41-44R; 118; CANR 22; DLB 16, 41
Kaufman, George S. 1889-1961**CLC 38; DAM DRAM**
  See also CA 108; 93-96; DLB 7; INT 108
Kaufman, Sue .... **CLC 3, 8**
  See also Barondess, Sue K(aufman)
Kavafis, Konstantinos Petrou 1863-1933
  See Cavafy, C(onstantine) P(eter)
  See also CA 104
Kavan, Anna 1901-1968 .... **CLC 5, 13, 82**
  See also CA 5-8R; CANR 6, 57; MTCW
Kavanagh, Dan
  See Barnes, Julian (Patrick)
Kavanagh, Patrick (Joseph) 1904-1967 **C L C 22**
  See also CA 123; 25-28R; DLB 15, 20; MTCW
Kawabata, Yasunari 1899-1972 **CLC 2, 5, 9, 18; DAM MULT; SSC 17**
  See also CA 93-96; 33-36R; DLB 180

Kaye, M(ary) M(argaret) 1909- .... **CLC 28**
  See also CA 89-92; CANR 24, 60; MTCW; SATA 62
Kaye, Mollie
  See Kaye, M(ary) M(argaret)
Kaye-Smith, Sheila 1887-1956 .... **TCLC 20**
  See also CA 118; DLB 36
Kaymor, Patrice Maguilene
  See Senghor, Leopold Sedar
Kazan, Elia 1909- .... **CLC 6, 16, 63**
  See also CA 21-24R; CANR 32
Kazantzakis, Nikos 1883(?)-1957 **TCLC 2, 5, 33**
  See also CA 105; 132; MTCW
Kazin, Alfred 1915- .... **CLC 34, 38**
  See also CA 1-4R; CAAS 7; CANR 1, 45; DLB 67
Keane, Mary Nesta (Skrine) 1904-1996
  See Keane, Molly
  See also CA 108; 114; 151
Keane, Molly ....**CLC 31**
  See also Keane, Mary Nesta (Skrine)
  See also INT 114
Keates, Jonathan 19(?)- .... **CLC 34**
Keaton, Buster 1895-1966 .... **CLC 20**
Keats, John 1795-1821 . **NCLC 8; DA; DAB; DAC; DAM MST, POET; PC 1; WLC**
  See also CDBLB 1789-1832; DLB 96, 110
Keene, Donald 1922- ....**CLC 34**
  See also CA 1-4R; CANR 5
Keillor, Garrison ....**CLC 40**
  See also Keillor, Gary (Edward)
  See also AAYA 2; BEST 89:3; DLBY 87; SATA 58
Keillor, Gary (Edward) 1942-
  See Keillor, Garrison
  See also CA 111; 117; CANR 36, 59; DAM POP; MTCW
Keith, Michael
  See Hubbard, L(afayette) Ron(ald)
Keller, Gottfried 1819-1890**NCLC 2; SSC 26**
  See also DLB 129
Kellerman, Jonathan 1949- ... **CLC 44; DAM POP**
  See also BEST 90:1; CA 106; CANR 29, 51; INT CANR-29
Kelley, William Melvin 1937-............**CLC 22**
  See also BW 1; CA 77-80; CANR 27; DLB 33
Kellogg, Marjorie 1922- .... **CLC 2**
  See also CA 81-84
Kellow, Kathleen
  See Hibbert, Eleanor Alice Burford
Kelly, M(ilton) T(erry) 1947- ....**CLC 55**
  See also CA 97-100; CAAS 22; CANR 19, 43
Kelman, James 1946- .... **CLC 58, 86**
  See also CA 148
Kemal, Yashar 1923- .... **CLC 14, 29**
  See also CA 89-92; CANR 44
Kemble, Fanny 1809-1893 .... **NCLC 18**
  See also DLB 32
Kemelman, Harry 1908-1996 .... **CLC 2**
  See also AITN 1; CA 9-12R; 155; CANR 6; DLB 28
Kempe, Margery 1373(?)-1440(?) .... **LC 6**
  See also DLB 146
Kempis, Thomas a 1380-1471 .... **LC 11**
Kendall, Henry 1839-1882 ....**NCLC 12**
Keneally, Thomas (Michael) 1935- **CLC 5, 8, 10, 14, 19, 27, 43; DAM NOV**
  See also CA 85-88; CANR 10, 50; MTCW
Kennedy, Adrienne (Lita) 1931- ..... **CLC 66; BLC; DAM MULT; DC 5**
  See also BW 2; CA 103; CAAS 20; CABS 3;

CANR 26, 53; DLB 38
Kennedy, John Pendleton 1795-1870**NCLC 2**
  See also DLB 3
Kennedy, Joseph Charles 1929-
  See Kennedy, X. J.
  See also CA 1-4R; CANR 4, 30, 40; SATA 14, 86
Kennedy, William 1928- ..**CLC 6, 28, 34, 53; DAM NOV**
  See also AAYA 1; CA 85-88; CANR 14, 31; DLB 143; DLBY 85; INT CANR-31; MTCW; SATA 57
Kennedy, X. J. .... **CLC 8, 42**
  See also Kennedy, Joseph Charles
  See also CAAS 9; CLR 27; DLB 5; SAAS 22
Kenny, Maurice (Francis) 1929- ..... **CLC 87; DAM MULT**
  See also CA 144; CAAS 22; DLB 175; NNAL
Kent, Kelvin
  See Kuttner, Henry
Kenton, Maxwell
  See Southern, Terry
Kenyon, Robert O.
  See Kuttner, Henry
Kerouac, Jack .... **CLC 1, 2, 3, 5, 14, 29, 61**
  See also Kerouac, Jean-Louis Lebris de
  See also CDALB 1941-1968; DLB 2, 16; DLBD 3; DLBY 95
Kerouac, Jean-Louis Lebris de 1922-1969
  See Kerouac, Jack
  See also AITN 1; CA 5-8R; 25-28R; CANR 26, 54; DA; DAB; DAC; DAM MST, NOV, POET, POP; MTCW; WLC
Kerr, Jean 1923- ....**CLC 22**
  See also CA 5-8R; CANR 7; INT CANR-7
Kerr, M. E. .... **CLC 12, 35**
  See also Meaker, Marijane (Agnes)
  See also AAYA 2; CLR 29; SAAS 1
Kerr, Robert ....**CLC 55**
Kerrigan, (Thomas) Anthony 1918-**CLC 4, 6**
  See also CA 49-52; CAAS 11; CANR 4
Kerry, Lois
  See Duncan, Lois
Kesey, Ken (Elton) 1935- **CLC 1, 3, 6, 11, 46, 64; DA; DAB; DAC; DAM MST, NOV, POP; WLC**
  See also CA 1-4R; CANR 22, 38; CDALB 1968-1988; DLB 2, 16; MTCW; SATA 66
Kesselring, Joseph (Otto) 1902-1967**CLC 45; DAM DRAM, MST**
  See also CA 150
Kessler, Jascha (Frederick) 1929-.......**CLC 4**
  See also CA 17-20R; CANR 8, 48
Kettelkamp, Larry (Dale) 1933- ....**CLC 12**
  See also CA 29-32R; CANR 16; SAAS 3; SATA 2
Key, Ellen 1849-1926 .... **TCLC 65**
Keyber, Conny
  See Fielding, Henry
Keyes, Daniel 1927-**CLC 80; DA; DAC; DAM MST, NOV**
  See also CA 17-20R; CANR 10, 26, 54; SATA 37
Keynes, John Maynard 1883-1946 **TCLC 64**
  See also CA 114; DLBD 10
Khanshendel, Chiron
  See Rose, Wendy
Khayyam, Omar 1048-1131**CMLC 11; DAM POET; PC 8**
Kherdian, David 1931-................... **CLC 6, 9**
  See also CA 21-24R; CAAS 2; CANR 39; CLR 24; JRDA; MAICYA; SATA 16, 74
Khlebnikov, Velimir .... **TCLC 20**

See also Khlebnikov, Viktor Vladimirovich

Khlebnikov, Viktor Vladimirovich 1885-1922
See Khlebnikov, Velimir
See also CA 117

Khodasevich, Vladislav (Felitsianovich) 1886-
1939 .... **TCLC 15**
See also CA 115

Kielland, Alexander Lange 1849-1906 **T C L C
5**
See also CA 104

Kiely, Benedict 1919- .... **CLC 23, 43**
See also CA 1-4R; CANR 2; DLB 15

Kienzle, William X(avier) 1928- ..... **CLC 25;
DAM POP**
See also CA 93-96; CAAS 1; CANR 9, 31, 59;
INT CANR-31; MTCW

Kierkegaard, Soren 1813-1855 ...... **NCLC 34**

Killens, John Oliver 1916-1987 .... **CLC 10**
See also BW 2; CA 77-80; 123; CAAS 2; CANR
26; DLB 33

Killigrew, Anne 1660-1685 .... **LC 4**
See also DLB 131

Kim
See Simenon, Georges (Jacques Christian)

Kincaid, Jamaica 1949- .. **CLC 43, 68; BLC;
DAM MULT, NOV**
See also AAYA 13; BW 2; CA 125; CANR 47,
59; DLB 157

King, Francis (Henry) 1923- **CLC 8, 53; DAM
NOV**
See also CA 1-4R; CANR 1, 33; DLB 15, 139;
MTCW

King, Martin Luther, Jr. 1929-1968 **CLC 83;
BLC; DA; DAB; DAC; DAM MST, MULT;
WLCS**
See also BW 2; CA 25-28; CANR 27, 44; CAP
2; MTCW; SATA 14

King, Stephen (Edwin) 1947- **CLC 12, 26, 37,
61; DAM NOV, POP; SSC 17**
See also AAYA 1, 17; BEST 90:1; CA 61-64;
CANR 1, 30, 52; DLB 143; DLBY 80;
JRDA; MTCW; SATA 9, 55

King, Steve
See King, Stephen (Edwin)

King, Thomas 1943- .... **CLC 89; DAC; DAM
MULT**
See also CA 144; DLB 175; NNAL; SATA 96

Kingman, Lee .... **CLC 17**
See also Natti, (Mary) Lee
See also SAAS 3; SATA 1, 67

Kingsley, Charles 1819-1875 .... **NCLC 35**
See also DLB 21, 32, 163; YABC 2

Kingsley, Sidney 1906-1995 .... **CLC 44**
See also CA 85-88; 147; DLB 7

Kingsolver, Barbara 1955- **CLC 55, 81; DAM
POP**
See also AAYA 15; CA 129; 134; CANR 60;
INT 134

Kingston, Maxine (Ting Ting) Hong 1940-
**CLC 12, 19, 58; DAM MULT, NOV;
WLCS**
See also AAYA 8; CA 69-72; CANR 13, 38;
DLB 173; DLBY 80; INT CANR-13;
MTCW; SATA 53

Kinnell, Galway 1927- **CLC 1, 2, 3, 5, 13, 29**
See also CA 9-12R; CANR 10, 34; DLB 5;
DLBY 87; INT CANR-34; MTCW

Kinsella, Thomas 1928- .... **CLC 4, 19**
See also CA 17-20R; CANR 15; DLB 27;
MTCW

Kinsella, W(illiam) P(atrick) 1935- **CLC 27,
43; DAC; DAM NOV, POP**
See also AAYA 7; CA 97-100; CAAS 7; CANR

21, 35; INT CANR-21; MTCW

Kipling, (Joseph) Rudyard 1865-1936 **T C L C
8, 17; DA; DAB; DAC; DAM MST, POET;
PC 3; SSC 5; WLC**
See also CA 105; 120; CANR 33; CDBLB
1890-1914; CLR 39; DLB 19, 34, 141, 156;
MAICYA; MTCW; YABC 2

Kirkup, James 1918- ....**CLC 1**
See also CA 1-4R; CAAS 4; CANR 2; DLB 27;
SATA 12

Kirkwood, James 1930(?)-1989 ....**CLC 9**
See also AITN 2; CA 1-4R; 128; CANR 6, 40

Kirshner, Sidney
See Kingsley, Sidney

Kis, Danilo 1935-1989 ....**CLC 57**
See also CA 109; 118; 129; CANR 61; DLB
181; MTCW

Kivi, Aleksis 1834-1872 ....**NCLC 30**

Kizer, Carolyn (Ashley) 1925- **CLC 15, 39, 80;
DAM POET**
See also CA 65-68; CAAS 5; CANR 24; DLB
5, 169

Klabund 1890-1928 ....**TCLC 44**
See also DLB 66

Klappert, Peter 1942- ....**CLC 57**
See also CA 33-36R; DLB 5

Klein, A(braham) M(oses) 1909-1972 **CLC 19;
DAB; DAC; DAM MST**
See also CA 101; 37-40R; DLB 68

Klein, Norma 1938-1989 ....**CLC 30**
See also AAYA 2; CA 41-44R; 128; CANR 15,
37; CLR 2, 19; INT CANR-15; JRDA;
MAICYA; SAAS 1; SATA 7, 57

Klein, T(heodore) E(ibon) D(onald) 1947-
CLC 34
See also CA 119; CANR 44

Kleist, Heinrich von 1777-1811 **NCLC 2, 37;
DAM DRAM; SSC 22**
See also DLB 90

Klima, Ivan 1931- .... **CLC 56; DAM NOV**
See also CA 25-28R; CANR 17, 50

Klimentov, Andrei Platonovich 1899-1951
See Platonov, Andrei
See also CA 108

Klinger, Friedrich Maximilian von 1752-1831
NCLC 1
See also DLB 94

Klingsor the Magician
See Hartmann, Sadakichi

Klopstock, Friedrich Gottlieb 1724-1803
NCLC 11
See also DLB 97

Knapp, Caroline 1959- ....**CLC 99**
See also CA 154

Knebel, Fletcher 1911-1993 ....**CLC 14**
See also AITN 1; CA 1-4R; 140; CAAS 3;
CANR 1, 36; SATA 36; SATA-Obit 75

Knickerbocker, Diedrich
See Irving, Washington

Knight, Etheridge 1931-1991 **CLC 40; BLC;
DAM POET; PC 14**
See also BW 1; CA 21-24R; 133; CANR 23;
DLB 41

Knight, Sarah Kemble 1666-1727 .... **LC 7**
See also DLB 24

Knister, Raymond 1899-1932 ....**TCLC 56**
See also DLB 68

Knowles, John 1926- .. **CLC 1, 4, 10, 26; DA;
DAC; DAM MST, NOV**
See also AAYA 10; CA 17-20R; CANR 40;
CDALB 1968-1988; DLB 6; MTCW; SATA
8, 89

Knox, Calvin M.

See Silverberg, Robert

Knox, John c. 1505-1572 .... **LC 37**
See also DLB 132

Knye, Cassandra
See Disch, Thomas M(ichael)

Koch, C(hristopher) J(ohn) 1932- ... **CLC 42**
See also CA 127

Koch, Christopher
See Koch, C(hristopher) J(ohn)

Koch, Kenneth 1925- .... **CLC 5, 8, 44; DAM
POET**
See also CA 1-4R; CANR 6, 36, 57; DLB 5;
INT CANR-36; SATA 65

Kochanowski, Jan 1530-1584 .... **LC 10**

Kock, Charles Paul de 1794-1871 ..**NCLC 16**

Koda Shigeyuki 1867-1947
See Rohan, Koda
See also CA 121

Koestler, Arthur 1905-1983 **CLC 1, 3, 6, 8, 15,
33**
See also CA 1-4R; 109; CANR 1, 33; CDBLB
1945-1960; DLBY 83; MTCW

Kogawa, Joy Nozomi 1935- .. **CLC 78; DAC;
DAM MST, MULT**
See also CA 101; CANR 19, 62

Kohout, Pavel 1928- .... **CLC 13**
See also CA 45-48; CANR 3

Koizumi, Yakumo
See Hearn, (Patricio) Lafcadio (Tessima Carlos)

Kolmar, Gertrud 1894-1943 .... **TCLC 40**

Komunyakaa, Yusef 1947- .... **CLC 86, 94**
See also CA 147; DLB 120

Konrad, George
See Konrad, Gyoergy

Konrad, Gyoergy 1933- .... **CLC 4, 10, 73**
See also CA 85-88

Konwicki, Tadeusz 1926- .... **CLC 8, 28, 54**
See also CA 101; CAAS 9; CANR 39, 59;
MTCW

Koontz, Dean R(ay) 1945- ..... **CLC 78; DAM
NOV, POP**
See also AAYA 9; BEST 89:3, 90:2; CA 108;
CANR 19, 36, 52; MTCW; SATA 92

Kopit, Arthur (Lee) 1937- **CLC 1, 18, 33; DAM
DRAM**
See also AITN 1; CA 81-84; CABS 3; DLB 7;
MTCW

Kops, Bernard 1926- .... **CLC 4**
See also CA 5-8R; DLB 13

Kornbluth, C(yril) M. 1923-1958 .... **TCLC 8**
See also CA 105; 160; DLB 8

Korolenko, V. G.
See Korolenko, Vladimir Galaktionovich

Korolenko, Vladimir
See Korolenko, Vladimir Galaktionovich

Korolenko, Vladimir G.
See Korolenko, Vladimir Galaktionovich

Korolenko, Vladimir Galaktionovich 1853-
1921 .... **TCLC 22**
See also CA 121

Korzybski, Alfred (Habdank Skarbek) 1879-
1950 .... **TCLC 61**
See also CA 123; 160

Kosinski, Jerzy (Nikodem) 1933-1991 **CLC 1,
2, 3, 6, 10, 15, 53, 70; DAM NOV**
See also CA 17-20R; 134; CANR 9, 46; DLB
2; DLBY 82; MTCW

Kostelanetz, Richard (Cory) 1940- .. **CLC 28**
See also CA 13-16R; CAAS 8; CANR 38

Kostrowitzki, Wilhelm Apollinaris de 1880-
1918
See Apollinaire, Guillaume
See also CA 104

Kotlowitz, Robert 1924- ....**CLC 4**
See also CA 33-36R; CANR 36
Kotzebue, August (Friedrich Ferdinand) von
1761-1819 ....**NCLC 25**
See also DLB 94
Kotzwinkle, William 1938- .....**CLC 5, 14, 35**
See also CA 45-48; CANR 3, 44; CLR 6; DLB
173; MAICYA; SATA 24, 70
Kowna, Stancy
See Szymborska, Wislawa
Kozol, Jonathan 1936- ....**CLC 17**
See also CA 61-64; CANR 16, 45
Kozoll, Michael 1940(?)- ....**CLC 35**
Kramer, Kathryn 19(?)- ....**CLC 34**
Kramer, Larry 1935-**CLC 42; DAM POP; DC**
8
See also CA 124; 126; CANR 60
Krasicki, Ignacy 1735-1801 ....**NCLC 8**
Krasinski, Zygmunt 1812-1859 ....**NCLC 4**
Kraus, Karl 1874-1936 ....**TCLC 5**
See also CA 104; DLB 118
Kreve (Mickevicius), Vincas 1882-1954**TCLC**
27
Kristeva, Julia 1941- ....**CLC 77**
See also CA 154
Kristofferson, Kris 1936-.................**CLC 26**
See also CA 104
Krizanc, John 1956- ....**CLC 57**
Krleza, Miroslav 1893-1981 ....**CLC 8**
See also CA 97-100; 105; CANR 50; DLB 147
Kroetsch, Robert 1927-**CLC 5, 23, 57; DAC;**
DAM POET
See also CA 17-20R; CANR 8, 38; DLB 53;
MTCW
Kroetz, Franz
See Kroetz, Franz Xaver
Kroetz, Franz Xaver 1946- ....**CLC 41**
See also CA 130
Kroker, Arthur (W.) 1945-................**CLC 77**
See also CA 161
Kropotkin, Peter (Aleksieevich) 1842-1921
TCLC 36
See also CA 119
Krotkov, Yuri 1917-...........................**CLC 19**
See also CA 102
Krumb
See Crumb, R(obert)
Krumgold, Joseph (Quincy) 1908-1980 **C L C**
12
See also CA 9-12R; 101; CANR 7; MAICYA;
SATA 1, 48; SATA-Obit 23
Krumwitz
See Crumb, R(obert)
Krutch, Joseph Wood 1893-1970 .....**CLC 24**
See also CA 1-4R; 25-28R; CANR 4; DLB 63
Krutzch, Gus
See Eliot, T(homas) S(tearns)
Krylov, Ivan Andreevich 1768(?)-1844**N C L C**
1
See also DLB 150
Kubin, Alfred (Leopold Isidor) 1877-1959
TCLC 23
See also CA 112; 149; DLB 81
Kubrick, Stanley 1928- ....**CLC 16**
See also CA 81-84; CANR 33; DLB 26
Kumin, Maxine (Winokur) 1925- **CLC 5, 13,**
28; DAM POET; PC 15
See also AITN 2; CA 1-4R; CAAS 8; CANR 1,
21; DLB 5; MTCW; SATA 12
Kundera, Milan 1929-...**CLC 4, 9, 19, 32, 68;**
DAM NOV; SSC 24
See also AAYA 2; CA 85-88; CANR 19, 52;
MTCW

Kunene, Mazisi (Raymond) 1930- ....**CLC 85**
See also BW 1; CA 125; DLB 117
Kunitz, Stanley (Jasspon) 1905-**CLC 6, 11, 14;**
PC 19
See also CA 41-44R; CANR 26, 57; DLB 48;
INT CANR-26; MTCW
Kunze, Reiner 1933-...........................**CLC 10**
See also CA 93-96; DLB 75
Kuprin, Aleksandr Ivanovich 1870-1938
TCLC 5
See also CA 104
Kureishi, Hanif 1954(?)- ....**CLC 64**
See also CA 139
Kurosawa, Akira 1910-**CLC 16; DAM MULT**
See also AAYA 11; CA 101; CANR 46
Kushner, Tony 1957(?)-**CLC 81; DAM DRAM**
See also CA 144
Kuttner, Henry 1915-1958 ....**TCLC 10**
See also Vance, Jack
See also CA 107; 157; DLB 8
Kuzma, Greg 1944- ....**CLC 7**
See also CA 33-36R
Kuzmin, Mikhail 1872(?)-1936 ......**TCLC 40**
Kyd, Thomas 1558-1594**LC 22; DAM DRAM;**
DC 3
See also DLB 62
Kyprianos, Iossif
See Samarakis, Antonis
La Bruyere, Jean de 1645-1696 ....**LC 17**
Lacan, Jacques (Marie Emile) 1901-1981
CLC 75
See also CA 121; 104
Laclos, Pierre Ambroise Francois Choderlos de
1741-1803 ....**NCLC 4**
La Colere, Francois
See Aragon, Louis
Lacolere, Francois
See Aragon, Louis
La Deshabilleuse
See Simenon, Georges (Jacques Christian)
Lady Gregory
See Gregory, Isabella Augusta (Persse)
Lady of Quality, A
See Bagnold, Enid
La Fayette, Marie (Madelaine Pioche de la
Vergne Comtes 1634-1693 ....**LC 2**
Lafayette, Rene
See Hubbard, L(afayette) Ron(ald)
Laforgue, Jules 1860-1887**NCLC 5, 53; PC 14;**
SSC 20
Lagerkvist, Paer (Fabian) 1891-1974 **CLC 7,**
10, 13, 54; DAM DRAM, NOV
See also Lagerkvist, Par
See also CA 85-88; 49-52; MTCW
Lagerkvist, Par ....**SSC 12**
See also Lagerkvist, Paer (Fabian)
Lagerloef, Selma (Ottiliana Lovisa) 1858-1940
TCLC 4, 36
See also Lagerlof, Selma (Ottiliana Lovisa)
See also CA 108; SATA 15
Lagerlof, Selma (Ottiliana Lovisa)
See Lagerloef, Selma (Ottiliana Lovisa)
See also CLR 7; SATA 15
La Guma, (Justin) Alex(ander) 1925-1985
CLC 19; DAM NOV
See also BW 1; CA 49-52; 118; CANR 25; DLB
117; MTCW
Laidlaw, A. K.
See Grieve, C(hristopher) M(urray)
Lainez, Manuel Mujica
See Mujica Lainez, Manuel
See also HW
Laing, R(onald) D(avid) 1927-1989 ..**CLC 95**

See also CA 107; 129; CANR 34; MTCW
Lamartine, Alphonse (Marie Louis Prat) de
1790-1869**NCLC 11; DAM POET; PC 16**
Lamb, Charles 1775-1834 .....**NCLC 10; DA;**
DAB; DAC; DAM MST; WLC
See also CDBLB 1789-1832; DLB 93, 107, 163;
SATA 17
Lamb, Lady Caroline 1785-1828 ...**NCLC 38**
See also DLB 116
Lamming, George (William) 1927-**CLC 2, 4,**
66; BLC; DAM MULT
See also BW 2; CA 85-88; CANR 26; DLB 125;
MTCW
L'Amour, Louis (Dearborn) 1908-1988 . **C L C**
25, 55; DAM NOV, POP
See also AAYA 16; AITN 2; BEST 89:2; CA 1-
4R; 125; CANR 3, 25, 40; DLBY 80; MTCW
Lampedusa, Giuseppe (Tomasi) di 1896-1957
TCLC 13
See also Tomasi di Lampedusa, Giuseppe
See also DLB 177
Lampman, Archibald 1861-1899 ...**NCLC 25**
See also DLB 92
Lancaster, Bruce 1896-1963 ....**CLC 36**
See also CA 9-10; CAP 1; SATA 9
Lanchester, John ....**CLC 99**
Landau, Mark Alexandrovich
See Aldanov, Mark (Alexandrovich)
Landau-Aldanov, Mark Alexandrovich
See Aldanov, Mark (Alexandrovich)
Landis, Jerry
See Simon, Paul (Frederick)
Landis, John 1950- ....**CLC 26**
See also CA 112; 122
Landolfi, Tommaso 1908-1979 ....**CLC 11, 49**
See also CA 127; 117; DLB 177
Landon, Letitia Elizabeth 1802-1838 . **N C L C**
15
See also DLB 96
Landor, Walter Savage 1775-1864 **NCLC 14**
See also DLB 93, 107
Landwirth, Heinz 1927-
See Lind, Jakov
See also CA 9-12R; CANR 7
Lane, Patrick 1939- .... **CLC 25; DAM POET**
See also CA 97-100; CANR 54; DLB 53; INT
97-100
Lang, Andrew 1844-1912 ....**TCLC 16**
See also CA 114; 137; DLB 98, 141, 184;
MAICYA; SATA 16
Lang, Fritz 1890-1976 ....**CLC 20, 103**
See also CA 77-80; 69-72; CANR 30
Lange, John
See Crichton, (John) Michael
Langer, Elinor 1939- ....**CLC 34**
See also CA 121
Langland, William 1330(?)-1400(?) ... **LC 19;**
DA; DAB; DAC; DAM MST, POET
See also DLB 146
Langstaff, Launcelot
See Irving, Washington
Lanier, Sidney 1842-1881 .....**NCLC 6; DAM**
POET
See also DLB 64; DLBD 13; MAICYA; SATA
18
Lanyer, Aemilia 1569-1645............**LC 10, 30**
See also DLB 121
Lao Tzu ....**CMLC 7**
Lapine, James (Elliot) 1949- ....**CLC 39**
See also CA 123; 130; CANR 54; INT 130
Larbaud, Valery (Nicolas) 1881-1957**TCLC 9**
See also CA 106; 152
Lardner, Ring

See Lardner, Ring(gold) W(ilmer)

Lardner, Ring W., Jr.
See Lardner, Ring(gold) W(ilmer)

Lardner, Ring(gold) W(ilmer) 1885-1933 TCLC 2, 14
See also CA 104; 131; CDALB 1917-1929; DLB 11, 25, 86; DLBD 16; MTCW

Laredo, Betty
See Codrescu, Andrei

Larkin, Maia
See Wojciechowska, Maia (Teresa)

Larkin, Philip (Arthur) 1922-1985CLC 3, 5, 8, 9, 13, 18, 33, 39, 64; DAB; DAM MST, POET
See also CA 5-8R; 117; CANR 24, 62; CDBLB 1960 to Present; DLB 27; MTCW

Larra (y Sanchez de Castro), Mariano Jose de 1809-1837 .... NCLC 17

Larsen, Eric 1941- .... CLC 55
See also CA 132

Larsen, Nella 1891-1964CLC 37; BLC; DAM MULT
See also BW 1; CA 125; DLB 51

Larson, Charles R(aymond) 1938- .. CLC 31
See also CA 53-56; CANR 4

Larson, Jonathan 1961(?)-1996 .... CLC 99

Las Casas, Bartolome de 1474-1566 ... LC 31

Lasch, Christopher 1932-1994 .... CLC 102
See also CA 73-76; 144; CANR 25; MTCW

Lasker-Schueler, Else 1869-1945 ... TCLC 57
See also DLB 66, 124

Latham, Jean Lee 1902- .... CLC 12
See also AITN 1; CA 5-8R; CANR 7; MAICYA; SATA 2, 68

Latham, Mavis
See Clark, Mavis Thorpe

Lathen, Emma .... CLC 2
See also Hennissart, Martha; Latsis, Mary J(ane)

Lathrop, Francis
See Leiber, Fritz (Reuter, Jr.)

Latsis, Mary J(ane)
See Lathen, Emma
See also CA 85-88

Lattimore, Richmond (Alexander) 1906-1984 CLC 3
See also CA 1-4R; 112; CANR 1

Laughlin, James 1914- .... CLC 49
See also CA 21-24R; CAAS 22; CANR 9, 47; DLB 48; DLBY 96

Laurence, (Jean) Margaret (Wemyss) 1926-1987 .. CLC 3, 6, 13, 50, 62; DAC; DAM MST; SSC 7
See also CA 5-8R; 121; CANR 33; DLB 53; MTCW; SATA-Obit 50

Laurent, Antoine 1952- .... CLC 50

Lauscher, Hermann
See Hesse, Hermann

Lautreamont, Comte de 1846-1870NCLC 12; SSC 14

Laverty, Donald
See Blish, James (Benjamin)

Lavin, Mary 1912-1996CLC 4, 18, 99; SSC 4
See also CA 9-12R; 151; CANR 33; DLB 15; MTCW

Lavond, Paul Dennis
See Kornbluth, C(yril) M.; Pohl, Frederik

Lawler, Raymond Evenor 1922- ...... CLC 58
See also CA 103

Lawrence, D(avid) H(erbert Richards) 1885-1930TCLC 2, 9, 16, 33, 48, 61; DA; DAB; DAC; DAM MST, NOV, POET; SSC 4, 19; WLC

See also CA 104; 121; CDBLB 1914-1945; DLB 10, 19, 36, 98, 162; MTCW

Lawrence, T(homas) E(dward) 1888-1935 TCLC 18
See also Dale, Colin
See also CA 115

Lawrence of Arabia
See Lawrence, T(homas) E(dward)

Lawson, Henry (Archibald Hertzberg) 1867-1922 .... TCLC 27; SSC 18
See also CA 120

Lawton, Dennis
See Faust, Frederick (Schiller)

Laxness, Halldor .... CLC 25
See also Gudjonsson, Halldor Kiljan

Layamon fl. c. 1200- .... CMLC 10
See also DLB 146

Laye, Camara 1928-1980 .. CLC 4, 38; BLC; DAM MULT
See also BW 1; CA 85-88; 97-100; CANR 25; MTCW

Layton, Irving (Peter) 1912-CLC 2, 15; DAC; DAM MST, POET
See also CA 1-4R; CANR 2, 33, 43; DLB 88; MTCW

Lazarus, Emma 1849-1887 .... NCLC 8

Lazarus, Felix
See Cable, George Washington

Lazarus, Henry
See Slavitt, David R(ytman)

Lea, Joan
See Neufeld, John (Arthur)

Leacock, Stephen (Butler) 1869-1944TCLC 2; DAC; DAM MST
See also CA 104; 141; DLB 92

Lear, Edward 1812-1888 .... NCLC 3
See also CLR 1; DLB 32, 163, 166; MAICYA; SATA 18

Lear, Norman (Milton) 1922- .... CLC 12
See also CA 73-76

Leavis, F(rank) R(aymond) 1895-1978CLC 24
See also CA 21-24R; 77-80; CANR 44; MTCW

Leavitt, David 1961- ...... CLC 34; DAM POP
See also CA 116; 122; CANR 50, 62; DLB 130; INT 122

Leblanc, Maurice (Marie Emile) 1864-1941 TCLC 49
See also CA 110

Lebowitz, Fran(ces Ann) 1951(?)-CLC 11, 36
See also CA 81-84; CANR 14, 60; INT CANR-14; MTCW

Lebrecht, Peter
See Tieck, (Johann) Ludwig

le Carre, John .... CLC 3, 5, 9, 15, 28
See also Cornwell, David (John Moore)
See also BEST 89:4; CDBLB 1960 to Present; DLB 87

Le Clezio, J(ean) M(arie) G(ustave) 1940- CLC 31
See also CA 116; 128; DLB 83

Leconte de Lisle, Charles-Marie-Rene 1818-1894 .... NCLC 29

Le Coq, Monsieur
See Simenon, Georges (Jacques Christian)

Leduc, Violette 1907-1972 .... CLC 22
See also CA 13-14; 33-36R; CAP 1

Ledwidge, Francis 1887(?)-1917 .... TCLC 23
See also CA 123; DLB 20

Lee, Andrea 1953-CLC 36; BLC; DAM MULT
See also BW 1; CA 125

Lee, Andrew
See Auchincloss, Louis (Stanton)

Lee, Chang-rae 1965- .... CLC 91

See also CA 148

Lee, Don L. .... CLC 2
See also Madhubuti, Haki R.

Lee, George W(ashington) 1894-1976CLC 52; BLC; DAM MULT
See also BW 1; CA 125; DLB 51

Lee, (Nelle) Harper 1926-.. CLC 12, 60; DA; DAB; DAC; DAM MST, NOV; WLC
See also AAYA 13; CA 13-16R; CANR 51; CDALB 1941-1968; DLB 6; MTCW; SATA 11

Lee, Helen Elaine 1959(?)- .... CLC 86
See also CA 148

Lee, Julian
See Latham, Jean Lee

Lee, Larry
See Lee, Lawrence

Lee, Laurie 1914-1997 CLC 90; DAB; DAM POP
See also CA 77-80; 158; CANR 33; DLB 27; MTCW

Lee, Lawrence 1941-1990 .... CLC 34
See also CA 131; CANR 43

Lee, Manfred B(ennington) 1905-1971CLC 11
See also Queen, Ellery
See also CA 1-4R; 29-32R; CANR 2; DLB 137

Lee, Shelton Jackson 1957(?)-CLC 105; DAM MULT
See also Lee, Spike
See also BW 2; CA 125; CANR 42

Lee, Spike
See Lee, Shelton Jackson
See also AAYA 4

Lee, Stan 1922- .... CLC 17
See also AAYA 5; CA 108; 111; INT 111

Lee, Tanith 1947- .... CLC 46
See also AAYA 15; CA 37-40R; CANR 53; SATA 8, 88

Lee, Vernon .... TCLC 5
See also Paget, Violet
See also DLB 57, 153, 156, 174, 178

Lee, William
See Burroughs, William S(eward)

Lee, Willy
See Burroughs, William S(eward)

Lee-Hamilton, Eugene (Jacob) 1845-1907 TCLC 22
See also CA 117

Leet, Judith 1935- .... CLC 11

Le Fanu, Joseph Sheridan 1814-1873NCLC 9, 58; DAM POP; SSC 14
See also DLB 21, 70, 159, 178

Leffland, Ella 1931- .... CLC 19
See also CA 29-32R; CANR 35; DLBY 84; INT CANR-35; SATA 65

Leger, Alexis
See Leger, (Marie-Rene Auguste) Alexis Saint-Leger

Leger, (Marie-Rene Auguste) Alexis Saint-Leger 1887-1975 CLC 11; DAM POET
See also Perse, St.-John
See also CA 13-16R; 61-64; CANR 43; MTCW

Leger, Saintleger
See Leger, (Marie-Rene Auguste) Alexis Saint-Leger

Le Guin, Ursula K(roeber) 1929- CLC 8, 13, 22, 45, 71; DAB; DAC; DAM MST, POP; SSC 12
See also AAYA 9; AITN 1; CA 21-24R; CANR 9, 32, 52; CDALB 1968-1988; CLR 3, 28; DLB 8, 52; INT CANR-32; JRDA; MAICYA; MTCW; SATA 4, 52

Lehmann, Rosamond (Nina) 1901-1990CLC 5

See also CA 77-80; 131; CANR 8; DLB 15
Leiber, Fritz (Reuter, Jr.) 1910-1992 **CLC 25**
　See also CA 45-48; 139; CANR 2, 40; DLB 8;
　MTCW; SATA 45; SATA-Obit 73
Leibniz, Gottfried Wilhelm von 1646-1716 **LC 35**
　See also DLB 168
Leimbach, Martha 1963-
　See Leimbach, Marti
　See also CA 130
Leimbach, Marti .... **CLC 65**
　See also Leimbach, Martha
Leino, Eino .... **TCLC 24**
　See also Loennbohm, Armas Eino Leopold
Leiris, Michel (Julien) 1901-1990 .... **CLC 61**
　See also CA 119; 128; 132
Leithauser, Brad 1953- .... **CLC 27**
　See also CA 107; CANR 27; DLB 120
Lelchuk, Alan 1938- .... **CLC 5**
　See also CA 45-48; CAAS 20; CANR 1
Lem, Stanislaw 1921- .... **CLC 8, 15, 40**
　See also CA 105; CAAS 1; CANR 32; MTCW
Lemann, Nancy 1956- .... **CLC 39**
　See also CA 118; 136
Lemonnier, (Antoine Louis) Camille 1844-1913 **TCLC 22**
　See also CA 121
Lenau, Nikolaus 1802-1850 .... **NCLC 16**
L'Engle, Madeleine (Camp Franklin) 1918- **CLC 12; DAM POP**
　See also AAYA 1; AITN 2; CA 1-4R; CANR 3,
　21, 39; CLR 1, 14; DLB 52; JRDA;
　MAICYA; MTCW; SAAS 15; SATA 1, 27,
　75
Lengyel, Jozsef 1896-1975 .... **CLC 7**
　See also CA 85-88; 57-60
Lenin 1870-1924
　See Lenin, V. I.
　See also CA 121
Lenin, V. I. .... **TCLC 67**
　See also Lenin
Lennon, John (Ono) 1940-1980 . **CLC 12, 35**
　See also CA 102
Lennox, Charlotte Ramsay 1729(?)-1804 **NCLC 23**
　See also DLB 39
Lentricchia, Frank (Jr.) 1940- .... **CLC 34**
　See also CA 25-28R; CANR 19
Lenz, Siegfried 1926- .... **CLC 27**
　See also CA 89-92; DLB 75
Leonard, Elmore (John, Jr.) 1925- **CLC 28, 34, 71; DAM POP**
　See also AAYA 22; AITN 1; BEST 89:1, 90:4;
　CA 81-84; CANR 12, 28, 53; DLB 173; INT
　CANR-28; MTCW
Leonard, Hugh .... **CLC 19**
　See also Byrne, John Keyes
　See also DLB 13
Leonov, Leonid (Maximovich) 1899-1994 **CLC 92; DAM NOV**
　See also CA 129; MTCW
Leopardi, (Conte) Giacomo 1798-1837 **NCLC 22**
Le Reveler
　See Artaud, Antonin (Marie Joseph)
Lerman, Eleanor 1952- .... **CLC 9**
　See also CA 85-88
Lerman, Rhoda 1936- .... **CLC 56**
　See also CA 49-52
Lermontov, Mikhail Yuryevich 1814-1841 **NCLC 47; PC 18**
Leroux, Gaston 1868-1927 .... **TCLC 25**
　See also CA 108; 136; SATA 65

Lesage, Alain-Rene 1668-1747 .... **LC 28**
Leskov, Nikolai (Semyonovich) 1831-1895 **NCLC 25**
Lessing, Doris (May) 1919- **CLC 1, 2, 3, 6, 10, 15, 22, 40, 94; DA; DAB; DAC; DAM MST, NOV; SSC 6; WLCS**
　See also CA 9-12R; CAAS 14; CANR 33, 54;
　CDBLB 1960 to Present; DLB 15, 139;
　DLBY 85; MTCW
Lessing, Gotthold Ephraim 1729-1781 **LC 8**
　See also DLB 97
Lester, Richard 1932- .... **CLC 20**
Lever, Charles (James) 1806-1872 . **NCLC 23**
　See also DLB 21
Leverson, Ada 1865(?)-1936(?) ...... **TCLC 18**
　See also Elaine
　See also CA 117; DLB 153
Levertov, Denise 1923- **CLC 1, 2, 3, 5, 8, 15, 28, 66; DAM POET; PC 11**
　See also CA 1-4R; CAAS 19; CANR 3, 29, 50;
　DLB 5, 165; INT CANR-29; MTCW
Levi, Jonathan .... **CLC 76**
Levi, Peter (Chad Tigar) 1931- .... **CLC 41**
　See also CA 5-8R; CANR 34; DLB 40
Levi, Primo 1919-1987 .. **CLC 37, 50; SSC 12**
　See also CA 13-16R; 122; CANR 12, 33, 61;
　DLB 177; MTCW
Levin, Ira 1929- .... **CLC 3, 6; DAM POP**
　See also CA 21-24R; CANR 17, 44; MTCW;
　SATA 66
Levin, Meyer 1905-1981 . **CLC 7; DAM POP**
　See also AITN 1; CA 9-12R; 104; CANR 15;
　DLB 9, 28; DLBY 81; SATA 21; SATA-Obit
　27
Levine, Norman 1924- .... **CLC 54**
　See also CA 73-76; CAAS 23; CANR 14; DLB
　88
Levine, Philip 1928- .. **CLC 2, 4, 5, 9, 14, 33; DAM POET**
　See also CA 9-12R; CANR 9, 37, 52; DLB 5
Levinson, Deirdre 1931- .... **CLC 49**
　See also CA 73-76
Levi-Strauss, Claude 1908- .... **CLC 38**
　See also CA 1-4R; CANR 6, 32, 57; MTCW
Levitin, Sonia (Wolff) 1934- .... **CLC 17**
　See also AAYA 13; CA 29-32R; CANR 14, 32;
　JRDA; MAICYA; SAAS 2; SATA 4, 68
Levon, O. U.
　See Kesey, Ken (Elton)
Levy, Amy 1861-1889 .... **NCLC 59**
　See also DLB 156
Lewes, George Henry 1817-1878 ... **NCLC 25**
　See also DLB 55, 144
Lewis, Alun 1915-1944 .... **TCLC 3**
　See also CA 104; DLB 20, 162
Lewis, C. Day
　See Day Lewis, C(ecil)
Lewis, C(live) S(taples) 1898-1963 **CLC 1, 3, 6, 14, 27; DA; DAB; DAC; DAM MST, NOV, POP; WLC**
　See also AAYA 3; CA 81-84; CANR 33;
　CDBLB 1945-1960; CLR 3, 27; DLB 15,
　100, 160; JRDA; MAICYA; MTCW; SATA
　13
Lewis, Janet 1899- .... **CLC 41**
　See also Winters, Janet Lewis
　See also CA 9-12R; CANR 29; CAP 1; DLBY
　87
Lewis, Matthew Gregory 1775-1818 **NCLC 11, 62**
　See also DLB 39, 158, 178
Lewis, (Harry) Sinclair 1885-1951 . **TCLC 4, 13, 23, 39; DA; DAB; DAC; DAM MST,**

NOV; WLC
　See also CA 104; 133; CDALB 1917-1929;
　DLB 9, 102; DLBD 1; MTCW
Lewis, (Percy) Wyndham 1882(?)-1957 **TCLC 2, 9**
　See also CA 104; 157; DLB 15
Lewisohn, Ludwig 1883-1955 .... **TCLC 19**
　See also CA 107; DLB 4, 9, 28, 102
Lewton, Val 1904-1951 .... **TCLC 76**
Leyner, Mark 1956- .... **CLC 92**
　See also CA 110; CANR 28, 53
Lezama Lima, Jose 1910-1976 **CLC 4, 10, 101; DAM MULT**
　See also CA 77-80; DLB 113; HW
L'Heureux, John (Clarke) 1934- .... **CLC 52**
　See also CA 13-16R; CANR 23, 45
Liddell, C. H.
　See Kuttner, Henry
Lie, Jonas (Lauritz Idemil) 1833-1908(?) **TCLC 5**
　See also CA 115
Lieber, Joel 1937-1971 .... **CLC 6**
　See also CA 73-76; 29-32R
Lieber, Stanley Martin
　See Lee, Stan
Lieberman, Laurence (James) 1935- . **CLC 4, 36**
　See also CA 17-20R; CANR 8, 36
Lieksman, Anders
　See Haavikko, Paavo Juhani
Li Fei-kan 1904-
　See Pa Chin
　See also CA 105
Lifton, Robert Jay 1926- .... **CLC 67**
　See also CA 17-20R; CANR 27; INT CANR-
　27; SATA 66
Lightfoot, Gordon 1938- .... **CLC 26**
　See also CA 109
Lightman, Alan P. 1948- .... **CLC 81**
　See also CA 141
Ligotti, Thomas (Robert) 1953- **CLC 44; SSC 16**
　See also CA 123; CANR 49
Li Ho 791-817 .... **PC 13**
Liliencron, (Friedrich Adolf Axel) Detlev von 1844-1909 .... **TCLC 18**
　See also CA 117
Lilly, William 1602-1681 .... **LC 27**
Lima, Jose Lezama
　See Lezama Lima, Jose
Lima Barreto, Afonso Henrique de 1881-1922 **TCLC 23**
　See also CA 117
Limonov, Edward 1944- .... **CLC 67**
　See also CA 137
Lin, Frank
　See Atherton, Gertrude (Franklin Horn)
Lincoln, Abraham 1809-1865 .... **NCLC 18**
Lind, Jakov .... **CLC 1, 2, 4, 27, 82**
　See also Landwirth, Heinz
　See also CAAS 4
Lindbergh, Anne (Spencer) Morrow 1906- **CLC 82; DAM NOV**
　See also CA 17-20R; CANR 16; MTCW; SATA
　33
Lindsay, David 1878-1945 .... **TCLC 15**
　See also CA 113
Lindsay, (Nicholas) Vachel 1879-1931 **TCLC 17; DA; DAC; DAM MST, POET; WLC**
　See also CA 114; 135; CDALB 1865-1917;
　DLB 54; SATA 40
Linke-Poot
　See Doeblin, Alfred

Linney, Romulus 1930- .... **CLC 51**
  See also CA 1-4R; CANR 40, 44
Linton, Eliza Lynn 1822-1898 .... **NCLC 41**
  See also DLB 18
Li Po 701-763 .... **CMLC 2**
Lipsius, Justus 1547-1606 .... **LC 16**
Lipsyte, Robert (Michael) 1938-**CLC 21; DA;**
  DAC; DAM MST, NOV
  See also AAYA 7; CA 17-20R; CANR 8, 57;
  CLR 23; JRDA; MAICYA; SATA 5, 68
Lish, Gordon (Jay) 1934- ... **CLC 45; SSC 18**
  See also CA 113; 117; DLB 130; INT 117
Lispector, Clarice 1925-1977 .... **CLC 43**
  See also CA 139; 116; DLB 113
Littell, Robert 1935(?)- .... **CLC 42**
  See also CA 109; 112
Little, Malcolm 1925-1965
  See Malcolm X
  See also BW 1; CA 125; 111; DA; DAB; DAC;
  DAM MST, MULT; MTCW
Littlewit, Humphrey Gent.
  See Lovecraft, H(oward) P(hillips)
Litwos
  See Sienkiewicz, Henryk (Adam Alexander
  Pius)
Liu E 1857-1909 .... **TCLC 15**
  See also CA 115
Lively, Penelope (Margaret) 1933- . **CLC 32,**
  50; DAM NOV
  See also CA 41-44R; CANR 29; CLR 7; DLB
  14, 161; JRDA; MAICYA; MTCW; SATA 7,
  60
Livesay, Dorothy (Kathleen) 1909-**CLC 4, 15,**
  79; DAC; DAM MST, POET
  See also AITN 2; CA 25-28R; CAAS 8; CANR
  36; DLB 68; MTCW
Livy c. 59B.C.-c. 17 .... **CMLC 11**
Lizardi, Jose Joaquin Fernandez de 1776-1827
  NCLC 30
Llewellyn, Richard
  See Llewellyn Lloyd, Richard Dafydd Vivian
  See also DLB 15
Llewellyn Lloyd, Richard Dafydd Vivian 1906-
  1983 .... **CLC 7, 80**
  See also Llewellyn, Richard
  See also CA 53-56; 111; CANR 7; SATA 11;
  SATA-Obit 37
Llosa, (Jorge) Mario (Pedro) Vargas
  See Vargas Llosa, (Jorge) Mario (Pedro)
Lloyd Webber, Andrew 1948-
  See Webber, Andrew Lloyd
  See also AAYA 1; CA 116; 149; DAM DRAM;
  SATA 56
Llull, Ramon c. 1235-c. 1316 .... **CMLC 12**
Locke, Alain (Le Roy) 1886-1954 .. **TCLC 43**
  See also BW 1; CA 106; 124; DLB 51
Locke, John 1632-1704 .... **LC 7, 35**
  See also DLB 101
Locke-Elliott, Sumner
  See Elliott, Sumner Locke
Lockhart, John Gibson 1794-1854 .. **NCLC 6**
  See also DLB 110, 116, 144
Lodge, David (John) 1935- .... **CLC 36; DAM**
  POP
  See also BEST 90:1; CA 17-20R; CANR 19,
  53; DLB 14; INT CANR-19; MTCW
Loennbohm, Armas Eino Leopold 1878-1926
  See Leino, Eino
  See also CA 123
Loewinsohn, Ron(ald William) 1937-**CLC 52**
  See also CA 25-28R
Logan, Jake
  See Smith, Martin Cruz

Logan, John (Burton) 1923-1987 .... **CLC 5**
  See also CA 77-80; 124; CANR 45; DLB 5
Lo Kuan-chung 1330(?)-1400(?) .... **LC 12**
Lombard, Nap
  See Johnson, Pamela Hansford
London, Jack .. **TCLC 9, 15, 39; SSC 4; WLC**
  See also London, John Griffith
  See also AAYA 13; AITN 2; CDALB 1865-
  1917; DLB 8, 12, 78; SATA 18
London, John Griffith 1876-1916
  See London, Jack
  See also CA 110; 119; DA; DAB; DAC; DAM
  MST, NOV; JRDA; MAICYA; MTCW
Long, Emmett
  See Leonard, Elmore (John, Jr.)
Longbaugh, Harry
  See Goldman, William (W.)
Longfellow, Henry Wadsworth 1807-1882
  NCLC 2, 45; DA; DAB; DAC; DAM MST,
  POET; WLCS
  See also CDALB 1640-1865; DLB 1, 59; SATA
  19
Longley, Michael 1939- .... **CLC 29**
  See also CA 102; DLB 40
Longus fl. c. 2nd cent. - .... **CMLC 7**
Longway, A. Hugh
  See Lang, Andrew
Lonnrot, Elias 1802-1884 .... **NCLC 53**
Lopate, Phillip 1943- .... **CLC 29**
  See also CA 97-100; DLBY 80; INT 97-100
Lopez Portillo (y Pacheco), Jose 1920-**CLC 46**
  See also CA 129; HW
Lopez y Fuentes, Gregorio 1897(?)-1966**CLC 32**
  See also CA 131; HW
Lorca, Federico Garcia
  See Garcia Lorca, Federico
Lord, Bette Bao 1938- .... **CLC 23**
  See also BEST 90:3; CA 107; CANR 41; INT
  107; SATA 58
Lord Auch
  See Bataille, Georges
Lord Byron
  See Byron, George Gordon (Noel)
Lorde, Audre (Geraldine) 1934-1992**CLC 18,**
  71; BLC; DAM MULT, POET; PC 12
  See also BW 1; CA 25-28R; 142; CANR 16,
  26, 46; DLB 41; MTCW
Lord Houghton
  See Milnes, Richard Monckton
Lord Jeffrey
  See Jeffrey, Francis
Lorenzini, Carlo 1826-1890
  See Collodi, Carlo
  See also MAICYA; SATA 29
Lorenzo, Heberto Padilla
  See Padilla (Lorenzo), Heberto
Loris
  See Hofmannsthal, Hugo von
Loti, Pierre .... **TCLC 11**
  See also Viaud, (Louis Marie) Julien
  See also DLB 123
Louie, David Wong 1954- .... **CLC 70**
  See also CA 139
Louis, Father M.
  See Merton, Thomas
Lovecraft, H(oward) P(hillips) 1890-1937
  TCLC 4, 22; DAM POP; SSC 3
  See also AAYA 14; CA 104; 133; MTCW
Lovelace, Earl 1935- .... **CLC 51**
  See also BW 2; CA 77-80; CANR 41; DLB 125;
  MTCW
Lovelace, Richard 1618-1657 .... **LC 24**

See also DLB 131
Lowell, Amy 1874-1925 .... **TCLC 1, 8; DAM**
  POET; PC 13
  See also CA 104; 151; DLB 54, 140
Lowell, James Russell 1819-1891 .... **NCLC 2**
  See also CDALB 1640-1865; DLB 1, 11, 64,
  79
Lowell, Robert (Traill Spence, Jr.) 1917-1977
  CLC 1, 2, 3, 4, 5, 8, 9, 11, 15, 37; DA; DAB;
  DAC; DAM MST, NOV; PC 3; WLC
  See also CA 9-12R; 73-76; CABS 2; CANR 26,
  60; DLB 5, 169; MTCW
Lowndes, Marie Adelaide (Belloc) 1868-1947
  TCLC 12
  See also CA 107; DLB 70
Lowry, (Clarence) Malcolm 1909-1957**TCLC**
  6, 40
  See also CA 105; 131; CANR 62; CDBLB
  1945-1960; DLB 15; MTCW
Lowry, Mina Gertrude 1882-1966
  See Loy, Mina
  See also CA 113
Loxsmith, John
  See Brunner, John (Kilian Houston)
Loy, Mina .... **CLC 28; DAM POET; PC 16**
  See also Lowry, Mina Gertrude
  See also DLB 4, 54
Loyson-Bridet
  See Schwob, (Mayer Andre) Marcel
Lucas, Craig 1951- .... **CLC 64**
  See also CA 137
Lucas, E(dward) V(errall) 1868-1938 **TCLC**
  73
  See also DLB 98, 149, 153; SATA 20
Lucas, George 1944- .... **CLC 16**
  See also AAYA 1; CA 77-80; CANR 30; SATA
  56
Lucas, Hans
  See Godard, Jean-Luc
Lucas, Victoria
  See Plath, Sylvia
Ludlam, Charles 1943-1987 .... **CLC 46, 50**
  See also CA 85-88; 122
Ludlum, Robert 1927-**CLC 22, 43; DAM NOV,**
  POP
  See also AAYA 10; BEST 89:1, 90:3; CA 33-
  36R; CANR 25, 41; DLBY 82; MTCW
Ludwig, Ken .... **CLC 60**
Ludwig, Otto 1813-1865 .... **NCLC 4**
  See also DLB 129
Lugones, Leopoldo 1874-1938 .... **TCLC 15**
  See also CA 116; 131; HW
Lu Hsun 1881-1936 .... **TCLC 3; SSC 20**
  See also Shu-Jen, Chou
Lukacs, George .... **CLC 24**
  See also Lukacs, Gyorgy (Szegeny von)
Lukacs, Gyorgy (Szegeny von) 1885-1971
  See Lukacs, George
  See also CA 101; 29-32R; CANR 62
Luke, Peter (Ambrose Cyprian) 1919-1995
  CLC 38
  See also CA 81-84; 147; DLB 13
Lunar, Dennis
  See Mungo, Raymond
Lurie, Alison 1926- .... **CLC 4, 5, 18, 39**
  See also CA 1-4R; CANR 2, 17, 50; DLB 2;
  MTCW; SATA 46
Lustig, Arnost 1926- .... **CLC 56**
  See also AAYA 3; CA 69-72; CANR 47; SATA
  56
Luther, Martin 1483-1546 .... **LC 9, 37**
  See also DLB 179
Luxemburg, Rosa 1870(?)-1919 ..... **TCLC 63**

See also CA 118
Luzi, Mario 1914- .... **CLC 13**
See also CA 61-64; CANR 9; DLB 128
Lyly, John 1554(?)-1606 .... **DC 7**
See also DAM DRAM; DLB 62, 167
L'Ymagier
See Gourmont, Remy (-Marie-Charles) de
Lynch, B. Suarez
See Bioy Casares, Adolfo; Borges, Jorge Luis
Lynch, David (K.) 1946- .... **CLC 66**
See also CA 124; 129
Lynch, James
See Andreyev, Leonid (Nikolaevich)
Lynch Davis, B.
See Bioy Casares, Adolfo; Borges, Jorge Luis
Lyndsay, Sir David 1490-1555 .... **LC 20**
Lynn, Kenneth S(chuyler) 1923-...... **CLC 50**
See also CA 1-4R; CANR 3, 27
Lynx
See West, Rebecca
Lyons, Marcus
See Blish, James (Benjamin)
Lyre, Pinchbeck
See Sassoon, Siegfried (Lorraine)
Lytle, Andrew (Nelson) 1902-1995 .. **CLC 22**
See also CA 9-12R; 150; DLB 6; DLBY 95
Lyttelton, George 1709-1773 .... **LC 10**
Maas, Peter 1929- .... **CLC 29**
See also CA 93-96; INT 93-96
Macaulay, Rose 1881-1958 .... **TCLC 7, 44**
See also CA 104; DLB 36
Macaulay, Thomas Babington 1800-1859
NCLC 42
See also CDBLB 1832-1890; DLB 32, 55
MacBeth, George (Mann) 1932-1992**CLC 2, 5,
9**
See also CA 25-28R; 136; CANR 61; DLB 40;
MTCW; SATA 4; SATA-Obit 70
MacCaig, Norman (Alexander) 1910-**CLC 36;
DAB; DAM POET**
See also CA 9-12R; CANR 3, 34; DLB 27
MacCarthy, (Sir Charles Otto) Desmond 1877-
1952 .... **TCLC 36**
MacDiarmid, Hugh**CLC 2, 4, 11, 19, 63; PC 9**
See also Grieve, C(hristopher) M(urray)
See also CDBLB 1945-1960; DLB 20
MacDonald, Anson
See Heinlein, Robert A(nson)
Macdonald, Cynthia 1928- .... **CLC 13, 19**
See also CA 49-52; CANR 4, 44; DLB 105
MacDonald, George 1824-1905 .... **TCLC 9**
See also CA 106; 137; DLB 18, 163, 178;
MAICYA; SATA 33
Macdonald, John
See Millar, Kenneth
MacDonald, John D(ann) 1916-1986 **CLC 3,
27, 44; DAM NOV, POP**
See also CA 1-4R; 121; CANR 1, 19, 60; DLB
8; DLBY 86; MTCW
Macdonald, John Ross
See Millar, Kenneth
Macdonald, Ross .... **CLC 1, 2, 3, 14, 34, 41**
See also Millar, Kenneth
See also DLBD 6
MacDougal, John
See Blish, James (Benjamin)
MacEwen, Gwendolyn (Margaret) 1941-1987
CLC 13, 55
See also CA 9-12R; 124; CANR 7, 22; DLB
53; SATA 50; SATA-Obit 55
Macha, Karel Hynek 1810-1846 ....**NCLC 46**
Machado (y Ruiz), Antonio 1875-1939**T C L C
3**

See also CA 104; DLB 108
Machado de Assis, Joaquim Maria 1839-1908
TCLC 10; BLC; SSC 24
See also CA 107; 153
Machen, Arthur .... **TCLC 4; SSC 20**
See also Jones, Arthur Llewellyn
See also DLB 36, 156, 178
Machiavelli, Niccolo 1469-1527**LC 8, 36; DA;
DAB; DAC; DAM MST; WLCS**
MacInnes, Colin 1914-1976 .... **CLC 4, 23**
See also CA 69-72; 65-68; CANR 21; DLB 14;
MTCW
MacInnes, Helen (Clark) 1907-1985**CLC 27,
39; DAM POP**
See also CA 1-4R; 117; CANR 1, 28, 58; DLB
87; MTCW; SATA 22; SATA-Obit 44
Mackay, Mary 1855-1924
See Corelli, Marie
See also CA 118
Mackenzie, Compton (Edward Montague)
1883-1972..................................... **CLC 18**
See also CA 21-22; 37-40R; CAP 2; DLB 34,
100
Mackenzie, Henry 1745-1831 .... **NCLC 41**
See also DLB 39
Mackintosh, Elizabeth 1896(?)-1952
See Tey, Josephine
See also CA 110
MacLaren, James
See Grieve, C(hristopher) M(urray)
Mac Laverty, Bernard 1942- .... **CLC 31**
See also CA 116; 118; CANR 43; INT 118
MacLean, Alistair (Stuart) 1922(?)-1987**C L C
3, 13, 50, 63; DAM POP**
See also CA 57-60; 121; CANR 28, 61; MTCW;
SATA 23; SATA-Obit 50
Maclean, Norman (Fitzroy) 1902-1990 . **C L C
78; DAM POP; SSC 13**
See also CA 102; 132; CANR 49
MacLeish, Archibald 1892-1982**CLC 3, 8, 14,
68; DAM POET**
See also CA 9-12R; 106; CANR 33; DLB 4, 7,
45; DLBY 82; MTCW
MacLennan, (John) Hugh 1907-1990 **CLC 2,
14, 92; DAC; DAM MST**
See also CA 5-8R; 142; CANR 33; DLB 68;
MTCW
MacLeod, Alistair 1936-**CLC 56; DAC; DAM
MST**
See also CA 123; DLB 60
Macleod, Fiona
See Sharp, William
MacNeice, (Frederick) Louis 1907-1963**C L C
1, 4, 10, 53; DAB; DAM POET**
See also CA 85-88; CANR 61; DLB 10, 20;
MTCW
MacNeill, Dand
See Fraser, George MacDonald
Macpherson, James 1736-1796 .... **LC 29**
See also DLB 109
Macpherson, (Jean) Jay 1931- .... **CLC 14**
See also CA 5-8R; DLB 53
MacShane, Frank 1927-..................... **CLC 39**
See also CA 9-12R; CANR 3, 33; DLB 111
Macumber, Mari
See Sandoz, Mari(e Susette)
Madach, Imre 1823-1864 .... **NCLC 19**
Madden, (Jerry) David 1933-....... **CLC 5, 15**
See also CA 1-4R; CAAS 3; CANR 4, 45; DLB
6; MTCW
Maddern, Al(an)
See Ellison, Harlan (Jay)
Madhubuti, Haki R. 1942- **CLC 6, 73; BLC;**

DAM MULT, POET; PC 5
See also Lee, Don L.
See also BW 2; CA 73-76; CANR 24, 51; DLB
5, 41; DLBD 8
Maepenn, Hugh
See Kuttner, Henry
Maepenn, K. H.
See Kuttner, Henry
Maeterlinck, Maurice 1862-1949 ....**TCLC 3;
DAM DRAM**
See also CA 104; 136; SATA 66
Maginn, William 1794-1842 .... **NCLC 8**
See also DLB 110, 159
Mahapatra, Jayanta 1928- ....**CLC 33; DAM
MULT**
See also CA 73-76; CAAS 9; CANR 15, 33
Mahfouz, Naguib (Abdel Aziz Al-Sabilgi)
1911(?)-
See Mahfuz, Najib
See also BEST 89:2; CA 128; CANR 55; DAM
NOV; MTCW
Mahfuz, Najib .... **CLC 52, 55**
See also Mahfouz, Naguib (Abdel Aziz Al-
Sabilgi)
See also DLBY 88
Mahon, Derek 1941- .... **CLC 27**
See also CA 113; 128; DLB 40
Mailer, Norman 1923-**CLC 1, 2, 3, 4, 5, 8, 11,
14, 28, 39, 74; DA; DAB; DAC; DAM MST,
NOV, POP**
See also AITN 2; CA 9-12R; CABS 1; CANR
28; CDALB 1968-1988; DLB 2, 16, 28;
DLBD 3; DLBY 80, 83; MTCW
Maillet, Antonine 1929- .... **CLC 54; DAC**
See also CA 115; 120; CANR 46; DLB 60; INT
120
Mais, Roger 1905-1955 .... **TCLC 8**
See also BW 1; CA 105; 124; DLB 125; MTCW
Maistre, Joseph de 1753-1821 .... **NCLC 37**
Maitland, Frederic 1850-1906 .... **TCLC 65**
Maitland, Sara (Louise) 1950- .... **CLC 49**
See also CA 69-72; CANR 13, 59
Major, Clarence 1936- **CLC 3, 19, 48; BLC;
DAM MULT**
See also BW 2; CA 21-24R; CAAS 6; CANR
13, 25, 53; DLB 33
Major, Kevin (Gerald) 1949-...**CLC 26; DAC**
See also AAYA 16; CA 97-100; CANR 21, 38;
CLR 11; DLB 60; INT CANR-21; JRDA;
MAICYA; SATA 32, 82
Maki, James
See Ozu, Yasujiro
Malabaila, Damiano
See Levi, Primo
Malamud, Bernard 1914-1986**CLC 1, 2, 3, 5,
8, 9, 11, 18, 27, 44, 78, 85; DA; DAB; DAC;
DAM MST, NOV, POP; SSC 15; WLC**
See also AAYA 16; CA 5-8R; 118; CABS 1;
CANR 28, 62; CDALB 1941-1968; DLB 2,
28, 152; DLBY 80, 86; MTCW
Malan, Herman
See Bosman, Herman Charles; Bosman, Herman
Charles
Malaparte, Curzio 1898-1957 .... **TCLC 52**
Malcolm, Dan
See Silverberg, Robert
Malcolm X .... **CLC 82; BLC; WLCS**
See also Little, Malcolm
Malherbe, Francois de 1555-1628 .... **LC 5**
Mallarme, Stephane 1842-1898 **NCLC 4, 41;
DAM POET; PC 4**
Mallet-Joris, Francoise 1930- .... **CLC 11**
See also CA 65-68; CANR 17; DLB 83

Malley, Ern
See McAuley, James Phillip
Mallowan, Agatha Christie
See Christie, Agatha (Mary Clarissa)
Maloff, Saul 1922- ....CLC **5**
See also CA 33-36R
Malone, Louis
See MacNeice, (Frederick) Louis
Malone, Michael (Christopher) 1942-CLC **43**
See also CA 77-80; CANR 14, 32, 57
Malory, (Sir) Thomas 1410(?)-1471(?)LC **11;**
DA; DAB; DAC; DAM MST; WLCS
See also CDBLB Before 1660; DLB 146; SATA
59; SATA-Brief 33
Malouf, (George Joseph) David 1934-CLC **28,**
86
See also CA 124; CANR 50
Malraux, (Georges-)Andre 1901-1976CLC **1,**
4, 9, 13, 15, 57; DAM NOV
See also CA 21-22; 69-72; CANR 34, 58; CAP
2; DLB 72; MTCW
Malzberg, Barry N(athaniel) 1939- ....CLC **7**
See also CA 61-64; CAAS 4; CANR 16; DLB
8
Mamet, David (Alan) 1947-CLC **9, 15, 34, 46,**
91; DAM DRAM; DC 4
See also AAYA 3; CA 81-84; CABS 3; CANR
15, 41; DLB 7; MTCW
Mamoulian, Rouben (Zachary) 1897-1987
CLC **16**
See also CA 25-28R; 124
Mandelstam, Osip (Emilievich) 1891(?)-1938(?)
TCLC **2, 6; PC 14**
See also CA 104; 150
Mander, (Mary) Jane 1877-1949 ... TCLC **31**
Mandeville, John fl. 1350- .... CMLC **19**
See also DLB 146
Mandiargues, Andre Pieyre de .... CLC **41**
See also Pieyre de Mandiargues, Andre
See also DLB 83
Mandrake, Ethel Belle
See Thurman, Wallace (Henry)
Mangan, James Clarence 1803-1849NCLC **27**
Maniere, J.-E.
See Giraudoux, (Hippolyte) Jean
Manley, (Mary) Delariviere 1672(?)-1724 L C
1
See also DLB 39, 80
Mann, Abel
See Creasey, John
Mann, Emily 1952-................................. DC **7**
See also CA 130; CANR 55
Mann, (Luiz) Heinrich 1871-1950 ... TCLC **9**
See also CA 106; DLB 66
Mann, (Paul) Thomas 1875-1955 TCLC **2, 8,**
14, 21, 35, 44, 60; DA; DAB; DAC; DAM
MST, NOV; SSC 5; WLC
See also CA 104; 128; DLB 66; MTCW
Mannheim, Karl 1893-1947 .... TCLC **65**
Manning, David
See Faust, Frederick (Schiller)
Manning, Frederic 1887(?)-1935 ... TCLC **25**
See also CA 124
Manning, Olivia 1915-1980 .... CLC **5, 19**
See also CA 5-8R; 101; CANR 29; MTCW
Mano, D. Keith 1942-.................... CLC **2, 10**
See also CA 25-28R; CAAS 6; CANR 26, 57;
DLB 6
Mansfield, KatherineTCLC **2, 8, 39; DAB; SSC**
9, 23; WLC
See also Beauchamp, Kathleen Mansfield
See also DLB 162
Manso, Peter 1940-........................... CLC **39**

See also CA 29-32R; CANR 44
Mantecon, Juan Jimenez
See Jimenez (Mantecon), Juan Ramon
Manton, Peter
See Creasey, John
Man Without a Spleen, A
See Chekhov, Anton (Pavlovich)
Manzoni, Alessandro 1785-1873 ....NCLC **29**
Mapu, Abraham (ben Jekutiel) 1808-1867
NCLC **18**
Mara, Sally
See Queneau, Raymond
Marat, Jean Paul 1743-1793 .... LC **10**
Marcel, Gabriel Honore 1889-1973 ..CLC **15**
See also CA 102; 45-48; MTCW
Marchbanks, Samuel
See Davies, (William) Robertson
Marchi, Giacomo
See Bassani, Giorgio
Margulies, Donald ....CLC **76**
Marie de France c. 12th cent. - .... CMLC **8**
Marie de l'Incarnation 1599-1672 ...... LC **10**
Marier, Captain Victor
See Griffith, D(avid Lewelyn) W(ark)
Mariner, Scott
See Pohl, Frederik
Marinetti, Filippo Tommaso 1876-1944TCLC
10
See also CA 107; DLB 114
Marivaux, Pierre Carlet de Chamblain de 1688-
1763 .... LC **4; DC 7**
Markandaya, Kamala .... CLC **8, 38**
See also Taylor, Kamala (Purnaiya)
Markfield, Wallace 1926- .... CLC **8**
See also CA 69-72; CAAS 3; DLB 2, 28
Markham, Edwin 1852-1940 .... TCLC **47**
See also CA 160; DLB 54
Markham, Robert
See Amis, Kingsley (William)
Marks, J
See Highwater, Jamake (Mamake)
Marks-Highwater, J
See Highwater, Jamake (Mamake)
Markson, David M(errill) 1927- .... CLC **67**
See also CA 49-52; CANR 1
Marley, Bob ....CLC **17**
See also Marley, Robert Nesta
Marley, Robert Nesta 1945-1981
See Marley, Bob
See also CA 107; 103
Marlowe, Christopher 1564-1593LC **22; DA;**
DAB; DAC; DAM DRAM, MST; DC 1;
WLC
See also CDBLB Before 1660; DLB 62
Marlowe, Stephen 1928-
See Queen, Ellery
See also CA 13-16R; CANR 6, 55
Marmontel, Jean-Francois 1723-1799 . LC **2**
Marquand, John P(hillips) 1893-1960CLC **2,**
10
See also CA 85-88; DLB 9, 102
Marques, Rene 1919-1979 .....CLC **96; DAM**
MULT; HLC
See also CA 97-100; 85-88; DLB 113; HW
Marquez, Gabriel (Jose) Garcia
See Garcia Marquez, Gabriel (Jose)
Marquis, Don(ald Robert Perry) 1878-1937
TCLC **7**
See also CA 104; DLB 11, 25
Marric, J. J.
See Creasey, John
Marrow, Bernard
See Moore, Brian

Marryat, Frederick 1792-1848 .... NCLC **3**
See also DLB 21, 163
Marsden, James
See Creasey, John
Marsh, (Edith) Ngaio 1899-1982 CLC **7, 53;**
DAM POP
See also CA 9-12R; CANR 6, 58; DLB 77;
MTCW
Marshall, Garry 1934-...................... CLC **17**
See also AAYA 3; CA 111; SATA 60
Marshall, Paule 1929-CLC **27, 72; BLC; DAM**
MULT; SSC 3
See also BW 2; CA 77-80; CANR 25; DLB 157;
MTCW
Marsten, Richard
See Hunter, Evan
Marston, John 1576-1634LC **33; DAM DRAM**
See also DLB 58, 172
Martha, Henry
See Harris, Mark
Marti, Jose 1853-1895NCLC **63; DAM MULT;**
HLC
Martial c. 40-c. 104 .... PC **10**
Martin, Ken
See Hubbard, L(afayette) Ron(ald)
Martin, Richard
See Creasey, John
Martin, Steve 1945- .... CLC **30**
See also CA 97-100; CANR 30; MTCW
Martin, Valerie 1948-....................... CLC **89**
See also BEST 90:2; CA 85-88; CANR 49
Martin, Violet Florence 1862-1915 TCLC **51**
Martin, Webber
See Silverberg, Robert
Martindale, Patrick Victor
See White, Patrick (Victor Martindale)
Martin du Gard, Roger 1881-1958 TCLC **24**
See also CA 118; DLB 65
Martineau, Harriet 1802-1876 .... NCLC **26**
See also DLB 21, 55, 159, 163, 166; YABC 2
Martines, Julia
See O'Faolain, Julia
Martinez, Enrique Gonzalez
See Gonzalez Martinez, Enrique
Martinez, Jacinto Benavente y
See Benavente (y Martinez), Jacinto
Martinez Ruiz, Jose 1873-1967
See Azorin; Ruiz, Jose Martinez
See also CA 93-96; HW
Martinez Sierra, Gregorio 1881-1947TCLC **6**
See also CA 115
Martinez Sierra, Maria (de la O'LeJarraga)
1874-1974 .... TCLC **6**
See also CA 115
Martinsen, Martin
See Follett, Ken(neth Martin)
Martinson, Harry (Edmund) 1904-1978C L C
14
See also CA 77-80; CANR 34
Marut, Ret
See Traven, B.
Marut, Robert
See Traven, B.
Marvell, Andrew 1621-1678LC **4; DA; DAB;**
DAC; DAM MST, POET; PC 10; WLC
See also CDBLB 1660-1789; DLB 131
Marx, Karl (Heinrich) 1818-1883 .NCLC **17**
See also DLB 129
Masaoka Shiki .... TCLC **18**
See also Masaoka Tsunenori
Masaoka Tsunenori 1867-1902
See Masaoka Shiki
See also CA 117

Masefield, John (Edward) 1878-1967CLC 11, 47; DAM POET
See also CA 19-20; 25-28R; CANR 33; CAP 2; CDBLB 1890-1914; DLB 10, 19, 153, 160; MTCW; SATA 19

Maso, Carole 19(?)- .... CLC 44

Mason, Bobbie Ann 1940-CLC 28, 43, 82; SSC 4
See also AAYA 5; CA 53-56; CANR 11, 31, 58; DLB 173; DLBY 87; INT CANR-31; MTCW

Mason, Ernst
See Pohl, Frederik

Mason, Lee W.
See Malzberg, Barry N(athaniel)

Mason, Nick 1945- .... CLC 35

Mason, Tally
See Derleth, August (William)

Mass, William
See Gibson, William

Masters, Edgar Lee 1868-1950 TCLC 2, 25; DA; DAC; DAM MST, POET; PC 1; WLCS
See also CA 104; 133; CDALB 1865-1917; DLB 54; MTCW

Masters, Hilary 1928- .... CLC 48
See also CA 25-28R; CANR 13, 47

Mastrosimone, William 19(?)- .... CLC 36

Mathe, Albert
See Camus, Albert

Mather, Cotton 1663-1728 .... LC 38
See also CDALB 1640-1865; DLB 24, 30, 140

Mather, Increase 1639-1723 .... LC 38
See also DLB 24

Matheson, Richard Burton 1926- .... CLC 37
See also CA 97-100; DLB 8, 44; INT 97-100

Mathews, Harry 1930- .... CLC 6, 52
See also CA 21-24R; CAAS 6; CANR 18, 40

Mathews, John Joseph 1894-1979 .. CLC 84; DAM MULT
See also CA 19-20; 142; CANR 45; CAP 2; DLB 175; NNAL

Mathias, Roland (Glyn) 1915- .... CLC 45
See also CA 97-100; CANR 19, 41; DLB 27

Matsuo Basho 1644-1694 .... PC 3
See also DAM POET

Mattheson, Rodney
See Creasey, John

Matthews, Greg 1949- .... CLC 45
See also CA 135

Matthews, William 1942- .... CLC 40
See also CA 29-32R; CAAS 18; CANR 12, 57; DLB 5

Matthias, John (Edward) 1941- .... CLC 9
See also CA 33-36R; CANR 56

Matthiessen, Peter 1927-CLC 5, 7, 11, 32, 64; DAM NOV
See also AAYA 6; BEST 90:4; CA 9-12R; CANR 21, 50; DLB 6, 173; MTCW; SATA 27

Maturin, Charles Robert 1780(?)-1824NCLC 6
See also DLB 178

Matute (Ausejo), Ana Maria 1925- .. CLC 11
See also CA 89-92; MTCW

Maugham, W. S.
See Maugham, W(illiam) Somerset

Maugham, W(illiam) Somerset 1874-1965
CLC 1, 11, 15, 67, 93; DA; DAB; DAC; DAM DRAM, MST, NOV; SSC 8; WLC
See also CA 5-8R; 25-28R; CANR 40; CDBLB 1914-1945; DLB 10, 36, 77, 100, 162; MTCW; SATA 54

Maugham, William Somerset
See Maugham, W(illiam) Somerset

Maupassant, (Henri Rene Albert) Guy de 1850-1893NCLC 1, 42; DA; DAB; DAC; DAM MST; SSC 1; WLC
See also DLB 123

Maupin, Armistead 1944-CLC 95; DAM POP
See also CA 125; 130; CANR 58; INT 130

Maurhut, Richard
See Traven, B.

Mauriac, Claude 1914-1996 .... CLC 9
See also CA 89-92; 152; DLB 83

Mauriac, Francois (Charles) 1885-1970 C L C 4, 9, 56; SSC 24
See also CA 25-28; CAP 2; DLB 65; MTCW

Mavor, Osborne Henry 1888-1951
See Bridie, James
See also CA 104

Maxwell, William (Keepers, Jr.) 1908-CLC 19
See also CA 93-96; CANR 54; DLBY 80; INT 93-96

May, Elaine 1932- .... CLC 16
See also CA 124; 142; DLB 44

Mayakovski, Vladimir (Vladimirovich) 1893-1930 .... TCLC 4, 18
See also CA 104; 158

Mayhew, Henry 1812-1887 .... NCLC 31
See also DLB 18, 55

Mayle, Peter 1939(?)- .... CLC 89
See also CA 139

Maynard, Joyce 1953- .... CLC 23
See also CA 111; 129

Mayne, William (James Carter) 1928-CLC 12
See also AAYA 20; CA 9-12R; CANR 37; CLR 25; JRDA; MAICYA; SAAS 11; SATA 6, 68

Mayo, Jim
See L'Amour, Louis (Dearborn)

Maysles, Albert 1926- .... CLC 16
See also CA 29-32R

Maysles, David 1932- .... CLC 16

Mazer, Norma Fox 1931- .... CLC 26
See also AAYA 5; CA 69-72; CANR 12, 32; CLR 23; JRDA; MAICYA; SAAS 1; SATA 24, 67

Mazzini, Guiseppe 1805-1872 .... NCLC 34

McAuley, James Phillip 1917-1976 ..CLC 45
See also CA 97-100

McBain, Ed
See Hunter, Evan

McBrien, William Augustine 1930- ..CLC 44
See also CA 107

McCaffrey, Anne (Inez) 1926-CLC 17; DAM NOV, POP
See also AAYA 6; AITN 2; BEST 89:2; CA 25-28R; CANR 15, 35, 55; DLB 8; JRDA; MAICYA; MTCW; SAAS 11; SATA 8, 70

McCall, Nathan 1955(?)- .... CLC 86
See also CA 146

McCann, Arthur
See Campbell, John W(ood, Jr.)

McCann, Edson
See Pohl, Frederik

McCarthy, Charles, Jr. 1933-
See McCarthy, Cormac
See also CANR 42; DAM POP

McCarthy, Cormac 1933- CLC 4, 57, 59, 101
See also McCarthy, Charles, Jr.
See also DLB 6, 143

McCarthy, Mary (Therese) 1912-1989CLC 1, 3, 5, 14, 24, 39, 59; SSC 24
See also CA 5-8R; 129; CANR 16, 50; DLB 2; DLBY 81; INT CANR-16; MTCW

McCartney, (James) Paul 1942-. CLC 12, 35

See also CA 146

McCauley, Stephen (D.) 1955- .... CLC 50
See also CA 141

McClure, Michael (Thomas) 1932-CLC 6, 10
See also CA 21-24R; CANR 17, 46; DLB 16

McCorkle, Jill (Collins) 1958- .... CLC 51
See also CA 121; DLBY 87

McCourt, James 1941- .... CLC 5
See also CA 57-60

McCoy, Horace (Stanley) 1897-1955TCLC 28
See also CA 108; 155; DLB 9

McCrae, John 1872-1918 .... TCLC 12
See also CA 109; DLB 92

McCreigh, James
See Pohl, Frederik

McCullers, (Lula) Carson (Smith) 1917-1967
CLC 1, 4, 10, 12, 48, 100; DA; DAB; DAC; DAM MST, NOV; SSC 9, 24; WLC
See also AAYA 21; CA 5-8R; 25-28R; CABS 1, 3; CANR 18; CDALB 1941-1968; DLB 2, 7, 173; MTCW; SATA 27

McCulloch, John Tyler
See Burroughs, Edgar Rice

McCullough, Colleen 1938(?)-CLC 27; DAM NOV, POP
See also CA 81-84; CANR 17, 46; MTCW

McDermott, Alice 1953- .... CLC 90
See also CA 109; CANR 40

McElroy, Joseph 1930- .... CLC 5, 47
See also CA 17-20R

McEwan, Ian (Russell) 1948- .... CLC 13, 66; DAM NOV
See also BEST 90:4; CA 61-64; CANR 14, 41; DLB 14; MTCW

McFadden, David 1940- ....CLC 48
See also CA 104; DLB 60; INT 104

McFarland, Dennis 1950- .... CLC 65

McGahern, John 1934-CLC 5, 9, 48; SSC 17
See also CA 17-20R; CANR 29; DLB 14; MTCW

McGinley, Patrick (Anthony) 1937- .CLC 41
See also CA 120; 127; CANR 56; INT 127

McGinley, Phyllis 1905-1978 ....CLC 14
See also CA 9-12R; 77-80; CANR 19; DLB 11, 48; SATA 2, 44; SATA-Obit 24

McGinniss, Joe 1942- .... CLC 32
See also AITN 2; BEST 89:2; CA 25-28R; CANR 26; INT CANR-26

McGivern, Maureen Daly
See Daly, Maureen

McGrath, Patrick 1950- .... CLC 55
See also CA 136

McGrath, Thomas (Matthew) 1916-1990CLC 28, 59; DAM POET
See also CA 9-12R; 132; CANR 6, 33; MTCW; SATA 41; SATA-Obit 66

McGuane, Thomas (Francis III) 1939-CLC 3, 7, 18, 45
See also AITN 2; CA 49-52; CANR 5, 24, 49; DLB 2; DLBY 80; INT CANR-24; MTCW

McGuckian, Medbh 1950- ..... CLC 48; DAM POET
See also CA 143; DLB 40

McHale, Tom 1942(?)-1982 .... CLC 3, 5
See also AITN 1; CA 77-80; 106

McIlvanney, William 1936- .... CLC 42
See also CA 25-28R; CANR 61; DLB 14

McIlwraith, Maureen Mollie Hunter
See Hunter, Mollie
See also SATA 2

McInerney, Jay 1955- ... CLC 34; DAM POP
See also AAYA 18; CA 116; 123; CANR 45; INT 123

McIntyre, Vonda N(eel) 1948- .... **CLC 18**
See also CA 81-84; CANR 17, 34; MTCW
McKay, Claude **TCLC 7, 41; BLC; DAB; PC 2**
See also McKay, Festus Claudius
See also DLB 4, 45, 51, 117
McKay, Festus Claudius 1889-1948
See McKay, Claude
See also BW 1; CA 104; 124; DA; DAC; DAM
MST, MULT, NOV, POET; MTCW; WLC
McKuen, Rod 1933- .... **CLC 1, 3**
See also AITN 1; CA 41-44R; CANR 40
McLoughlin, R. B.
See Mencken, H(enry) L(ouis)
McLuhan, (Herbert) Marshall 1911-1980
CLC 37, 83
See also CA 9-12R; 102; CANR 12, 34, 61;
DLB 88; INT CANR-12; MTCW
McMillan, Terry (L.) 1951- **CLC 50, 61; DAM
MULT, NOV, POP**
See also AAYA 21; BW 2; CA 140; CANR 60
McMurtry, Larry (Jeff) 1936- **CLC 2, 3, 7, 11,
27, 44; DAM NOV, POP**
See also AAYA 15; AITN 2; BEST 89:2; CA 5-
8R; CANR 19, 43; CDALB 1968-1988; DLB
2, 143; DLBY 80, 87; MTCW
McNally, T. M. 1961- .... **CLC 82**
McNally, Terrence 1939- ... **CLC 4, 7, 41, 91;
DAM DRAM**
See also CA 45-48; CANR 2, 56; DLB 7
McNamer, Deirdre 1950- .... **CLC 70**
McNeile, Herman Cyril 1888-1937
See Sapper
See also DLB 77
McNickle, (William) D'Arcy 1904-1977 **C L C
89; DAM MULT**
See also CA 9-12R; 85-88; CANR 5, 45; DLB
175; NNAL; SATA-Obit 22
McPhee, John (Angus) 1931- .... **CLC 36**
See also BEST 90:1; CA 65-68; CANR 20, 46;
MTCW
McPherson, James Alan 1943- ... **CLC 19, 77**
See also BW 1; CA 25-28R; CAAS 17; CANR
24; DLB 38; MTCW
McPherson, William (Alexander) 1933- **C L C
34**
See also CA 69-72; CANR 28; INT CANR-28
Mead, Margaret 1901-1978 .... **CLC 37**
See also AITN 1; CA 1-4R; 81-84; CANR 4;
MTCW; SATA-Obit 20
Meaker, Marijane (Agnes) 1927-
See Kerr, M. E.
See also CA 107; CANR 37; INT 107; JRDA;
MAICYA; MTCW; SATA 20, 61
Medoff, Mark (Howard) 1940- ... **CLC 6, 23;
DAM DRAM**
See also AITN 1; CA 53-56; CANR 5; DLB 7;
INT CANR-5
Medvedev, P. N.
See Bakhtin, Mikhail Mikhailovich
Meged, Aharon
See Megged, Aharon
Meged, Aron
See Megged, Aharon
Megged, Aharon 1920- .... **CLC 9**
See also CA 49-52; CAAS 13; CANR 1
Mehta, Ved (Parkash) 1934- .... **CLC 37**
See also CA 1-4R; CANR 2, 23; MTCW
Melanter
See Blackmore, R(ichard) D(oddridge)
Melikow, Loris
See Hofmannsthal, Hugo von
Melmoth, Sebastian
See Wilde, Oscar (Fingal O'Flahertie Wills)

Meltzer, Milton 1915- .... **CLC 26**
See also AAYA 8; CA 13-16R; CANR 38; CLR
13; DLB 61; JRDA; MAICYA; SAAS 1;
SATA 1, 50, 80
Melville, Herman 1819-1891 **NCLC 3, 12, 29,
45, 49; DA; DAB; DAC; DAM MST, NOV;
SSC 1, 17; WLC**
See also CDALB 1640-1865; DLB 3, 74; SATA
59
Menander c. 342B.C.-c. 292B.C. .... **CMLC 9;
DAM DRAM; DC 3**
See also DLB 176
Mencken, H(enry) L(ouis) 1880-1956 **T C L C
13**
See also CA 105; 125; CDALB 1917-1929;
DLB 11, 29, 63, 137; MTCW
Mendelsohn, Jane 1965(?)- .... **CLC 99**
See also CA 154
Mercer, David 1928-1980 **CLC 5; DAM DRAM**
See also CA 9-12R; 102; CANR 23; DLB 13;
MTCW
Merchant, Paul
See Ellison, Harlan (Jay)
Meredith, George 1828-1909 .. **TCLC 17, 43;
DAM POET**
See also CA 117; 153; CDBLB 1832-1890;
DLB 18, 35, 57, 159
Meredith, William (Morris) 1919- **CLC 4, 13,
22, 55; DAM POET**
See also CA 9-12R; CAAS 14; CANR 6, 40;
DLB 5
Merezhkovsky, Dmitry Sergeyevich 1865-1941
TCLC 29
Merimee, Prosper 1803-1870 **NCLC 6, 65; SSC
7**
See also DLB 119
Merkin, Daphne 1954- .... **CLC 44**
See also CA 123
Merlin, Arthur
See Blish, James (Benjamin)
Merrill, James (Ingram) 1926-1995 **CLC 2, 3,
6, 8, 13, 18, 34, 91; DAM POET**
See also CA 13-16R; 147; CANR 10, 49; DLB
5, 165; DLBY 85; INT CANR-10; MTCW
Merriman, Alex
See Silverberg, Robert
Merritt, E. B.
See Waddington, Miriam
Merton, Thomas 1915-1968 **CLC 1, 3, 11, 34,
83; PC 10**
See also CA 5-8R; 25-28R; CANR 22, 53; DLB
48; DLBY 81; MTCW
Merwin, W(illiam) S(tanley) 1927- **CLC 1, 2,
3, 5, 8, 13, 18, 45, 88; DAM POET**
See also CA 13-16R; CANR 15, 51; DLB 5,
169; INT CANR-15; MTCW
Metcalf, John 1938- .... **CLC 37**
See also CA 113; DLB 60
Metcalf, Suzanne
See Baum, L(yman) Frank
Mew, Charlotte (Mary) 1870-1928 .. **TCLC 8**
See also CA 105; DLB 19, 135
Mewshaw, Michael 1943- .... **CLC 9**
See also CA 53-56; CANR 7, 47; DLBY 80
Meyer, June
See Jordan, June
Meyer, Lynn
See Slavitt, David R(ytman)
Meyer-Meyrink, Gustav 1868-1932
See Meyrink, Gustav
See also CA 117
Meyers, Jeffrey 1939- .... **CLC 39**
See also CA 73-76; CANR 54; DLB 111

Meynell, Alice (Christina Gertrude Thompson)
1847-1922 ....
TCLC 6
See also CA 104; DLB 19, 98
Meyrink, Gustav .... **TCLC 21**
See also Meyer-Meyrink, Gustav
See also DLB 81
Michaels, Leonard 1933- **CLC 6, 25; SSC 16**
See also CA 61-64; CANR 21, 62; DLB 130;
MTCW
Michaux, Henri 1899-1984 .... **CLC 8, 19**
See also CA 85-88; 114
Micheaux, Oscar 1884-1951 .... **TCLC 76**
See also DLB 50
Michelangelo 1475-1564 .... **LC 12**
Michelet, Jules 1798-1874 .... **NCLC 31**
Michener, James A(lbert) 1907(?)-1997 **C L C
1, 5, 11, 29, 60; DAM NOV, POP**
See also AITN 1; BEST 90:1; CA 5-8R; 161;
CANR 21, 45; DLB 6; MTCW
Mickiewicz, Adam 1798-1855 .... **NCLC 3**
Middleton, Christopher 1926- .... **CLC 13**
See also CA 13-16R; CANR 29, 54; DLB 40
Middleton, Richard (Barham) 1882-1911
TCLC 56
See also DLB 156
Middleton, Stanley 1919- .... **CLC 7, 38**
See also CA 25-28R; CAAS 23; CANR 21, 46;
DLB 14
Middleton, Thomas 1580-1627 **LC 33; DAM
DRAM, MST; DC 5**
See also DLB 58
Migueis, Jose Rodrigues 1901- .... **CLC 10**
Mikszath, Kalman 1847-1910 .... **TCLC 31**
Miles, Jack .... **CLC 100**
Miles, Josephine (Louise) 1911-1985 **CLC 1, 2,
14, 34, 39; DAM POET**
See also CA 1-4R; 116; CANR 2, 55; DLB 48
Militant
See Sandburg, Carl (August)
Mill, John Stuart 1806-1873 .... **NCLC 11, 58**
See also CDBLB 1832-1890; DLB 55
Millar, Kenneth 1915-1983 .... **CLC 14; DAM
POP**
See also Macdonald, Ross
See also CA 9-12R; 110; CANR 16; DLB 2;
DLBD 6; DLBY 83; MTCW
Millay, E. Vincent
See Millay, Edna St. Vincent
Millay, Edna St. Vincent 1892-1950 **TCLC 4,
49; DA; DAB; DAC; DAM MST, POET;
PC 6; WLCS**
See also CA 104; 130; CDALB 1917-1929;
DLB 45; MTCW
Miller, Arthur 1915- **CLC 1, 2, 6, 10, 15, 26, 47,
78; DA; DAB; DAC; DAM DRAM, MST;
DC 1; WLC**
See also AAYA 15; AITN 1; CA 1-4R; CABS
3; CANR 2, 30, 54; CDALB 1941-1968;
DLB 7; MTCW
Miller, Henry (Valentine) 1891-1980 **CLC 1, 2,
4, 9, 14, 43, 84; DA; DAB; DAC; DAM
MST, NOV; WLC**
See also CA 9-12R; 97-100; CANR 33; CDALB
1929-1941; DLB 4, 9; DLBY 80; MTCW
Miller, Jason 1939(?)- .... **CLC 2**
See also AITN 1; CA 73-76; DLB 7
Miller, Sue 1943- .... **CLC 44; DAM POP**
See also BEST 90:3; CA 139; CANR 59; DLB
143
Miller, Walter M(ichael, Jr.) 1923- **CLC 4, 30**
See also CA 85-88; DLB 8
Millett, Kate 1934- .... **CLC 67**

See also AITN 1; CA 73-76; CANR 32, 53; MTCW

Millhauser, Steven 1943- .... **CLC 21, 54**
See also CA 110; 111; DLB 2; INT 111

Millin, Sarah Gertrude 1889-1968 .. **CLC 49**
See also CA 102; 93-96

Milne, A(lan) A(lexander) 1882-1956**TCLC 6; DAB; DAC; DAM MST**
See also CA 104; 133; CLR 1, 26; DLB 10, 77, 100, 160; MAICYA; MTCW; YABC 1

Milner, Ron(ald) 1938- **CLC 56; BLC; DAM MULT**
See also AITN 1; BW 1; CA 73-76; CANR 24; DLB 38; MTCW

Milnes, Richard Monckton 1809-1885 **N C L C 61**
See also DLB 32, 184

Milosz, Czeslaw 1911- **CLC 5, 11, 22, 31, 56, 82; DAM MST, POET; PC 8; WLCS**
See also CA 81-84; CANR 23, 51; MTCW

Milton, John 1608-1674 ..... **LC 9; DA; DAB; DAC; DAM MST, POET; PC 19; WLC**
See also CDBLB 1660-1789; DLB 131, 151

Min, Anchee 1957-.............................. **CLC 86**
See also CA 146

Minehaha, Cornelius
See Wedekind, (Benjamin) Frank(lin)

Miner, Valerie 1947-........................... **CLC 40**
See also CA 97-100; CANR 59

Minimo, Duca
See D'Annunzio, Gabriele

Minot, Susan 1956-.............................. **CLC 44**
See also CA 134

Minus, Ed 1938- .... **CLC 39**

Miranda, Javier
See Bioy Casares, Adolfo

Mirbeau, Octave 1848-1917 .... **TCLC 55**
See also DLB 123

Miro (Ferrer), Gabriel (Francisco Victor) 1879-1930 .... **TCLC 5**
See also CA 104

Mishima, Yukio 1925-1970**CLC 2, 4, 6, 9, 27; DC 1; SSC 4**
See also Hiraoka, Kimitake
See also DLB 182

Mistral, Frederic 1830-1914 .... **TCLC 51**
See also CA 122

Mistral, Gabriela .... **TCLC 2; HLC**
See also Godoy Alcayaga, Lucila

Mistry, Rohinton 1952-........... **CLC 71; DAC**
See also CA 141

Mitchell, Clyde
See Ellison, Harlan (Jay); Silverberg, Robert

Mitchell, James Leslie 1901-1935
See Gibbon, Lewis Grassic
See also CA 104; DLB 15

Mitchell, Joni 1943- .... **CLC 12**
See also CA 112

Mitchell, Joseph (Quincy) 1908-1996**CLC 98**
See also CA 77-80; 152; DLBY 96

Mitchell, Margaret (Munnerlyn) 1900-1949 **TCLC 11; DAM NOV, POP**
See also CA 109; 125; CANR 55; DLB 9; MTCW

Mitchell, Peggy
See Mitchell, Margaret (Munnerlyn)

Mitchell, S(ilas) Weir 1829-1914 ... **TCLC 36**

Mitchell, W(illiam) O(rmond) 1914-**CLC 25; DAC; DAM MST**
See also CA 77-80; CANR 15, 43; DLB 88

Mitford, Mary Russell 1787-1855 ... **NCLC 4**
See also DLB 110, 116

Mitford, Nancy 1904-1973 .... **CLC 44**

See also CA 9-12R

Miyamoto, Yuriko 1899-1951 .... **TCLC 37**
See also DLB 180

Miyazawa Kenji 1896-1933 .... **TCLC 76**
See also CA 157

Mizoguchi, Kenji 1898-1956 .... **TCLC 72**

Mo, Timothy (Peter) 1950(?)-............. **CLC 46**
See also CA 117; MTCW

Modarressi, Taghi (M.) 1931- .... **CLC 44**
See also CA 121; 134; INT 134

Modiano, Patrick (Jean) 1945- .... **CLC 18**
See also CA 85-88; CANR 17, 40; DLB 83

Moerck, Paal
See Roelvaag, O(le) E(dvart)

Mofolo, Thomas (Mokopu) 1875(?)-1948 **TCLC 22; BLC; DAM MULT**
See also CA 121; 153

Mohr, Nicholasa 1935-**CLC 12; DAM MULT; HLC**
See also AAYA 8; CA 49-52; CANR 1, 32; CLR 22; DLB 145; HW; JRDA; SAAS 8; SATA 8

Mojtabai, A(nn) G(race) 1938- **CLC 5, 9, 15, 29**
See also CA 85-88

Moliere 1622-1673 . **LC 28; DA; DAB; DAC; DAM DRAM, MST; WLC**

Molin, Charles
See Mayne, William (James Carter)

Molnar, Ferenc 1878-1952 .. **TCLC 20; DAM DRAM**
See also CA 109; 153

Momaday, N(avarre) Scott 1934- **CLC 2, 19, 85, 95; DA; DAB; DAC; DAM MST, MULT, NOV, POP; WLCS**
See also AAYA 11; CA 25-28R; CANR 14, 34; DLB 143, 175; INT CANR-14; MTCW; NNAL; SATA 48; SATA-Brief 30

Monette, Paul 1945-1995 .... **CLC 82**
See also CA 139; 147

Monroe, Harriet 1860-1936 .... **TCLC 12**
See also CA 109; DLB 54, 91

Monroe, Lyle
See Heinlein, Robert A(nson)

Montagu, Elizabeth 1917- .... **NCLC 7**
See also CA 9-12R

Montagu, Mary (Pierrepont) Wortley 1689-1762 .... **LC 9; PC 16**
See also DLB 95, 101

Montagu, W. H.
See Coleridge, Samuel Taylor

Montague, John (Patrick) 1929- **CLC 13, 46**
See also CA 9-12R; CANR 9; DLB 40; MTCW

Montaigne, Michel (Eyquem) de 1533-1592 **LC 8; DA; DAB; DAC; DAM MST; WLC**

Montale, Eugenio 1896-1981**CLC 7, 9, 18; PC 13**
See also CA 17-20R; 104; CANR 30; DLB 114; MTCW

Montesquieu, Charles-Louis de Secondat 1689-1755 .... **LC 7**

Montgomery, (Robert) Bruce 1921-1978
See Crispin, Edmund
See also CA 104

Montgomery, L(ucy) M(aud) 1874-1942 **TCLC 51; DAC; DAM MST**
See also AAYA 12; CA 108; 137; CLR 8; DLB 92; DLBD 14; JRDA; MAICYA; YABC 1

Montgomery, Marion H., Jr. 1925- .... **CLC 7**
See also AITN 1; CA 1-4R; CANR 3, 48; DLB 6

Montgomery, Max
See Davenport, Guy (Mattison, Jr.)

Montherlant, Henry (Milon) de 1896-1972

CLC 8, 19; DAM DRAM
See also CA 85-88; 37-40R; DLB 72; MTCW

Monty Python
See Chapman, Graham; Cleese, John (Marwood); Gilliam, Terry (Vance); Idle, Eric; Jones, Terence Graham Parry; Palin, Michael (Edward)
See also AAYA 7

Moodie, Susanna (Strickland) 1803-1885 **NCLC 14**
See also DLB 99

Mooney, Edward 1951-
See Mooney, Ted
See also CA 130

Mooney, Ted .... **CLC 25**
See also Mooney, Edward

Moorcock, Michael (John) 1939-**CLC 5, 27, 58**
See also CA 45-48; CAAS 5; CANR 2, 17, 38; DLB 14; MTCW; SATA 93

Moore, Brian 1921- **CLC 1, 3, 5, 7, 8, 19, 32, 90; DAB; DAC; DAM MST**
See also CA 1-4R; CANR 1, 25, 42; MTCW

Moore, Edward
See Muir, Edwin

Moore, George Augustus 1852-1933**TCLC 7; SSC 19**
See also CA 104; DLB 10, 18, 57, 135

Moore, Lorrie .... **CLC 39, 45, 68**
See also Moore, Marie Lorena

Moore, Marianne (Craig) 1887-1972**CLC 1, 2, 4, 8, 10, 13, 19, 47; DA; DAB; DAC; DAM MST, POET; PC 4; WLCS**
See also CA 1-4R; 33-36R; CANR 3, 61; CDALB 1929-1941; DLB 45; DLBD 7; MTCW; SATA 20

Moore, Marie Lorena 1957-
See Moore, Lorrie
See also CA 116; CANR 39

Moore, Thomas 1779-1852 .... **NCLC 6**
See also DLB 96, 144

Morand, Paul 1888-1976 .... **CLC 41; SSC 22**
See also CA 69-72; DLB 65

Morante, Elsa 1918-1985 .... **CLC 8, 47**
See also CA 85-88; 117; CANR 35; DLB 177; MTCW

Moravia, Alberto 1907-1990**CLC 2, 7, 11, 27, 46; SSC 26**
See also Pincherle, Alberto
See also DLB 177

More, Hannah 1745-1833 .... **NCLC 27**
See also DLB 107, 109, 116, 158

More, Henry 1614-1687 .... **LC 9**
See also DLB 126

More, Sir Thomas 1478-1535 .... **LC 10, 32**

Moreas, Jean .... **TCLC 18**
See also Papadiamantopoulos, Johannes

Morgan, Berry 1919- .... **CLC 6**
See also CA 49-52; DLB 6

Morgan, Claire
See Highsmith, (Mary) Patricia

Morgan, Edwin (George) 1920- .... **CLC 31**
See also CA 5-8R; CANR 3, 43; DLB 27

Morgan, (George) Frederick 1922- .. **CLC 23**
See also CA 17-20R; CANR 21

Morgan, Harriet
See Mencken, H(enry) L(ouis)

Morgan, Jane
See Cooper, James Fenimore

Morgan, Janet 1945- .... **CLC 39**
See also CA 65-68

Morgan, Lady 1776(?)-1859 .... **NCLC 29**
See also DLB 116, 158

Morgan, Robin 1941- .... **CLC 2**

See also CA 69-72; CANR 29; MTCW; SATA 80

Morgan, Scott
See Kuttner, Henry

Morgan, Seth 1949(?)-1990 .... **CLC 65**
See also CA 132

Morgenstern, Christian 1871-1914 . **TCLC 8**
See also CA 105

Morgenstern, S.
See Goldman, William (W.)

Moricz, Zsigmond 1879-1942 .... **TCLC 33**

Morike, Eduard (Friedrich) 1804-1875 **NCLC 10**
See also DLB 133

Mori Ogai .... **TCLC 14**
See also Mori Rintaro

Mori Rintaro 1862-1922
See Mori Ogai
See also CA 110

Moritz, Karl Philipp 1756-1793 .... **LC 2**
See also DLB 94

Morland, Peter Henry
See Faust, Frederick (Schiller)

Morren, Theophil
See Hofmannsthal, Hugo von

Morris, Bill 1952- .... **CLC 76**

Morris, Julian
See West, Morris L(anglo)

Morris, Steveland Judkins 1950(?)-
See Wonder, Stevie
See also CA 111

Morris, William 1834-1896 .... **NCLC 4**
See also CDBLB 1832-1890; DLB 18, 35, 57, 156, 178, 184

Morris, Wright 1910- ...... **CLC 1, 3, 7, 18, 37**
See also CA 9-12R; CANR 21; DLB 2; DLBY 81; MTCW

Morrison, Arthur 1863-1945 .... **TCLC 72**
See also CA 120; 157; DLB 70, 135

Morrison, Chloe Anthony Wofford
See Morrison, Toni

Morrison, James Douglas 1943-1971
See Morrison, Jim
See also CA 73-76; CANR 40

Morrison, Jim .... **CLC 17**
See also Morrison, James Douglas

Morrison, Toni 1931-**CLC 4, 10, 22, 55, 81, 87; BLC; DA; DAB; DAC; DAM MST, MULT, NOV, POP**
See also AAYA 1, 22; BW 2; CA 29-32R; CANR 27, 42; CDALB 1968-1988; DLB 6, 33, 143; DLBY 81; MTCW; SATA 57

Morrison, Van 1945- .... **CLC 21**
See also CA 116

Morrissy, Mary 1958- .... **CLC 99**

Mortimer, John (Clifford) 1923-**CLC 28, 43; DAM DRAM, POP**
See also CA 13-16R; CANR 21; CDBLB 1960 to Present; DLB 13; INT CANR-21; MTCW

Mortimer, Penelope (Ruth) 1918- .... **CLC 5**
See also CA 57-60; CANR 45

Morton, Anthony
See Creasey, John

Mosca, Gaetano 1858-1941 .... **TCLC 75**

Mosher, Howard Frank 1943- .... **CLC 62**
See also CA 139

Mosley, Nicholas 1923- .... **CLC 43, 70**
See also CA 69-72; CANR 41, 60; DLB 14

Mosley, Walter 1952- **CLC 97; DAM MULT, POP**
See also AAYA 17; BW 2; CA 142; CANR 57

Moss, Howard 1922-1987 **CLC 7, 14, 45, 50; DAM POET**

See also CA 1-4R; 123; CANR 1, 44; DLB 5

Mossgiel, Rab
See Burns, Robert

Motion, Andrew (Peter) 1952- .... **CLC 47**
See also CA 146; DLB 40

Motley, Willard (Francis) 1909-1965 **CLC 18**
See also BW 1; CA 117; 106; DLB 76, 143

Motoori, Norinaga 1730-1801 .... **NCLC 45**

Mott, Michael (Charles Alston) 1930-**CLC 15, 34**
See also CA 5-8R; CAAS 7; CANR 7, 29

Mountain Wolf Woman 1884-1960 ... **CLC 92**
See also CA 144; NNAL

Moure, Erin 1955- .... **CLC 88**
See also CA 113; DLB 60

Mowat, Farley (McGill) 1921-**CLC 26; DAC; DAM MST**
See also AAYA 1; CA 1-4R; CANR 4, 24, 42; CLR 20; DLB 68; INT CANAR-24; JRDA; MAICYA; MTCW; SATA 3, 55

Moyers, Bill 1934- .... **CLC 74**
See also AITN 2; CA 61-64; CANR 31, 52

Mphahlele, Es'kia
See Mphahlele, Ezekiel
See also DLB 125

Mphahlele, Ezekiel 1919-**CLC 25; BLC; DAM MULT**
See also Mphahlele, Es'kia
See also BW 2; CA 81-84; CANR 26

Mqhayi, S(amuel) E(dward) K(rune Loliwe) 1875-1945 **TCLC 25; BLC; DAM MULT**
See also CA 153

Mrozek, Slawomir 1930- .... **CLC 3, 13**
See also CA 13-16R; CAAS 10; CANR 29; MTCW

Mrs. Belloc-Lowndes
See Lowndes, Marie Adelaide (Belloc)

Mtwa, Percy (?)- .... **CLC 47**

Mueller, Lisel 1924- .... **CLC 13, 51**
See also CA 93-96; DLB 105

Muir, Edwin 1887-1959 .... **TCLC 2**
See also CA 104; DLB 20, 100

Muir, John 1838-1914 .... **TCLC 28**

Mujica Lainez, Manuel 1910-1984 ... **CLC 31**
See also Lainez, Manuel Mujica
See also CA 81-84; 112; CANR 32; HW

Mukherjee, Bharati 1940-**CLC 53; DAM NOV**
See also BEST 89:2; CA 107; CANR 45; DLB 60; MTCW

Muldoon, Paul 1951-**CLC 32, 72; DAM POET**
See also CA 113; 129; CANR 52; DLB 40; INT 129

Mulisch, Harry 1927- .... **CLC 42**
See also CA 9-12R; CANR 6, 26, 56

Mull, Martin 1943- .... **CLC 17**
See also CA 105

Mulock, Dinah Maria
See Craik, Dinah Maria (Mulock)

Munford, Robert 1737(?)-1783 .... **LC 5**
See also DLB 31

Mungo, Raymond 1946- .... **CLC 72**
See also CA 49-52; CANR 2

Munro, Alice 1931-.... **CLC 6, 10, 19, 50, 95; DAC; DAM MST, NOV; SSC 3; WLCS**
See also AITN 2; CA 33-36R; CANR 33, 53; DLB 53; MTCW; SATA 29

Munro, H(ector) H(ugh) 1870-1916
See Saki
See also CA 104; 130; CDBLB 1890-1914; DA; DAB; DAC; DAM MST, NOV; DLB 34, 162; MTCW; WLC

Murasaki, Lady .... **CMLC 1**

Murdoch, (Jean) Iris 1919-**CLC 1, 2, 3, 4, 6, 8,** 11, 15, 22, 31, 51; DAB; DAC; DAM MST, NOV
See also CA 13-16R; CANR 8, 43; CDBLB 1960 to Present; DLB 14; INT CANR-8; MTCW

Murfree, Mary Noailles 1850-1922 ... **SSC 22**
See also CA 122; DLB 12, 74

Murnau, Friedrich Wilhelm
See Plumpe, Friedrich Wilhelm

Murphy, Richard 1927- .... **CLC 41**
See also CA 29-32R; DLB 40

Murphy, Sylvia 1937- .... **CLC 34**
See also CA 121

Murphy, Thomas (Bernard) 1935- .. **CLC 51**
See also CA 101

Murray, Albert L. 1916- .... **CLC 73**
See also BW 2; CA 49-52; CANR 26, 52; DLB 38

Murray, Judith Sargent 1751-1820 **NCLC 63**
See also DLB 37

Murray, Les(lie) A(llan) 1938-**CLC 40; DAM POET**
See also CA 21-24R; CANR 11, 27, 56

Murry, J. Middleton
See Murry, John Middleton

Murry, John Middleton 1889-1957 **TCLC 16**
See also CA 118; DLB 149

Musgrave, Susan 1951- .... **CLC 13, 54**
See also CA 69-72; CANR 45

Musil, Robert (Edler von) 1880-1942 . **T C L C 12, 68; SSC 18**
See also CA 109; CANR 55; DLB 81, 124

Muske, Carol 1945- .... **CLC 90**
See also Muske-Dukes, Carol (Anne)

Muske-Dukes, Carol (Anne) 1945-
See Muske, Carol
See also CA 65-68; CANR 32

Musset, (Louis Charles) Alfred de 1810-1857 **NCLC 7**

My Brother's Brother
See Chekhov, Anton (Pavlovich)

Myers, L(eopold) H(amilton) 1881-1944 **TCLC 59**
See also CA 157; DLB 15

Myers, Walter Dean 1937-.....**CLC 35; BLC; DAM MULT, NOV**
See also AAYA 4; BW 2; CA 33-36R; CANR 20, 42; CLR 4, 16, 35; DLB 33; INT CANR-20; JRDA; MAICYA; SAAS 2; SATA 41, 71; SATA-Brief 27

Myers, Walter M.
See Myers, Walter Dean

Myles, Symon
See Follett, Ken(neth Martin)

Nabokov, Vladimir (Vladimirovich) 1899-1977 **CLC 1, 2, 3, 6, 8, 11, 15, 23, 44, 46, 64; DA; DAB; DAC; DAM MST, NOV; SSC 11; WLC**
See also CA 5-8R; 69-72; CANR 20; CDALB 1941-1968; DLB 2; DLBD 3; DLBY 80, 91; MTCW

Nagai Kafu 1879-1959 .... **TCLC 51**
See also Nagai Sokichi
See also DLB 180

Nagai Sokichi 1879-1959
See Nagai Kafu
See also CA 117

Nagy, Laszlo 1925-1978 .... **CLC 7**
See also CA 129; 112

Naipaul, Shiva(dhar Srinivasa) 1945-1985 **CLC 32, 39; DAM NOV**
See also CA 110; 112; 116; CANR 33; DLB 157; DLBY 85; MTCW

Naipaul, V(idiadhar) S(urajprasad) 1932-
    CLC 4, 7, 9, 13, 18, 37, 105; DAB; DAC;
    DAM MST, NOV
    See also CA 1-4R; CANR 1, 33, 51; CDBLB
        1960 to Present; DLB 125; DLBY 85;
        MTCW
Nakos, Lilika 1899(?)- .... **CLC 29**
Narayan, R(asipuram) K(rishnaswami) 1906-
    CLC 7, 28, 47; DAM NOV; SSC 25
    See also CA 81-84; CANR 33, 61; MTCW;
        SATA 62
Nash, (Frediric) Ogden 1902-1971 . **CLC 23;**
    DAM POET
    See also CA 13-14; 29-32R; CANR 34, 61; CAP
        1; DLB 11; MAICYA; MTCW; SATA 2, 46
Nathan, Daniel
    See Dannay, Frederic
Nathan, George Jean 1882-1958 .... **TCLC 18**
    See also Hatteras, Owen
    See also CA 114; DLB 137
Natsume, Kinnosuke 1867-1916
    See Natsume, Soseki
    See also CA 104
Natsume, Soseki 1867-1916 .... **TCLC 2, 10**
    See also Natsume, Kinnosuke
    See also DLB 180
Natti, (Mary) Lee 1919-
    See Kingman, Lee
    See also CA 5-8R; CANR 2
Naylor, Gloria 1950- **CLC 28, 52; BLC; DA;**
    DAC; DAM MST, MULT, NOV, POP;
    WLCS
    See also AAYA 6; BW 2; CA 107; CANR 27,
        51; DLB 173; MTCW
Neihardt, John Gneisenau 1881-1973**CLC 32**
    See also CA 13-14; CAP 1; DLB 9, 54
Nekrasov, Nikolai Alekseevich 1821-1878
    NCLC 11
Nelligan, Emile 1879-1941 .... **TCLC 14**
    See also CA 114; DLB 92
Nelson, Willie 1933- .... **CLC 17**
    See also CA 107
Nemerov, Howard (Stanley) 1920-1991**CLC 2,**
    6, 9, 36; DAM POET
    See also CA 1-4R; 134; CABS 2; CANR 1, 27,
        53; DLB 5, 6; DLBY 83; INT CANR-27;
        MTCW
Neruda, Pablo 1904-1973**CLC 1, 2, 5, 7, 9, 28,**
    62; DA; DAB; DAC; DAM MST, MULT,
    POET; HLC; PC 4; WLC
    See also CA 19-20; 45-48; CAP 2; HW; MTCW
Nerval, Gerard de 1808-1855**NCLC 1; PC 13;**
    SSC 18
Nervo, (Jose) Amado (Ruiz de) 1870-1919
    TCLC 11
    See also CA 109; 131; HW
Nessi, Pio Baroja y
    See Baroja (y Nessi), Pio
Nestroy, Johann 1801-1862 .... **NCLC 42**
    See also DLB 133
Netterville, Luke
    See O'Grady, Standish (James)
Neufeld, John (Arthur) 1938- .... **CLC 17**
    See also AAYA 11; CA 25-28R; CANR 11, 37,
        56; MAICYA; SAAS 3; SATA 6, 81
Neville, Emily Cheney 1919- .... **CLC 12**
    See also CA 5-8R; CANR 3, 37; JRDA;
        MAICYA; SAAS 2; SATA 1
Newbound, Bernard Slade 1930-
    See Slade, Bernard
    See also CA 81-84; CANR 49; DAM DRAM
Newby, P(ercy) H(oward) 1918-1997 **CLC 2,**
    13; DAM NOV

    See also CA 5-8R; 161; CANR 32; DLB 15;
        MTCW
Newlove, Donald 1928- .... **CLC 6**
    See also CA 29-32R; CANR 25
Newlove, John (Herbert) 1938-........ **CLC 14**
    See also CA 21-24R; CANR 9, 25
Newman, Charles 1938- .... **CLC 2, 8**
    See also CA 21-24R
Newman, Edwin (Harold) 1919- .... **CLC 14**
    See also AITN 1; CA 69-72; CANR 5
Newman, John Henry 1801-1890 ... **NCLC 38**
    See also DLB 18, 32, 55
Newton, Suzanne 1936- .... **CLC 35**
    See also CA 41-44R; CANR 14; JRDA; SATA
        5, 77
Nexo, Martin Andersen 1869-1954 **TCLC 43**
Nezval, Vitezslav 1900-1958 .... **TCLC 44**
    See also CA 123
Ng, Fae Myenne 1957(?)- .... **CLC 81**
    See also CA 146
Ngema, Mbongeni 1955- .... **CLC 57**
    See also BW 2; CA 143
Ngugi, James T(hiong'o) .... **CLC 3, 7, 13**
    See also Ngugi wa Thiong'o
Ngugi wa Thiong'o 1938-**CLC 36; BLC; DAM**
    MULT, NOV
    See also Ngugi, James T(hiong'o)
    See also BW 2; CA 81-84; CANR 27, 58; DLB
        125; MTCW
Nichol, B(arrie) P(hillip) 1944-1988 .**CLC 18**
    See also CA 53-56; DLB 53; SATA 66
Nichols, John (Treadwell) 1940- .... **CLC 38**
    See also CA 9-12R; CAAS 2; CANR 6; DLBY
        82
Nichols, Leigh
    See Koontz, Dean R(ay)
Nichols, Peter (Richard) 1927- **CLC 5, 36, 65**
    See also CA 104; CANR 33; DLB 13; MTCW
Nicolas, F. R. E.
    See Freeling, Nicolas
Niedecker, Lorine 1903-1970 .... **CLC 10, 42;**
    DAM POET
    See also CA 25-28; CAP 2; DLB 48
Nietzsche, Friedrich (Wilhelm) 1844-1900
    TCLC 10, 18, 55
    See also CA 107; 121; DLB 129
Nievo, Ippolito 1831-1861 .... **NCLC 22**
Nightingale, Anne Redmon 1943-
    See Redmon, Anne
    See also CA 103
Nik. T. O.
    See Annensky, Innokenty (Fyodorovich)
Nin, Anais 1903-1977 **CLC 1, 4, 8, 11, 14, 60;**
    DAM NOV, POP; SSC 10
    See also AITN 2; CA 13-16R; 69-72; CANR
        22, 53; DLB 2, 4, 152; MTCW
Nishiwaki, Junzaburo 1894-1982 .... **PC 15**
    See also CA 107
Nissenson, Hugh 1933- .... **CLC 4, 9**
    See also CA 17-20R; CANR 27; DLB 28
Niven, Larry .... **CLC 8**
    See also Niven, Laurence Van Cott
    See also DLB 8
Niven, Laurence Van Cott 1938-
    See Niven, Larry
    See also CA 21-24R; CAAS 12; CANR 14, 44;
        DAM POP; MTCW; SATA 95
Nixon, Agnes Eckhardt 1927- .... **CLC 21**
    See also CA 110
Nizan, Paul 1905-1940 .... **TCLC 40**
    See also CA 161; DLB 72
Nkosi, Lewis 1936- ...... **CLC 45; BLC; DAM**
    MULT

    See also BW 1; CA 65-68; CANR 27; DLB 157
Nodier, (Jean) Charles (Emmanuel) 1780-1844
    NCLC 19
    See also DLB 119
Nolan, Christopher 1965- .... **CLC 58**
    See also CA 111
Noon, Jeff 1957- .... **CLC 91**
    See also CA 148
Norden, Charles
    See Durrell, Lawrence (George)
Nordhoff, Charles (Bernard) 1887-1947
    TCLC 23
    See also CA 108; DLB 9; SATA 23
Norfolk, Lawrence 1963- .... **CLC 76**
    See also CA 144
Norman, Marsha 1947-**CLC 28; DAM DRAM;**
    DC 8
    See also CA 105; CABS 3; CANR 41; DLBY
        84
Norris, Frank 1870-1902 .... **SSC 28**
    See also Norris, (Benjamin) Frank(lin, Jr.)
    See also CDALB 1865-1917; DLB 12, 71
Norris, (Benjamin) Frank(lin, Jr.) 1870-1902
    TCLC 24
    See also Norris, Frank
    See also CA 110; 160
Norris, Leslie 1921- .... **CLC 14**
    See also CA 11-12; CANR 14; CAP 1; DLB 27
North, Andrew
    See Norton, Andre
North, Anthony
    See Koontz, Dean R(ay)
North, Captain George
    See Stevenson, Robert Louis (Balfour)
North, Milou
    See Erdrich, Louise
Northrup, B. A.
    See Hubbard, L(afayette) Ron(ald)
North Staffs
    See Hulme, T(homas) E(rnest)
Norton, Alice Mary
    See Norton, Andre
    See also MAICYA; SATA 1, 43
Norton, Andre 1912- .... **CLC 12**
    See also Norton, Alice Mary
    See also AAYA 14; CA 1-4R; CANR 2, 31; DLB
        8, 52; JRDA; MTCW; SATA 91
Norton, Caroline 1808-1877 .... **NCLC 47**
    See also DLB 21, 159
Norway, Nevil Shute 1899-1960
    See Shute, Nevil
    See also CA 102; 93-96
Norwid, Cyprian Kamil 1821-1883 **NCLC 17**
Nosille, Nabrah
    See Ellison, Harlan (Jay)
Nossack, Hans Erich 1901-1978 .... **CLC 6**
    See also CA 93-96; 85-88; DLB 69
Nostradamus 1503-1566 .... **LC 27**
Nosu, Chuji
    See Ozu, Yasujiro
Notenburg, Eleanora (Genrikhovna) von
    See Guro, Elena
Nova, Craig 1945-........................... **CLC 7, 31**
    See also CA 45-48; CANR 2, 53
Novak, Joseph
    See Kosinski, Jerzy (Nikodem)
Novalis 1772-1801 .... **NCLC 13**
    See also DLB 90
Novis, Emile
    See Weil, Simone (Adolphine)
Nowlan, Alden (Albert) 1933-1983 . **CLC 15;**
    DAC; DAM MST
    See also CA 9-12R; CANR 5; DLB 53

Noyes, Alfred 1880-1958 .... **TCLC 7**
  See also CA 104; DLB 20
Nunn, Kem .... **CLC 34**
  See also CA 159
Nye, Robert 1939-... **CLC 13, 42; DAM NOV**
  See also CA 33-36R; CANR 29; DLB 14;
  MTCW; SATA 6
Nyro, Laura 1947- .... **CLC 17**
Oates, Joyce Carol 1938-**CLC 1, 2, 3, 6, 9, 11,
  15, 19, 33, 52; DA; DAB; DAC; DAM MST,
  NOV, POP; SSC 6; WLC**
  See also AAYA 15; AITN 1; BEST 89:2; CA 5-
  8R; CANR 25, 45; CDALB 1968-1988; DLB
  2, 5, 130; DLBY 81; INT CANR-25; MTCW
O'Brien, Darcy 1939- .... **CLC 11**
  See also CA 21-24R; CANR 8, 59
O'Brien, E. G.
  See Clarke, Arthur C(harles)
O'Brien, Edna 1936- **CLC 3, 5, 8, 13, 36, 65;
  DAM NOV; SSC 10**
  See also CA 1-4R; CANR 6, 41; CDBLB 1960
  to Present; DLB 14; MTCW
O'Brien, Fitz-James 1828-1862 ..... **NCLC 21**
  See also DLB 74
O'Brien, Flann .... **CLC 1, 4, 5, 7, 10, 47**
  See also O Nuallain, Brian
O'Brien, Richard 1942- .... **CLC 17**
  See also CA 124
O'Brien, (William) Tim(othy) 1946- **CLC 7,
  19, 40, 103; DAM POP**
  See also AAYA 16; CA 85-88; CANR 40, 58;
  DLB 152; DLBD 9; DLBY 80
Obstfelder, Sigbjoern 1866-1900 ... **TCLC 23**
  See also CA 123
O'Casey, Sean 1880-1964**CLC 1, 5, 9, 11, 15,
  88; DAB; DAC; DAM DRAM, MST;
  WLCS**
  See also CA 89-92; CANR 62; CDBLB 1914-
  1945; DLB 10; MTCW
O'Cathasaigh, Sean
  See O'Casey, Sean
Ochs, Phil 1940-1976 .... **CLC 17**
  See also CA 65-68
O'Connor, Edwin (Greene) 1918-1968**CLC 14**
  See also CA 93-96; 25-28R
O'Connor, (Mary) Flannery 1925-1964 **C L C
  1, 2, 3, 6, 10, 13, 15, 21, 66, 104; DA; DAB;
  DAC; DAM MST, NOV; SSC 1, 23; WLC**
  See also AAYA 7; CA 1-4R; CANR 3, 41;
  CDALB 1941-1968; DLB 2, 152; DLBD 12;
  DLBY 80; MTCW
O'Connor, Frank .... **CLC 23; SSC 5**
  See also O'Donovan, Michael John
  See also DLB 162
O'Dell, Scott 1898-1989 .... **CLC 30**
  See also AAYA 3; CA 61-64; 129; CANR 12,
  30; CLR 1, 16; DLB 52; JRDA; MAICYA;
  SATA 12, 60
Odets, Clifford 1906-1963**CLC 2, 28, 98; DAM
  DRAM; DC 6**
  See also CA 85-88; CANR 62; DLB 7, 26;
  MTCW
O'Doherty, Brian 1934- .... **CLC 76**
  See also CA 105
O'Donnell, K. M.
  See Malzberg, Barry N(athaniel)
O'Donnell, Lawrence
  See Kuttner, Henry
O'Donovan, Michael John 1903-1966**CLC 14**
  See also O'Connor, Frank
  See also CA 93-96
Oe, Kenzaburo 1935- **CLC 10, 36, 86; DAM
  NOV; SSC 20**

  See also CA 97-100; CANR 36, 50; DLB 182;
  DLBY 94; MTCW
O'Faolain, Julia 1932- .... **CLC 6, 19, 47**
  See also CA 81-84; CAAS 2; CANR 12, 61;
  DLB 14; MTCW
O'Faolain, Sean 1900-1991 **CLC 1, 7, 14, 32,
  70; SSC 13**
  See also CA 61-64; 134; CANR 12; DLB 15,
  162; MTCW
O'Flaherty, Liam 1896-1984**CLC 5, 34; SSC 6**
  See also CA 101; 113; CANR 35; DLB 36, 162;
  DLBY 84; MTCW
Ogilvy, Gavin
  See Barrie, J(ames) M(atthew)
O'Grady, Standish (James) 1846-1928**T C L C
  5**
  See also CA 104; 157
O'Grady, Timothy 1951- .... **CLC 59**
  See also CA 138
O'Hara, Frank 1926-1966 . **CLC 2, 5, 13, 78;
  DAM POET**
  See also CA 9-12R; 25-28R; CANR 33; DLB
  5, 16; MTCW
O'Hara, John (Henry) 1905-1970**CLC 1, 2, 3,
  6, 11, 42; DAM NOV; SSC 15**
  See also CA 5-8R; 25-28R; CANR 31, 60;
  CDALB 1929-1941; DLB 9, 86; DLBD 2;
  MTCW
O Hehir, Diana 1922- .... **CLC 41**
  See also CA 93-96
Okigbo, Christopher (Ifenayichukwu) 1932-
  1967 ... **CLC 25, 84; BLC; DAM MULT,
  POET; PC 7**
  See also BW 1; CA 77-80; DLB 125; MTCW
Okri, Ben 1959- .... **CLC 87**
  See also BW 2; CA 130; 138; DLB 157; INT
  138
Olds, Sharon 1942- .... **CLC 32, 39, 85; DAM
  POET**
  See also CA 101; CANR 18, 41; DLB 120
Oldstyle, Jonathan
  See Irving, Washington
Olesha, Yuri (Karlovich) 1899-1960 ... **CLC 8**
  See also CA 85-88
Oliphant, Laurence 1829(?)-1888 .. **NCLC 47**
  See also DLB 18, 166
Oliphant, Margaret (Oliphant Wilson) 1828-
  1897 .... **NCLC 11, 61; SSC 25**
  See also DLB 18, 159
Oliver, Mary 1935- .... **CLC 19, 34, 98**
  See also CA 21-24R; CANR 9, 43; DLB 5
Olivier, Laurence (Kerr) 1907-1989 . **CLC 20**
  See also CA 111; 150; 129
Olsen, Tillie 1913-**CLC 4, 13; DA; DAB; DAC;
  DAM MST; SSC 11**
  See also CA 1-4R; CANR 1, 43; DLB 28; DLBY
  80; MTCW
Olson, Charles (John) 1910-1970**CLC 1, 2, 5,
  6, 9, 11, 29; DAM POET; PC 19**
  See also CA 13-16; 25-28R; CABS 2; CANR
  35, 61; CAP 1; DLB 5, 16; MTCW
Olson, Toby 1937- .... **CLC 28**
  See also CA 65-68; CANR 9, 31
Olyesha, Yuri
  See Olesha, Yuri (Karlovich)
Ondaatje, (Philip) Michael 1943-**CLC 14, 29,
  51, 76; DAB; DAC; DAM MST**
  See also CA 77-80; CANR 42; DLB 60
Oneal, Elizabeth 1934-
  See Oneal, Zibby
  See also CA 106; CANR 28; MAICYA; SATA
  30, 82
Oneal, Zibby .... **CLC 30**

  See also Oneal, Elizabeth
  See also AAYA 5; CLR 13; JRDA
O'Neill, Eugene (Gladstone) 1888-1953**TCLC
  1, 6, 27, 49; DA; DAB; DAC; DAM DRAM,
  MST; WLC**
  See also AITN 1; CA 110; 132; CDALB 1929-
  1941; DLB 7; MTCW
Onetti, Juan Carlos 1909-1994 ... **CLC 7, 10;
  DAM MULT, NOV; SSC 23**
  See also CA 85-88; 145; CANR 32; DLB 113;
  HW; MTCW
O Nuallain, Brian 1911-1966
  See O'Brien, Flann
  See also CA 21-22; 25-28R; CAP 2
Opie, Amelia 1769-1853 .... **NCLC 65**
  See also DLB 116, 159
Oppen, George 1908-1984 ...... **CLC 7, 13, 34**
  See also CA 13-16R; 113; CANR 8; DLB 5,
  165
Oppenheim, E(dward) Phillips 1866-1946
  TCLC 45
  See also CA 111; DLB 70
Origen c. 185-c. 254 .... **CMLC 19**
Orlovitz, Gil 1918-1973 .... **CLC 22**
  See also CA 77-80; 45-48; DLB 2, 5
Orris
  See Ingelow, Jean
Ortega y Gasset, Jose 1883-1955 .... **TCLC 9;
  DAM MULT; HLC**
  See also CA 106; 130; HW; MTCW
Ortese, Anna Maria 1914- .... **CLC 89**
  See also DLB 177
Ortiz, Simon J(oseph) 1941-.. **CLC 45; DAM
  MULT, POET; PC 17**
  See also CA 134; DLB 120, 175; NNAL
Orton, Joe .... **CLC 4, 13, 43; DC 3**
  See also Orton, John Kingsley
  See also CDBLB 1960 to Present; DLB 13
Orton, John Kingsley 1933-1967
  See Orton, Joe
  See also CA 85-88; CANR 35; DAM DRAM;
  MTCW
Orwell, George **TCLC 2, 6, 15, 31, 51; DAB;
  WLC**
  See also Blair, Eric (Arthur)
  See also CDBLB 1945-1960; DLB 15, 98
Osborne, David
  See Silverberg, Robert
Osborne, George
  See Silverberg, Robert
Osborne, John (James) 1929-1994**CLC 1, 2, 5,
  11, 45; DA; DAB; DAC; DAM DRAM,
  MST; WLC**
  See also CA 13-16R; 147; CANR 21, 56;
  CDBLB 1945-1960; DLB 13; MTCW
Osborne, Lawrence 1958-................. **CLC 50**
Oshima, Nagisa 1932- .... **CLC 20**
  See also CA 116; 121
Oskison, John Milton 1874-1947 . **TCLC 35;
  DAM MULT**
  See also CA 144; DLB 175; NNAL
Ossoli, Sarah Margaret (Fuller marchesa d')
  1810-1850
  See Fuller, Margaret
  See also SATA 25
Ostrovsky, Alexander 1823-1886**NCLC 30, 57**
Otero, Blas de 1916-1979 .... **CLC 11**
  See also CA 89-92; DLB 134
Otto, Whitney 1955-......................... **CLC 70**
  See also CA 140
Ouida .... **TCLC 43**
  See also De La Ramee, (Marie) Louise
  See also DLB 18, 156

Ousmane, Sembene 1923- .... **CLC 66; BLC**
  See also BW 1; CA 117; 125; MTCW
Ovid 43B.C.-18(?)**CMLC 7; DAM POET; PC 2**
Owen, Hugh
  See Faust, Frederick (Schiller)
Owen, Wilfred (Edward Salter) 1893-1918
  TCLC 5, 27; DA; DAB; DAC; DAM MST, POET; PC 19; WLC
  See also CA 104; 141; CDBLB 1914-1945; DLB 20
Owens, Rochelle 1936- .... **CLC 8**
  See also CA 17-20R; CAAS 2; CANR 39
Oz, Amos 1939-**CLC 5, 8, 11, 27, 33, 54; DAM NOV**
  See also CA 53-56; CANR 27, 47; MTCW
Ozick, Cynthia 1928-**CLC 3, 7, 28, 62; DAM NOV, POP; SSC 15**
  See also BEST 90:1; CA 17-20R; CANR 23, 58; DLB 28, 152; DLBY 82; INT CANR-23; MTCW
Ozu, Yasujiro 1903-1963 .... **CLC 16**
  See also CA 112
Pacheco, C.
  See Pessoa, Fernando (Antonio Nogueira)
Pa Chin .... **CLC 18**
  See also Li Fei-kan
Pack, Robert 1929- .... **CLC 13**
  See also CA 1-4R; CANR 3, 44; DLB 5
Padgett, Lewis
  See Kuttner, Henry
Padilla (Lorenzo), Heberto 1932- .... **CLC 38**
  See also AITN 1; CA 123; 131; HW
Page, Jimmy 1944- .... **CLC 12**
Page, Louise 1955- .... **CLC 40**
  See also CA 140
Page, P(atricia) K(athleen) 1916- **CLC 7, 18; DAC; DAM MST; PC 12**
  See also CA 53-56; CANR 4, 22; DLB 68; MTCW
Page, Thomas Nelson 1853-1922 .... **SSC 23**
  See also CA 118; DLB 12, 78; DLBD 13
Pagels, Elaine Hiesey 1943- .... **CLC 104**
  See also CA 45-48; CANR 2, 24, 51
Paget, Violet 1856-1935
  See Lee, Vernon
  See also CA 104
Paget-Lowe, Henry
  See Lovecraft, H(oward) P(hillips)
Paglia, Camille (Anna) 1947- .... **CLC 68**
  See also CA 140
Paige, Richard
  See Koontz, Dean R(ay)
Paine, Thomas 1737-1809 .... **NCLC 62**
  See also CDALB 1640-1865; DLB 31, 43, 73, 158
Pakenham, Antonia
  See Fraser, (Lady) Antonia (Pakenham)
Palamas, Kostes 1859-1943 .... **TCLC 5**
  See also CA 105
Palazzeschi, Aldo 1885-1974 .... **CLC 11**
  See also CA 89-92; 53-56; DLB 114
Paley, Grace 1922-**CLC 4, 6, 37; DAM POP; SSC 8**
  See also CA 25-28R; CANR 13, 46; DLB 28; INT CANR-13; MTCW
Palin, Michael (Edward) 1943- .... **CLC 21**
  See also Monty Python
  See also CA 107; CANR 35; SATA 67
Palliser, Charles 1947- .... **CLC 65**
  See also CA 136
Palma, Ricardo 1833-1919 .... **TCLC 29**
Pancake, Breece Dexter 1952-1979

See Pancake, Breece D'J
  See also CA 123; 109
Pancake, Breece D'J .... **CLC 29**
  See also Pancake, Breece Dexter
  See also DLB 130
Panko, Rudy
  See Gogol, Nikolai (Vasilyevich)
Papadiamantis, Alexandros 1851-1911**T C L C 29**
Papadiamantopoulos, Johannes 1856-1910
  See Moreas, Jean
  See also CA 117
Papini, Giovanni 1881-1956 .... **TCLC 22**
  See also CA 121
Paracelsus 1493-1541 .... **LC 14**
  See also DLB 179
Parasol, Peter
  See Stevens, Wallace
Pareto, Vilfredo 1848-1923 .... **TCLC 69**
Parfenie, Maria
  See Codrescu, Andrei
Parini, Jay (Lee) 1948- ....**CLC 54**
  See also CA 97-100; CAAS 16; CANR 32
Park, Jordan
  See Kornbluth, C(yril) M.; Pohl, Frederik
Park, Robert E(zra) 1864-1944 ...... **TCLC 73**
  See also CA 122
Parker, Bert
  See Ellison, Harlan (Jay)
Parker, Dorothy (Rothschild) 1893-1967**C L C 15, 68; DAM POET; SSC 2**
  See also CA 19-20; 25-28R; CAP 2; DLB 11, 45, 86; MTCW
Parker, Robert B(rown) 1932-**CLC 27; DAM NOV, POP**
  See also BEST 89:4; CA 49-52; CANR 1, 26, 52; INT CANR-26; MTCW
Parkin, Frank 1940- ....**CLC 43**
  See also CA 147
Parkman, Francis, Jr. 1823-1893 ... **NCLC 12**
  See also DLB 1, 30
Parks, Gordon (Alexander Buchanan) 1912-
  CLC 1, 16; BLC; DAM MULT
  See also AITN 2; BW 2; CA 41-44R; CANR 26; DLB 33; SATA 8
Parmenides c. 515B.C.-c. 450B.C. **CMLC 22**
  See also DLB 176
Parnell, Thomas 1679-1718 .... **LC 3**
  See also DLB 94
Parra, Nicanor 1914- ....**CLC 2, 102; DAM MULT; HLC**
  See also CA 85-88; CANR 32; HW; MTCW
Parrish, Mary Frances
  See Fisher, M(ary) F(rances) K(ennedy)
Parson
  See Coleridge, Samuel Taylor
Parson Lot
  See Kingsley, Charles
Partridge, Anthony
  See Oppenheim, E(dward) Phillips
Pascal, Blaise 1623-1662 .... **LC 35**
Pascoli, Giovanni 1855-1912 .... **TCLC 45**
Pasolini, Pier Paolo 1922-1975 . **CLC 20, 37, 106; PC 17**
  See also CA 93-96; 61-64; DLB 128, 177; MTCW
Pasquini
  See Silone, Ignazio
Pastan, Linda (Olenik) 1932- **CLC 27; DAM POET**
  See also CA 61-64; CANR 18, 40, 61; DLB 5
Pasternak, Boris (Leonidovich) 1890-1960
  CLC 7, 10, 18, 63; DA; DAB; DAC; DAM

MST, NOV, POET; PC 6; WLC
  See also CA 127; 116; MTCW
Patchen, Kenneth 1911-1972 ... **CLC 1, 2, 18; DAM POET**
  See also CA 1-4R; 33-36R; CANR 3, 35; DLB 16, 48; MTCW
Pater, Walter (Horatio) 1839-1894 ..**NCLC 7**
  See also CDBLB 1832-1890; DLB 57, 156
Paterson, A(ndrew) B(arton) 1864-1941
  TCLC 32
  See also CA 155
Paterson, Katherine (Womeldorf) 1932-**C L C 12, 30**
  See also AAYA 1; CA 21-24R; CANR 28, 59; CLR 7; DLB 52; JRDA; MAICYA; MTCW; SATA 13, 53, 92
Patmore, Coventry Kersey Dighton 1823-1896
  NCLC 9
  See also DLB 35, 98
Paton, Alan (Stewart) 1903-1988 **CLC 4, 10, 25, 55, 106; DA; DAB; DAC; DAM MST, NOV; WLC**
  See also CA 13-16; 125; CANR 22; CAP 1; MTCW; SATA 11; SATA-Obit 56
Paton Walsh, Gillian 1937-
  See Walsh, Jill Paton
  See also CANR 38; JRDA; MAICYA; SAAS 3; SATA 4, 72
Paulding, James Kirke 1778-1860 ... **NCLC 2**
  See also DLB 3, 59, 74
Paulin, Thomas Neilson 1949-
  See Paulin, Tom
  See also CA 123; 128
Paulin, Tom ....**CLC 37**
  See also Paulin, Thomas Neilson
  See also DLB 40
Paustovsky, Konstantin (Georgievich) 1892-
  1968 ....**CLC 40**
  See also CA 93-96; 25-28R
Pavese, Cesare 1908-1950 ... **TCLC 3; PC 13; SSC 19**
  See also CA 104; DLB 128, 177
Pavic, Milorad 1929- ....**CLC 60**
  See also CA 136; DLB 181
Payne, Alan
  See Jakes, John (William)
Paz, Gil
  See Lugones, Leopoldo
Paz, Octavio 1914-**CLC 3, 4, 6, 10, 19, 51, 65; DA; DAB; DAC; DAM MST, MULT, POET; HLC; PC 1; WLC**
  See also CA 73-76; CANR 32; DLBY 90; HW; MTCW
p'Bitek, Okot 1931-1982**CLC 96; BLC; DAM MULT**
  See also BW 2; CA 124; 107; DLB 125; MTCW
Peacock, Molly 1947- ....**CLC 60**
  See also CA 103; CAAS 21; CANR 52; DLB 120
Peacock, Thomas Love 1785-1866 . **NCLC 22**
  See also DLB 96, 116
Peake, Mervyn 1911-1968 .... **CLC 7, 54**
  See also CA 5-8R; 25-28R; CANR 3; DLB 15, 160; MTCW; SATA 23
Pearce, Philippa ....**CLC 21**
  See also Christie, (Ann) Philippa
  See also CLR 9; DLB 161; MAICYA; SATA 1, 67
Pearl, Eric
  See Elman, Richard
Pearson, T(homas) R(eid) 1956- ....**CLC 39**
  See also CA 120; 130; INT 130
Peck, Dale 1967- ....**CLC 81**

See also CA 146

Peck, John 1941- ....**CLC 3**
See also CA 49-52; CANR 3

Peck, Richard (Wayne) 1934-........... **CLC 21**
See also AAYA 1; CA 85-88; CANR 19, 38;
CLR 15; INT CANR-19; JRDA; MAICYA;
SAAS 2; SATA 18, 55

Peck, Robert Newton 1928- ..... **CLC 17; DA;
DAC; DAM MST**
See also AAYA 3; CA 81-84; CANR 31; CLR
45; JRDA; MAICYA; SAAS 1; SATA 21, 62

Peckinpah, (David) Sam(uel) 1925-1984 **C L C
20**
See also CA 109; 114

Pedersen, Knut 1859-1952
See Hamsun, Knut
See also CA 104; 119; MTCW

Peeslake, Gaffer
See Durrell, Lawrence (George)

Peguy, Charles Pierre 1873-1914 ... **TCLC 10**
See also CA 107

Pena, Ramon del Valle y
See Valle-Inclan, Ramon (Maria) del

Pendennis, Arthur Esquir
See Thackeray, William Makepeace

Penn, William 1644-1718 .... **LC 25**
See also DLB 24

PEPECE
See Prado (Calvo), Pedro

Pepys, Samuel 1633-1703 **LC 11; DA; DAB;
DAC; DAM MST; WLC**
See also CDBLB 1660-1789; DLB 101

Percy, Walker 1916-1990 **CLC 2, 3, 6, 8, 14, 18,
47, 65; DAM NOV, POP**
See also CA 1-4R; 131; CANR 1, 23; DLB 2;
DLBY 80, 90; MTCW

Perec, Georges 1936-1982 .... **CLC 56**
See also CA 141; DLB 83

Pereda (y Sanchez de Porrua), Jose Maria de
1833-1906 .... **TCLC 16**
See also CA 117

Pereda y Porrua, Jose Maria de
See Pereda (y Sanchez de Porrua), Jose Maria
de

Peregoy, George Weems
See Mencken, H(enry) L(ouis)

Perelman, S(idney) J(oseph) 1904-1979 **C L C
3, 5, 9, 15, 23, 44, 49; DAM DRAM**
See also AITN 1, 2; CA 73-76; 89-92; CANR
18; DLB 11, 44; MTCW

Peret, Benjamin 1899-1959 .... **TCLC 20**
See also CA 117

Peretz, Isaac Loeb 1851(?)-1915 .. **TCLC 16;
SSC 26**
See also CA 109

Peretz, Yitzkhok Leibush
See Peretz, Isaac Loeb

Perez Galdos, Benito 1843-1920 .... **TCLC 27**
See also CA 125; 153; HW

Perrault, Charles 1628-1703 .... **LC 2**
See also MAICYA; SATA 25

Perry, Brighton
See Sherwood, Robert E(mmet)

Perse, St.-John .... **CLC 4, 11, 46**
See also Leger, (Marie-Rene Auguste) Alexis
Saint-Leger

Perutz, Leo 1882-1957 .... **TCLC 60**
See also DLB 81

Peseenz, Tulio F.
See Lopez y Fuentes, Gregorio

Pesetsky, Bette 1932- .... **CLC 28**
See also CA 133; DLB 130

Peshkov, Alexei Maximovich 1868-1936

See Gorky, Maxim
See also CA 105; 141; DA; DAC; DAM DRAM,
MST, NOV

Pessoa, Fernando (Antonio Nogueira) 1888-
1935 .... **TCLC 27; HLC; PC 20**
See also CA 125

Peterkin, Julia Mood 1880-1961 .... **CLC 31**
See also CA 102; DLB 9

Peters, Joan K(aren) 1945- .... **CLC 39**
See also CA 158

Peters, Robert L(ouis) 1924- .... **CLC 7**
See also CA 13-16R; CAAS 8; DLB 105

Petofi, Sandor 1823-1849 .... **NCLC 21**

Petrakis, Harry Mark 1923- .... **CLC 3**
See also CA 9-12R; CANR 4, 30

Petrarch 1304-1374 **CMLC 20; DAM POET;
PC 8**

Petrov, Evgeny .... **TCLC 21**
See also Kataev, Evgeny Petrovich

Petry, Ann (Lane) 1908-1997 ... **CLC 1, 7, 18**
See also BW 1; CA 5-8R; 157; CAAS 6; CANR
4, 46; CLR 12; DLB 76; JRDA; MAICYA;
MTCW; SATA 5; SATA-Obit 94

Petursson, Halligrimur 1614-1674 .... **LC 8**

Phaedrus 18(?)B.C.-55(?) .... **CMLC 24**

Philips, Katherine 1632-1664 .... **LC 30**
See also DLB 131

Philipson, Morris H. 1926- .... **CLC 53**
See also CA 1-4R; CANR 4

Phillips, Caryl 1958- . **CLC 96; DAM MULT**
See also BW 2; CA 141; DLB 157

Phillips, David Graham 1867-1911 **TCLC 44**
See also CA 108; DLB 9, 12

Phillips, Jack
See Sandburg, Carl (August)

Phillips, Jayne Anne 1952- **CLC 15, 33; SSC 16**
See also CA 101; CANR 24, 50; DLBY 80; INT
CANR-24; MTCW

Phillips, Richard
See Dick, Philip K(indred)

Phillips, Robert (Schaeffer) 1938- .... **CLC 28**
See also CA 17-20R; CAAS 13; CANR 8; DLB
105

Phillips, Ward
See Lovecraft, H(oward) P(hillips)

Piccolo, Lucio 1901-1969 .... **CLC 13**
See also CA 97-100; DLB 114

Pickthall, Marjorie L(owry) C(hristie) 1883-
1922 .... **TCLC 21**
See also CA 107; DLB 92

Pico della Mirandola, Giovanni 1463-1494 **LC
15**

Piercy, Marge 1936- **CLC 3, 6, 14, 18, 27, 62**
See also CA 21-24R; CAAS 1; CANR 13, 43;
DLB 120; MTCW

Piers, Robert
See Anthony, Piers

Pieyre de Mandiargues, Andre 1909-1991
See Mandiargues, Andre Pieyre de
See also CA 103; 136; CANR 22

Pilnyak, Boris .... **TCLC 23**
See also Vogau, Boris Andreyevich

Pincherle, Alberto 1907-1990 ... **CLC 11, 18;
DAM NOV**
See also Moravia, Alberto
See also CA 25-28R; 132; CANR 33; MTCW

Pinckney, Darryl 1953- .... **CLC 76**
See also BW 2; CA 143

Pindar 518B.C.-446B.C...... **CMLC 12; PC 19**
See also DLB 176

Pineda, Cecile 1942- .... **CLC 39**
See also CA 118

Pinero, Arthur Wing 1855-1934 .. **TCLC 32;**

DAM DRAM
See also CA 110; 153; DLB 10

Pinero, Miguel (Antonio Gomez) 1946-1988
CLC 4, 55
See also CA 61-64; 125; CANR 29; HW

Pinget, Robert 1919-1997 .... **CLC 7, 13, 37**
See also CA 85-88; 160; DLB 83

Pink Floyd
See Barrett, (Roger) Syd; Gilmour, David; Mason, Nick; Waters, Roger; Wright, Rick

Pinkney, Edward 1802-1828 .... **NCLC 31**

Pinkwater, Daniel Manus 1941- .... **CLC 35**
See also Pinkwater, Manus
See also AAYA 1; CA 29-32R; CANR 12, 38;
CLR 4; JRDA; MAICYA; SAAS 3; SATA 46,
76

Pinkwater, Manus
See Pinkwater, Daniel Manus
See also SATA 8

Pinsky, Robert 1940- **CLC 9, 19, 38, 94; DAM
POET**
See also CA 29-32R; CAAS 4; CANR 58;
DLBY 82

Pinta, Harold
See Pinter, Harold

Pinter, Harold 1930- **CLC 1, 3, 6, 9, 11, 15, 27,
58, 73; DA; DAB; DAC; DAM DRAM,
MST; WLC**
See also CA 5-8R; CANR 33; CDBLB 1960 to
Present; DLB 13; MTCW

Piozzi, Hester Lynch (Thrale) 1741-1821
NCLC 57
See also DLB 104, 142

Pirandello, Luigi 1867-1936 **TCLC 4, 29; DA;
DAB; DAC; DAM DRAM, MST; DC 5;
SSC 22; WLC**
See also CA 104; 153

Pirsig, Robert M(aynard) 1928- **CLC 4, 6, 73;
DAM POP**
See also CA 53-56; CANR 42; MTCW; SATA
39

Pisarev, Dmitry Ivanovich 1840-1868 **N C L C
25**

Pix, Mary (Griffith) 1666-1709 .... **LC 8**
See also DLB 80

Pixerecourt, Guilbert de 1773-1844 **NCLC 39**

Plaatje, Sol(omon) T(shekisho) 1876-1932
TCLC 73
See also BW 2; CA 141

Plaidy, Jean
See Hibbert, Eleanor Alice Burford

Planche, James Robinson 1796-1880 **NCLC 42**

Plant, Robert 1948- .... **CLC 12**

Plante, David (Robert) 1940- **CLC 7, 23, 38;
DAM NOV**
See also CA 37-40R; CANR 12, 36, 58; DLBY
83; INT CANR-12; MTCW

Plath, Sylvia 1932-1963 **CLC 1, 2, 3, 5, 9, 11,
14, 17, 50, 51, 62; DA; DAB; DAC; DAM
MST, POET; PC 1; WLC**
See also AAYA 13; CA 19-20; CANR 34; CAP
2; CDALB 1941-1968; DLB 5, 6, 152;
MTCW; SATA 96

Plato 428(?)B.C.-348(?)B.C..... **CMLC 8; DA;
DAB; DAC; DAM MST; WLCS**
See also DLB 176

Platonov, Andrei .... **TCLC 14**
See also Klimentov, Andrei Platonovich

Platt, Kin 1911- .... **CLC 26**
See also AAYA 11; CA 17-20R; CANR 11;
JRDA; SAAS 17; SATA 21, 86

Plautus c. 251B.C.-184B.C. .... **DC 6**

Plick et Plock

See Simenon, Georges (Jacques Christian)
Plimpton, George (Ames) 1927- .... **CLC 36**
See also AITN 1; CA 21-24R; CANR 32;
MTCW; SATA 10
Pliny the Elder c. 23-79 .... **CMLC 23**
Plomer, William Charles Franklin 1903-1973
CLC 4, 8
See also CA 21-22; CANR 34; CAP 2; DLB
20, 162; MTCW; SATA 24
Plowman, Piers
See Kavanagh, Patrick (Joseph)
Plum, J.
See Wodehouse, P(elham) G(renville)
Plumly, Stanley (Ross) 1939- .... **CLC 33**
See also CA 108; 110; DLB 5; INT 110
Plumpe, Friedrich Wilhelm 1888-1931**T C L C
53**
See also CA 112
Po Chu-i 772-846 .... **CMLC 24**
Poe, Edgar Allan 1809-1849**NCLC 1, 16, 55;
DA; DAB; DAC; DAM MST, POET; PC
1; SSC 1, 22; WLC**
See also AAYA 14; CDALB 1640-1865; DLB
3, 59, 73, 74; SATA 23
Poet of Titchfield Street, The
See Pound, Ezra (Weston Loomis)
Pohl, Frederik 1919- .... **CLC 18; SSC 25**
See also CA 61-64; CAAS 1; CANR 11, 37;
DLB 8; INT CANR-11; MTCW; SATA 24
Poirier, Louis 1910-
See Gracq, Julien
See also CA 122; 126
Poitier, Sidney 1927- .... **CLC 26**
See also BW 1; CA 117
Polanski, Roman 1933- .... **CLC 16**
See also CA 77-80
Poliakoff, Stephen 1952- .... **CLC 38**
See also CA 106; DLB 13
Police, The
See Copeland, Stewart (Armstrong); Summers,
Andrew James; Sumner, Gordon Matthew
Polidori, John William 1795-1821 . **NCLC 51**
See also DLB 116
Pollitt, Katha 1949- .... **CLC 28**
See also CA 120; 122; MTCW
Pollock, (Mary) Sharon 1936-**CLC 50; DAC;
DAM DRAM, MST**
See also CA 141; DLB 60
Polo, Marco 1254-1324 .... **CMLC 15**
Polonsky, Abraham (Lincoln) 1910- **CLC 92**
See also CA 104; DLB 26; INT 104
Polybius c. 200B.C.-c. 118B.C. ...... **CMLC 17**
See also DLB 176
Pomerance, Bernard 1940-.... **CLC 13; DAM
DRAM**
See also CA 101; CANR 49
Ponge, Francis (Jean Gaston Alfred) 1899-1988
CLC 6, 18; DAM POET
See also CA 85-88; 126; CANR 40
Pontoppidan, Henrik 1857-1943 .... **TCLC 29**
Poole, Josephine .... **CLC 17**
See also Helyar, Jane Penelope Josephine
See also SAAS 2; SATA 5
Popa, Vasko 1922-1991 .... **CLC 19**
See also CA 112; 148; DLB 181
Pope, Alexander 1688-1744 **LC 3; DA; DAB;
DAC; DAM MST, POET; WLC**
See also CDBLB 1660-1789; DLB 95, 101
Porter, Connie (Rose) 1959(?)- .... **CLC 70**
See also BW 2; CA 142; SATA 81
Porter, Gene(va Grace) Stratton 1863(?)-1924
TCLC 21
See also CA 112

Porter, Katherine Anne 1890-1980**CLC 1, 3, 7,
10, 13, 15, 27, 101; DA; DAB; DAC; DAM
MST, NOV; SSC 4**
See also AITN 2; CA 1-4R; 101; CANR 1; DLB
4, 9, 102; DLBD 12; DLBY 80; MTCW;
SATA 39; SATA-Obit 23
Porter, Peter (Neville Frederick) 1929-**CLC 5,
13, 33**
See also CA 85-88; DLB 40
Porter, William Sydney 1862-1910
See Henry, O.
See also CA 104; 131; CDALB 1865-1917; DA;
DAB; DAC; DAM MST; DLB 12, 78, 79;
MTCW; YABC 2
Portillo (y Pacheco), Jose Lopez
See Lopez Portillo (y Pacheco), Jose
Post, Melville Davisson 1869-1930 **TCLC 39**
See also CA 110
Potok, Chaim 1929- . **CLC 2, 7, 14, 26; DAM
NOV**
See also AAYA 15; AITN 1, 2; CA 17-20R;
CANR 19, 35; DLB 28, 152; INT CANR-
19; MTCW; SATA 33
Potter, (Helen) Beatrix 1866-1943
See Webb, (Martha) Beatrice (Potter)
See also MAICYA
Potter, Dennis (Christopher George) 1935-1994
CLC 58, 86
See also CA 107; 145; CANR 33, 61; MTCW
Pound, Ezra (Weston Loomis) 1885-1972**CLC
1, 2, 3, 4, 5, 7, 10, 13, 18, 34, 48, 50; DA;
DAB; DAC; DAM MST, POET; PC 4;
WLC**
See also CA 5-8R; 37-40R; CANR 40; CDALB
1917-1929; DLB 4, 45, 63; DLBD 15;
MTCW
Povod, Reinaldo 1959-1994 .... **CLC 44**
See also CA 136; 146
Powell, Adam Clayton, Jr. 1908-1972**CLC 89;
BLC; DAM MULT**
See also BW 1; CA 102; 33-36R
Powell, Anthony (Dymoke) 1905-**CLC 1, 3, 7,
9, 10, 31**
See also CA 1-4R; CANR 1, 32, 62; CDBLB
1945-1960; DLB 15; MTCW
Powell, Dawn 1897-1965 .... **CLC 66**
See also CA 5-8R
Powell, Padgett 1952-......................... **CLC 34**
See also CA 126
Power, Susan 1961- .... **CLC 91**
Powers, J(ames) F(arl) 1917-**CLC 1, 4, 8, 57;
SSC 4**
See also CA 1-4R; CANR 2, 61; DLB 130;
MTCW
Powers, John J(ames) 1945-
See Powers, John R.
See also CA 69-72
Powers, John R. .... **CLC 66**
See also Powers, John J(ames)
Powers, Richard (S.) 1957- .... **CLC 93**
See also CA 148
Pownall, David 1938- .... **CLC 10**
See also CA 89-92; CAAS 18; CANR 49; DLB
14
Powys, John Cowper 1872-1963**CLC 7, 9, 15,
46**
See also CA 85-88; DLB 15; MTCW
Powys, T(heodore) F(rancis) 1875-1953
TCLC 9
See also CA 106; DLB 36, 162
Prado (Calvo), Pedro 1886-1952 .... **TCLC 75**
See also CA 131; HW
Prager, Emily 1952- .... **CLC 56**

Pratt, E(dwin) J(ohn) 1883(?)-1964 **CLC 19;
DAC; DAM POET**
See also CA 141; 93-96; DLB 92
Premchand .... **TCLC 21**
See also Srivastava, Dhanpat Rai
Preussler, Otfried 1923- .... **CLC 17**
See also CA 77-80; SATA 24
Prevert, Jacques (Henri Marie) 1900-1977
CLC 15
See also CA 77-80; 69-72; CANR 29, 61;
MTCW; SATA-Obit 30
Prevost, Abbe (Antoine Francois) 1697-1763
LC 1
Price, (Edward) Reynolds 1933-**CLC 3, 6, 13,
43, 50, 63; DAM NOV; SSC 22**
See also CA 1-4R; CANR 1, 37, 57; DLB 2;
INT CANR-37
Price, Richard 1949- .... **CLC 6, 12**
See also CA 49-52; CANR 3; DLBY 81
Prichard, Katharine Susannah 1883-1969
CLC 46
See also CA 11-12; CANR 33; CAP 1; MTCW;
SATA 66
Priestley, J(ohn) B(oynton) 1894-1984**CLC 2,
5, 9, 34; DAM DRAM, NOV**
See also CA 9-12R; 113; CANR 33; CDBLB
1914-1945; DLB 10, 34, 77, 100, 139; DLBY
84; MTCW
Prince 1958(?)- .... **CLC 35**
Prince, F(rank) T(empleton) 1912-... **CLC 22**
See also CA 101; CANR 43; DLB 20
Prince Kropotkin
See Kropotkin, Peter (Aleksieevich)
Prior, Matthew 1664-1721 .... **LC 4**
See also DLB 95
Prishvin, Mikhail 1873-1954 .... **TCLC 75**
Pritchard, William H(arrison) 1932- **CLC 34**
See also CA 65-68; CANR 23; DLB 111
Pritchett, V(ictor) S(awdon) 1900-1997 **C L C
5, 13, 15, 41; DAM NOV; SSC 14**
See also CA 61-64; 157; CANR 31; DLB 15,
139; MTCW
Private 19022
See Manning, Frederic
Probst, Mark 1925- .... **CLC 59**
See also CA 130
Prokosch, Frederic 1908-1989 ..... **CLC 4, 48**
See also CA 73-76; 128; DLB 48
Prophet, The
See Dreiser, Theodore (Herman Albert)
Prose, Francine 1947- ....**CLC 45**
See also CA 109; 112; CANR 46
Proudhon
See Cunha, Euclides (Rodrigues Pimenta) da
Proulx, E. Annie 1935- ....**CLC 81**
**Proust, (Valentin-Louis-George-Eugene-)
Marcel** 1871-1922 **TCLC 7, 13, 33; DA;
DAB; DAC; DAM MST, NOV; WLC**
See also CA 104; 120; DLB 65; MTCW
Prowler, Harley
See Masters, Edgar Lee
Prus, Boleslaw 1845-1912 .... **TCLC 48**
Pryor, Richard (Franklin Lenox Thomas) 1940-
CLC 26
See also CA 122
Przybyszewski, Stanislaw 1868-1927**TCLC 36**
See also CA 160; DLB 66
Pteleon
See Grieve, C(hristopher) M(urray)
See also DAM POET
Puckett, Lute
See Masters, Edgar Lee
Puig, Manuel 1932-1990**CLC 3, 5, 10, 28, 65;**

DAM MULT; HLC
See also CA 45-48; CANR 2, 32; DLB 113; HW;
MTCW

Pulitzer, Joseph 1847-1911 .... **TCLC 76**
See also CA 114; DLB 23

Purdy, Al(fred Wellington) 1918-**CLC 3, 6, 14, 50; DAC; DAM MST, POET**
See also CA 81-84; CAAS 17; CANR 42; DLB 88

Purdy, James (Amos) 1923-**CLC 2, 4, 10, 28, 52**
See also CA 33-36R; CAAS 1; CANR 19, 51;
DLB 2; INT CANR-19; MTCW

Pure, Simon
See Swinnerton, Frank Arthur

Pushkin, Alexander (Sergeyevich) 1799-1837
NCLC 3, 27; DA; DAB; DAC; DAM DRAM, MST, POET; PC 10; SSC 27; WLC
See also SATA 61

P'u Sung-ling 1640-1715 .... **LC 3**

Putnam, Arthur Lee
See Alger, Horatio, Jr.

Puzo, Mario 1920-**CLC 1, 2, 6, 36; DAM NOV, POP**
See also CA 65-68; CANR 4, 42; DLB 6;
MTCW

Pygge, Edward
See Barnes, Julian (Patrick)

Pyle, Ernest Taylor 1900-1945
See Pyle, Ernie
See also CA 115; 160

Pyle, Ernie 1900-1945 .... **TCLC 75**
See also Pyle, Ernest Taylor
See also DLB 29

Pym, Barbara (Mary Crampton) 1913-1980
CLC 13, 19, 37
See also CA 13-14; 97-100; CANR 13, 34; CAP
1; DLB 14; DLBY 87; MTCW

Pynchon, Thomas (Ruggles, Jr.) 1937-**CLC 2, 3, 6, 9, 11, 18, 33, 62, 72; DA; DAB; DAC; DAM MST, NOV, POP; SSC 14; WLC**
See also BEST 90:2; CA 17-20R; CANR 22,
46; DLB 2, 173; MTCW

Pythagoras c. 570B.C.-c. 500B.C. . **CMLC 22**
See also DLB 176

Qian Zhongshu
See Ch'ien Chung-shu

Qroll
See Dagerman, Stig (Halvard)

Quarrington, Paul (Lewis) 1953-..... **CLC 65**
See also CA 129; CANR 62

Quasimodo, Salvatore 1901-1968 .... **CLC 10**
See also CA 13-16; 25-28R; CAP 1; DLB 114;
MTCW

Quay, Stephen 1947- .... **CLC 95**

Quay, The Brothers
See Quay, Stephen; Quay, Timothy

Quay, Timothy 1947-......................... **CLC 95**

Queen, Ellery .... **CLC 3, 11**
See also Dannay, Frederic; Davidson, Avram;
Lee, Manfred B(ennington); Marlowe,
Stephen; Sturgeon, Theodore (Hamilton);
Vance, John Holbrook

Queen, Ellery, Jr.
See Dannay, Frederic; Lee, Manfred
B(ennington)

Queneau, Raymond 1903-1976 **CLC 2, 5, 10, 42**
See also CA 77-80; 69-72; CANR 32; DLB 72;
MTCW

Quevedo, Francisco de 1580-1645 ...... **LC 23**

Quiller-Couch, Arthur Thomas 1863-1944
TCLC 53
See also CA 118; DLB 135, 153

Quin, Ann (Marie) 1936-1973 .... **CLC 6**
See also CA 9-12R; 45-48; DLB 14

Quinn, Martin
See Smith, Martin Cruz

Quinn, Peter 1947- .... **CLC 91**

Quinn, Simon
See Smith, Martin Cruz

Quiroga, Horacio (Sylvestre) 1878-1937
TCLC 20; DAM MULT; HLC
See also CA 117; 131; HW; MTCW

Quoirez, Francoise 1935-.................... **CLC 9**
See also Sagan, Francoise
See also CA 49-52; CANR 6, 39; MTCW

Raabe, Wilhelm 1831-1910 .... **TCLC 45**
See also DLB 129

Rabe, David (William) 1940-... **CLC 4, 8, 33; DAM DRAM**
See also CA 85-88; CABS 3; CANR 59; DLB 7

Rabelais, Francois 1483-1553**LC 5; DA; DAB; DAC; DAM MST; WLC**

Rabinovitch, Sholem 1859-1916
See Aleichem, Sholom
See also CA 104

Rachilde 1860-1953 .... **TCLC 67**
See also DLB 123

Racine, Jean 1639-1699 . **LC 28; DAB; DAM MST**

Radcliffe, Ann (Ward) 1764-1823**NCLC 6, 55**
See also DLB 39, 178

Radiguet, Raymond 1903-1923 ...... **TCLC 29**
See also DLB 65

Radnoti, Miklos 1909-1944 .... **TCLC 16**
See also CA 118

Rado, James 1939- ....**CLC 17**
See also CA 105

Radvanyi, Netty 1900-1983
See Seghers, Anna
See also CA 85-88; 110

Rae, Ben
See Griffiths, Trevor

Raeburn, John (Hay) 1941- .... **CLC 34**
See also CA 57-60

Ragni, Gerome 1942-1991 .... **CLC 17**
See also CA 105; 134

Rahv, Philip 1908-1973 .... **CLC 24**
See also Greenberg, Ivan
See also DLB 137

Raine, Craig 1944- .... **CLC 32, 103**
See also CA 108; CANR 29, 51; DLB 40

Raine, Kathleen (Jessie) 1908- ..... **CLC 7, 45**
See also CA 85-88; CANR 46; DLB 20; MTCW

Rainis, Janis 1865-1929 .... **TCLC 29**

Rakosi, Carl ....**CLC 47**
See also Rawley, Callman
See also CAAS 5

Raleigh, Richard
See Lovecraft, H(oward) P(hillips)

Raleigh, Sir Walter 1554(?)-1618 . **LC 31, 39**
See also CDBLB Before 1660; DLB 172

Rallentando, H. P.
See Sayers, Dorothy L(eigh)

Ramal, Walter
See de la Mare, Walter (John)

Ramon, Juan
See Jimenez (Mantecon), Juan Ramon

Ramos, Graciliano 1892-1953 .... **TCLC 32**

Rampersad, Arnold 1941- .... **CLC 44**
See also BW 2; CA 127; 133; DLB 111; INT
133

Rampling, Anne
See Rice, Anne

Ramsay, Allan 1684(?)-1758 .... **LC 29**
See also DLB 95

Ramuz, Charles-Ferdinand 1878-1947**T C L C 33**

Rand, Ayn 1905-1982**CLC 3, 30, 44, 79; DA; DAC; DAM MST, NOV, POP; WLC**
See also AAYA 10; CA 13-16R; 105; CANR
27; MTCW

Randall, Dudley (Felker) 1914-**CLC 1; BLC; DAM MULT**
See also BW 1; CA 25-28R; CANR 23; DLB
41

Randall, Robert
See Silverberg, Robert

Ranger, Ken
See Creasey, John

Ransom, John Crowe 1888-1974**CLC 2, 4, 5, 11, 24; DAM POET**
See also CA 5-8R; 49-52; CANR 6, 34; DLB
45, 63; MTCW

Rao, Raja 1909- ...... **CLC 25, 56; DAM NOV**
See also CA 73-76; CANR 51; MTCW

Raphael, Frederic (Michael) 1931-**CLC 2, 14**
See also CA 1-4R; CANR 1; DLB 14

Ratcliffe, James P.
See Mencken, H(enry) L(ouis)

Rathbone, Julian 1935-..................... **CLC 41**
See also CA 101; CANR 34

Rattigan, Terence (Mervyn) 1911-1977**CLC 7; DAM DRAM**
See also CA 85-88; 73-76; CDBLB 1945-1960;
DLB 13; MTCW

Ratushinskaya, Irina 1954- .... **CLC 54**
See also CA 129

Raven, Simon (Arthur Noel) 1927-.. **CLC 14**
See also CA 81-84

Rawley, Callman 1903-
See Rakosi, Carl
See also CA 21-24R; CANR 12, 32

Rawlings, Marjorie Kinnan 1896-1953**T C L C 4**
See also AAYA 20; CA 104; 137; DLB 9, 22,
102; JRDA; MAICYA; YABC 1

Ray, Satyajit 1921-1992 .. **CLC 16, 76; DAM MULT**
See also CA 114; 137

Read, Herbert Edward 1893-1968 ..... **CLC 4**
See also CA 85-88; 25-28R; DLB 20, 149

Read, Piers Paul 1941- .... **CLC 4, 10, 25**
See also CA 21-24R; CANR 38; DLB 14; SATA
21

Reade, Charles 1814-1884 .... **NCLC 2**
See also DLB 21

Reade, Hamish
See Gray, Simon (James Holliday)

Reading, Peter 1946- .... **CLC 47**
See also CA 103; CANR 46; DLB 40

Reaney, James 1926- ... **CLC 13; DAC; DAM MST**
See also CA 41-44R; CAAS 15; CANR 42; DLB
68; SATA 43

Rebreanu, Liviu 1885-1944 .... **TCLC 28**

Rechy, John (Francisco) 1934- **CLC 1, 7, 14, 18; DAM MULT; HLC**
See also CA 5-8R; CAAS 4; CANR 6, 32; DLB
122; DLBY 82; HW; INT CANR-6

Redcam, Tom 1870-1933 .... **TCLC 25**

Reddin, Keith .... **CLC 67**

Redgrove, Peter (William) 1932- . **CLC 6, 41**
See also CA 1-4R; CANR 3, 39; DLB 40

Redmon, Anne .... **CLC 22**
See also Nightingale, Anne Redmon
See also DLBY 86

Reed, Eliot
See Ambler, Eric
Reed, Ishmael 1938-**CLC 2, 3, 5, 6, 13, 32, 60;
BLC; DAM MULT**
See also BW 2; CA 21-24R; CANR 25, 48; DLB
2, 5, 33, 169; DLBD 8; MTCW
Reed, John (Silas) 1887-1920 .... **TCLC 9**
See also CA 106
Reed, Lou .... **CLC 21**
See also Firbank, Louis
Reeve, Clara 1729-1807 .... **NCLC 19**
See also DLB 39
Reich, Wilhelm 1897-1957 .... **TCLC 57**
Reid, Christopher (John) 1949- .... **CLC 33**
See also CA 140; DLB 40
Reid, Desmond
See Moorcock, Michael (John)
Reid Banks, Lynne 1929-
See Banks, Lynne Reid
See also CA 1-4R; CANR 6, 22, 38; CLR 24;
JRDA; MAICYA; SATA 22, 75
Reilly, William K.
See Creasey, John
Reiner, Max
See Caldwell, (Janet Miriam) Taylor (Holland)
Reis, Ricardo
See Pessoa, Fernando (Antonio Nogueira)
Remarque, Erich Maria 1898-1970 **CLC 21;
DA; DAB; DAC; DAM MST, NOV**
See also CA 77-80; 29-32R; DLB 56; MTCW
Remizov, A.
See Remizov, Aleksei (Mikhailovich)
Remizov, A. M.
See Remizov, Aleksei (Mikhailovich)
Remizov, Aleksei (Mikhailovich) 1877-1957
TCLC 27
See also CA 125; 133
Renan, Joseph Ernest 1823-1892 ... **NCLC 26**
Renard, Jules 1864-1910 .... **TCLC 17**
See also CA 117
Renault, Mary .... **CLC 3, 11, 17**
See also Challans, Mary
See also DLBY 83
Rendell, Ruth (Barbara) 1930- . **CLC 28, 48;
DAM POP**
See also Vine, Barbara
See also CA 109; CANR 32, 52; DLB 87; INT
CANR-32; MTCW
Renoir, Jean 1894-1979 .... **CLC 20**
See also CA 129; 85-88
Resnais, Alain 1922- .... **CLC 16**
Reverdy, Pierre 1889-1960 .... **CLC 53**
See also CA 97-100; 89-92
Rexroth, Kenneth 1905-1982 **CLC 1, 2, 6, 11,
22, 49; DAM POET; PC 20**
See also CA 5-8R; 107; CANR 14, 34; CDALB
1941-1968; DLB 16, 48, 165; DLBY 82; INT
CANR-14; MTCW
Reyes, Alfonso 1889-1959 .... **TCLC 33**
See also CA 131; HW
Reyes y Basoalto, Ricardo Eliecer Neftali
See Neruda, Pablo
Reymont, Wladyslaw (Stanislaw) 1868(?)-1925
TCLC 5
See also CA 104
Reynolds, Jonathan 1942- .... **CLC 6, 38**
See also CA 65-68; CANR 28
Reynolds, Joshua 1723-1792 .... **LC 15**
See also DLB 104
Reynolds, Michael Shane 1937- .... **CLC 44**
See also CA 65-68; CANR 9
Reznikoff, Charles 1894-1976 .... **CLC 9**
See also CA 33-36; 61-64; CAP 2; DLB 28, 45

Rezzori (d'Arezzo), Gregor von 1914-**CLC 25**
See also CA 122; 136
Rhine, Richard
See Silverstein, Alvin
Rhodes, Eugene Manlove 1869-1934**TCLC 53**
R'hoone
See Balzac, Honore de
Rhys, Jean 1890(?)-1979 **CLC 2, 4, 6, 14, 19,
51; DAM NOV; SSC 21**
See also CA 25-28R; 85-88; CANR 35, 62;
CDBLB 1945-1960; DLB 36, 117, 162;
MTCW
Ribeiro, Darcy 1922-1997 .... **CLC 34**
See also CA 33-36R; 156
Ribeiro, Joao Ubaldo (Osorio Pimentel) 1941-
CLC 10, 67
See also CA 81-84
Ribman, Ronald (Burt) 1932- .... **CLC 7**
See also CA 21-24R; CANR 46
Ricci, Nino 1959- .... **CLC 70**
See also CA 137
Rice, Anne 1941- .... **CLC 41; DAM POP**
See also AAYA 9; BEST 89:2; CA 65-68; CANR
12, 36, 53
Rice, Elmer (Leopold) 1892-1967 **CLC 7, 49;
DAM DRAM**
See also CA 21-22; 25-28R; CAP 2; DLB 4, 7;
MTCW
Rice, Tim(othy Miles Bindon) 1944- **CLC 21**
See also CA 103; CANR 46
Rich, Adrienne (Cecile) 1929-**CLC 3, 6, 7, 11,
18, 36, 73, 76; DAM POET; PC 5**
See also CA 9-12R; CANR 20, 53; DLB 5, 67;
MTCW
Rich, Barbara
See Graves, Robert (von Ranke)
Rich, Robert
See Trumbo, Dalton
Richard, Keith .... **CLC 17**
See also Richards, Keith
Richards, David Adams 1950- **CLC 59; DAC**
See also CA 93-96; CANR 60; DLB 53
Richards, I(vor) A(rmstrong) 1893-1979**CLC
14, 24**
See also CA 41-44R; 89-92; CANR 34; DLB
27
Richards, Keith 1943-
See Richard, Keith
See also CA 107
Richardson, Anne
See Roiphe, Anne (Richardson)
Richardson, Dorothy Miller 1873-1957**TCLC
3**
See also CA 104; DLB 36
Richardson, Ethel Florence (Lindesay) 1870-
1946
See Richardson, Henry Handel
See also CA 105
Richardson, Henry Handel .... **TCLC 4**
See also Richardson, Ethel Florence (Lindesay)
Richardson, John 1796-1852**NCLC 55; DAC**
See also DLB 99
Richardson, Samuel 1689-1761 .... **LC 1; DA;
DAB; DAC; DAM MST, NOV; WLC**
See also CDBLB 1660-1789; DLB 39
Richler, Mordecai 1931-**CLC 3, 5, 9, 13, 18, 46,
70; DAC; DAM MST, NOV**
See also AITN 1; CA 65-68; CANR 31, 62; CLR
17; DLB 53; MAICYA; MTCW; SATA 44;
SATA-Brief 27
Richter, Conrad (Michael) 1890-1968**CLC 30**
See also AAYA 21; CA 5-8R; 25-28R; CANR
23; DLB 9; MTCW; SATA 3

Ricostranza, Tom
See Ellis, Trey
Riddell, J. H. 1832-1906 .... **TCLC 40**
Riding, Laura .... **CLC 3, 7**
See also Jackson, Laura (Riding)
Riefenstahl, Berta Helene Amalia 1902-
See Riefenstahl, Leni
See also CA 108
Riefenstahl, Leni .... **CLC 16**
See also Riefenstahl, Berta Helene Amalia
Riffe, Ernest
See Bergman, (Ernst) Ingmar
Riggs, (Rolla) Lynn 1899-1954 ..... **TCLC 56;
DAM MULT**
See also CA 144; DLB 175; NNAL
Riley, James Whitcomb 1849-1916**TCLC 51;
DAM POET**
See also CA 118; 137; MAICYA; SATA 17
Riley, Tex
See Creasey, John
Rilke, Rainer Maria 1875-1926**TCLC 1, 6, 19;
DAM POET; PC 2**
See also CA 104; 132; CANR 62; DLB 81;
MTCW
Rimbaud, (Jean Nicolas) Arthur 1854-1891
**NCLC 4, 35; DA; DAB; DAC; DAM MST,
POET; PC 3; WLC**
Rinehart, Mary Roberts 1876-1958**TCLC 52**
See also CA 108
Ringmaster, The
See Mencken, H(enry) L(ouis)
Ringwood, Gwen(dolyn Margaret) Pharis
1910-1984 .... **CLC 48**
See also CA 148; 112; DLB 88
Rio, Michel 19(?)- .... **CLC 43**
Ritsos, Giannes
See Ritsos, Yannis
Ritsos, Yannis 1909-1990 .... **CLC 6, 13, 31**
See also CA 77-80; 133; CANR 39, 61; MTCW
Ritter, Erika 1948(?)- .... **CLC 52**
Rivera, Jose Eustasio 1889-1928 ... **TCLC 35**
See also HW
Rivers, Conrad Kent 1933-1968 .... **CLC 1**
See also BW 1; CA 85-88; DLB 41
Rivers, Elfrida
See Bradley, Marion Zimmer
Riverside, John
See Heinlein, Robert A(nson)
Rizal, Jose 1861-1896 .... **NCLC 27**
Roa Bastos, Augusto (Antonio) 1917-**CLC 45;
DAM MULT; HLC**
See also CA 131; DLB 113; HW
Robbe-Grillet, Alain 1922- **CLC 1, 2, 4, 6, 8,
10, 14, 43**
See also CA 9-12R; CANR 33; DLB 83; MTCW
Robbins, Harold 1916- ... **CLC 5; DAM NOV**
See also CA 73-76; CANR 26, 54; MTCW
Robbins, Thomas Eugene 1936-
See Robbins, Tom
See also CA 81-84; CANR 29, 59; DAM NOV,
POP; MTCW
Robbins, Tom .... **CLC 9, 32, 64**
See also Robbins, Thomas Eugene
See also BEST 90:3; DLBY 80
Robbins, Trina 1938- .... **CLC 21**
See also CA 128
Roberts, Charles G(eorge) D(ouglas) 1860-1943
TCLC 8
See also CA 105; CLR 33; DLB 92; SATA 88;
SATA-Brief 29
Roberts, Elizabeth Madox 1886-1941 **TCLC
68**
See also CA 111; DLB 9, 54, 102; SATA 33;

SATA-Brief 27

Roberts, Kate 1891-1985 .... **CLC 15**
See also CA 107; 116

Roberts, Keith (John Kingston) 1935-**CLC 14**
See also CA 25-28R; CANR 46

Roberts, Kenneth (Lewis) 1885-1957**TCLC 23**
See also CA 109; DLB 9

Roberts, Michele (B.) 1949- .... **CLC 48**
See also CA 115; CANR 58

Robertson, Ellis
See Ellison, Harlan (Jay); Silverberg, Robert

Robertson, Thomas William 1829-1871**NCLC 35; DAM DRAM**

Robeson, Kenneth
See Dent, Lester

Robinson, Edwin Arlington 1869-1935**TCLC 5; DA; DAC; DAM MST, POET; PC 1**
See also CA 104; 133; CDALB 1865-1917;
DLB 54; MTCW

Robinson, Henry Crabb 1775-1867**NCLC 15**
See also DLB 107

Robinson, Jill 1936- .... **CLC 10**
See also CA 102; INT 102

Robinson, Kim Stanley 1952- .... **CLC 34**
See also CA 126

Robinson, Lloyd
See Silverberg, Robert

Robinson, Marilynne 1944- .... **CLC 25**
See also CA 116

Robinson, Smokey .... **CLC 21**
See also Robinson, William, Jr.

Robinson, William, Jr. 1940-
See Robinson, Smokey
See also CA 116

Robison, Mary 1949- .... **CLC 42, 98**
See also CA 113; 116; DLB 130; INT 116

Rod, Edouard 1857-1910 .... **TCLC 52**

Roddenberry, Eugene Wesley 1921-1991
See Roddenberry, Gene
See also CA 110; 135; CANR 37; SATA 45;
SATA-Obit 69

Roddenberry, Gene .... **CLC 17**
See also Roddenberry, Eugene Wesley
See also AAYA 5; SATA-Obit 69

Rodgers, Mary 1931- .... **CLC 12**
See also CA 49-52; CANR 8, 55; CLR 20; INT
CANR-8; JRDA; MAICYA; SATA 8

Rodgers, W(illiam) R(obert) 1909-1969**CLC 7**
See also CA 85-88; DLB 20

Rodman, Eric
See Silverberg, Robert

Rodman, Howard 1920(?)-1985 .... **CLC 65**
See also CA 118

Rodman, Maia
See Wojciechowska, Maia (Teresa)

Rodriguez, Claudio 1934- .... **CLC 10**
See also DLB 134

Roelvaag, O(le) E(dvart) 1876-1931**TCLC 17**
See also CA 117; DLB 9

Roethke, Theodore (Huebner) 1908-1963**CLC 1, 3, 8, 11, 19, 46, 101; DAM POET; PC 15**
See also CA 81-84; CABS 2; CDALB 1941-1968; DLB 5; MTCW

Rogers, Thomas Hunton 1927- .... **CLC 57**
See also CA 89-92; INT 89-92

Rogers, Will(iam Penn Adair) 1879-1935
TCLC 8, 71; DAM MULT
See also CA 105; 144; DLB 11; NNAL

Rogin, Gilbert 1929- .... **CLC 18**
See also CA 65-68; CANR 15

Rohan, Koda .... **TCLC 22**
See also Koda Shigeyuki

Rohlfs, Anna Katharine Green
See Green, Anna Katharine

Rohmer, Eric ....**CLC 16**
See also Scherer, Jean-Marie Maurice

Rohmer, Sax .... **TCLC 28**
See also Ward, Arthur Henry Sarsfield
See also DLB 70

Roiphe, Anne (Richardson) 1935- . **CLC 3, 9**
See also CA 89-92; CANR 45; DLBY 80; INT 89-92

Rojas, Fernando de 1465-1541 .... **LC 23**

Rolfe, Frederick (William Serafino Austin Lewis Mary) 1860-1913 .... **TCLC 12**
See also CA 107; DLB 34, 156

Rolland, Romain 1866-1944 .... **TCLC 23**
See also CA 118; DLB 65

Rolle, Richard c. 1300-c. 1349 ...... **CMLC 21**
See also DLB 146

Rolvaag, O(le) E(dvart)
See Roelvaag, O(le) E(dvart)

Romain Arnaud, Saint
See Aragon, Louis

Romains, Jules 1885-1972 .... **CLC 7**
See also CA 85-88; CANR 34; DLB 65; MTCW

Romero, Jose Ruben 1890-1952 ..... **TCLC 14**
See also CA 114; 131; HW

Ronsard, Pierre de 1524-1585 ... **LC 6; PC 11**

Rooke, Leon 1934- .. **CLC 25, 34; DAM POP**
See also CA 25-28R; CANR 23, 53

Roosevelt, Theodore 1858-1919 ..... **TCLC 69**
See also CA 115; DLB 47

Roper, William 1498-1578 .... **LC 10**

Roquelaure, A. N.
See Rice, Anne

Rosa, Joao Guimaraes 1908-1967 ....**CLC 23**
See also CA 89-92; DLB 113

Rose, Wendy 1948-**CLC 85; DAM MULT; PC 13**
See also CA 53-56; CANR 5, 51; DLB 175;
NNAL; SATA 12

Rosen, R. D.
See Rosen, Richard (Dean)

Rosen, Richard (Dean) 1949- ....**CLC 39**
See also CA 77-80; CANR 62; INT CANR-30

Rosenberg, Isaac 1890-1918 .... **TCLC 12**
See also CA 107; DLB 20

Rosenblatt, Joe ....**CLC 15**
See also Rosenblatt, Joseph

Rosenblatt, Joseph 1933-
See Rosenblatt, Joe
See also CA 89-92; INT 89-92

Rosenfeld, Samuel 1896-1963
See Tzara, Tristan
See also CA 89-92

Rosenstock, Sami
See Tzara, Tristan

Rosenstock, Samuel
See Tzara, Tristan

Rosenthal, M(acha) L(ouis) 1917-1996 . **C L C 28**
See also CA 1-4R; 152; CAAS 6; CANR 4, 51;
DLB 5; SATA 59

Ross, Barnaby
See Dannay, Frederic

Ross, Bernard L.
See Follett, Ken(neth Martin)

Ross, J. H.
See Lawrence, T(homas) E(dward)

Ross, Martin
See Martin, Violet Florence
See also DLB 135

Ross, (James) Sinclair 1908- **CLC 13; DAC; DAM MST; SSC 24**
See also CA 73-76; DLB 88

Rossetti, Christina (Georgina) 1830-1894
NCLC 2, 50, 66; DA; DAB; DAC; DAM MST, POET; PC 7; WLC
See also DLB 35, 163; MAICYA; SATA 20

Rossetti, Dante Gabriel 1828-1882 **NCLC 4; DA; DAB; DAC; DAM MST, POET; WLC**
See also CDBLB 1832-1890; DLB 35

Rossner, Judith (Perelman) 1935-**CLC 6, 9, 29**
See also AITN 2; BEST 90:3; CA 17-20R;
CANR 18, 51; DLB 6; INT CANR-18;
MTCW

Rostand, Edmond (Eugene Alexis) 1868-1918
TCLC 6, 37; DA; DAB; DAC; DAM DRAM, MST
See also CA 104; 126; MTCW

Roth, Henry 1906-1995 ..... **CLC 2, 6, 11, 104**
See also CA 11-12; 149; CANR 38; CAP 1;
DLB 28; MTCW

Roth, Philip (Milton) 1933-**CLC 1, 2, 3, 4, 6, 9, 15, 22, 31, 47, 66, 86; DA; DAB; DAC; DAM MST, NOV, POP; SSC 26**
See also BEST 90:3; CA 1-4R; CANR 1, 22, 36, 55; CDALB 1968-1988; DLB 2, 28, 173;
DLBY 82; MTCW

Rothenberg, Jerome 1931- .... **CLC 6, 57**
See also CA 45-48; CANR 1; DLB 5

Roumain, Jacques (Jean Baptiste) 1907-1944
TCLC 19; BLC; DAM MULT
See also BW 1; CA 117; 125

Rourke, Constance (Mayfield) 1885-1941
TCLC 12
See also CA 107; YABC 1

Rousseau, Jean-Baptiste 1671-1741 ..... **LC 9**

Rousseau, Jean-Jacques 1712-1778**LC 14, 36; DA; DAB; DAC; DAM MST; WLC**

Roussel, Raymond 1877-1933 .... **TCLC 20**
See also CA 117

Rovit, Earl (Herbert) 1927- .... **CLC 7**
See also CA 5-8R; CANR 12

Rowe, Nicholas 1674-1718 .... **LC 8**
See also DLB 84

Rowley, Ames Dorrance
See Lovecraft, H(oward) P(hillips)

Rowson, Susanna Haswell 1762(?)-1824
NCLC 5
See also DLB 37

Roy, Gabrielle 1909-1983 **CLC 10, 14; DAB; DAC; DAM MST**
See also CA 53-56; 110; CANR 5, 61; DLB 68;
MTCW

Rozewicz, Tadeusz 1921- ...**CLC 9, 23; DAM POET**
See also CA 108; CANR 36; MTCW

Ruark, Gibbons 1941- ....**CLC 3**
See also CA 33-36R; CAAS 23; CANR 14, 31, 57; DLB 120

Rubens, Bernice (Ruth) 1923- .... **CLC 19, 31**
See also CA 25-28R; CANR 33; DLB 14;
MTCW

Rubin, Harold
See Robbins, Harold

Rudkin, (James) David 1936- .... **CLC 14**
See also CA 89-92; DLB 13

Rudnik, Raphael 1933- ....**CLC 7**
See also CA 29-32R

Ruffian, M.
See Hasek, Jaroslav (Matej Frantisek)

Ruiz, Jose Martinez ....**CLC 11**
See also Martinez Ruiz, Jose

Rukeyser, Muriel 1913-1980**CLC 6, 10, 15, 27; DAM POET; PC 12**
See also CA 5-8R; 93-96; CANR 26, 60; DLB 48; MTCW; SATA-Obit 22

Rule, Jane (Vance) 1931- .... **CLC 27**
See also CA 25-28R; CAAS 18; CANR 12; DLB 60

Rulfo, Juan 1918-1986 .... **CLC 8, 80; DAM MULT; HLC; SSC 25**
See also CA 85-88; 118; CANR 26; DLB 113; HW; MTCW

Rumi, Jalal al-Din 1297-1373 .... **CMLC 20**

Runeberg, Johan 1804-1877 .... **NCLC 41**

Runyon, (Alfred) Damon 1884(?)-1946**T C L C 10**
See also CA 107; DLB 11, 86, 171

Rush, Norman 1933- .... **CLC 44**
See also CA 121; 126; INT 126

Rushdie, (Ahmed) Salman 1947-**CLC 23, 31, 55, 100; DAB; DAC; DAM MST, NOV, POP; WLCS**
See also BEST 89:3; CA 108; 111; CANR 33, 56; INT 111; MTCW

Rushforth, Peter (Scott) 1945- .... **CLC 19**
See also CA 101

Ruskin, John 1819-1900 .... **TCLC 63**
See also CA 114; 129; CDBLB 1832-1890; DLB 55, 163; SATA 24

Russ, Joanna 1937- .... **CLC 15**
See also CA 25-28R; CANR 11, 31; DLB 8; MTCW

Russell, George William 1867-1935
See Baker, Jean H.
See also CA 104; 153; CDBLB 1890-1914; DAM POET

Russell, (Henry) Ken(neth Alfred) 1927-**C L C 16**
See also CA 105

Russell, Willy 1947- .... **CLC 60**

Rutherford, Mark .... **TCLC 25**
See also White, William Hale
See also DLB 18

Ruyslinck, Ward 1929- .... **CLC 14**
See also Belser, Reimond Karel Maria de

Ryan, Cornelius (John) 1920-1974 ..... **CLC 7**
See also CA 69-72; 53-56; CANR 38

Ryan, Michael 1946- .... **CLC 65**
See also CA 49-52; DLBY 82

Ryan, Tim
See Dent, Lester

Rybakov, Anatoli (Naumovich) 1911-**CLC 23, 53**
See also CA 126; 135; SATA 79

Ryder, Jonathan
See Ludlum, Robert

Ryga, George 1932-1987**CLC 14; DAC; DAM MST**
See also CA 101; 124; CANR 43; DLB 60

S. H.
See Hartmann, Sadakichi

S. S.
See Sassoon, Siegfried (Lorraine)

Saba, Umberto 1883-1957 .... **TCLC 33**
See also CA 144; DLB 114

Sabatini, Rafael 1875-1950 .... **TCLC 47**

Sabato, Ernesto (R.) 1911-**CLC 10, 23; DAM MULT; HLC**
See also CA 97-100; CANR 32; DLB 145; HW; MTCW

Sacastru, Martin
See Bioy Casares, Adolfo

Sacher-Masoch, Leopold von 1836(?)-1895 **NCLC 31**

Sachs, Marilyn (Stickle) 1927- .... **CLC 35**
See also AAYA 2; CA 17-20R; CANR 13, 47; CLR 2; JRDA; MAICYA; SAAS 2; SATA 3, 68

Sachs, Nelly 1891-1970 .... **CLC 14, 98**
See also CA 17-18; 25-28R; CAP 2

Sackler, Howard (Oliver) 1929-1982 **CLC 14**
See also CA 61-64; 108; CANR 30; DLB 7

Sacks, Oliver (Wolf) 1933- .... **CLC 67**
See also CA 53-56; CANR 28, 50; INT CANR-28; MTCW

Sadakichi
See Hartmann, Sadakichi

Sade, Donatien Alphonse Francois Comte 1740-1814 .... **NCLC 47**

Sadoff, Ira 1945- .... **CLC 9**
See also CA 53-56; CANR 5, 21; DLB 120

Saetone
See Camus, Albert

Safire, William 1929- .... **CLC 10**
See also CA 17-20R; CANR 31, 54

Sagan, Carl (Edward) 1934-1996 ...... **CLC 30**
See also AAYA 2; CA 25-28R; 155; CANR 11, 36; MTCW; SATA 58; SATA-Obit 94

Sagan, Francoise .... **CLC 3, 6, 9, 17, 36**
See also Quoirez, Francoise
See also DLB 83

Sahgal, Nayantara (Pandit) 1927- .... **CLC 41**
See also CA 9-12R; CANR 11

Saint, H(arry) F. 1941- .... **CLC 50**
See also CA 127

St. Aubin de Teran, Lisa 1953-
See Teran, Lisa St. Aubin de
See also CA 118; 126; INT 126

Saint Birgitta of Sweden c. 1303-1373**C M L C 24**

Sainte-Beuve, Charles Augustin 1804-1869 **NCLC 5**

Saint-Exupery, Antoine (Jean Baptiste Marie Roger) de 1900-1944**TCLC 2, 56; DAM NOV; WLC**
See also CA 108; 132; CLR 10; DLB 72; MAICYA; MTCW; SATA 20

St. John, David
See Hunt, E(verette) Howard, (Jr.)

Saint-John Perse
See Leger, (Marie-Rene Auguste) Alexis Saint-Leger

Saintsbury, George (Edward Bateman) 1845-1933 .... **TCLC 31**
See also CA 160; DLB 57, 149

Sait Faik .... **TCLC 23**
See also Abasiyanik, Sait Faik

Saki .... **TCLC 3; SSC 12**
See also Munro, H(ector) H(ugh)

Sala, George Augustus .... **NCLC 46**

Salama, Hannu 1936- .... **CLC 18**

Salamanca, J(ack) R(ichard) 1922-**CLC 4, 15**
See also CA 25-28R

Sale, J. Kirkpatrick
See Sale, Kirkpatrick

Sale, Kirkpatrick 1937- .... **CLC 68**
See also CA 13-16R; CANR 10

Salinas, Luis Omar 1937- ...... **CLC 90; DAM MULT; HLC**
See also CA 131; DLB 82; HW

Salinas (y Serrano), Pedro 1891(?)-1951 **TCLC 17**
See also CA 117; DLB 134

Salinger, J(erome) D(avid) 1919-**CLC 1, 3, 8, 12, 55, 56; DA; DAB; DAC; DAM MST, NOV, POP; SSC 2, 28; WLC**
See also AAYA 2; CA 5-8R; CANR 39; CDALB 1941-1968; CLR 18; DLB 2, 102, 173; MAICYA; MTCW; SATA 67

Salisbury, John
See Caute, David

Salter, James 1925- .... **CLC 7, 52, 59**
See also CA 73-76; DLB 130

Saltus, Edgar (Everton) 1855-1921 . **TCLC 8**
See also CA 105

Saltykov, Mikhail Evgrafovich 1826-1889 **NCLC 16**

Samarakis, Antonis 1919- .... **CLC 5**
See also CA 25-28R; CAAS 16; CANR 36

Sanchez, Florencio 1875-1910 .... **TCLC 37**
See also CA 153; HW

Sanchez, Luis Rafael 1936- .... **CLC 23**
See also CA 128; DLB 145; HW

Sanchez, Sonia 1934- ..... **CLC 5; BLC; DAM MULT; PC 9**
See also BW 2; CA 33-36R; CANR 24, 49; CLR 18; DLB 41; DLBD 8; MAICYA; MTCW; SATA 22

Sand, George 1804-1876**NCLC 2, 42, 57; DA; DAB; DAC; DAM MST, NOV; WLC**
See also DLB 119

Sandburg, Carl (August) 1878-1967**CLC 1, 4, 10, 15, 35; DA; DAB; DAC; DAM MST, POET; PC 2; WLC**
See also CA 5-8R; 25-28R; CANR 35; CDALB 1865-1917; DLB 17, 54; MAICYA; MTCW; SATA 8

Sandburg, Charles
See Sandburg, Carl (August)

Sandburg, Charles A.
See Sandburg, Carl (August)

Sanders, (James) Ed(ward) 1939- .... **CLC 53**
See also CA 13-16R; CAAS 21; CANR 13, 44; DLB 16

Sanders, Lawrence 1920-**CLC 41; DAM POP**
See also BEST 89:4; CA 81-84; CANR 33, 62; MTCW

Sanders, Noah
See Blount, Roy (Alton), Jr.

Sanders, Winston P.
See Anderson, Poul (William)

Sandoz, Mari(e Susette) 1896-1966 ..**CLC 28**
See also CA 1-4R; 25-28R; CANR 17; DLB 9; MTCW; SATA 5

Saner, Reg(inald Anthony) 1931- .... **CLC 9**
See also CA 65-68

Sannazaro, Jacopo 1456(?)-1530 .... **LC 8**

Sansom, William 1912-1976 **CLC 2, 6; DAM NOV; SSC 21**
See also CA 5-8R; 65-68; CANR 42; DLB 139; MTCW

Santayana, George 1863-1952 .... **TCLC 40**
See also CA 115; DLB 54, 71; DLBD 13

Santiago, Danny .... **CLC 33**
See also James, Daniel (Lewis)
See also DLB 122

Santmyer, Helen Hoover 1895-1986 . **CLC 33**
See also CA 1-4R; 118; CANR 15, 33; DLBY 84; MTCW

Santoka, Taneda 1882-1940 .... **TCLC 72**

Santos, Bienvenido N(uqui) 1911-1996 . **C L C 22; DAM MULT**
See also CA 101; 151; CANR 19, 46

Sapper .... **TCLC 44**
See also McNeile, Herman Cyril

Sapphire 1950- .... **CLC 99**

Sappho fl. 6th cent. B.C.- ...... **CMLC 3; DAM POET; PC 5**
See also DLB 176

Sarduy, Severo 1937-1993 .... **CLC 6, 97**
See also CA 89-92; 142; CANR 58; DLB 113; HW

Sargeson, Frank 1903-1982 .... **CLC 31**
See also CA 25-28R; 106; CANR 38

Sarmiento, Felix Ruben Garcia
　　See Dario, Ruben
Saroyan, William 1908-1981CLC 1, 8, 10, 29,
　　34, 56; DA; DAB; DAC; DAM DRAM,
　　MST, NOV; SSC 21; WLC
　　See also CA 5-8R; 103; CANR 30; DLB 7, 9,
　　86; DLBY 81; MTCW; SATA 23; SATA-Obit
　　24
Sarraute, Nathalie 1900-CLC 1, 2, 4, 8, 10, 31,
　　80
　　See also CA 9-12R; CANR 23; DLB 83; MTCW
Sarton, (Eleanor) May 1912-1995CLC 4, 14,
　　49, 91; DAM POET
　　See also CA 1-4R; 149; CANR 1, 34, 55; DLB
　　48; DLBY 81; INT CANR-34; MTCW;
　　SATA 36; SATA-Obit 86
Sartre, Jean-Paul 1905-1980CLC 1, 4, 7, 9, 13,
　　18, 24, 44, 50, 52; DA; DAB; DAC; DAM
　　DRAM, MST, NOV; DC 3; WLC
　　See also CA 9-12R; 97-100; CANR 21; DLB
　　72; MTCW
Sassoon, Siegfried (Lorraine) 1886-1967C L C
　　36; DAB; DAM MST, NOV, POET; PC 12
　　See also CA 104; 25-28R; CANR 36; DLB 20;
　　MTCW
Satterfield, Charles
　　See Pohl, Frederik
Saul, John (W. III) 1942-CLC 46; DAM NOV,
　　POP
　　See also AAYA 10; BEST 90:4; CA 81-84;
　　CANR 16, 40
Saunders, Caleb
　　See Heinlein, Robert A(nson)
Saura (Atares), Carlos 1932- .... CLC 20
　　See also CA 114; 131; HW
Sauser-Hall, Frederic 1887-1961 ..... CLC 18
　　See also Cendrars, Blaise
　　See also CA 102; 93-96; CANR 36, 62; MTCW
Saussure, Ferdinand de 1857-1913 TCLC 49
Savage, Catharine
　　See Brosman, Catharine Savage
Savage, Thomas 1915- .... CLC 40
　　See also CA 126; 132; CAAS 15; INT 132
Savan, Glenn 19(?)- .... CLC 50
Sayers, Dorothy L(eigh) 1893-1957 TCLC 2,
　　15; DAM POP
　　See also CA 104; 119; CANR 60; CDBLB 1914-
　　1945; DLB 10, 36, 77, 100; MTCW
Sayers, Valerie 1952- .... CLC 50
　　See also CA 134; CANR 61
Sayles, John (Thomas) 1950- . CLC 7, 10, 14
　　See also CA 57-60; CANR 41; DLB 44
Scammell, Michael 1935- .... CLC 34
　　See also CA 156
Scannell, Vernon 1922- .... CLC 49
　　See also CA 5-8R; CANR 8, 24, 57; DLB 27;
　　SATA 59
Scarlett, Susan
　　See Streatfeild, (Mary) Noel
Schaeffer, Susan Fromberg 1941- CLC 6, 11,
　　22
　　See also CA 49-52; CANR 18; DLB 28; MTCW;
　　SATA 22
Schary, Jill
　　See Robinson, Jill
Schell, Jonathan 1943- .... CLC 35
　　See also CA 73-76; CANR 12
Schelling, Friedrich Wilhelm Joseph von 1775-
　　1854 .... NCLC 30
　　See also DLB 90
Schendel, Arthur van 1874-1946 ... TCLC 56
Scherer, Jean-Marie Maurice 1920-
　　See Rohmer, Eric

See also CA 110
Schevill, James (Erwin) 1920- .... CLC 7
　　See also CA 5-8R; CAAS 12
Schiller, Friedrich 1759-1805NCLC 39; DAM
　　DRAM
　　See also DLB 94
Schisgal, Murray (Joseph) 1926- .... CLC 6
　　See also CA 21-24R; CANR 48
Schlee, Ann 1934- .... CLC 35
　　See also CA 101; CANR 29; SATA 44; SATA-
　　Brief 36
Schlegel, August Wilhelm von 1767-1845
　　NCLC 15
　　See also DLB 94
Schlegel, Friedrich 1772-1829 .... NCLC 45
　　See also DLB 90
Schlegel, Johann Elias (von) 1719(?)-1749L C
　　5
Schlesinger, Arthur M(eier), Jr. 1917-CLC 84
　　See also AITN 1; CA 1-4R; CANR 1, 28, 58;
　　DLB 17; INT CANR-28; MTCW; SATA 61
Schmidt, Arno (Otto) 1914-1979 ..... CLC 56
　　See also CA 128; 109; DLB 69
Schmitz, Aron Hector 1861-1928
　　See Svevo, Italo
　　See also CA 104; 122; MTCW
Schnackenberg, Gjertrud 1953- .... CLC 40
　　See also CA 116; DLB 120
Schneider, Leonard Alfred 1925-1966
　　See Bruce, Lenny
　　See also CA 89-92
Schnitzler, Arthur 1862-1931TCLC 4; SSC 15
　　See also CA 104; DLB 81, 118
Schoenberg, Arnold 1874-1951 ...... TCLC 75
　　See also CA 109
Schonberg, Arnold
　　See Schoenberg, Arnold
Schopenhauer, Arthur 1788-1860 .. NCLC 51
　　See also DLB 90
Schor, Sandra (M.) 1932(?)-1990 ...... CLC 65
　　See also CA 132
Schorer, Mark 1908-1977 .... CLC 9
　　See also CA 5-8R; 73-76; CANR 7; DLB 103
Schrader, Paul (Joseph) 1946- .... CLC 26
　　See also CA 37-40R; CANR 41; DLB 44
Schreiner, Olive (Emilie Albertina) 1855-1920
　　TCLC 9
　　See also CA 105; DLB 18, 156
Schulberg, Budd (Wilson) 1914-.. CLC 7, 48
　　See also CA 25-28R; CANR 19; DLB 6, 26,
　　28; DLBY 81
Schulz, Bruno 1892-1942TCLC 5, 51; SSC 13
　　See also CA 115; 123
Schulz, Charles M(onroe) 1922- .... CLC 12
　　See also CA 9-12R; CANR 6; INT CANR-6;
　　SATA 10
Schumacher, E(rnst) F(riedrich) 1911-1977
　　CLC 80
　　See also CA 81-84; 73-76; CANR 34
Schuyler, James Marcus 1923-1991CLC 5, 23;
　　DAM POET
　　See also CA 101; 134; DLB 5, 169; INT 101
Schwartz, Delmore (David) 1913-1966CLC 2,
　　4, 10, 45, 87; PC 8
　　See also CA 17-18; 25-28R; CANR 35; CAP 2;
　　DLB 28, 48; MTCW
Schwartz, Ernst
　　See Ozu, Yasujiro
Schwartz, John Burnham 1965- .... CLC 59
　　See also CA 132
Schwartz, Lynne Sharon 1939- .... CLC 31
　　See also CA 103; CANR 44
Schwartz, Muriel A.

See Eliot, T(homas) S(tearns)
Schwarz-Bart, Andre 1928- .... CLC 2, 4
　　See also CA 89-92
Schwarz-Bart, Simone 1938- .... CLC 7
　　See also BW 2; CA 97-100
Schwob, (Mayer Andre) Marcel 1867-1905
　　TCLC 20
　　See also CA 117; DLB 123
Sciascia, Leonardo 1921-1989 . CLC 8, 9, 41
　　See also CA 85-88; 130; CANR 35; DLB 177;
　　MTCW
Scoppettone, Sandra 1936- .... CLC 26
　　See also AAYA 11; CA 5-8R; CANR 41; SATA
　　9, 92
Scorsese, Martin 1942- .... CLC 20, 89
　　See also CA 110; 114; CANR 46
Scotland, Jay
　　See Jakes, John (William)
Scott, Duncan Campbell 1862-1947 TCLC 6;
　　DAC
　　See also CA 104; 153; DLB 92
Scott, Evelyn 1893-1963 .... CLC 43
　　See also CA 104; 112; DLB 9, 48
Scott, F(rancis) R(eginald) 1899-1985CLC 22
　　See also CA 101; 114; DLB 88; INT 101
Scott, Frank
　　See Scott, F(rancis) R(eginald)
Scott, Joanna 1960- .... CLC 50
　　See also CA 126; CANR 53
Scott, Paul (Mark) 1920-1978 ...... CLC 9, 60
　　See also CA 81-84; 77-80; CANR 33; DLB 14;
　　MTCW
Scott, Walter 1771-1832NCLC 15; DA; DAB;
　　DAC; DAM MST, NOV, POET; PC 13;
　　WLC
　　See also AAYA 22; CDBLB 1789-1832; DLB
　　93, 107, 116, 144, 159; YABC 2
Scribe, (Augustin) Eugene 1791-1861 N C L C
　　16; DAM DRAM; DC 5
Scrum, R.
　　See Crumb, R(obert)
Scudery, Madeleine de 1607-1701 .... LC 2
Scum
　　See Crumb, R(obert)
Scumbag, Little Bobby
　　See Crumb, R(obert)
Seabrook, John
　　See Hubbard, L(afayette) Ron(ald)
Sealy, I. Allan 1951- .... CLC 55
Search, Alexander
　　See Pessoa, Fernando (Antonio Nogueira)
Sebastian, Lee
　　See Silverberg, Robert
Sebastian Owl
　　See Thompson, Hunter S(tockton)
Sebestyen, Ouida 1924-.................... CLC 30
　　See also AAYA 8; CA 107; CANR 40; CLR 17;
　　JRDA; MAICYA; SAAS 10; SATA 39
Secundus, H. Scriblerus
　　See Fielding, Henry
Sedges, John
　　See Buck, Pearl S(ydenstricker)
Sedgwick, Catharine Maria 1789-1867N C L C
　　19
　　See also DLB 1, 74
Seelye, John 1931- .... CLC 7
Seferiades, Giorgos Stylianou 1900-1971
　　See Seferis, George
　　See also CA 5-8R; 33-36R; CANR 5, 36;
　　MTCW
Seferis, George .... CLC 5, 11
　　See also Seferiades, Giorgos Stylianou
Segal, Erich (Wolf) 1937- ..CLC 3, 10; DAM

POP
See also BEST 89:1; CA 25-28R; CANR 20, 36; DLBY 86; INT CANR-20; MTCW

Seger, Bob 1945- .... **CLC 35**

Seghers, Anna ....**CLC 7**
See also Radvanyi, Netty
See also DLB 69

Seidel, Frederick (Lewis) 1936- .... **CLC 18**
See also CA 13-16R; CANR 8; DLBY 84

Seifert, Jaroslav 1901-1986 .. **CLC 34, 44, 93**
See also CA 127; MTCW

Sei Shonagon c. 966-1017(?) .... **CMLC 6**

Selby, Hubert, Jr. 1928-**CLC 1, 2, 4, 8; SSC 20**
See also CA 13-16R; CANR 33; DLB 2

Selzer, Richard 1928- .... **CLC 74**
See also CA 65-68; CANR 14

Sembene, Ousmane
See Ousmane, Sembene

Senancour, Etienne Pivert de 1770-1846
NCLC 16
See also DLB 119

Sender, Ramon (Jose) 1902-1982**CLC 8; DAM MULT; HLC**
See also CA 5-8R; 105; CANR 8; HW; MTCW

Seneca, Lucius Annaeus 4B.C.-65 **CMLC 6; DAM DRAM; DC 5**

Senghor, Leopold Sedar 1906-**CLC 54; BLC; DAM MULT, POET**
See also BW 2; CA 116; 125; CANR 47; MTCW

Serling, (Edward) Rod(man) 1924-1975**C L C 30**
See also AAYA 14; AITN 1; CA 65-68; 57-60; DLB 26

Serna, Ramon Gomez de la
See Gomez de la Serna, Ramon

Serpieres
See Guillevic, (Eugene)

Service, Robert
See Service, Robert W(illiam)
See also DAB; DLB 92

Service, Robert W(illiam) 1874(?)-1958**TCLC 15; DA; DAC; DAM MST, POET; WLC**
See also Service, Robert
See also CA 115; 140; SATA 20

Seth, Vikram 1952-**CLC 43, 90; DAM MULT**
See also CA 121; 127; CANR 50; DLB 120; INT 127

Seton, Cynthia Propper 1926-1982 . **CLC 27**
See also CA 5-8R; 108; CANR 7

Seton, Ernest (Evan) Thompson 1860-1946
TCLC 31
See also CA 109; DLB 92; DLBD 13; JRDA; SATA 18

Seton-Thompson, Ernest
See Seton, Ernest (Evan) Thompson

Settle, Mary Lee 1918- .... **CLC 19, 61**
See also CA 89-92; CAAS 1; CANR 44; DLB 6; INT 89-92

Seuphor, Michel
See Arp, Jean

Sevigne, Marie (de Rabutin-Chantal) Marquise de 1626-1696 .... **LC 11**

Sewall, Samuel 1652-1730 .... **LC 38**
See also DLB 24

Sexton, Anne (Harvey) 1928-1974**CLC 2, 4, 6, 8, 10, 15, 53; DA; DAB; DAC; DAM MST, POET; PC 2; WLC**
See also CA 1-4R; 53-56; CABS 2; CANR 3, 36; CDALB 1941-1968; DLB 5, 169; MTCW; SATA 10

Shaara, Michael (Joseph, Jr.) 1929-1988**C L C 15; DAM POP**
See also AITN 1; CA 102; 125; CANR 52;

DLBY 83

Shackleton, C. C.
See Aldiss, Brian W(ilson)

Shacochis, Bob ....**CLC 39**
See also Shacochis, Robert G.

Shacochis, Robert G. 1951-
See Shacochis, Bob
See also CA 119; 124; INT 124

Shaffer, Anthony (Joshua) 1926- .... **CLC 19; DAM DRAM**
See also CA 110; 116; DLB 13

Shaffer, Peter (Levin) 1926-**CLC 5, 14, 18, 37, 60; DAB; DAM DRAM, MST; DC 7**
See also CA 25-28R; CANR 25, 47; CDBLB 1960 to Present; DLB 13; MTCW

Shakey, Bernard
See Young, Neil

Shalamov, Varlam (Tikhonovich) 1907(?)-1982
CLC 18
See also CA 129; 105

Shamlu, Ahmad 1925- ....**CLC 10**

Shammas, Anton 1951- ....**CLC 55**

Shange, Ntozake 1948-**CLC 8, 25, 38, 74; BLC; DAM DRAM, MULT; DC 3**
See also AAYA 9; BW 2; CA 85-88; CABS 3; CANR 27, 48; DLB 38; MTCW

Shanley, John Patrick 1950- ....**CLC 75**
See also CA 128; 133

Shapcott, Thomas W(illiam) 1935- ... **CLC 38**
See also CA 69-72; CANR 49

Shapiro, Jane ....**CLC 76**

Shapiro, Karl (Jay) 1913-... **CLC 4, 8, 15, 53**
See also CA 1-4R; CAAS 6; CANR 1, 36; DLB 48; MTCW

Sharp, William 1855-1905 ....**TCLC 39**
See also CA 160; DLB 156

Sharpe, Thomas Ridley 1928-
See Sharpe, Tom
See also CA 114; 122; INT 122

Sharpe, Tom ....**CLC 36**
See also Sharpe, Thomas Ridley
See also DLB 14

Shaw, Bernard ....**TCLC 45**
See also Shaw, George Bernard
See also BW 1

Shaw, G. Bernard
See Shaw, George Bernard

Shaw, George Bernard 1856-1950**TCLC 3, 9, 21; DA; DAB; DAC; DAM DRAM, MST; WLC**
See also Shaw, Bernard
See also CA 104; 128; CDBLB 1914-1945; DLB 10, 57; MTCW

Shaw, Henry Wheeler 1818-1885 ..**NCLC 15**
See also DLB 11

Shaw, Irwin 1913-1984 **CLC 7, 23, 34; DAM DRAM, POP**
See also AITN 1; CA 13-16R; 112; CANR 21; CDALB 1941-1968; DLB 6, 102; DLBY 84; MTCW

Shaw, Robert 1927-1978 ....**CLC 5**
See also AITN 1; CA 1-4R; 81-84; CANR 4; DLB 13, 14

Shaw, T. E.
See Lawrence, T(homas) E(dward)

Shawn, Wallace 1943- ....**CLC 41**
See also CA 112

Shea, Lisa 1953- ....**CLC 86**
See also CA 147

Sheed, Wilfrid (John Joseph) 1930-**CLC 2, 4, 10, 53**
See also CA 65-68; CANR 30; DLB 6; MTCW

Sheldon, Alice Hastings Bradley 1915(?)-1987

See Tiptree, James, Jr.
See also CA 108; 122; CANR 34; INT 108; MTCW

Sheldon, John
See Bloch, Robert (Albert)

Shelley, Mary Wollstonecraft (Godwin) 1797-1851**NCLC 14, 59; DA; DAB; DAC; DAM MST, NOV; WLC**
See also AAYA 20; CDBLB 1789-1832; DLB 110, 116, 159, 178; SATA 29

Shelley, Percy Bysshe 1792-1822 . **NCLC 18; DA; DAB; DAC; DAM MST, POET; PC 14; WLC**
See also CDBLB 1789-1832; DLB 96, 110, 158

Shepard, Jim 1956- ....**CLC 36**
See also CA 137; CANR 59; SATA 90

Shepard, Lucius 1947- ....**CLC 34**
See also CA 128; 141

Shepard, Sam 1943-**CLC 4, 6, 17, 34, 41, 44; DAM DRAM; DC 5**
See also AAYA 1; CA 69-72; CABS 3; CANR 22; DLB 7; MTCW

Shepherd, Michael
See Ludlum, Robert

Sherburne, Zoa (Morin) 1912- ....**CLC 30**
See also AAYA 13; CA 1-4R; CANR 3, 37; MAICYA; SAAS 18; SATA 3

Sheridan, Frances 1724-1766 ....**LC 7**
See also DLB 39, 84

Sheridan, Richard Brinsley 1751-1816**N C L C 5; DA; DAB; DAC; DAM DRAM, MST; DC 1; WLC**
See also CDBLB 1660-1789; DLB 89

Sherman, Jonathan Marc ....**CLC 55**

Sherman, Martin 1941(?)- ....**CLC 19**
See also CA 116; 123

Sherwin, Judith Johnson 1936- ... **CLC 7, 15**
See also CA 25-28R; CANR 34

Sherwood, Frances 1940- ....**CLC 81**
See also CA 146

Sherwood, Robert E(mmet) 1896-1955**T C L C 3; DAM DRAM**
See also CA 104; 153; DLB 7, 26

Shestov, Lev 1866-1938 ....**TCLC 56**

Shevchenko, Taras 1814-1861 ....**NCLC 54**

Shiel, M(atthew) P(hipps) 1865-1947**TCLC 8**
See also Holmes, Gordon
See also CA 106; 160; DLB 153

Shields, Carol 1935- ....**CLC 91; DAC**
See also CA 81-84; CANR 51

Shields, David 1956- ....**CLC 97**
See also CA 124; CANR 48

Shiga, Naoya 1883-1971 ..... **CLC 33; SSC 23**
See also CA 101; 33-36R; DLB 180

Shilts, Randy 1951-1994 ....**CLC 85**
See also AAYA 19; CA 115; 127; 144; CANR 45; INT 127

Shimazaki, Haruki 1872-1943
See Shimazaki Toson
See also CA 105; 134

Shimazaki Toson 1872-1943 .... **TCLC 5**
See also Shimazaki, Haruki
See also DLB 180

Sholokhov, Mikhail (Aleksandrovich) 1905-1984 .... **CLC 7, 15**
See also CA 101; 112; MTCW; SATA-Obit 36

Shone, Patric
See Hanley, James

Shreve, Susan Richards 1939-...........**CLC 23**
See also CA 49-52; CAAS 5; CANR 5, 38; MAICYA; SATA 46, 95; SATA-Brief 41

Shue, Larry 1946-1985**CLC 52; DAM DRAM**
See also CA 145; 117

Shu-Jen, Chou 1881-1936
See Lu Hsun
See also CA 104
Shulman, Alix Kates 1932- .... **CLC 2, 10**
See also CA 29-32R; CANR 43; SATA 7
Shuster, Joe 1914- .... **CLC 21**
Shute, Nevil .... **CLC 30**
See also Norway, Nevil Shute
Shuttle, Penelope (Diane) 1947- .... **CLC 7**
See also CA 93-96; CANR 39; DLB 14, 40
Sidney, Mary 1561-1621 .... **LC 19, 39**
Sidney, Sir Philip 1554-1586 **LC 19, 39; DA;**
DAB; DAC; DAM MST, POET
See also CDBLB Before 1660; DLB 167
Siegel, Jerome 1914-1996 .... **CLC 21**
See also CA 116; 151
Siegel, Jerry
See Siegel, Jerome
Sienkiewicz, Henryk (Adam Alexander Pius)
1846-1916 .... **TCLC 3**
See also CA 104; 134
Sierra, Gregorio Martinez
See Martinez Sierra, Gregorio
Sierra, Maria (de la O'LeJarraga) Martinez
See Martinez Sierra, Maria (de la O'LeJarraga)
Sigal, Clancy 1926- .... **CLC 7**
See also CA 1-4R
Sigourney, Lydia Howard (Huntley) 1791-1865
NCLC 21
See also DLB 1, 42, 73
Siguenza y Gongora, Carlos de 1645-1700 **LC 8**
Sigurjonsson, Johann 1880-1919 ... **TCLC 27**
Sikelianos, Angelos 1884-1951 .... **TCLC 39**
Silkin, Jon 1930- .... **CLC 2, 6, 43**
See also CA 5-8R; CAAS 5; DLB 27
Silko, Leslie (Marmon) 1948- **CLC 23, 74; DA;**
DAC; DAM MST, MULT, POP; WLCS
See also AAYA 14; CA 115; 122; CANR 45;
DLB 143, 175; NNAL
Sillanpaa, Frans Eemil 1888-1964 ... **CLC 19**
See also CA 129; 93-96; MTCW
Sillitoe, Alan 1928- .... **CLC 1, 3, 6, 10, 19, 57**
See also AITN 1; CA 9-12R; CAAS 2; CANR
8, 26, 55; CDBLB 1960 to Present; DLB 14,
139; MTCW; SATA 61
Silone, Ignazio 1900-1978 .... **CLC 4**
See also CA 25-28; 81-84; CANR 34; CAP 2;
MTCW
Silver, Joan Micklin 1935- .... **CLC 20**
See also CA 114; 121; INT 121
Silver, Nicholas
See Faust, Frederick (Schiller)
Silverberg, Robert 1935- **CLC 7; DAM POP**
See also CA 1-4R; CAAS 3; CANR 1, 20, 36;
DLB 8; INT CANR-20; MAICYA; MTCW;
SATA 13, 91
Silverstein, Alvin 1933- .... **CLC 17**
See also CA 49-52; CANR 2; CLR 25; JRDA;
MAICYA; SATA 8, 69
Silverstein, Virginia B(arbara Opshelor) 1937-
CLC 17
See also CA 49-52; CANR 2; CLR 25; JRDA;
MAICYA; SATA 8, 69
Sim, Georges
See Simenon, Georges (Jacques Christian)
Simak, Clifford D(onald) 1904-1988 **CLC 1, 55**
See also CA 1-4R; 125; CANR 1, 35; DLB 8;
MTCW; SATA-Obit 56
Simenon, Georges (Jacques Christian) 1903-
1989 .. **CLC 1, 2, 3, 8, 18, 47; DAM POP**
See also CA 85-88; 129; CANR 35; DLB 72;
DLBY 89; MTCW

Simic, Charles 1938- .... **CLC 6, 9, 22, 49, 68;**
DAM POET
See also CA 29-32R; CAAS 4; CANR 12, 33,
52, 61; DLB 105
Simmel, Georg 1858-1918 .... **TCLC 64**
See also CA 157
Simmons, Charles (Paul) 1924- .... **CLC 57**
See also CA 89-92; INT 89-92
Simmons, Dan 1948- ...... **CLC 44; DAM POP**
See also AAYA 16; CA 138; CANR 53
Simmons, James (Stewart Alexander) 1933-
CLC 43
See also CA 105; CAAS 21; DLB 40
Simms, William Gilmore 1806-1870 **NCLC 3**
See also DLB 3, 30, 59, 73
Simon, Carly 1945- .... **CLC 26**
See also CA 105
Simon, Claude 1913- **CLC 4, 9, 15, 39; DAM**
NOV
See also CA 89-92; CANR 33; DLB 83; MTCW
Simon, (Marvin) Neil 1927- **CLC 6, 11, 31, 39,**
70; DAM DRAM
See also AITN 1; CA 21-24R; CANR 26, 54;
DLB 7; MTCW
Simon, Paul (Frederick) 1941(?)- ...... **CLC 17**
See also CA 116; 153
Simonon, Paul 1956(?)- .... **CLC 30**
Simpson, Harriette
See Arnow, Harriette (Louisa) Simpson
Simpson, Louis (Aston Marantz) 1923- **CLC 4,**
7, 9, 32; DAM POET
See also CA 1-4R; CAAS 4; CANR 1, 61; DLB
5; MTCW
Simpson, Mona (Elizabeth) 1957- .... **CLC 44**
See also CA 122; 135
Simpson, N(orman) F(rederick) 1919- **CLC 29**
See also CA 13-16R; DLB 13
Sinclair, Andrew (Annandale) 1935- . **CLC 2,**
14
See also CA 9-12R; CAAS 5; CANR 14, 38;
DLB 14; MTCW
Sinclair, Emil
See Hesse, Hermann
Sinclair, Iain 1943- .... **CLC 76**
See also CA 132
Sinclair, Iain MacGregor
See Sinclair, Iain
Sinclair, Irene
See Griffith, D(avid Lewelyn) W(ark)
Sinclair, Mary Amelia St. Clair 1865(?)-1946
See Sinclair, May
See also CA 104
Sinclair, May .... **TCLC 3, 11**
See also Sinclair, Mary Amelia St. Clair
See also DLB 36, 135
Sinclair, Roy
See Griffith, D(avid Lewelyn) W(ark)
Sinclair, Upton (Beall) 1878-1968 **CLC 1, 11,**
15, 63; DA; DAB; DAC; DAM MST, NOV;
WLC
See also CA 5-8R; 25-28R; CANR 7; CDALB
1929-1941; DLB 9; INT CANR-7; MTCW;
SATA 9
Singer, Isaac
See Singer, Isaac Bashevis
Singer, Isaac Bashevis 1904-1991 **CLC 1, 3, 6,**
9, 11, 15, 23, 38, 69; DA; DAB; DAC; DAM
MST, NOV; SSC 3; WLC
See also AITN 1, 2; CA 1-4R; 134; CANR 1,
39; CDALB 1941-1968; CLR 1; DLB 6, 28,
52; DLBY 91; JRDA; MAICYA; MTCW;
SATA 3, 27; SATA-Obit 68
Singer, Israel Joshua 1893-1944 .... **TCLC 33**

Singh, Khushwant 1915- .... **CLC 11**
See also CA 9-12R; CAAS 9; CANR 6
Singleton, Ann
See Benedict, Ruth (Fulton)
Sinjohn, John
See Galsworthy, John
Sinyavsky, Andrei (Donatevich) 1925-1997
CLC 8
See also CA 85-88; 159
Sirin, V.
See Nabokov, Vladimir (Vladimirovich)
Sissman, L(ouis) E(dward) 1928-1976 **CLC 9,**
18
See also CA 21-24R; 65-68; CANR 13; DLB 5
Sisson, C(harles) H(ubert) 1914- .... **CLC 8**
See also CA 1-4R; CAAS 3; CANR 3, 48; DLB
27
Sitwell, Dame Edith 1887-1964 **CLC 2, 9, 67;**
DAM POET; PC 3
See also CA 9-12R; CANR 35; CDBLB 1945-
1960; DLB 20; MTCW
Siwaarmill, H. P.
See Sharp, William
Sjoewall, Maj 1935- .... **CLC 7**
See also CA 65-68
Sjowall, Maj
See Sjoewall, Maj
Skelton, Robin 1925-1997 .... **CLC 13**
See also AITN 2; CA 5-8R; 160; CAAS 5;
CANR 28; DLB 27, 53
Skolimowski, Jerzy 1938- .... **CLC 20**
See also CA 128
Skram, Amalie (Bertha) 1847-1905 **TCLC 25**
Skvorecky, Josef (Vaclav) 1924- **CLC 15, 39,**
69; DAC; DAM NOV
See also CA 61-64; CAAS 1; CANR 10, 34;
MTCW
Slade, Bernard .... **CLC 11, 46**
See also Newbound, Bernard Slade
See also CAAS 9; DLB 53
Slaughter, Carolyn 1946- .... **CLC 56**
See also CA 85-88
Slaughter, Frank G(ill) 1908- .... **CLC 29**
See also AITN 2; CA 5-8R; CANR 5; INT
CANR-5
Slavitt, David R(ytman) 1935- ..... **CLC 5, 14**
See also CA 21-24R; CAAS 3; CANR 41; DLB
5, 6
Slesinger, Tess 1905-1945 .... **TCLC 10**
See also CA 107; DLB 102
Slessor, Kenneth 1901-1971 .... **CLC 14**
See also CA 102; 89-92
Slowacki, Juliusz 1809-1849 .... **NCLC 15**
Smart, Christopher 1722-1771 ... **LC 3; DAM**
POET; PC 13
See also DLB 109
Smart, Elizabeth 1913-1986 .... **CLC 54**
See also CA 81-84; 118; DLB 88
Smiley, Jane (Graves) 1949- **CLC 53, 76; DAM**
POP
See also CA 104; CANR 30, 50; INT CANR-
30
Smith, A(rthur) J(ames) M(arshall) 1902-1980
CLC 15; DAC
See also CA 1-4R; 102; CANR 4; DLB 88
Smith, Adam 1723-1790 .... **LC 36**
See also DLB 104
Smith, Alexander 1829-1867 .... **NCLC 59**
See also DLB 32, 55
Smith, Anna Deavere 1950- .... **CLC 86**
See also CA 133
Smith, Betty (Wehner) 1896-1972 .... **CLC 19**
See also CA 5-8R; 33-36R; DLBY 82; SATA 6

Smith, Charlotte (Turner) 1749-1806 **N C L C 23**
  See also DLB 39, 109
Smith, Clark Ashton 1893-1961 .... **CLC 43**
  See also CA 143
Smith, Dave .... **CLC 22, 42**
  See also Smith, David (Jeddie)
  See also CAAS 7; DLB 5
Smith, David (Jeddie) 1942-
  See Smith, Dave
  See also CA 49-52; CANR 1, 59; DAM POET
Smith, Florence Margaret 1902-1971
  See Smith, Stevie
  See also CA 17-18; 29-32R; CANR 35; CAP 2;
    DAM POET; MTCW
Smith, Iain Crichton 1928- .... **CLC 64**
  See also CA 21-24R; DLB 40, 139
Smith, John 1580(?)-1631 .... **LC 9**
Smith, Johnston
  See Crane, Stephen (Townley)
Smith, Joseph, Jr. 1805-1844 .... **NCLC 53**
Smith, Lee 1944- .... **CLC 25, 73**
  See also CA 114; 119; CANR 46; DLB 143;
    DLBY 83; INT 119
Smith, Martin
  See Smith, Martin Cruz
Smith, Martin Cruz 1942- ..... **CLC 25; DAM
    MULT, POP**
  See also BEST 89:4; CA 85-88; CANR 6, 23,
    43; INT CANR-23; NNAL
Smith, Mary-Ann Tirone 1944- .... **CLC 39**
  See also CA 118; 136
Smith, Patti 1946- .... **CLC 12**
  See also CA 93-96
Smith, Pauline (Urmson) 1882-1959 **TCLC 25**
Smith, Rosamond
  See Oates, Joyce Carol
Smith, Sheila Kaye
  See Kaye-Smith, Sheila
Smith, Stevie .... **CLC 3, 8, 25, 44; PC 12**
  See also Smith, Florence Margaret
  See also DLB 20
Smith, Wilbur (Addison) 1933- .... **CLC 33**
  See also CA 13-16R; CANR 7, 46; MTCW
Smith, William Jay 1918- .... **CLC 6**
  See also CA 5-8R; CANR 44; DLB 5; MAICYA;
    SAAS 22; SATA 2, 68
Smith, Woodrow Wilson
  See Kuttner, Henry
Smolenskin, Peretz 1842-1885 .... **NCLC 30**
Smollett, Tobias (George) 1721-1771 ... **LC 2**
  See also CDBLB 1660-1789; DLB 39, 104
Snodgrass, W(illiam) D(e Witt) 1926- **CLC 2,
    6, 10, 18, 68; DAM POET**
  See also CA 1-4R; CANR 6, 36; DLB 5; MTCW
Snow, C(harles) P(ercy) 1905-1980 **CLC 1, 4,
    6, 9, 13, 19; DAM NOV**
  See also CA 5-8R; 101; CANR 28; CDBLB
    1945-1960; DLB 15, 77; MTCW
Snow, Frances Compton
  See Adams, Henry (Brooks)
Snyder, Gary (Sherman) 1930- **CLC 1, 2, 5, 9,
    32; DAM POET**
  See also CA 17-20R; CANR 30, 60; DLB 5,
    16, 165
Snyder, Zilpha Keatley 1927- .... **CLC 17**
  See also AAYA 15; CA 9-12R; CANR 38; CLR
    31; JRDA; MAICYA; SAAS 2; SATA 1, 28,
    75
Soares, Bernardo
  See Pessoa, Fernando (Antonio Nogueira)
Sobh, A.
  See Shamlu, Ahmad

Sobol, Joshua .... **CLC 60**
Soderberg, Hjalmar 1869-1941 ..... **TCLC 39**
Sodergran, Edith (Irene)
  See Soedergran, Edith (Irene)
Soedergran, Edith (Irene) 1892-1923 . **T C L C
    31**
Softly, Edgar
  See Lovecraft, H(oward) P(hillips)
Softly, Edward
  See Lovecraft, H(oward) P(hillips)
Sokolov, Raymond 1941- .... **CLC 7**
  See also CA 85-88
Solo, Jay
  See Ellison, Harlan (Jay)
Sologub, Fyodor .... **TCLC 9**
  See also Teternikov, Fyodor Kuzmich
Solomons, Ikey Esquir
  See Thackeray, William Makepeace
Solomos, Dionysios 1798-1857 .... **NCLC 15**
Solwoska, Mara
  See French, Marilyn
Solzhenitsyn, Aleksandr I(sayevich) 1918-
    **CLC 1, 2, 4, 7, 9, 10, 18, 26, 34, 78; DA;
    DAB; DAC; DAM MST, NOV; WLC**
  See also AITN 1; CA 69-72; CANR 40; MTCW
Somers, Jane
  See Lessing, Doris (May)
Somerville, Edith 1858-1949 .... **TCLC 51**
  See also DLB 135
Somerville & Ross
  See Martin, Violet Florence; Somerville, Edith
Sommer, Scott 1951- .... **CLC 25**
  See also CA 106
Sondheim, Stephen (Joshua) 1930- . **CLC 30,
    39; DAM DRAM**
  See also AAYA 11; CA 103; CANR 47
Sontag, Susan 1933- **CLC 1, 2, 10, 13, 31, 105;
    DAM POP**
  See also CA 17-20R; CANR 25, 51; DLB 2,
    67; MTCW
Sophocles 496(?)B.C.-406(?)B.C. .. **CMLC 2;
    DA; DAB; DAC; DAM DRAM, MST; DC
    1; WLCS**
  See also DLB 176
Sordello 1189-1269 .... **CMLC 15**
Sorel, Julia
  See Drexler, Rosalyn
Sorrentino, Gilbert 1929- **CLC 3, 7, 14, 22, 40**
  See also CA 77-80; CANR 14, 33; DLB 5, 173;
    DLBY 80; INT CANR-14
Soto, Gary 1952- . **CLC 32, 80; DAM MULT;
    HLC**
  See also AAYA 10; CA 119; 125; CANR 50;
    CLR 38; DLB 82; HW; INT 125; JRDA;
    SATA 80
Soupault, Philippe 1897-1990 .... **CLC 68**
  See also CA 116; 147; 131
Souster, (Holmes) Raymond 1921- **CLC 5, 14;
    DAC; DAM POET**
  See also CA 13-16R; CAAS 14; CANR 13, 29,
    53; DLB 88; SATA 63
Southern, Terry 1924(?)-1995 .... **CLC 7**
  See also CA 1-4R; 150; CANR 1, 55; DLB 2
Southey, Robert 1774-1843 .... **NCLC 8**
  See also DLB 93, 107, 142; SATA 54
Southworth, Emma Dorothy Eliza Nevitte
    1819-1899 .... **NCLC 26**
Souza, Ernest
  See Scott, Evelyn
Soyinka, Wole 1934- **CLC 3, 5, 14, 36, 44; BLC;
    DA; DAB; DAC; DAM DRAM, MST,
    MULT; DC 2; WLC**
  See also BW 2; CA 13-16R; CANR 27, 39; DLB

125; MTCW
Spackman, W(illiam) M(ode) 1905-1990 **C L C
    46**
  See also CA 81-84; 132
Spacks, Barry (Bernard) 1931- .... **CLC 14**
  See also CA 154; CANR 33; DLB 105
Spanidou, Irini 1946- .... **CLC 44**
Spark, Muriel (Sarah) 1918- **CLC 2, 3, 5, 8, 13,
    18, 40, 94; DAB; DAC; DAM MST, NOV;
    SSC 10**
  See also CA 5-8R; CANR 12, 36; CDBLB 1945-
    1960; DLB 15, 139; INT CANR-12; MTCW
Spaulding, Douglas
  See Bradbury, Ray (Douglas)
Spaulding, Leonard
  See Bradbury, Ray (Douglas)
Spence, J. A. D.
  See Eliot, T(homas) S(tearns)
Spencer, Elizabeth 1921- .... **CLC 22**
  See also CA 13-16R; CANR 32; DLB 6;
    MTCW; SATA 14
Spencer, Leonard G.
  See Silverberg, Robert
Spencer, Scott 1945- .... **CLC 30**
  See also CA 113; CANR 51; DLBY 86
Spender, Stephen (Harold) 1909-1995 **CLC 1,
    2, 5, 10, 41, 91; DAM POET**
  See also CA 9-12R; 149; CANR 31, 54; CDBLB
    1945-1960; DLB 20; MTCW
Spengler, Oswald (Arnold Gottfried) 1880-1936
    TCLC 25
  See also CA 118
Spenser, Edmund 1552(?)-1599 **LC 5, 39; DA;
    DAB; DAC; DAM MST, POET; PC 8;
    WLC**
  See also CDBLB Before 1660; DLB 167
Spicer, Jack 1925-1965 **CLC 8, 18, 72; DAM
    POET**
  See also CA 85-88; DLB 5, 16
Spiegelman, Art 1948- .... **CLC 76**
  See also AAYA 10; CA 125; CANR 41, 55
Spielberg, Peter 1929- .... **CLC 6**
  See also CA 5-8R; CANR 4, 48; DLBY 81
Spielberg, Steven 1947- .... **CLC 20**
  See also AAYA 8; CA 77-80; CANR 32; SATA
    32
Spillane, Frank Morrison 1918-
  See Spillane, Mickey
  See also CA 25-28R; CANR 28; MTCW; SATA
    66
Spillane, Mickey .... **CLC 3, 13**
  See also Spillane, Frank Morrison
Spinoza, Benedictus de 1632-1677 .... **LC 9**
Spinrad, Norman (Richard) 1940- ... **CLC 46**
  See also CA 37-40R; CAAS 19; CANR 20; DLB
    8; INT CANR-20
Spitteler, Carl (Friedrich Georg) 1845-1924
    TCLC 12
  See also CA 109; DLB 129
Spivack, Kathleen (Romola Drucker) 1938-
    CLC 6
  See also CA 49-52
Spoto, Donald 1941- .... **CLC 39**
  See also CA 65-68; CANR 11, 57
Springsteen, Bruce (F.) 1949- .... **CLC 17**
  See also CA 111
Spurling, Hilary 1940- .... **CLC 34**
  See also CA 104; CANR 25, 52
Spyker, John Howland
  See Elman, Richard
Squires, (James) Radcliffe 1917-1993 **CLC 51**
  See also CA 1-4R; 140; CANR 6, 21
Srivastava, Dhanpat Rai 1880(?)-1936

See Premchand
See also CA 118
Stacy, Donald
See Pohl, Frederik
Stael, Germaine de
See Stael-Holstein, Anne Louise Germaine
Necker Baronn
See also DLB 119
**Stael-Holstein, Anne Louise Germaine Necker
Baronn** 1766-1817 .... NCLC 3
See also Stael, Germaine de
Stafford, Jean 1915-1979CLC 4, 7, 19, 68; SSC
26
See also CA 1-4R; 85-88; CANR 3; DLB 2, 173;
MTCW; SATA-Obit 22
Stafford, William (Edgar) 1914-1993 CLC 4,
7, 29; DAM POET
See also CA 5-8R; 142; CAAS 3; CANR 5, 22;
DLB 5; INT CANR-22
Stagnelius, Eric Johan 1793-1823 . NCLC 61
Staines, Trevor
See Brunner, John (Kilian Houston)
Stairs, Gordon
See Austin, Mary (Hunter)
Stannard, Martin 1947- .... CLC 44
See also CA 142; DLB 155
Stanton, Elizabeth Cady 1815-1902TCLC 73
See also DLB 79
Stanton, Maura 1946- .... CLC 9
See also CA 89-92; CANR 15; DLB 120
Stanton, Schuyler
See Baum, L(yman) Frank
Stapledon, (William) Olaf 1886-1950 . T C L C
22
See also CA 111; DLB 15
Starbuck, George (Edwin) 1931-1996CLC 53;
DAM POET
See also CA 21-24R; 153; CANR 23
Stark, Richard
See Westlake, Donald E(dwin)
Staunton, Schuyler
See Baum, L(yman) Frank
Stead, Christina (Ellen) 1902-1983 CLC 2, 5,
8, 32, 80
See also CA 13-16R; 109; CANR 33, 40;
MTCW
Stead, William Thomas 1849-1912 TCLC 48
Steele, Richard 1672-1729 .... LC 18
See also CDBLB 1660-1789; DLB 84, 101
Steele, Timothy (Reid) 1948- .... CLC 45
See also CA 93-96; CANR 16, 50; DLB 120
Steffens, (Joseph) Lincoln 1866-1936 . T C L C
20
See also CA 117
Stegner, Wallace (Earle) 1909-1993CLC 9, 49,
81; DAM NOV; SSC 27
See also AITN 1; BEST 90:3; CA 1-4R; 141;
CAAS 9; CANR 1, 21, 46; DLB 9; DLBY
93; MTCW
Stein, Gertrude 1874-1946TCLC 1, 6, 28, 48;
DA; DAB; DAC; DAM MST, NOV, POET;
PC 18; WLC
See also CA 104; 132; CDALB 1917-1929;
DLB 4, 54, 86; DLBD 15; MTCW
Steinbeck, John (Ernst) 1902-1968 CLC 1, 5,
9, 13, 21, 34, 45, 75; DA; DAB; DAC; DAM
DRAM, MST, NOV; SSC 11; WLC
See also AAYA 12; CA 1-4R; 25-28R; CANR
1, 35; CDALB 1929-1941; DLB 7, 9; DLBD
2; MTCW; SATA 9
Steinem, Gloria 1934- .... CLC 63
See also CA 53-56; CANR 28, 51; MTCW
Steiner, George 1929- ... CLC 24; DAM NOV

See also CA 73-76; CANR 31; DLB 67; MTCW;
SATA 62
Steiner, K. Leslie
See Delany, Samuel R(ay, Jr.)
Steiner, Rudolf 1861-1925 .... TCLC 13
See also CA 107
Stendhal 1783-1842NCLC 23, 46; DA; DAB;
DAC; DAM MST, NOV; SSC 27; WLC
See also DLB 119
Stephen, Leslie 1832-1904 .... TCLC 23
See also CA 123; DLB 57, 144
Stephen, Sir Leslie
See Stephen, Leslie
Stephen, Virginia
See Woolf, (Adeline) Virginia
Stephens, James 1882(?)-1950 .... TCLC 4
See also CA 104; DLB 19, 153, 162
Stephens, Reed
See Donaldson, Stephen R.
Steptoe, Lydia
See Barnes, Djuna
Sterchi, Beat 1949- .... CLC 65
Sterling, Brett
See Bradbury, Ray (Douglas); Hamilton,
Edmond
Sterling, Bruce 1954- .... CLC 72
See also CA 119; CANR 44
Sterling, George 1869-1926 .... TCLC 20
See also CA 117; DLB 54
Stern, Gerald 1925- .... CLC 40, 100
See also CA 81-84; CANR 28; DLB 105
Stern, Richard (Gustave) 1928- ... CLC 4, 39
See also CA 1-4R; CANR 1, 25, 52; DLBY 87;
INT CANR-25
Sternberg, Josef von 1894-1969 ....CLC 20
See also CA 81-84
Sterne, Laurence 1713-1768LC 2; DA; DAB;
DAC; DAM MST, NOV; WLC
See also CDBLB 1660-1789; DLB 39
Sternheim, (William Adolf) Carl 1878-1942
TCLC 8
See also CA 105; DLB 56, 118
Stevens, Mark 1951- .... CLC 34
See also CA 122
Stevens, Wallace 1879-1955 TCLC 3, 12, 45;
DA; DAB; DAC; DAM MST, POET; PC
6; WLC
See also CA 104; 124; CDALB 1929-1941;
DLB 54; MTCW
Stevenson, Anne (Katharine) 1933-CLC 7, 33
See also CA 17-20R; CAAS 9; CANR 9, 33;
DLB 40; MTCW
Stevenson, Robert Louis (Balfour) 1850-1894
NCLC 5, 14, 63; DA; DAB; DAC; DAM
MST, NOV; SSC 11; WLC
See also CDBLB 1890-1914; CLR 10, 11; DLB
18, 57, 141, 156, 174; DLBD 13; JRDA;
MAICYA; YABC 2
Stewart, J(ohn) I(nnes) M(ackintosh) 1906-
1994 .... CLC 7, 14, 32
See also CA 85-88; 147; CAAS 3; CANR 47;
MTCW
Stewart, Mary (Florence Elinor) 1916-CLC 7,
35; DAB
See also CA 1-4R; CANR 1, 59; SATA 12
Stewart, Mary Rainbow
See Stewart, Mary (Florence Elinor)
Stifle, June
See Campbell, Maria
Stifter, Adalbert 1805-1868NCLC 41; SSC 28
See also DLB 133
Still, James 1906- .... CLC 49
See also CA 65-68; CAAS 17; CANR 10, 26;

DLB 9; SATA 29
Sting
See Sumner, Gordon Matthew
Stirling, Arthur
See Sinclair, Upton (Beall)
Stitt, Milan 1941-............................... CLC 29
See also CA 69-72
Stockton, Francis Richard 1834-1902
See Stockton, Frank R.
See also CA 108; 137; MAICYA; SATA 44
Stockton, Frank R. .... TCLC 47
See also Stockton, Francis Richard
See also DLB 42, 74; DLBD 13; SATA-Brief
32
Stoddard, Charles
See Kuttner, Henry
Stoker, Abraham 1847-1912
See Stoker, Bram
See also CA 105; DA; DAC; DAM MST, NOV;
SATA 29
Stoker, Bram 1847-1912TCLC 8; DAB; WLC
See also Stoker, Abraham
See also CA 150; CDBLB 1890-1914; DLB 36,
70, 178
Stolz, Mary (Slattery) 1920- .... CLC 12
See also AAYA 8; AITN 1; CA 5-8R; CANR
13, 41; JRDA; MAICYA; SAAS 3; SATA 10,
71
Stone, Irving 1903-1989 ..CLC 7; DAM POP
See also AITN 1; CA 1-4R; 129; CAAS 3;
CANR 1, 23; INT CANR-23; MTCW; SATA
3; SATA-Obit 64
Stone, Oliver (William) 1946- .... CLC 73
See also AAYA 15; CA 110; CANR 55
Stone, Robert (Anthony) 1937-CLC 5, 23, 42
See also CA 85-88; CANR 23; DLB 152; INT
CANR-23; MTCW
Stone, Zachary
See Follett, Ken(neth Martin)
Stoppard, Tom 1937-CLC 1, 3, 4, 5, 8, 15, 29,
34, 63, 91; DA; DAB; DAC; DAM DRAM,
MST; DC 6; WLC
See also CA 81-84; CANR 39; CDBLB 1960
to Present; DLB 13; DLBY 85; MTCW
Storey, David (Malcolm) 1933-CLC 2, 4, 5, 8;
DAM DRAM
See also CA 81-84; CANR 36; DLB 13, 14;
MTCW
Storm, Hyemeyohsts 1935- ...... CLC 3; DAM
MULT
See also CA 81-84; CANR 45; NNAL
Storm, (Hans) Theodor (Woldsen) 1817-1888
NCLC 1; SSC 27
Storni, Alfonsina 1892-1938 . TCLC 5; DAM
MULT; HLC
See also CA 104; 131; HW
Stoughton, William 1631-1701 .... LC 38
See also DLB 24
Stout, Rex (Todhunter) 1886-1975 .....CLC 3
See also AITN 2; CA 61-64
Stow, (Julian) Randolph 1935- .. CLC 23, 48
See also CA 13-16R; CANR 33; MTCW
Stowe, Harriet (Elizabeth) Beecher 1811-1896
NCLC 3, 50; DA; DAB; DAC; DAM MST,
NOV; WLC
See also CDALB 1865-1917; DLB 1, 12, 42,
74; JRDA; MAICYA; YABC 1
Strachey, (Giles) Lytton 1880-1932 TCLC 12
See also CA 110; DLB 149; DLBD 10
Strand, Mark 1934- CLC 6, 18, 41, 71; DAM
POET
See also CA 21-24R; CANR 40; DLB 5; SATA
41

Straub, Peter (Francis) 1943- **CLC 28; DAM POP**
See also BEST 89:1; CA 85-88; CANR 28; DLBY 84; MTCW

Strauss, Botho 1944- .... **CLC 22**
See also CA 157; DLB 124

Streatfeild, (Mary) Noel 1895(?)-1986**CLC 21**
See also CA 81-84; 120; CANR 31; CLR 17; DLB 160; MAICYA; SATA 20; SATA-Obit 48

Stribling, T(homas) S(igismund) 1881-1965 **CLC 23**
See also CA 107; DLB 9

Strindberg, (Johan) August 1849-1912**TCLC 1, 8, 21, 47; DA; DAB; DAC; DAM DRAM, MST; WLC**
See also CA 104; 135

Stringer, Arthur 1874-1950 .... **TCLC 37**
See also CA 161; DLB 92

Stringer, David
See Roberts, Keith (John Kingston)

Stroheim, Erich von 1885-1957 ..... **TCLC 71**

Strugatskii, Arkadii (Natanovich) 1925-1991 **CLC 27**
See also CA 106; 135

Strugatskii, Boris (Natanovich) 1933-**CLC 27**
See also CA 106

Strummer, Joe 1953(?)- .... **CLC 30**

Stuart, Don A.
See Campbell, John W(ood, Jr.)

Stuart, Ian
See MacLean, Alistair (Stuart)

Stuart, Jesse (Hilton) 1906-1984**CLC 1, 8, 11, 14, 34**
See also CA 5-8R; 112; CANR 31; DLB 9, 48, 102; DLBY 84; SATA 2; SATA-Obit 36

Sturgeon, Theodore (Hamilton) 1918-1985 **CLC 22, 39**
See also Queen, Ellery
See also CA 81-84; 116; CANR 32; DLB 8; DLBY 85; MTCW

Sturges, Preston 1898-1959 .... **TCLC 48**
See also CA 114; 149; DLB 26

Styron, William 1925-**CLC 1, 3, 5, 11, 15, 60; DAM NOV, POP; SSC 25**
See also BEST 90:4; CA 5-8R; CANR 6, 33; CDALB 1968-1988; DLB 2, 143; DLBY 80; INT CANR-6; MTCW

Suarez Lynch, B.
See Bioy Casares, Adolfo; Borges, Jorge Luis

Su Chien 1884-1918
See Su Man-shu
See also CA 123

Suckow, Ruth 1892-1960 .... **SSC 18**
See also CA 113; DLB 9, 102

Sudermann, Hermann 1857-1928 .. **TCLC 15**
See also CA 107; DLB 118

Sue, Eugene 1804-1857 .... **NCLC 1**
See also DLB 119

Sueskind, Patrick 1949- .... **CLC 44**
See also Suskind, Patrick

Sukenick, Ronald 1932- .... **CLC 3, 4, 6, 48**
See also CA 25-28R; CAAS 8; CANR 32; DLB 173; DLBY 81

Suknaski, Andrew 1942- .... **CLC 19**
See also CA 101; DLB 53

Sullivan, Vernon
See Vian, Boris

Sully Prudhomme 1839-1907 .... **TCLC 31**

Su Man-shu .... **TCLC 24**
See also Su Chien

Summerforest, Ivy B.
See Kirkup, James

Summers, Andrew James 1942- .... **CLC 26**

Summers, Andy
See Summers, Andrew James

Summers, Hollis (Spurgeon, Jr.) 1916-**CLC 10**
See also CA 5-8R; CANR 3; DLB 6

Summers, (Alphonsus Joseph-Mary Augustus) Montague 1880-1948 .... **TCLC 16**
See also CA 118

Sumner, Gordon Matthew 1951- ...... **CLC 26**

Surtees, Robert Smith 1803-1864 .. **NCLC 14**
See also DLB 21

Susann, Jacqueline 1921-1974 .... **CLC 3**
See also AITN 1; CA 65-68; 53-56; MTCW

Su Shih 1036-1101 .... **CMLC 15**

Suskind, Patrick
See Sueskind, Patrick
See also CA 145

Sutcliff, Rosemary 1920-1992**CLC 26; DAB; DAC; DAM MST, POP**
See also AAYA 10; CA 5-8R; 139; CANR 37; CLR 1, 37; JRDA; MAICYA; SATA 6, 44, 78; SATA-Obit 73

Sutro, Alfred 1863-1933 .... **TCLC 6**
See also CA 105; DLB 10

Sutton, Henry
See Slavitt, David R(ytman)

Svevo, Italo 1861-1928 . **TCLC 2, 35; SSC 25**
See also Schmitz, Aron Hector

Swados, Elizabeth (A.) 1951- .... **CLC 12**
See also CA 97-100; CANR 49; INT 97-100

Swados, Harvey 1920-1972 .... **CLC 5**
See also CA 5-8R; 37-40R; CANR 6; DLB 2

Swan, Gladys 1934- .... **CLC 69**
See also CA 101; CANR 17, 39

Swarthout, Glendon (Fred) 1918-1992**CLC 35**
See also CA 1-4R; 139; CANR 1, 47; SATA 26

Sweet, Sarah C.
See Jewett, (Theodora) Sarah Orne

Swenson, May 1919-1989**CLC 4, 14, 61, 106; DA; DAB; DAC; DAM MST, POET; PC 14**
See also CA 5-8R; 130; CANR 36, 61; DLB 5; MTCW; SATA 15

Swift, Augustus
See Lovecraft, H(oward) P(hillips)

Swift, Graham (Colin) 1949- ...... **CLC 41, 88**
See also CA 117; 122; CANR 46

Swift, Jonathan 1667-1745 **LC 1; DA; DAB; DAC; DAM MST, NOV, POET; PC 9; WLC**
See also CDBLB 1660-1789; DLB 39, 95, 101; SATA 19

Swinburne, Algernon Charles 1837-1909 **TCLC 8, 36; DA; DAB; DAC; DAM MST, POET; WLC**
See also CA 105; 140; CDBLB 1832-1890; DLB 35, 57

Swinfen, Ann .... **CLC 34**

Swinnerton, Frank Arthur 1884-1982**CLC 31**
See also CA 108; DLB 34

Swithen, John
See King, Stephen (Edwin)

Sylvia
See Ashton-Warner, Sylvia (Constance)

Symmes, Robert Edward
See Duncan, Robert (Edward)

Symonds, John Addington 1840-1893 **NCLC 34**
See also DLB 57, 144

Symons, Arthur 1865-1945 .... **TCLC 11**
See also CA 107; DLB 19, 57, 149

Symons, Julian (Gustave) 1912-1994 **CLC 2, 14, 32**

See also CA 49-52; 147; CAAS 3; CANR 3, 33, 59; DLB 87, 155; DLBY 92; MTCW

Synge, (Edmund) J(ohn) M(illington) 1871-1909 .. **TCLC 6, 37; DAM DRAM; DC 2**
See also CA 104; 141; CDBLB 1890-1914; DLB 10, 19

Syruc, J.
See Milosz, Czeslaw

Szirtes, George 1948- ....**CLC 46**
See also CA 109; CANR 27, 61

Szymborska, Wislawa 1923-...............**CLC 99**
See also CA 154; DLBY 96

T. O., Nik
See Annensky, Innokenty (Fyodorovich)

Tabori, George 1914- ....**CLC 19**
See also CA 49-52; CANR 4

Tagore, Rabindranath 1861-1941**TCLC 3, 53; DAM DRAM, POET; PC 8**
See also CA 104; 120; MTCW

Taine, Hippolyte Adolphe 1828-1893 . **NCLC 15**

Talese, Gay 1932- ....**CLC 37**
See also AITN 1; CA 1-4R; CANR 9, 58; INT CANR-9; MTCW

Tallent, Elizabeth (Ann) 1954- ....**CLC 45**
See also CA 117; DLB 130

Tally, Ted 1952- ....**CLC 42**
See also CA 120; 124; INT 124

Tamayo y Baus, Manuel 1829-1898 . **NCLC 1**

Tammsaare, A(nton) H(ansen) 1878-1940 **TCLC 27**

Tam'si, Tchicaya U
See Tchicaya, Gerald Felix

Tan, Amy (Ruth) 1952-**CLC 59; DAM MULT, NOV, POP**
See also AAYA 9; BEST 89:3; CA 136; CANR 54; DLB 173; SATA 75

Tandem, Felix
See Spitteler, Carl (Friedrich Georg)

Tanizaki, Jun'ichiro 1886-1965**CLC 8, 14, 28; SSC 21**
See also CA 93-96; 25-28R; DLB 180

Tanner, William
See Amis, Kingsley (William)

Tao Lao
See Storni, Alfonsina

Tarassoff, Lev
See Troyat, Henri

Tarbell, Ida M(inerva) 1857-1944 . **TCLC 40**
See also CA 122; DLB 47

Tarkington, (Newton) Booth 1869-1946**TCLC 9**
See also CA 110; 143; DLB 9, 102; SATA 17

Tarkovsky, Andrei (Arsenyevich) 1932-1986 **CLC 75**
See also CA 127

Tartt, Donna 1964(?)- ....**CLC 76**
See also CA 142

Tasso, Torquato 1544-1595 .... **LC 5**

Tate, (John Orley) Allen 1899-1979**CLC 2, 4, 6, 9, 11, 14, 24**
See also CA 5-8R; 85-88; CANR 32; DLB 4, 45, 63; MTCW

Tate, Ellalice
See Hibbert, Eleanor Alice Burford

Tate, James (Vincent) 1943- ..... **CLC 2, 6, 25**
See also CA 21-24R; CANR 29, 57; DLB 5, 169

Tavel, Ronald 1940- ....**CLC 6**
See also CA 21-24R; CANR 33

Taylor, C(ecil) P(hilip) 1929-1981 .....**CLC 27**
See also CA 25-28R; 105; CANR 47

Taylor, Edward 1642(?)-1729 ..... **LC 11; DA;**

DAB; DAC; DAM MST, POET
See also DLB 24

Taylor, Eleanor Ross 1920- .... **CLC 5**
See also CA 81-84

Taylor, Elizabeth 1912-1975 ..... **CLC 2, 4, 29**
See also CA 13-16R; CANR 9; DLB 139;
MTCW; SATA 13

Taylor, Frederick Winslow 1856-1915 **T C L C
76**

Taylor, Henry (Splawn) 1942- .... **CLC 44**
See also CA 33-36R; CAAS 7; CANR 31; DLB
5

Taylor, Kamala (Purnaiya) 1924-
See Markandaya, Kamala
See also CA 77-80

Taylor, Mildred D. .... **CLC 21**
See also AAYA 10; BW 1; CA 85-88; CANR
25; CLR 9; DLB 52; JRDA; MAICYA; SAAS
5; SATA 15, 70

Taylor, Peter (Hillsman) 1917-1994**CLC 1, 4,
18, 37, 44, 50, 71; SSC 10**
See also CA 13-16R; 147; CANR 9, 50; DLBY
81, 94; INT CANR-9; MTCW

Taylor, Robert Lewis 1912- .... **CLC 14**
See also CA 1-4R; CANR 3; SATA 10

Tchekhov, Anton
See Chekhov, Anton (Pavlovich)

Tchicaya, Gerald Felix 1931-1988 . **CLC 101**
See also CA 129; 125

Tchicaya U Tam'si
See Tchicaya, Gerald Felix

Teasdale, Sara 1884-1933 .... **TCLC 4**
See also CA 104; DLB 45; SATA 32

Tegner, Esaias 1782-1846 .... **NCLC 2**

Teilhard de Chardin, (Marie Joseph) Pierre
1881-1955 .... **TCLC 9**
See also CA 105

Temple, Ann
See Mortimer, Penelope (Ruth)

Tennant, Emma (Christina) 1937-**CLC 13, 52**
See also CA 65-68; CAAS 9; CANR 10, 38,
59; DLB 14

Tenneshaw, S. M.
See Silverberg, Robert

Tennyson, Alfred 1809-1892 ... **NCLC 30, 65;
DA; DAB; DAC; DAM MST, POET; PC
6; WLC**
See also CDBLB 1832-1890; DLB 32

Teran, Lisa St. Aubin de .... **CLC 36**
See also St. Aubin de Teran, Lisa

Terence 195(?)B.C.-159B.C. **CMLC 14; DC 7**

Teresa de Jesus, St. 1515-1582 .... **LC 18**

Terkel, Louis 1912-
See Terkel, Studs
See also CA 57-60; CANR 18, 45; MTCW

Terkel, Studs .... **CLC 38**
See also Terkel, Louis
See also AITN 1

Terry, C. V.
See Slaughter, Frank G(ill)

Terry, Megan 1932- .... **CLC 19**
See also CA 77-80; CABS 3; CANR 43; DLB 7

Tertz, Abram
See Sinyavsky, Andrei (Donatevich)

Tesich, Steve 1943(?)-1996 .... **CLC 40, 69**
See also CA 105; 152; DLBY 83

Teternikov, Fyodor Kuzmich 1863-1927
See Sologub, Fyodor
See also CA 104

Tevis, Walter 1928-1984 .... **CLC 42**
See also CA 113

Tey, Josephine .... **TCLC 14**
See also Mackintosh, Elizabeth

See also DLB 77

Thackeray, William Makepeace 1811-1863
**NCLC 5, 14, 22, 43; DA; DAB; DAC; DAM
MST, NOV; WLC**
See also CDBLB 1832-1890; DLB 21, 55, 159,
163; SATA 23

Thakura, Ravindranatha
See Tagore, Rabindranath

Tharoor, Shashi 1956- .... **CLC 70**
See also CA 141

Thelwell, Michael Miles 1939- .... **CLC 22**
See also BW 2; CA 101

Theobald, Lewis, Jr.
See Lovecraft, H(oward) P(hillips)

Theodorescu, Ion N. 1880-1967
See Arghezi, Tudor
See also CA 116

Theriault, Yves 1915-1983 .... **CLC 79; DAC;
DAM MST**
See also CA 102; DLB 88

Theroux, Alexander (Louis) 1939-**CLC 2, 25**
See also CA 85-88; CANR 20

Theroux, Paul (Edward) 1941- **CLC 5, 8, 11,
15, 28, 46; DAM POP**
See also BEST 89:4; CA 33-36R; CANR 20,
45; DLB 2; MTCW; SATA 44

Thesen, Sharon 1946- .... **CLC 56**

Thevenin, Denis
See Duhamel, Georges

Thibault, Jacques Anatole Francois 1844-1924
See France, Anatole
See also CA 106; 127; DAM NOV; MTCW

Thiele, Colin (Milton) 1920- .... **CLC 17**
See also CA 29-32R; CANR 12, 28, 53; CLR
27; MAICYA; SAAS 2; SATA 14, 72

Thomas, Audrey (Callahan) 1935-**CLC 7, 13,
37; SSC 20**
See also AITN 2; CA 21-24R; CAAS 19; CANR
36, 58; DLB 60; MTCW

Thomas, D(onald) M(ichael) 1935- . **CLC 13,
22, 31**
See also CA 61-64; CAAS 11; CANR 17, 45;
CDBLB 1960 to Present; DLB 40; INT
CANR-17; MTCW

Thomas, Dylan (Marlais) 1914-1953**TCLC 1,
8, 45; DA; DAB; DAC; DAM DRAM,
MST, POET; PC 2; SSC 3; WLC**
See also CA 104; 120; CDBLB 1945-1960;
DLB 13, 20, 139; MTCW; SATA 60

Thomas, (Philip) Edward 1878-1917 . **T C L C
10; DAM POET**
See also CA 106; 153; DLB 19

Thomas, Joyce Carol 1938- .... **CLC 35**
See also AAYA 12; BW 2; CA 113; 116; CANR
48; CLR 19; DLB 33; INT 116; JRDA;
MAICYA; MTCW; SAAS 7; SATA 40, 78

Thomas, Lewis 1913-1993 .... **CLC 35**
See also CA 85-88; 143; CANR 38, 60; MTCW

Thomas, Paul
See Mann, (Paul) Thomas

Thomas, Piri 1928- .... **CLC 17**
See also CA 73-76; HW

Thomas, R(onald) S(tuart) 1913- **CLC 6, 13,
48; DAB; DAM POET**
See also CA 89-92; CAAS 4; CANR 30;
CDBLB 1960 to Present; DLB 27; MTCW

Thomas, Ross (Elmore) 1926-1995 ... **CLC 39**
See also CA 33-36R; 150; CANR 22

Thompson, Francis Clegg
See Mencken, H(enry) L(ouis)

Thompson, Francis Joseph 1859-1907**TCLC 4**
See also CA 104; CDBLB 1890-1914; DLB 19

Thompson, Hunter S(tockton) 1939- . **CLC 9,**

17, 40, 104; DAM POP
See also BEST 89:1; CA 17-20R; CANR 23,
46; MTCW

Thompson, James Myers
See Thompson, Jim (Myers)

Thompson, Jim (Myers) 1906-1977(?)**CLC 69**
See also CA 140

Thompson, Judith .... **CLC 39**

Thomson, James 1700-1748 .... **LC 16, 29, 40;
DAM POET**
See also DLB 95

Thomson, James 1834-1882 **NCLC 18; DAM
POET**
See also DLB 35

Thoreau, Henry David 1817-1862**NCLC 7, 21,
61; DA; DAB; DAC; DAM MST; WLC**
See also CDALB 1640-1865; DLB 1

Thornton, Hall
See Silverberg, Robert

Thucydides c. 455B.C.-399B.C. ...... **CMLC 17**
See also DLB 176

Thurber, James (Grover) 1894-1961 . **CLC 5,
11, 25; DA; DAB; DAC; DAM DRAM,
MST, NOV; SSC 1**
See also CA 73-76; CANR 17, 39; CDALB
1929-1941; DLB 4, 11, 22, 102; MAICYA;
MTCW; SATA 13

Thurman, Wallace (Henry) 1902-1934**T C L C
6; BLC; DAM MULT**
See also BW 1; CA 104; 124; DLB 51

Ticheburn, Cheviot
See Ainsworth, William Harrison

Tieck, (Johann) Ludwig 1773-1853 **NCLC 5,
46**
See also DLB 90

Tiger, Derry
See Ellison, Harlan (Jay)

Tilghman, Christopher 1948(?)- ...... **CLC 65**
See also CA 159

Tillinghast, Richard (Williford) 1940-**CLC 29**
See also CA 29-32R; CAAS 23; CANR 26, 51

Timrod, Henry 1828-1867 .... **NCLC 25**
See also DLB 3

Tindall, Gillian 1938- .... **CLC 7**
See also CA 21-24R; CANR 11

Tiptree, James, Jr. .... **CLC 48, 50**
See also Sheldon, Alice Hastings Bradley
See also DLB 8

Titmarsh, Michael Angelo
See Thackeray, William Makepeace

Tocqueville, Alexis (Charles Henri Maurice
Clerel Comte) 1805-1859 ...**NCLC 7, 63**

Tolkien, J(ohn) R(onald) R(euel) 1892-1973
**CLC 1, 2, 3, 8, 12, 38; DA; DAB; DAC;
DAM MST, NOV, POP; WLC**
See also AAYA 10; AITN 1; CA 17-18; 45-48;
CANR 36; CAP 2; CDBLB 1914-1945; DLB
15, 160; JRDA; MAICYA; MTCW; SATA 2,
32; SATA-Obit 24

Toller, Ernst 1893-1939 .... **TCLC 10**
See also CA 107; DLB 124

Tolson, M. B.
See Tolson, Melvin B(eaunorus)

Tolson, Melvin B(eaunorus) 1898(?)-1966
CLC 36, 105; BLC; DAM MULT, POET
See also BW 1; CA 124; 89-92; DLB 48, 76

Tolstoi, Aleksei Nikolaevich
See Tolstoy, Alexey Nikolaevich

Tolstoy, Alexey Nikolaevich 1882-1945**T C L C
18**
See also CA 107; 158

Tolstoy, Count Leo
See Tolstoy, Leo (Nikolaevich)

Tolstoy, Leo (Nikolaevich) 1828-1910TCLC 4, 11, 17, 28, 44; DA; DAB; DAC; DAM MST, NOV; SSC 9; WLC
See also CA 104; 123; SATA 26

Tomasi di Lampedusa, Giuseppe 1896-1957
See Lampedusa, Giuseppe (Tomasi) di
See also CA 111

Tomlin, Lily .... CLC 17
See also Tomlin, Mary Jean

Tomlin, Mary Jean 1939(?)-
See Tomlin, Lily
See also CA 117

Tomlinson, (Alfred) Charles 1927-CLC 2, 4, 6, 13, 45; DAM POET; PC 17
See also CA 5-8R; CANR 33; DLB 40

Tomlinson, H(enry) M(ajor) 1873-1958TCLC 71
See also CA 118; 161; DLB 36, 100

Tonson, Jacob
See Bennett, (Enoch) Arnold

Toole, John Kennedy 1937-1969 CLC 19, 64
See also CA 104; DLBY 81

Toomer, Jean 1894-1967 .... CLC 1, 4, 13, 22; BLC; DAM MULT; PC 7; SSC 1; WLCS
See also BW 1; CA 85-88; CDALB 1917-1929; DLB 45, 51; MTCW

Torley, Luke
See Blish, James (Benjamin)

Tornimparte, Alessandra
See Ginzburg, Natalia

Torre, Raoul della
See Mencken, H(enry) L(ouis)

Torrey, E(dwin) Fuller 1937- .... CLC 34
See also CA 119

Torsvan, Ben Traven
See Traven, B.

Torsvan, Benno Traven
See Traven, B.

Torsvan, Berick Traven
See Traven, B.

Torsvan, Berwick Traven
See Traven, B.

Torsvan, Bruno Traven
See Traven, B.

Torsvan, Traven
See Traven, B.

Tournier, Michel (Edouard) 1924-CLC 6, 23, 36, 95
See also CA 49-52; CANR 3, 36; DLB 83; MTCW; SATA 23

Tournimparte, Alessandra
See Ginzburg, Natalia

Towers, Ivar
See Kornbluth, C(yril) M.

Towne, Robert (Burton) 1936(?)-..... CLC 87
See also CA 108; DLB 44

Townsend, Sue 1946-.... CLC 61; DAB; DAC
See also CA 119; 127; INT 127; MTCW; SATA 55, 93; SATA-Brief 48

Townshend, Peter (Dennis Blandford) 1945-CLC 17, 42
See also CA 107

Tozzi, Federigo 1883-1920 .... TCLC 31
See also CA 160

Traill, Catharine Parr 1802-1899 ..NCLC 31
See also DLB 99

Trakl, Georg 1887-1914 .... TCLC 5; PC 20
See also CA 104

Transtroemer, Tomas (Goesta) 1931-CLC 52, 65; DAM POET
See also CA 117; 129; CAAS 17

Transtromer, Tomas Gosta
See Transtroemer, Tomas (Goesta)

Traven, B. (?)-1969 .... CLC 8, 11
See also CA 19-20; 25-28R; CAP 2; DLB 9, 56; MTCW

Treitel, Jonathan 1959- .... CLC 70

Tremain, Rose 1943- .... CLC 42
See also CA 97-100; CANR 44; DLB 14

Tremblay, Michel 1942- CLC 29, 102; DAC; DAM MST
See also CA 116; 128; DLB 60; MTCW

Trevanian .... CLC 29
See also Whitaker, Rod(ney)

Trevor, Glen
See Hilton, James

Trevor, William 1928- ..CLC 7, 9, 14, 25, 71; SSC 21
See also Cox, William Trevor
See also DLB 14, 139

Trifonov, Yuri (Valentinovich) 1925-1981 CLC 45
See also CA 126; 103; MTCW

Trilling, Lionel 1905-1975 ...... CLC 9, 11, 24
See also CA 9-12R; 61-64; CANR 10; DLB 28, 63; INT CANR-10; MTCW

Trimball, W. H.
See Mencken, H(enry) L(ouis)

Tristan
See Gomez de la Serna, Ramon

Tristram
See Housman, A(lfred) E(dward)

Trogdon, William (Lewis) 1939-
See Heat-Moon, William Least
See also CA 115; 119; CANR 47; INT 119

Trollope, Anthony 1815-1882NCLC 6, 33; DA; DAB; DAC; DAM MST, NOV; SSC 28; WLC
See also CDBLB 1832-1890; DLB 21, 57, 159; SATA 22

Trollope, Frances 1779-1863 .... NCLC 30
See also DLB 21, 166

Trotsky, Leon 1879-1940 .... TCLC 22
See also CA 118

Trotter (Cockburn), Catharine 1679-1749L C 8
See also DLB 84

Trout, Kilgore
See Farmer, Philip Jose

Trow, George W. S. 1943- .... CLC 52
See also CA 126

Troyat, Henri 1911- .... CLC 23
See also CA 45-48; CANR 2, 33; MTCW

Trudeau, G(arretson) B(eekman) 1948-
See Trudeau, Garry B.
See also CA 81-84; CANR 31; SATA 35

Trudeau, Garry B. .... CLC 12
See also Trudeau, G(arretson) B(eekman)
See also AAYA 10; AITN 2

Truffaut, Francois 1932-1984 .. CLC 20, 101
See also CA 81-84; 113; CANR 34

Trumbo, Dalton 1905-1976 .... CLC 19
See also CA 21-24R; 69-72; CANR 10; DLB 26

Trumbull, John 1750-1831 .... NCLC 30
See also DLB 31

Trundlett, Helen B.
See Eliot, T(homas) S(tearns)

Tryon, Thomas 1926-1991 . CLC 3, 11; DAM POP
See also AITN 1; CA 29-32R; 135; CANR 32; MTCW

Tryon, Tom
See Tryon, Thomas

Ts'ao Hsueh-ch'in 1715(?)-1763 .... LC 1

Tsushima, Shuji 1909-1948

See Dazai, Osamu
See also CA 107

Tsvetaeva (Efron), Marina (Ivanovna) 1892-1941 .... TCLC 7, 35; PC 14
See also CA 104; 128; MTCW

Tuck, Lily 1938- .... CLC 70
See also CA 139

Tu Fu 712-770 .... PC 9
See also DAM MULT

Tunis, John R(oberts) 1889-1975 ...... CLC 12
See also CA 61-64; CANR 62; DLB 22, 171; JRDA; MAICYA; SATA 37; SATA-Brief 30

Tuohy, Frank .... CLC 37
See also Tuohy, John Francis
See also DLB 14, 139

Tuohy, John Francis 1925-
See Tuohy, Frank
See also CA 5-8R; CANR 3, 47

Turco, Lewis (Putnam) 1934- ...... CLC 11, 63
See also CA 13-16R; CAAS 22; CANR 24, 51; DLBY 84

Turgenev, Ivan 1818-1883 .... NCLC 21; DA; DAB; DAC; DAM MST, NOV; DC 7; SSC 7; WLC

Turgot, Anne-Robert-Jacques 1727-1781 L C 26

Turner, Frederick 1943- .... CLC 48
See also CA 73-76; CAAS 10; CANR 12, 30, 56; DLB 40

Tutu, Desmond M(pilo) 1931-CLC 80; BLC; DAM MULT
See also BW 1; CA 125

Tutuola, Amos 1920-1997CLC 5, 14, 29; BLC; DAM MULT
See also BW 2; CA 9-12R; 159; CANR 27; DLB 125; MTCW

Twain, Mark TCLC 6, 12, 19, 36, 48, 59; SSC 26; WLC
See also Clemens, Samuel Langhorne
See also AAYA 20; DLB 11, 12, 23, 64, 74

Tyler, Anne 1941- . CLC 7, 11, 18, 28, 44, 59, 103; DAM NOV, POP
See also AAYA 18; BEST 89:1; CA 9-12R; CANR 11, 33, 53; DLB 6, 143; DLBY 82; MTCW; SATA 7, 90

Tyler, Royall 1757-1826 .... NCLC 3
See also DLB 37

Tynan, Katharine 1861-1931 .... TCLC 3
See also CA 104; DLB 153

Tyutchev, Fyodor 1803-1873 .... NCLC 34

Tzara, Tristan 1896-1963 ...... CLC 47; DAM POET
See also Rosenfeld, Samuel; Rosenstock, Sami; Rosenstock, Samuel
See also CA 153

Uhry, Alfred 1936- .. CLC 55; DAM DRAM, POP
See also CA 127; 133; INT 133

Ulf, Haerved
See Strindberg, (Johan) August

Ulf, Harved
See Strindberg, (Johan) August

Ulibarri, Sabine R(eyes) 1919-CLC 83; DAM MULT
See also CA 131; DLB 82; HW

Unamuno (y Jugo), Miguel de 1864-1936 TCLC 2, 9; DAM MULT, NOV; HLC; SSC 11
See also CA 104; 131; DLB 108; HW; MTCW

Undercliffe, Errol
See Campbell, (John) Ramsey

Underwood, Miles
See Glassco, John

Undset, Sigrid 1882-1949TCLC 3; DA; DAB;
　　DAC; DAM MST, NOV; WLC
　　See also CA 104; 129; MTCW
Ungaretti, Giuseppe 1888-1970CLC 7, 11, 15
　　See also CA 19-20; 25-28R; CAP 2; DLB 114
Unger, Douglas 1952- .... CLC 34
　　See also CA 130
Unsworth, Barry (Forster) 1930- .... CLC 76
　　See also CA 25-28R; CANR 30, 54
Updike, John (Hoyer) 1932-CLC 1, 2, 3, 5, 7,
　　9, 13, 15, 23, 34, 43, 70; DA; DAB; DAC;
　　DAM MST, NOV, POET, POP; SSC 13, 27;
　　WLC
　　See also CA 1-4R; CABS 1; CANR 4, 33, 51;
　　CDALB 1968-1988; DLB 2, 5, 143; DLBD
　　3; DLBY 80, 82; MTCW
Upshaw, Margaret Mitchell
　　See Mitchell, Margaret (Munnerlyn)
Upton, Mark
　　See Sanders, Lawrence
Urdang, Constance (Henriette) 1922-CLC 47
　　See also CA 21-24R; CANR 9, 24
Uriel, Henry
　　See Faust, Frederick (Schiller)
Uris, Leon (Marcus) 1924- CLC 7, 32; DAM
　　NOV, POP
　　See also AITN 1, 2; BEST 89:2; CA 1-4R;
　　CANR 1, 40; MTCW; SATA 49
Urmuz
　　See Codrescu, Andrei
Urquhart, Jane 1949- .... CLC 90; DAC
　　See also CA 113; CANR 32
Ustinov, Peter (Alexander) 1921- .... CLC 1
　　See also AITN 1; CA 13-16R; CANR 25, 51;
　　DLB 13
U Tam'si, Gerald Felix Tchicaya
　　See Tchicaya, Gerald Felix
U Tam'si, Tchicaya
　　See Tchicaya, Gerald Felix
Vachss, Andrew (Henry) 1942- ...... CLC 106
　　See also CA 118; CANR 44
Vachss, Andrew H.
　　See Vachss, Andrew (Henry)
Vaculik, Ludvik 1926- .... CLC 7
　　See also CA 53-56
Vaihinger, Hans 1852-1933 .... TCLC 71
　　See also CA 116
Valdez, Luis (Miguel) 1940- ..CLC 84; DAM
　　MULT; HLC
　　See also CA 101; CANR 32; DLB 122; HW
Valenzuela, Luisa 1938- CLC 31, 104; DAM
　　MULT; SSC 14
　　See also CA 101; CANR 32; DLB 113; HW
Valera y Alcala-Galiano, Juan 1824-1905
　　TCLC 10
　　See also CA 106
Valery, (Ambroise) Paul (Toussaint Jules) 1871-
　　1945 .... TCLC 4, 15; DAM POET; PC 9
　　See also CA 104; 122; MTCW
Valle-Inclan, Ramon (Maria) del 1866-1936
　　TCLC 5; DAM MULT; HLC
　　See also CA 106; 153; DLB 134
Vallejo, Antonio Buero
　　See Buero Vallejo, Antonio
Vallejo, Cesar (Abraham) 1892-1938TCLC 3,
　　56; DAM MULT; HLC
　　See also CA 105; 153; HW
Vallette, Marguerite Eymery
　　See Rachilde
Valle Y Pena, Ramon del
　　See Valle-Inclan, Ramon (Maria) del
Van Ash, Cay 1918- .... CLC 34
Vanbrugh, Sir John 1664-1726 LC 21; DAM

DRAM
　　See also DLB 80
Van Campen, Karl
　　See Campbell, John W(ood, Jr.)
Vance, Gerald
　　See Silverberg, Robert
Vance, Jack ....CLC 35
　　See also Kuttner, Henry; Vance, John Holbrook
　　See also DLB 8
Vance, John Holbrook 1916-
　　See Queen, Ellery; Vance, Jack
　　See also CA 29-32R; CANR 17; MTCW
Van Den Bogarde, Derek Jules Gaspard Ulric
　　Niven 1921-
　　See Bogarde, Dirk
　　See also CA 77-80
Vandenburgh, Jane ....CLC 59
Vanderhaeghe, Guy 1951- ....CLC 41
　　See also CA 113
van der Post, Laurens (Jan) 1906-1996CLC 5
　　See also CA 5-8R; 155; CANR 35
van de Wetering, Janwillem 1931- ...CLC 47
　　See also CA 49-52; CANR 4, 62
Van Dine, S. S. .... TCLC 23
　　See also Wright, Willard Huntington
Van Doren, Carl (Clinton) 1885-1950 T C L C
　　18
　　See also CA 111
Van Doren, Mark 1894-1972 .... CLC 6, 10
　　See also CA 1-4R; 37-40R; CANR 3; DLB 45;
　　MTCW
Van Druten, John (William) 1901-1957TCLC
　　2
　　See also CA 104; 161; DLB 10
Van Duyn, Mona (Jane) 1921- CLC 3, 7, 63;
　　DAM POET
　　See also CA 9-12R; CANR 7, 38, 60; DLB 5
Van Dyne, Edith
　　See Baum, L(yman) Frank
van Itallie, Jean-Claude 1936- .... CLC 3
　　See also CA 45-48; CAAS 2; CANR 1, 48; DLB
　　7
van Ostaijen, Paul 1896-1928 .... TCLC 33
Van Peebles, Melvin 1932- .CLC 2, 20; DAM
　　MULT
　　See also BW 2; CA 85-88; CANR 27
Vansittart, Peter 1920- .... CLC 42
　　See also CA 1-4R; CANR 3, 49
Van Vechten, Carl 1880-1964 ....CLC 33
　　See also CA 89-92; DLB 4, 9, 51
Van Vogt, A(lfred) E(lton) 1912- ....CLC 1
　　See also CA 21-24R; CANR 28; DLB 8; SATA
　　14
Varda, Agnes 1928- ....CLC 16
　　See also CA 116; 122
Vargas Llosa, (Jorge) Mario (Pedro) 1936-
　　CLC 3, 6, 9, 10, 15, 31, 42, 85; DA; DAB;
　　DAC; DAM MST, MULT, NOV; HLC
　　See also CA 73-76; CANR 18, 32, 42; DLB 145;
　　HW; MTCW
Vasiliu, Gheorghe 1881-1957
　　See Bacovia, George
　　See also CA 123
Vassa, Gustavus
　　See Equiano, Olaudah
Vassilikos, Vassilis 1933- .... CLC 4, 8
　　See also CA 81-84
Vaughan, Henry 1621-1695 .... LC 27
　　See also DLB 131
Vaughn, Stephanie ....CLC 62
Vazov, Ivan (Minchov) 1850-1921 . TCLC 25
　　See also CA 121; DLB 147
Veblen, Thorstein (Bunde) 1857-1929 T C L C

31
　　See also CA 115
Vega, Lope de 1562-1635 .... LC 23
Venison, Alfred
　　See Pound, Ezra (Weston Loomis)
Verdi, Marie de
　　See Mencken, H(enry) L(ouis)
Verdu, Matilde
　　See Cela, Camilo Jose
Verga, Giovanni (Carmelo) 1840-1922T C L C
　　3; SSC 21
　　See also CA 104; 123
Vergil 70B.C.-19B.C. .... CMLC 9; DA; DAB;
　　DAC; DAM MST, POET; PC 12; WLCS
Verhaeren, Emile (Adolphe Gustave) 1855-1916
　　TCLC 12
　　See also CA 109
Verlaine, Paul (Marie) 1844-1896NCLC 2, 51;
　　DAM POET; PC 2
Verne, Jules (Gabriel) 1828-1905TCLC 6, 52
　　See also AAYA 16; CA 110; 131; DLB 123;
　　JRDA; MAICYA; SATA 21
Very, Jones 1813-1880 .... NCLC 9
　　See also DLB 1
Vesaas, Tarjei 1897-1970 .... CLC 48
　　See also CA 29-32R
Vialis, Gaston
　　See Simenon, Georges (Jacques Christian)
Vian, Boris 1920-1959 .... TCLC 9
　　See also CA 106; DLB 72
Viaud, (Louis Marie) Julien 1850-1923
　　See Loti, Pierre
　　See also CA 107
Vicar, Henry
　　See Felsen, Henry Gregor
Vicker, Angus
　　See Felsen, Henry Gregor
Vidal, Gore 1925-CLC 2, 4, 6, 8, 10, 22, 33, 72;
　　DAM NOV, POP
　　See also AITN 1; BEST 90:2; CA 5-8R; CANR
　　13, 45; DLB 6, 152; INT CANR-13; MTCW
Viereck, Peter (Robert Edwin) 1916- .CLC 4
　　See also CA 1-4R; CANR 1, 47; DLB 5
Vigny, Alfred (Victor) de 1797-1863NCLC 7;
　　DAM POET
　　See also DLB 119
Vilakazi, Benedict Wallet 1906-1947TCLC 37
Villiers de l'Isle Adam, Jean Marie Mathias
　　Philippe Auguste Comte 1838-1889
　　NCLC 3; SSC 14
　　See also DLB 123
Villon, Francois 1431-1463(?) ....PC 13
Vinci, Leonardo da 1452-1519 .... LC 12
Vine, Barbara .... CLC 50
　　See also Rendell, Ruth (Barbara)
　　See also BEST 90:4
Vinge, Joan D(ennison) 1948-CLC 30; SSC 24
　　See also CA 93-96; SATA 36
Violis, G.
　　See Simenon, Georges (Jacques Christian)
Visconti, Luchino 1906-1976 .... CLC 16
　　See also CA 81-84; 65-68; CANR 39
Vittorini, Elio 1908-1966 .... CLC 6, 9, 14
　　See also CA 133; 25-28R
Vizenor, Gerald Robert 1934-CLC 103; DAM
　　MULT
　　See also CA 13-16R; CAAS 22; CANR 5, 21,
　　44; DLB 175; NNAL
Vizinczey, Stephen 1933- .... CLC 40
　　See also CA 128; INT 128
Vliet, R(ussell) G(ordon) 1929-1984 CLC 22
　　See also CA 37-40R; 112; CANR 18
Vogau, Boris Andreyevich 1894-1937(?)

See Pilnyak, Boris
See also CA 123
Vogel, Paula A(nne) 1951- .... **CLC 76**
See also CA 108
Voight, Ellen Bryant 1943- .... **CLC 54**
See also CANR 11, 29, 55; DLB 120
Voigt, Cynthia 1942- .... **CLC 30**
See also AAYA 3; CA 106; CANR 18, 37, 40;
CLR 13,48; INT CANR-18; JRDA;
MAICYA; SATA 48, 79; SATA-Brief 33
Voinovich, Vladimir (Nikolaevich) 1932-**CLC 10, 49**
See also CA 81-84; CAAS 12; CANR 33;
MTCW
Vollmann, William T. 1959-...**CLC 89; DAM NOV, POP**
See also CA 134
Voloshinov, V. N.
See Bakhtin, Mikhail Mikhailovich
Voltaire 1694-1778 **LC 14; DA; DAB; DAC; DAM DRAM, MST; SSC 12; WLC**
von Daeniken, Erich 1935- .... **CLC 30**
See also AITN 1; CA 37-40R; CANR 17, 44
von Daniken, Erich
See von Daeniken, Erich
von Heidenstam, (Carl Gustaf) Verner
See Heidenstam, (Carl Gustaf) Verner von
von Heyse, Paul (Johann Ludwig)
See Heyse, Paul (Johann Ludwig von)
von Hofmannsthal, Hugo
See Hofmannsthal, Hugo von
von Horvath, Odon
See Horvath, Oedoen von
von Horvath, Oedoen
See Horvath, Oedoen von
von Liliencron, (Friedrich Adolf Axel) Detlev
See Liliencron, (Friedrich Adolf Axel) Detlev von
Vonnegut, Kurt, Jr. 1922-**CLC 1, 2, 3, 4, 5, 8, 12, 22, 40, 60; DA; DAB; DAC; DAM MST, NOV, POP; SSC 8; WLC**
See also AAYA 6; AITN 1; BEST 90:4; CA 1-4R; CANR 1, 25, 49; CDALB 1968-1988;
DLB 2, 8, 152; DLBD 3; DLBY 80; MTCW
Von Rachen, Kurt
See Hubbard, L(afayette) Ron(ald)
von Rezzori (d'Arezzo), Gregor
See Rezzori (d'Arezzo), Gregor von
von Sternberg, Josef
See Sternberg, Josef von
Vorster, Gordon 1924- .... **CLC 34**
See also CA 133
Vosce, Trudie
See Ozick, Cynthia
Voznesensky, Andrei (Andreievich) 1933-**CLC 1, 15, 57; DAM POET**
See also CA 89-92; CANR 37; MTCW
Waddington, Miriam 1917- .... **CLC 28**
See also CA 21-24R; CANR 12, 30; DLB 68
Wagman, Fredrica 1937- .... **CLC 7**
See also CA 97-100; INT 97-100
Wagner, Linda W.
See Wagner-Martin, Linda (C.)
Wagner, Linda Welshimer
See Wagner-Martin, Linda (C.)
Wagner, Richard 1813-1883 .... **NCLC 9**
See also DLB 129
Wagner-Martin, Linda (C.) 1936- ... **CLC 50**
See also CA 159
Wagoner, David (Russell) 1926- **CLC 3, 5, 15**
See also CA 1-4R; CAAS 3; CANR 2; DLB 5;
SATA 14
Wah, Fred(erick James) 1939- .... **CLC 44**

See also CA 107; 141; DLB 60
Wahloo, Per 1926-1975 ....**CLC 7**
See also CA 61-64
Wahloo, Peter
See Wahloo, Per
Wain, John (Barrington) 1925-1994 .**CLC 2, 11, 15, 46**
See also CA 5-8R; 145; CAAS 4; CANR 23, 54; CDBLB 1960 to Present; DLB 15, 27, 139, 155; MTCW
Wajda, Andrzej 1926- ....**CLC 16**
See also CA 102
Wakefield, Dan 1932- ....**CLC 7**
See also CA 21-24R; CAAS 7
Wakoski, Diane 1937-.**CLC 2, 4, 7, 9, 11, 40; DAM POET; PC 15**
See also CA 13-16R; CAAS 1; CANR 9, 60;
DLB 5; INT CANR-9
Wakoski-Sherbell, Diane
See Wakoski, Diane
Walcott, Derek (Alton) 1930-**CLC 2, 4, 9, 14, 25, 42, 67, 76; BLC; DAB; DAC; DAM MST, MULT, POET; DC 7**
See also BW 2; CA 89-92; CANR 26, 47; DLB 117; DLBY 81; MTCW
Waldman, Anne 1945-..........................**CLC 7**
See also CA 37-40R; CAAS 17; CANR 34; DLB 16
Waldo, E. Hunter
See Sturgeon, Theodore (Hamilton)
Waldo, Edward Hamilton
See Sturgeon, Theodore (Hamilton)
Walker, Alice (Malsenior) 1944- **CLC 5, 6, 9, 19, 27, 46, 58, 103; BLC; DA; DAB; DAC; DAM MST, MULT, NOV, POET, POP; SSC 5; WLCS**
See also AAYA 3; BEST 89:4; BW 2; CA 37-40R; CANR 9, 27, 49; CDALB 1968-1988;
DLB 6, 33, 143; INT CANR-27; MTCW;
SATA 31
Walker, David Harry 1911-1992 ....**CLC 14**
See also CA 1-4R; 137; CANR 1; SATA 8;
SATA-Obit 71
Walker, Edward Joseph 1934-
See Walker, Ted
See also CA 21-24R; CANR 12, 28, 53
Walker, George F. 1947- . **CLC 44, 61; DAB; DAC; DAM MST**
See also CA 103; CANR 21, 43, 59; DLB 60
Walker, Joseph A. 1935- .... **CLC 19; DAM DRAM, MST**
See also BW 1; CA 89-92; CANR 26; DLB 38
Walker, Margaret (Abigail) 1915- **CLC 1, 6; BLC; DAM MULT; PC 20**
See also BW 2; CA 73-76; CANR 26, 54; DLB 76, 152; MTCW
Walker, Ted ....**CLC 13**
See also Walker, Edward Joseph
See also DLB 40
Wallace, David Foster 1962- ....**CLC 50**
See also CA 132; CANR 59
Wallace, Dexter
See Masters, Edgar Lee
Wallace, (Richard Horatio) Edgar 1875-1932 **TCLC 57**
See also CA 115; DLB 70
Wallace, Irving 1916-1990 .**CLC 7, 13; DAM NOV, POP**
See also AITN 1; CA 1-4R; 132; CAAS 1;
CANR 1, 27; INT CANR-27; MTCW
Wallant, Edward Lewis 1926-1962**CLC 5, 10**
See also CA 1-4R; CANR 22; DLB 2, 28, 143;
MTCW

Walley, Byron
See Card, Orson Scott
Walpole, Horace 1717-1797 .... **LC 2**
See also DLB 39, 104
Walpole, Hugh (Seymour) 1884-1941**TCLC 5**
See also CA 104; DLB 34
Walser, Martin 1927- ....**CLC 27**
See also CA 57-60; CANR 8, 46; DLB 75, 124
Walser, Robert 1878-1956 **TCLC 18; SSC 20**
See also CA 118; DLB 66
Walsh, Jill Paton ....**CLC 35**
See also Paton Walsh, Gillian
See also AAYA 11; CLR 2; DLB 161; SAAS 3
Walter, Villiam Christian
See Andersen, Hans Christian
Wambaugh, Joseph (Aloysius, Jr.) 1937-**CLC 3, 18; DAM NOV, POP**
See also AITN 1; BEST 89:3; CA 33-36R;
CANR 42; DLB 6; DLBY 83; MTCW
Wang Wei 699(?)-761(?) ....**PC 18**
Ward, Arthur Henry Sarsfield 1883-1959
See Rohmer, Sax
See also CA 108
Ward, Douglas Turner 1930- ....**CLC 19**
See also BW 1; CA 81-84; CANR 27; DLB 7, 38
Ward, Mary Augusta
See Ward, Mrs. Humphry
Ward, Mrs. Humphry 1851-1920 .. **TCLC 55**
See also DLB 18
Ward, Peter
See Faust, Frederick (Schiller)
Warhol, Andy 1928(?)-1987 ....**CLC 20**
See also AAYA 12; BEST 89:4; CA 89-92; 121;
CANR 34
Warner, Francis (Robert le Plastrier) 1937-**CLC 14**
See also CA 53-56; CANR 11
Warner, Marina 1946- ....**CLC 59**
See also CA 65-68; CANR 21, 55
Warner, Rex (Ernest) 1905-1986 ......**CLC 45**
See also CA 89-92; 119; DLB 15
Warner, Susan (Bogert) 1819-1885 **NCLC 31**
See also DLB 3, 42
Warner, Sylvia (Constance) Ashton
See Ashton-Warner, Sylvia (Constance)
Warner, Sylvia Townsend 1893-1978 **CLC 7, 19; SSC 23**
See also CA 61-64; 77-80; CANR 16, 60; DLB 34, 139; MTCW
Warren, Mercy Otis 1728-1814 ......**NCLC 13**
See also DLB 31
Warren, Robert Penn 1905-1989**CLC 1, 4, 6, 8, 10, 13, 18, 39, 53, 59; DA; DAB; DAC; DAM MST, NOV, POET; SSC 4; WLC**
See also AITN 1; CA 13-16R; 129; CANR 10, 47; CDALB 1968-1988; DLB 2, 48, 152;
DLBY 80, 89; INT CANR-10; MTCW; SATA 46; SATA-Obit 63
Warshofsky, Isaac
See Singer, Isaac Bashevis
Warton, Thomas 1728-1790 ..... **LC 15; DAM POET**
See also DLB 104, 109
Waruk, Kona
See Harris, (Theodore) Wilson
Warung, Price 1855-1911 .... **TCLC 45**
Warwick, Jarvis
See Garner, Hugh
Washington, Alex
See Harris, Mark
Washington, Booker T(aliaferro) 1856-1915 **TCLC 10; BLC; DAM MULT**

See also BW 1; CA 114; 125; SATA 28
Washington, George 1732-1799 .... **LC 25**
See also DLB 31
Wassermann, (Karl) Jakob 1873-1934 **T C L C 6**
See also CA 104; DLB 66
Wasserstein, Wendy 1950- ... **CLC 32, 59, 90; DAM DRAM; DC 4**
See also CA 121; 129; CABS 3; CANR 53; INT 129; SATA 94
Waterhouse, Keith (Spencer) 1929-. **CLC 47**
See also CA 5-8R; CANR 38; DLB 13, 15; MTCW
Waters, Frank (Joseph) 1902-1995 .. **CLC 88**
See also CA 5-8R; 149; CAAS 13; CANR 3, 18; DLBY 86
Waters, Roger 1944-........................... **CLC 35**
Watkins, Frances Ellen
See Harper, Frances Ellen Watkins
Watkins, Gerrold
See Malzberg, Barry N(athaniel)
Watkins, Gloria 1955(?)-
See hooks, bell
See also BW 2; CA 143
Watkins, Paul 1964- .... **CLC 55**
See also CA 132; CANR 62
Watkins, Vernon Phillips 1906-1967 **CLC 43**
See also CA 9-10; 25-28R; CAP 1; DLB 20
Watson, Irving S.
See Mencken, H(enry) L(ouis)
Watson, John H.
See Farmer, Philip Jose
Watson, Richard F.
See Silverberg, Robert
Waugh, Auberon (Alexander) 1939- ..**CLC 7**
See also CA 45-48; CANR 6, 22; DLB 14
Waugh, Evelyn (Arthur St. John) 1903-1966 **CLC 1, 3, 8, 13, 19, 27, 44; DA; DAB; DAC; DAM MST, NOV, POP; WLC**
See also CA 85-88; 25-28R; CANR 22; CDBLB 1914-1945; DLB 15, 162; MTCW
Waugh, Harriet 1944- ....**CLC 6**
See also CA 85-88; CANR 22
Ways, C. R.
See Blount, Roy (Alton), Jr.
Waystaff, Simon
See Swift, Jonathan
Webb, (Martha) Beatrice (Potter) 1858-1943 **TCLC 22**
See also Potter, (Helen) Beatrix
See also CA 117
Webb, Charles (Richard) 1939- ....**CLC 7**
See also CA 25-28R
Webb, James H(enry), Jr. 1946- ...... **CLC 22**
See also CA 81-84
Webb, Mary (Gladys Meredith) 1881-1927 **TCLC 24**
See also CA 123; DLB 34
Webb, Mrs. Sidney
See Webb, (Martha) Beatrice (Potter)
Webb, Phyllis 1927-........................... **CLC 18**
See also CA 104; CANR 23; DLB 53
Webb, Sidney (James) 1859-1947 .. **TCLC 22**
See also CA 117
Webber, Andrew Lloyd .... **CLC 21**
See also Lloyd Webber, Andrew
Weber, Lenora Mattingly 1895-1971 **CLC 12**
See also CA 19-20; 29-32R; CAP 1; SATA 2; SATA-Obit 26
Weber, Max 1864-1920 .... **TCLC 69**
See also CA 109
Webster, John 1579(?)-1634(?) ... **LC 33; DA; DAB; DAC; DAM DRAM, MST; DC 2;**

WLC
See also CDBLB Before 1660; DLB 58
Webster, Noah 1758-1843 ....**NCLC 30**
Wedekind, (Benjamin) Frank(lin) 1864-1918 **TCLC 7; DAM DRAM**
See also CA 104; 153; DLB 118
Weidman, Jerome 1913- ....**CLC 7**
See also AITN 2; CA 1-4R; CANR 1; DLB 28
Weil, Simone (Adolphine) 1909-1943**TCLC 23**
See also CA 117; 159
Weinstein, Nathan
See West, Nathanael
Weinstein, Nathan von Wallenstein
See West, Nathanael
Weir, Peter (Lindsay) 1944- ....**CLC 20**
See also CA 113; 123
Weiss, Peter (Ulrich) 1916-1982**CLC 3, 15, 51; DAM DRAM**
See also CA 45-48; 106; CANR 3; DLB 69, 124
Weiss, Theodore (Russell) 1916-**CLC 3, 8, 14**
See also CA 9-12R; CAAS 2; CANR 46; DLB 5
Welch, (Maurice) Denton 1915-1948**TCLC 22**
See also CA 121; 148
Welch, James 1940- ..... **CLC 6, 14, 52; DAM MULT, POP**
See also CA 85-88; CANR 42; DLB 175; NNAL
Weldon, Fay 1933-..**CLC 6, 9, 11, 19, 36, 59; DAM POP**
See also CA 21-24R; CANR 16, 46; CDBLB 1960 to Present; DLB 14; INT CANR-16; MTCW
Wellek, Rene 1903-1995 .... **CLC 28**
See also CA 5-8R; 150; CAAS 7; CANR 8; DLB 63; INT CANR-8
Weller, Michael 1942- .... **CLC 10, 53**
See also CA 85-88
Weller, Paul 1958-............................... **CLC 26**
Wellershoff, Dieter 1925-...................**CLC 46**
See also CA 89-92; CANR 16, 37
Welles, (George) Orson 1915-1985**CLC 20, 80**
See also CA 93-96; 117
Wellman, Mac 1945- .... **CLC 65**
Wellman, Manly Wade 1903-1986 ....**CLC 49**
See also CA 1-4R; 118; CANR 6, 16, 44; SATA 6; SATA-Obit 47
Wells, Carolyn 1869(?)-1942 .... **TCLC 35**
See also CA 113; DLB 11
Wells, H(erbert) G(eorge) 1866-1946**TCLC 6, 12, 19; DA; DAB; DAC; DAM MST, NOV; SSC 6; WLC**
See also AAYA 18; CA 110; 121; CDBLB 1914-1945; DLB 34, 70, 156, 178; MTCW; SATA 20
Wells, Rosemary 1943-.......................**CLC 12**
See also AAYA 13; CA 85-88; CANR 48; CLR 16; MAICYA; SAAS 1; SATA 18, 69
Welty, Eudora 1909- **CLC 1, 2, 5, 14, 22, 33, 105; DA; DAB; DAC; DAM MST, NOV; SSC 1, 27; WLC**
See also CA 9-12R; CABS 1; CANR 32; CDALB 1941-1968; DLB 2, 102, 143; DLBD 12; DLBY 87; MTCW
Wen I-to 1899-1946 .... **TCLC 28**
Wentworth, Robert
See Hamilton, Edmond
Werfel, Franz (Viktor) 1890-1945 ... **TCLC 8**
See also CA 104; 161; DLB 81, 124
Wergeland, Henrik Arnold 1808-1845**N C L C 5**

SATA 1, 58
Wertmueller, Lina 1928- .... **CLC 16**
See also CA 97-100; CANR 39
Wescott, Glenway 1901-1987 .... **CLC 13**
See also CA 13-16R; 121; CANR 23; DLB 4, 9, 102
Wesker, Arnold 1932-.... **CLC 3, 5, 42; DAB; DAM DRAM**
See also CA 1-4R; CAAS 7; CANR 1, 33; CDBLB 1960 to Present; DLB 13; MTCW
Wesley, Richard (Errol) 1945- ....**CLC 7**
See also BW 1; CA 57-60; CANR 27; DLB 38
Wessel, Johan Herman 1742-1785 .... **LC 7**
West, Anthony (Panther) 1914-1987 **CLC 50**
See also CA 45-48; 124; CANR 3, 19; DLB 15
West, C. P.
See Wodehouse, P(elham) G(renville)
West, (Mary) Jessamyn 1902-1984**CLC 7, 17**
See also CA 9-12R; 112; CANR 27; DLB 6; DLBY 84; MTCW; SATA-Obit 37
West, Morris L(anglo) 1916- .... **CLC 6, 33**
See also CA 5-8R; CANR 24, 49; MTCW
West, Nathanael 1903-1940 **TCLC 1, 14, 44; SSC 16**
See also CA 104; 125; CDALB 1929-1941; DLB 4, 9, 28; MTCW
West, Owen
See Koontz, Dean R(ay)
West, Paul 1930- .... **CLC 7, 14, 96**
See also CA 13-16R; CAAS 7; CANR 22, 53; DLB 14; INT CANR-22
West, Rebecca 1892-1983 ... **CLC 7, 9, 31, 50**
See also CA 5-8R; 109; CANR 19; DLB 36; DLBY 83; MTCW
Westall, Robert (Atkinson) 1929-1993**CLC 17**
See also AAYA 12; CA 69-72; 141; CANR 18; CLR 13; JRDA; MAICYA; SAAS 2; SATA 23, 69; SATA-Obit 75
Westlake, Donald E(dwin) 1933- **CLC 7, 33; DAM POP**
See also CA 17-20R; CAAS 13; CANR 16, 44; INT CANR-16
Westmacott, Mary
See Christie, Agatha (Mary Clarissa)
Weston, Allen
See Norton, Andre
Wetcheek, J. L.
See Feuchtwanger, Lion
Wetering, Janwillem van de
See van de Wetering, Janwillem
Wetherell, Elizabeth
See Warner, Susan (Bogert)
Whale, James 1889-1957 .... **TCLC 63**
Whalen, Philip 1923-...................... **CLC 6, 29**
See also CA 9-12R; CANR 5, 39; DLB 16
Wharton, Edith (Newbold Jones) 1862-1937 **TCLC 3, 9, 27, 53; DA; DAB; DAC; DAM MST, NOV; SSC 6; WLC**
See also CA 104; 132; CDALB 1865-1917; DLB 4, 9, 12, 78; DLBD 13; MTCW
Wharton, James
See Mencken, H(enry) L(ouis)
Wharton, William (a pseudonym)CLC 18, 37
See also CA 93-96; DLBY 80; INT 93-96
Wheatley (Peters), Phillis 1754(?)-1784**LC 3; BLC; DA; DAC; DAM MST, MULT, POET; PC 3; WLC**
See also CDALB 1640-1865; DLB 31, 50
Wheelock, John Hall 1886-1978 ...... **CLC 14**
See also CA 13-16R; 77-80; CANR 14; DLB 45
White, E(lwyn) B(rooks) 1899-1985 **CLC 10, 34, 39; DAM POP**

See also AITN 2; CA 13-16R; 116; CANR 16, 37; CLR 1, 21; DLB 11, 22; MAICYA; MTCW; SATA 2, 29; SATA-Obit 44

White, Edmund (Valentine III) 1940-CLC 27; DAM POP
See also AAYA 7; CA 45-48; CANR 3, 19, 36, 62; MTCW

White, Patrick (Victor Martindale) 1912-1990 CLC 3, 4, 5, 7, 9, 18, 65, 69
See also CA 81-84; 132; CANR 43; MTCW

White, Phyllis Dorothy James 1920-
See James, P. D.
See also CA 21-24R; CANR 17, 43; DAM POP; MTCW

White, T(erence) H(anbury) 1906-1964 C L C 30
See also AAYA 22; CA 73-76; CANR 37; DLB 160; JRDA; MAICYA; SATA 12

White, Terence de Vere 1912-1994 .. CLC 49
See also CA 49-52; 145; CANR 3

White, Walter F(rancis) 1893-1955 TCLC 15
See also White, Walter
See also BW 1; CA 115; 124; DLB 51

White, William Hale 1831-1913
See Rutherford, Mark
See also CA 121

Whitehead, E(dward) A(nthony) 1933-CLC 5
See also CA 65-68; CANR 58

Whitemore, Hugh (John) 1936- .... CLC 37
See also CA 132; INT 132

Whitman, Sarah Helen (Power) 1803-1878 NCLC 19
See also DLB 1

Whitman, Walt(er) 1819-1892 .. NCLC 4, 31; DA; DAB; DAC; DAM MST, POET; PC 3; WLC
See also CDALB 1640-1865; DLB 3, 64; SATA 20

Whitney, Phyllis A(yame) 1903- ..... CLC 42; DAM POP
See also AITN 2; BEST 90:3; CA 1-4R; CANR 3, 25, 38, 60; JRDA; MAICYA; SATA 1, 30

Whittemore, (Edward) Reed (Jr.) 1919-CLC 4
See also CA 9-12R; CAAS 8; CANR 4; DLB 5

Whittier, John Greenleaf 1807-1892NCLC 8, 59
See also DLB 1

Whittlebot, Hernia
See Coward, Noel (Peirce)

Wicker, Thomas Grey 1926-
See Wicker, Tom
See also CA 65-68; CANR 21, 46

Wicker, Tom .... CLC 7
See also Wicker, Thomas Grey

Wideman, John Edgar 1941- CLC 5, 34, 36, 67; BLC; DAM MULT
See also BW 2; CA 85-88; CANR 14, 42; DLB 33, 143

Wiebe, Rudy (Henry) 1934-... CLC 6, 11, 14; DAC; DAM MST
See also CA 37-40R; CANR 42; DLB 60

Wieland, Christoph Martin 1733-1813N C L C 17
See also DLB 97

Wiene, Robert 1881-1938 .... TCLC 56

Wieners, John 1934-............................CLC 7
See also CA 13-16R; DLB 16

Wiesel, Elie(zer) 1928- CLC 3, 5, 11, 37; DA; DAB; DAC; DAM MST, NOV; WLCS 2
See also AAYA 7; AITN 1; CA 5-8R; CAAS 4; CANR 8, 40; DLB 83; DLBY 87; INT CANR-8; MTCW; SATA 56

Wiggins, Marianne 1947- .... CLC 57

See also BEST 89:3; CA 130; CANR 60

Wight, James Alfred 1916-
See Herriot, James
See also CA 77-80; SATA 55; SATA-Brief 44

Wilbur, Richard (Purdy) 1921-CLC 3, 6, 9, 14, 53; DA; DAB; DAC; DAM MST, POET
See also CA 1-4R; CABS 2; CANR 2, 29; DLB 5, 169; INT CANR-29; MTCW; SATA 9

Wild, Peter 1940- .... CLC 14
See also CA 37-40R; DLB 5

Wilde, Oscar (Fingal O'Flahertie Wills) 1854(?)-1900TCLC 1, 8, 23, 41; DA; DAB; DAC; DAM DRAM, MST, NOV; SSC 11; WLC
See also CA 104; 119; CDBLB 1890-1914; DLB 10, 19, 34, 57, 141, 156; SATA 24

Wilder, Billy .... CLC 20
See also Wilder, Samuel
See also DLB 26

Wilder, Samuel 1906-
See Wilder, Billy
See also CA 89-92

Wilder, Thornton (Niven) 1897-1975CLC 1, 5, 6, 10, 15, 35, 82; DA; DAB; DAC; DAM DRAM, MST, NOV; DC 1; WLC
See also AITN 2; CA 13-16R; 61-64; CANR 40; DLB 4, 7, 9; MTCW

Wilding, Michael 1942-....................... CLC 73
See also CA 104; CANR 24, 49

Wiley, Richard 1944- .... CLC 44
See also CA 121; 129

Wilhelm, Kate .... CLC 7
See also Wilhelm, Katie Gertrude
See also AAYA 20; CAAS 5; DLB 8; INT CANR-17

Wilhelm, Katie Gertrude 1928-
See Wilhelm, Kate
See also CA 37-40R; CANR 17, 36, 60; MTCW

Wilkins, Mary
See Freeman, Mary Eleanor Wilkins

Willard, Nancy 1936- .... CLC 7, 37
See also CA 89-92; CANR 10, 39; CLR 5; DLB 5, 52; MAICYA; MTCW; SATA 37, 71; SATA-Brief 30

Williams, C(harles) K(enneth) 1936-CLC 33, 56; DAM POET
See also CA 37-40R; CAAS 26; CANR 57; DLB 5

Williams, Charles
See Collier, James L(incoln)

Williams, Charles (Walter Stansby) 1886-1945 TCLC 1, 11
See also CA 104; DLB 100, 153

Williams, (George) Emlyn 1905-1987CLC 15; DAM DRAM
See also CA 104; 123; CANR 36; DLB 10, 77; MTCW

Williams, Hugo 1942-.......................... CLC 42
See also CA 17-20R; CANR 45; DLB 40

Williams, J. Walker
See Wodehouse, P(elham) G(renville)

Williams, John A(lfred) 1925-..... CLC 5, 13; BLC; DAM MULT
See also BW 2; CA 53-56; CAAS 3; CANR 6, 26, 51; DLB 2, 33; INT CANR-6

Williams, Jonathan (Chamberlain) 1929- CLC 13
See also CA 9-12R; CAAS 12; CANR 8; DLB 5

Williams, Joy 1944- .... CLC 31
See also CA 41-44R; CANR 22, 48

Williams, Norman 1952- .... CLC 39
See also CA 118

Williams, Sherley Anne 1944-CLC 89; BLC; DAM MULT, POET
See also BW 2; CA 73-76; CANR 25; DLB 41; INT CANR-25; SATA 78

Williams, Shirley
See Williams, Sherley Anne

Williams, Tennessee 1911-1983CLC 1, 2, 5, 7, 8, 11, 15, 19, 30, 39, 45, 71; DA; DAB; DAC; DAM DRAM, MST; DC 4; WLC
See also AITN 1, 2; CA 5-8R; 108; CABS 3; CANR 31; CDALB 1941-1968; DLB 7; DLBD 4; DLBY 83; MTCW

Williams, Thomas (Alonzo) 1926-1990CLC 14
See also CA 1-4R; 132; CANR 2

Williams, William C.
See Williams, William Carlos

Williams, William Carlos 1883-1963CLC 1, 2, 5, 9, 13, 22, 42, 67; DA; DAB; DAC; DAM MST, POET; PC 7
See also CA 89-92; CANR 34; CDALB 1917-1929; DLB 4, 16, 54, 86; MTCW

Williamson, David (Keith) 1942- ...... CLC 56
See also CA 103; CANR 41

Williamson, Ellen Douglas 1905-1984
See Douglas, Ellen
See also CA 17-20R; 114; CANR 39

Williamson, Jack .... CLC 29
See also Williamson, John Stewart
See also CAAS 8; DLB 8

Williamson, John Stewart 1908-
See Williamson, Jack
See also CA 17-20R; CANR 23

Willie, Frederick
See Lovecraft, H(oward) P(hillips)

Willingham, Calder (Baynard, Jr.) 1922-1995 CLC 5, 51
See also CA 5-8R; 147; CANR 3; DLB 2, 44; MTCW

Willis, Charles
See Clarke, Arthur C(harles)

Willy
See Colette, (Sidonie-Gabrielle)

Willy, Colette
See Colette, (Sidonie-Gabrielle)

Wilson, A(ndrew) N(orman) 1950- ...CLC 33
See also CA 112; 122; DLB 14, 155

Wilson, Angus (Frank Johnstone) 1913-1991 CLC 2, 3, 5, 25, 34; SSC 21
See also CA 5-8R; 134; CANR 21; DLB 15, 139, 155; MTCW

Wilson, August 1945- CLC 39, 50, 63; BLC; DA; DAB; DAC; DAM DRAM, MST, MULT; DC 2; WLCS
See also AAYA 16; BW 2; CA 115; 122; CANR 42, 54; MTCW

Wilson, Brian 1942- .... CLC 12

Wilson, Colin 1931-....................... CLC 3, 14
See also CA 1-4R; CAAS 5; CANR 1, 22, 33; DLB 14; MTCW

Wilson, Dirk
See Pohl, Frederik

Wilson, Edmund 1895-1972CLC 1, 2, 3, 8, 24
See also CA 1-4R; 37-40R; CANR 1, 46; DLB 63; MTCW

Wilson, Ethel Davis (Bryant) 1888(?)-1980 CLC 13; DAC; DAM POET
See also CA 102; DLB 68; MTCW

Wilson, John 1785-1854 ....NCLC 5

Wilson, John (Anthony) Burgess 1917-1993
See Burgess, Anthony
See also CA 1-4R; 143; CANR 2, 46; DAC; DAM NOV; MTCW

Wilson, Lanford 1937- CLC 7, 14, 36; DAM

DRAM
See also CA 17-20R; CABS 3; CANR 45; DLB 7

Wilson, Robert M. 1944- .... **CLC 7, 9**
See also CA 49-52; CANR 2, 41; MTCW

Wilson, Robert McLiam 1964-......... **CLC 59**
See also CA 132

Wilson, Sloan 1920-........................... **CLC 32**
See also CA 1-4R; CANR 1, 44

Wilson, Snoo 1948-............................ **CLC 33**
See also CA 69-72

Wilson, William S(mith) 1932-......... **CLC 49**
See also CA 81-84

Wilson, Woodrow 1856-1924 .... **TCLC 73**
See also DLB 47

Winchilsea, Anne (Kingsmill) Finch Counte
1661-1720 .... **LC 3**

Windham, Basil
See Wodehouse, P(elham) G(renville)

Wingrove, David (John) 1954- .... **CLC 68**
See also CA 133

Wintergreen, Jane
See Duncan, Sara Jeannette

Winters, Janet Lewis .... **CLC 41**
See also Lewis, Janet
See also DLBY 87

Winters, (Arthur) Yvor 1900-1968 **CLC 4, 8, 32**
See also CA 11-12; 25-28R; CAP 1; DLB 48; MTCW

Winterson, Jeanette 1959-**CLC 64; DAM POP**
See also CA 136; CANR 58

Winthrop, John 1588-1649 .... **LC 31**
See also DLB 24, 30

Wiseman, Frederick 1930-................ **CLC 20**
See also CA 159

Wister, Owen 1860-1938 .... **TCLC 21**
See also CA 108; DLB 9, 78; SATA 62

Witkacy
See Witkiewicz, Stanislaw Ignacy

Witkiewicz, Stanislaw Ignacy 1885-1939
TCLC 8
See also CA 105

Wittgenstein, Ludwig (Josef Johann) 1889-1951
TCLC 59
See also CA 113

Wittig, Monique 1935(?)-.................. **CLC 22**
See also CA 116; 135; DLB 83

Wittlin, Jozef 1896-1976 .... **CLC 25**
See also CA 49-52; 65-68; CANR 3

Wodehouse, P(elham) G(renville) 1881-1975
CLC 1, 2, 5, 10, 22; DAB; DAC; DAM NOV; SSC 2
See also AITN 2; CA 45-48; 57-60; CANR 3, 33; CDBLB 1914-1945; DLB 34, 162; MTCW; SATA 22

Woiwode, L.
See Woiwode, Larry (Alfred)

Woiwode, Larry (Alfred) 1941- ... **CLC 6, 10**
See also CA 73-76; CANR 16; DLB 6; INT CANR-16

Wojciechowska, Maia (Teresa) 1927-**CLC 26**
See also AAYA 8; CA 9-12R; CANR 4, 41; CLR 1; JRDA; MAICYA; SAAS 1; SATA 1, 28, 83

Wolf, Christa 1929- .... **CLC 14, 29, 58**
See also CA 85-88; CANR 45; DLB 75; MTCW

Wolfe, Gene (Rodman) 1931- **CLC 25; DAM POP**
See also CA 57-60; CAAS 9; CANR 6, 32, 60; DLB 8

Wolfe, George C. 1954- .... **CLC 49**
See also CA 149

Wolfe, Thomas (Clayton) 1900-1938**TCLC 4, 13, 29, 61; DA; DAB; DAC; DAM MST, NOV; WLC**
See also CA 104; 132; CDALB 1929-1941; DLB 9, 102; DLBD 2, 16; DLBY 85; MTCW

Wolfe, Thomas Kennerly, Jr. 1931-
See Wolfe, Tom
See also CA 13-16R; CANR 9, 33; DAM POP; INT CANR-9; MTCW

Wolfe, Tom .... **CLC 1, 2, 9, 15, 35, 51**
See also Wolfe, Thomas Kennerly, Jr.
See also AAYA 8; AITN 2; BEST 89:1; DLB 152

Wolff, Geoffrey (Ansell) 1937- .... **CLC 41**
See also CA 29-32R; CANR 29, 43

Wolff, Sonia
See Levitin, Sonia (Wolff)

Wolff, Tobias (Jonathan Ansell) 1945-.. **C L C 39, 64**
See also AAYA 16; BEST 90:2; CA 114; 117; CAAS 22; CANR 54; DLB 130; INT 117

Wolfram von Eschenbach c. 1170-c. 1220
CMLC 5
See also DLB 138

Wolitzer, Hilma 1930- ....**CLC 17**
See also CA 65-68; CANR 18, 40; INT CANR-18; SATA 31

Wollstonecraft, Mary 1759-1797 .... **LC 5**
See also CDBLB 1789-1832; DLB 39, 104, 158

Wonder, Stevie ....**CLC 12**
See also Morris, Steveland Judkins

Wong, Jade Snow 1922- ....**CLC 17**
See also CA 109

Woodberry, George Edward 1855-1930
TCLC 73
See also DLB 71, 103

Woodcott, Keith
See Brunner, John (Kilian Houston)

Woodruff, Robert W.
See Mencken, H(enry) L(ouis)

Woolf, (Adeline) Virginia 1882-1941**TCLC 1, 5, 20, 43, 56; DA; DAB; DAC; DAM MST, NOV; SSC 7; WLC**
See also CA 104; 130; CDBLB 1914-1945; DLB 36, 100, 162; DLBD 10; MTCW

Woollcott, Alexander (Humphreys) 1887-1943
TCLC 5
See also CA 105; 161; DLB 29

Woolrich, Cornell 1903-1968 .... **CLC 77**
See also Hopley-Woolrich, Cornell George

Wordsworth, Dorothy 1771-1855 .. **NCLC 25**
See also DLB 107

Wordsworth, William 1770-1850 ..**NCLC 12, 38; DA; DAB; DAC; DAM MST, POET; PC 4; WLC**
See also CDBLB 1789-1832; DLB 93, 107

Wouk, Herman 1915-**CLC 1, 9, 38; DAM NOV, POP**
See also CA 5-8R; CANR 6, 33; DLBY 82; INT CANR-6; MTCW

Wright, Charles (Penzel, Jr.) 1935-**CLC 6, 13, 28**
See also CA 29-32R; CAAS 7; CANR 23, 36, 62; DLB 165; DLBY 82; MTCW

Wright, Charles Stevenson 1932- ... **CLC 49; BLC 3; DAM MULT, POET**
See also BW 1; CA 9-12R; CANR 26; DLB 33

Wright, Jack R.
See Harris, Mark

Wright, James (Arlington) 1927-1980**CLC 3, 5, 10, 28; DAM POET**
See also AITN 2; CA 49-52; 97-100; CANR 4, 34; DLB 5, 169; MTCW

Wright, Judith (Arandell) 1915- **CLC 11, 53; PC 14**
See also CA 13-16R; CANR 31; MTCW; SATA 14

Wright, L(aurali) R. 1939- .... **CLC 44**
See also CA 138

Wright, Richard (Nathaniel) 1908-1960 **C L C 1, 3, 4, 9, 14, 21, 48, 74; BLC; DA; DAB; DAC; DAM MST, MULT, NOV; SSC 2; WLC**
See also AAYA 5; BW 1; CA 108; CDALB 1929-1941; DLB 76, 102; DLBD 2; MTCW

Wright, Richard B(ruce) 1937-.......... **CLC 6**
See also CA 85-88; DLB 53

Wright, Rick 1945- .... **CLC 35**

Wright, Rowland
See Wells, Carolyn

Wright, Stephen Caldwell 1946- ...... **CLC 33**
See also BW 2

Wright, Willard Huntington 1888-1939
See Van Dine, S. S.
See also CA 115; DLBD 16

Wright, William 1930- .... **CLC 44**
See also CA 53-56; CANR 7, 23

Wroth, LadyMary 1587-1653(?) .... **LC 30**
See also DLB 121

Wu Ch'eng-en 1500(?)-1582(?) .... **LC 7**

Wu Ching-tzu 1701-1754 .... **LC 2**

Wurlitzer, Rudolph 1938(?)- .... **CLC 2, 4, 15**
See also CA 85-88; DLB 173

Wycherley, William 1641-1715**LC 8, 21; DAM DRAM**
See also CDBLB 1660-1789; DLB 80

Wylie, Elinor (Morton Hoyt) 1885-1928
TCLC 8
See also CA 105; DLB 9, 45

Wylie, Philip (Gordon) 1902-1971 ... **CLC 43**
See also CA 21-22; 33-36R; CAP 2; DLB 9

Wyndham, John .... **CLC 19**
See also Harris, John (Wyndham Parkes Lucas) Beynon

Wyss, Johann David Von 1743-1818**NCLC 10**
See also JRDA; MAICYA; SATA 29; SATA-Brief 27

Xenophon c. 430B.C.-c. 354B.C. ... **CMLC 17**
See also DLB 176

Yakumo Koizumi
See Hearn, (Patricio) Lafcadio (Tessima Carlos)

Yanez, Jose Donoso
See Donoso (Yanez), Jose

Yanovsky, Basile S.
See Yanovsky, V(assily) S(emenovich)

Yanovsky, V(assily) S(emenovich) 1906-1989
CLC 2, 18
See also CA 97-100; 129

Yates, Richard 1926-1992 .... **CLC 7, 8, 23**
See also CA 5-8R; 139; CANR 10, 43; DLB 2; DLBY 81, 92; INT CANR-10

Yeats, W. B.
See Yeats, William Butler

Yeats, William Butler 1865-1939**TCLC 1, 11, 18, 31; DA; DAB; DAC; DAM DRAM, MST, POET; PC 20; WLC**
See also CA 104; 127; CANR 45; CDBLB 1890-1914; DLB 10, 19, 98, 156; MTCW

Yehoshua, A(braham) B. 1936-.. **CLC 13, 31**
See also CA 33-36R; CANR 43

Yep, Laurence Michael 1948-.......... **CLC 35**
See also AAYA 5; CA 49-52; CANR 1, 46; CLR 3, 17; DLB 52; JRDA; MAICYA; SATA 7, 69

Yerby, Frank G(arvin) 1916-1991 **CLC 1, 7, 22; BLC; DAM MULT**

See also BW 1; CA 9-12R; 136; CANR 16, 52; DLB 76; INT CANR-16; MTCW

Yesenin, Sergei Alexandrovich
See Esenin, Sergei (Alexandrovich)

Yevtushenko, Yevgeny (Alexandrovich) 1933- **CLC 1, 3, 13, 26, 51; DAM POET**
See also CA 81-84; CANR 33, 54; MTCW

Yezierska, Anzia 1885(?)-1970 .... **CLC 46**
See also CA 126; 89-92; DLB 28; MTCW

Yglesias, Helen 1915- .... **CLC 7, 22**
See also CA 37-40R; CAAS 20; CANR 15; INT CANR-15; MTCW

Yokomitsu Riichi 1898-1947 .... **TCLC 47**

Yonge, Charlotte (Mary) 1823-1901 **TCLC 48**
See also CA 109; DLB 18, 163; SATA 17

York, Jeremy
See Creasey, John

York, Simon
See Heinlein, Robert A(nson)

Yorke, Henry Vincent 1905-1974 ..... **CLC 13**
See also Green, Henry
See also CA 85-88; 49-52

Yosano Akiko 1878-1942 .... **TCLC 59; PC 11**
See also CA 161

Yoshimoto, Banana .... **CLC 84**
See also Yoshimoto, Mahoko

Yoshimoto, Mahoko 1964-
See Yoshimoto, Banana
See also CA 144

Young, Al(bert James) 1939- . **CLC 19; BLC; DAM MULT**
See also BW 2; CA 29-32R; CANR 26; DLB 33

Young, Andrew (John) 1885-1971 ...... **CLC 5**
See also CA 5-8R; CANR 7, 29

Young, Collier
See Bloch, Robert (Albert)

Young, Edward 1683-1765 .... **LC 3, 40**
See also DLB 95

Young, Marguerite (Vivian) 1909-1995 **C L C 82**
See also CA 13-16; 150; CAP 1

Young, Neil 1945- .... **CLC 17**
See also CA 110

Young Bear, Ray A. 1950- ..... **CLC 94; DAM MULT**
See also CA 146; DLB 175; NNAL

Yourcenar, Marguerite 1903-1987 **CLC 19, 38, 50, 87; DAM NOV**
See also CA 69-72; CANR 23, 60; DLB 72; DLBY 88; MTCW

Yurick, Sol 1925- .... **CLC 6**
See also CA 13-16R; CANR 25

Zabolotskii, Nikolai Alekseevich 1903-1958 **TCLC 52**
See also CA 116

Zamiatin, Yevgenii
See Zamyatin, Evgeny Ivanovich

Zamora, Bernice (B. Ortiz) 1938-... **CLC 89; DAM MULT; HLC**
See also CA 151; DLB 82; HW

Zamyatin, Evgeny Ivanovich 1884-1937 **TCLC 8, 37**
See also CA 105

Zangwill, Israel 1864-1926 .... **TCLC 16**
See also CA 109; DLB 10, 135

Zappa, Francis Vincent, Jr. 1940-1993
See Zappa, Frank
See also CA 108; 143; CANR 57

Zappa, Frank .... **CLC 17**
See also Zappa, Francis Vincent, Jr.

Zaturenska, Marya 1902-1982 ...... **CLC 6, 11**
See also CA 13-16R; 105; CANR 22

Zeami 1363-1443 .... **DC 7**

Zelazny, Roger (Joseph) 1937-1995 . **CLC 21**
See also AAYA 7; CA 21-24R; 148; CANR 26, 60; DLB 8; MTCW; SATA 57; SATA-Brief 39

Zhdanov, Andrei A(lexandrovich) 1896-1948 **TCLC 18**
See also CA 117

Zhukovsky, Vasily 1783-1852 .... **NCLC 35**

Ziegenhagen, Eric .... **CLC 55**

Zimmer, Jill Schary
See Robinson, Jill

Zimmerman, Robert
See Dylan, Bob

Zindel, Paul 1936- **CLC 6, 26; DA; DAB; DAC; DAM DRAM, MST, NOV; DC 5**
See also AAYA 2; CA 73-76; CANR 31; CLR 3, 45; DLB 7, 52; JRDA; MAICYA; MTCW; SATA 16, 58

Zinov'Ev, A. A.
See Zinoviev, Alexander (Aleksandrovich)

Zinoviev, Alexander (Aleksandrovich) 1922- **CLC 19**
See also CA 116; 133; CAAS 10

Zoilus
See Lovecraft, H(oward) P(hillips)

Zola, Emile (Edouard Charles Antoine) 1840-1902 **TCLC 1, 6, 21, 41; DA; DAB; DAC; DAM MST, NOV; WLC**
See also CA 104; 138; DLB 123

Zoline, Pamela 1941- .... **CLC 62**
See also CA 161

Zorrilla y Moral, Jose 1817-1893 .... **NCLC 6**

Zoshchenko, Mikhail (Mikhailovich) 1895-1958 **TCLC 15; SSC 15**
See also CA 115; 160

Zuckmayer, Carl 1896-1977 .... **CLC 18**
See also CA 69-72; DLB 56, 124

Zuk, Georges
See Skelton, Robin

Zukofsky, Louis 1904-1978 **CLC 1, 2, 4, 7, 11, 18; DAM POET; PC 11**
See also CA 9-12R; 77-80; CANR 39; DLB 5, 165; MTCW

Zweig, Paul 1935-1984 .... **CLC 34, 42**
See also CA 85-88; 113

Zweig, Stefan 1881-1942 .... **TCLC 17**
See also CA 112; DLB 81, 118

Zwingli, Huldreich 1484-1531 .... **LC 37**
See also DLB 179

Literary Criticism Series
Cumulative Topic Index

This index lists all topic entries in Gale's *Classical and Medieval Literature Criticism, Contemporary Literary Criticism, Literature Criticism from 1400 to 1800, Nineteenth-Century Literature Criticism,* and *Twentieth-Century Literary Criticism.*

Age of Johnson LC 15: 1-87
Johnson's London, 3-15
aesthetics of neoclassicism, 15-36
"age of prose and reason," 36-45
clubmen and bluestockings, 45-56
printing technology, 56-62
periodicals: "a map of busy life," 62-74
transition, 74-86

Age of Spenser LC 39: 1-70
Overviews, 2-21
Literary Style, 22-34
Poets and the Crown, 34-70

AIDS in Literature CLC 81: 365-416

Alcohol and Literature TCLC 70: 1-58
overview, 2-8
fiction, 8-48
poetry and drama, 48-58

American Abolitionism NCLC 44: 1-73
overviews, 2-26
abolitionist ideals, 26-46
the literature of abolitionism, 46-72

American Black Humor Fiction TCLC 54: 1-85
characteristics of black humor, 2-13
origins and development, 13-38
black humor distinguished from related literary trends, 38-60
black humor and society, 60-75
black humor reconsidered, 75-83

American Civil War in Literature NCLC 32: 1-109
overviews, 2-20
regional perspectives, 20-54
fiction popular during the war, 54-79
the historical novel, 79-108

American Frontier in Literature NCLC 28: 1-103
definitions, 2-12
development, 12-17
nonfiction writing about the frontier, 17-30
frontier fiction, 30-45
frontier protagonists, 45-66
portrayals of Native Americans, 66-86
feminist readings, 86-98
twentieth-century reaction against frontier literature, 98-100

American Humor Writing NCLC 52: 1-59
overviews, 2-12
the Old Southwest, 12-42
broader impacts, 42-5
women humorists, 45-58

***American Mercury,* The** TCLC 74: 1-80

American Popular Song, Golden Age of TCLC 42: 1-49
background and major figures, 2-34
the lyrics of popular songs, 34-47

American Proletarian Literature TCLC 54: 86-175
overviews, 87-95
American proletarian literature and the American Communist Party, 95-111
ideology and literary merit, 111-7
novels, 117-36
Gastonia, 136-48
drama, 148-54
journalism, 154-9
proletarian literature in the United States, 159-74

American Romanticism NCLC 44: 74-138
overviews, 74-84
sociopolitical influences, 84-104
Romanticism and the American frontier, 104-15
thematic concerns, 115-37

American Western Literature TCLC 46: 1-100
definition and development of American Western literature, 2-7
characteristics of the Western novel, 8-23
Westerns as history and fiction, 23-34
critical reception of American Western literature, 34-41
the Western hero, 41-73
women in Western fiction, 73-91
later Western fiction, 91-9

Art and Literature TCLC 54: 176-248
overviews, 176-93
definitions, 193-219
influence of visual arts on literature, 219-31
spatial form in literature, 231-47

Arthurian Literature CMLC 10: 1-127
historical context and literary beginnings, 2-27
development of the legend through Malory, 27-64
development of the legend from Malory to the Victorian Age, 65-81
themes and motifs, 81-95
principal characters, 95-125

Arthurian Revival NCLC 36: 1-77
overviews, 2-12
Tennyson and his influence, 12-43
other leading figures, 43-73
the Arthurian legend in the visual arts, 73-6

Australian Literature TCLC 50: 1-94
origins and development, 2-21
characteristics of Australian literature, 21-33

historical and critical perspectives, 33-41
poetry, 41-58
fiction, 58-76
drama, 76-82
Aboriginal literature, 82-91

Beat Generation, Literature of the TCLC 42: 50-102
overviews, 51-9
the Beat generation as a social phenomenon, 59-62
development, 62-5
Beat literature, 66-96
influence, 97-100

The Bell Curve Controversy CLC 91: 281-330

Bildungsroman in Nineteenth-Century Literature NCLC 20: 92-168
surveys, 93-113
in Germany, 113-40
in England, 140-56
female *Bildungsroman*, 156-67

Bloomsbury Group TCLC 34: 1-73
history and major figures, 2-13
definitions, 13-7
influences, 17-27
thought, 27-40
prose, 40-52
and literary criticism, 52-4
political ideals, 54-61
response to, 61-71

Bly, Robert, *Iron John: A Book about Men and Men's Work* CLC 70: 414-62

The Book of J CLC 65: 289-311

Buddhism and Literature TCLC 70: 59-164
eastern literature, 60-113
western literature, 113-63

Businessman in American Literature TCLC 26: 1-48
portrayal of the businessman, 1-32
themes and techniques in business fiction, 32-47

Catholicism in Nineteenth-Century American Literature NCLC 64: 1-58
overviews, 3-14
polemical literature, 14-46
Catholicism in literature, 47-57

Celtic Twilight
See **Irish Literary Renaissance**

Chartist Movement and Literature, The NCLC 60: 1-84
overview: nineteenth-century working-class fiction, 2-19
Chartist fiction and poetry, 19-73
the Chartist press, 73-84

Children's Literature, Nineteenth-Century NCLC 52: 60-135
overviews, 61-72
moral tales, 72-89
fairy tales and fantasy, 90-119
making men/making women, 119-34

Civic Critics, Russian NCLC 20: 402-46
principal figures and background, 402-9
and Russian Nihilism, 410-6
aesthetic and critical views, 416-45

Colonial America: The Intellectual Background LC 25: 1-98
overviews, 2-17
philosophy and politics, 17-31
early religious influences in Colonial America, 31-60
consequences of the Revolution, 60-78
religious influences in post-revolutionary America, 78-87
colonial literary genres, 87-97

Colonialism in Victorian English Literature NCLC 56: 1-77
overviews, 2-34
colonialism and gender, 34-51
monsters and the occult, 51-76

Columbus, Christopher, Books on the Quincentennial of His Arrival in the New World CLC 70: 329-60

Comic Books TCLC 66: 1-139
historical and critical perspectives, 2-48
superheroes, 48-67

underground comix, 67-88
comic books and society, 88-122
adult comics and graphic novels, 122-36

Connecticut Wits NCLC 48: 1-95
general overviews, 2-40
major works, 40-76
intellectual context, 76-95

Crime in Literature TCLC 54: 249-307
evolution of the criminal figure in literature, 250-61
crime and society, 261-77
literary perspectives on crime and punishment, 277-88
writings by criminals, 288-306

Czechoslovakian Literature of the Twentieth Century TCLC 42: 103-96
through World War II, 104-35
de-Stalinization, the Prague Spring, and contemporary literature, 135-72
Slovak literature, 172-85
Czech science fiction, 185-93

Dadaism TCLC 46: 101-71
background and major figures, 102-16
definitions, 116-26
manifestos and commentary by Dadaists, 126-40
theater and film, 140-58
nature and characteristics of Dadaist writing, 158-70

Darwinism and Literature NCLC 32: 110-206
background, 110-31
direct responses to Darwin, 131-71
collateral effects of Darwinism, 171-205

de Man, Paul, Wartime Journalism of CLC 55: 382-424

Detective Fiction, Nineteenth-Century NCLC 36: 78-148
origins of the genre, 79-100
history of nineteenth-century detective fiction, 101-33
significance of nineteenth-century detective fiction, 133-46

Detective Fiction, Twentieth-Century

TCLC 38: 1-96
  genesis and history of the detective
    story, 3-22
  defining detective fiction, 22-32
  evolution and varieties, 32-77
  the appeal of detective fiction, 77-90

Disease and Literature TCLC 66: 140-283
  overviews, 141-65
  disease in nineteenth-century literature,
    165-81
  tuberculosis and literature, 181-94
  women and disease in literature, 194-
    221
  plague literature, 221-53
  AIDS in literature, 253-82

**The Double in Nineteenth-Century
Literature** NCLC 40: 1-95
  genesis and development of the theme,
    2-15
  the double and Romanticism, 16-27
  sociological views, 27-52
  psychological interpretations, 52-87
  philosophical considerations, 87-95

Dramatic Realism NCLC 44: 139-202
  overviews, 140-50
  origins and definitions, 150-66
  impact and influence, 166-93
  realist drama and tragedy, 193-201

**Electronic "Books": Hypertext and
Hyperfiction** CLC 86: 367-404
  books vs. CD-ROMS, 367-76
  hypertext and hyperfiction, 376-95
  implications for publishing, libraries,
    and the public, 395-403

Eliot, T. S., Centenary of Birth CLC 55:
345-75

Elizabethan Drama LC 22: 140-240
  origins and influences, 142-67
  characteristics and conventions, 167-83
  theatrical production, 184-200
  histories, 200-12
  comedy, 213-20
  tragedy, 220-30

The Encyclopedists LC 26: 172-253
  overviews, 173-210

intellectual background, 210-32
views on esthetics, 232-41
views on women, 241-52

English Caroline Literature LC 13: 221-
307
  background, 222-41
  evolution and varieties, 241-62
  the Cavalier mode, 262-75
  court and society, 275-91
  politics and religion, 291-306

English Decadent Literature of the 1890s
NCLC 28: 104-200
  fin de siècle: the Decadent period, 105-
    19
  definitions, 120-37
  major figures: "the tragic generation,"
    137-50
  French literature and English literary
    Decadence, 150-7
  themes, 157-61
  poetry, 161-82
  periodicals, 182-96

English Essay, Rise of the LC 18: 238-308
  definitions and origins, 236-54
  influence on the essay, 254-69
  historical background, 269-78
  the essay in the seventeenth century,
    279-93
  the essay in the eighteenth century, 293-
    307

English Mystery Cycle Dramas LC 34: 1-
88
  overviews, 1-27
  the nature of dramatic performances, 27-
    42
  the medieval worldview and the mystery
    cycles, 43-67
  the doctrine of repentance and the
    mystery cycles, 67-76
  the fall from grace in the mystery cycles,
    76-88

English Romantic Poetry NCLC 28: 201-
327
  overviews and reputation, 202-37
  major subjects and themes, 237-67
  forms of Romantic poetry, 267-78
  politics, society, and Romantic poetry,
    278-99
  philosophy, religion, and Romantic
    poetry, 299-324

Espionage Literature TCLC 50: 95-159
  overviews, 96-113
  espionage fiction/formula fiction, 113-
    26
  spies in fact and fiction, 126-38
  the female spy, 138-44
  social and psychological perspectives,
    144-58

European Romanticism NCLC 36: 149-
284
  definitions, 149-77
  origins of the movement, 177-82
  Romantic theory, 182-200
  themes and techniques, 200-23
  Romanticism in Germany, 223-39
  Romanticism in France, 240-61
  Romanticism in Italy, 261-4
  Romanticism in Spain, 264-8
  impact and legacy, 268-82

Existentialism and Literature TCLC 42:
197-268
  overviews and definitions, 198-209
  history and influences, 209-19
  Existentialism critiqued and defended,
    220-35
  philosophical and religious perspectives,
    235-41
  Existentialist fiction and drama, 241-67

Familiar Essay NCLC 48: 96-211
  definitions and origins, 97-130
  overview of the genre, 130-43
  elements of form and style, 143-59
  elements of content, 159-73
  the Cockneys: Hazlitt, Lamb, and Hunt,
    173-91
  status of the genre, 191-210

Fear in Literature TCLC 74: 81-258
  overviews, 81
  pre-twentieth-century literature, 123
  twentieth-century literature, 182

**Feminism in the 1990s: Commentary on
Works by Naomi Wolf, Susan Faludi, and
Camille Paglia** CLC 76: 377-415

Feminist Criticism in 1990 CLC 65: 312-
60

Fifteenth-Century English Literature LC

17: 248-334
  background, 249-72
  poetry, 272-315
  drama, 315-23
  prose, 323-33

Film and Literature TCLC 38: 97-226
  overviews, 97-119
  film and theater, 119-34
  film and the novel, 134-45
  the art of the screenplay, 145-66
  genre literature/genre film, 167-79
  the writer and the film industry, 179-90
  authors on film adaptations of their
    works, 190-200
  fiction into film: comparative essays,
    200-23

French Drama in the Age of Louis XIV LC
28: 94-185
  overview, 95-127
  tragedy, 127-46
  comedy, 146-66
  tragicomedy, 166-84

French Enlightenment LC 14: 81-145
  the question of definition, 82-9
  Le siècle des lumières, 89-94
  women and the salons, 94-105
  censorship, 105-15
  the philosophy of reason, 115-31
  influence and legacy, 131-44

French Realism NCLC 52: 136-216
  origins and definitions, 137-70
  issues and influence, 170-98
  realism and representation, 198-215

French Revolution and English Literature
NCLC 40: 96-195
  history and theory, 96-123
  romantic poetry, 123-50
  the novel, 150-81
  drama, 181-92
  children's literature, 192-5

Futurism, Italian TCLC 42: 269-354
  principles and formative influences,
    271-9
  manifestos, 279-88
  literature, 288-303
  theater, 303-19
  art, 320-30
  music, 330-6

architecture, 336-9
and politics, 339-46
reputation and significance, 346-51

Gaelic Revival
See **Irish Literary Renaissance**

**Gates, Henry Louis, Jr., and African-
American Literary Criticism** CLC 65:
361-405

Gay and Lesbian Literature CLC 76:
416-39

German Exile Literature TCLC 30: 1-58
  the writer and the Nazi state, 1-10
  definition of, 10-4
  life in exile, 14-32
  surveys, 32-50
  Austrian literature in exile, 50-2
  German publishing in the United States,
    52-7

German Expressionism TCLC 34: 74-160
  history and major figures, 76-85
  aesthetic theories, 85-109
  drama, 109-26
  poetry, 126-38
  film, 138-42
  painting, 142-7
  music, 147-53
  and politics, 153-8

***Glasnost* and Contemporary Soviet
Literature** CLC 59: 355-97

Gothic Novel NCLC 28: 328-402
  development and major works, 328-34
  definitions, 334-50
  themes and techniques, 350-78
  in America, 378-85
  in Scotland, 385-91
  influence and legacy, 391-400

Graphic Narratives CLC 86: 405-32
  history and overviews, 406-21
  the "Classics Illustrated" series, 421-2
  reviews of recent works, 422-32

Greek Historiography CMLC 17: 1-49

Harlem Renaissance TCLC 26: 49-125
  principal issues and figures, 50-67
  the literature and its audience, 67-74
  theme and technique in poetry, fiction,
    and drama, 74-115
  and American society, 115-21
  achievement and influence, 121-2

Havel, Václav, Playwright and President
CLC 65: 406-63

Historical Fiction, Nineteenth-Century
NCLC 48: 212-307
  definitions and characteristics, 213-36
  Victorian historical fiction, 236-65
  American historical fiction, 265-88
  realism in historical fiction, 288-306

**Holocaust and the Atomic Bomb: Fifty
Years Later** CLC 91: 331-82
  the Holocaust remembered, 333-52
  Anne Frank revisited, 352-62
  the atomic bomb and American memory,
    362-81

Holocaust Denial Literature TCLC 58: 1-
110
  overviews, 1-30
  Robert Faurisson and Noam Chomsky,
    30-52
  Holocaust denial literature in America,
    52-71
  library access to Holocaust denial
    literature, 72-5
  the authenticity of Anne Frank's diary,
    76-90
  David Irving and the "normalization" of
    Hitler, 90-109

Holocaust, Literature of the TCLC 42:
355-450
  historical overview, 357-61
  critical overview, 361-70
  diaries and memoirs, 370-95
  novels and short stories, 395-425
  poetry, 425-41
  drama, 441-8

**Homosexuality in Nineteenth-Century
Literature** NCLC 56: 78-182
  defining homosexuality, 80-111
  Greek love, 111-44
  trial and danger, 144-81

Hungarian Literature of the Twentieth Century TCLC 26: 126-88
    surveys of, 126-47
    Nyugat and early twentieth-century literature, 147-56
    mid-century literature, 156-68
    and politics, 168-78
    since the 1956 revolt, 178-87

Hysteria in Nineteenth-Century Literature NCLC 64: 59-184
    the history of hysteria, 60-75
    the gender of hysteria, 75-103
    hysteria and women's narratives, 103-57
    hysteria in nineteenth-century poetry, 157-83

Imagism TCLC 74: 259-454
    history and development, 260
    major figures, 288
    sources and influences, 352
    Imagism and other movements, 397
    influence and legacy, 431

Indian Literature in English TCLC 54: 308-406
    overview, 309-13
    origins and major figures, 313-25
    the Indo-English novel, 325-55
    Indo-English poetry, 355-67
    Indo-English drama, 367-72
    critical perspectives on Indo-English literature, 372-80
    modern Indo-English literature, 380-9
    Indo-English authors on their work, 389-404

Industrial Revolution in Literature, The NCLC 56: 183-273
    historical and cultural perspectives, 184-201
    contemporary reactions to the machine, 201-21
    themes and symbols in literature, 221-73

The Irish Famine as Represented in Nineteenth-Century Literature NCLC 64: 185-261
    overviews, 187-98
    historical background, 198-212
    famine novels, 212-34
    famine poetry, 234-44
    famine letters and eye-witness accounts, 245-61

Irish Literary Renaissance TCLC 46: 172-287
    overview, 173-83
    development and major figures, 184-202
    influence of Irish folklore and mythology, 202-22
    Irish poetry, 222-34
    Irish drama and the Abbey Theatre, 234-56
    Irish fiction, 256-86

Irish Nationalism and Literature NCLC 44: 203-73
    the Celtic element in literature, 203-19
    anti-Irish sentiment and the Celtic response, 219-34
    literary ideals in Ireland, 234-45
    literary expressions, 245-73

Italian Futurism
See **Futurism, Italian**

Italian Humanism LC 12: 205-77
    origins and early development, 206-18
    revival of classical letters, 218-23
    humanism and other philosophies, 224-39
    humanisms and humanists, 239-46
    the plastic arts, 246-57
    achievement and significance, 258-76

Italian Romanticism NCLC 60: 85-145
    origins and overviews, 86-101
    Italian Romantic theory, 101-25
    the language of Romanticism, 125-45

Jacobean Drama LC 33: 1-37
    the Jacobean worldview: an era of transition, 2-14
    the moral vision of Jacobean drama, 14-22
    Jacobean tragedy, 22-3
    the Jacobean masque, 23-36

Jewish-American Fiction TCLC 62: 1-181
    overviews, 2-24
    major figures, 24-48
    Jewish writers and American life, 48-78
    Jewish characters in American fiction, 78-108
    themes in Jewish-American fiction, 108-43
    Jewish-American women writers, 143-59
    the Holocaust and Jewish-American fiction, 159-81

Knickerbocker Group, The NCLC 56: 274-341
    overviews, 276-314
    Knickerbocker periodicals, 314-26
    writers and artists, 326-40

Lake Poets, The NCLC 52: 217-304
    characteristics of the Lake Poets and their works, 218-27
    literary influences and collaborations, 227-66
    defining and developing Romantic ideals, 266-84
    embracing Conservatism, 284-303

Larkin, Philip, Controversy CLC 81: 417-64

Latin American Literature, Twentieth-Century TCLC 58: 111-98
    historical and critical perspectives, 112-36
    the novel, 136-45
    the short story, 145-9
    drama, 149-60
    poetry, 160-7
    the writer and society, 167-86
    Native Americans in Latin American literature, 186-97

Madness in Twentieth-Century Literature TCLC 50: 160-225
    overviews, 161-71
    madness and the creative process, 171-86
    suicide, 186-91
    madness in American literature, 191-207
    madness in German literature, 207-13
    madness and feminist artists, 213-24

Metaphysical Poets LC 24: 356-439
    early definitions, 358-67
    surveys and overviews, 367-92
    cultural and social influences, 392-406
    stylistic and thematic variations, 407-38

Modern Essay, The TCLC 58: 199-273
    overview, 200-7
    the essay in the early twentieth century, 207-19

Topic Index

characteristics of the modern essay, 219-
32
modern essayists, 232-45
the essay as a literary genre, 245-73

Modern Japanese Literature TCLC 66:
284-389
poetry, 285-305
drama, 305-29
fiction, 329-61
western influences, 361-87

Modernism TCLC 70: 165-275
definitions, 166-184
Modernism and earlier influences, 184-
200
stylistic and thematic traits, 200-229
poetry and drama, 229-242
redefining Modernism, 242-275

**Muckraking Movement in American
Journalism** TCLC 34: 161-242
development, principles, and major
figures, 162-70
publications, 170-9
social and political ideas, 179-86
targets, 186-208
fiction, 208-19
decline, 219-29
impact and accomplishments, 229-40

**Multiculturalism in Literature and
Education** CLC 70: 361-413

Music and Modern Literature TCLC 62:
182-329
overviews, 182-211
musical form/literary form, 211-32
music in literature, 232-50
the influence of music on literature,
250-73
literature and popular music, 273-303
jazz and poetry, 303-28

Native American Literature CLC 76: 440-
76

Natural School, Russian NCLC 24: 205-40
history and characteristics, 205-25
contemporary criticism, 225-40

Naturalism NCLC 36: 285-382
definitions and theories, 286-305

critical debates on Naturalism, 305-16
Naturalism in theater, 316-32
European Naturalism, 332-61
American Naturalism, 361-72
the legacy of Naturalism, 372-81

Negritude TCLC 50: 226-361
origins and evolution, 227-56
definitions, 256-91
Negritude in literature, 291-343
Negritude reconsidered, 343-58

New Criticism TCLC 34: 243-318
development and ideas, 244-70
debate and defense, 270-99
influence and legacy, 299-315

The New World in Renaissance Literature
LC 31: 1-51
overview, 1-18
utopia vs. terror, 18-31
explorers and Native Americans, 31-51

**New York Intellectuals and *Partisan
Review*** TCLC 30: 117-98
development and major figures, 118-28
influence of Judaism, 128-39
Partisan Review, 139-57
literary philosophy and practice, 157-75
political philosophy, 175-87
achievement and significance, 187-97

The New Yorker TCLC 58: 274-357
overviews, 274-95
major figures, 295-304
New Yorker style, 304-33
fiction, journalism, and humor at *The
New Yorker,* 333-48
the new *New Yorker,* 348-56

Newgate Novel NCLC 24: 166-204
development of Newgate literature, 166-
73
Newgate Calendar, 173-7
Newgate fiction, 177-95
Newgate drama, 195-204

**Nigerian Literature of the Twentieth
Century** TCLC 30: 199-265
surveys of, 199-227
English language and African life, 227-
45
politics and the Nigerian writer, 245-54

Nigerian writers and society, 255-62

**Nineteenth-Century Native American
Autobiography** NCLC 64: 262-389
overview, 263-8
problems of authorship, 268-81
the evolution of Native American
autobiography, 281-304
political issues, 304-15
gender and autobiography, 316-62
autobiographical works during the turn
of the century, 362-88

Northern Humanism LC 16: 281-356
background, 282-305
precursor of the Reformation, 305-14
the Brethren of the Common Life, the
Devotio Moderna, and education,
314-40
the impact of printing, 340-56

Novel of Manners, The NCLC 56: 342-96
social and political order, 343-53
domestic order, 353-73
depictions of gender, 373-83
the American novel of manners, 383-95

**Nuclear Literature: Writings and
Criticism in the Nuclear Age** TCLC 46:
288-390
overviews, 290-301
fiction, 301-35
poetry, 335-8
nuclear war in Russo-Japanese literature, 338-55
nuclear war and women writers, 355-67
the nuclear referent and literary
criticism, 367-88

Occultism in Modern Literature TCLC 50:
362-406
influence of occultism on literature,
363-72
occultism, literature, and society, 372-87
fiction, 387-96
drama, 396-405

**Opium and the Nineteenth-Century
Literary Imagination** NCLC 20: 250-301
original sources, 250-62
historical background, 262-71
and literary society, 271-9
and literary creativity, 279-300

Periodicals, Nineteenth-Century British
NCLC 24: 100-65
    overviews, 100-30
    in the Romantic Age, 130-41
    in the Victorian era, 142-54
    and the reviewer, 154-64

Plath, Sylvia, and the Nature of Biography
CLC 86: 433-62
    the nature of biography, 433-52
    reviews of *The Silent Woman,* 452-61

Political Theory from the 15th to the 18th Century LC 36: 1-55
    <Overview, 1-26
    Natural Law, 26-42
    Empiricism, 42-55

Polish Romanticism NCLC 52: 305-71
    overviews, 306-26
    major figures, 326-40
    Polish Romantic drama, 340-62
    influences, 362-71

Popular Literature TCLC 70: 279-382
    overviews, 280-324
    "formula" fiction, 324-336
    readers of popular literature, 336-351
    evolution of popular literature, 351-382

Pre-Raphaelite Movement NCLC 20: 302-401
    overview, 302-4
    genesis, 304-12
    Germ and *Oxford and Cambridge Magazine,* 312-20
    Robert Buchanan and the "Fleshly School of Poetry," 320-31
    satires and parodies, 331-4
    surveys, 334-51
    aesthetics, 351-75
    sister arts of poetry and painting, 375-94
    influence, 394-9

Preromanticism LC 40: 1-56
    overviews, 2-14
    defining the period, 14-23
    new directions in poetry and prose, 23-45
    the focus on the self, 45-56

Presocratic Philosophy CMLC 22: 1-56
    overviews, 3-24
    the Ionians and the Pythagoreans, 25-35

    Heraclitus, the Eleatics, and the Atomists, 36-47
    the Sophists, 47-55

Protestant Reformation, Literature of the
LC 37: 1-83
    overviews, 1-49
    humanism and scholasticism, 49-69
    the reformation and literature, 69-82

Psychoanalysis and Literature TCLC 38: 227-338
    overviews, 227-46
    Freud on literature, 246-51
    psychoanalytic views of the literary process, 251-61
    psychoanalytic theories of response to literature, 261-88
    psychoanalysis and literary criticism, 288-312
    psychoanalysis as literature/literature as psychoanalysis, 313-34

Rap Music CLC 76: 477-50

Renaissance Natural Philosophy LC 27: 201-87
    cosmology, 201-28
    astrology, 228-54
    magic, 254-86

Restoration Drama LC 21: 184-275
    general overviews, 185-230
    Jeremy Collier stage controversy, 230-9
    other critical interpretations, 240-75

Revising the Literary Canon CLC 81: 465-509

Robin Hood, Legend of LC 19: 205-58
    origins and development of the Robin Hood legend, 206-20
    representations of Robin Hood, 220-44
    Robin Hood as hero, 244-56

Rushdie, Salman, *Satanic Verses* Controversy CLC 55 214-63; 59: 404-56

Russian Nihilism NCLC 28: 403-47
    definitions and overviews, 404-17
    women and Nihilism, 417-27

    literature as reform: the Civic Critics, 427-33
    Nihilism and the Russian novel: Turgenev and Dostoevsky, 433-47

Russian Thaw TCLC 26: 189-247
    literary history of the period, 190-206
    theoretical debate of socialist realism, 206-11
    Novy Mir, 211-7
    Literary Moscow, 217-24
    Pasternak, *Zhivago,* and the Nobel Prize, 224-7
    poetry of liberation, 228-31
    Brodsky trial and the end of the Thaw, 231-6
    achievement and influence, 236-46

Salem Witch Trials LC-38: 1-145
    overviews, 2-30
    historical background, 30-65
    judicial background, 65-78
    the search for causes, 78-115
    the role of women in the trials, 115-44

Salinger, J. D., Controversy Surrounding *In Search of J. D. Salinger* CLC 55: 325-44

Science Fiction, Nineteenth-Century
NCLC 24: 241-306
    background, 242-50
    definitions of the genre, 251-6
    representative works and writers, 256-75
    themes and conventions, 276-305

Scottish Chaucerians LC 20: 363-412

Scottish Poetry, Eighteenth-Century LC 29: 95-167
    overviews, 96-114
    the Scottish Augustans, 114-28
    the Scots Vernacular Revival, 132-63
    Scottish poetry after Burns, 163-6

Sentimental Novel, The NCLC 60: 146-245
    overviews, 147-58
    the politics of domestic fiction, 158-79
    a literature of resistance and repression, 179-212
    the reception of sentimental fiction, 213-

Topic Index

44

Sherlock Holmes Centenary TCLC 26: 248-310
 Doyle's life and the composition of the Holmes stories, 248-59
 life and character of Holmes, 259-78
 method, 278-9
 Holmes and the Victorian world, 279-92
 Sherlockian scholarship, 292-301
 Doyle and the development of the detective story, 301-7
 Holmes's continuing popularity, 307-9

Slave Narratives, American NCLC 20: 1-91
 background, 2-9
 overviews, 9-24
 contemporary responses, 24-7
 language, theme, and technique, 27-70
 historical authenticity, 70-5
 antecedents, 75-83
 role in development of Black American literature, 83-8

Spanish Civil War Literature TCLC 26: 311-85
 topics in, 312-33
 British and American literature, 333-59
 French literature, 359-62
 Spanish literature, 362-73
 German literature, 373-5
 political idealism and war literature, 375-83

Spanish Golden Age Literature LC 23: 262-332
 overviews, 263-81
 verse drama, 281-304
 prose fiction, 304-19
 lyric poetry, 319-31

Spasmodic School of Poetry NCLC 24: 307-52
 history and major figures, 307-21
 the Spasmodics on poetry, 321-7
 Firmilian and critical disfavor, 327-39
 theme and technique, 339-47
 influence, 347-51

Steinbeck, John, Fiftieth Anniversary of *The Grapes of Wrath* CLC 59: 311-54

Sturm und Drang NCLC 40: 196-276
 definitions, 197-238
 poetry and poetics, 238-58
 drama, 258-75

Supernatural Fiction in the Nineteenth Century NCLC 32: 207-87
 major figures and influences, 208-35
 the Victorian ghost story, 236-54
 the influence of science and occultism, 254-66
 supernatural fiction and society, 266-86

Supernatural Fiction, Modern TCLC 30: 59-116
 evolution and varieties, 60-74
 "decline" of the ghost story, 74-86
 as a literary genre, 86-92
 technique, 92-101
 nature and appeal, 101-15

Surrealism TCLC 30: 334-406
 history and formative influences, 335-43
 manifestos, 343-54
 philosophic, aesthetic, and political principles, 354-75
 poetry, 375-81
 novel, 381-6
 drama, 386-92
 film, 392-8
 painting and sculpture, 398-403
 achievement, 403-5

Symbolism, Russian TCLC 30: 266-333
 doctrines and major figures, 267-92
 theories, 293-8
 and French Symbolism, 298-310
 themes in poetry, 310-4
 theater, 314-20
 and the fine arts, 320-32

Symbolist Movement, French NCLC 20: 169-249
 background and characteristics, 170-86
 principles, 186-91
 attacked and defended, 191-7
 influences and predecessors, 197-211
 and Decadence, 211-6
 theater, 216-26
 prose, 226-33
 decline and influence, 233-47

Theater of the Absurd TCLC 38: 339-415
 "The Theater of the Absurd," 340-7

 major plays and playwrights, 347-58
 and the concept of the absurd, 358-86
 theatrical techniques, 386-94
 predecessors of, 394-402
 influence of, 402-13

Tin Pan Alley
See **American Popular Song, Golden Age of**

Transcendentalism, American NCLC 24: 1-99
 overviews, 3-23
 contemporary documents, 23-41
 theological aspects of, 42-52
 and social issues, 52-74
 literature of, 74-96

Travel Writing in the Nineteenth Century NCLC 44: 274-392
 the European grand tour, 275-303
 the Orient, 303-47
 North America, 347-91

Travel Writing in the Twentieth Century TCLC 30: 407-56
 conventions and traditions, 407-27
 and fiction writing, 427-43
 comparative essays on travel writers, 443-54

True-Crime Literature CLC 99: 333-433
 history and analysis, 334-407
 reviews of true-crime publications, 407-23
 writing instruction, 424-29
 author profiles, 429-33

Ulysses **and the Process of Textual Reconstruction** TCLC 26: 386-416
 evaluations of the new *Ulysses,* 386-94
 editorial principles and procedures, 394-401
 theoretical issues, 401-16

Utopian Literature, Nineteenth-Century NCLC 24: 353-473
 definitions, 354-74
 overviews, 374-88
 theory, 388-408
 communities, 409-26
 fiction, 426-53
 women and fiction, 454-71

Utopian Literature, Renaissance LC-32: 1-63
  overviews, 2-25
  classical background, 25-33
  utopia and the social contract, 33-9
  origins in mythology, 39-48
  utopia and the Renaissance country
    house, 48-52
  influence of millenarianism, 52-62

Vampire in Literature TCLC 46: 391-454
  origins and evolution, 392-412
  social and psychological perspectives,
    413-44
  vampire fiction and science fiction, 445-
    53

Victorian Autobiography NCLC 40: 277-
363
  development and major characteristics,
    278-88
  themes and techniques, 289-313
  the autobiographical tendency in
    Victorian prose and poetry, 313-47
  Victorian women's autobiographies,
    347-62

Victorian Fantasy Literature NCLC 60:
246-384
  overviews, 247-91
  major figures, 292-366
  women in Victorian fantasy literature,
    366-83

Victorian Novel NCLC 32: 288-454
  development and major characteristics,
    290-310
  themes and techniques, 310-58
  social criticism in the Victorian novel,
    359-97
  urban and rural life in the Victorian
    novel, 397-406
  women in the Victorian novel, 406-25
  Mudie's Circulating Library, 425-34
  the late-Victorian novel, 434-51

Vietnam War in Literature and Film CLC
91: 383-437
  overview, 384-8
  prose, 388-412
  film and drama, 412-24
  poetry, 424-35

Vorticism TCLC 62: 330-426
  Wyndham Lewis and Vorticism, 330-8
  characteristics and principles of
    Vorticism, 338-65
  Lewis and Pound, 365-82
  Vorticist writing, 382-416
  Vorticist painting, 416-26

Women's Diaries, Nineteenth-Century
NCLC 48: 308-
54
  overview, 308-13
  diary as history, 314-25

  sociology of diaries, 325-34
  diaries as psychological scholarship,
    334-43
  diary as autobiography, 343-8
  diary as literature, 348-53

Women Writers, Seventeenth-Century LC
30: 2-58
  overview, 2-15
  women and education, 15-9
  women and autobiography, 19-31
  women's diaries, 31-9
  early feminists, 39-58

World War I Literature TCLC 34: 392-486
  overview, 393-403
  English, 403-27
  German, 427-50
  American, 450-66
  French, 466-74
  and modern history, 474-82

Yellow Journalism NCLC 36: 383-456
  overviews, 384-96
  major figures, 396-413

Young Playwrights Festival
  1988—CLC 55: 376-81
  1989—CLC 59: 398-403
  1990—CLC 65: 444-8

Topic Index

Contemporary Literary Criticism
Cumulative Nationality Index

ALBANIAN

Kadare, Ismail 52

ALGERIAN

Althusser, Louis 106
Camus, Albert 1, 2, 4, 9, 11, 14, 32, 63, 69
Cixous, Helene 92
Cohen-Solal, Annie 50

AMERICAN

Abbey, Edward 36, 59
Abbott, Lee K(ittredge) 48
Abish, Walter 22
Abrams, M(eyer) H(oward) 24
Acker, Kathy 45
Adams, Alice (Boyd) 6, 13, 46
Addams, Charles (Samuel) 30
Adler, C(arole) S(chwerdtfeger) 35
Adler, Renata 8, 31
Ai 4, 14, 69
Aiken, Conrad (Potter) 1, 3, 5, 10, 52
Albee, Edward (Franklin III) 1, 2, 3, 5, 9, 11, 13, 25, 53, 86
Alexander, Lloyd (Chudley) 35
Alexie, Sherman (Joseph Jr.) 96
Algren, Nelson 4, 10, 33
Allen, Edward 59
Allen, Paula Gunn 84
Allen, Woody 16, 52
Allison, Dorothy E. 78
Alta 19
Alter, Robert B(ernard) 34
Alther, Lisa 7, 41
Altman, Robert 16
Alvarez, Julia 93
Ammons, A(rchie) R(andolph) 2, 3, 5, 8, 9, 25, 57
Anaya, Rudolfo A(lfonso) 23
Anderson, Jon (Victor) 9
Anderson, Poul (William) 15
Anderson, Robert (Woodruff) 23
Angell, Roger 26
Angelou, Maya 12, 35, 64, 77
Anthony, Piers 35
Apple, Max (Isaac) 9, 33
Appleman, Philip (Dean) 51
Archer, Jules 12
Arendt, Hannah 66, 98
Arnow, Harriette (Louisa) Simpson 2, 7, 18
Arrick, Fran 30
Arzner, Dorothy 98
Ashbery, John (Lawrence) 2, 3, 4, 6, 9, 13, 15, 25, 41, 77
Asimov, Isaac 1, 3, 9, 19, 26, 76, 92
Attaway, William (Alexander) 92
Auchincloss, Louis (Stanton) 4, 6, 9, 18, 45
Auden, W(ystan) H(ugh) 1, 2, 3, 4, 6, 9, 11, 14, 43
Auel, Jean M(arie) 31
Auster, Paul 47
Bach, Richard (David) 14
Badanes, Jerome 59
Baker, Elliott 8
Baker, Nicholson 61

Baker, Russell (Wayne) 31
Bakshi, Ralph 26
Baldwin, James (Arthur) 1, 2, 3, 4, 5, 8, 13, 15, 17, 42, 50, 67, 90
Bambara, Toni Cade 19, 88
Banks, Russell 37, 72
Baraka, Amiri 1, 2, 3, 5, 10, 14, 33
Barbera, Jack (Vincent) 44
Barnard, Mary (Ethel) 48
Barnes, Djuna 3, 4, 8, 11, 29
Barondess, Sue K(aufman) 8
Barrett, William (Christopher) 27
Barth, John (Simmons) 1, 2, 3, 5, 7, 9, 10, 14, 27, 51, 89
Barthelme, Donald 1, 2, 3, 5, 6, 8, 13, 23, 46, 59
Barthelme, Frederick 36
Barzun, Jacques (Martin) 51
Bass, Rick 79
Baumbach, Jonathan 6, 23
Bausch, Richard (Carl) 51
Baxter, Charles 45, 78
Beagle, Peter S(oyer) 7, 104
Beattie, Ann 8, 13, 18, 40, 63
Becker, Walter 26
Beecher, John 6
Begiebing, Robert J(ohn) 70
Behrman, S(amuel) N(athaniel) 40
Belitt, Ben 22
Bell, Madison Smartt 41, 102
Bell, Marvin (Hartley) 8, 31
Bellow, Saul 1, 2, 3, 6, 8, 10, 13, 15, 25, 33, 34, 63, 79
Benary-Isbert, Margot 12
Benchley, Peter (Bradford) 4, 8
Benedikt, Michael 4, 14
Benford, Gregory (Albert) 52
Bennett, Hal 5
Bennett, Jay 35
Benson, Jackson J. 34
Benson, Sally 17
Bentley, Eric (Russell) 24
Berendt, John (Lawrence) 86
Berger, Melvin H. 12
Berger, Thomas (Louis) 3, 5, 8, 11, 18, 38
Bergstein, Eleanor 4
Bernard, April 59
Berriault, Gina 54
Berrigan, Daniel 4
Berrigan, Ted 37
Berry, Chuck 17
Berry, Wendell (Erdman) 4, 6, 8, 27, 46
Berryman, John 1, 2, 3, 4, 6, 8, 10, 13, 25, 62
Bessie, Alvah 23
Bettelheim, Bruno 79
Betts, Doris (Waugh) 3, 6, 28
Bidart, Frank 33
Bishop, Elizabeth 1, 4, 9, 13, 15, 32
Bishop, John 10
Blackburn, Paul 9, 43
Blackmur, R(ichard) P(almer) 2, 24
Blaise, Clark 29
Blatty, William Peter 2
Blessing, Lee 54

Blish, James (Benjamin) 14
Bloch, Robert (Albert) 33
Bloom, Harold 24, 103
Blount, Roy (Alton) Jr. 38
Blume, Judy (Sussman) 12, 30
Bly, Robert (Elwood) 1, 2, 5, 10, 15, 38
Bochco, Steven 35
Bogan, Louise 4, 39, 46, 93
Bogosian, Eric 45
Bograd, Larry 35
Bonham, Frank 12
Bontemps, Arna(ud Wendell) 1, 18
Booth, Philip 23
Booth, Wayne C(layson) 24
Bottoms, David 53
Bourjaily, Vance (Nye) 8, 62
Bova, Ben(jamin William) 45
Bowers, Edgar 9
Bowles, Jane (Sydney) 3, 68
Bowles, Paul (Frederick) 1, 2, 19, 53
Boyle, Kay 1, 5, 19, 58
Boyle, T(homas) Coraghessan 36, 55, 90
Bradbury, Ray (Douglas) 1, 3, 10, 15, 42, 98
Bradley, David (Henry Jr.) 23
Bradley, John Ed(mund Jr.) 55
Bradley, Marion Zimmer 30
Brady, Joan 86
Brammer, William 31
Brancato, Robin F(idler) 35
Brand, Millen 7
Branden, Barbara 44
Branley, Franklyn M(ansfield) 21
Brautigan, Richard (Gary) 1, 3, 5, 9, 12, 34, 42
Braverman, Kate 67
Brennan, Maeve 5
Breslin, Jimmy 4, 43
Bridgers, Sue Ellen 26
Brin, David 34
Brodkey, Harold (Roy) 56
Brodsky, Joseph 4, 6, 13, 36, 100
Brodsky, Michael (Mark) 19
Bromell, Henry 5
Bronk, William 10
Broner, E(sther) M(asserman) 19
Brooks, Cleanth 24, 86
Brooks, Gwendolyn 1, 2, 4, 5, 15, 49
Brooks, Mel 12
Brooks, Peter 34
Brooks, Van Wyck 29
Brosman, Catharine Savage 9
Broughton, T(homas) Alan 19
Broumas, Olga 10, 73
Brown, Alan 99
Brown, Claude 30
Brown, Dee (Alexander) 18, 47
Brown, Rita Mae 18, 43, 79
Brown, Rosellen 32
Brown, Sterling Allen 1, 23, 59
Brown, (William) Larry 73
Browne, (Clyde) Jackson 21
Browning, Tod 16
Bruccoli, Matthew J(oseph) 34
Bruce, Lenny 21

Bryan, C(ourtlandt) D(ixon) B(arnes) 29
Buchwald, Art(hur) 33
Buck, Pearl S(ydenstricker) 7, 11, 18
Buckley, William F(rank) Jr. 7, 18, 37
Buechner, (Carl) Frederick 2, 4, 6, 9
Bukowski, Charles 2, 5, 9, 41, 82
Bullins, Ed 1, 5, 7
Burke, Kenneth (Duva) 2, 24
Burnshaw, Stanley 3, 13, 44
Burr, Anne 6
Burroughs, William S(eward) 1, 2, 5, 15, 22, 42, 75
Busch, Frederick 7, 10, 18, 47
Bush, Ronald 34
Butler, Octavia E(stelle) 38
Butler, Robert Olen (Jr.) 81
Byars, Betsy (Cromer) 35
Byrne, David 26
Cage, John (Milton Jr.) 41
Cain, James M(allahan) 3, 11, 28
Caldwell, Erskine (Preston) 1, 8, 14, 50, 60
Caldwell, (Janet Miriam) Taylor (Holland) 2, 28, 39
Calisher, Hortense 2, 4, 8, 38
Cameron, Carey 59
Cameron, Peter 44
Campbell, John W(ood Jr.) 32
Campbell, Joseph 69
Campion, Jane 95
Canby, Vincent 13
Canin, Ethan 55
Capote, Truman 1, 3, 8, 13, 19, 34, 38, 58
Capra, Frank 16
Caputo, Philip 32
Card, Orson Scott 44, 47, 50
Carey, Ernestine Gilbreth 17
Carlisle, Henry (Coffin) 33
Carlson, Ron(ald F.) 54
Carpenter, Don(ald Richard) 41
Carr, Caleb 86
Carr, John Dickson 3
Carr, Virginia Spencer 34
Carroll, James P. 38
Carroll, Jim 35
Carruth, Hayden 4, 7, 10, 18, 84
Carson, Rachel Louise 71
Carver, Raymond 22, 36, 53, 55
Casey, John (Dudley) 59
Casey, Michael 2
Casey, Warren (Peter) 12
Cassavetes, John 20
Cassill, R(onald) V(erlin) 4, 23
Cassity, (Allen) Turner 6, 42
Castaneda, Carlos 12
Castedo, Elena 65
Catton, (Charles) Bruce 35
Caunitz, William J. 34
Cavanna, Betty 12
Chabon, Michael 55
Chappell, Fred (Davis) 40, 78
Charyn, Jerome 5, 8, 18
Chase, Mary Ellen 2
Chayefsky, Paddy 23
Cheever, John 3, 7, 8, 11, 15, 25, 64
Cheever, Susan 18, 48
Cherryh, C. J. 35
Chester, Alfred 49
Childress, Alice 12, 15, 86, 96
Chute, Carolyn 39
Ciardi, John (Anthony) 10, 40, 44
Cimino, Michael 16
Cisneros, Sandra 69
Clampitt, Amy 32

Clancy, Tom 45
Clark, Eleanor 5, 19
Clark, Walter Van Tilburg 28
Clarke, Shirley 16
Clavell, James (duMaresq) 6, 25, 87
Cleaver, (Leroy) Eldridge 30
Clifton, (Thelma) Lucille 19, 66
Coburn, D(onald) L(ee) 10
Codrescu, Andrei 46
Cohen, Arthur A(llen) 7, 31
Collier, Christopher 30
Collier, James L(incoln) 30
Collins, Linda 44
Colter, Cyrus 58
Colum, Padraic 28
Colwin, Laurie (E.) 5, 13, 23, 84
Condon, Richard (Thomas) 4, 6, 8, 10, 45, 100
Connell, Evan S(helby) Jr. 4, 6, 45
Connelly, Marc(us Cook) 7
Conroy, Donald Pat(rick) 30, 74
Cook, Robin 14
Cooke, Elizabeth 55
Cook-Lynn, Elizabeth 93
Cooper, J(oan) California 56
Coover, Robert (Lowell) 3, 7, 15, 32, 46, 87
Coppola, Francis Ford 16
Corcoran, Barbara 17
Corman, Cid 9
Cormier, Robert (Edmund) 12, 30
Corn, Alfred (DeWitt III) 33
Corso, (Nunzio) Gregory 1, 11
Costain, Thomas B(ertram) 30
Cowley, Malcolm 39
Cozzens, James Gould 1, 4, 11, 92
Crane, R(onald) S(almon) 27
Crase, Douglas 58
Creeley, Robert (White) 1, 2, 4, 8, 11, 15, 36, 78
Crews, Harry (Eugene) 6, 23, 49
Crichton, (John) Michael 2, 6, 54, 90
Cristofer, Michael 28
Crow Dog, Mary (Ellen) 93
Crowley, John 57
Crumb, R(obert) 17
Cryer, Gretchen (Kiger) 21
Cudlip, David 34
Cummings, E(dward) E(stlin) 1, 3, 8, 12, 15, 68
Cunningham, J(ames) V(incent) 3, 31
Cunningham, Julia (Woolfolk) 12
Cunningham, Michael 34
Currie, Ellen 44
Dacey, Philip 51
Dahlberg, Edward 1, 7, 14
Daitch, Susan 103
Daly, Elizabeth 52
Daly, Maureen 17
Dannay, Frederic 11
Danticat, Edwidge 94
Danvers, Dennis 70
Danziger, Paula 21
Davenport, Guy (Mattison Jr.) 6, 14, 38
Davidson, Donald (Grady) 2, 13, 19
Davidson, Sara 9
Davis, Angela (Yvonne) 77
Davis, Harold Lenoir 49
Davison, Peter (Hubert) 28
Dawson, Fielding 6
Deer, Sandra 45
Delany, Samuel R(ay Jr.) 8, 14, 38
Delbanco, Nicholas (Franklin) 6, 13
DeLillo, Don 8, 10, 13, 27, 39, 54, 76

Deloria, Vine (Victor) Jr. 21
Del Vecchio, John M(ichael) 29
de Man, Paul (Adolph Michel) 55
De Marinis, Rick 54
Demby, William 53
Denby, Edwin (Orr) 48
De Palma, Brian (Russell) 20
Deren, Maya 16, 102
Derleth, August (William) 31
Deutsch, Babette 18
De Vries, Peter 1, 2, 3, 7, 10, 28, 46
Dexter, Pete 34, 55
Diamond, Neil 30
Dick, Philip K(indred) 10, 30, 72
Dickey, James (Lafayette) 1, 2, 4, 7, 10, 15, 47
Dickey, William 3, 28
Dickinson, Charles 49
Didion, Joan 1, 3, 8, 14, 32
Dillard, Annie 9, 60
Dillard, R(ichard) H(enry) W(ilde) 5
Disch, Thomas M(ichael) 7, 36
Dixon, Stephen 52
Dobyns, Stephen 37
Doctorow, E(dgar) L(aurence) 6, 11, 15, 18, 37, 44, 65
Dodson, Owen (Vincent) 79
Doerr, Harriet 34
Donaldson, Stephen R. 46
Donleavy, J(ames) P(atrick) 1, 4, 6, 10, 45
Donovan, John 35
Doolittle, Hilda 3, 8, 14, 31, 34, 73
Dorn, Edward (Merton) 10, 18
Dos Passos, John (Roderigo) 1, 4, 8, 11, 15, 25, 34, 82
Douglas, Ellen 73
Dove, Rita (Frances) 50, 81
Dowell, Coleman 60
Drexler, Rosalyn 2, 6
Drury, Allen (Stuart) 37
Duberman, Martin 8
Dubie, Norman (Evans) 36
Du Bois, W(illiam) E(dward) B(urghardt) 1, 2, 13, 64, 96
Dubus, Andre 13, 36, 97
Duffy, Bruce 50
Dugan, Alan 2, 6
Dumas, Henry L. 6, 62
Duncan, Lois 26
Duncan, Robert (Edward) 1, 2, 4, 7, 15, 41, 55
Dunn, Katherine (Karen) 71
Dunn, Stephen 36
Dunne, John Gregory 28
Durang, Christopher (Ferdinand) 27, 38
Durban, (Rosa) Pam 39
Dworkin, Andrea 43
Dylan, Bob 3, 4, 6, 12, 77
Eastlake, William (Derry) 8
Eberhart, Richard (Ghormley) 3, 11, 19, 56
Eberstadt, Fernanda 39
Eckert, Allan W. 17
Edel, (Joseph) Leon 29, 34
Edgerton, Clyde (Carlyle) 39
Edmonds, Walter D(umaux) 35
Edson, Russell 13
Edwards, Gus 43
Ehle, John (Marsden Jr.) 27
Eigner, Larry 9
Eiseley, Loren Corey 7
Eisenstadt, Jill 50
Eliade, Mircea 19
Eliot, T(homas) S(tearns) 1, 2, 3, 6, 9, 10, 13, 15, 24, 34, 41, 55, 57
Elkin, Stanley L(awrence) 4, 6, 9, 14, 27, 51,

91

Elledge, Scott 34
Elliott, George P(aul) 2
Ellis, Bret Easton 39, 71
Ellison, Harlan (Jay) 1, 13, 42
Ellison, Ralph (Waldo) 1, 3, 11, 54, 86
Ellmann, Lucy (Elizabeth) 61
Ellmann, Richard (David) 50
Elman, Richard 19
Ephron, Nora 17, 31
Epstein, Daniel Mark 7
Epstein, Jacob 19
Epstein, Joseph 39
Epstein, Leslie 27
Erdman, Paul E(mil) 25
Erdrich, Louise 39, 54
Erickson, Steve 64
Eshleman, Clayton 7
Estleman, Loren D. 48
Eugenides, Jeffrey 81
Everett, Percival L. 57
Everson, William (Oliver) 1, 5, 14
Exley, Frederick (Earl) 6, 11
Ezekiel, Tish O'Dowd 34
Fagen, Donald 26
Fair, Ronald L. 18
Fante, John (Thomas) 60
Farina, Richard 9
Farley, Walter (Lorimer) 17
Farmer, Philip Jose 1, 19
Farrell, James T(homas) 1, 4, 8, 11, 66
Fast, Howard (Melvin) 23
Faulkner, William (Cuthbert) 1, 3, 6, 8, 9, 11,
    14, 18, 28, 52, 68
Fauset, Jessie Redmon 19, 54
Faust, Irvin 8
Fearing, Kenneth (Flexner) 51
Federman, Raymond 6, 47
Feiffer, Jules (Ralph) 2, 8, 64
Feinberg, David B. 59
Feldman, Irving (Mordecai) 7
Felsen, Henry Gregor 17
Ferber, Edna 18, 93
Ferlinghetti, Lawrence (Monsanto) 2, 6, 10,
    27
Ferrigno, Robert 65
Fiedler, Leslie A(aron) 4, 13, 24
Field, Andrew 44
Fierstein, Harvey (Forbes) 33
Fisher, M(ary) F(rances) K(ennedy) 76, 87
Fisher, Vardis (Alvero) 7
Fitzgerald, Robert (Stuart) 39
Flanagan, Thomas (James Bonner) 25, 52
Fleming, Thomas (James) 37
Foote, Horton 51, 91
Foote, Shelby 75
Forbes, Esther 12
Forche, Carolyn (Louise) 25, 83, 86
Ford, John 16
Ford, Richard 46
Ford, Richard 99
Foreman, Richard 50
Forman, James Douglas 21
Fornes, Maria Irene 39, 61
Forrest, Leon 4
Fosse, Bob 20
Fox, Paula 2, 8
Fox, William Price (Jr.) 22
Francis, Robert (Churchill) 15
Frank, Elizabeth 39
Fraze, Candida (Merrill) 50
Frazier, Ian 46
Freeman, Judith 55

French, Albert 86
French, Marilyn 10, 18, 60
Friedan, Betty (Naomi) 74
Friedman, B(ernard) H(arper) 7
Friedman, Bruce Jay 3, 5, 56
Frost, Robert (Lee) 1, 3, 4, 9, 10, 13, 15, 26,
    34, 44
Fuchs, Daniel 34
Fuchs, Daniel 8, 22
Fuller, Charles (H. Jr.) 25
Fulton, Alice 52
Fussell, Paul 74
Gaddis, William 1, 3, 6, 8, 10, 19, 43, 86
Gaines, Ernest J(ames) 3, 11, 18, 86
Gaitskill, Mary 69
Gallagher, Tess 18, 63
Gallant, Roy A(rthur) 17
Gallico, Paul (William) 2
Galvin, James 38
Gann, Ernest Kellogg 23
Garcia, Cristina 76
Gardner, Herb(ert) 44
Gardner, John (Champlin) Jr. 2, 3, 5, 7, 8, 10,
    18, 28, 34
Garrett, George (Palmer) 3, 11, 51
Garrigue, Jean 2, 8
Gass, William H(oward) 1, 2, 8, 11, 15, 39
Gates, Henry Louis Jr. 65
Gaye, Marvin (Penze) 26
Gelbart, Larry (Simon) 21, 61
Gelber, Jack 1, 6, 14, 79
Gellhorn, Martha (Ellis) 14, 60
Gent, Peter 29
George, Jean Craighead 35
Gertler, T. 34
Ghiselin, Brewster 23
Gibbons, Kaye 50, 88
Gibson, William 23
Gibson, William (Ford) 39, 63
Gifford, Barry (Colby) 34
Gilbreth, Frank B. Jr. 17
Gilchrist, Ellen 34, 48
Giles, Molly 39
Gilliam, Terry (Vance) 21
Gilroy, Frank D(aniel) 2
Gilstrap, John 99
Ginsberg, Allen 1, 2, 3, 4, 6, 13, 36, 69
Giovanni, Nikki 2, 4, 19, 64
Glasser, Ronald J. 37
Gluck, Louise (Elisabeth) 7, 22, 44, 81
Godwin, Gail (Kathleen) 5, 8, 22, 31, 69
Goines, Donald 80
Gold, Herbert 4, 7, 14, 42
Goldbarth, Albert 5, 38
Goldman, Francisco 76
Goldman, William (W.) 1, 48
Goldsberry, Steven 34
Goodman, Paul 1, 2, 4, 7
Gordon, Caroline 6, 13, 29, 83
Gordon, Mary (Catherine) 13, 22
Gordon, Sol 26
Gordone, Charles 1, 4
Gould, Lois 4, 10
Goyen, (Charles) William 5, 8, 14, 40
Graham, Jorie 48
Grau, Shirley Ann 4, 9
Graver, Elizabeth 70
Gray, Amlin 29
Gray, Francine du Plessix 22
Gray, Spalding 49
Grayson, Richard (A.) 38
Greeley, Andrew M(oran) 28
Green, Hannah 3

Green, Julien 3, 11, 77
Green, Paul (Eliot) 25
Greenberg, Joanne (Goldenberg) 7, 30
Greenberg, Richard 57
Greene, Bette 30
Greene, Gael 8
Gregor, Arthur 9
Griffin, John Howard 68
Griffin, Peter 39
Grisham, John 84
Grumbach, Doris (Isaac) 13, 22, 64
Grunwald, Lisa 44
Guare, John 8, 14, 29, 67
Guest, Barbara 34
Guest, Judith (Ann) 8, 30
Guild, Nicholas M. 33
Gunn, Bill 5
Gurganus, Allan 70
Gurney, A(lbert) R(amsdell) Jr. 32, 50, 54
Gustafson, James M(oody) 100
Guterson, David 91
Guthrie, A(lfred) B(ertram) Jr. 23
Guthrie, Woody 35
Guy, Rosa (Cuthbert) 26
Hacker, Marilyn 5, 9, 23, 72, 91
Hailey, Elizabeth Forsythe 40
Haines, John (Meade) 58
Haldeman, Joe (William) 61
Haley, Alex(ander Murray Palmer) 8, 12, 76
Hall, Donald (Andrew Jr.) 1, 13, 37, 59
Halpern, Daniel 14
Hamill, Pete 10
Hamilton, Edmond 1
Hamilton, Virginia 26
Hammett, (Samuel) Dashiell 3, 5, 10, 19, 47
Hamner, Earl (Henry) Jr. 12
Hannah, Barry 23, 38, 90
Hansberry, Lorraine (Vivian) 17, 62
Hansen, Joseph 38
Hanson, Kenneth O(stlin) 13
Hardwick, Elizabeth 13
Harjo, Joy 83
Harlan, Louis R(udolph) 34
Harling, Robert 53
Harmon, William (Ruth) 38
Harper, Michael S(teven) 7, 22
Harris, MacDonald 9
Harris, Mark 19
Harrison, Harry (Max) 42
Harrison, James (Thomas) 6, 14, 33, 66
Harrison, Kathryn 70
Harriss, Will(ard Irvin) 34
Hart, Moss 66
Hartman, Geoffrey H. 27
Haruf, Kent 34
Hass, Robert 18, 39, 99
Haviaras, Stratis 33
Hawkes, John (Clendennin Burne Jr.) 1, 2, 3,
    4, 7, 9, 14, 15, 27, 49
Hayden, Robert E(arl) 5, 9, 14, 37
Hayman, Ronald 44
H. D. 3, 8, 14, 31, 34, 73
Hearne, Vicki 56
Hearon, Shelby 63
Heat-Moon, William Least 29
Hecht, Anthony (Evan) 8, 13, 19
Hecht, Ben 8
Heifner, Jack 11
Heilbrun, Carolyn G(old) 25
Heinemann, Larry (Curtiss) 50
Heinlein, Robert A(nson) 1, 3, 8, 14, 26, 55
Heller, Joseph 1, 3, 5, 8, 11, 36, 63
Hellman, Lillian (Florence) 2, 4, 8, 14, 18, 34,

44, 52
Helprin, Mark 7, 10, 22, 32
Hemingway, Ernest (Miller) 1, 3, 6, 8, 10, 13, 19, 30, 34, 39, 41, 44, 50, 61, 80
Hempel, Amy 39
Henley, Beth 23
Hentoff, Nat(han Irving) 26
Herbert, Frank (Patrick) 12, 23, 35, 44, 85
Herbst, Josephine (Frey) 34
Herlihy, James Leo 6
Herrmann, Dorothy 44
Hersey, John (Richard) 1, 2, 7, 9, 40, 81, 97
Heyen, William 13, 18
Higgins, George V(incent) 4, 7, 10, 18
Highsmith, (Mary) Patricia 2, 4, 14, 42, 102
Highwater, Jamake (Mamake) 12
Hijuelos, Oscar 65
Hill, George Roy 26
Hillerman, Tony 62
Himes, Chester (Bomar) 2, 4, 7, 18, 58
Hinton, S(usan) E(loise) 30
Hirsch, Edward 31, 50
Hirsch, E(ric) D(onald) Jr. 79
Hoagland, Edward 28
Hoban, Russell (Conwell) 7, 25
Hobson, Laura Z(ametkin) 7, 25
Hochman, Sandra 3, 8
Hoffman, Alice 51
Hoffman, Daniel (Gerard) 6, 13, 23
Hoffman, Stanley 5
Hoffman, William M(oses) 40
Hogan, Linda 73
Holland, Isabelle 21
Hollander, John 2, 5, 8, 14
Holleran, Andrew 38
Holmes, John Clellon 56
Honig, Edwin 33
hooks, bell 94
Horgan, Paul (George Vincent O'Shaughnessy) 9, 53
Horovitz, Israel (Arthur) 56
Horwitz, Julius 14
Hougan, Carolyn 34
Howard, Maureen 5, 14, 46
Howard, Richard 7, 10, 47
Howe, Fanny 47
Howe, Irving 85
Howe, Susan 72
Howe, Tina 48
Howes, Barbara 15
Hubbard, L(afayette) Ron(ald) 43
Huddle, David 49
Hughart, Barry 39
Hughes, (James) Langston 1, 5, 10, 15, 35, 44
Hugo, Richard F(ranklin) 6, 18, 32
Humphrey, William 45
Humphreys, Josephine 34, 57
Hunt, E(verette) Howard (Jr.) 3
Hunt, Marsha 70
Hunter, Evan 11, 31
Hunter, Kristin (Eggleston) 35
Hurston, Zora Neale 7, 30, 61
Huston, John (Marcellus) 20
Hustvedt, Siri 76
Hwang, David Henry 55
Hyde, Margaret O(ldroyd) 21
Hynes, James 65
Ian, Janis 21
Ignatow, David 4, 7, 14, 40
Ingalls, Rachel (Holmes) 42
Inge, William (Motter) 1, 8, 19
Innaurato, Albert (F.) 21, 60
Irving, John (Winslow) 13, 23, 38

Isaacs, Susan 32
Isler, Alan (David) 91
Ivask, Ivar Vidrik 14
Jackson, Jesse 12
Jackson, Shirley 11, 60, 87
Jacobs, Jim 12
Jacobsen, Josephine 48, 102
Jakes, John (William) 29
Janowitz, Tama 43
Jarrell, Randall 1, 2, 6, 9, 13, 49
Jeffers, (John) Robinson 2, 3, 11, 15, 54
Jen, Gish 70
Jennings, Waylon 21
Jensen, Laura (Linnea) 37
Joel, Billy 26
Johnson, Charles (Richard) 7, 51, 65
Johnson, Denis 52
Johnson, Diane 5, 13, 48
Johnson, Joyce 58
Jones, Edward P. 76
Jones, Gayl 6, 9
Jones, James 1, 3, 10, 39
Jones, LeRoi 1, 2, 3, 5, 10, 14
Jones, Louis B. 65
Jones, Madison (Percy Jr.) 4
Jones, Nettie (Pearl) 34
Jones, Preston 10
Jones, Robert F(rancis) 7
Jones, Thom 81
Jong, Erica 4, 6, 8, 18, 83
Jordan, June 5, 11, 23
Jordan, Pat(rick M.) 37
Just, Ward (Swift) 4, 27
Justice, Donald (Rodney) 6, 19, 102
Kadohata, Cynthia 59
Kahn, Roger 30
Kaletski, Alexander 39
Kallman, Chester (Simon) 2
Kaminsky, Stuart M(elvin) 59
Kanin, Garson 22
Kantor, MacKinlay 7
Kaplan, David Michael 50
Kaplan, James 59
Karl, Frederick R(obert) 34
Katz, Steve 47
Kauffman, Janet 42
Kaufman, Bob (Garnell) 49
Kaufman, George S. 38
Kaufman, Sue 3, 8
Kazan, Elia 6, 16, 63
Kazin, Alfred 34, 38
Keaton, Buster 20
Keene, Donald 34
Keillor, Garrison 40
Kellerman, Jonathan 44
Kelley, William Melvin 22
Kellogg, Marjorie 2
Kemelman, Harry 2
Kennedy, Adrienne (Lita) 66
Kennedy, William 6, 28, 34, 53
Kennedy, X. J. 8, 42
Kenny, Maurice (Francis) 87
Kerouac, Jack 1, 2, 3, 5, 14, 29, 61
Kerr, Jean 22
Kerr, M. E. 12, 35
Kerr, Robert 55
Kerrigan, (Thomas) Anthony 4, 6
Kesey, Ken (Elton) 1, 3, 6, 11, 46, 64
Kesselring, Joseph (Otto) 45
Kessler, Jascha (Frederick) 4
Kettelkamp, Larry (Dale) 12
Keyes, Daniel 80
Kherdian, David 6, 9

Kienzle, William X(avier) 25
Killens, John Oliver 10
Kincaid, Jamaica 43, 68
King, Martin Luther Jr. 83
King, Stephen (Edwin) 12, 26, 37, 61
King, Thomas 89
Kingman, Lee 17
Kingsley, Sidney 44
Kingsolver, Barbara 55, 81
Kingston, Maxine (Ting Ting) Hong 12, 19, 58
Kinnell, Galway 1, 2, 3, 5, 13, 29
Kirkwood, James 9
Kizer, Carolyn (Ashley) 15, 39, 80
Klappert, Peter 57
Klein, Norma 30
Klein, T(heodore) E(ibon) D(onald) 34
Knapp, Caroline 99
Knebel, Fletcher 14
Knight, Etheridge 40
Knowles, John 1, 4, 10, 26
Koch, Kenneth 5, 8, 44
Komunyakaa, Yusef 86, 94
Koontz, Dean R(ay) 78
Kopit, Arthur (Lee) 1, 18, 33
Kosinski, Jerzy (Nikodem) 1, 2, 3, 6, 10, 15, 53, 70
Kostelanetz, Richard (Cory) 28
Kotlowitz, Robert 4
Kotzwinkle, William 5, 14, 35
Kozol, Jonathan 17
Kozoll, Michael 35
Kramer, Kathryn 34
Kramer, Larry 42
Kristofferson, Kris 26
Krumgold, Joseph (Quincy) 12
Krutch, Joseph Wood 24
Kubrick, Stanley 16
Kumin, Maxine (Winokur) 5, 13, 28
Kunitz, Stanley (Jasspon) 6, 11, 14
Kushner, Tony 81
Kuzma, Greg 7
L'Amour, Louis (Dearborn) 25, 55
Lancaster, Bruce 36
Landis, John 26
Langer, Elinor 34
Lapine, James (Elliot) 39
Larsen, Eric 55
Larsen, Nella 37
Larson, Charles R(aymond) 31
Larson, Jonathan 99
Lasch, Christopher 102
Latham, Jean Lee 12
Lattimore, Richmond (Alexander) 3
Laughlin, James 49
Lear, Norman (Milton) 12
Leavitt, David 34
Lebowitz, Fran(ces Ann) 11, 36
Lee, Andrea 36
Lee, Chang-rae 91
Lee, Don L. 2
Lee, George W(ashington) 52
Lee, Helen Elaine 86
Lee, Lawrence 34
Lee, Manfred B(ennington) 11
Lee, (Nelle) Harper 12, 60
Lee, Shelton Jackson 105
Lee, Stan 17
Leet, Judith 11
Leffland, Ella 19
Le Guin, Ursula K(roeber) 8, 13, 22, 45, 71
Leiber, Fritz (Reuter Jr.) 25
Leimbach, Marti 65

Leithauser, Brad 27
Lelchuk, Alan 5
Lemann, Nancy 39
L'Engle, Madeleine (Camp Franklin) 12
Lentricchia, Frank (Jr.) 34
Leonard, Elmore (John Jr.) 28, 34, 71
Lerman, Eleanor 9
Lerman, Rhoda 56
Lester, Richard 20
Levertov, Denise 1, 2, 3, 5, 8, 15, 28, 66
Levi, Jonathan 76
Levin, Ira 3, 6
Levin, Meyer 7
Levine, Philip 2, 4, 5, 9, 14, 33
Levinson, Deirdre 49
Levitin, Sonia (Wolff) 17
Lewis, Janet 41
Leyner, Mark 92
L'Heureux, John (Clarke) 52
Lieber, Joel 6
Lieberman, Laurence (James) 4, 36
Lifton, Robert Jay 67
Lightman, Alan P. 81
Ligotti, Thomas (Robert) 44
Lindbergh, Anne (Spencer) Morrow 82
Linney, Romulus 51
Lipsyte, Robert (Michael) 21
Lish, Gordon (Jay) 45
Littell, Robert 42
Loewinsohn, Ron(ald William) 52
Logan, John (Burton) 5
Lopate, Phillip 29
Lord, Bette Bao 23
Lorde, Audre (Geraldine) 18, 71
Louie, David Wong 70
Lowell, Robert (Traill Spence Jr.) 1, 2, 3, 4, 5,
    8, 9, 11, 15, 37
Loy, Mina 28
Lucas, Craig 64
Lucas, George 16
Ludlam, Charles 46, 50
Ludlum, Robert 22, 43
Ludwig, Ken 60
Lurie, Alison 4, 5, 18, 39
Lynch, David (K.) 66
Lynn, Kenneth S(chuyler) 50
Lytle, Andrew (Nelson) 22
Maas, Peter 29
Macdonald, Cynthia 13, 19
MacDonald, John D(ann) 3, 27, 44
Macdonald, Ross 1, 2, 3, 14, 34, 41
MacInnes, Helen (Clark) 27, 39
Maclean, Norman (Fitzroy) 78
MacLeish, Archibald 3, 8, 14, 68
MacShane, Frank 39
Madden, (Jerry) David 5, 15
Madhubuti, Haki R. 6, 73
Mailer, Norman 1, 2, 3, 4, 5, 8, 11, 14, 28, 39,
    74
Major, Clarence 3, 19, 48
Malamud, Bernard 1, 2, 3, 5, 8, 9, 11, 18, 27,
    44, 78, 85
Malcolm X 82
Maloff, Saul 5
Malone, Michael (Christopher) 43
Malzberg, Barry N(athaniel) 7
Mamet, David (Alan) 9, 15, 34, 46, 91
Mamoulian, Rouben (Zachary) 16
Mano, D. Keith 2, 10
Manso, Peter 39
Margulies, Donald 76
Markfield, Wallace 8
Markson, David M(errill) 67

Marquand, John P(hillips) 2, 10
Marques, Rene 96
Marshall, Garry 17
Marshall, Paule 27, 72
Martin, Steve 30
Martin, Valerie 89
Maso, Carole 44
Mason, Bobbie Ann 28, 43, 82
Masters, Hilary 48
Mastrosimone, William 36
Matheson, Richard Burton 37
Mathews, Harry 6, 52
Mathews, John Joseph 84
Matthews, William 40
Matthias, John (Edward) 9
Matthiessen, Peter 5, 7, 11, 32, 64
Maupin, Armistead 95
Maxwell, William (Keepers Jr.) 19
May, Elaine 16
Maynard, Joyce 23
Maysles, Albert 16
Maysles, David 16
Mazer, Norma Fox 26
McBrien, William Augustine 44
McCaffrey, Anne (Inez) 17
McCall, Nathan 86
McCarthy, Cormac 4, 57, 59, 101
McCarthy, Mary (Therese) 1, 3, 5, 14, 24, 39,
    59
McCauley, Stephen (D.) 50
McClure, Michael (Thomas) 6, 10
McCorkle, Jill (Collins) 51
McCourt, James 5
McCullers, (Lula) Carson (Smith) 1, 4, 10, 12,
    48, 100
McDermott, Alice 90
McElroy, Joseph 5, 47
McFarland, Dennis 65
McGinley, Phyllis 14
McGinniss, Joe 32
McGrath, Thomas (Matthew) 28, 59
McGuane, Thomas (Francis III) 3, 7, 18, 45
McHale, Tom 3, 5
McInerney, Jay 34
McIntyre, Vonda N(eel) 18
McKuen, Rod 1, 3
McMillan, Terry (L.) 50, 61
McMurtry, Larry (Jeff) 2, 3, 7, 11, 27, 44
McNally, Terrence 4, 7, 41, 91
McNally, T. M. 82
McNamer, Deirdre 70
McNickle, (William) D'Arcy 89
McPhee, John (Angus) 36
McPherson, James Alan 19, 77
McPherson, William (Alexander) 34
Mead, Margaret 37
Medoff, Mark (Howard) 6, 23
Mehta, Ved (Parkash) 37
Meltzer, Milton 26
Mendelsohn, Jane 99
Meredith, William (Morris) 4, 13, 22, 55
Merkin, Daphne 44
Merrill, James (Ingram) 2, 3, 6, 8, 13, 18, 34,
    91
Merton, Thomas 1, 3, 11, 34, 83
Merwin, W(illiam) S(tanley) 1, 2, 3, 5, 8, 13,
    18, 45, 88
Mewshaw, Michael 9
Meyers, Jeffrey 39
Michaels, Leonard 6, 25
Michener, James A(lbert) 1, 5, 11, 29, 60
Miles, Jack 100
Miles, Josephine (Louise) 1, 2, 14, 34, 39

Millar, Kenneth 14
Miller, Arthur 1, 2, 6, 10, 15, 26, 47, 78
Miller, Henry (Valentine) 1, 2, 4, 9, 14, 43, 84
Miller, Jason 2
Miller, Sue 44
Miller, Walter M(ichael Jr.) 4, 30
Millett, Kate 67
Millhauser, Steven 21, 54
Milner, Ron(ald) 56
Miner, Valerie 40
Minot, Susan 44
Minus, Ed 39
Mitchell, Joseph (Quincy) 98
Modarressi, Taghi (M.) 44
Mohr, Nicholasa 12
Mojtabai, A(nn) G(race) 5, 9, 15, 29
Momaday, N(avarre) Scott 2, 19, 85, 95
Monette, Paul 82
Montague, John (Patrick) 13, 46
Montgomery, Marion H. Jr. 7
Mooney, Ted 25
Moore, Lorrie 39, 45, 68
Moore, Marianne (Craig) 1, 2, 4, 8, 10, 13, 19,
    47
Morgan, Berry 6
Morgan, (George) Frederick 23
Morgan, Robin 2
Morgan, Seth 65
Morris, Bill 76
Morris, Wright 1, 3, 7, 18, 37
Morrison, Jim 17
Morrison, Toni 4, 10, 22, 55, 81, 87
Mosher, Howard Frank 62
Mosley, Walter 97
Moss, Howard 7, 14, 45, 50
Motley, Willard (Francis) 18
Mountain Wolf Woman 92
Moyers, Bill 74
Mueller, Lisel 13, 51
Mukherjee, Bharati 53
Mull, Martin 17
Mungo, Raymond 72
Murphy, Sylvia 34
Murray, Albert L. 73
Muske, Carol 90
Myers, Walter Dean 35
Nabokov, Vladimir (Vladimirovich) 1, 2, 3, 6,
    8, 11, 15, 23, 44, 46, 64
Nash, (Frediric) Ogden 23
Naylor, Gloria 28, 52
Neihardt, John Gneisenau 32
Nelson, Willie 17
Nemerov, Howard (Stanley) 2, 6, 9, 36
Neufeld, John (Arthur) 17
Neville, Emily Cheney 12
Newlove, Donald 6
Newman, Charles 2, 8
Newman, Edwin (Harold) 14
Newton, Suzanne 35
Nichols, John (Treadwell) 38
Niedecker, Lorine 10, 42
Nin, Anais 1, 4, 8, 11, 14, 60
Nissenson, Hugh 4, 9
Niven, Larry 8
Nixon, Agnes Eckhardt 21
Norman, Marsha 28
Norton, Andre 12
Nova, Craig 7, 31
Nunn, Kem 34
Nyro, Laura 17
Oates, Joyce Carol 1, 2, 3, 6, 9, 11, 15, 19, 33,
    52
O'Brien, Darcy 11

O'Brien, (William) Tim(othy) 7, 19, 40, 103
Ochs, Phil 17
O'Connor, Edwin (Greene) 14
O'Connor, (Mary) Flannery 1, 2, 3, 6, 10, 13, 15, 21, 66, 104
O'Dell, Scott 30
Odets, Clifford 2, 28, 98
O'Donovan, Michael John 14
O'Grady, Timothy 59
O'Hara, Frank 2, 5, 13, 78
O'Hara, John (Henry) 1, 2, 3, 6, 11, 42
O Hehir, Diana 41
Olds, Sharon 32, 39, 85
Oliver, Mary 19, 34, 98
Olsen, Tillie 4, 13
Olson, Charles (John) 1, 2, 5, 6, 9, 11, 29
Olson, Toby 28
Oneal, Zibby 30
Oppen, George 7, 13, 34
Orlovitz, Gil 22
Ortiz, Simon J(oseph) 45
Otto, Whitney 70
Owens, Rochelle 8
Ozick, Cynthia 3, 7, 28, 62
Pack, Robert 13
Pagels, Elaine Hiesey 104
Paglia, Camille (Anna) 68
Paley, Grace 4, 6, 37
Palliser, Charles 65
Pancake, Breece D'J 29
Parini, Jay (Lee) 54
Parker, Dorothy (Rothschild) 15, 68
Parker, Robert B(rown) 27
Parks, Gordon (Alexander Buchanan) 1, 16
Pastan, Linda (Olenik) 27
Patchen, Kenneth 1, 2, 18
Paterson, Katherine (Womeldorf) 12, 30
Peacock, Molly 60
Pearson, T(homas) R(eid) 39
Peck, John 3
Peck, Richard (Wayne) 21
Peck, Robert Newton 17
Peckinpah, (David) Sam(uel) 20
Percy, Walker 2, 3, 6, 8, 14, 18, 47, 65
Perelman, S(idney) J(oseph) 3, 5, 9, 15, 23, 44, 49
Pesetsky, Bette 28
Peterkin, Julia Mood 31
Peters, Joan K(aren) 39
Peters, Robert L(ouis) 7
Petrakis, Harry Mark 3
Petry, Ann (Lane) 1, 7, 18
Philipson, Morris H. 53
Phillips, Jayne Anne 15, 33
Phillips, Robert (Schaeffer) 28
Piercy, Marge 3, 6, 14, 18, 27, 62
Pinckney, Darryl 76
Pineda, Cecile 39
Pinkwater, Daniel Manus 35
Pinsky, Robert 9, 19, 38, 94
Pirsig, Robert M(aynard) 4, 6, 73
Plante, David (Robert) 7, 23, 38
Plath, Sylvia 1, 2, 3, 5, 9, 11, 14, 17, 50, 51, 62
Platt, Kin 26
Plimpton, George (Ames) 36
Plumly, Stanley (Ross) 33
Pohl, Frederik 18
Poitier, Sidney 26
Pollitt, Katha 28
Polonsky, Abraham (Lincoln) 92
Pomerance, Bernard 13
Porter, Connie (Rose) 70

Porter, Katherine Anne 1, 3, 7, 10, 13, 15, 27, 101
Potok, Chaim 2, 7, 14, 26
Pound, Ezra (Weston Loomis) 1, 2, 3, 4, 5, 7, 10, 13, 18, 34, 48, 50
Povod, Reinaldo 44
Powell, Adam Clayton Jr. 89
Powell, Dawn 66
Powell, Padgett 34
Power, Susan 91
Powers, J(ames) F(arl) 1, 4, 8, 57
Powers, John R. 66
Powers, Richard (S.) 93
Prager, Emily 56
Price, (Edward) Reynolds 3, 6, 13, 43, 50, 63
Price, Richard 6, 12
Prince 35
Pritchard, William H(arrison) 34
Probst, Mark 59
Prokosch, Frederic 4, 48
Prose, Francine 45
Proulx, E. Annie 81
Pryor, Richard (Franklin Lenox Thomas) 26
Purdy, James (Amos) 2, 4, 10, 28, 52
Puzo, Mario 1, 2, 6, 36
Pynchon, Thomas (Ruggles Jr.) 2, 3, 6, 9, 11, 18, 33, 62, 72
Quay, Stephen 95
Quay, Timothy 95
Queen, Ellery 3, 11
Quinn, Peter 91
Rabe, David (William) 4, 8, 33
Rado, James 17
Raeburn, John (Hay) 34
Ragni, Gerome 17
Rahv, Philip 24
Rakosi, Carl 47
Rampersad, Arnold 44
Rand, Ayn 3, 30, 44, 79
Randall, Dudley (Felker) 1
Ransom, John Crowe 2, 4, 5, 11, 24
Raphael, Frederic (Michael) 2, 14
Rechy, John (Francisco) 1, 7, 14, 18
Reddin, Keith 67
Redmon, Anne 22
Reed, Ishmael 2, 3, 5, 6, 13, 32, 60
Reed, Lou 21
Remarque, Erich Maria 21
Rexroth, Kenneth 1, 2, 6, 11, 22, 49
Reynolds, Jonathan 6, 38
Reynolds, Michael Shane 44
Reznikoff, Charles 9
Ribman, Ronald (Burt) 7
Rice, Anne 41
Rice, Elmer (Leopold) 7, 49
Rich, Adrienne (Cecile) 3, 6, 7, 11, 18, 36, 73, 76
Richter, Conrad (Michael) 30
Riding, Laura 3, 7
Ringwood, Gwen(dolyn Margaret) Pharis 48
Rivers, Conrad Kent 1
Robbins, Harold 5
Robbins, Tom 9, 32, 64
Robbins, Trina 21
Robinson, Jill 10
Robinson, Kim Stanley 34
Robinson, Marilynne 25
Robinson, Smokey 21
Robison, Mary 42, 98
Roddenberry, Gene 17
Rodgers, Mary 12
Rodman, Howard 65
Roethke, Theodore (Huebner) 1, 3, 8, 11, 19,

46, 101
Rogers, Thomas Hunton 57
Rogin, Gilbert 18
Roiphe, Anne (Richardson) 3, 9
Rooke, Leon 25, 34
Rose, Wendy 85
Rosen, Richard (Dean) 39
Rosenthal, M(acha) L(ouis) 28
Rossner, Judith (Perelman) 6, 9, 29
Roth, Henry 2, 6, 11, 104
Roth, Philip (Milton) 1, 2, 3, 4, 6, 9, 15, 22, 31, 47, 66, 86
Rothenberg, Jerome 6, 57
Rovit, Earl (Herbert) 7
Ruark, Gibbons 3
Rudnik, Raphael 7
Rukeyser, Muriel 6, 10, 15, 27
Rule, Jane (Vance) 27
Rush, Norman 44
Russ, Joanna 15
Ryan, Cornelius (John) 7
Ryan, Michael 65
Sachs, Marilyn (Stickle) 35
Sackler, Howard (Oliver) 14
Sadoff, Ira 9
Safire, William 10
Sagan, Carl (Edward) 30
Saint, H(arry) F. 50
Salamanca, J(ack) R(ichard) 4, 15
Sale, Kirkpatrick 68
Salinas, Luis Omar 90
Salinger, J(erome) D(avid) 1, 3, 8, 12, 55, 56
Salter, James 7, 52, 59
Sanchez, Sonia 5
Sandburg, Carl (August) 1, 4, 10, 15, 35
Sanders, (James) Ed(ward) 53
Sanders, Lawrence 41
Sandoz, Mari(e Susette) 28
Saner, Reg(inald Anthony) 9
Santiago, Danny 33
Santmyer, Helen Hoover 33
Santos, Bienvenido N(uqui) 22
Sapphire 99
Saroyan, William 1, 8, 10, 29, 34, 56
Sarton, (Eleanor) May 4, 14, 49, 91
Saul, John (W. III) 46
Savage, Thomas 40
Savan, Glenn 50
Sayers, Valerie 50
Sayles, John (Thomas) 7, 10, 14
Schaeffer, Susan Fromberg 6, 11, 22
Schell, Jonathan 35
Schevill, James (Erwin) 7
Schisgal, Murray (Joseph) 6
Schlesinger, Arthur M(eier) Jr. 84
Schnackenberg, Gjertrud 40
Schor, Sandra (M.) 65
Schorer, Mark 9
Schrader, Paul (Joseph) 26
Schulberg, Budd (Wilson) 7, 48
Schulz, Charles M(onroe) 12
Schuyler, James Marcus 5, 23
Schwartz, Delmore (David) 2, 4, 10, 45, 87
Schwartz, John Burnham 59
Schwartz, Lynne Sharon 31
Scoppettone, Sandra 26
Scorsese, Martin 20, 89
Scott, Evelyn 43
Scott, Joanna 50
Sebestyen, Ouida 30
Seelye, John 7
Segal, Erich (Wolf) 3, 10
Seger, Bob 35

Seidel, Frederick (Lewis) 18
Selby, Hubert Jr. 1, 2, 4, 8
Selzer, Richard 74
Serling, (Edward) Rod(man) 30
Seton, Cynthia Propper 27
Settle, Mary Lee 19, 61
Sexton, Anne (Harvey) 2, 4, 6, 8, 10, 15, 53
Shaara, Michael (Joseph Jr.) 15
Shacochis, Bob 39
Shange, Ntozake 8, 25, 38, 74
Shanley, John Patrick 75
Shapiro, Jane 76
Shapiro, Karl (Jay) 4, 8, 15, 53
Shaw, Irwin 7, 23, 34
Shawn, Wallace 41
Shea, Lisa 86
Sheed, Wilfrid (John Joseph) 2, 4, 10, 53
Shepard, Jim 36
Shepard, Lucius 34
Shepard, Sam 4, 6, 17, 34, 41, 44
Sherburne, Zoa (Morin) 30
Sherman, Jonathan Marc 55
Sherman, Martin 19
Sherwin, Judith Johnson 7, 15
Shields, Carol 91
Shields, David 97
Shilts, Randy 85
Shreve, Susan Richards 23
Shue, Larry 52
Shulman, Alix Kates 2, 10
Shuster, Joe 21
Siegel, Jerome 21
Sigal, Clancy 7
Silko, Leslie (Marmon) 23, 74
Silver, Joan Micklin 20
Silverberg, Robert 7
Silverstein, Alvin 17
Silverstein, Virginia B(arbara Opshelor) 17
Simak, Clifford D(onald) 1, 55
Simic, Charles 6, 9, 22, 49, 68
Simmons, Charles (Paul) 57
Simmons, Dan 44
Simon, Carly 26
Simon, (Marvin) Neil 6, 11, 31, 39, 70
Simon, Paul (Frederick) 17
Simpson, Louis (Aston Marantz) 4, 7, 9, 32
Simpson, Mona (Elizabeth) 44
Sinclair, Upton (Beall) 1, 11, 15, 63
Singer, Isaac Bashevis 1, 3, 6, 9, 11, 15, 23, 38, 69
Sissman, L(ouis) E(dward) 9, 18
Slaughter, Frank G(ill) 29
Slavitt, David R(ytman) 5, 14
Smiley, Jane (Graves) 53, 76
Smith, Anna Deavere 86
Smith, Betty (Wehner) 19
Smith, Clark Ashton 43
Smith, Dave 22, 42
Smith, Lee 25, 73
Smith, Martin Cruz 25
Smith, Mary-Ann Tirone 39
Smith, Patti 12
Smith, William Jay 6
Snodgrass, W(illiam) D(e Witt) 2, 6, 10, 18, 68
Snyder, Gary (Sherman) 1, 2, 5, 9, 32
Snyder, Zilpha Keatley 17
Sokolov, Raymond 7
Sommer, Scott 25
Sondheim, Stephen (Joshua) 30, 39
Sontag, Susan 1, 2, 10, 13, 31, 105
Sorrentino, Gilbert 3, 7, 14, 22, 40
Soto, Gary 32, 80

Southern, Terry 7
Spackman, W(illiam) M(ode) 46
Spacks, Barry (Bernard) 14
Spanidou, Irini 44
Spencer, Elizabeth 22
Spencer, Scott 30
Spicer, Jack 8, 18, 72
Spiegelman, Art 76
Spielberg, Peter 6
Spielberg, Steven 20
Spillane, Mickey 3, 13
Spinrad, Norman (Richard) 46
Spivack, Kathleen (Romola Drucker) 6
Spoto, Donald 39
Springsteen, Bruce (F.) 17
Squires, (James) Radcliffe 51
Stafford, Jean 4, 7, 19, 68
Stafford, William (Edgar) 4, 7, 29
Stanton, Maura 9
Starbuck, George (Edwin) 53
Steele, Timothy (Reid) 45
Stegner, Wallace (Earle) 9, 49, 81
Steinbeck, John (Ernst) 1, 5, 9, 13, 21, 34, 45, 75
Steinem, Gloria 63
Steiner, George 24
Sterling, Bruce 72
Stern, Gerald 40, 100
Stern, Richard (Gustave) 4, 39
Sternberg, Josef von 20
Stevens, Mark 34
Stevenson, Anne (Katharine) 7, 33
Still, James 49
Stitt, Milan 29
Stolz, Mary (Slattery) 12
Stone, Irving 7
Stone, Oliver (William) 73
Stone, Robert (Anthony) 5, 23, 42
Storm, Hyemeyohsts 3
Stout, Rex (Todhunter) 3
Strand, Mark 6, 18, 41, 71
Straub, Peter (Francis) 28
Stribling, T(homas) S(igismund) 23
Stuart, Jesse (Hilton) 1, 8, 11, 14, 34
Sturgeon, Theodore (Hamilton) 22, 39
Styron, William 1, 3, 5, 11, 15, 60
Sukenick, Ronald 3, 4, 6, 48
Summers, Hollis (Spurgeon Jr.) 10
Susann, Jacqueline 3
Swados, Elizabeth (A.) 12
Swados, Harvey 5
Swan, Gladys 69
Swarthout, Glendon (Fred) 35
Swenson, May 4, 14, 61, 106
Talese, Gay 37
Tallent, Elizabeth (Ann) 45
Tally, Ted 42
Tan, Amy (Ruth) 59
Tartt, Donna 76
Tate, James (Vincent) 2, 6, 25
Tate, (John Orley) Allen 2, 4, 6, 9, 11, 14, 24
Tavel, Ronald 6
Taylor, Eleanor Ross 5
Taylor, Henry (Splawn) 44
Taylor, Mildred D. 21
Taylor, Peter (Hillsman) 1, 4, 18, 37, 44, 50, 71
Taylor, Robert Lewis 14
Terkel, Studs 38
Terry, Megan 19
Tesich, Steve 40, 69
Tevis, Walter 42
Theroux, Alexander (Louis) 2, 25

Theroux, Paul (Edward) 5, 8, 11, 15, 28, 46
Thomas, Audrey (Callahan) 7, 13, 37
Thomas, Joyce Carol 35
Thomas, Lewis 35
Thomas, Piri 17
Thomas, Ross (Elmore) 39
Thompson, Hunter S(tockton) 9, 17, 40, 104
Thompson, Jim (Myers) 69
Thurber, James (Grover) 5, 11, 25
Tilghman, Christopher 65
Tillinghast, Richard (Williford) 29
Tiptree, James Jr. 48, 50
Tolson, Melvin B(eaunorus) 36, 105
Tomlin, Lily 17
Toole, John Kennedy 19, 64
Toomer, Jean 1, 4, 13, 22
Torrey, E(dwin) Fuller 34
Towne, Robert (Burton) 87
Traven, B. 8, 11
Trevanian 29
Trilling, Lionel 9, 11, 24
Trow, George W. S. 52
Trudeau, Garry B. 12
Trumbo, Dalton 19
Tryon, Thomas 3, 11
Tuck, Lily 70
Tunis, John R(oberts) 12
Turco, Lewis (Putnam) 11, 63
Turner, Frederick 48
Tyler, Anne 7, 11, 18, 28, 44, 59, 103
Uhry, Alfred 55
Ulibarri, Sabine R(eyes) 83
Unger, Douglas 34
Updike, John (Hoyer) 1, 2, 3, 5, 7, 9, 13, 15, 23, 34, 43, 70
Urdang, Constance (Henriette) 47
Uris, Leon (Marcus) 7, 32
Vachss, Andrew (Henry) 106
Valdez, Luis (Miguel) 84
Van Ash, Cay 34
Vance, Jack 35
Vandenburgh, Jane 59
Van Doren, Mark 6, 10
Van Duyn, Mona (Jane) 3, 7, 63
Van Peebles, Melvin 2, 20
Van Vechten, Carl 33
Vaughn, Stephanie 62
Vidal, Gore 2, 4, 6, 8, 10, 22, 33, 72
Viereck, Peter (Robert Edwin) 4
Vinge, Joan D(ennison) 30
Vizenor, Gerald Robert 103
Vliet, R(ussell) G(ordon) 22
Vogel, Paula A(nne) 76
Voight, Ellen Bryant 54
Voigt, Cynthia 30
Vollmann, William T. 89
Vonnegut, Kurt Jr. 1, 2, 3, 4, 5, 8, 12, 22, 40, 60
Wagman, Fredrica 7
Wagner-Martin, Linda (C.) 50
Wagoner, David (Russell) 3, 5, 15
Wakefield, Dan 7
Wakoski, Diane 2, 4, 7, 9, 11, 40
Waldman, Anne 7
Walker, Alice (Malsenior) 5, 6, 9, 19, 27, 46, 58, 103
Walker, Joseph A. 19
Walker, Margaret (Abigail) 1, 6
Wallace, David Foster 50
Wallace, Irving 7, 13
Wallant, Edward Lewis 5, 10
Wambaugh, Joseph (Aloysius Jr.) 3, 18
Ward, Douglas Turner 19

Nationality Index

Warhol, Andy **20**
Warren, Robert Penn **1, 4, 6, 8, 10, 13, 18, 39,
53, 59**
Wasserstein, Wendy **32, 59, 90**
Waters, Frank (Joseph) **88**
Watkins, Paul **55**
Webb, Charles (Richard) **7**
Webb, James H(enry) Jr. **22**
Weber, Lenora Mattingly **12**
Weidman, Jerome **7**
Weiss, Theodore (Russell) **3, 8, 14**
Welch, James **6, 14, 52**
Wellek, Rene **28**
Weller, Michael **10, 53**
Welles, (George) Orson **20, 80**
Wellman, Mac **65**
Wellman, Manly Wade **49**
Wells, Rosemary **12**
Welty, Eudora **1, 2, 5, 14, 22, 33, 105**
Wersba, Barbara **30**
Wescott, Glenway **13**
Wesley, Richard (Errol) **7**
West, (Mary) Jessamyn **7, 17**
West, Paul **7, 14, 96**
Westlake, Donald E(dwin) **7, 33**
Whalen, Philip **6, 29**
Wharton, William (a pseudonym) **18, 37**
Wheelock, John Hall **14**
White, Edmund (Valentine III) **27**
White, E(lwyn) B(rooks) **10, 34, 39**
Whitney, Phyllis A(yame) **42**
Whittemore, (Edward) Reed (Jr.) **4**
Wicker, Tom **7**
Wideman, John Edgar **5, 34, 36, 67**
Wieners, John **7**
Wiesel, Elie(zer) **3, 5, 11, 37**
Wiggins, Marianne **57**
Wilbur, Richard (Purdy) **3, 6, 9, 14, 53**
Wild, Peter **14**
Wilder, Billy **20**
Wilder, Thornton (Niven) **1, 5, 6, 10, 15, 35,
82**
Wiley, Richard **44**
Wilhelm, Kate **7**
Willard, Nancy **7, 37**
Williams, C(harles) K(enneth) **33, 56**
Williams, John A(lfred) **5, 13**
Williams, Jonathan (Chamberlain) **13**
Williams, Joy **31**
Williams, Norman **39**
Williams, Sherley Anne **89**
Williams, Tennessee **1, 2, 5, 7, 8, 11, 15, 19,
30, 39, 45, 71**
Williams, Thomas (Alonzo) **14**
Williams, William Carlos **1, 2, 5, 9, 13, 22,
42, 67**
Williamson, Jack **29**
Willingham, Calder (Baynard Jr.) **5, 51**
Wilson, August **39, 50, 63**
Wilson, Brian **12**
Wilson, Edmund **1, 2, 3, 8, 24**
Wilson, Lanford **7, 14, 36**
Wilson, Robert M. **7, 9**
Wilson, Sloan **32**
Wilson, William S(mith) **49**
Winters, (Arthur) Yvor **4, 8, 32**
Winters, Janet Lewis **41**
Wiseman, Frederick **20**
Wodehouse, P(elham) G(renville) **1, 2, 5, 10,
22**
Woiwode, Larry (Alfred) **6, 10**
Wojciechowska, Maia (Teresa) **26**
Wolfe, Gene (Rodman) **25**

Wolfe, George C. **49**
Wolfe, Tom **1, 2, 9, 15, 35, 51**
Wolff, Geoffrey (Ansell) **41**
Wolff, Tobias (Jonathan Ansell) **39, 64**
Wolitzer, Hilma **17**
Wonder, Stevie **12**
Wong, Jade Snow **17**
Woolrich, Cornell **77**
Wouk, Herman **1, 9, 38**
Wright, Charles (Penzel Jr.) **6, 13, 28**
Wright, Charles Stevenson **49**
Wright, James (Arlington) **3, 5, 10, 28**
Wright, Richard (Nathaniel) **1, 3, 4, 9, 14, 21,
48, 74**
Wright, Stephen Caldwell **33**
Wright, William **44**
Wurlitzer, Rudolph **2, 4, 15**
Wylie, Philip (Gordon) **43**
Yates, Richard **7, 8, 23**
Yep, Laurence Michael **35**
Yerby, Frank G(arvin) **1, 7, 22**
Yglesias, Helen **7, 22**
Young, Al(bert James) **19**
Young, Marguerite (Vivian) **82**
Young Bear, Ray A. **94**
Yurick, Sol **6**
Zamora, Bernice (B. Ortiz) **89**
Zappa, Frank **17**
Zaturenska, Marya **6, 11**
Zelazny, Roger (Joseph) **21**
Ziegenhagen, Eric **55**
Zindel, Paul **6, 26**
Zoline, Pamela **62**
Zukofsky, Louis **1, 2, 4, 7, 11, 18**
Zweig, Paul **34, 42**

ANTIGUAN
Edwards, Gus **43**
Kincaid, Jamaica **43, 68**

ARGENTINIAN
Bioy Casares, Adolfo **4, 8, 13, 88**
Borges, Jorge Luis **1, 2, 3, 4, 6, 8, 9, 10, 13,
19, 44, 48, 83**
Cortazar, Julio **2, 3, 5, 10, 13, 15, 33, 34, 92**
Costantini, Humberto **49**
Dorfman, Ariel **48, 77**
Guevara, Che **87**
Mujica Lainez, Manuel **31**
Puig, Manuel **3, 5, 10, 28, 65**
Sabato, Ernesto (R.) **10, 23**
Valenzuela, Luisa **31, 104**

ARMENIAN
Mamoulian, Rouben (Zachary) **16**

AUSTRALIAN
Anderson, Jessica (Margaret) Queale **37**
Astley, Thea (Beatrice May) **41**
Brinsmead, H(esba) F(ay) **21**
Buckley, Vincent (Thomas) **57**
Buzo, Alexander (John) **61**
Carey, Peter **40, 55, 96**
Clark, Mavis Thorpe **12**
Clavell, James (duMaresq) **6, 25, 87**
Courtenay, Bryce **59**
Davison, Frank Dalby **15**
Elliott, Sumner Locke **38**
FitzGerald, Robert D(avid) **19**
Grenville, Kate **61**
Hall, Rodney **51**
Hazzard, Shirley **18**
Hope, A(lec) D(erwent) **3, 51**

Hospital, Janette Turner **42**
Jolley, (Monica) Elizabeth **46**
Jones, Rod **50**
Keneally, Thomas (Michael) **5, 8, 10, 14, 19,
27, 43**
Koch, C(hristopher) J(ohn) **42**
Lawler, Raymond Evenor **58**
Malouf, (George Joseph) David **28, 86**
Matthews, Greg **45**
McAuley, James Phillip **45**
McCullough, Colleen **27**
Murray, Les(lie) A(llan) **40**
Porter, Peter (Neville Frederick) **5, 13, 33**
Prichard, Katharine Susannah **46**
Shapcott, Thomas W(illiam) **38**
Slessor, Kenneth **14**
Stead, Christina (Ellen) **2, 5, 8, 32, 80**
Stow, (Julian) Randolph **23, 48**
Thiele, Colin (Milton) **17**
Weir, Peter (Lindsay) **20**
West, Morris L(anglo) **6, 33**
White, Patrick (Victor Martindale) **3, 4, 5, 7,
9, 18, 65, 69**
Wilding, Michael **73**
Williamson, David (Keith) **56**
Wright, Judith (Arandell) **11, 53**

AUSTRIAN
Adamson, Joy(-Friederike Victoria) **17**
Bachmann, Ingeborg **69**
Bernhard, Thomas **3, 32, 61**
Bettelheim, Bruno **79**
Frankl, Viktor E(mil) **93**
Gregor, Arthur **9**
Handke, Peter **5, 8, 10, 15, 38**
Hochwaelder, Fritz **36**
Jandl, Ernst **34**
Lang, Fritz **20, 103**
Lind, Jakov **1, 2, 4, 27, 82**
Sternberg, Josef von **20**
Wellek, Rene **28**
Wilder, Billy **20**

BARBADIAN
Brathwaite, Edward Kamau **11**
Clarke, Austin C(hesterfield) **8, 53**
Kennedy, Adrienne (Lita) **66**
Lamming, George (William) **2, 4, 66**

BELGIAN
Crommelynck, Fernand **75**
Ghelderode, Michel de **6, 11**
Levi-Strauss, Claude **38**
Mallet-Joris, Francoise **11**
Michaux, Henri **8, 19**
Sarton, (Eleanor) May **4, 14, 49, 91**
Simenon, Georges (Jacques Christian) **1, 2, 3,
8, 18, 47**
van Itallie, Jean-Claude **3**
Yourcenar, Marguerite **19, 38, 50, 87**

BOTSWANAN
Head, Bessie **25, 67**

BRAZILIAN
Amado, Jorge **13, 40, 106**
Andrade, Carlos Drummond de **18**
Cabral de Melo Neto, Joao **76**
Dourado, (Waldomiro Freitas) Autran **23, 60**
Drummond de Andrade, Carlos **18**
Lispector, Clarice **43**
Ribeiro, Darcy **34**
Ribeiro, Joao Ubaldo (Osorio Pimentel) **10,**

67
Rosa, Joao Guimaraes 23

BULGARIAN
Bagryana, Elisaveta 10
Belcheva, Elisaveta 10
Canetti, Elias 3, 14, 25, 75, 86
Kristeva, Julia 77

CAMEROONIAN
Beti, Mongo 27

CANADIAN
Acorn, Milton 15
Aquin, Hubert 15
Atwood, Margaret (Eleanor) 2, 3, 4, 8, 13, 15, 25, 44, 84
Avison, Margaret 2, 4, 97
Barfoot, Joan 18
Bellow, Saul 1, 2, 3, 6, 8, 10, 13, 15, 25, 33, 34, 63, 79
Berton, Pierre (Francis De Marigny) 104
Birney, (Alfred) Earle 1, 4, 6, 11
Bissett, Bill 18
Blais, Marie-Claire 2, 4, 6, 13, 22
Blaise, Clark 29
Bowering, George 15, 47
Bowering, Marilyn R(uthe) 32
Buckler, Ernest 13
Buell, John (Edward) 10
Callaghan, Morley Edward 3, 14, 41, 65
Campbell, Maria 85
Carrier, Roch 13, 78
Child, Philip 19, 68
Chislett, (Margaret) Anne 34
Clarke, Austin C(hesterfield) 8, 53
Cohen, Leonard (Norman) 3, 38
Cohen, Matt 19
Coles, Don 46
Cook, Michael 58
Cooper, Douglas 86
Coupland, Douglas 85
Craven, Margaret 17
Davies, (William) Robertson 2, 7, 13, 25, 42, 75, 91
de la Roche, Mazo 14
Donnell, David 34
Ducharme, Rejean 74
Dudek, Louis 11, 19
Engel, Marian 36
Everson, R(onald) G(ilmour) 27
Faludy, George 42
Ferron, Jacques 94
Finch, Robert (Duer Claydon) 18
Findley, Timothy 27, 102
Fraser, Sylvia 64
Frye, (Herman) Northrop 24, 70
Gallant, Mavis 7, 18, 38
Garner, Hugh 13
Gilmour, David 35
Glassco, John 9
Gotlieb, Phyllis Fay (Bloom) 18
Govier, Katherine 51
Gunnars, Kristjana 69
Gustafson, Ralph (Barker) 36
Haig-Brown, Roderick (Langmere) 21
Hailey, Arthur 5
Harris, Christie (Lucy) Irwin 12
Hebert, Anne 4, 13, 29
Highway, Tomson 92
Hillis, Rick 66
Hine, (William) Daryl 15
Hodgins, Jack 23

Hood, Hugh (John Blagdon) 15, 28
Hospital, Janette Turner 42
Hyde, Anthony 42
Jacobsen, Josephine 48, 102
Jiles, Paulette 13, 58
Johnston, George (Benson) 51
Jones, D(ouglas) G(ordon) 10
Kelly, M(ilton) T(erry) 55
King, Thomas 89
Kinsella, W(illiam) P(atrick) 27, 43
Klein, A(braham) M(oses) 19
Kogawa, Joy Nozomi 78
Krizanc, John 57
Kroetsch, Robert 5, 23, 57
Kroker, Arthur (W.) 77
Lane, Patrick 25
Laurence, (Jean) Margaret (Wemyss) 3, 6, 13, 50, 62
Layton, Irving (Peter) 2, 15
Levine, Norman 54
Lightfoot, Gordon 26
Livesay, Dorothy (Kathleen) 4, 15, 79
MacEwen, Gwendolyn (Margaret) 13, 55
MacLennan, (John) Hugh 2, 14, 92
MacLeod, Alistair 56
Macpherson, (Jean) Jay 14
Maillet, Antonine 54
Major, Kevin (Gerald) 26
McFadden, David 48
McLuhan, (Herbert) Marshall 37, 83
Metcalf, John 37
Mitchell, Joni 12
Mitchell, W(illiam) O(rmond) 25
Moore, Brian 1, 3, 5, 7, 8, 19, 32, 90
Morgan, Janet 39
Moure, Erin 88
Mowat, Farley (McGill) 26
Munro, Alice 6, 10, 19, 50, 95
Musgrave, Susan 13, 54
Newlove, John (Herbert) 14
Nichol, B(arrie) P(hillip) 18
Nowlan, Alden (Albert) 15
Ondaatje, (Philip) Michael 14, 29, 51, 76
Page, P(atricia) K(athleen) 7, 18
Pollock, (Mary) Sharon 50
Pratt, E(dwin) J(ohn) 19
Purdy, Al(fred Wellington) 3, 6, 14, 50
Quarrington, Paul (Lewis) 65
Reaney, James 13
Ricci, Nino 70
Richards, David Adams 59
Richler, Mordecai 3, 5, 9, 13, 18, 46, 70
Ringwood, Gwen(dolyn Margaret) Pharis 48
Ritter, Erika 52
Rooke, Leon 25, 34
Rosenblatt, Joe 15
Ross, (James) Sinclair 13
Roy, Gabrielle 10, 14
Rule, Jane (Vance) 27
Ryga, George 14
Scott, F(rancis) R(eginald) 22
Shields, Carol 91
Skelton, Robin 13
Skvorecky, Josef (Vaclav) 15, 39, 69
Slade, Bernard 11, 46
Smart, Elizabeth 54
Smith, A(rthur) J(ames) M(arshall) 15
Souster, (Holmes) Raymond 5, 14
Suknaski, Andrew 19
Theriault, Yves 79
Thesen, Sharon 56
Thomas, Audrey (Callahan) 7, 13, 37
Thompson, Judith 39

Tremblay, Michel 29, 102
Urquhart, Jane 90
Vanderhaeghe, Guy 41
Van Vogt, A(lfred) E(lton) 1
Vizinczey, Stephen 40
Waddington, Miriam 28
Wah, Fred(erick James) 44
Walker, David Harry 14
Walker, George F. 44, 61
Webb, Phyllis 18
Wiebe, Rudy (Henry) 6, 11, 14
Wilson, Ethel Davis (Bryant) 13
Wright, L(aurali) R. 44
Wright, Richard B(ruce) 6
Young, Neil 17

CHILEAN
Alegria, Fernando 57
Allende, Isabel 39, 57, 97
Donoso (Yanez), Jose 4, 8, 11, 32, 99
Dorfman, Ariel 48, 77
Neruda, Pablo 1, 2, 5, 7, 9, 28, 62
Parra, Nicanor 2, 102

CHINESE
Chang, Jung 71
Ch'ien Chung-shu 22
Ding Ling 68
Lord, Bette Bao 23
Mo, Timothy (Peter) 46
Pa Chin 18
Peake, Mervyn 7, 54
Wong, Jade Snow 17

COLOMBIAN
Garcia Marquez, Gabriel (Jose) 2, 3, 8, 10, 15, 27, 47, 55, 68

CONGOLESE
Tchicaya, Gerald Felix 101

CUBAN
Arenas, Reinaldo 41
Cabrera Infante, G(uillermo) 5, 25, 45
Calvino, Italo 5, 8, 11, 22, 33, 39, 73
Carpentier (y Valmont), Alejo 8, 11, 38
Fornes, Maria Irene 39, 61
Garcia, Cristina 76
Guevara, Che 87
Guillen, Nicolas (Cristobal) 48, 79
Lezama Lima, Jose 4, 10, 101
Padilla (Lorenzo), Heberto 38
Sarduy, Severo 6, 97

CZECH
Friedlander, Saul 90
Havel, Vaclav 25, 58, 65
Holub, Miroslav 4
Hrabal, Bohumil 13, 67
Klima, Ivan 56
Kohout, Pavel 13
Kundera, Milan 4, 9, 19, 32, 68
Lustig, Arnost 56
Seifert, Jaroslav 34, 44, 93
Skvorecky, Josef (Vaclav) 15, 39, 69
Vaculik, Ludvik 7

DANISH
Abell, Kjeld 15
Bodker, Cecil 21
Dinesen, Isak 10, 29, 95
Dreyer, Carl Theodor 16
Hoeg, Peter 95

Nationality Index

DUTCH

de Hartog, Jan 19
Mulisch, Harry 42
Ruyslinck, Ward 14
van de Wetering, Janwillem 47

EGYPTIAN

Chedid, Andree 47
Mahfuz, Najib 52, 55

ENGLISH

Ackroyd, Peter 34, 52
Adams, Douglas (Noel) 27, 60
Adams, Richard (George) 4, 5, 18
Adcock, Fleur 41
Aickman, Robert (Fordyce) 57
Aiken, Joan (Delano) 35
Aldington, Richard 49
Aldiss, Brian W(ilson) 5, 14, 40
Allingham, Margery (Louise) 19
Almedingen, E. M. 12
Alvarez, A(lfred) 5, 13
Ambler, Eric 4, 6, 9
Amis, Kingsley (William) 1, 2, 3, 5, 8, 13, 40, 44
Amis, Martin (Louis) 4, 9, 38, 62, 101
Anderson, Lindsay (Gordon) 20
Anthony, Piers 35
Archer, Jeffrey (Howard) 28
Arden, John 6, 13, 15
Armatrading, Joan 17
Arthur, Ruth M(abel) 12
Arundel, Honor (Morfydd) 17
Atkinson, Kate 99
Auden, W(ystan) H(ugh) 1, 2, 3, 4, 6, 9, 11, 14, 43
Ayckbourn, Alan 5, 8, 18, 33, 74
Ayrton, Michael 7
Bagnold, Enid 25
Bailey, Paul 45
Bainbridge, Beryl (Margaret) 4, 5, 8, 10, 14, 18, 22, 62
Ballard, J(ames) G(raham) 3, 6, 14, 36
Banks, Lynne Reid 23
Barker, Clive 52
Barker, George Granville 8, 48
Barker, Howard 37
Barker, Pat(ricia) 32, 94
Barnes, Julian (Patrick) 42
Barnes, Peter 5, 56
Barrett, (Roger) Syd 35
Bates, H(erbert) E(rnest) 46
Beer, Patricia 58
Bennett, Alan 45, 77
Berger, John (Peter) 2, 19
Berkoff, Steven 56
Bermant, Chaim (Icyk) 40
Betjeman, John 2, 6, 10, 34, 43
Billington, (Lady) Rachel (Mary) 43
Binyon, T(imothy) J(ohn) 34
Blunden, Edmund (Charles) 2, 56
Bogarde, Dirk 19
Bolt, Robert (Oxton) 14
Bond, Edward 4, 6, 13, 23
Booth, Martin 13
Bowen, Elizabeth (Dorothea Cole) 1, 3, 6, 11, 15, 22
Bowie, David 17
Boyd, William 28, 53, 70
Bradbury, Malcolm (Stanley) 32, 61
Bragg, Melvyn 10
Braine, John (Gerard) 1, 3, 41
Brenton, Howard 31

Brittain, Vera (Mary) 23
Brooke-Rose, Christine 40
Brookner, Anita 32, 34, 51
Brophy, Brigid (Antonia) 6, 11, 29, 105
Brunner, John (Kilian Houston) 8, 10
Bunting, Basil 10, 39, 47
Burgess, Anthony 1, 2, 4, 5, 8, 10, 13, 15, 22, 40, 62, 81, 94
Byatt, A(ntonia) S(usan Drabble) 19, 65
Caldwell, (Janet Miriam) Taylor (Holland) 2, 28, 39
Campbell, (John) Ramsey 42
Carter, Angela (Olive) 5, 41, 76
Causley, Charles (Stanley) 7
Caute, David 29
Chambers, Aidan 35
Chaplin, Charles Spencer 16
Chapman, Graham 21
Chatwin, (Charles) Bruce 28, 57, 59
Chitty, Thomas Willes 11
Christie, Agatha (Mary Clarissa) 1, 6, 8, 12, 39, 48
Churchill, Caryl 31, 55
Clark, (Robert) Brian 29
Clarke, Arthur C(harles) 1, 4, 13, 18, 35
Cleese, John (Marwood) 21
Colegate, Isabel 36
Comfort, Alex(ander) 7
Compton-Burnett, I(vy) 1, 3, 10, 15, 34
Cooney, Ray 62
Copeland, Stewart (Armstrong) 26
Cornwell, David (John Moore) 9, 15
Costello, Elvis 21
Coward, Noel (Peirce) 1, 9, 29, 51
Creasey, John 11
Crispin, Edmund 22
Dabydeen, David 34
Dahl, Roald 1, 6, 18, 79
Daryush, Elizabeth 6, 19
Davie, Donald (Alfred) 5, 8, 10, 31
Davies, Rhys 23
Day Lewis, C(ecil) 1, 6, 10
Deighton, Len 4, 7, 22, 46
Delaney, Shelagh 29
Dennis, Nigel (Forbes) 8
Dickinson, Peter (Malcolm) 12, 35
Drabble, Margaret 2, 3, 5, 8, 10, 22, 53
Duffy, Maureen 37
du Maurier, Daphne 6, 11, 59
Durrell, Lawrence (George) 1, 4, 6, 8, 13, 27, 41
Eagleton, Terry 63
Edgar, David 42
Edwards, G(erald) B(asil) 25
Eliot, T(homas) S(tearns) 1, 2, 3, 6, 9, 10, 13, 15, 24, 34, 41, 55, 57
Elliott, Janice 47
Ellis, A. E. 7
Ellis, Alice Thomas 40
Empson, William 3, 8, 19, 33, 34
Enright, D(ennis) J(oseph) 4, 8, 31
Ewart, Gavin (Buchanan) 13, 46
Fairbairns, Zoe (Ann) 32
Farrell, J(ames) G(ordon) 6
Feinstein, Elaine 36
Fenton, James Martin 32
Figes, Eva 31
Fisher, Roy 25
Fitzgerald, Penelope 19, 51, 61
Fleming, Ian (Lancaster) 3, 30
Follett, Ken(neth Martin) 18
Forester, C(ecil) S(cott) 35
Forster, E(dward) M(organ) 1, 2, 3, 4, 9, 10,

13, 15, 22, 45, 77
Forsyth, Frederick 2, 5, 36
Fowles, John 1, 2, 3, 4, 6, 9, 10, 15, 33, 87
Francis, Dick 2, 22, 42, 102
Fraser, George MacDonald 7
Fraser, (Lady) Antonia (Pakenham) 32
Frayn, Michael 3, 7, 31, 47
Freeling, Nicolas 38
Fry, Christopher 2, 10, 14
Fugard, Sheila 48
Fuller, John (Leopold) 62
Fuller, Roy (Broadbent) 4, 28
Gardam, Jane 43
Gardner, John (Edmund) 30
Garfield, Leon 12
Garner, Alan 17
Garnett, David 3
Gascoyne, David (Emery) 45
Gee, Maggie (Mary) 57
Gerhardie, William Alexander 5
Gilliatt, Penelope (Ann Douglass) 2, 10, 13, 53
Glanville, Brian (Lester) 6
Glendinning, Victoria 50
Gloag, Julian 40
Godden, (Margaret) Rumer 53
Golding, William (Gerald) 1, 2, 3, 8, 10, 17, 27, 58, 81
Graham, Winston (Mawdsley) 23
Graves, Richard Perceval 44
Graves, Robert (von Ranke) 1, 2, 6, 11, 39, 44, 45
Gray, Simon (James Holliday) 9, 14, 36
Green, Henry 2, 13, 97
Greene, Graham (Henry) 1, 3, 6, 9, 14, 18, 27, 37, 70, 72
Griffiths, Trevor 13, 52
Grigson, Geoffrey (Edward Harvey) 7, 39
Gunn, Thom(son William) 3, 6, 18, 32, 81
Haig-Brown, Roderick (Langmere) 21
Hailey, Arthur 5
Hall, Rodney 51
Hamburger, Michael (Peter Leopold) 5, 14
Hamilton, (Anthony Walter) Patrick 51
Hampton, Christopher (James) 4
Hare, David 29, 58
Harrison, Tony 43
Hartley, L(eslie) P(oles) 2, 22
Harwood, Ronald 32
Hastings, Selina 44
Hawking, Stephen W(illiam) 63, 105
Headon, (Nicky) Topper 30
Heppenstall, (John) Rayner 10
Herriot, James 12
Hibbert, Eleanor Alice Burford 7
Hill, Geoffrey (William) 5, 8, 18, 45
Hill, Susan (Elizabeth) 4
Hinde, Thomas 6, 11
Hitchcock, Alfred (Joseph) 16
Hocking, Mary (Eunice) 13
Holden, Ursula 18
Holdstock, Robert P. 39
Hollinghurst, Alan 55, 91
Hooker, (Peter) Jeremy 43
Hopkins, John (Richard) 4
Household, Geoffrey (Edward West) 11
Howard, Elizabeth Jane 7, 29
Hughes, David (John) 48
Hughes, Richard (Arthur Warren) 1, 11
Hughes, Ted 2, 4, 9, 14, 37
Huxley, Aldous (Leonard) 1, 3, 4, 5, 8, 11, 18, 35, 79
Idle, Eric 21

Ingalls, Rachel (Holmes) **42**
Isherwood, Christopher (William Bradshaw) **1, 9, 11, 14, 44**
Ishiguro, Kazuo **27, 56, 59**
Jacobson, Dan **4, 14**
Jagger, Mick **17**
James, C(yril) L(ionel) R(obert) **33**
James, P. D. **18, 46**
Jellicoe, (Patricia) Ann **27**
Jennings, Elizabeth (Joan) **5, 14**
Jhabvala, Ruth Prawer **4, 8, 29, 94**
Johnson, B(ryan) S(tanley William) **6, 9**
Johnson, Pamela Hansford **1, 7, 27**
Jolley, (Monica) Elizabeth **46**
Jones, David (Michael) **2, 4, 7, 13, 42**
Jones, Diana Wynne **26**
Jones, Mervyn **10, 52**
Jones, Mick **30**
Josipovici, Gabriel **6, 43**
Kavan, Anna **5, 13, 82**
Kaye, M(ary) M(argaret) **28**
Keates, Jonathan **34**
King, Francis (Henry) **8, 53**
Kirkup, James **1**
Koestler, Arthur **1, 3, 6, 8, 15, 33**
Kops, Bernard **4**
Kureishi, Hanif **64**
Lanchester, John **99**
Larkin, Philip (Arthur) **3, 5, 8, 9, 13, 18, 33, 39, 64**
Leavis, F(rank) R(aymond) **24**
le Carré, John **3, 5, 9, 15, 28**
Lee, Laurie **90**
Lee, Tanith **46**
Lehmann, Rosamond (Nina) **5**
Lennon, John (Ono) **12, 35**
Lessing, Doris (May) **1, 2, 3, 6, 10, 15, 22, 40, 94**
Levertov, Denise **1, 2, 3, 5, 8, 15, 28, 66**
Levi, Peter (Chad Tigar) **41**
Lewis, C(live) S(taples) **1, 3, 6, 14, 27**
Lively, Penelope (Margaret) **32, 50**
Lodge, David (John) **36**
Loy, Mina **28**
Luke, Peter (Ambrose Cyprian) **38**
MacInnes, Colin **4, 23**
Mackenzie, Compton (Edward Montague) **18**
Macpherson, (Jean) Jay **14**
Maitland, Sara (Louise) **49**
Manning, Olivia **5, 19**
Markandaya, Kamala **8, 38**
Masefield, John (Edward) **11, 47**
Mason, Nick **35**
Maugham, W(illiam) Somerset **1, 11, 15, 67, 93**
Mayle, Peter **89**
Mayne, William (James Carter) **12**
McEwan, Ian (Russell) **13, 66**
McGrath, Patrick **55**
Mercer, David **5**
Metcalf, John **37**
Middleton, Christopher **13**
Middleton, Stanley **7, 38**
Mitford, Nancy **44**
Mo, Timothy (Peter) **46**
Moorcock, Michael (John) **5, 27, 58**
Mortimer, John (Clifford) **28, 43**
Mortimer, Penelope (Ruth) **5**
Mosley, Nicholas **43, 70**
Mott, Michael (Charles Alston) **15, 34**
Murdoch, (Jean) Iris **1, 2, 3, 4, 6, 8, 11, 15, 22, 31, 51**
Naipaul, V(idiadhar) S(urajprasad) **4, 7, 9, 13,**

18, 37, 105
Newby, P(ercy) H(oward) **2, 13**
Nichols, Peter (Richard) **5, 36, 65**
Noon, Jeff **91**
Norfolk, Lawrence **76**
Nye, Robert **13, 42**
O'Brien, Richard **17**
O'Faolain, Julia **6, 19, 47**
Olivier, Laurence (Kerr) **20**
Orton, Joe **4, 13, 43**
Osborne, John (James) **1, 2, 5, 11, 45**
Osborne, Lawrence **50**
Page, Jimmy **12**
Page, Louise **40**
Page, P(atricia) K(athleen) **7, 18**
Palin, Michael (Edward) **21**
Parkin, Frank **43**
Paulin, Tom **37**
Peake, Mervyn **7, 54**
Pearce, Philippa **21**
Phillips, Caryl **96**
Pinter, Harold **1, 3, 6, 9, 11, 15, 27, 58, 73**
Plant, Robert **12**
Poliakoff, Stephen **38**
Poole, Josephine **17**
Potter, Dennis (Christopher George) **58, 86**
Powell, Anthony (Dymoke) **1, 3, 7, 9, 10, 31**
Pownall, David **10**
Powys, John Cowper **7, 9, 15, 46**
Priestley, J(ohn) B(oynton) **2, 5, 9, 34**
Prince, F(rank) T(empleton) **22**
Pritchett, V(ictor) S(awdon) **5, 13, 15, 41**
Pym, Barbara (Mary Crampton) **13, 19, 37**
Quin, Ann (Marie) **6**
Raine, Craig **32, 103**
Raine, Kathleen (Jessie) **7, 45**
Rathbone, Julian **41**
Rattigan, Terence (Mervyn) **7**
Raven, Simon (Arthur Noel) **14**
Read, Herbert Edward **4**
Read, Piers Paul **4, 10, 25**
Reading, Peter **47**
Redgrove, Peter (William) **6, 41**
Reid, Christopher (John) **33**
Renault, Mary **3, 11, 17**
Rendell, Ruth (Barbara) **28, 48**
Rhys, Jean **2, 4, 6, 14, 19, 51**
Rice, Tim(othy Miles Bindon) **21**
Richard, Keith **17**
Richards, I(vor) A(rmstrong) **14, 24**
Roberts, Keith (John Kingston) **14**
Roberts, Michele (B.) **48**
Rudkin, (James) David **14**
Rushdie, (Ahmed) Salman **23, 31, 55, 100**
Rushforth, Peter (Scott) **19**
Russell, (Henry) Ken(neth Alfred) **16**
Russell, Willy **60**
Sacks, Oliver (Wolf) **67**
Sansom, William **2, 6**
Sassoon, Siegfried (Lorraine) **36**
Scammell, Michael **34**
Scannell, Vernon **49**
Schlee, Ann **35**
Schumacher, E(rnst) F(riedrich) **80**
Scott, Paul (Mark) **9, 60**
Shaffer, Anthony (Joshua) **19**
Shaffer, Peter (Levin) **5, 14, 18, 37, 60**
Sharpe, Tom **36**
Shaw, Robert **5**
Sheed, Wilfrid (John Joseph) **2, 4, 10, 53**
Shute, Nevil **30**
Shuttle, Penelope (Diane) **7**
Silkin, Jon **2, 6, 43**

Sillitoe, Alan **1, 3, 6, 10, 19, 57**
Simonon, Paul **30**
Simpson, N(orman) F(rederick) **29**
Sinclair, Andrew (Annandale) **2, 14**
Sinclair, Iain **76**
Sisson, C(harles) H(ubert) **8**
Sitwell, Dame Edith **2, 9, 67**
Slaughter, Carolyn **56**
Smith, Stevie **3, 8, 25, 44**
Snow, C(harles) P(ercy) **1, 4, 6, 9, 13, 19**
Spender, Stephen (Harold) **1, 2, 5, 10, 41, 91**
Spurling, Hilary **34**
Stannard, Martin **44**
Stewart, J(ohn) I(nnes) M(ackintosh) **7, 14, 32**
Stewart, Mary (Florence Elinor) **7, 35**
Stoppard, Tom **1, 3, 4, 5, 8, 15, 29, 34, 63, 91**
Storey, David (Malcolm) **2, 4, 5, 8**
Streatfeild, (Mary) Noel **21**
Strummer, Joe **30**
Summers, Andrew James **26**
Sumner, Gordon Matthew **26**
Sutcliff, Rosemary **26**
Swift, Graham (Colin) **41, 88**
Swinfen, Ann **34**
Swinnerton, Frank Arthur **31**
Symons, Julian (Gustave) **2, 14, 32**
Szirtes, George **46**
Taylor, Elizabeth **2, 4, 29**
Tennant, Emma (Christina) **13, 52**
Teran, Lisa St. Aubin de **36**
Thomas, D(onald) M(ichael) **13, 22, 31**
Tindall, Gillian **7**
Tolkien, J(ohn) R(onald) R(euel) **1, 2, 3, 8, 12, 38**
Tomlinson, (Alfred) Charles **2, 4, 6, 13, 45**
Townsend, Sue **61**
Townshend, Peter (Dennis Blandford) **17, 42**
Treitel, Jonathan **70**
Tremain, Rose **42**
Tuohy, Frank **37**
Turner, Frederick **48**
Unsworth, Barry (Forster) **76**
Ustinov, Peter (Alexander) **1**
Vansittart, Peter **42**
Vine, Barbara **50**
Wain, John (Barrington) **2, 11, 15, 46**
Walker, Ted **13**
Walsh, Jill Paton **35**
Warner, Francis (Robert le Plastrier) **14**
Warner, Marina **59**
Warner, Rex (Ernest) **45**
Warner, Sylvia Townsend **7, 19**
Waterhouse, Keith (Spencer) **47**
Waters, Roger **35**
Waugh, Auberon (Alexander) **7**
Waugh, Evelyn (Arthur St. John) **1, 3, 8, 13, 19, 27, 44**
Waugh, Harriet **6**
Webber, Andrew Lloyd **21**
Weldon, Fay **6, 9, 11, 19, 36, 59**
Weller, Paul **26**
Wesker, Arnold **3, 5, 42**
West, Anthony (Panther) **50**
West, Paul **7, 14, 96**
West, Rebecca **7, 9, 31, 50**
Westall, Robert (Atkinson) **17**
White, Patrick (Victor Martindale) **3, 4, 5, 7, 9, 18, 65, 69**
White, T(erence) H(anbury) **30**
Whitehead, E(dward) A(nthony) **5**
Whitemore, Hugh (John) **37**
Wilding, Michael **73**
Williams, Hugo **42**

Nationality Index

CONTEMPORARY LITERARY CRITICISM

Wilson, A(ndrew) N(orman) 33
Wilson, Angus (Frank Johnstone) 2, 3, 5, 25, 34
Wilson, Colin 3, 14
Wilson, Snoo 33
Wingrove, David (John) 68
Winterson, Jeanette 64
Wodehouse, P(elham) G(renville) 1, 2, 5, 10, 22
Wright, Rick 35
Wyndham, John 19
Yorke, Henry Vincent 13
Young, Andrew (John) 5

ESTONIAN
Ivask, Ivar Vidrik 14

FIJI ISLANDER
Prichard, Katharine Susannah 46

FILIPINO
Santos, Bienvenido N(uqui) 22

FINNISH
Haavikko, Paavo Juhani 18, 34
Salama, Hannu 18
Sillanpaa, Frans Eemil 19

FRENCH
Adamov, Arthur 4, 25
Anouilh, Jean (Marie Lucien Pierre) 1, 3, 8, 13, 40, 50
Aragon, Louis 3, 22
Audiberti, Jacques 38
Ayme, Marcel (Andre) 11
Barthes, Roland (Gerard) 24, 83
Bataille, Georges 29
Baudrillard, Jean 60
Beauvoir, Simone (Lucie Ernestine Marie Bertrand) de 1, 2, 4, 8, 14, 31, 44, 50, 71
Beckett, Samuel (Barclay) 1, 2, 3, 4, 6, 9, 10, 11, 14, 18, 29, 57, 59, 83
Bonnefoy, Yves 9, 15, 58
Bresson, Robert 16
Breton, Andre 2, 9, 15, 54
Butor, Michel (Marie Francois) 1, 3, 8, 11, 15
Camus, Albert 1, 2, 4, 9, 11, 14, 32, 63, 69
Carrere, Emmanuel 89
Cayrol, Jean 11
Celine, Louis-Ferdinand 1, 3, 4, 7, 9, 15, 47
Cendrars, Blaise 18, 106
Chabrol, Claude 16
Char, Rene(-Emile) 9, 11, 14, 55
Chedid, Andree 47
Cixous, Helene 92
Clair, Rene 20
Cocteau, Jean (Maurice Eugene Clement) 1, 8, 15, 16, 43
Cousteau, Jacques-Yves 30
del Castillo, Michel 38
Derrida, Jacques 24, 87
Destouches, Louis-Ferdinand 9, 15
Duhamel, Georges 8
Duras, Marguerite 3, 6, 11, 20, 34, 40, 68, 100
Ernaux, Annie 88
Federman, Raymond 6, 47
Foucault, Michel 31, 34, 69
Fournier, Pierre 11
Francis, Claude 50
Gallo, Max Louis 95
Gary, Romain 25
Gascar, Pierre 11
Genet, Jean 1, 2, 5, 10, 14, 44, 46

Giono, Jean 4, 11
Godard, Jean-Luc 20
Goldmann, Lucien 24
Gontier, Fernande 50
Gracq, Julien 11, 48
Gray, Francine du Plessix 22
Green, Julien 3, 11, 77
Guillevic, (Eugene) 33
Ionesco, Eugene 1, 4, 6, 9, 11, 15, 41, 86
Japrisot, Sebastien 90
Jouve, Pierre Jean 47
Kristeva, Julia 77
Lacan, Jacques (Marie Emile) 75
Laurent, Antoine 50
Le Clezio, J(ean) M(arie) G(ustave) 31
Leduc, Violette 22
Leger, (Marie-Rene Auguste) Alexis Saint-Leger 11
Leiris, Michel (Julien) 61
Levi-Strauss, Claude 38
Mallet-Joris, Francoise 11
Malraux, (Georges-)Andre 1, 4, 9, 13, 15, 57
Mandiargues, Andre Pieyre de 41
Marcel, Gabriel Honore 15
Mauriac, Claude 9
Mauriac, Francois (Charles) 4, 9, 56
Merton, Thomas 1, 3, 11, 34, 83
Modiano, Patrick (Jean) 18
Montherlant, Henry (Milon) de 8, 19
Morand, Paul 41
Nin, Anais 1, 4, 8, 11, 14, 60
Perec, Georges 56
Perse, St.-John 4, 11, 46
Pinget, Robert 7, 13, 37
Ponge, Francis (Jean Gaston Alfred) 6, 18
Prevert, Jacques (Henri Marie) 15
Queneau, Raymond 2, 5, 10, 42
Quoirez, Francoise 9
Renoir, Jean 20
Resnais, Alain 16
Reverdy, Pierre 53
Rio, Michel 43
Robbe-Grillet, Alain 1, 2, 4, 6, 8, 10, 14, 43
Rohmer, Eric 16
Romains, Jules 7
Sachs, Nelly 14, 98
Sagan, Francoise 3, 6, 9, 17, 36
Sarduy, Severo 6, 97
Sarraute, Nathalie 1, 2, 4, 8, 10, 31, 80
Sartre, Jean-Paul 1, 4, 7, 9, 13, 18, 24, 44, 50, 52
Sauser-Hall, Frederic 18
Schwarz-Bart, Andre 2, 4
Schwarz-Bart, Simone 7
Simenon, Georges (Jacques Christian) 1, 2, 3, 8, 18, 47
Simon, Claude 4, 9, 15, 39
Soupault, Philippe 68
Steiner, George 24
Tournier, Michel (Edouard) 6, 23, 36, 95
Troyat, Henri 23
Truffaut, Francois 20, 101
Tuck, Lily 70
Tzara, Tristan 47
Varda, Agnes 16
Wittig, Monique 22
Yourcenar, Marguerite 19, 38, 50, 87

FRENCH GUINEAN
Damas, Leon-Gontran 84

GERMAN
Amichai, Yehuda 9, 22, 57

Arendt, Hannah 66, 98
Arp, Jean 5
Becker, Jurek 7, 19
Benary-Isbert, Margot 12
Bienek, Horst 7, 11
Boell, Heinrich (Theodor) 2, 3, 6, 9, 11, 15, 27, 32, 72
Buchheim, Lothar-Guenther 6
Bukowski, Charles 2, 5, 9, 41, 82
Eich, Guenter 15
Ende, Michael (Andreas Helmuth) 31
Enzensberger, Hans Magnus 43
Fassbinder, Rainer Werner 20
Figes, Eva 31
Grass, Guenter (Wilhelm) 1, 2, 4, 6, 11, 15, 22, 32, 49, 88
Habermas, Juergen 104
Hamburger, Michael (Peter Leopold) 5, 14
Heidegger, Martin 24
Herzog, Werner 16
Hesse, Hermann 1, 2, 3, 6, 11, 17, 25, 69
Heym, Stefan 41
Hildesheimer, Wolfgang 49
Hochhuth, Rolf 4, 11, 18
Hofmann, Gert 54
Johnson, Uwe 5, 10, 15, 40
Kroetz, Franz Xaver 41
Kunze, Reiner 10
Lenz, Siegfried 27
Levitin, Sonia (Wolff) 17
Mueller, Lisel 13, 51
Nossack, Hans Erich 6
Preussler, Otfried 17
Remarque, Erich Maria 21
Riefenstahl, Leni 16
Sachs, Nelly 14, 98
Schmidt, Arno (Otto) 56
Schumacher, E(rnst) F(riedrich) 80
Seghers, Anna 7
Strauss, Botho 22
Sueskind, Patrick 44
Walser, Martin 27
Weiss, Peter (Ulrich) 3, 15, 51
Wellershoff, Dieter 46
Wolf, Christa 14, 29, 58
Zuckmayer, Carl 18

GHANIAN
Armah, Ayi Kwei 5, 33

GREEK
Broumas, Olga 10, 73
Elytis, Odysseus 15, 49, 100
Haviaras, Stratis 33
Karapanou, Margarita 13
Nakos, Lilika 29
Ritsos, Yannis 6, 13, 31
Samarakis, Antonis 5
Seferis, George 5, 11
Spanidou, Irini 44
Vassilikos, Vassilis 4, 8

GUADELOUPEAN
Conde, Maryse 52, 92
Schwarz-Bart, Simone 7

GUATEMALAN
Asturias, Miguel Angel 3, 8, 13

GUINEAN
Laye, Camara 4, 38

GUYANESE

Dabydeen, David **34**
Harris, (Theodore) Wilson **25**

HUNGARIAN
Faludy, George **42**
Koestler, Arthur **1, 3, 6, 8, 15, 33**
Konrad, Gyoergy **4, 10, 73**
Lengyel, Jozsef **7**
Lukacs, George **24**
Nagy, Laszlo **7**
Szirtes, George **46**
Tabori, George **19**
Vizinczey, Stephen **40**

ICELANDIC
Gunnars, Kristjana **69**
Laxness, Halldor **25**

INDIAN
Ali, Ahmed **69**
Anand, Mulk Raj **23, 93**
Desai, Anita **19, 37, 97**
Ezekiel, Nissim **61**
Ghosh, Amitav **44**
Mahapatra, Jayanta **33**
Markandaya, Kamala **8, 38**
Mehta, Ved (Parkash) **37**
Mistry, Rohinton **71**
Mukherjee, Bharati **53**
Narayan, R(asipuram) K(rishnaswami) **7, 28, 47**
Rao, Raja **25, 56**
Ray, Satyajit **16, 76**
Rushdie, (Ahmed) Salman **23, 31, 55, 100**
Sahgal, Nayantara (Pandit) **41**
Sealy, I. Allan **55**
Seth, Vikram **43, 90**
Singh, Khushwant **11**
Tharoor, Shashi **70**
White, T(erence) H(anbury) **30**

IRANIAN
Modarressi, Taghi (M.) **44**
Shamlu, Ahmad **10**

IRISH
Banville, John **46**
Beckett, Samuel (Barclay) **1, 2, 3, 4, 6, 9, 10, 11, 14, 18, 29, 57, 59, 83**
Behan, Brendan **1, 8, 11, 15, 79**
Blackwood, Caroline **6, 9, 100**
Boland, Eavan (Aisling) **40, 67**
Bowen, Elizabeth (Dorothea Cole) **1, 3, 6, 11, 15, 22**
Boyle, Patrick **19**
Brennan, Maeve **5**
Brown, Christy **63**
Carroll, Paul Vincent **10**
Clarke, Austin **6, 9**
Colum, Padraic **28**
Cox, William Trevor **9, 14, 71**
Day Lewis, C(ecil) **1, 6, 10**
Dillon, Eilis **17**
Donleavy, J(ames) P(atrick) **1, 4, 6, 10, 45**
Doyle, Roddy **81**
Durcan, Paul **43, 70**
Friel, Brian **5, 42, 59**
Gebler, Carlo (Ernest) **39**
Hanley, James **3, 5, 8, 13**
Hart, Josephine **70**
Heaney, Seamus (Justin) **5, 7, 14, 25, 37, 74, 91**
Johnston, Jennifer **7**

Kavanagh, Patrick (Joseph) **22**
Keane, Molly **31**
Kiely, Benedict **23, 43**
Kinsella, Thomas **4, 19**
Lavin, Mary **4, 18, 99**
Leonard, Hugh **19**
Longley, Michael **29**
Mac Laverty, Bernard **31**
MacNeice, (Frederick) Louis **1, 4, 10, 53**
Mahon, Derek **27**
McGahern, John **5, 9, 48**
McGinley, Patrick (Anthony) **41**
McGuckian, Medbh **48**
Montague, John (Patrick) **13, 46**
Moore, Brian **1, 3, 5, 7, 8, 19, 32, 90**
Morrison, Van **21**
Morrissy, Mary **99**
Muldoon, Paul **32, 72**
Murphy, Richard **41**
Murphy, Thomas (Bernard) **51**
Nolan, Christopher **58**
O'Brien, Edna **3, 5, 8, 13, 36, 65**
O'Brien, Flann **1, 4, 5, 7, 10, 47**
O'Casey, Sean **1, 5, 9, 11, 15, 88**
O'Connor, Frank **23**
O'Doherty, Brian **76**
O'Faolain, Julia **6, 19, 47**
O'Faolain, Sean **1, 7, 14, 32, 70**
O'Flaherty, Liam **5, 34**
Paulin, Tom **37**
Rodgers, W(illiam) R(obert) **7**
Simmons, James (Stewart Alexander) **43**
Trevor, William **7, 9, 14, 25, 71**
White, Terence de Vere **49**
Wilson, Robert McLiam **59**

ISRAELI
Agnon, S(hmuel) Y(osef Halevi) **4, 8, 14**
Amichai, Yehuda **9, 22, 57**
Appelfeld, Aharon **23, 47**
Bakshi, Ralph **26**
Friedlander, Saul **90**
Grossman, David **67**
Kaniuk, Yoram **19**
Levin, Meyer **7**
Megged, Aharon **9**
Oz, Amos **5, 8, 11, 27, 33, 54**
Shammas, Anton **55**
Sobol, Joshua **60**
Yehoshua, A(braham) B. **13, 31**

ITALIAN
Antonioni, Michelangelo **20**
Bacchelli, Riccardo **19**
Bassani, Giorgio **9**
Bertolucci, Bernardo **16**
Bufalino, Gesualdo **74**
Buzzati, Dino **36**
Calasso, Roberto **81**
Calvino, Italo **5, 8, 11, 22, 33, 39, 73**
De Sica, Vittorio **20**
Eco, Umberto **28, 60**
Fallaci, Oriana **11**
Fellini, Federico **16, 85**
Fo, Dario **32**
Gadda, Carlo Emilio **11**
Ginzburg, Natalia **5, 11, 54, 70**
Giovene, Andrea **7**
Landolfi, Tommaso **11, 49**
Levi, Primo **37, 50**
Luzi, Mario **13**
Montale, Eugenio **7, 9, 18**
Morante, Elsa **8, 47**

Moravia, Alberto **2, 7, 11, 27, 46**
Ortese, Anna Maria **89**
Palazzeschi, Aldo **11**
Pasolini, Pier Paolo **20, 37, 106**
Piccolo, Lucio **13**
Pincherle, Alberto **11, 18**
Quasimodo, Salvatore **10**
Ricci, Nino **70**
Sciascia, Leonardo **8, 9, 41**
Silone, Ignazio **4**
Ungaretti, Giuseppe **7, 11, 15**
Visconti, Luchino **16**
Vittorini, Elio **6, 9, 14**
Wertmueller, Lina **16**

JAMAICAN
Bennett, Louise (Simone) **28**
Cliff, Jimmy **21**
Marley, Bob **17**
Thelwell, Michael Miles **22**

JAPANESE
Abe, Kobo **8, 22, 53, 81**
Enchi Fumiko (Ueda) **31**
Endo, Shusaku **7, 14, 19, 54, 99**
Ibuse Masuji **22**
Ichikawa, Kon **20**
Ishiguro, Kazuo **27, 56, 59**
Kawabata, Yasunari **2, 5, 9, 18**
Kurosawa, Akira **16**
Mishima, Yukio **2, 4, 6, 9, 27**
Oe, Kenzaburo **10, 36, 86**
Oshima, Nagisa **20**
Ozu, Yasujiro **16**
Shiga, Naoya **33**
Tanizaki, Jun'ichiro **8, 14, 28**
Yoshimoto, Banana **84**

KENYAN
Ngugi, James T(hiong'o) **3, 7, 13**
Ngugi wa Thiong'o **36**

MARTINICAN
Cesaire, Aime (Fernand) **19, 32**
Fanon, Frantz **74**
Glissant, Edouard **10, 68**

MEXICAN
Castellanos, Rosario **66**
Fuentes, Carlos **3, 8, 10, 13, 22, 41, 60**
Ibarguengoitia, Jorge **37**
Lopez Portillo (y Pacheco), Jose **46**
Lopez y Fuentes, Gregorio **32**
Paz, Octavio **3, 4, 6, 10, 19, 51, 65**
Rulfo, Juan **8, 80**

MOROCCAN
Arrabal, Fernando **2, 9, 18, 58**

NEW ZEALANDER
Adcock, Fleur **41**
Ashton-Warner, Sylvia (Constance) **19**
Baxter, James K(eir) **14**
Campion, Jane **95**
Frame, Janet **2, 3, 6, 22, 66, 96**
Gee, Maurice (Gough) **29**
Grace, Patricia **56**
Hilliard, Noel (Harvey) **15**
Hulme, Keri **39**
Ihimaera, Witi **46**
Marsh, (Edith) Ngaio **7, 53**
Sargeson, Frank **31**

NICARAGUAN
Alegria, Claribel 75
Cardenal, Ernesto 31

NIGERIAN
Achebe, (Albert) Chinua(lumogu) **1, 3, 5, 7, 11, 26, 51, 75**
Clark, John Pepper 38
Ekwensi, Cyprian (Odiatu Duaka) 4
Emecheta, (Florence Onye) Buchi **14, 48**
Okigbo, Christopher (Ifenayichukwu) **25, 84**
Okri, Ben 87
Soyinka, Wole **3, 5, 14, 36, 44**
Tutuola, Amos **5, 14, 29**

NORTHERN IRISH
Simmons, James (Stewart Alexander) 43
Wilson, Robert McLiam 59

NORWEGIAN
Friis-Baastad, Babbis Ellinor 12
Heyerdahl, Thor 26
Vesaas, Tarjei 48

PAKISTANI
Ali, Ahmed 69
Ghose, Zulfikar 42

PARAGUAYAN
Roa Bastos, Augusto (Antonio) 45

PERUVIAN
Allende, Isabel **39, 57, 97**
Arguedas, Jose Maria **10, 18**
Goldemberg, Isaac 52
Vargas Llosa, (Jorge) Mario (Pedro) **3, 6, 9, 10, 15, 31, 42, 85**

POLISH
Agnon, S(hmuel) Y(osef Halevi) **4, 8, 14**
Becker, Jurek **7, 19**
Bermant, Chaim (Icyk) 40
Bienek, Horst **7, 11**
Brandys, Kazimierz 62
Dabrowska, Maria (Szumska) 15
Gombrowicz, Witold **4, 7, 11, 49**
Herbert, Zbigniew **9, 43**
Konwicki, Tadeusz **8, 28, 54**
Kosinski, Jerzy (Nikodem) **1, 2, 3, 6, 10, 15, 53, 70**
Lem, Stanislaw **8, 15, 40**
Milosz, Czeslaw **5, 11, 22, 31, 56, 82**
Mrozek, Slawomir **3, 13**
Polanski, Roman 16
Rozewicz, Tadeusz **9, 23**
Singer, Isaac Bashevis **1, 3, 6, 9, 11, 15, 23, 38, 69**
Skolimowski, Jerzy 20
Szymborska, Wislawa 99
Wajda, Andrzej 16
Wittlin, Jozef 25
Wojciechowska, Maia (Teresa) 26

PORTUGUESE
Migueis, Jose Rodrigues 10

PUERTO RICAN
Marques, Rene 96
Pinero, Miguel (Antonio Gomez) **4, 55**
Sanchez, Luis Rafael 23

ROMANIAN
Appelfeld, Aharon **23, 47**

Arghezi, Tudor 80
Blaga, Lucian 75
Celan, Paul **10, 19, 53, 82**
Cioran, E(mil) M. 64
Codrescu, Andrei 46
Ionesco, Eugene **1, 4, 6, 9, 11, 15, 41, 86**
Rezzori (d'Arezzo), Gregor von 25
Tzara, Tristan 47
Wiesel, Elie(zer) **3, 5, 11, 37**

RUSSIAN
Aitmatov, Chingiz (Torekulovich) 71
Akhmadulina, Bella Akhatovna 53
Akhmatova, Anna **11, 25, 64**
Aksyonov, Vassily (Pavlovich) **22, 37, 101**
Aleshkovsky, Yuz 44
Almedingen, E. M. 12
Asimov, Isaac **1, 3, 9, 19, 26, 76, 92**
Bakhtin, Mikhail Mikhailovich 83
Bitov, Andrei (Georgievich) 57
Brodsky, Joseph **4, 6, 13, 36, 100**
Deren, Maya **16, 102**
Ehrenburg, Ilya (Grigoryevich) **18, 34, 62**
Eliade, Mircea 19
Gary, Romain 25
Goldberg, Anatol 34
Grade, Chaim 10
Grossman, Vasily (Semenovich) 41
Iskander, Fazil 47
Kaletski, Alexander 39
Krotkov, Yuri 19
Leonov, Leonid (Maximovich) 92
Limonov, Edward 67
Nabokov, Vladimir (Vladimirovich) **1, 2, 3, 6, 8, 11, 15, 23, 44, 46, 64**
Olesha, Yuri (Karlovich) 8
Pasternak, Boris (Leonidovich) **7, 10, 18, 63**
Paustovsky, Konstantin (Georgievich) 40
Rahv, Philip 24
Rand, Ayn **3, 30, 44, 79**
Ratushinskaya, Irina 54
Rybakov, Anatoli (Naumovich) **23, 53**
Sarraute, Nathalie **1, 2, 4, 8, 10, 31, 80**
Shalamov, Varlam (Tikhonovich) 18
Sholokhov, Mikhail (Aleksandrovich) **7, 15**
Sinyavsky, Andrei (Donatevich) 8
Solzhenitsyn, Aleksandr I(sayevich) **1, 2, 4, 7, 9, 10, 18, 26, 34, 78**
Strugatskii, Arkadii (Natanovich) 27
Strugatskii, Boris (Natanovich) 27
Tarkovsky, Andrei (Arsenyevich) 75
Trifonov, Yuri (Valentinovich) 45
Troyat, Henri 23
Voinovich, Vladimir (Nikolaevich) **10, 49**
Voznesensky, Andrei (Andreievich) **1, 15, 57**
Yanovsky, V(assily) S(emenovich) **2, 18**
Yevtushenko, Yevgeny (Alexandrovich) **1, 3, 13, 26, 51**
Yezierska, Anzia 46
Zaturenska, Marya **6, 11**
Zinoviev, Alexander (Aleksandrovich) 19

SALVADORAN
Alegria, Claribel 75
Argueta, Manlio 31

SCOTTISH
Banks, Iain M(enzies) 34
Brown, George Mackay **5, 48, 100**
Cronin, A(rchibald) J(oseph) 32
Dunn, Douglas (Eaglesham) **6, 40**
Graham, W(illiam) S(ydney) 29
Gray, Alasdair (James) 41

Grieve, C(hristopher) M(urray) **11, 19**
Hunter, Mollie 21
Jenkins, (John) Robin 52
Kelman, James **58, 86**
Laing, R(onald) D(avid) 95
MacBeth, George (Mann) **2, 5, 9**
MacCaig, Norman (Alexander) 36
MacDiarmid, Hugh **2, 4, 11, 19, 63**
MacInnes, Helen (Clark) **27, 39**
MacLean, Alistair (Stuart) **3, 13, 50, 63**
McIlvanney, William 42
Morgan, Edwin (George) 31
Smith, Iain Crichton 64
Spark, Muriel (Sarah) **2, 3, 5, 8, 13, 18, 40, 94**
Taylor, C(ecil) P(hilip) 27
Walker, David Harry 14
Young, Andrew (John) 5

SENEGALESE
Ousmane, Sembene 66
Senghor, Leopold Sedar 54

SOMALIAN
Farah, Nuruddin 53

SOUTH AFRICAN
Abrahams, Peter (Henry) 4
Breytenbach, Breyten **23, 37**
Brink, Andre (Philippus) **18, 36, 106**
Brutus, Dennis 43
Coetzee, J(ohn) M(ichael) **23, 33, 66**
Courtenay, Bryce 59
Fugard, (Harold) Athol **5, 9, 14, 25, 40, 80**
Fugard, Sheila 48
Gordimer, Nadine **3, 5, 7, 10, 18, 33, 51, 70**
Harwood, Ronald 32
Head, Bessie **25, 67**
Hope, Christopher (David Tully) 52
Kunene, Mazisi (Raymond) 85
La Guma, (Justin) Alex(ander) 19
Millin, Sarah Gertrude 49
Mphahlele, Ezekiel 25
Mtwa, Percy 47
Ngema, Mbongeni 57
Nkosi, Lewis 45
Paton, Alan (Stewart) **4, 10, 25, 55, 106**
Plomer, William Charles Franklin **4, 8**
Prince, F(rank) T(empleton) 22
Smith, Wilbur (Addison) 33
Tolkien, J(ohn) R(onald) R(euel) **1, 2, 3, 8, 12, 38**
Tutu, Desmond M(pilo) 80
van der Post, Laurens (Jan) 5
Vorster, Gordon 34

SPANISH
Alberti, Rafael 7
Aleixandre, Vicente **9, 36**
Alfau, Felipe 66
Alonso, Damaso 14
Arrabal, Fernando **2, 9, 18, 58**
Azorin 11
Benet, Juan 28
Buero Vallejo, Antonio **15, 46**
Bunuel, Luis **16, 80**
Casona, Alejandro 49
Castedo, Elena 65
Cela, Camilo Jose **4, 13, 59**
Cernuda (y Bidon), Luis 54
del Castillo, Michel 38
Delibes, Miguel **8, 18**
Espriu, Salvador 9
Gironella, Jose Maria 11

Gomez de la Serna, Ramon 9
Goytisolo, Juan **5, 10, 23**
Guillen, Jorge **11**
Matute (Ausejo), Ana Maria **11**
Otero, Blas de **11**
Rodriguez, Claudio **10**
Ruiz, Jose Martinez **11**
Saura (Atares), Carlos **20**
Sender, Ramon (Jose) **8**

SRI LANKAN
Gunesekera, Romesh **91**

ST. LUCIAN
Walcott, Derek (Alton) **2, 4, 9, 14, 25, 42, 67, 76**

SWEDISH
Beckman, Gunnel **26**
Bergman, (Ernst) Ingmar **16, 72**
Ekeloef, (Bengt) Gunnar **27**
Johnson, Eyvind (Olof Verner) **14**
Lagerkvist, Paer (Fabian) **7, 10, 13, 54**
Martinson, Harry (Edmund) **14**
Sjoewall, Maj **7**
Spiegelman, Art **76**
Transtroemer, Tomas (Goesta) **52, 65**
Wahloo, Per **7**
Weiss, Peter (Ulrich) **3, 15, 51**

SWISS
Canetti, Elias **3, 14, 25, 75, 86**
Cendrars, Blaise **18, 106**
Duerrenmatt, Friedrich **1, 4, 8, 11, 15, 43, 102**
Frisch, Max (Rudolf) **3, 9, 14, 18, 32, 44**
Hesse, Hermann **1, 2, 3, 6, 11, 17, 25, 69**
Pinget, Robert **7, 13, 37**
Sauser-Hall, Frederic **18**
Sterchi, Beat **65**
von Daeniken, Erich **30**

TRINIDADIAN
Guy, Rosa (Cuthbert) **26**
James, C(yril) L(ionel) R(obert) **33**
Lovelace, Earl **51**
Naipaul, Shiva(dhar Srinivasa) **32, 39**
Naipaul, V(idiadhar) S(urajprasad) **4, 7, 9, 13, 18, 37, 105**

TURKISH
Hikmet, Nazim **40**
Kemal, Yashar **14, 29**
Seferis, George **5, 11**

UGANDAN
p'Bitek, Okot **96**

URUGUAYAN
Galeano, Eduardo (Hughes) **72**
Onetti, Juan Carlos **7, 10**

WELSH
Abse, Dannie **7, 29**
Arundel, Honor (Morfydd) **17**
Clarke, Gillian **61**
Dahl, Roald **1, 6, 18, 79**
Davies, Rhys **23**
Francis, Dick **2, 22, 42, 102**
Hughes, Richard (Arthur Warren) **1, 11**
Humphreys, Emyr Owen **47**
Jones, David (Michael) **2, 4, 7, 13, 42**
Jones, Terence Graham Parry **21**
Levinson, Deirdre **49**

Llewellyn Lloyd, Richard Dafydd Vivian **7, 80**
Mathias, Roland (Glyn) **45**
Norris, Leslie **14**
Roberts, Kate **15**
Rubens, Bernice (Ruth) **19, 31**
Thomas, R(onald) S(tuart) **6, 13, 48**
Watkins, Vernon Phillips **43**
Williams, (George) Emlyn **15**

YUGOSLAVIAN
Andric, Ivo **8**
Cosic, Dobrica **14**
Kis, Danilo **57**
Krleza, Miroslav **8**
Pavic, Milorad **60**
Popa, Vasko **19**
Simic, Charles **6, 9, 22, 49, 68**
Tesich, Steve **40, 69**

Nationality Index

CLC-106 Title Index

The 120 Days of Sodoma (Pasolini)
See *Salo: 120 Days of Sodom*
The ABC's of Cinema (Cendrars) **106**:194
Accattone (Pasolini) **106**:206, 208-09, 219, 221-22, 225-26, 248, 251, 253, 263, 273
An Act of Terror (Brink) **106**:117-18, 133, 137
"The Adventures of My Seven Uncles" (Cendrars)
See "Le Panama ou les aventures de mes sept oncles"
"Advertising=Poetry" (Cendrars) **106**:179
Ah, but Your Land Is Beautiful (Paton) **106**:294-95, 298, 300
"Aleluja" (Pasolini) **106**:233
"All That Time" (Swenson) **106**:337
Amado mio (Pasolini) **106**:254-55
The Ambassador (Brink) **106**:105-06, 124, 136
"Analysis of Baseball" (Swenson) **106**:331, 339
"Annual" (Swenson) **106**:347
"Another Animal" (Swenson) **106**:347
Another Animal (Swenson) **106**:317, 324, 331, 336, 340, 345-46
Antarctic Fugue (Cendrars)
See *Le plan de l'aiguille*
Anthologie Nègre (Cendrars) **106**:149, 185
"Appearances" (Swenson) **106**:345
"L'Appennino" (Pasolini) **106**:265
The Arabian Nights (Pasolini)
See *Il fiore della Mille e una notte*
Archives de ma tour d'ivoire (Cendrars) **106**:170
"As Mortes e o Triunfo de Rosalinda" (Amado) **106**:74, 77
As sete portas du Bahia (Amado) **106**:62
The Ashes of Gramsci (Pasolini)
See *Le ceneri di Gramscí*
Os ásperos tempos (Amado) **106**:59
The Astonished Man (Cendrars)
See *L'homme foudroyé*
"At Breakfast" (Swenson) **106**:318-19
"At East River" (Swenson) **106**:325
Atti impuri (Pasolini) **106**:254-55
"August Night" (Swenson) **106**:347
L'avenir dure longtemps (Althusser) **106**:12, 16-17, 28, 31-2, 37-40, 42
Bahia de todos os santos (Amado) **106**:57, 62
Le Banlieue de Paris (Cendrars) **106**:167, 173
Batman: The Ultimate Evil (Vachss) **106**:366-67
The Beach Waifs (Amado)
See *Capitaes da areia*
"The Beauty of the Head" (Swenson) **106**:329, 344
Berro Dágua (Amado)
See "A Morte e a morte de Quincas Berro Dágua"
Biciclettone (Pasolini) **106**:222, 224
"Big My Secret, But It's Bandaged" (Swenson) **106**:341
"Birth of the Virgin" (Swenson) **106**:349
Black African Poems (Cendrars) **106**:190
"Black Tuesday" (Swenson) **106**:321
"Bleeding" (Swenson) **106**:328, 349
Blossom (Vachss) **106**:361-62
"Blue" (Swenson) **106**:344
Blue Belle (Vachss) **106**:355-61
Born Bad (Vachss) **106**:364

Bourlinguer (Cendrars) **106**:167, 173, 181-84, 186-87, 190
"The Bubus" (Cendrars) **106**:159
"By Morning" (Swenson) **106**:319
"Cabal" (Swenson) **106**:331
Cacao (Amado)
See *Cacáu*
Cacáu (Amado) **106**:71
"Café Tableau" (Swenson) **106**:338
A Cage of Spines (Swenson) **106**:314-16, 319, 325, 340, 347
"Camping in Madera Canyon" (Swenson) **106**:351
The Canterbury Tales (Pasolini)
See *I racconti di Canterbury*
Cape of Storms (Brink) **106**:126-33
Capitaes da areia (Amado) **106**:60
"Captain Holm" (Swenson) **106**:329
Carnival Country (Amado)
See *O país do carnaval*
Carnival Land (Amado)
See *O país do carnaval*
A Carnival Story (Amado)
See "História do Carnaval"
"Le ceneri di Gramscí" (Pasolini) **106**:244-45, 253
Le ceneri di Gramscí (Pasolini) **106**:220, 232, 241, 243-44, 250, 262-63, 267
"Censorship and Literature" (Brink) **106**:119
"The Centaur" (Swenson) **106**:316, 344, 346
A Chain of Voices (Brink) **106**:123-24, 126-27
"Ciant da li ciampanis" (Pasolini) **106**:233
"Ciants di muart" (Pasolini) **106**:233
"A City Garden in April" (Swenson) **106**:326
"Colors without Objects" (Swenson) **106**:331
"The Communist Party to Youth" (Pasolini) **106**:225
"De como o Mulato Porciúncula Descarregou seu Defunto" (Amado) **106**:74-76
A Completa verdade sobre as discutides aventuras do comandante Vasco Moscoso d'Aragao (Amado) **106**:57
Complete Poems (Cendrars) **106**:188
Les confessions de Dan Yack (Cendrars) **106**:169, 183, 185-86, 190
"La confusione degli stili" (Pasolini) **106**:245
"Contrasts" (Cendrars) **106**:180
"A Couple" (Swenson) **106**:337
La Création de Monde (Cendrars) **106**:190
Cry, the Beloved Country: A Story of Comfort in Desolation (Paton) **106**:278-79, 281-83, 288, 293-94, 297-300, 304-06, 311
"El cuòr su l'agua" (Pasolini) **106**:260
"Daffodildo" (Swenson) **106**:341
"Dal laboratorio" (Pasolini) **106**:247
Dan Yack (Cendrars)
See *Les confessions de Dan Yack*
"Dark Wild Honey" (Swenson) **106**:339
Darkness (Brink)
See *Kennis van die Aand*
"David" (Pasolini) **106**:228
"The Dead Lad" (Pasolini) **106**:260
"Dear Elizabeth" (Swenson) **106**:321
"Death, Great Smoothener" (Swenson) **106**:350

"Death Invited" (Swenson) **106**:350
"Deaths" (Swenson) **106**:350
"The Deaths and the Victory of Rosalinda" (Amado)
See "As Mortes e o Triunfo de Rosalinda"
The Decameron (Pasolini)
See *Il Decamerone*
Il Decamerone (Pasolini) **106**:224, 226
Dedica (Pasolini) **106**:233
Les dernières paroles d'un impie (Pasolini) **106**:254-55
A Descoberta de América pelos Turcos (Amado) **106**:91
"A Desperate Vitality" (Pasolini)
See "Una Disperata Vitalita"
"Dili" (Pasolini) **106**:228
"The Disappearance of the Fireflies" (Pasolini) **106**:251
"Una Disperata Vitalita" (Pasolini) **106**:220, 239, 241, 249, 253, 264
"Distance and a Certain Light" (Swenson) **106**:326
The Divine Mimesis (Pasolini) **106**:265
Dix-neuf poèmes élastiques (Cendrars) **106**:163, 177, 181, 185-86, 190-91, 197-98
Documentaires (Cendrars)
See *Kodak*
"La Domenica Uliva" (Pasolini) **106**:233
Dona Flor and Her Two Husbands (Amado)
See *Dona Flor e seus dois maridos*
Dona Flor e seus dois maridos (Amado) **106**:54-5, 57, 61, 65, 73, 78-9, 81, 84, 86
"Double Exposure" (Swenson) **106**:332
Dov'è la mia patria (Pasolini) **106**:232
Down in the Zero (Vachss) **106**:364-65
A Dry White Season (Brink) **106**:98-9, 104, 119, 124, 130, 133, 137, 139, 142, 143, 145
"Each Day of Summer" (Swenson) **106**:339
"Early Morning: Cape Cod" (Swenson) **106**:339
"Earth Your Dancing Place" (Swenson) **106**:346
Easter in New York (Cendrars)
See *Les pâques*
Edipo Re (Pasolini) **106**:226, 256
"Elephant Hunt" (Cendrars) **106**:158
Emmène-moi au bout du monde! (Cendrars) **106**:176, 178, 187
Empirismo eretico (Pasolini) **106**:224-25, 235, 245-47
"The End of the Avant-Garde" (Pasolini) **106**:258
The End of the World Filmed by the Angel of Notre Dame (Cendrars) **106**:191
"Ending" (Swenson) **106**:335
"Equilibrist" (Swenson) **106**:336-37, 347
Essays in Self-Criticism (Althusser) **106**:41
"L'Eubage" (Cendrars) **106**:170
"The Even Sea" (Swenson) **106**:315
"Evolution" (Swenson) **106**:314, 337, 346, 348-49
"The Experience of Poetry in a Scientific Age" (Swenson) **106**:334
"Facing" (Swenson) **106**:348-49
"The Facts" (Althusser) **106**:32, 37
The Facts (Althusser) **106**:40-1
Les Faits (Althusser) **106**:12

"Far West" (Cendrars) **106**:175
"Fashion in the 70's" (Swenson) **106**:330
"Feel Me" (Swenson) **106**:344-45
Feuilles de route (Cendrars) **106**:185, 198
"Fiesta" (Pasolini) **106**:230
File on a Diplomat (Brink) **106**:99, 124, 126-27, 136-37
Il fiore della Mille e una notte (Pasolini) **106**:226, 241, 248, 250, 266, 270
"Fire Island" (Swenson) **106**:349-50
Flood (Vachss) **106**:354, 357-59, 361, 365
Footsteps of the Hawk (Vachss) **106**:365-66
For Marx (Althusser)
　　See *Pour Marx*
"Forest" (Swenson) **106**:334
"Fountain Piece" (Swenson) **106**:325
"The Fountains of Aix" (Swenson) **106**:320-21, 349-50
"Four-Word Lines" (Swenson) **106**:337
"From a Daybook" (Swenson) **106**:333
"Frontispiece" (Swenson) **106**:315
The Future Lasts a Long Time (Althusser)
　　See *L'avenir dure longtemps*
The Future Lasts Forever (Althusser)
　　See *L'avenir dure longtemps*
Gabriela, Clove and Cinnamon (Amado)
　　See *Gabriela, cravo e canela*
Gabriela, cravo e canela (Amado) **106**:54-5, 57, 60-2, 65, 73, 77-8, 84-6, 89
"The Garden at St. John's" (Swenson) **106**:317
"God" (Swenson) **106**:316, 327, 345-46, 350
Gold (Cendrars)
　　See *L'or*
The Golden Harvest (Amado) **106**:86, 89
The Gospel according to St. Matthew (Pasolini)
　　See *Il vangelo secondo Matteo*
Half Sun Half Sleep (Swenson) **106**:320-21, 348-49
Hard Candy (Vachss) **106**:359-61, 365
The Hawks and the Sparrows (Pasolini)
　　See *Uccellacci e uccellini*
"He that None could Capture" (Swenson) **106**:337
"The Heart on the Water" (Pasolini) **106**:260
"Her Early Work" (Swenson) **106**:340-41
"História do Carnaval" (Amado) **106**:74-5
"Holding the Towel" (Swenson) **106**:337
Hollywood (Cendrars) **106**:190, 193-94
Home Is the Sailor (Amado)
　　See *Os velhos marinheiros*
L'homme foudroyé (Cendrars) **106**:167, 169, 172-73, 179, 182-83, 185, 187-88, 190, 192
"Horse and Swan Feeding" (Swenson) **106**:313, 324-25, 340
"How Everything Happens (Based on a Study of the Wave)" (Swenson) **106**:335, 339, 351
"How the Mulatto Porciúncula Got the Corpse Off His Back" (Amado)
　　See "De como o Mulato Porciúncula Descarregou seu Defunto"
"How to Be Old" (Swenson) **106**:319
"A Hurricane at Sea" (Swenson) **106**:326
I Have Killed (Cendrars) **106**:191
"I Look at My Hand" (Swenson) **106**:344
"I Will Lie Down" (Swenson) **106**:350
Iconographs (Swenson) **106**:320-21, 325, 327-28, 338, 342, 344, 349-50
"If I Had Children" (Swenson) **106**:342
"Il cinema di poesia" (Pasolini) **106**:237
"Il diaul cu la mari" (Pasolini) **106**:230
"Il neo-sperimentalismo" (Pasolini) **106**:212
"Il nini muart" (Pasolini) **106**:227-28, 233, 260-61
Il sogno di una cosa (Pasolini) **106**:231, 254

Imaginings of Sand (Brink) **106**:134-38
"In Love Made Visible" (Swenson) **106**:337, 347-48
In Other Words (Swenson) **106**:323, 333, 336, 340, 342-43, 346
In Praise of the Dangerous Life (Cendrars) **106**:191
"Incantation" (Swenson) **106**:351
"The Indivisible Incompatibles" (Swenson) **106**:348
An Instant in the Wind (Brink)
　　See *File on a Diplomat*
"Instead of Camargue" (Swenson) **106**:320
Journey Continued (Paton) **106**:305-06
Jubiabá (Amado) **106**:57-8, 62-3, 71
Kennis van die Aand (Brink) **106**:95-7, 99, 101, 122-25, 137
"The Key to Everything" (Swenson) **106**:314, 345
Kodak (Cendrars) **106**:153, 158-59, 175, 185-86, 190-91, 198
Kodak Documentaires (Cendrars)
　　See *Kodak*
"A Lake Scene" (Swenson) **106**:326
Land of Carnival (Amado)
　　See *O país do carnaval*
"Languages and Culture" (Brink) **106**:120
"Li letanis dal biel fì" (Pasolini) **106**:261
"La libertà stilistica" (Pasolini) **106**:246
Lice (Cendrars)
　　See *La Main Coupée*
"The Lightning" (Swenson) **106**:349
"La lingua seritta della realtà" (Pasolini) **106**:235
"Lion" (Swenson) **106**:326
Lire "Le Capital" (Althusser) **106**:12, 17-19, 21, 29, 31, 38, 42-3
"The Litanies of the Beautiful Bay" (Pasolini) **106**:261
Literatuur in die strydperk (Brink) **106**:109
"Little Lion Face" (Swenson) **106**:343
Looking on Darkness (Brink)
　　See *Kennis van die Aand*
Le lotissement du ciel (Cendrars) **106**:167, 172, 190
"Love Is" (Swenson) **106**:347
The Love Poems of May Swenson (Swenson) **106**:336-37, 343-44, 347-48
"The Lowering" (Swenson) **106**:320-21
Lutheran Letters (Pasolini) **106**:259
La Main Coupée (Cendrars) **106**:167, 183, 187-88, 190
Mamma Roma (Pasolini) **106**:206-08, 221-22, 226, 253, 273
"Manyone Flying" (Swenson) **106**:344, 346
Mapmakers (Brink) **106**:109, 119-20
Mar morto (Amado) **106**:58-60, 63
May Out West (Swenson) **106**:351
Medea (Pasolini) **106**:226, 256
"Mee Too Buggi" (Cendrars) **106**:190
La meglio gioventù (Pasolini) **106**:227, 231, 243
"Menus" (Cendrars) **106**:191
The Milk-Cheese (Pasolini)
　　See *La Ricotta*
"The Miracle of the Birds" (Amado) **106**:73
Modernities and Other Writings (Cendrars) **106**:190-91
Moravagine (Cendrars) **106**:166, 183-85, 187-90, 192
More Poems to Solve (Swenson) **106**:340
"A Morte e a morte de Quincas Berro Dágua" (Amado) **106**:65-6, 70-1, 73, 77
"Mostru o pavea" (Pasolini) **106**:229
"Motherhood" (Swenson) **106**:335
Nature: Poems Old and New (Swenson) **106**:346,

351
Navegaçao de Cabotagem (Amado) **106**:91
"Neither Wanting More" (Swenson) **106**:347
New and Selected Things Taking Place (Swenson) **106**:321-22, 324, 328-29, 331, 336, 338, 343-45
The New Youth (Pasolini)
　　See *La nuova gioventù*
"News Flash" (Cendrars) **106**:197
"News from the Cabin" (Swenson) **106**:325
"Night Visits with the Family" (Swenson) **106**:344
The Nightingale of the Catholic Church (Pasolini)
　　See *L'usignuolo della Chiesa Cattolica*
"Nightwind" (Swenson) **106**:318
Nineteen Elastic Poems (Cendrars)
　　See *Dix-neuf poèmes élastiques*
"nNight Before the Journey" (Swenson) **106**:337
"No Swan so Fine" (Swenson) **106**:340
"The North Rim" (Swenson) **106**:329
"A Nosty Fright" (Swenson) **106**:323
"La not di maj" (Pasolini) **106**:229
"Notes on the Road: The SS. Formosa" (Cendrars) **106**:158
Notre pain quotidien (Cendrars) **106**:173
Un Nouveau Patron pour l'Aviation (Cendrars) **106**:172
Une nuit dans la fôret (Cendrars) **106**:166
La nuova gioventù (Pasolini) **106**:265, 267
O Gato Malhado e a Andorinha Sinhá (Amado) **106**:73
"O me donzel" (Pasolini) **106**:228
"October" (Swenson) **106**:322
Oedipus Rex (Pasolini)
　　See *Edipo Re*
"Of Rounds" (Swenson) **106**:339
Officina (Pasolini) **106**:232
On the Contrary (Brink) **106**:130, 132-33, 137
"On the Materialist Dialectic" (Althusser) **106**:23
"One Morning in New Hampshire" (Swenson) **106**:321, 338
"One of Many Epilogs" (Pasolini)
　　See "Uno dei tanti epiloghi"
L'or (Cendrars) **106**:149, 153-54, 167, 182-83, 185, 190, 194
"Organelle" (Swenson) **106**:314
"Organs" (Swenson) **106**:339
Orgie (Brink) **106**:101
"Our Forward Shadows" (Swenson) **106**:339
"Out of My Head" (Swenson) **106**:345
O país do carnaval (Amado) **106**:55, 57, 89-90
"Panama, etc." (Cendrars) **106**:158
"Le Panama ou les aventures de mes sept oncles" (Cendrars) **106**:152, 154, 158-59, 163, 167, 177, 181, 184, 186, 190-92, 196-97
Les pâques (Cendrars) **106**:159, 163, 177-78, 180, 184, 189-90, 195
"Pascoli e Montale" (Pasolini) **106**:232
"La passione" (Pasolini) **106**:268
Passione e ideologia (Pasolini) **106**:245
"Pastorela di Narcis" (Pasolini) **106**:230
Os pastores da noite (Amado) **106**:64, 73, 77
Petrolio (Pasolini) **106**:272, 274
Le plan de l'aiguille (Cendrars) **106**:169, 185-86
"Plan of Future Works" (Pasolini) **106**:241, 250
Planus (Cendrars)
　　See *Bourlinguer*
"Ploja fòur di dut" (Pasolini) **106**:267
"Ploja tai cunfins" (Pasolini) **106**:226-28, 267
Poems (Pasolini)
　　See *Poesi*
Poems in the Shape of a Rose (Pasolini)
　　See *Poems in the Shape of a Rose*

Poems to Solve (Swenson)　**106**:320, 339
Poesi (Pasolini)　**106**:250, 253
La poesia dialettale del Novecento (Pasolini)　**106**:226, 231,
Poesia in forma di rosa (Pasolini)　**106**:220, 253, 263
"La poesia popolaine italiana" (Pasolini)　**106**:231, 245
Poesie a Casarsa (Pasolini)　**106**:228-29, 231, 234, 243, 271
"Poet to Tiger" (Swenson)　**106**:329, 343
"The Poetry of Tradition" (Pasolini)　**106**:265
Porcilè (Pasolini)　**106**:241, 256
"Porciúncula" (Amado)
　　See "De como o Mulato Porciúncula Descarregou seu Defunto"
Pour Marx (Althusser)　**106**:3, 17, 19, 29, 31, 39, 42
"The Pregnant Dream" (Swenson)　**106**:337
Profound Today (Cendrars)　**106**:191-92
"Prose du transsibérien et de la petite Jeanne de France" (Cendrars)　**106**:151, 158-59, 163, 167, 177, 180-81, 184, 186, 189-90, 192, 196-97
"Prose of the Trans-Siberian" (Cendrars)
　　See "Prose du transsibérien et de la petite Jeanne de France"
"Prosody of the Transsiberian" (Cendrars)
　　See "Prose du transsibérien et de la petite Jeanne de France"
"The Pure Suit of Happiness" (Swenson)　**106**:322
"Question" (Swenson)　**106**:346, 350
"La rabbia" (Pasolini)　**106**:265
I racconti di Canterbury (Pasolini)　**106**:226, 266
The Ragazzi (Pasolini)
　　See *Ragazzi di vita*
Ragazzi di vita (Pasolini)　**106**:211, 216-18, 231, 242, 251, 253-54, 271
Rain (Brink)
　　See *Rumours of Rain*
Reading Capital (Althusser)
　　See *Lire "Le Capital"*
"Reality" (Pasolini)　**106**:241, 250
Red Harvest (Amado)
　　See *Seára vermelha*
Reinventing a Continent: Essays on South African Writing and Politics (Brink)　**106**:138
"The Religion of My Time" (Pasolini)　**106**:239, 241, 253
La religione del mio tempo (Pasolini)　**106**:220, 263, 265
"Reperdiation of the *Trilogy of Life*" (Pasolini)　**106**:268
La Ricotta (Pasolini)　**106**:206-208, 221
"Riding the `A'" (Swenson)　**106**:328
"Rital and Raton" (Pasolini)　**106**:270
RoGoPaG (Pasolini)　**106**:226
Romancero (Pasolini)　**106**:230-31
Rumours of Rain (Brink)　**106**:96-7, 99, 123-24, 130, 146
Sacrifice (Vachss)　**106**:362
Salo: 120 Days of Sodom (Pasolini)　**106**:238-39, 241, 248-50, 257, 268, 273
Sao Jorge dos Ilhéus (Amado)　**106**:60-1, 89
"Satanic Form" (Swenson)　**106**:337
"La sceneggiatura come `struttura che vuol essene altia struttura'" (Pasolini)　**106**:237
"The School of Desire" (Swenson)　**106**:339, 347
Scritti corsair (Pasolini)　**106**:245
Sea of Death (Amado)
　　See *Mar morto*
Sea of the Dead (Amado)
　　See *Mar morto*

Seára vermelha (Amado)　**106**:57-59
"Un secolo di studi sulla poesia popolare" (Pasolini)　**106**:245
"The Seed of My Father" (Swenson)　**106**:351
Selected Writings (Cendrars)　**106**:177
"The Shape of Death" (Swenson)　**106**:328, 350
Shella (Vachss)　**106**:363-64
Shepherds of the Night (Amado)
　　See *Os pastores da noite*
Showdown (Amado)
　　See *Tocaia grande*
"Shuttles" (Swenson)　**106**:333
"Sketch for a Landscape" (Swenson)　**106**:313
"'So Long' to the Moon from the Men of Apollo" (Swenson)　**106**:327
"Some Quadrangles" (Swenson)　**106**:335
"The Sonnet Hobby" (Pasolini)　**106**:265-66
"Southbound on the Freeway" (Swenson)　**106**:319
Spiritual (Pasolini)　**106**:230
St. George of Ilhéus (Amado)
　　See *Sao Jorge dos Ilhéus*
"Staring at the Sea on the Day of the Death of Another" (Swenson)　**106**:328
States of Emergency (Brink)　**106**:107-08, 119-20, 123-25, 137
"Still Turning" (Swenson)　**106**:351
"Stone or Flame" (Swenson)　**106**:337
La strada (Pasolini)　**106**:230
"Strawberrying" (Swenson)　**106**:333
Strega (Vachss)　**106**:355-59, 361, 365
"Studies on the Life of Testaccio (Pasolini)　**106**:270
Os subterrâneos da liberdade (Amado)　**106**:57, 59
Suite furlana (Pasolini)　**106**:229, 233
"The Surface" (Swenson)　**106**:346
Sutter's Gold (Cendrars)
　　See *L'or*
The Swallow and the Tom Cat: A Love Story (Amado)
　　See *O Gato Malhado e a Andorinha Sinhá*
"Swimmers" (Swenson)　**106**:339
"Symmetrical Companion" (Swenson)　**106**:336, 348
"Tears of an Excavator" (Pasolini)　**106**:241-249
"Teddy Bears" (Swenson)　**106**:333
Tenda dos milagres (Amado)　**106**:56, 60, 62, 65
Tent of Miracles (Amado)
　　See *Tenda dos milagres*
Teorema (Pasolini)　**106**:226, 248, 256, 265, 273
"Teoria delle giunte" (Pasolini)　**106**:236
Tereza Batista cansada de guerra (Amado)　**106**:55, 59, 62, 73, 76, 86
Tereza Batista Home from the Wars (Amado)
　　See *Tereza Batista cansada de guerra*
Terras do sem fim (Amado)　**106**:58, 61-2
"Testament Coran" (Pasolini)　**106**:243
"A Thank-You Letter" (Swenson)　**106**:323
"That the Soul May Wax Plump" (Swenson)　**106**:329, 344
Theorem (Pasolini)
　　See *Teorema*
Things Taking Place (Swenson)
　　See *New and Selected Things Taking Place*
"Thou Art Lovelier Than the Sky and Sea" (Cendrars)　**106**:159
"The Thousand Islands" (Cendrars)　**106**:190
"Three White Vases" (Swenson)　**106**:333
"The Tide at Long Point" (Swenson)　**106**:315
Tieta do Agreste, pastora de cabras; ou, A volta da filha pródiga (Amado)　**106**:86
Tieta, the Goat Girl; or, The Return of the Prodigal Daughter (Amado)

　　See *Tieta do Agreste, pastora de cabras; ou, A volta da filha pródiga*
"To Confirm a Thing" (Swenson)　**106**:314, 341
"To F." (Swenson)　**106**:343
"To Make a Play" (Swenson)　**106**:339
To Mix with Time: New and Selected Poems (Swenson)　**106**:316, 319-20, 327, 336, 341, 345, 349
To the End of the World (Cendrars)
　　See *Emmène-moi au bout du monde!*
To Transfigure, To Organize (Pasolini)
　　See *Trasumanar e organizzar*
Tocaia grande (Amado)　**106**:84-5, 91
Too Late the Phalarope (Paton)　**106**:288-89, 292-94, 296-97, 300, 304-06
Too Much Is Too Much (Cendrars)　**106**:177-78
"Tornant al pais" (Pasolini)　**106**:229
Towards the Mountain (Paton)　**106**:299, 305
"Transsiberian" (Cendrars)
　　See "Prose du transsibérien et de la petite Jeanne de France"
Trasumanar e organizzar (Pasolini)　**106**:253, 265-66
Travel Notes (Cendrars)　**106**:190-91, 194, 198
"A Trellis for R." (Swenson)　**106**:321, 344
Trilogia della vita (Pasolini)　**106**:248, 266, 268
Trilogy of Life (Pasolini)
　　See *Trilogy of Life*
Two Deaths (Amado)
　　See "A Morte e a morte de Quincas Berro Dágua"
The Two Deaths of Quincas Wateryell (Amado)
　　See "A Morte e a morte de Quincas Berro Dágua"
"Two-Part Pear Able" (Swenson)　**106**:325
Uccellacci e uccellini (Pasolini)　**106**:220, 226, 273
"L'umile Itallia" (Pasolini)　**106**:265
"The Universe" (Swenson)　**106**:316, 345
"Uno dei tanti epiloghi" (Pasolini)　**106**:266
"Untitled" (Swenson)　**106**:336, 349
L'usignuolo della Chiesa Cattolica (Pasolini)　**106**:228, 242, 250, 263, 265, 267-68
Il vangelo secondo Matteo (Pasolini)　**106**:202-05, 207-09, 221, 226, 248-49, 265, 272-73
"Vegnerà el vero Cristo" (Pasolini)　**106**:230
Os velhos marinheiros (Amado)　**106**:57, 63-4
"Vilota" (Pasolini)　**106**:228
The Violent Land (Amado)
　　See *Terras do sem fim*
Una vita violenta (Pasolini)　**106**:209, 216, 218-19, 242, 253, 254, 269-70
"Waiting for It" (Swenson)　**106**:326
The Wall of the Plague (Brink)　**106**:119-22, 124
The War of the Saints (Amado)　**106**:86-91
"Watching the Jets Lose to Buffalo at Shea" (Swenson)　**106**:330
"Wednesday at the Waldorf" (Swenson)　**106**:339
The Wheel (Cendrars)　**106**:185
"While Seated on a Plane" (Swenson)　**106**:335
"While Sitting in the Tuileries and Facing the Slanting Sun" (Swenson)　**106**:349
"White Moon" (Swenson)　**106**:351
"Why We Die" (Swenson)　**106**:314
"Wild Water" (Swenson)　**106**:337, 347
"The Willets" (Swenson)　**106**:324-25, 337
"Women" (Swenson)　**106**:342
"The Writer in a State of Siege" (Brink)　**106**:103
Writing in a State of Siege (Brink)　**106**:101, 103
"The Year of the Double Spring" (Swenson)　**106**:338
"You Are" (Swenson)　**106**:337, 347-48
"Zambesi and Ranee" (Swenson)　**106**:340

ISBN 0-7876-2029-7

90000

9 780787 620295